The Stoddart colour visual dictionary

JEAN-CLAUDE CORBEIL • ARIANE ARCHAMBAULT

The Stoddart colour visual dictionary

Canadian Cataloguing in Publication Data

Corbeil, Jean-Claude, 1932-

Stoddart colour visual dictionary

  Includes bibliographical references and index.

  ISBN 0-7737-2648-9

  1. Picture dictionaries, English. 2. English language - Dictionaries. I. Archambault, Ariane, 1936-   . II. Title

PEl629.C67 1992   423'.1   C92-094477-9

Created and produced
by Québec/Amérique International
a division of
Éditions Québec/Amérique Inc.
425, rue Saint-Jean-Baptiste, Montréal, Québec H2Y 2Z7
Tél. : (514) 393-1450 Fax : (514) 866-2430

First published in 1992 by
Stoddart Publishing Co. Limited
34 Lesmill Road
Toronto, Canada
M3B 2T6

Stoddart Publishing gratefully acknowledges the support of the Canada Council, Ontario Arts Council
and Ontario Publishing Centre in the development of writing and publishing in Canada.

Printed and Bound in Canada

ACKNOWLEDGMENTS

In preparing *The Stoddart Colour Visual Dictionary,* we have benefitted from the help of numerous groups, organizations and companies, which have provided us with up-to-date technical documents. We have also received judicious advice from various specialists, colleagues, terminologists and translators. We extend a special thank-you to our initial contributors, Édith Girard, René St-Pierre, Marielle Hébert, Christiane Vachon and Anik Lapointe. In addition, we wish to express our sincere gratitude to the following individuals and organizations:

A.C. Delco
Aérospatiale (France)
Aérospatiale Canada (ACI) inc.
Air Canada (Linguistic Policy and Services)
Amity-Leather Products Company
Animat inc.
Archambault Musique
International Association of Lighthouse
    Authorities (Marie-Hélène Grillet)
Association des groupes d'astronomes amateurs
    (Jean-Marc Richard)
Atlas Copco
Atomic Energy of Canada Ltd. (Pierre Giguère)
Bell Canada
Bell Helicopter Textron
Bellefontaine
Benoît, Richard
Beretta
Black & Decker
Bombardier Inc.
Boutique de harnais Pépin
British Hovercraft Corporation Ltd. (Division of
    Westland Aerospace)
C. Plath North American Division
Caloritech inc.
Cambridge Instruments (Canada) Inc.
CAMIF (Direction relations extérieures)
Canada Billard & Bowling inc. (Bernard Monsec)
Canadian National (Information and Linguistic
    Services)
Canadian Kenworth Company
Canadian Coleman Supply Inc.
Canadian Liquid Air Ltd.
Canadian Curling Association
Canadian Coast Guard
Canadian Broadcasting Corporation (Gilles
    Amyot, Pierre Beaucage, Claude L'Hérault,
    Pierre Laroche)
Carpentier, Jean-Marc
Casavant Frères Limitée (Gilbert Lemieux)
Centre de Tissage Leclerc inc.
Chromalox inc.
Clerc, Redjean
Club de tir à l'arc de Montréal
Club de planeur Champlain
Collège Jean de Brébeuf (Paul-Émile Tremblay)
Collège militaire royal de Saint-Jean
Communauté urbaine de Montréal (Bureau de
    transport métropolitain)
Complexe sportif Claude-Robillard
Control Data Canada Ltd.
Cycles Performance
David M. Stewart Museum (Philippe Butler)
Department of National Defence of Canada
    (Public Relations)
Detson
Direction des constructions navales
    (Programmes internationaux) (France)
Distributions TTI inc.
Energy, Mines and Resources Canada (Canada
    Centre for Remote Sensing)
Environment Canada (Atmospheric Environment
    Service, Gilles Sanscartier)
FACOM
Fédération québécoise des échecs
Fédération québécoise de tennis
Fédération québécoise de luge et bobsleigh
Fédération québécoise de canot-camping
Fédération québécoise de boxe olympique
Fédération québécoise de badminton
Fédération québécoise d'haltérophilie

Fédération québécoise d'escrime
Fédération de patinage de vitesse du Québec
Festival des Montolfières du Haut-Richelieu
Fincantieri Naval Shipbuilding Division
Fisher Scientific Ltd.
Ford New-Holland Inc.
Gadbois, Alain
GAM Pro Plongée
G.E. Astro-Space Division
G.T.E. Sylvania Canada Ltd.
General Electric Canada Inc. (Dominion
    Engineering Works, Mony Schinasi)
General Motors of Canada Ltd.
GIAT Industries
Government of Canada Terminology Bank
Gym Plus
Harrison (1985) inc.
Hewitt Equipment Ltd.
Hippodrome Blue Bonnets (Robert Perez)
Honeywell Ltd.
Hortipro
Hughes Aircraft Company
Hydro-Québec (Centre de documentation, Anne
    Crépeau)
IBM Canada Ltd.
Imperial Oil Ltd.
Institut de recherche d'Hydro-Québec (IREQ)
International Telecommunications Satellite
    Organisation (Intelsat)
International Civil Aviation Organization (IATA)
Jardin Botanique de Montréal
John Deere Ltd.
Johnson & Johnson Inc.
La Maison Olympique (Sylvia Doucette)
La Cordée
Le Beau Voyage
Le Coz, Jean-Pierre
Lee Valley Tools Ltd.
Leica Camera
Les Manufacturiers Draco ltée
Les Instruments de Musique Twigg inc.
Les Équipements Chalin ltée
Les Appareils orthopédiques BBG inc.
Leviton Manufacturing of Canada Ltd.
Liebherr-Québec
Manac inc.
Manutan
Marcoux, Jean-Marie
Marrazza Musique
MATRA S.A.
Matra Défense (Direction de la communication)
Mazda Canada
Médiatel
Mendes inc. (François Caron)
Michelin
MIL Tracy (Henri Vacher)
Ministère des transports du Québec (Sécurité
    routière, Signalisation routière)
Monette Sport inc.
Moto Internationale
National Oceanic and Atmospheric
    Administration (NOAA) — National
    Environmental Satelite and Information
    Service (Frank Lepore)
National Aeronautics and Space Administration
    (N.A.S.A.)
Nikon Canada Inc.
Northern Telecom Canada Ltd.
Office de la langue française du Québec
    (Chantal Robinson)
Ogilvie Mills Ltd. (Michel Ladouceur)

Olivetti Systems and Networks Canada Ltd.
Ontario Hydro
Paterson Darkroom Necessities
Petro-Canada (Calgary)
Philips Electronics Ltd. (Philips Lighting)
Philips Electronics Ltd. (Scientific and Analytical
    Equipment)
Pierre-Olivier Decor
Planétarium Dow (Pierre Lacombe)
Plastimo
Port of Montreal (Public Affairs)
Pratt & Whitney Canada Inc.
Quincaillerie A.C.L. inc.
Radio-Québec
Remington Products (Canada) Inc.
Russell Rinfret
Rodriguez Cantieri navali S.p.A.
S.A. Redoute Catalogue (Relations extérieures)
Samsonite
Secretary of State of Canada (Translation
    Bureau)
Shell Canada
SIAL Poterie
Smith-Corona (Canada) Ltd.
SNC Defence Products Ltd.
Société Nationale des Chemins de Fer français
    (S.N.C.F.) (Direction de la communication)
Société de transport de la Communauté urbaine
    de Montréal
Spalding Canada
Spar Aerospace Ltd. (Hélène Lapierre)
St. Lawrence Seaway Authority (Normand
    Dodier)
Sunbeam Corporation (Canada) Ltd.
Swimming Canada
Teleglobe Canada Inc. (Roger Leblanc)
Telesat Canada (Yves Comtois)
The Coal Association of Canada
The British Petroleum Company p.l.c.
    (Photographic Services)
Thibault
Tideland Signal Canada Ltd.
Transport Canada (Montreal Airports, Gilbert
    L'Espérance, Koos R. Van der Peijl)
Ultramar Canada Inc.
United States Department of Defense
    (Department of the Navy, Office of
    Information)
Université du Québec à Montréal (Module des
    arts, Michel Fournier)
Université du Québec (Institut national de la
    recherche scientifique, Benoît Jean)
Varin, Claude
Via Rail Canada Inc.
Viala L.R. inc. (Jean Beaudin)
Ville de Montréal (Bureau du cinéma; Service de
    l'habitation et du développement urbain;
    Service de la prévention des incendies,
    Robert Gilbert, Réal Audet; Service des
    travaux publics)
Volcano inc.
Volkswagen Canada Inc.
Volvo Canada Ltd.
Water Ski Canada
Weider
Wild Leitz Canada ltée
Xerox Canada Inc.
Yamaha Canada Music Ltd.

Often, we find ourselves unable to name or describe an object. Failing the exact vocabulary, we fall back on words like "thing" or "gizmo"; obviously, these terms convey little information. *The Stoddart Colour Visual Dictionary*, an original reference tool quite unlike any language or encyclopædic dictionaries, has been designed to remedy just such situations.

This dictionary uses pictures to define words. Illustrations have been assigned a key role; indeed, their documentary value is invaluable. It has been proven that pictures are quickly committed to memory. An amazing source of emotion, they pique people's curiosity. This is why, with the help of precise modern-day technology, we have chosen to pair vocabulary with high-quality, computer-assisted illustrations.

The Stoddart Colour Visual Dictionary covers all aspects of everyday life. It is aimed at all those who wish to enrich their vocabulary and enhance communication by using the correct terms for objects. The quality of its illustrations, the exactness of its terminology, the scope of its contents and the ease with which it may be consulted make this dictionary a truly revolutionary work of reference.

Given new developments in the fields of technology and communications, today's readers require quick access to efficient, concise information. By creating a direct link between pictures and words, *The Stoddart Colour Visual Dictionary* answers this twofold need for speed and precision. This full-colour dictionary is an abundant source of information, rivalling conventional reference works.

This visual dictionary is the fruit of collaboration. Over the past three years, a team of linguists, terminologists, researchers, proof-readers, illustrators, computer and non-computer graphic artists, computer technicians, and programmers have pooled their skills to create this exceptional cultural tool, adapted to today's dynamic world. Readers who feel the need to better understand, increase their knowledge, or enhance their communication skills will soon acquire the habit of consulting *The Stoddart Colour Visual Dictionary*.

Jacques Fortin
Publisher

INTRODUCTION

The *Stoddart Colour Visual Dictionary* is quite unlike other dictionaries, in both its contents and presentation. Given its uniqueness, a few words of explanation will help you appreciate its usefulness and the quality of the information it contains. The following introduction explains how and why *The Stoddart Colour Visual Dictionary* differs from language dictionaries and encyclopædias. For dictionary "fans" and professional lexicographers, we have included a brief description of the principles and methods that guided us in producing the dictionary.

A PICTURE/WORD DICTIONARY

The Stoddart Colour Visual Dictionary closely links pictures and words. The pictures offer a visual description and analysis of today's world: the objects of everyday life, our physical environment, the animal and plant life that surround us, the communication and work techniques that are changing our lifestyles, the weapons that preoccupy us, the means of transportation that are breaking down geographical barriers, the sources of energy on which we depend.

Illustrations play a specific role in this dictionary: they serve to define words, enabling dictionary users to "see" immediately the meaning of each term. Users can thus recognize the objects they are looking for and, at a single glance, find the corresponding vocabulary.

The Stoddart Colour Visual Dictionary provides users with the words they need to accurately name the objects that make up the world around them. The terms in the dictionary have been carefully selected from the latest documentation written by experts in each area. The vocabulary has been studied by specialists and cross-checked in encyclopædias and language dictionaries. We have used all means available to ensure the accuracy of each word and a high level of standardization.

A DICTIONARY FOR ONE AND ALL

The Stoddart Colour Visual Dictionary is aimed at those in modern society who need to know and use technical terms from a wide range of fields. Not designed only for specialists, it thus addresses the needs and curiosity of each and every one of us.

People's degree of knowledge differs from one field to another, and the complexity of the topics dealt with varies widely. Therefore, rather than arbitrarily providing a uniform breakdown of each subject, the authors have varied the depth of analysis according to the subject. For example, most people are more familiar with clothing and automobiles than with atomic energy or telecommunications satellites, and find the former subjects simpler to understand. Terms used to describe human anatomy seem more complicated than those used for fruits and vegetables. In addition, our world is changing: photographic vocabulary, for example, has become much more complicated with camera automation. Similarly, although microcomputer fans are familiar with computer terminology, the field remains a mystery for much of the rest of the population.

The Stoddart Colour Visual Dictionary allows for these differences, and thus highlights the specialized vocabulary commonly used in each field.

AN EASY-TO-CONSULT DICTIONARY

With its Summary, Detailed Table of Contents, and Index *The Stoddart Colour Visual Dictionary* can be used in several different ways.

Users may consult the dictionary:

By going from an idea to a word, if they are familiar with an object and can clearly visualize it, but do not know the name for it. The Detailed Table of Contents breaks each subject down using an easy-to-consult, stratified classification system. The Stoddart Colour Visual Dictionary is the only dictionary that allows users to find a word from its meaning.

By going from a word to an idea, if they want to check the meaning of a term. The Index refers users to the illustrations, which provide the names for the individual features.

At a glance, by using the Summary. The coloured page edges help users find the chapters they are looking for.

For sheer pleasure, by flipping from one illustration to another, or from one word to another, for the sole purpose of enriching their knowledge and enjoying the illustrations.

A DICTIONARY WITH A DIFFERENCE

We are all familiar with several types of dictionaries and encyclopædias. It is not always easy, however, to grasp their distinguishing features. The following overview highlights the main differences between *The Stoddart Colour Visual Dictionary* and other reference works.

a) Language dictionaries

These dictionaries describe the meanings given by speakers to the general vocabulary of their language.

They provide two major types of information: headwords (vocabulary), and a list of the meanings of each term (dictionary entries).

The vocabulary constitutes the framework of the dictionary. Arranged in alphabetical order, the vocabulary includes common, contemporary language, archaic words useful for understanding the texts or history of a civilization, and a certain number of widely used technical terms.

Each dictionary entry provides an itemized, semantic description of the corresponding headword. Generally, the entry indicates the part of speech for the headword, its etymology and various meanings as well as the word's social usage (familiar, colloquial, vulgar, etc.) according to criteria that, even today, remain somewhat vague.

In general, language dictionaries are classified by their target users and the number of terms in the vocabulary. A 5,000-word dictionary is intended for younger children, one with 15,000 words is suitable for elementary schools and a 50,000-word dictionary covers the needs of the general public.

b) Encyclopædic dictionaries

In addition to the information included in language dictionaries, encyclopædic dictionaries provide details about the nature, functioning, and history of things, thus enabling both laymen with solid general knowledge and specialists to understand the scope of a word. They devote much more space to technical terms and reflect current scientific and technological developments. Generally speaking, pictures play an important role in illustrating the text. The size of encyclopædic dictionaries varies according to the breadth of the vocabulary, the length of the entries, the emphasis placed on proper nouns, and the number of fields of specialization covered.

c) Encyclopædias

Encyclopædias do not deal with language; they provide scientific, technical, economic, historical, and geographic descriptions. The entries may be arranged alphabetically, conceptually, chronologically, or by field of specialization. The number of different encyclopædias is virtually unlimited, given the fragmentation of civilization into multiple categories. There is, however, a distinction between universal encyclopædias and specialized encyclopædias.

d) Specialized lexicons and vocabularies

These works usually address specific needs created by scientific and technological progress. They focus on ensuring efficient communication through precise, standardized terminology. They vary in all respects: the method of compilation, the authors' approach to the subject matter, the scope of the vocabulary, the number of languages, and the means of establishing equivalents in the various languages (i.e., by simple translation or by a comparison of unilingual terminologies). Specialized lexicography has become an area of intense activity. The number of works is multiplying in all sectors and in all language combinations.

e) *The Stoddart Colour Visual Dictionary*

The Stoddart Colour Visual Dictionary is a terminology-oriented dictionary. It is aimed at providing members of the general public with the specific terms they need to name the objects of daily life, and helping them grasp the meaning of words through illustrations. Grouped together in interlocking categories, the various elements are interdefined. The dictionary is thus organized according to themes, subjects, specific objects, and features of these objects. Depending on a person's degree of familiarity with a given theme, the terminology may seem simple or technical. The fundamental goal, however, is to provide non-specialists with a coherent analysis of useful, necessary vocabulary for each subject.

The Stoddart Colour Visual Dictionary is not an encyclopædia, for at least two reasons: rather than describing objects, it names them; in addition, it avoids listing all the objects in a given category. For example, rather than enumerating the various types of trees, it focuses on a typical representative of the category, and examines its structure and individual parts.

It bears even less resemblance to a language dictionary, for it contains no written definitions and covers only nouns and, in particular, noun phrases.

Nor is it a compendium of specialized vocabularies; it avoids terminology used only by specialists, focusing instead on more widespread terms—at the risk of being considered simplistic by experts in specific fields.

This is the first terminology-oriented dictionary to group together in a single volume the thousands of technical and not-so-technical terms most commonly used in a society where science, technology, and their end products are part of everyday life.

Such is the editorial policy that has guided us in creating this dictionary. Consequently, the number of words it contains does not have the same significance as for a language dictionary, for several reasons: in keeping with our editorial policy, we have deliberately chosen to limit the number of words; unlike conventional dictionaries, this work focuses exclusively on nouns, the most significant words in the language; and finally, no one is sure exactly how to count compound terms!

COMPUTER-PRODUCED ILLUSTRATIONS

The illustrations in *The Stoddart Colour Visual Dictionary* have been created by computer from recent documents and original photographs. The use of computers has given the illustrations a highly realistic, almost photographic look, allowing us to highlight the essential features corresponding to the vocabulary. The graphic precision of this dictionary is one of the main reasons for its excellence as an encyclopædic and lexicographical reference tool.

In addition, thanks to computers, we have been able to improve the accuracy of the lines joining objects to their names, thus enhancing the clarity of the link between words and the things they describe.

CAREFULLY ESTABLISHED VOCABULARY

In creating this dictionary, we have used the method of systematic and comparative terminological research, which is standard practice among professionals who prepare works of this type. This method comprises several logical steps, briefly described in the following paragraphs.

Field delimitation

First of all, we defined the scope and contents of the proposed work. We began by choosing the themes we felt it should cover. We then divided each theme into fields and subfields, taking care to abide by our editorial policy of avoiding overspecialization and the temptation to cover all subjects in detail. This step resulted in a working table of contents, the framework of the dictionary, which guided our subsequent steps and was refined as the work progressed. The Detailed Table of Contents is the result of this process.

Documentary research

Next, we assembled pertinent documents likely to provide us with the required information about words and notions in each subject matter. In order of reliability, our documentary sources were as follows:

• Articles and books by experts in the various fields, written in their native language, with an acceptable degree of specialization. (Translations of such texts provide revealing information about vocabulary usage, but must be used with caution.)

• Technical documents, such as national standards or the guidelines of the International Standard Organization (ISO), product instructions, technical documents provided by manufacturers, official government publications, etc.

• Catalogues, commercial texts, advertisements from specialized magazines and major newspapers;

• Encyclopædias, encyclopædic dictionaries, and unilingual language dictionaries.

• Unilingual, bilingual, and multilingual specialized vocabularies and dictionaries.

• Bilingual and multilingual language dictionaries.

In all, we consulted four to five thousand references. The selected bibliography included in the dictionary indicates only the general documentary sources consulted and does not include specialized sources.

Sifting through the documents

A terminologist went through the documents for each subject, searching for specific notions and the words used to express them by different authors and works. Gradually, a framework was established as the terminologist noted the use of the same term for a given concept from one source to another. Where there were several terms for the same idea, the terminologist continued his research until he was able to form a well-documented opinion of each competing term. All of this research was recorded, with reference notes.

Creation of terminology files

The preceding step enabled us to assemble all of the elements for our terminology files. Each notion, identified and defined by an illustration, was paired with the term most frequently used to describe it by the leading authors or in the most reliable sources. Where several competing terms were found in the reference material, the terminologist and the scientific director assessed each and agreed on a single term.

Terminological variants

Frequently, several words may be used to designate the same notion. We dealt with such situations as follows:

• In some cases, a term was used by one author only or appeared just once in our documentary sources. We retained the most frequently used competing term.

• Technical terms are often compound words, with or without a hyphen, or several-word expressions. This results in at least two types of terminological variants:

a) The compound technical term may be shortened by the deletion of one or more of its elements, especially where the meaning is clear in the context. The shortened expression may even become the normal term for the notion. In such cases, we retained the compound form, leaving users the freedom to abbreviate it according to the context.

b) An element of the compound term may itself have equivalents (most often synonyms from the commonly spoken language). We retained the most frequently used form.

• Variants may stem from the evolution of the language, without terminological consequences. We therefore retained the most contemporary or well-known form.

TERMINOLOGICAL APPROACH

Language dictionaries have a long history and a well-established, widely known and accepted tradition. They are familiar reference works, used by most people since early school age. We all know how to consult a dictionary and interpret the information it provides—or fails to provide.

Terminological dictionaries are either very recent or intended for a specialized public. There is no solid tradition to guide those who design and produce such works. Although specialists know how to interpret dictionaries pertaining to their own fields, the same cannot be said for laymen, who are confused by variants. Whereas language dictionaries have, to a certain extent, established standard word usage among their users, specialized vocabularies are characterized by competing terms in new fields of specialization.

Users of a reference work such as *The Stoddart Colour Visual Dictionary* should take into account these elements in assessing this new type of reference tool.

Jean-Claude Corbeil
Ariane Archambault

THE HEADING •
identifies the subject matter of each page.

THE SUBHEADING •
indicates the object analysed by the vocabulary.

THE THEME •
of the dictionary section is shown in the side margin on each page.

Find the correct term for an object by flipping to the Table of Contents, which lists the dictionary themes, headings, and subheadings, with the first-page reference for each heading.

THE COLOUR ILLUSTRATION •
realistically depicts the object and its component parts.

You may also flip through the dictionary for sheer pleasure and to enhance your vocabulary.

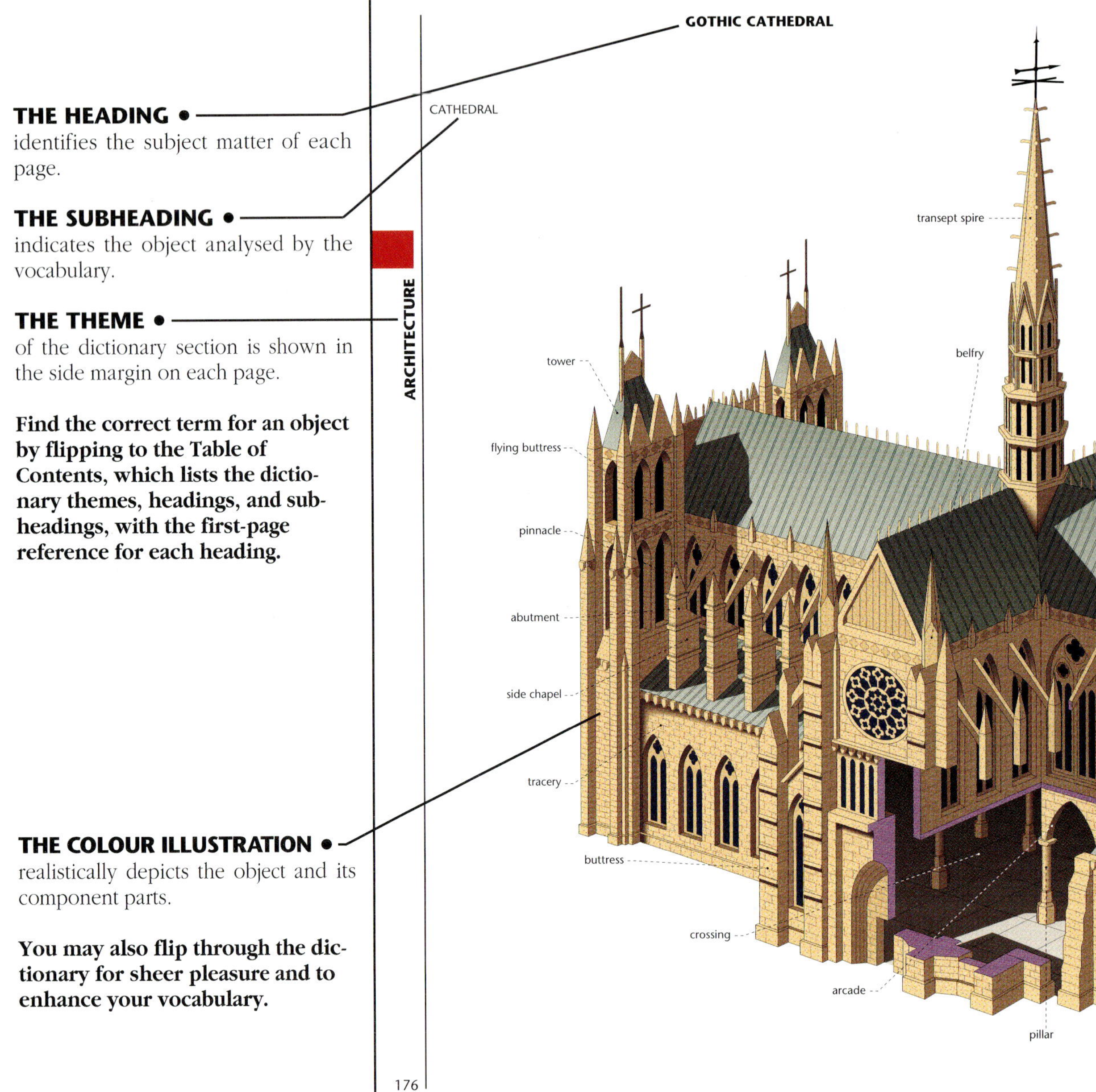

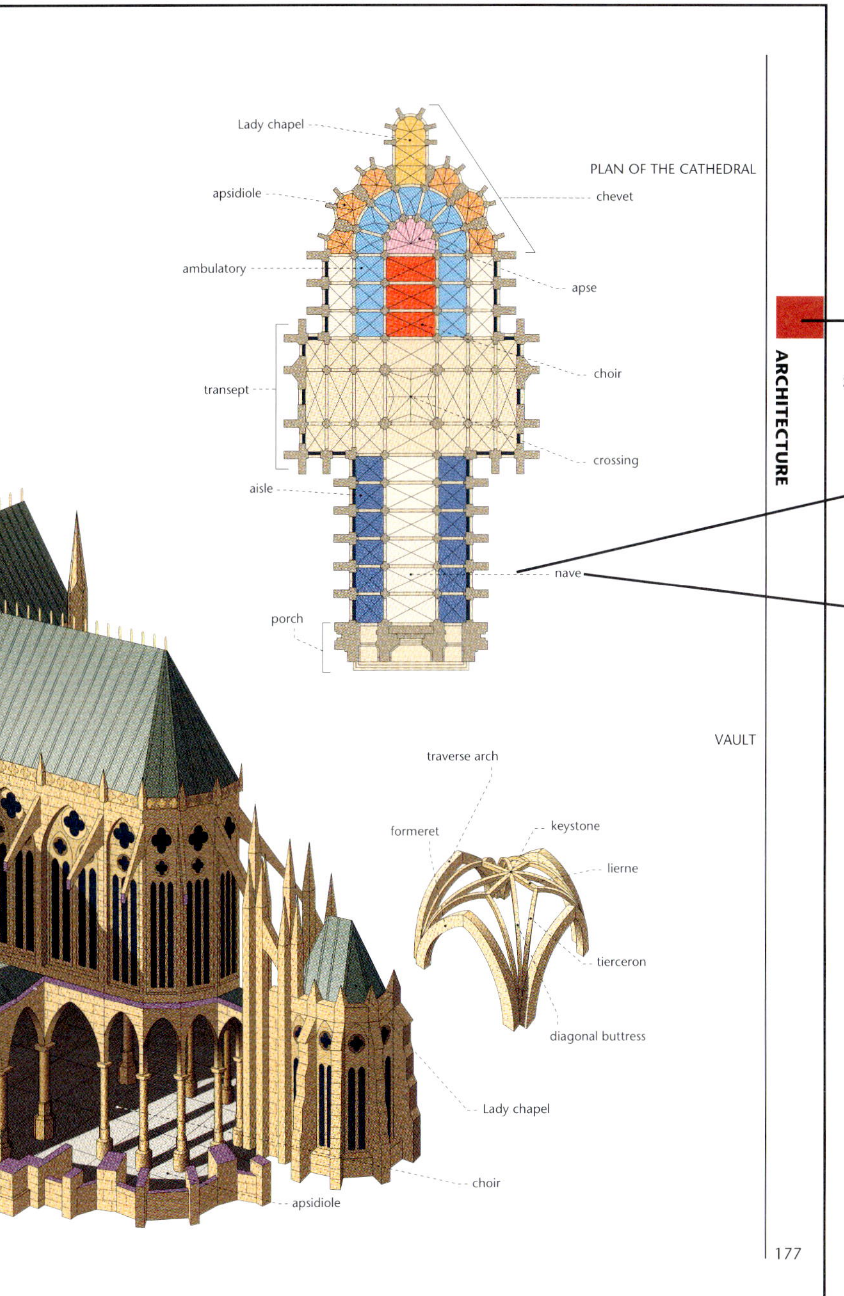

• THE COLOURED PAGE EDGE

corresponds to the individual theme, as shown in the Summary. This colour-coding allows you to find the subject you are looking for, at a glance.

• THE LINE

links the word with the object it describes.

• EACH WORD

is included in the Index, with references to all the pages where it appears.

Find the object described by a word, by consulting the Index.

177

REFERENCE BOOKS

DICTIONARIES
• *Gage Canadian Dictionary,* Toronto, Gage Publishing
  Limited, 1983, 1313 p.
• *The New Britannica/Webster Dictionary and Reference Guide,*
  Chicago, Toronto, Encyclopedia Britannica, 1981, 1505 p.
• *The Oxford English Dictionary,* second edition, Oxford,
  Clarendon Press, 1989, 20 vol.
• *The Oxford Illustrated Dictionary,* Oxford, Clarendon Press,
  1967, 974 p.
• *Oxford American Dictionary,* Eugene Ehrlich and al.,
  New York, Oxford, Oxford University Press, 1980, 816 p.
• *The Random House Dictionary of the English Language,*
  the unabridged edition, New York, 1983, 2059 p.
• *Webster's Encyclopedic Unabridged Dictionary of the English
  Language,* New York, Portland House, 1989, 2078 p.
• *Webster's Third New International Dictionary,* Springfield,
  Merriam-Webster, 1986, 2662 p.
• *Webster's Ninth New Collegiate Dictionary,* Springfield,
  Merriam-Webster, 1984, 1563 p.
• *Webster's New World Dictionary of American Language,*
  New York, The World Pub., 1953.

ENCYCLOPÆDIAS
• *Academic American Encyclopedia,* Princeton,
  Arete Publishing Company, 1980, 21 vol.
• *Architectural Graphic Standards,* eighth edition,
  New York, John Wiley & Sons, 1988, 854 p.
• *Chamber's Encyclopedia,* new rev. edition, London,
  International Learning System, !989.
• *Collier's Encyclopedia,* New York, Macmillan Educational
  Company, 1984, 24 vol.
• *Compton's Encyclopedia,* Chicago, F.E. Compton Company,
  Division of Encyclopedia Britannica Inc., 1982, 26 vol.
• *Encyclopedia Americana,* Danbury, Internationaled.,
  Conn.: Grolier, 1981, 30 vol.
• *How it works, The illustrated science and invention
  encyclopedia,* New York, H.S. Stuttman, 1977, 21 vol.
• *McGraw-Hill Encyclopedia of Science & Technology,*
  New York, McGraw-Hill Book Company, 1982, 15 vol.
• *Merit Students Encyclopedia,* New York, Macmillan
  Educational Company, 1984, 20 vol.
• *New Encyclopedia Britannica,* Chicago, Toronto,
  Encyclopedia Britannica, 1985, 32 vol.
• *The Joy of Knowledge Encyclopedia,* London, Mitchell
  Beazley Encyclopedias, 1976, 7 vol.
• *The Random House Encyclopedia,* New York, Random
  House, 1977, 2 vol.
• *The World Book Encyclopedia,* Chicago, Field Enterprises
  Educational Corporation, 1973.

FRENCH AND ENGLISH DICTIONARIES:
• Collins-Robert, *French-English, English-French Dictionary,*
  London, Glasgow, Cleveland, Toronto, 1978, 781 p.
• Dubois, Marguerite, *Dictionnaire moderne français-anglais,*
  Paris, Larousse, 1978, 752 p.
• Harrap's *New Standard French and English Dictionary,*
  part one, French-English, London, 1977, 2 vol.,
  part two, English-French, London, 1983, 2 vol.
• Harrap's *Shorter French and English Dictionary,* London,
  Toronto, Willington, Sydney, 1953, 940 p.

CONTENTS

CONTENTS

CONTENTS

XX

CONTENTS

CONTENTS

CONTENTS

CONTENTS

CONTENTS

LIST OF CHAPTERS

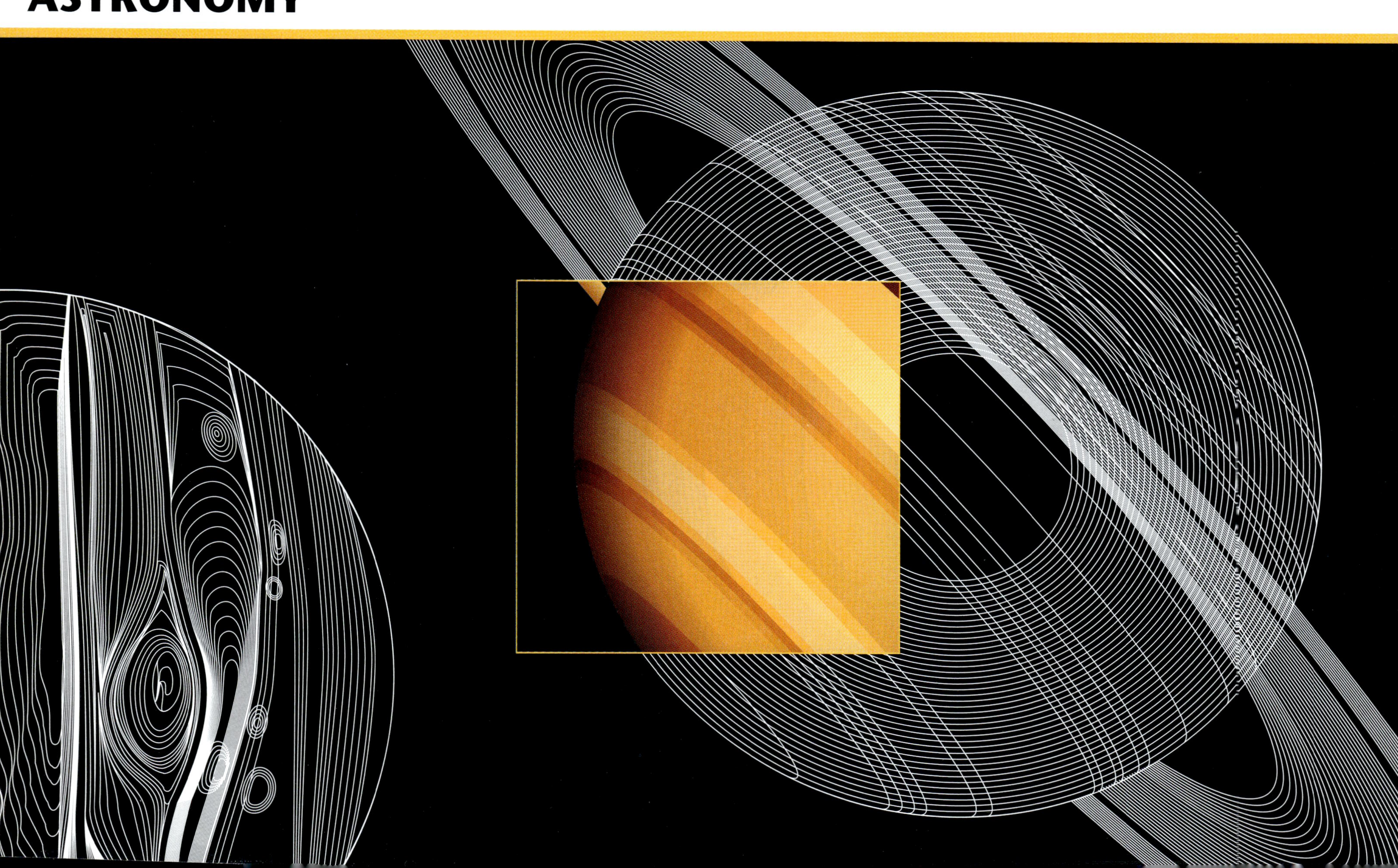

ASTRONOMY

CONTENTS

CELESTIAL COORDINATE SYSTEM

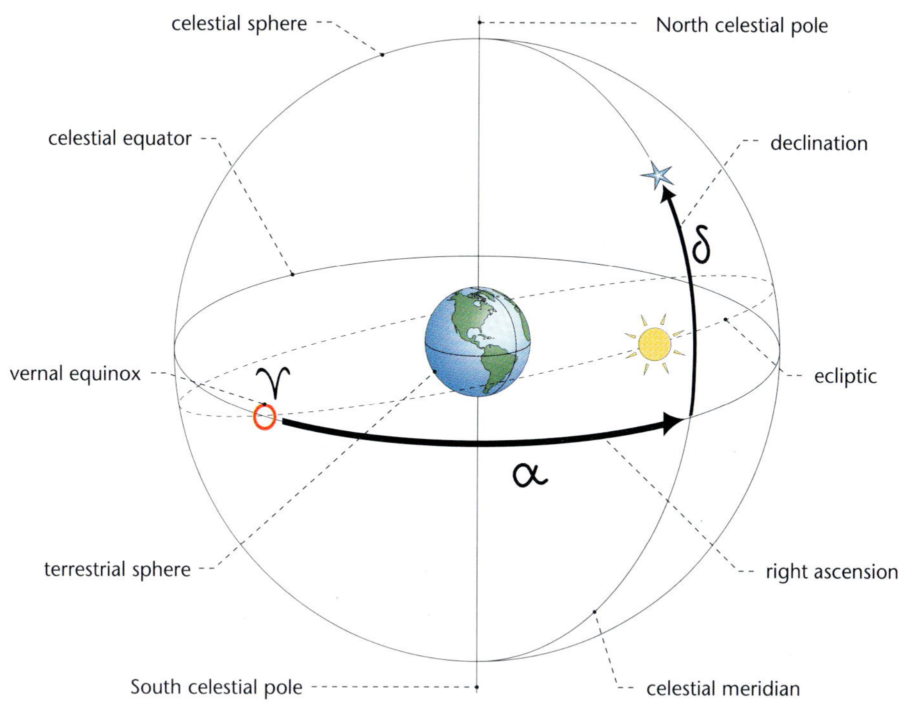

EARTH COORDINATE SYSTEM

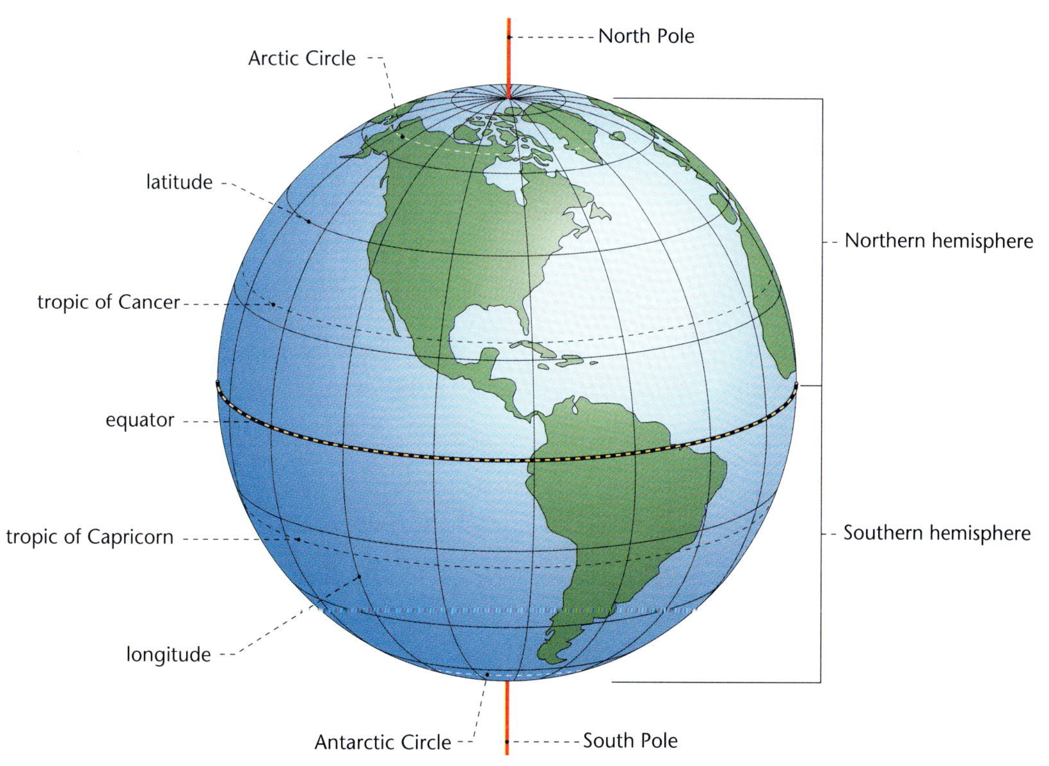

PLANETS AND MOONS

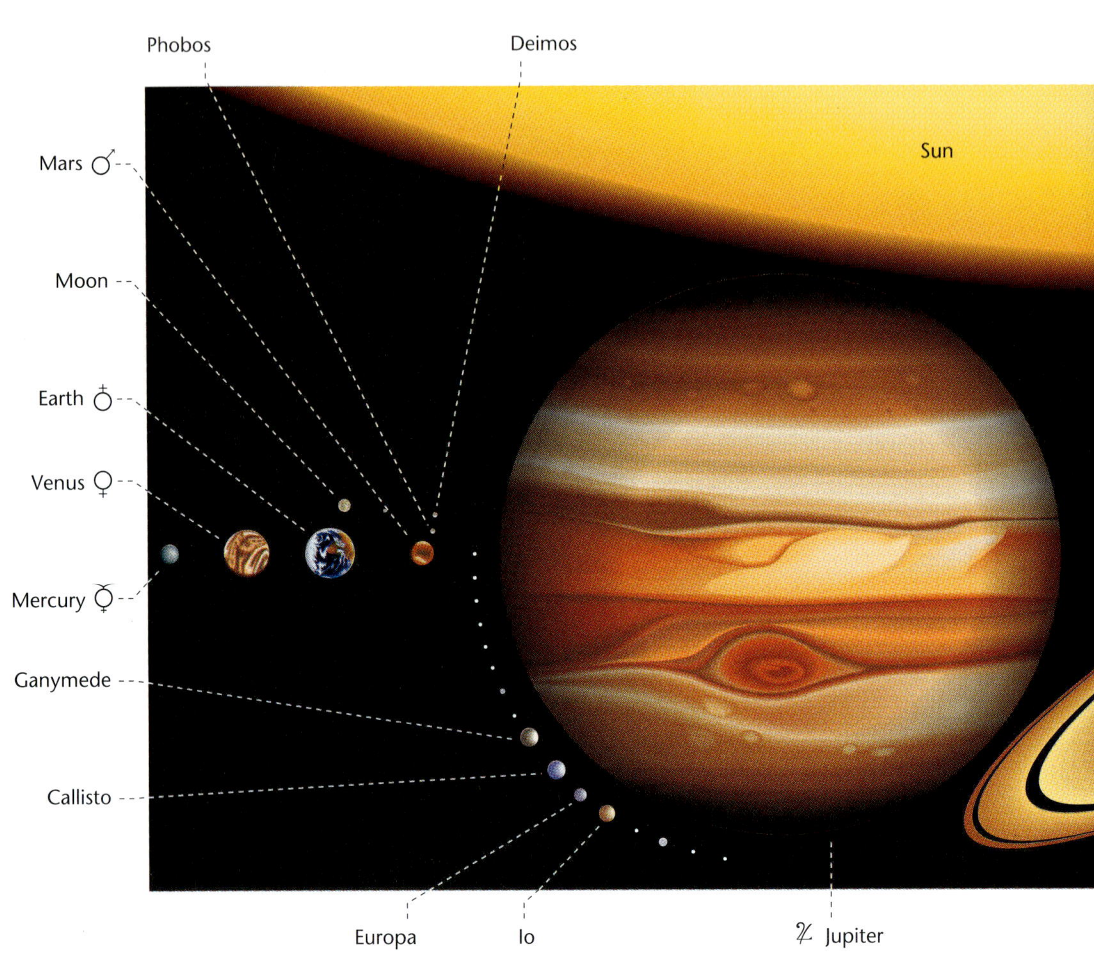

ORBITS OF THE PLANETS

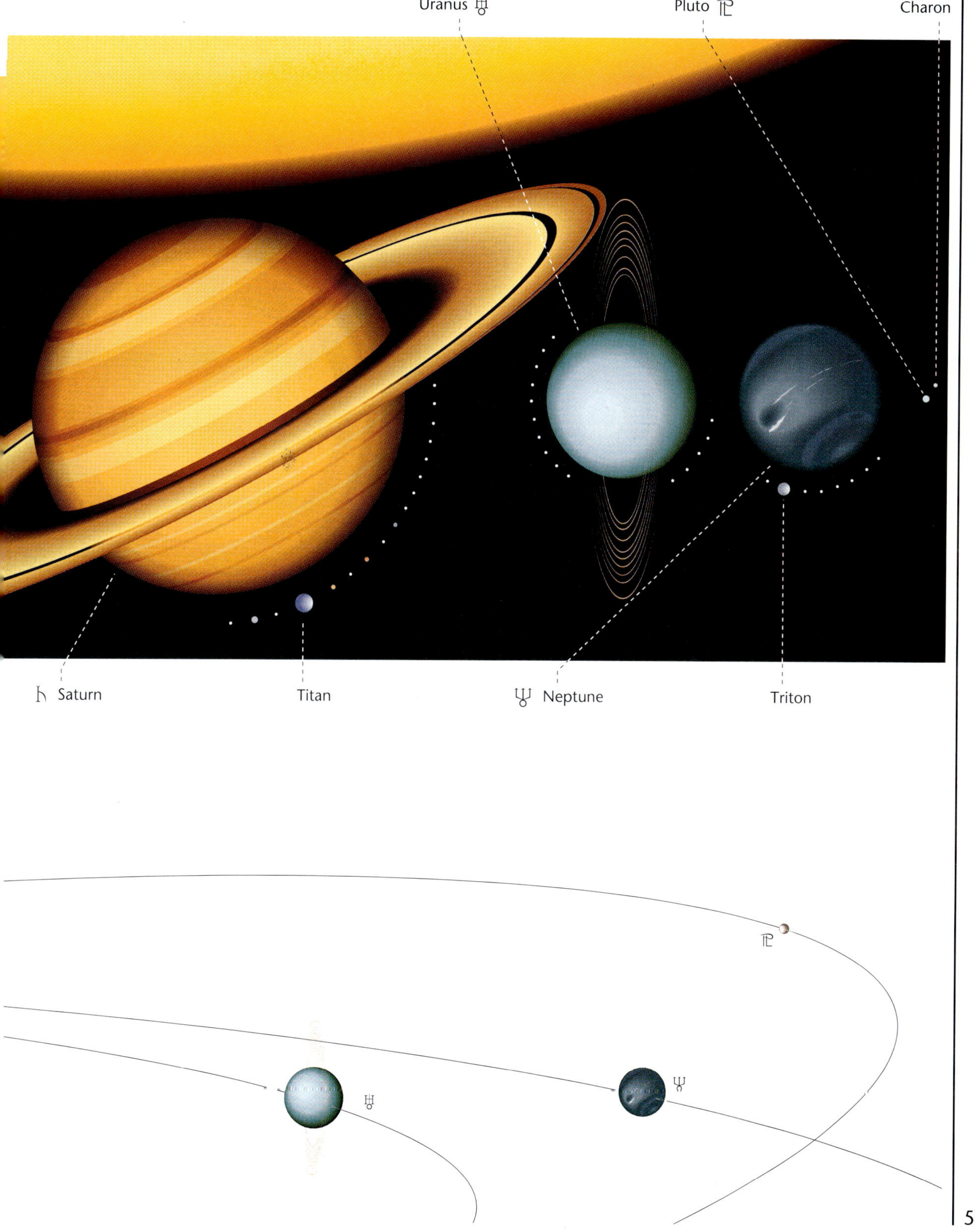

Uranus ⛢
Pluto ♇
Charon
♄ Saturn
Titan
♆ Neptune
Triton
♇
⛢
♆

SUN

STRUCTURE OF THE SUN

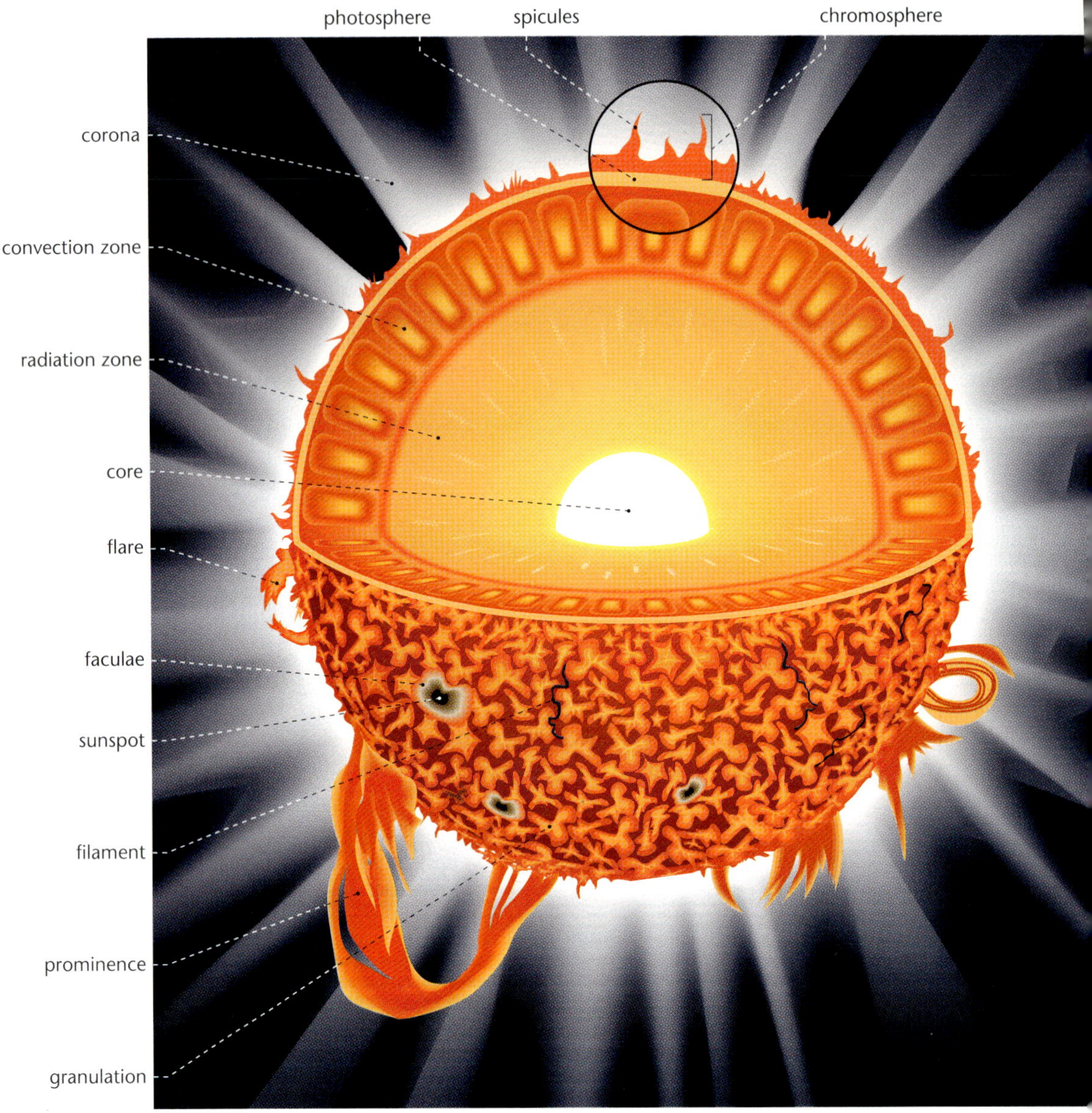

PHASES OF THE MOON

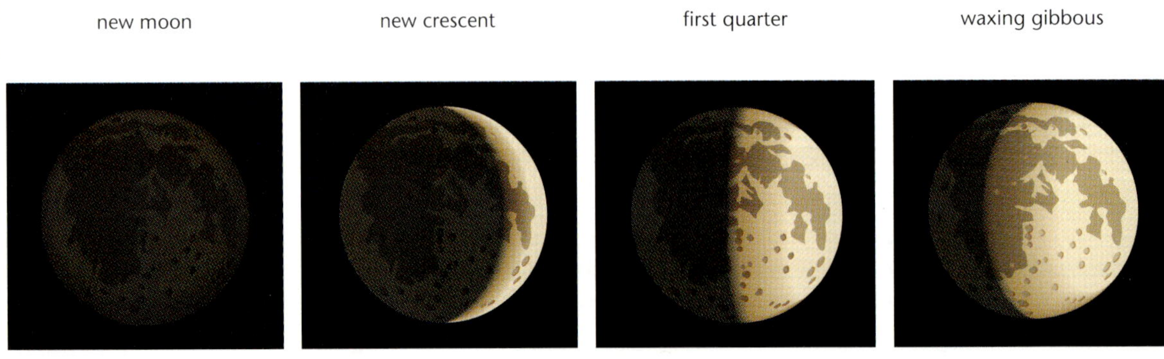

MOON

LUNAR FEATURES

cliff
bay
ocean
lake
sea
mountain range
cirque
wall
crater

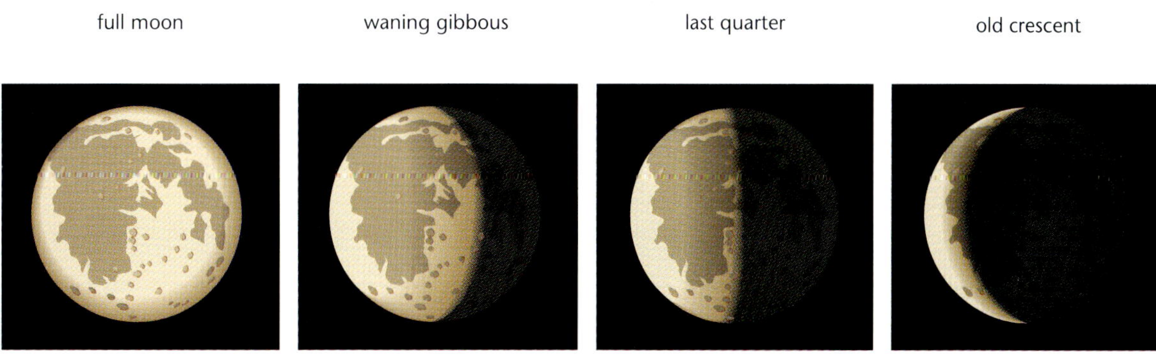

full moon
waning gibbous
last quarter
old crescent

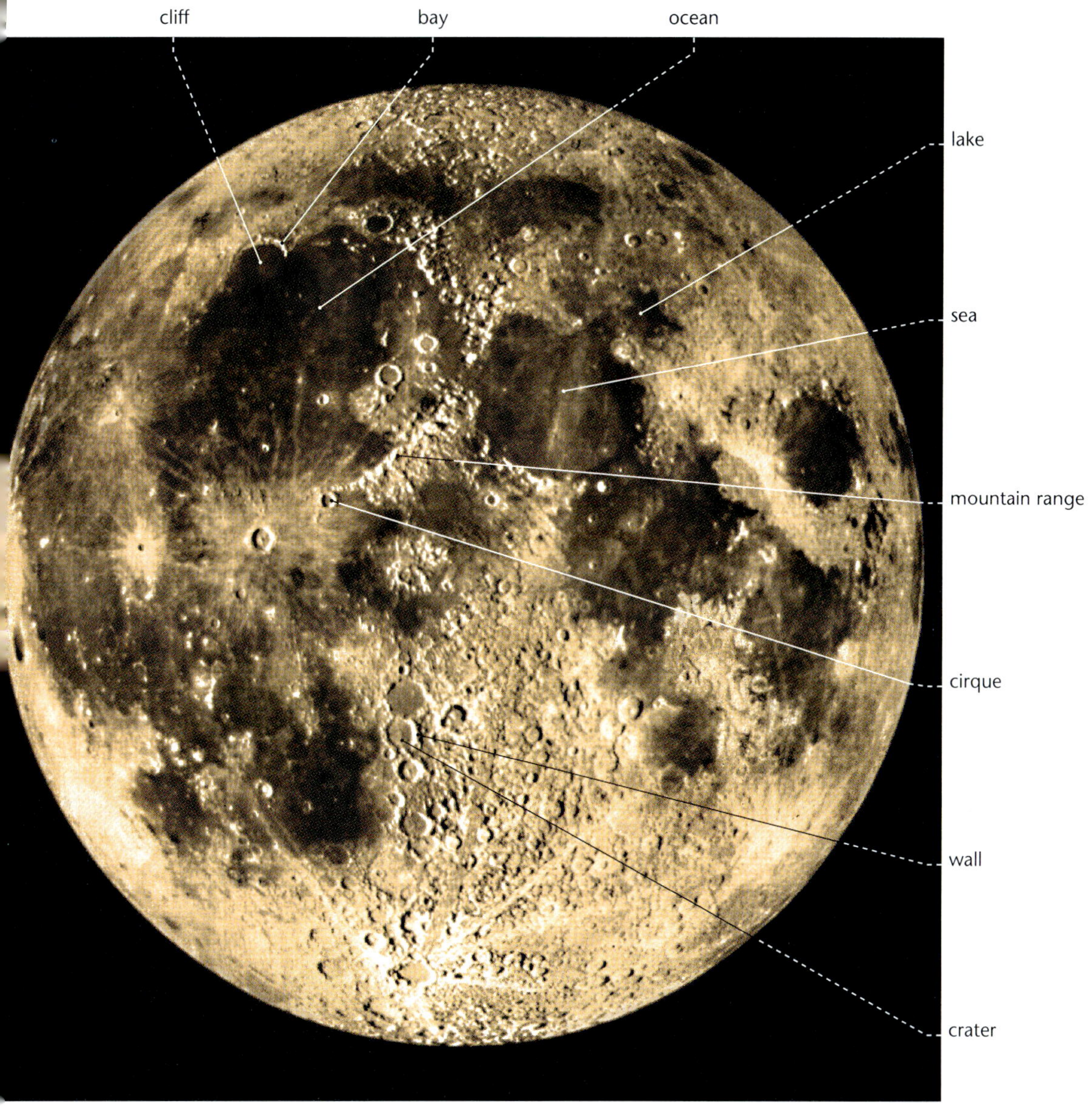

SOLAR ECLIPSE

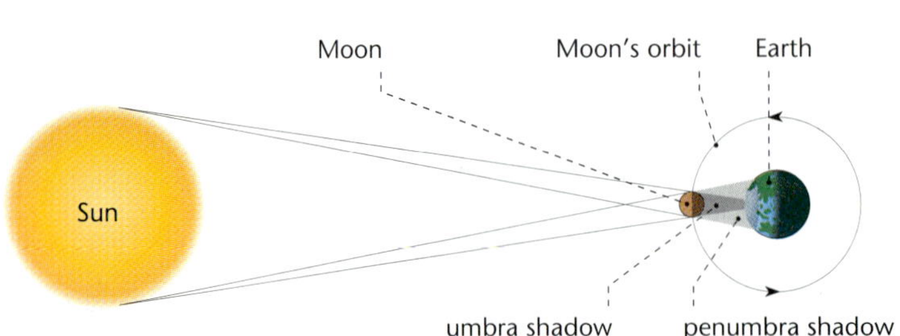

TYPES OF ECLIPSES

total eclipse 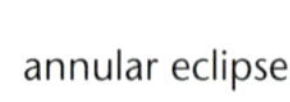 

annular eclipse  

partial eclipse

LUNAR ECLIPSE

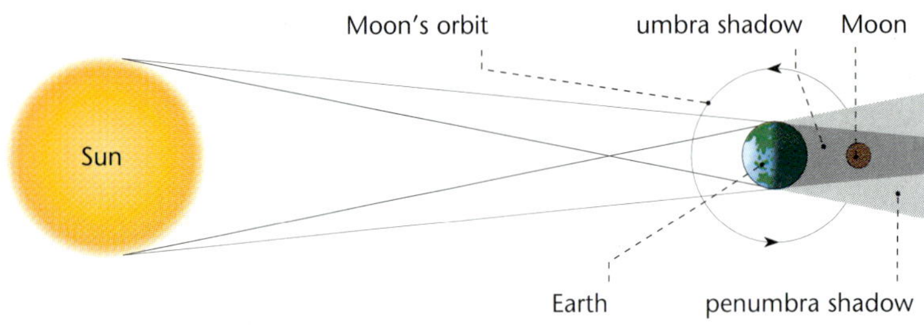

TYPES OF ECLIPSES

partial eclipse  

total eclipse 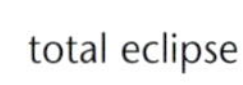 

SEASONS OF THE YEAR

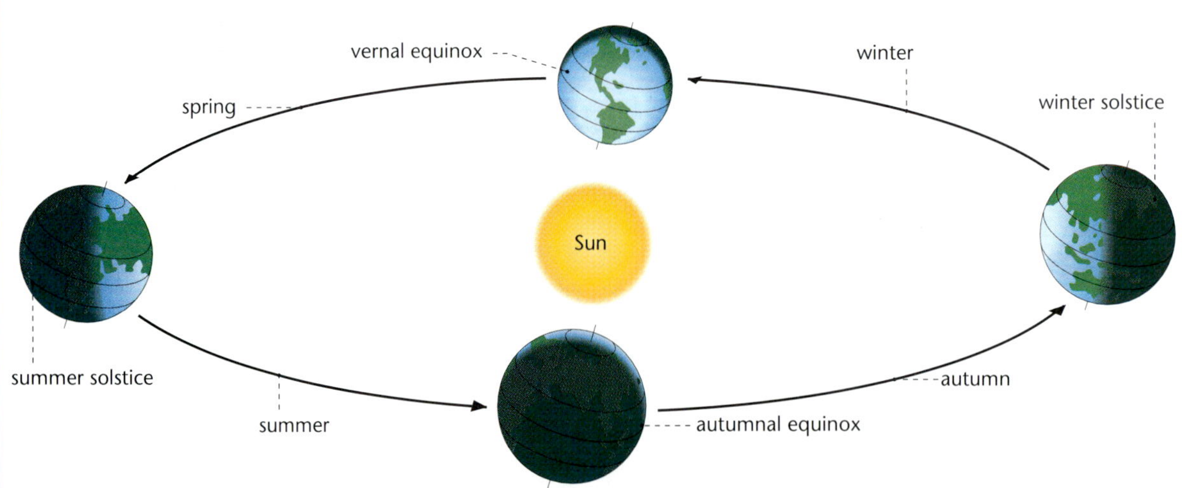

COMET

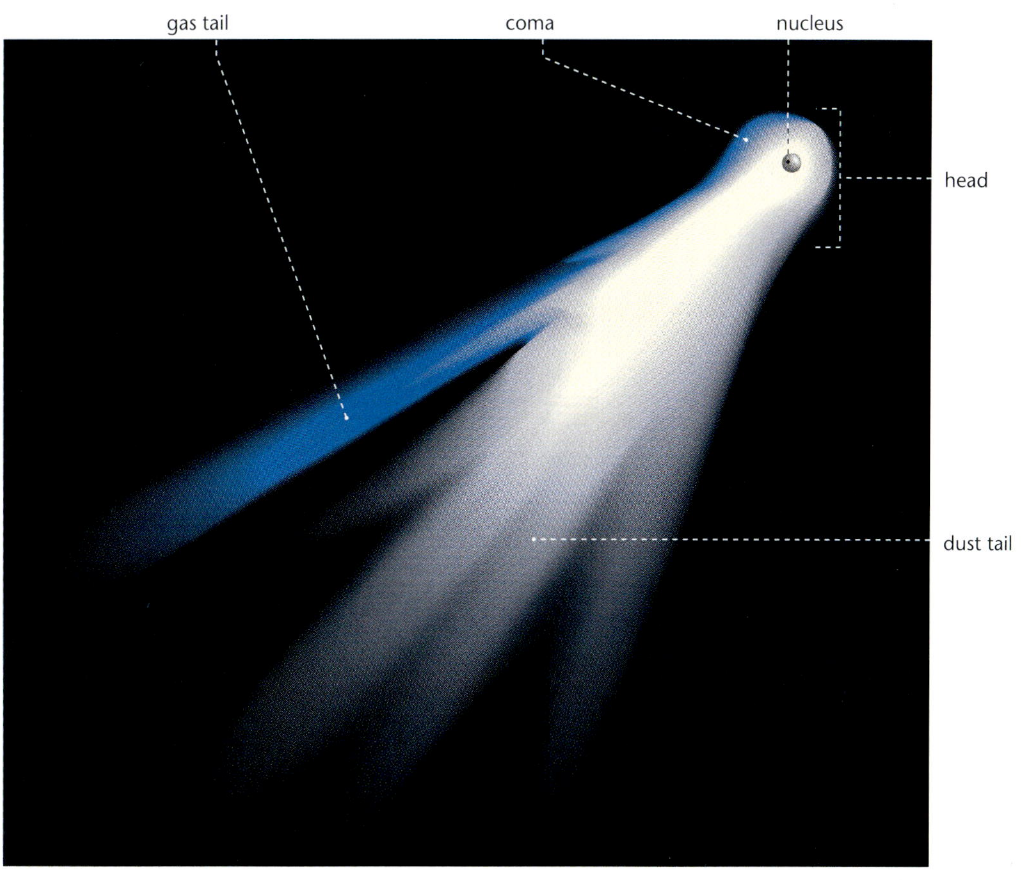

GALAXY

HUBBLE'S CLASSIFICATION

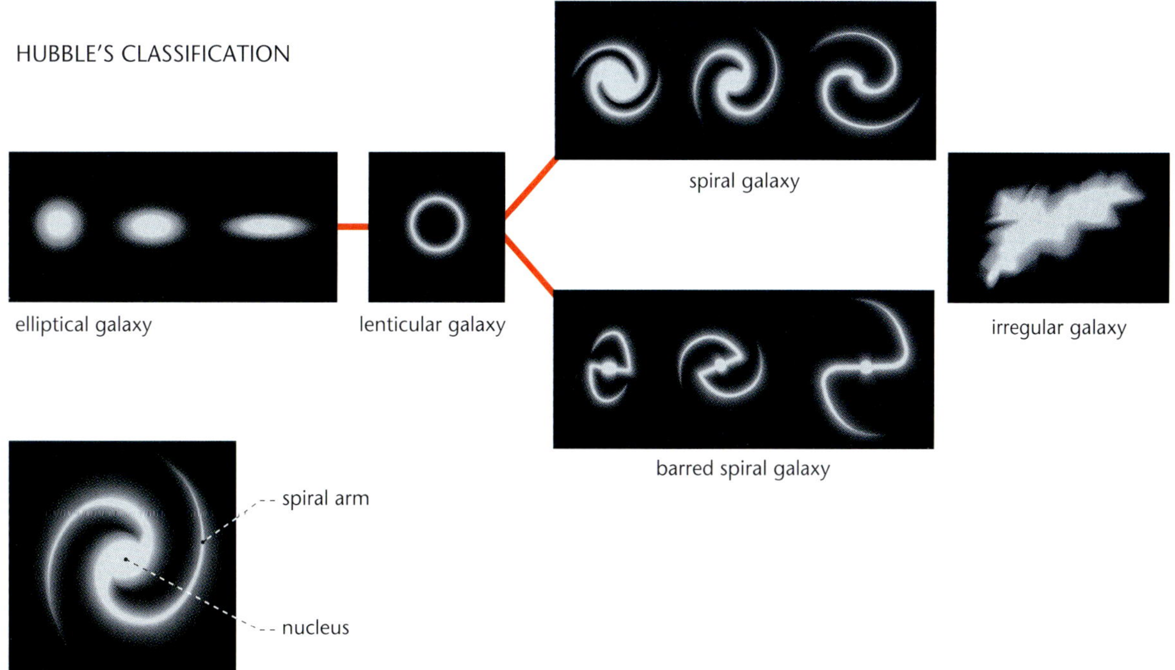

CONSTELLATIONS OF THE NORTHERN HEMISPHERE

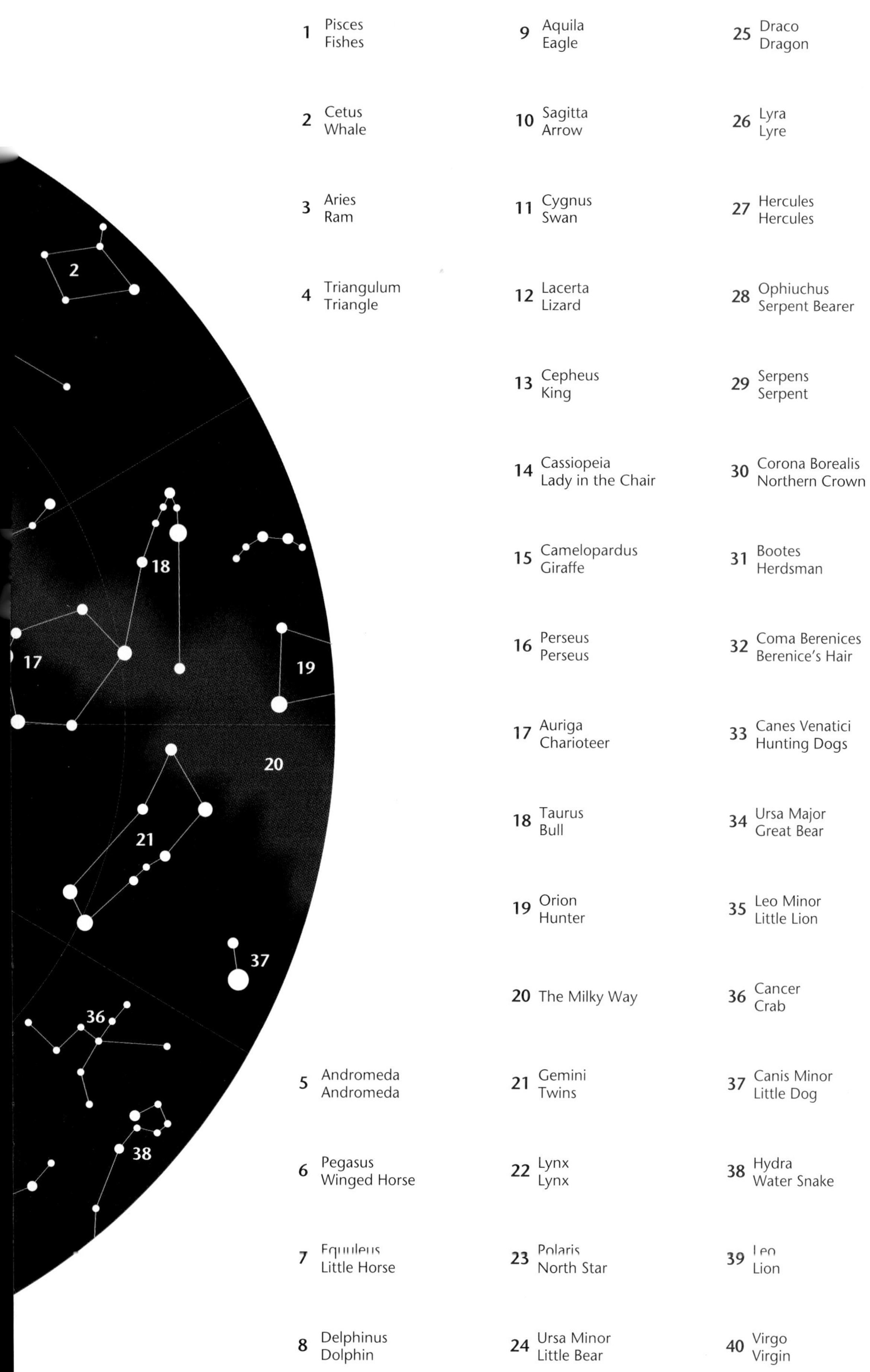

1	Pisces / Fishes	9	Aquila / Eagle	25	Draco / Dragon
2	Cetus / Whale	10	Sagitta / Arrow	26	Lyra / Lyre
3	Aries / Ram	11	Cygnus / Swan	27	Hercules / Hercules
4	Triangulum / Triangle	12	Lacerta / Lizard	28	Ophiuchus / Serpent Bearer
		13	Cepheus / King	29	Serpens / Serpent
		14	Cassiopeia / Lady in the Chair	30	Corona Borealis / Northern Crown
		15	Camelopardus / Giraffe	31	Bootes / Herdsman
		16	Perseus / Perseus	32	Coma Berenices / Berenice's Hair
		17	Auriga / Charioteer	33	Canes Venatici / Hunting Dogs
		18	Taurus / Bull	34	Ursa Major / Great Bear
		19	Orion / Hunter	35	Leo Minor / Little Lion
		20	The Milky Way	36	Cancer / Crab
5	Andromeda / Andromeda	21	Gemini / Twins	37	Canis Minor / Little Dog
6	Pegasus / Winged Horse	22	Lynx / Lynx	38	Hydra / Water Snake
7	Equuleus / Little Horse	23	Polaris / North Star	39	Leo / Lion
8	Delphinus / Dolphin	24	Ursa Minor / Little Bear	40	Virgo / Virgin

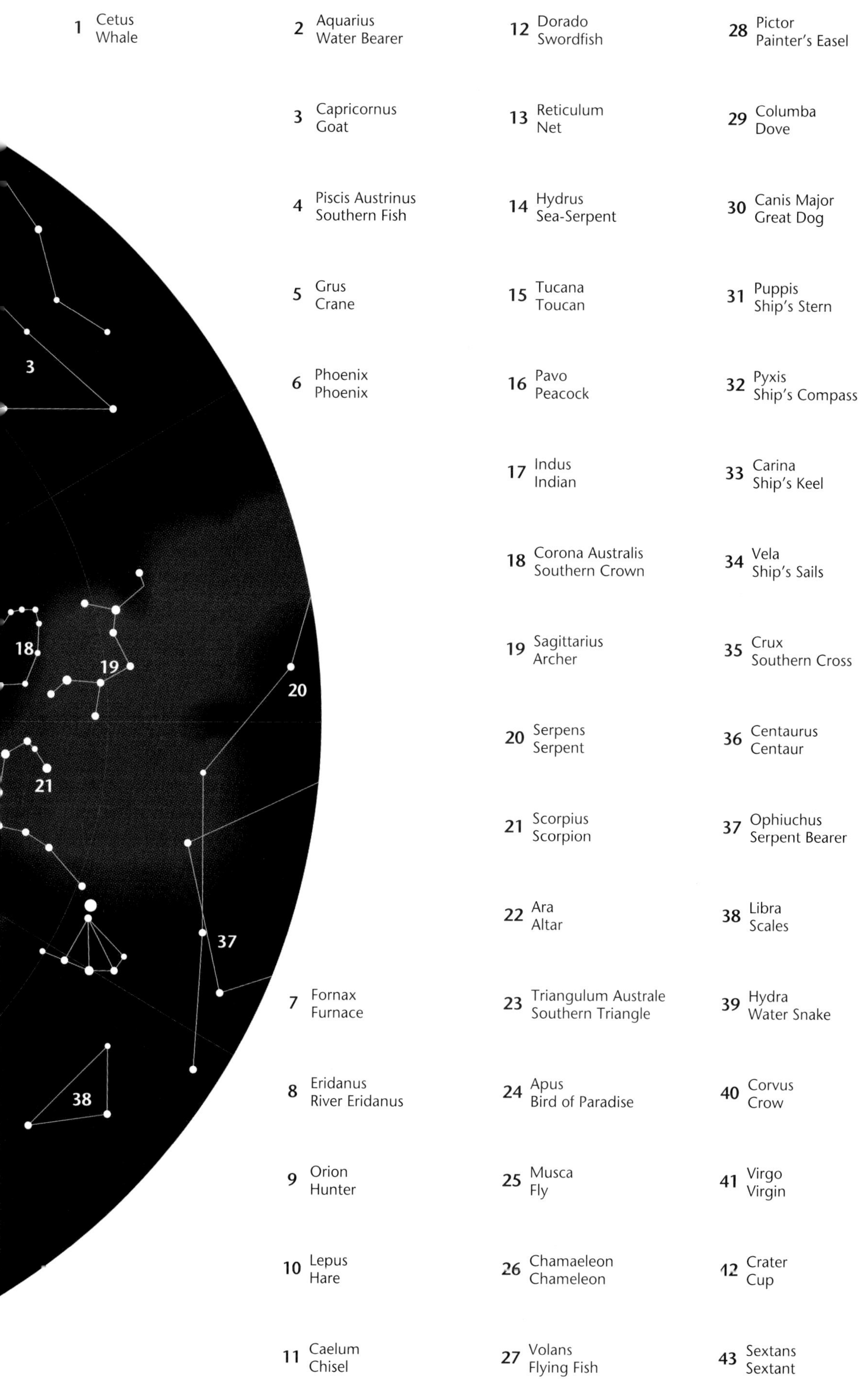

1 Cetus / Whale	2 Aquarius / Water Bearer	12 Dorado / Swordfish	28 Pictor / Painter's Easel
	3 Capricornus / Goat	13 Reticulum / Net	29 Columba / Dove
	4 Piscis Austrinus / Southern Fish	14 Hydrus / Sea-Serpent	30 Canis Major / Great Dog
	5 Grus / Crane	15 Tucana / Toucan	31 Puppis / Ship's Stern
	6 Phoenix / Phoenix	16 Pavo / Peacock	32 Pyxis / Ship's Compass
		17 Indus / Indian	33 Carina / Ship's Keel
		18 Corona Australis / Southern Crown	34 Vela / Ship's Sails
		19 Sagittarius / Archer	35 Crux / Southern Cross
		20 Serpens / Serpent	36 Centaurus / Centaur
		21 Scorpius / Scorpion	37 Ophiuchus / Serpent Bearer
		22 Ara / Altar	38 Libra / Scales
	7 Fornax / Furnace	23 Triangulum Australe / Southern Triangle	39 Hydra / Water Snake
	8 Eridanus / River Eridanus	24 Apus / Bird of Paradise	40 Corvus / Crow
	9 Orion / Hunter	25 Musca / Fly	41 Virgo / Virgin
	10 Lepus / Hare	26 Chamaeleon / Chameleon	42 Crater / Cup
	11 Caelum / Chisel	27 Volans / Flying Fish	43 Sextans / Sextant

13

ASTRONOMICAL OBSERVATORY

TELESCOPE

OBSERVATORY

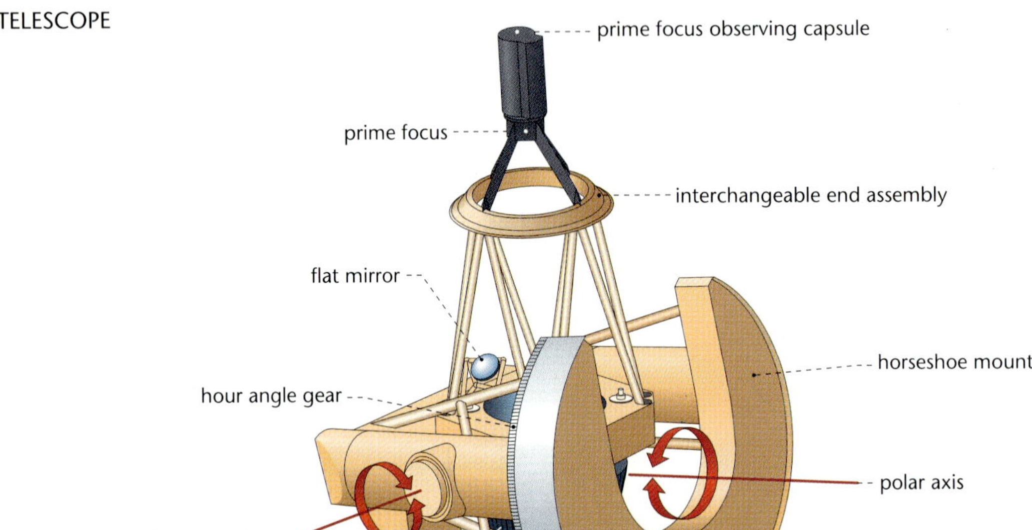

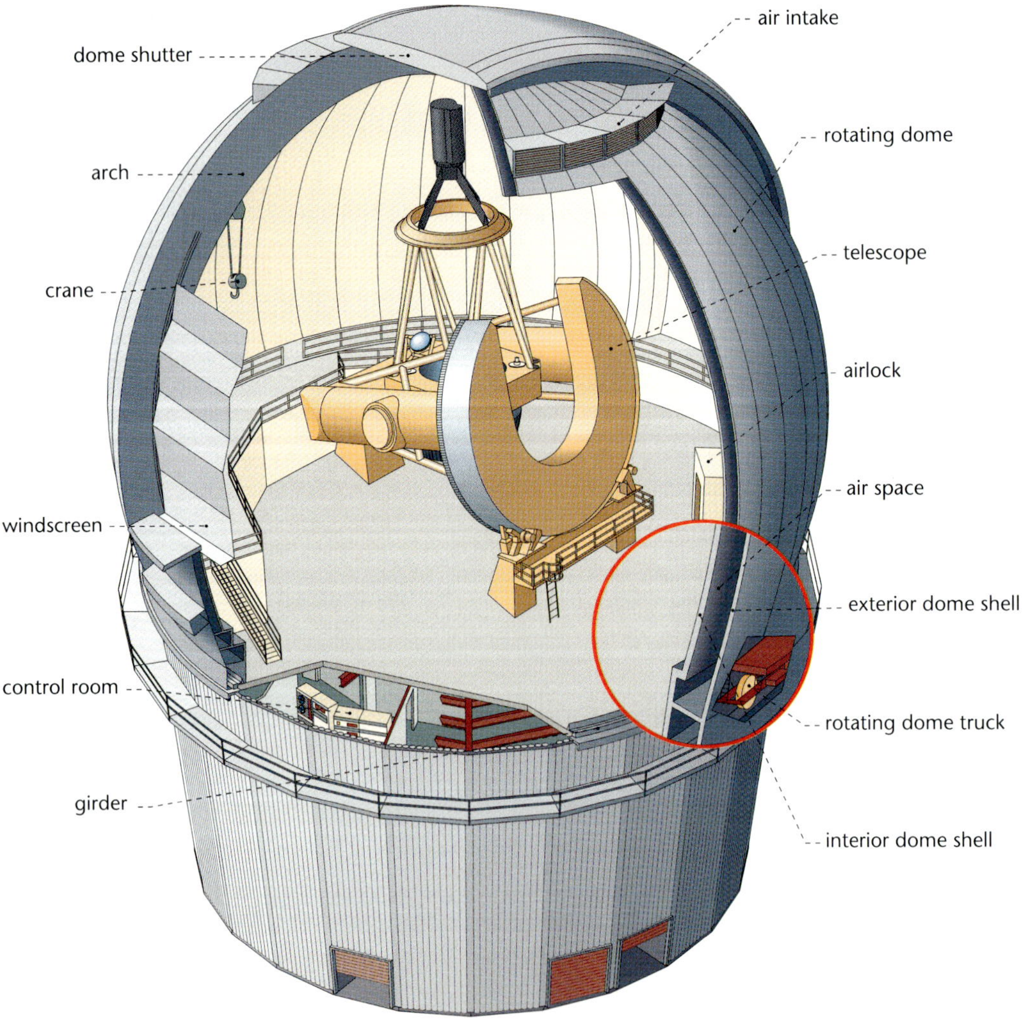

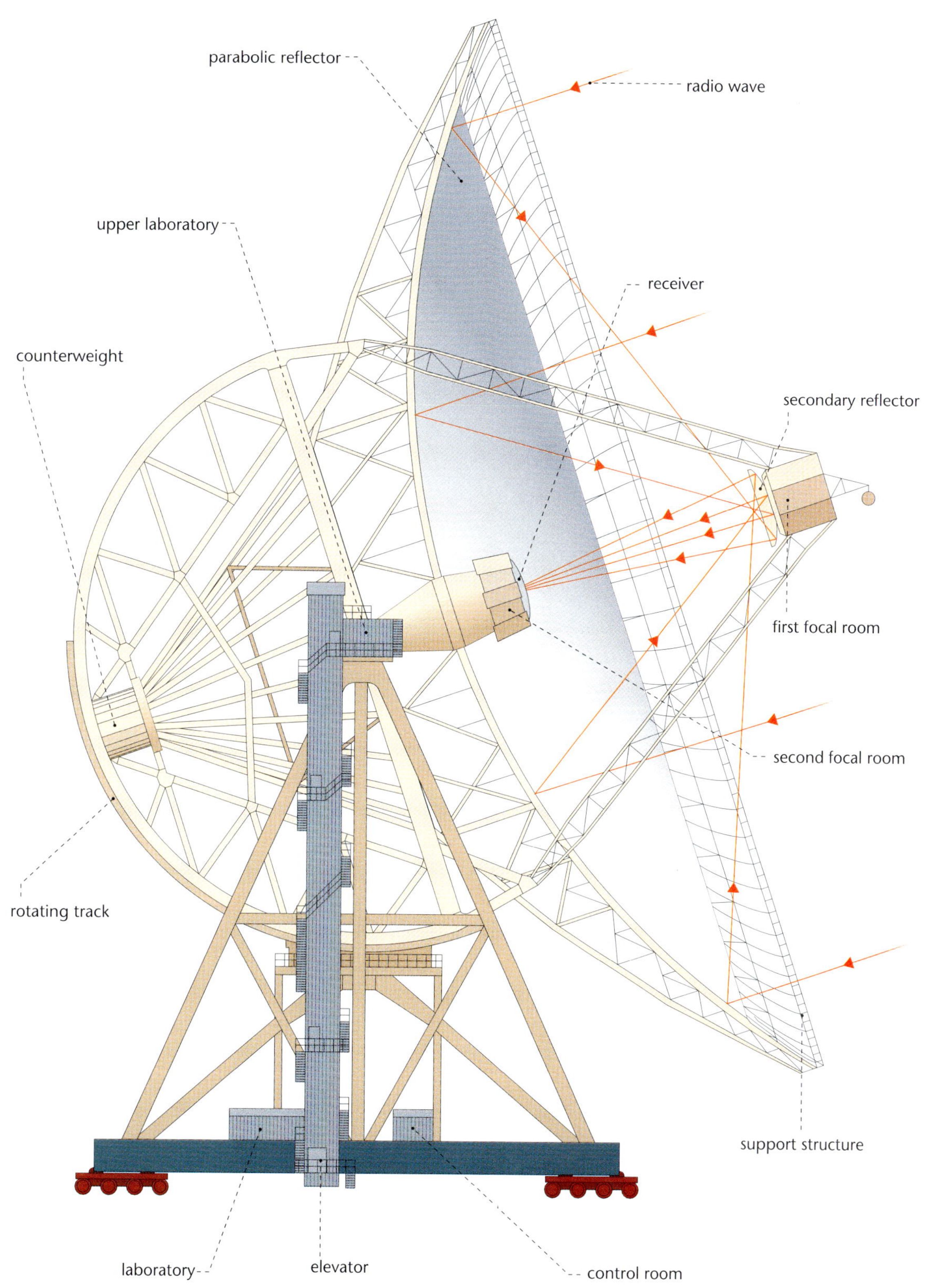
ALTAZIMUTH MOUNTING
parabolic reflector
radio wave
upper laboratory
receiver
counterweight
secondary reflector
first focal room
second focal room
rotating track
support structure
laboratory
elevator
control room

HUBBLE SPACE TELESCOPE

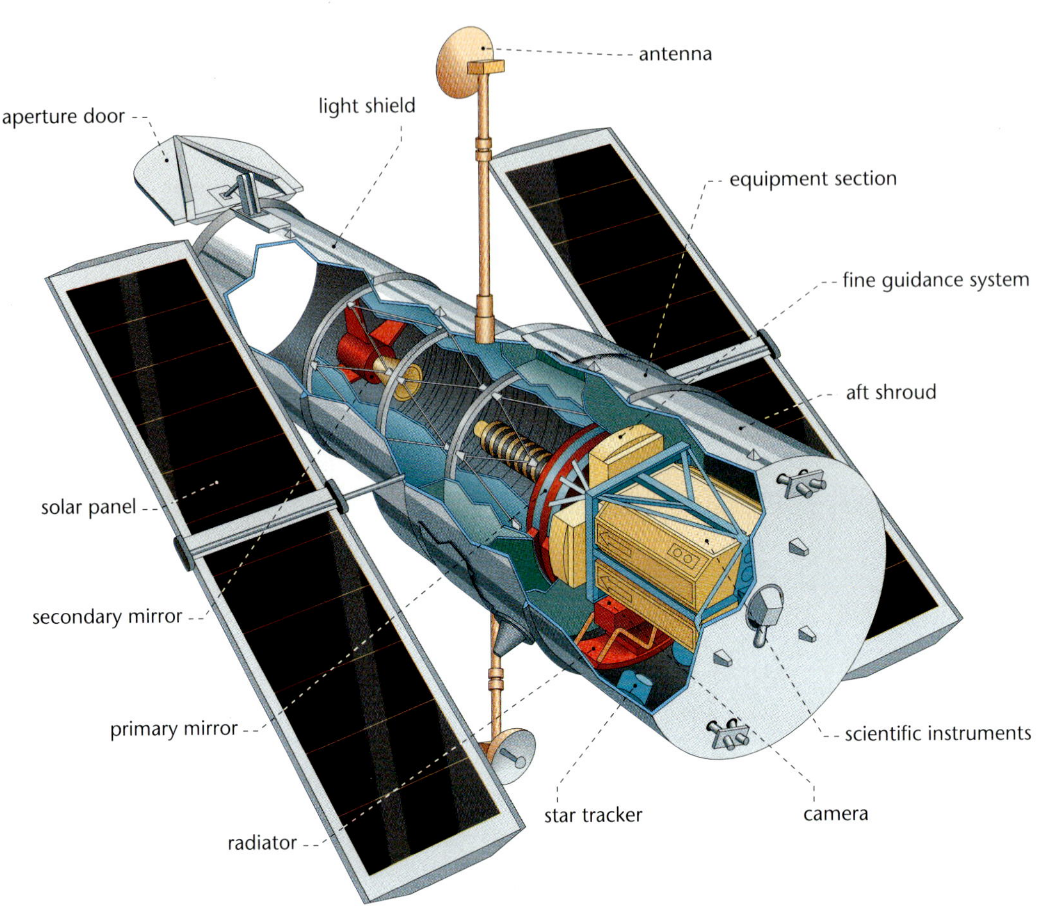

PLANETARIUM

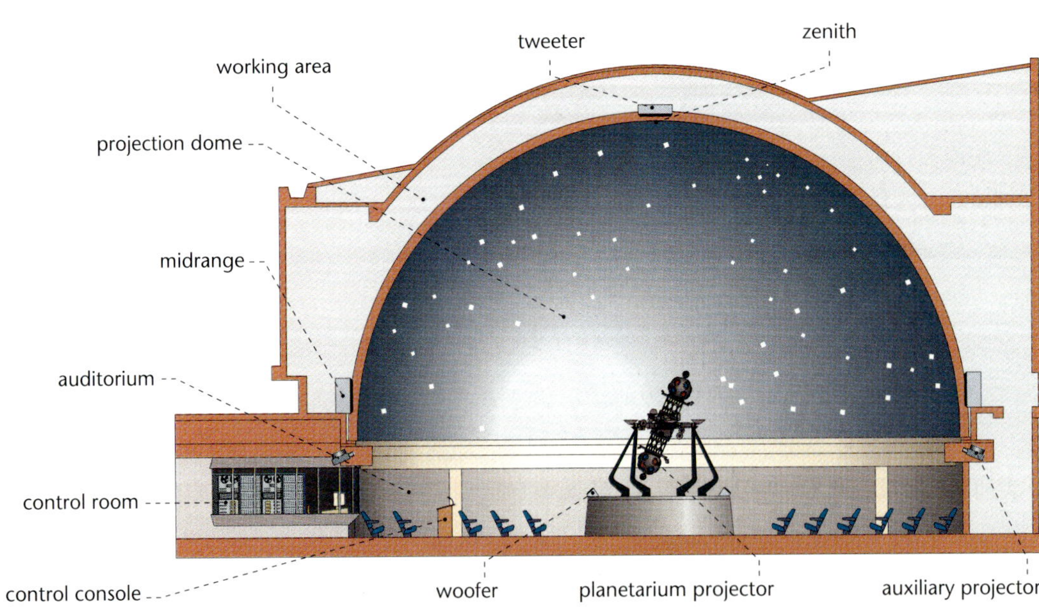

GEOGRAPHY
Wilmington
Pinehurst
Burlington
Woburn
Winchester
Lexington
Arlington
Belmont
Waltham
Watertown
Newton
Brookline
Cambridge
Somerville
Medford
Stoneham
Reading
Lynnfield
Wakefield
Melrose
Malden
Everett
Saugus
Chelsea
Revere
Winth
Lynn Harbo
Boston
Boston Harbor
Quincy Bay
Quincy
Dedham
Milton
Islington
Norwood
Braintree
Needham
Lake

CONTENTS

PROFILE OF THE EARTH'S ATMOSPHERE

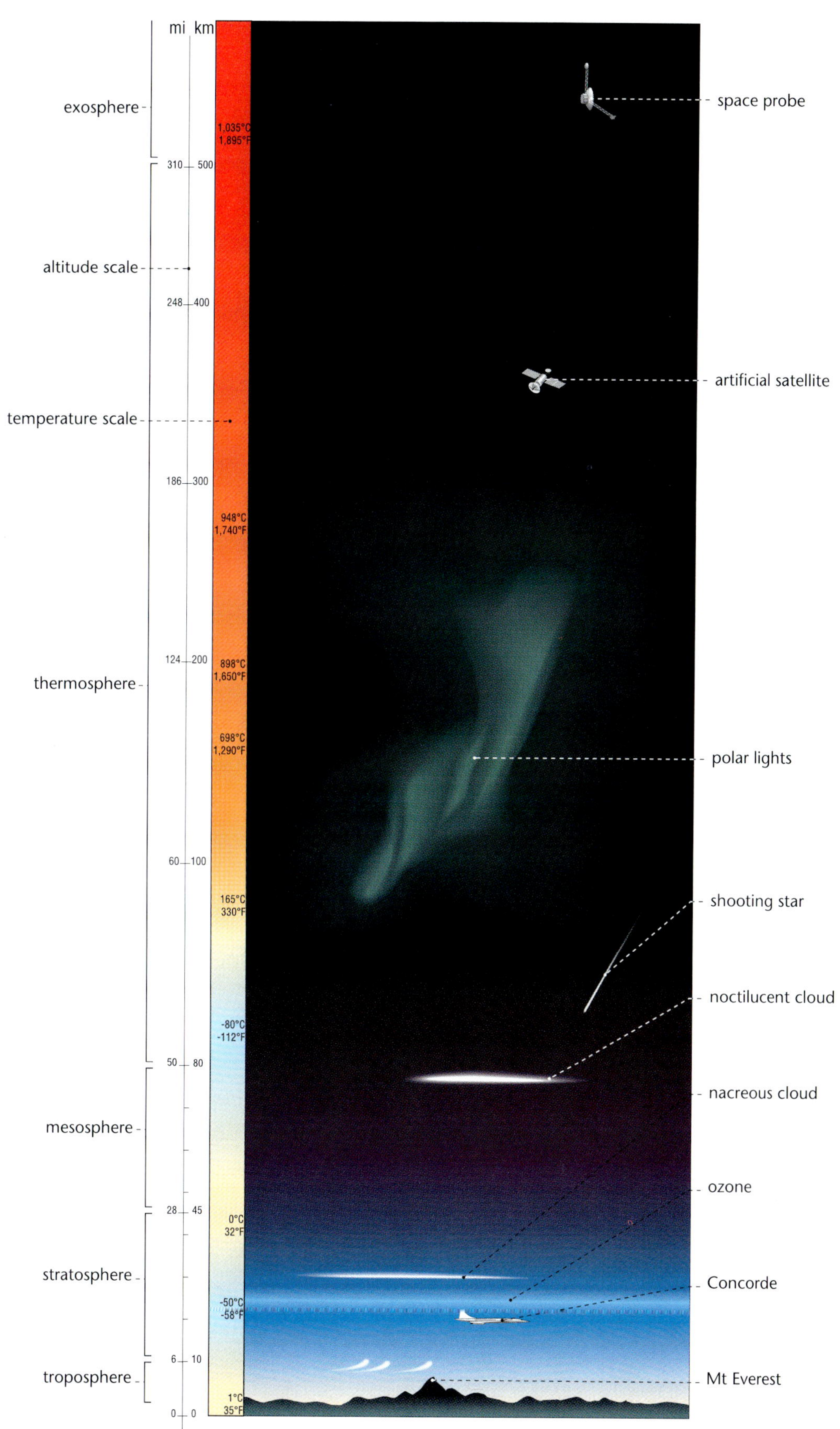

CONFIGURATION OF THE CONTINENTS

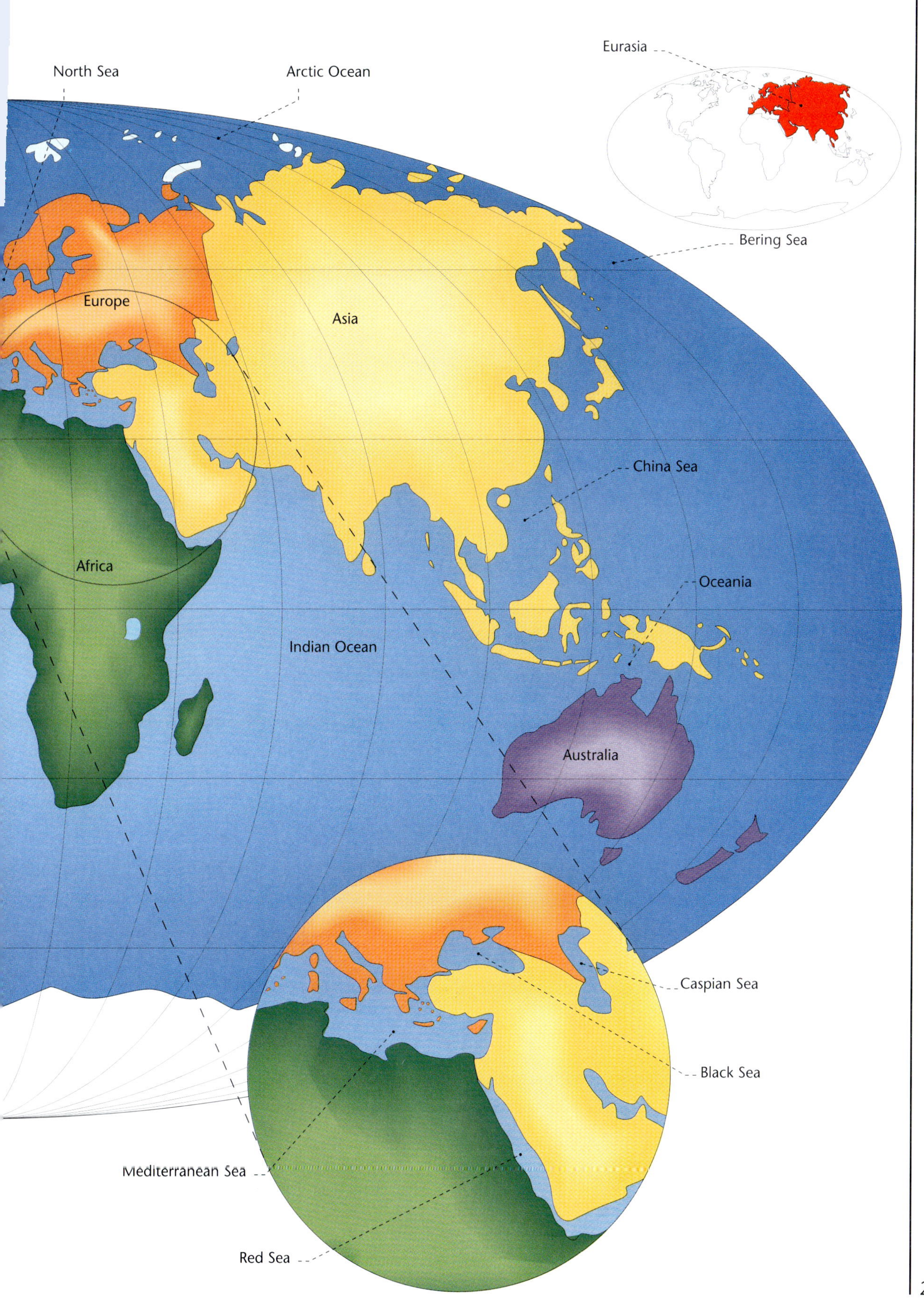
North Sea
Arctic Ocean
Eurasia
Bering Sea
Europe
Asia
China Sea
Africa
Oceania
Indian Ocean
Australia
Caspian Sea
Black Sea
Mediterranean Sea
Red Sea

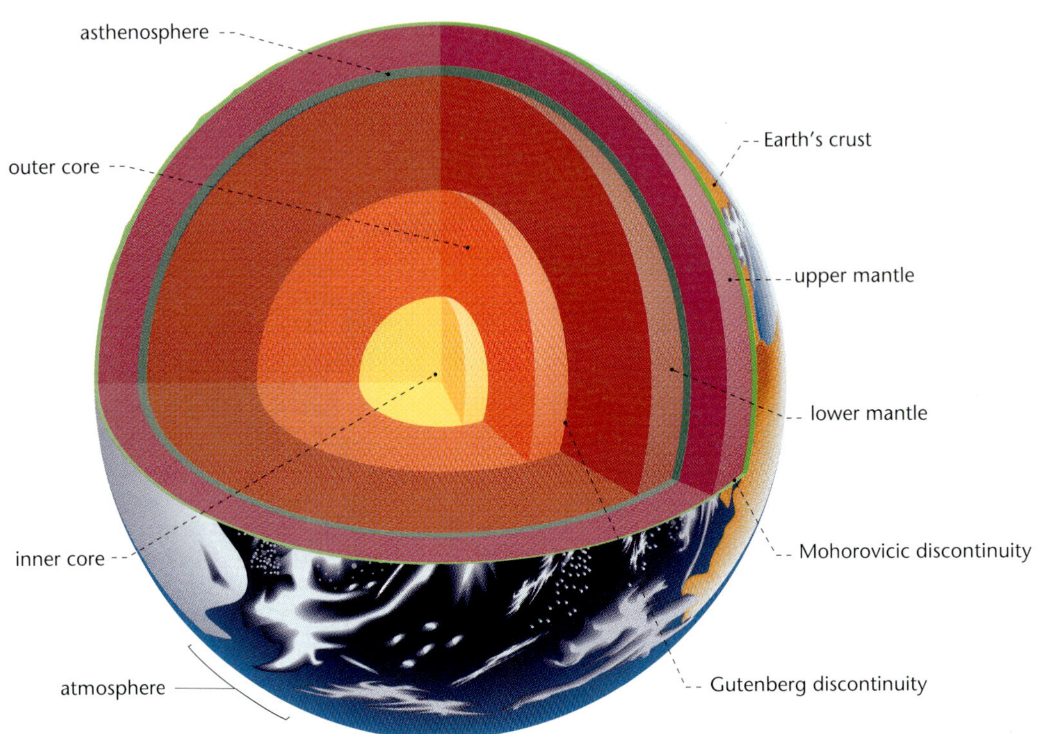

SECTION OF THE EARTH'S CRUST

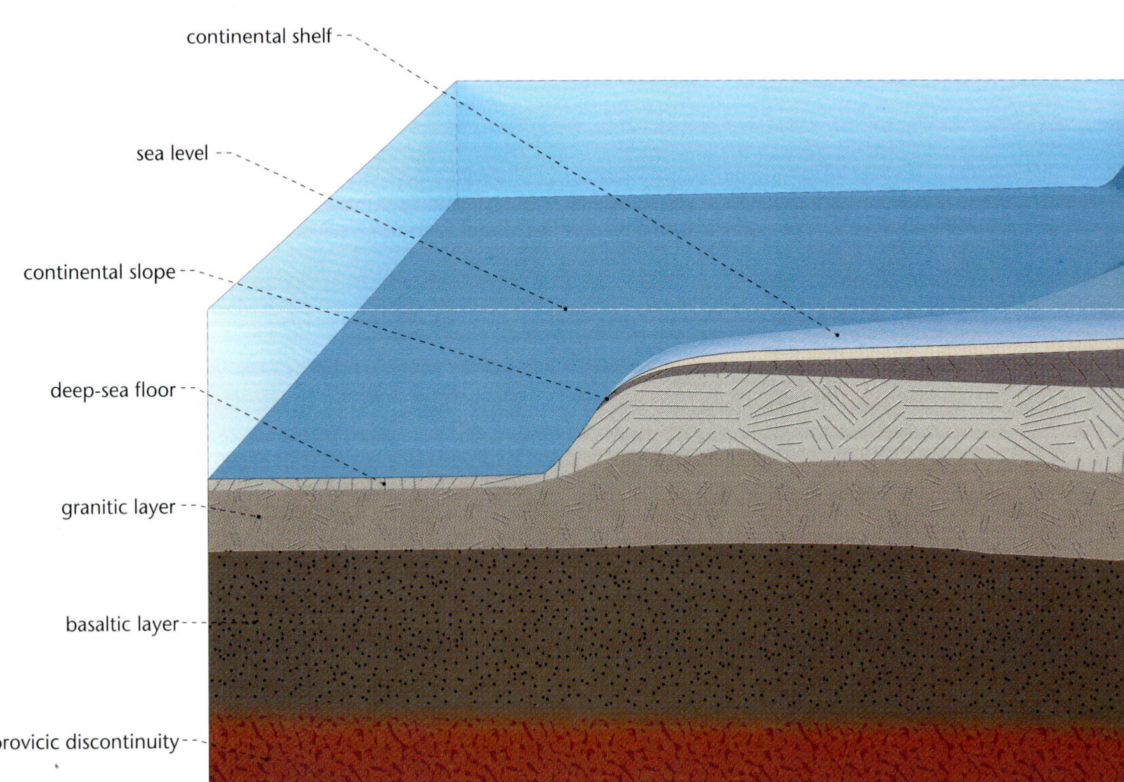

EARTHQUAKE

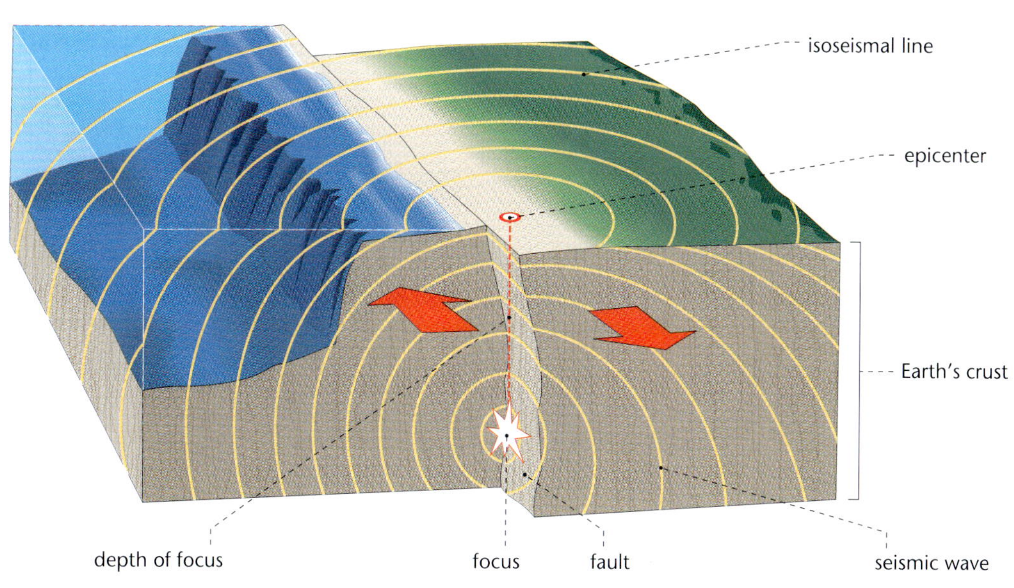

isoseismal line
epicenter
Earth's crust
depth of focus
focus
fault
seismic wave

cliff
beach
volcano
mountain range
fault
sedimentary rocks
metamorphic rocks
igneous rocks
intrusive rocks

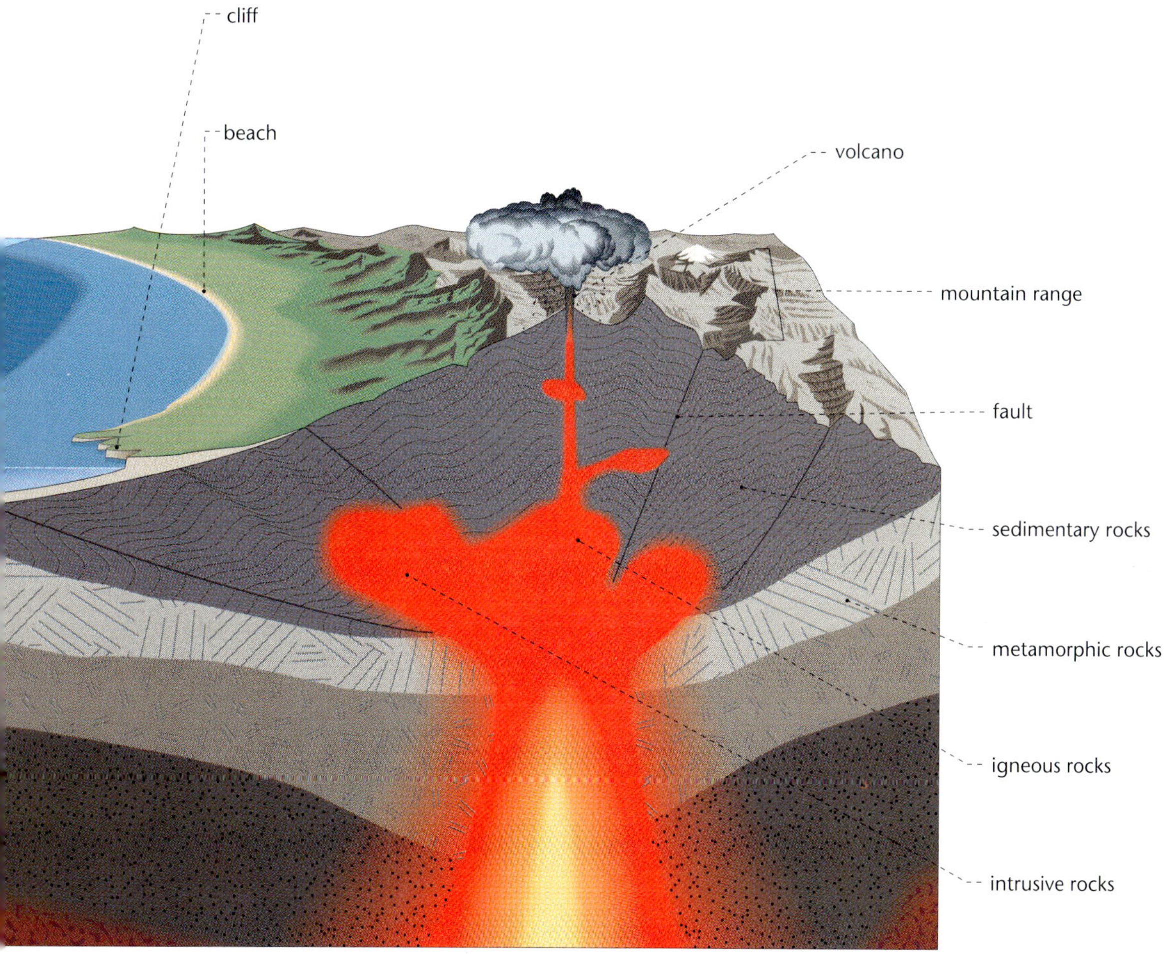

CAVE

gorge
stalactite
sinkhole
pothole
lapiaz
swallow hole
dry gallery
column
gour
siphon
water table
stalagmite
subterranean stream
cone
dormant volcano
fumarole
sill

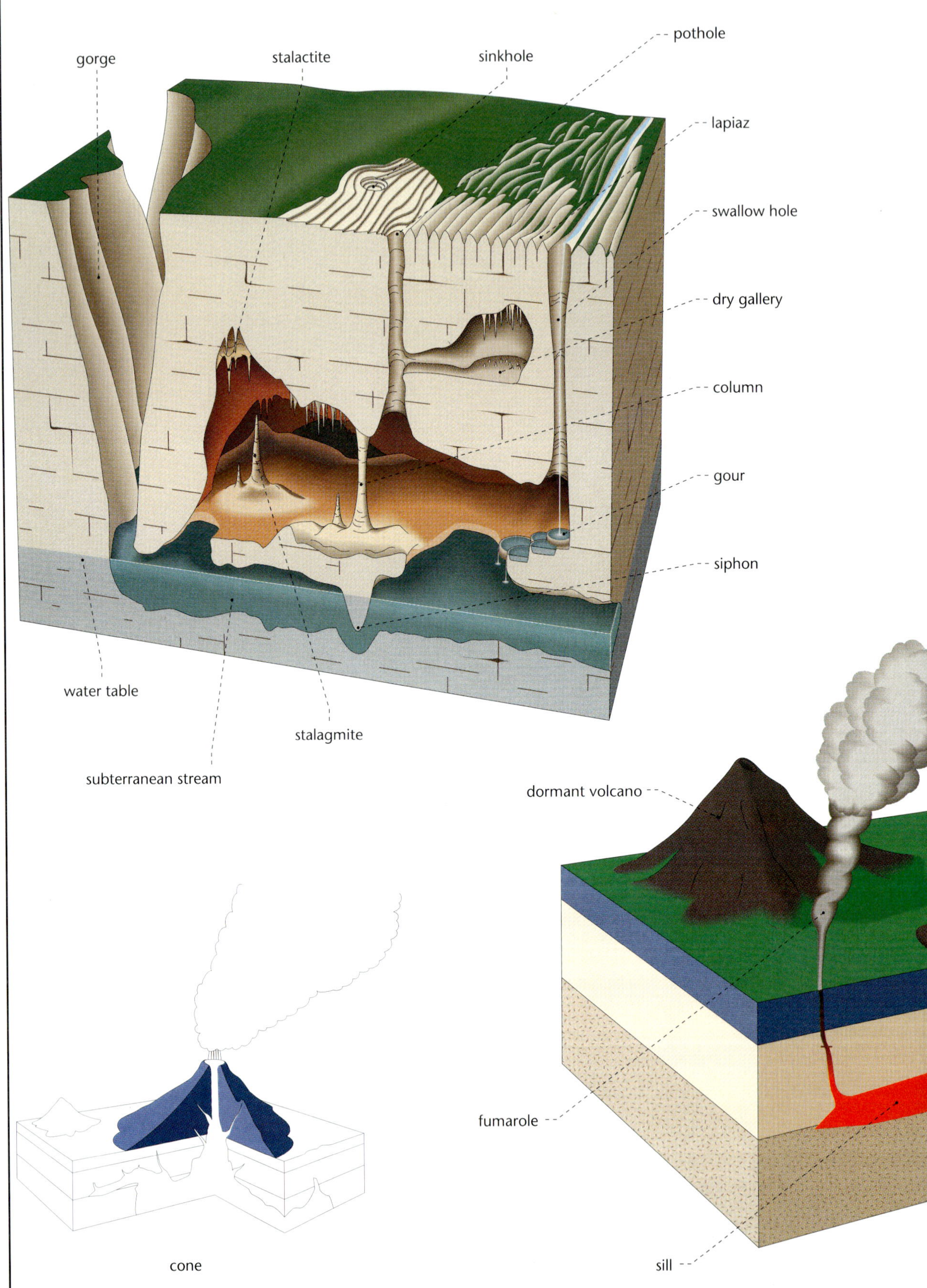

VOLCANO DURING ERUPTION

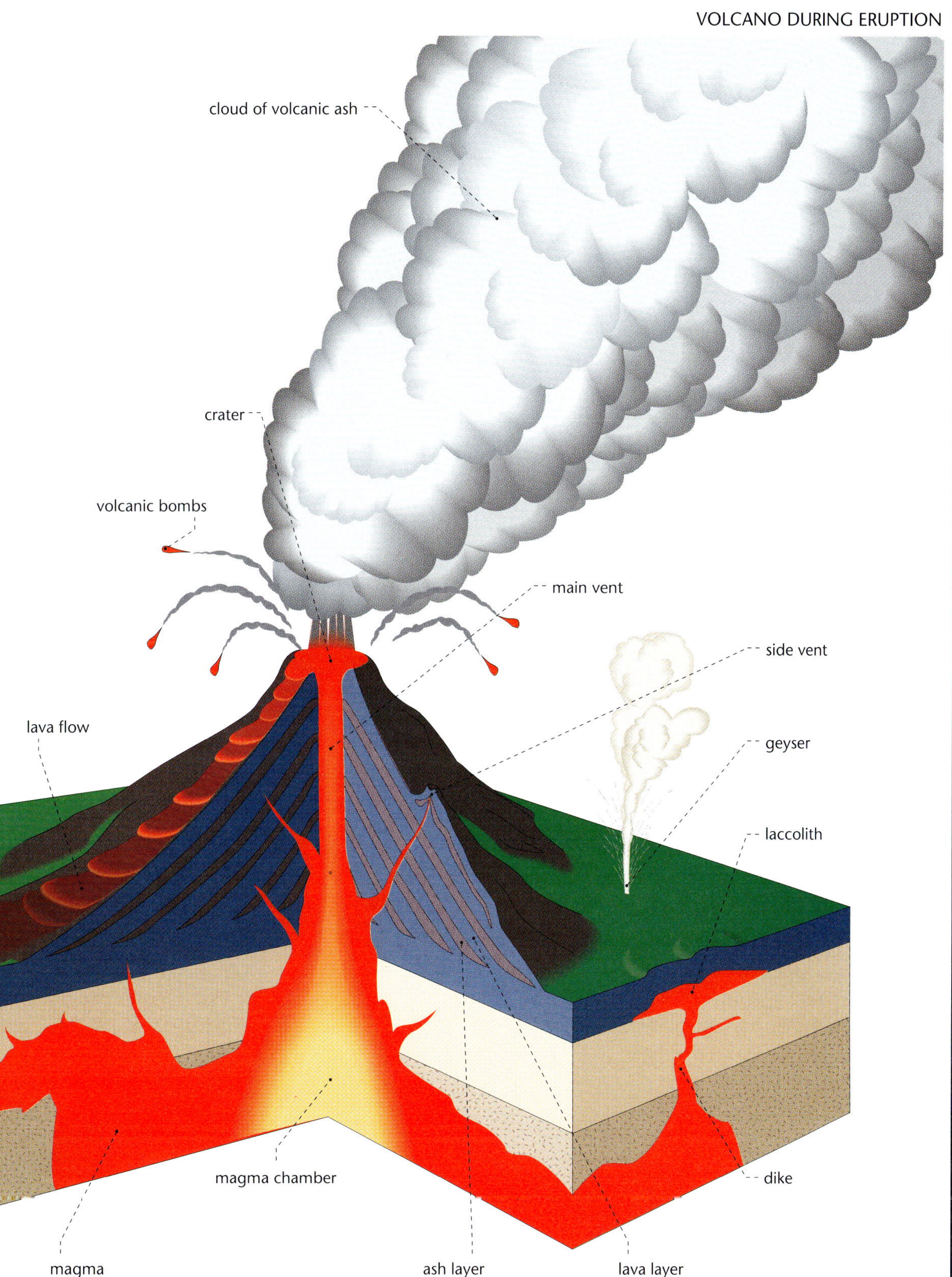

GLACIER

firn
bergschrund
serac
glacial cirque
hanging glacier
rock basin
rock step
crevasse
glacier tongue
ground moraine
medial moraine

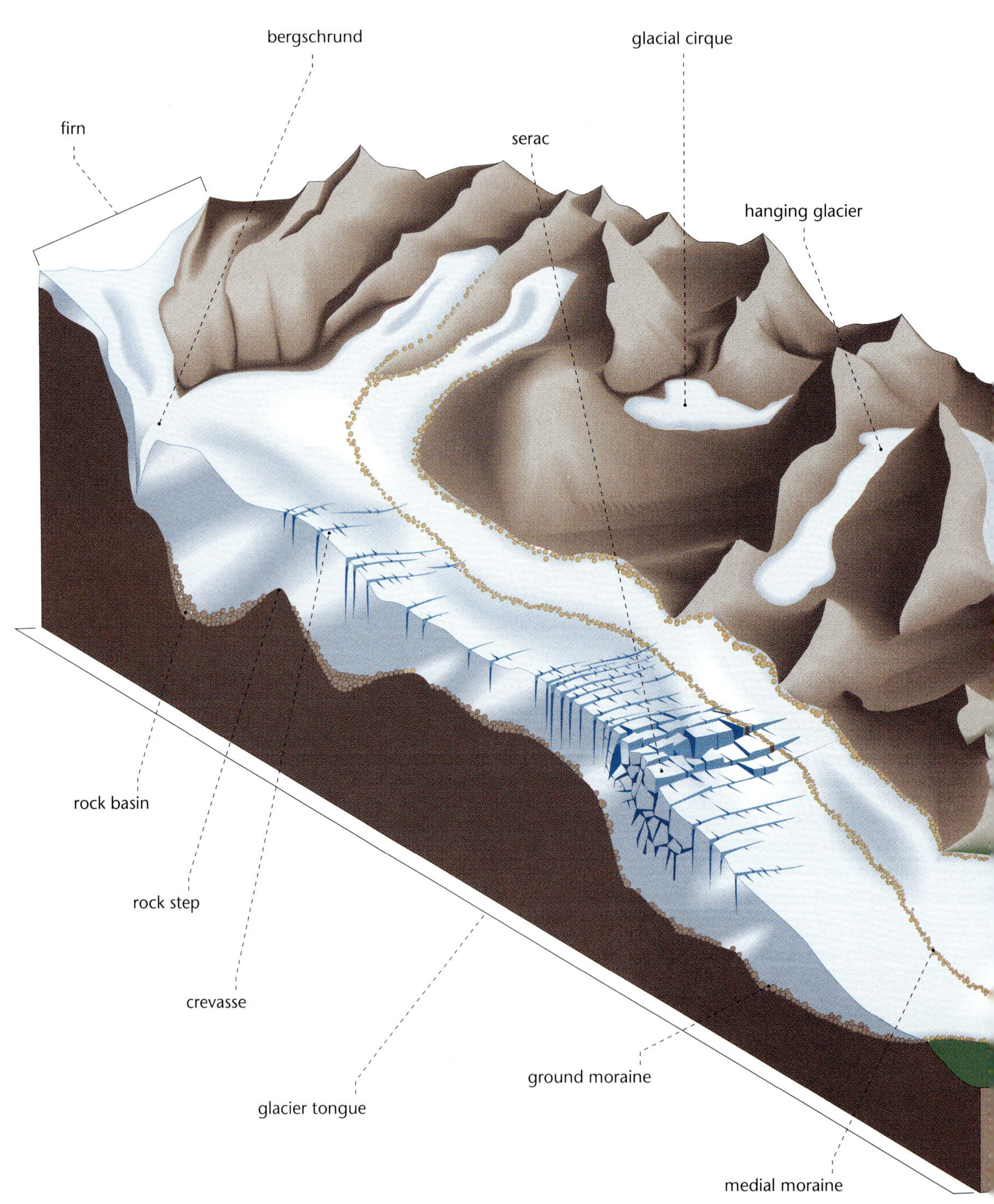

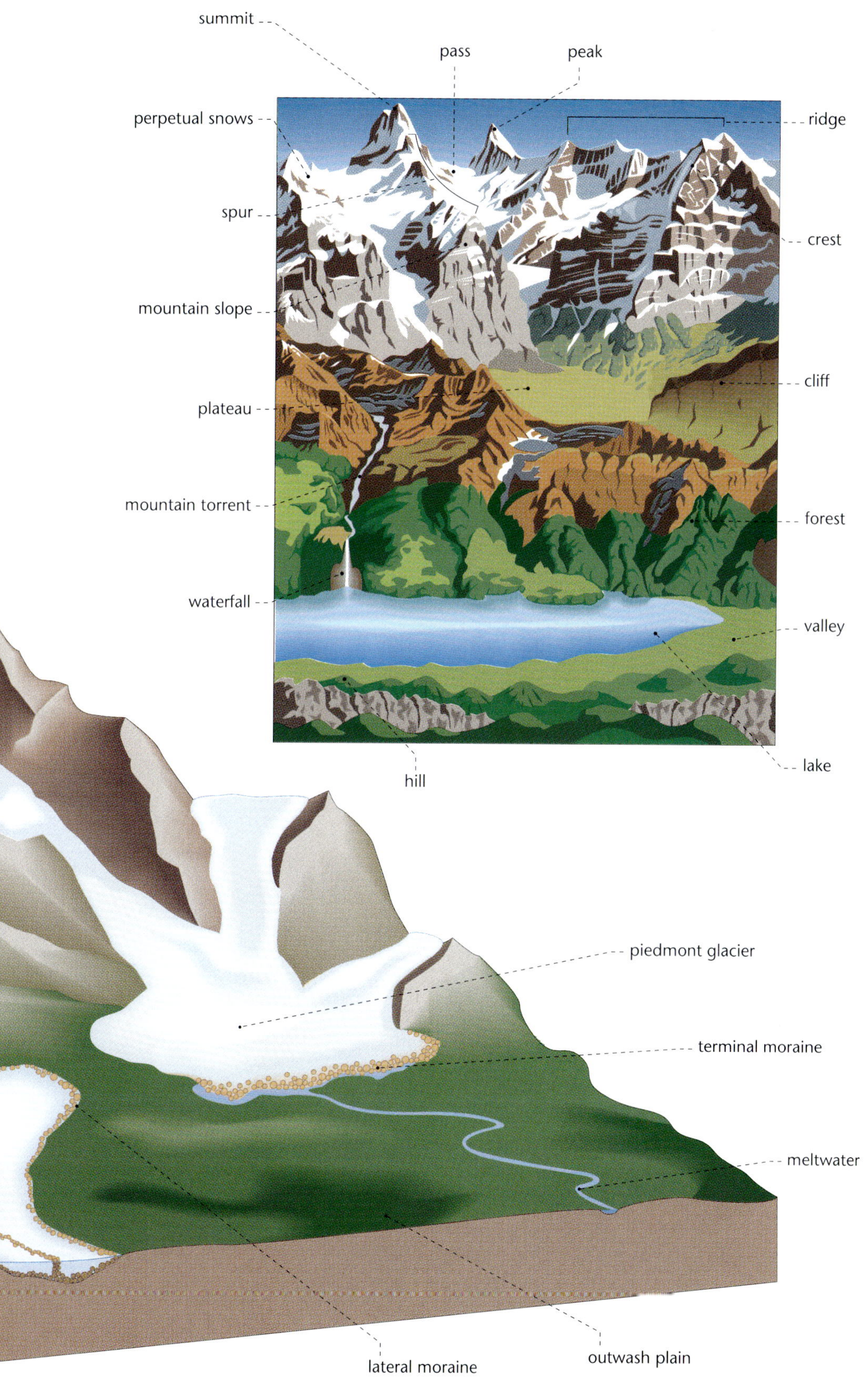

summit
pass
peak
perpetual snows
ridge
spur
crest
mountain slope
cliff
plateau
mountain torrent
forest
waterfall
valley
hill
lake
piedmont glacier
terminal moraine
meltwater
lateral moraine
outwash plain

MID-OCEAN RIDGE

TOPOGRAPHIC FEATURES

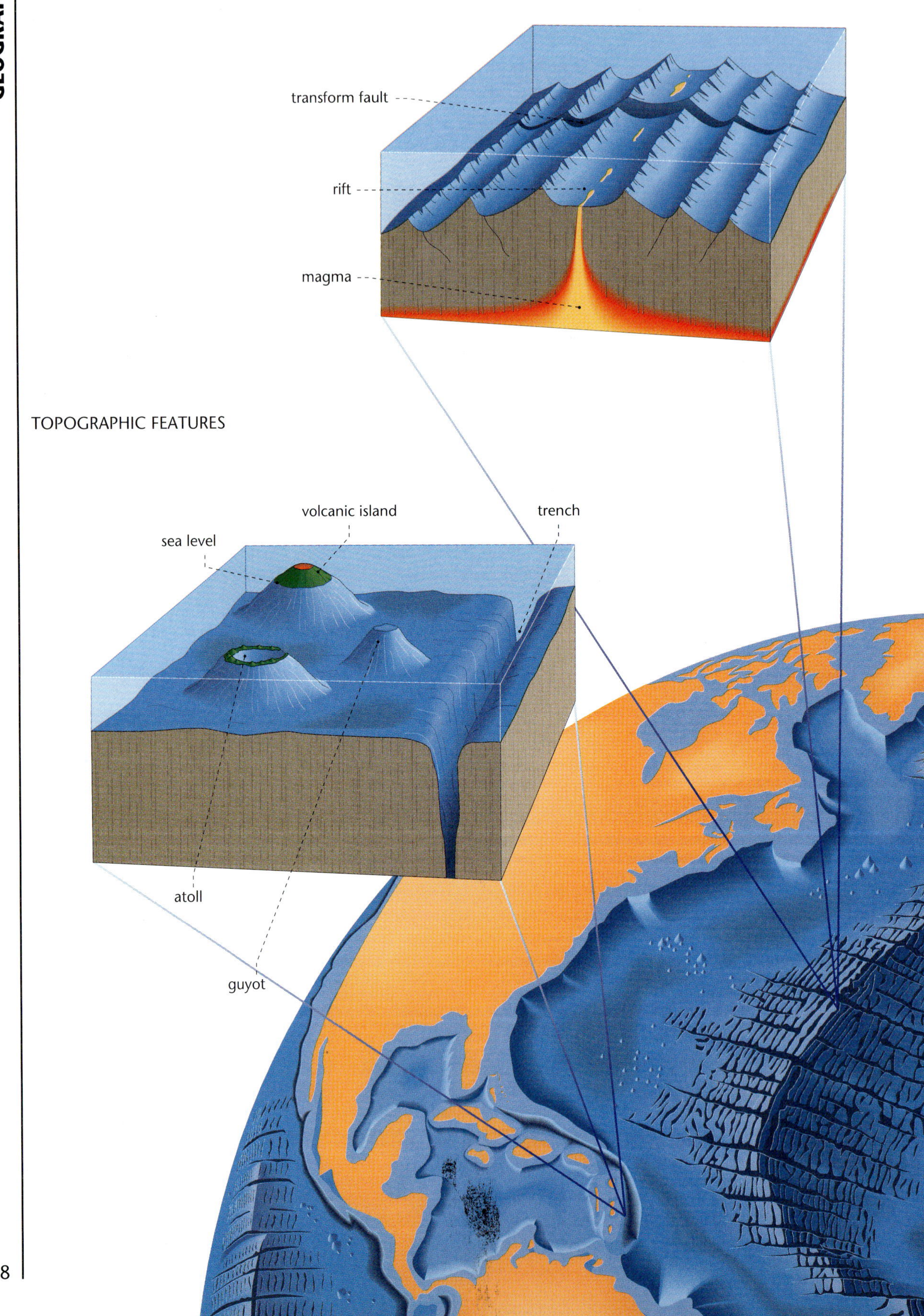

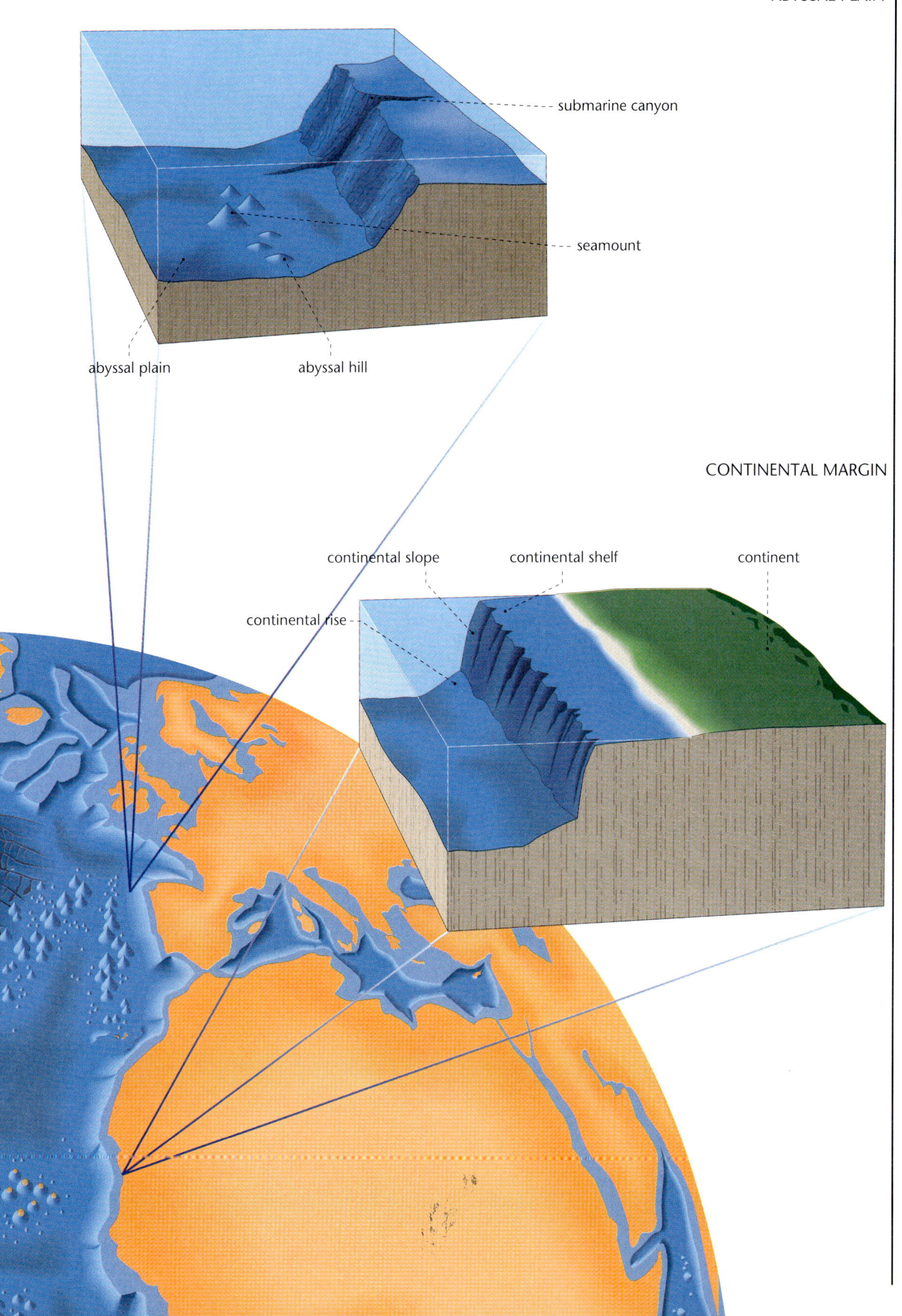
ABYSSAL PLAIN
submarine canyon
seamount
abyssal plain
abyssal hill
CONTINENTAL MARGIN
continental slope
continental shelf
continent
continental rise

WAVE

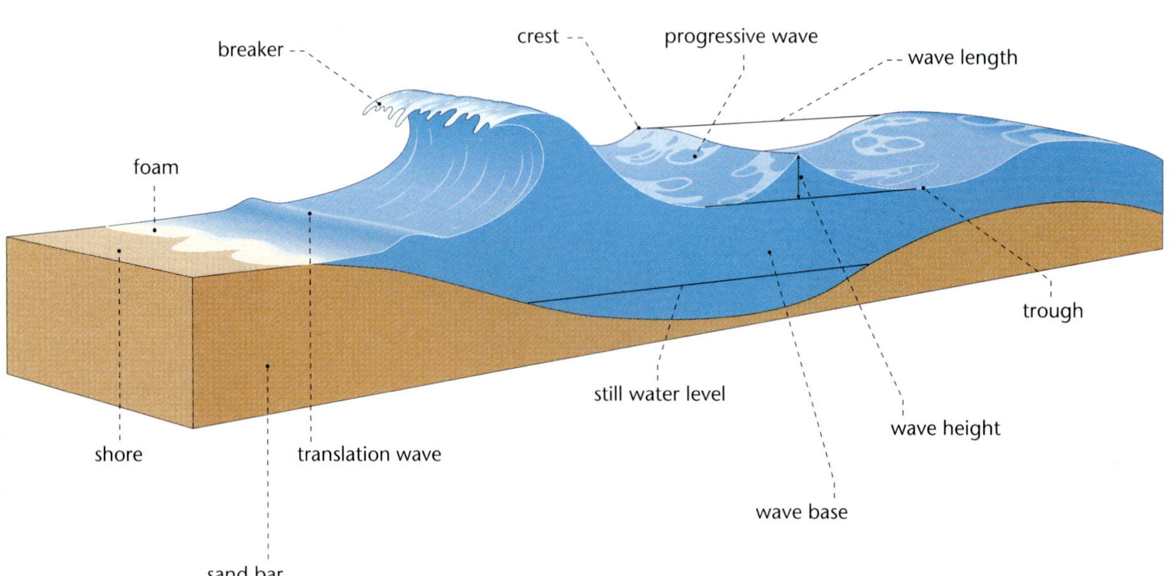

COMMON COASTAL FEATURES

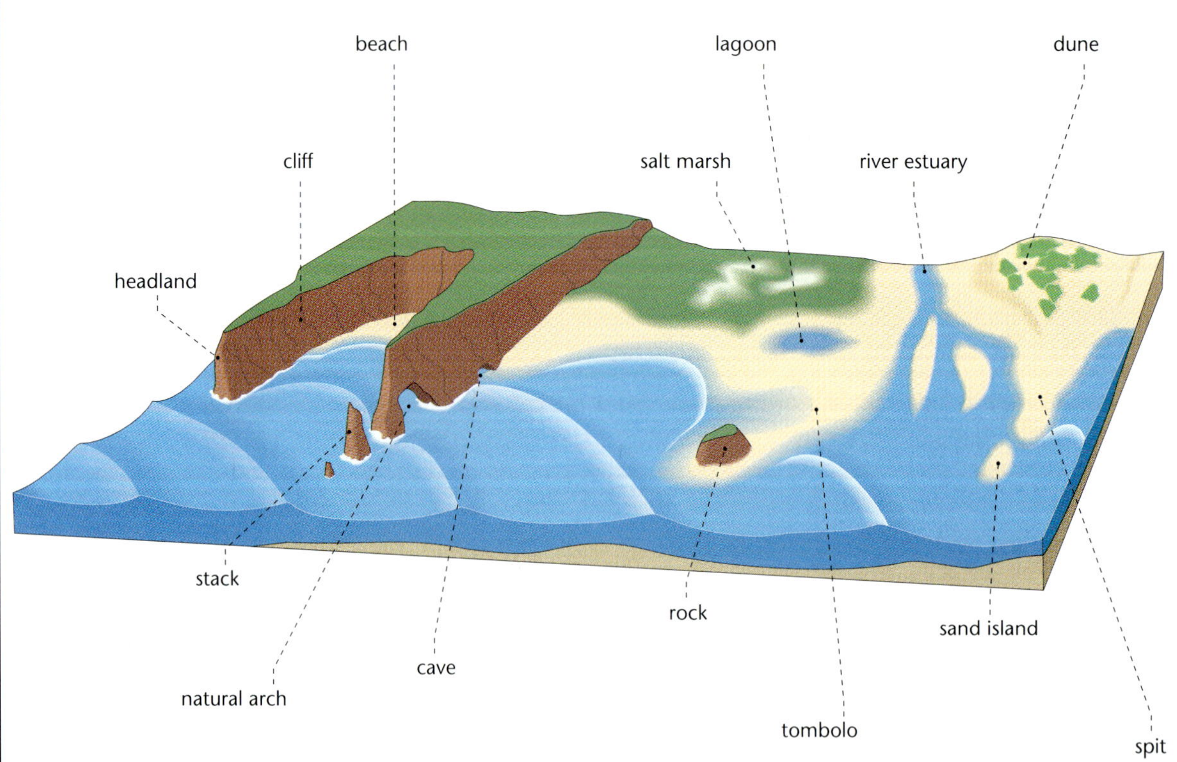

ECOLOGY

STRUCTURE OF THE BIOSPHERE

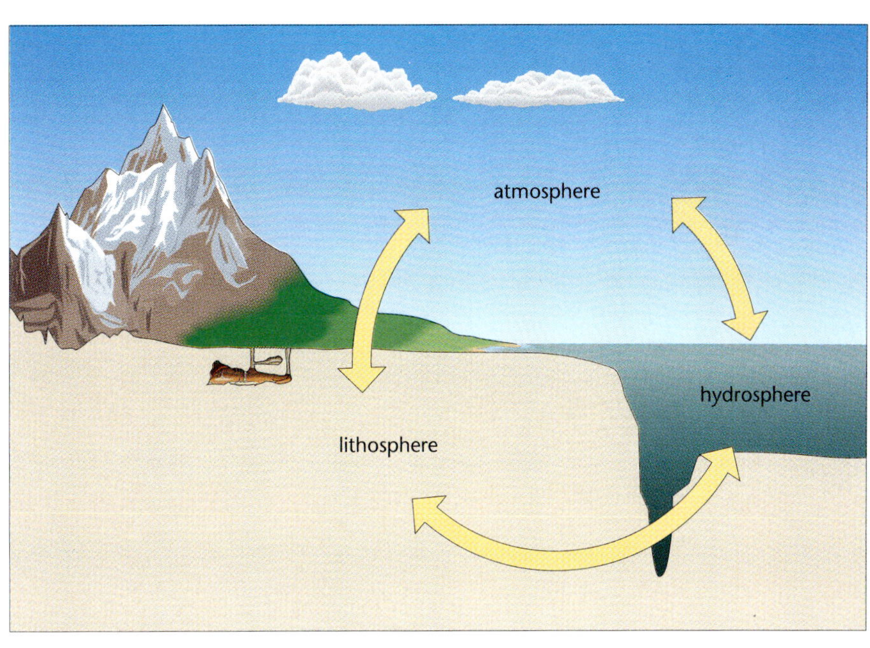

FOOD CHAIN

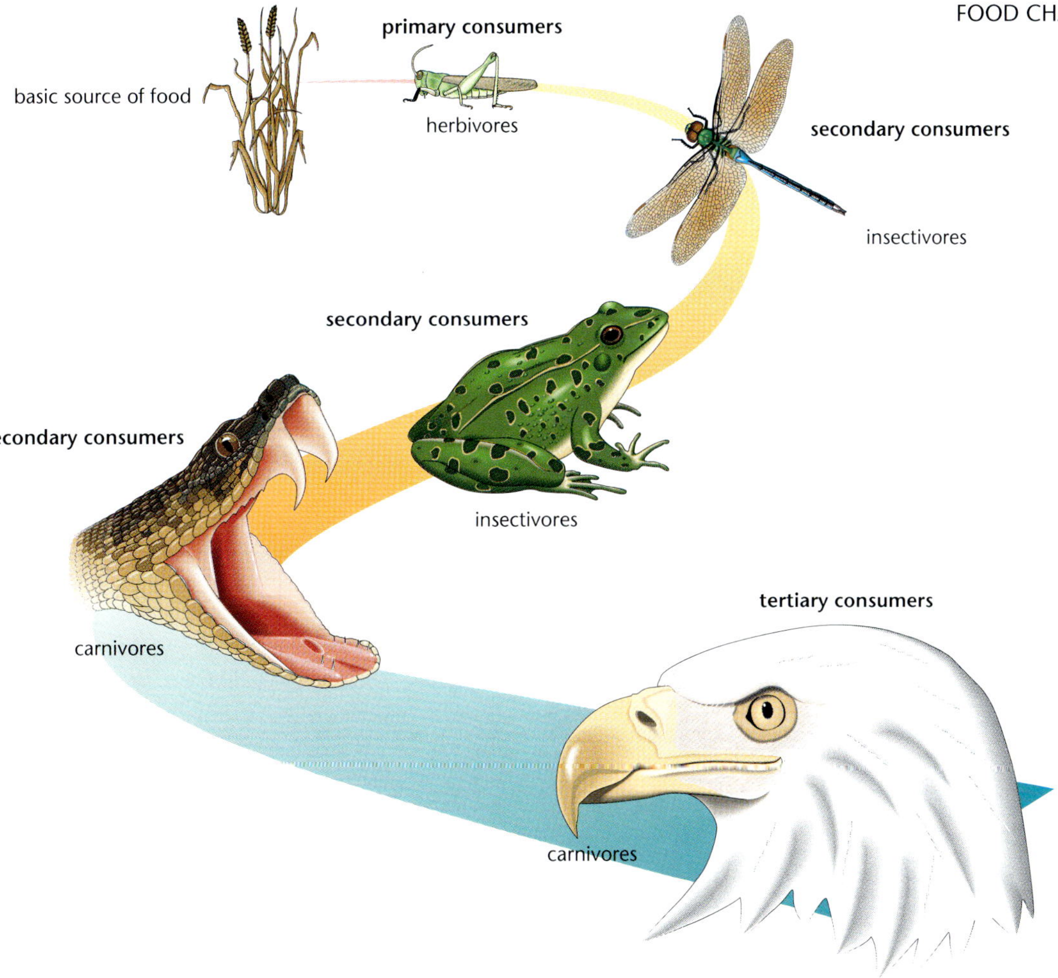

POLLUTION OF FOOD ON GROUND

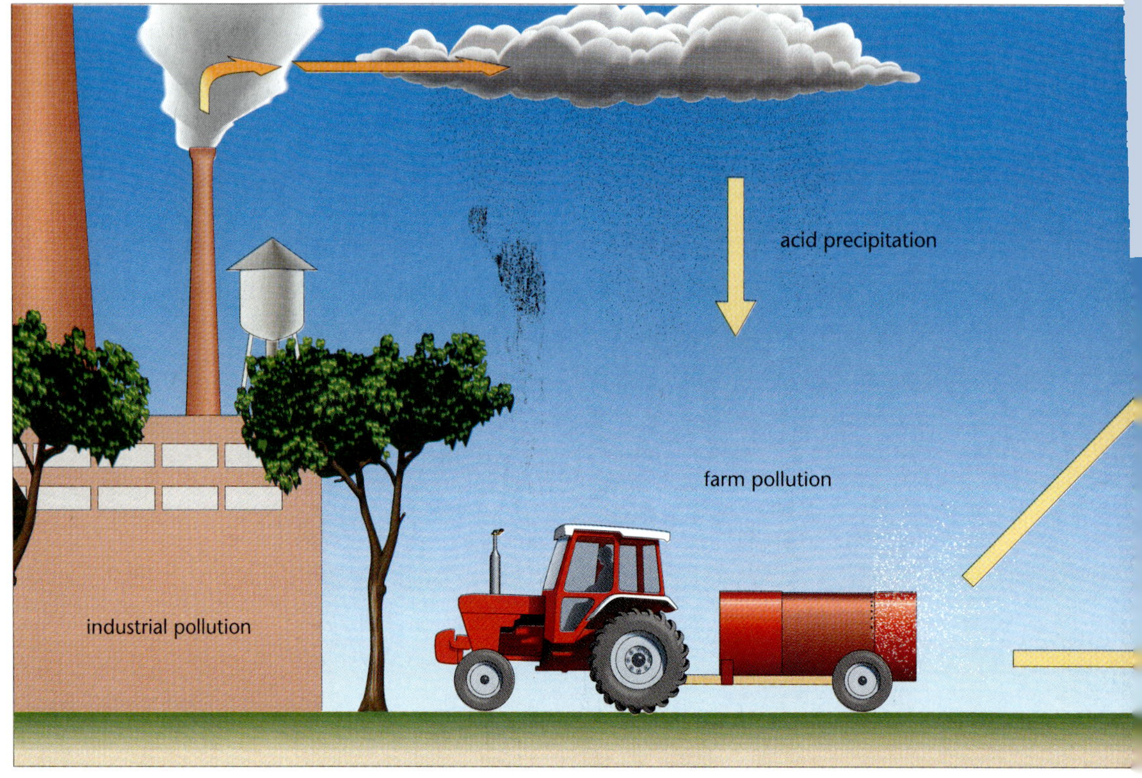

POLLUTION OF FOOD IN WATER

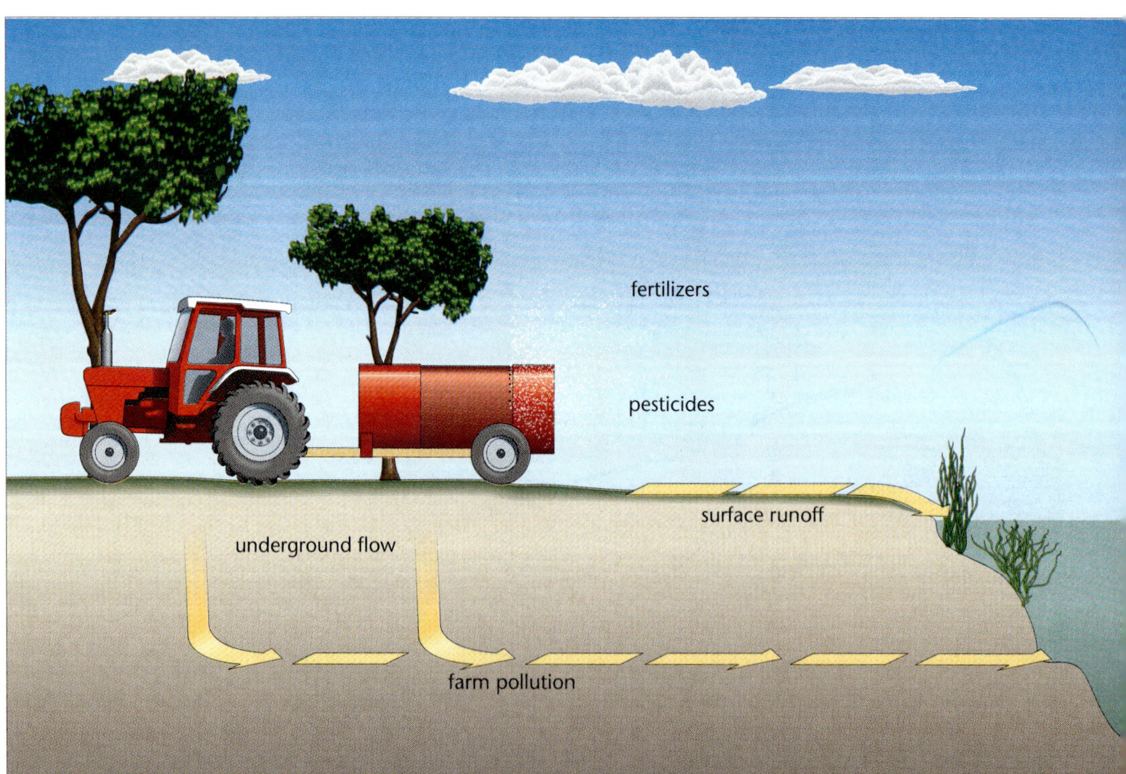

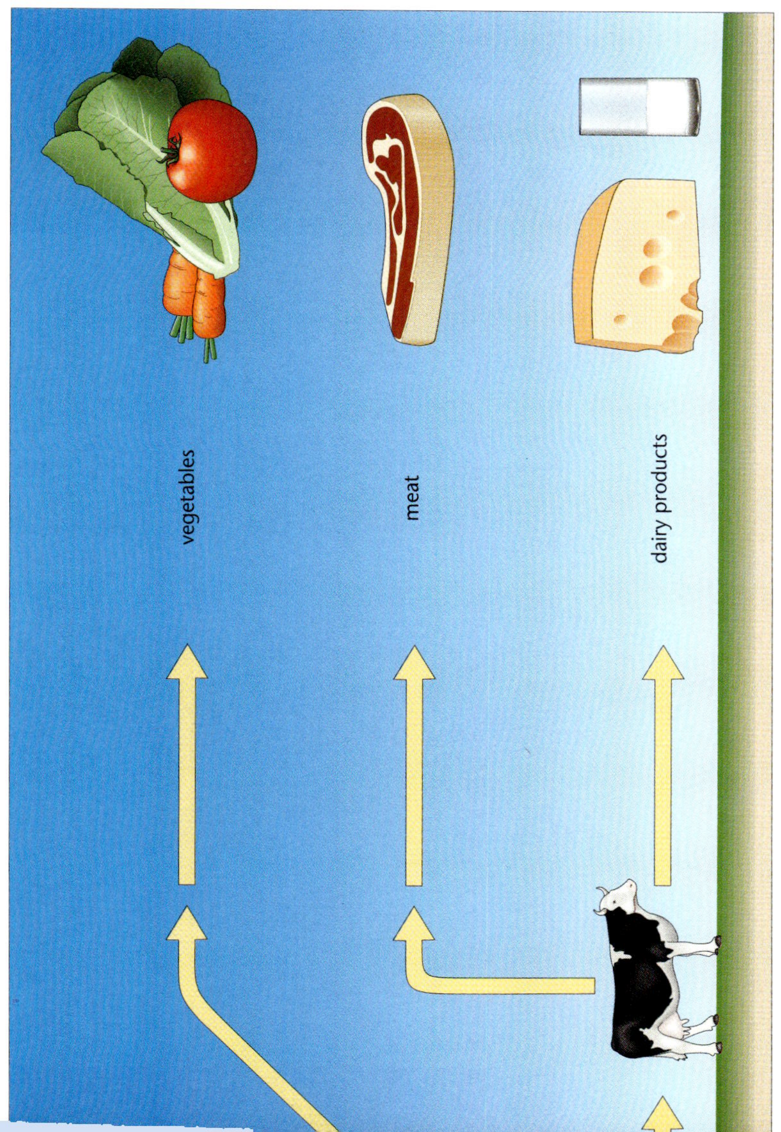

vegetables
meat
dairy products

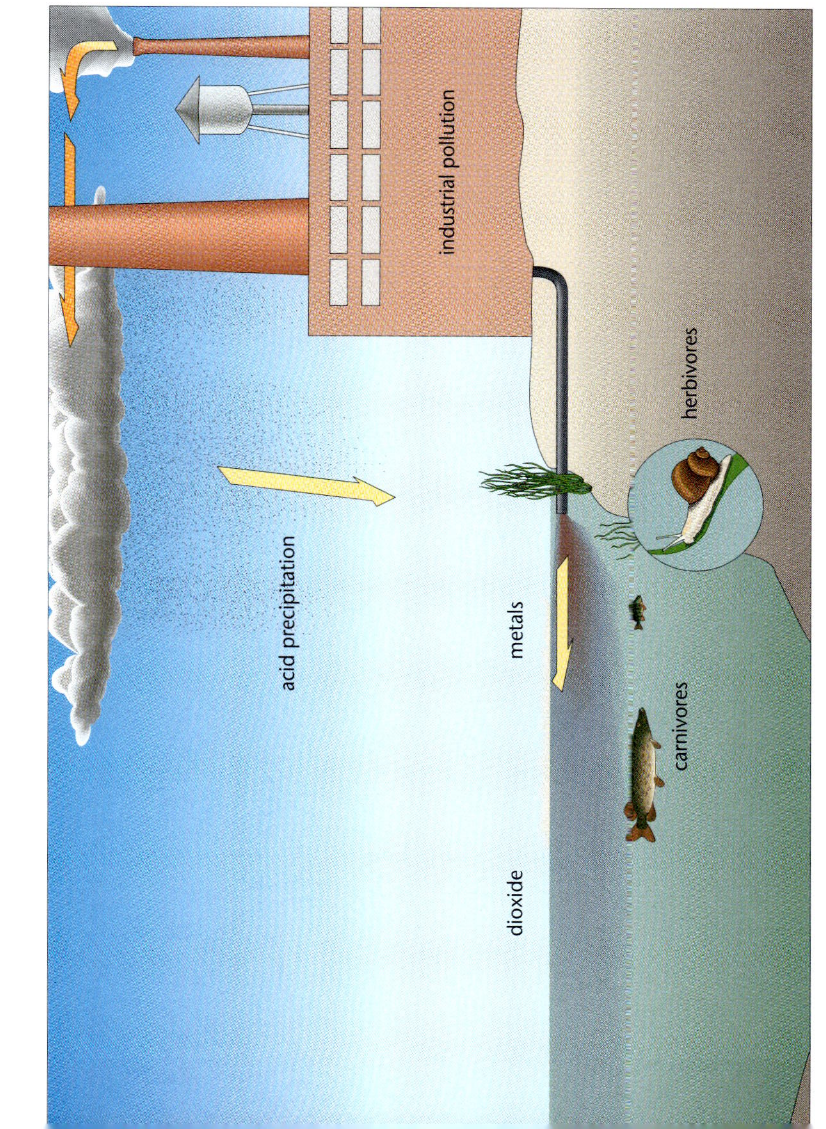

industrial pollution
acid precipitation
metals
dioxide
herbivores
carnivores

ATMOSPHERIC POLLUTION

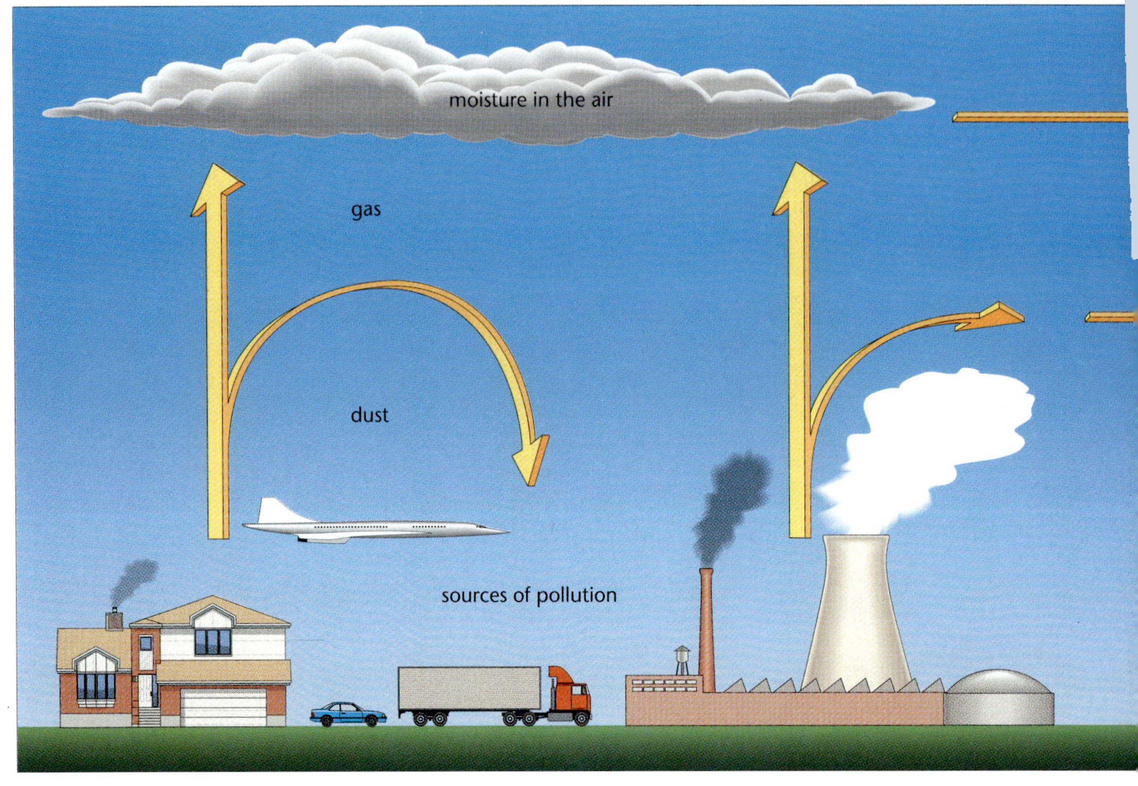

HYDROLOGIC CYCLE

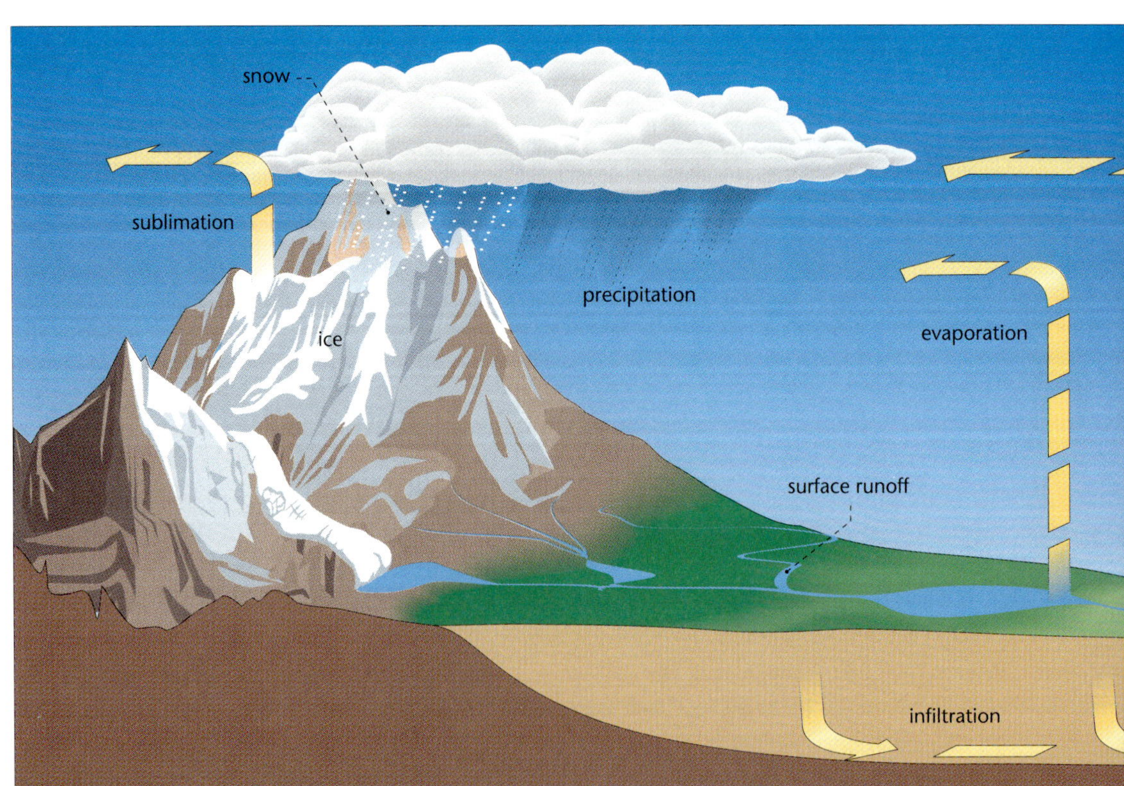

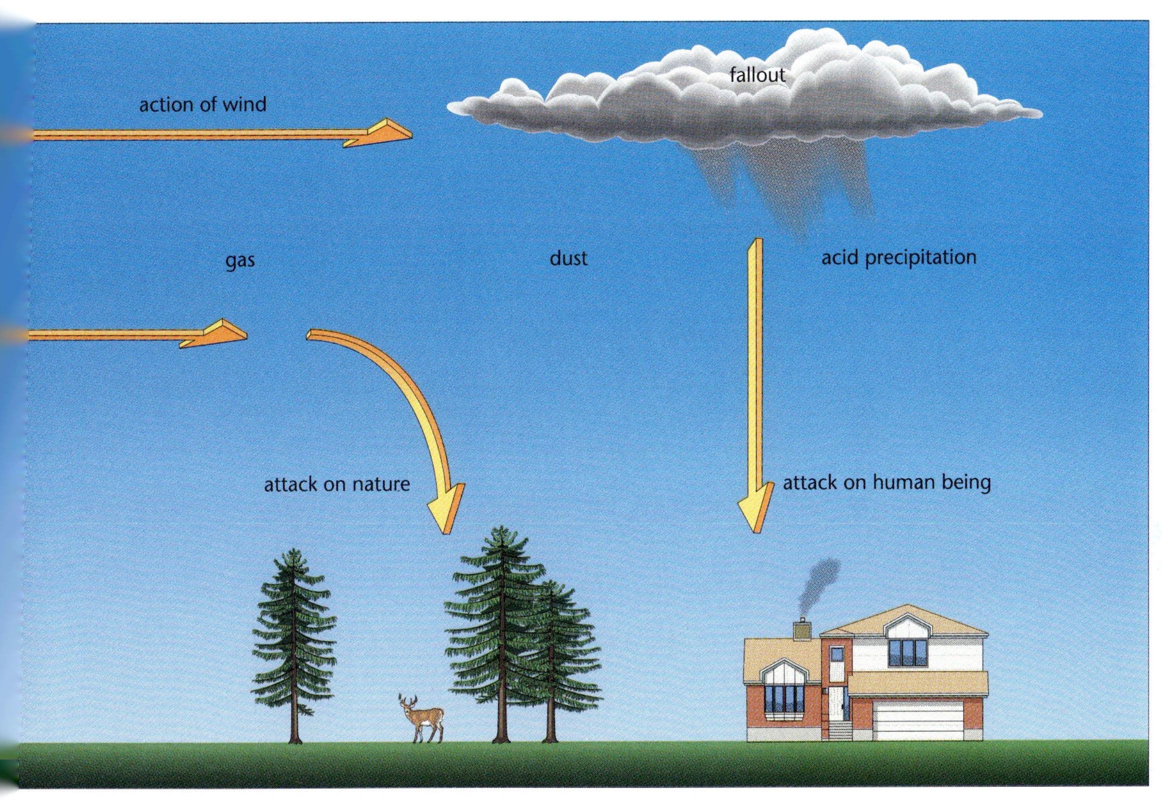

action of wind
fallout
gas
dust
acid precipitation
attack on nature
attack on human being

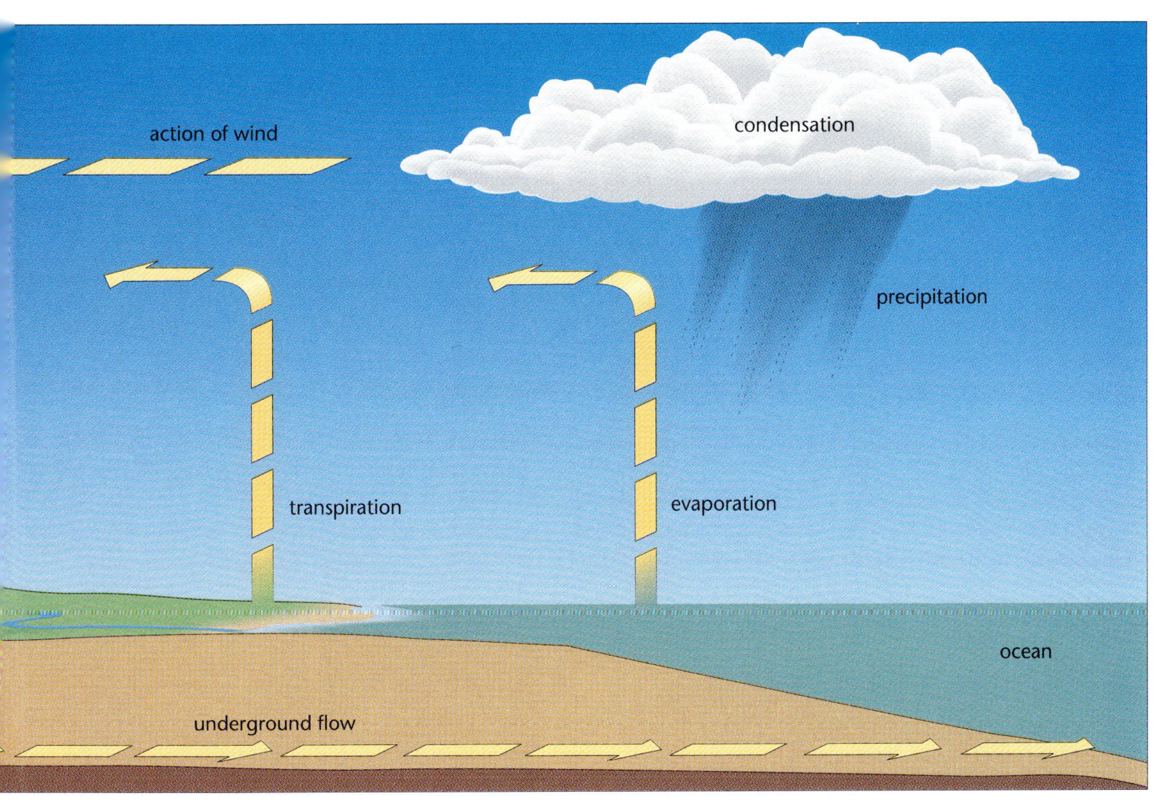

action of wind
condensation
precipitation
transpiration
evaporation
ocean
underground flow

GEOGRAPHY

STORMY SKY

rainbow

rain

lightning

cloud

raindrop

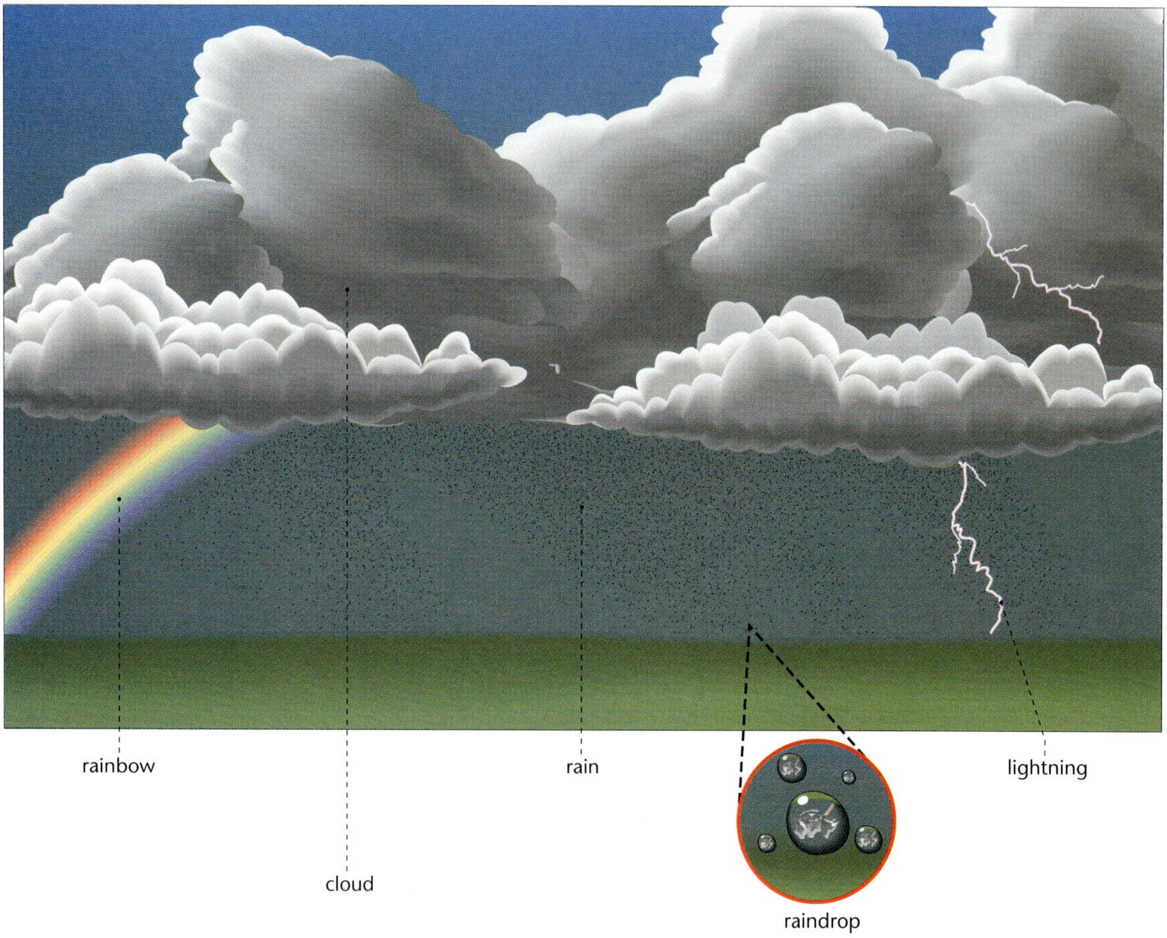

CLASSIFICATION OF SNOW CRYSTALS

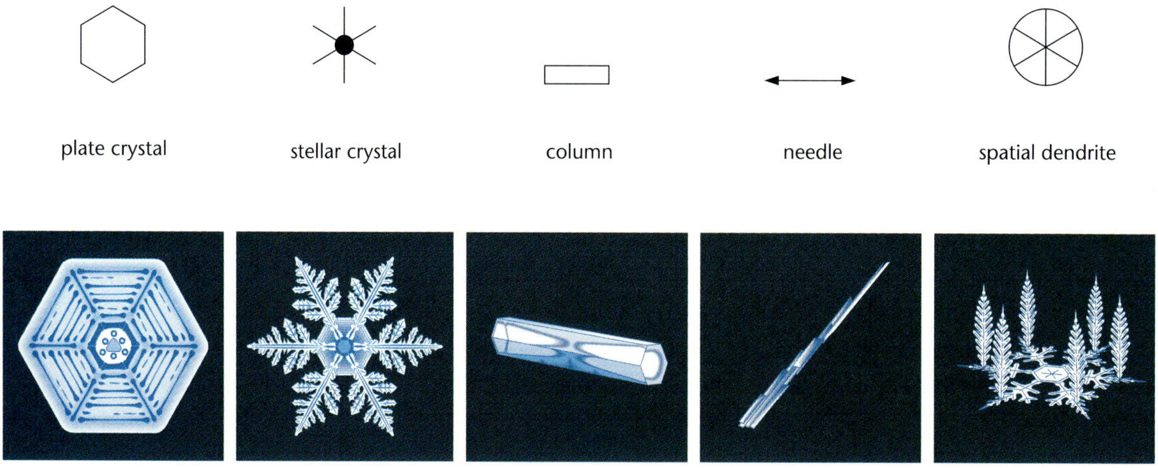

plate crystal

stellar crystal

column

needle

spatial dendrite

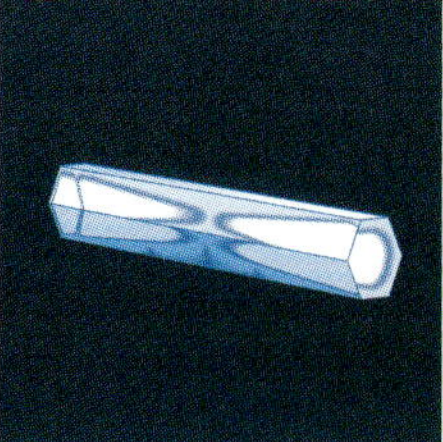

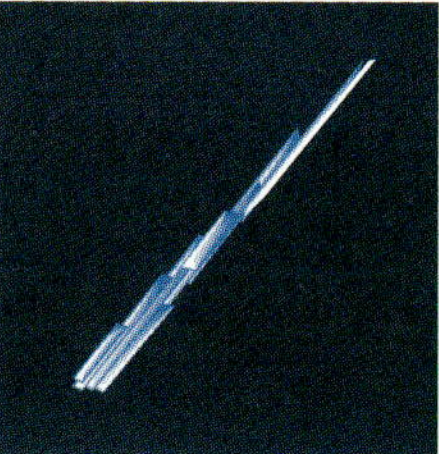

mist

fog

dew

frost

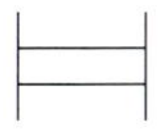

capped column

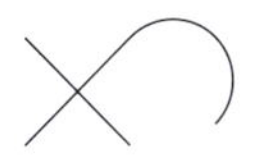

irregular crystal

snow pellet

sleet

hail

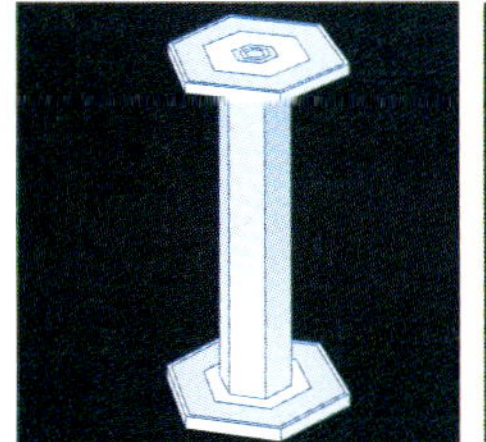

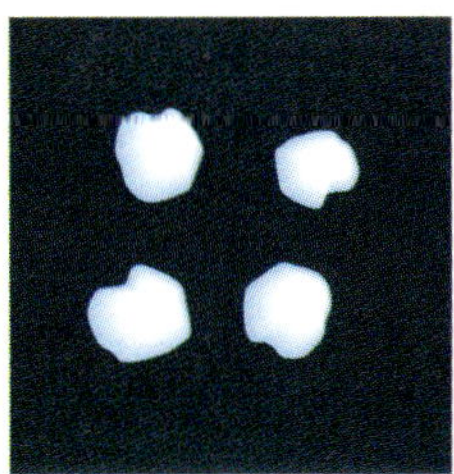

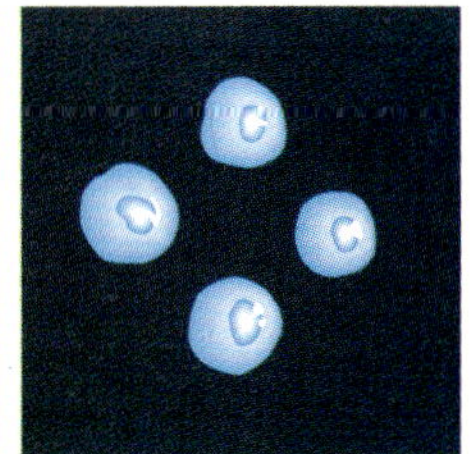

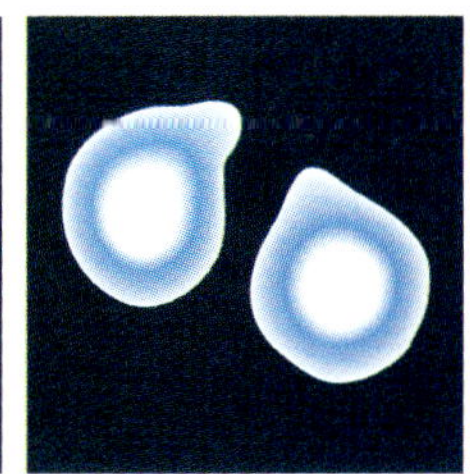

WEATHER MAP

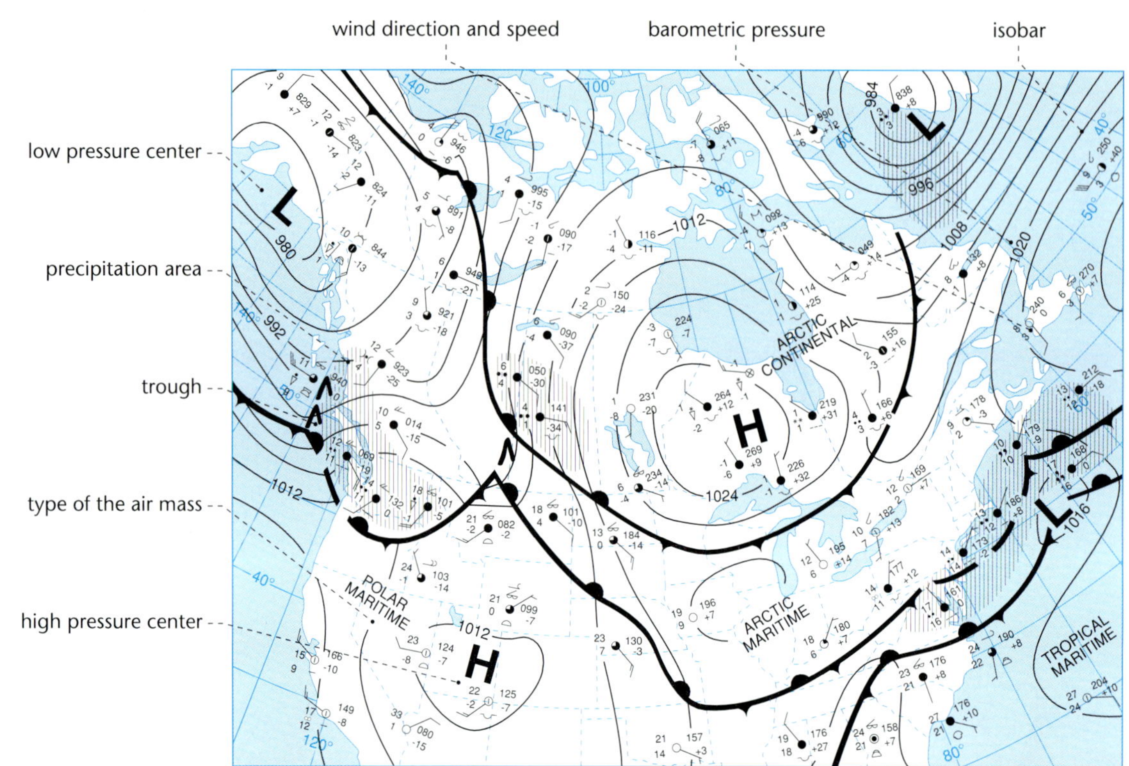

STATION MODEL

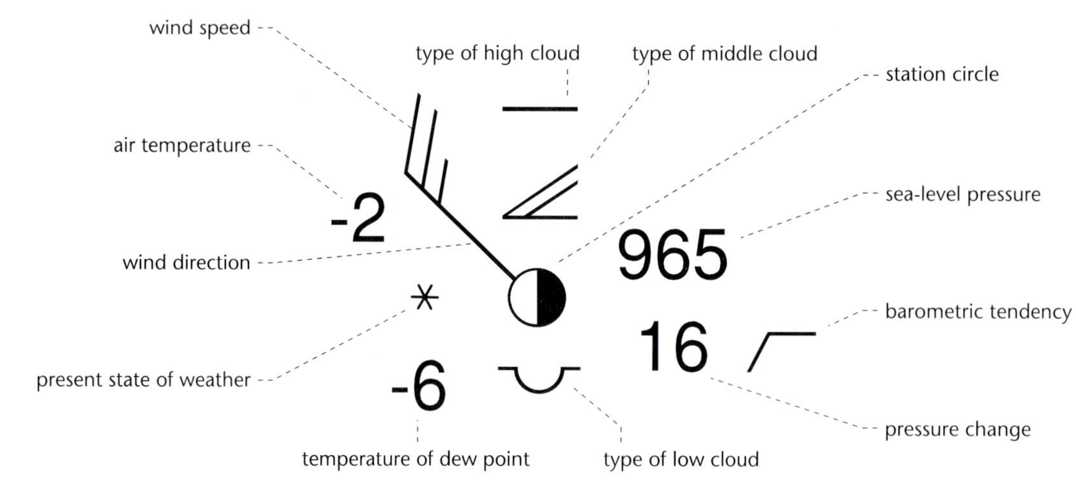

WIND

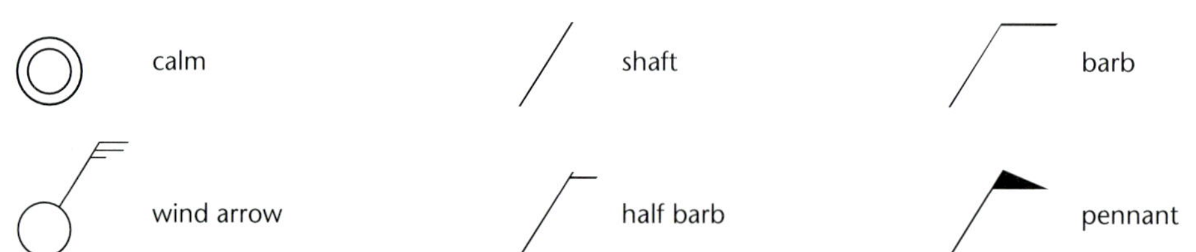

INTERNATIONAL WEATHER SYMBOLS

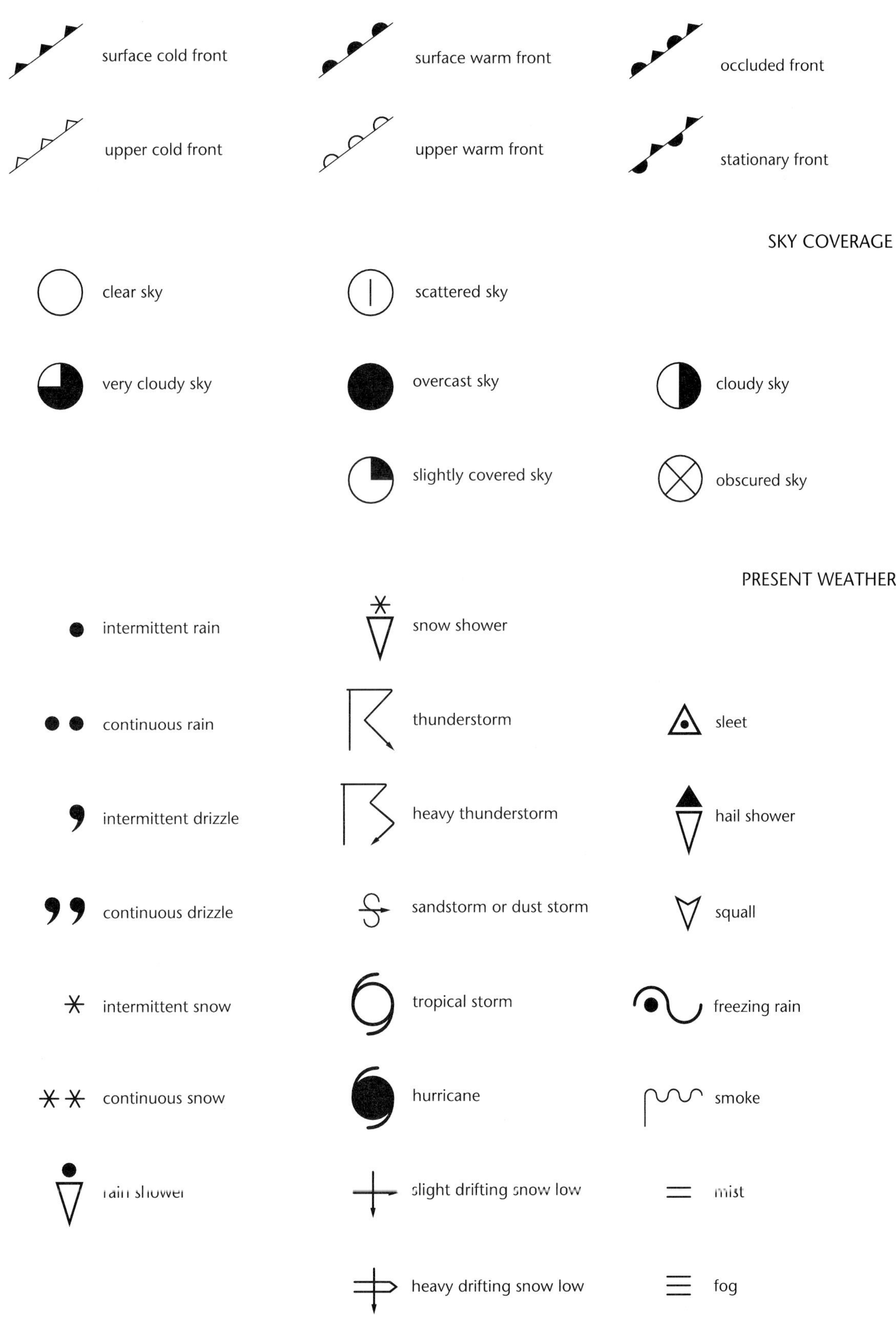

METEOROLOGICAL MEASURING INSTRUMENTS

MEASURE OF SUNSHINE

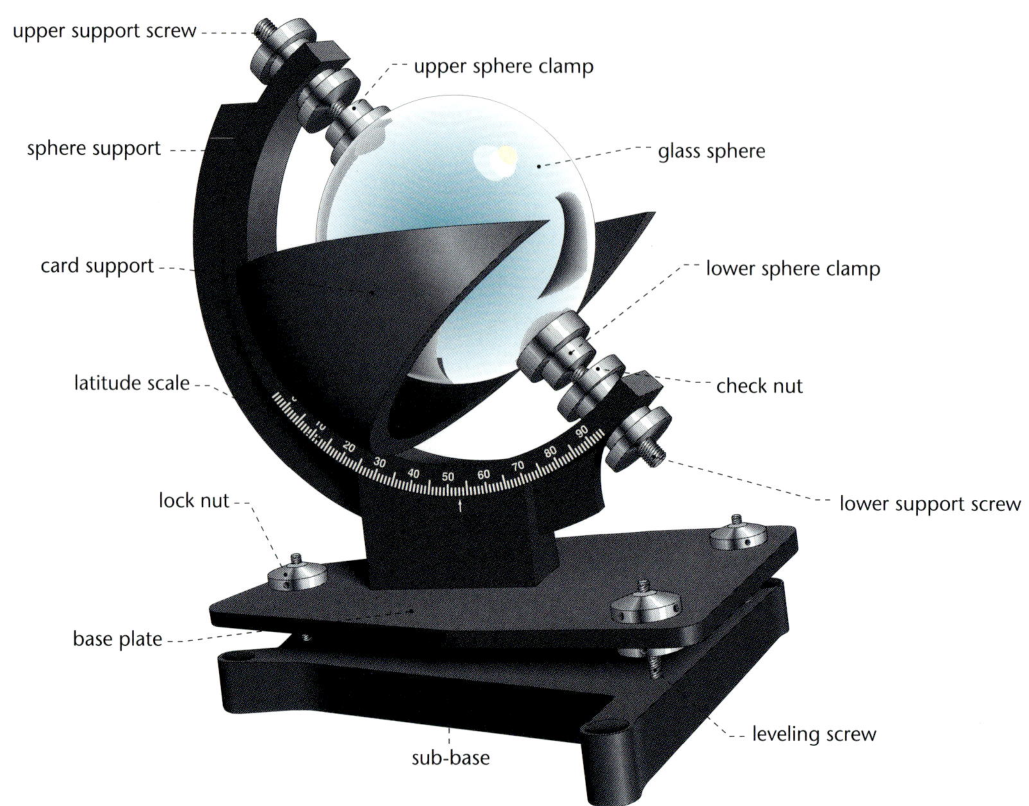

MEASURE OF RAINFALL

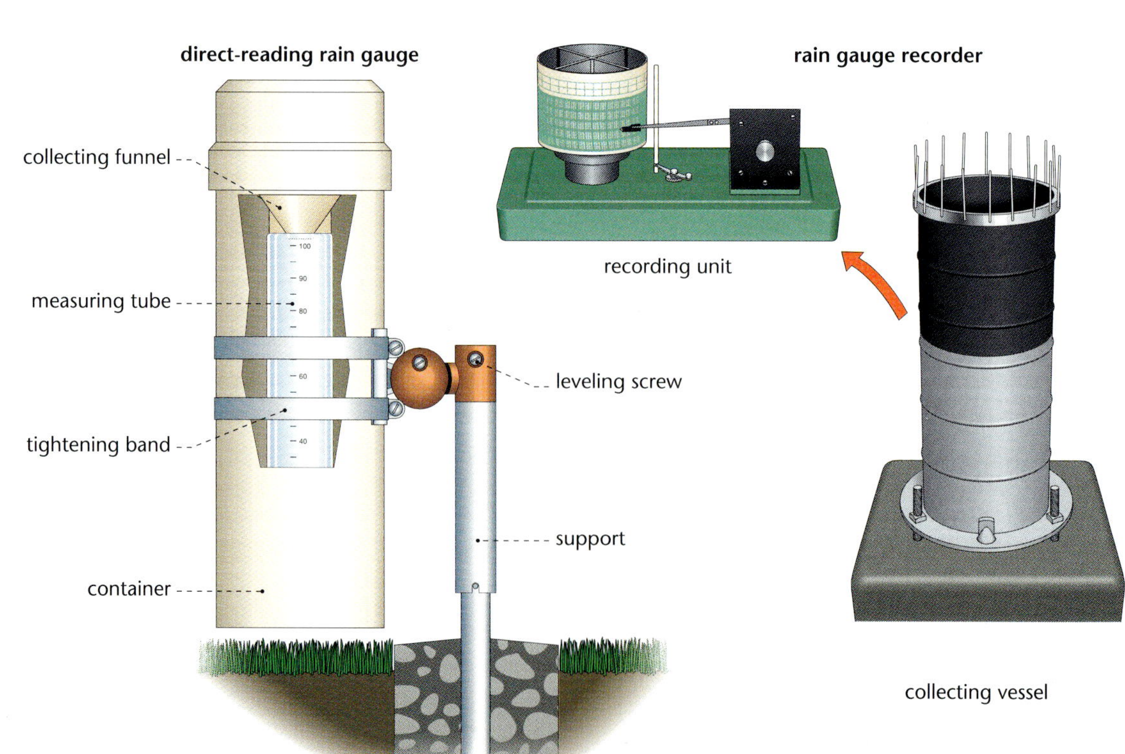

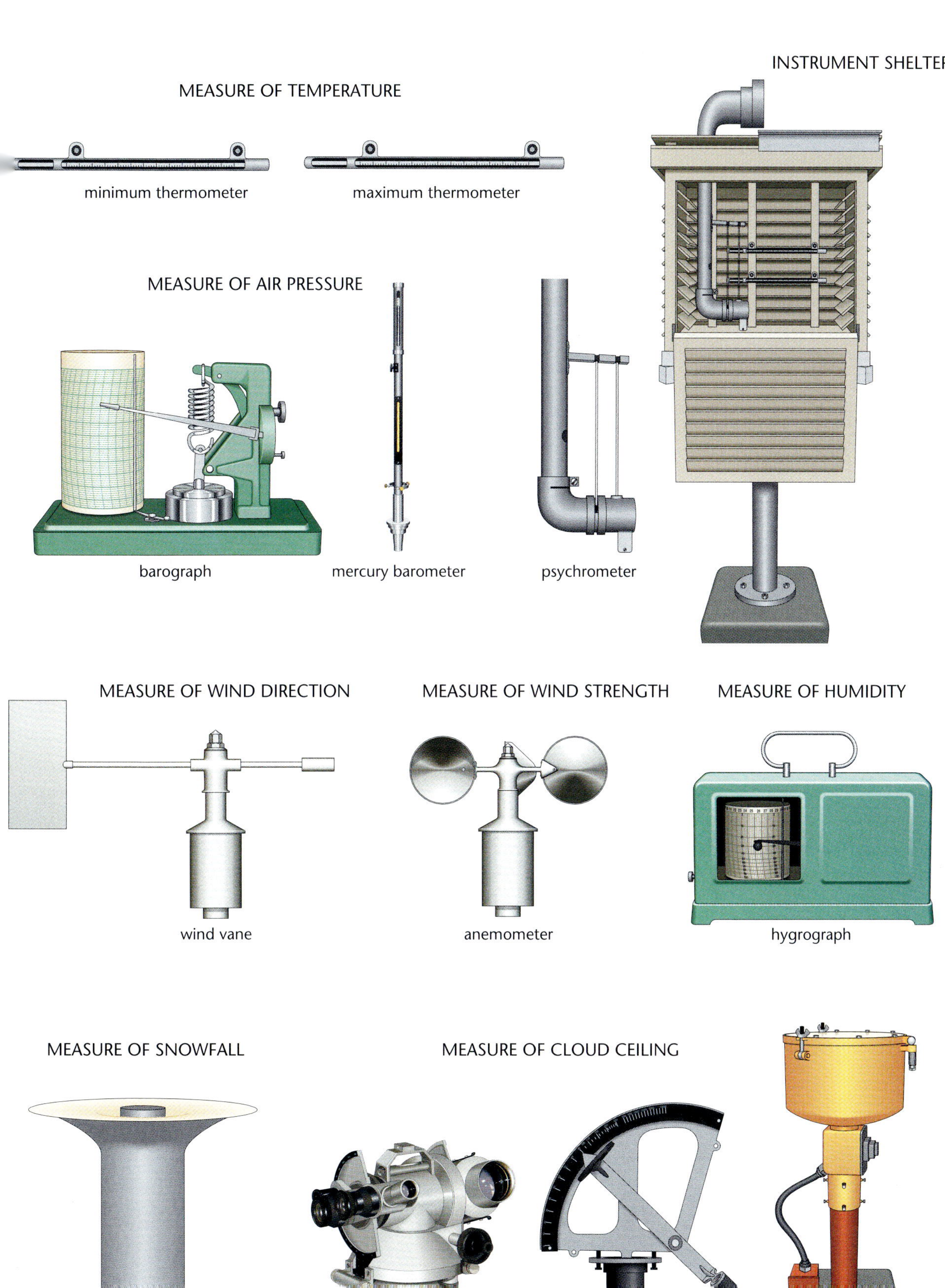

MEASURE OF TEMPERATURE
minimum thermometer
maximum thermometer
INSTRUMENT SHELTER
MEASURE OF AIR PRESSURE
barograph
mercury barometer
psychrometer
MEASURE OF WIND DIRECTION
MEASURE OF WIND STRENGTH
MEASURE OF HUMIDITY
wind vane
anemometer
hygrograph
MEASURE OF SNOWFALL
MEASURE OF CLOUD CEILING
snow gauge
theodolite
alidade
ceiling projector

GEOSTATIONARY SATELLITE

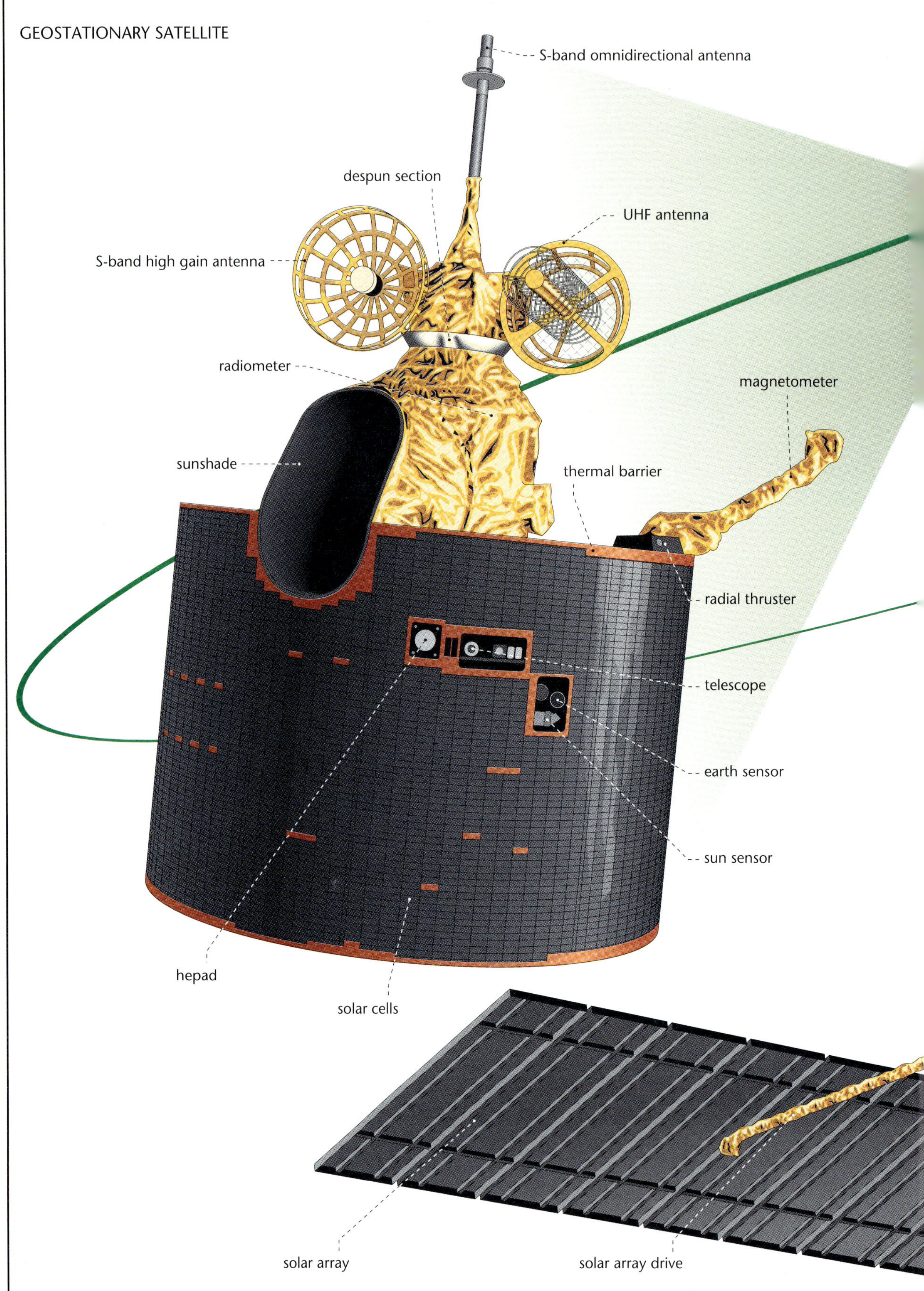

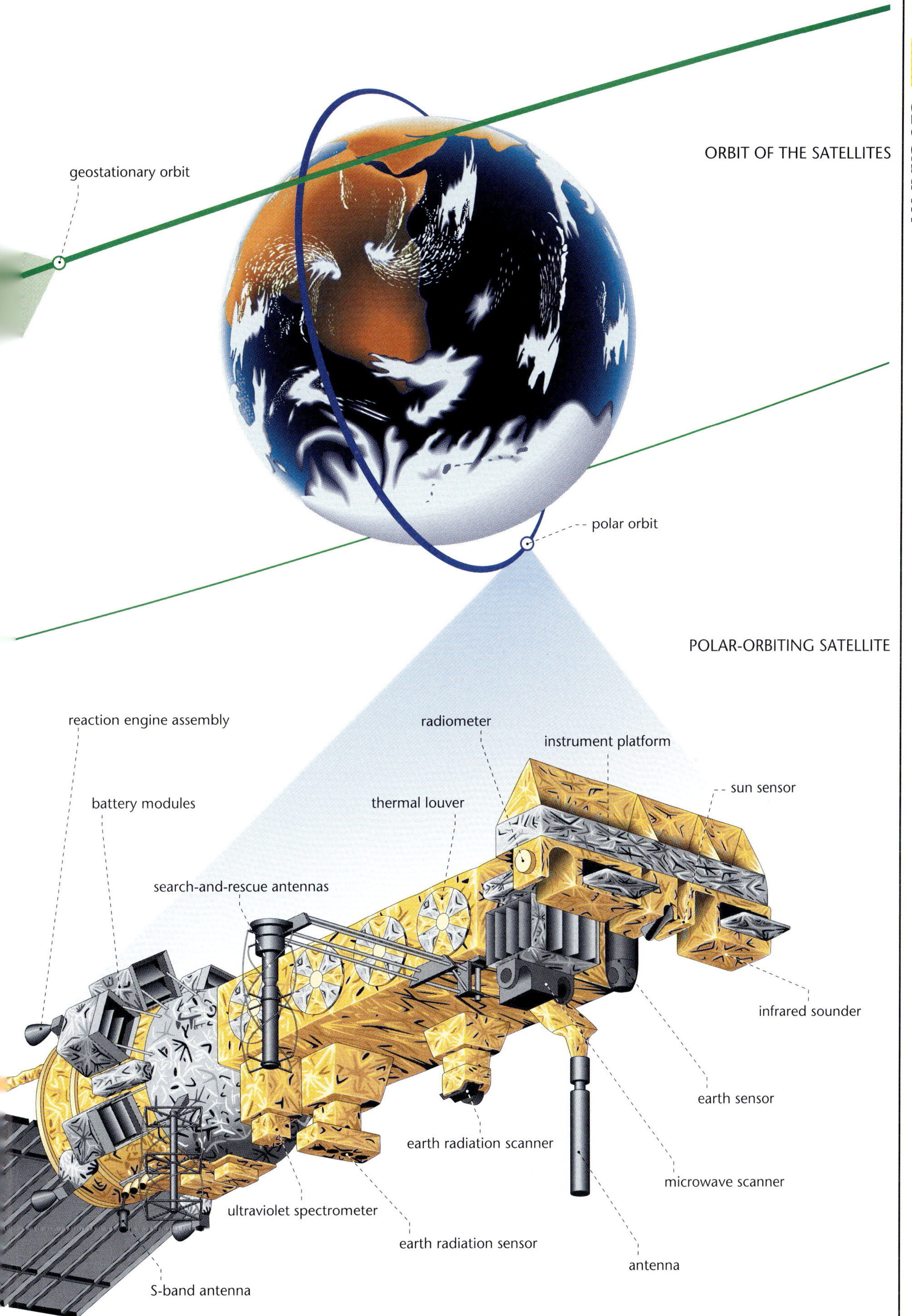

geostationary orbit
ORBIT OF THE SATELLITES
polar orbit
POLAR-ORBITING SATELLITE
reaction engine assembly
radiometer
instrument platform
sun sensor
battery modules
thermal louver
search-and-rescue antennas
infrared sounder
earth sensor
earth radiation scanner
microwave scanner
ultraviolet spectrometer
earth radiation sensor
antenna
S-band antenna

CLOUDS AND METEOROLOGICAL SYMBOLS

CLIMATES OF THE WORLD

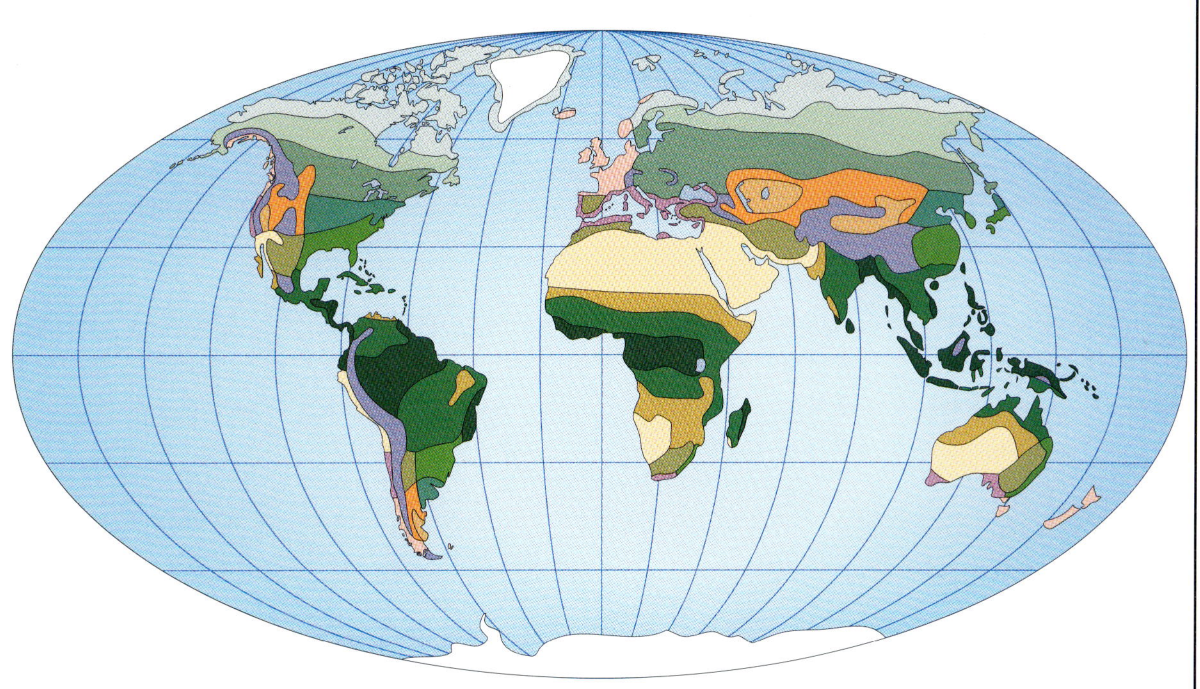

TROPICAL CLIMATES

- tropical rain forest
- tropical savanna
- steppe
- desert

CONTINENTAL CLIMATES

- dry continental - arid
- dry continental - semiarid

TEMPERATE CLIMATES

- humid - long summer
- humid - short summer
- marine

SUBTROPICAL CLIMATES

- Mediterranean subtropical
- humid subtropical
- dry subtropical

POLAR CLIMATES

- polar tundra
- polar ice cap

HIGHLAND CLIMATES

- highland climates

SUBARCTIC CLIMATES

- subarctic climates

oasis palm grove

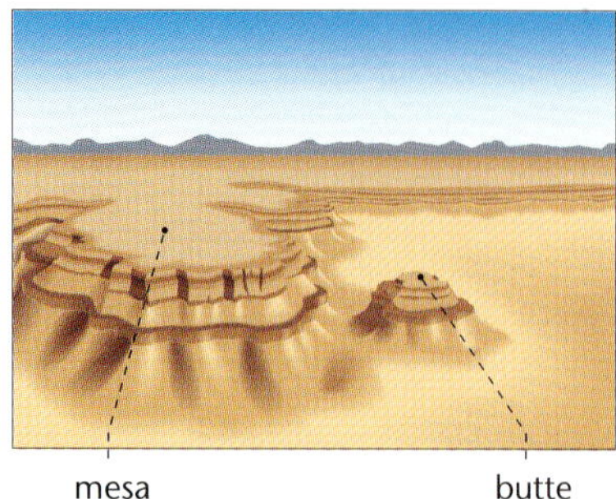

mesa butte

rocky desert

saline lake

sandy desert

crescentic dune

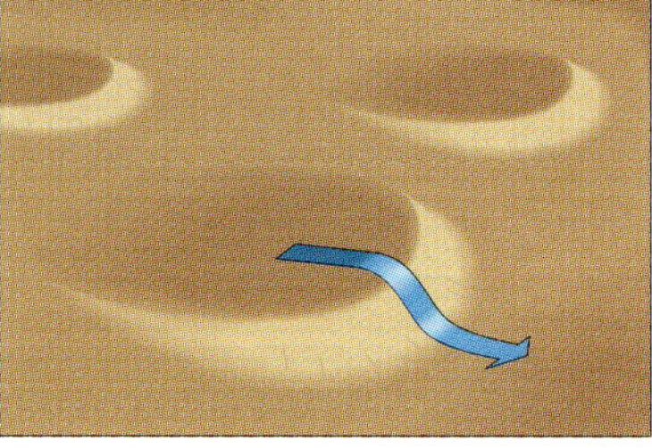

parabolic dune

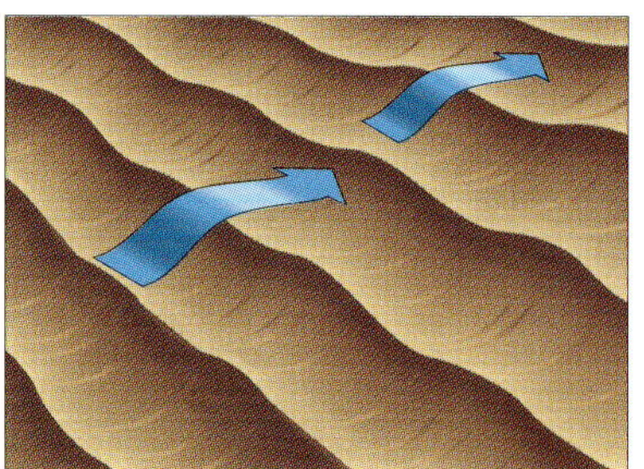

transverse dunes

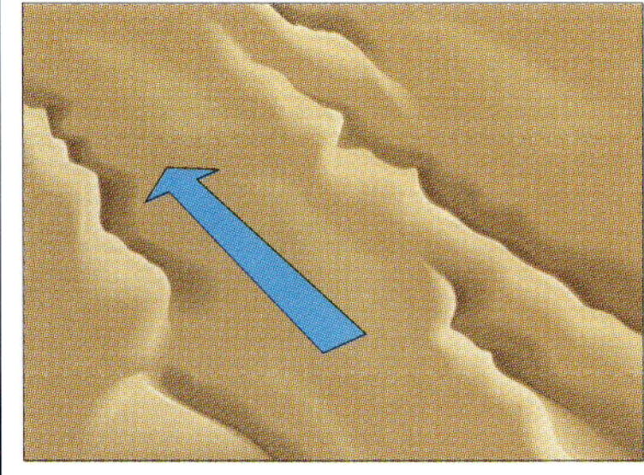

chain of dunes

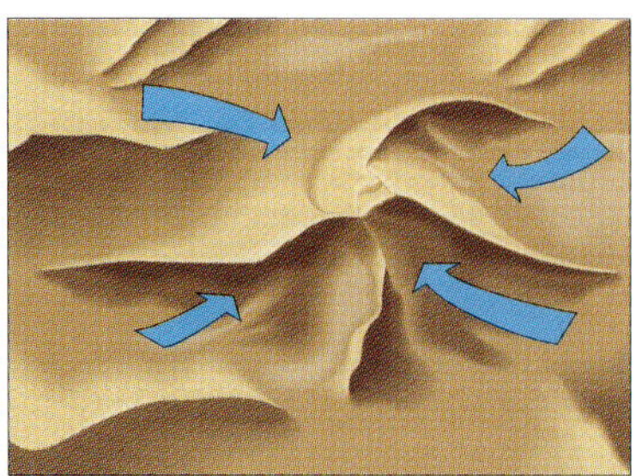

complex dune

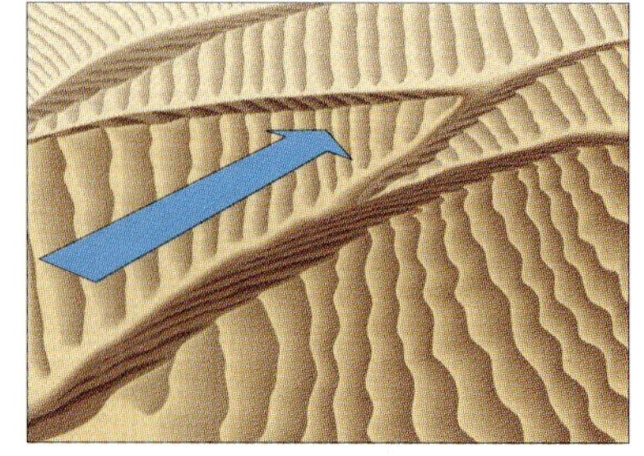

longitudinal dunes

CARTOGRAPHY

HEMISPHERES

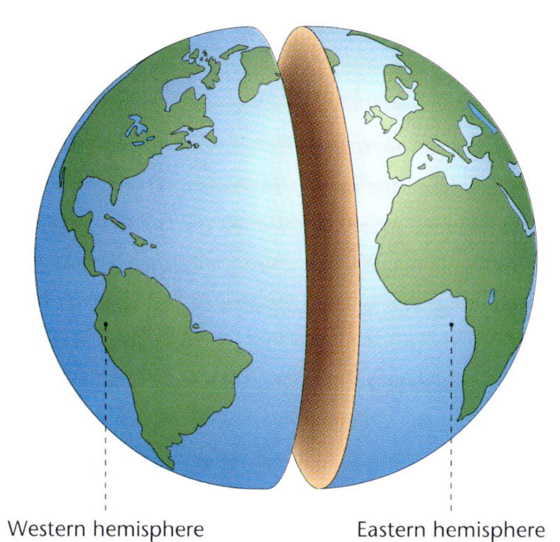

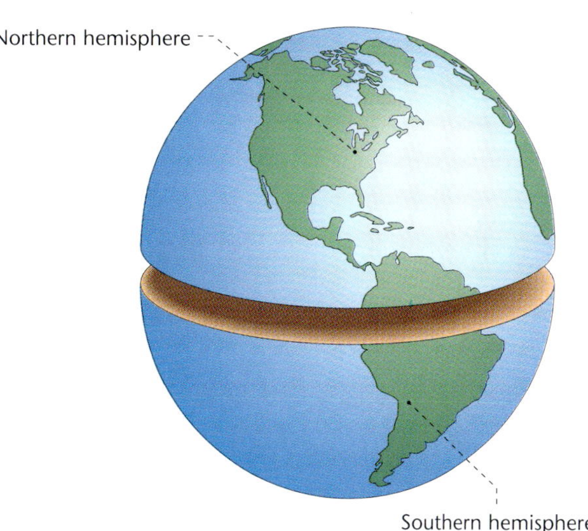

GRID SYSTEM

lines of latitude

lines of longitude

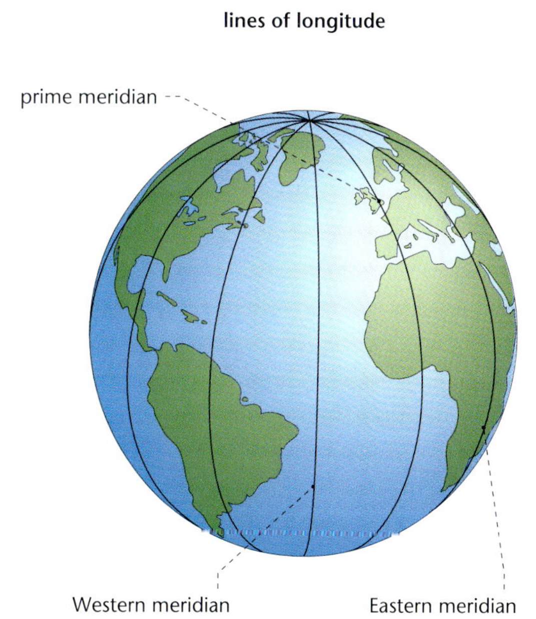

REMOTE DETECTION SATELLITE

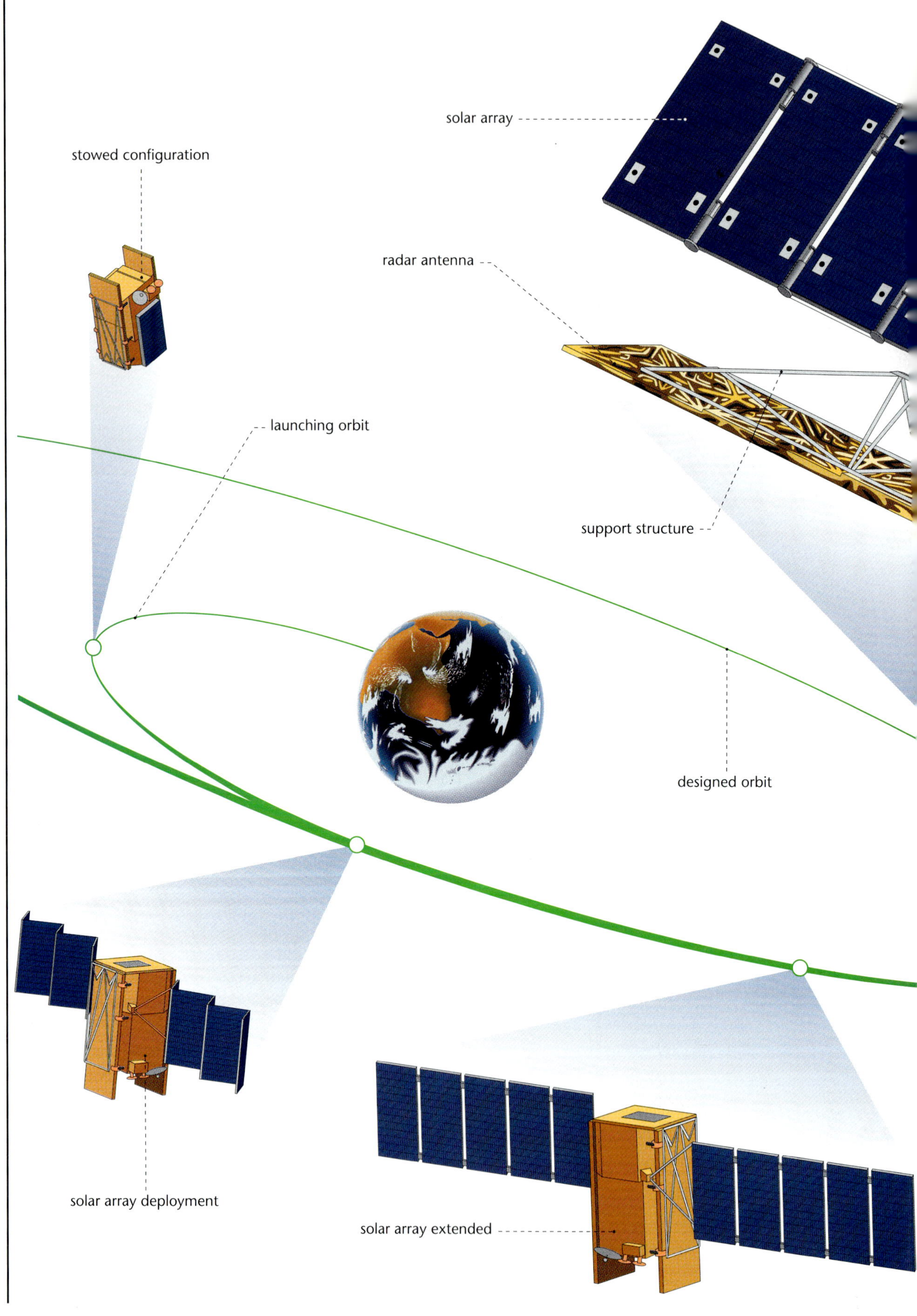

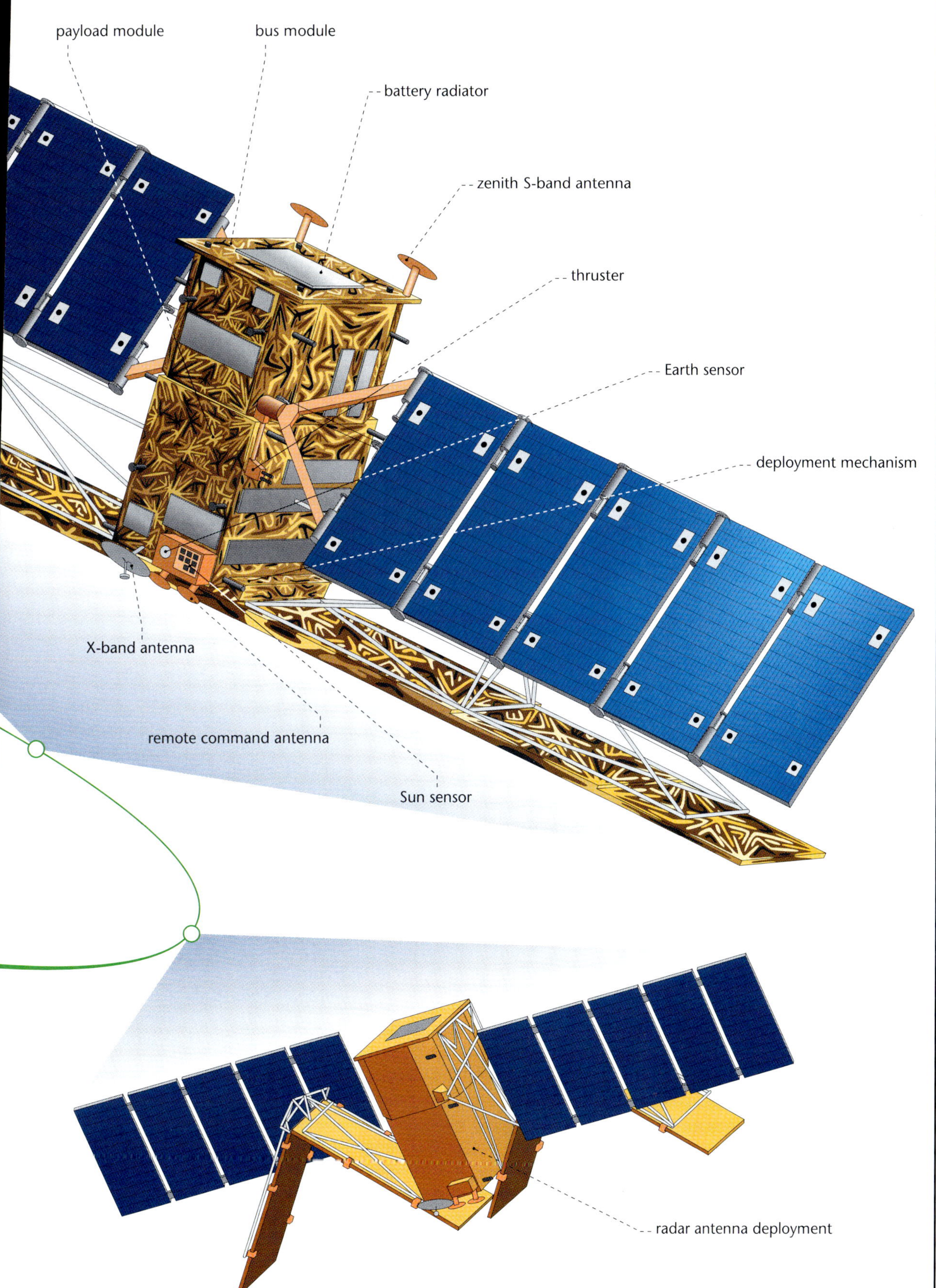
payload module
bus module
battery radiator
zenith S-band antenna
thruster
Earth sensor
deployment mechanism
X-band antenna
remote command antenna
Sun sensor
radar antenna deployment

MAP PROJECTIONS

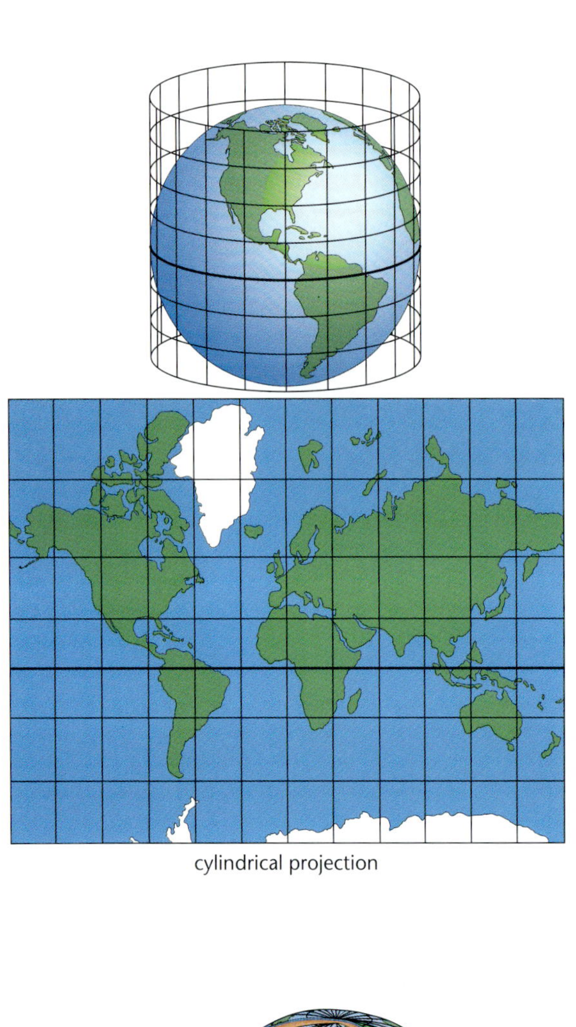

cylindrical projection

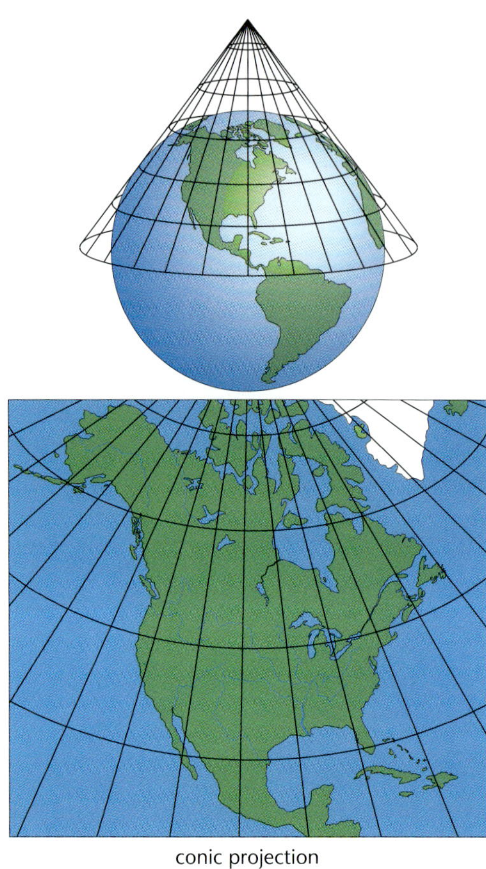

conic projection

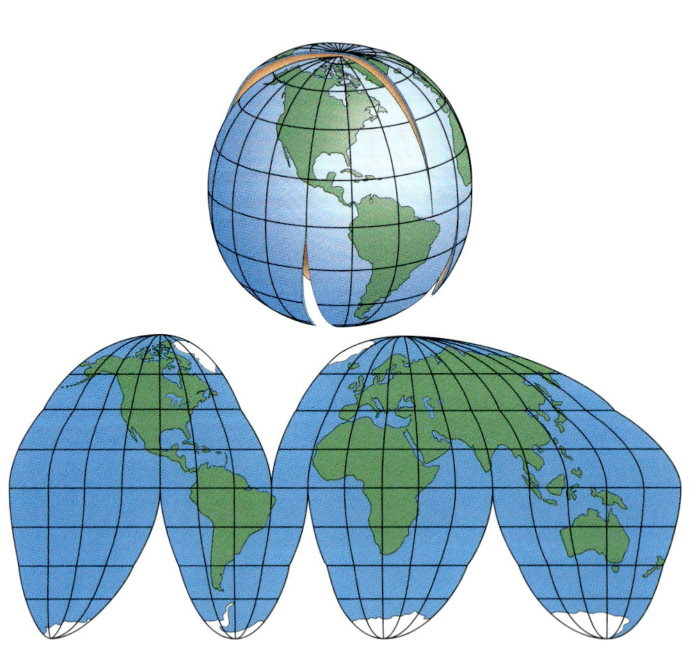

interrupted projection

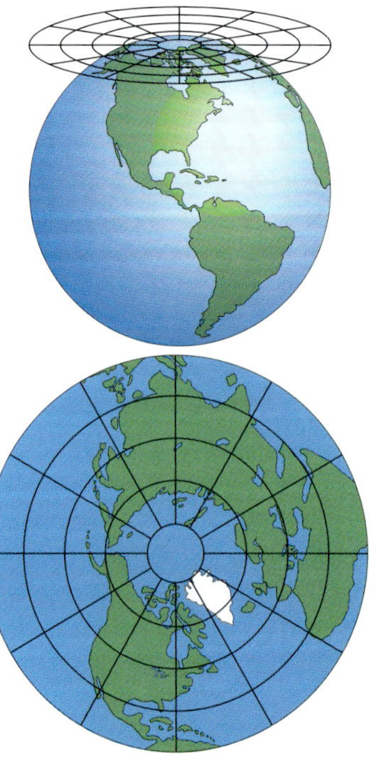

plane projection

POLITICAL MAP

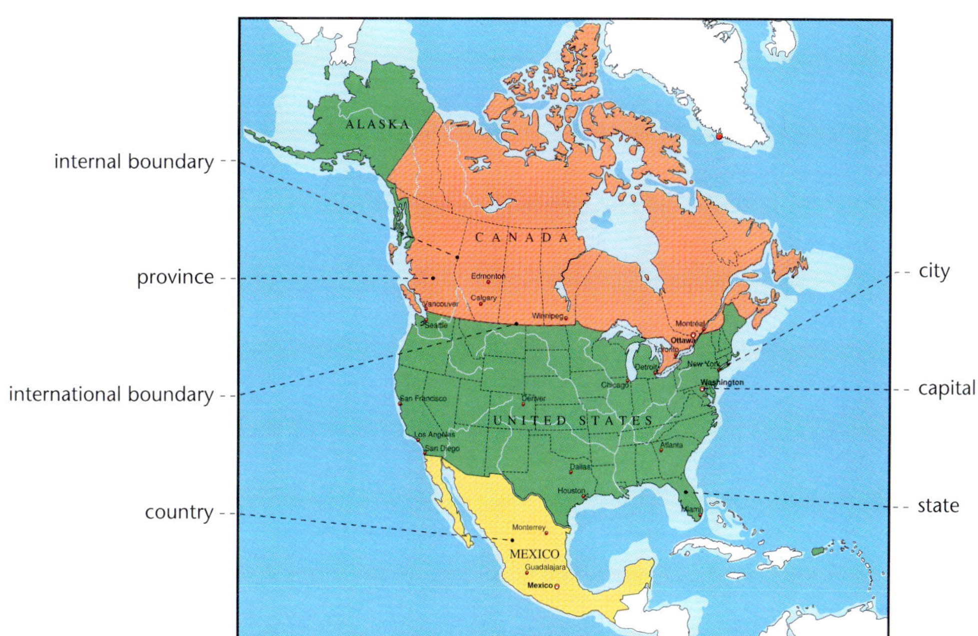

PHYSICAL MAP

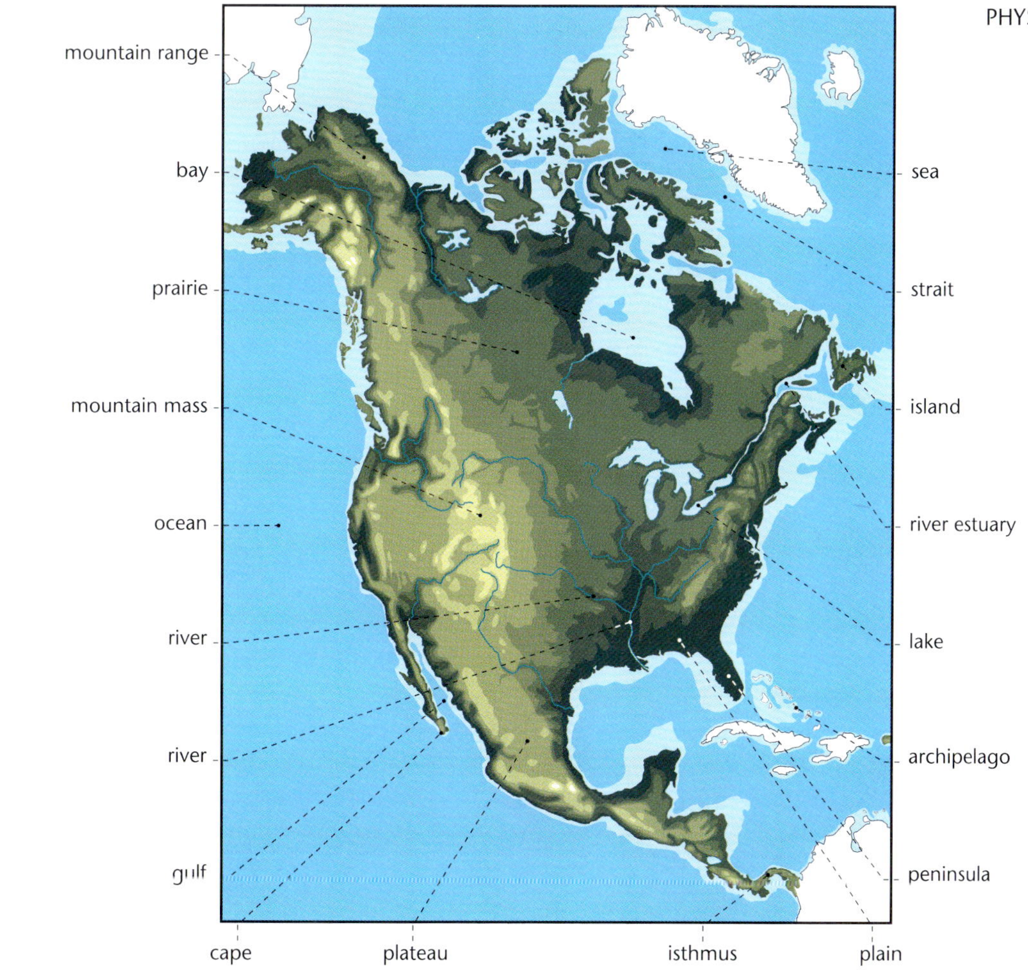

GEOGRAPHY

URBAN MAP

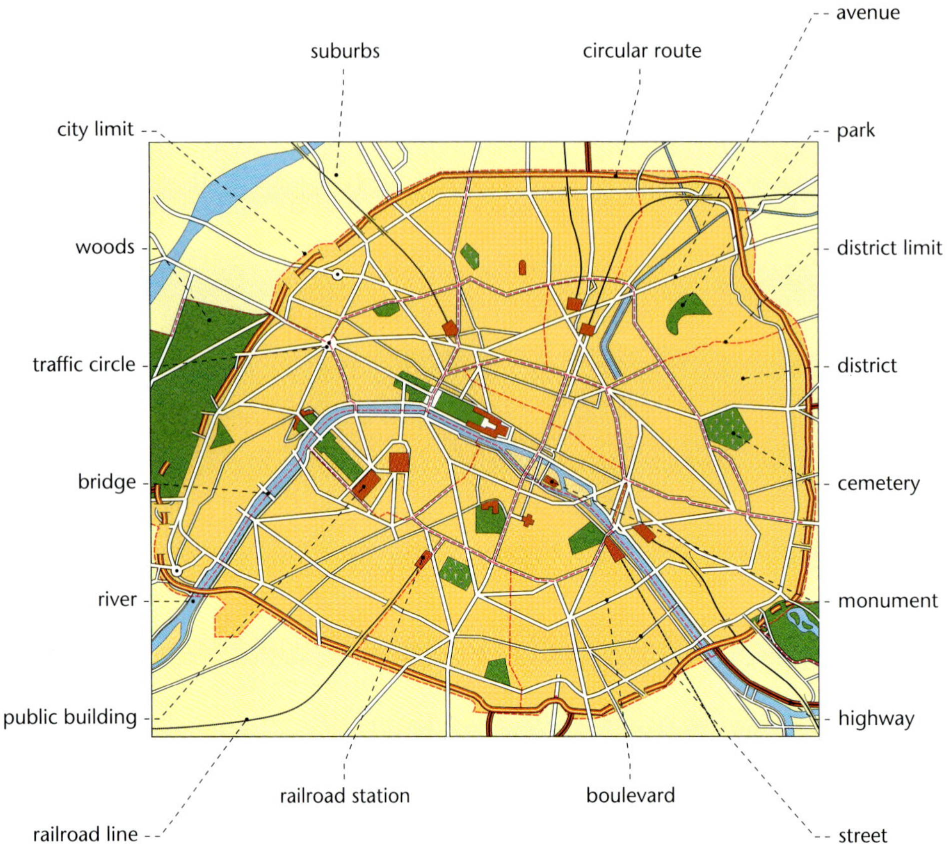

ROAD MAP

VEGETABLE KINGDOM

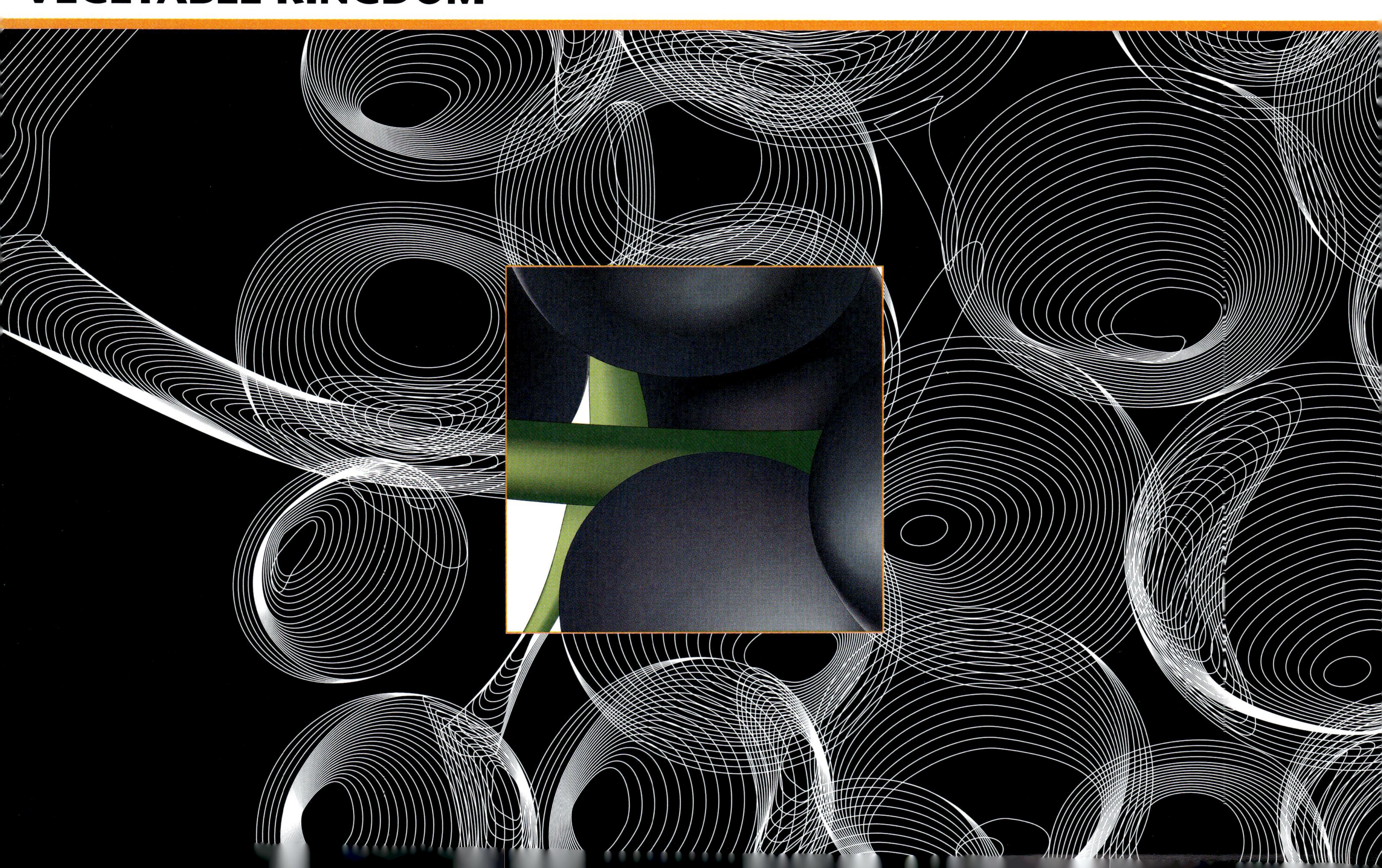

CONTENTS

MUSHROOM

STRUCTURE OF A MUSHROOM
cap
gill
ring
stem
volva
spores
hypha
mycelium
EDIBLE MUSHROOMS
truffle
cultivated mushroom
morel
DEADLY POISONOUS MUSHROOM
royal agaric
delicious lactarius
green russula
destroying angel
POISONOUS MUSHROOM
chanterelle
boletus
oyster mushroom
fly agaric

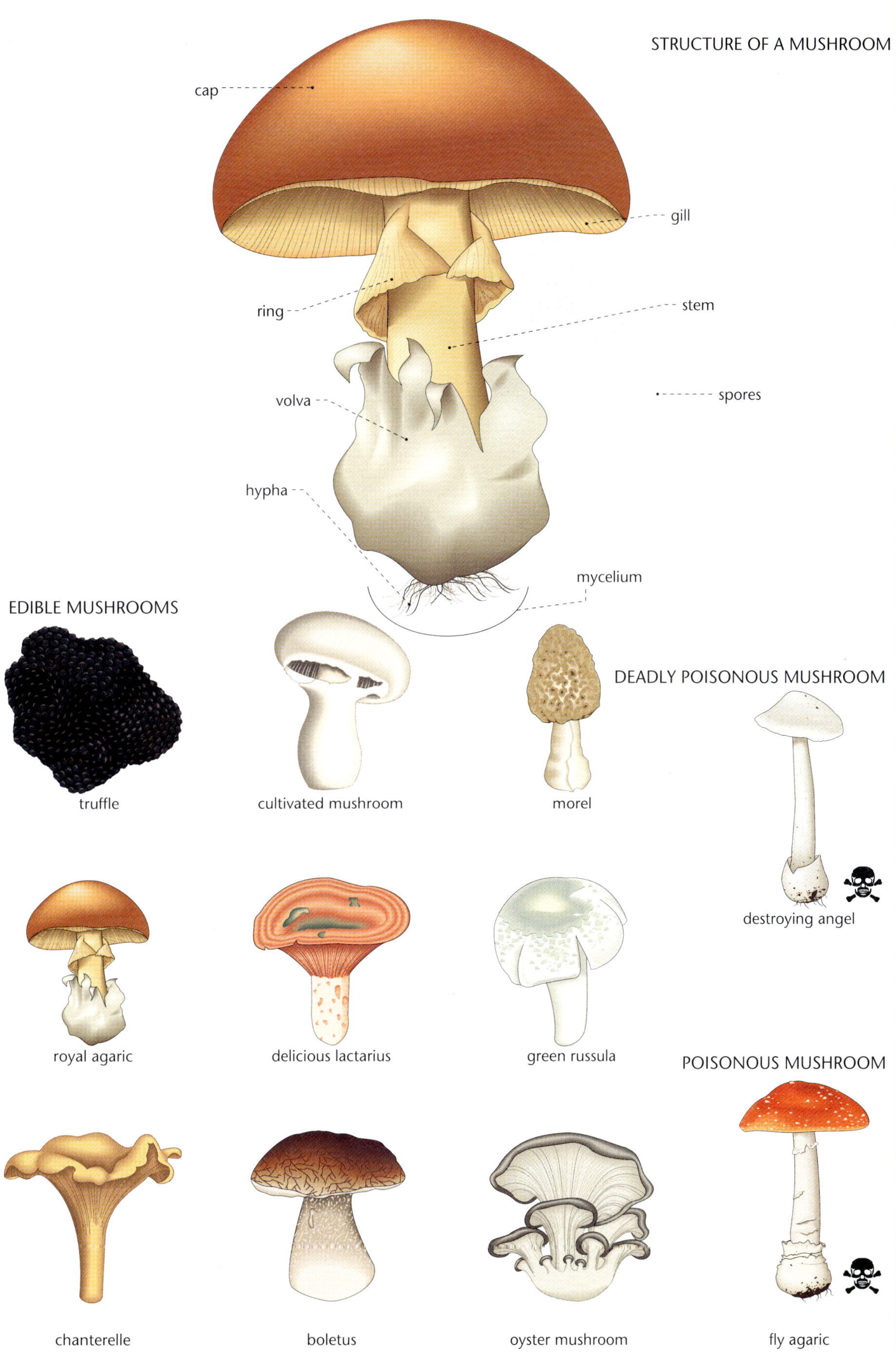

VEGETABLE KINGDOM
LEAF MARGIN
dentate
doubly dentate
crenate
ciliate
entire
lobate
LEAF
COMPOUND LEAVES
trifoliolate
palmate
pinnatifid
odd pinnate
abruptly pinnate
SIMPLE LEAVES
orbiculate
reniform
linear
peltate
hastate
ovate
cordate
spatulate
lanceolate
stipule
sheath
leaf axil
petiole
vein
midrib

STRUCTURE OF A PLANT

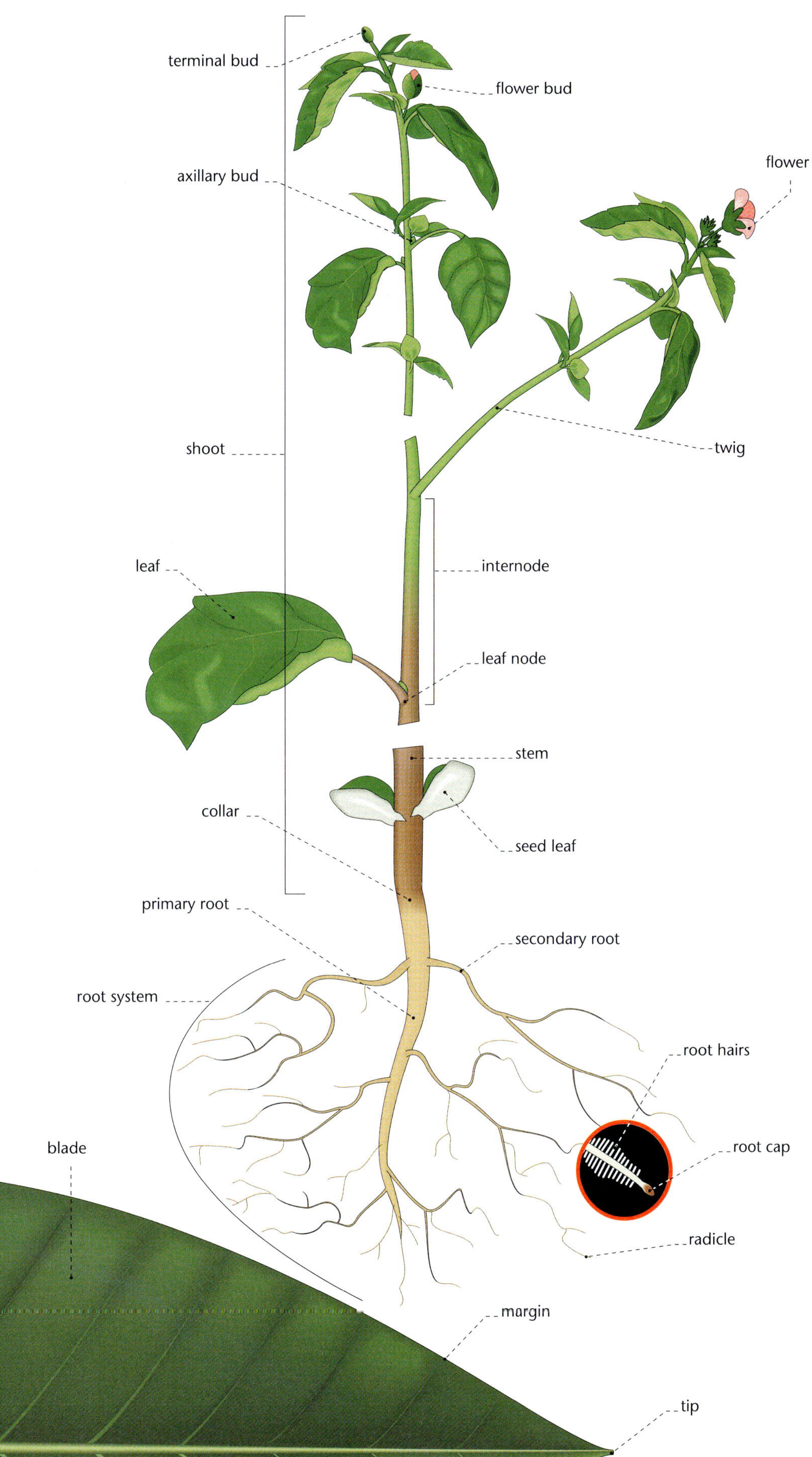

cone
umbrella pine
pine seed
BRANCH
female cone
male cone
larch
TYPES OF LEAVES
fir needles
cypress scalelike leaves
pine needles

STRUCTURE OF A TREE

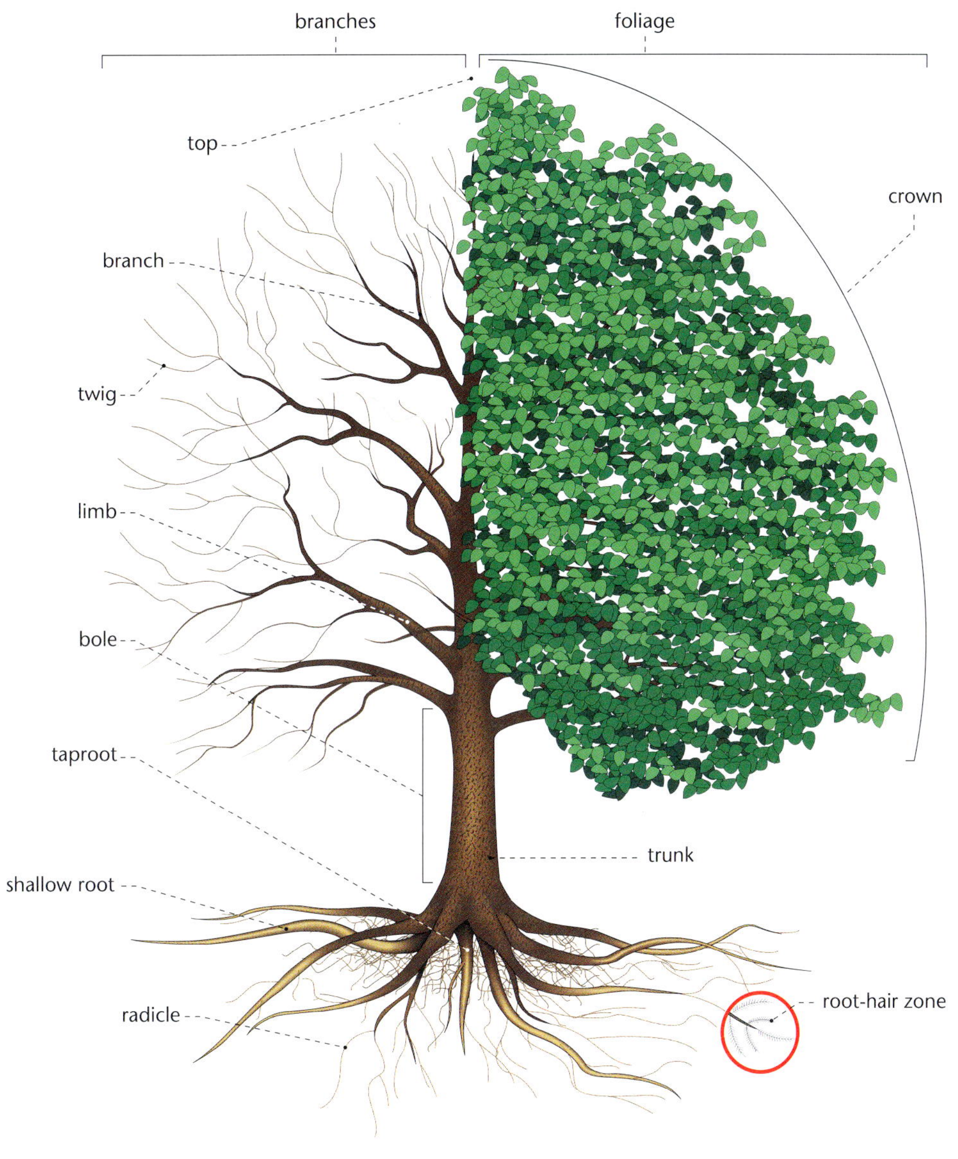

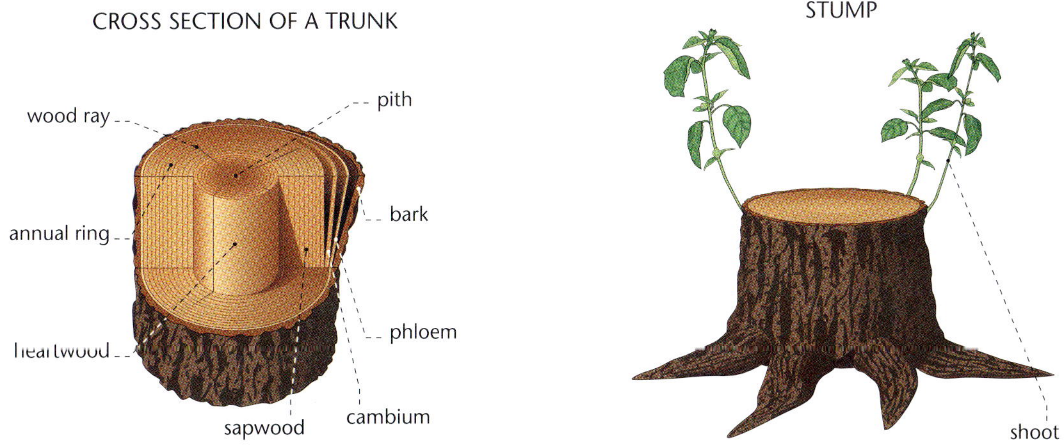

CROSS SECTION OF A TRUNK

STUMP

STRUCTURE OF A FLOWER

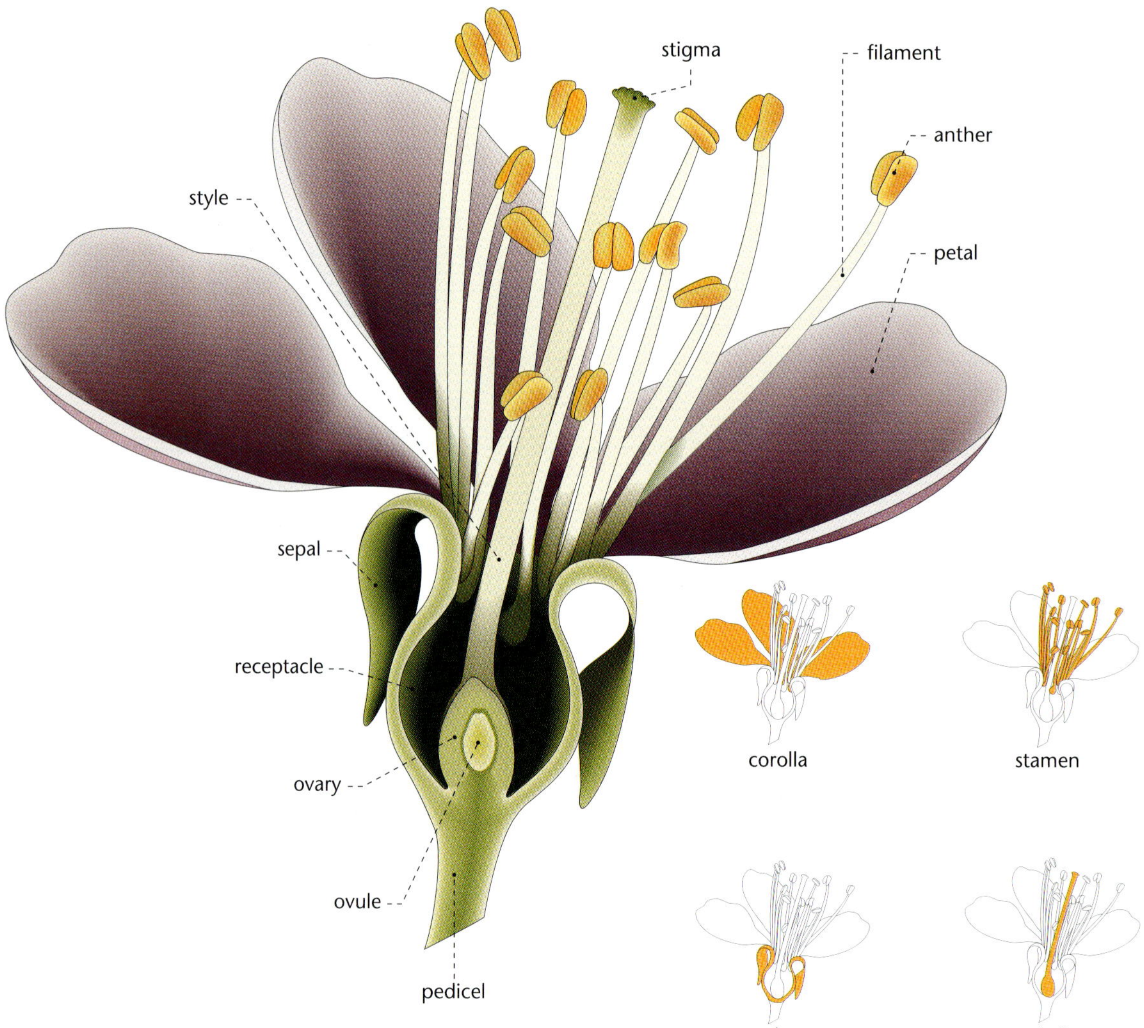

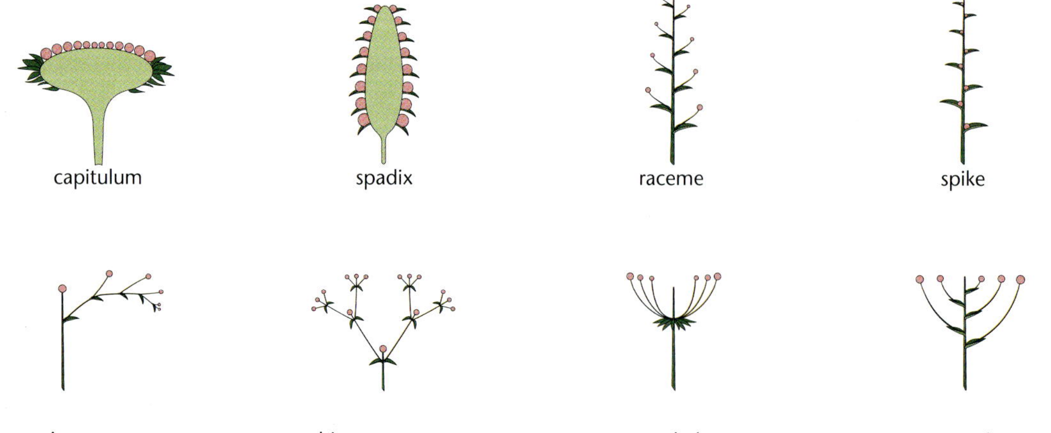

TYPES OF INFLORESCENCES

GRAPE

MATURING STEPS
flowering
fruition
ripening
ripeness
VINE STOCK
fruit branch
vine shoot
sucker
trunk
root system
BUNCH OF GRAPES
main stalk
tendril
pedicel
branch
grape
GRAPE LEAF
terminal lobe
upper lateral sinus
upper lateral lobe
lower lateral sinus
petiolar sinus
lower lateral lobe

SECTION OF A BERRY

MAJOR TYPES OF BERRIES

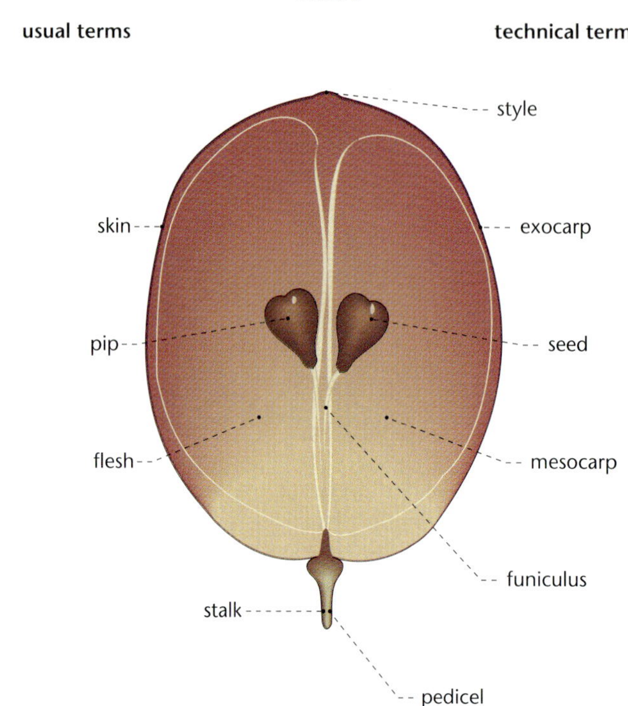

GRAPE

usual terms

technical terms

SECTION OF A RASPBERRY

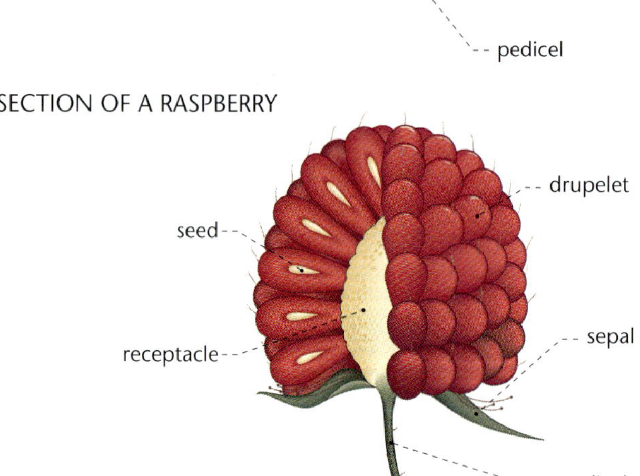

SECTION OF A STRAWBERRY

black currant

currant

grape

gooseberry

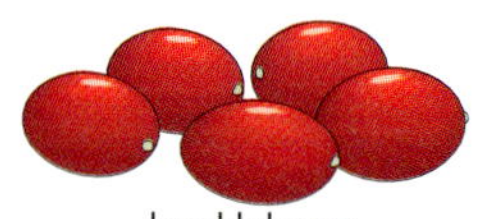

blueberry

huckleberry

cranberry

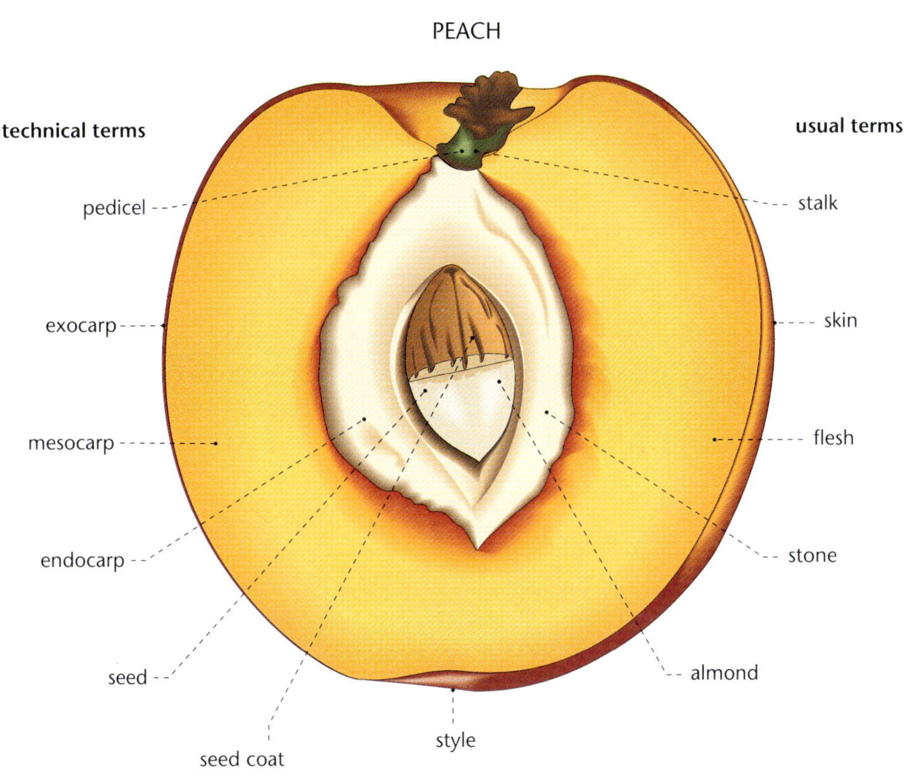

SECTION OF A STONE FRUIT
PEACH
technical terms
usual terms
pedicel
stalk
exocarp
skin
mesocarp
flesh
endocarp
stone
seed
almond
seed coat
style

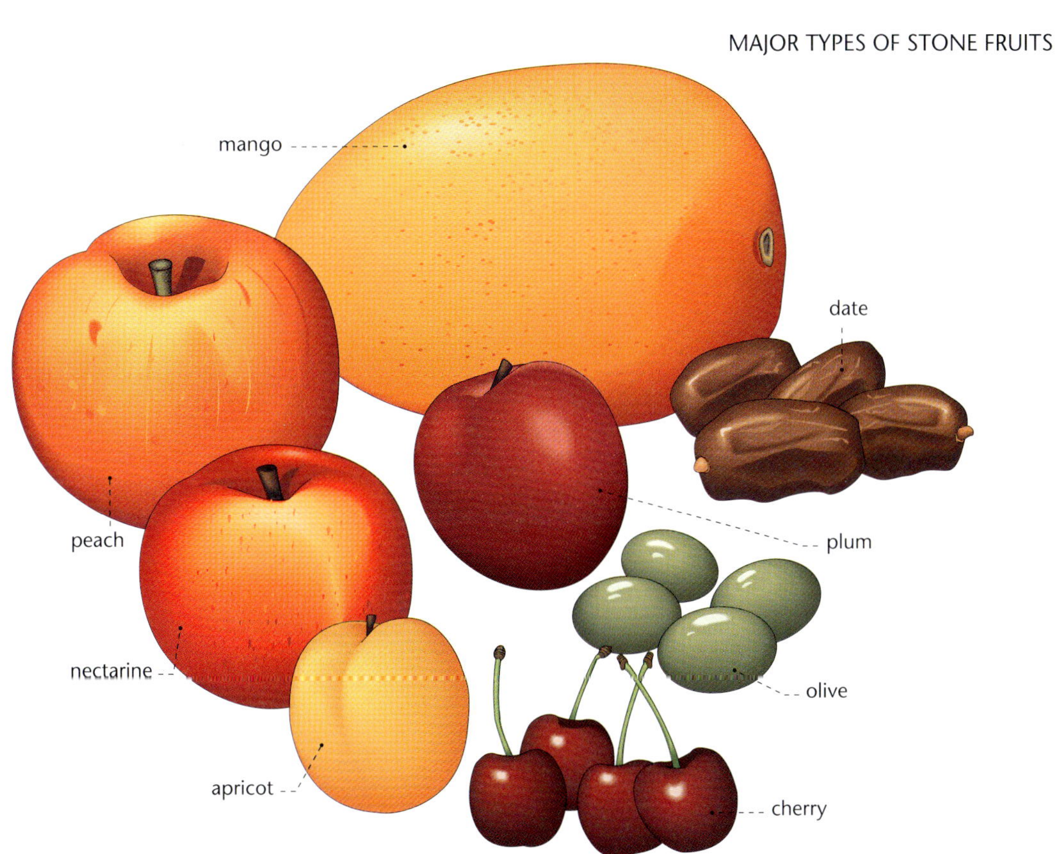

MAJOR TYPES OF STONE FRUITS
mango
date
peach
plum
nectarine
olive
apricot
cherry

POME FLESHY FRUITS

SECTION OF A POME FRUIT

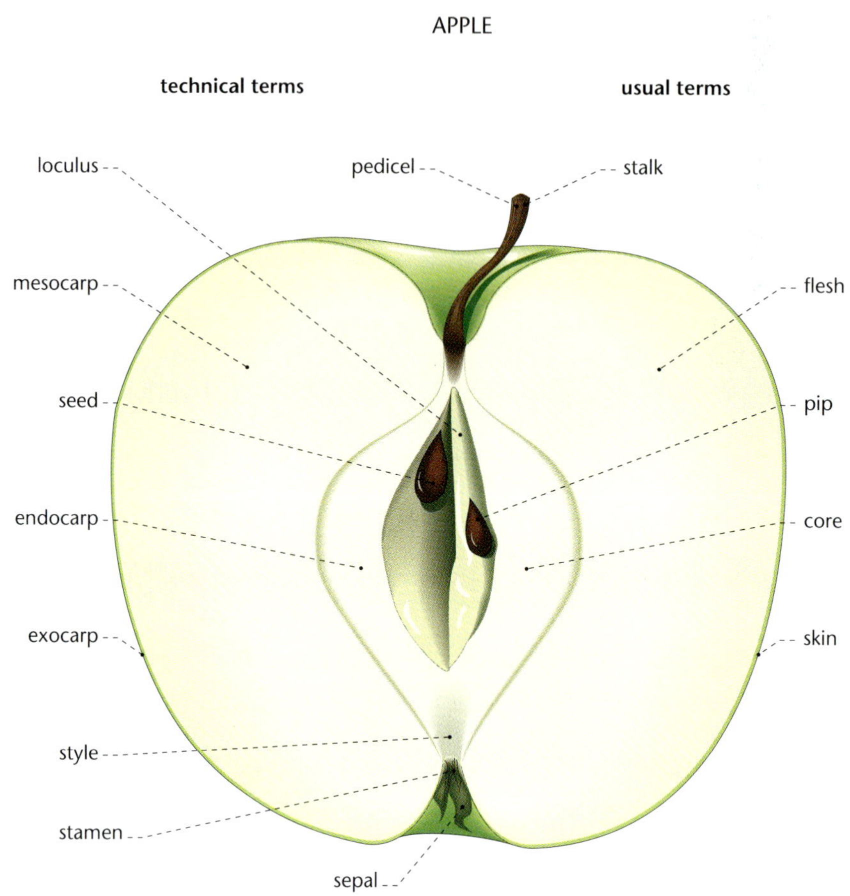

MAJOR TYPES OF POME FRUITS

SECTION OF A CITRUS FRUIT

ORANGE

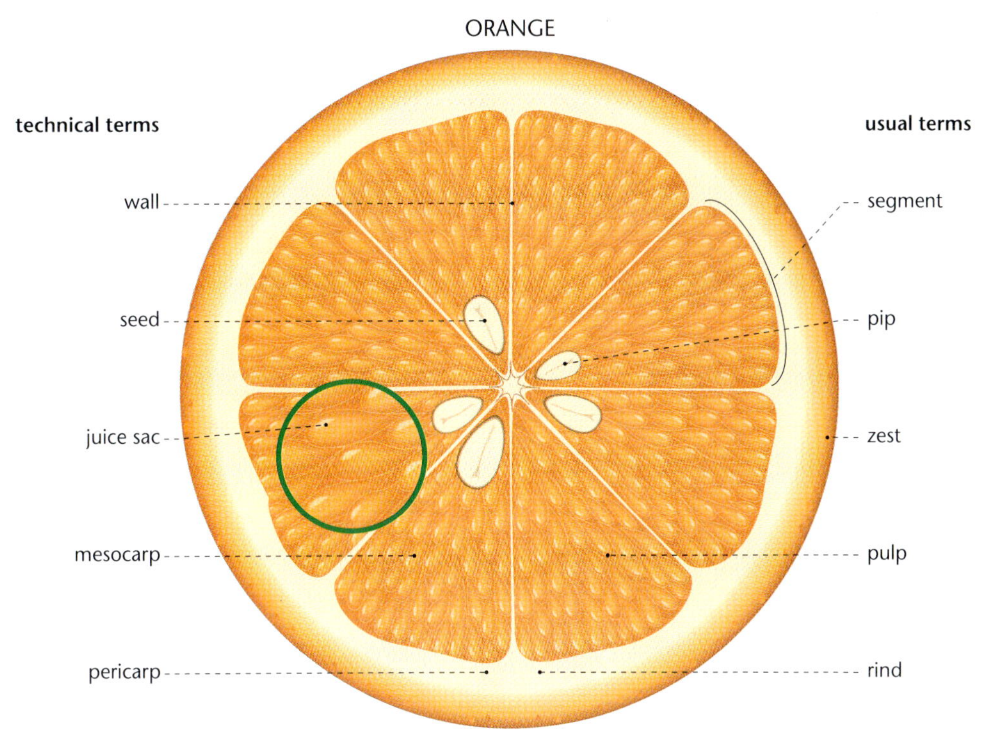

MAJOR TYPES OF CITRUS FRUITS

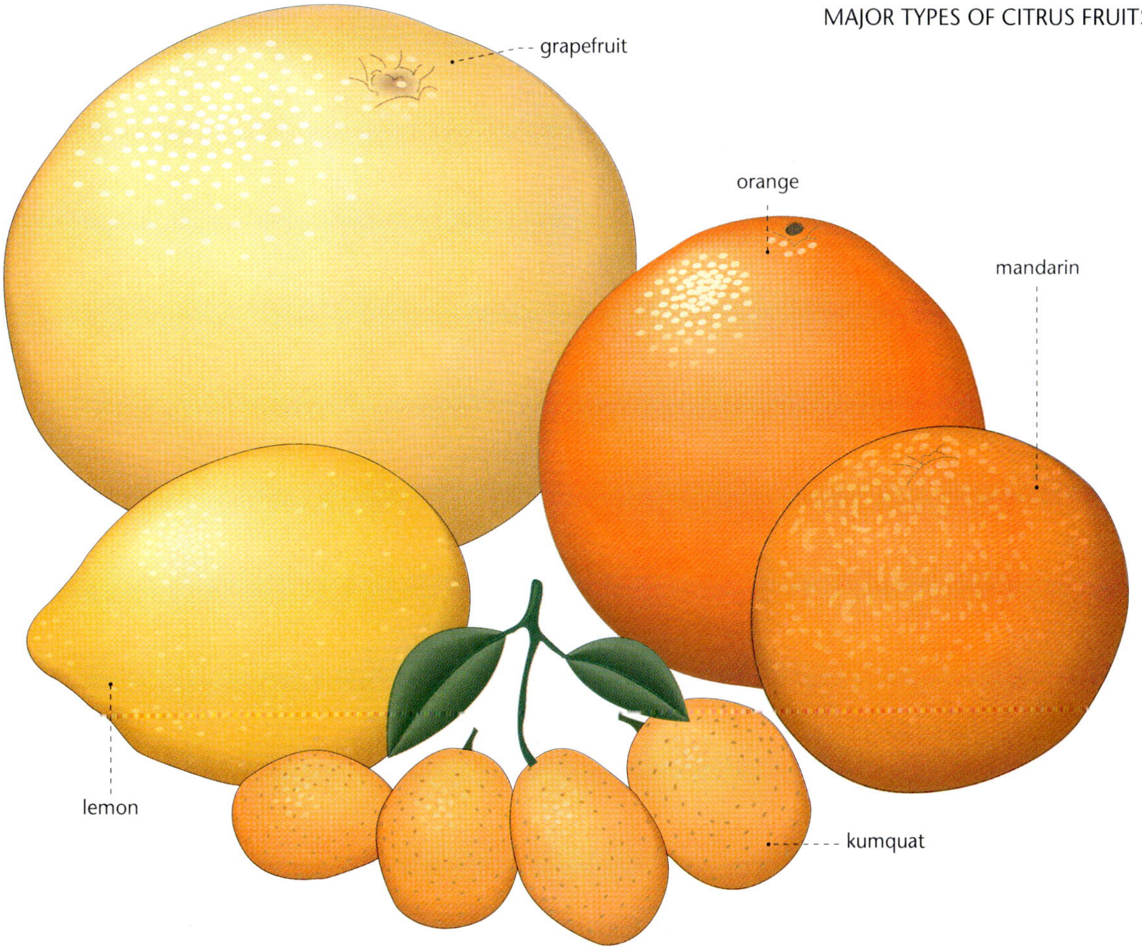

DRY FRUITS: NUTS

SECTION OF A HAZELNUT

SECTION OF A WALNUT

MAJOR TYPES OF NUTS

HUSK

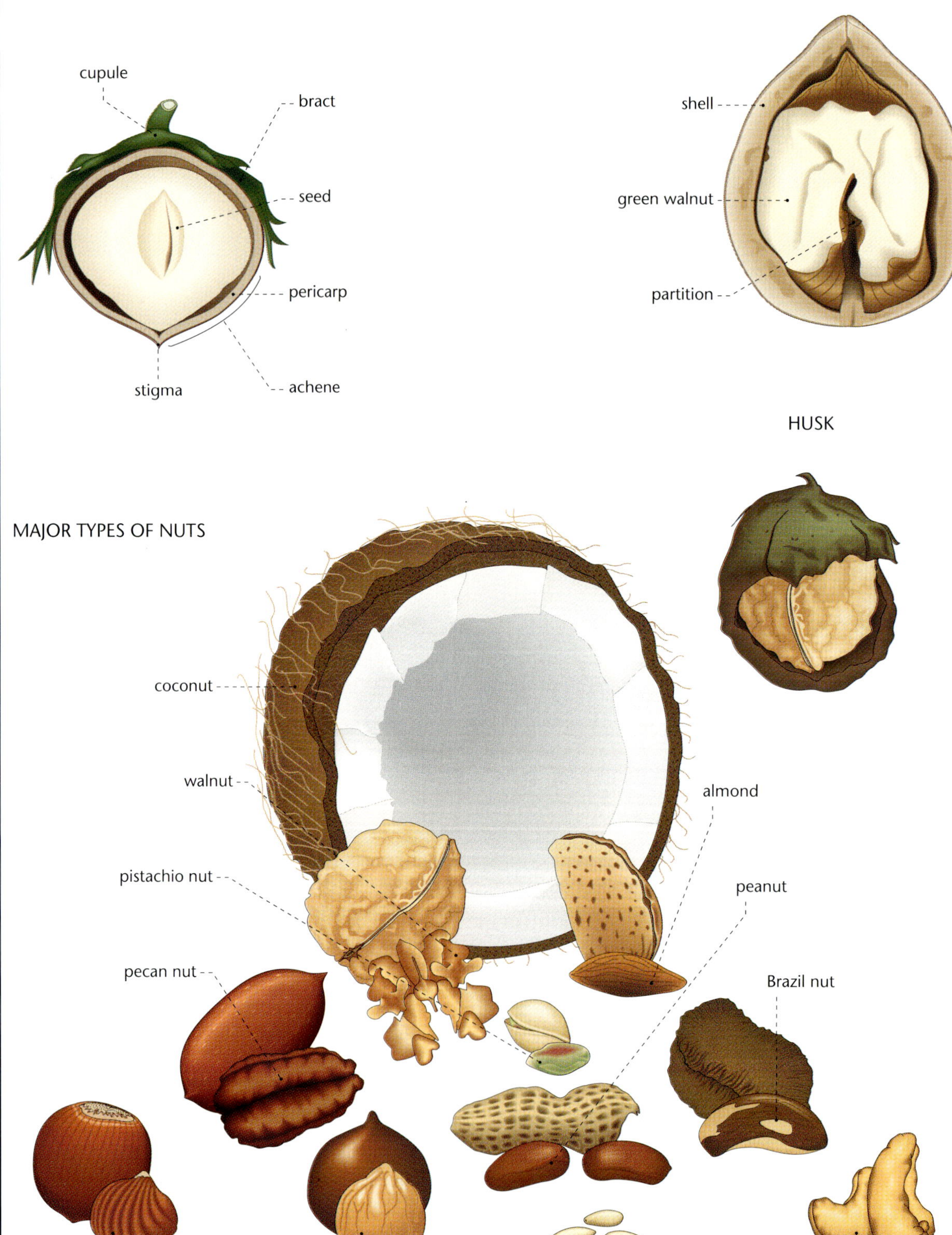

VARIOUS DRY FRUITS

SECTION OF A FOLLICLE

star anise

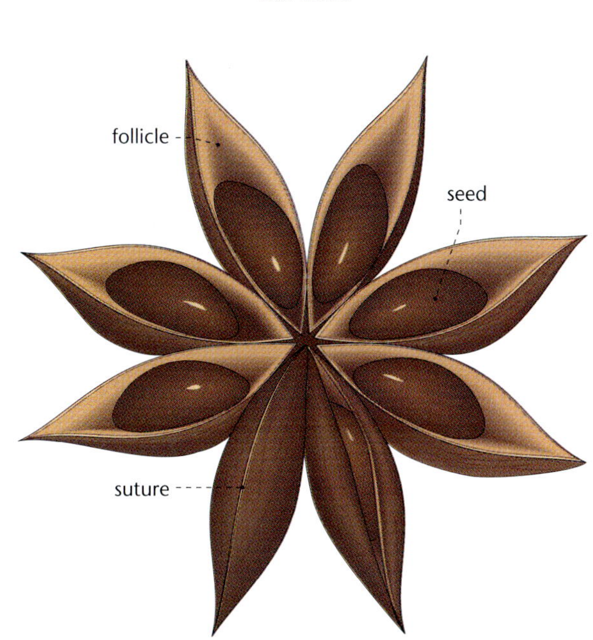

SECTION OF A SILIQUE

mustard

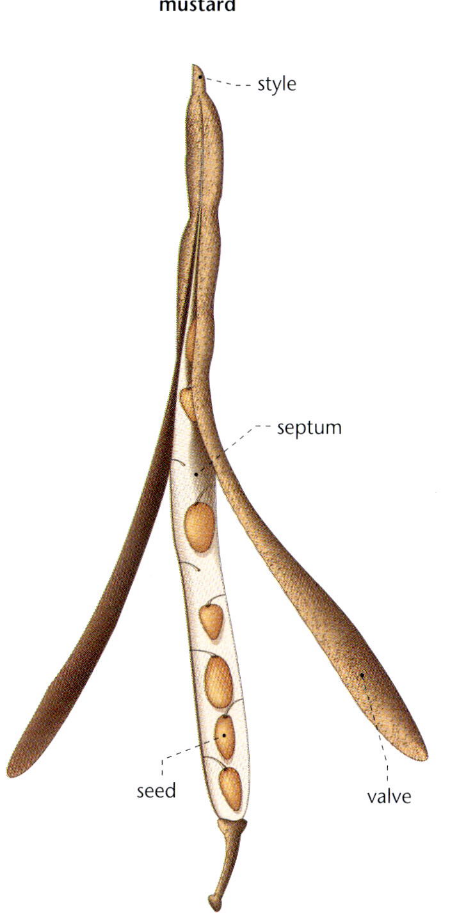

SECTION OF A LEGUME

pea

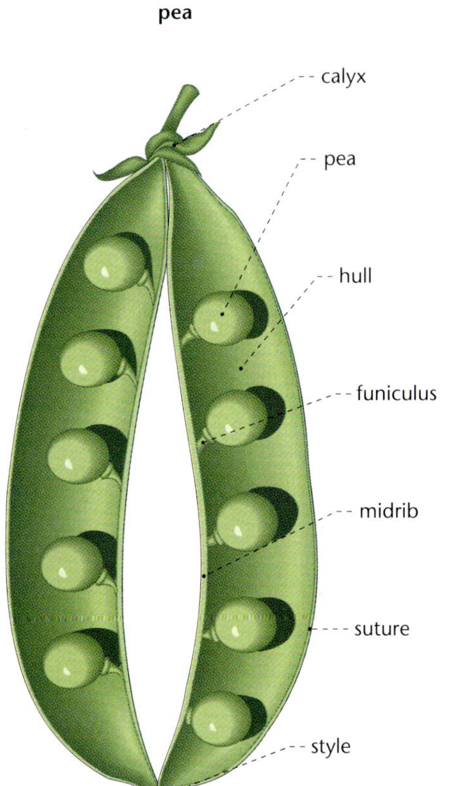

SECTION OF A CAPSULE

poppy

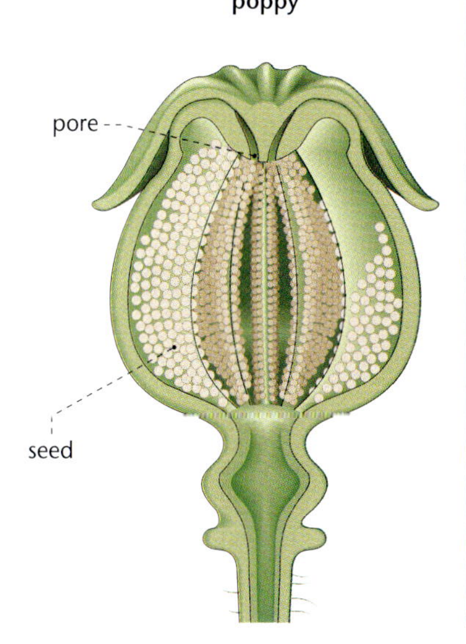

MAJOR TYPES OF TROPICAL FRUITS

VEGETABLES

FRUIT VEGETABLES

INFLORESCENT VEGETABLES

SECTION OF A BULB

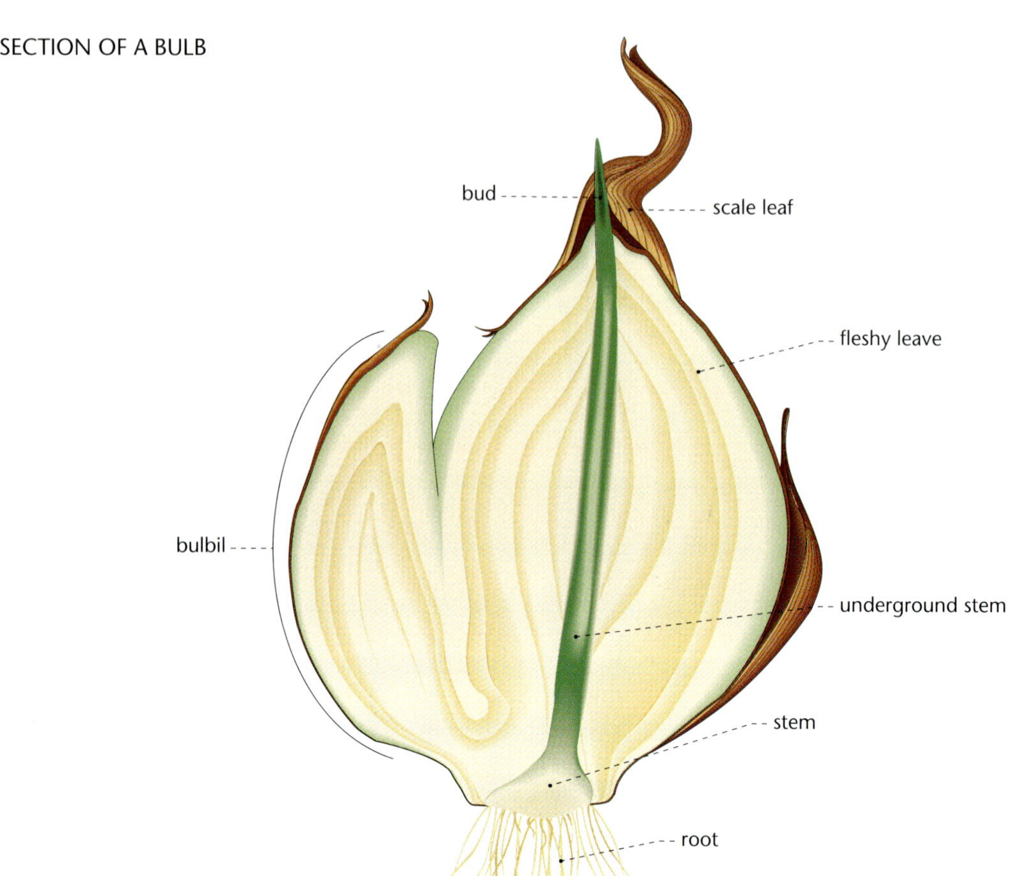

BULB VEGETABLES

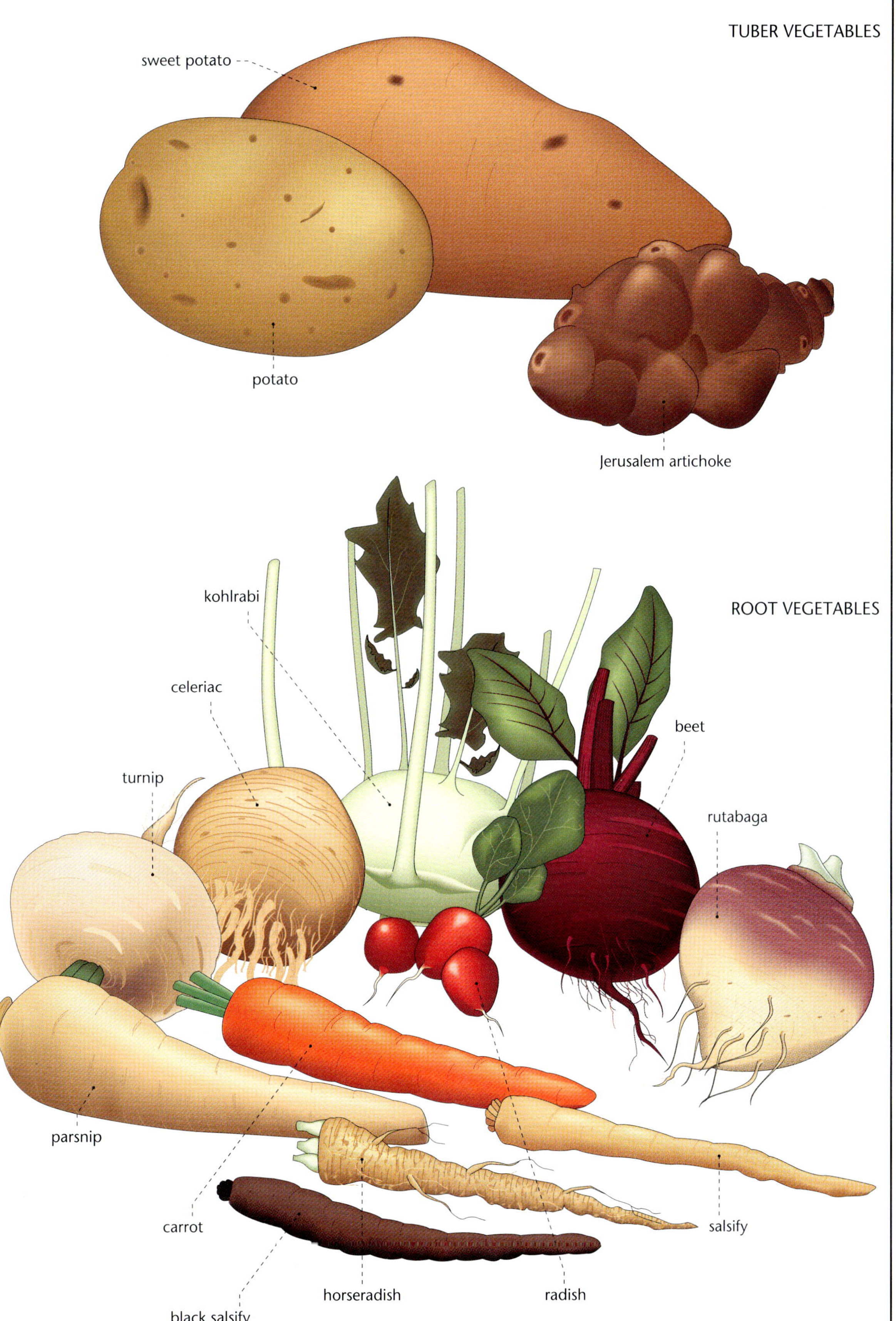

TUBER VEGETABLES

ROOT VEGETABLES

VEGETABLE KINGDOM

71

STALK VEGETABLES
rhubarb
asparagus
spear
bundle
tip
celery
cardoon
Swiss chard
leaf
branch
head
fennel
stalk
bulb
rib
SEED VEGETABLES
broad beans
sweet peas
green peas
CORN
lentils
chick peas
silk
cob
husk
soybeans
bean sprouts
kernel

72

LEAF VEGETABLES

corn salad

watercress

chicory

Brussels sprouts

curled kale

grape leaf

garden sorrel

spinach

curled endive

broad-leaved endive

romaine lettuce

dandelion

white cabbage

cabbage lettuce

green cabbage

Chinese cabbage

HERBS

dill
basil
borage
chervil
coriander
tarragon
hyssop
sweet bay
lovage
mint
oregano
parsley
rosemary
savory
sage
thyme

CONTENTS

spider

dragonfly

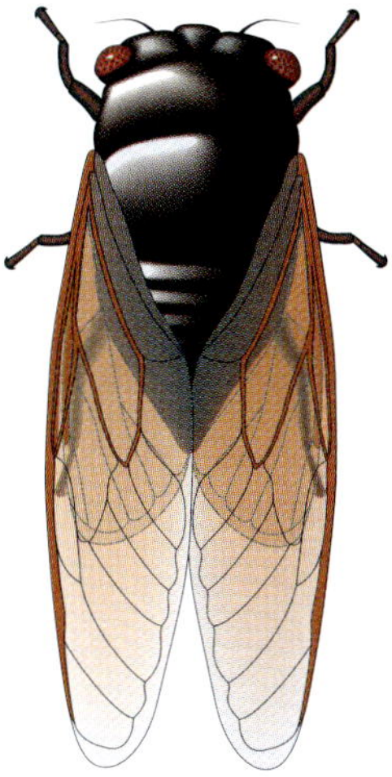

cicada

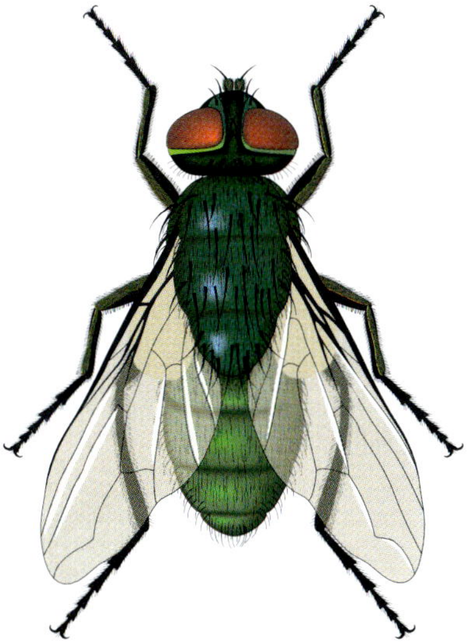

fly

ladybug

ant

grasshopper

ANIMAL KINGDOM

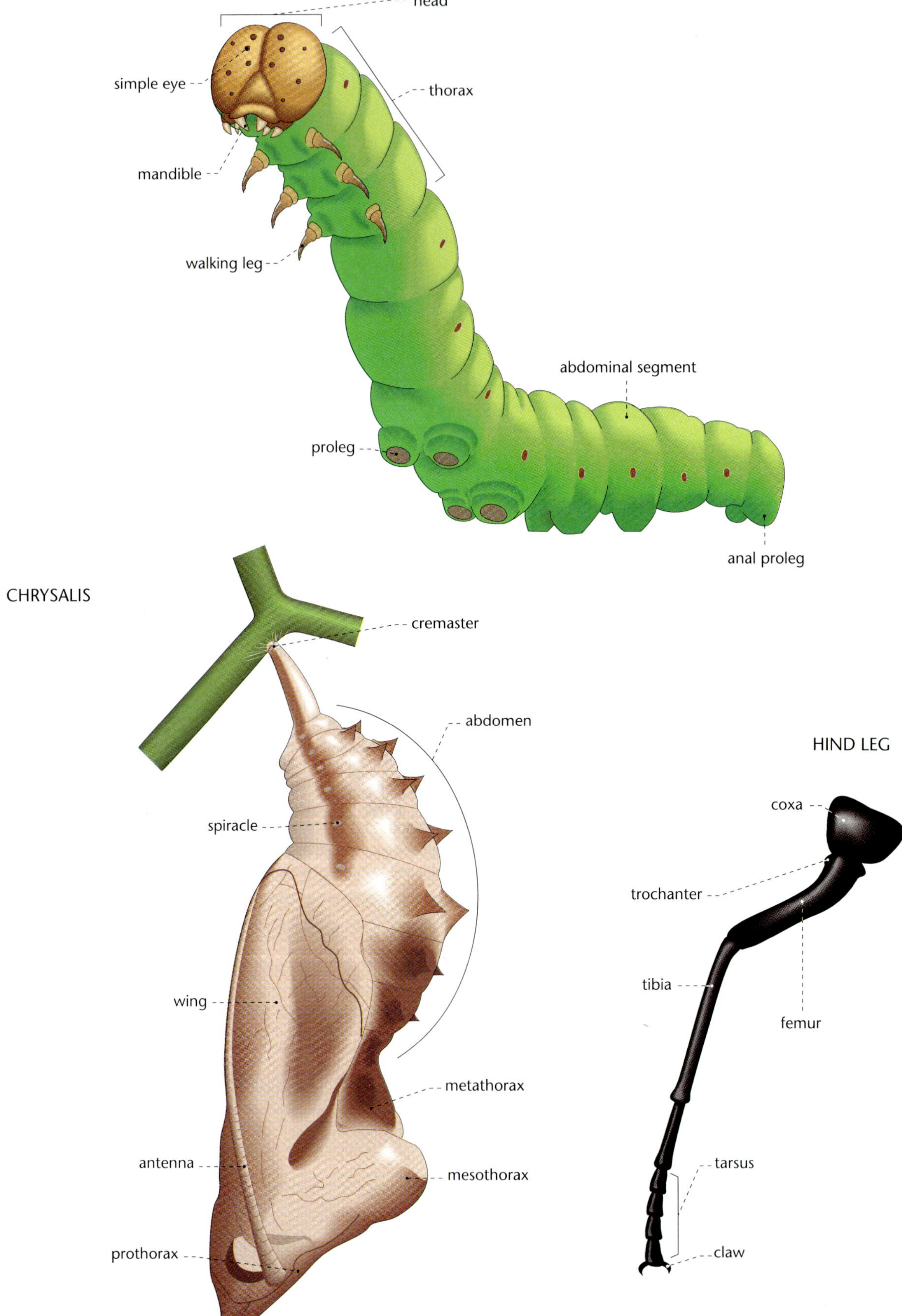
CATERPILLAR
head
simple eye
thorax
mandible
walking leg
abdominal segment
proleg
anal proleg
CHRYSALIS
cremaster
abdomen
HIND LEG
spiracle
coxa
trochanter
tibia
femur
wing
metathorax
antenna
mesothorax
tarsus
prothorax
claw

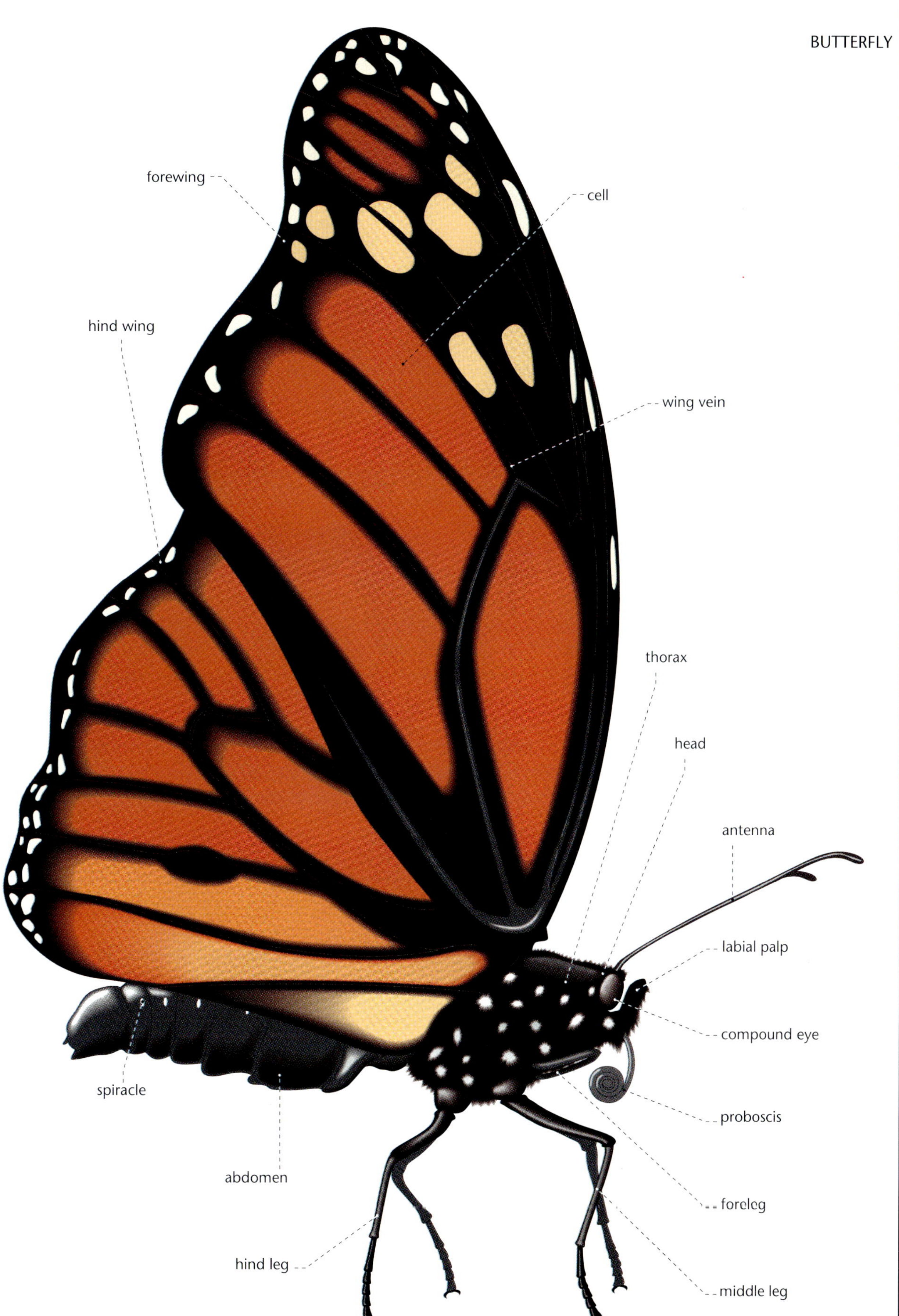
forewing
hind wing
cell
wing vein
thorax
head
antenna
labial palp
compound eye
proboscis
spiracle
abdomen
foreleg
hind leg
middle leg

WORKER

simple eye
head
thorax
compound eye
antenna
mandible
foreleg
middle leg

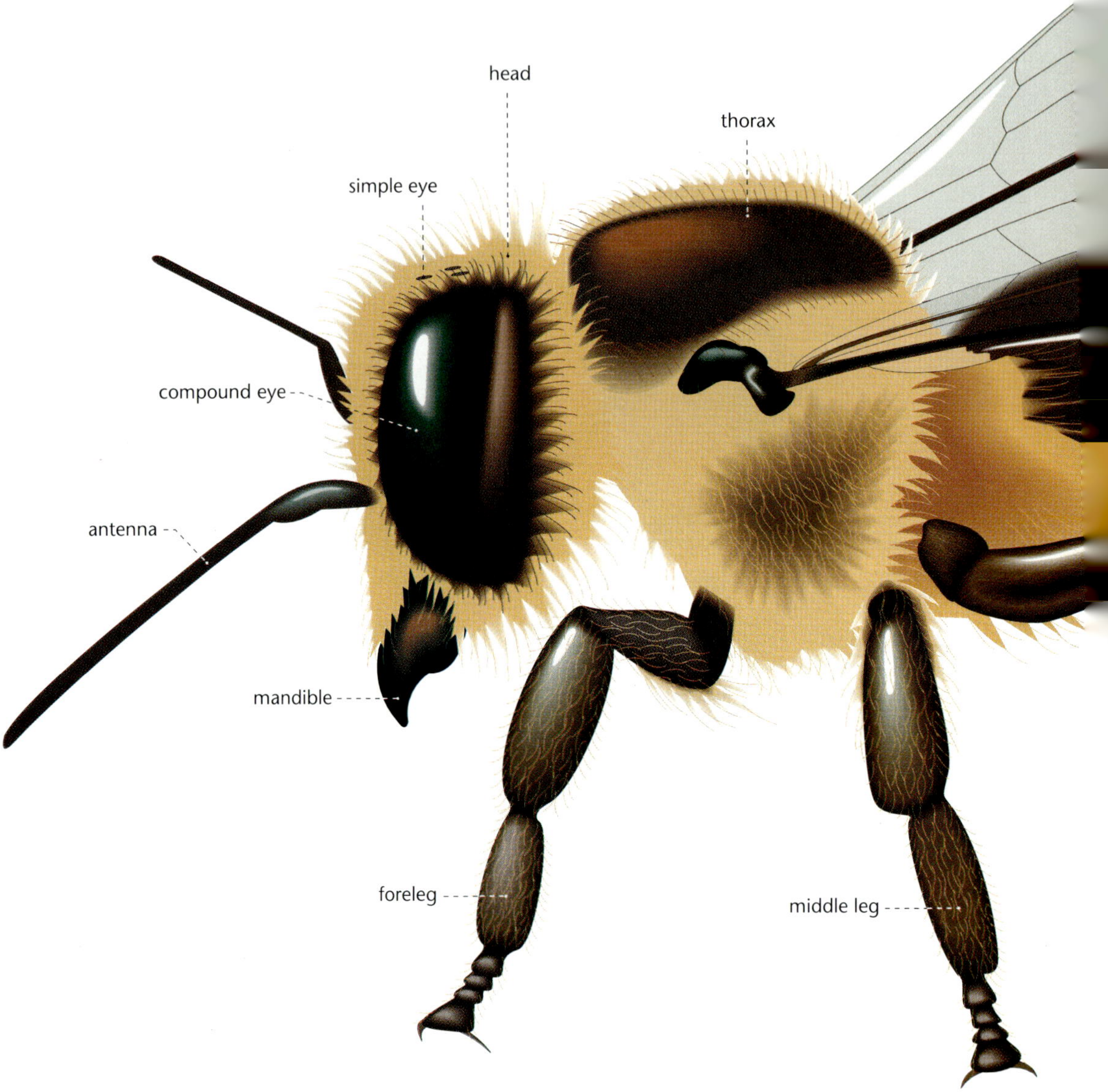

FORELEG (OUTER SURFACE)

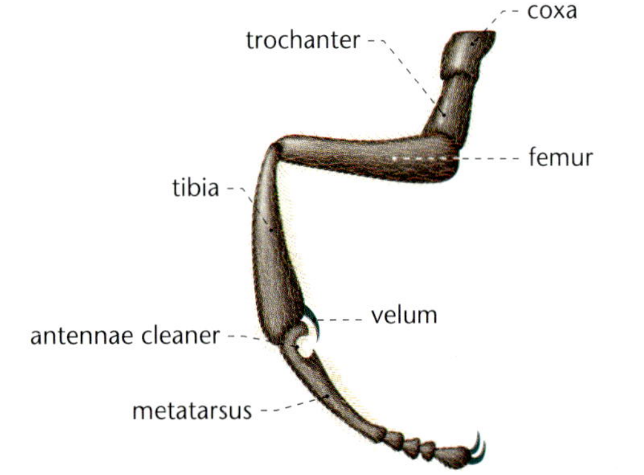

MIDDLE LEG (OUTER SURFACE)

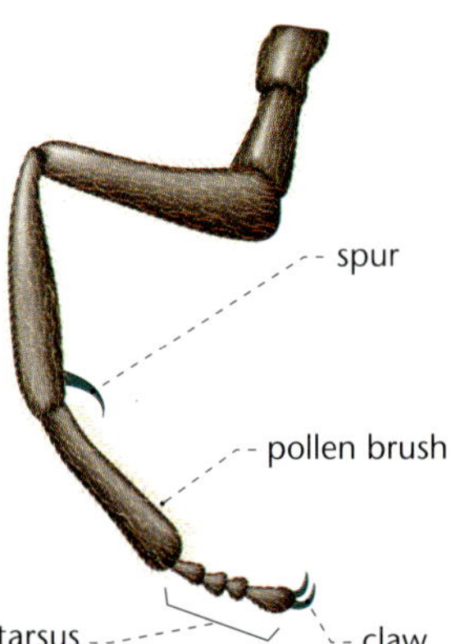

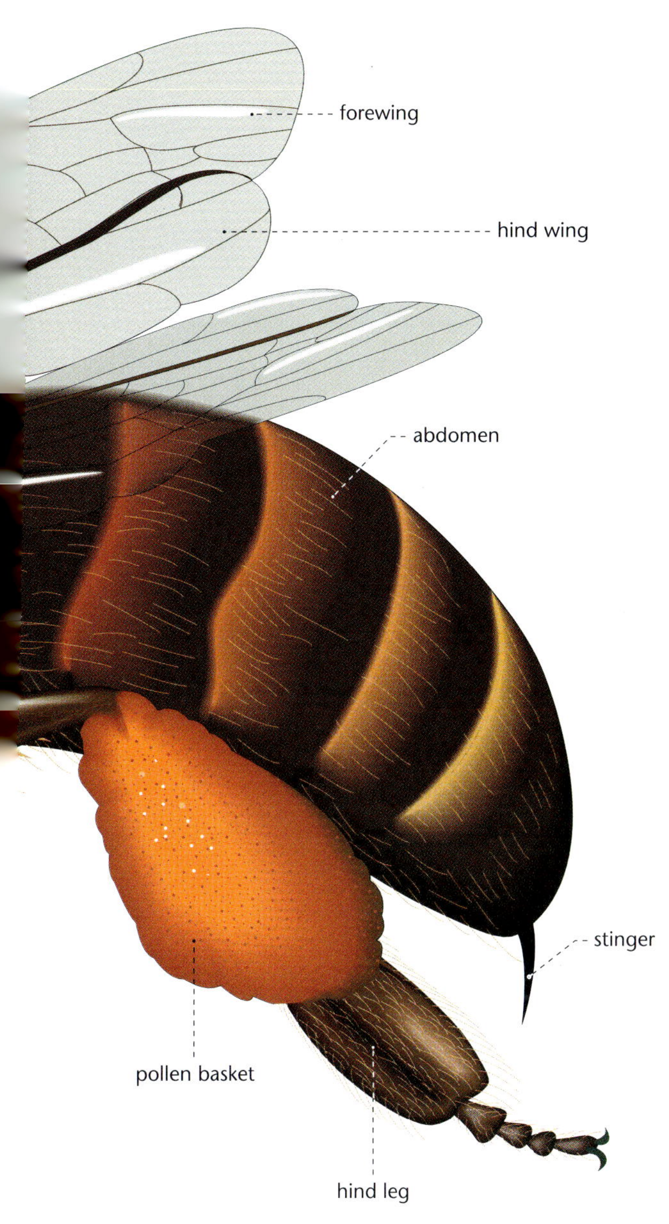

MOUTHPARTS

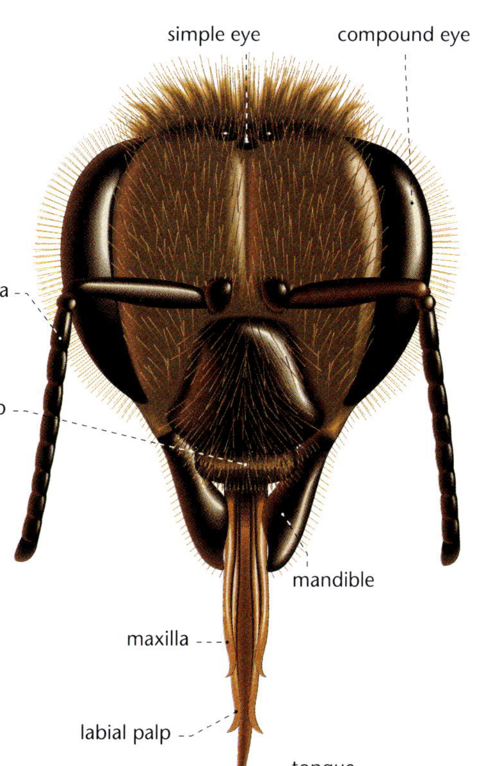

HIND LEG (INNER SURFACE)

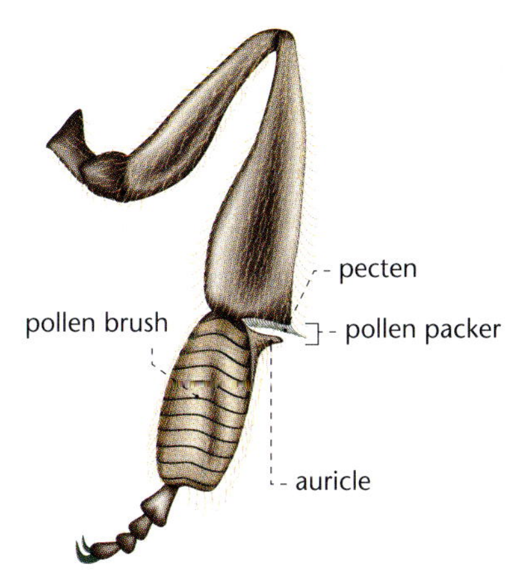

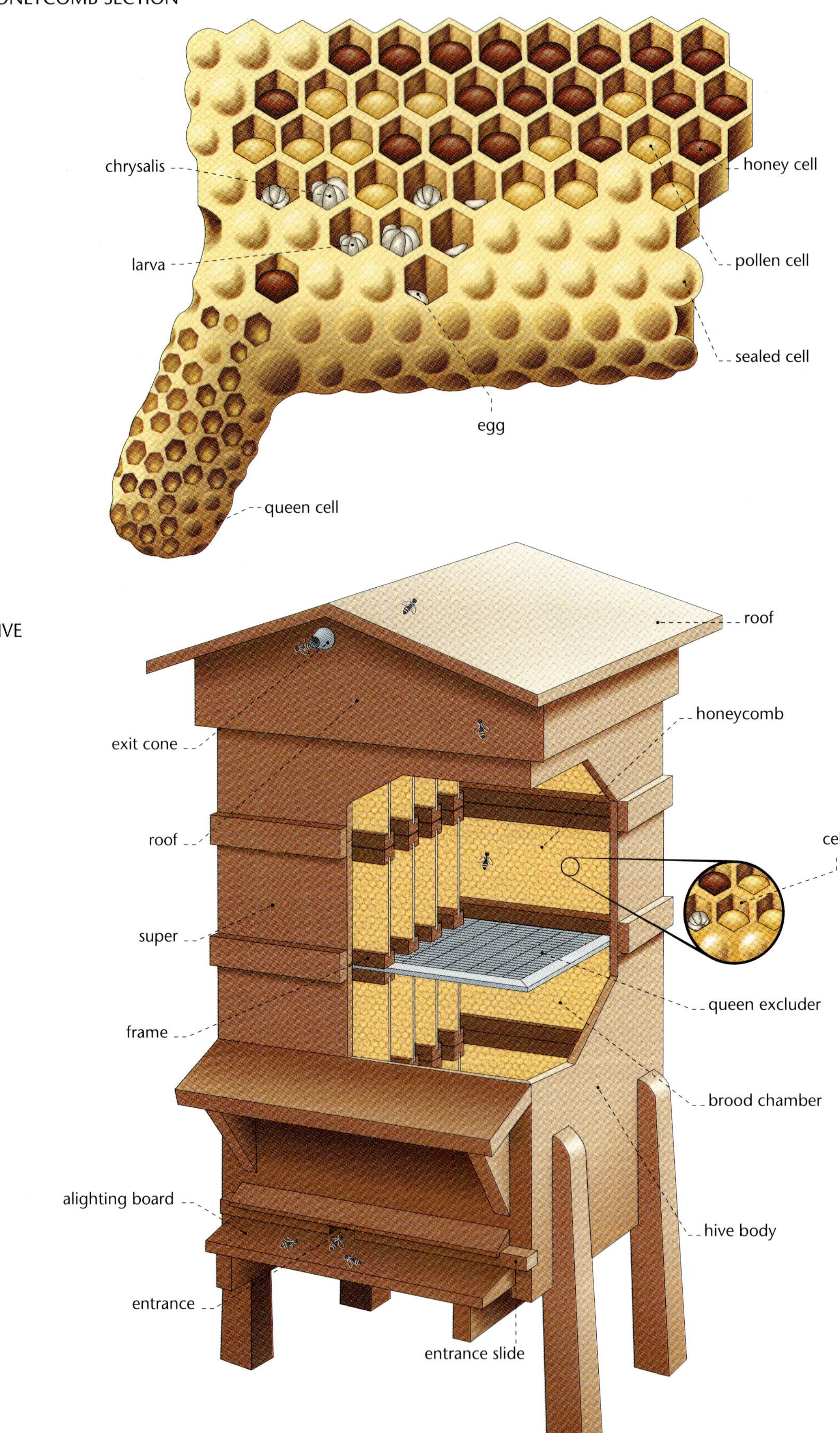
HONEYCOMB SECTION
chrysalis
larva
honey cell
pollen cell
sealed cell
egg
queen cell
HIVE
roof
exit cone
honeycomb
roof
cell
super
frame
queen excluder
brood chamber
alighting board
hive body
entrance
entrance slide

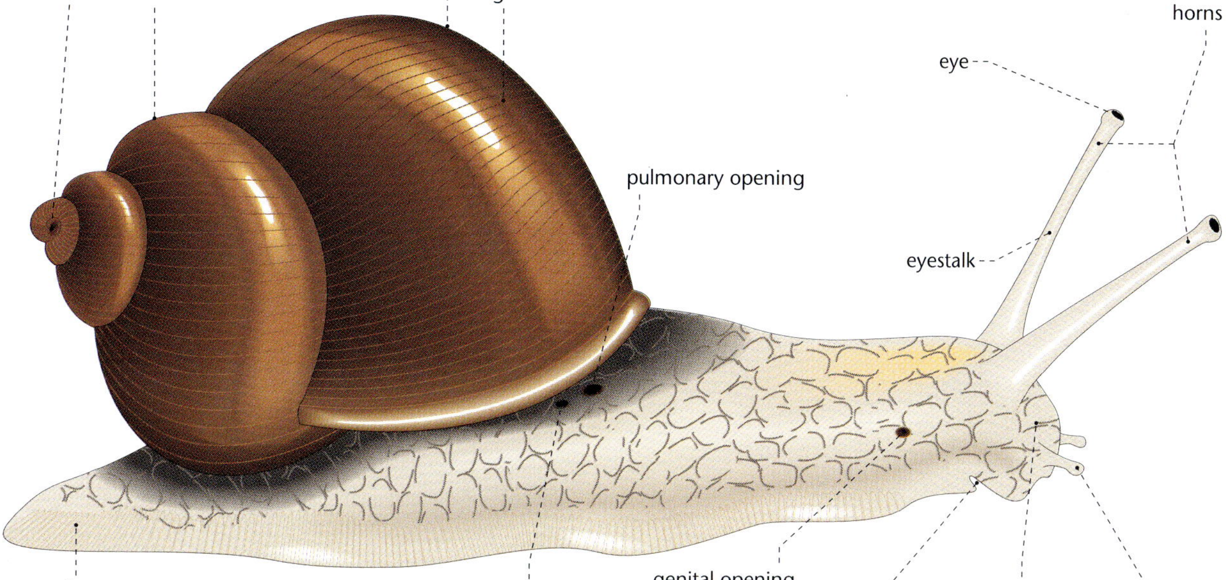

MAJOR EDIBLE GASTROPODS

AMPHIBIANS

FROG

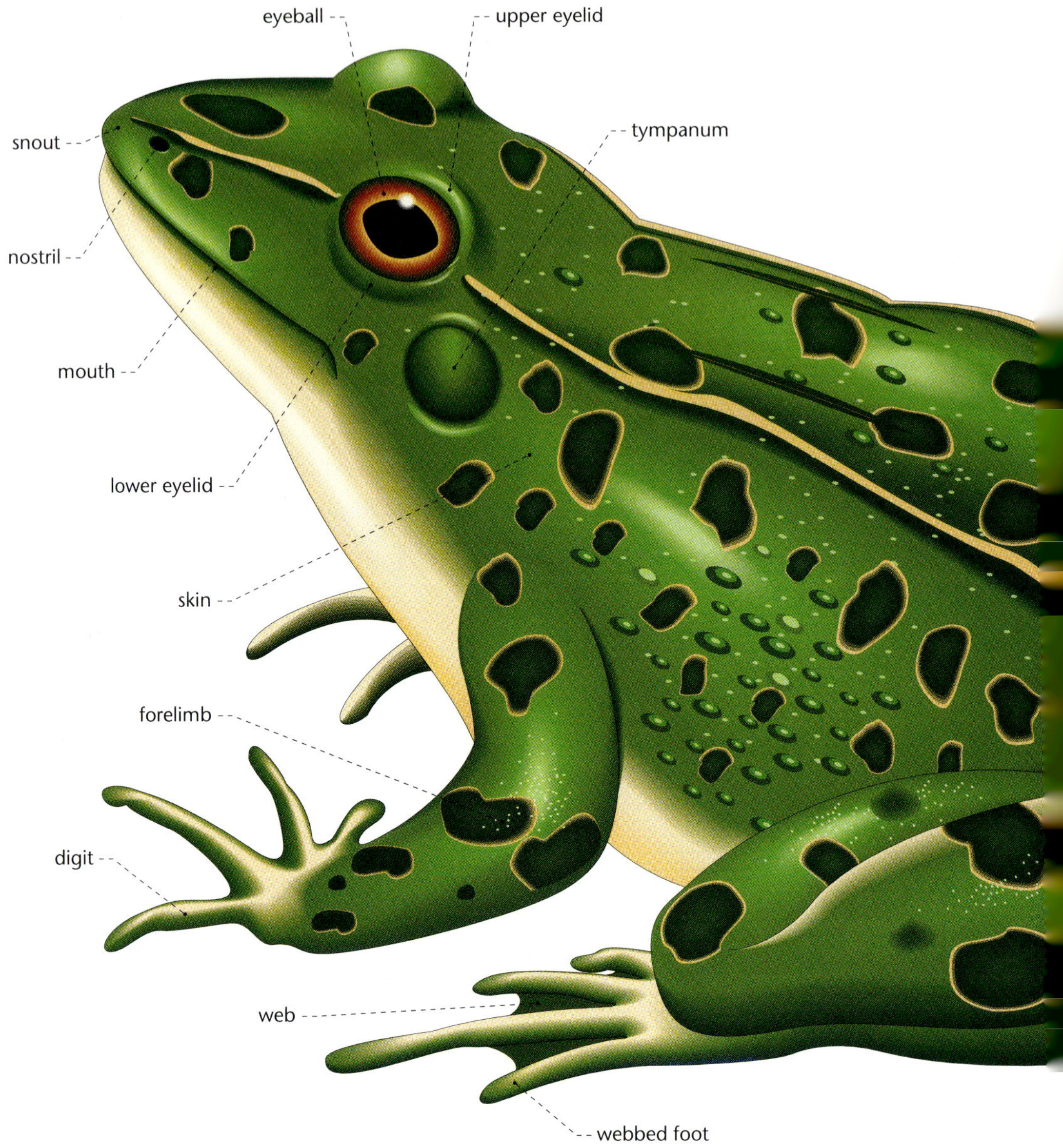

LIFE CYCLE OF THE FROG

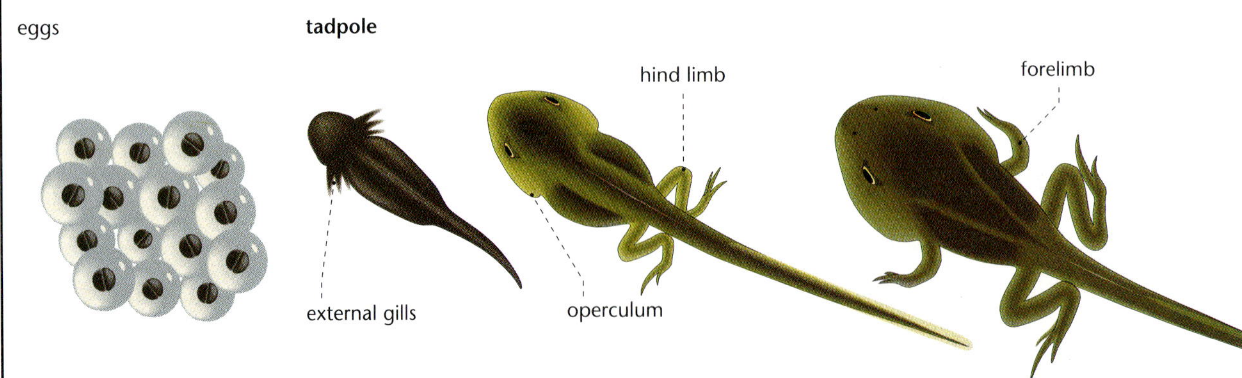

toad  
warty skin
hind limb
tree frog 
adhesive disk
salamander

FISH

MORPHOLOGY

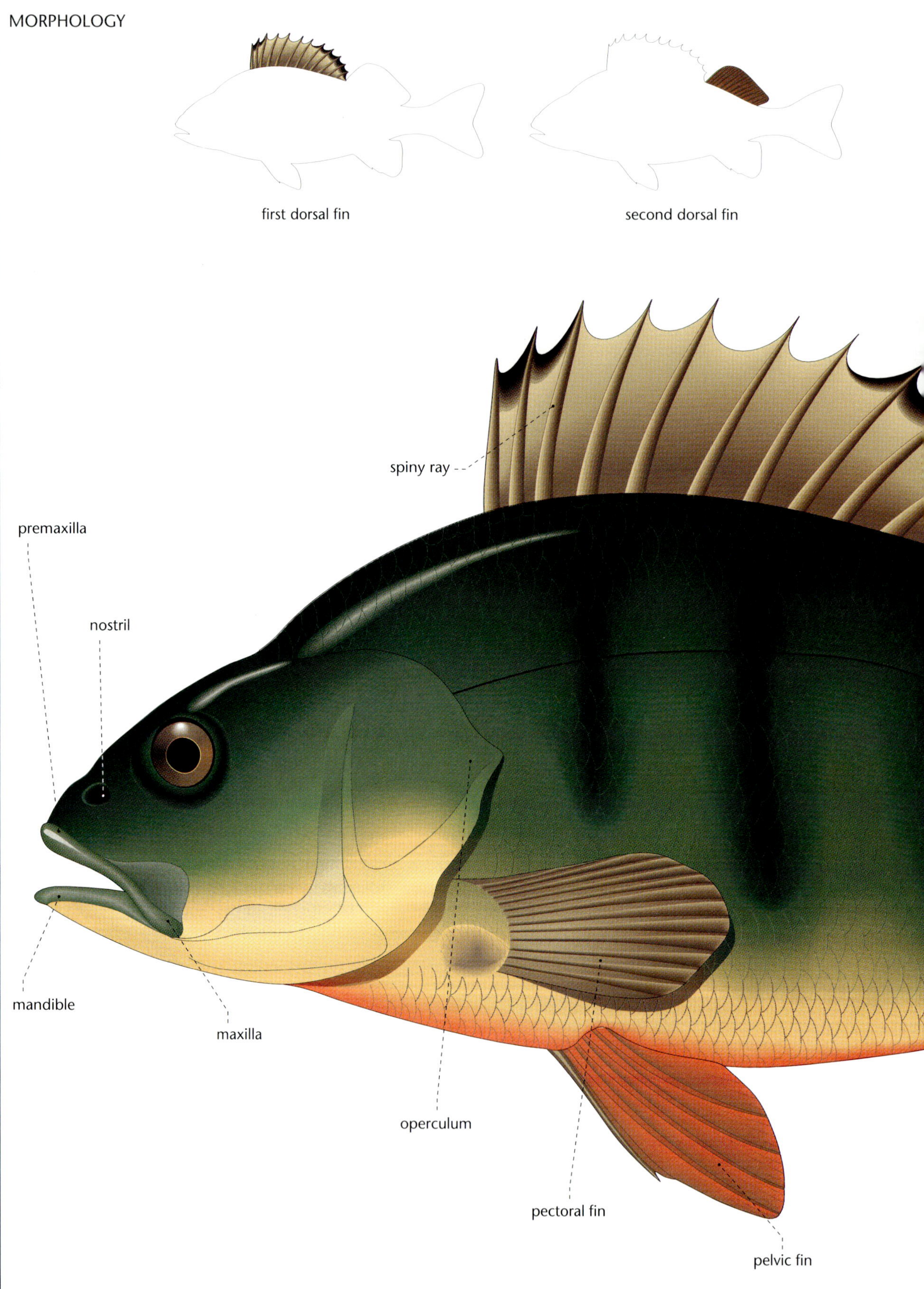

upper gill arch
gill raker
lower gill arch
gill filament
soft ray
lateral line
caudal fin
scale
anal fin

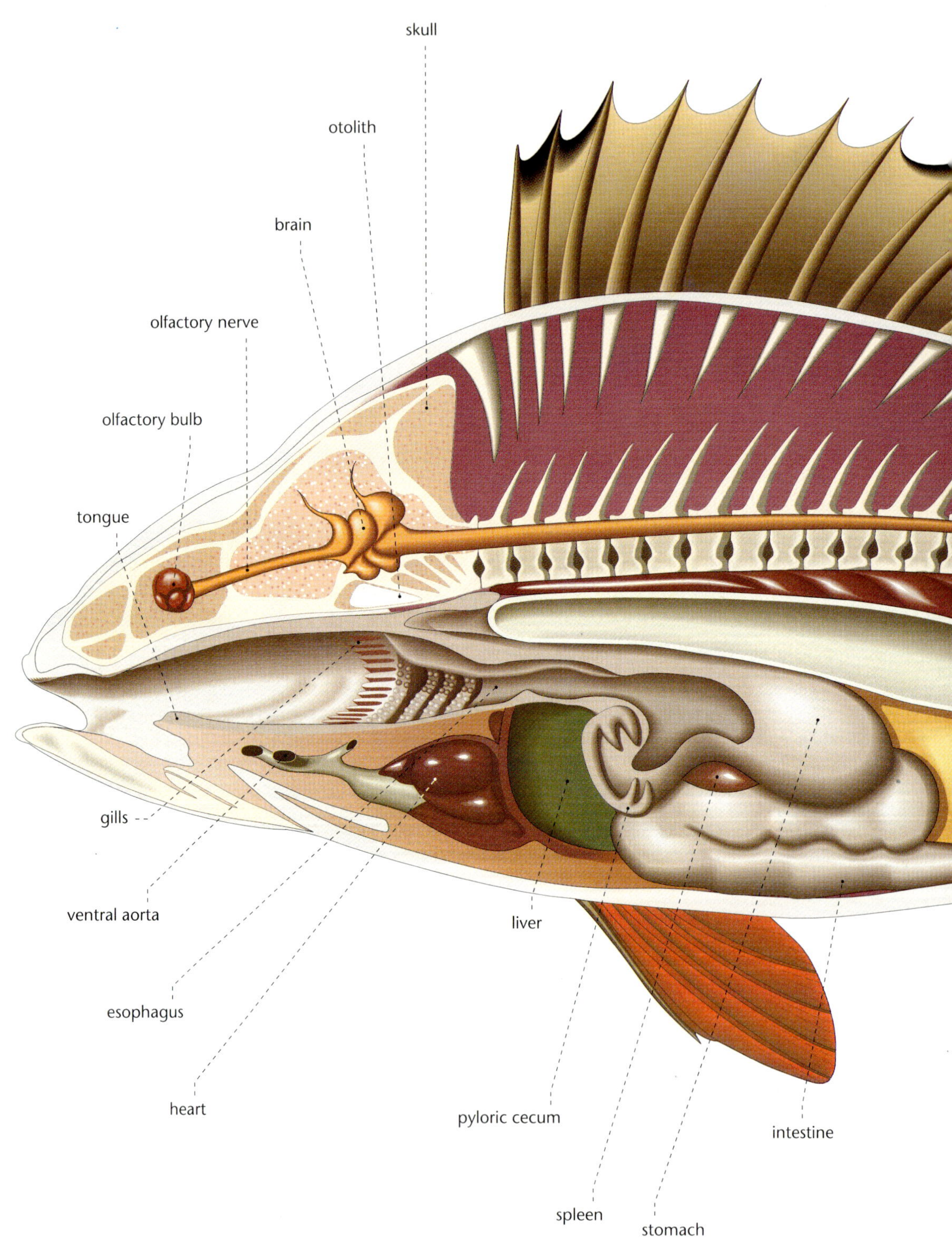
skull
otolith
brain
olfactory nerve
olfactory bulb
tongue
gills
ventral aorta
esophagus
heart
liver
pyloric cecum
spleen
stomach
intestine

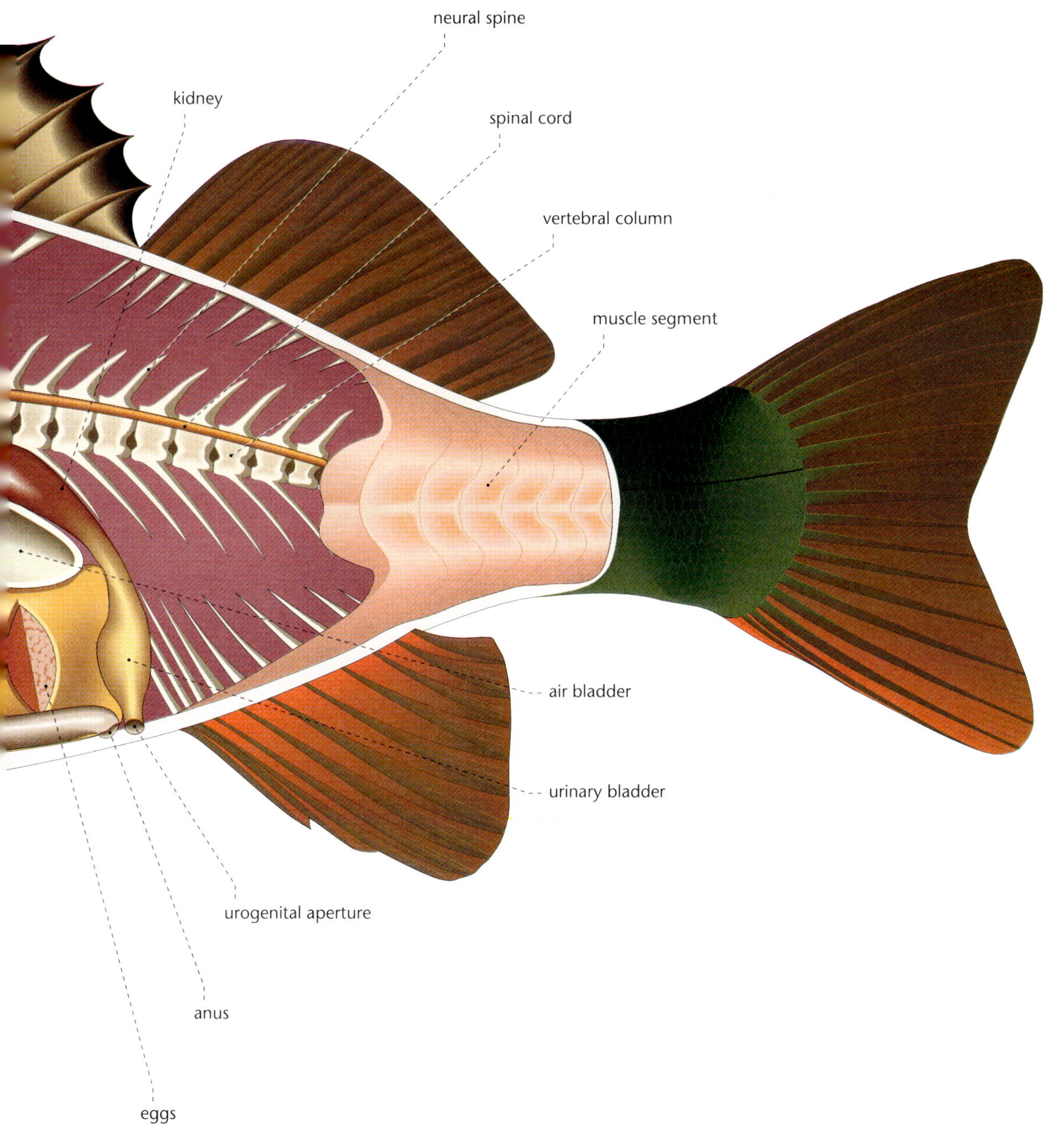

neural spine
kidney
spinal cord
vertebral column
muscle segment
air bladder
urinary bladder
urogenital aperture
anus
eggs

CRUSTACEAN

LOBSTER

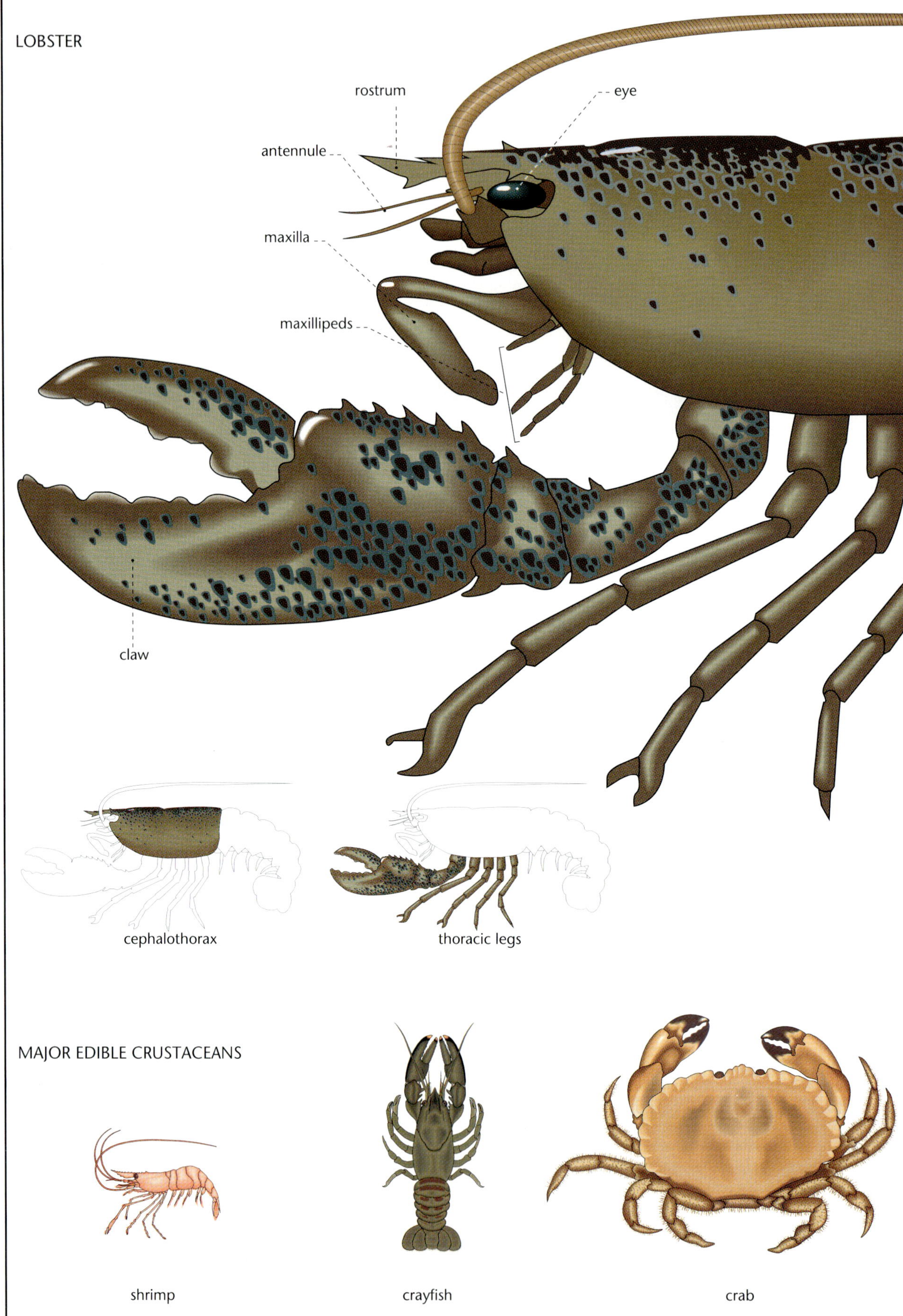

MAJOR EDIBLE CRUSTACEANS

shrimp

crayfish

crab

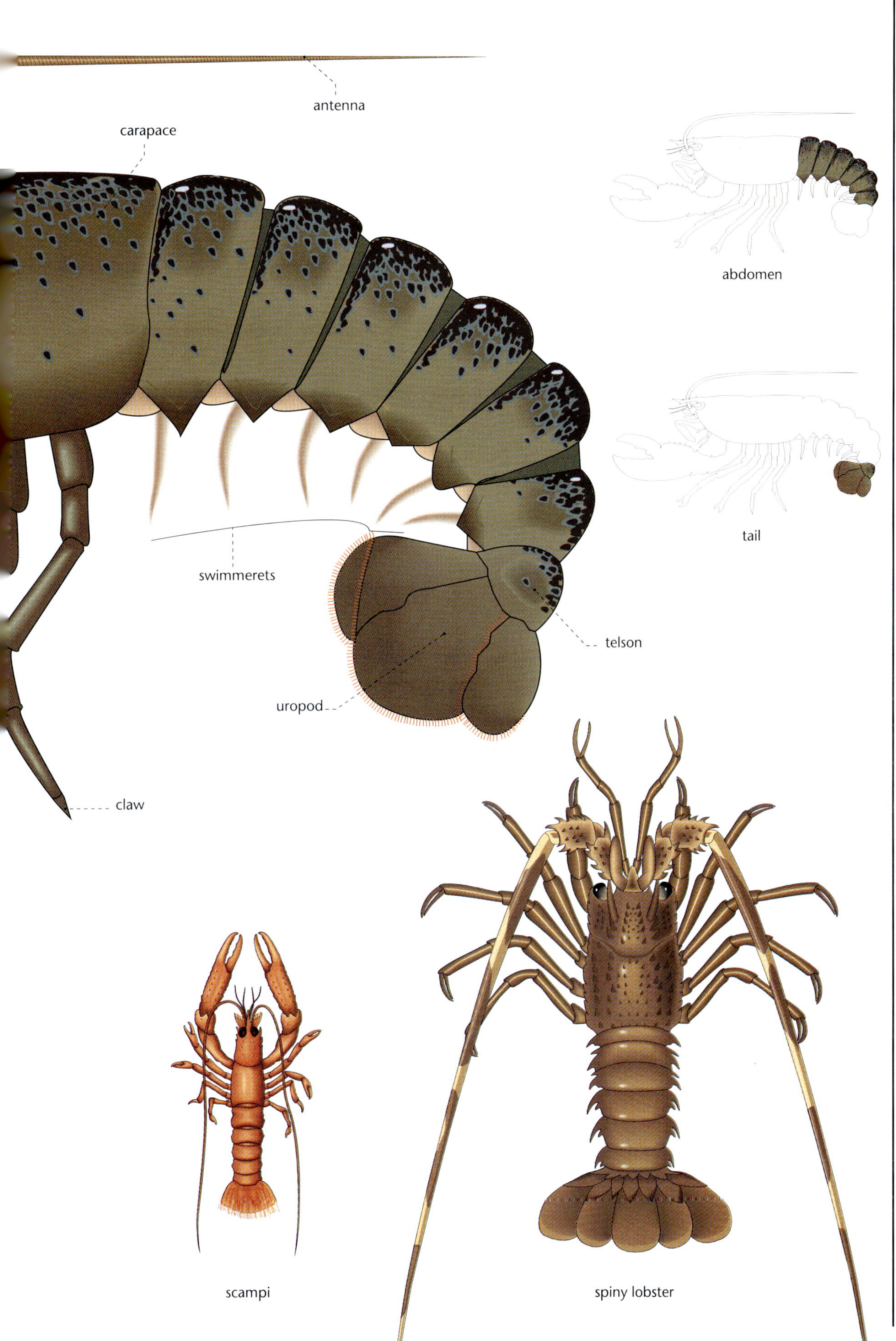

antenna
carapace
swimmerets
uropod
telson
claw
abdomen
tail
scampi
spiny lobster

OYSTER

shell
mouth
elastic ligament
labial palp
esophagus
stomach
intestine
digestive gland
heart
anus
adductor muscle
gills
mantle edge

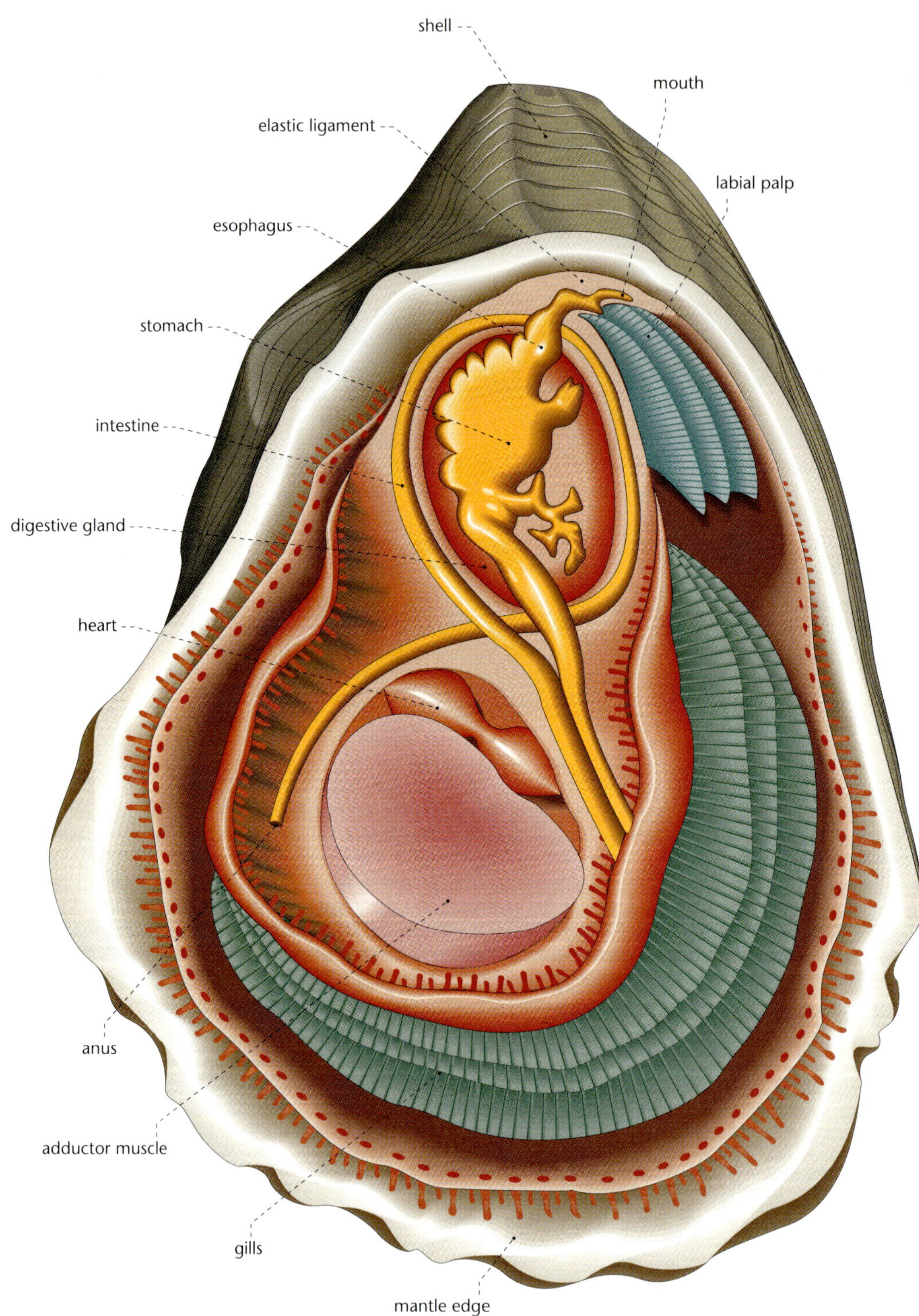

oyster
soft shell clam
razor clam
scallop
blue mussel
cockle
hard shell clam
great scallop
clam

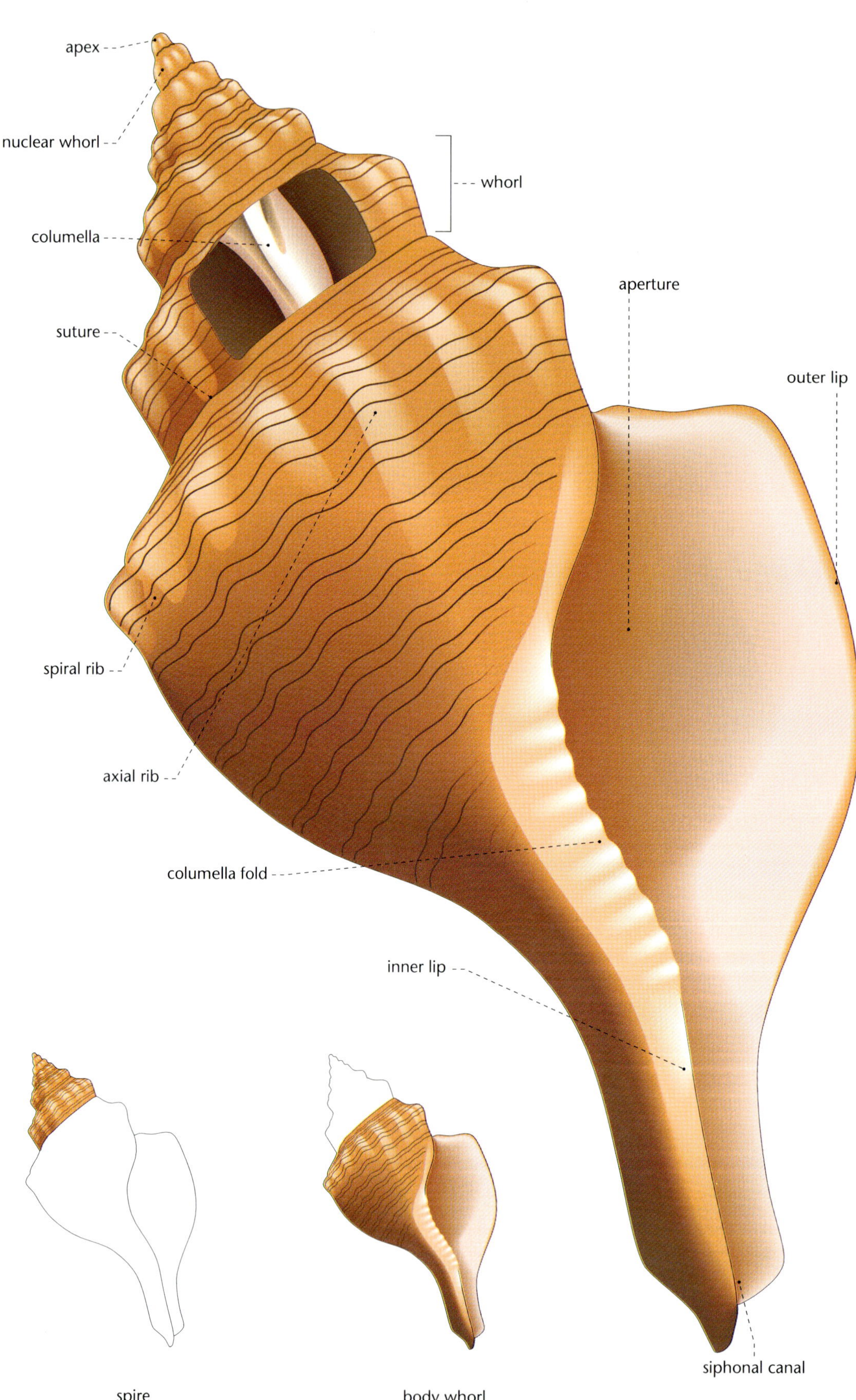

apex
nuclear whorl
columella
whorl
suture
aperture
outer lip
spiral rib
axial rib
columella fold
inner lip
siphonal canal
spire
body whorl

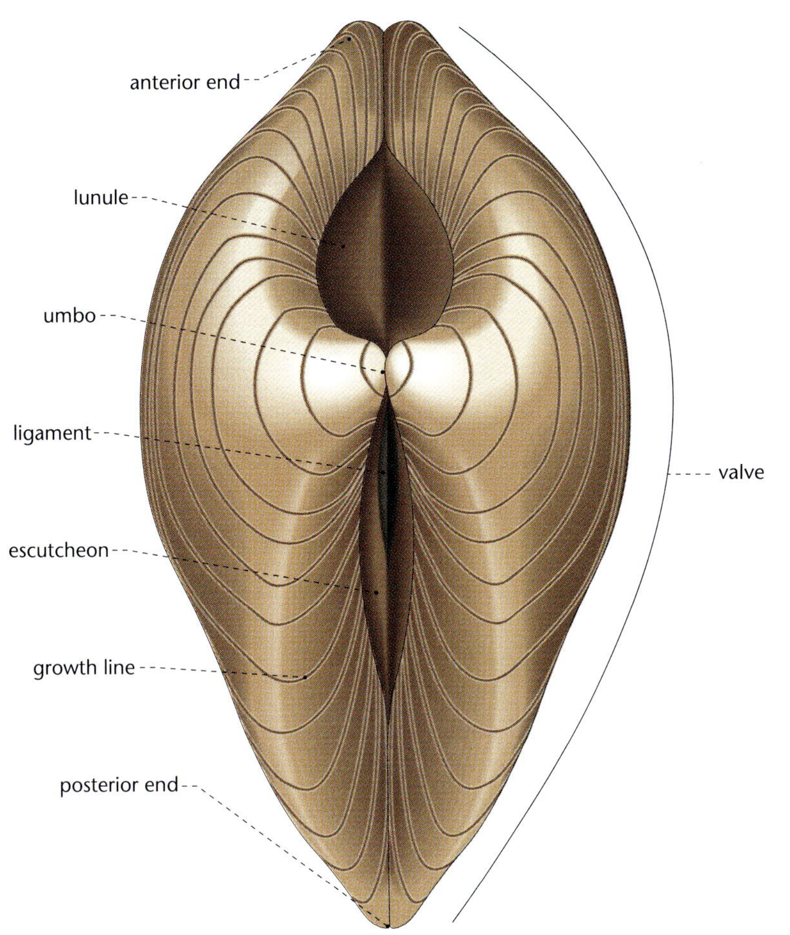
DORSAL VIEW
anterior end
lunule
umbo
ligament
escutcheon
growth line
posterior end
valve

ANIMAL KINGDOM

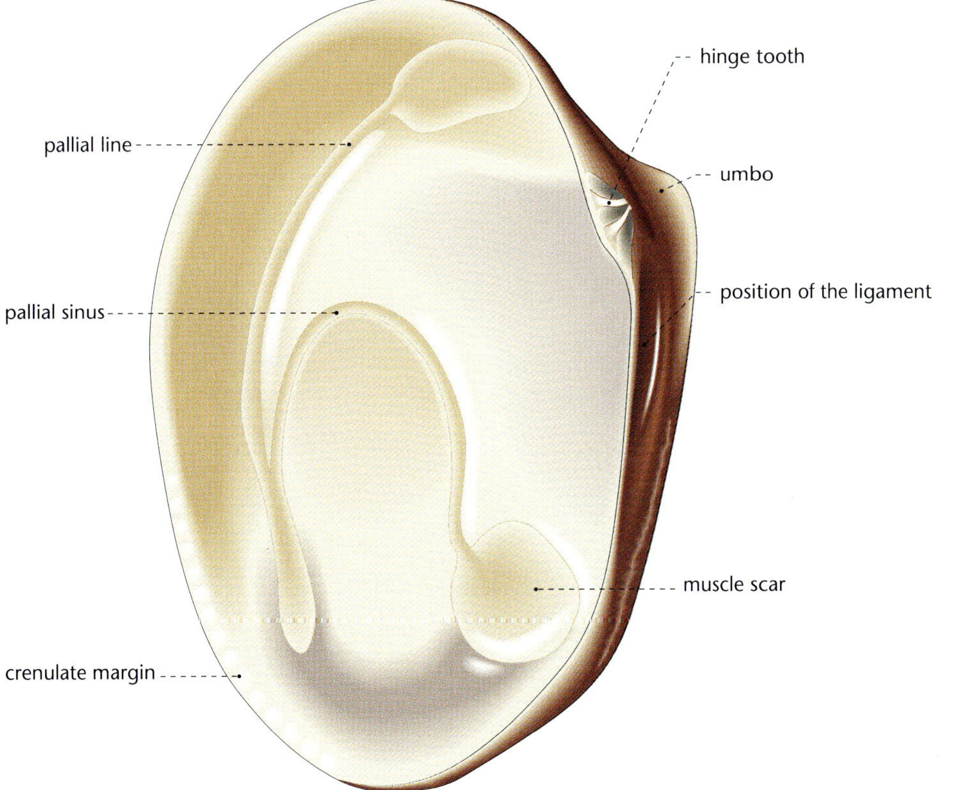
LEFT VALVE
pallial line
pallial sinus
crenulate margin
hinge tooth
umbo
position of the ligament
muscle scar

VENOMOUS SNAKE'S HEAD

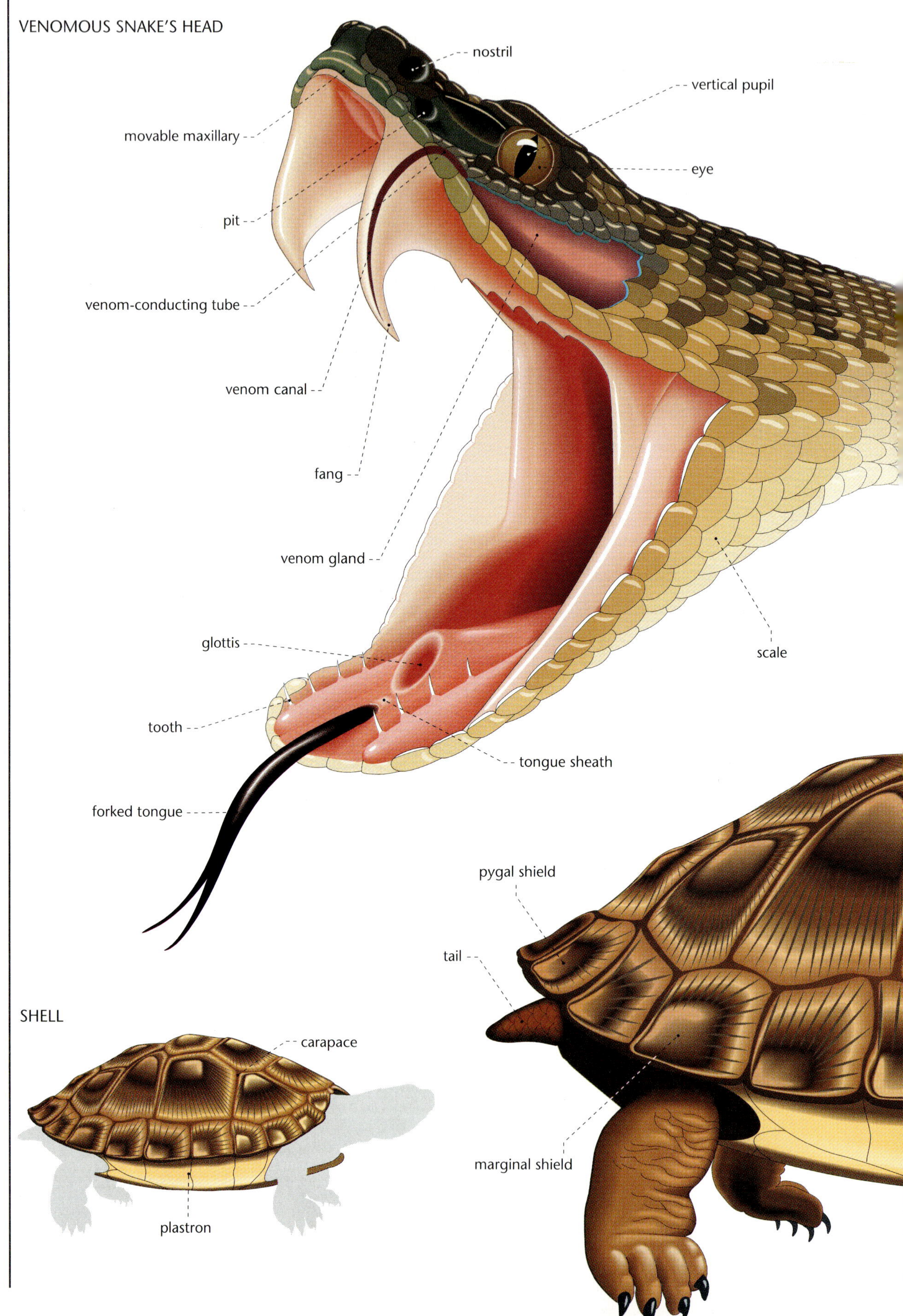

ANIMAL KINGDOM

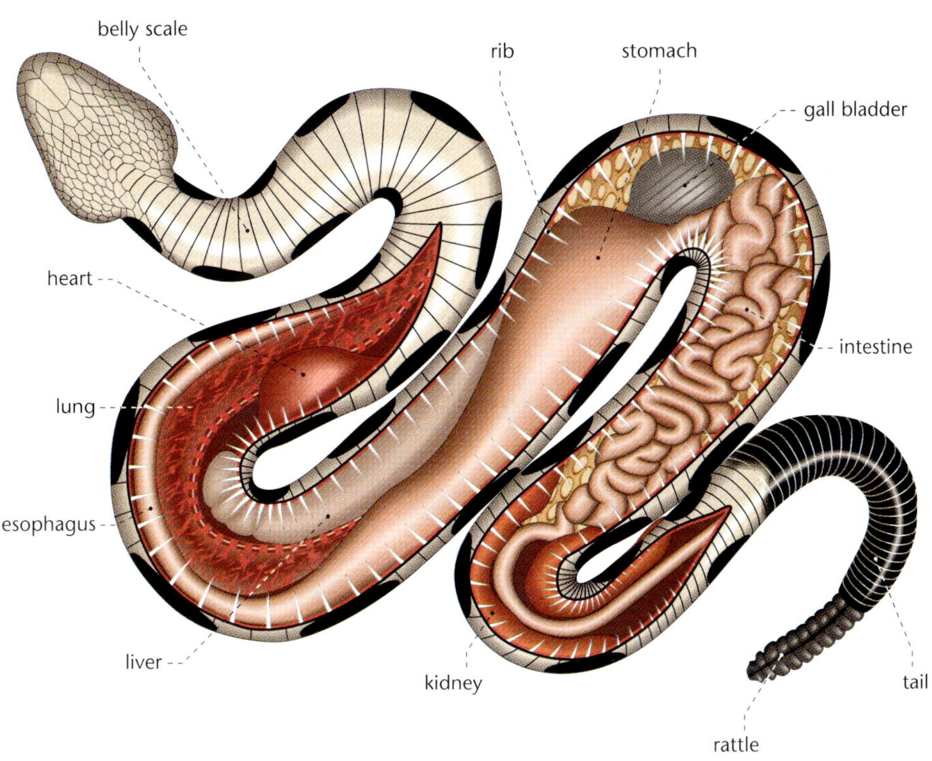

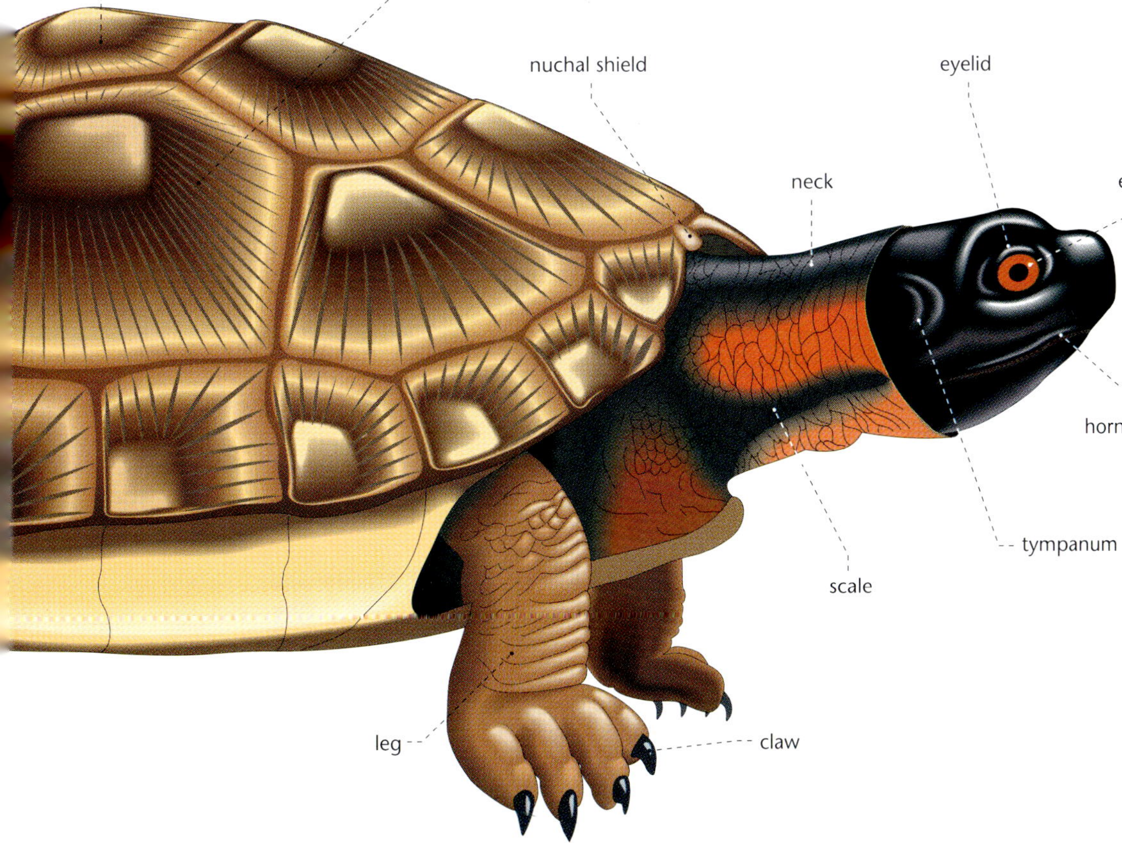

TYPES OF JAWS

BEAVER

RODENT'S JAW

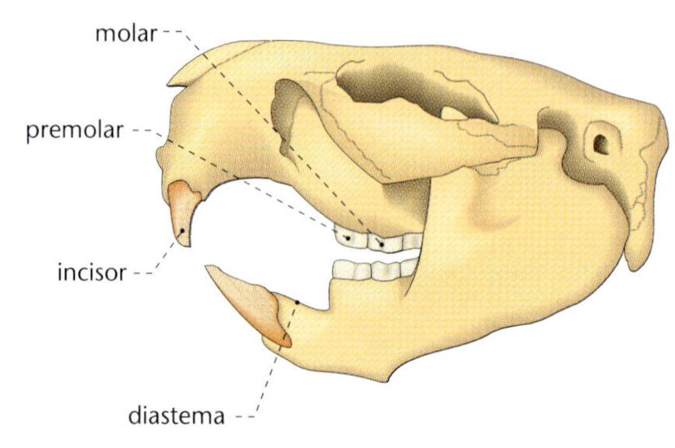

LION

CARNIVORE'S JAW

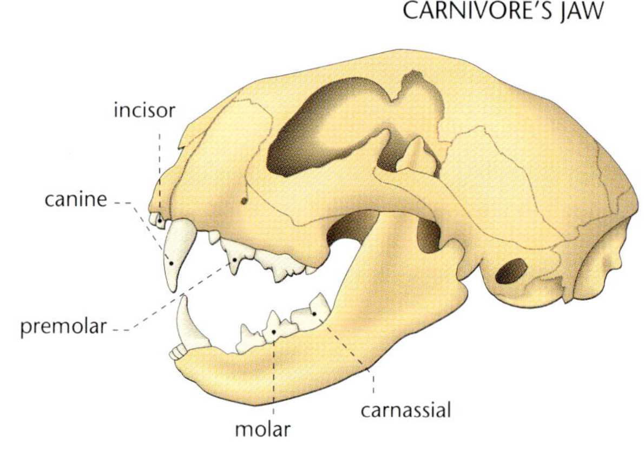

HERBIVORE'S JAW

HORSE

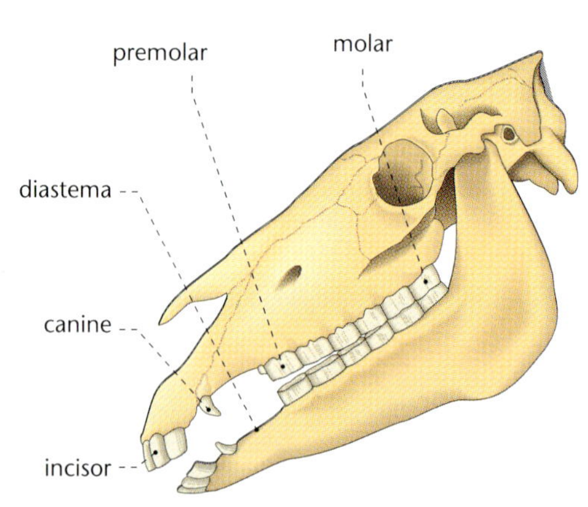

MAJOR TYPES OF HORNS

horns of mouflon

horns of giraffe

horns of rhinoceros

MAJOR TYPES OF TUSKS

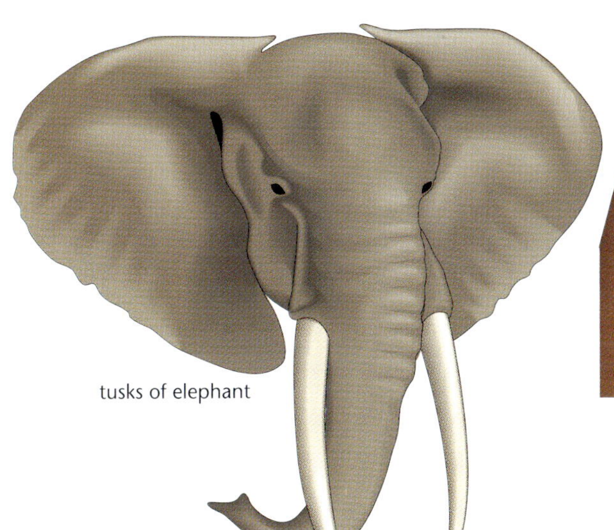

tusks of elephant

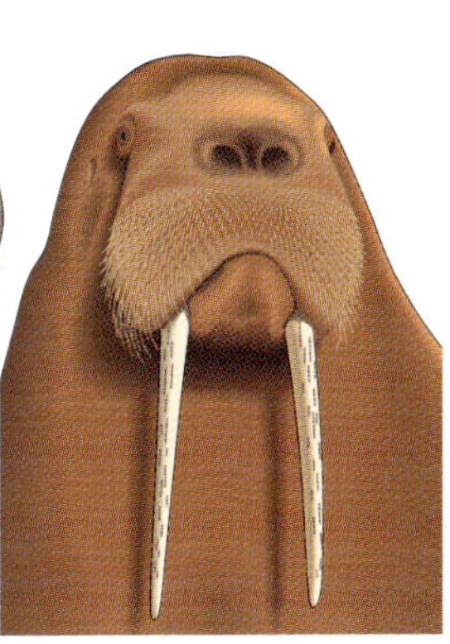

tusks of walrus

tusks of wart hog

TYPES OF HOOFS

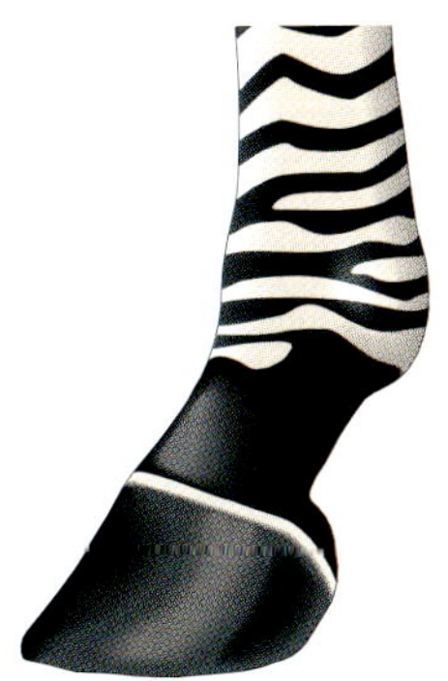

one-toe hoof

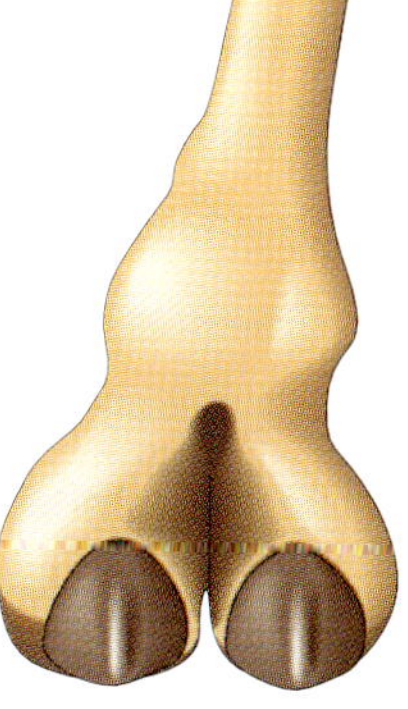

two-toed hoof

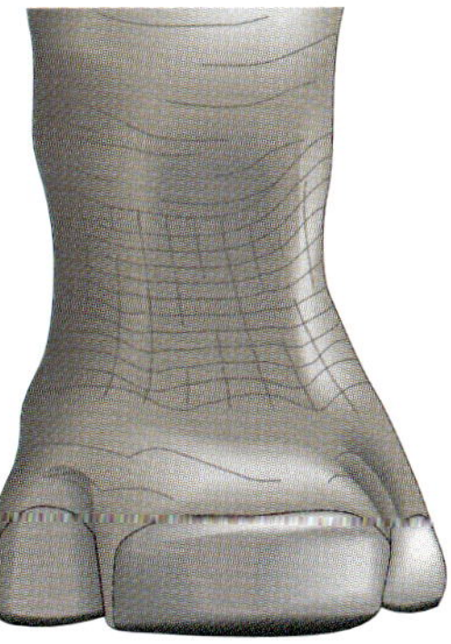

three-toed hoof

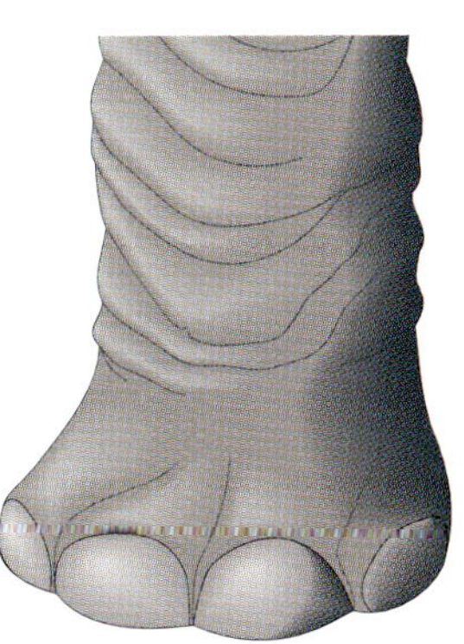

four-toed hoof

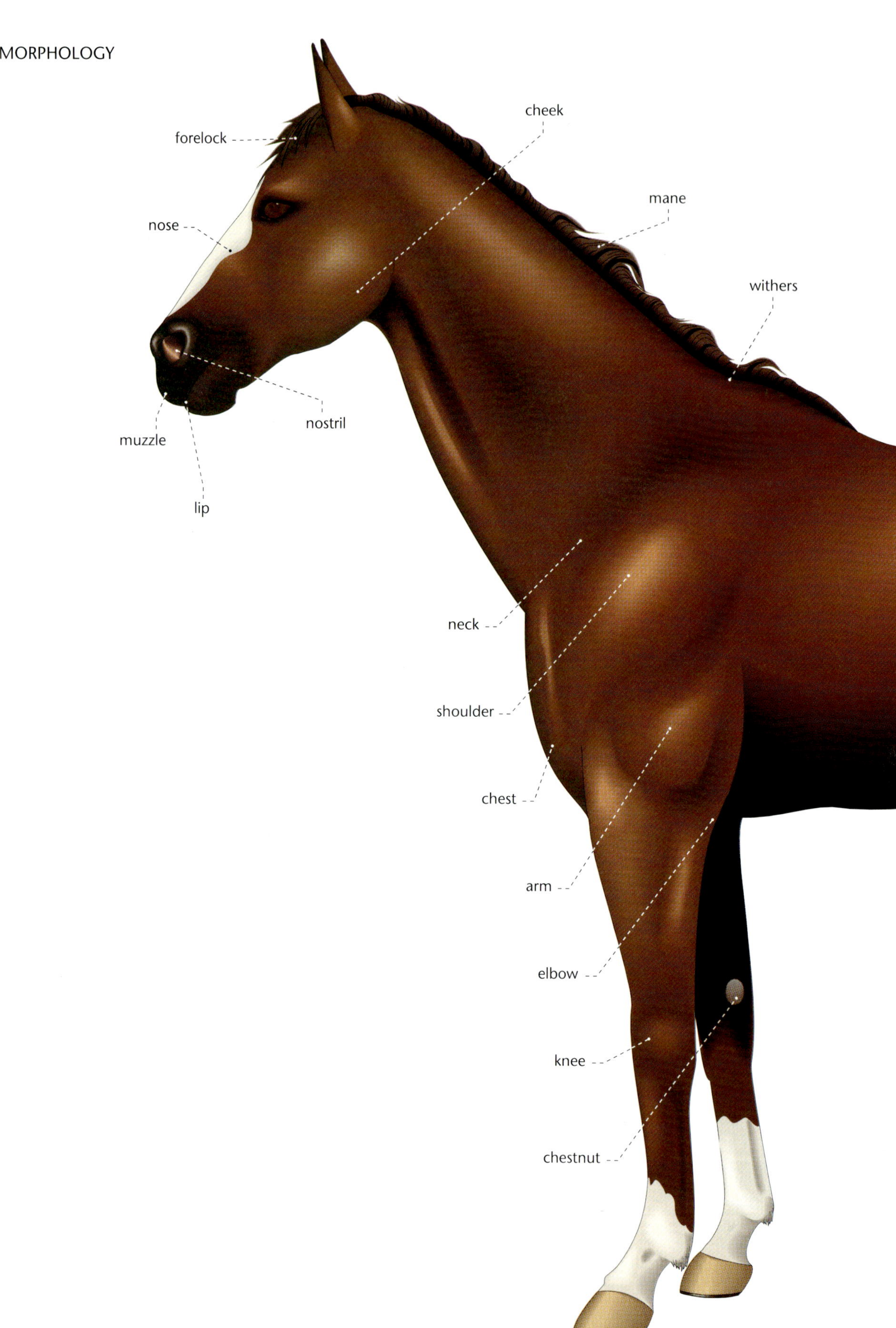

forelock
cheek
nose
mane
withers
muzzle
nostril
lip
neck
shoulder
chest
arm
elbow
knee
chestnut

GAITS

pace
walk
trot
gallop

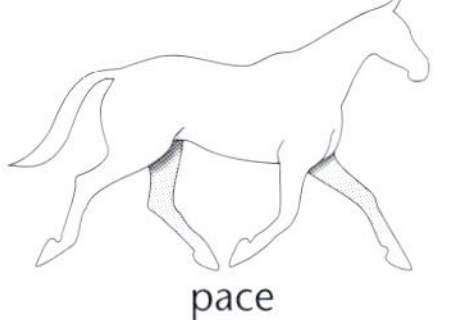

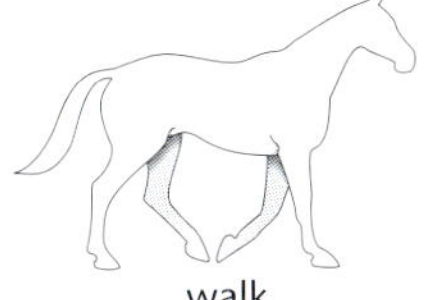

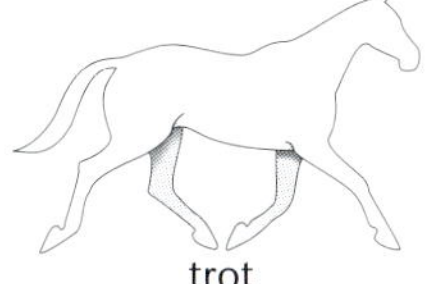

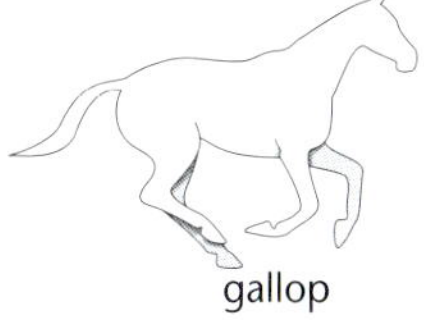

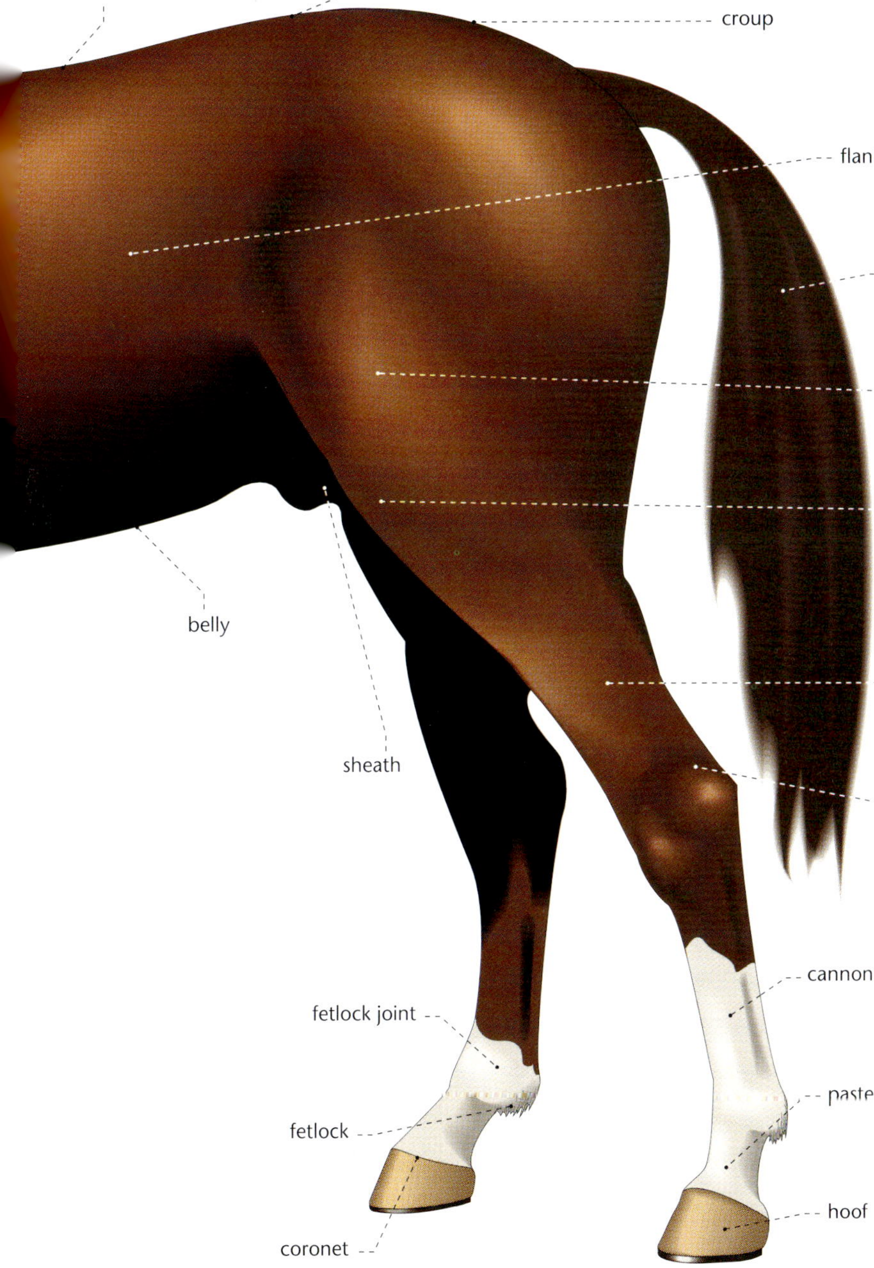

back
loin
croup
flank
tail
thigh
stifle
belly
gaskin
sheath
hock
cannon
fetlock joint
pastern
fetlock
hoof
coronet

SKELETON

atlas
skull
rib
scapula
mandible
skull
humerus
olecranon
sternum
radius
cervical vertebrae
ulna
carpus
metacarpus
proximal sesamoid
distal sesamoid
thoracic vertebrae

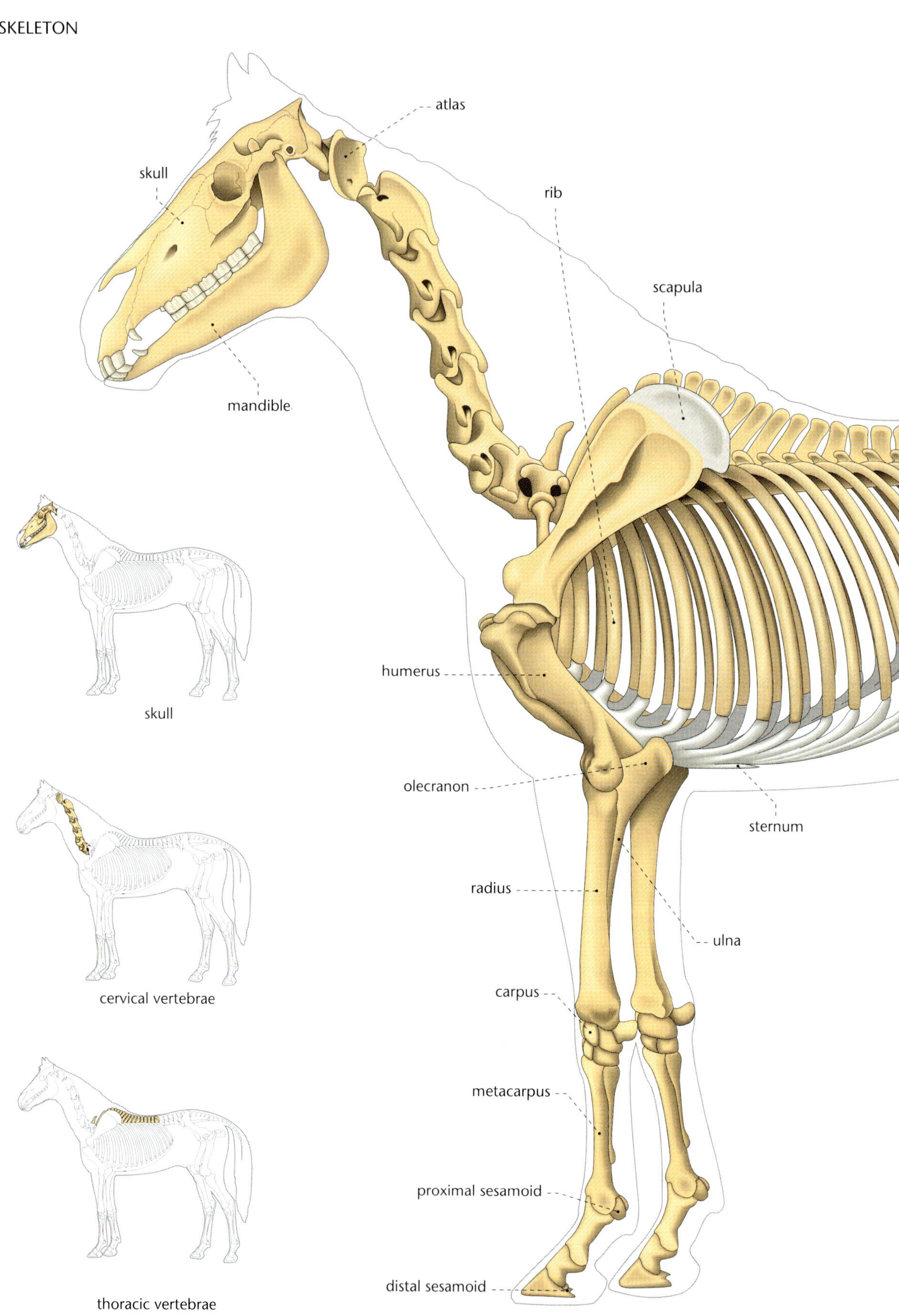

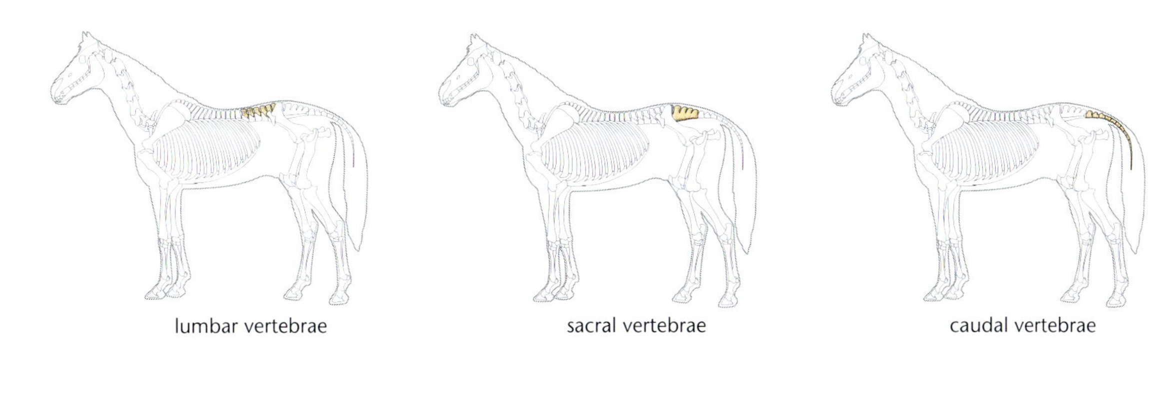

lumbar vertebrae
sacral vertebrae
caudal vertebrae

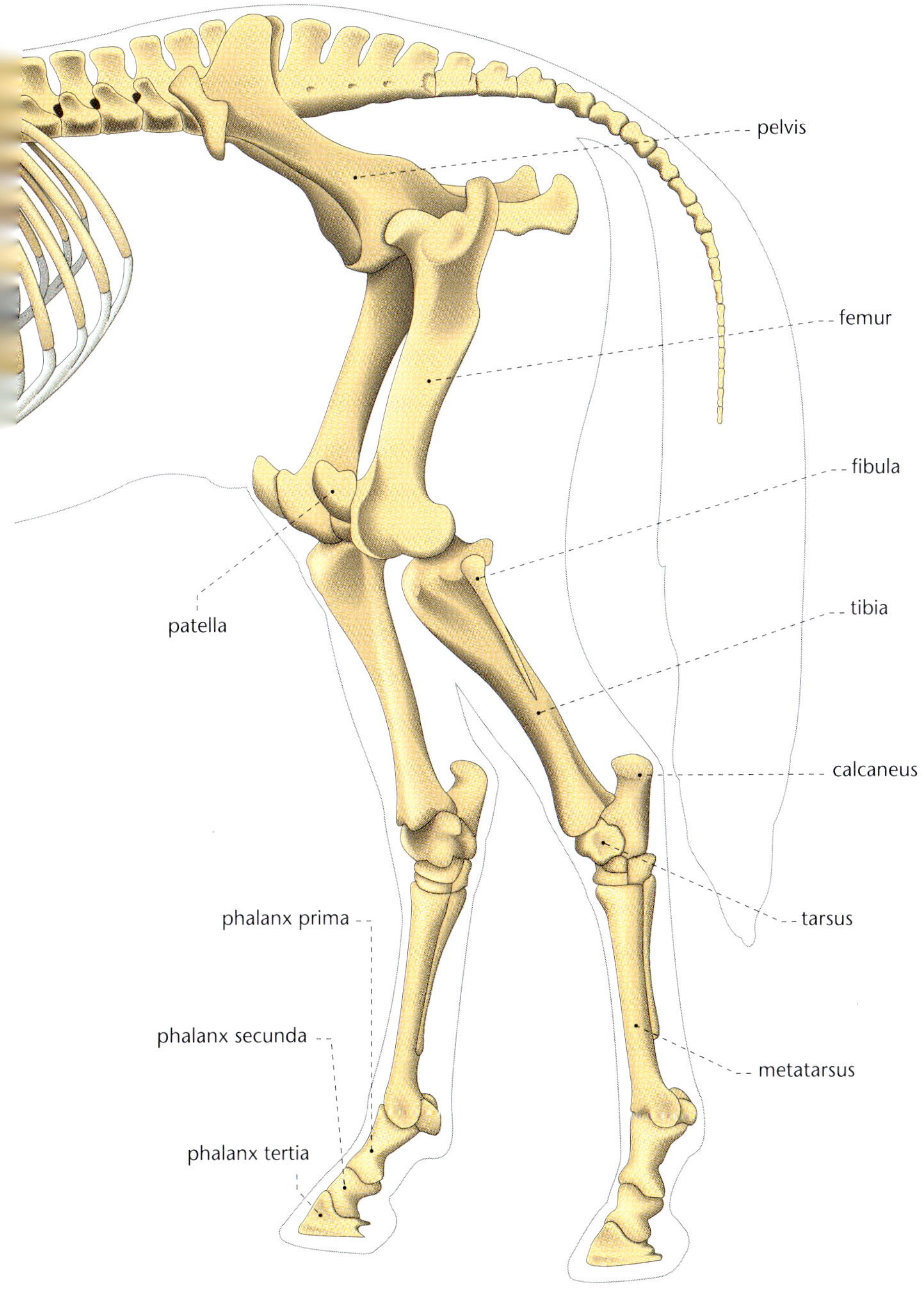

pelvis
femur
fibula
tibia
calcaneus
patella
tarsus
phalanx prima
phalanx secunda
metatarsus
phalanx tertia

PLANTAR SURFACE OF THE HOOF

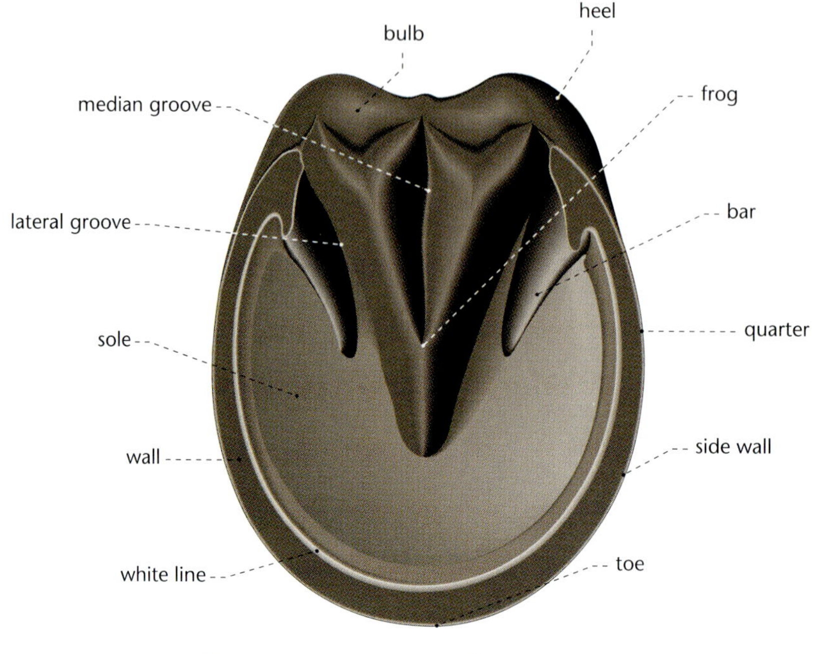

HORSESHOE

HOOF

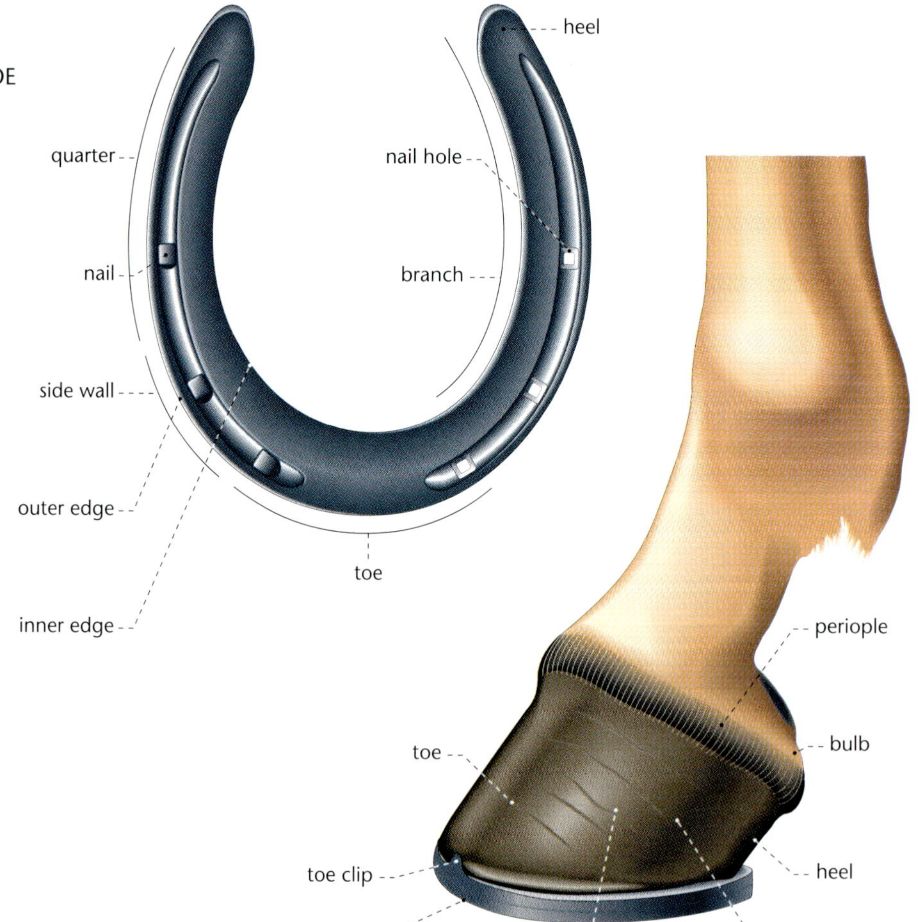

DEER FAMILY

DEER ANTLERS

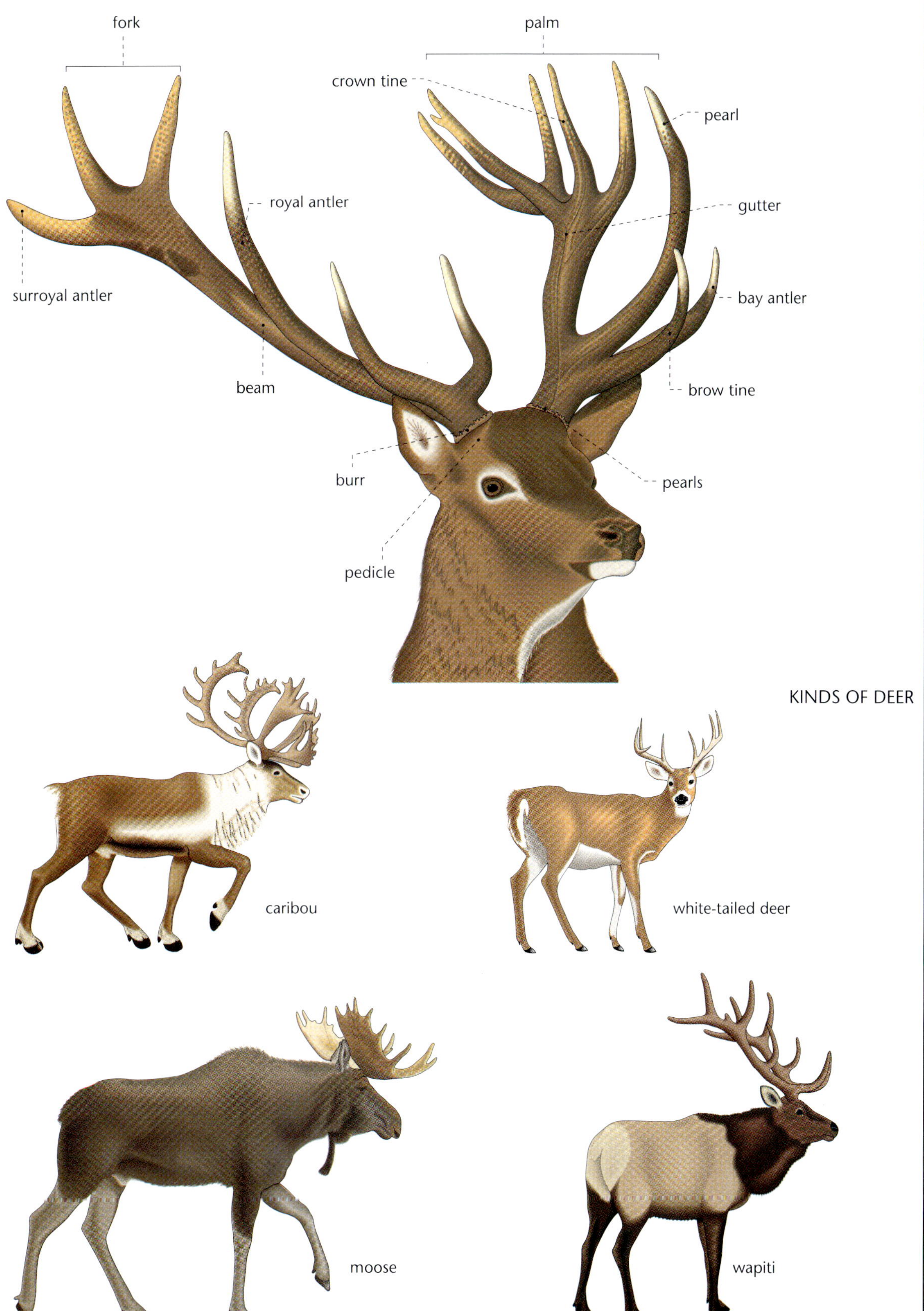

KINDS OF DEER

105

DOG

MORPHOLOGY

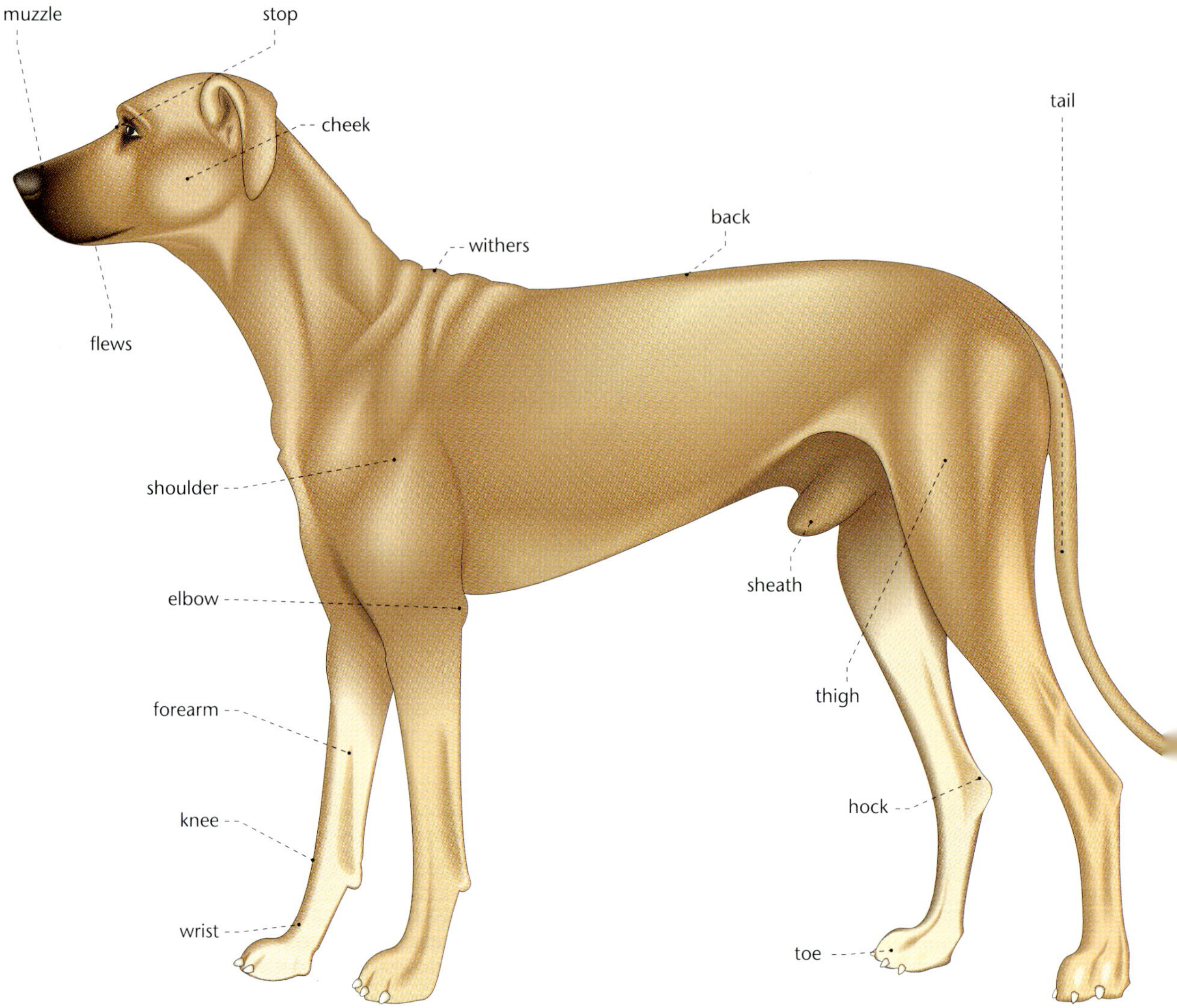

DOG'S FOREPAW

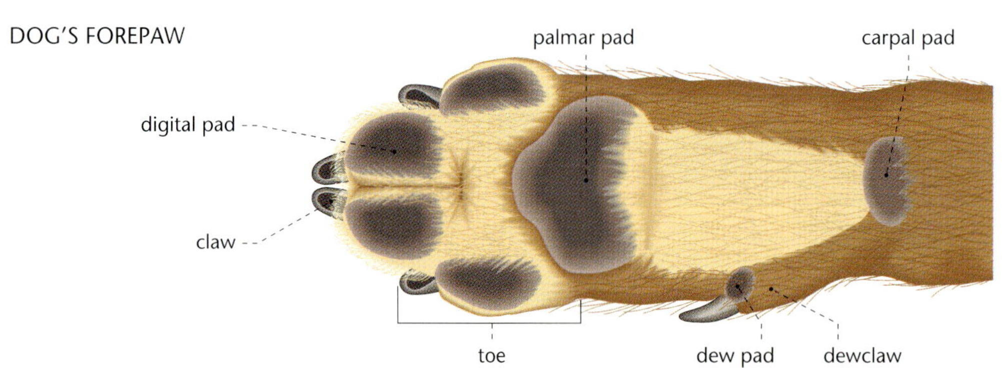

CAT

CAT'S HEAD

EXTENDED CLAW

RETRACTED CLAW

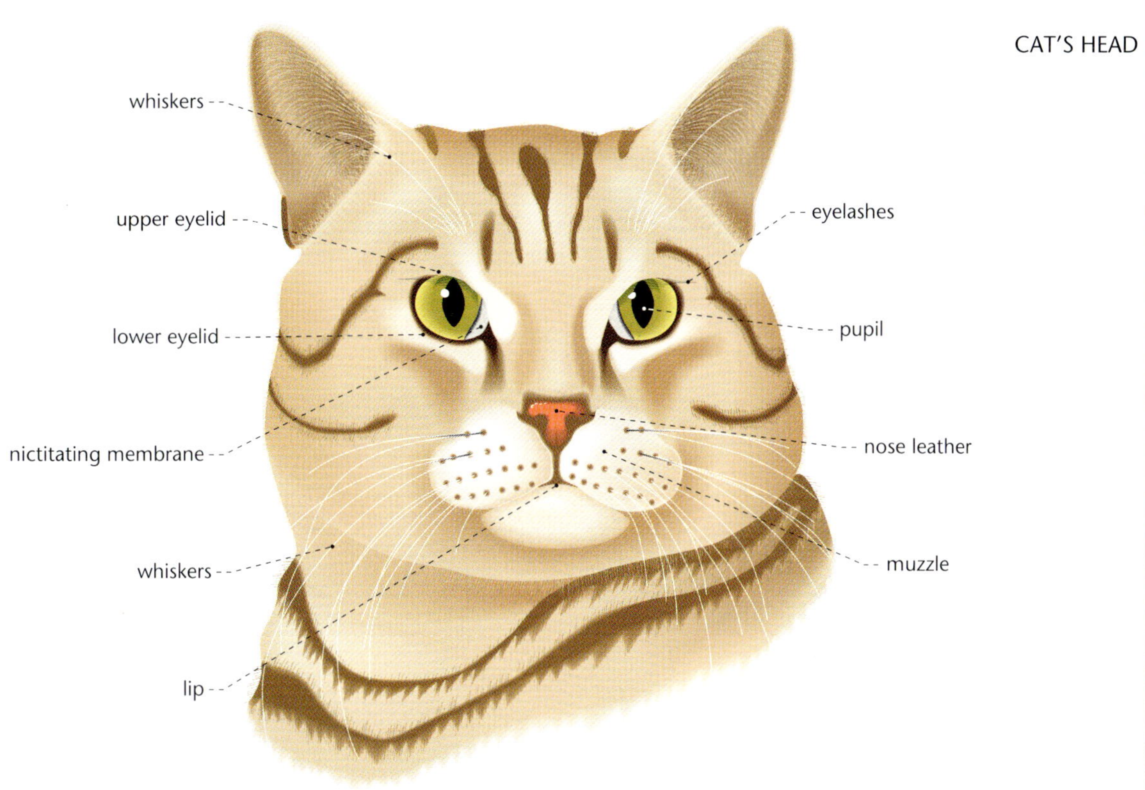

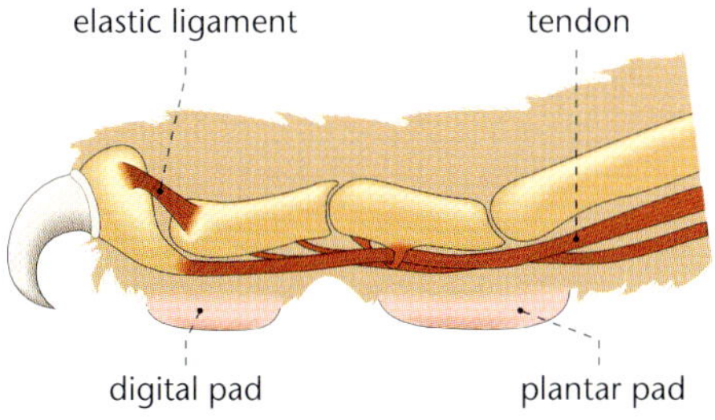

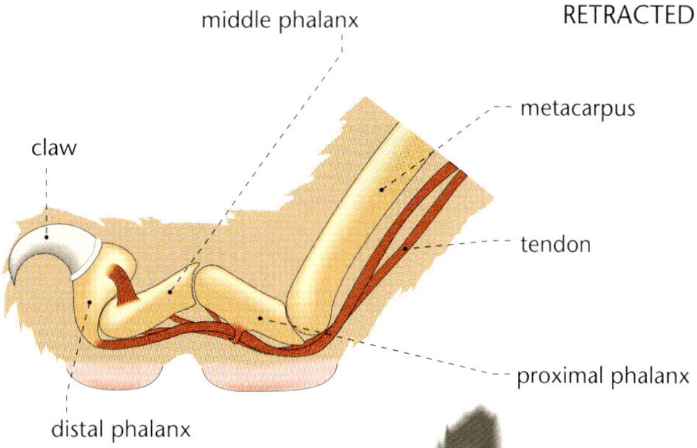

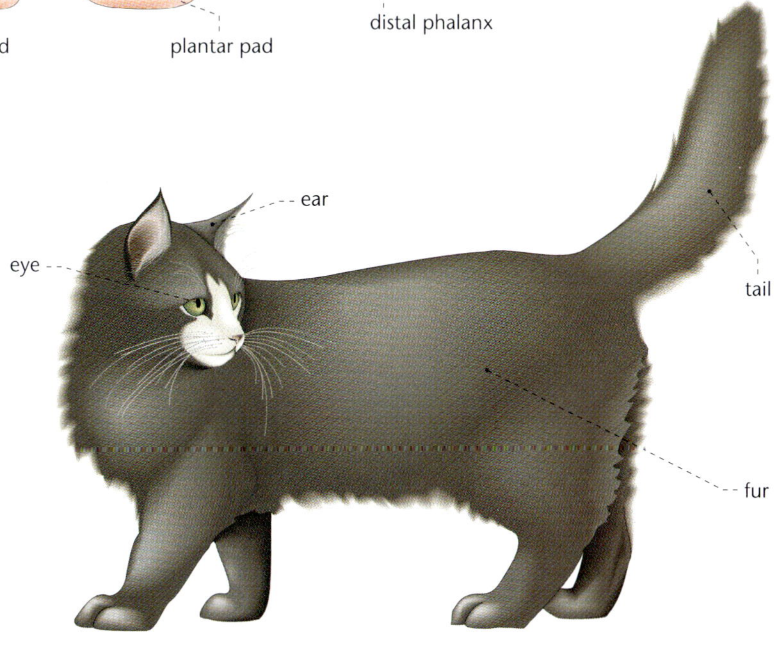

MORPHOLOGY

bill
chin
throat
wing covert
breast
wing
abdomen
tarsus
inner toe
middle toe
outer toe
claw
hind toe
thigh
flank
nape
back

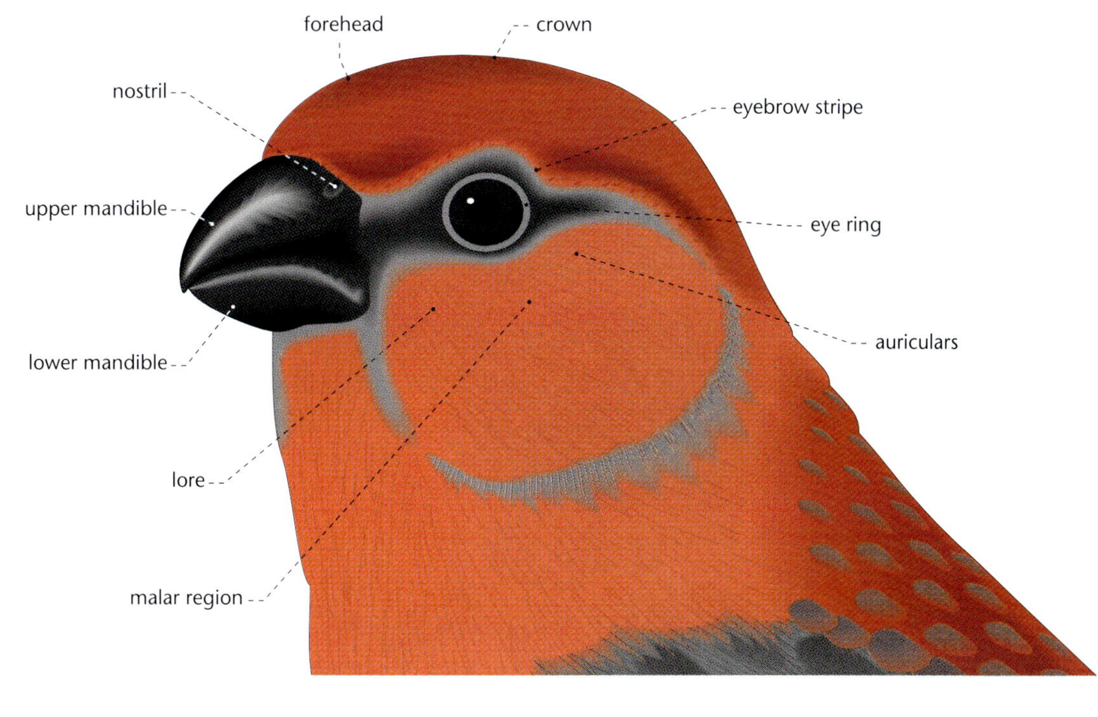

forehead
crown
nostril
eyebrow stripe
upper mandible
eye ring
lower mandible
auriculars
lore
malar region

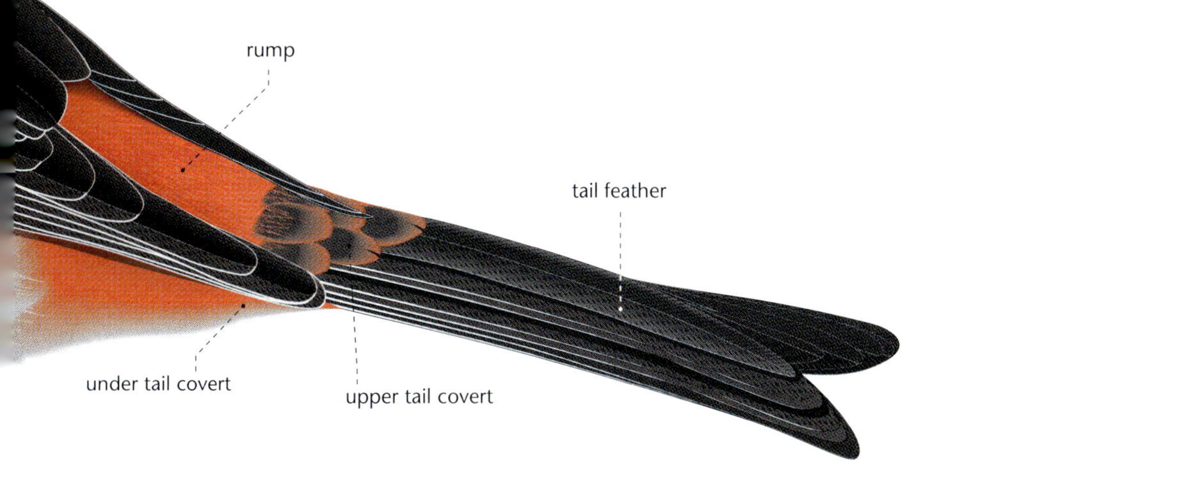

rump
tail feather
under tail covert
upper tail covert

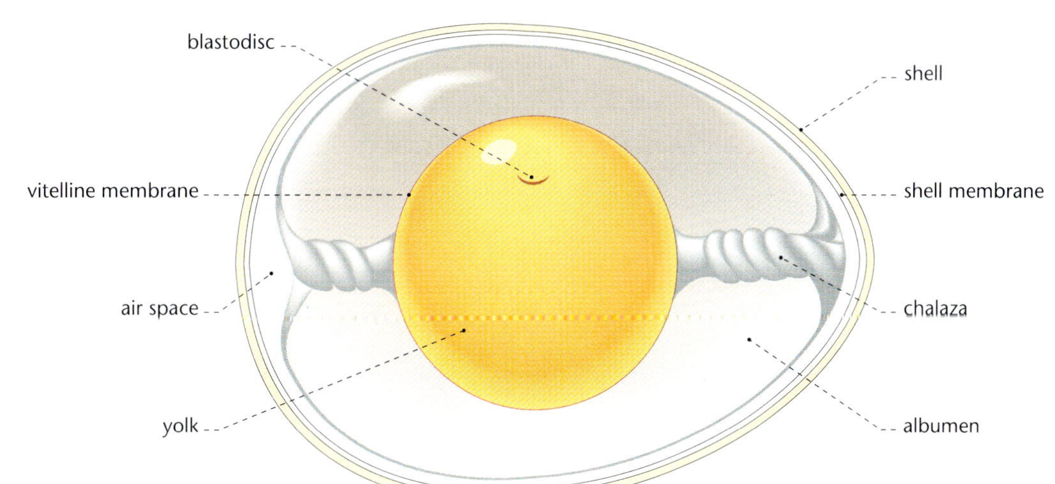

blastodisc
shell
vitelline membrane
shell membrane
air space
chalaza
yolk
albumen

ANIMAL KINGDOM

WING

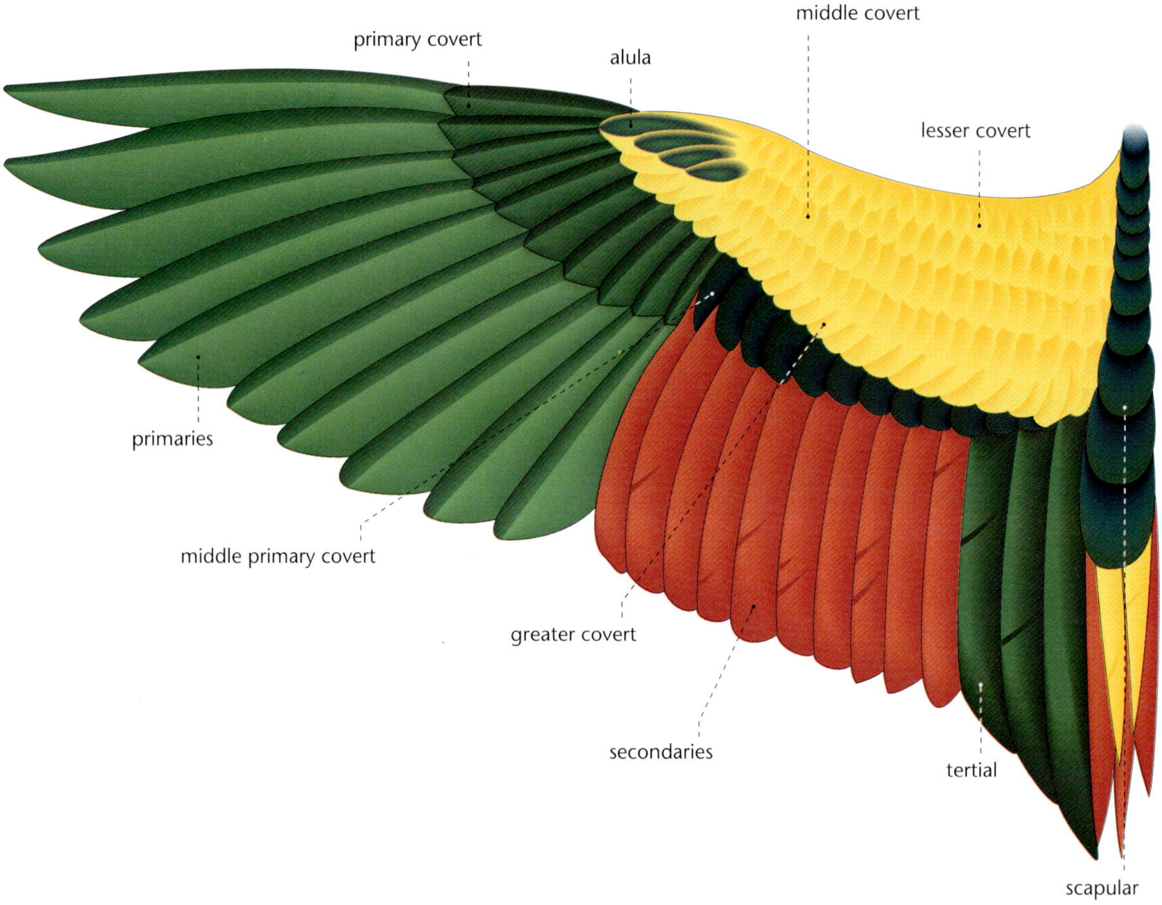

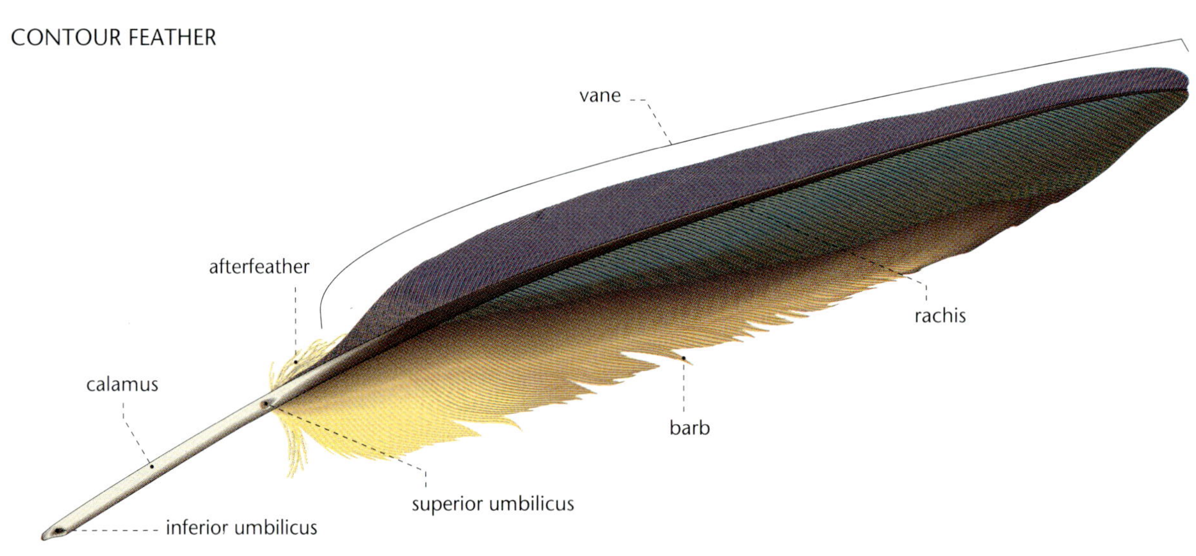

CONTOUR FEATHER

PRINCIPAL TYPES OF BILLS

bird of prey

aquatic bird

wading bird

granivorous bird

insectivorous bird

PRINCIPAL TYPES OF FEET

perching bird

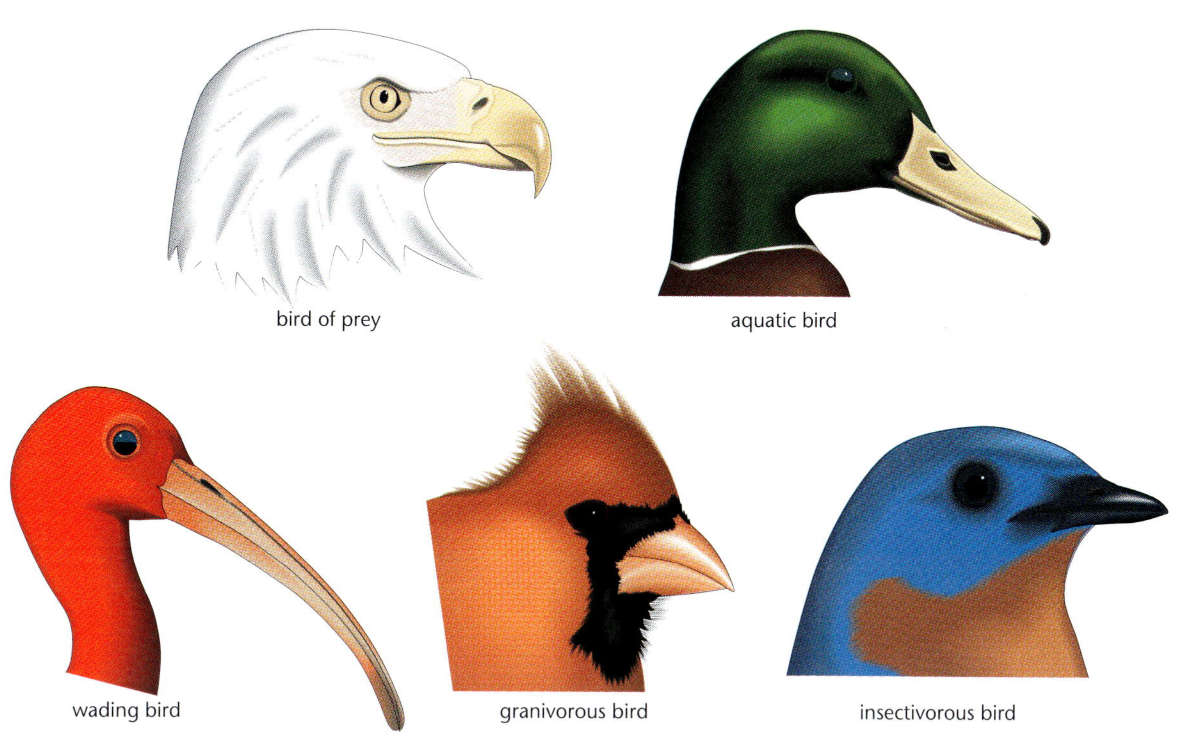

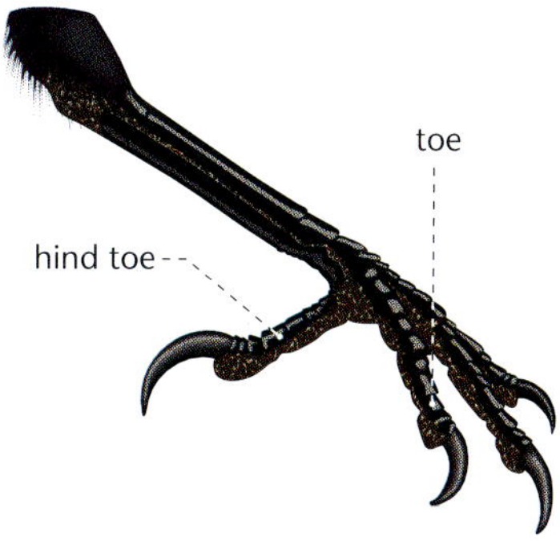

bird of prey

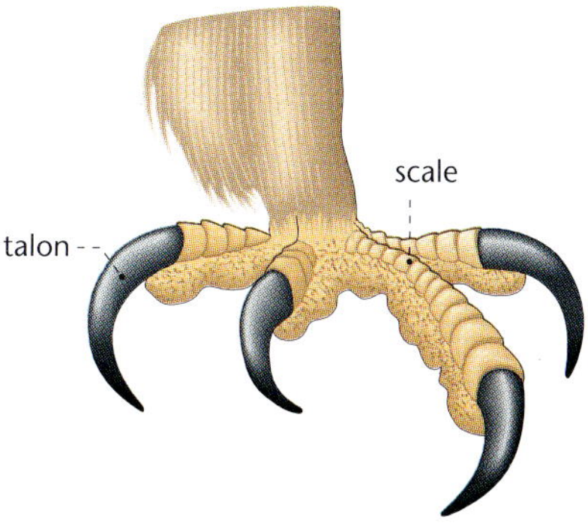

aquatic bird

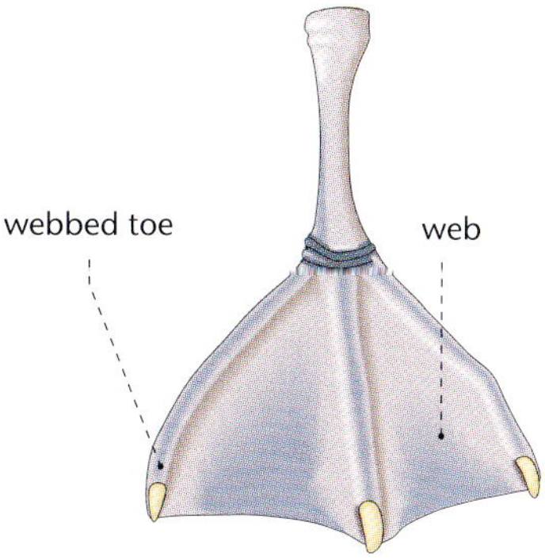

aquatic bird

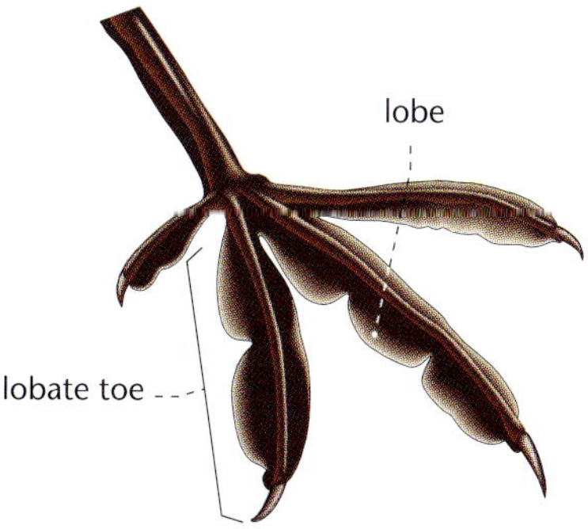

BAT

blood vessels
wing membrane
wrist
calcar
interfemoral membrane
tail
tibia
foot
claw
5th metacarpal
4th metacarpal
3rd metacarpal
2nd metacarpal
elbow
radius
thumb
wings
BAT'S HEAD
ear
tragus
nose leaf

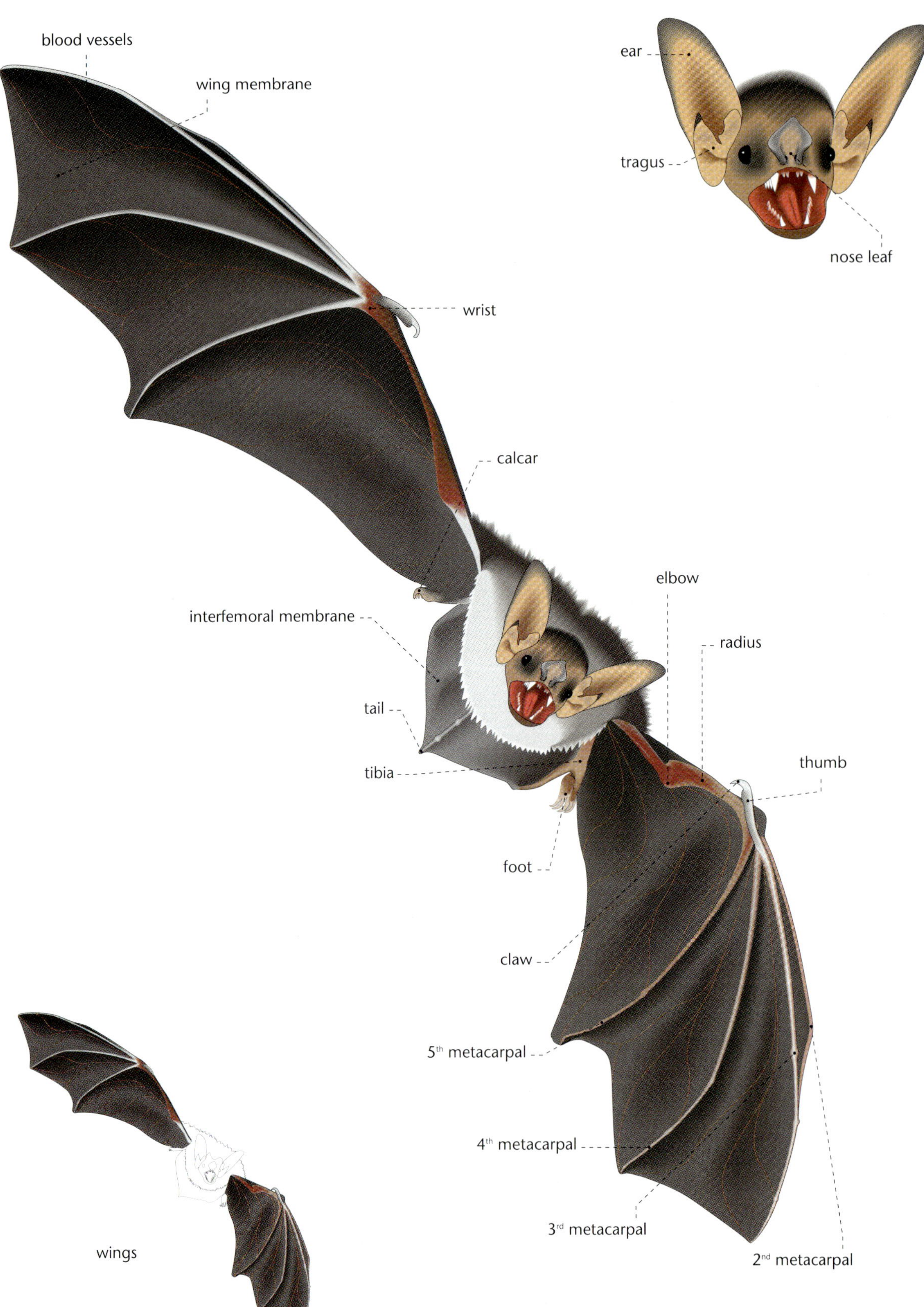

CONTENTS

PLANT CELL

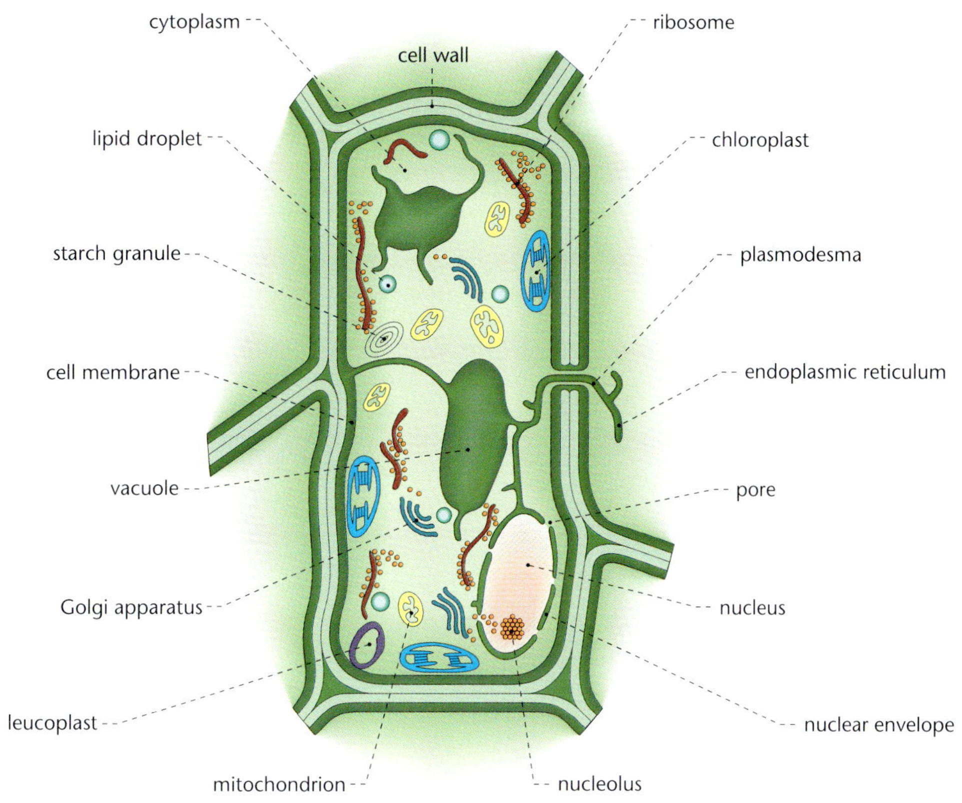

ANIMAL CELL

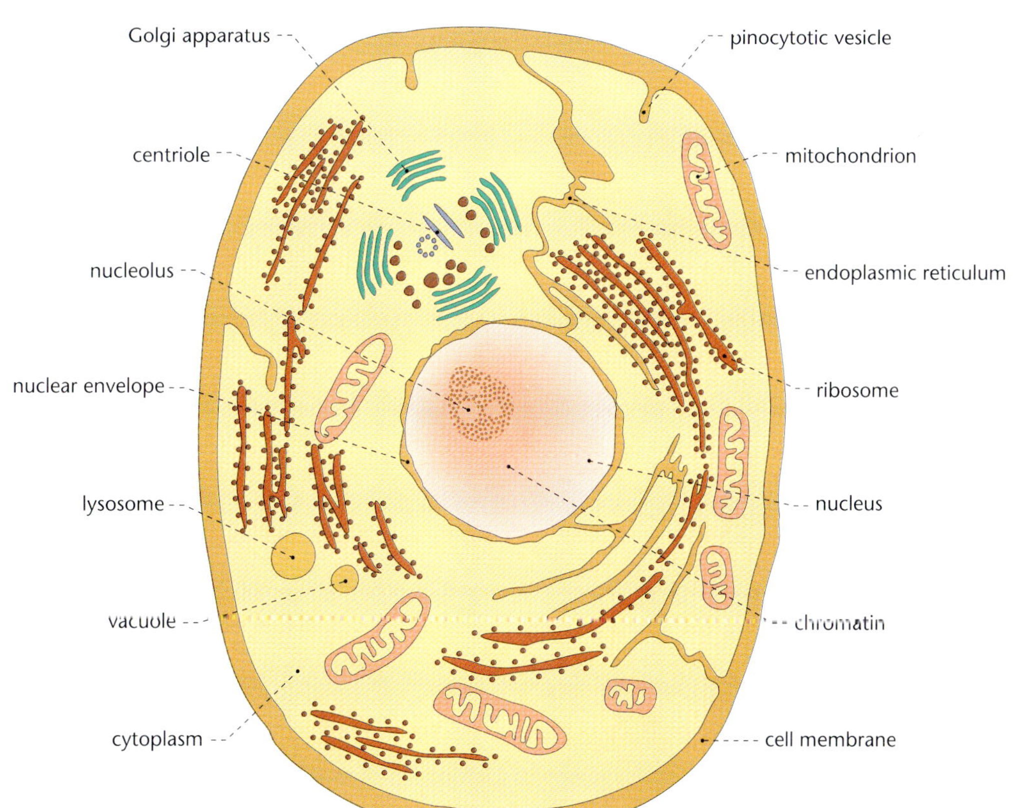

HUMAN BODY

forehead
skull
temple
face
ear
Adam's apple
shoulder
nipple
armpit
breast
chest
thorax
navel
abdomen
pubis
penis
groin
scrotum
knee
foot
ankle
toe

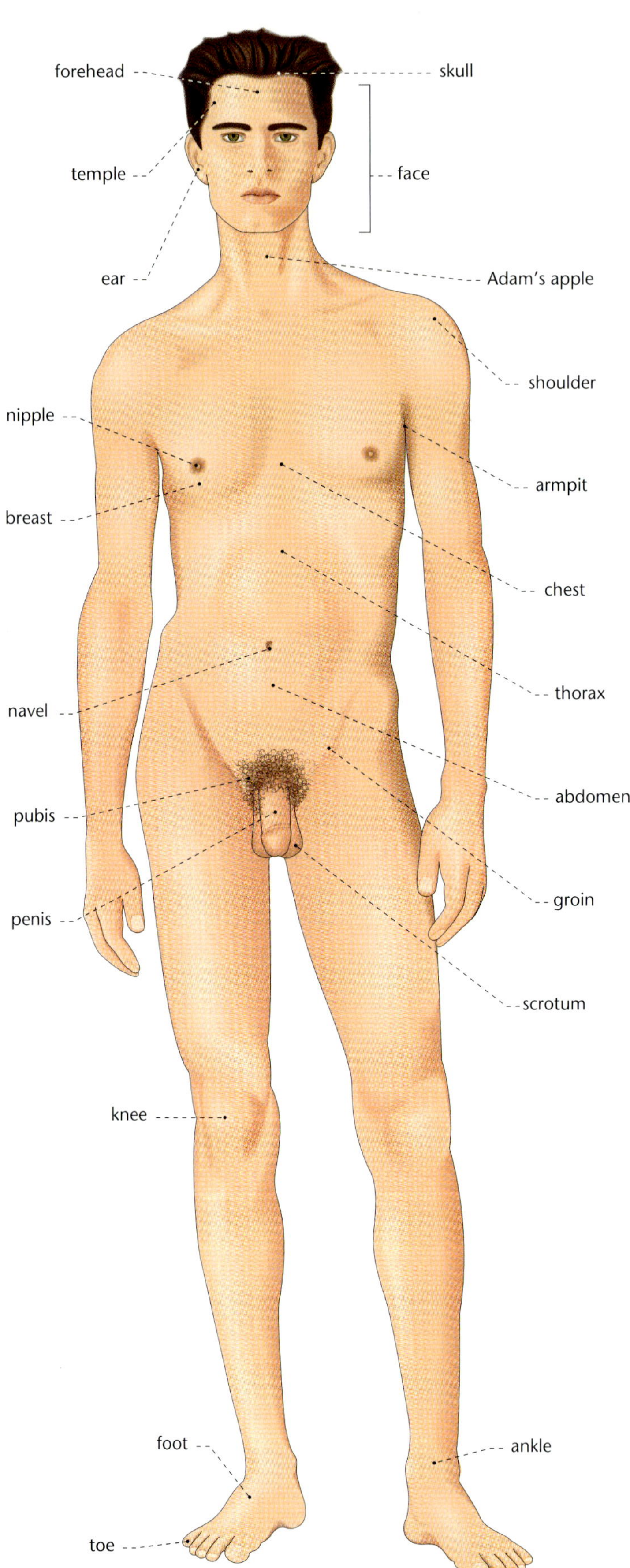

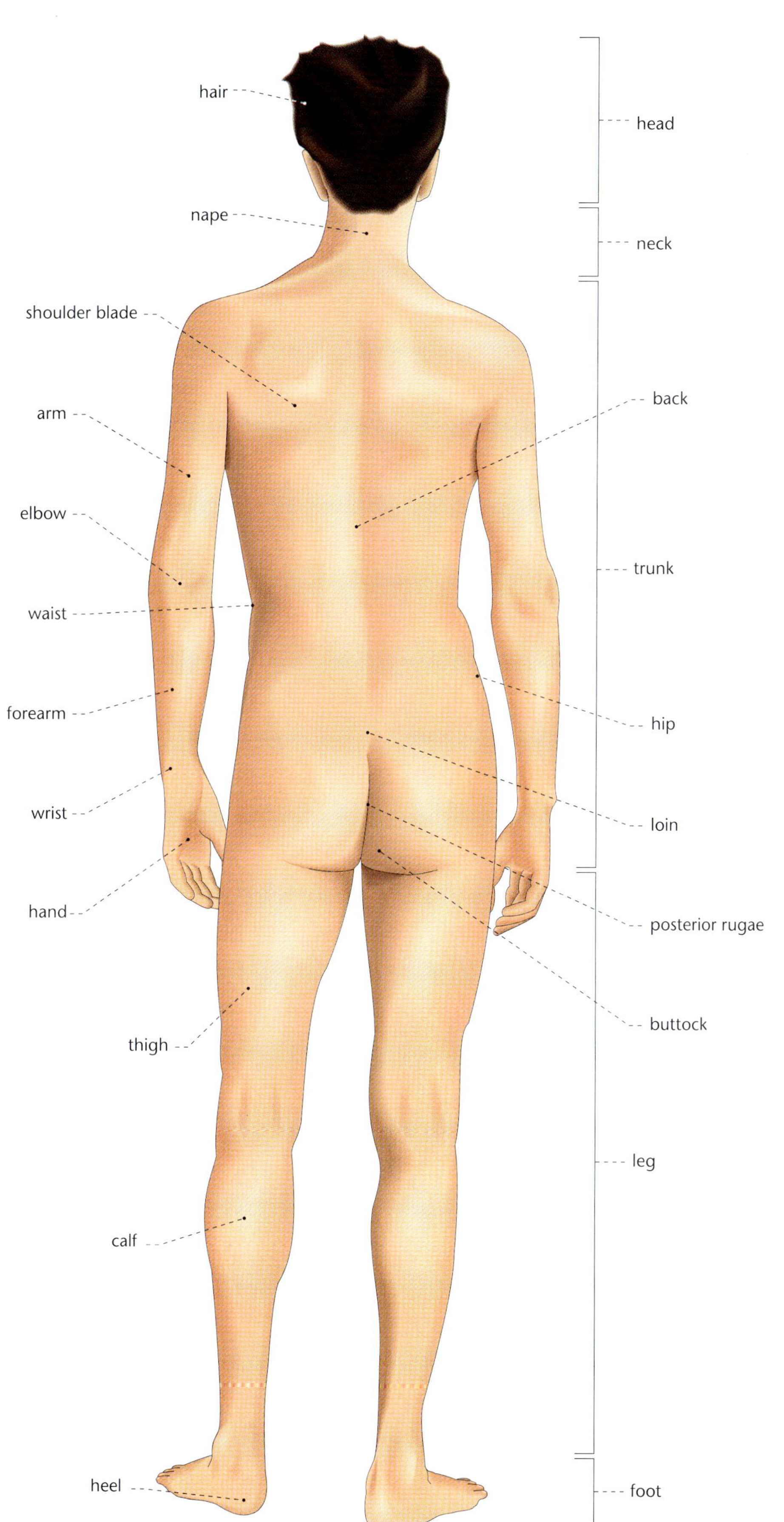

hair
nape
shoulder blade
arm
elbow
waist
forearm
wrist
hand
thigh
calf
heel
head
neck
back
trunk
hip
loin
posterior rugae
buttock
leg
foot

HUMAN BODY

eye
nose
cheek
mouth
neck
chin
shoulder
nipple
armpit
breast
chest
thorax
navel
abdomen
pubis
groin
vulva
knee
foot
ankle
toe

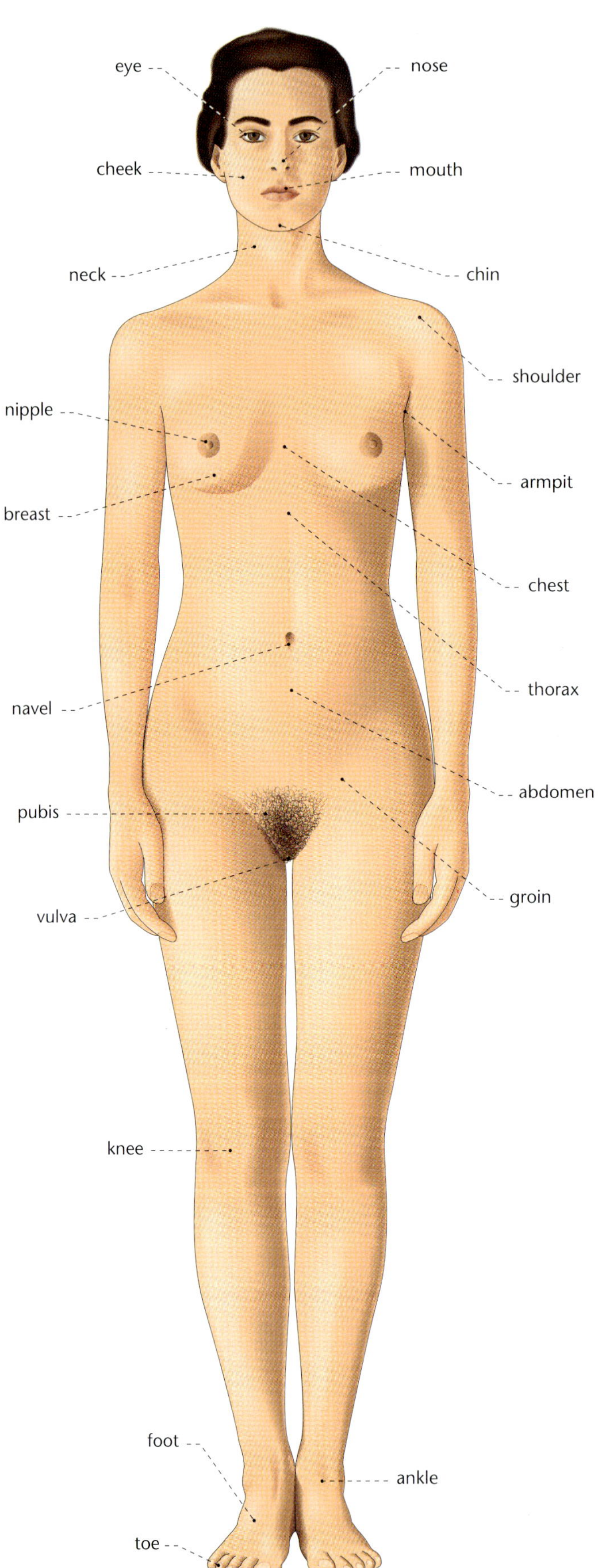

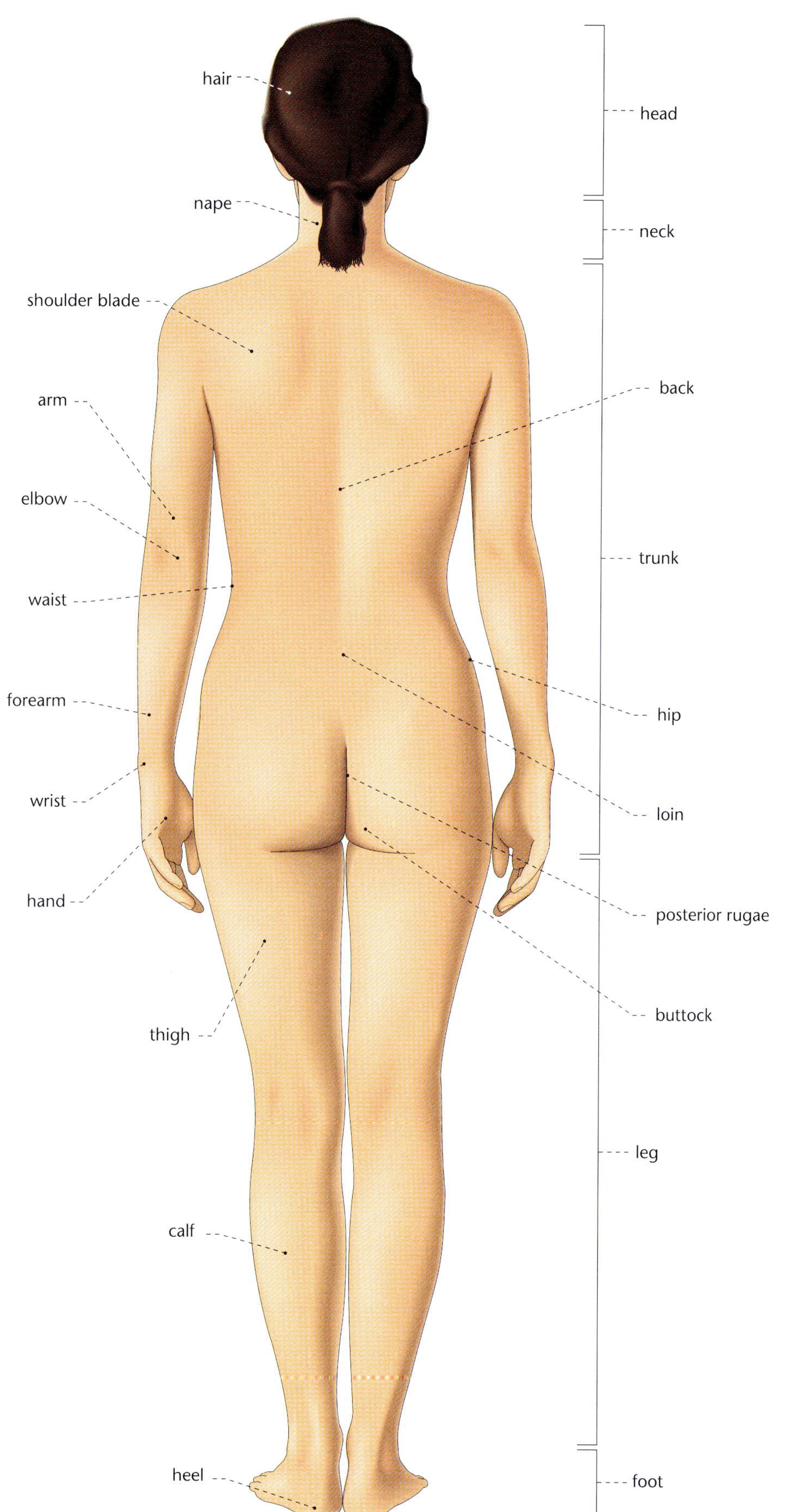

hair
nape
shoulder blade
arm
elbow
waist
forearm
wrist
hand
thigh
calf
heel
head
neck
back
trunk
hip
loin
posterior rugae
buttock
leg
foot

ANTERIOR VIEW

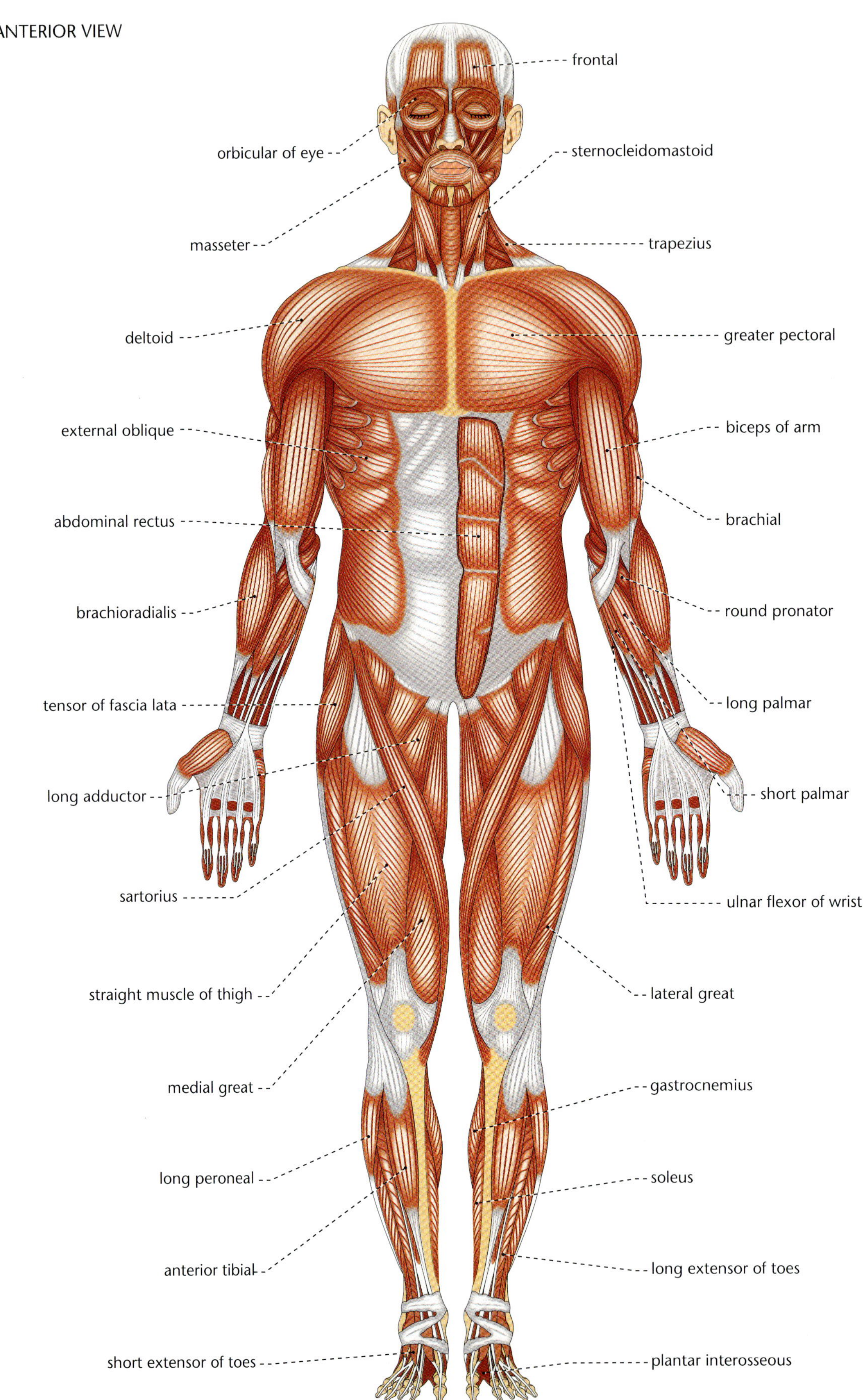

HUMAN BEING

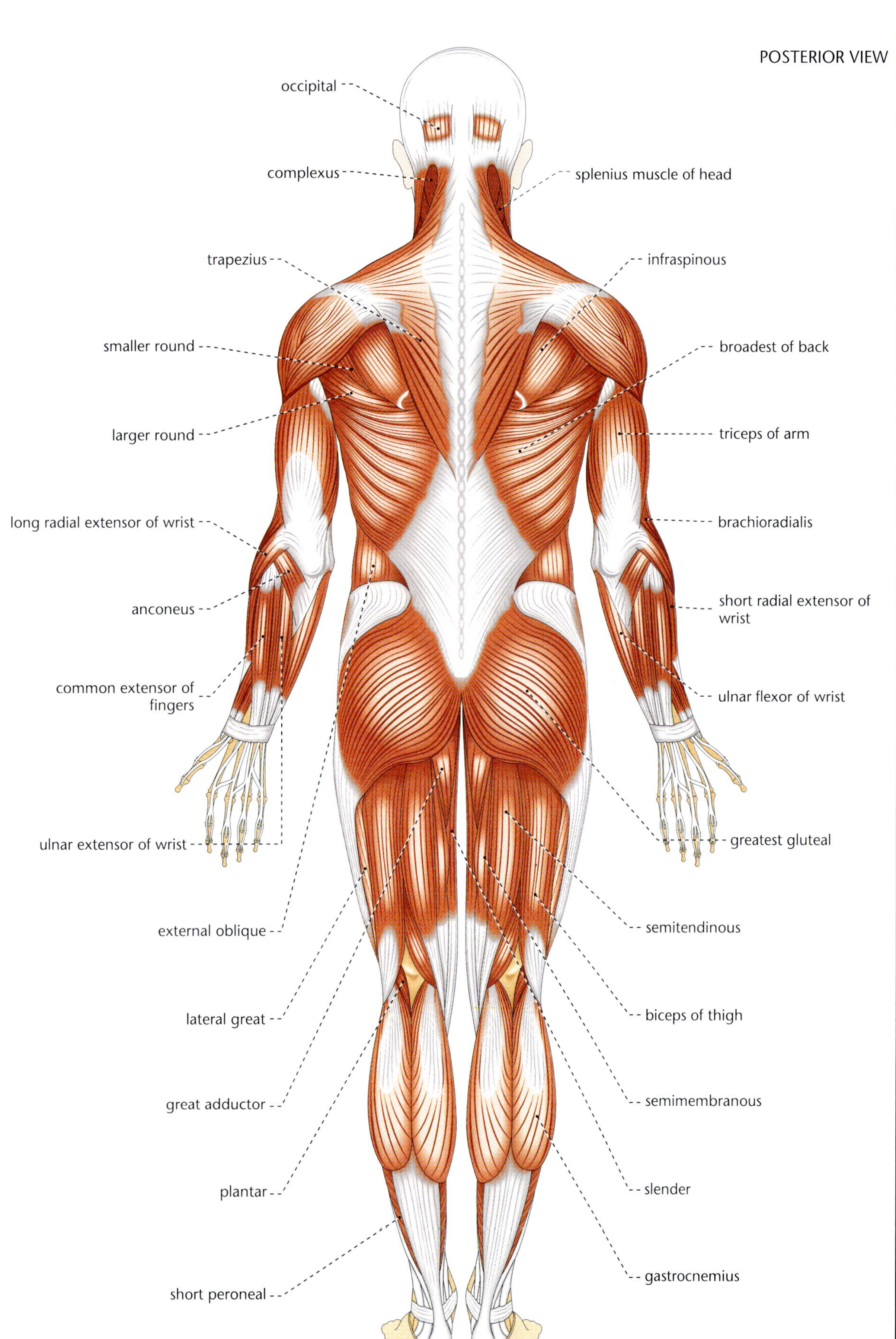

121

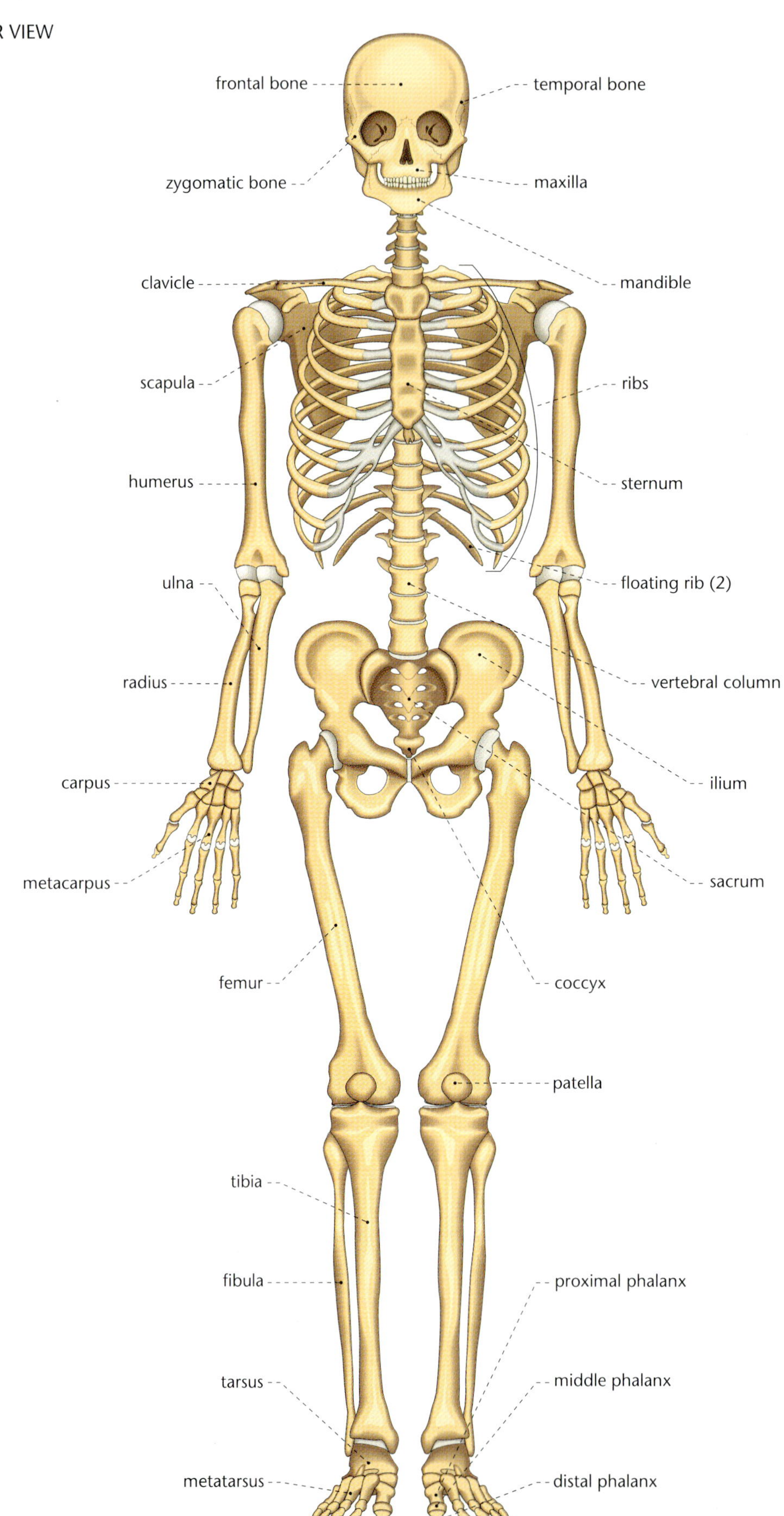

SKELETON
ANTERIOR VIEW
frontal bone
temporal bone
zygomatic bone
maxilla
mandible
clavicle
scapula
ribs
humerus
sternum
ulna
radius
floating rib (2)
vertebral column
carpus
ilium
metacarpus
sacrum
femur
coccyx
patella
tibia
fibula
proximal phalanx
tarsus
middle phalanx
metatarsus
distal phalanx

occipital bone
parietal bone
atlas
axis
cervical vertebra (7)
acromion
head of humerus
spine of scapula
scapula
thoracic vertebra (12)
epicondyle
false rib (3)
olecranon
lumbar vertebra (5)
epitrochlea
sacrum
greater trochanter
proximal phalanx
middle phalanx
neck of femur
distal phalanx
head of femur
lateral condyle of femur
ischium
medial condyle of femur
talus
calcaneus

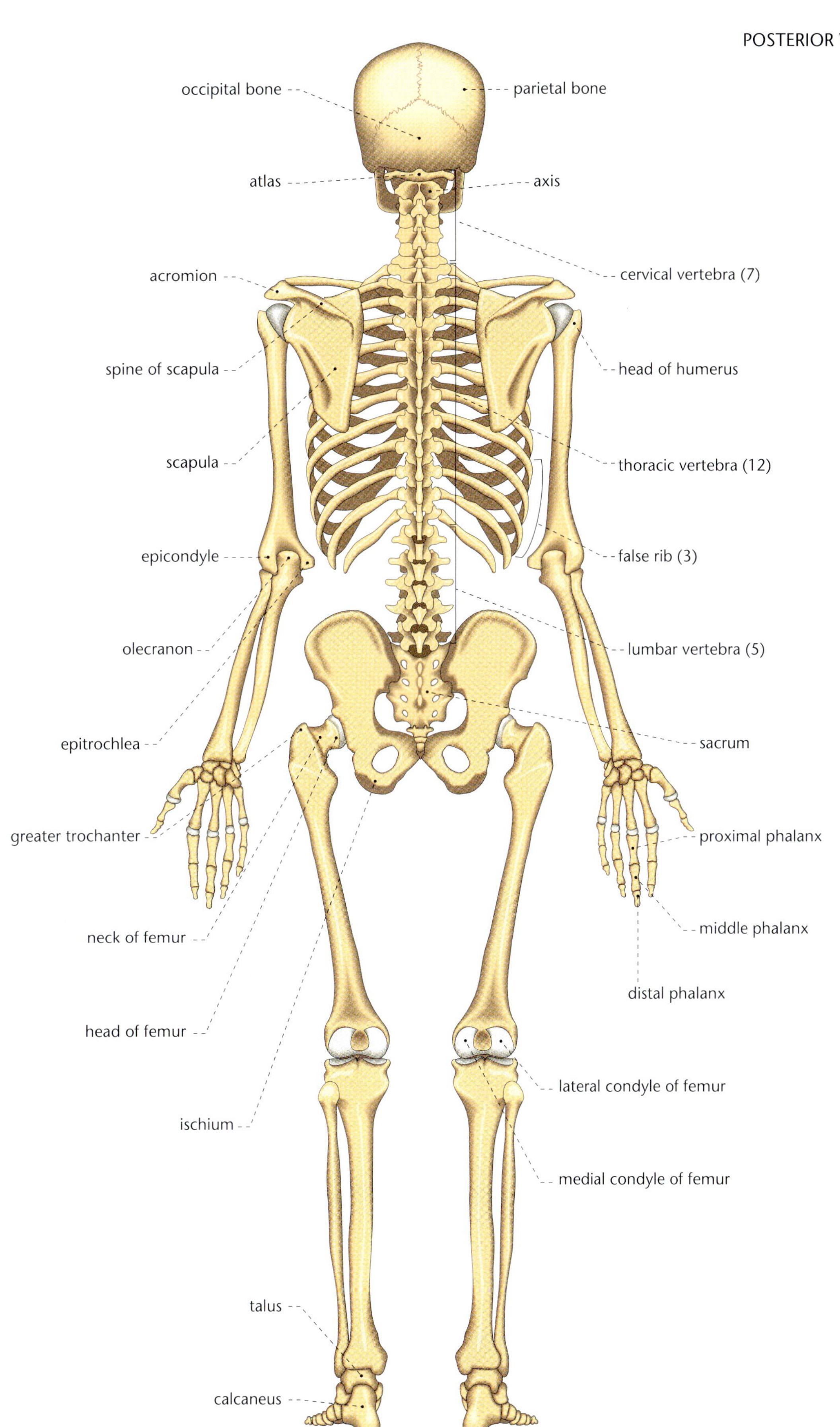

HUMAN BEING

SCHEMA OF CIRCULATION

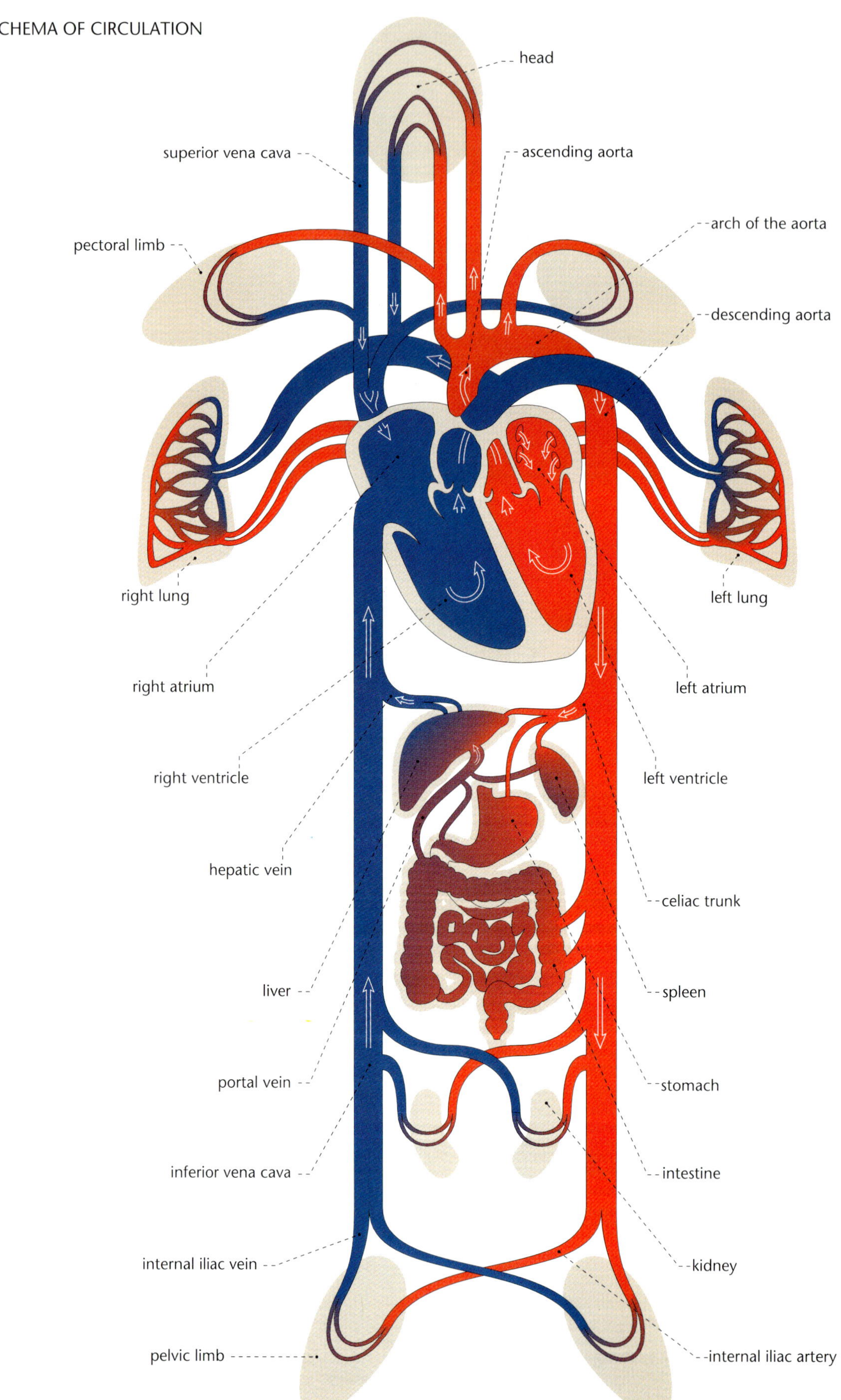

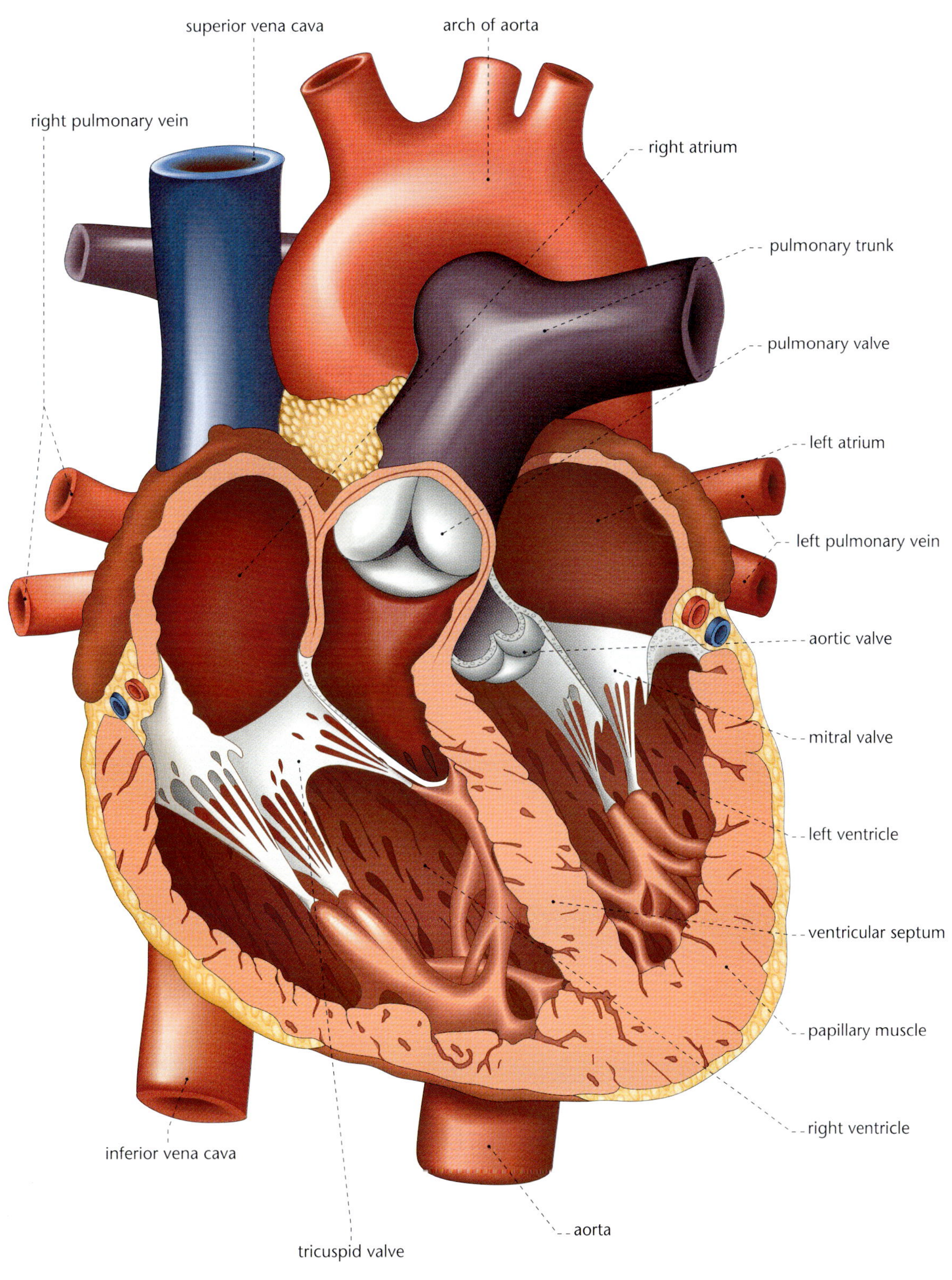

superior vena cava
arch of aorta
right pulmonary vein
right atrium
pulmonary trunk
pulmonary valve
left atrium
left pulmonary vein
aortic valve
mitral valve
left ventricle
ventricular septum
papillary muscle
right ventricle
inferior vena cava
tricuspid valve
aorta

BLOOD CIRCULATION

PRINCIPAL VEINS AND ARTERIES

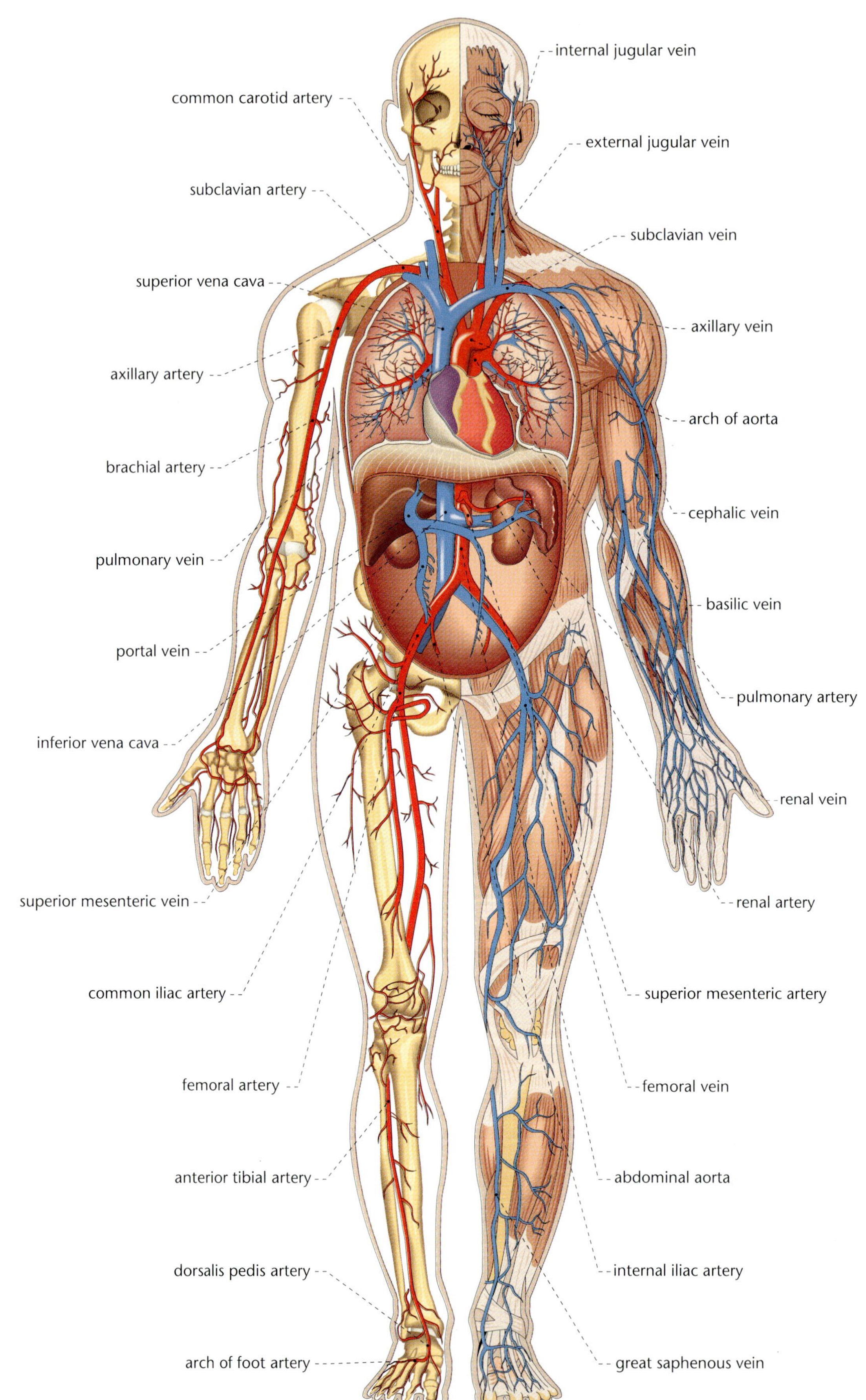

MALE GENITAL ORGANS

SAGITTAL SECTION

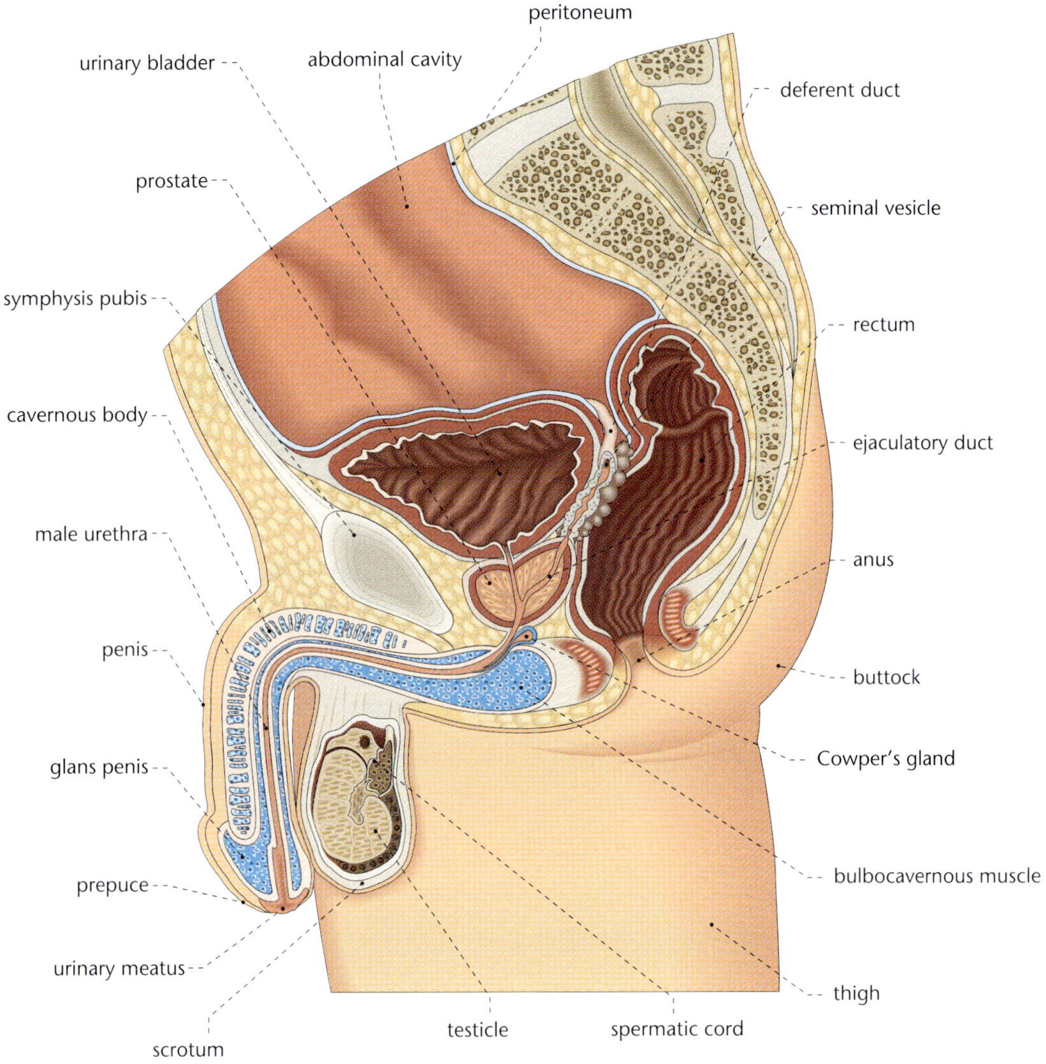

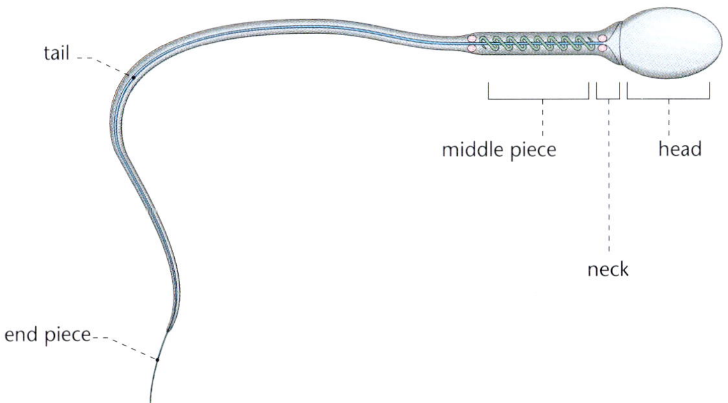

SPERMATOZOON

FEMALE GENITAL ORGANS

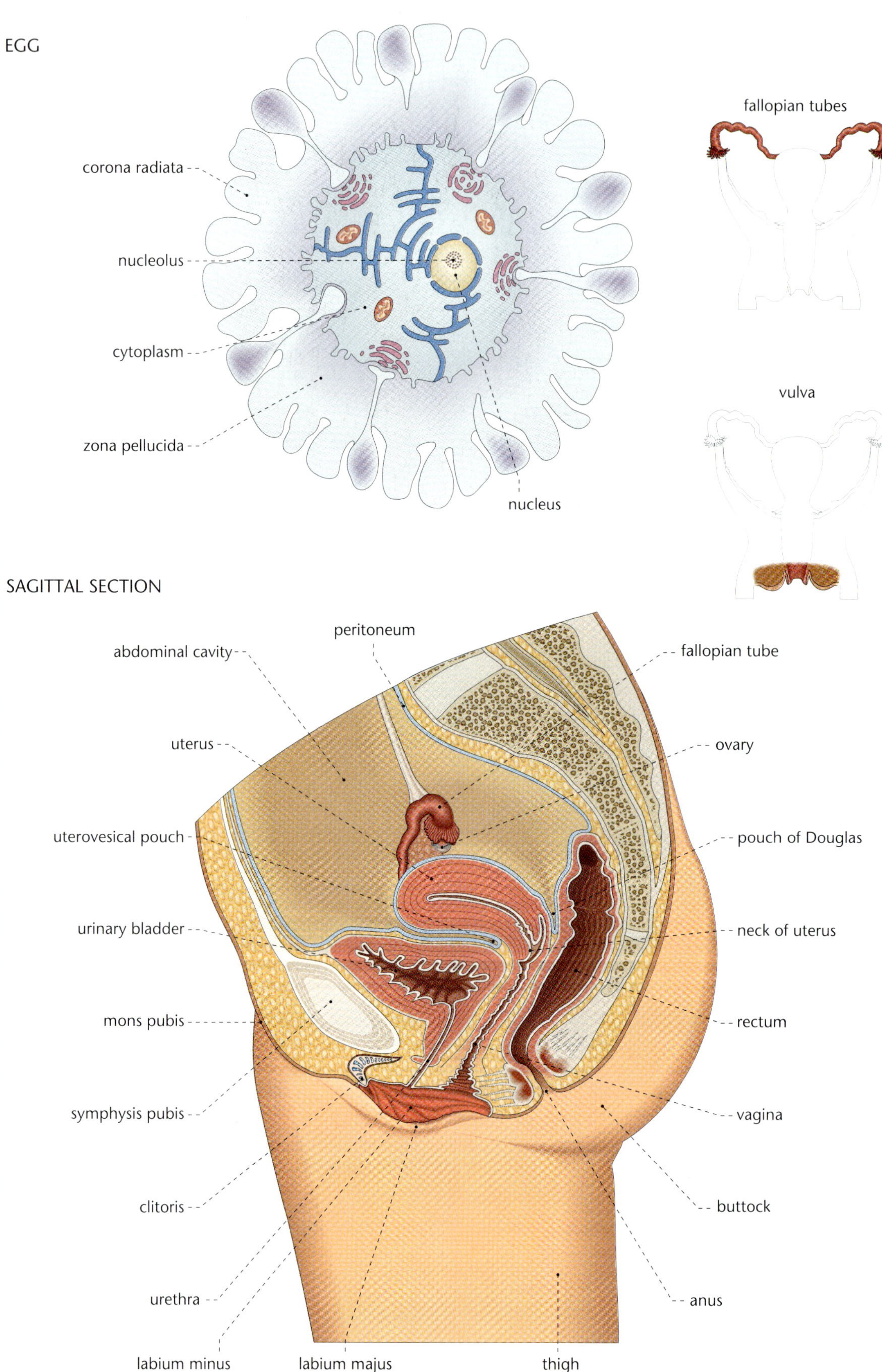

FEMALE GENITAL ORGANS

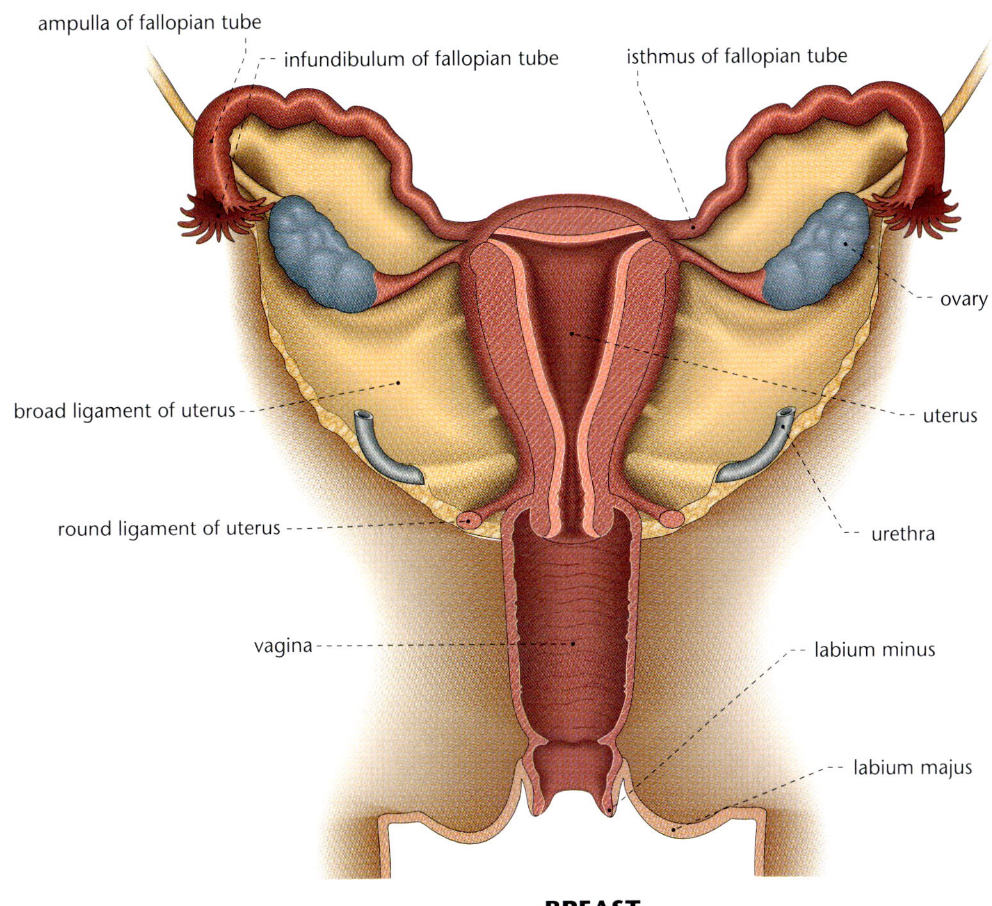

BREAST

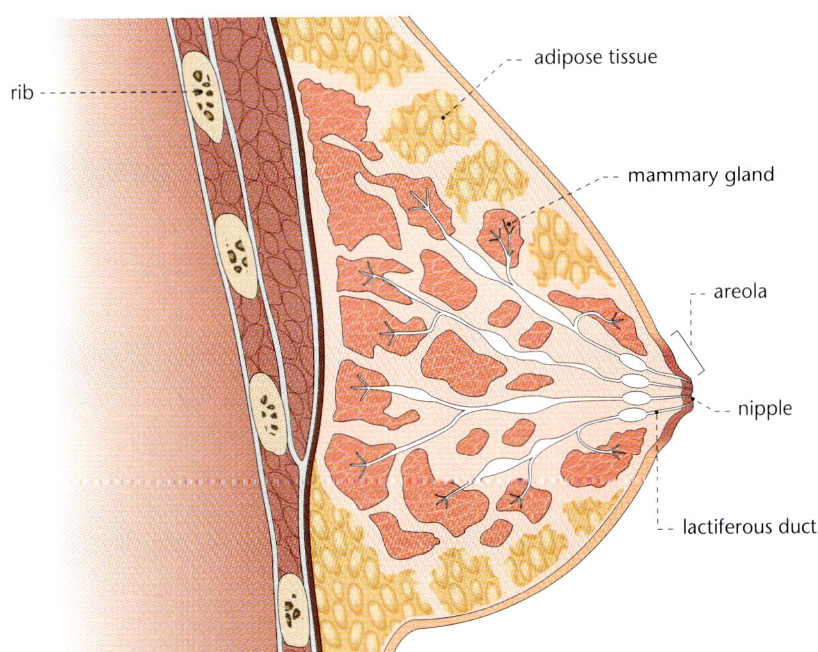

RESPIRATORY SYSTEM

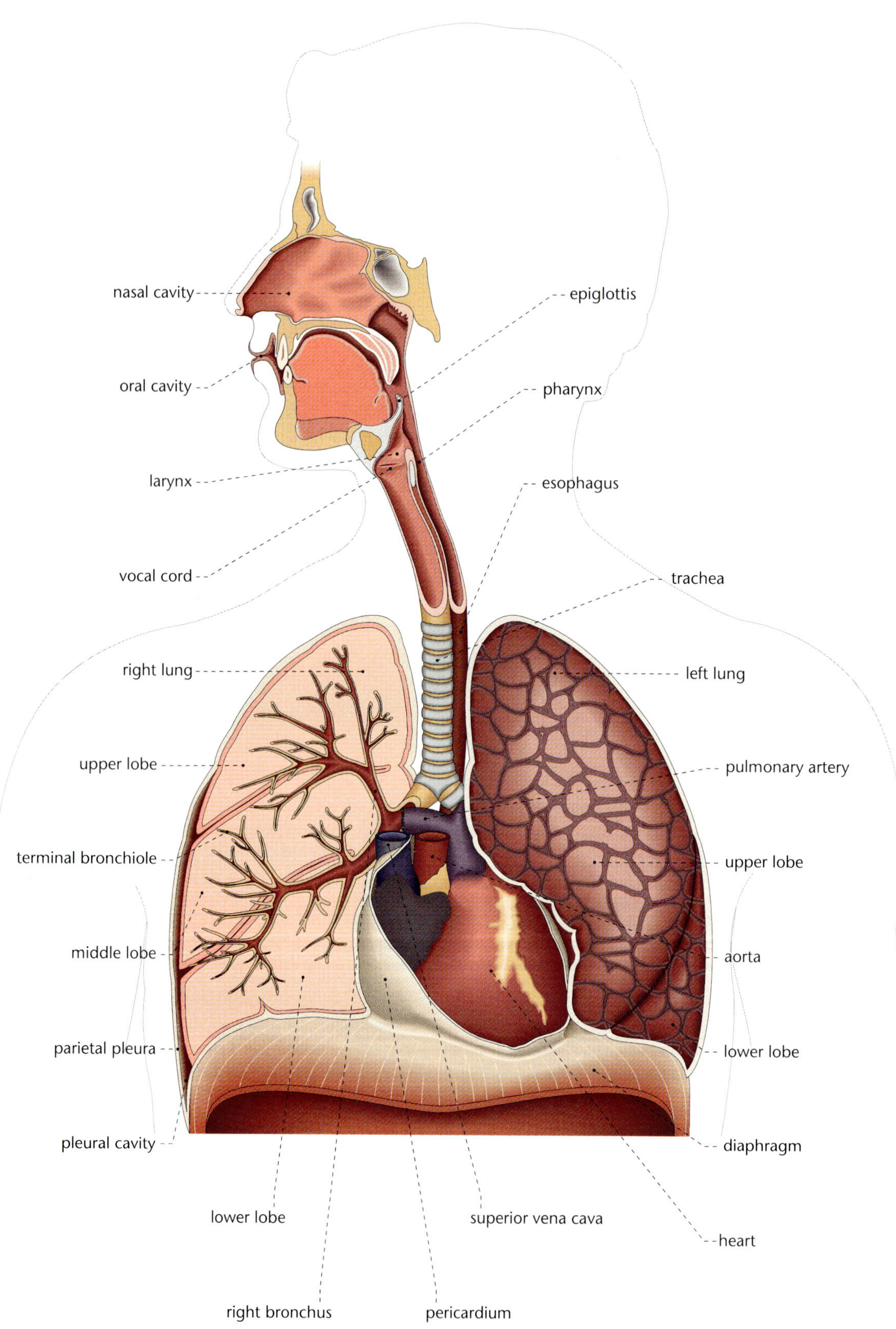

DIGESTIVE SYSTEM

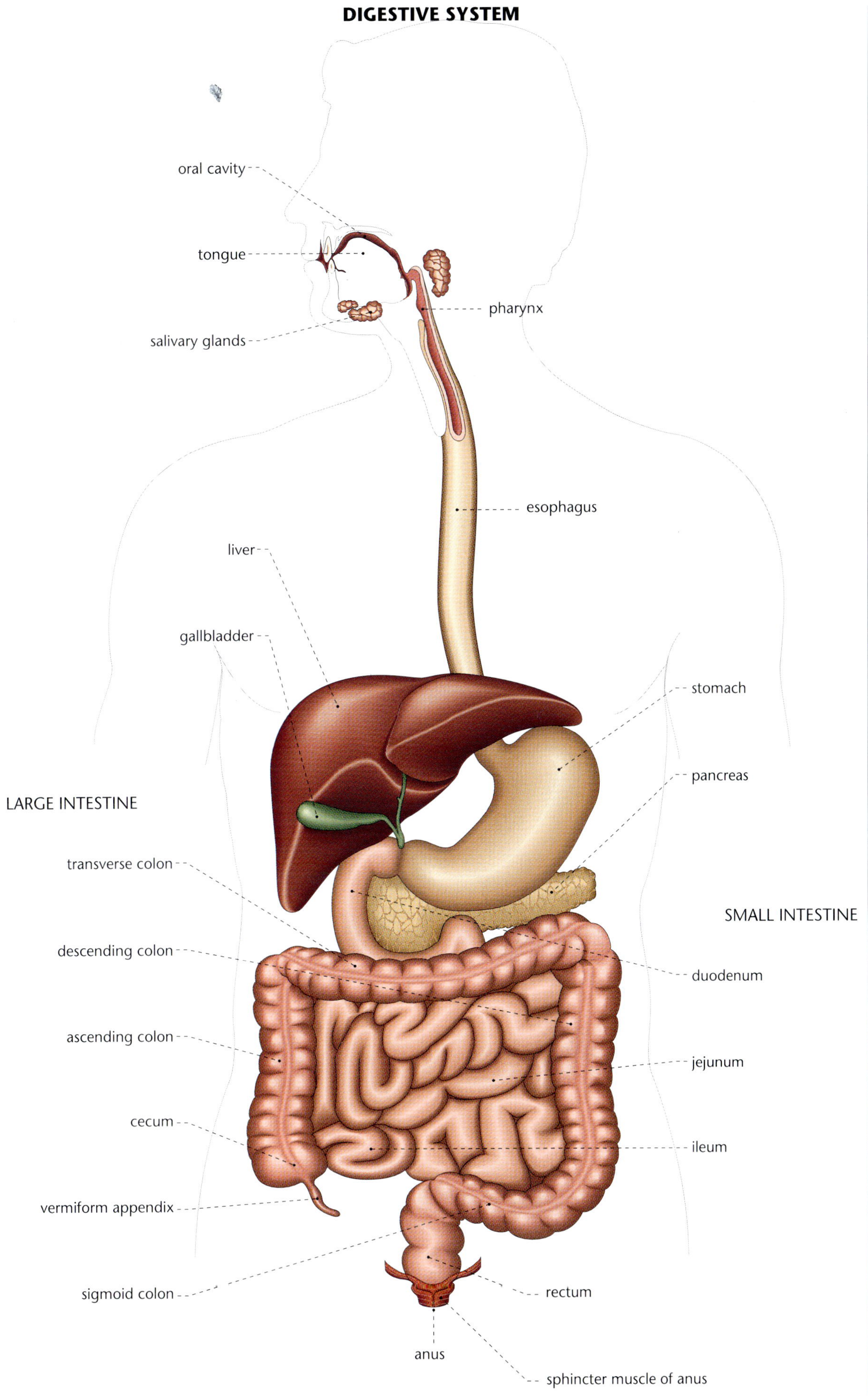

URINARY SYSTEM

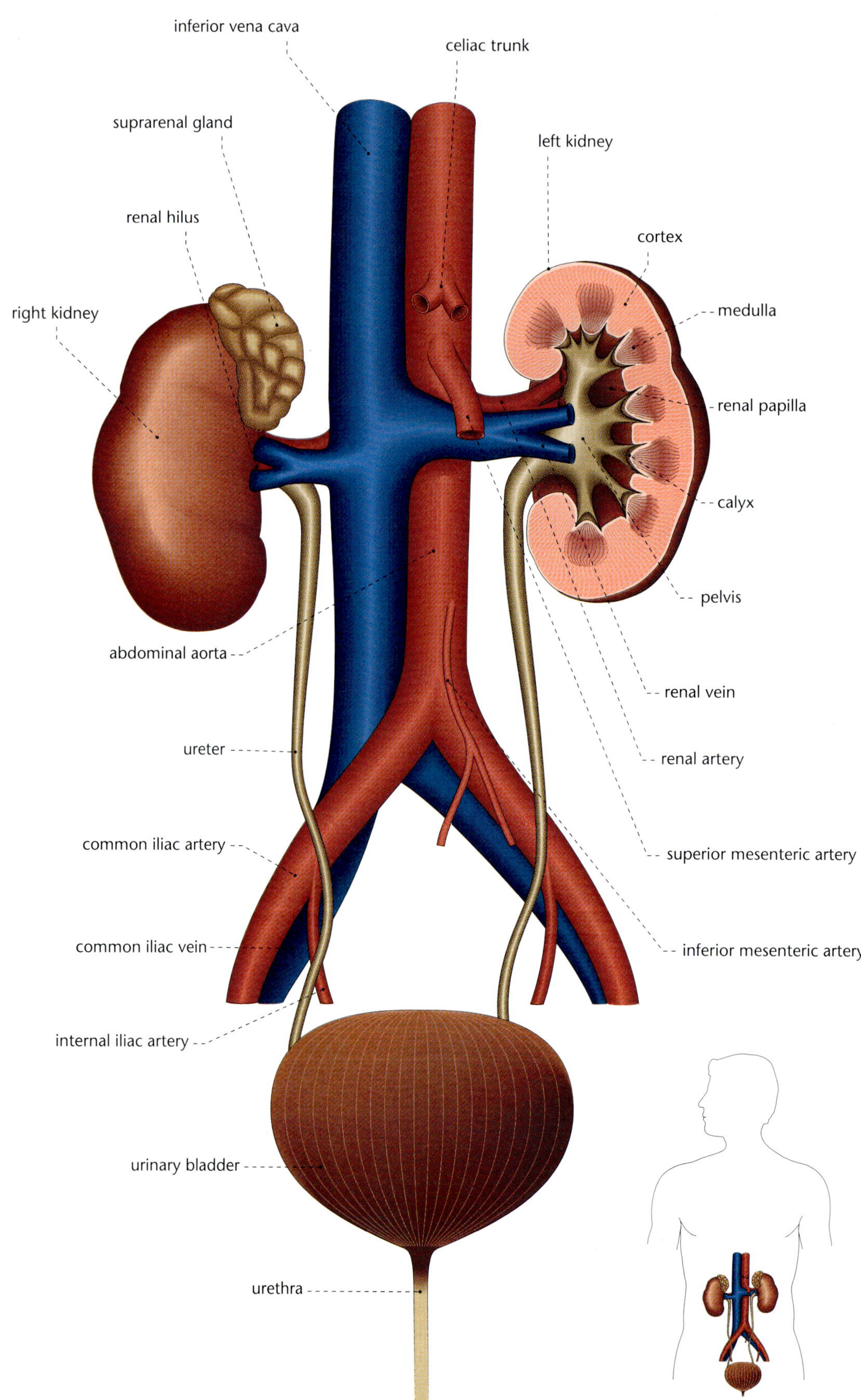

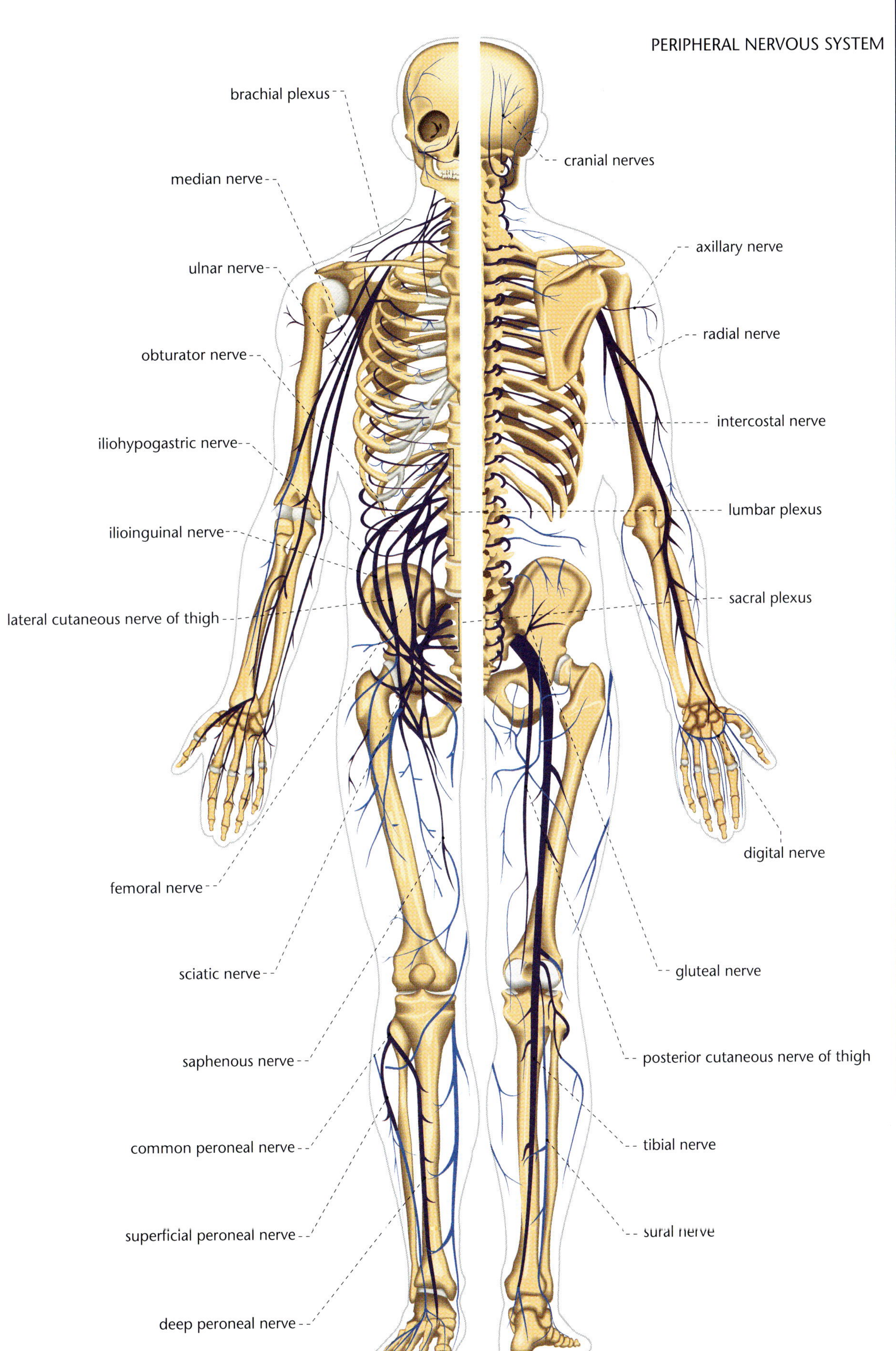
PERIPHERAL NERVOUS SYSTEM
brachial plexus
cranial nerves
median nerve
ulnar nerve
axillary nerve
obturator nerve
radial nerve
iliohypogastric nerve
intercostal nerve
ilioinguinal nerve
lumbar plexus
lateral cutaneous nerve of thigh
sacral plexus
femoral nerve
digital nerve
sciatic nerve
gluteal nerve
saphenous nerve
posterior cutaneous nerve of thigh
common peroneal nerve
tibial nerve
superficial peroneal nerve
sural nerve
deep peroneal nerve

CENTRAL NERVOUS SYSTEM

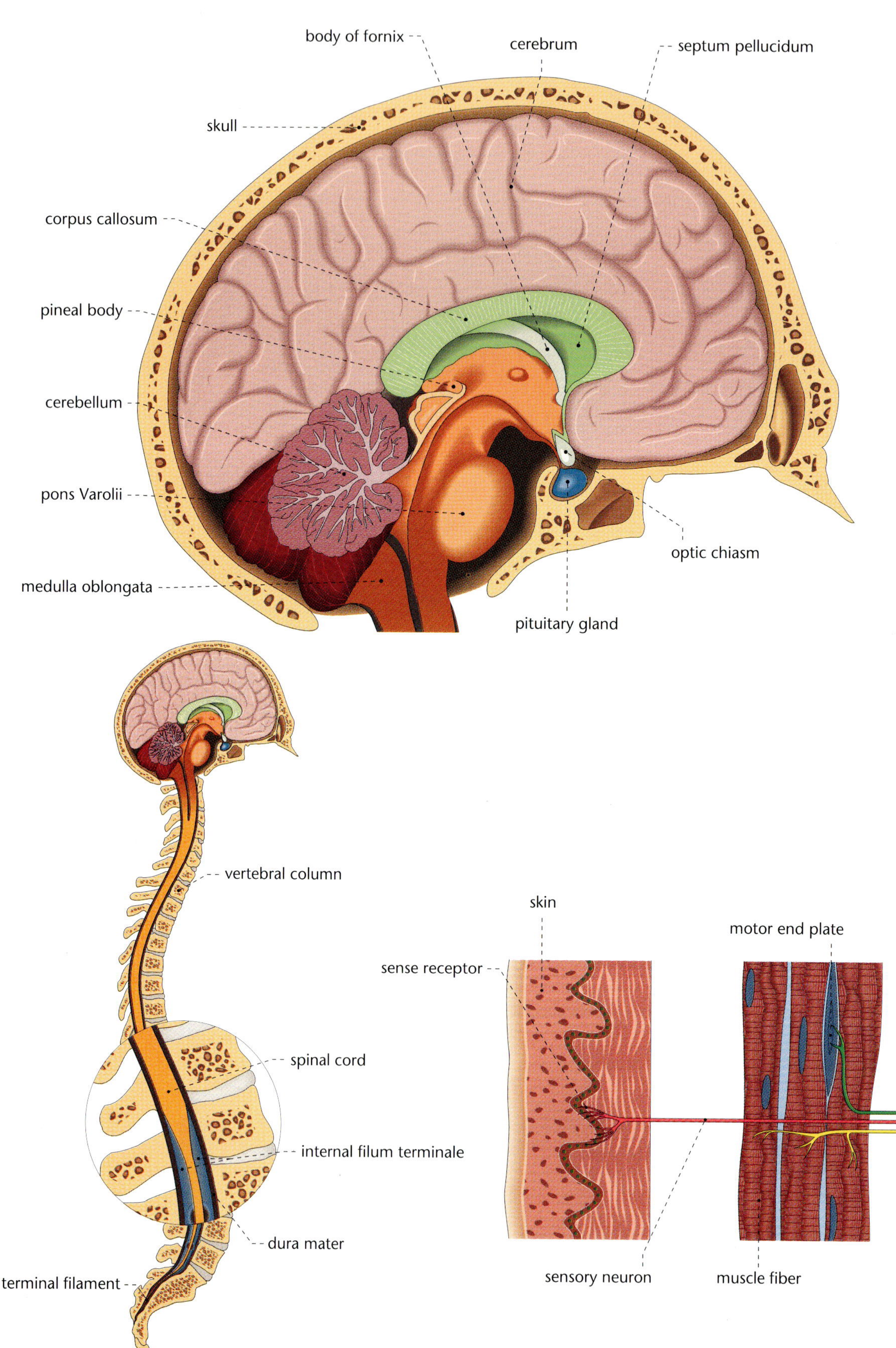

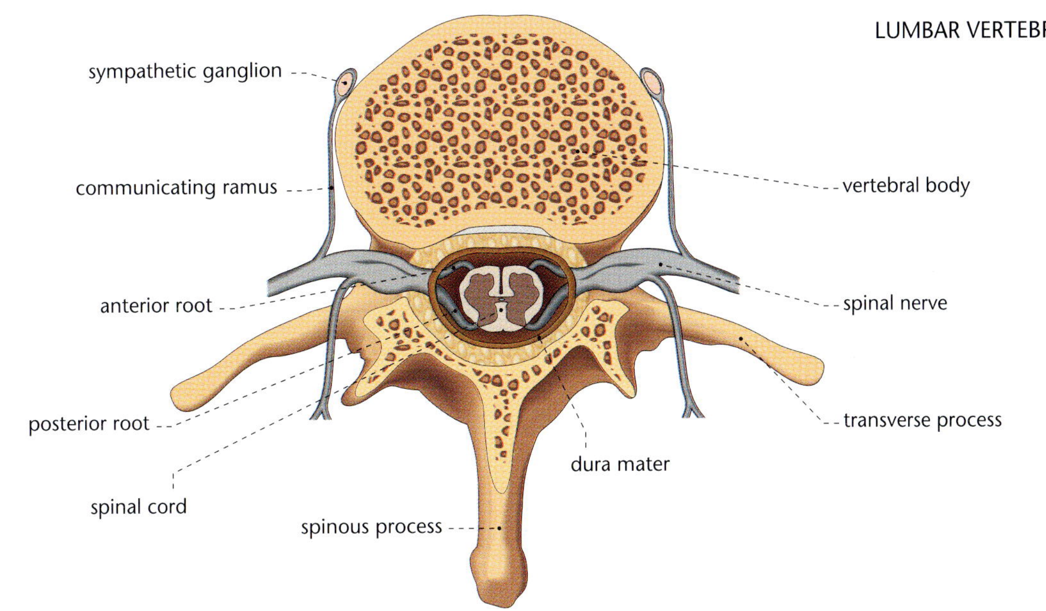

LUMBAR VERTEBRA
sympathetic ganglion
communicating ramus
anterior root
posterior root
spinal cord
spinous process
vertebral body
spinal nerve
transverse process
dura mater

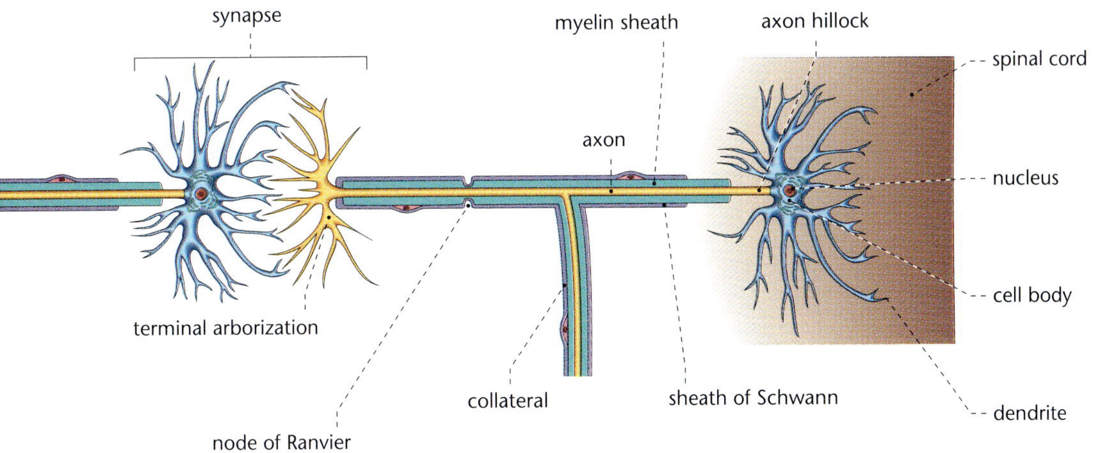

CHAIN OF NEURONS
synapse
myelin sheath
axon hillock
spinal cord
axon
nucleus
terminal arborization
cell body
collateral
sheath of Schwann
dendrite
node of Ranvier

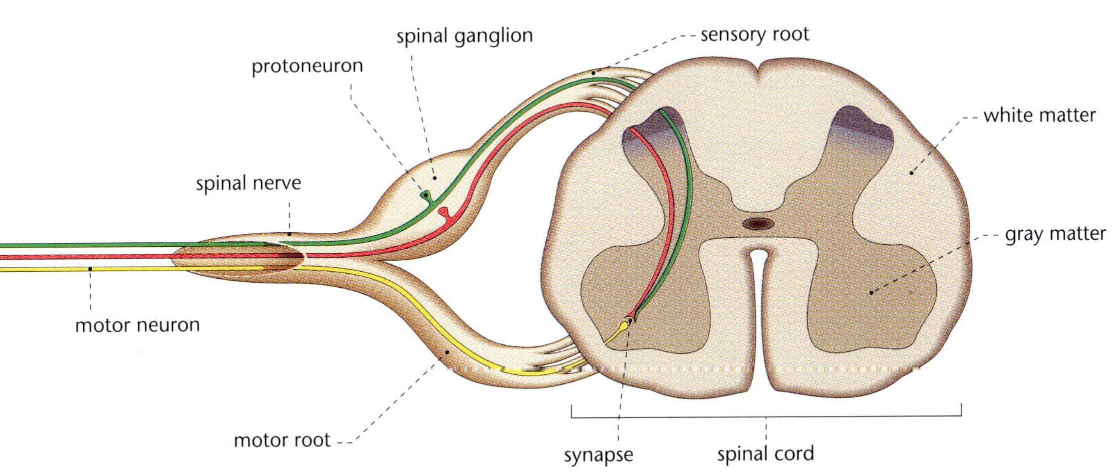

SENSORY IMPULSE
protoneuron
spinal ganglion
sensory root
white matter
spinal nerve
gray matter
motor neuron
motor root
synapse
spinal cord

SKIN

hair shaft
hair
pore
Ruffini's corpuscle
Meissner's corpuscle
stratum corneum
stratum lucidum
stratum granulosum
stratum spinosum
stratum basale
nerve termination
muscle arrector pili
sebaceous gland
hair follicle
hair bulb
nerve fiber
papilla
nerve
blood vessel
apocrine sweat gland
sudoriferous duct
Pacinian corpuscle
eccrine sweat gland
adipose tissue

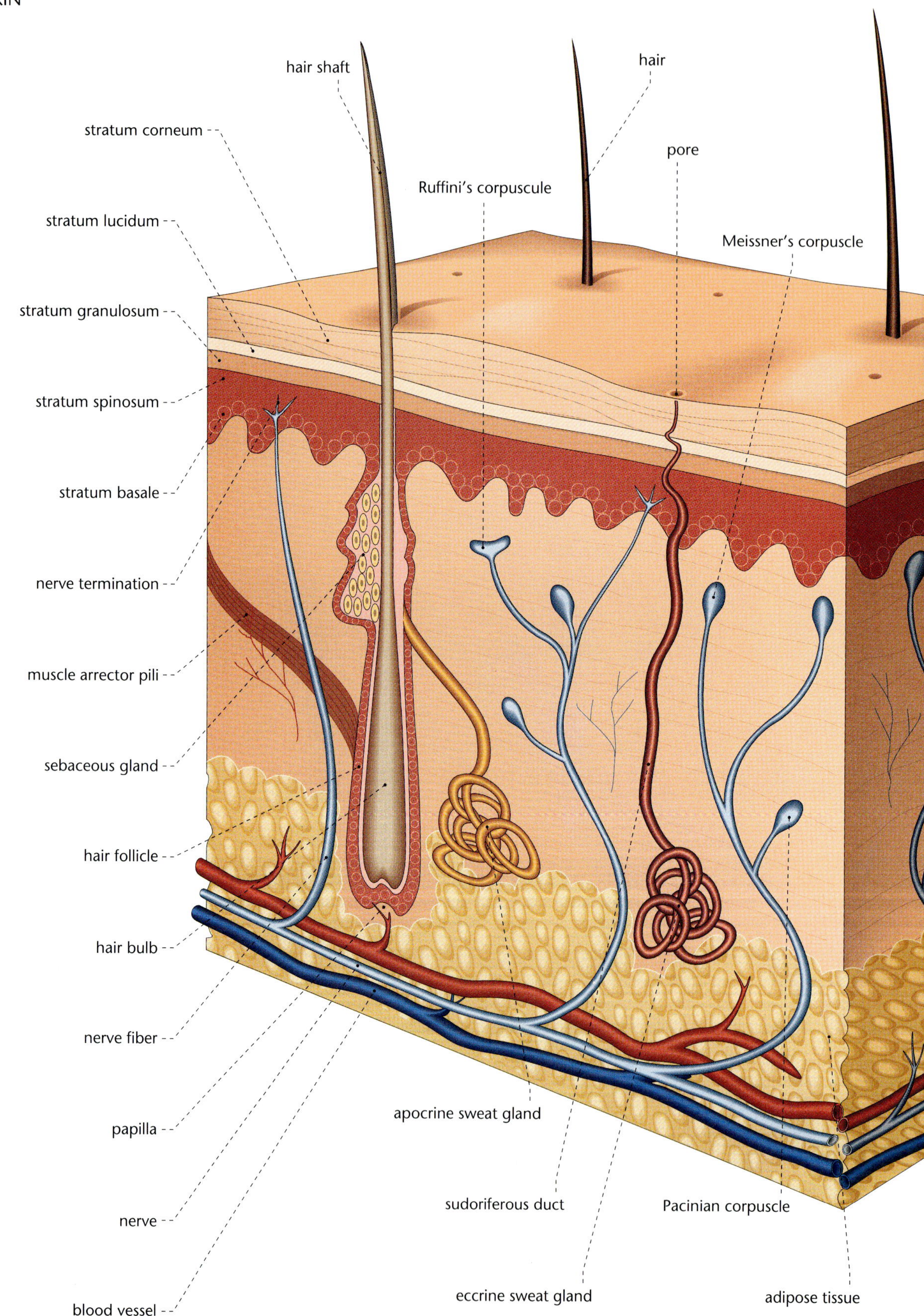

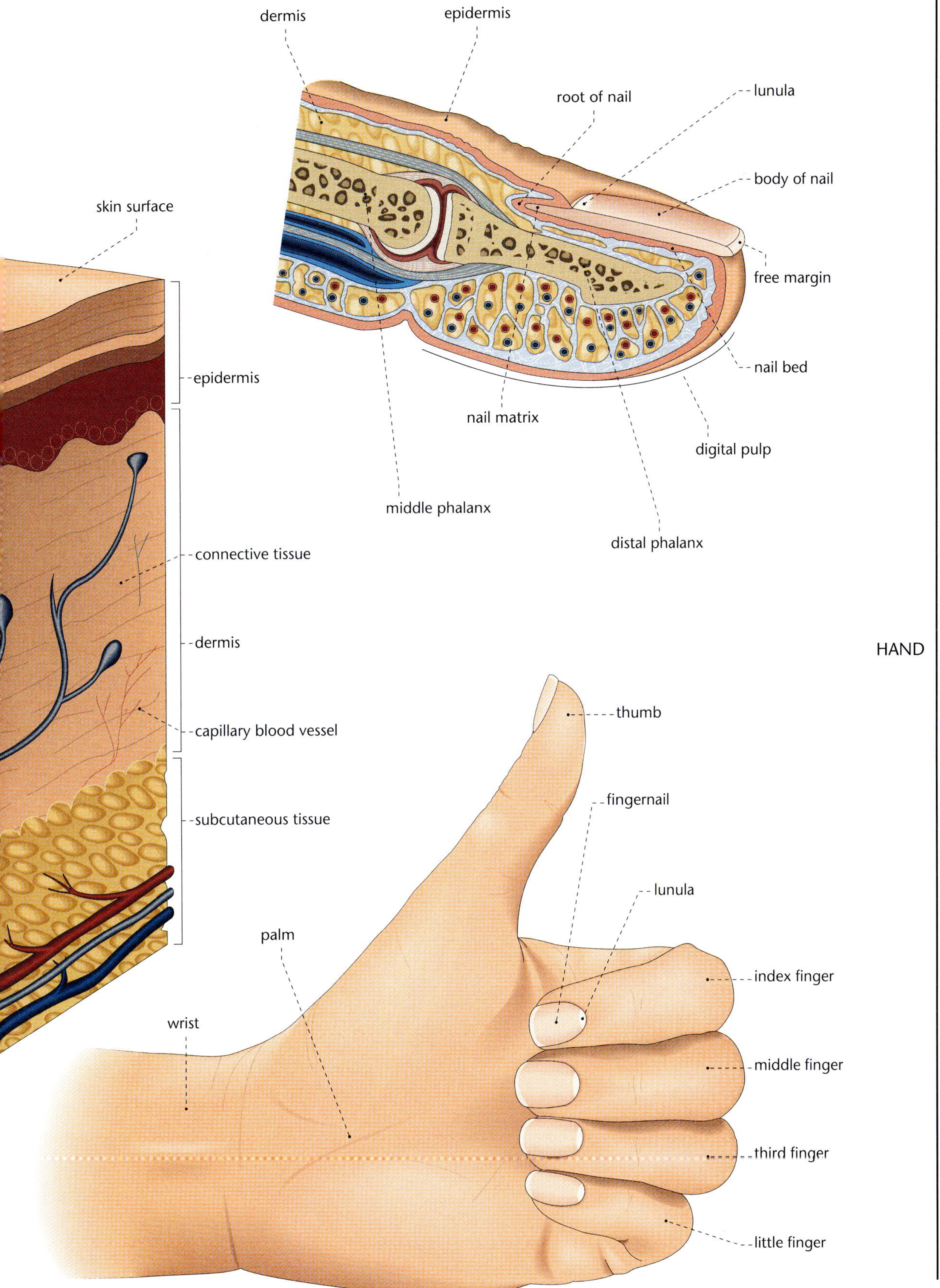
dermis
epidermis
root of nail
lunula
body of nail
skin surface
free margin
nail bed
epidermis
nail matrix
digital pulp
connective tissue
middle phalanx
distal phalanx
dermis
capillary blood vessel
subcutaneous tissue
palm
thumb
fingernail
lunula
index finger
middle finger
wrist
third finger
little finger

PARTS OF THE EAR

AUDITORY OSSICLES

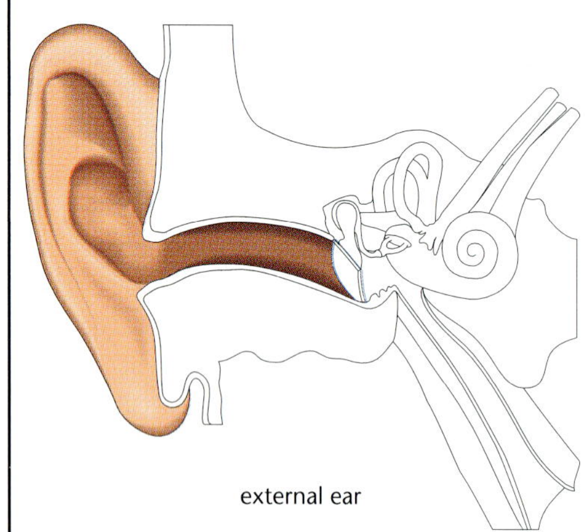

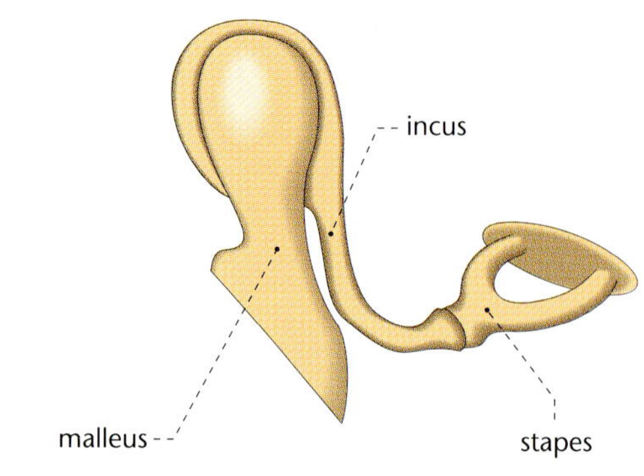

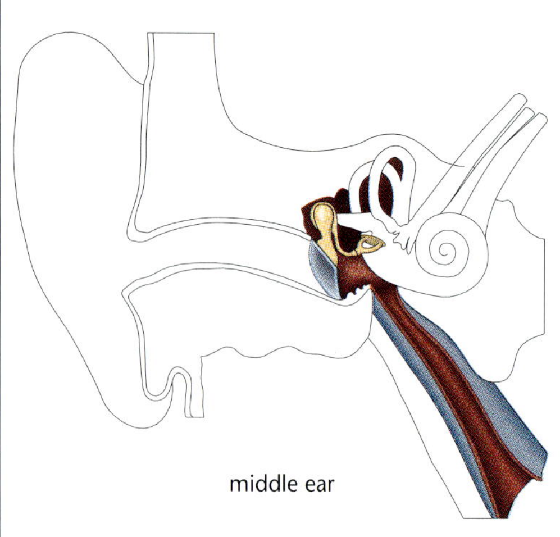

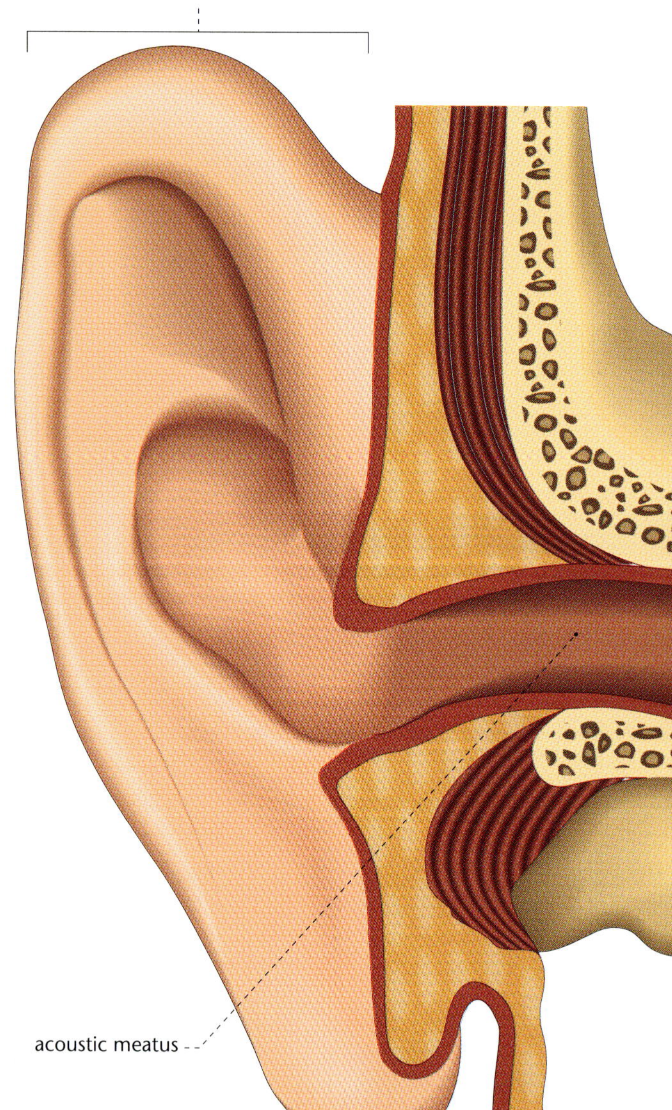

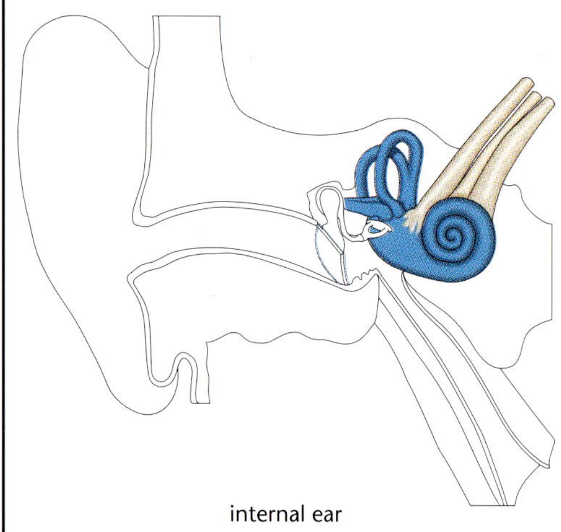

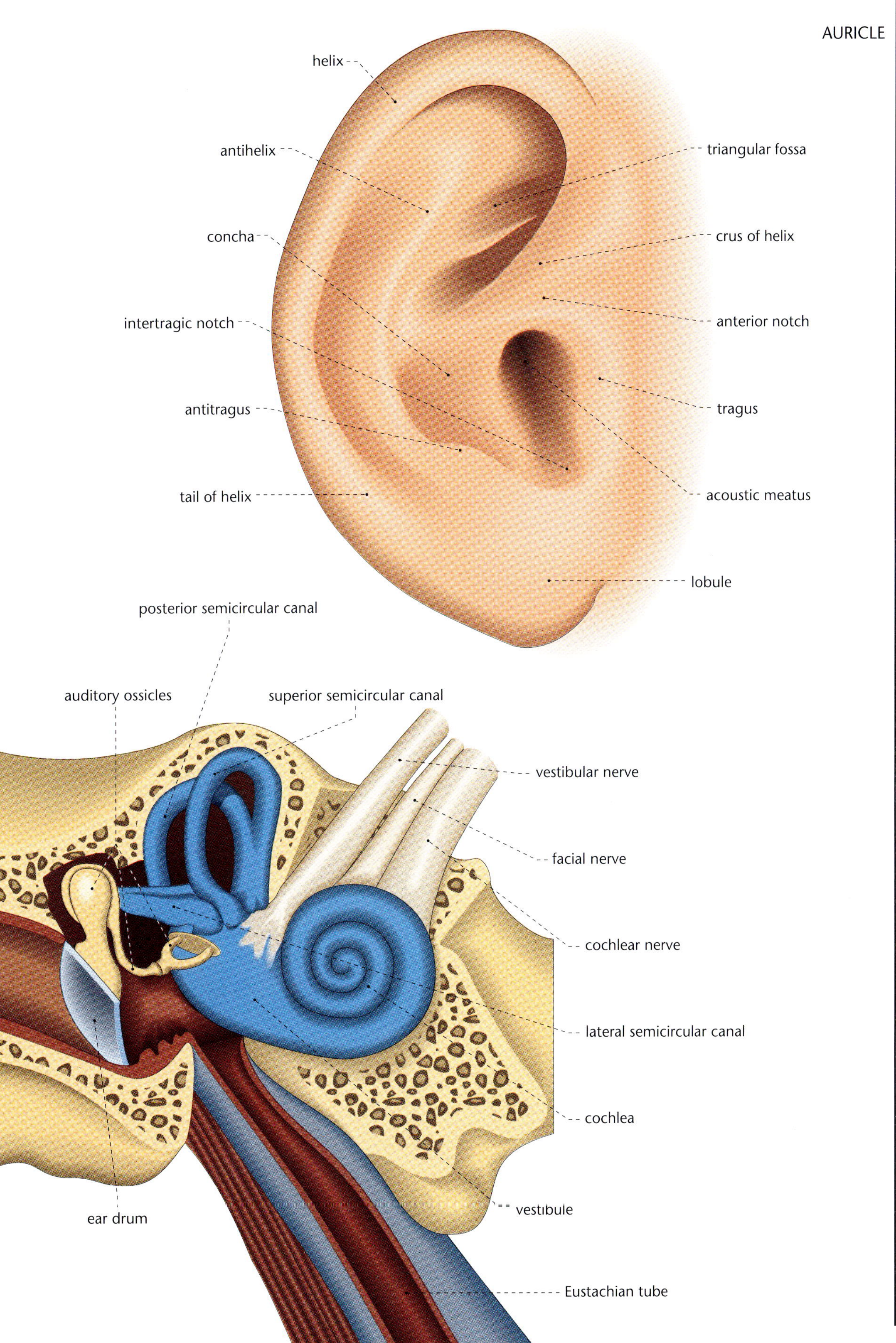

helix
antihelix
concha
intertragic notch
antitragus
tail of helix
triangular fossa
crus of helix
anterior notch
tragus
acoustic meatus
lobule
posterior semicircular canal
auditory ossicles
superior semicircular canal
vestibular nerve
facial nerve
cochlear nerve
lateral semicircular canal
cochlea
ear drum
vestibule
Eustachian tube

EYE

eyebrow
upper eyelid
eyelash
pupil
lacrimal duct
sclera
iris
lower eyelid

EYEBALL

medial rectus muscle
lens
sclera
posterior chamber
choroid
anterior chamber
retina
cornea
fovea
pupil
aqueous humor
conjunctiva
optic nerve
iris
papilla
suspensory ligament
ciliary body
lateral rectus muscle
vitreous body

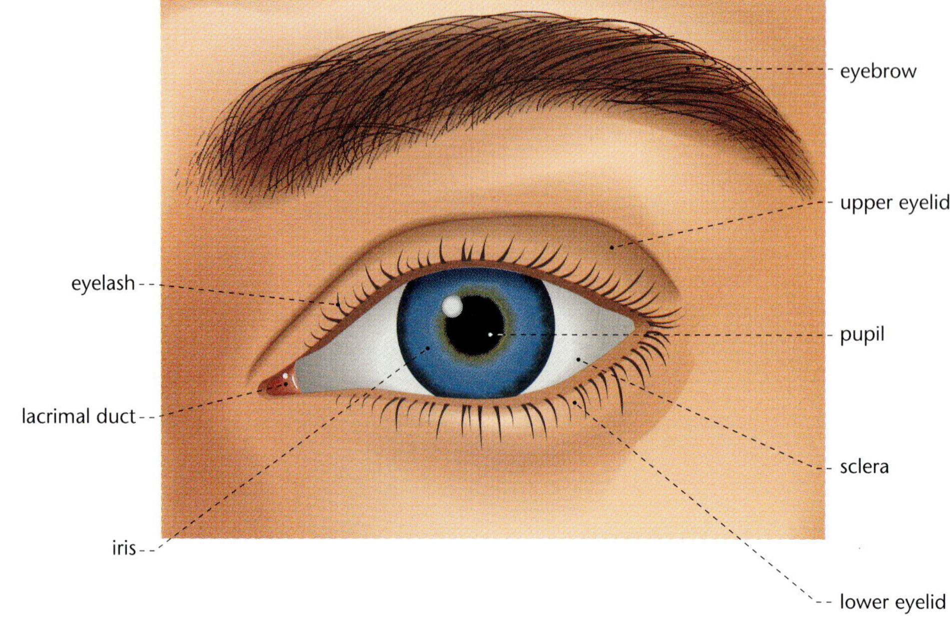

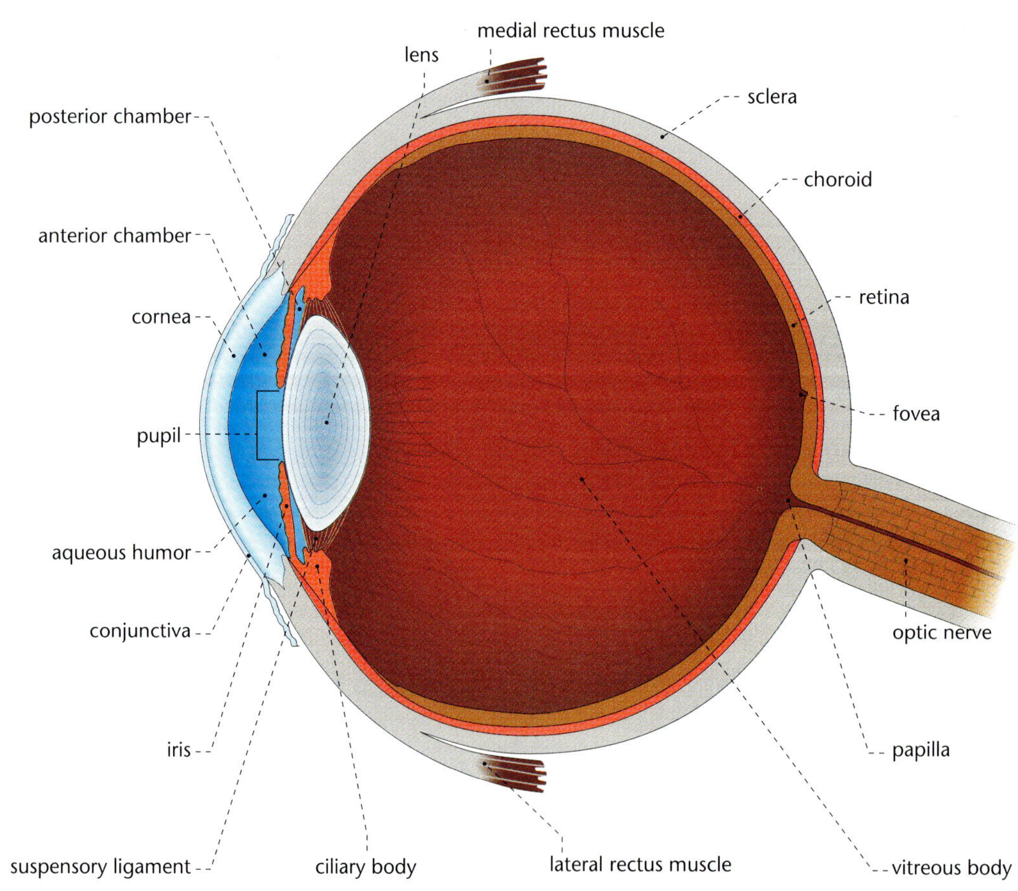

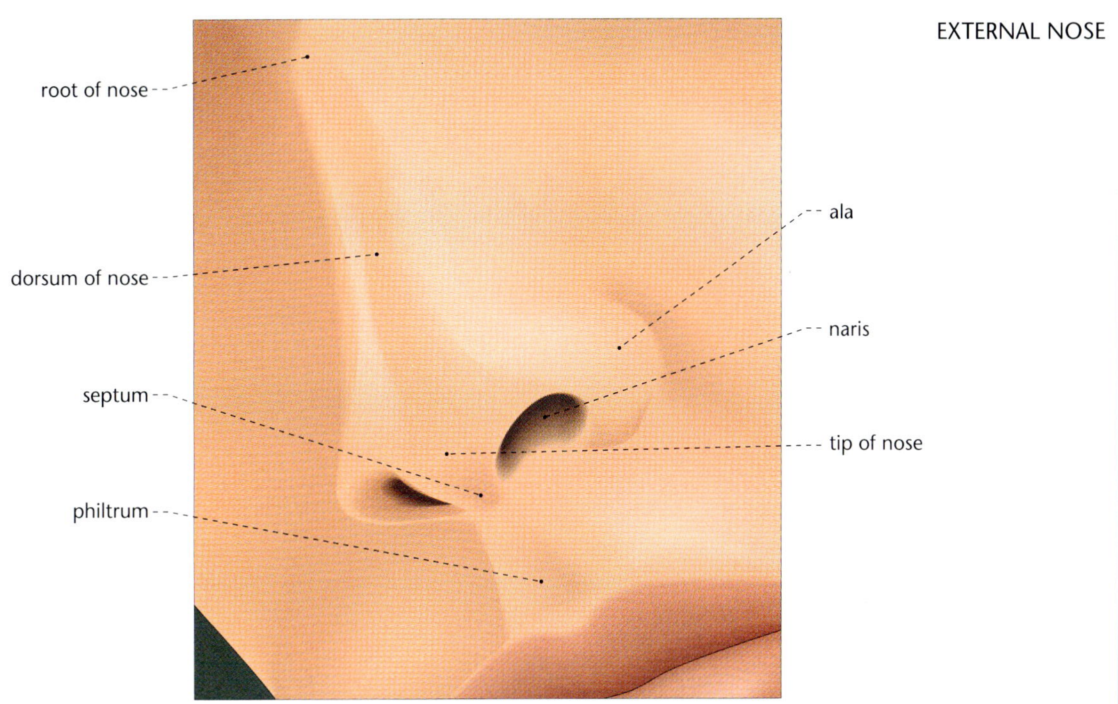
EXTERNAL NOSE
root of nose
dorsum of nose
septum
philtrum
ala
naris
tip of nose
NASAL FOSSAE
frontal sinus
cribriform plate of ethmoid
nasal bone
superior nasal concha
middle nasal concha
sphenoidal sinus
septal cartilage of nose
inferior nasal concha
greater alar cartilage
maxilla
hard palate
nasopharynx
Eustachian tube
soft palate
uvula

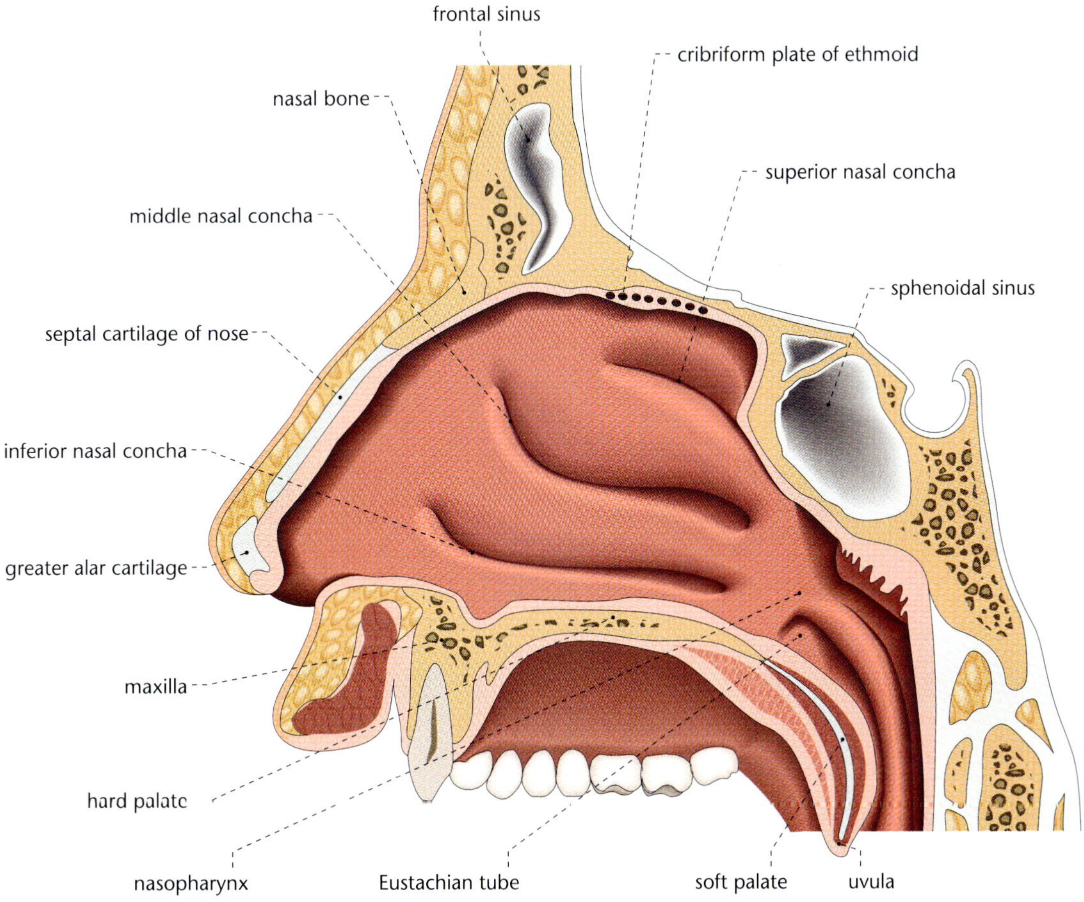

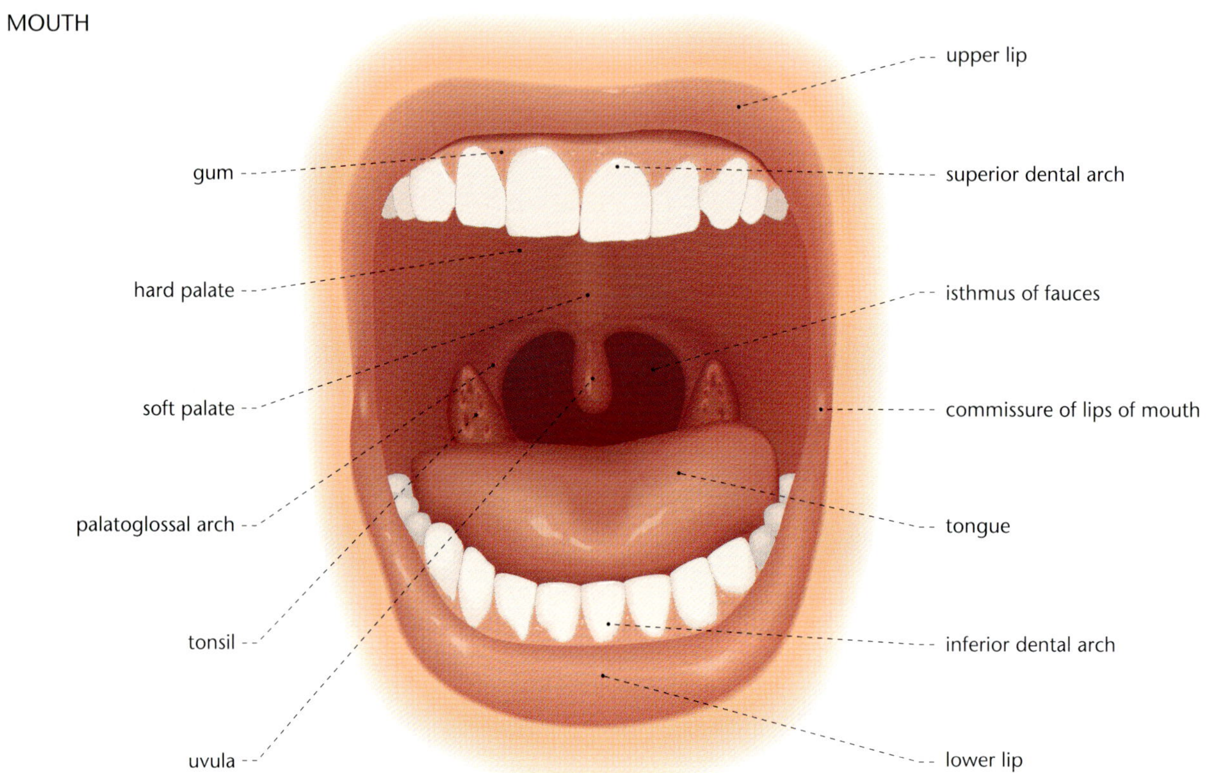

MOUTH
gum
hard palate
soft palate
palatoglossal arch
tonsil
uvula
upper lip
superior dental arch
isthmus of fauces
commissure of lips of mouth
tongue
inferior dental arch
lower lip
SAGITTAL SECTION
Brunn's membrane
olfactory bulb
olfactory nerve
olfactory membrane
tongue
epiglottis
glottis
larynx
esophagus

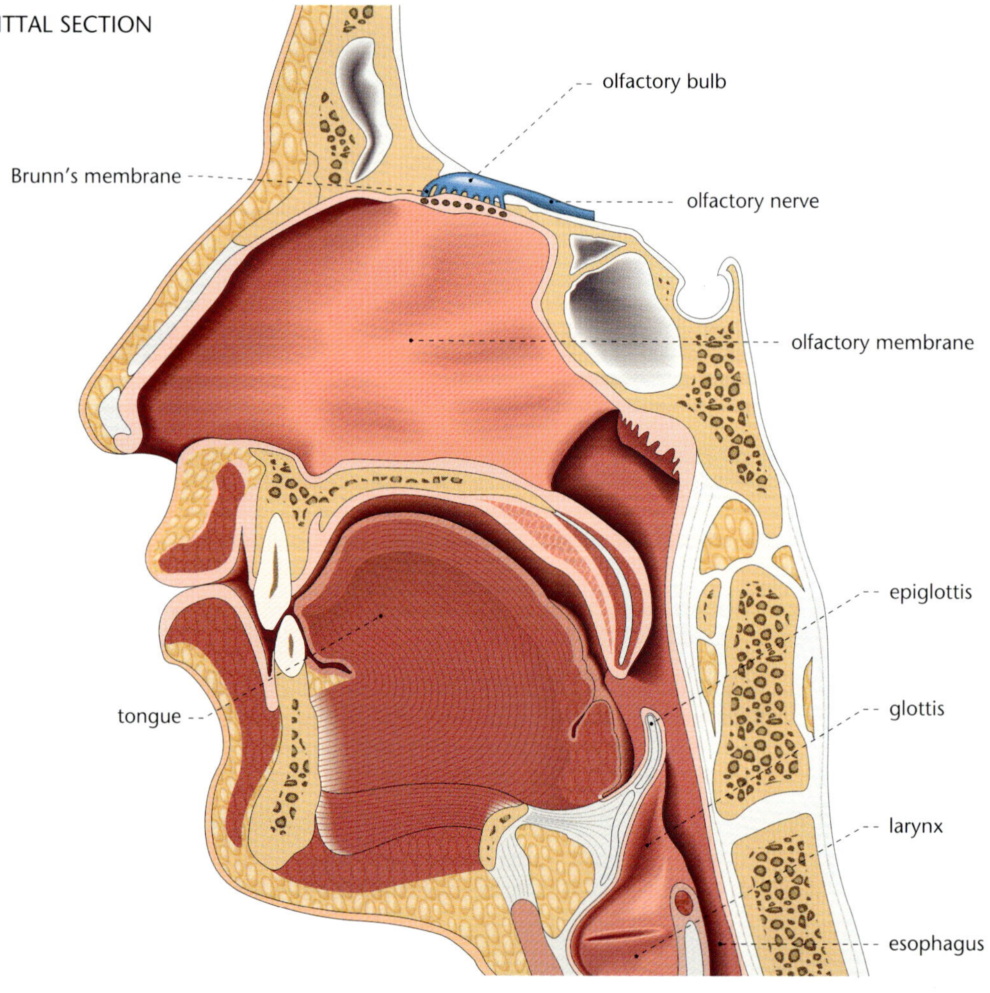

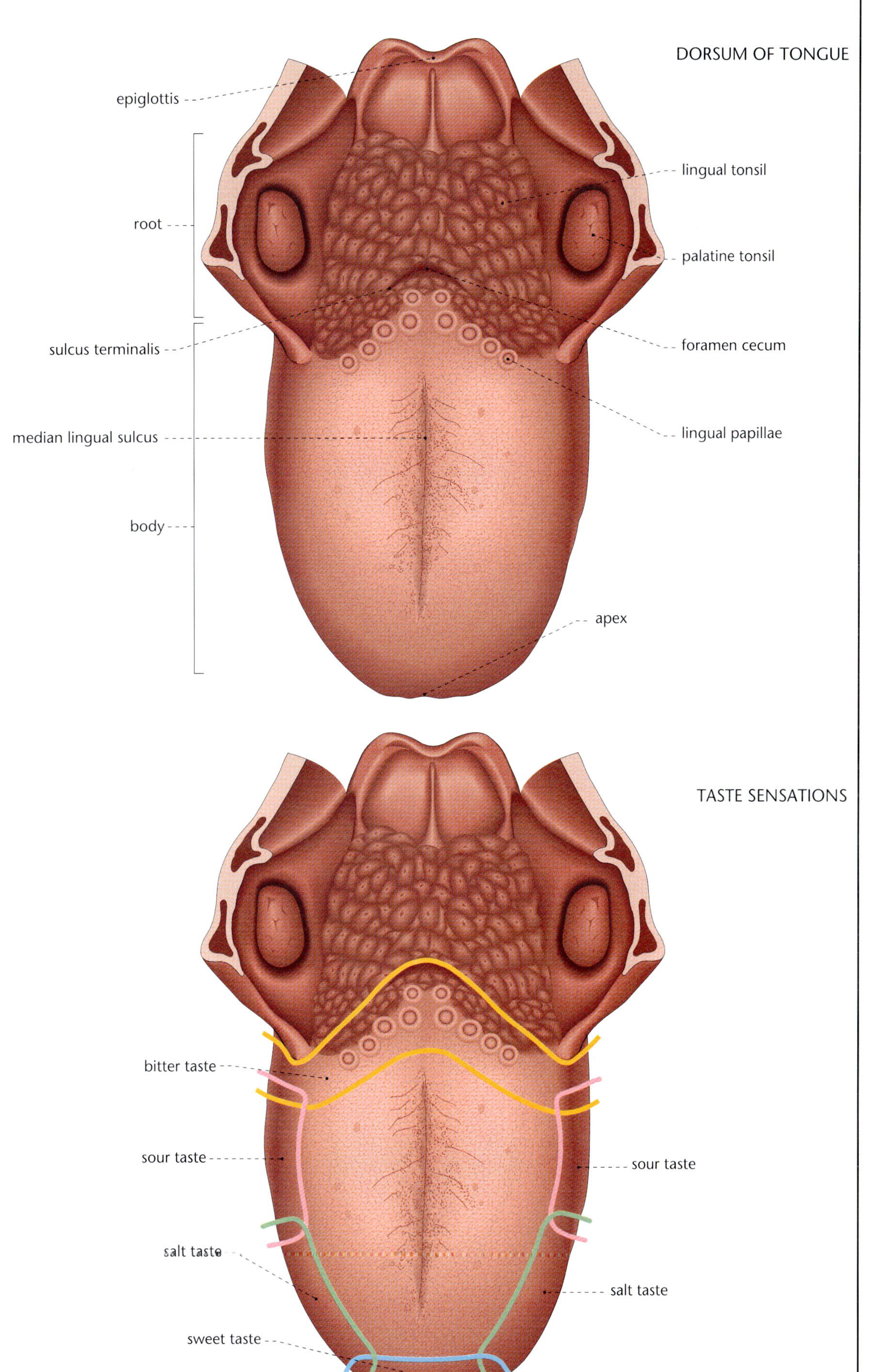
DORSUM OF TONGUE
epiglottis
lingual tonsil
root
palatine tonsil
sulcus terminalis
foramen cecum
median lingual sulcus
lingual papillae
body
apex
TASTE SENSATIONS
bitter taste
sour taste
sour taste
salt taste
salt taste
sweet taste

HUMAN DENTURE

CROSS SECTION OF A MOLAR

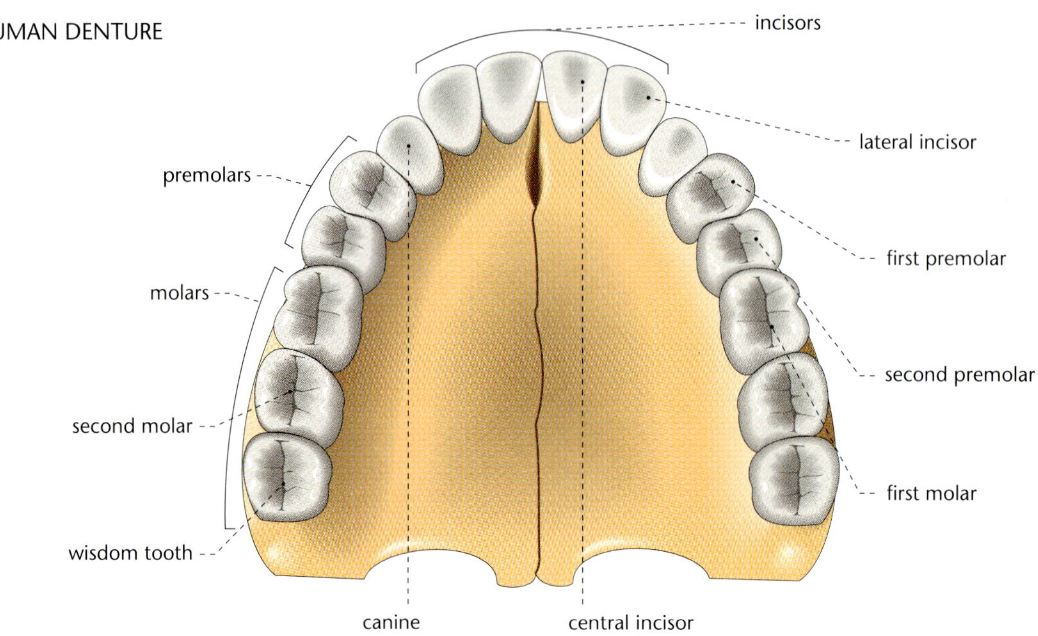

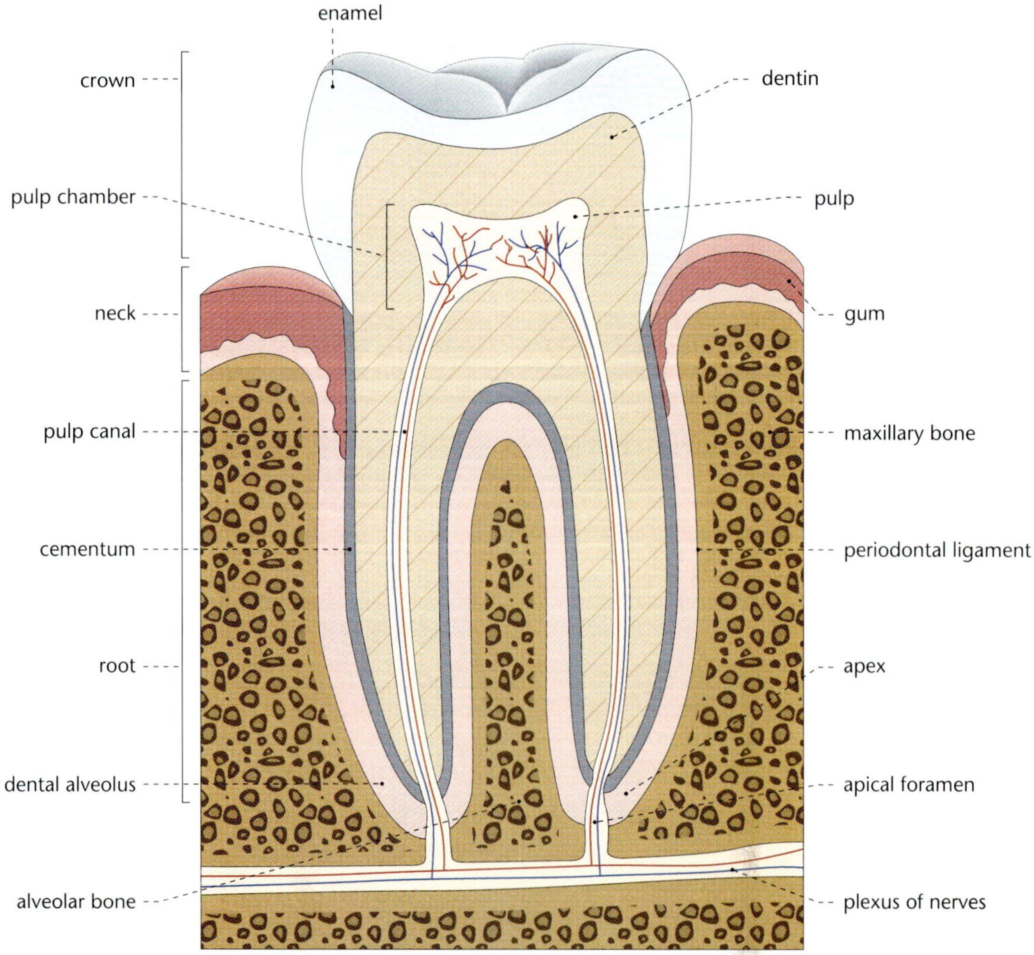

FARMING

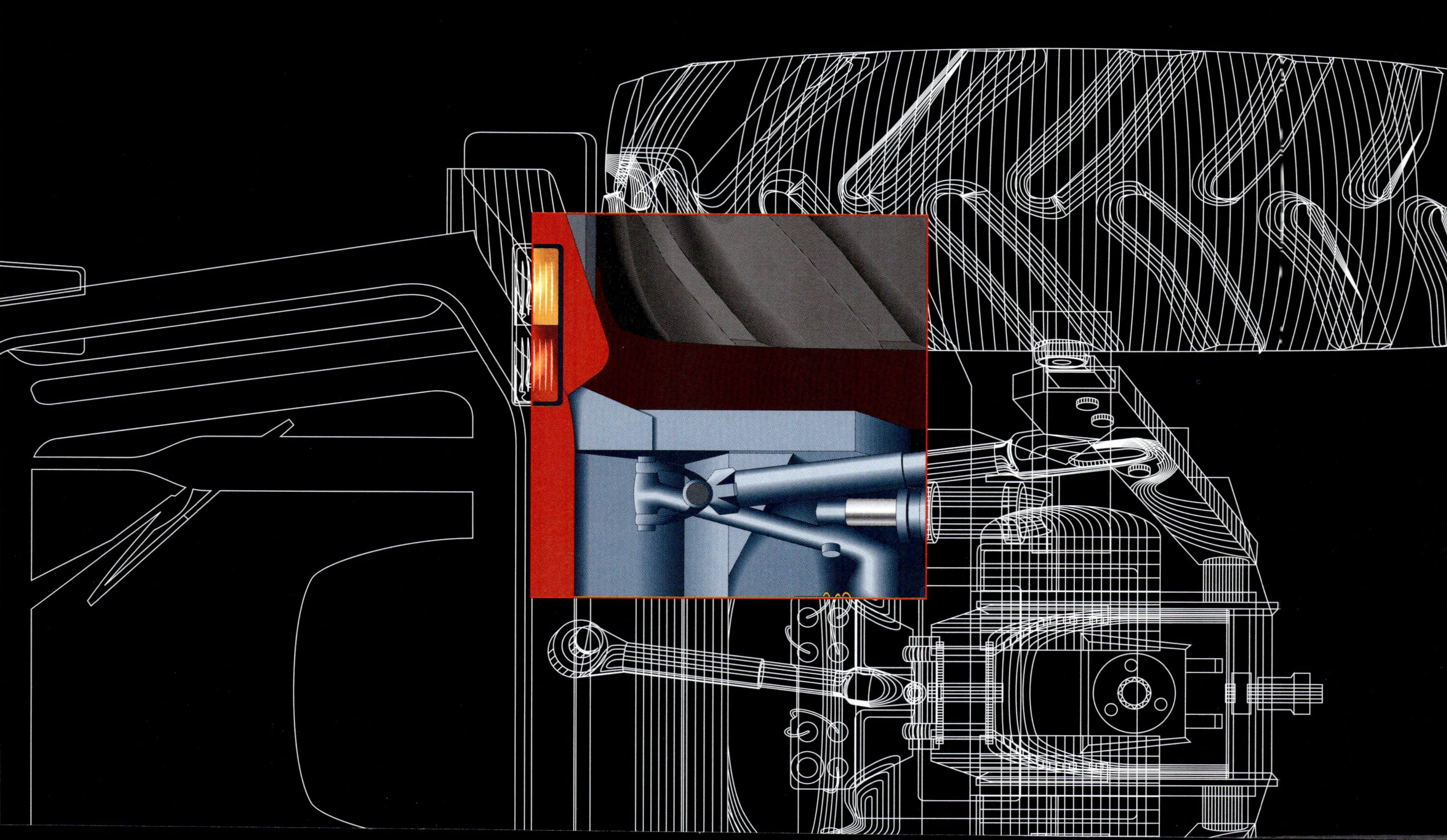

CONTENTS

REAR VIEW

FARMING

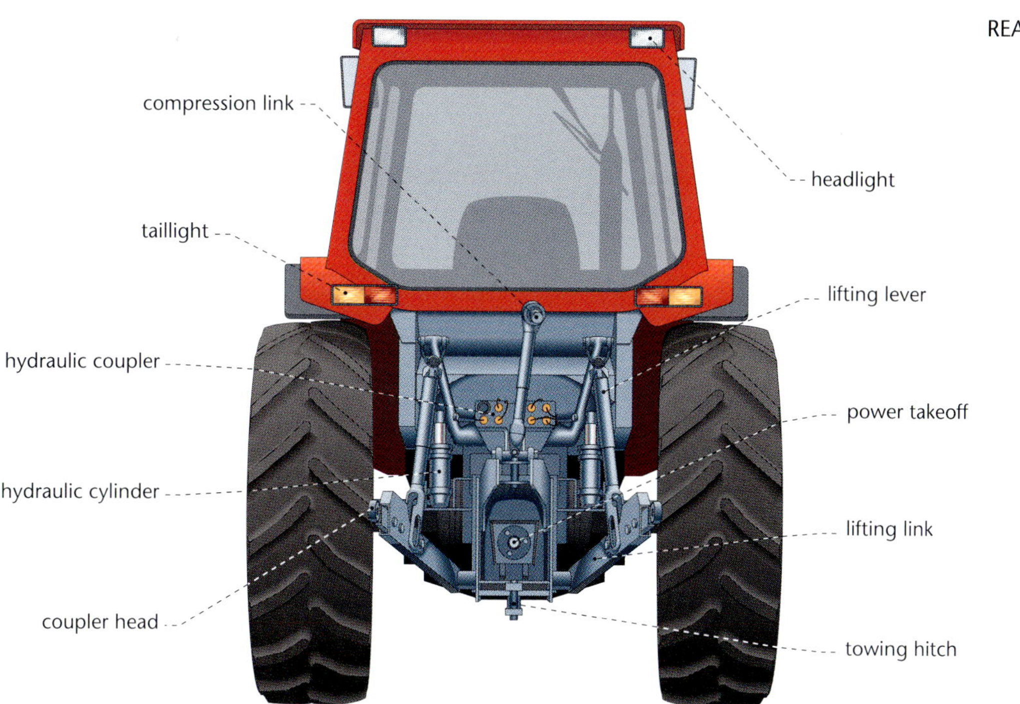

FRONT VIEW

FARMSTEAD

fallow
permanent pasture
fence
hayloft
barn
machinery shed
farmyard
hen house
vegetable garden
ornamental tree
farmhouse

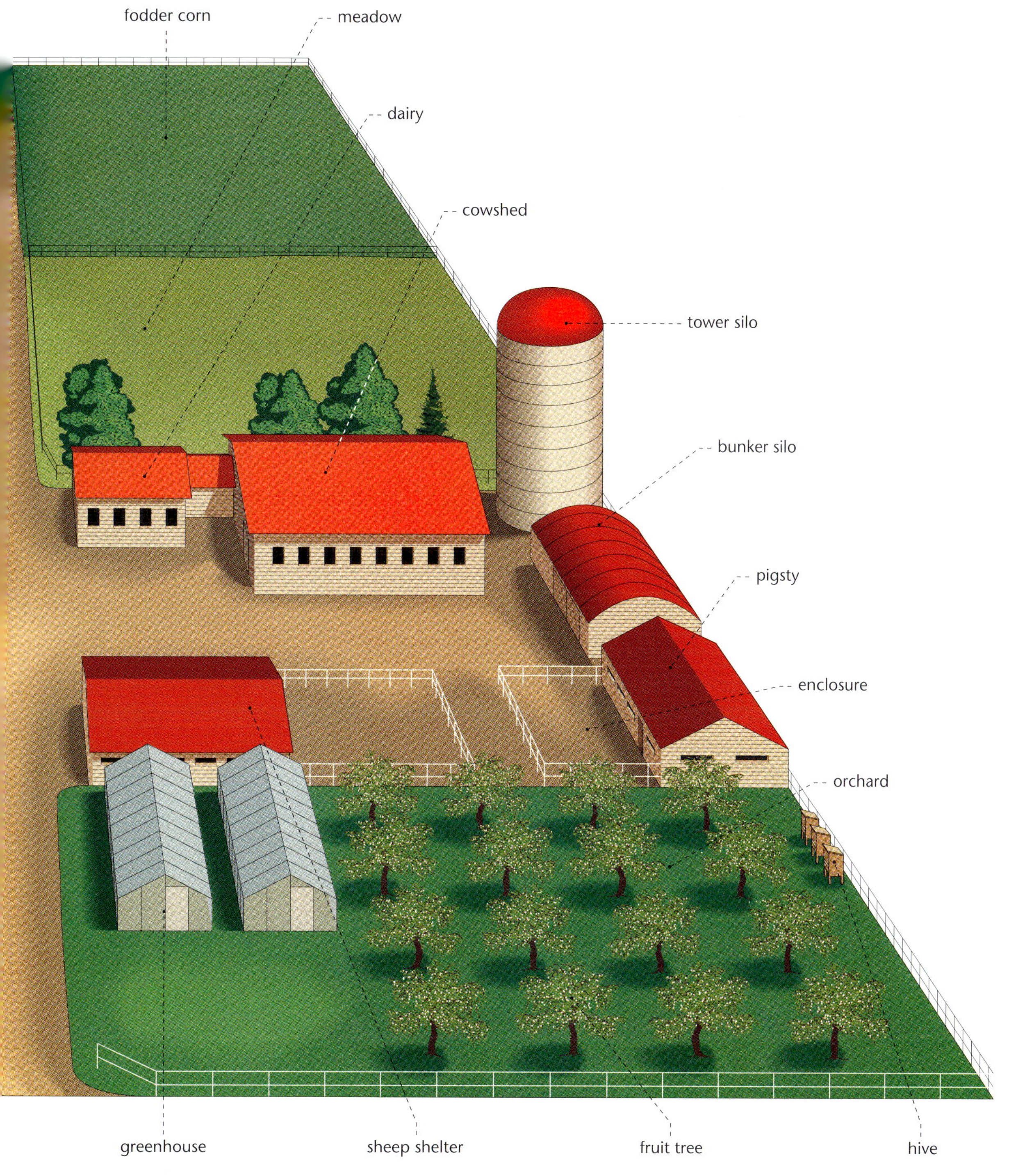

fodder corn
meadow
dairy
cowshed
tower silo
bunker silo
pigsty
enclosure
orchard
greenhouse
sheep shelter
fruit tree
hive

hen

chick

rooster

duck

goose

turkey

goat

lamb

sheep

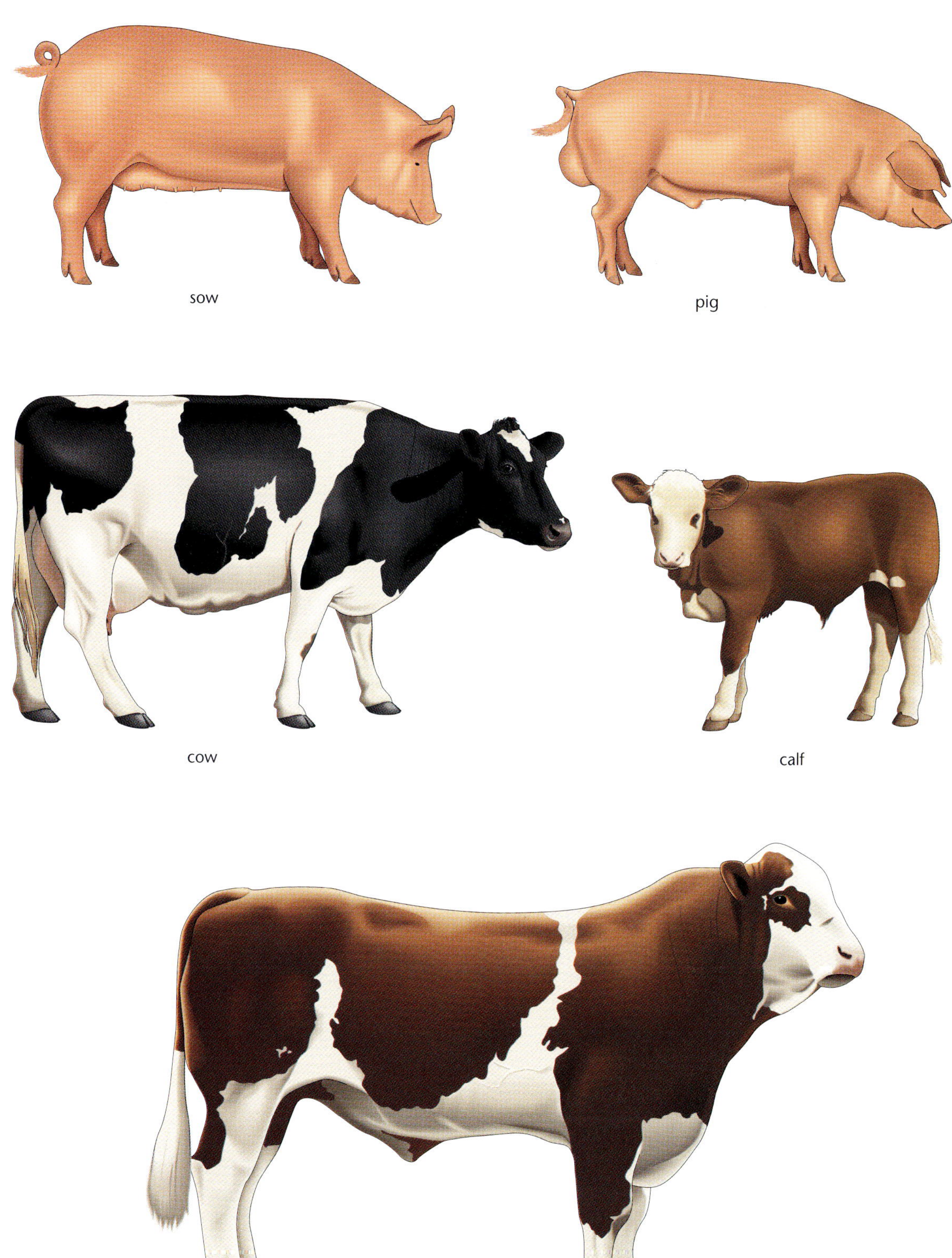

sow
pig
cow
calf
ox

FARMING

SECTION OF A GRAIN OF WHEAT
brush
starch
seed coat
germ
wheat
corn
barley
rye
rice
sorghum
oats
millet
buckwheat

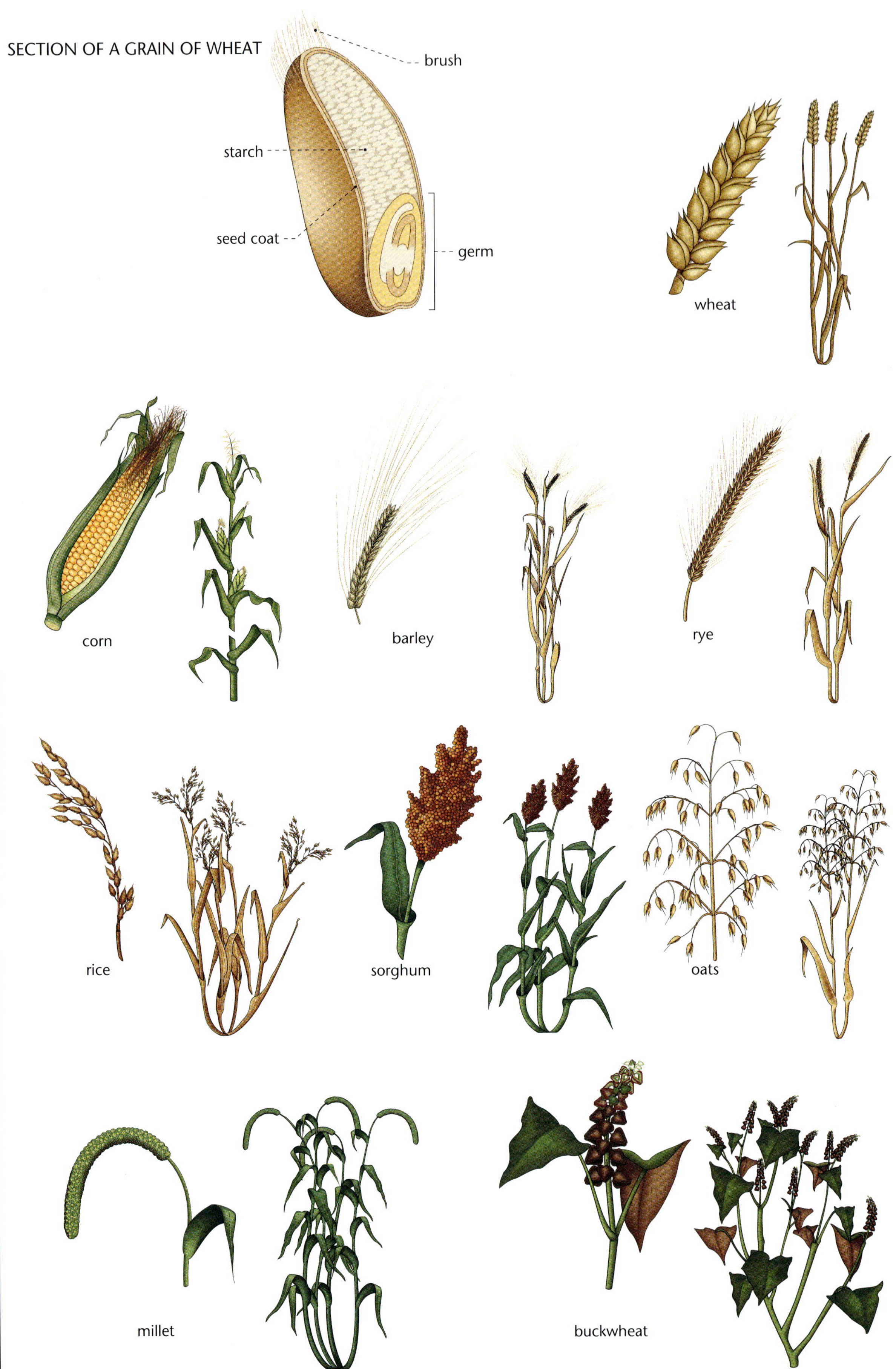

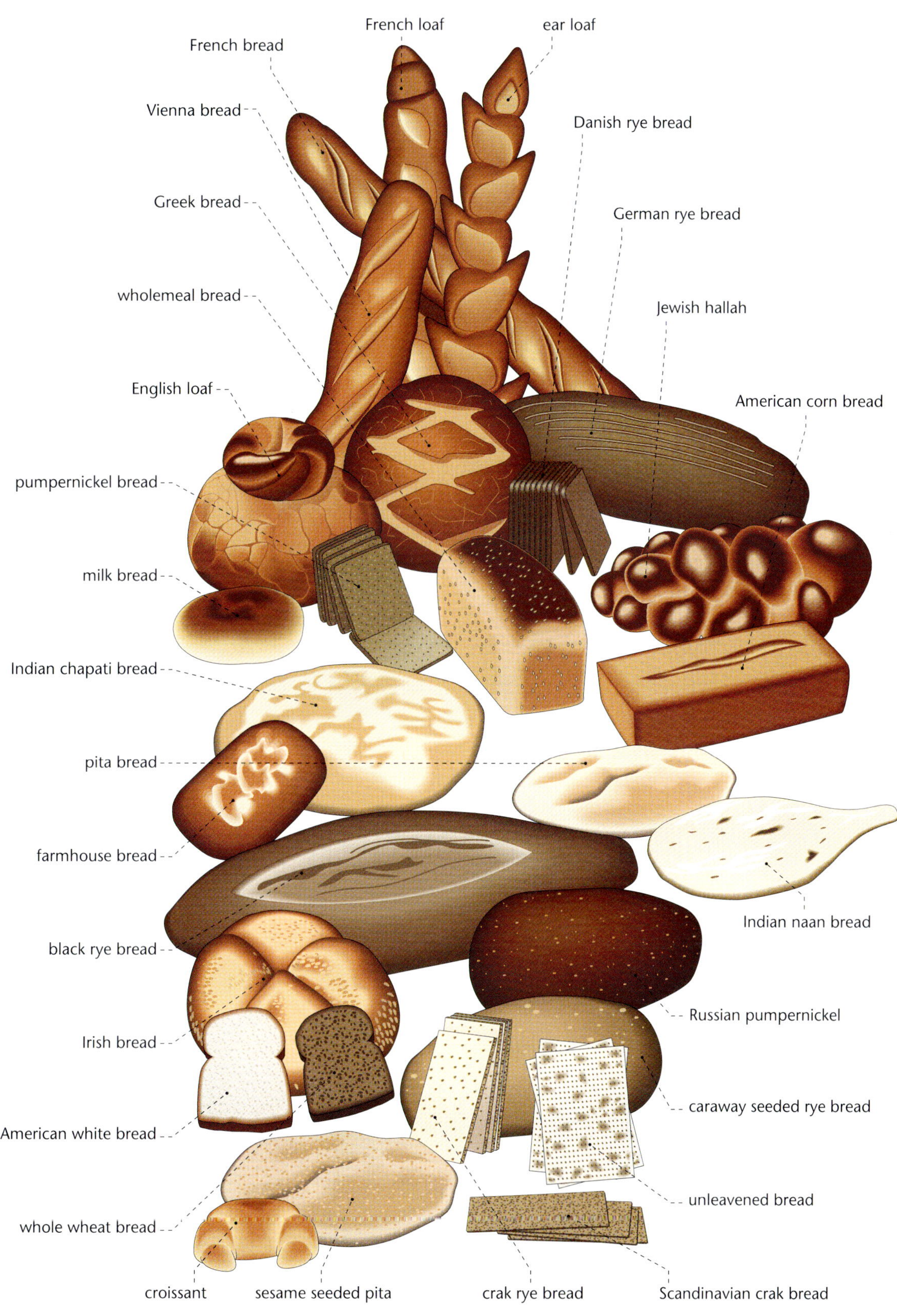
French bread
French loaf
ear loaf
Vienna bread
Danish rye bread
Greek bread
German rye bread
wholemeal bread
Jewish hallah
English loaf
American corn bread
pumpernickel bread
milk bread
Indian chapati bread
pita bread
farmhouse bread
Indian naan bread
black rye bread
Russian pumpernickel
Irish bread
caraway seeded rye bread
American white bread
unleavened bread
whole wheat bread
croissant
sesame seeded pita
crak rye bread
Scandinavian crak bread

STEPS FOR CULTIVATING SOIL

PLOWING SOIL

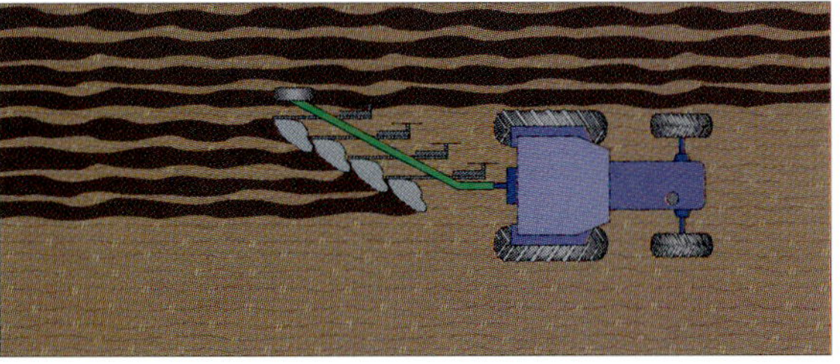

ribbing plow

FERTILIZING SOIL

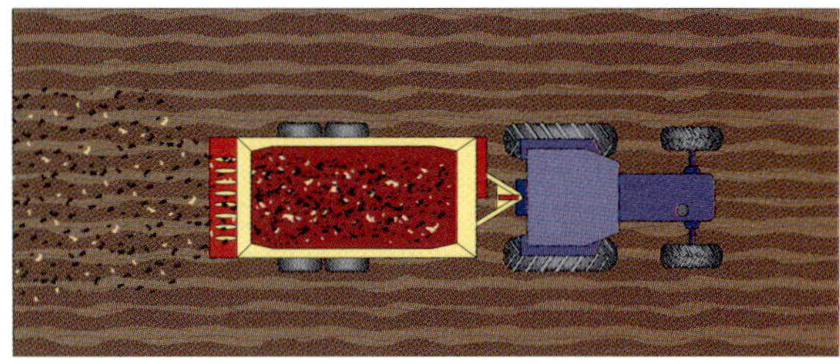

manure spreader

PULVERIZING SOIL

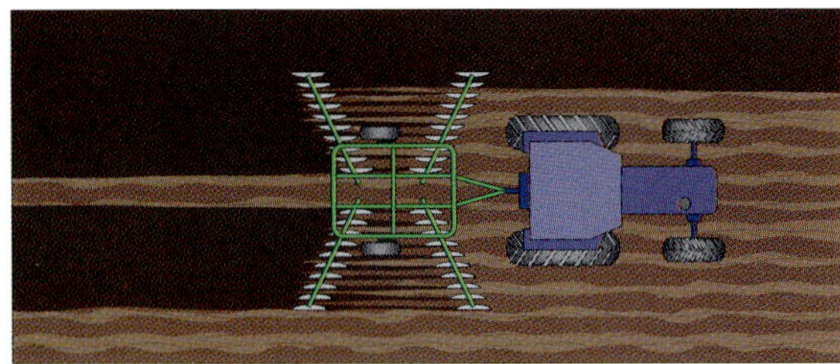

tandem disk harrow

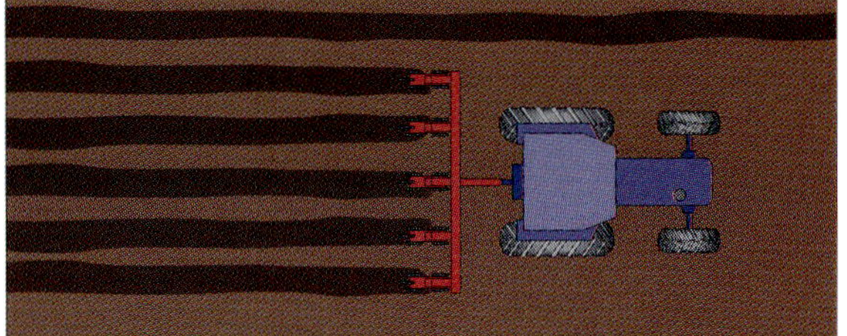

cultivator

PLANTING

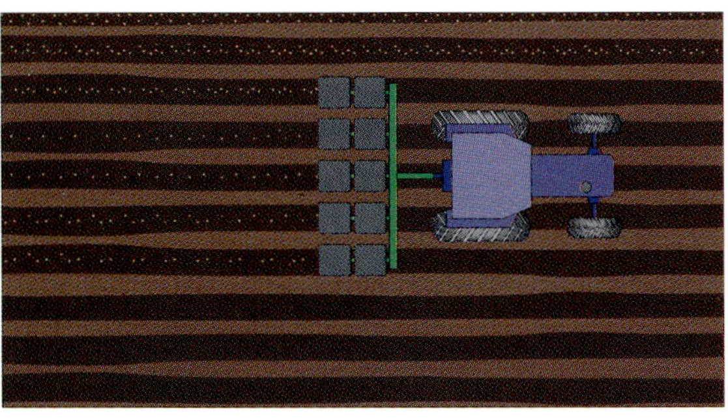

seed drill

MOWING

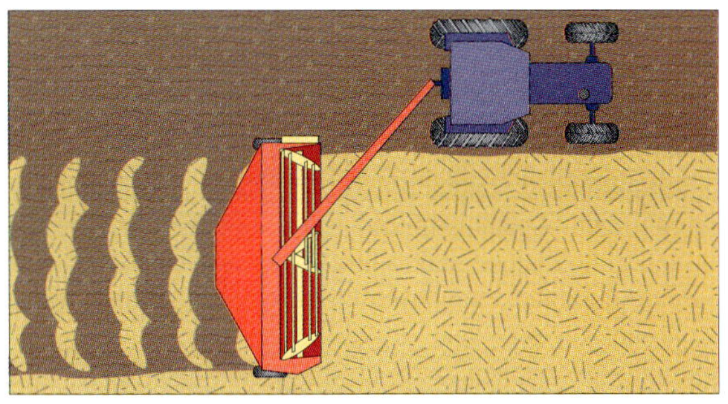

flail mower

TEDDING

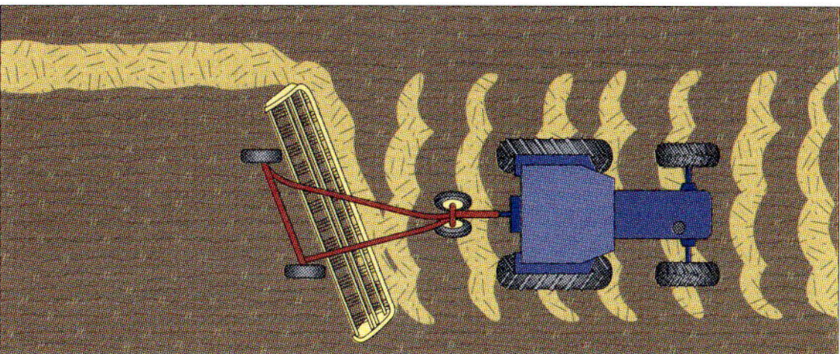

rake

HARVESTING

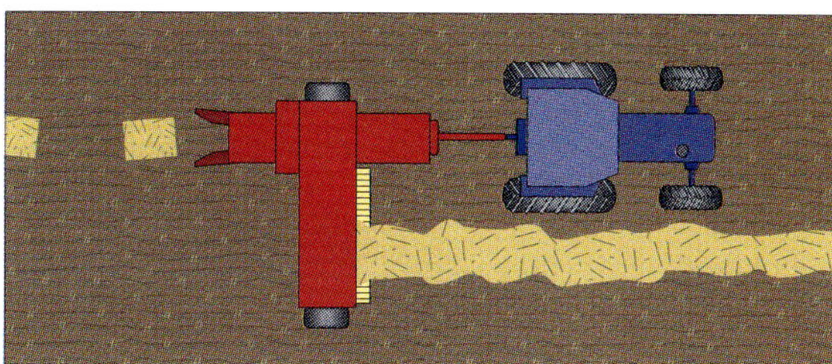

hay baler

HARVESTING

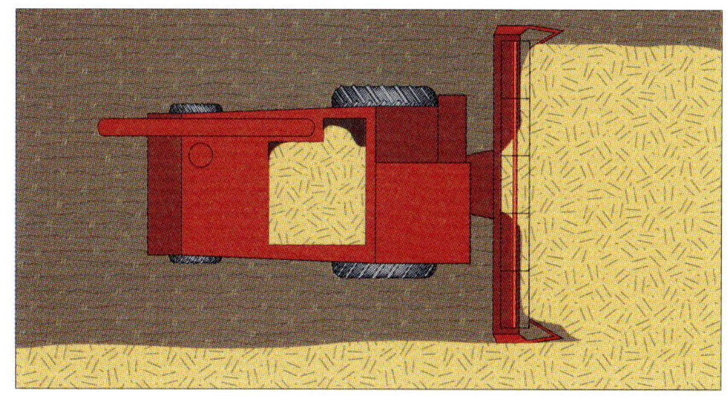

combine harvester

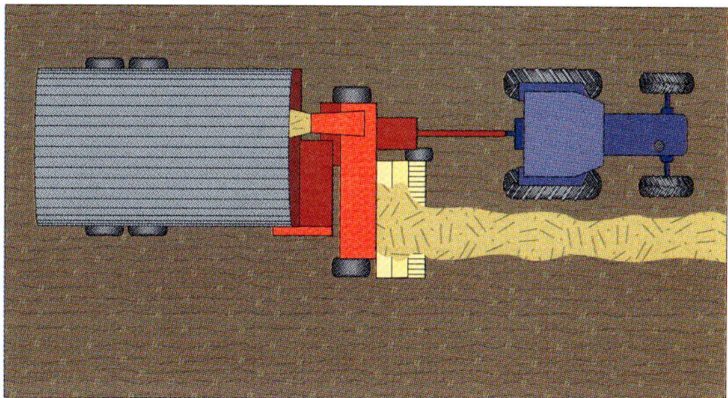

forage harvester

ENSILING

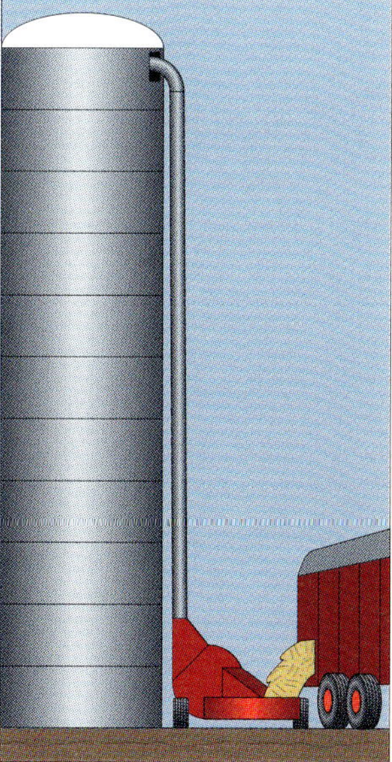

forage blower

RIBBING PLOW

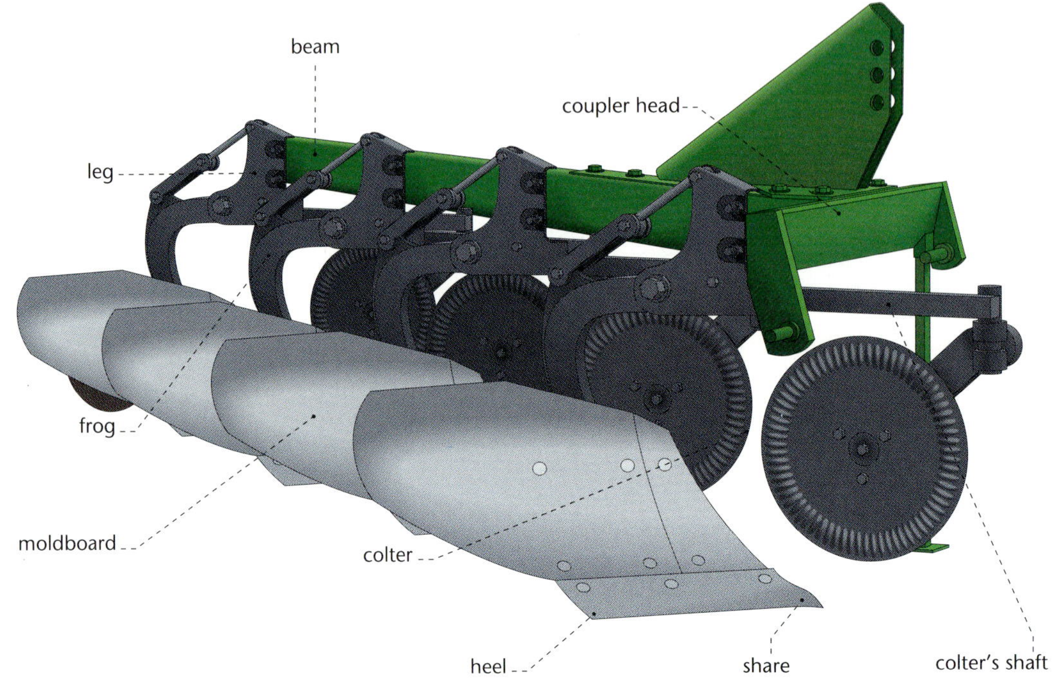

FERTILIZING SOIL

MANURE SPREADER

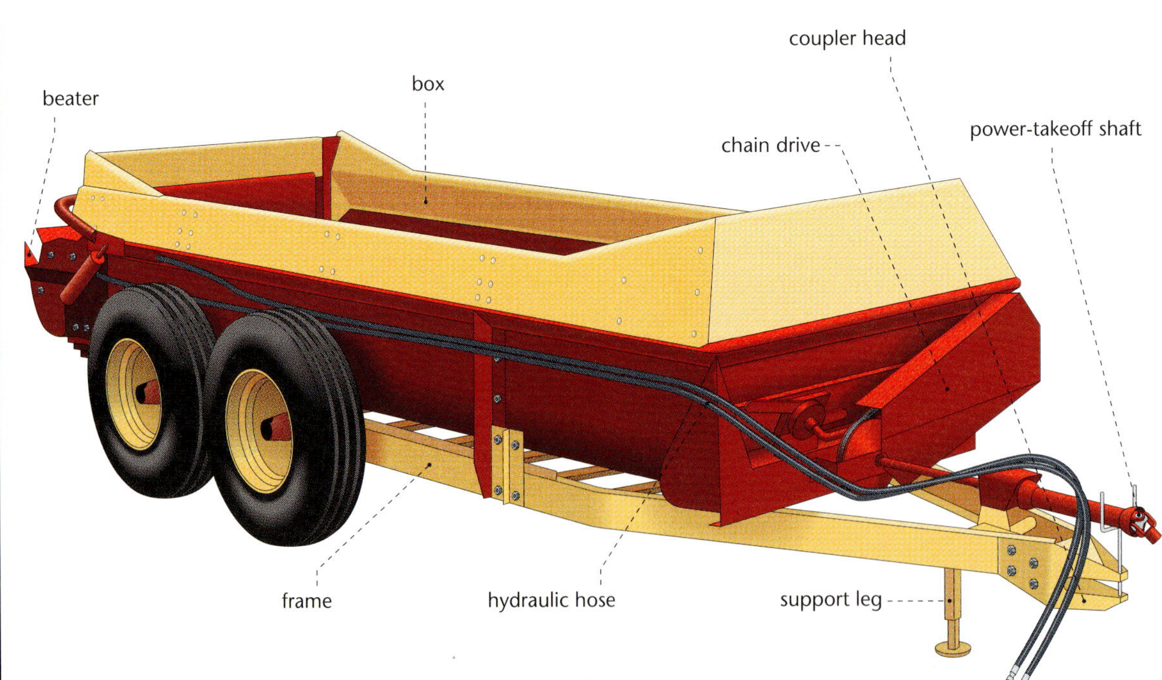

TANDEM DISK HARROW

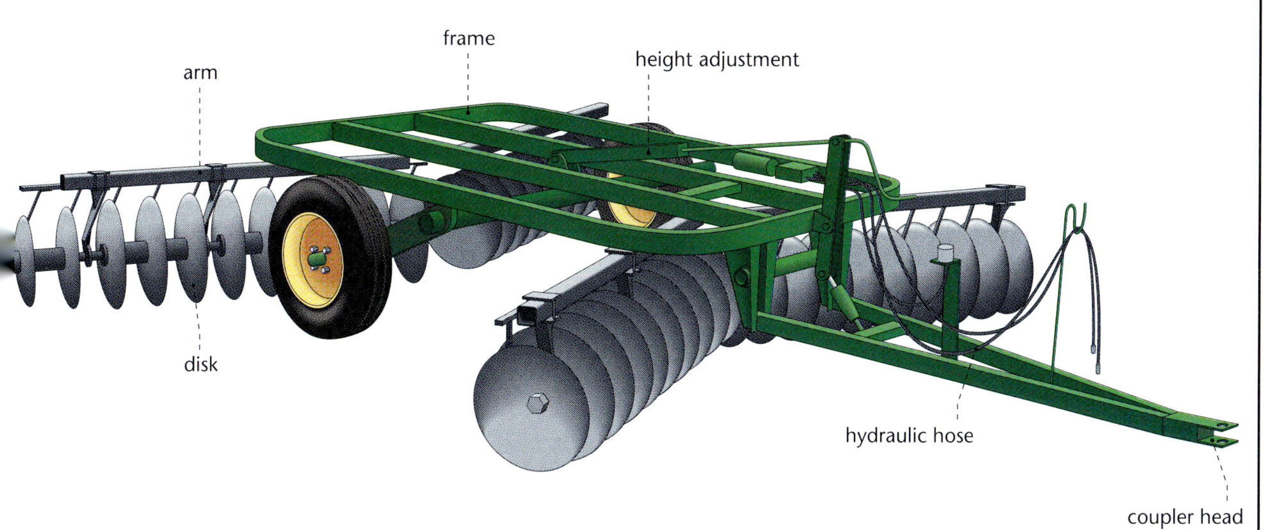

CULTIVATOR

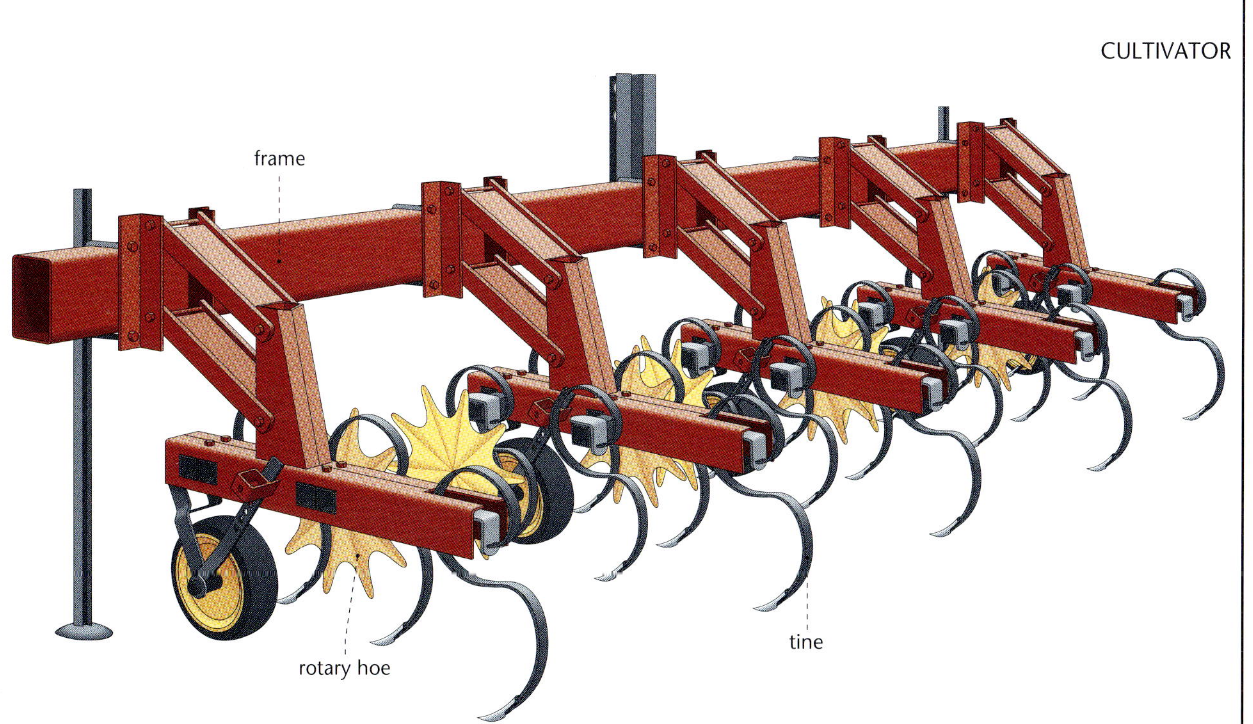

SEED DRILL

MOWING

FLAIL MOWER

TEDDING

RAKE

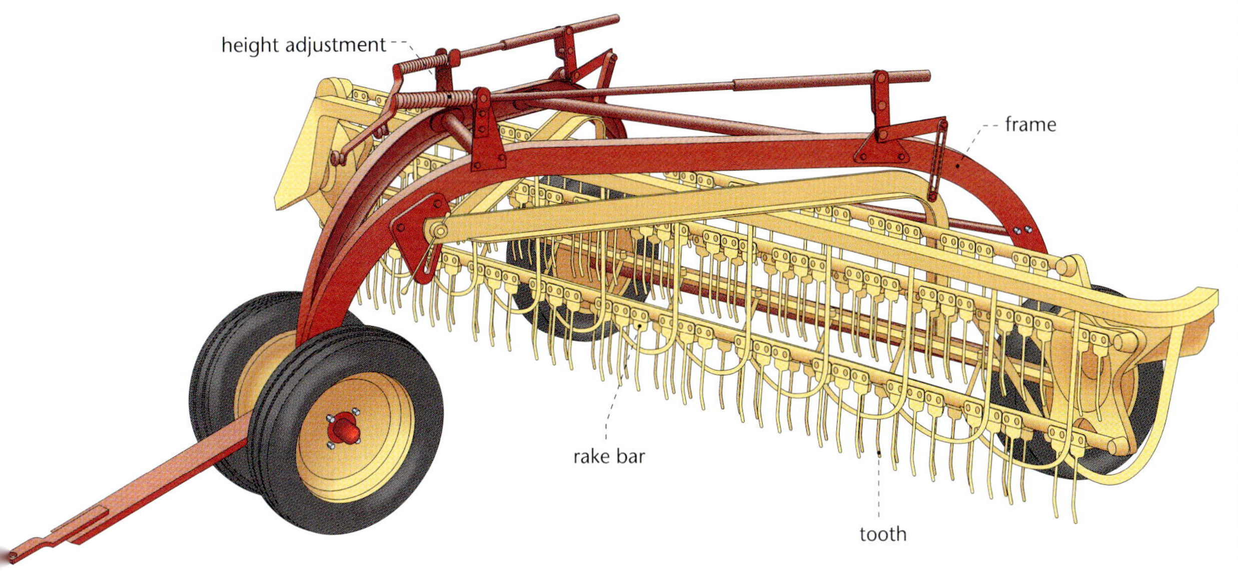

HARVESTING

HAY BALER

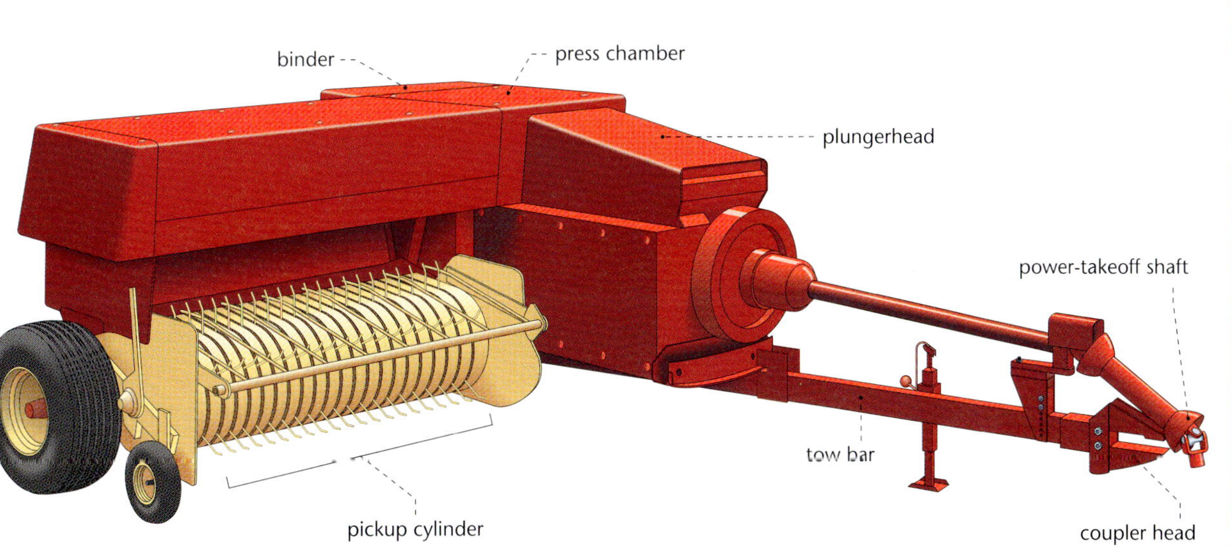

COMBINE HARVESTER

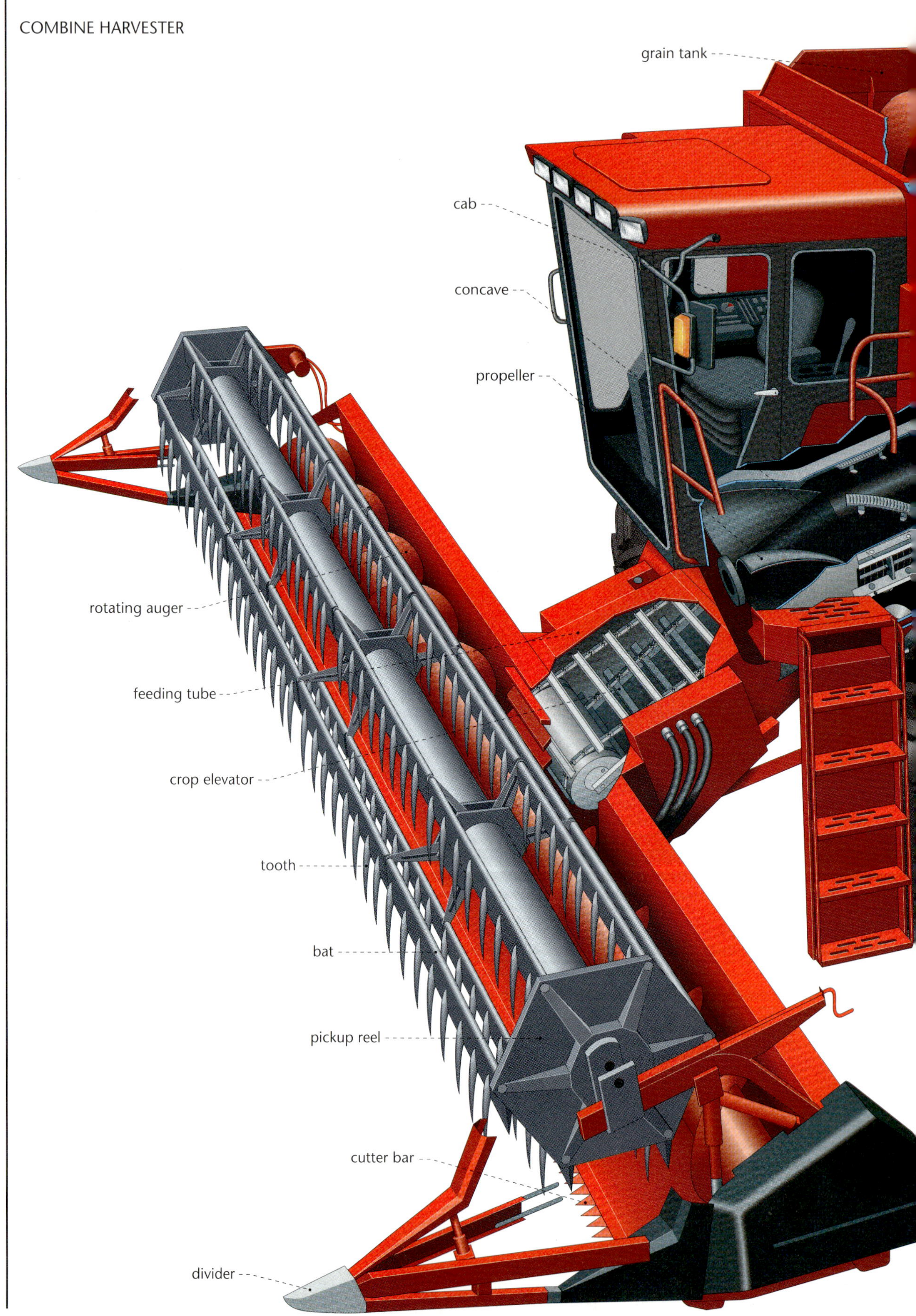

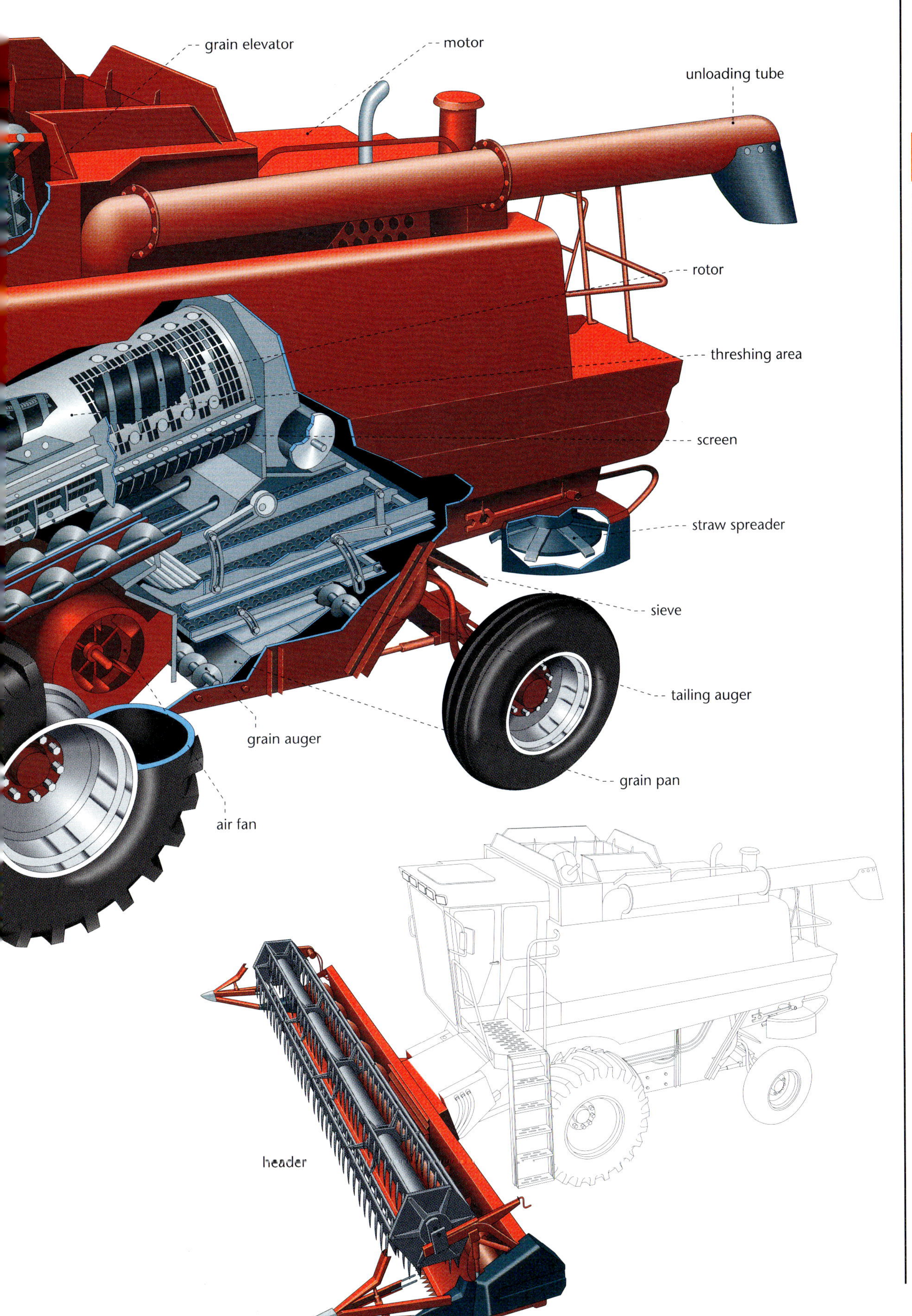

grain elevator
motor
unloading tube
rotor
threshing area
screen
straw spreader
sieve
tailing auger
grain pan
grain auger
air fan
header

FORAGE HARVESTER

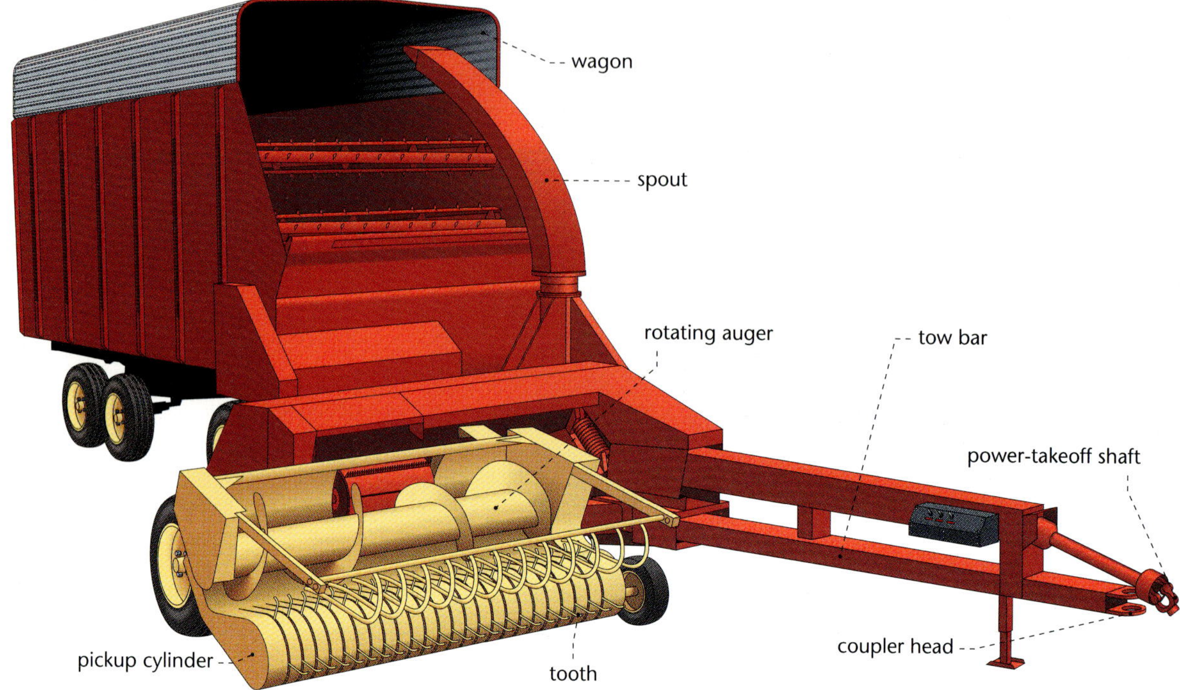

ENSILING

FORAGE BLOWER

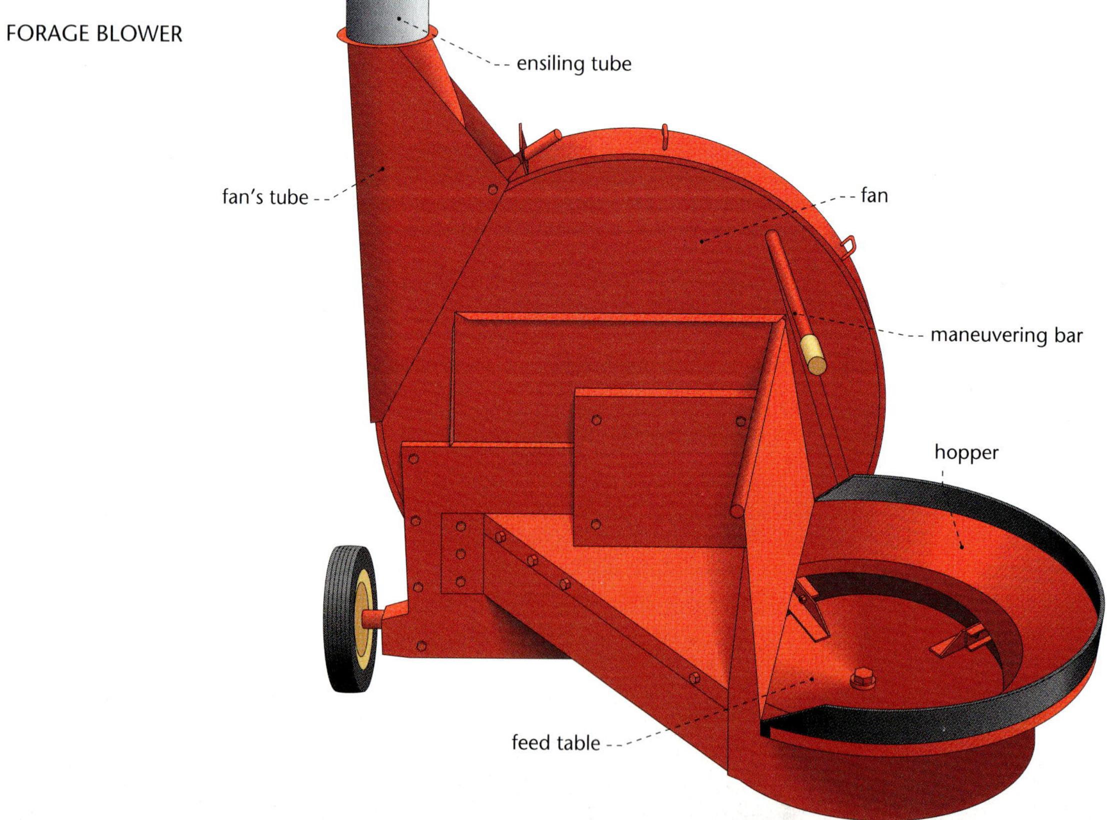

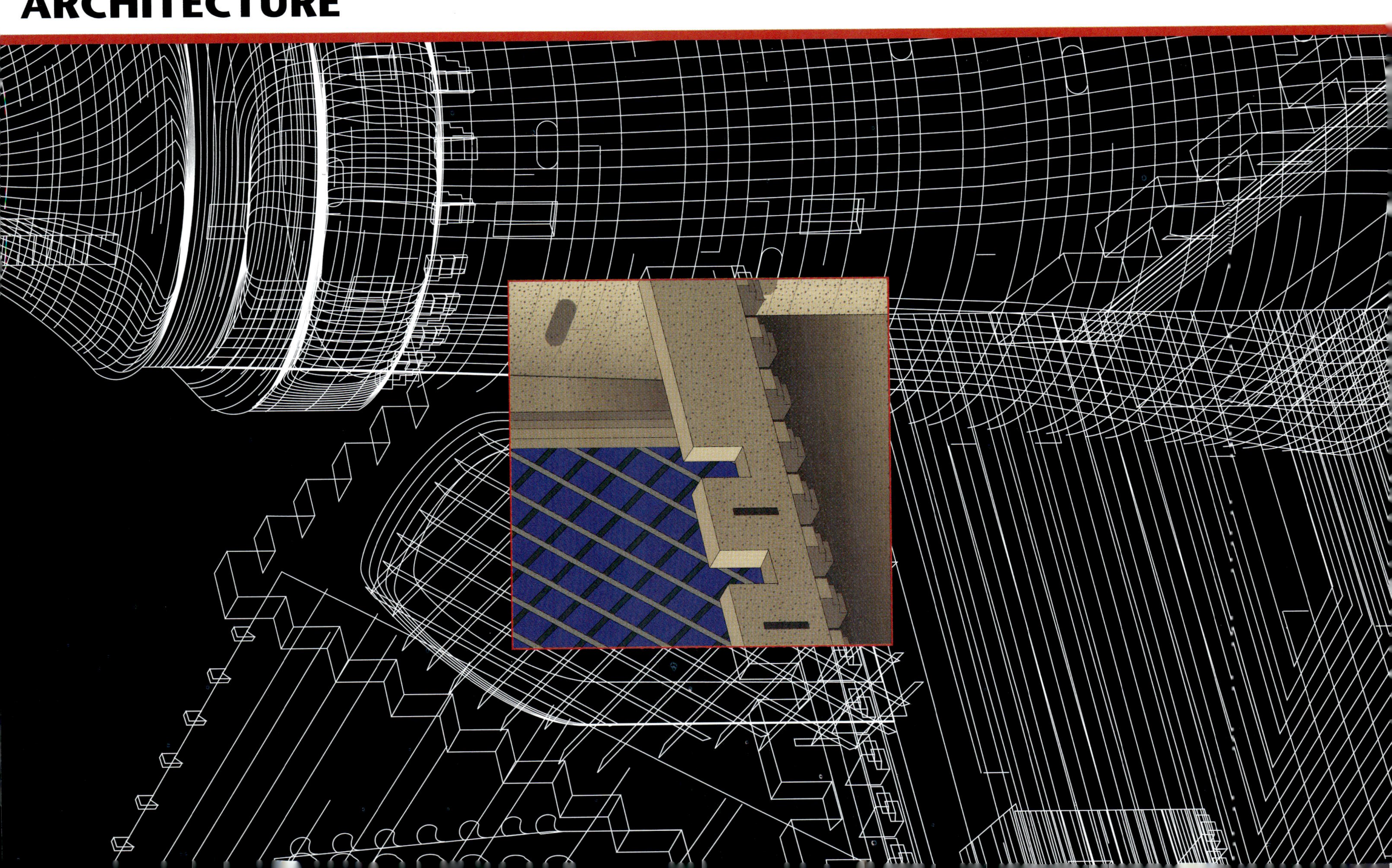

CONTENTS

ARCHITECTURE

igloo

wigwam

yurt

isba

hut

hut

tepee

pile dwelling

IONIC ORDER

tympanum
sima
pediment
cornice
entablature
frieze
architrave
dentil
abacus
fascia
capital
volute
flute
shaft
fillet
column
torus
scotia
base
stylobate
crepidoma
euthynteria

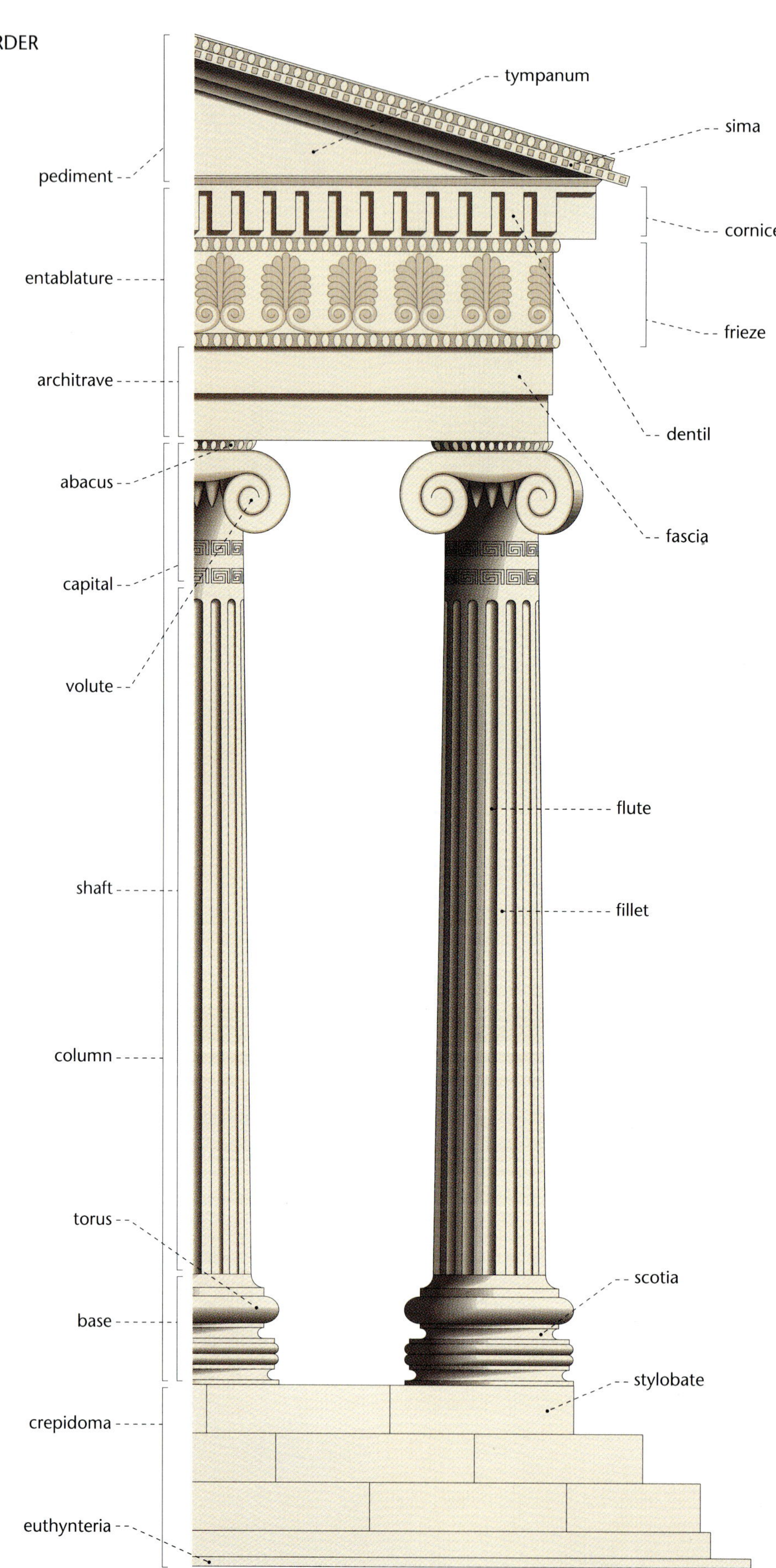

DORIC ORDER

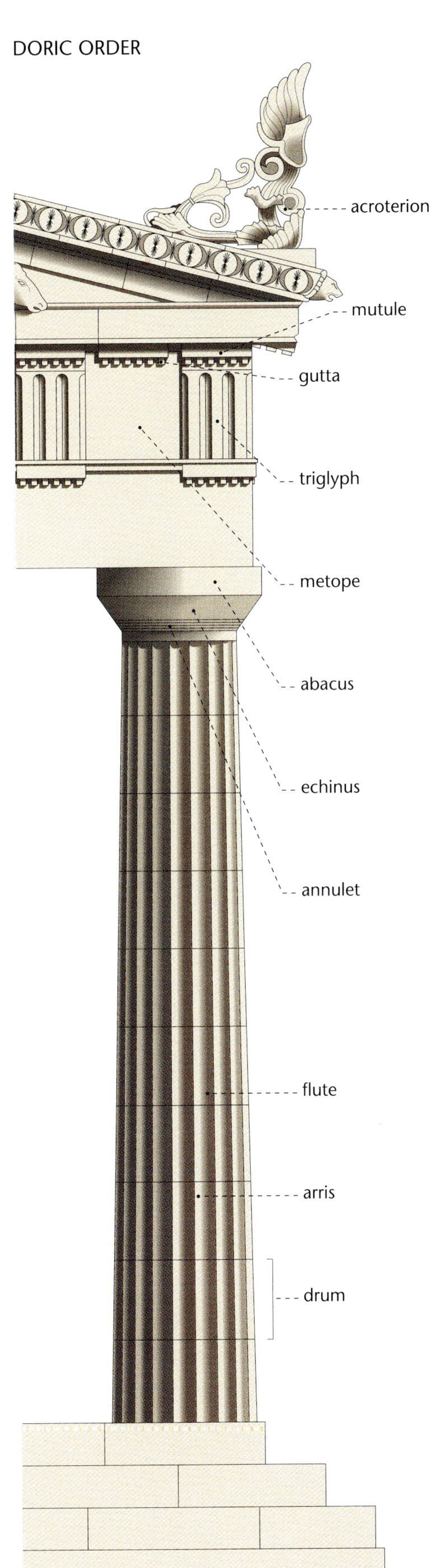

CORINTHIAN ORDER

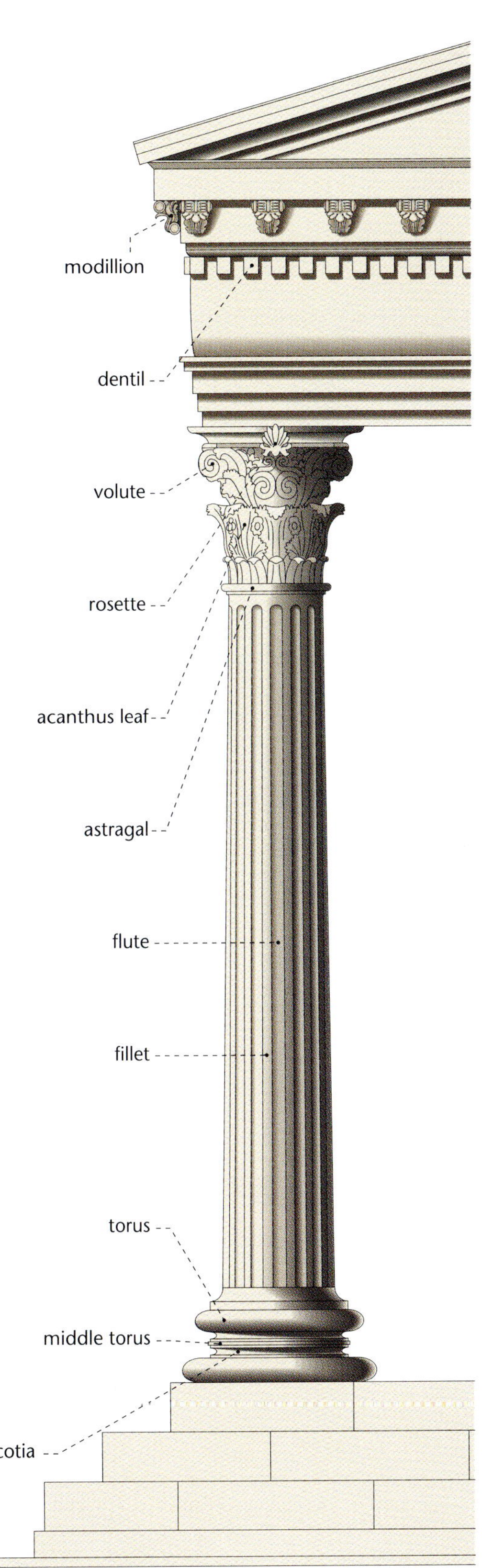

GREEK TEMPLE

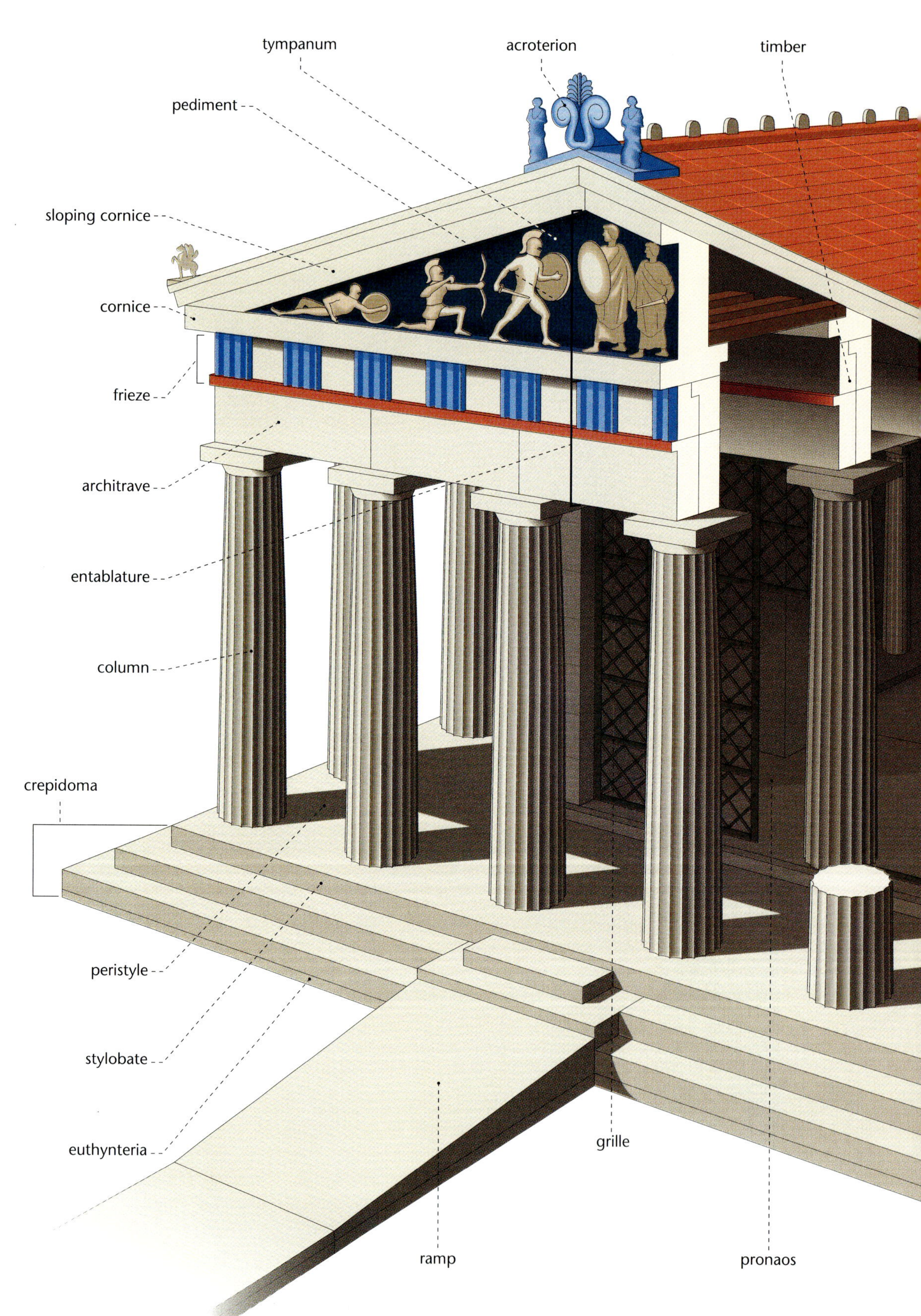

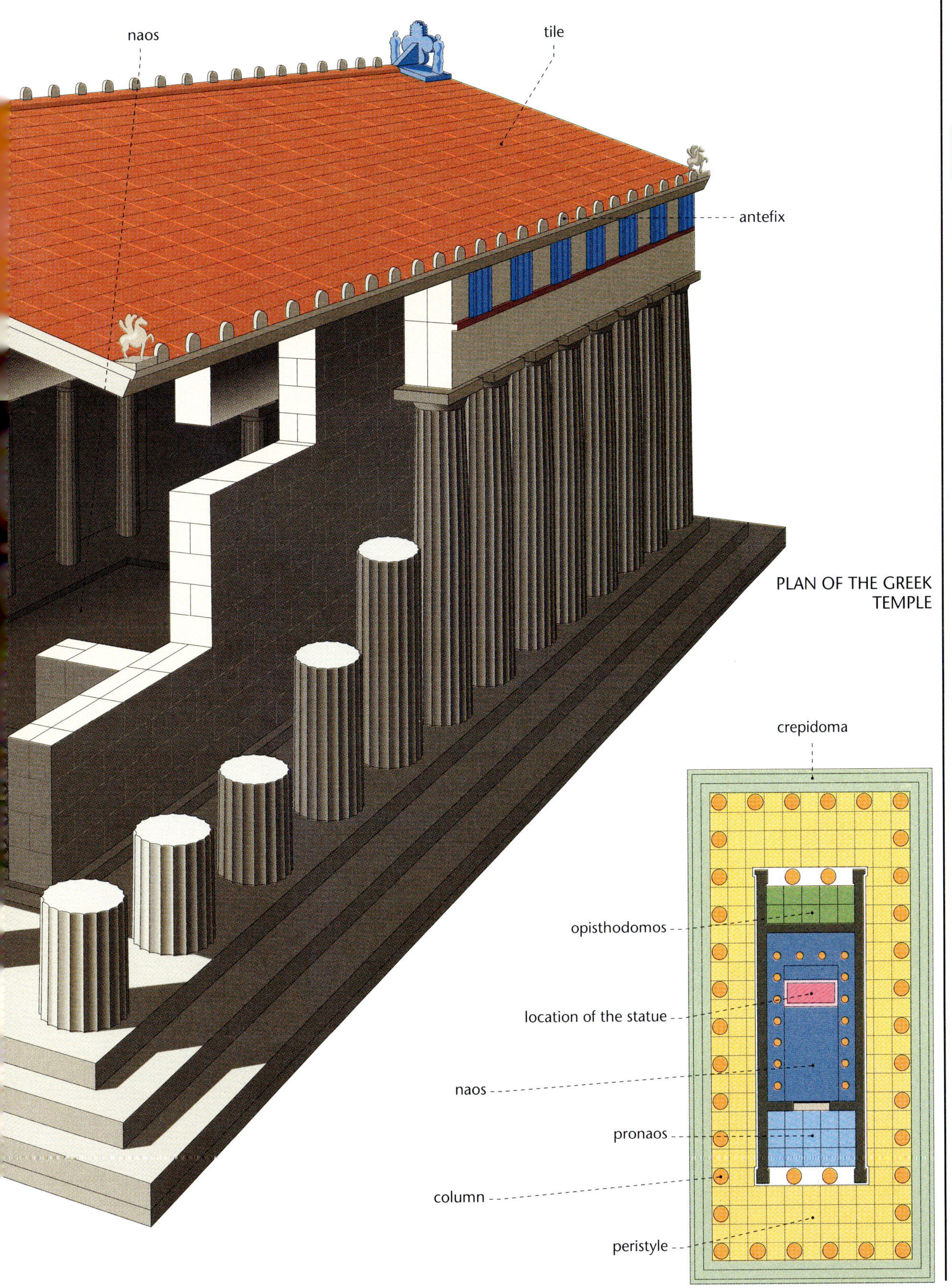
naos
tile
antefix
PLAN OF THE GREEK TEMPLE
crepidoma
opisthodomos
location of the statue
naos
pronaos
column
peristyle

ROMAN HOUSE

fresco
tile
compluvium
tablinum
timber
vestibule
atrium
impluvium
shop
bed chamber

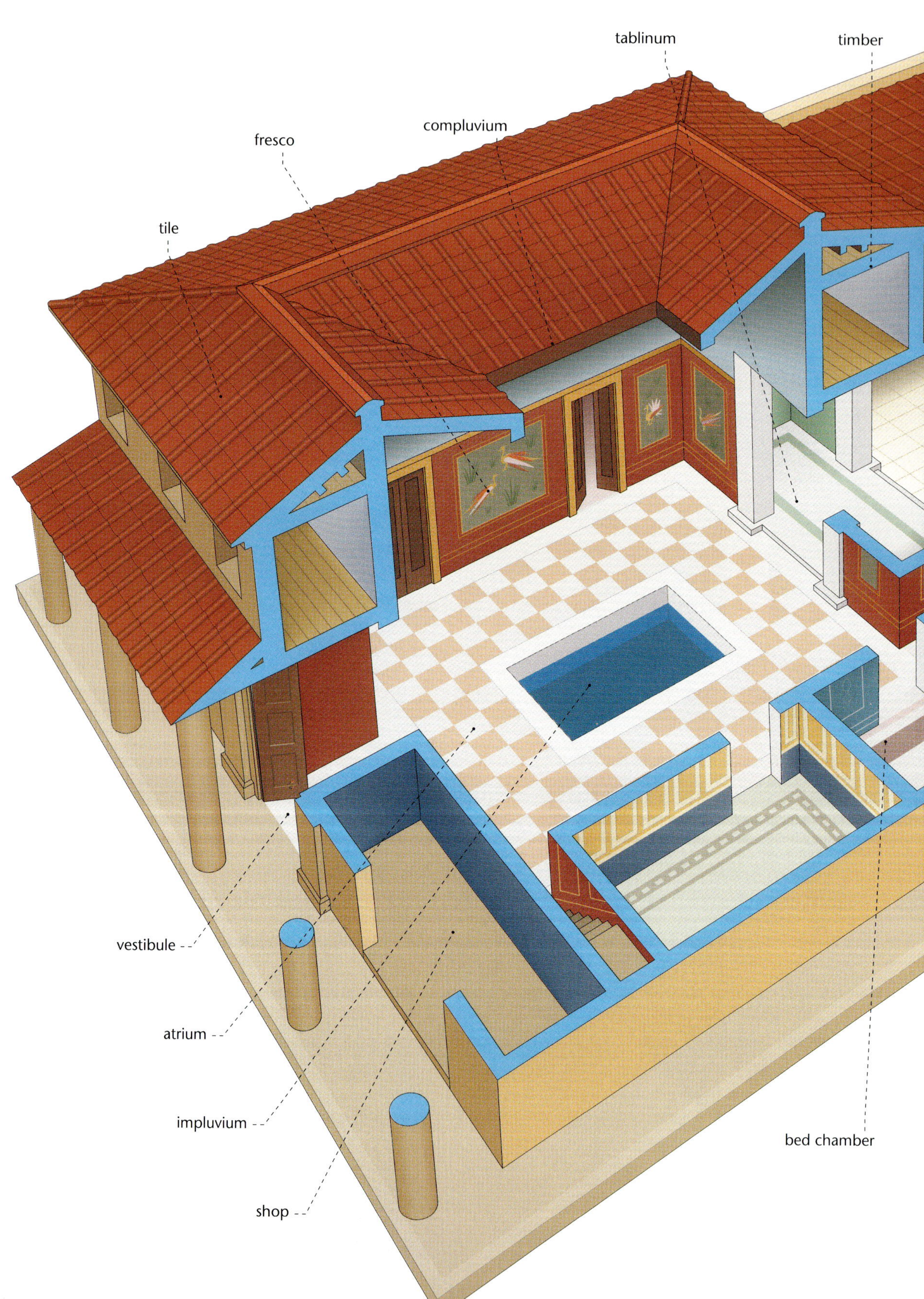

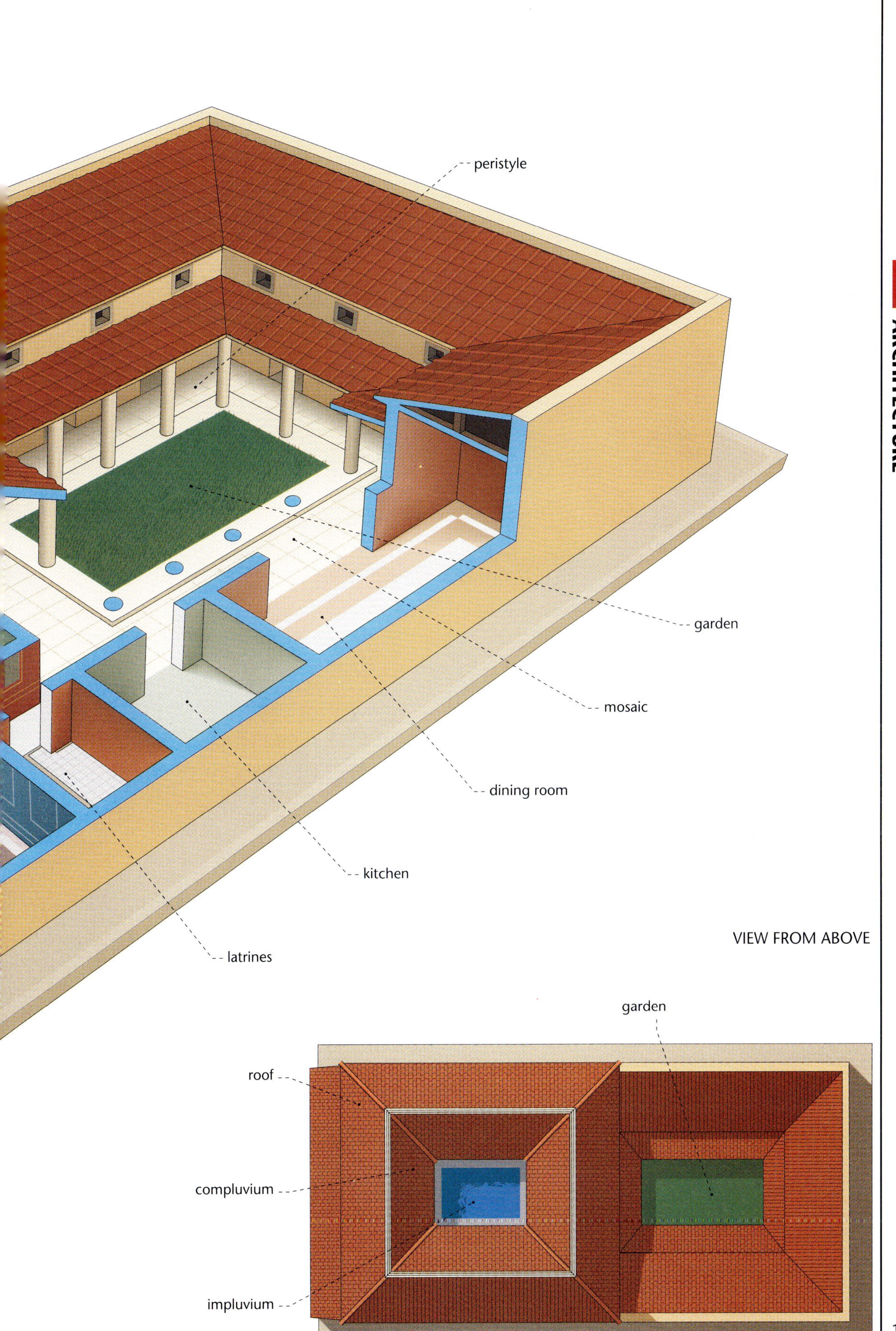
peristyle
garden
mosaic
dining room
kitchen
latrines
VIEW FROM ABOVE
garden
roof
compluvium
impluvium

MOSQUE

porch dome
prayer hall
porch
service room
minaret
shady arcades
reception hall
ablutions fountain
courtyard
fortified wall

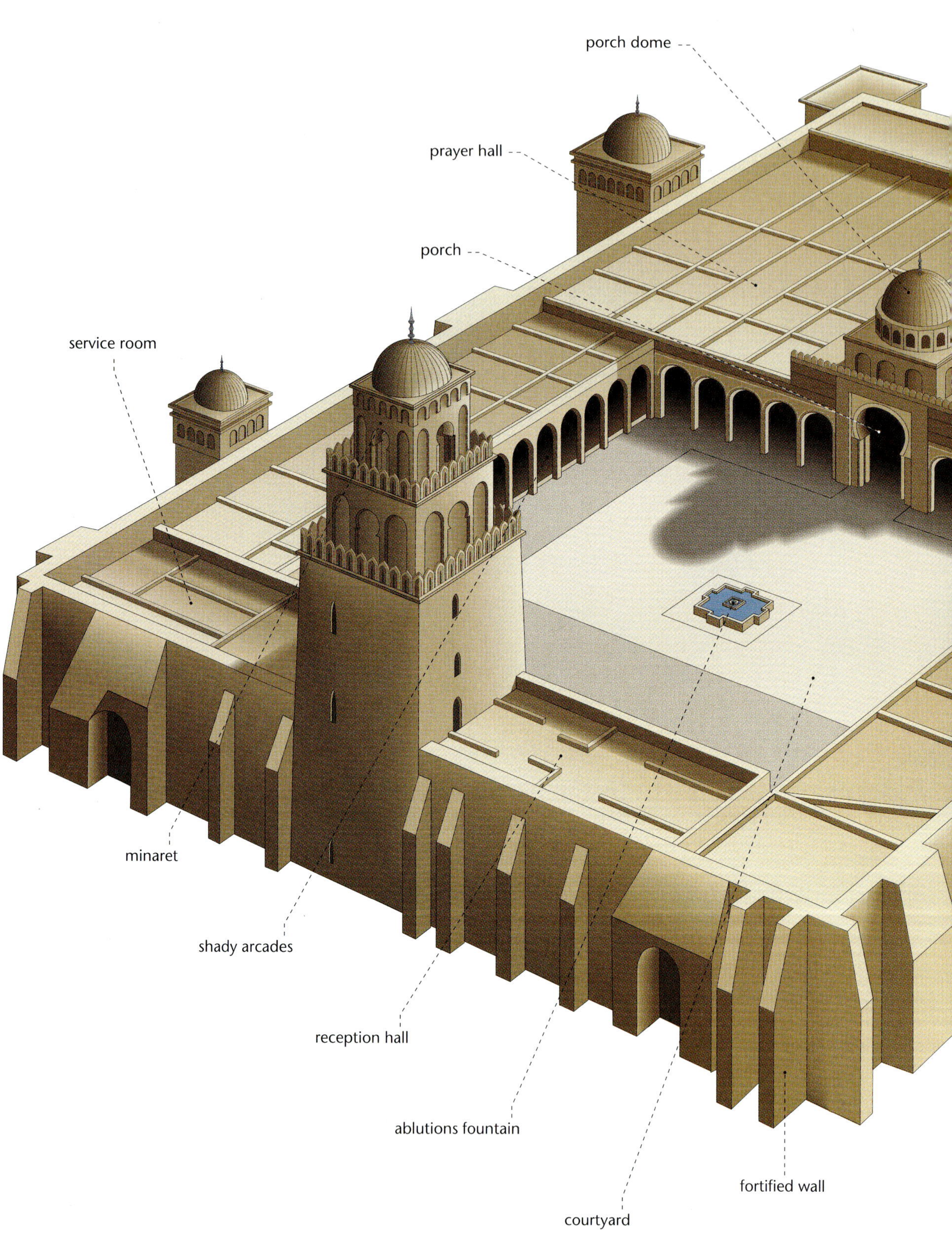

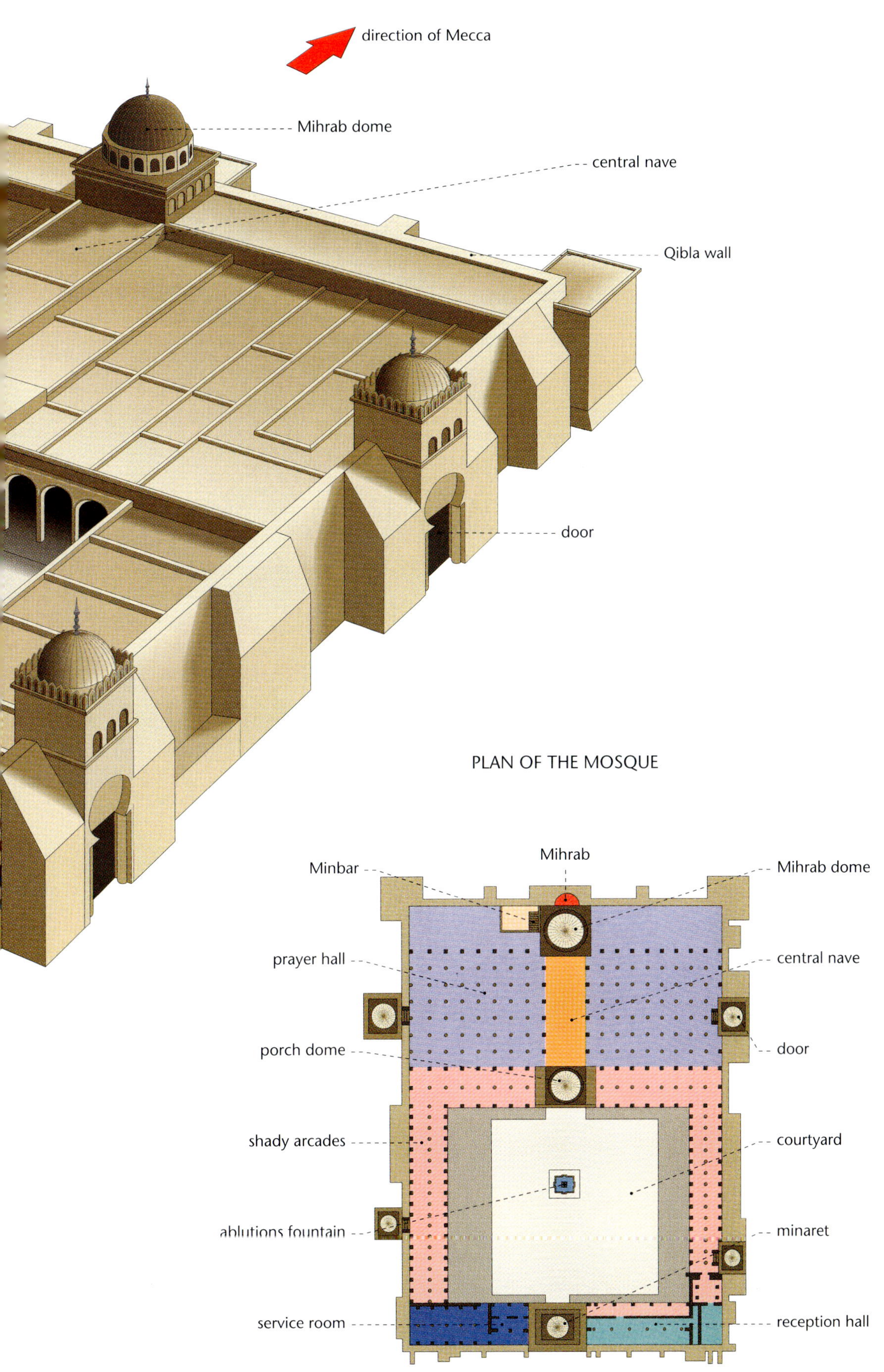

direction of Mecca
Mihrab dome
central nave
Qibla wall
door
PLAN OF THE MOSQUE
Minbar
Mihrab
Mihrab dome
prayer hall
central nave
porch dome
door
shady arcades
courtyard
ablutions fountain
minaret
service room
reception hall

SEMICIRCULAR ARCH

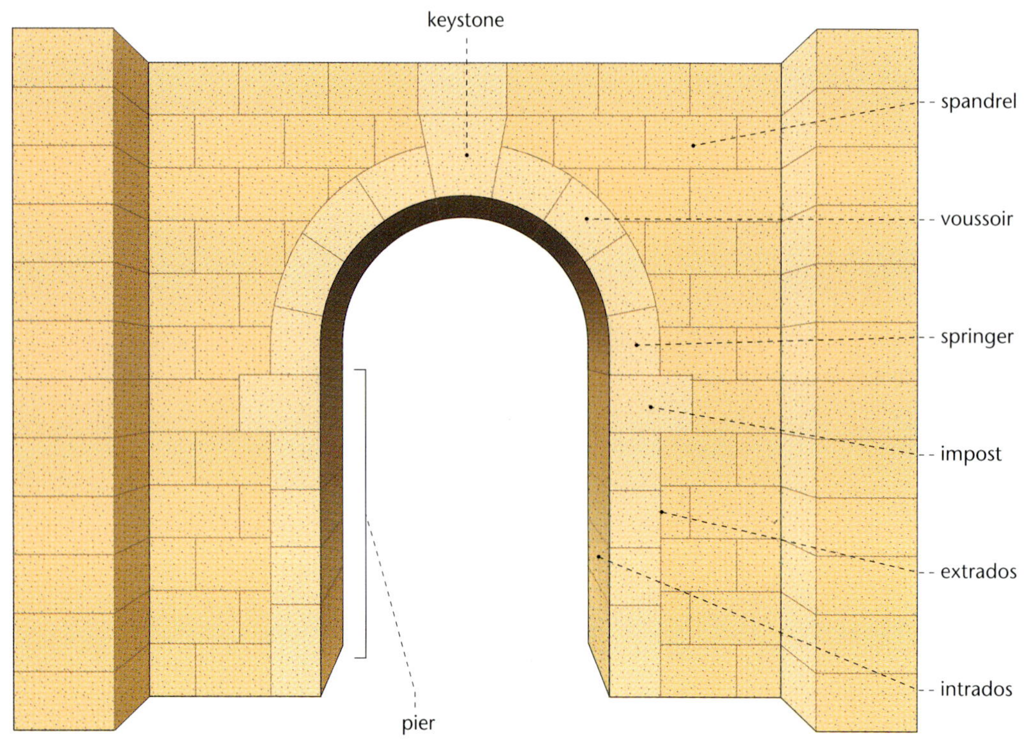

TYPES OF ARCHES

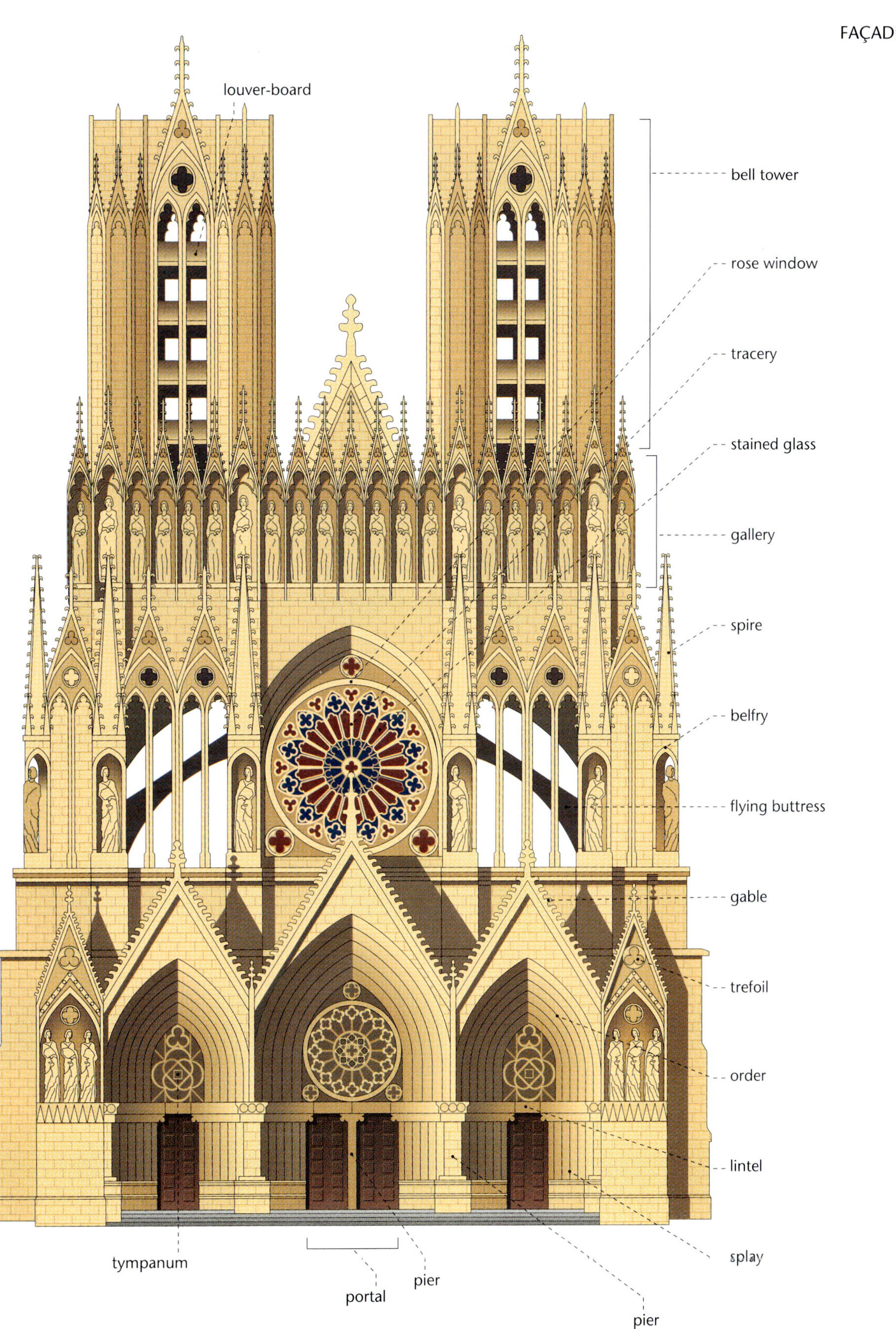

louver-board
bell tower
rose window
tracery
stained glass
gallery
spire
belfry
flying buttress
gable
trefoil
order
lintel
splay
tympanum
portal
pier
pier

GOTHIC CATHEDRAL

CATHEDRAL

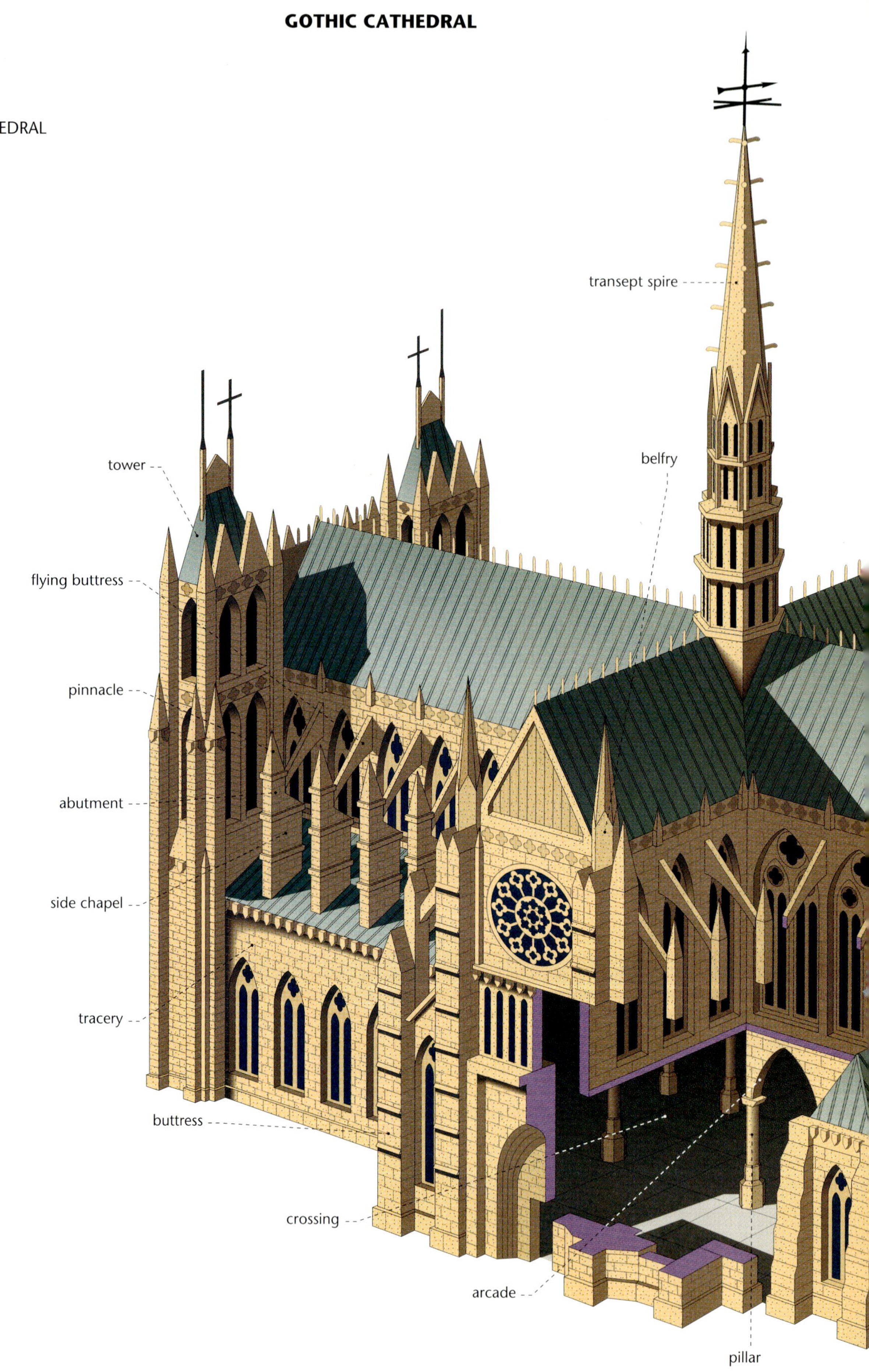

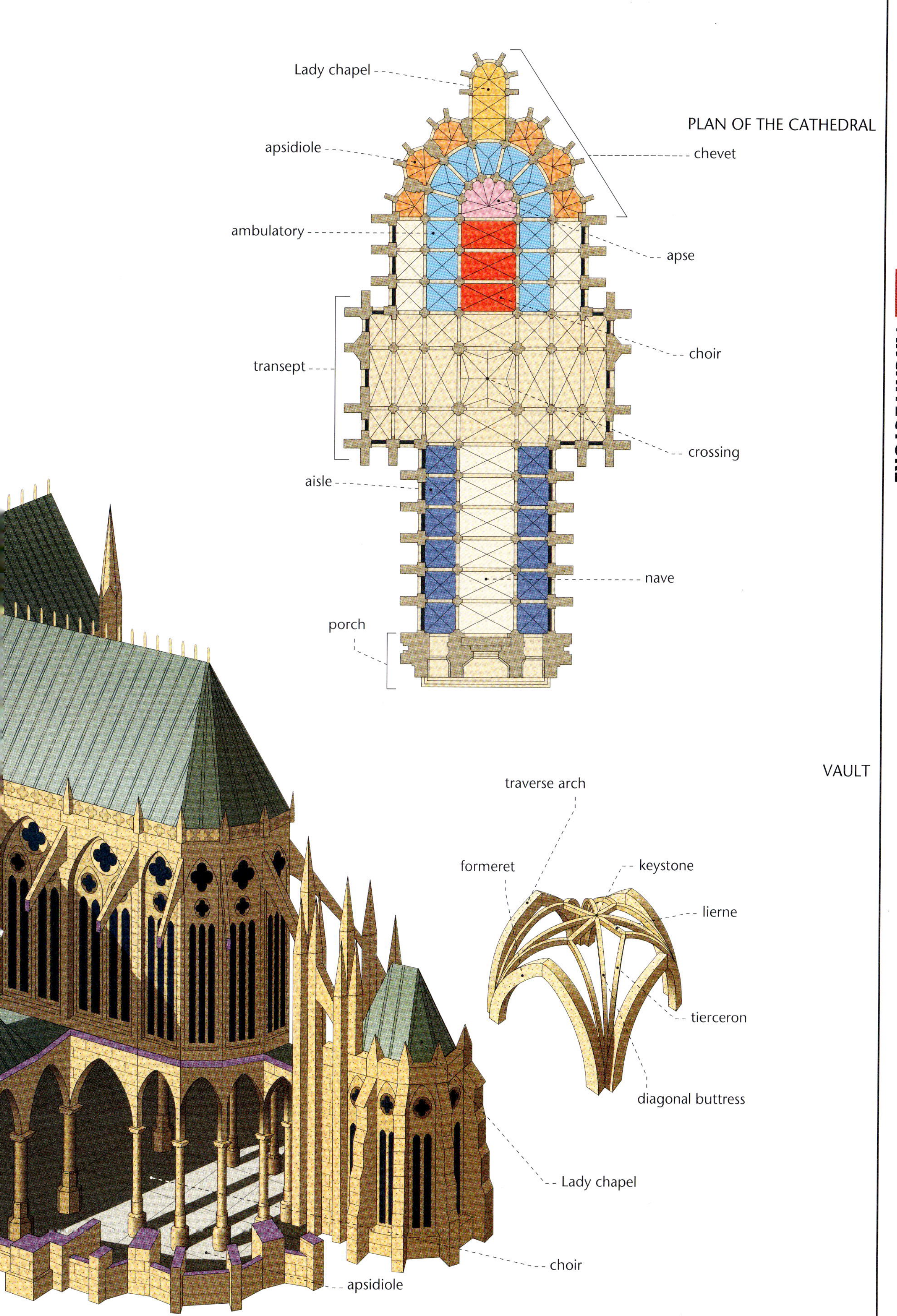
PLAN OF THE CATHEDRAL
Lady chapel
apsidiole
ambulatory
transept
aisle
porch
chevet
apse
choir
crossing
nave
VAULT
traverse arch
formeret
keystone
lierne
tierceron
diagonal buttress
Lady chapel
choir
apsidiole

VAUBAN FORTIFICATION

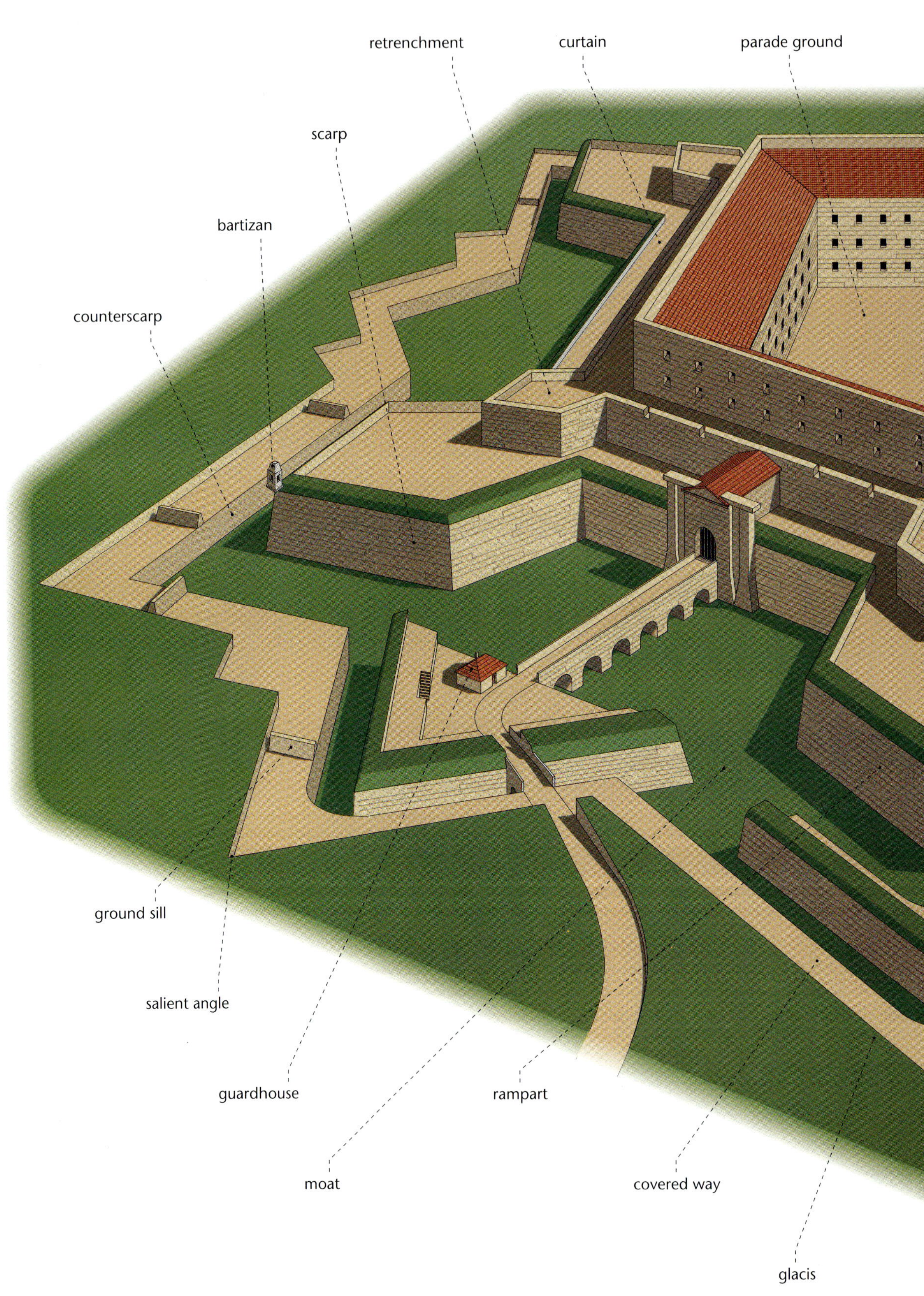

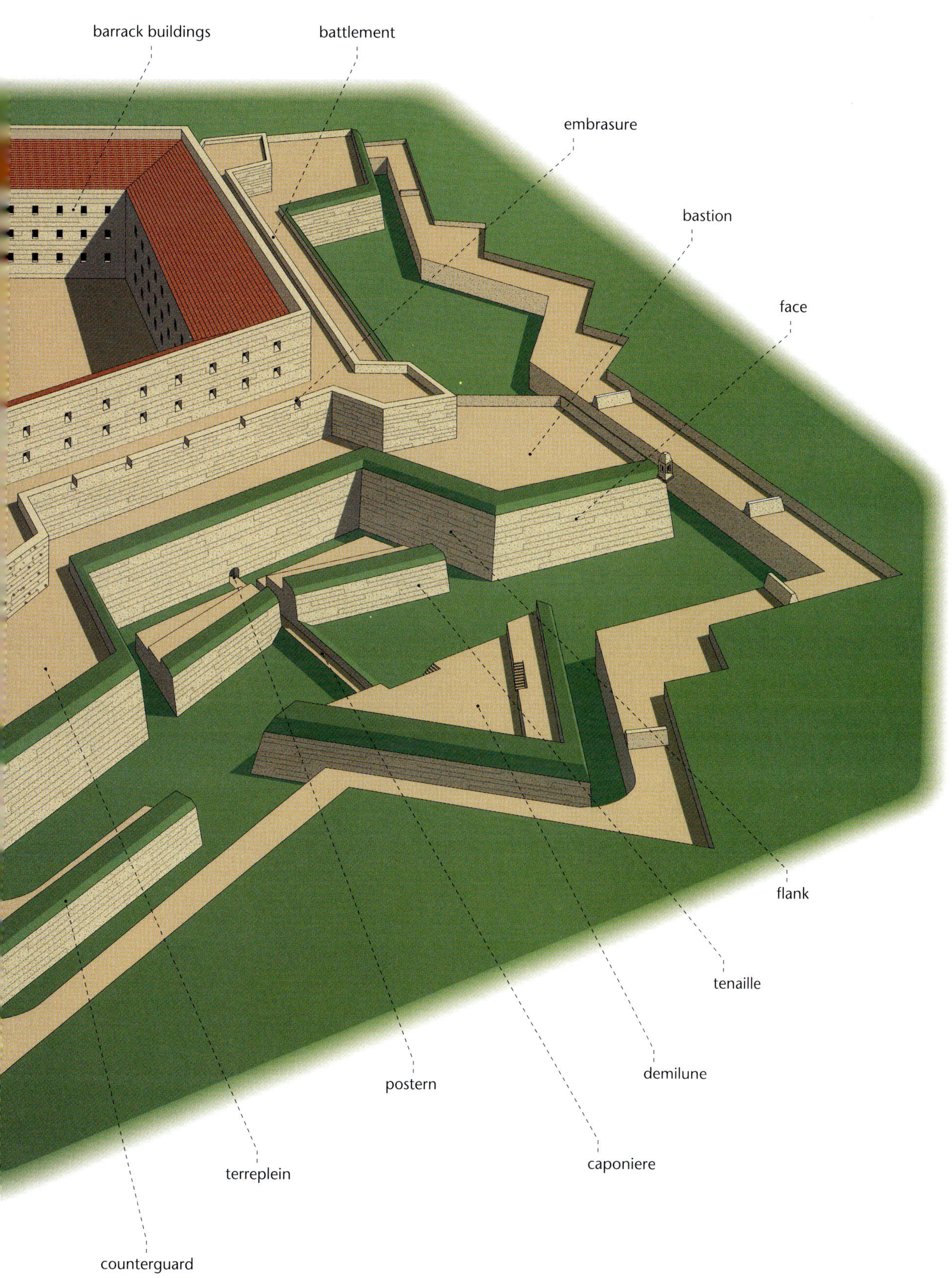

barrack buildings
battlement
embrasure
bastion
face
flank
tenaille
demilune
caponiere
postern
terreplein
counterguard

CASTLE

corner tower
castle
turret
flanking tower
covered parapet walk
bailey
curtain wall
corbel
guardhouse
machicolation
drawbridge
rampart
barbican
footbridge

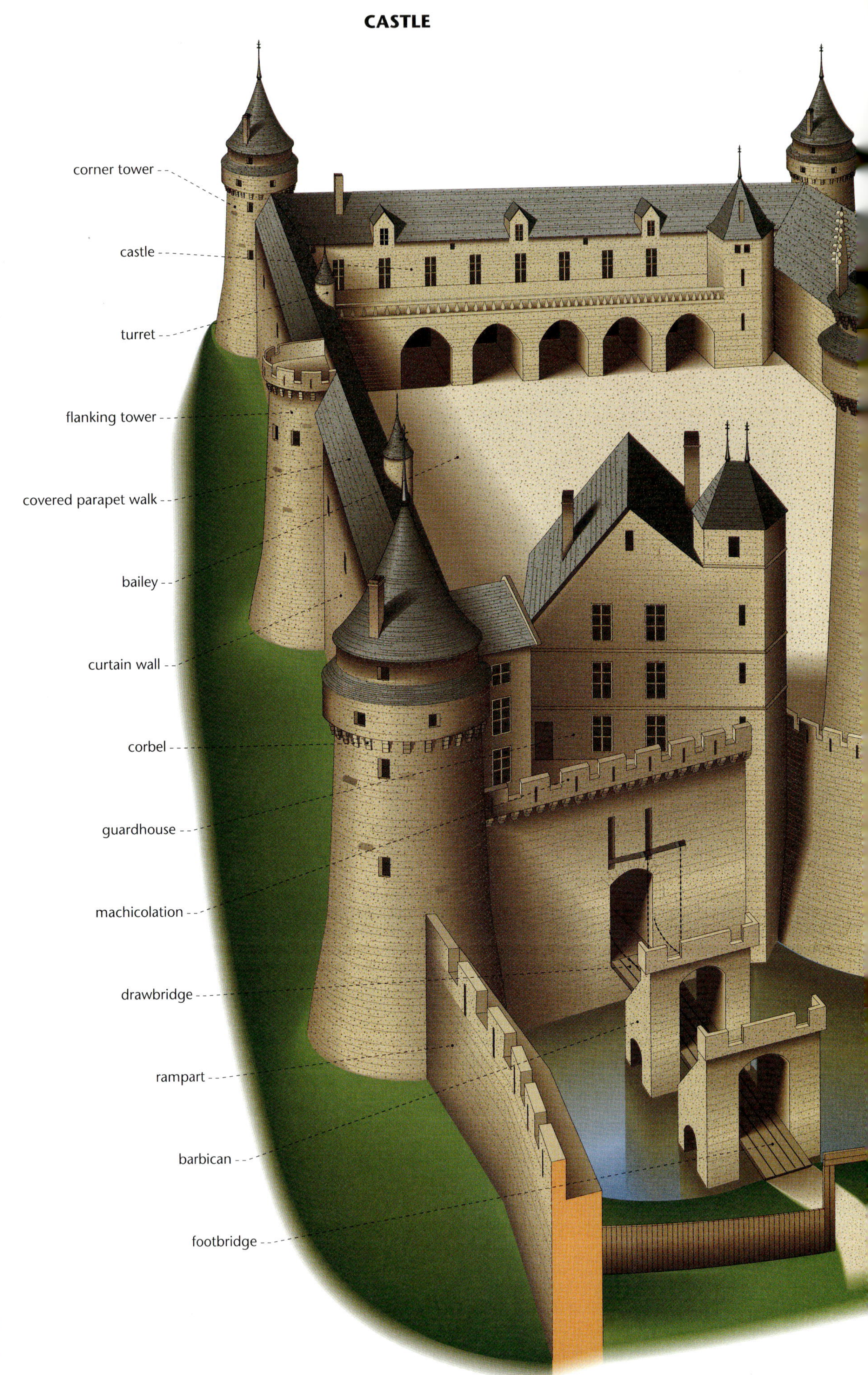

ARCHITECTURE

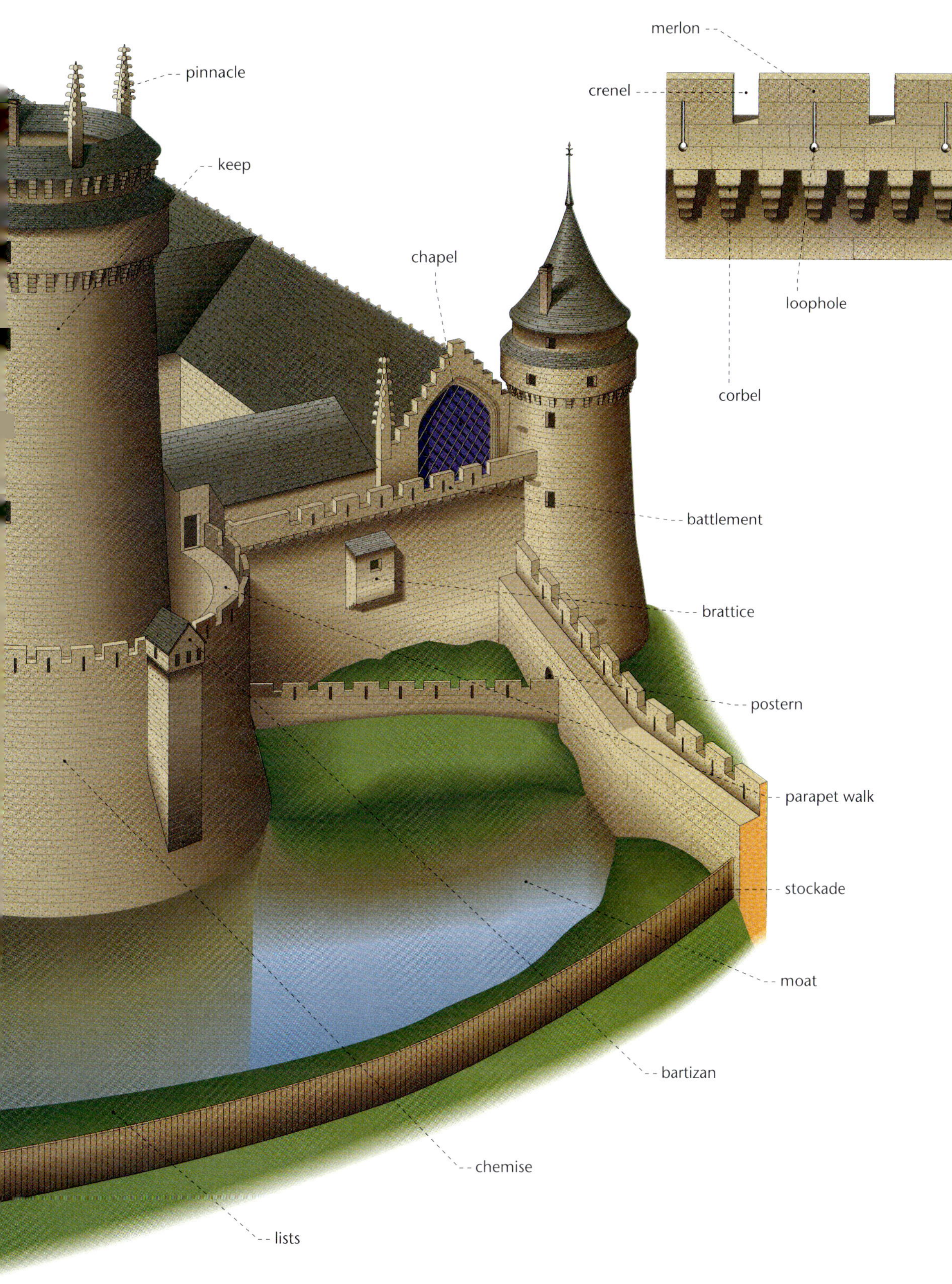

ROOFS

pitched roof
gable roof
hip roof
lean-to roof
flat roof
sawtooth roof
monitor roof
ogee roof

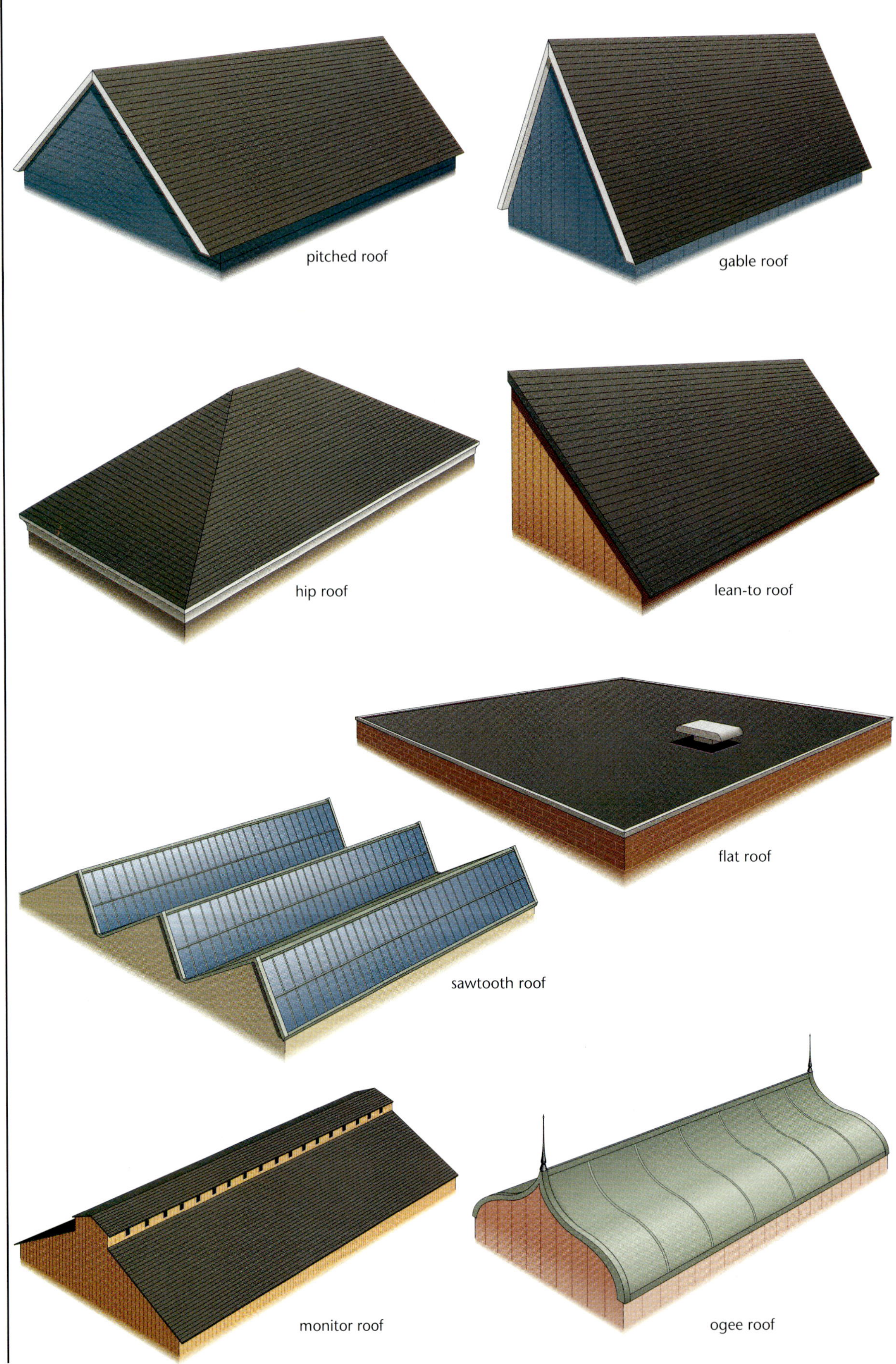

bell roof

dome roof

helm roof

sloped turret

hip-and-valley roof

conical broach roof

pavilion roof

rotunda roof

imperial roof

mansard roof

ARCHITECTURE

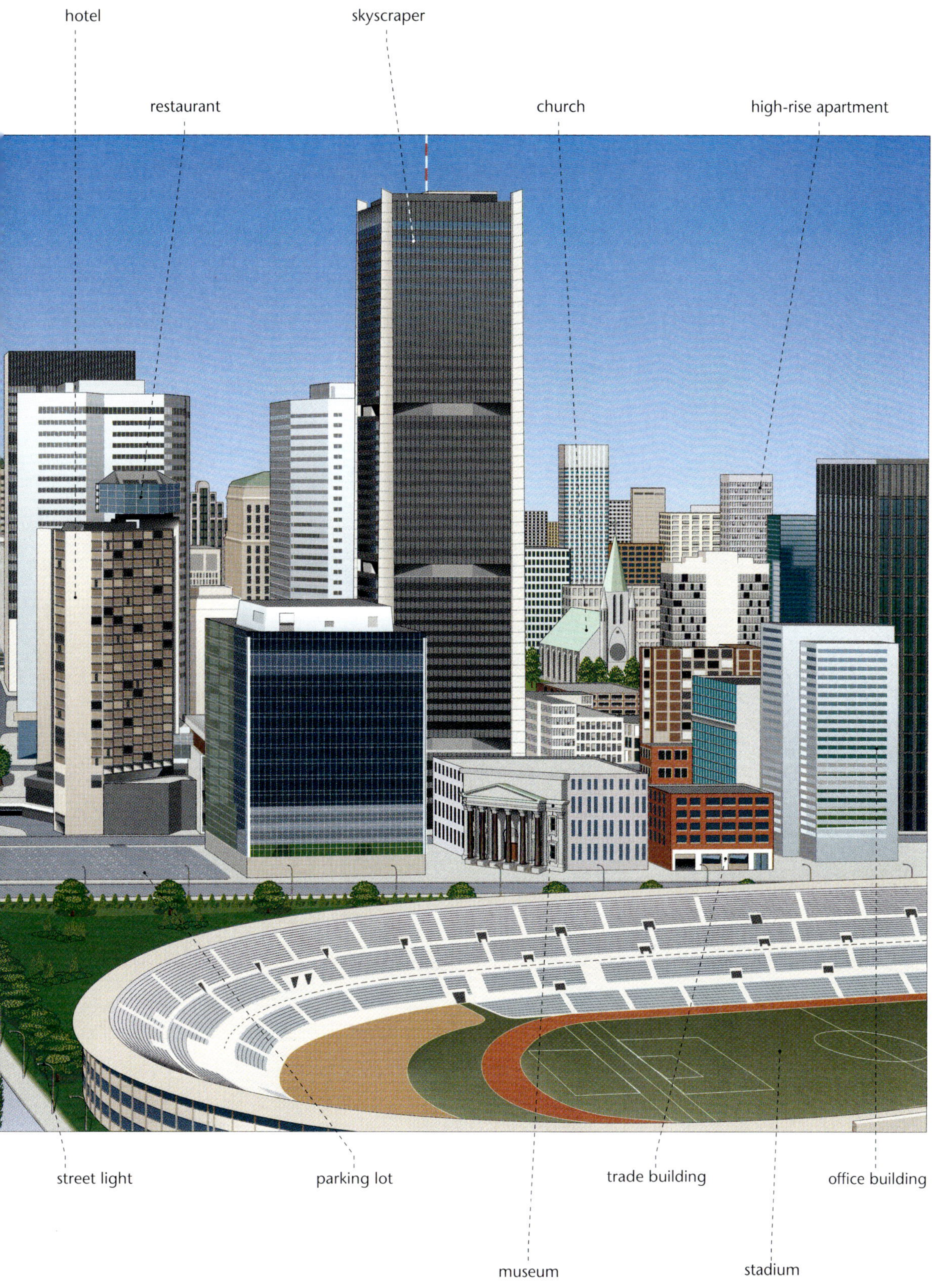

hotel
restaurant
skyscraper
church
high-rise apartment
street light
parking lot
museum
trade building
stadium
office building

CROSS SECTION OF A STREET

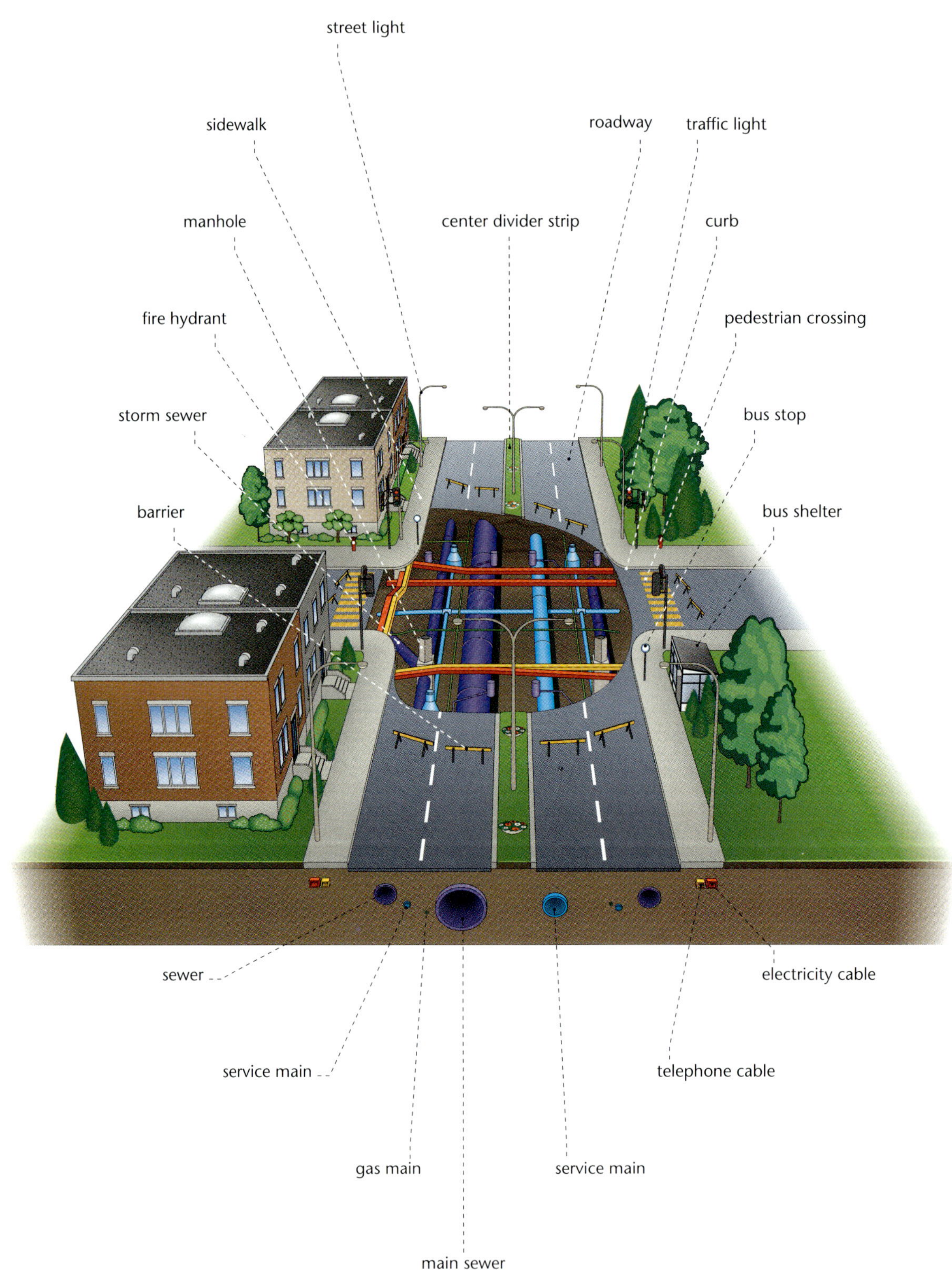

CITY HOUSES

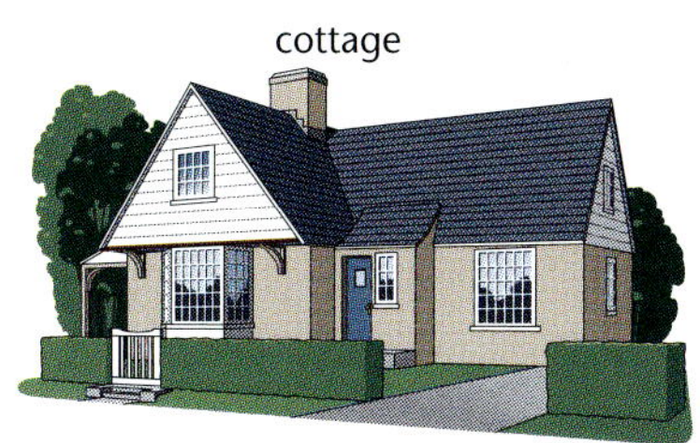

cottage

single-family home

condominiums

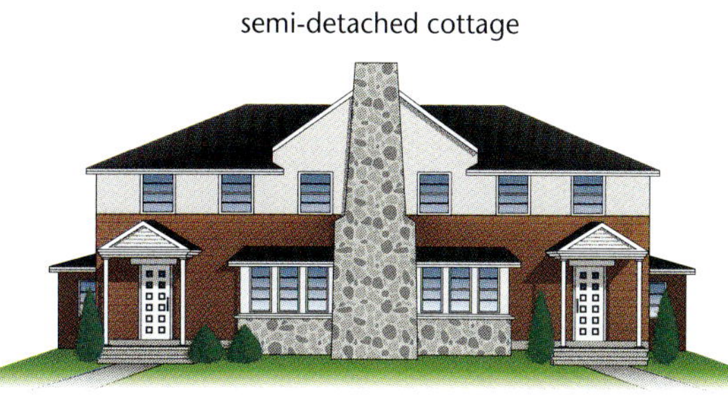

semi-detached cottage

town houses

high-rise apartment

THEATER

grid
catwalk
flies
batten
upstage
footlights
backdrop
border
stage curtain
iron curtain
rehearsing room
scenery storage
slot
stage
scenery lift
prompt box
proscenium
hoist
orchestra pit
orchestra seats

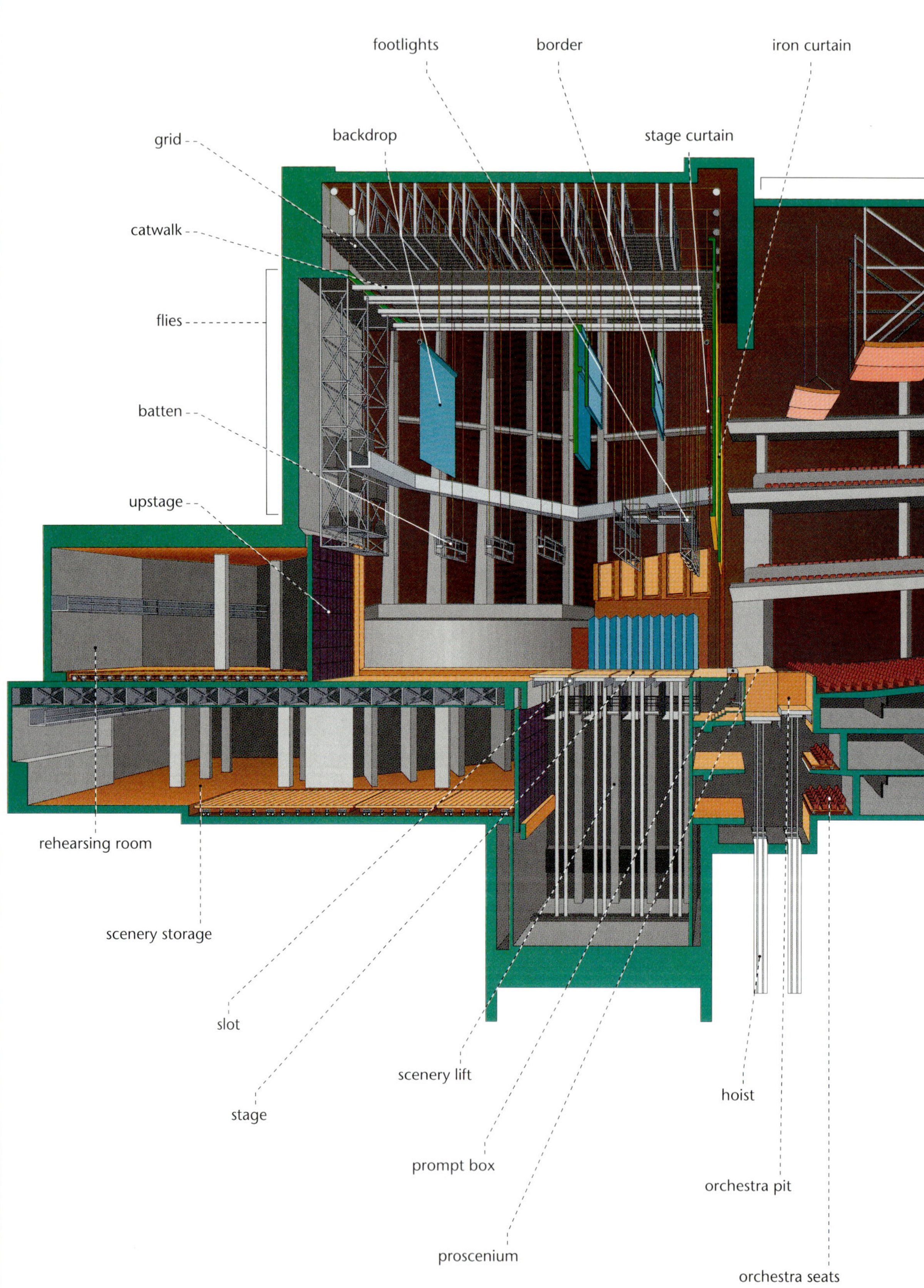

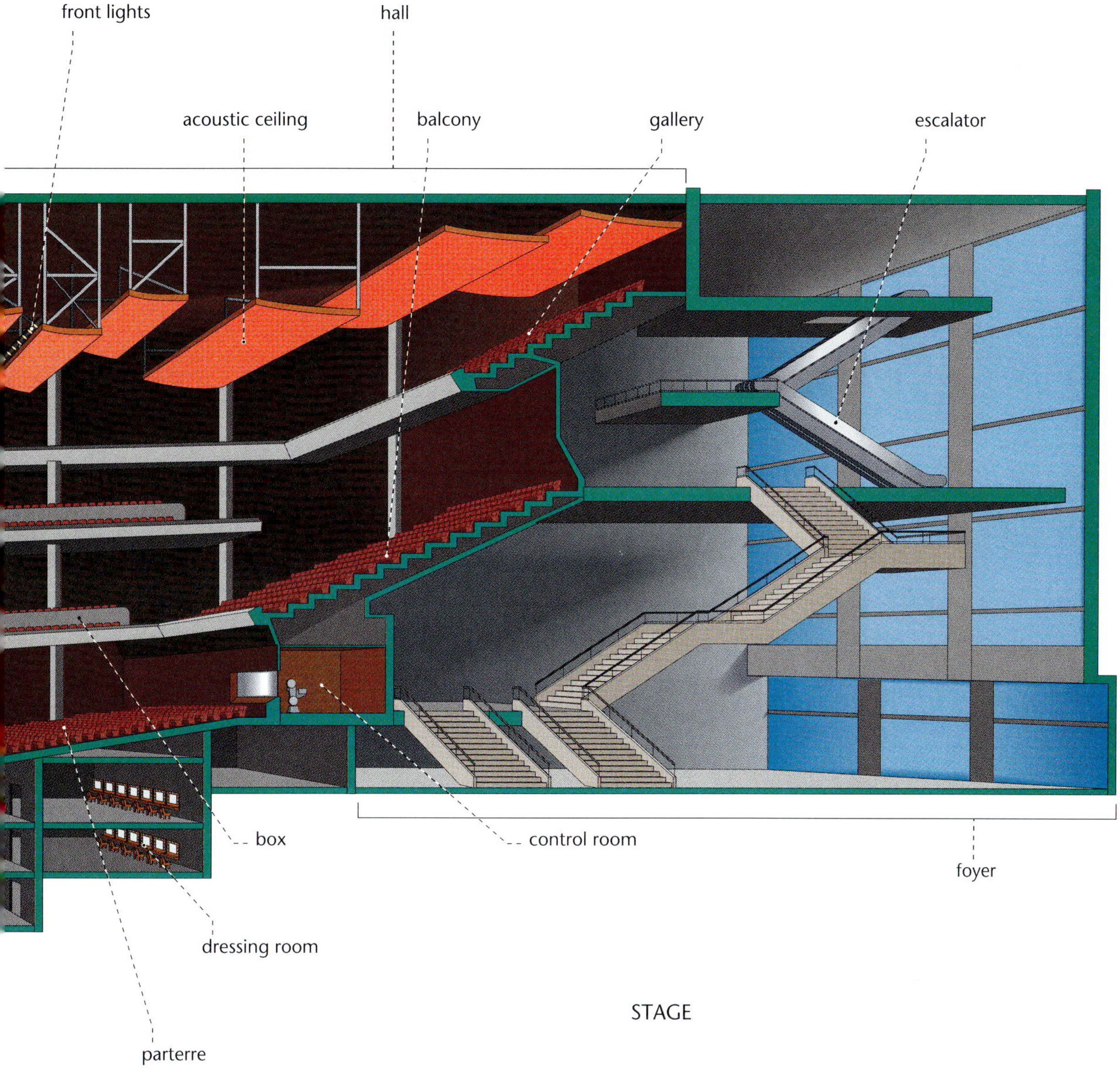

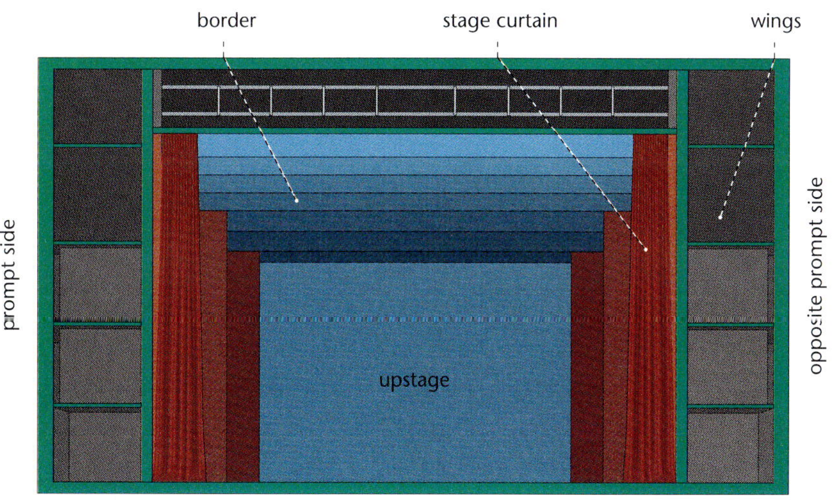

front lights
hall
acoustic ceiling
balcony
gallery
escalator
box
control room
foyer
dressing room
parterre
STAGE
border
stage curtain
wings
prompt side
opposite prompt side
upstage

OFFICE BUILDING

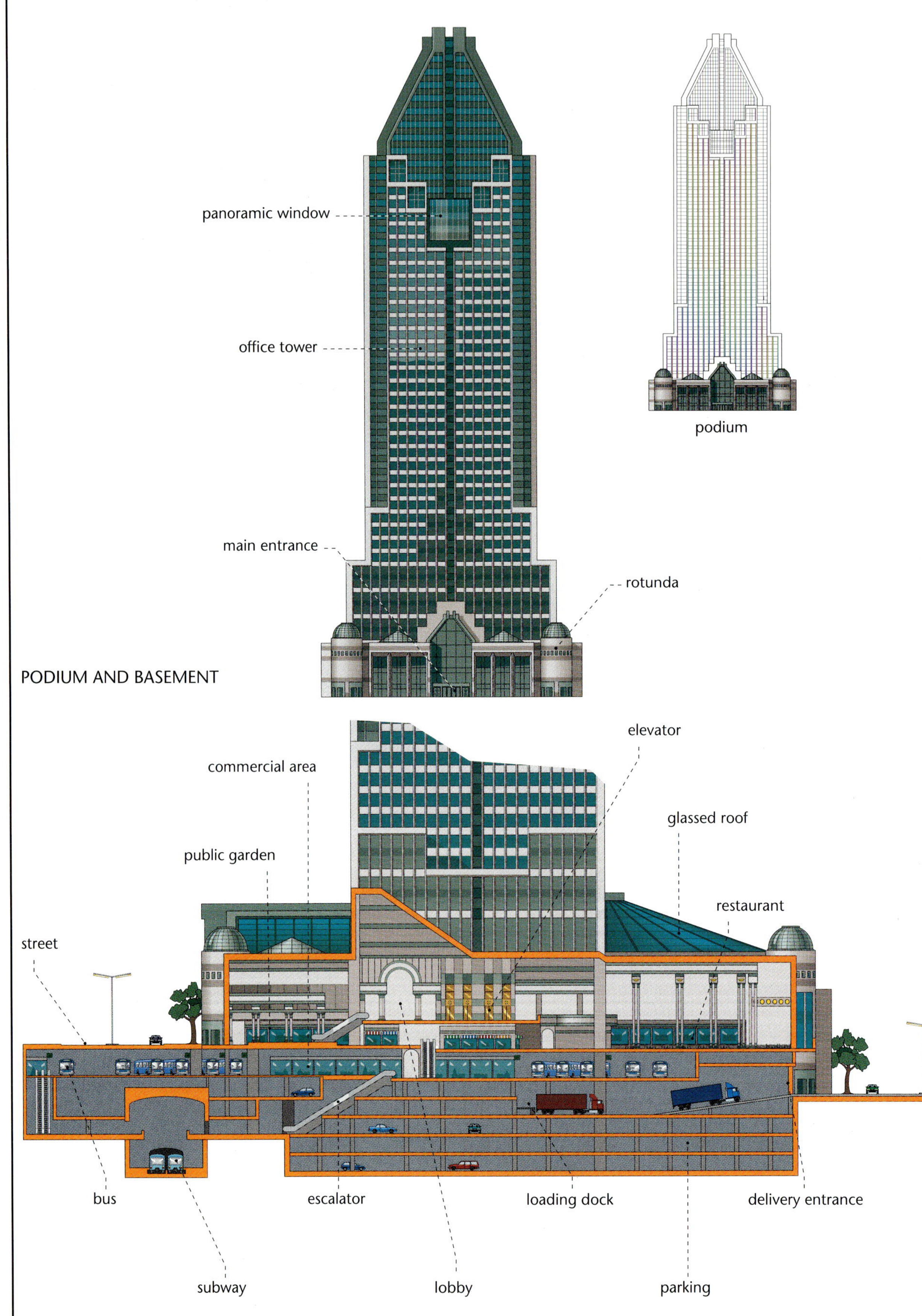

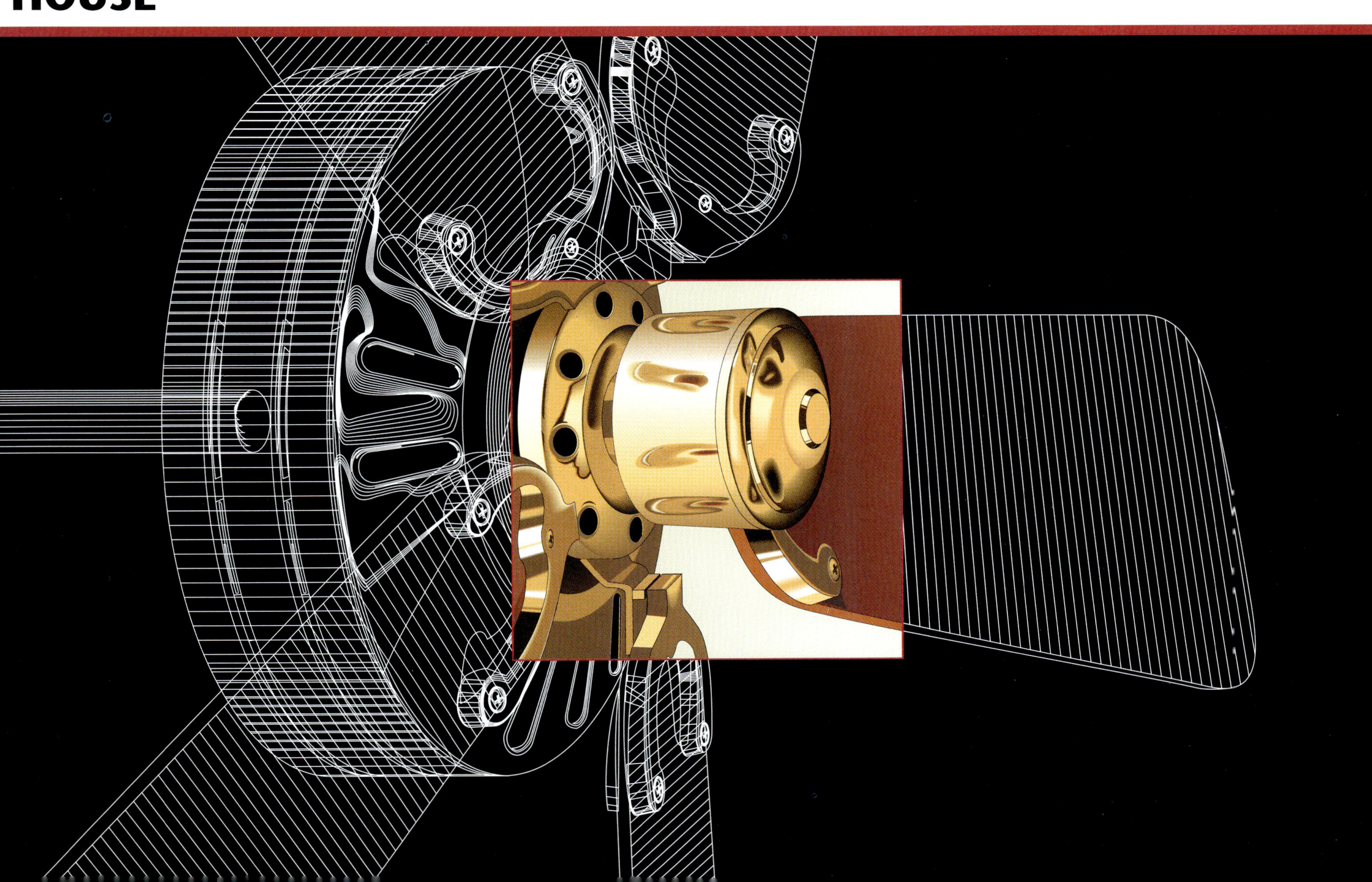

CONTENTS

ELEVATION

SITE PLAN

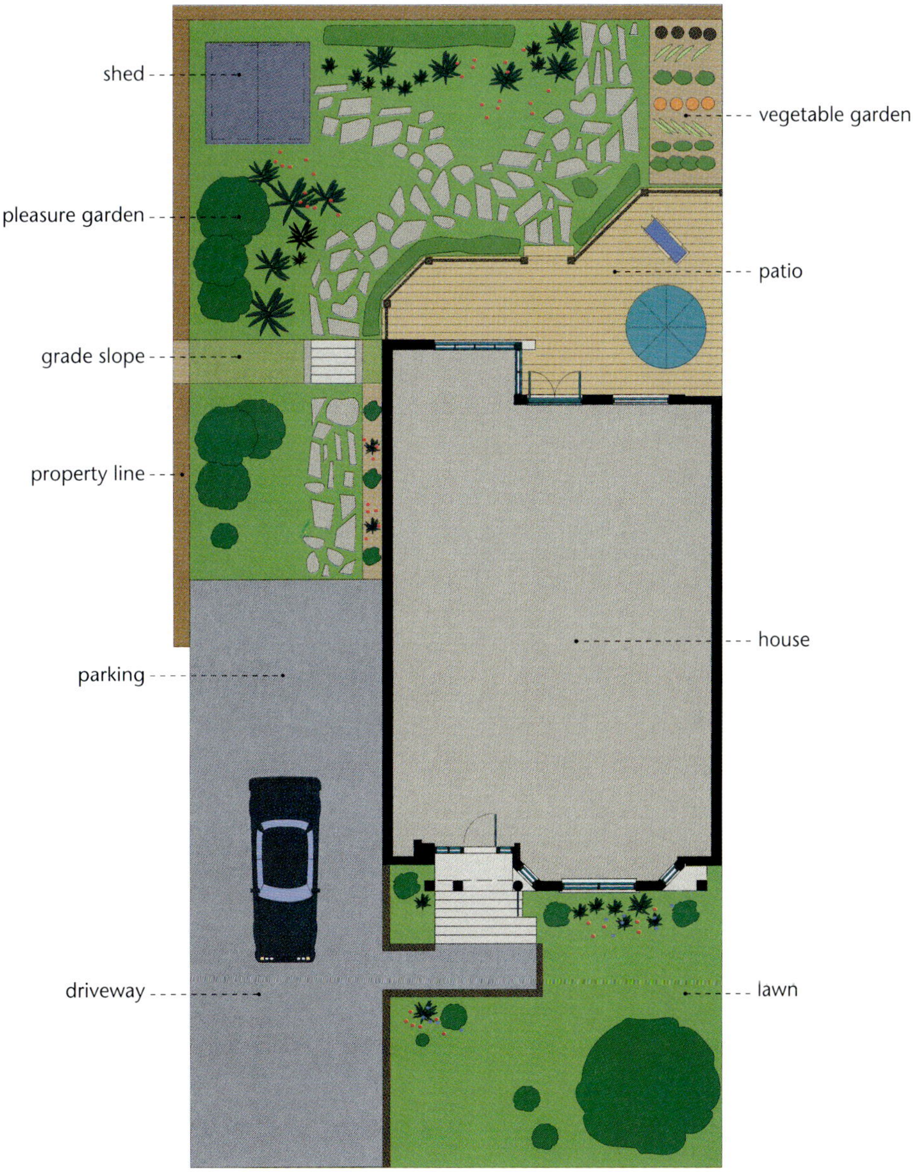

MEZZANINE FLOOR

SECOND FLOOR

FIRST FLOOR

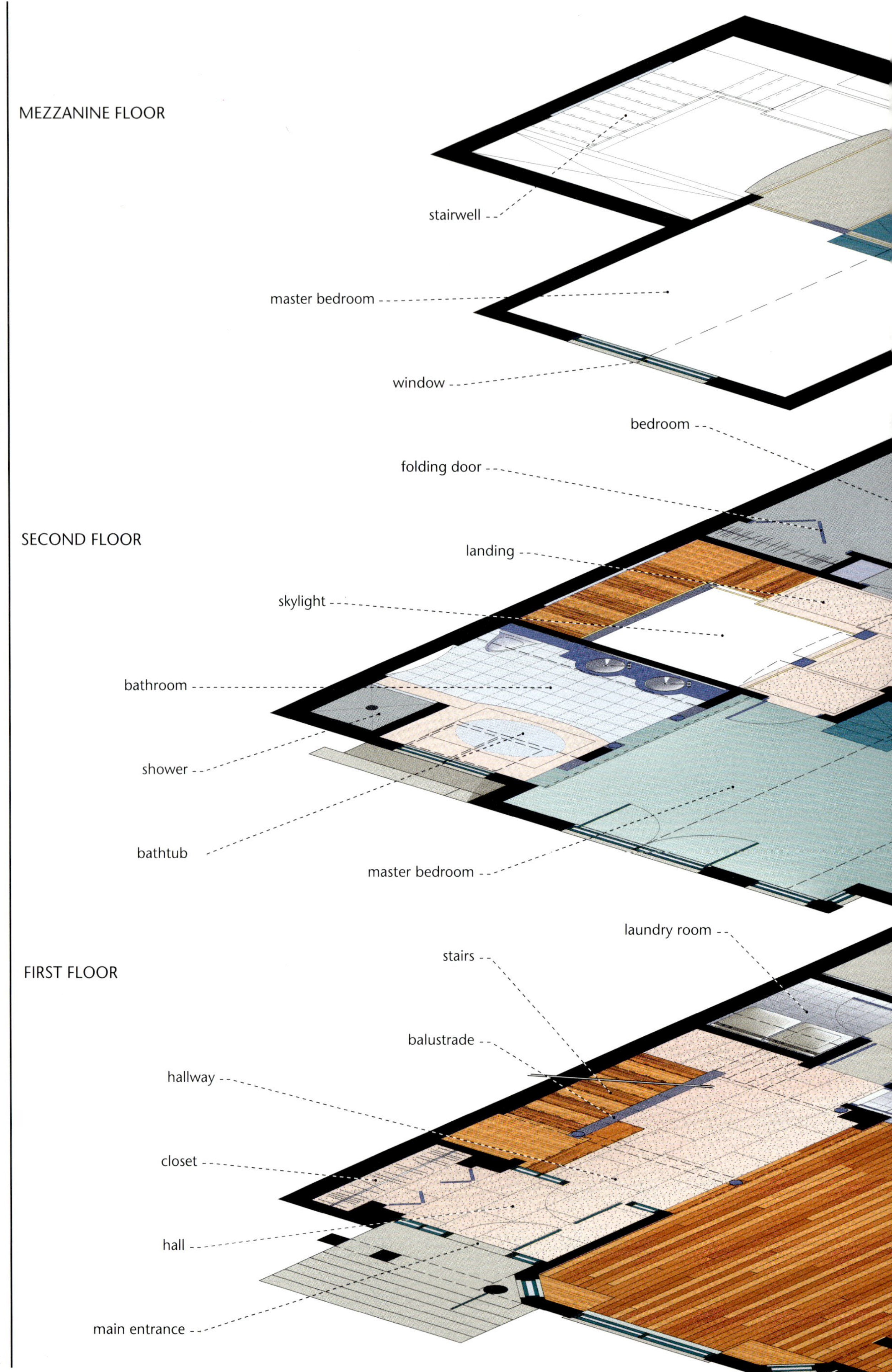

BLUEPRINT READING

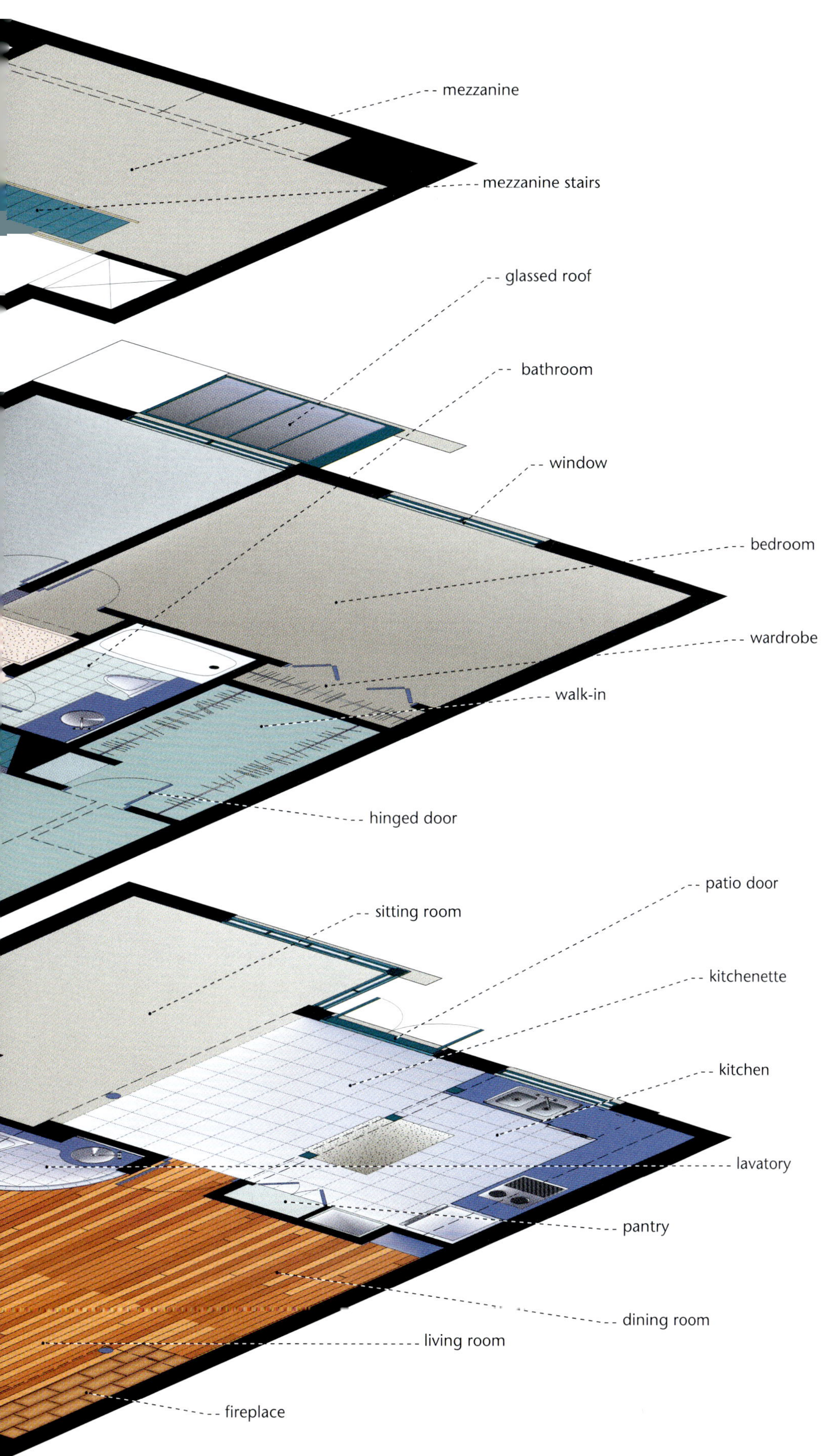

roof vent
cornice
second floor
garage
driveway
perron
outdoor light

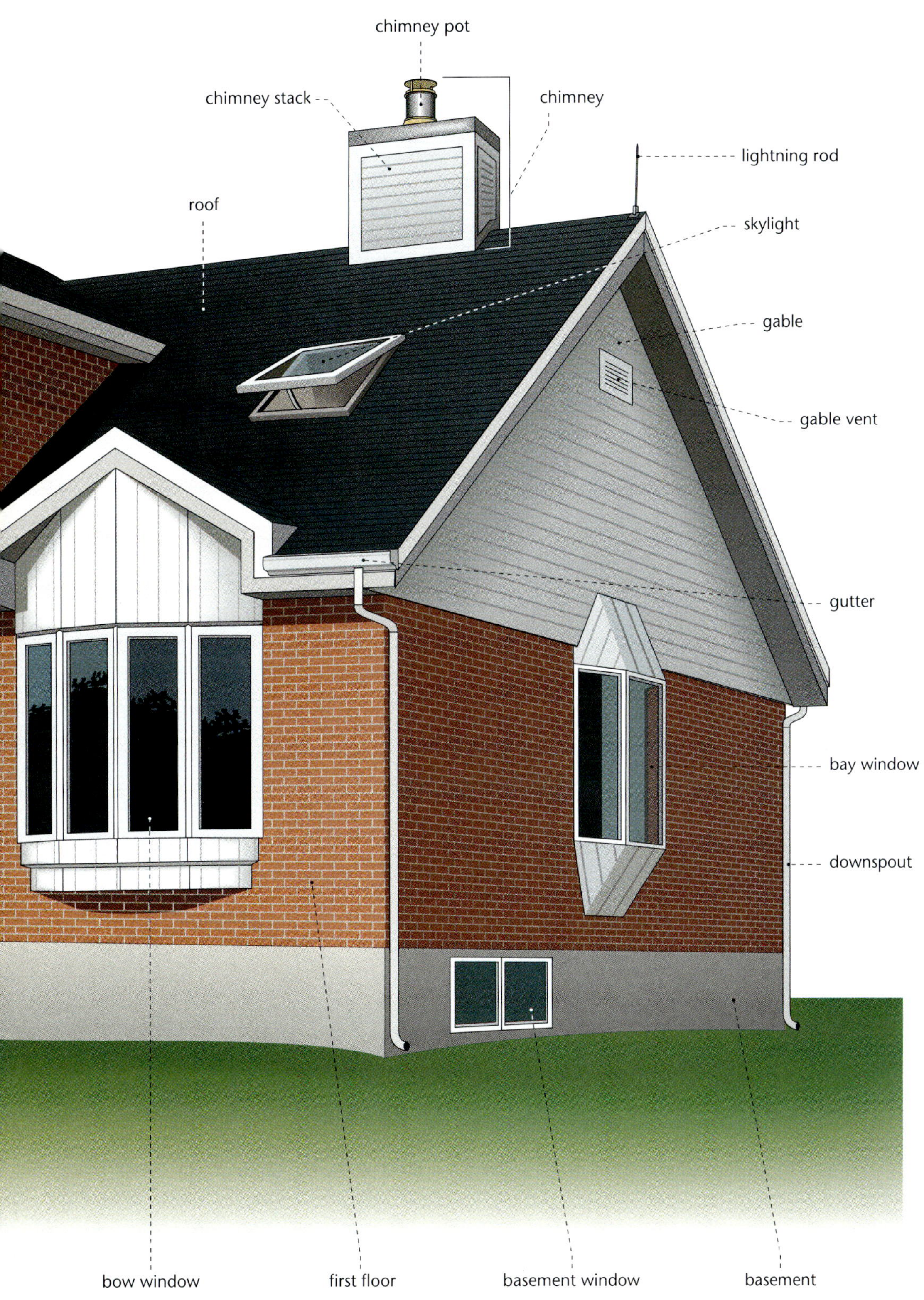

chimney pot
chimney stack
chimney
roof
lightning rod
skylight
gable
gable vent
gutter
bay window
downspout
bow window
first floor
basement window
basement

STRUCTURE OF A HOUSE

FRAME

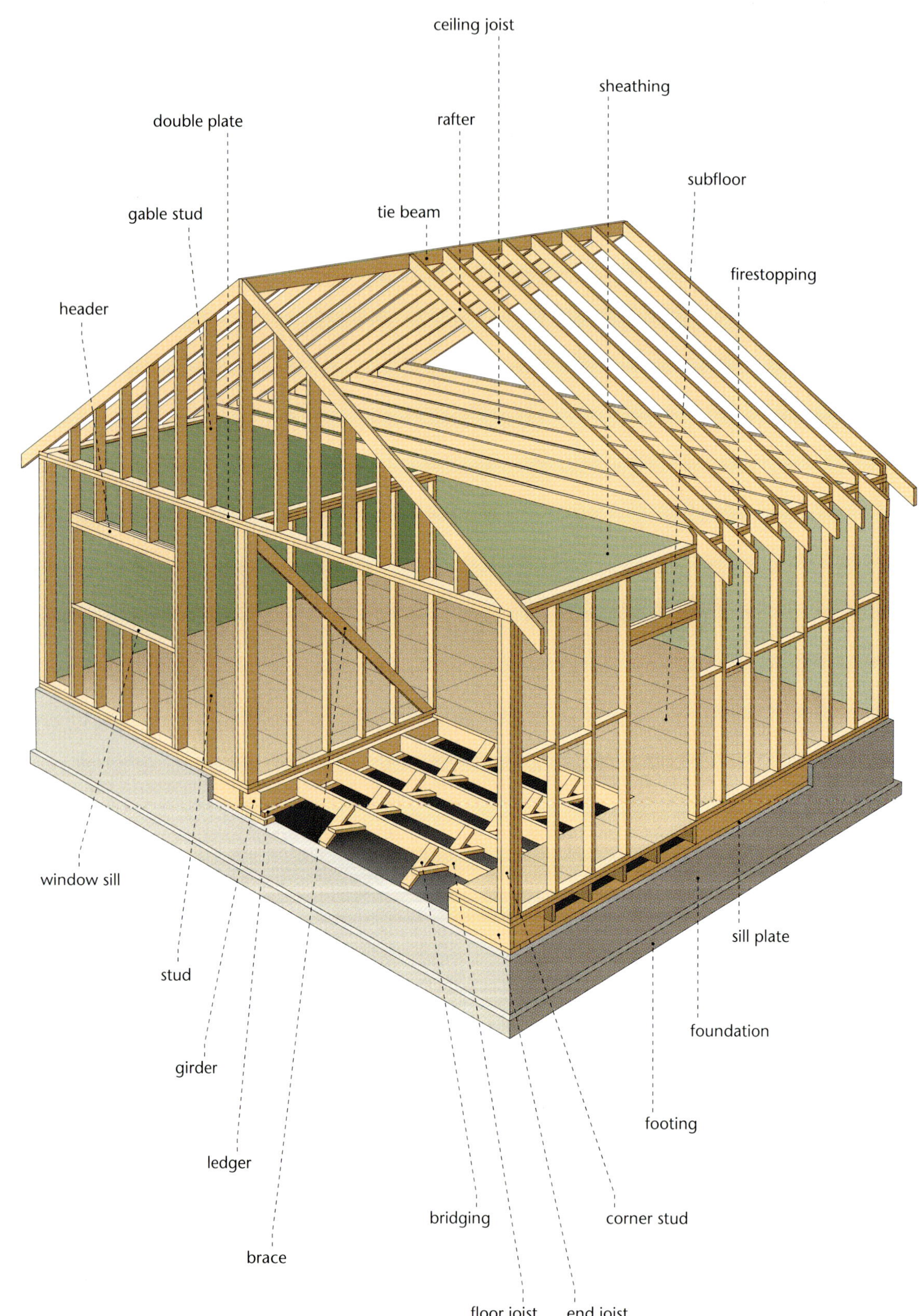

king post
side post
principal rafter
ridge beam
strut

HOUSE

sheathing
subfloor
wall stud
baseboard
brick wall
molding
insulating material
wood flooring
sill
foundation
floor joist
end joist
sill plate
footing
gravel
drain tile

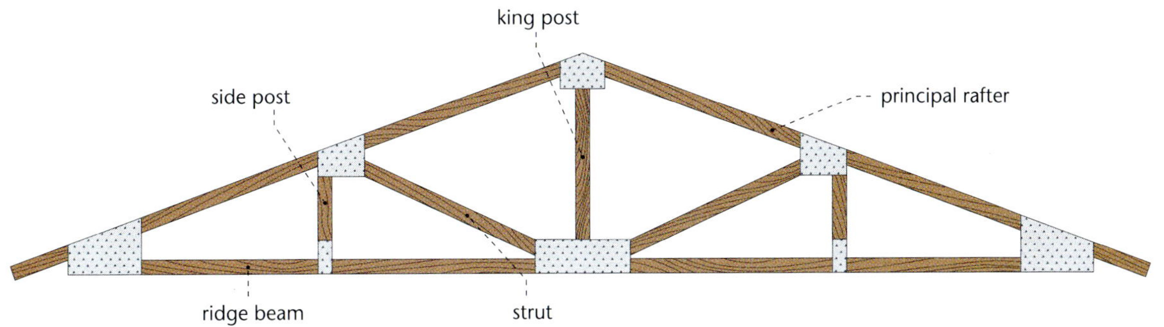

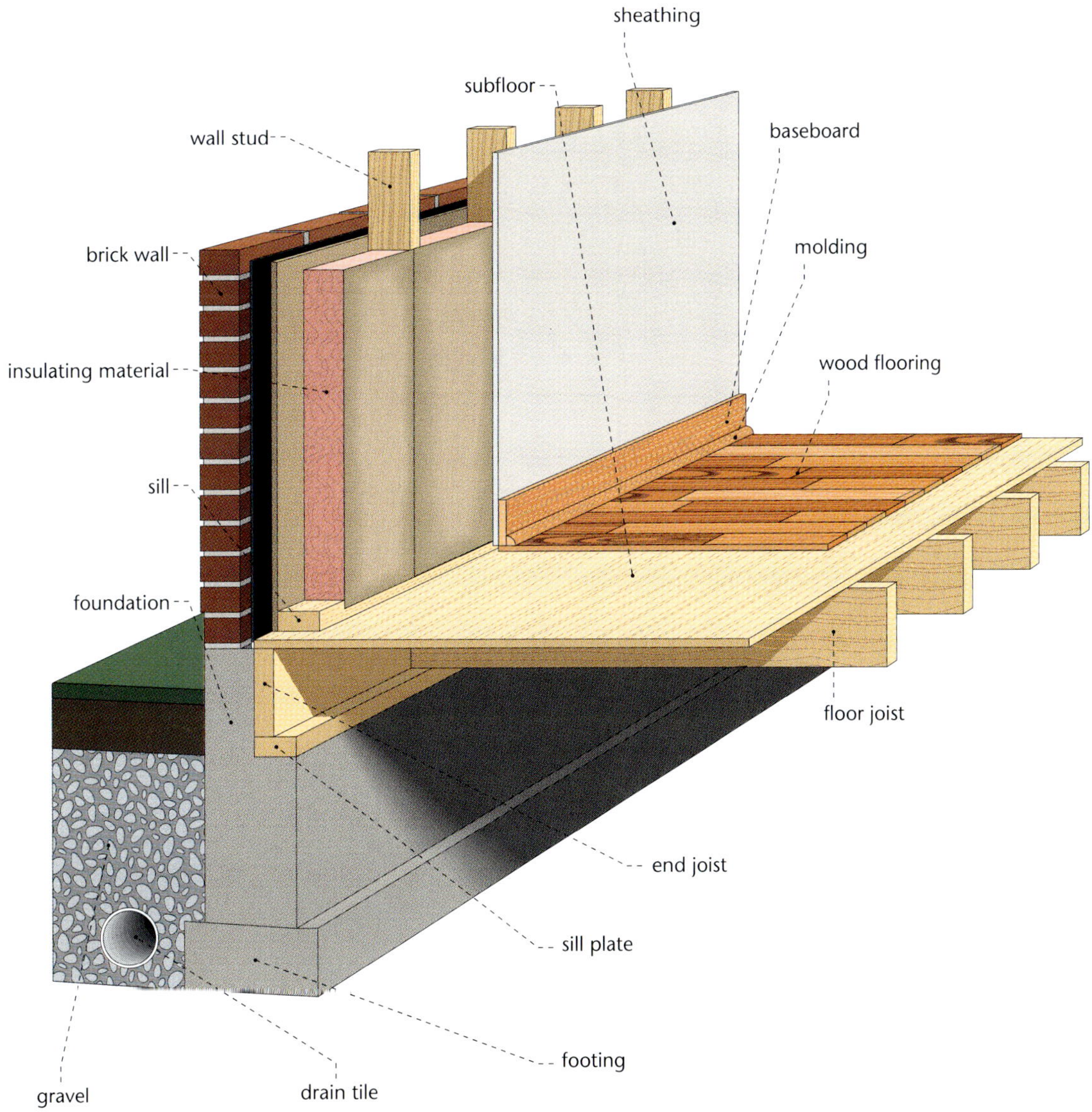

WOOD FLOORING ON CEMENT SCREED

WOOD FLOORING ON WOODEN STRUCTURE

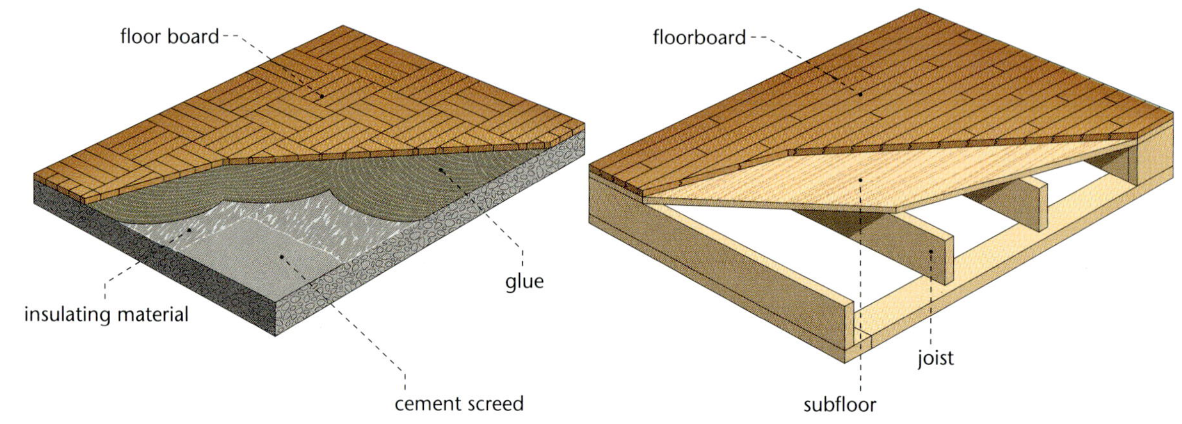

WOOD FLOORING ARRANGEMENTS

overlay flooring

strip flooring with alternate joints

herringbone parquet

herringbone pattern

inlaid parquet

basket weave pattern

Arenberg parquet

Chantilly parquet

Versailles parquet

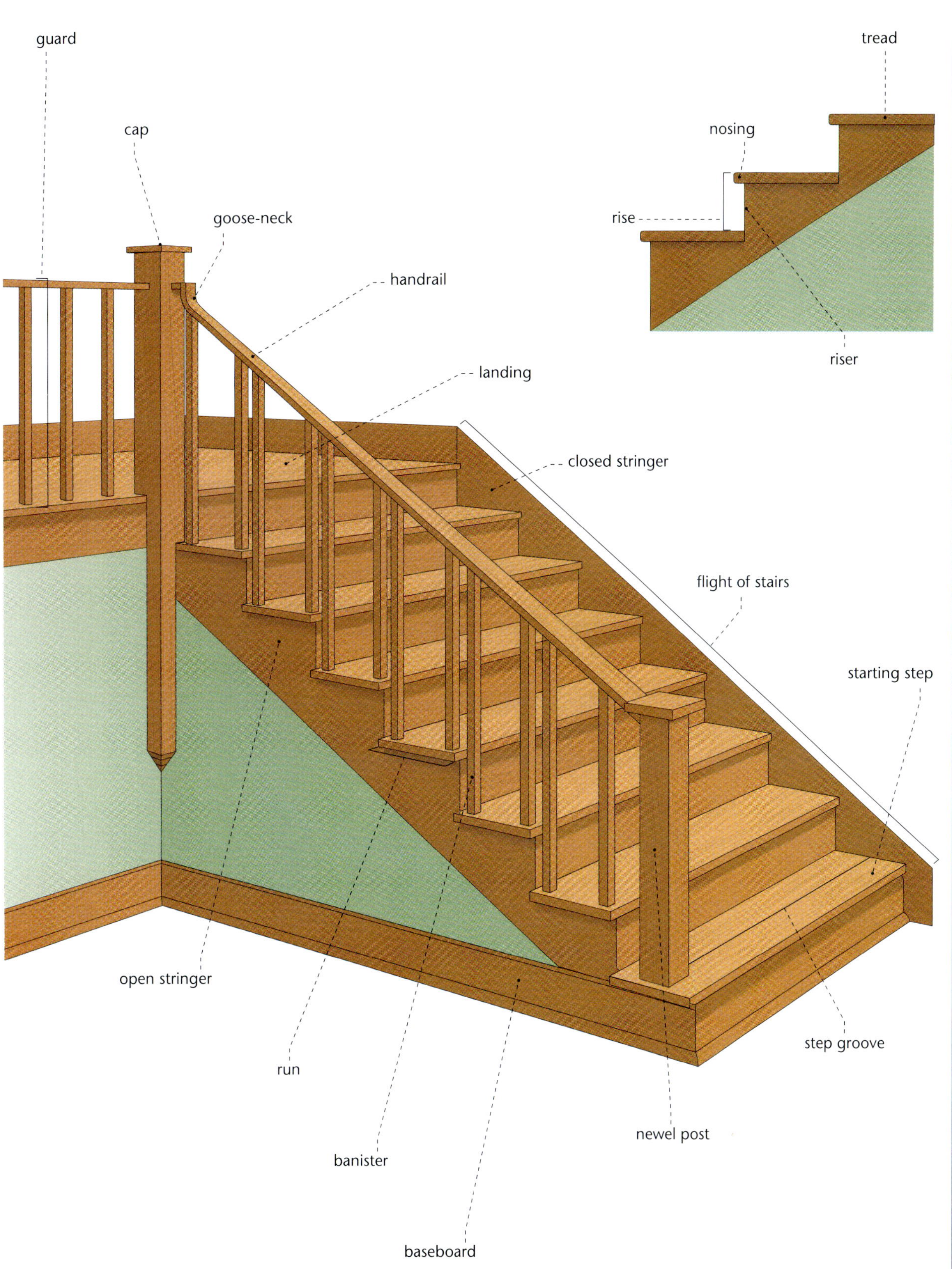

guard
cap
goose-neck
handrail
landing
closed stringer
flight of stairs
starting step
open stringer
run
banister
baseboard
newel post
step groove
tread
nosing
rise
riser

DOOR

EXTERIOR DOOR

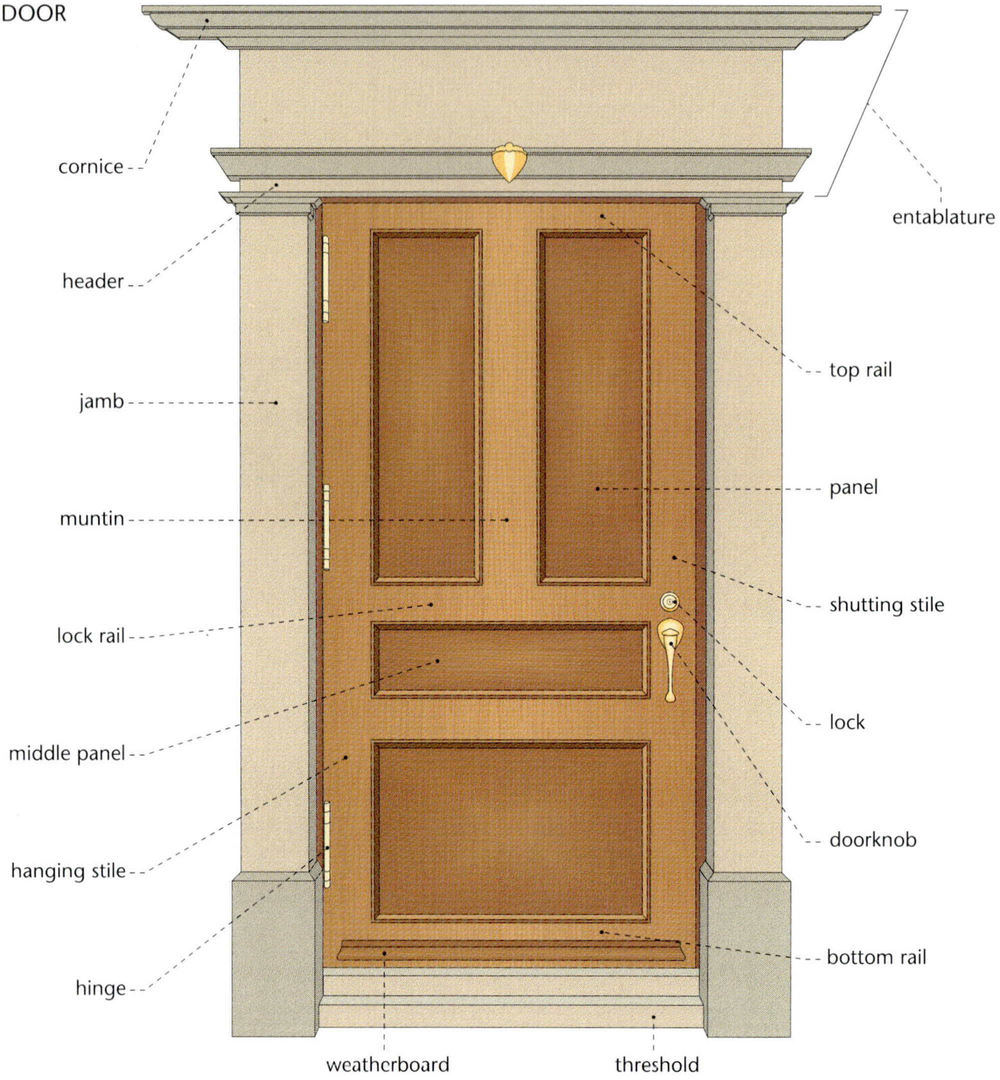

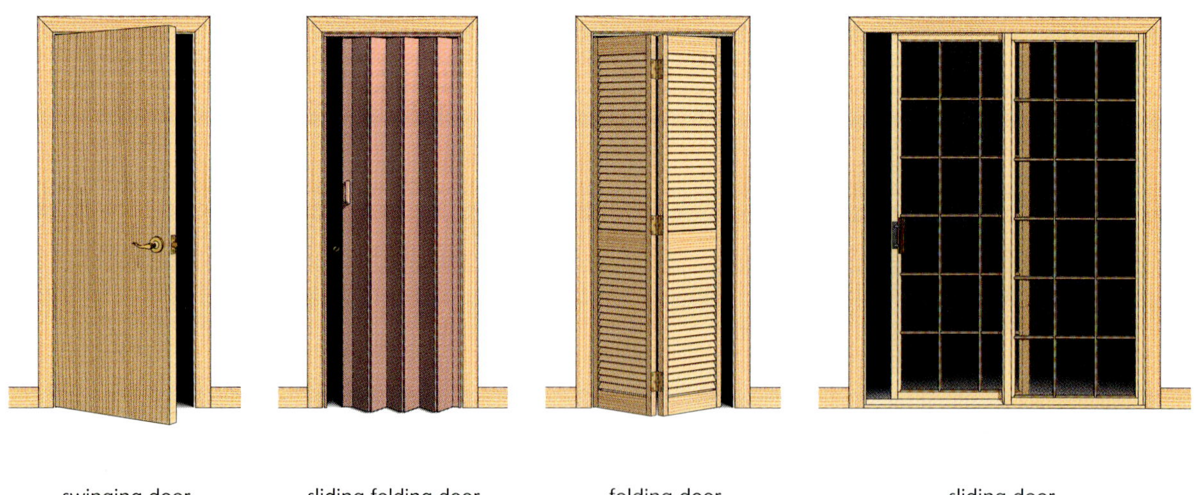

cornice
header
jamb
muntin
lock rail
middle panel
hanging stile
hinge
weatherboard
threshold
entablature
top rail
panel
shutting stile
lock
doorknob
bottom rail

TYPES OF DOORS

swinging door

sliding folding door

folding door

sliding door

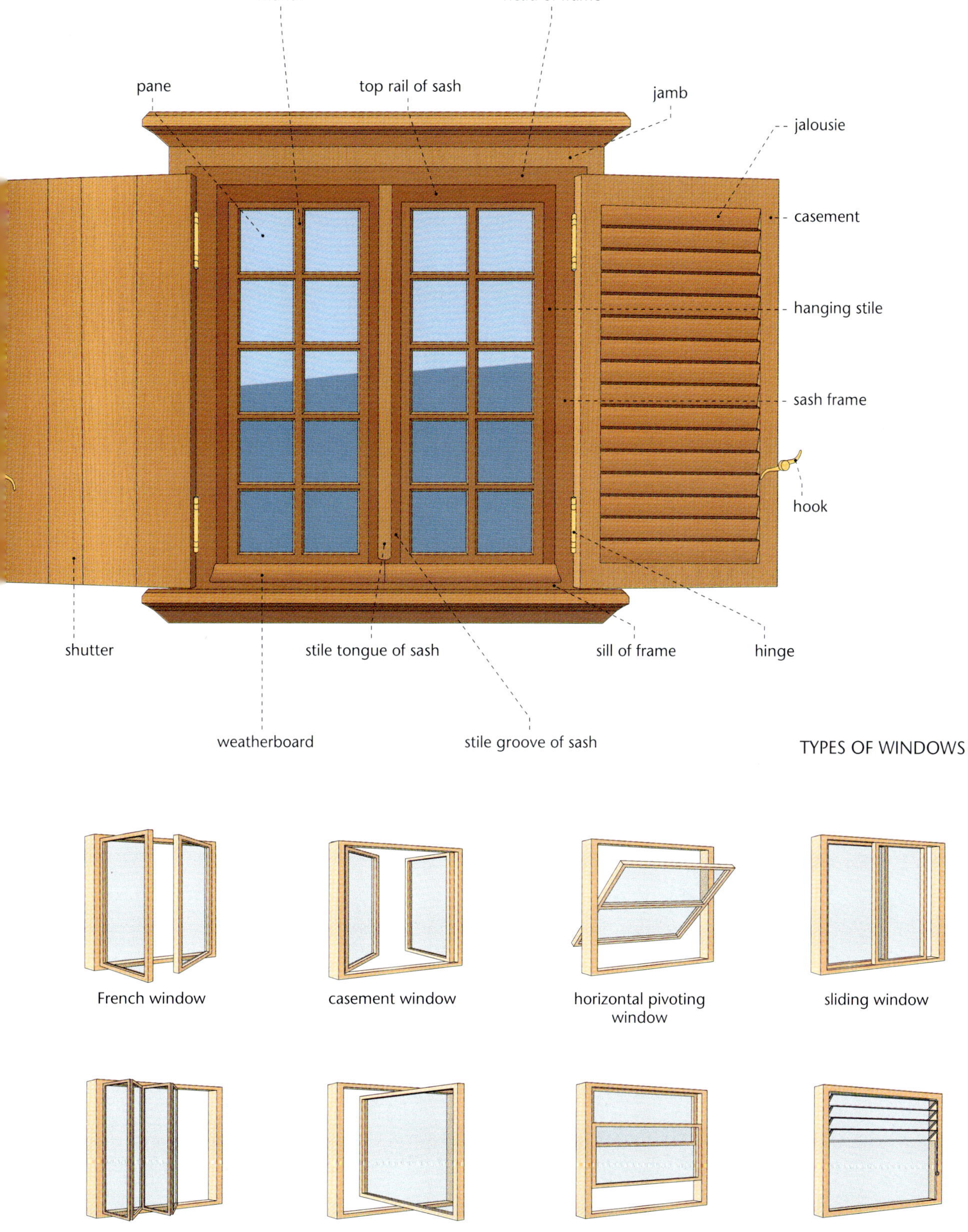

TYPES OF WINDOWS

French window

casement window

horizontal pivoting window

sliding window

sliding folding window

vertical pivoting window

sash window

louvered window

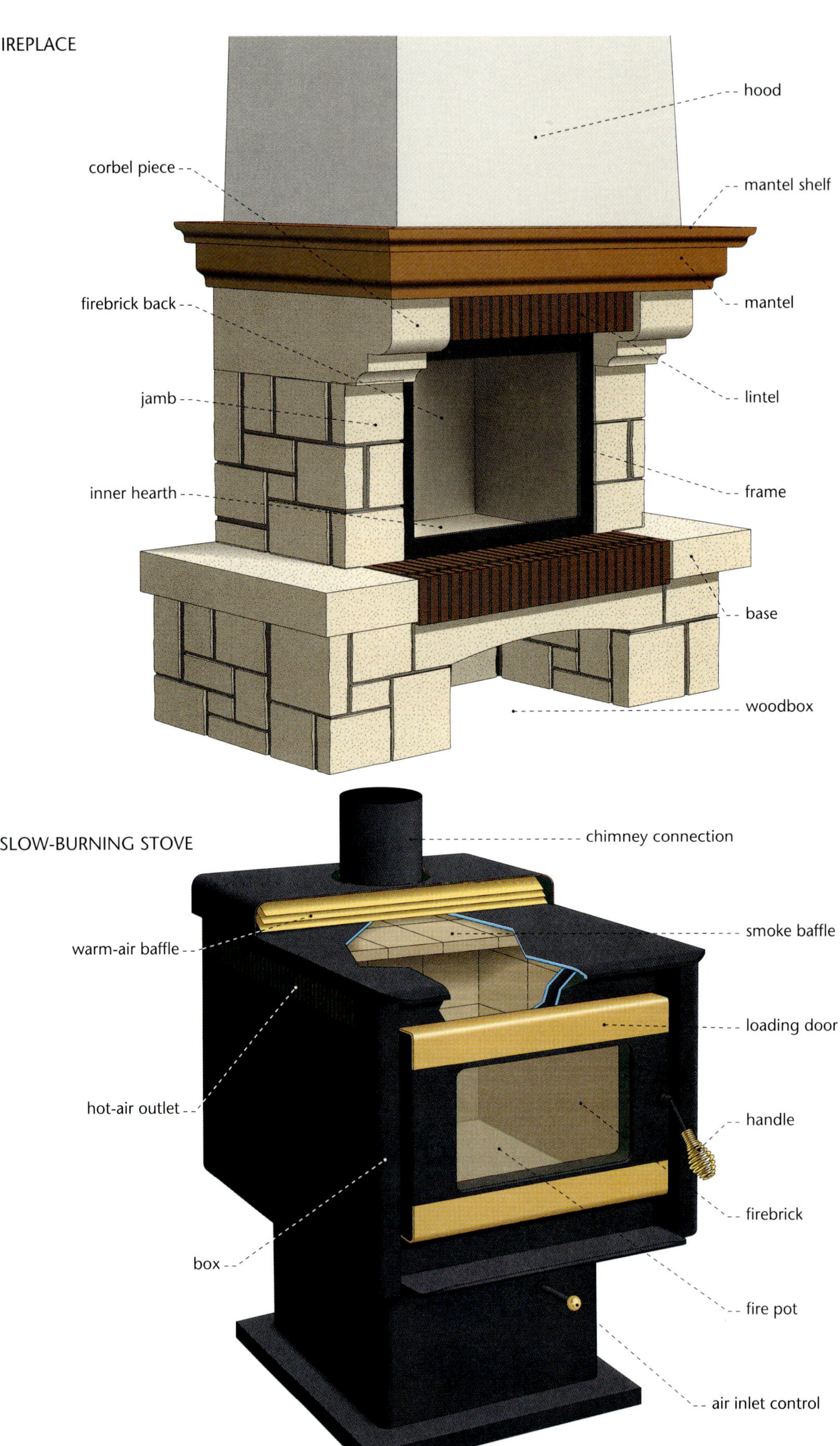
FIREPLACE
hood
corbel piece
mantel shelf
firebrick back
mantel
jamb
lintel
inner hearth
frame
base
woodbox
SLOW-BURNING STOVE
chimney connection
smoke baffle
warm-air baffle
loading door
hot-air outlet
handle
firebrick
box
fire pot
air inlet control

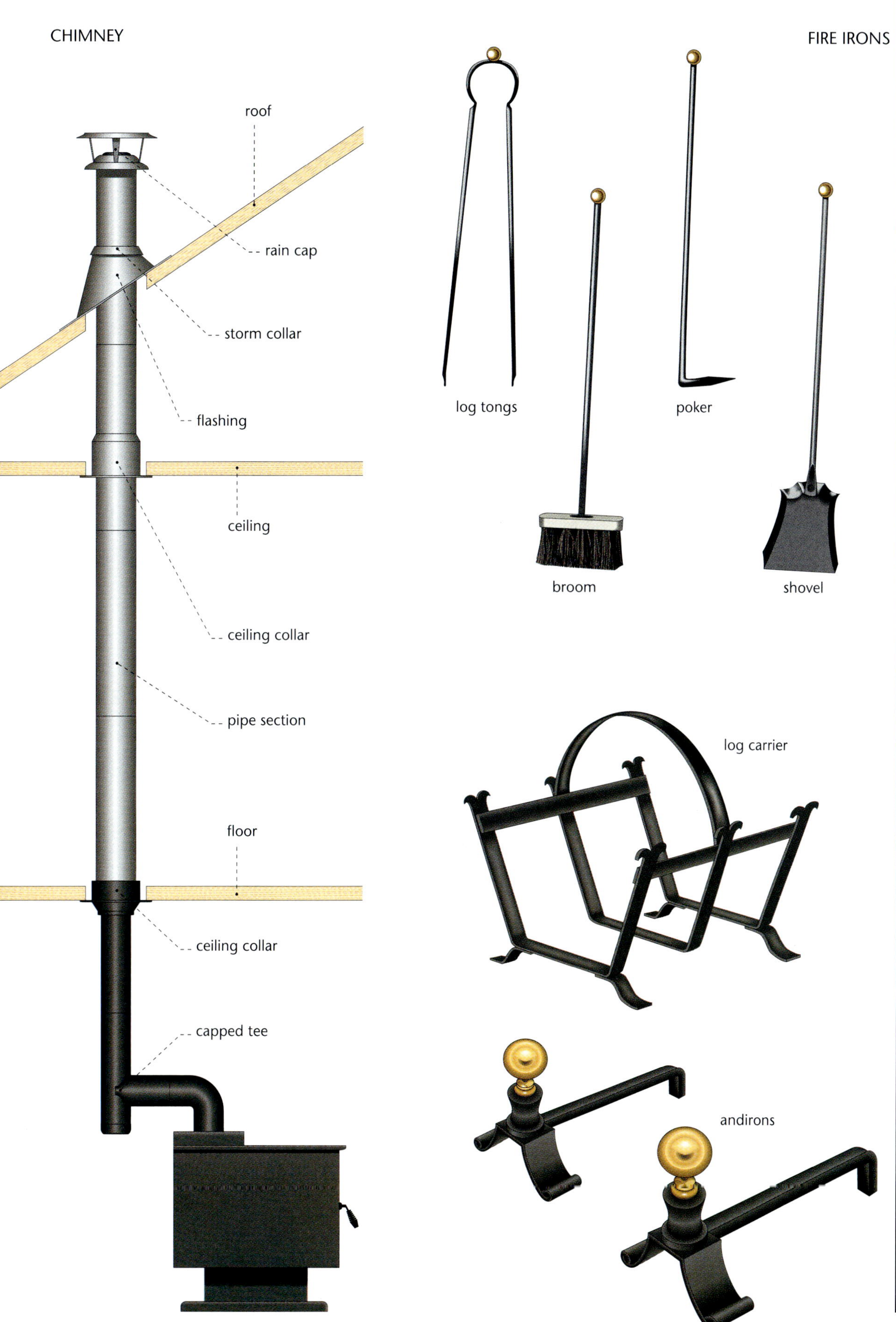
roof
rain cap
storm collar
flashing
ceiling
ceiling collar
pipe section
floor
ceiling collar
capped tee
log tongs
poker
broom
shovel
log carrier
andirons

FORCED WARM-AIR SYSTEM

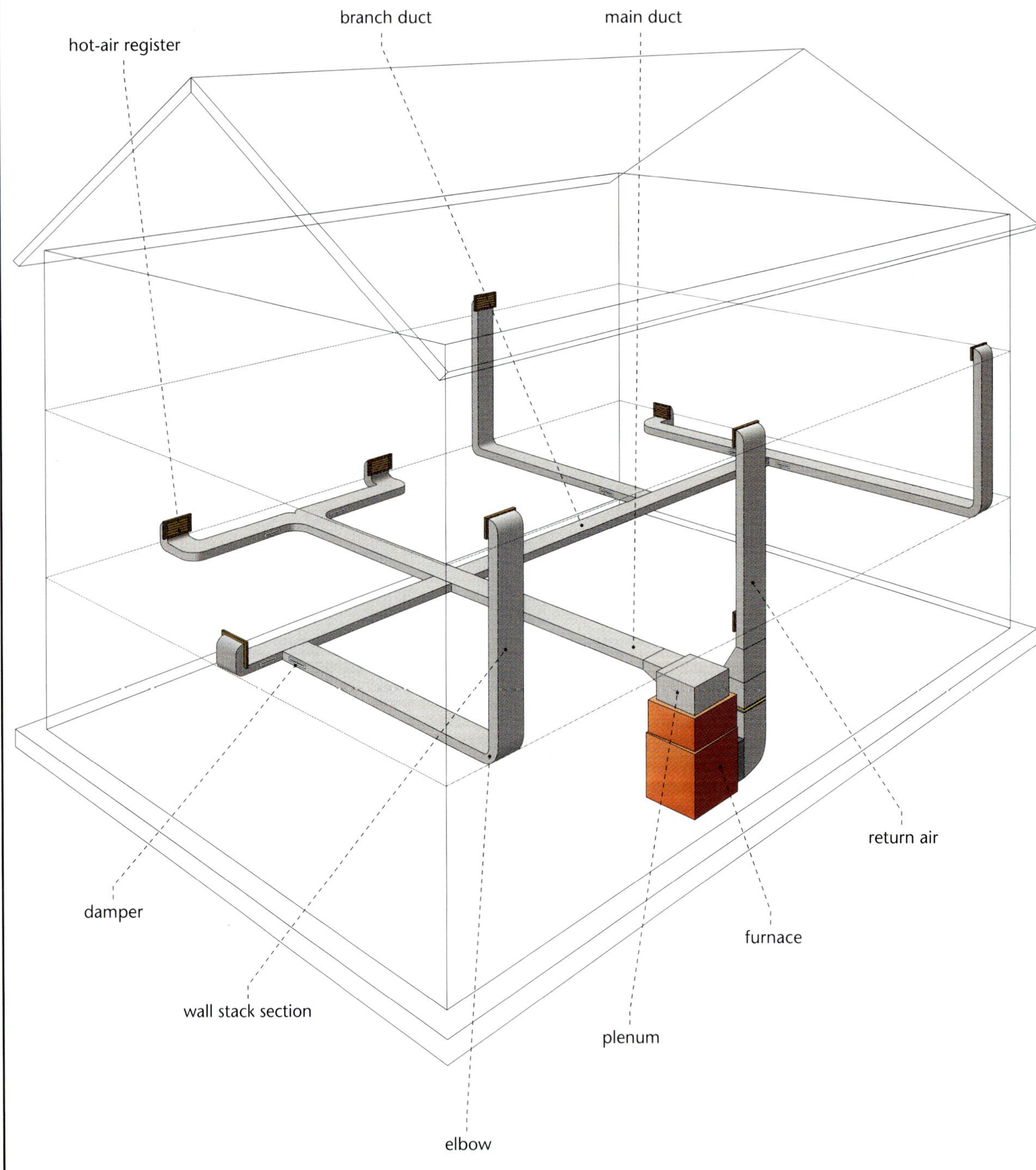

ELECTRIC FURNACE

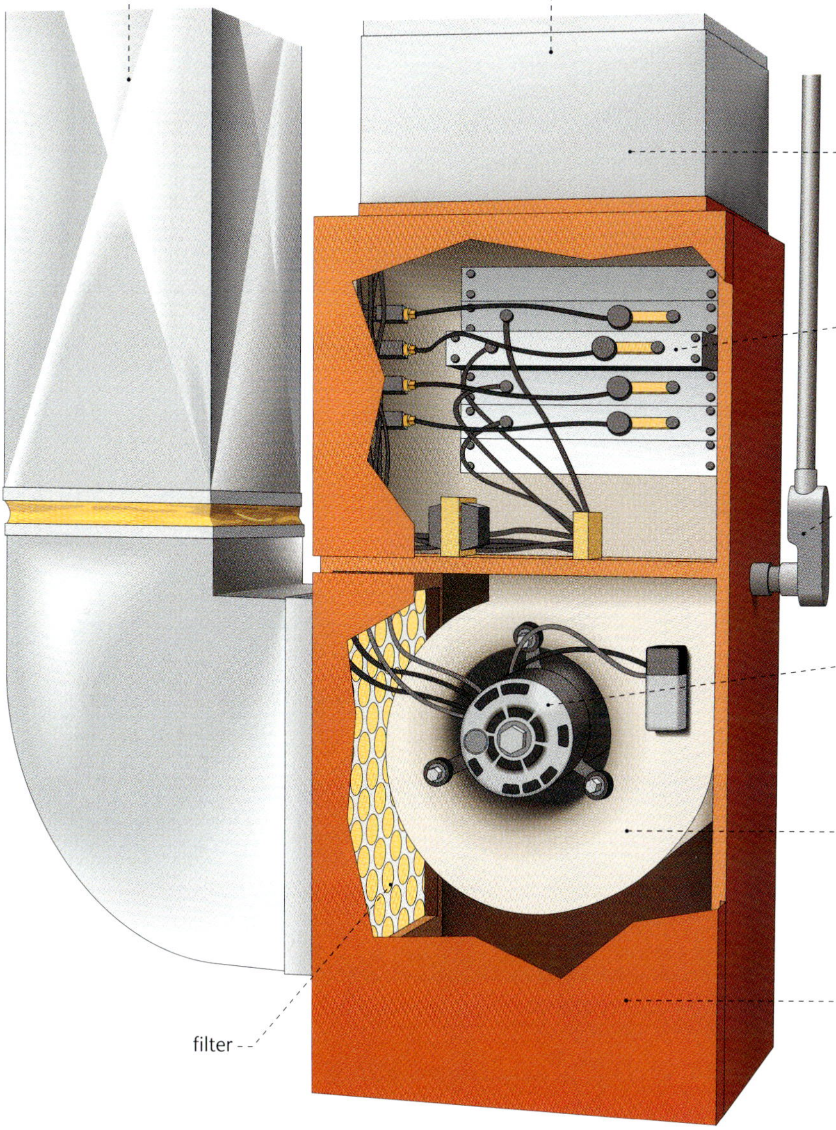

TYPES OF REGISTERS

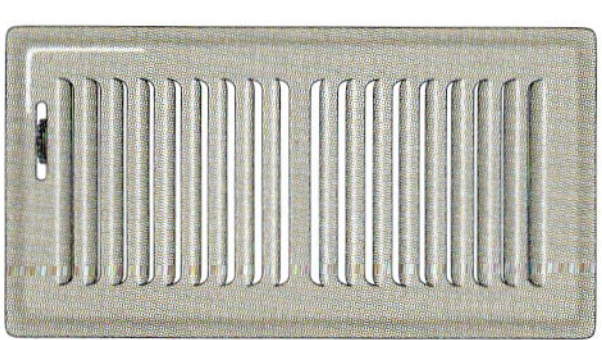

baseboard register

ceiling register

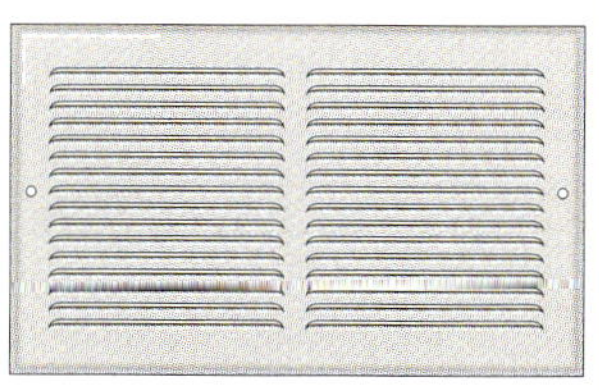

wall register

FORCED HOT-WATER SYSTEM

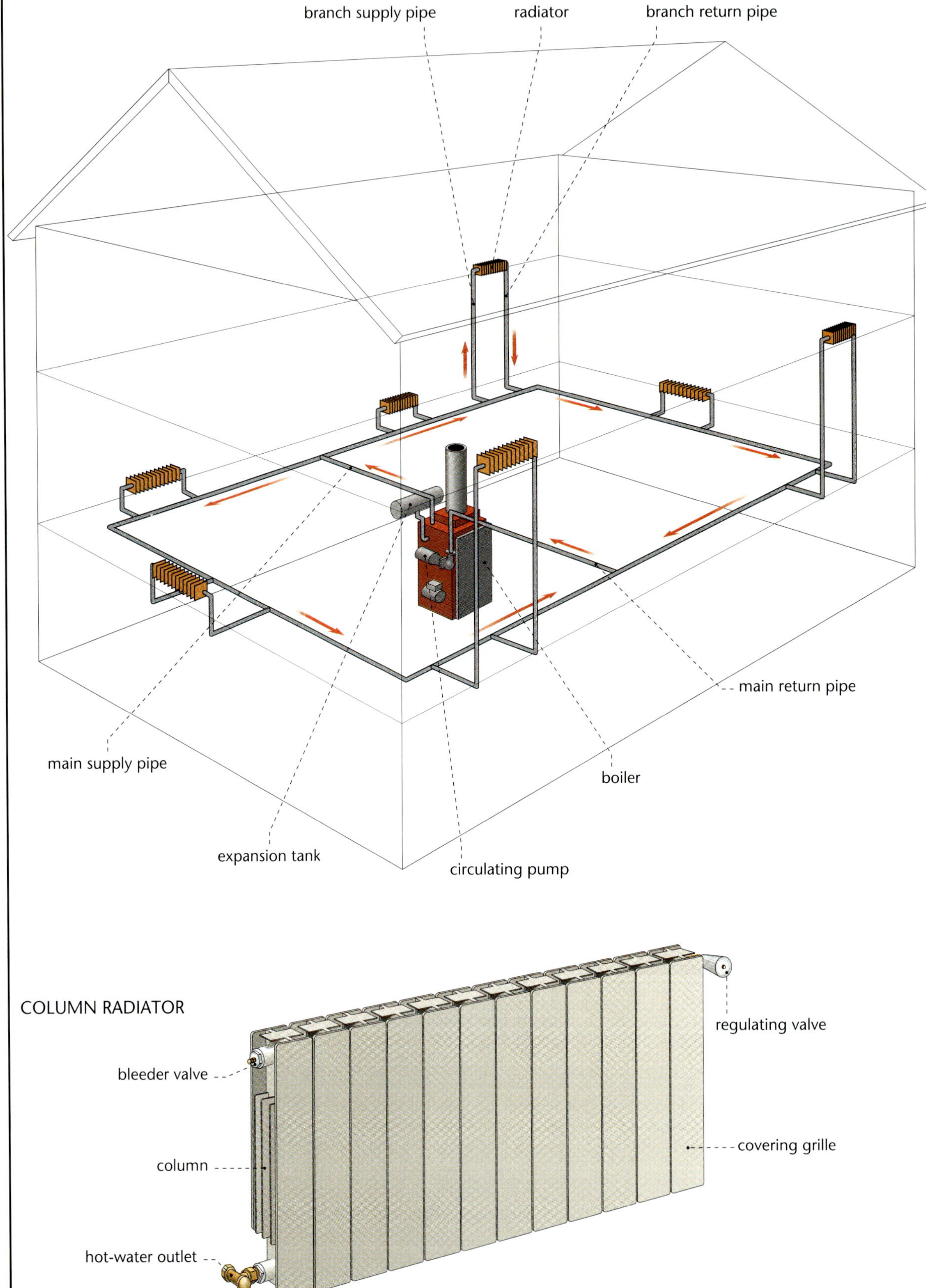

COLUMN RADIATOR

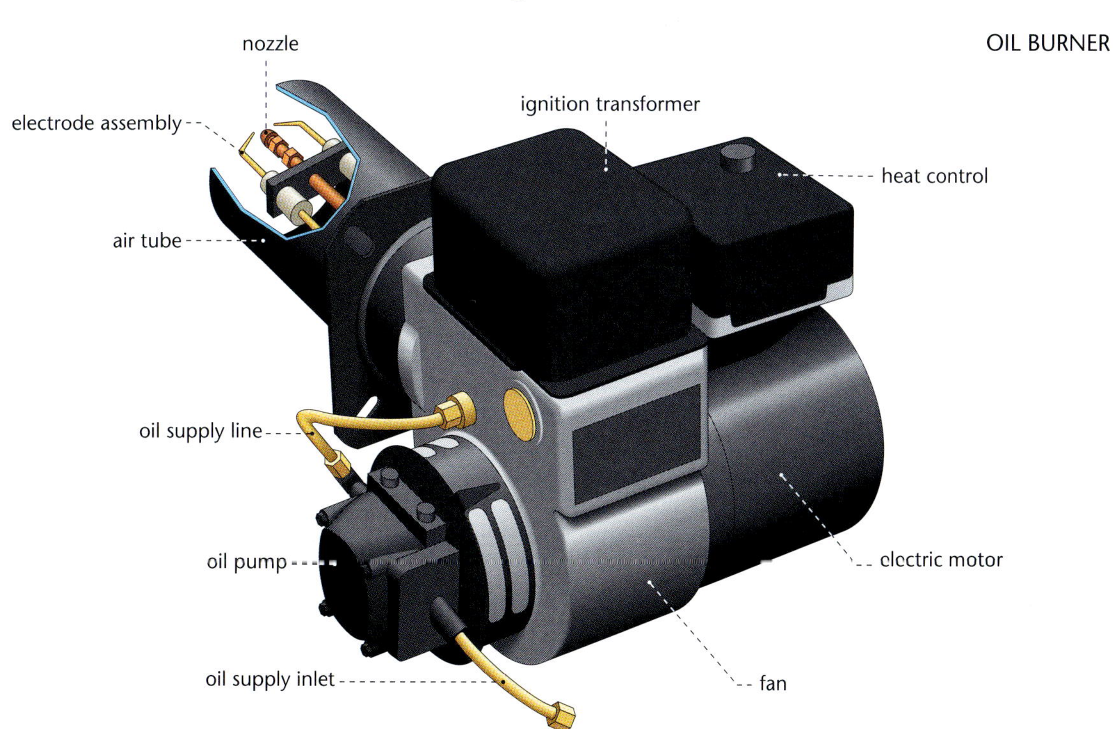
BOILER 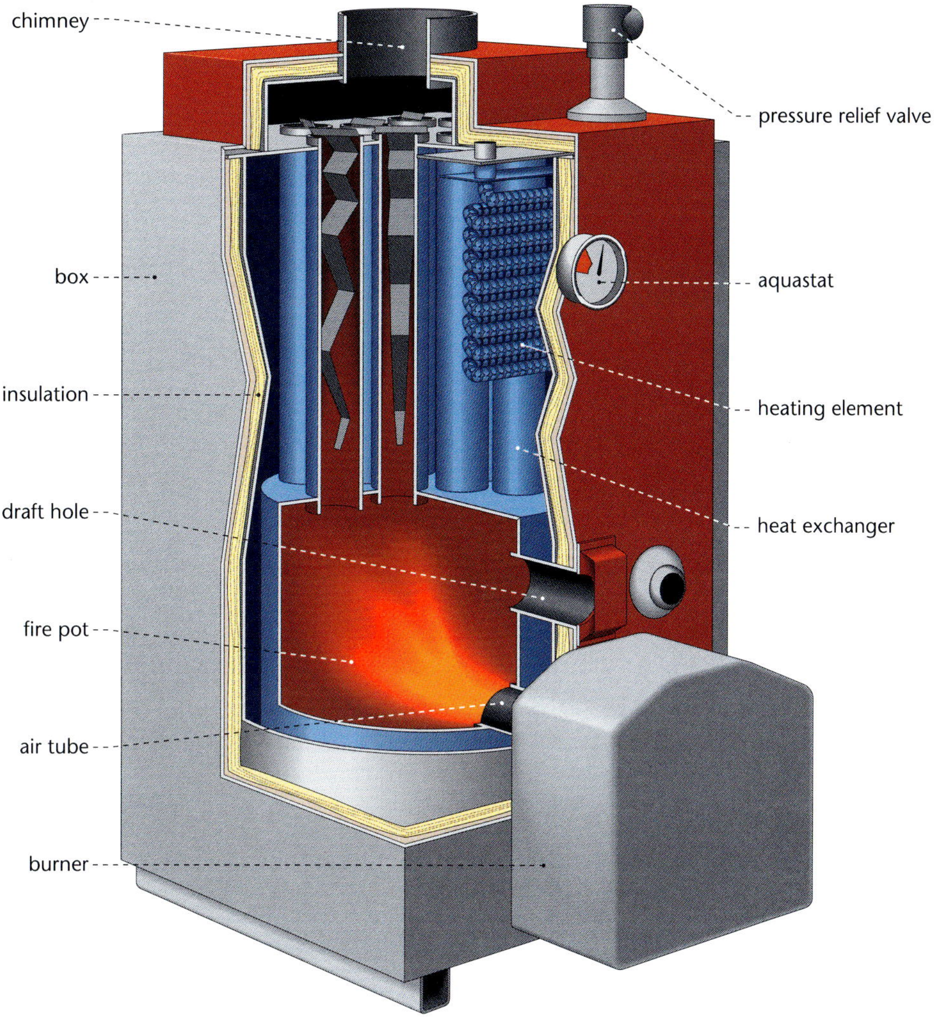
chimney
pressure relief valve
box
aquastat
insulation
heating element
draft hole
heat exchanger
fire pot
air tube
burner
OIL BURNER
nozzle
electrode assembly
ignition transformer
heat control
air tube
oil supply line
oil pump
electric motor
oil supply inlet
fan

HUMIDIFIER

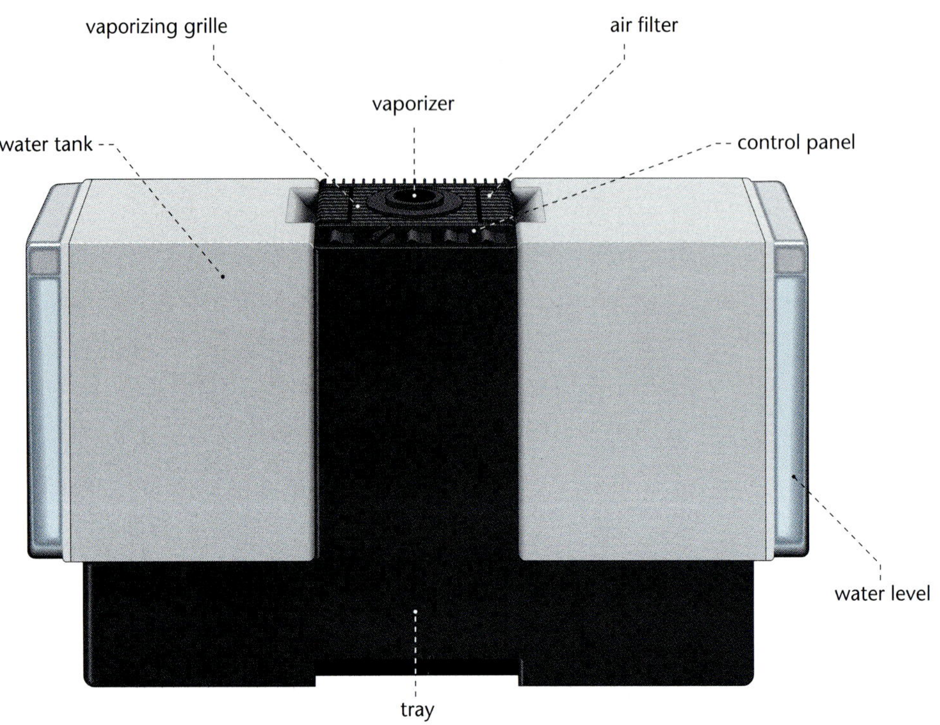

HYGROMETER

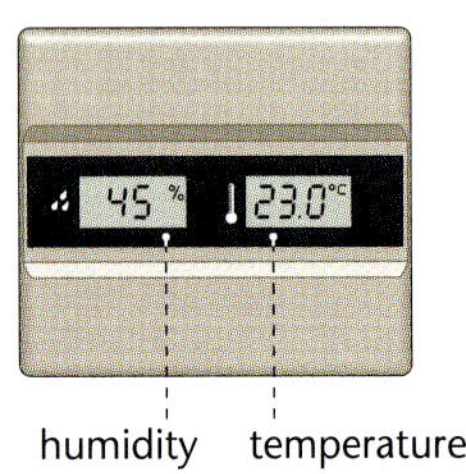

ELECTRIC BASEBOARD RADIATOR

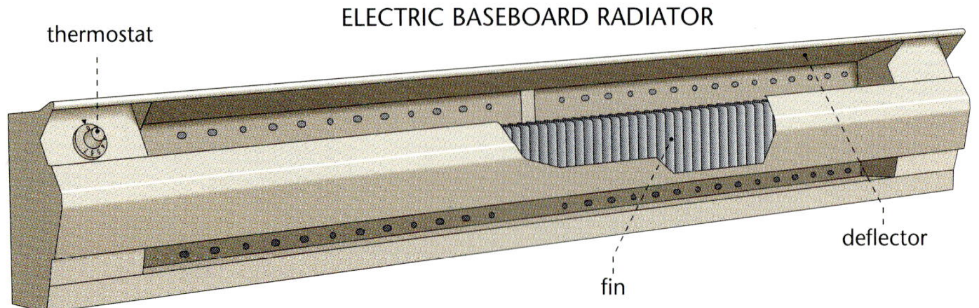

CONVECTOR

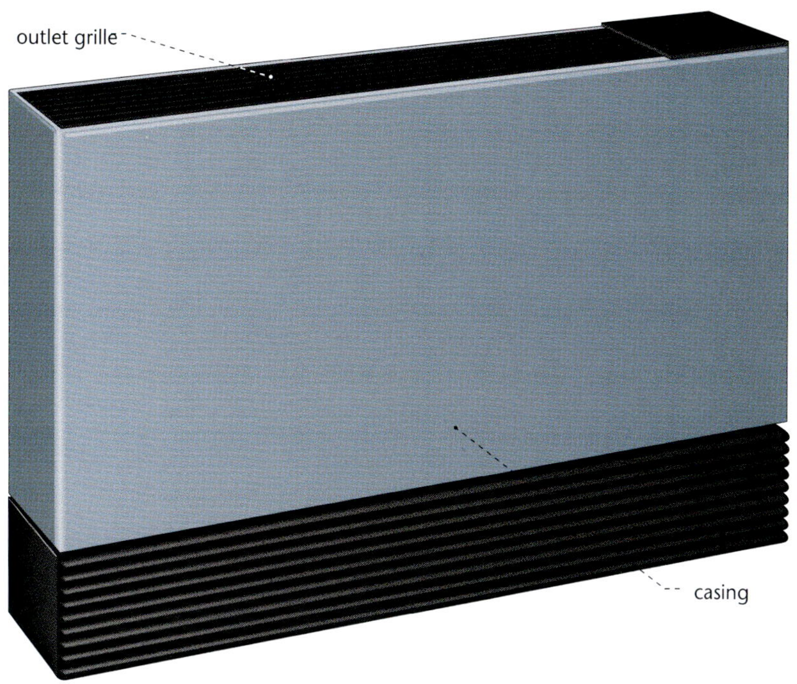

AUXILIARY HEATING

radiant heater

oil-filled heater

fan heater

HEAT PUMP

OUTDOOR UNIT

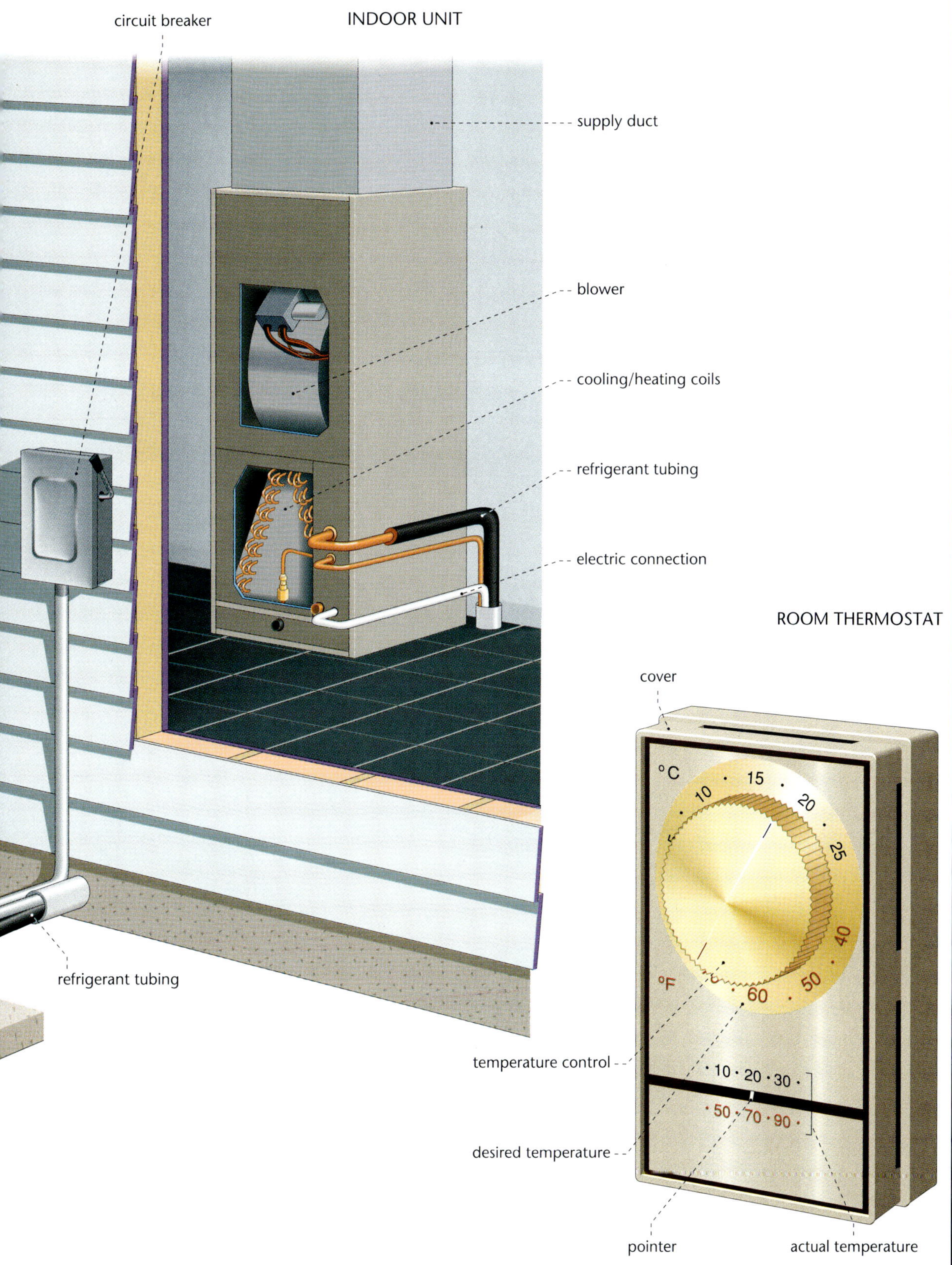

circuit breaker
INDOOR UNIT
supply duct
blower
cooling/heating coils
refrigerant tubing
electric connection
refrigerant tubing
ROOM THERMOSTAT
cover
°C
°F
temperature control
desired temperature
pointer
actual temperature

AIR CONDITIONING

CEILING FAN

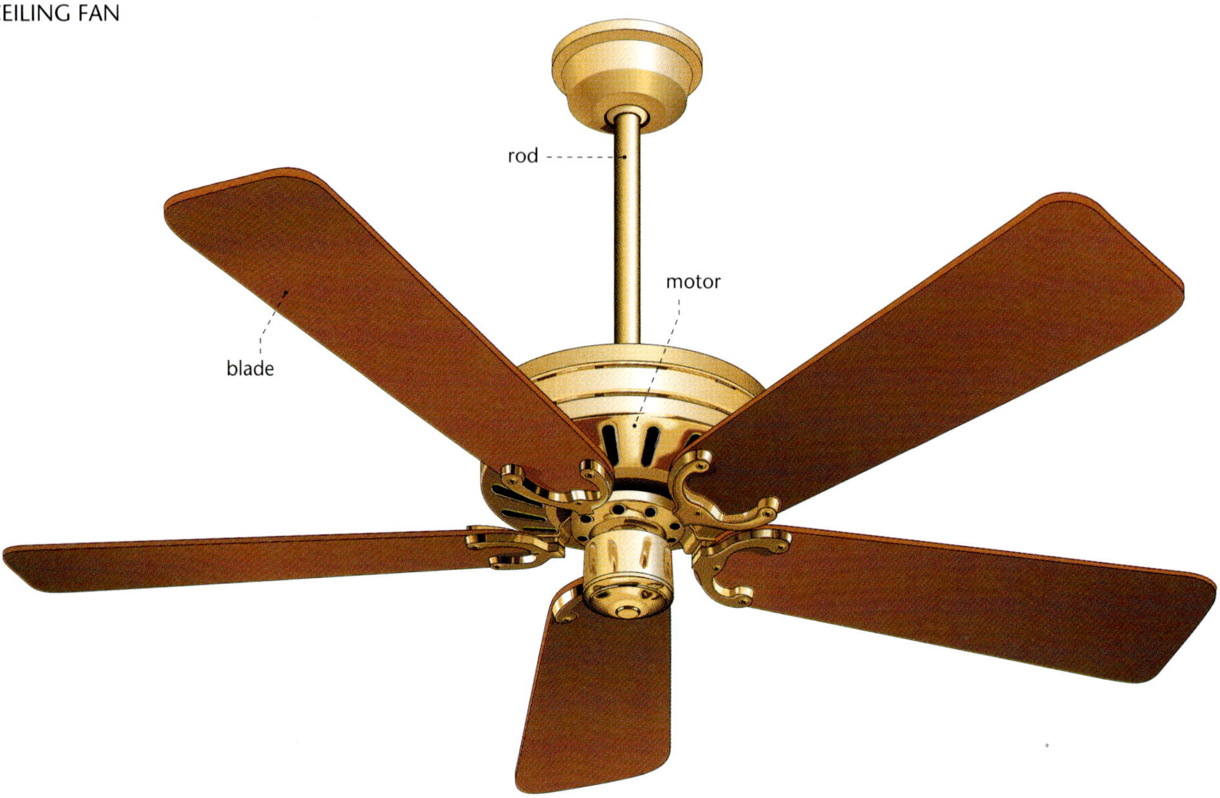

ROOM AIR CONDITIONER

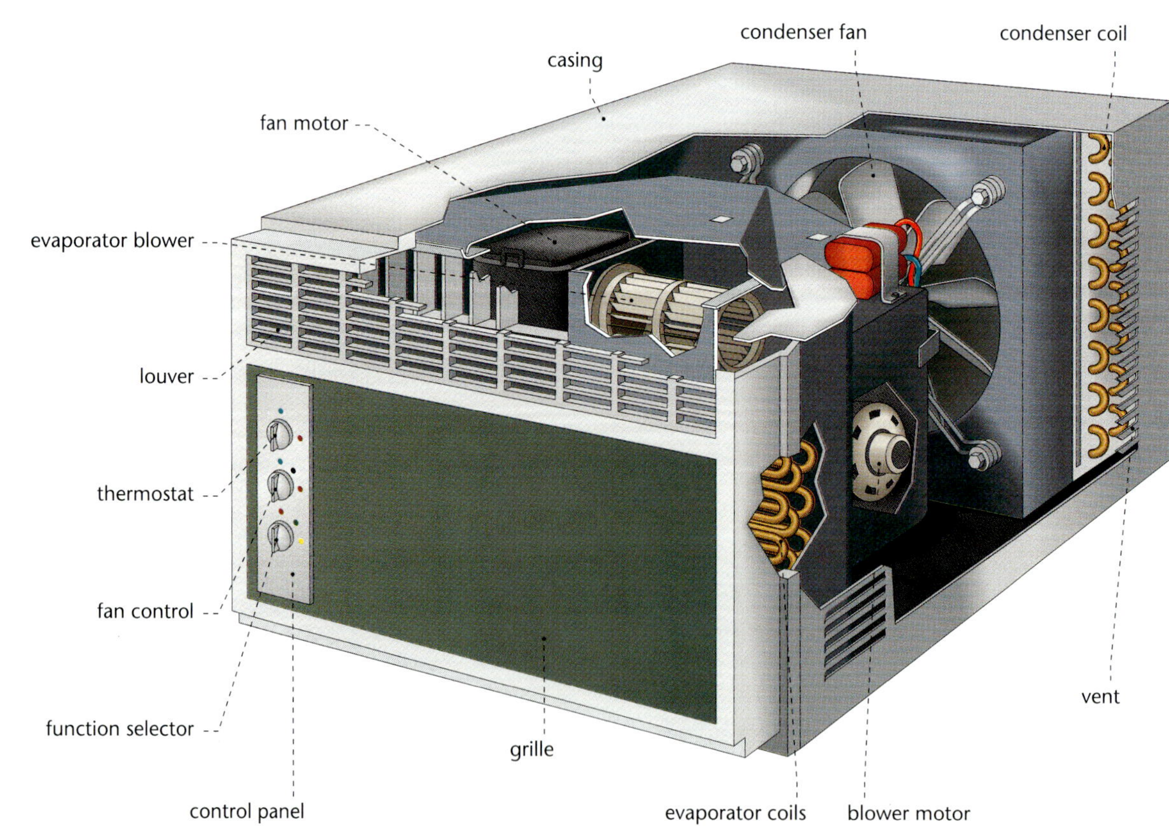

PLUMBING SYSTEM

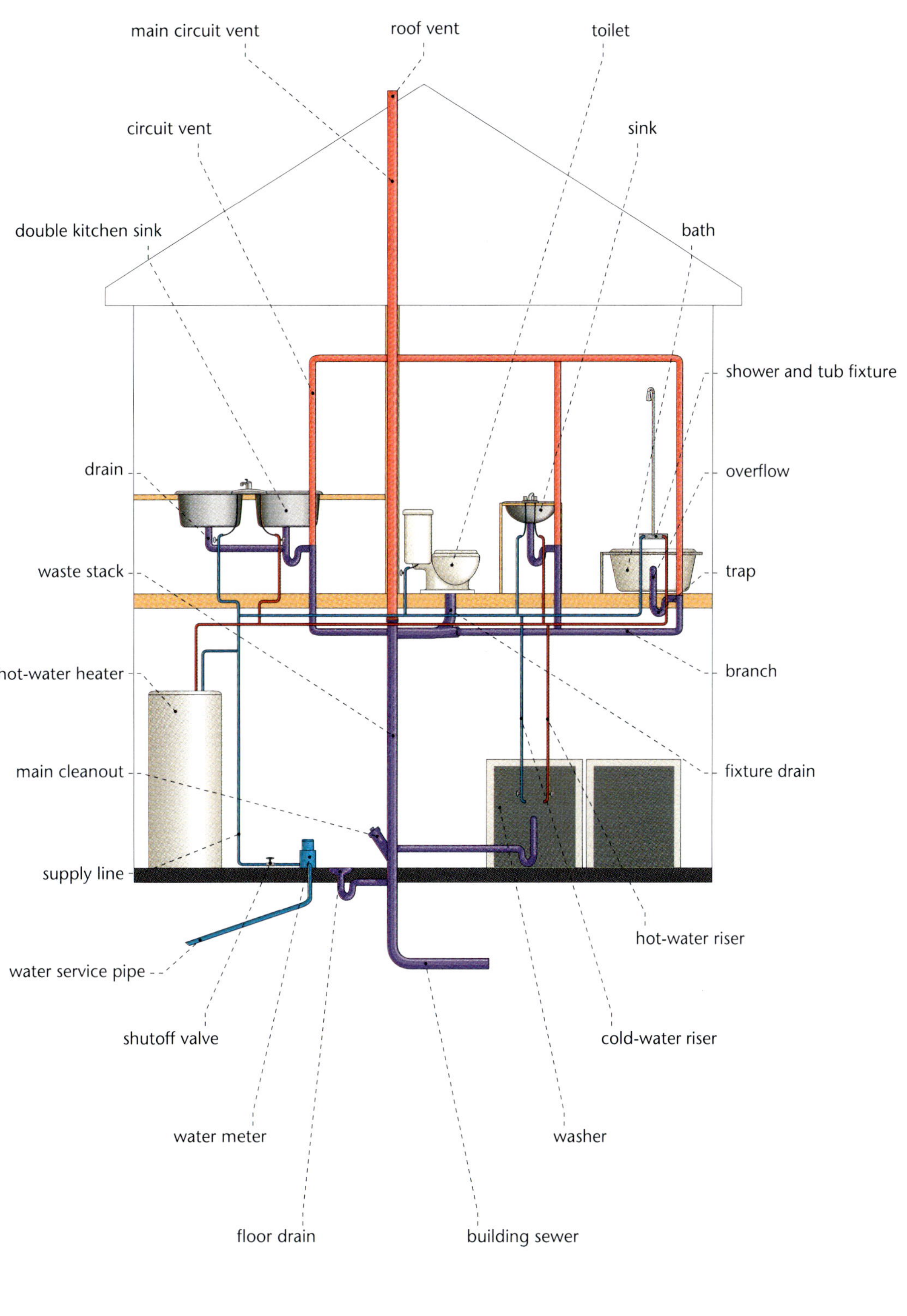

PEDESTAL-TYPE SUMP PUMP

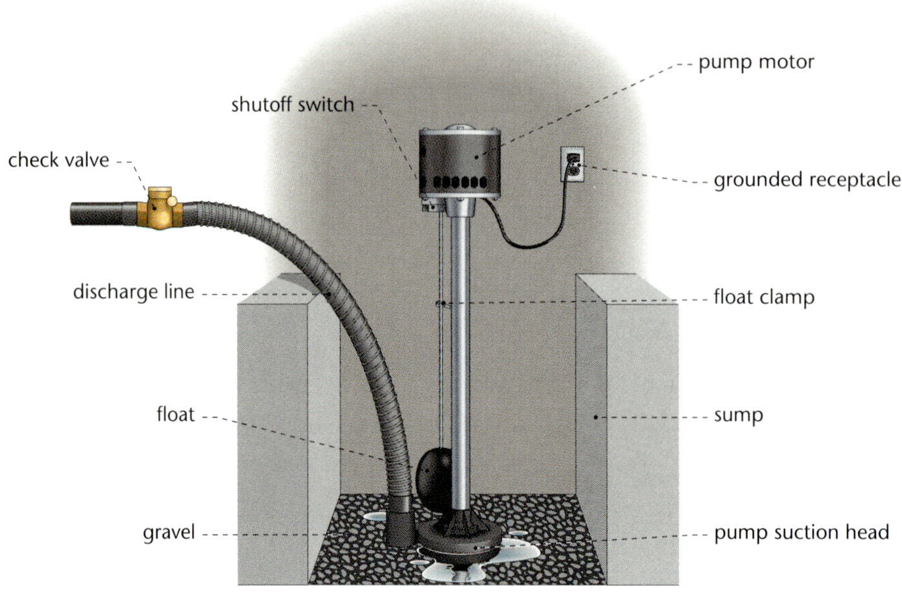

SEPTIC TANK

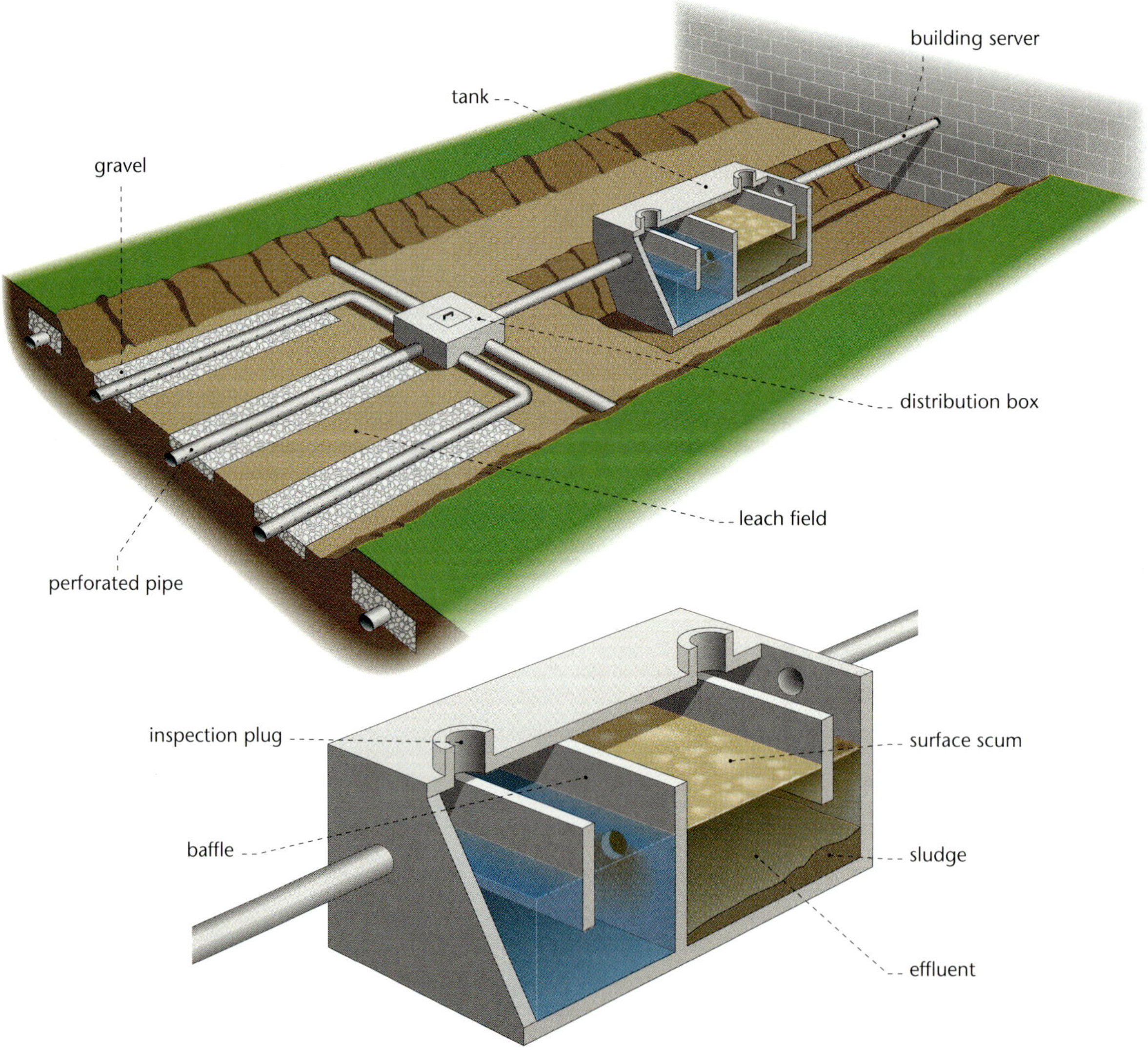

HOUSE FURNITURE

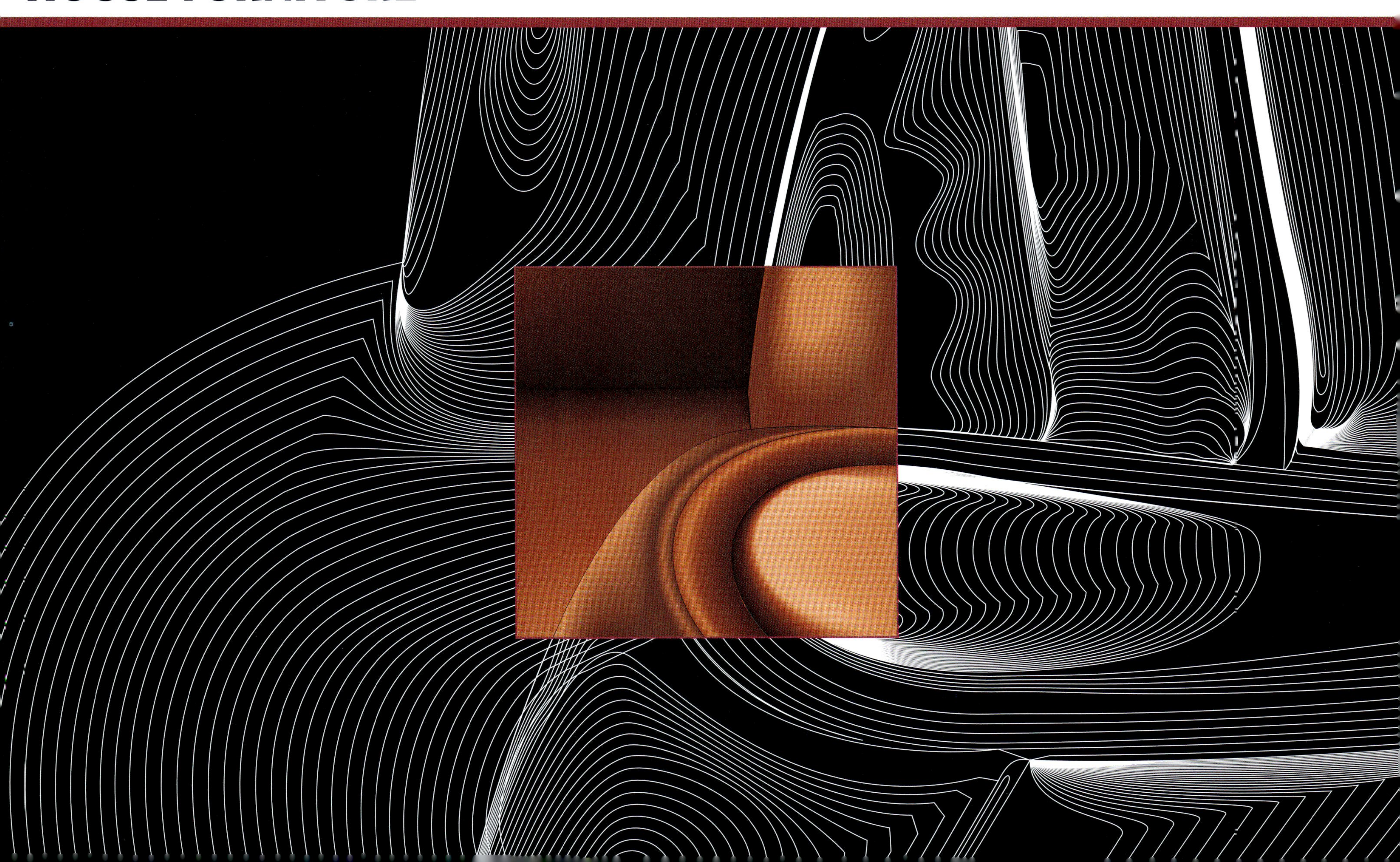

CONTENTS

TABLE

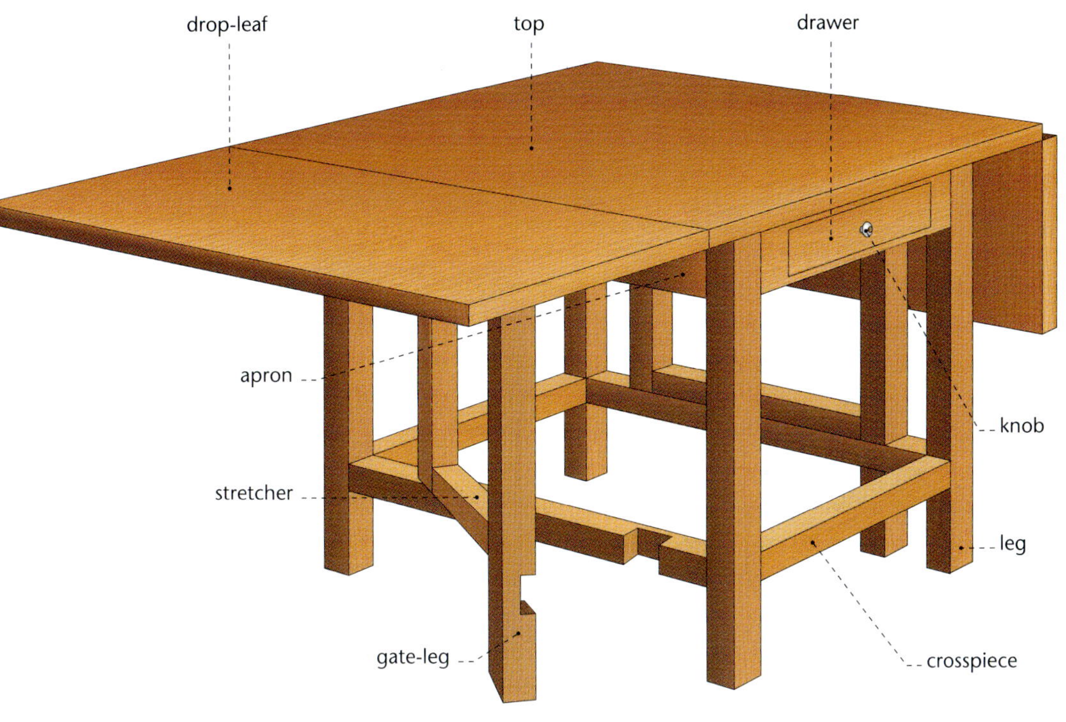

GATE-LEG TABLE

drop-leaf
top
drawer
apron
knob
stretcher
leg
gate-leg
crosspiece

MAJOR TYPES OF TABLES

extension table

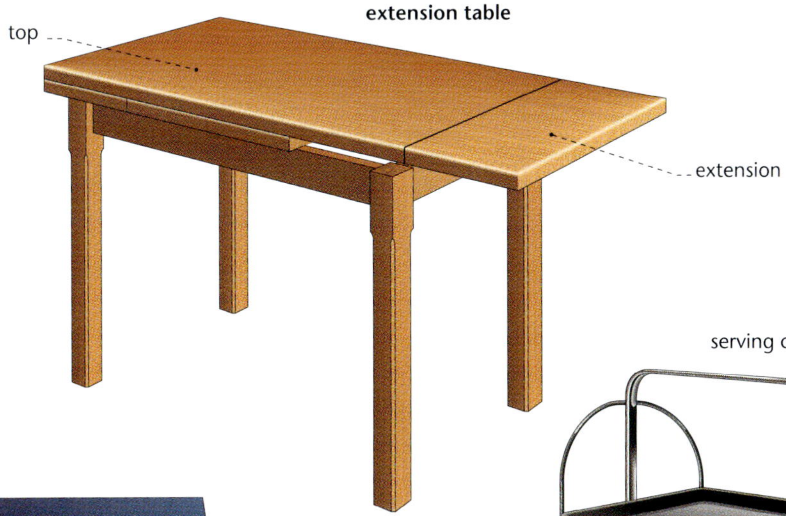

top
extension

serving cart

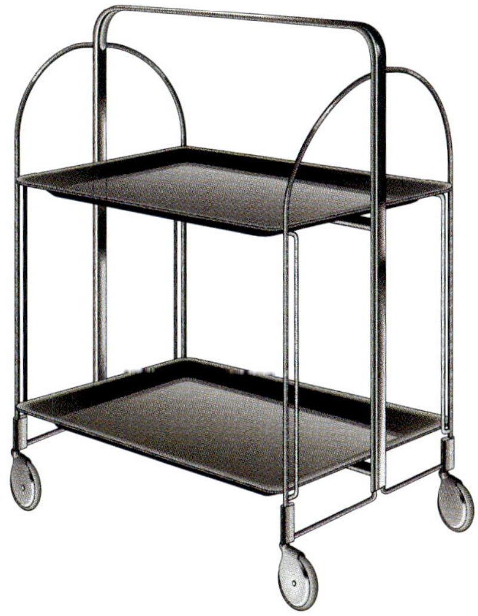

nest of tables

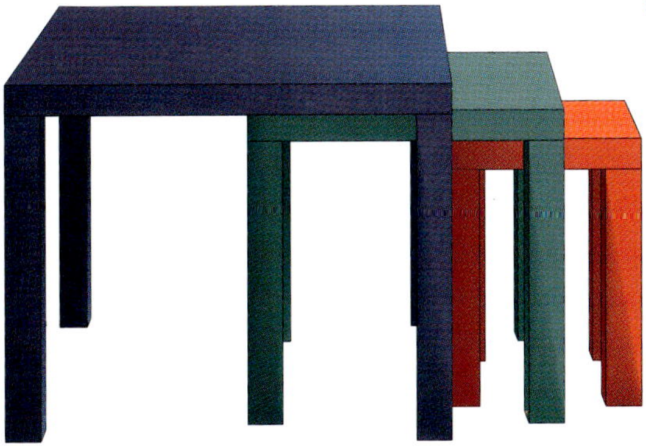

HOUSE FURNITURE

PARTS

PRINCIPAL TYPES OF ARMCHAIRS

bergère

cabriolet

director's chair

sofa

love seat

récamier

chesterfield

méridienne

Wassily chair

rocking chair

club chair

banquette

ottoman

bean bag chair

bench

bar stool

footstool

step chair

SIDE CHAIR

TYPES OF CHAIRS

HOUSE FURNITURE

PARTS

footboard
handle
mattress cover
mattress
headboard
pillow protector
bolster
elastic
box spring
pillow
leg

LINEN

sham
pillowcase
scatter cushion
neckroll
comforter
blanket
valance
flat sheet
fitted sheet

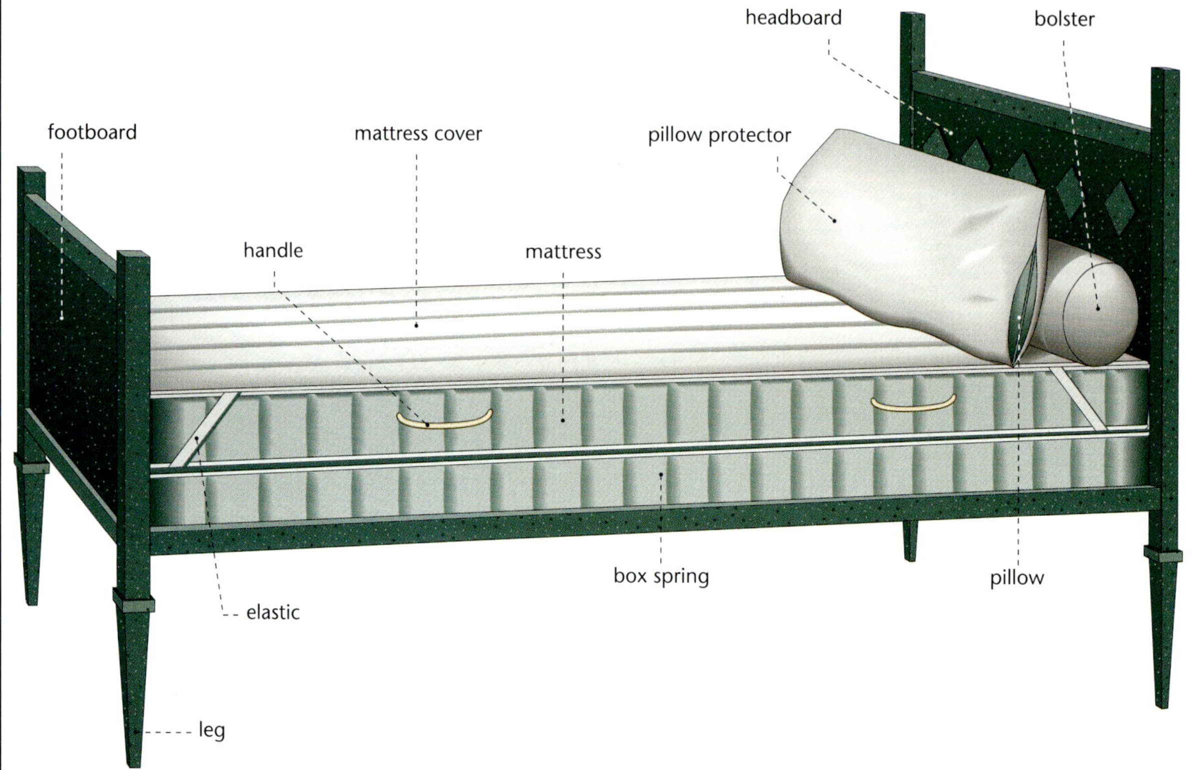

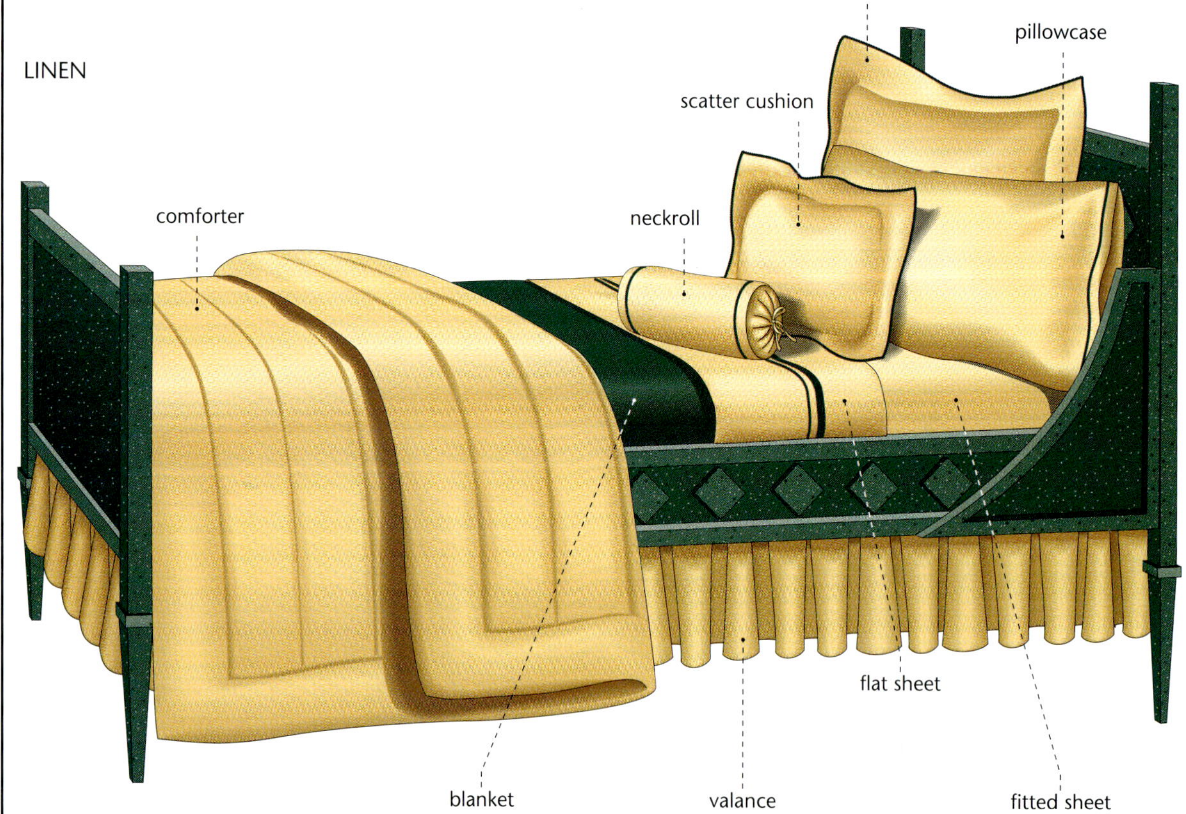

frieze
center post
cornice
top rail
door panel
diamond point
lock
hanging stile
rail
frame stile
hinge
peg
bottom rail
foot
bracket base
frame
door

ARMOIRE

linen chest

dresser

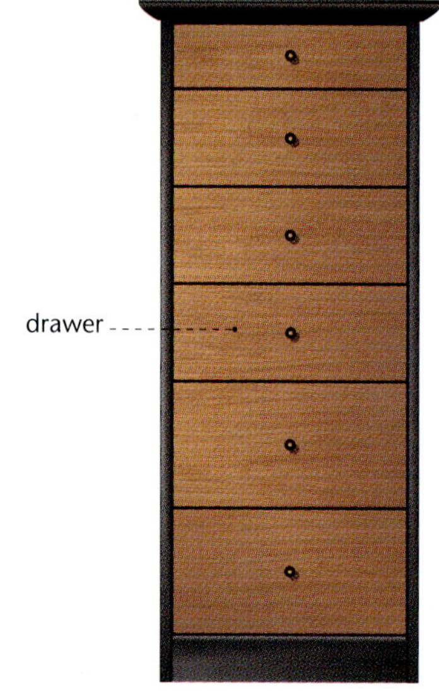

chiffonier

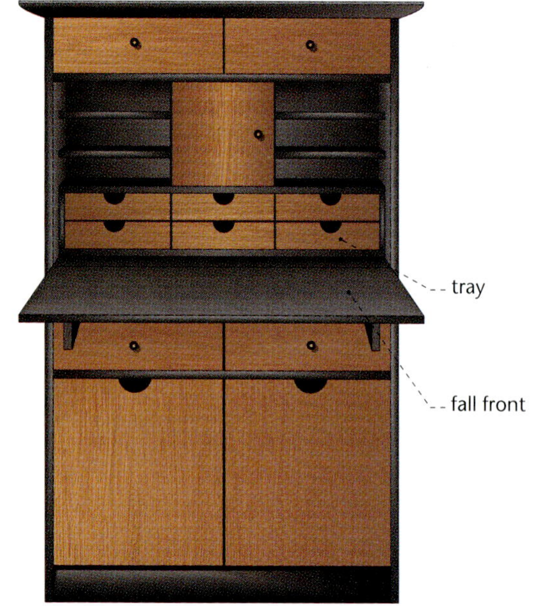

secretary

wardrobe

display cabinet

cocktail cabinet

glass-fronted display cabinet

corner cupboard

buffet

TYPES OF CURTAINS

GLASS CURTAIN

ATTACHED CURTAIN

LOOSE CURTAIN

TYPES OF PLEATS

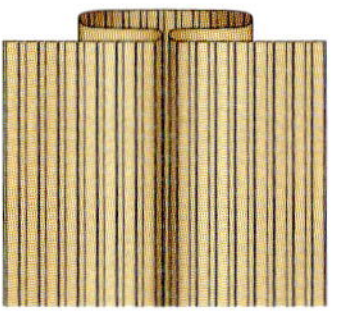

box pleat

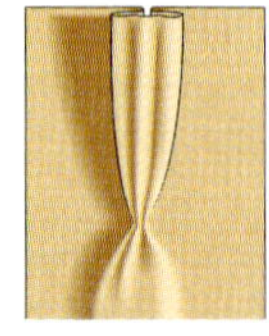

pinch pleat

inverted pleat

CURTAIN

BALLOON CURTAIN

CRISSCROSS CURTAINS

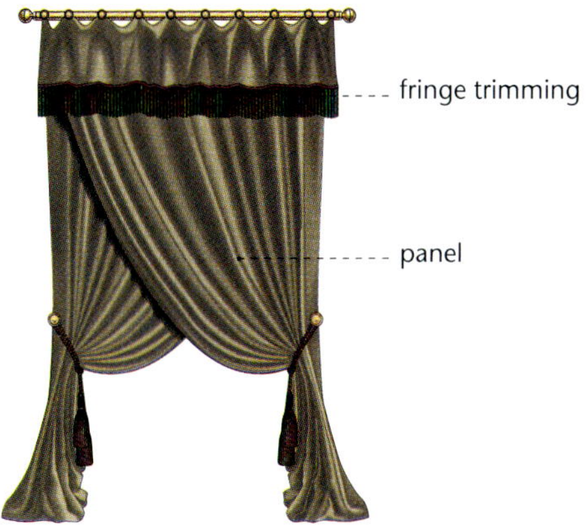

TYPES OF HEADINGS

draped swag

pencil pleat heading

pleated heading

shirred heading

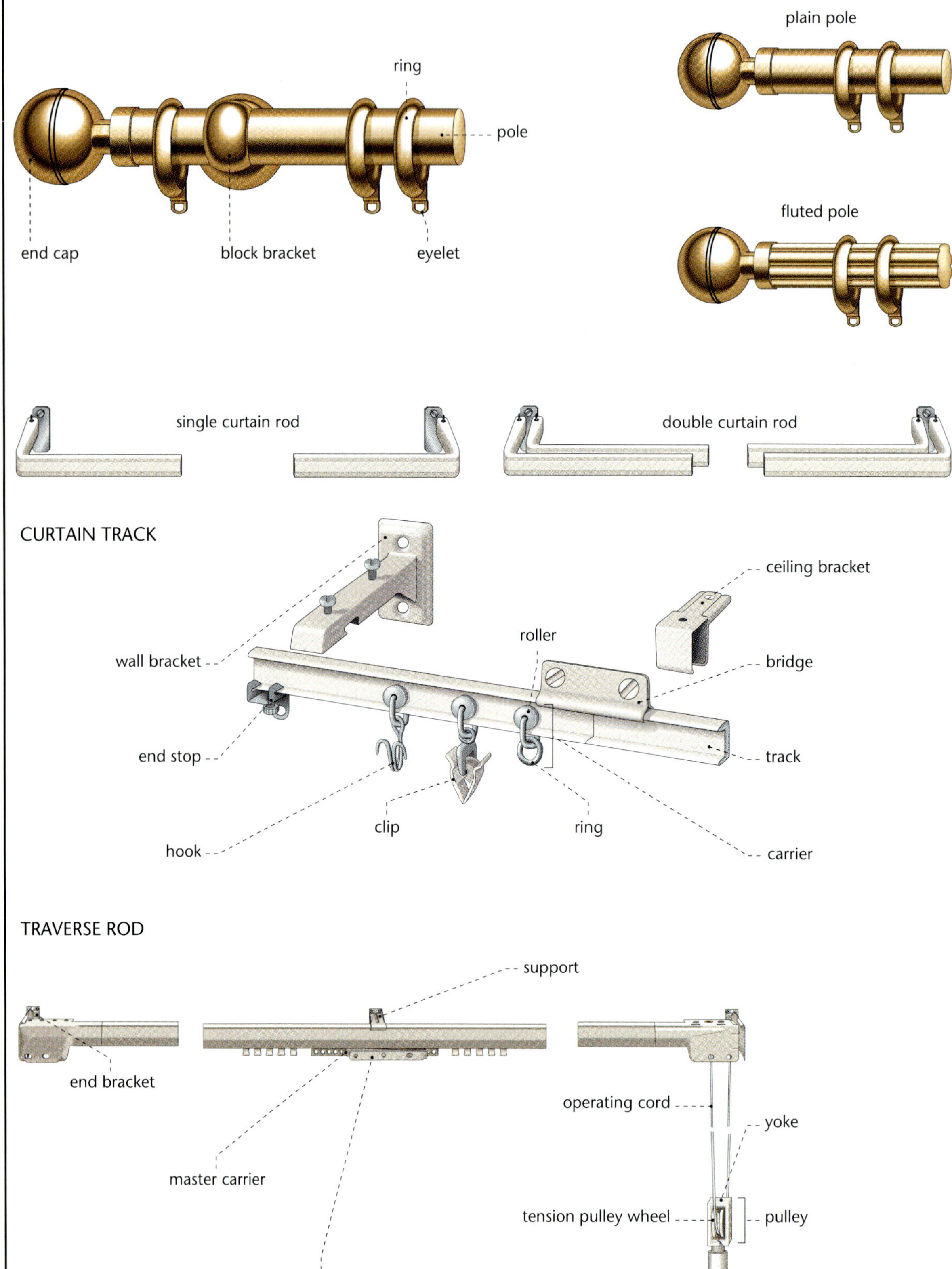
CURTAIN POLE
plain pole
ring
pole
fluted pole
end cap
block bracket
eyelet
single curtain rod
double curtain rod
CURTAIN TRACK
ceiling bracket
roller
wall bracket
bridge
end stop
track
clip
ring
hook
carrier
TRAVERSE ROD
support
end bracket
operating cord
yoke
master carrier
tension pulley wheel
pulley
overlap carrier
spring housing
fastening device

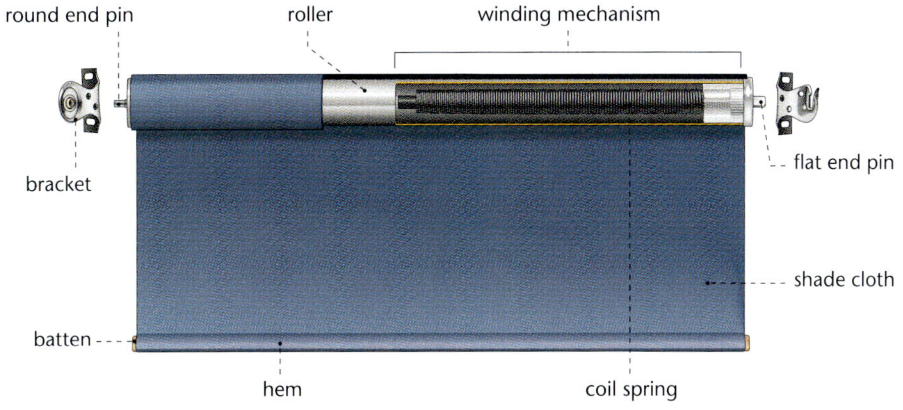

VENETIAN BLIND

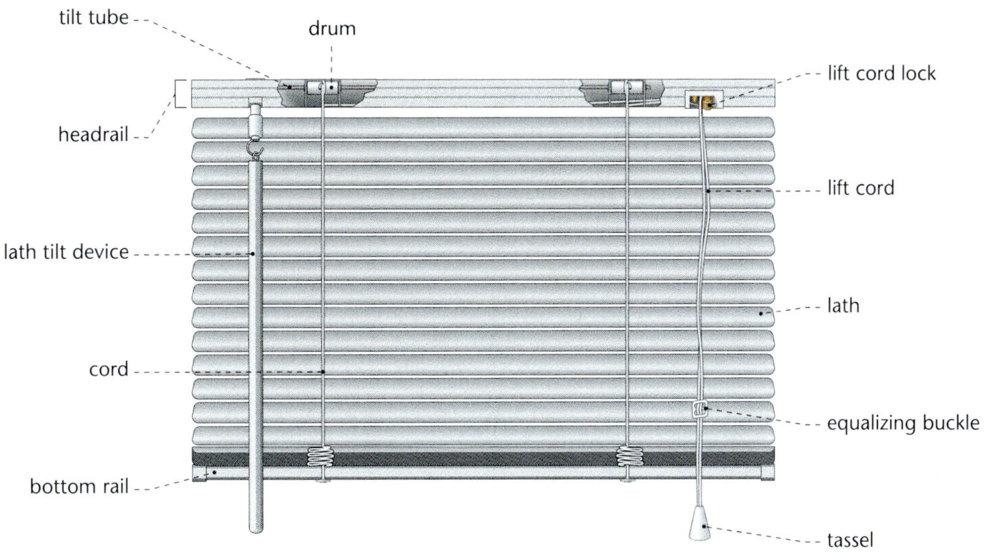

roll-up blind

roman shade

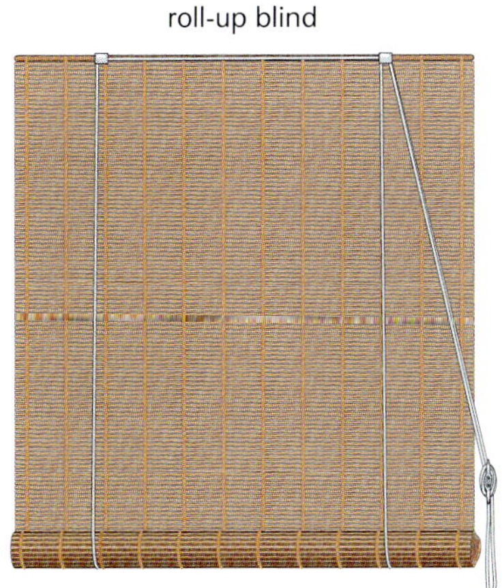

indoor shutters

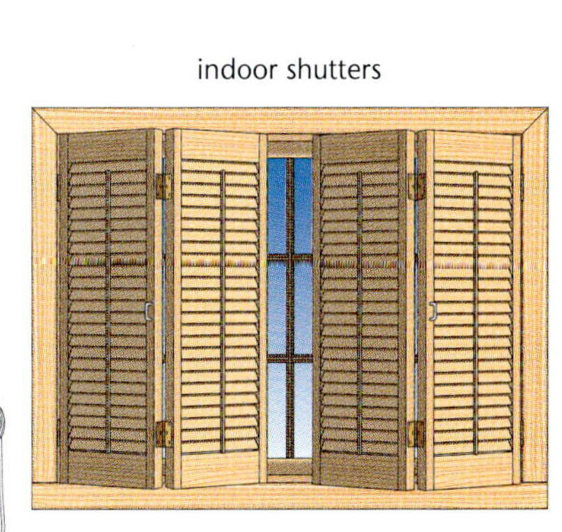

LIGHTS

INCANDESCENT LAMP

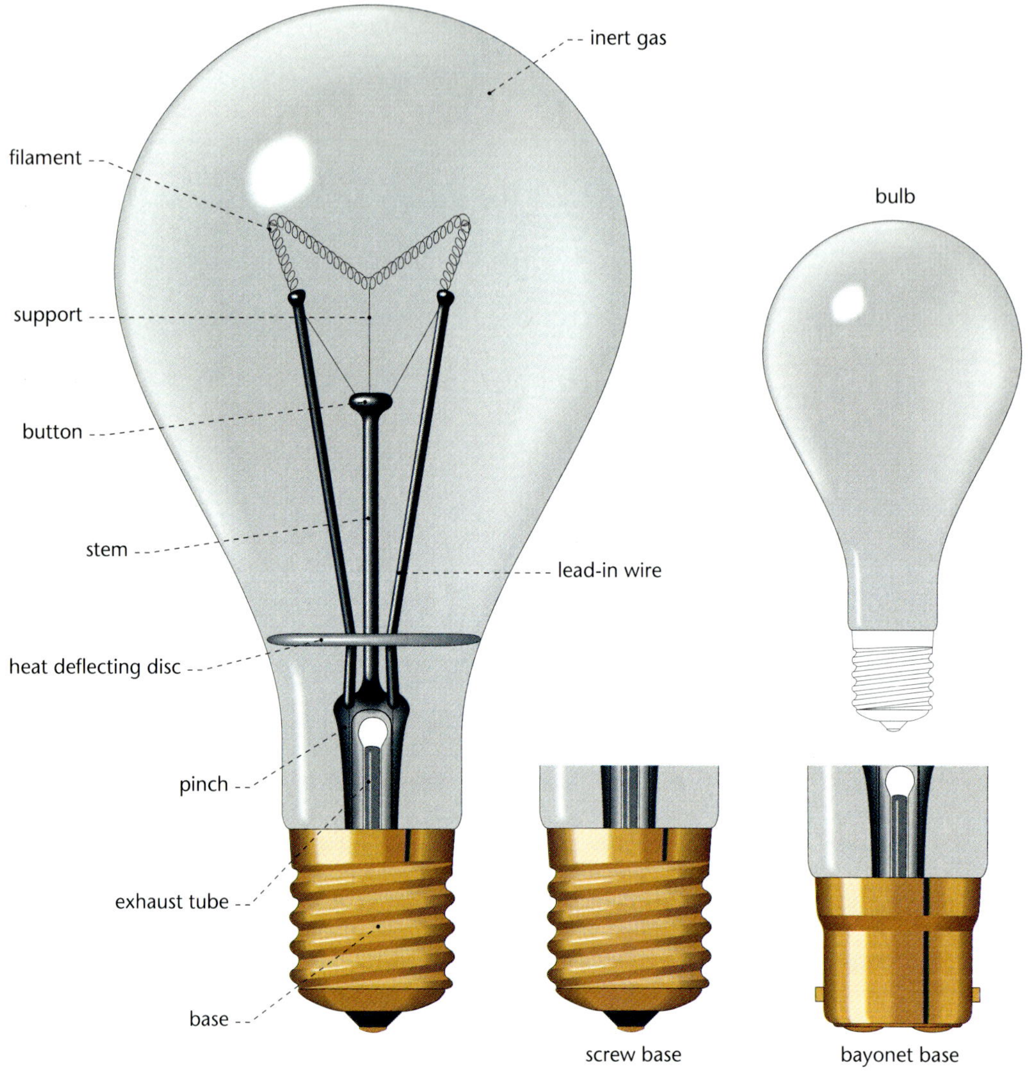

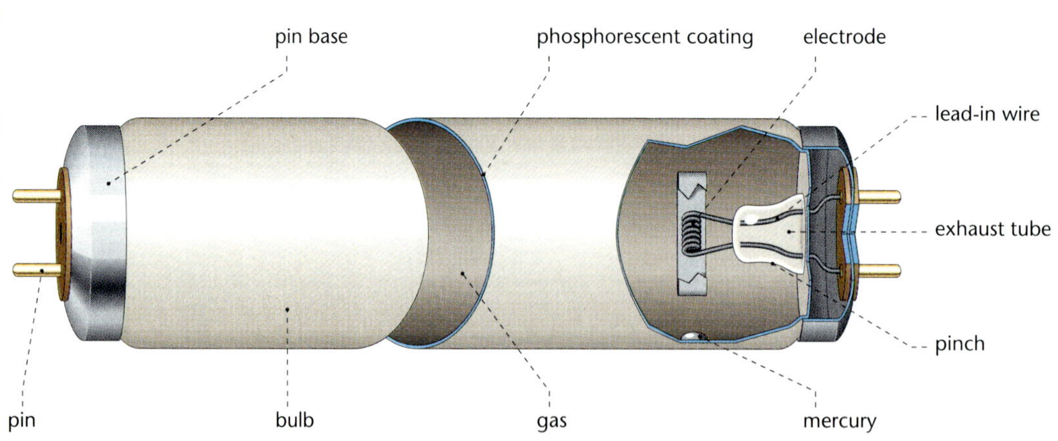

FLUORESCENT TUBE

TUNGSTEN-HALOGEN LAMP

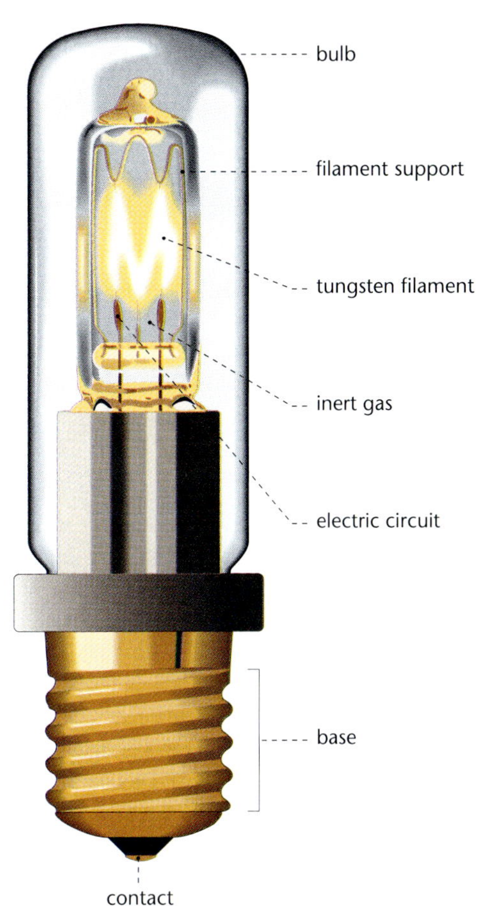

TUNGSTEN-HALOGEN LAMP

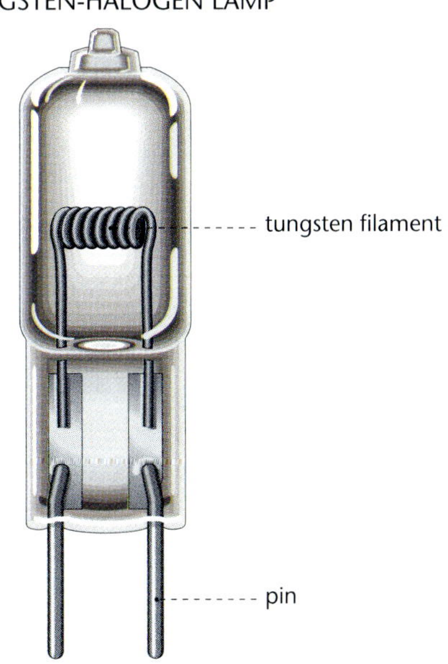

ENERGY SAVING BULB

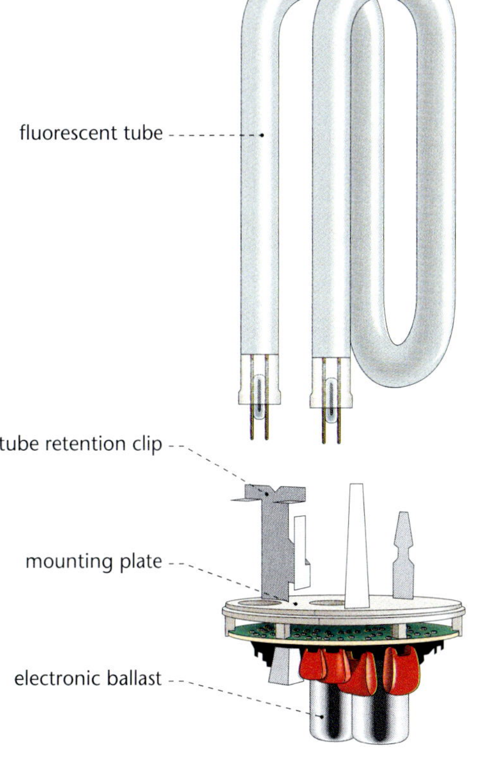

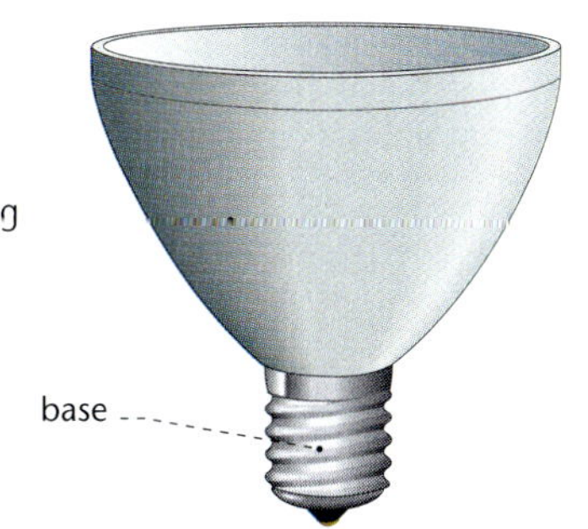

wall fitting
swivel wall lamp
ADJUSTABLE LAMP
on-off switch
arm
shade
spring
adjustable clamp
desk lamp
bed lamp

TRACK LIGHTING

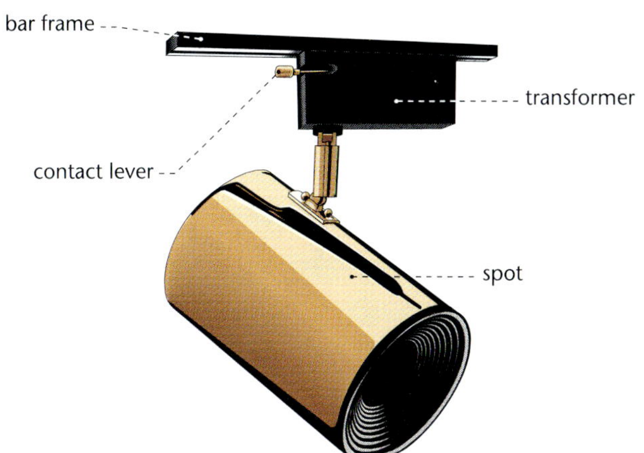

clamp spotlight

wall lantern

strip light

CHANDELIER

floor lamp

hanging pendant

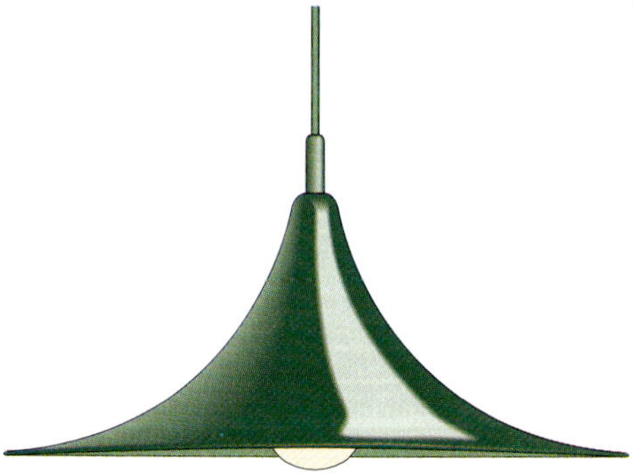

ceiling fitting

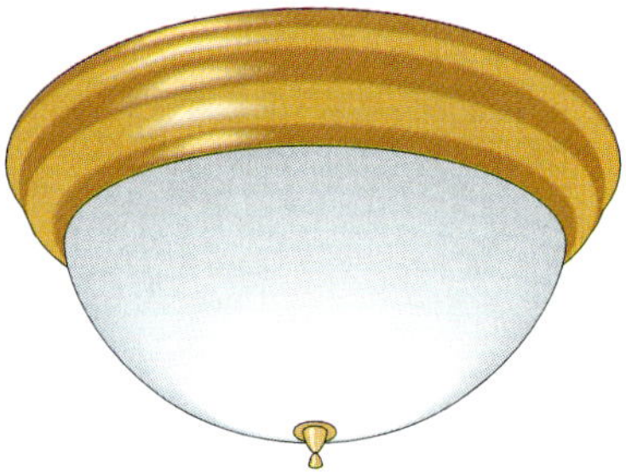

table lamp

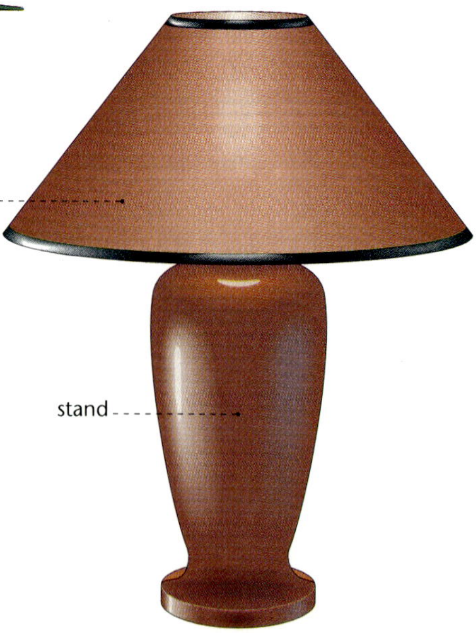

shade

stand

base

port glass

sparkling wine glass

brandy snifter

liqueur glass

white wine glass

bordeaux glass

burgundy glass

Alsace glass

old-fashioned glass

highball glass

cocktail glass

water goblet

decanter

small decanter

champagne flute

beer mug

demitasse

cup

coffee mug

creamer

sugar bowl

pepper shaker

salt shaker

gravy boat

butter dish

ramekin

soup bowl

rim soup bowl

dinner plate

salad plate

bread and butter plate

teapot

platter

vegetable bowl

fish platter

hors d'oeuvre dish

water pitcher

salad bowl

serving bowl

soup tureen

SILVERWARE

KNIFE

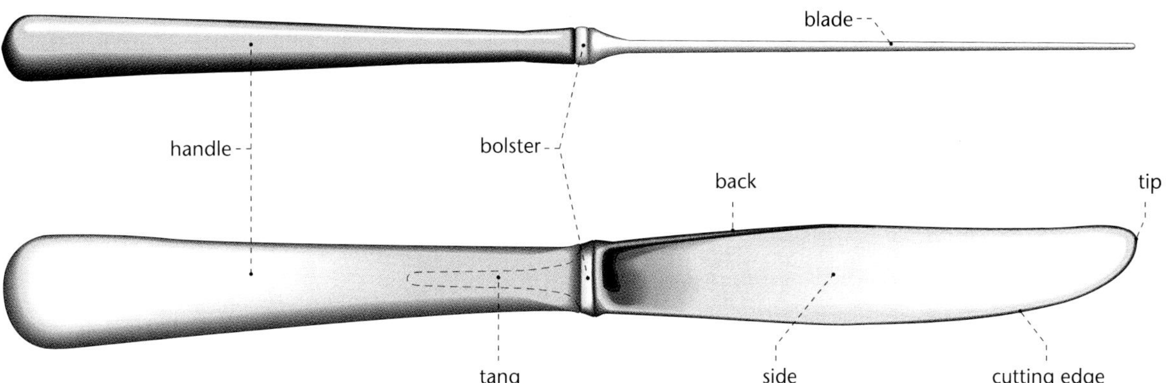

MAJOR TYPES OF KNIVES

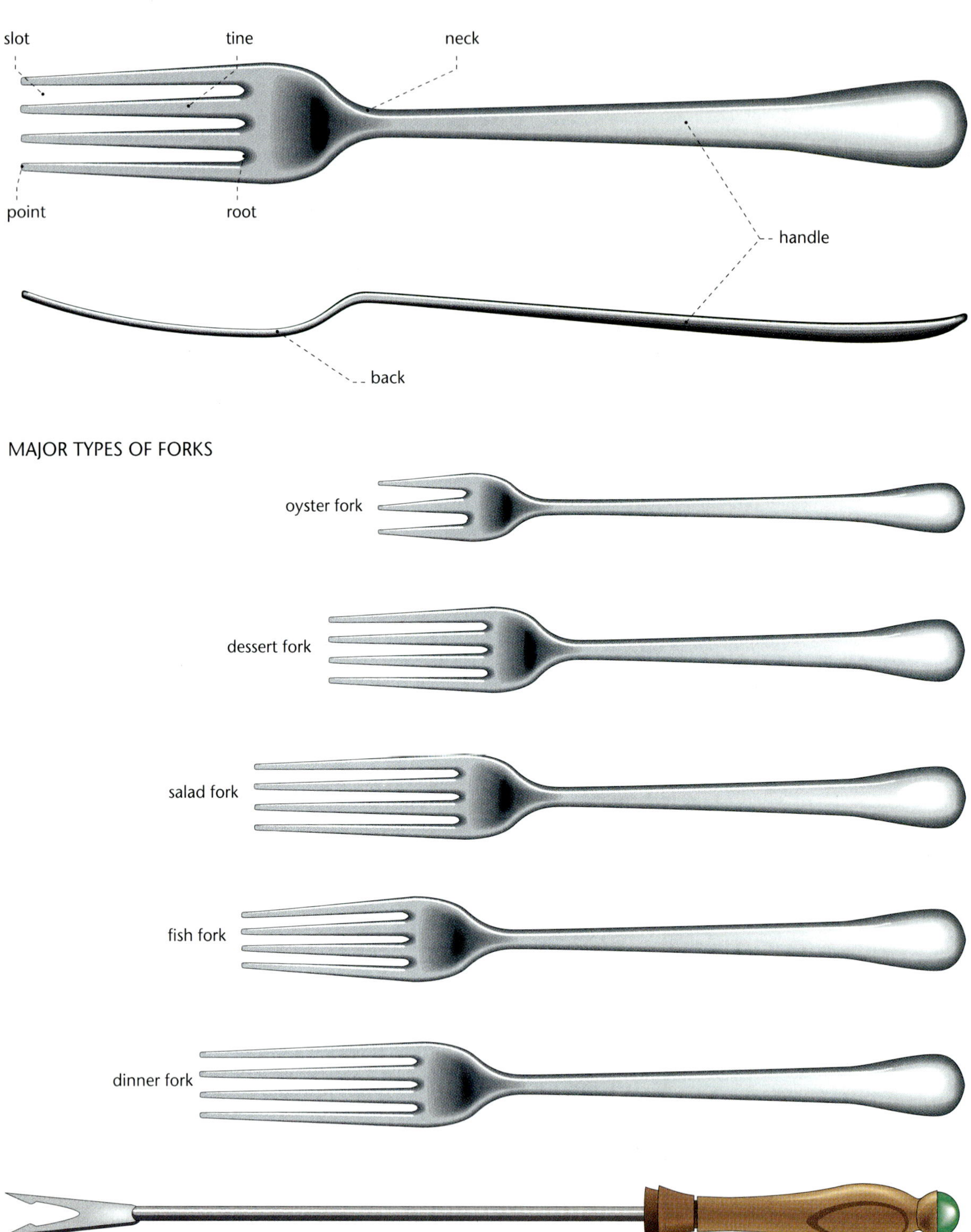

FORK
slot
tine
neck
point
root
handle
back
MAJOR TYPES OF FORKS
oyster fork
dessert fork
salad fork
fish fork
dinner fork
fondue fork

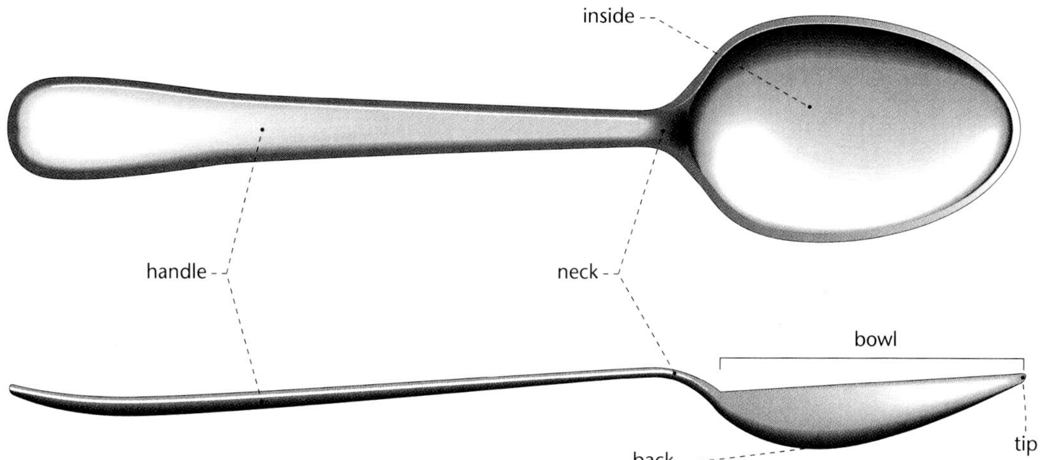

MAJOR TYPES OF SPOONS

coffee spoon

teaspoon

soup spoon

dessert spoon

sundae spoon

tablespoon

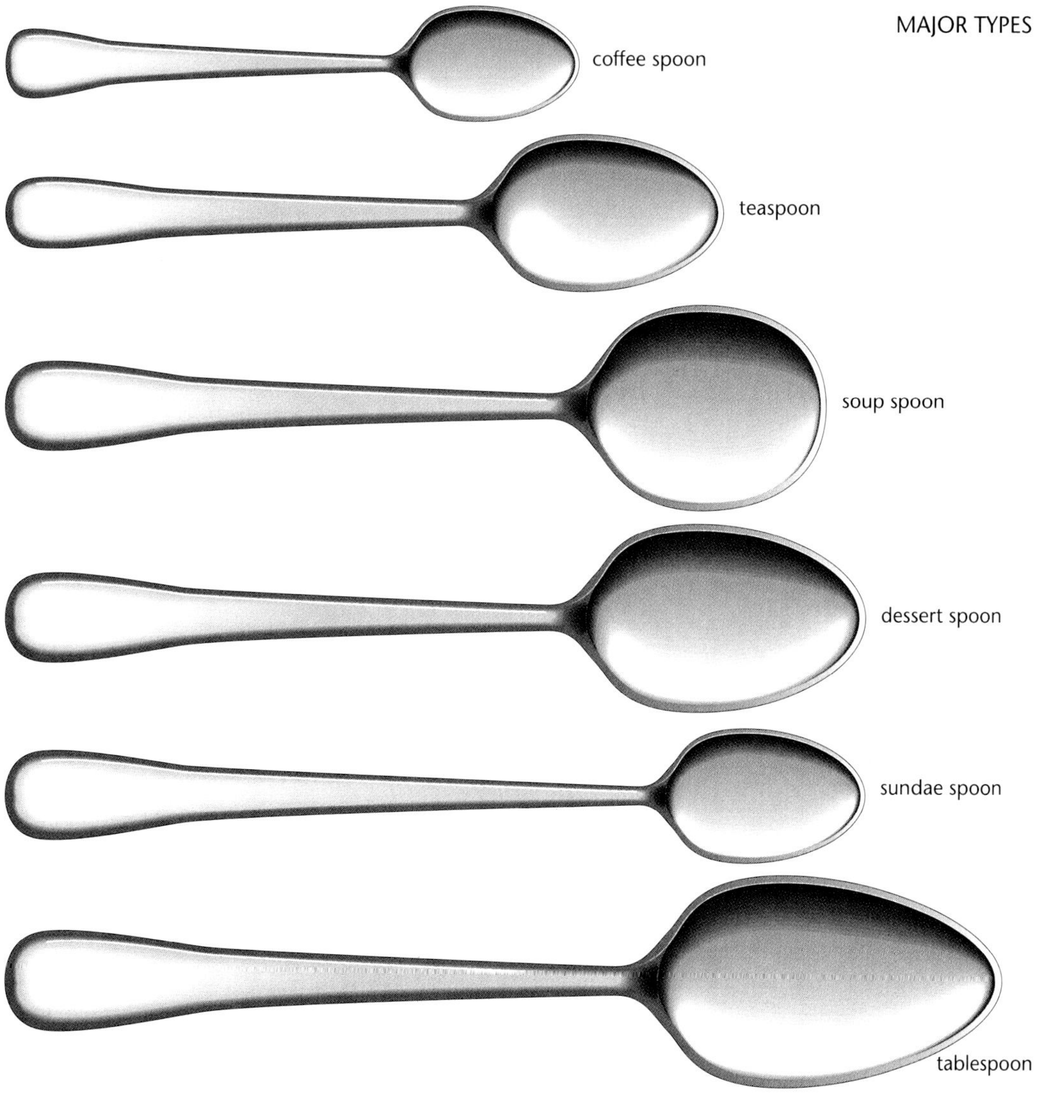

HOUSE FURNITURE

KITCHEN KNIFE

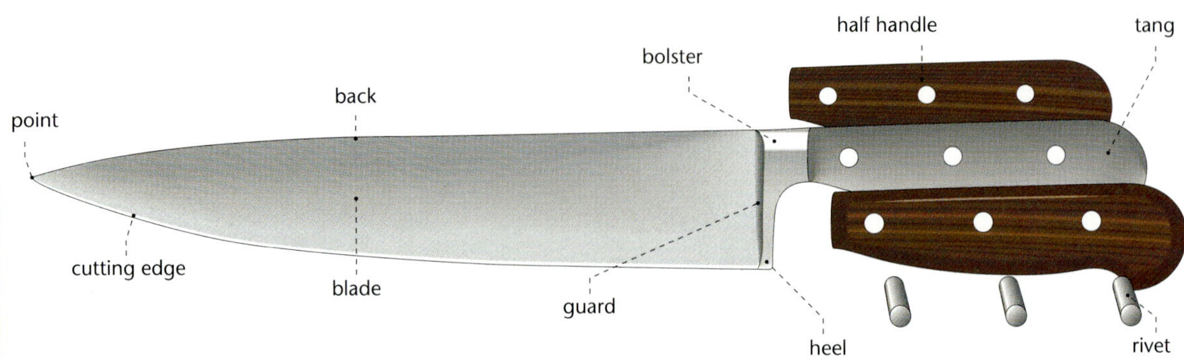

TYPES OF KITCHEN KNIVES

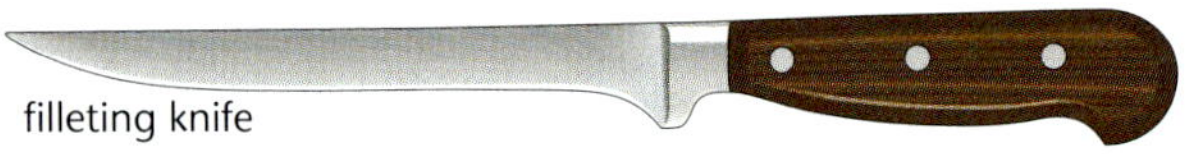

filleting knife

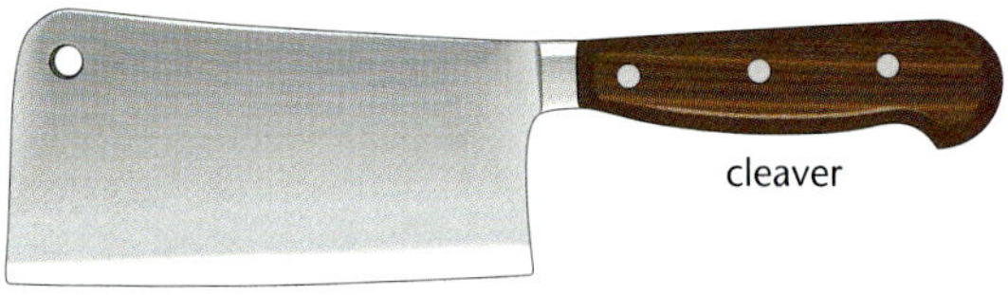

cleaver

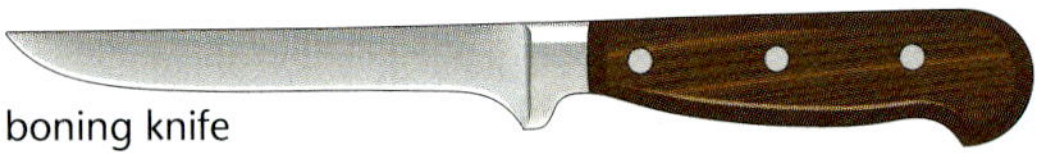

boning knife

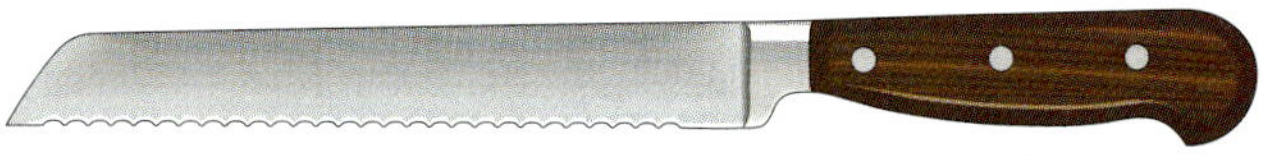

bread knife

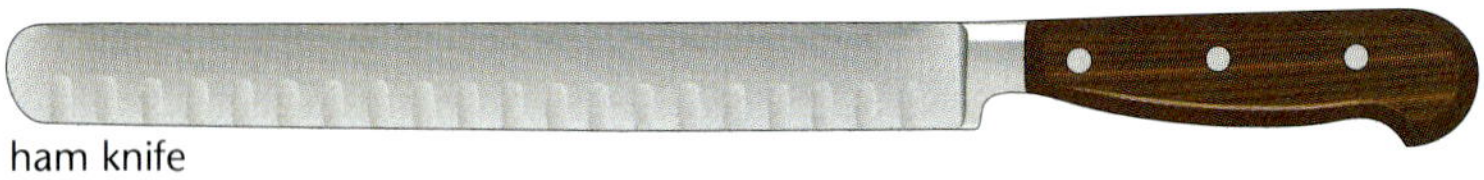

ham knife

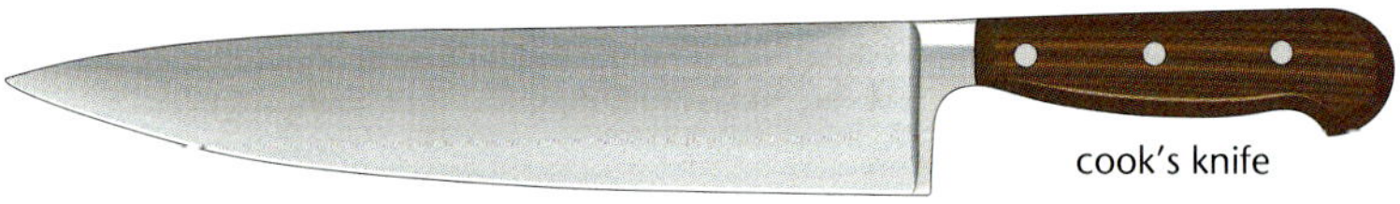

cook's knife

carving knife

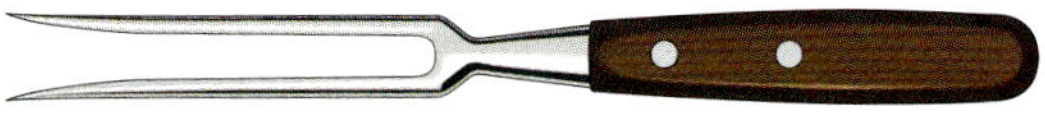

carving fork

sharpening steel

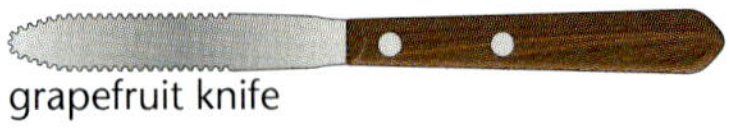

grapefruit knife

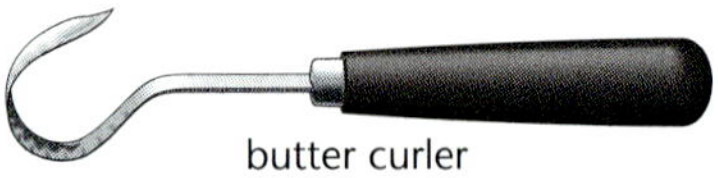

butter curler

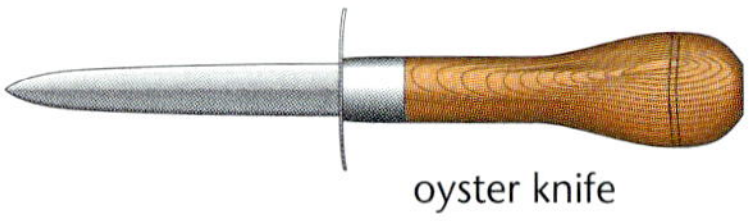

oyster knife

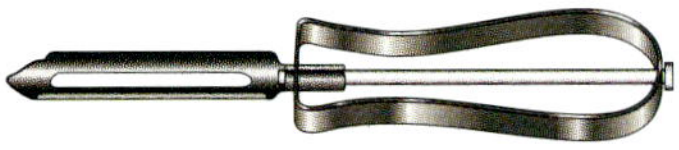

peeler

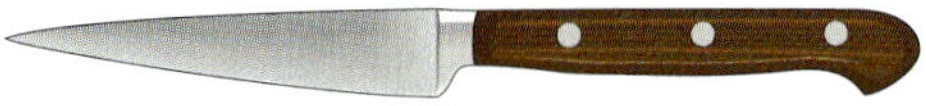

paring knife

zester

funnel
colander
strainer
salad spinner
FOR GRINDING AND GRATING
pestle
mortar
nutcracker
garlic press
citrus juicer
meat grinder
grater
pasta maker

KITCHEN UTENSILS

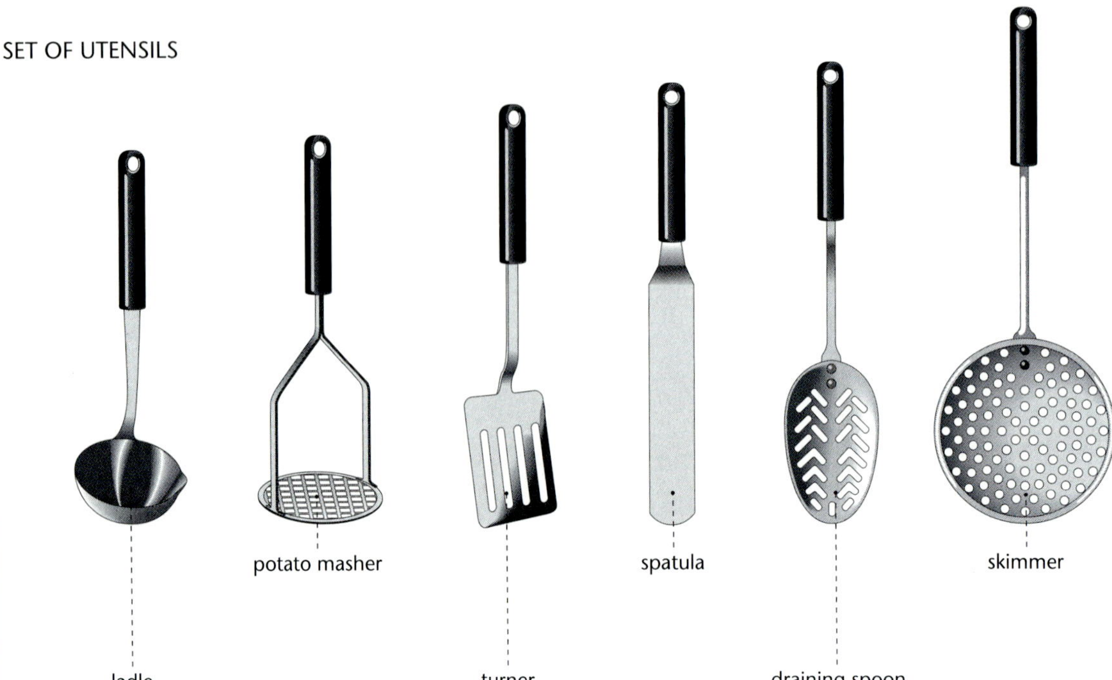

SET OF UTENSILS

ladle
potato masher
turner
spatula
draining spoon
skimmer

FOR OPENING

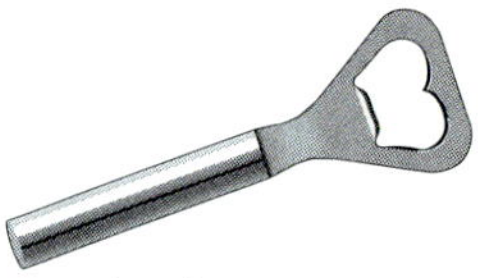
bottle opener

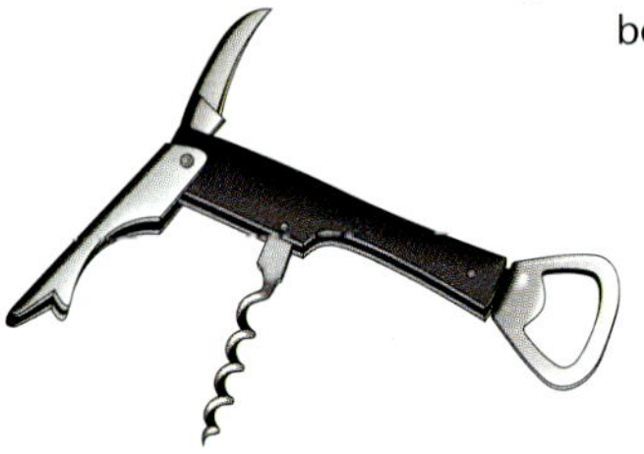
wine waiter corkscrew

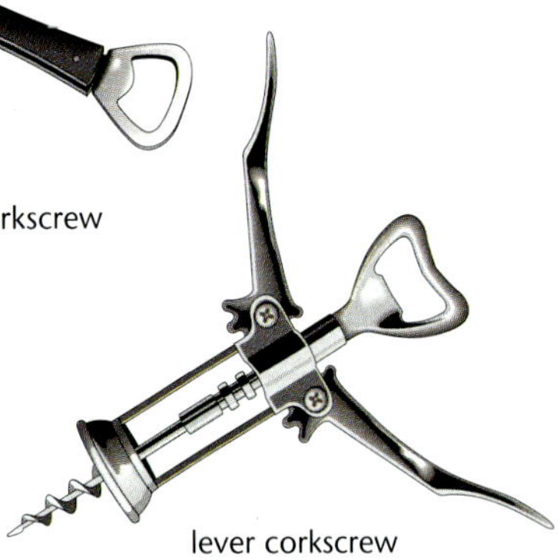
lever corkscrew

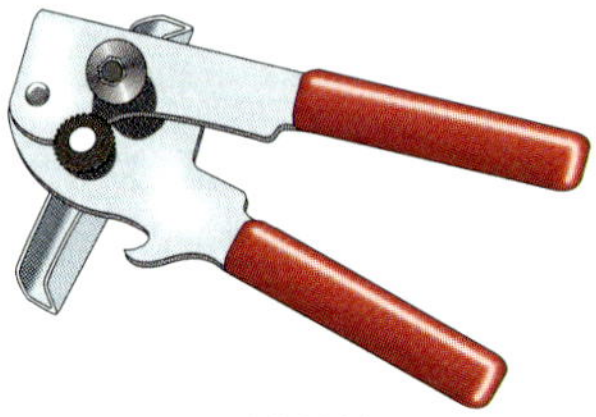
can opener

FOR MEASURING

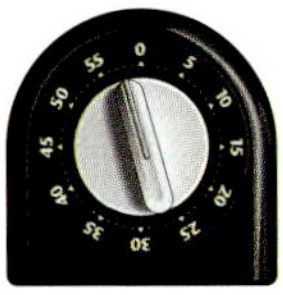
kitchen timer

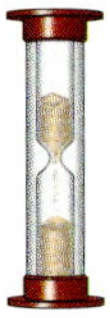
egg timer

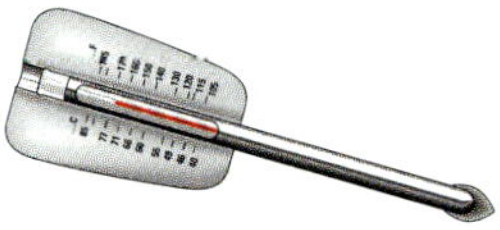
meat thermometer

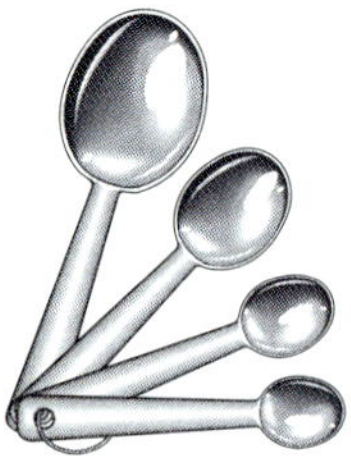
measuring spoons

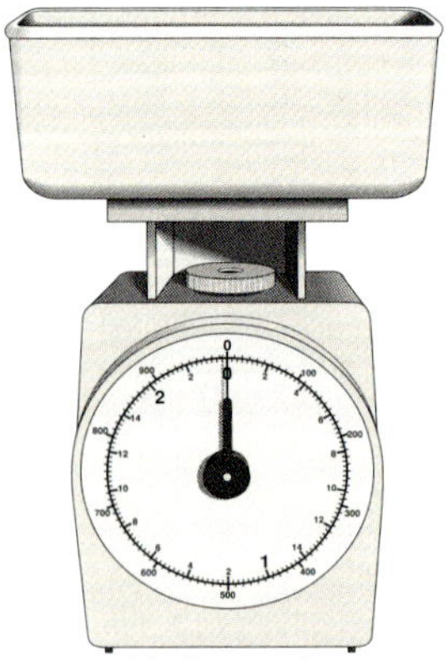
kitchen scale

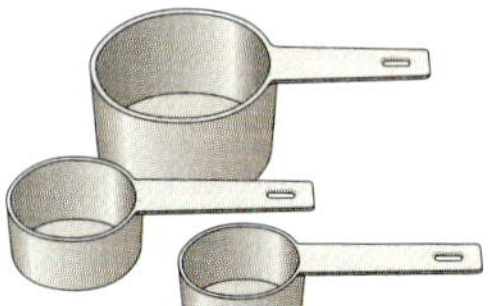
measuring cups

pastry brush
icing syringe
whisk
egg beater
sifter
pastry cutting wheel
muffin pan
pastry bag and nozzles
cookie sheet
rolling pin
mixing bowls
cookie cutters
removable-bottomed pan
pie pan
quiche plate
cake pan

MISCELLANEOUS UTENSILS

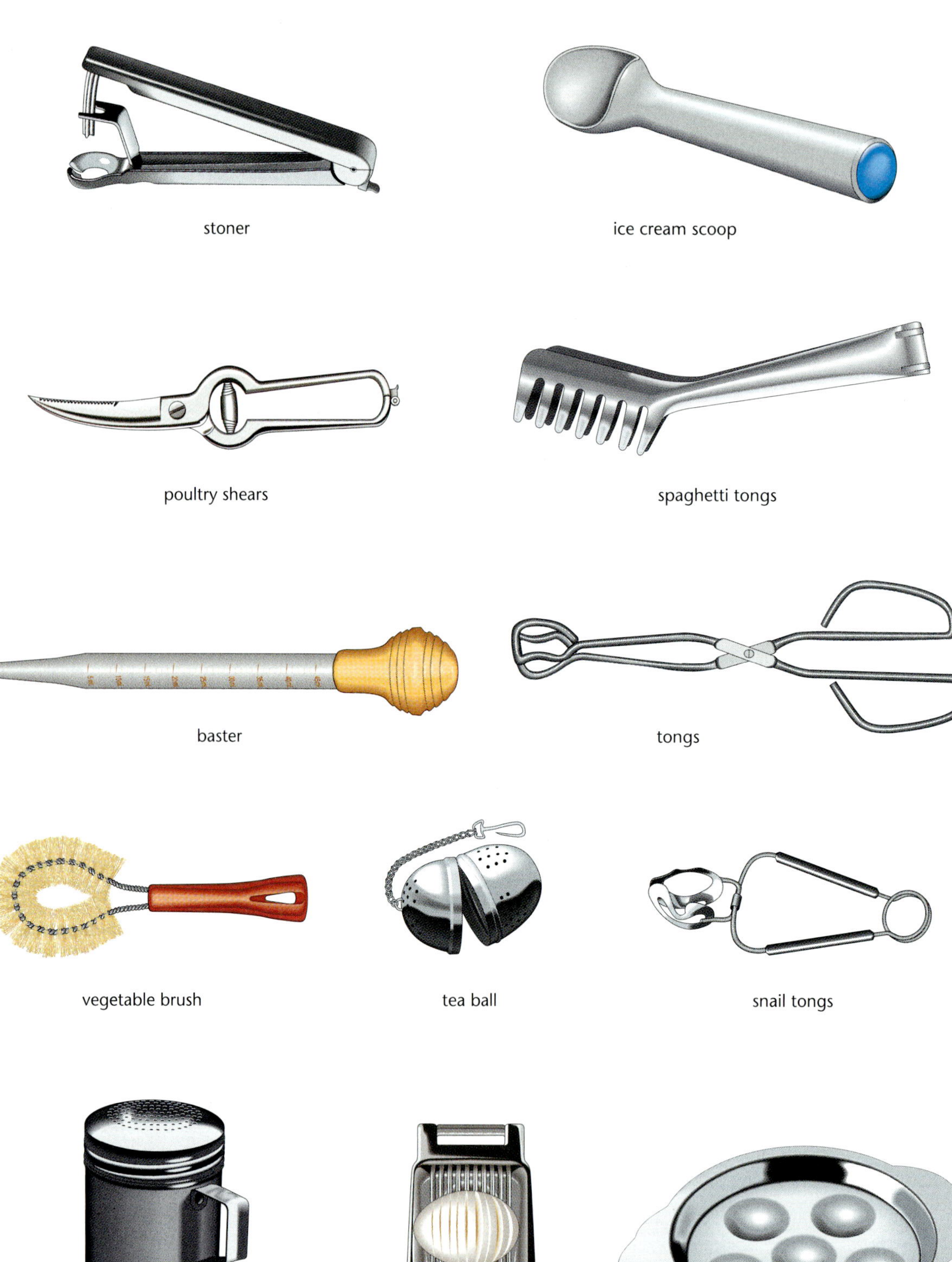

stoner

ice cream scoop

poultry shears

spaghetti tongs

baster

tongs

vegetable brush

tea ball

snail tongs

dredger

egg slicer

snail dish

COFFEE MAKERS

AUTOMATIC DRIP COFFEE MAKER

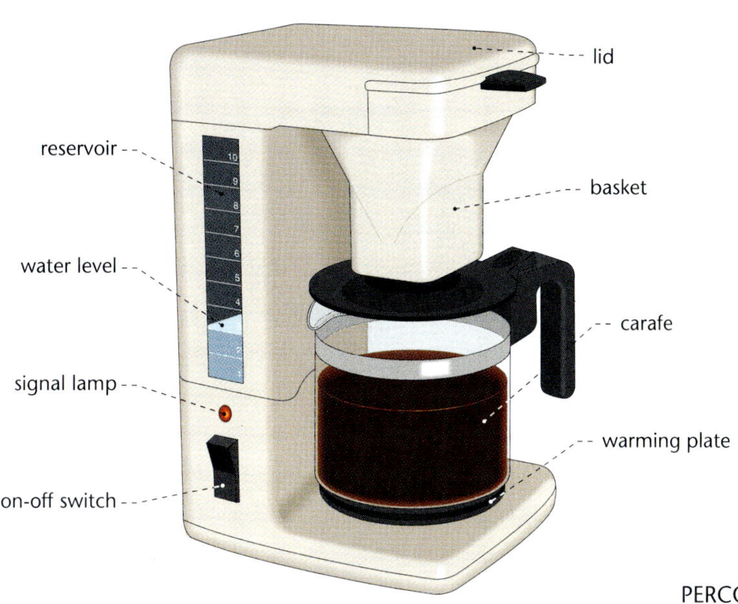

VACUUM COFFEE MAKER

PERCOLATOR

plunger

Neapolitan coffee maker

espresso coffee maker

COOKING UTENSILS

WOK SET

FISH POACHER

FONDUE SET

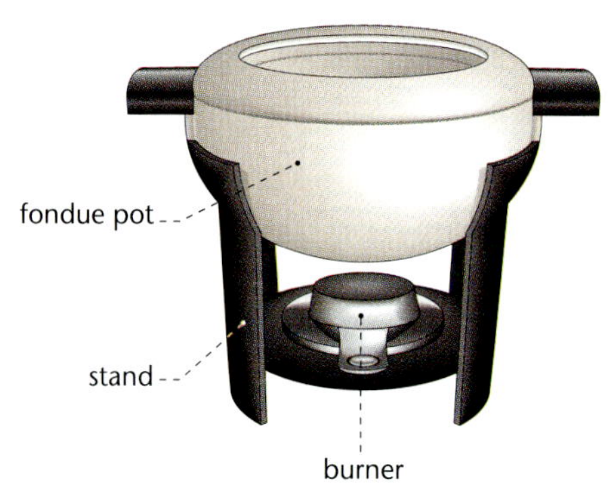

PRESSURE COOKER

roasting pans

Dutch oven

stock pot

frying pan

pancake pan

couscous kettle

egg poacher

sauté pan

vegetable steamer

double boiler

saucepan

DOMESTIC APPLIANCES

BLENDER

HAND MIXER

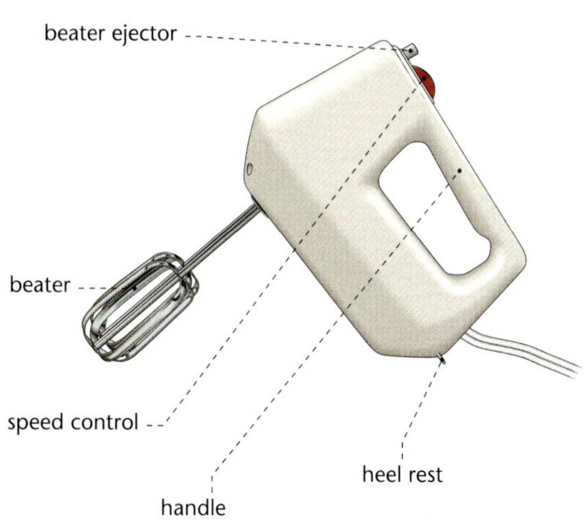

HAND BLENDER

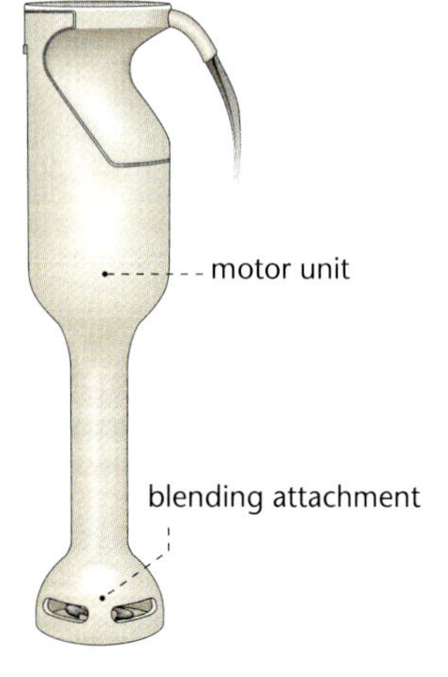

TABLE MIXER

BEATERS

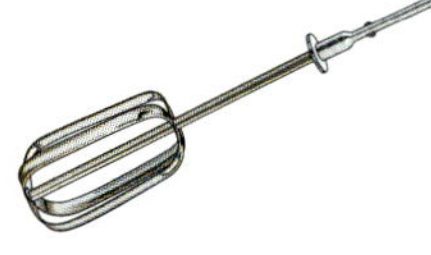

four blade beater

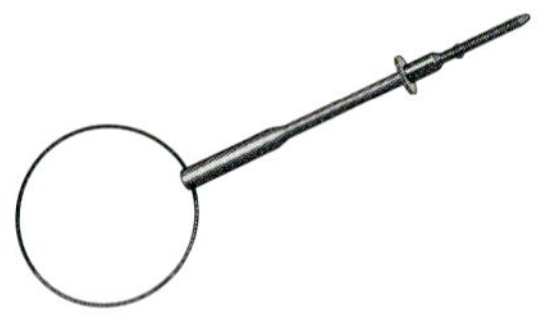

spiral beater

wire beater

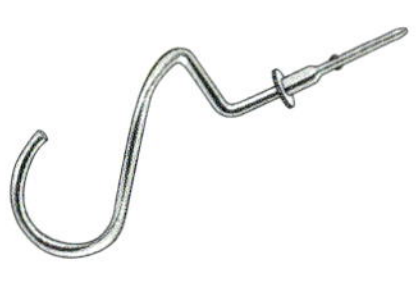

dough hook

FOOD PROCESSOR

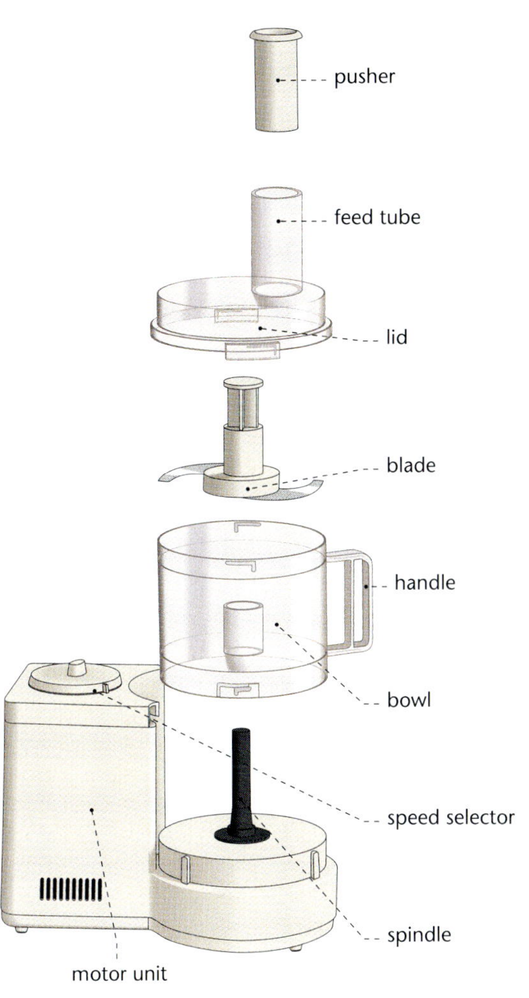

disks

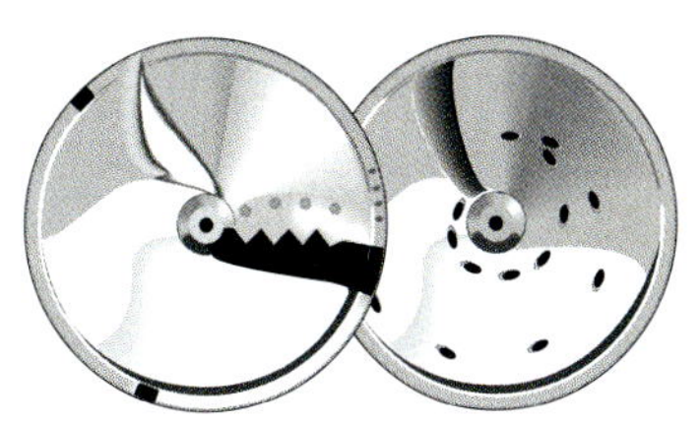

CITRUS JUICER

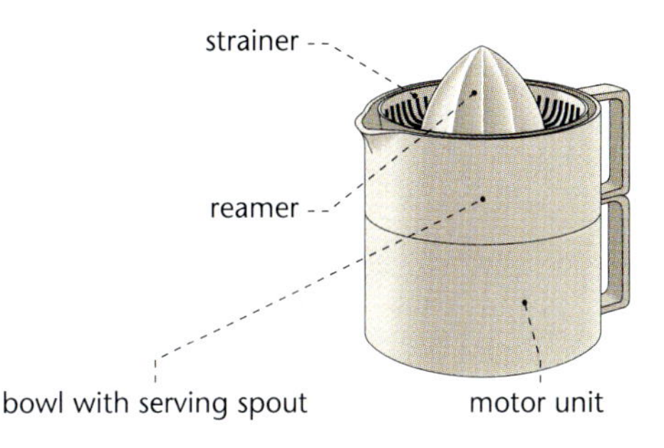

JUICER

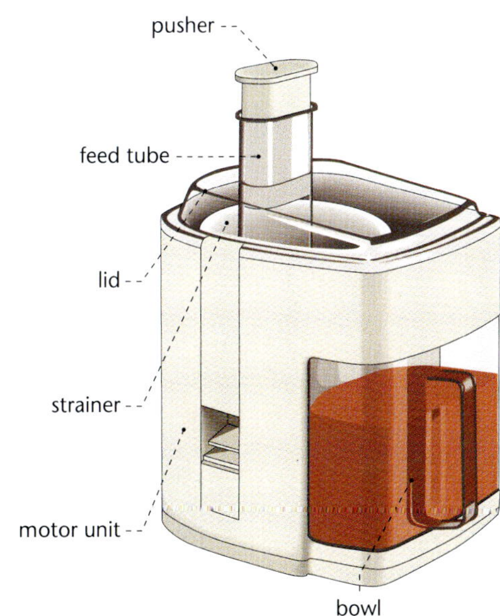

ICE CREAM FREEZER

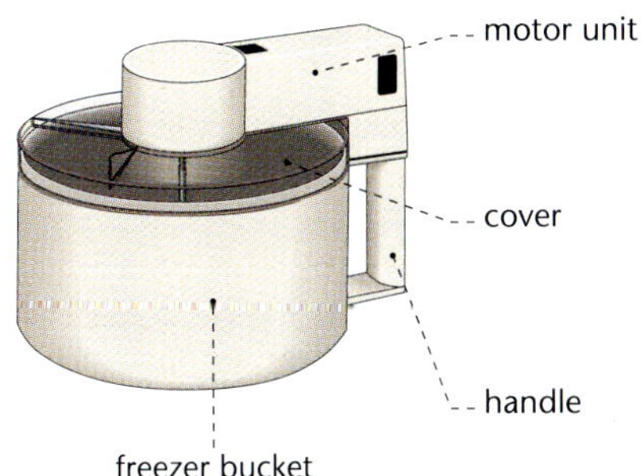

DOMESTIC APPLIANCES

KETTLE

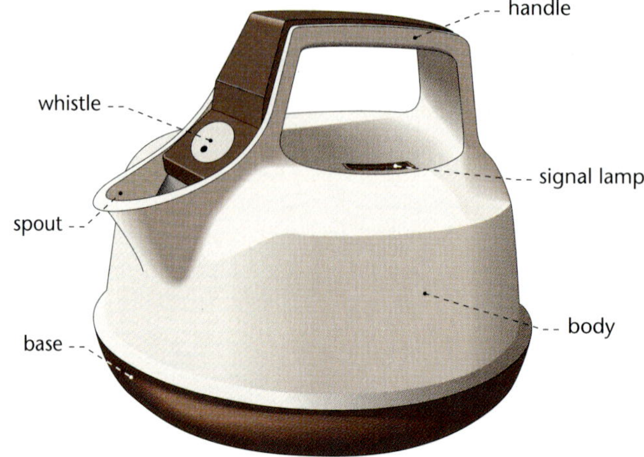

TOASTER

DEEP FRYER

WAFFLE IRON

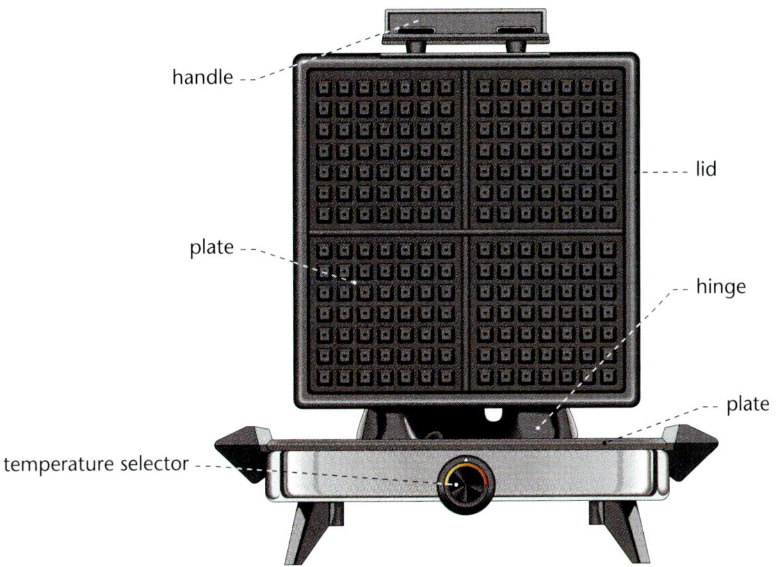

MICROWAVE OVEN

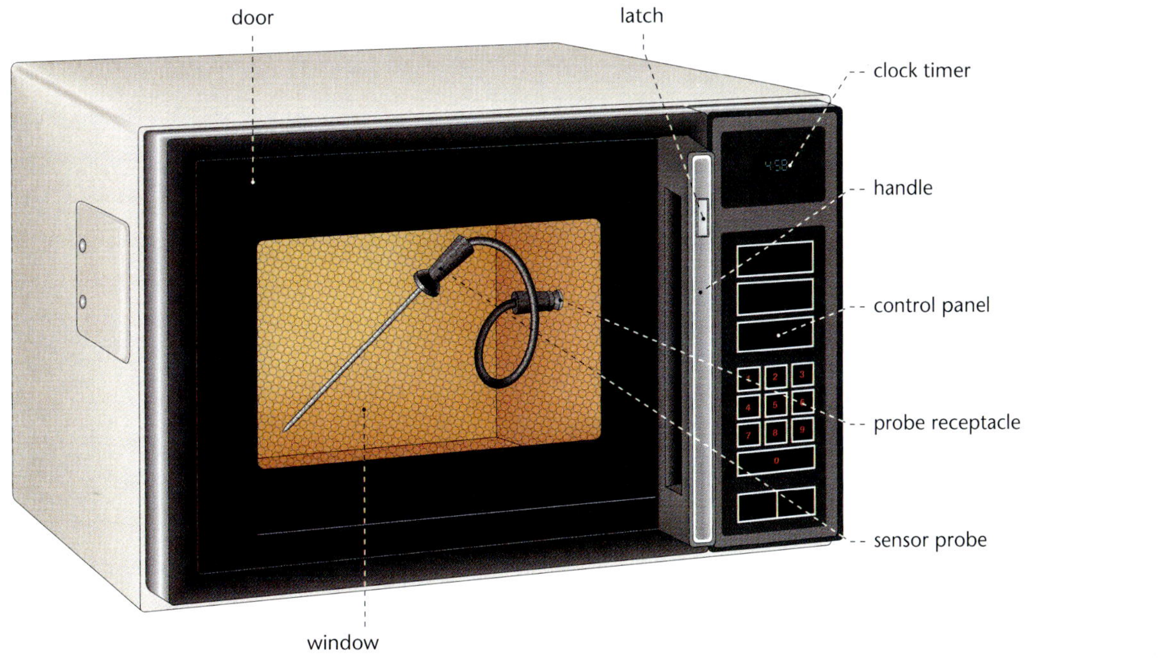

GRIDDLE

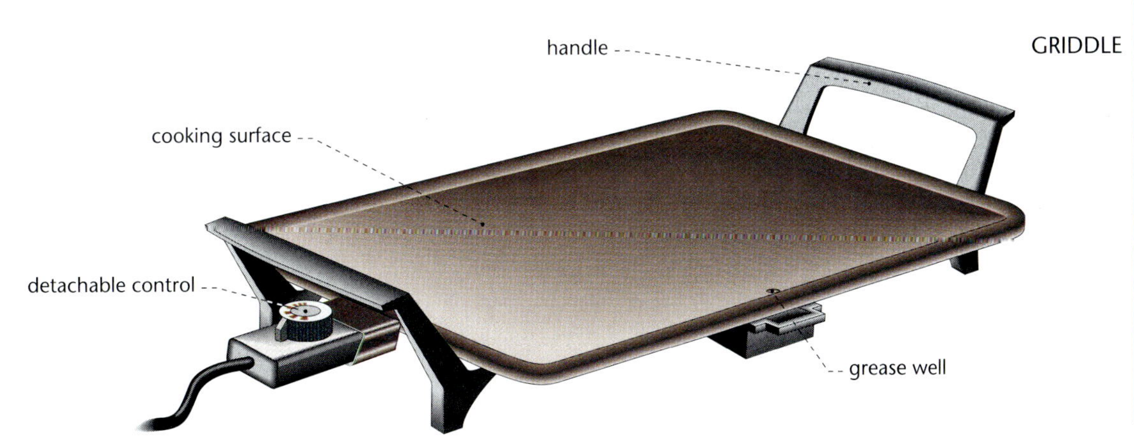

REFRIGERATOR

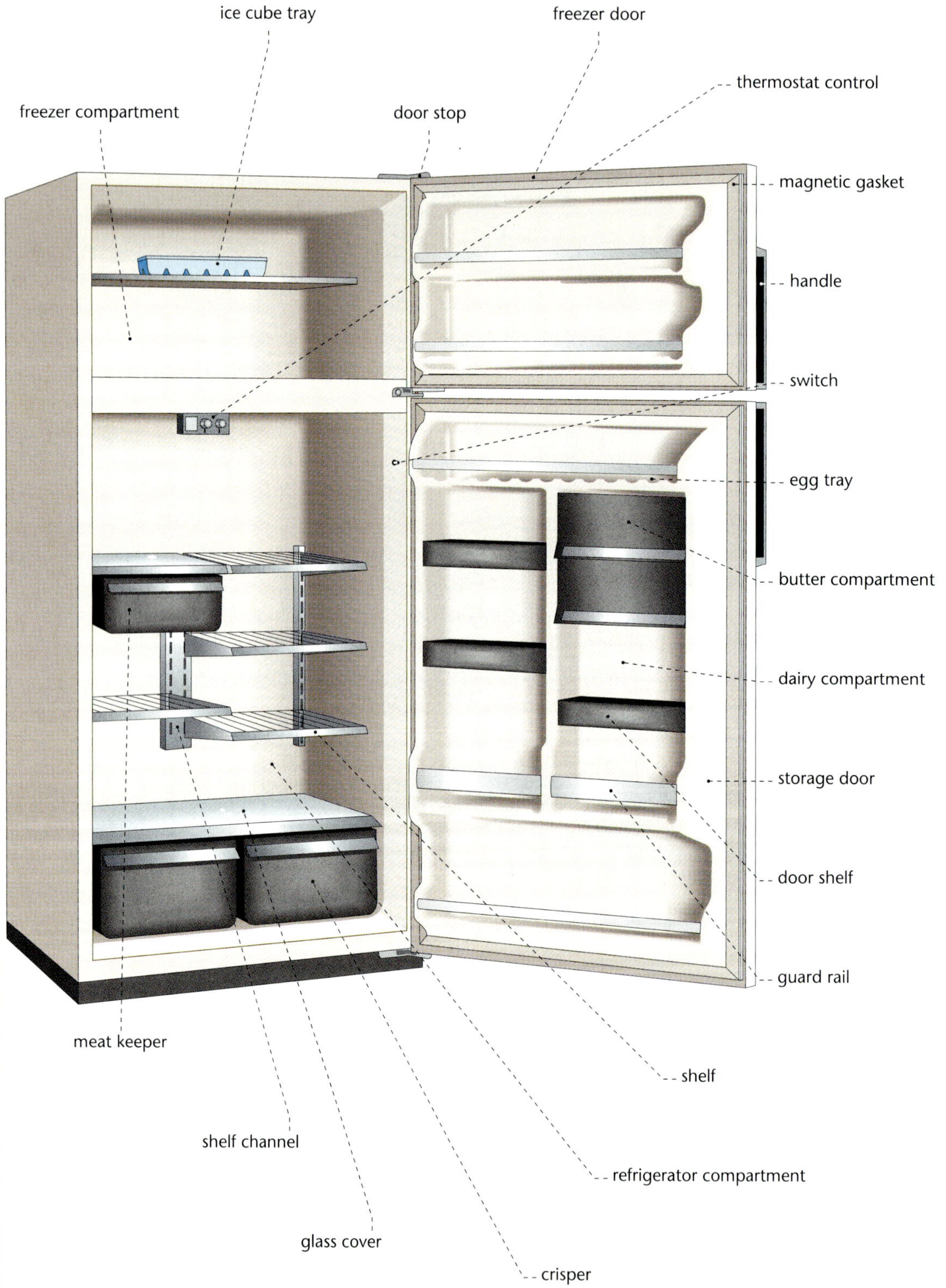

RANGE HOOD

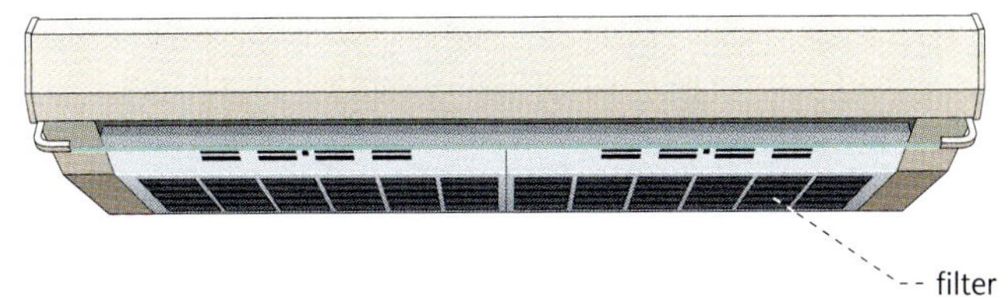

ELECTRIC RANGE

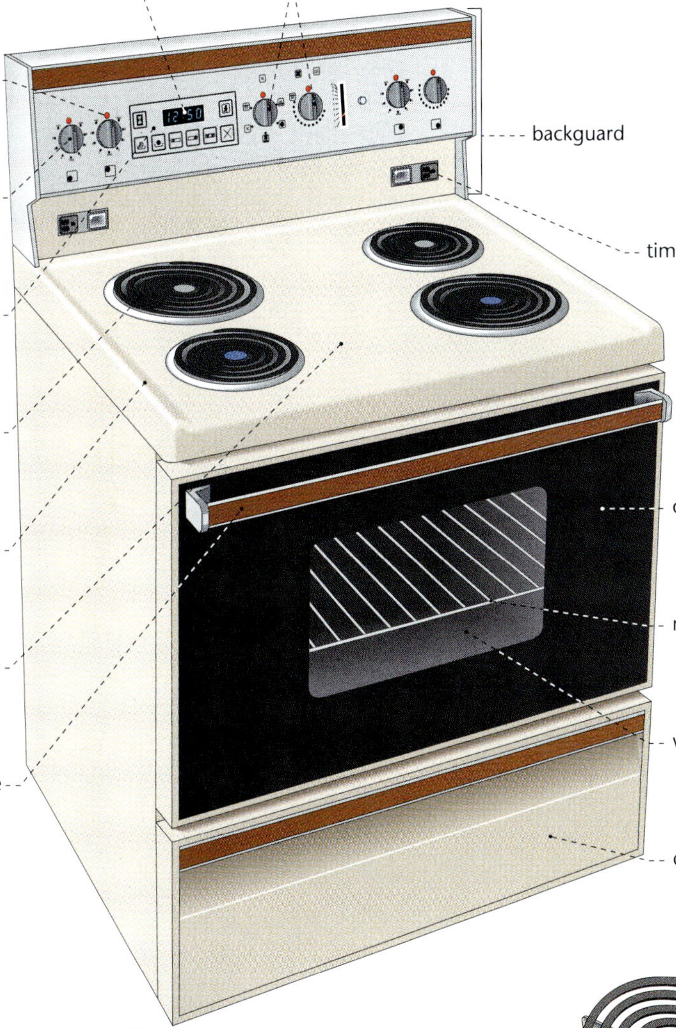

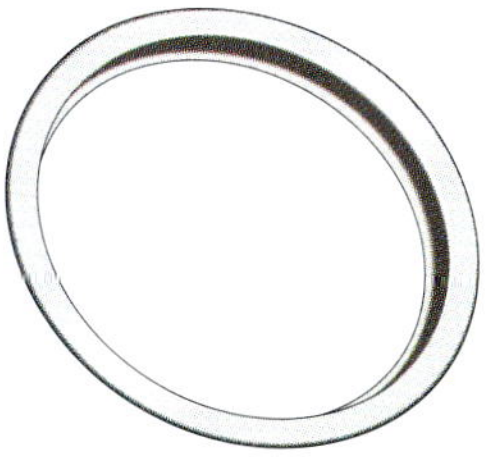

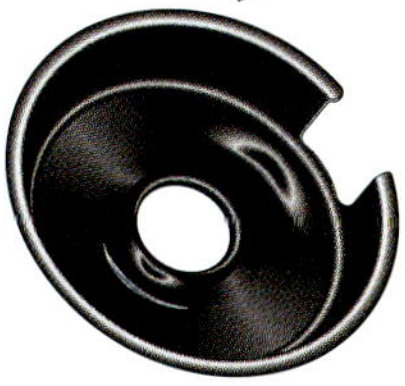

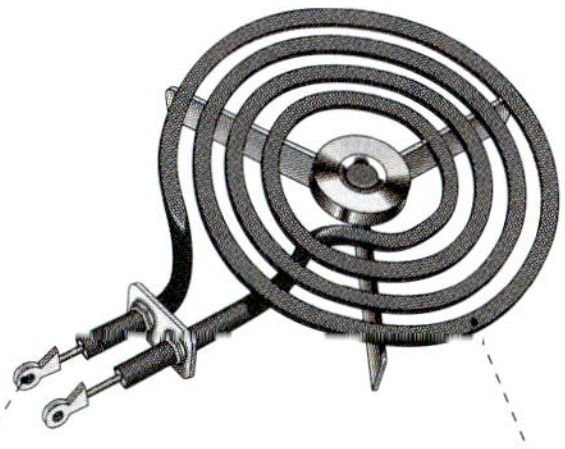

STEAM IRON
front tip
shell
fill opening
water-level tube
spray
spray button
spray control
fabric guide
soleplate
handle
temperature control
vertical cord lift
heel rest
cord
signal lamp
COFFEE MILL
lid
CAN OPENER
pierce lever
blade
magnetic lid holder
on-off button
cutting blade
motor unit
drive wheel

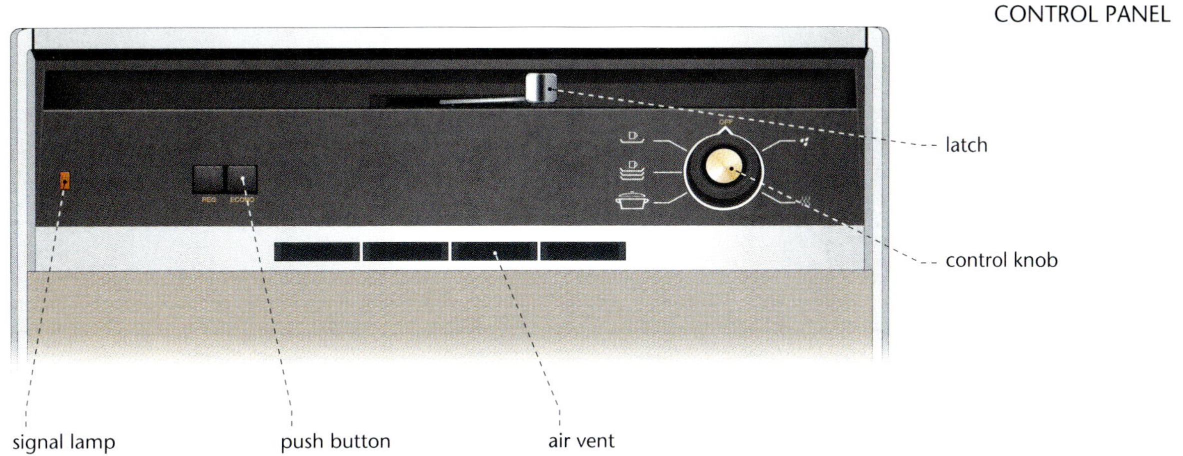

HOUSE FURNITURE

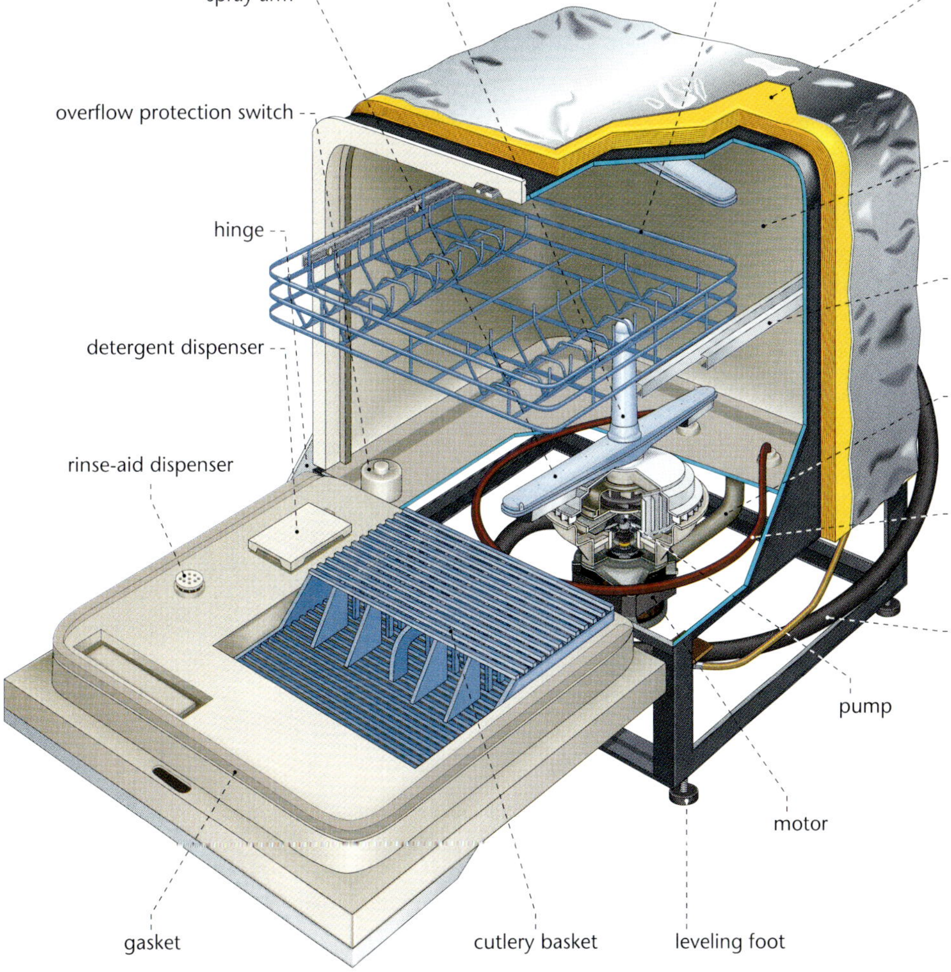

WASHER

water-level selector
temperature selector
control panel
control knob
backguard
lid
tub rim
agitator
basket
cabinet
tub
lint filter
transmission
suspension arm
motor
drain hose
emptying hose
torque converter
pump
leveling foot
drive belt
spring

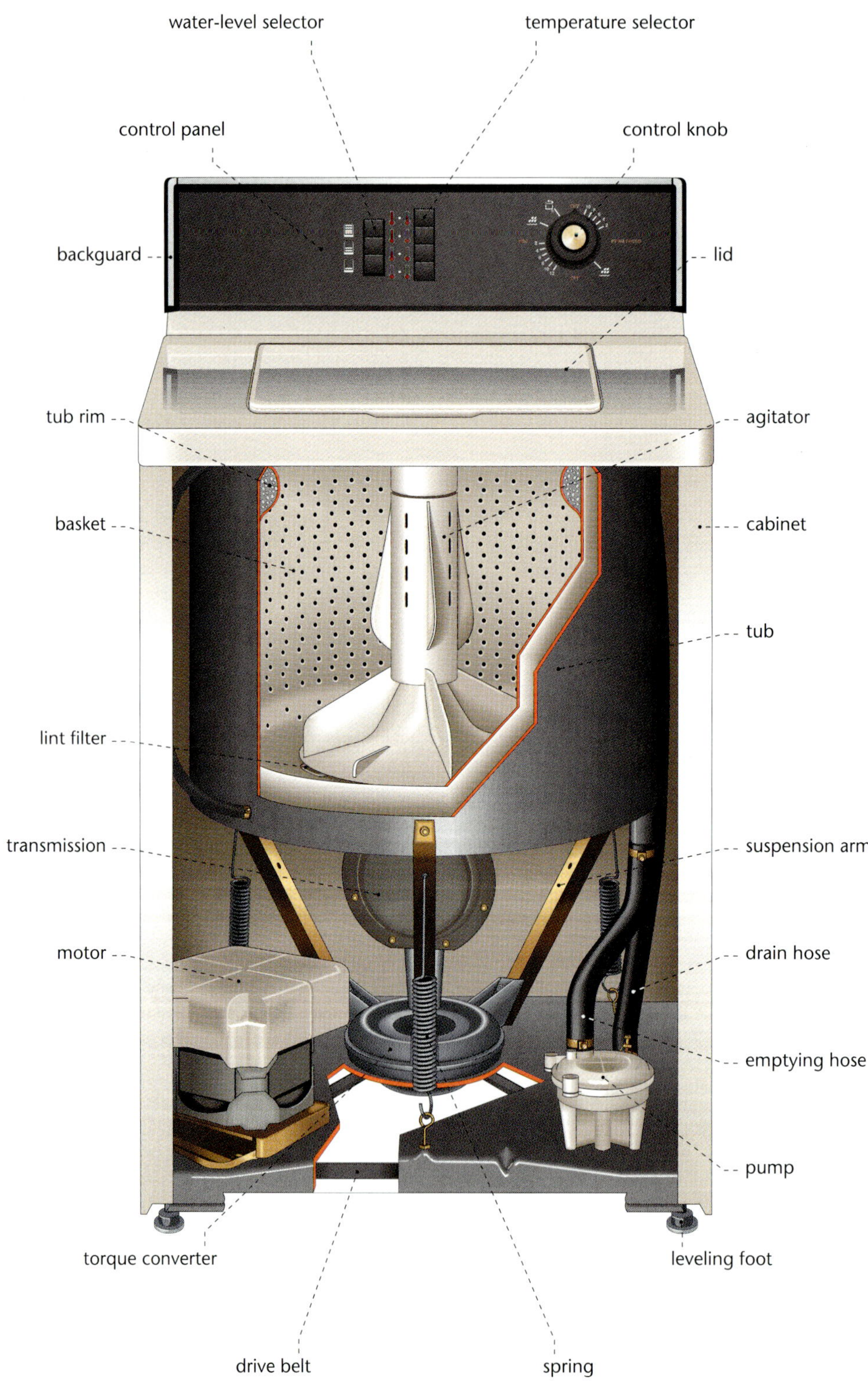

HOUSE FURNITURE

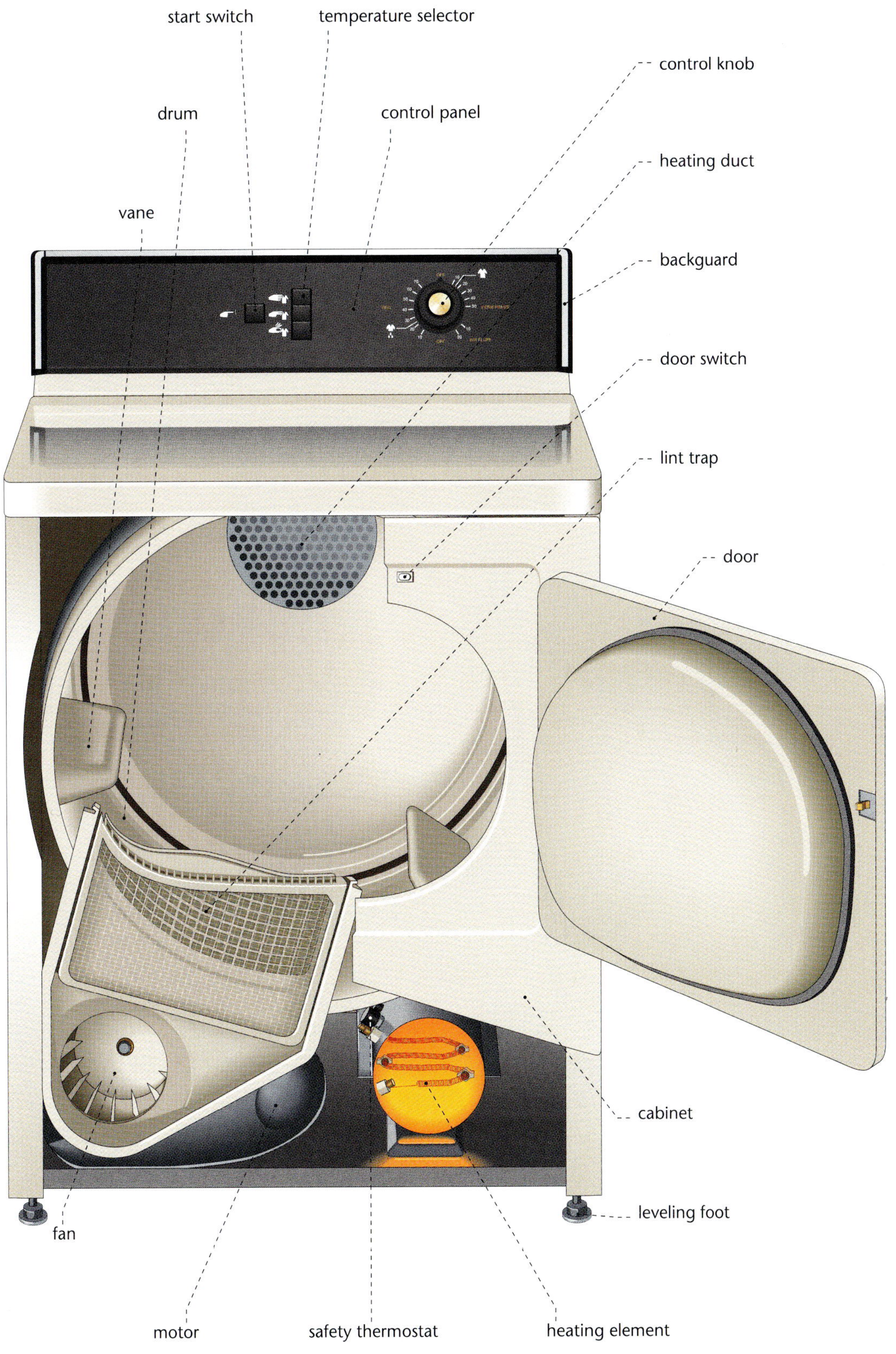

HAND VACUUM CLEANER

locking button
dust receiver
on-off switch
motor unit
recharging base

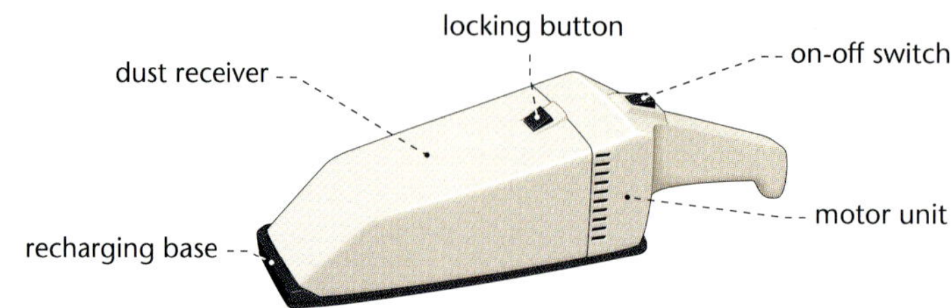

CANISTER VACUUM CLEANER

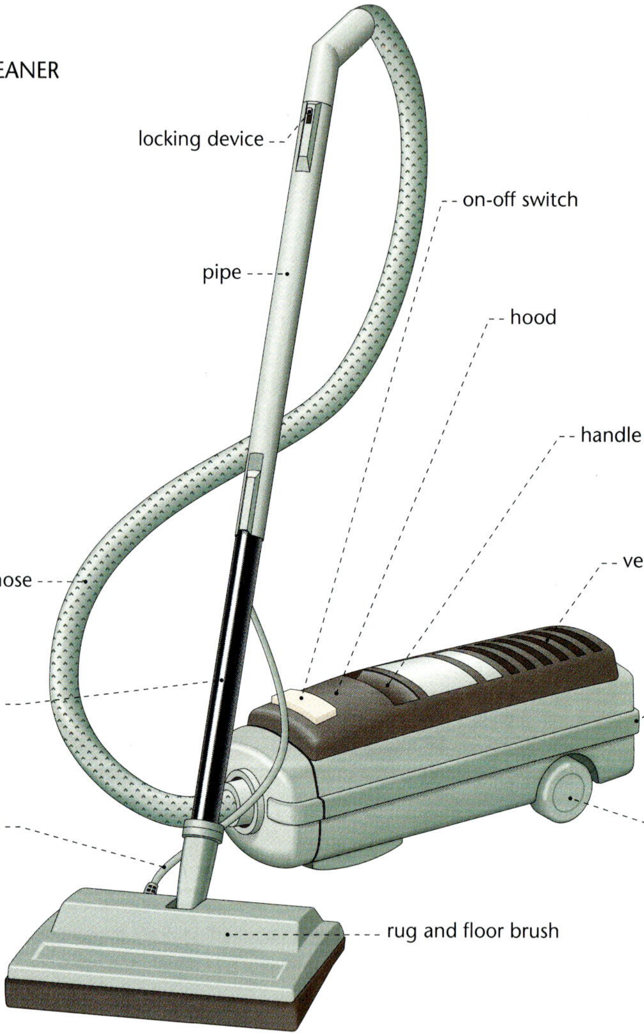

locking device
on-off switch
pipe
hood
handle
ventilating grille
flexible hose
extension pipe
bumper
cord
caster
rug and floor brush

CLEANING TOOLS

upholstery nozzle
crevice tool
floor brush
dusting brush

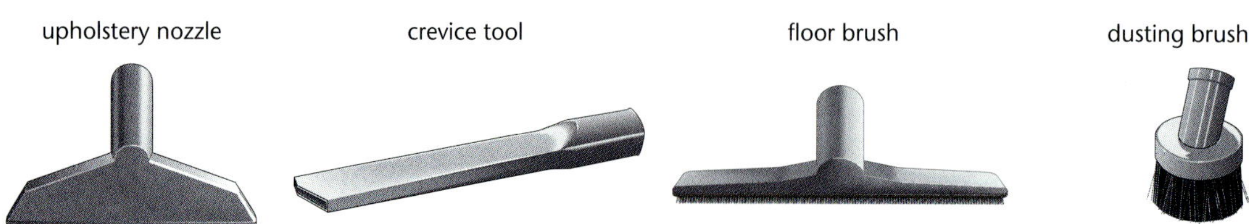

GARDENING

CONTENTS

PLEASURE GARDEN

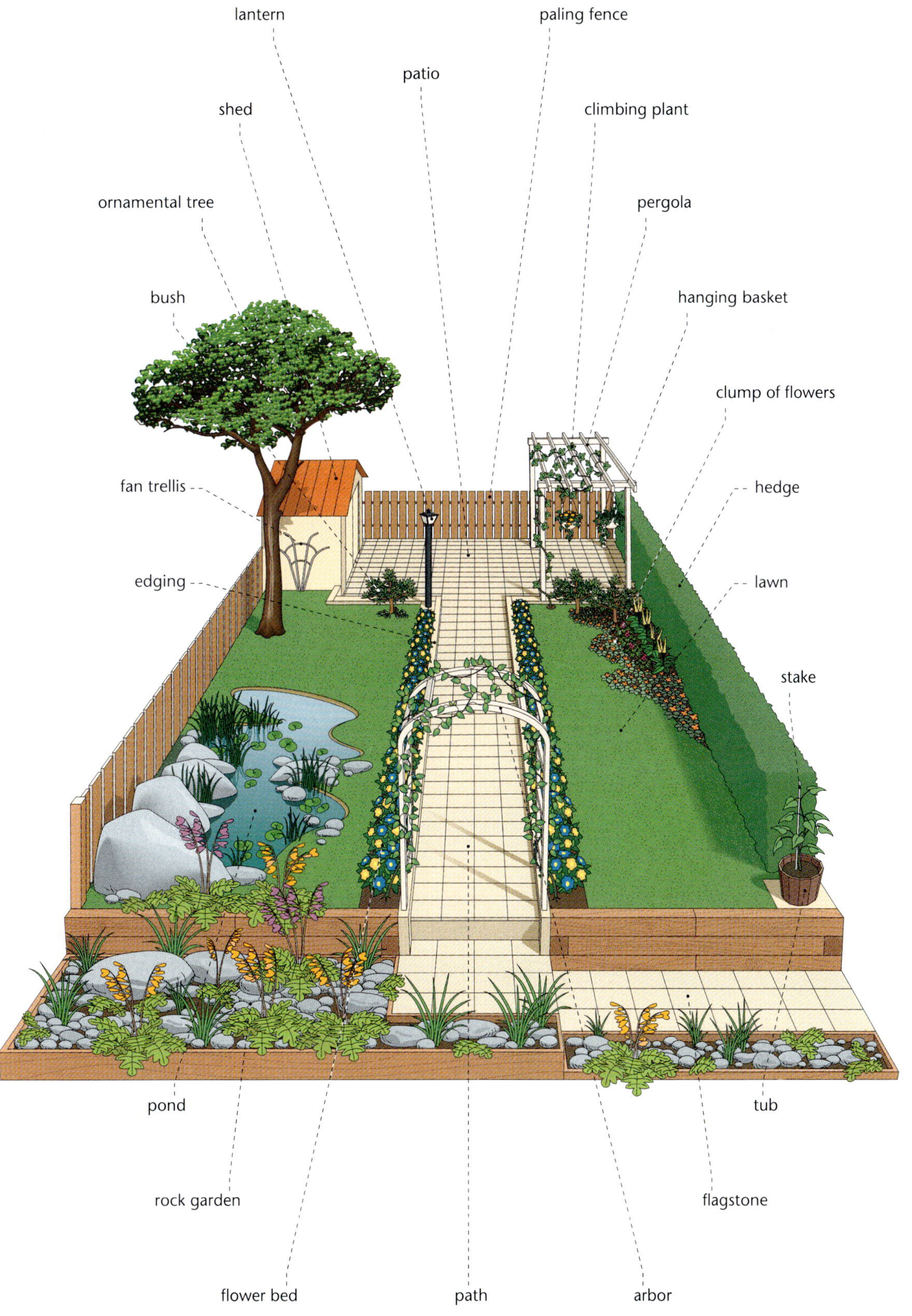

TOOLS AND EQUIPMENT

pistol nozzle

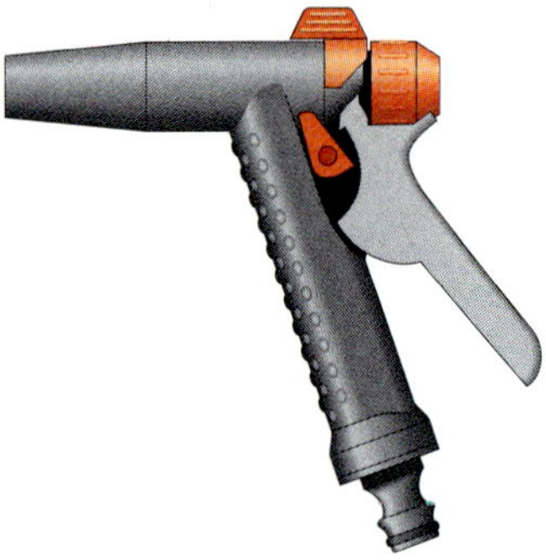

sprayer

spray nozzle

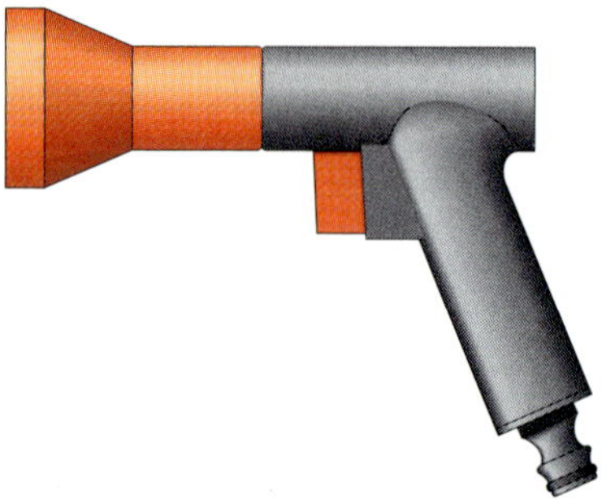

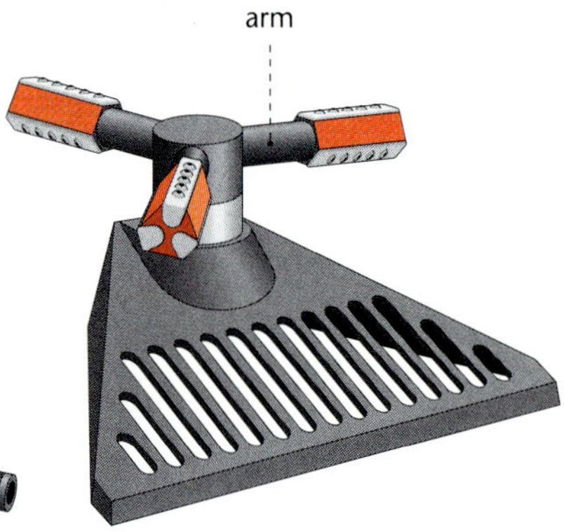

arm

REVOLVING SPRINKLER

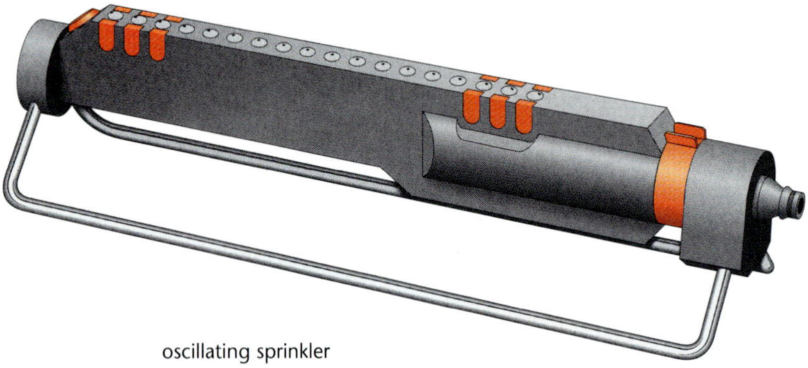

oscillating sprinkler

IMPULSE SPRINKLER

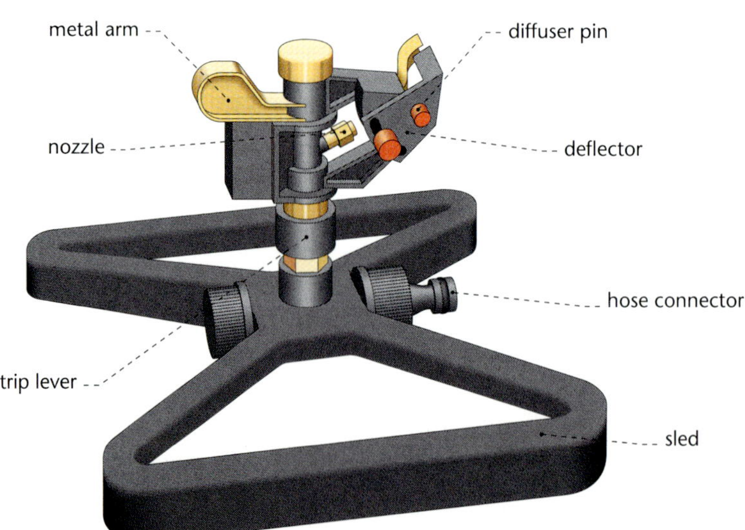

HOSE TROLLEY

sprinkler hose

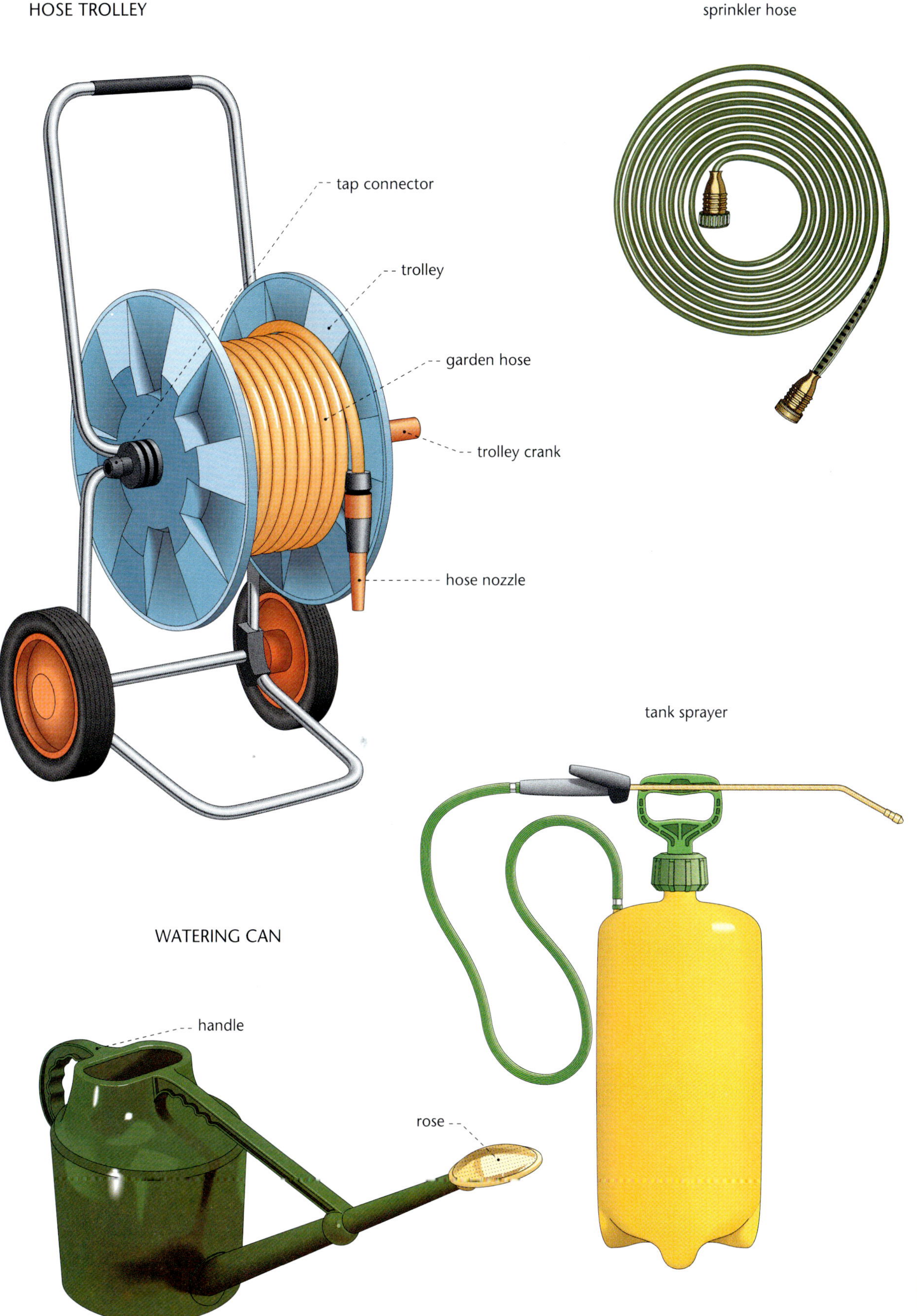

shovel
spade
spading fork
lawn edger
scuffle hoe
lawn aerator
draw hoe
hoe-fork
weeding hoe

hook
rake
lawn rake
scythe
hoe
pick

hand fork
weeder
trowel
small hand cultivator
seeder
garden line
dibble
bulb dibble
HEDGE TRIMMER
cord
hand protector
trigger
tooth
electric motor
blade

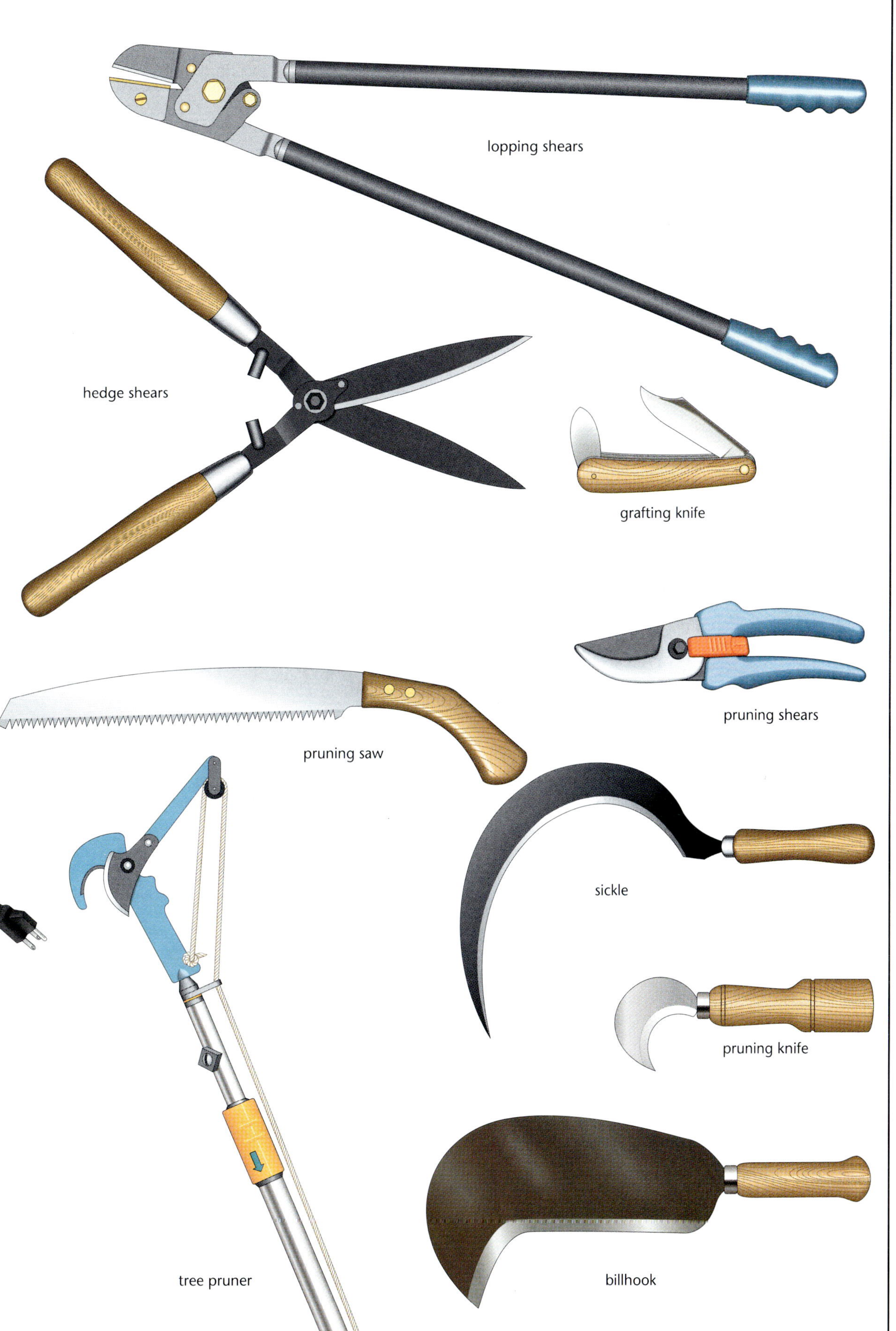

lopping shears
hedge shears
grafting knife
pruning shears
pruning saw
sickle
pruning knife
tree pruner
billhook

spreader
MOTORIZED EARTH AUGER
handle
control cable
auger bit
starting cable
motor
WHEELBARROW
tray
handle
leg
wheel
roller

HAND MOWER
EDGER
cord
blade
electric motor
security casing
nylon yarn
cutting cylinder

POWER MOWER
handle
speed control
safety handle
ignition key
grassbox
motor
starter
accelerator cable
filler cap
spark plug
deflector
casing

CHAINSAW

TILLER

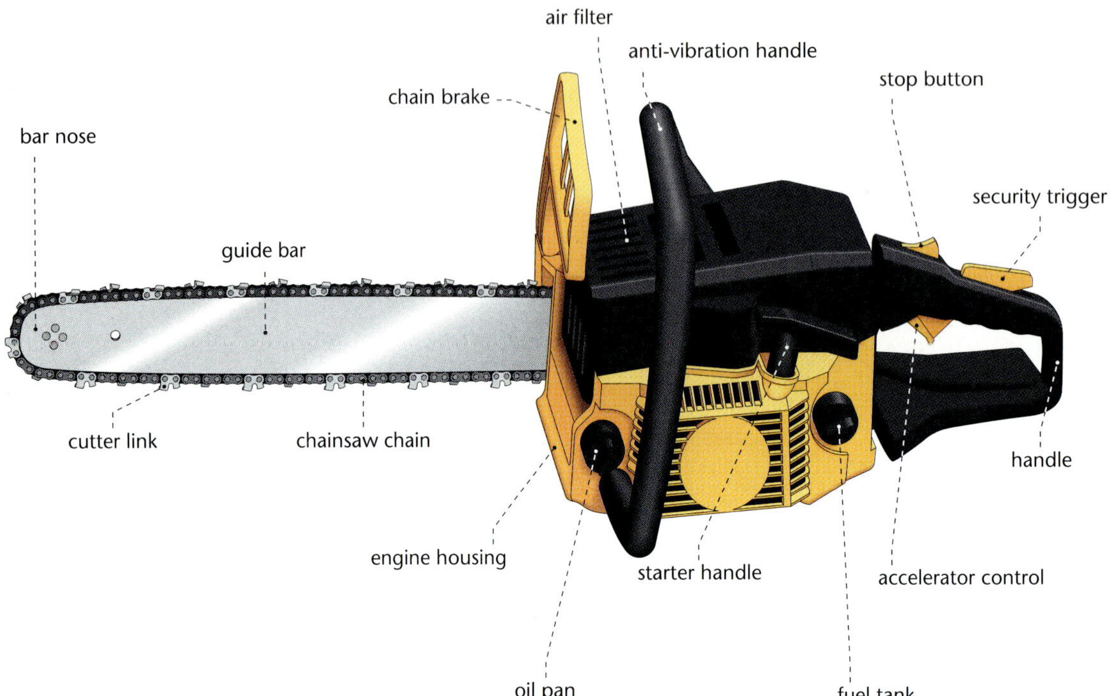

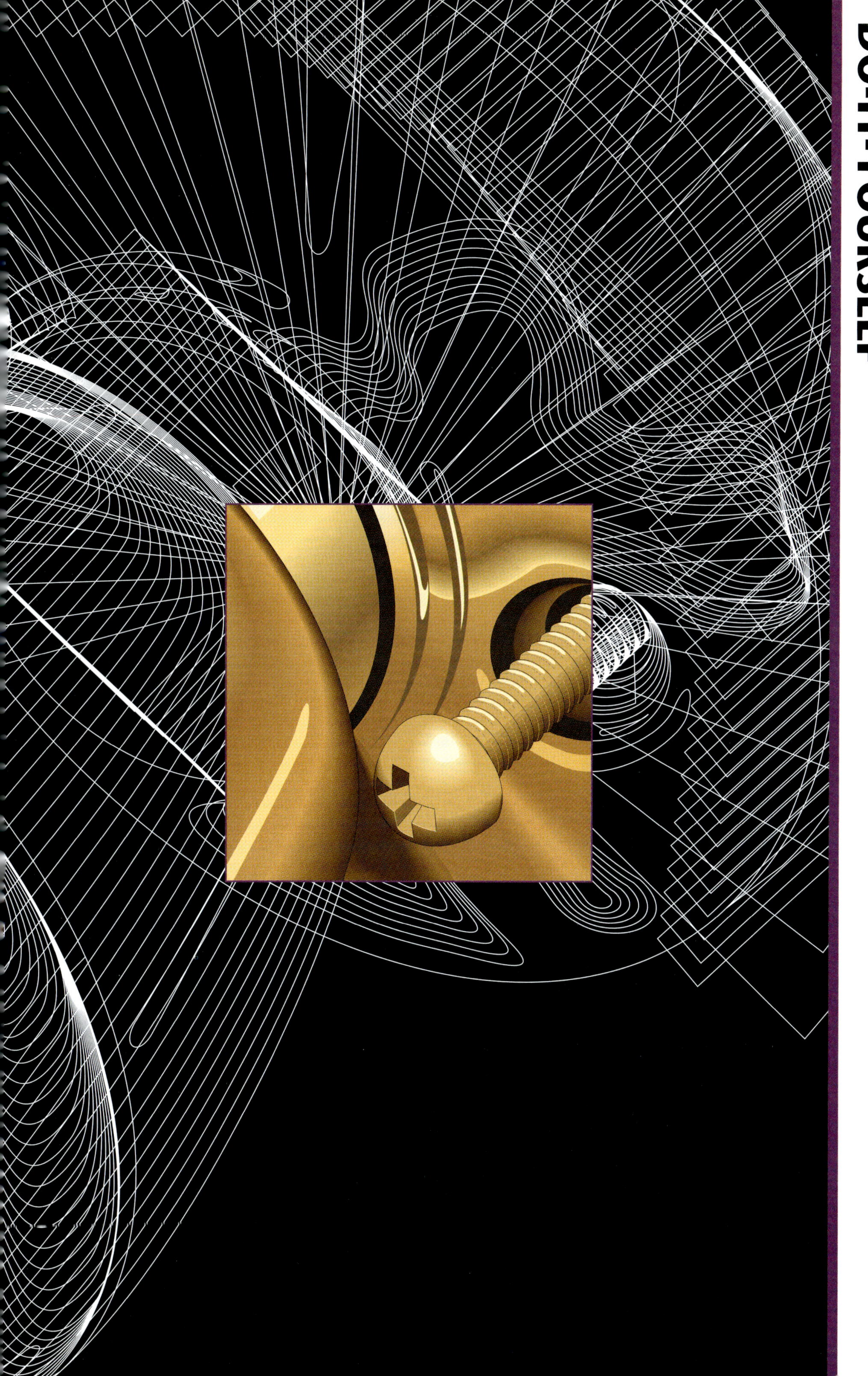

DO-IT-YOURSELF

CONTENTS

DO-IT-YOURSELF

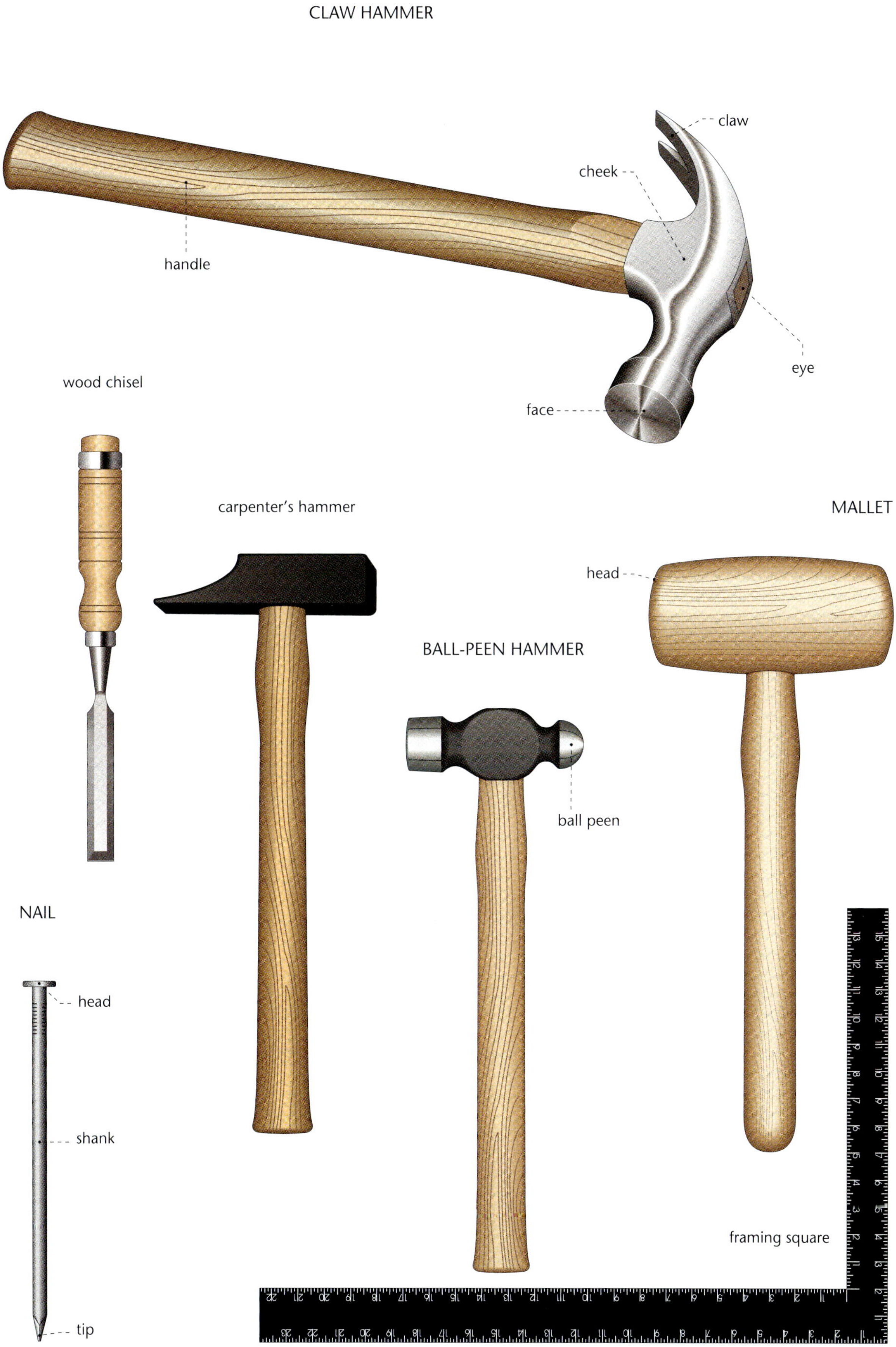

CLAW HAMMER

claw

cheek

handle

eye

face

wood chisel

carpenter's hammer

MALLET

head

BALL-PEEN HAMMER

ball peen

NAIL

head

shank

tip

framing square

DO-IT-YOURSELF

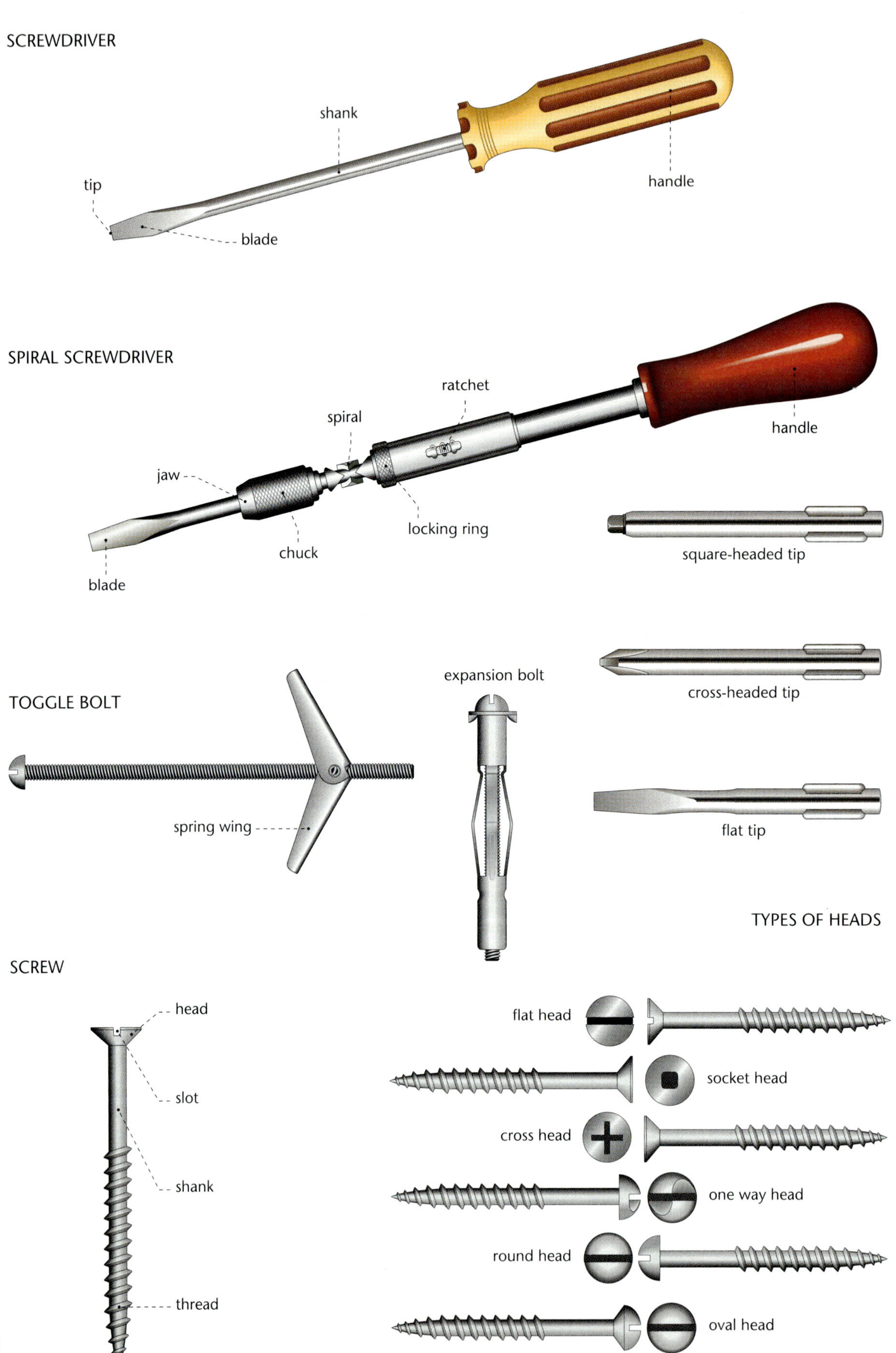

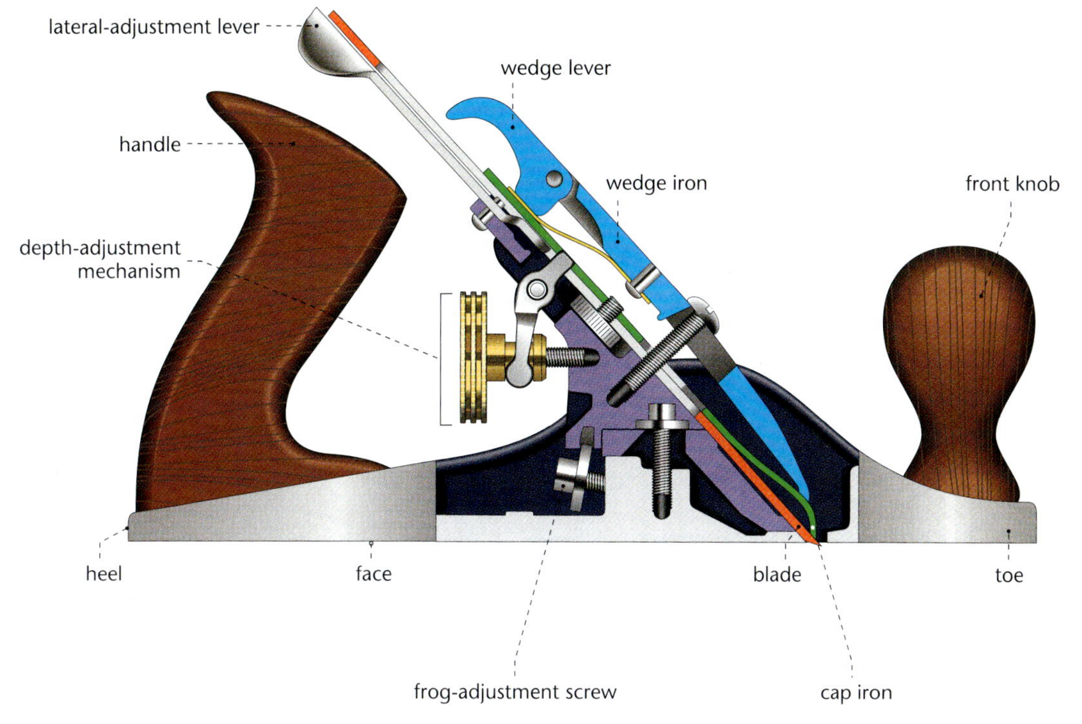

HACKSAW

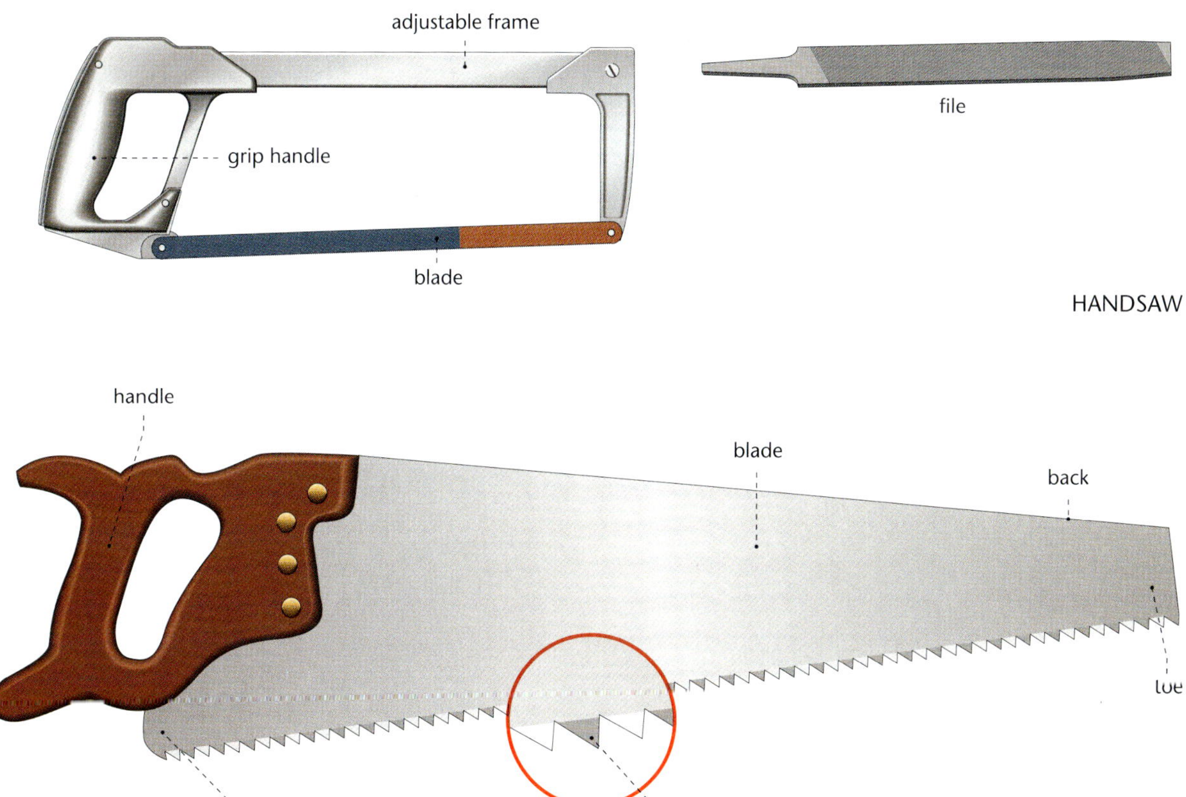

HANDSAW

DO-IT-YOURSELF

SLIP JOINT PLIERS

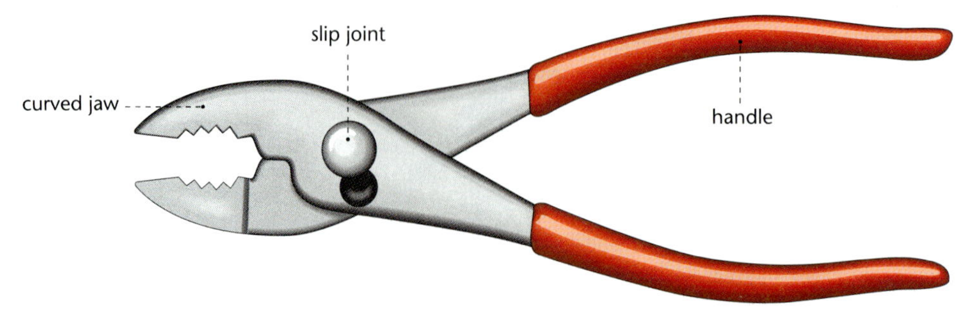

RIB JOINT PLIERS

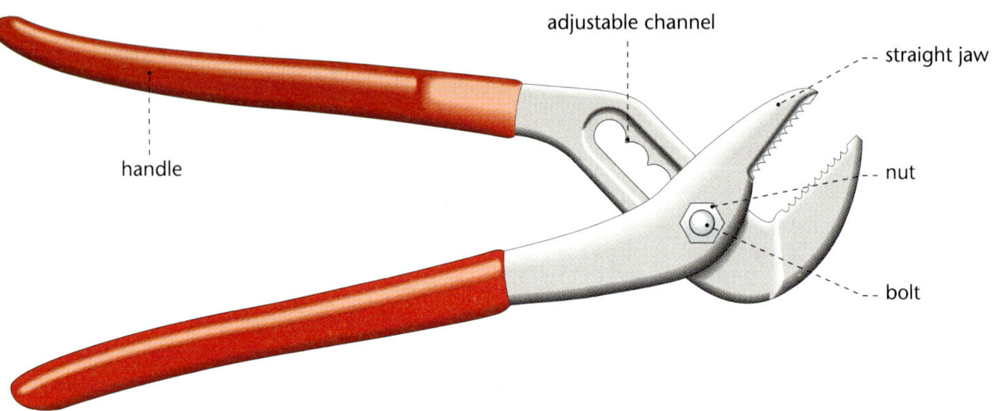

LOCKING PLIERS

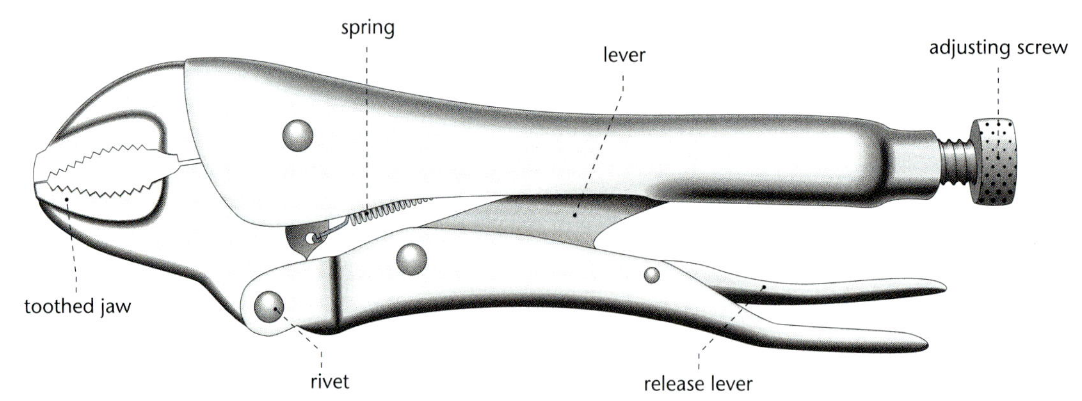

WASHERS

flat washer 

lock washer 

internal tooth lock washer 

external tooth lock washer 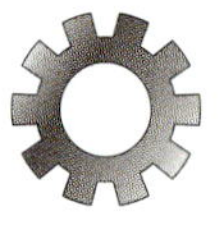

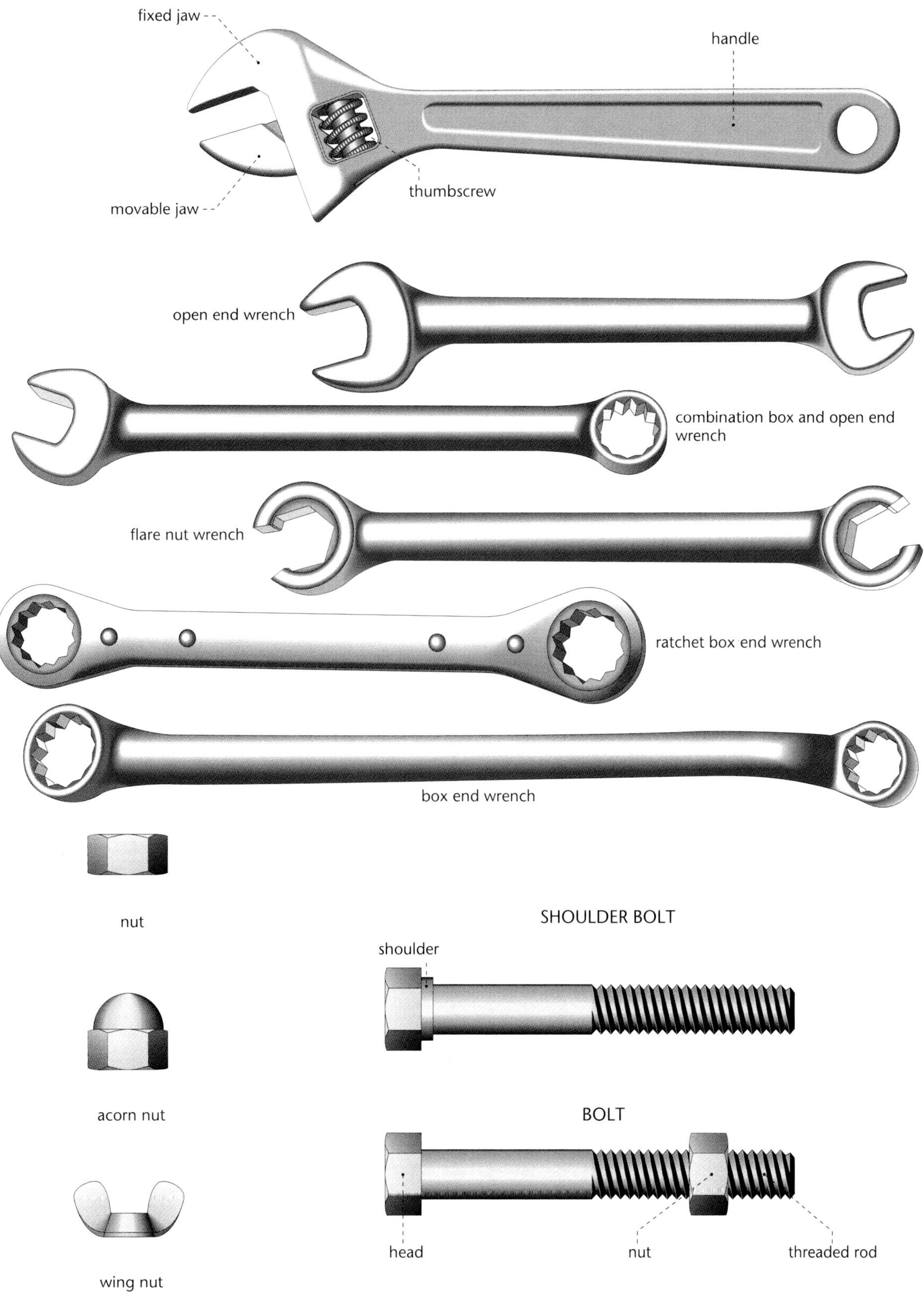

CRESCENT WRENCH
fixed jaw
handle
movable jaw
thumbscrew
open end wrench
combination box and open end wrench
flare nut wrench
ratchet box end wrench
box end wrench
nut
acorn nut
wing nut
SHOULDER BOLT
shoulder
BOLT
head
nut
threaded rod

ELECTRIC DRILL

HAND DRILL

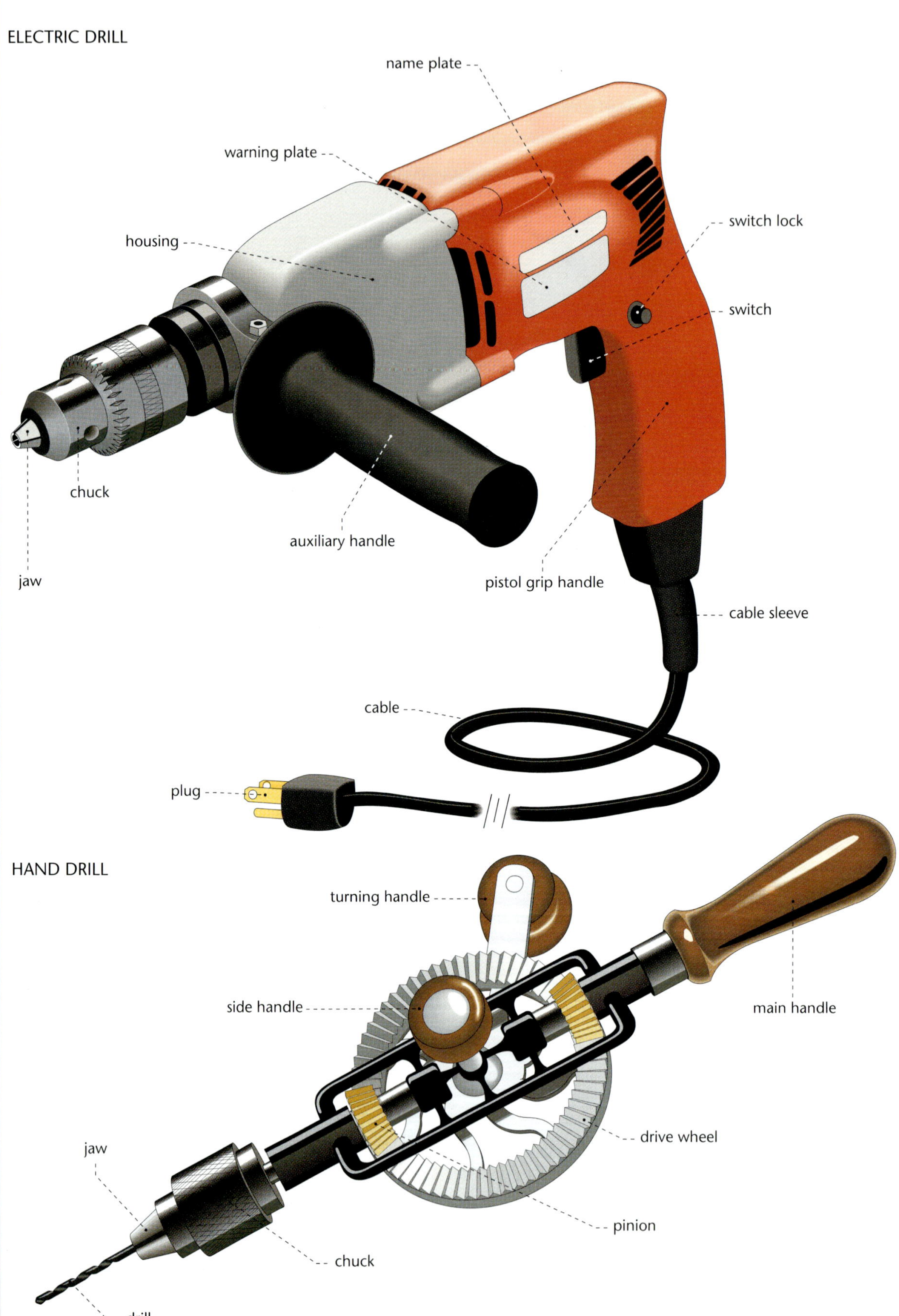

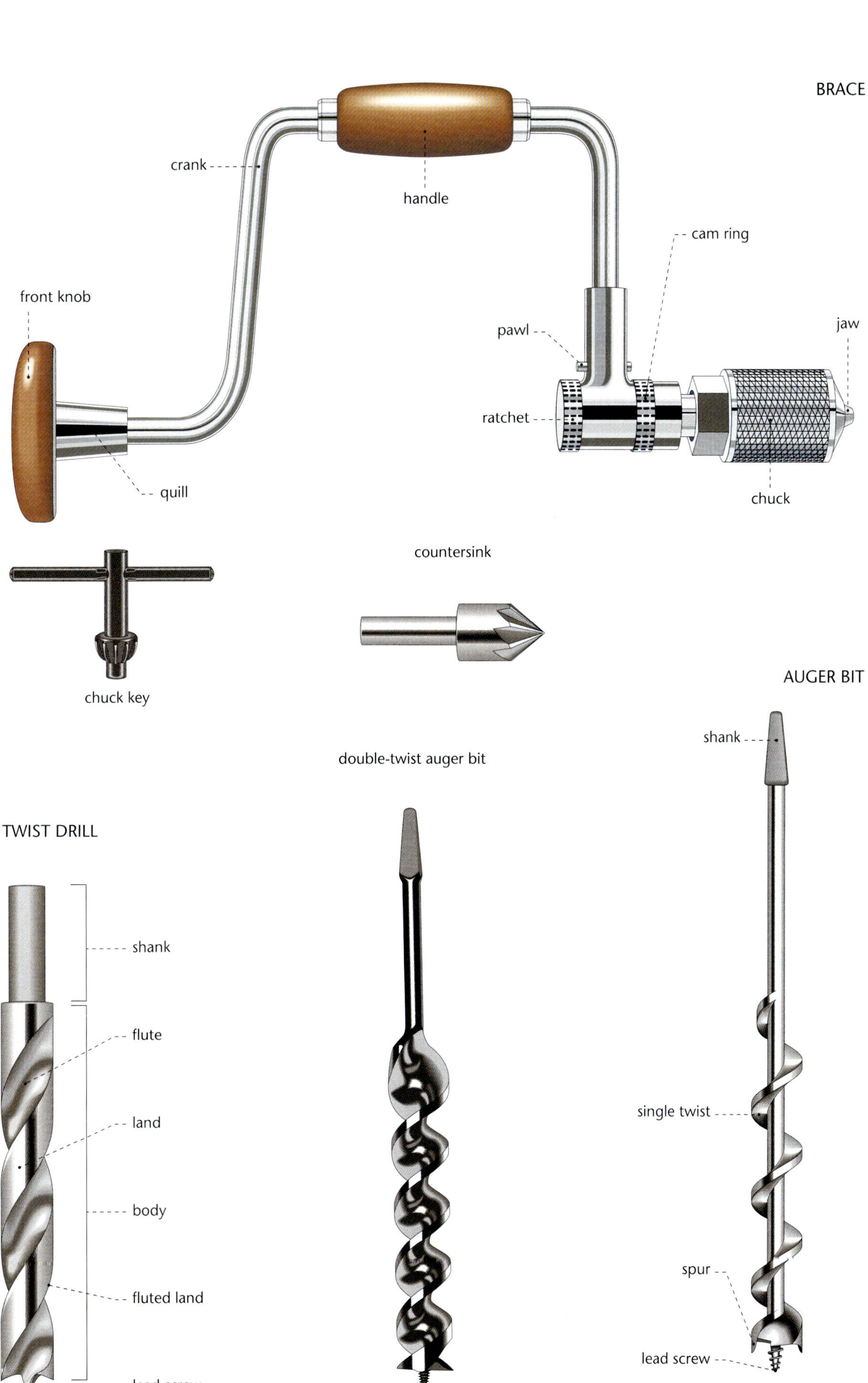

BRACE
crank
handle
cam ring
front knob
pawl
jaw
quill
ratchet
chuck
countersink
chuck key
AUGER BIT
shank
double-twist auger bit
TWIST DRILL
shank
flute
single twist
land
body
fluted land
spur
lead screw
lead screw

C-CLAMP

fixed jaw
movable jaw
swivel head
adjusting screw
throat
frame
handle

VISE

movable jaw
fixed jaw
adjusting screw
swivel lock
handle
bolt
swivel base
fixed base

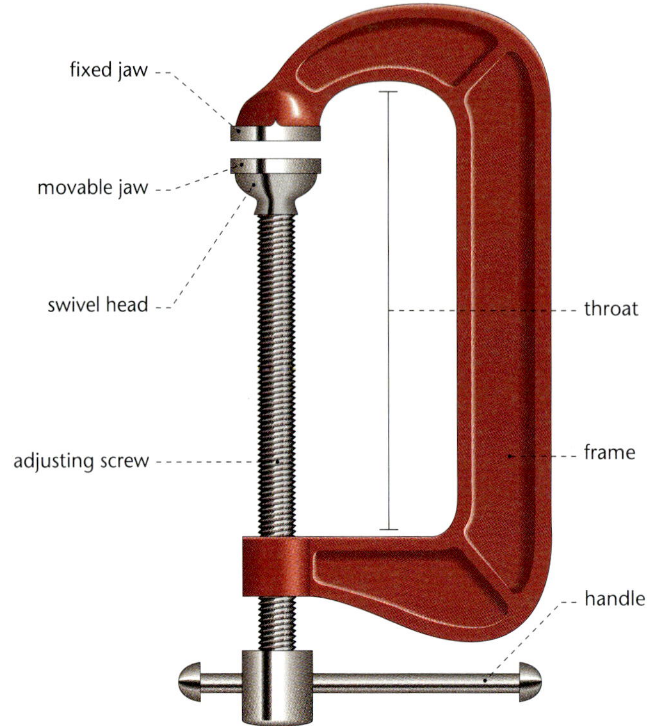

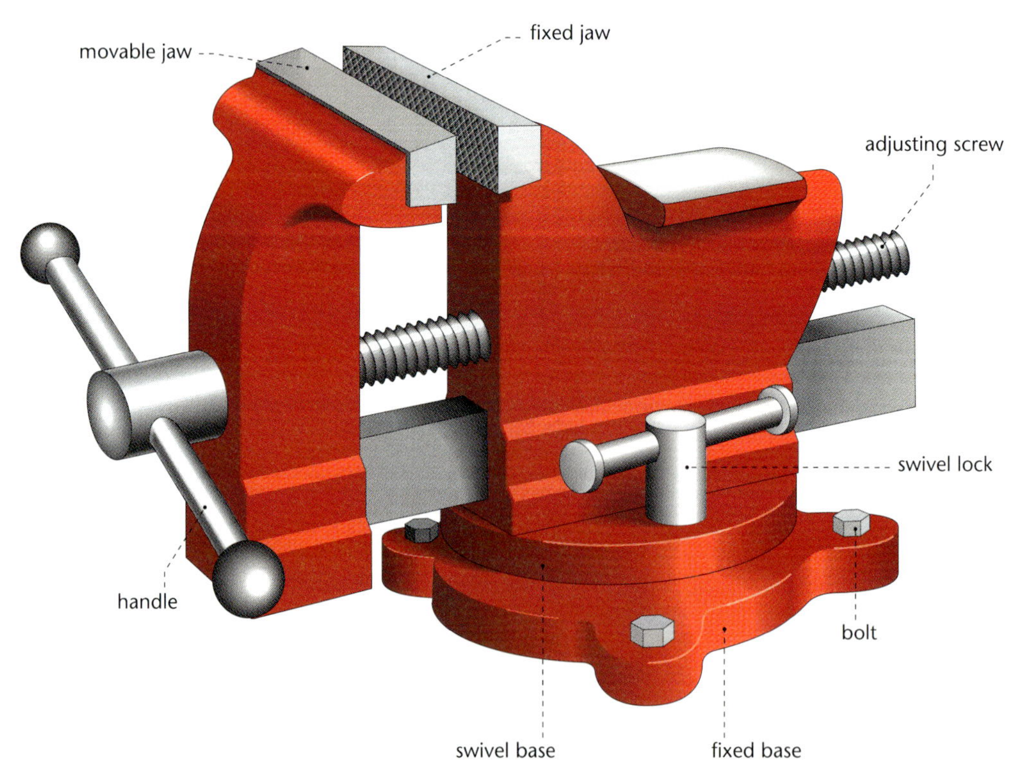

DO-IT-YOURSELF

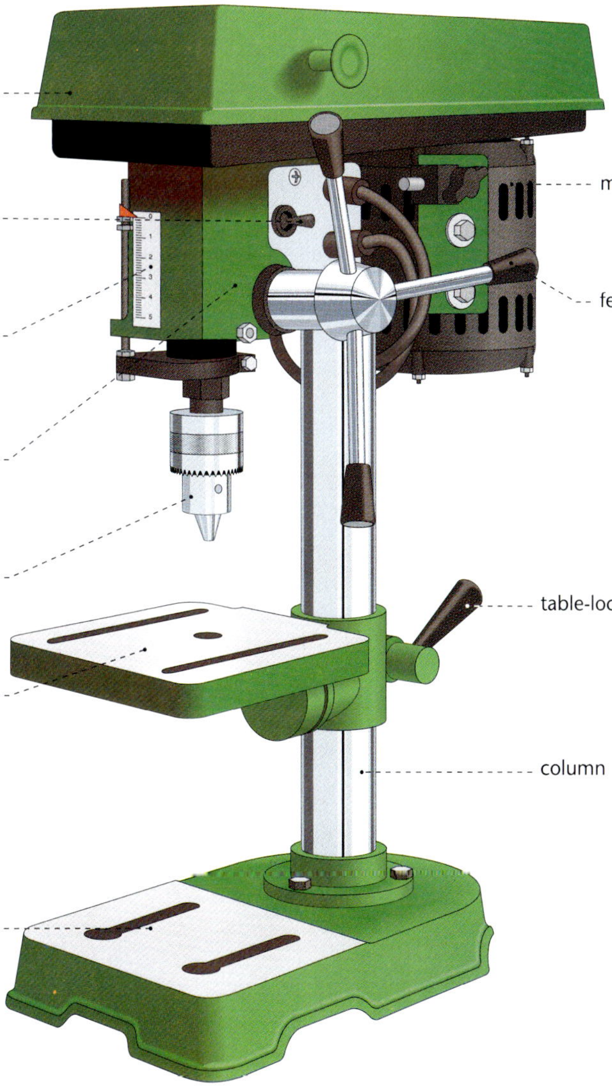

CIRCULAR SAW BLADE

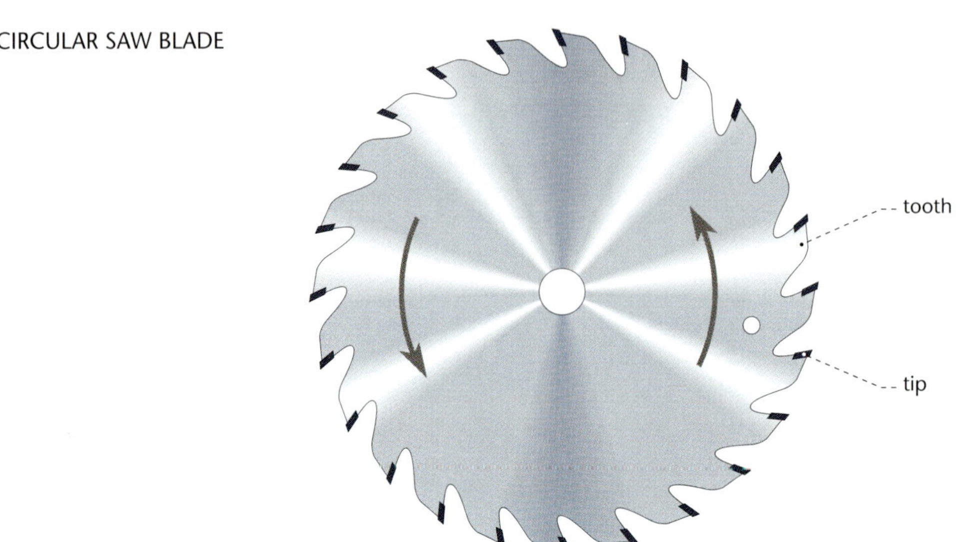

CIRCULAR SAW

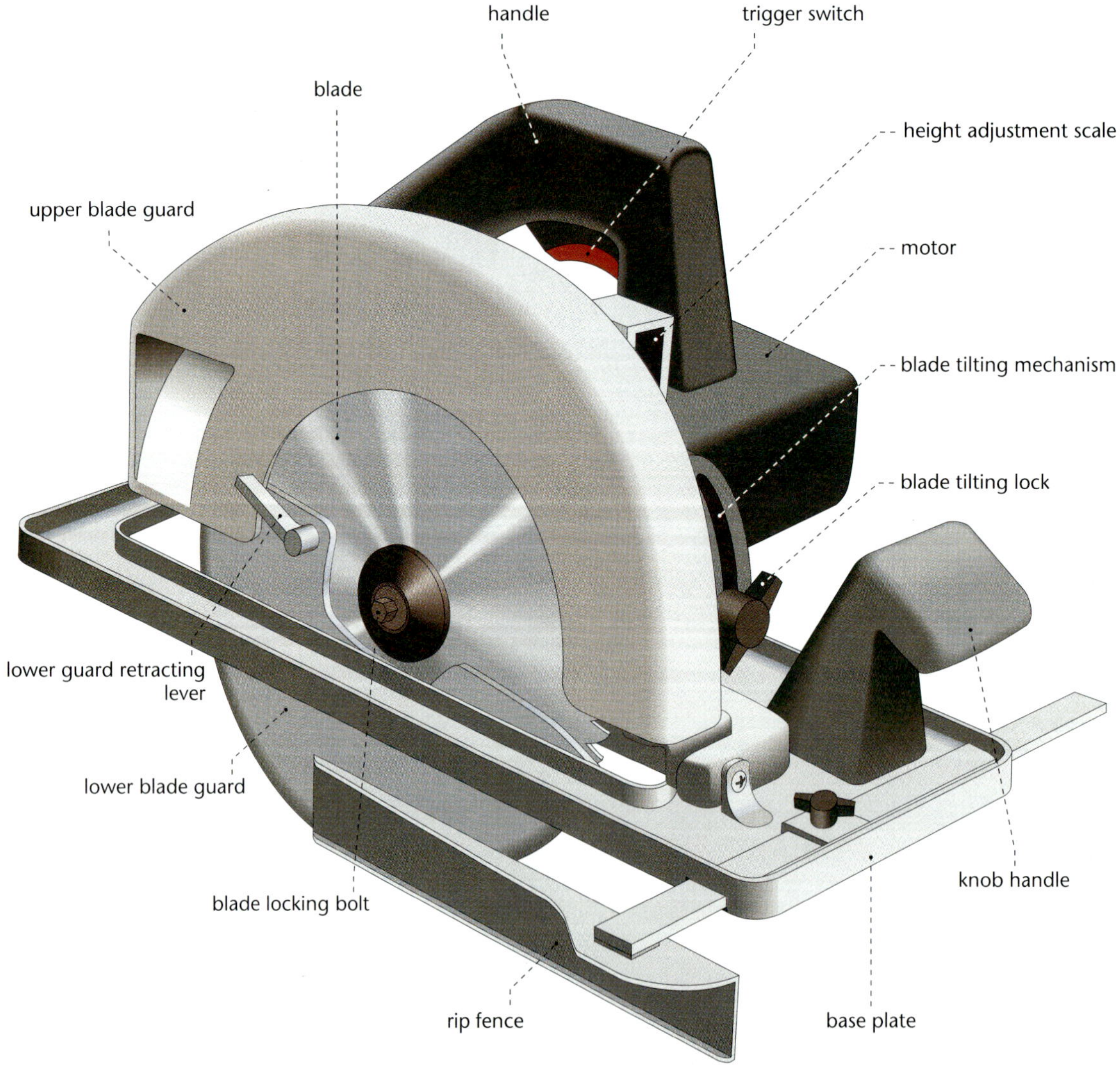

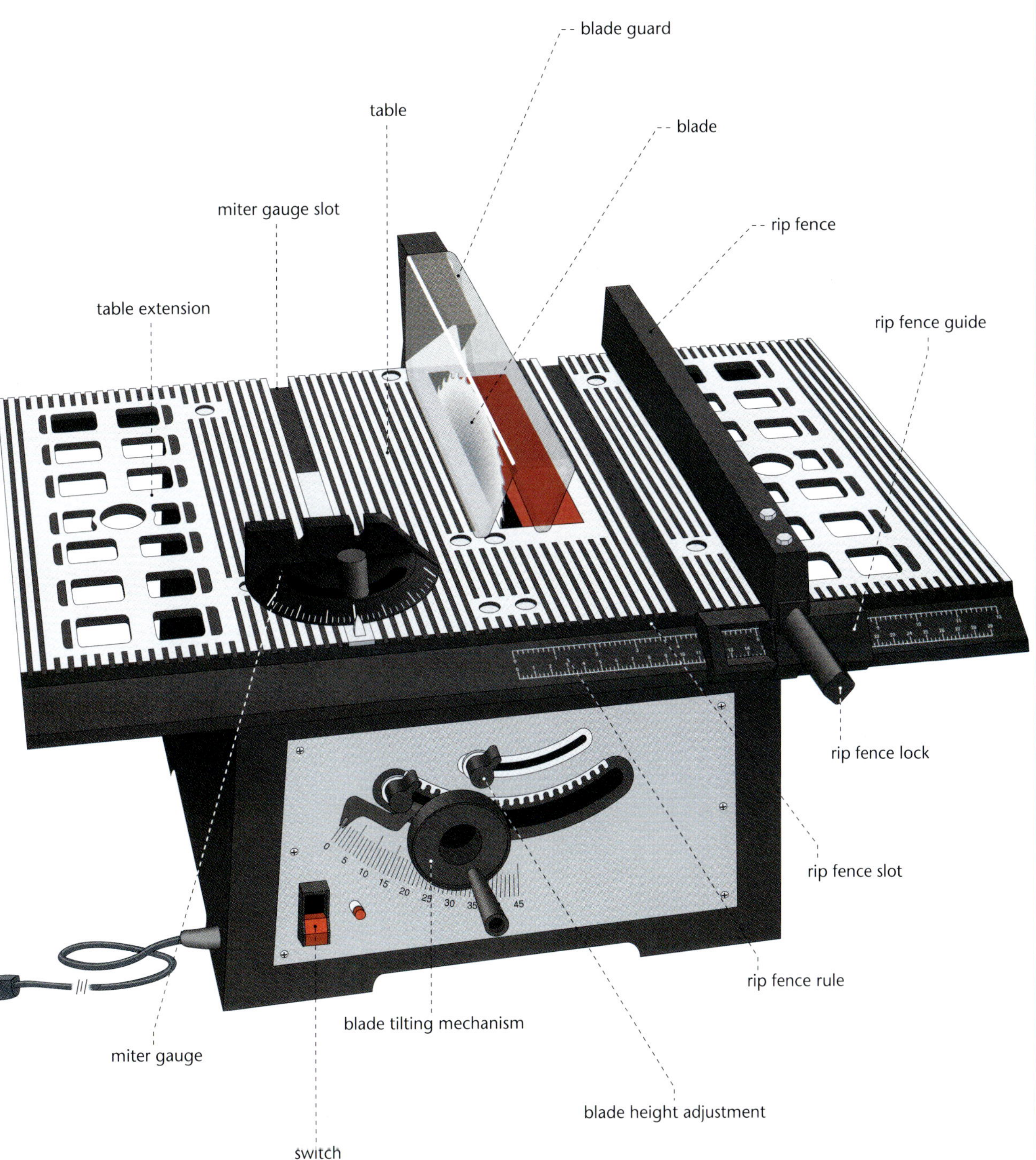
blade guard
table
blade
rip fence
miter gauge slot
table extension
rip fence guide
rip fence lock
rip fence slot
rip fence rule
blade height adjustment
blade tilting mechanism
miter gauge
switch

DO-IT-YOURSELF

spring-metal insulation

foam insulation

molded insulation

foam-rubber insulation

vinyl insulation

board insulation

pipe-wrapping insulation

loose fill insulation

blanket insulation

WOOD

SECTION OF A LOG

hardboard

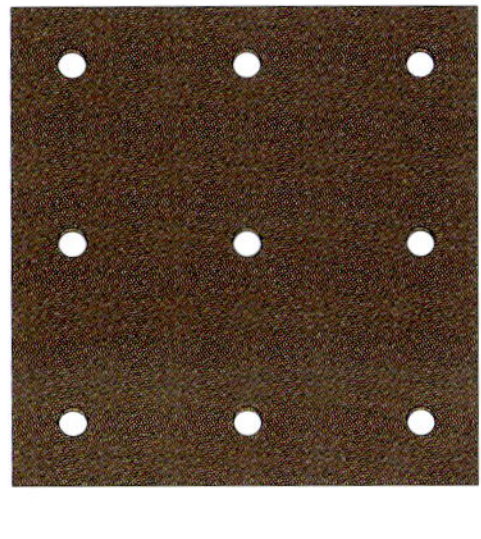

perforated hardboard

plastic-laminated particle board

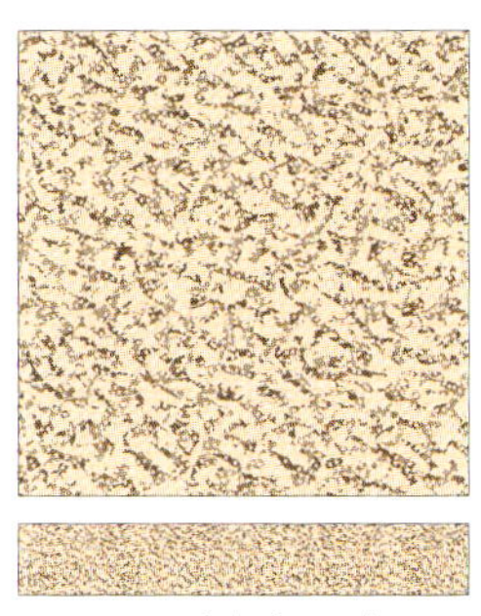

particle board

LOCK

GENERAL VIEW

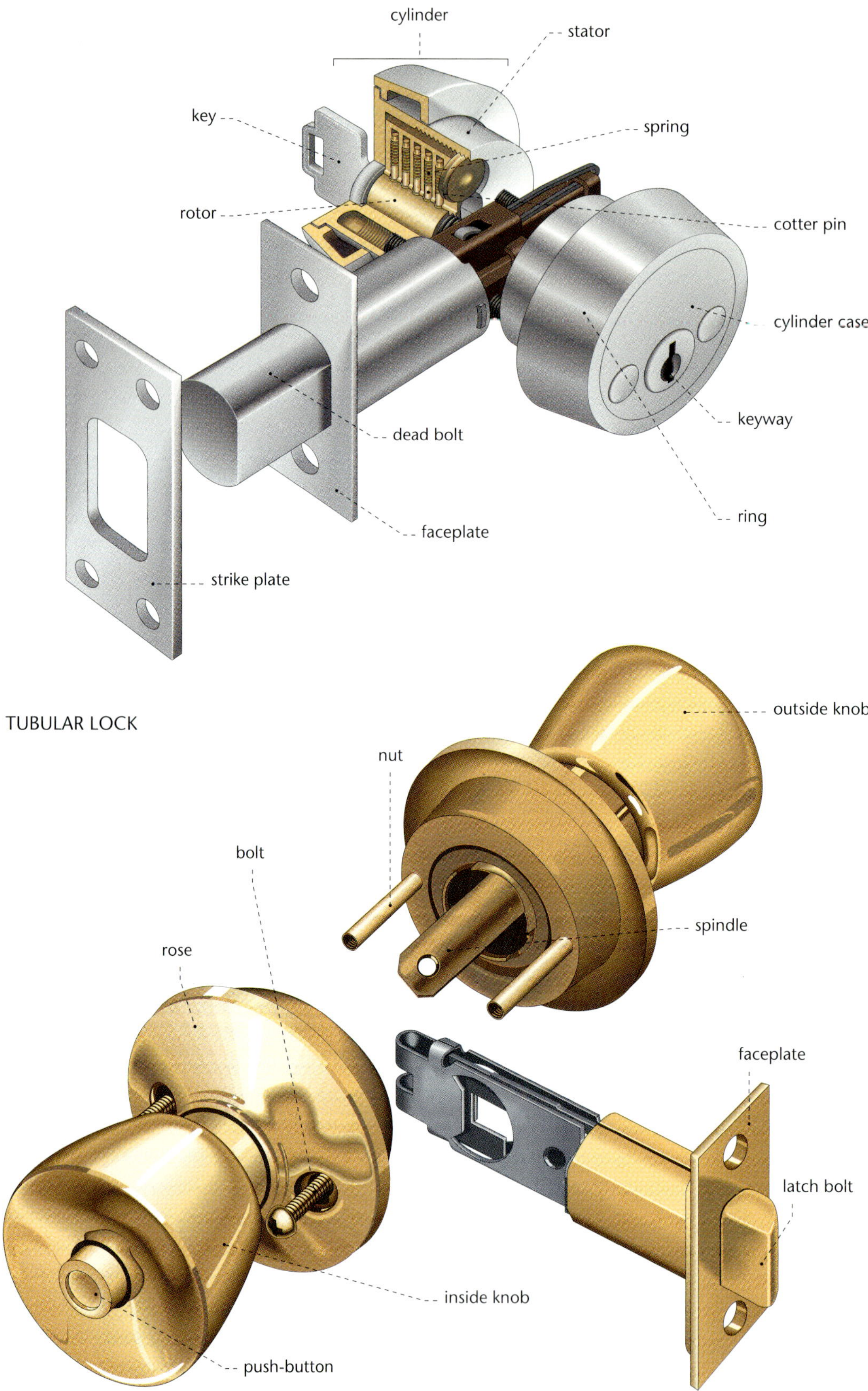
MORTISE LOCK
cylinder
stator
key
spring
rotor
cotter pin
cylinder case
dead bolt
keyway
faceplate
ring
strike plate
TUBULAR LOCK
outside knob
nut
bolt
spindle
rose
faceplate
latch bolt
inside knob
push-button

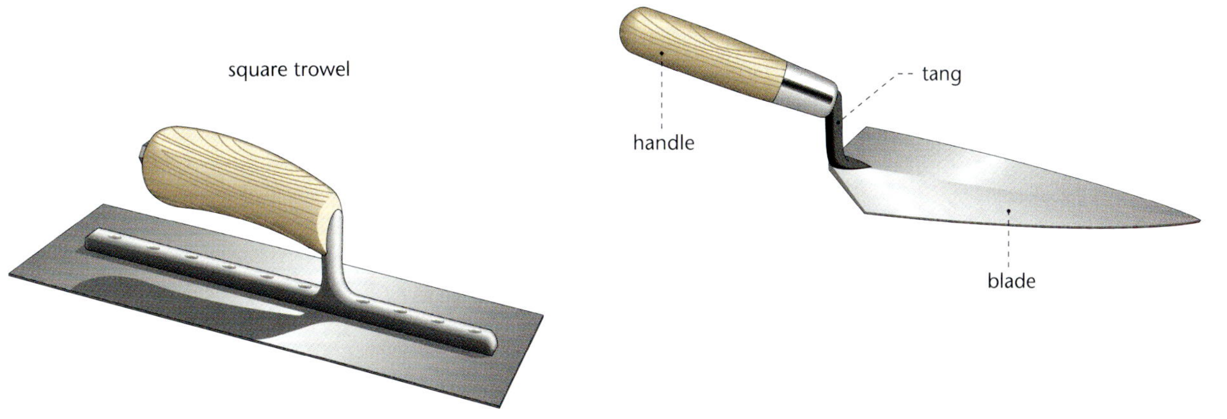

MASON'S TROWEL
square trowel
tang
handle
blade

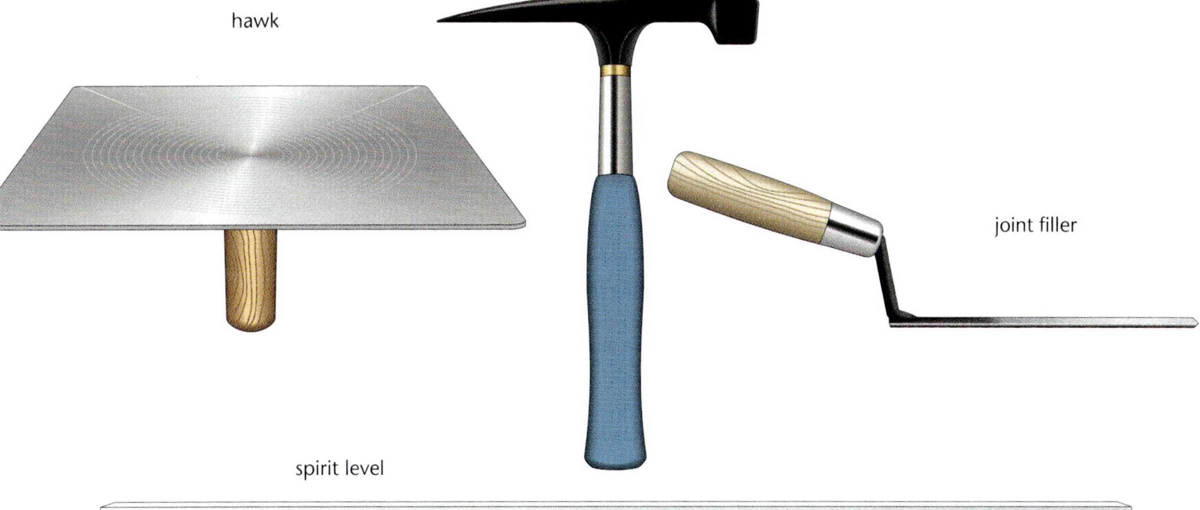

bricklayer's hammer
hawk
joint filler

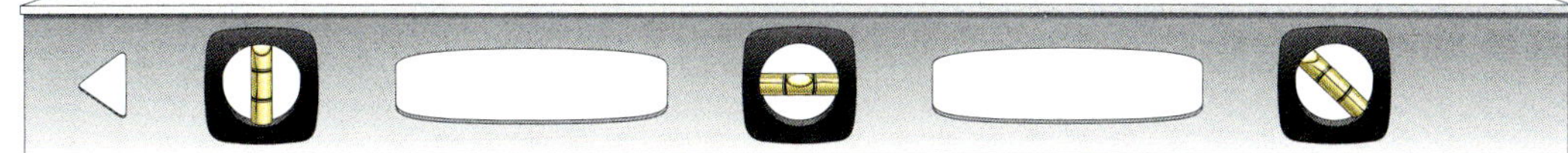

spirit level

CAULKING GUN

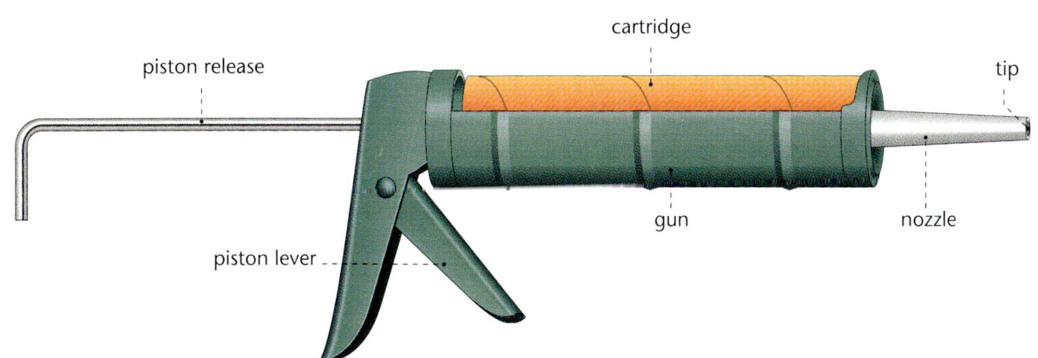

cartridge
piston release
tip
gun
nozzle
piston lever

DO-IT-YOURSELF

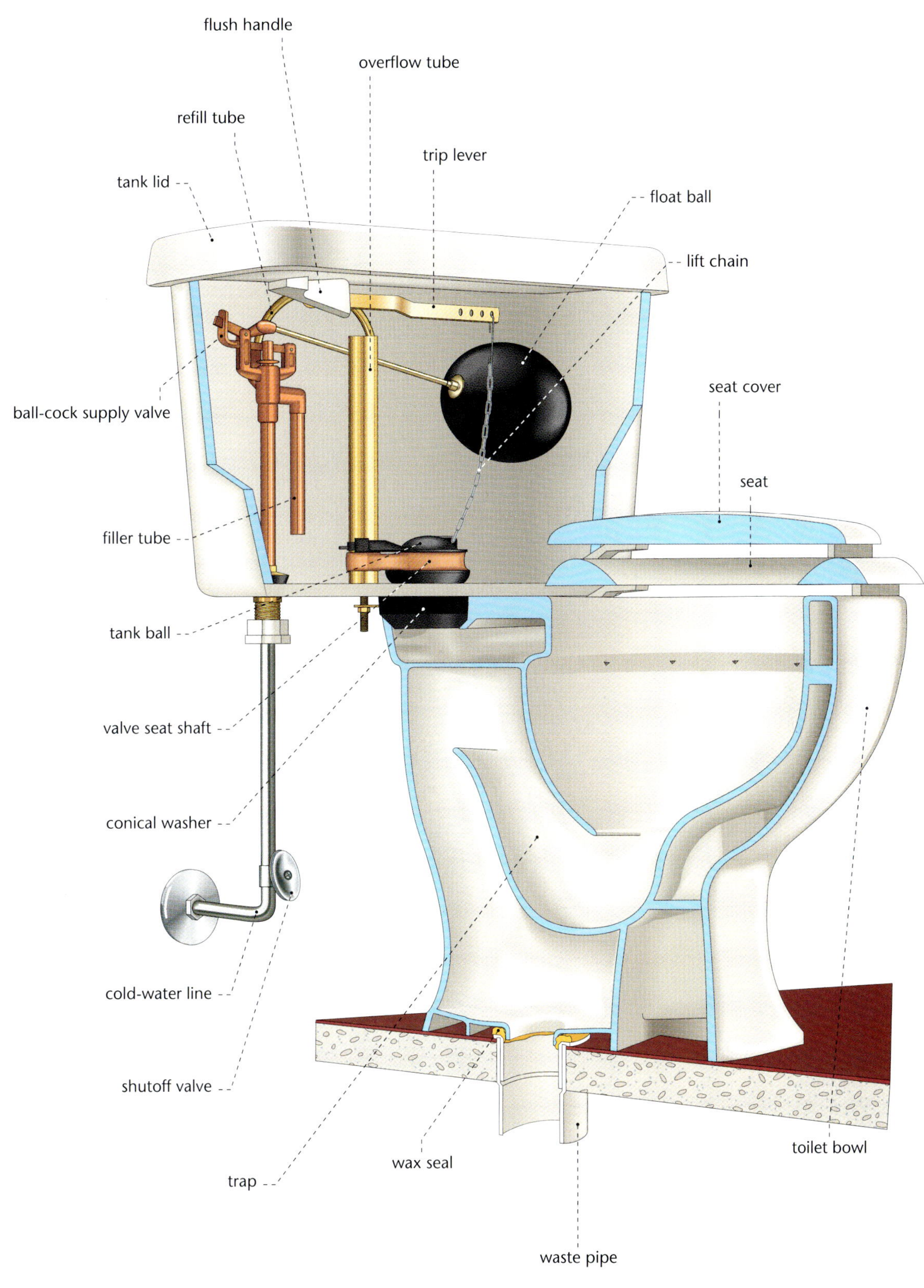
flush handle
overflow tube
refill tube
trip lever
tank lid
float ball
lift chain
ball-cock supply valve
seat cover
seat
filler tube
tank ball
valve seat shaft
conical washer
cold-water line
shutoff valve
trap
wax seal
toilet bowl
waste pipe

STEM FAUCET

BALL-TYPE FAUCET

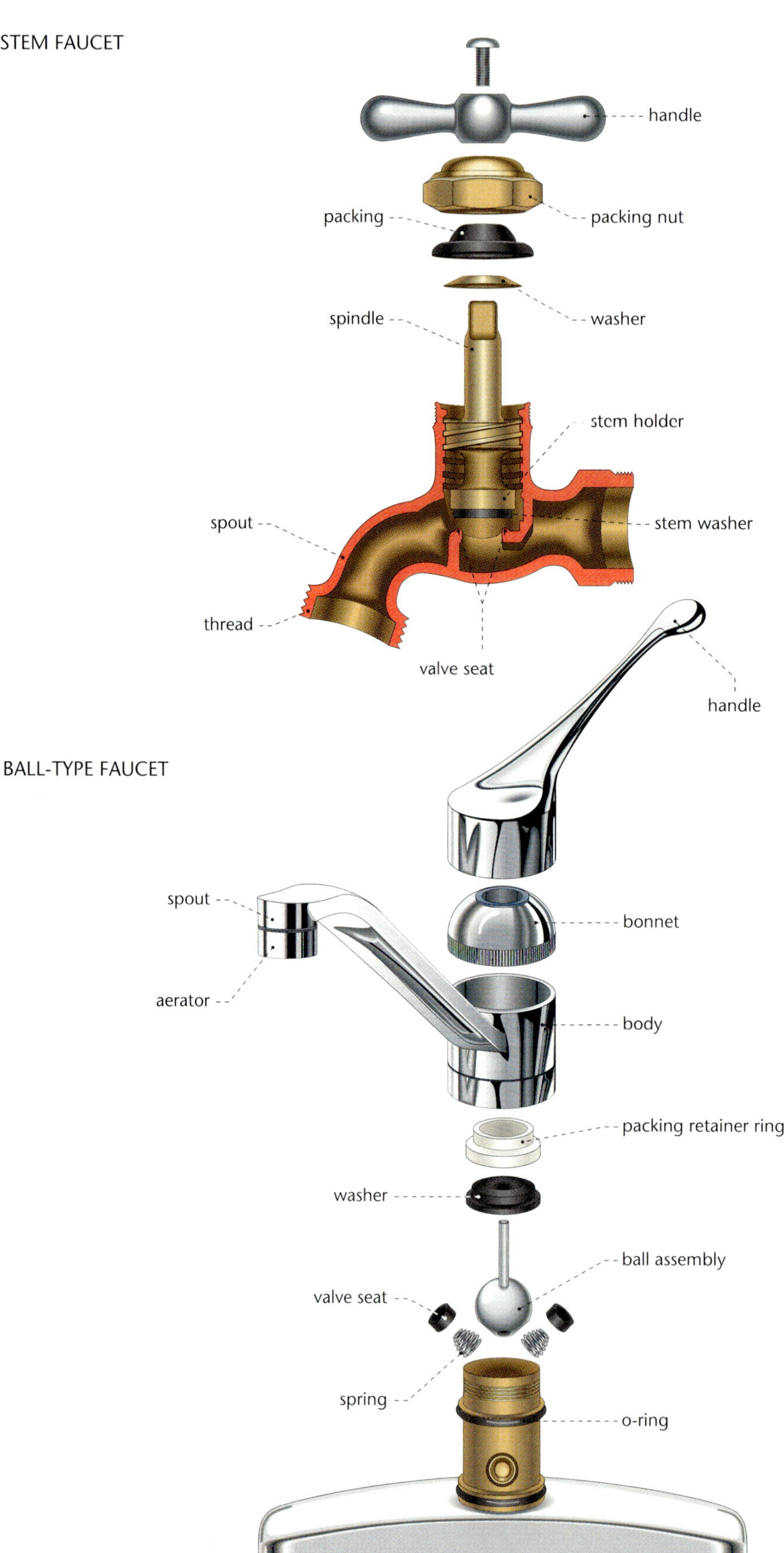

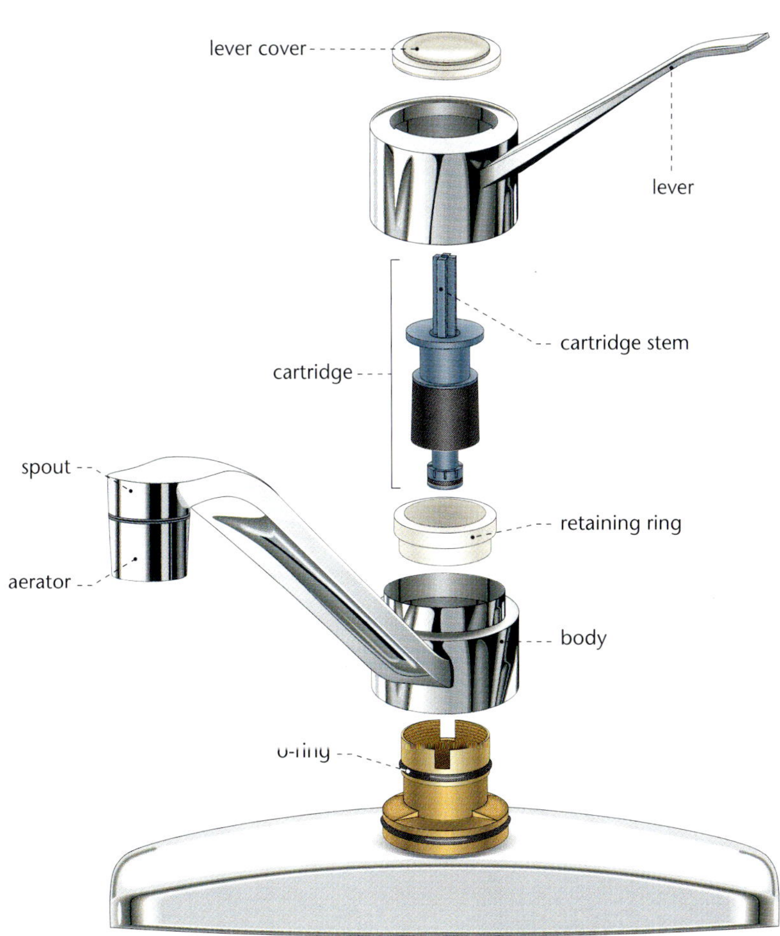

DO-IT-YOURSELF

GARBAGE DISPOSAL SINK

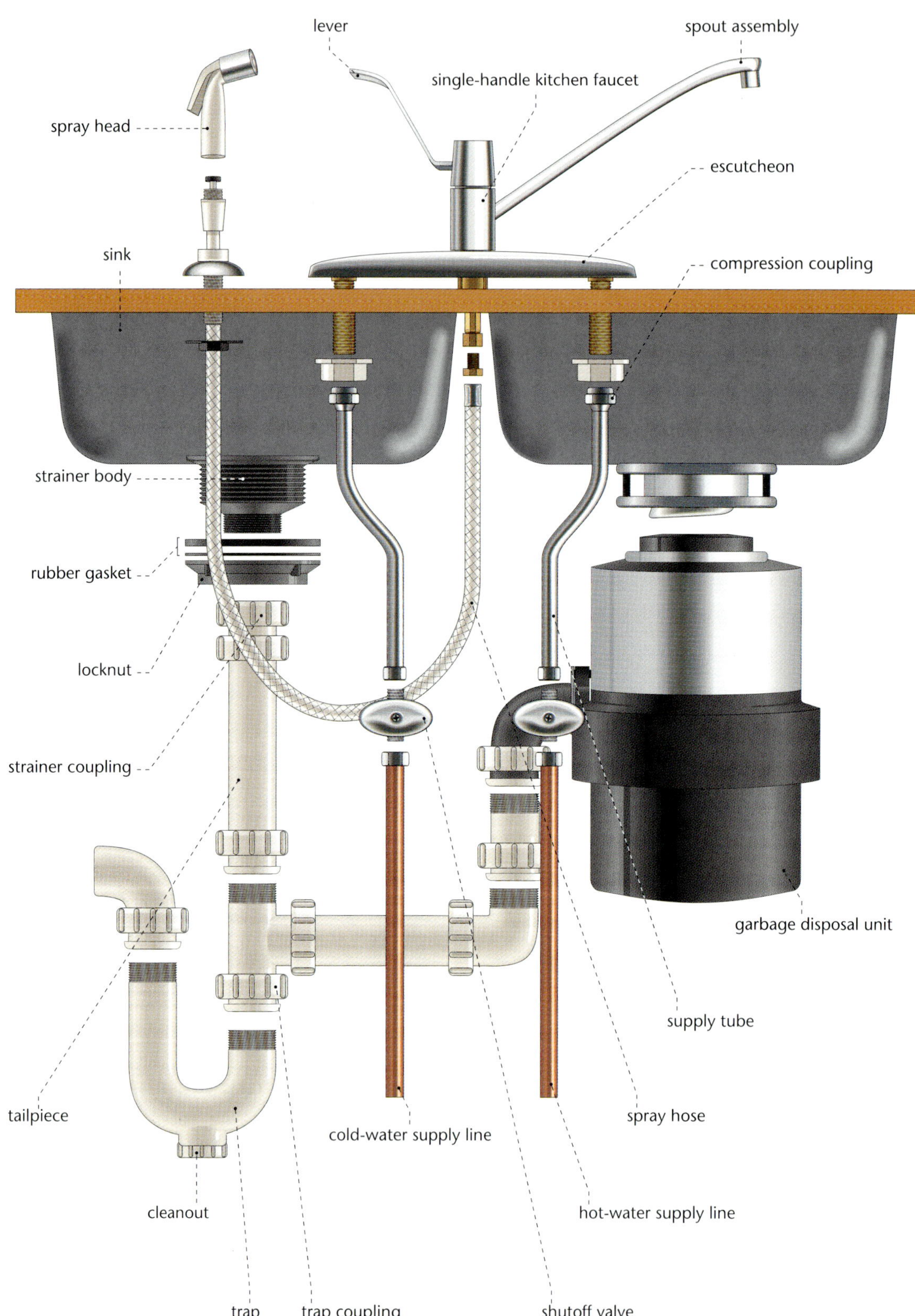

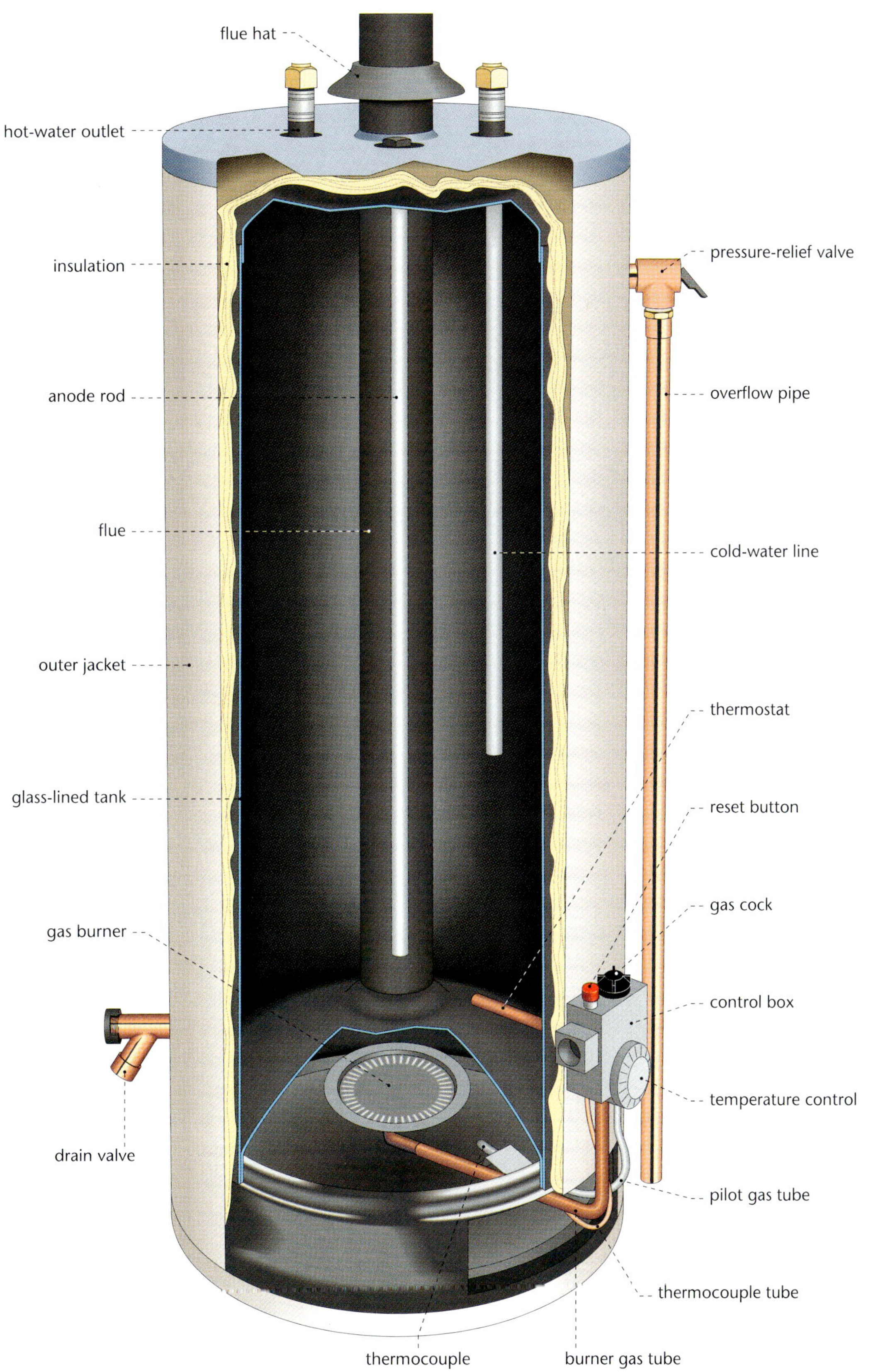

GAS WATER-HEATER TANK
flue hat
hot-water outlet
insulation
anode rod
flue
outer jacket
glass-lined tank
gas burner
drain valve
pressure-relief valve
overflow pipe
cold-water line
thermostat
reset button
gas cock
control box
temperature control
pilot gas tube
thermocouple tube
thermocouple
burner gas tube

WASHER

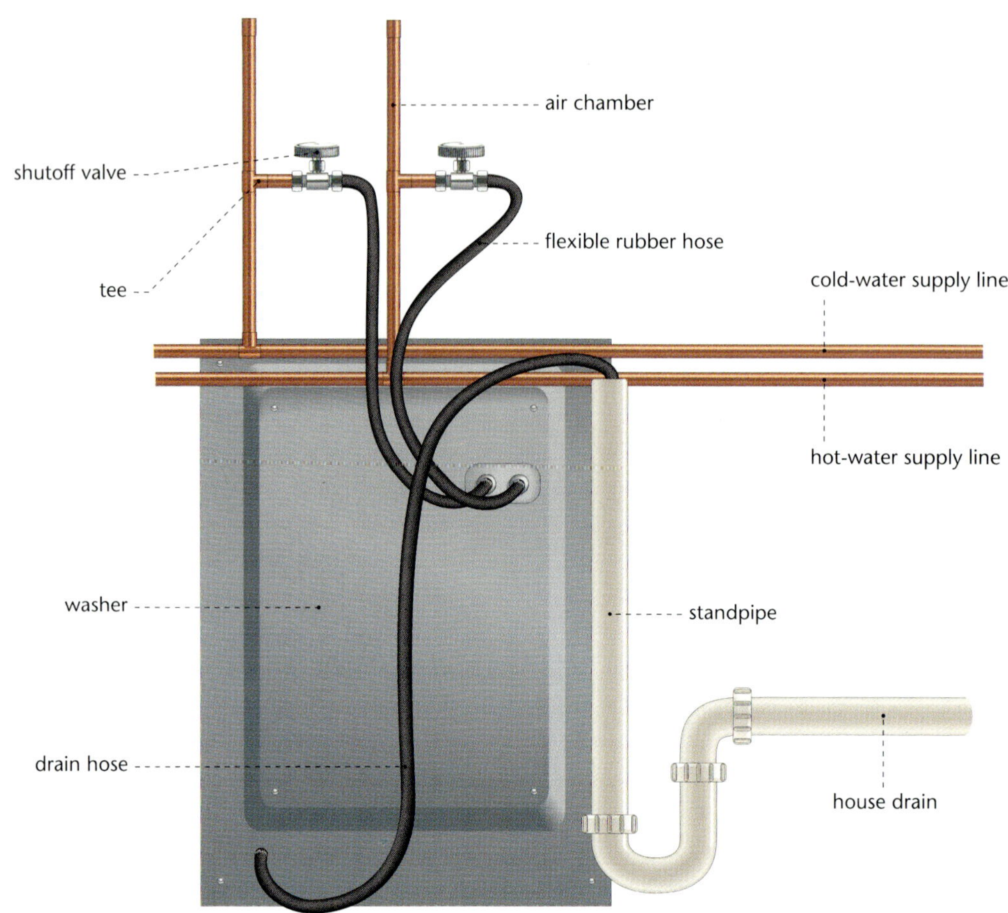

DISHWASHER

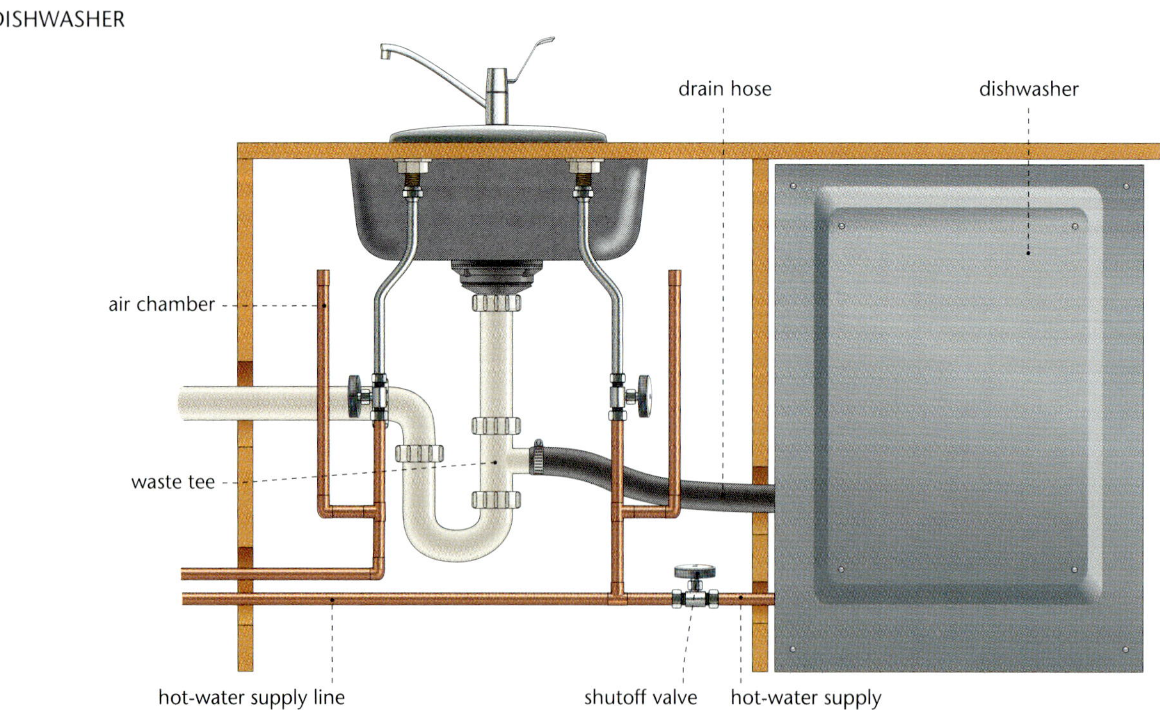

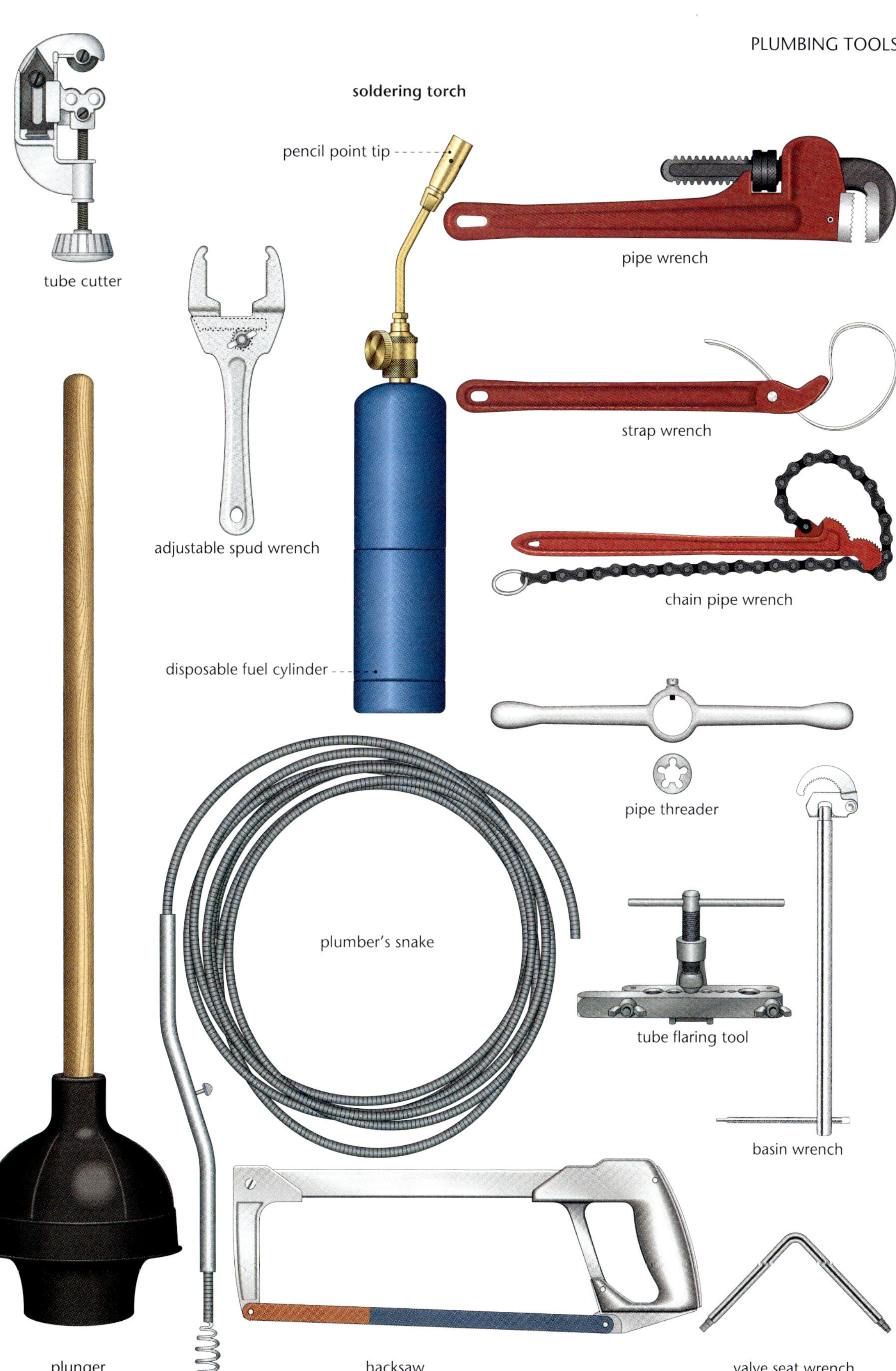

PLUMBING TOOLS
soldering torch
pencil point tip
pipe wrench
tube cutter
adjustable spud wrench
strap wrench
chain pipe wrench
disposable fuel cylinder
pipe threader
plumber's snake
tube flaring tool
basin wrench
plunger
hacksaw
valve seat wrench

MECHANICAL CONNECTORS

compression fitting

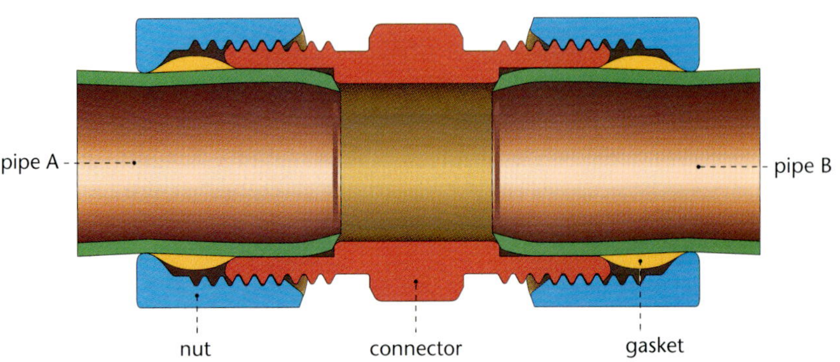

flare joint

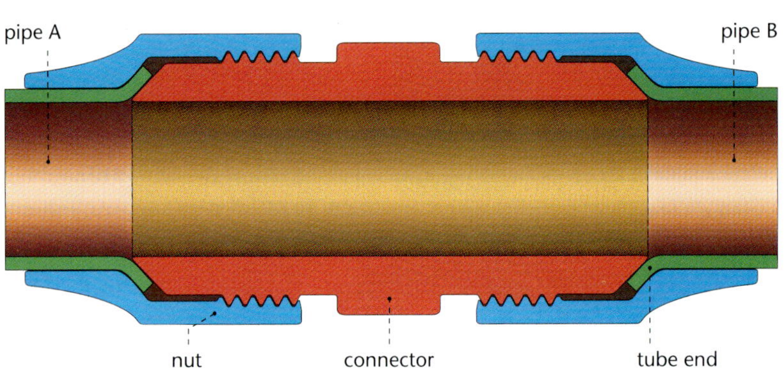

union

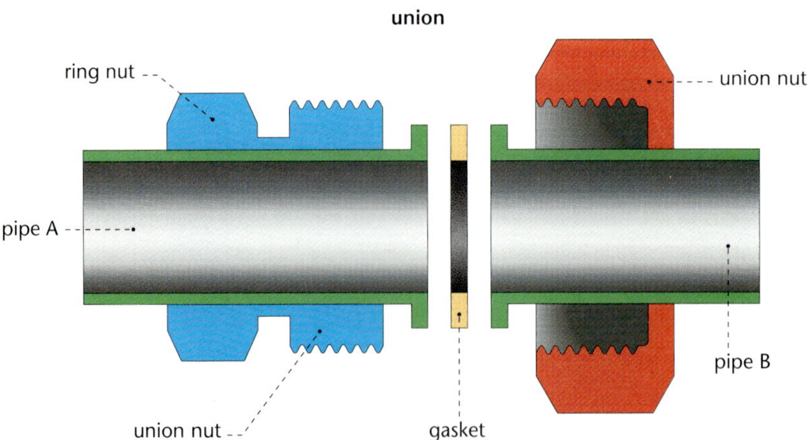

steel to plastic

copper to plastic

copper to steel

FITTINGS

45° elbow

elbow

U-bend

tee

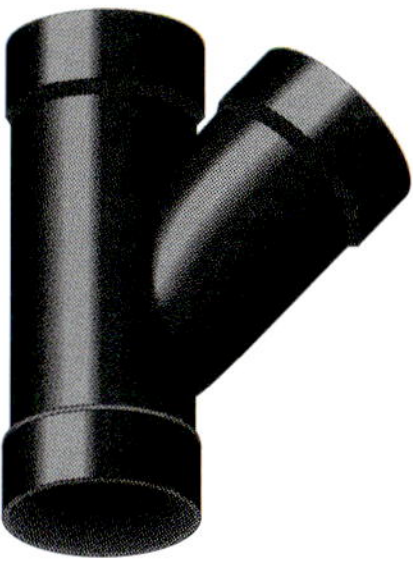

Y-branch

offset

trap

square head plug

cap

flush bushing

nipple

reducing coupling

threaded cap

pipe coupling

hexagon bushing

DO-IT-YOURSELF

STEPLADDER
top
tool tray
step
step stool
brace
PLATFORM LADDER
safety rail
shelf
platform
frame
step
rubber tip
EXTENSION LADDER
rung
side rail
pulley
locking device
hoisting rope
anti-slip shoe

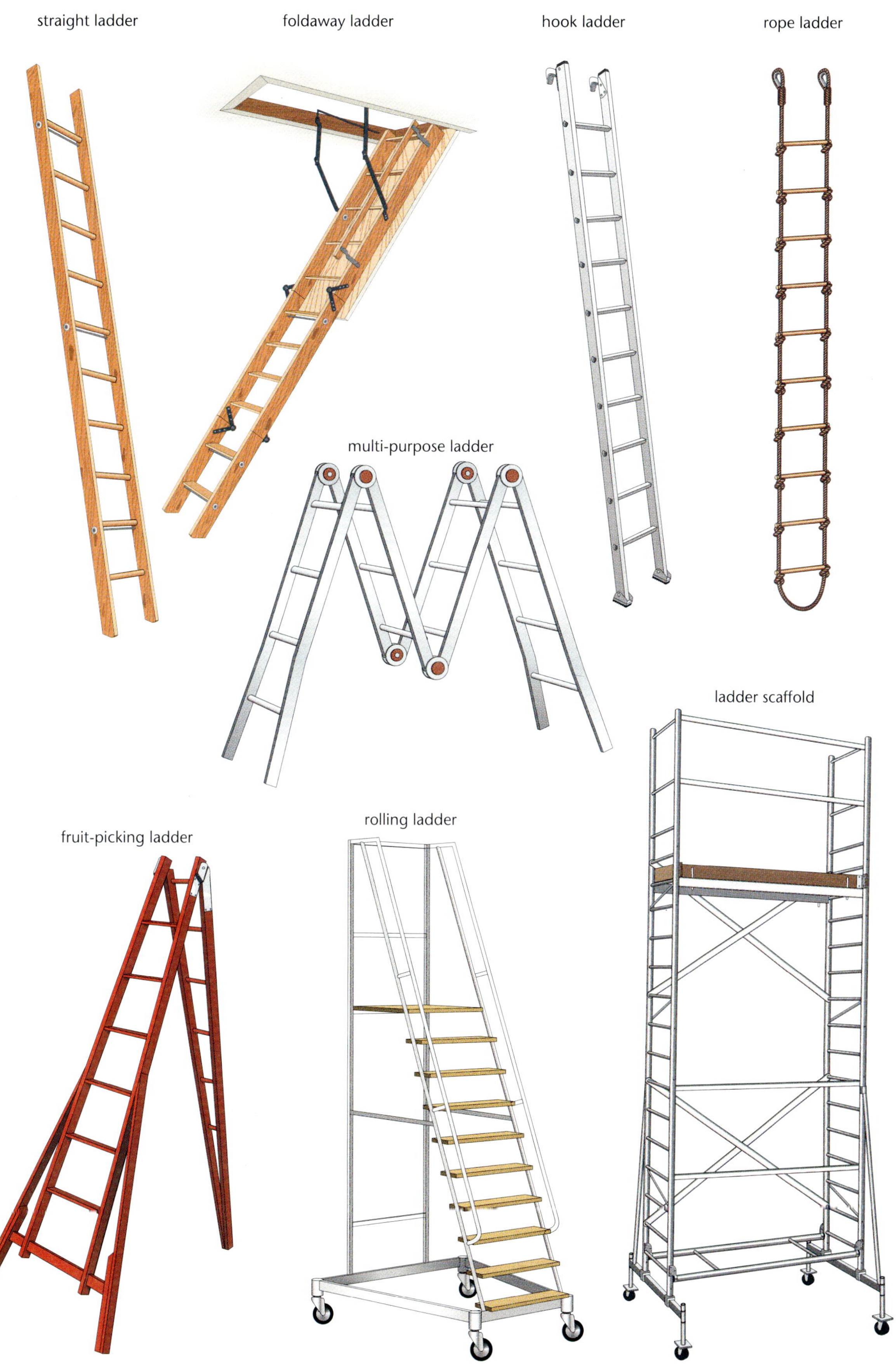

straight ladder
foldaway ladder
hook ladder
rope ladder
multi-purpose ladder
ladder scaffold
fruit-picking ladder
rolling ladder

SPRAY PAINT GUN

SCRAPER

BRUSH

PAINT ROLLER

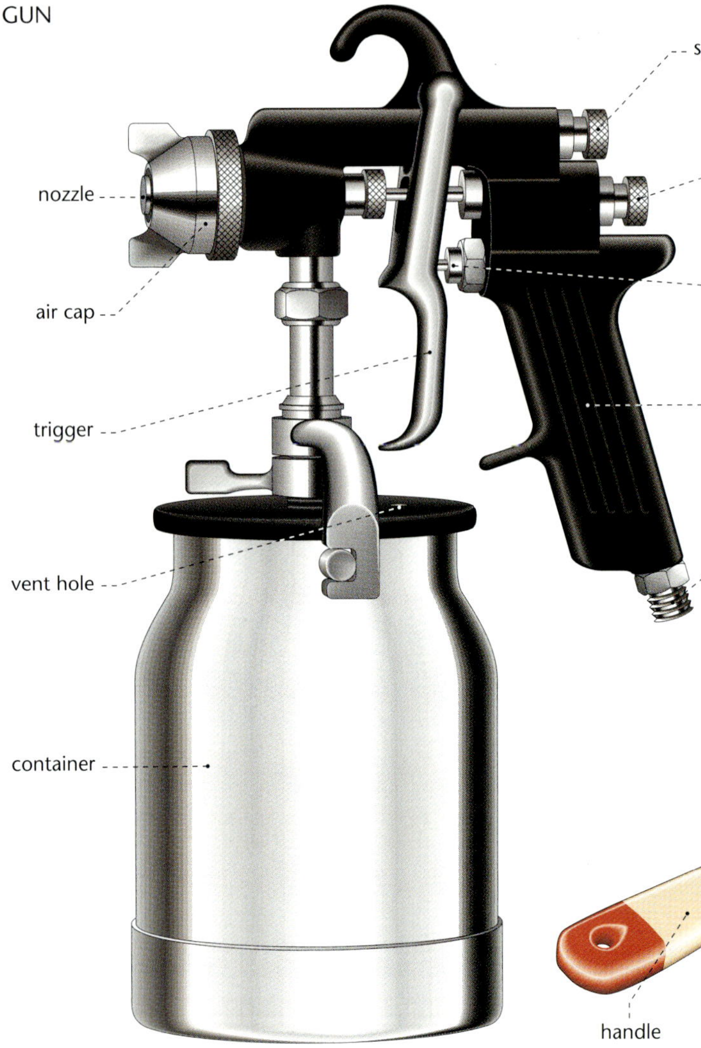

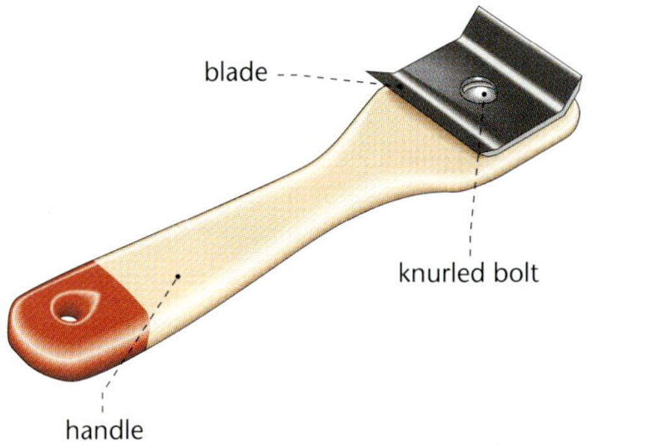

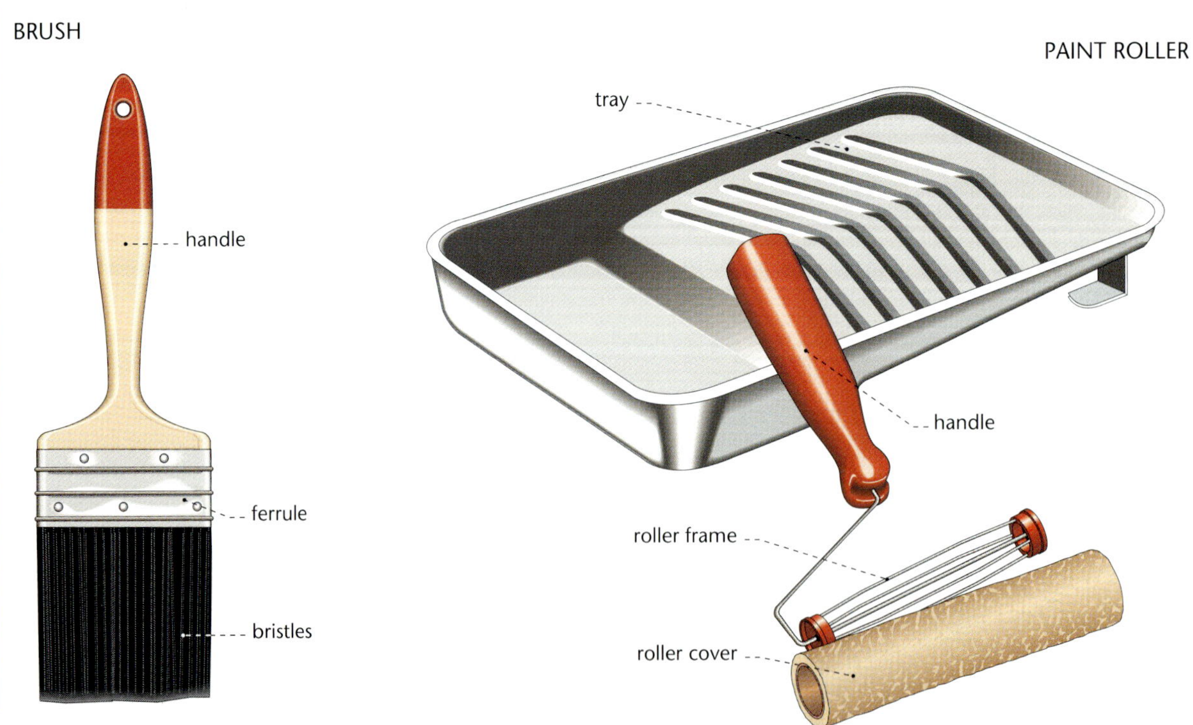

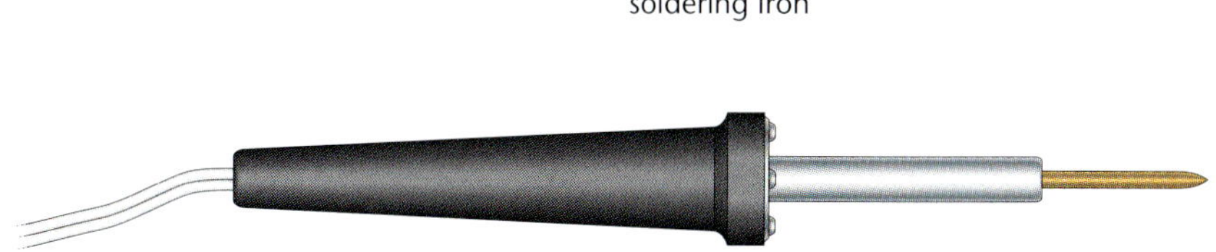

soldering iron

SOLDERING GUN

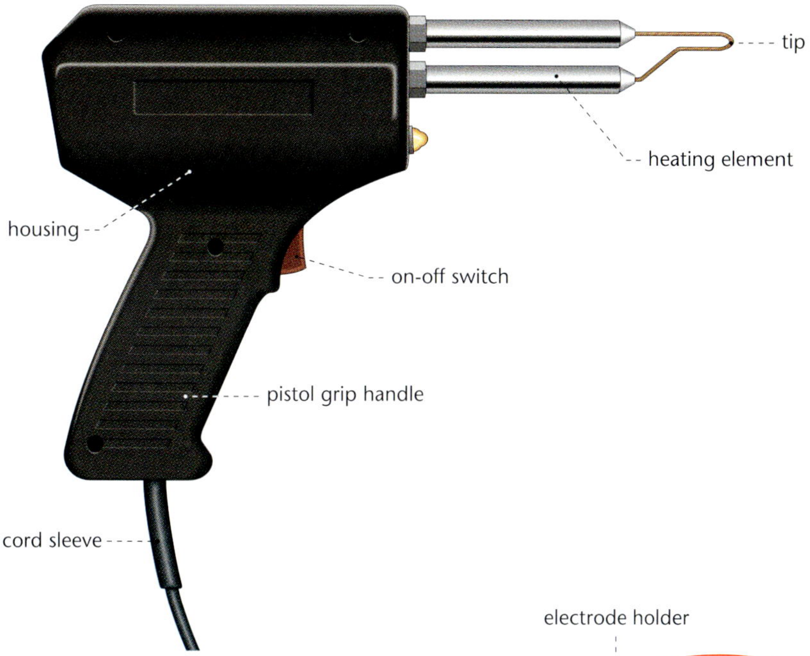

ARC WELDING

CUTTING TORCH

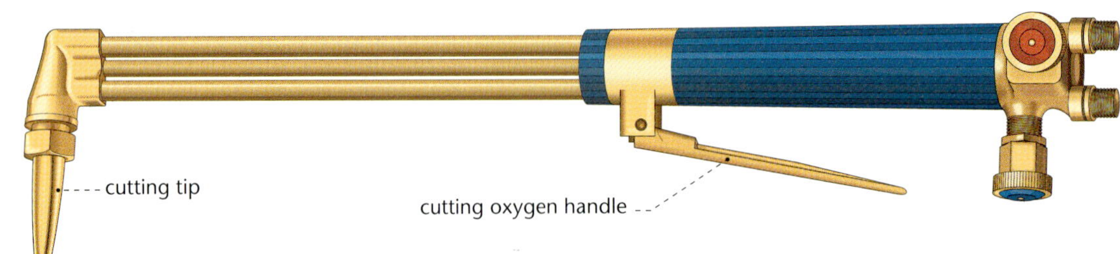

WELDING TORCH

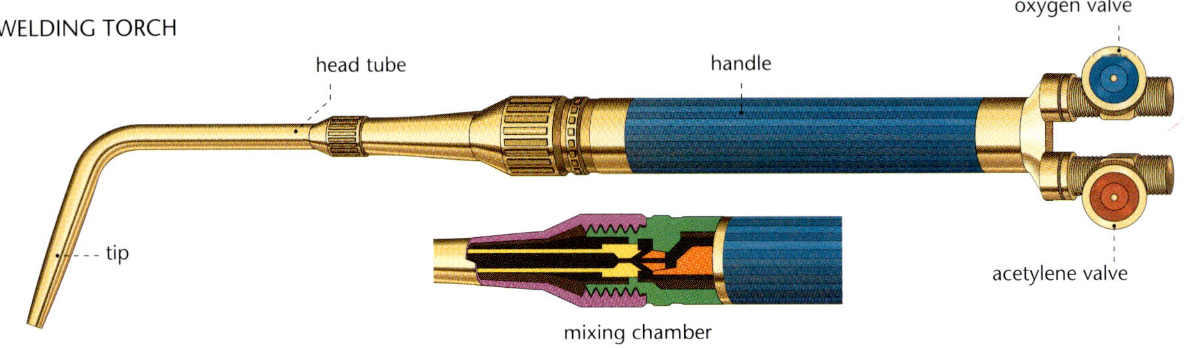

OXYACETYLENE WELDING

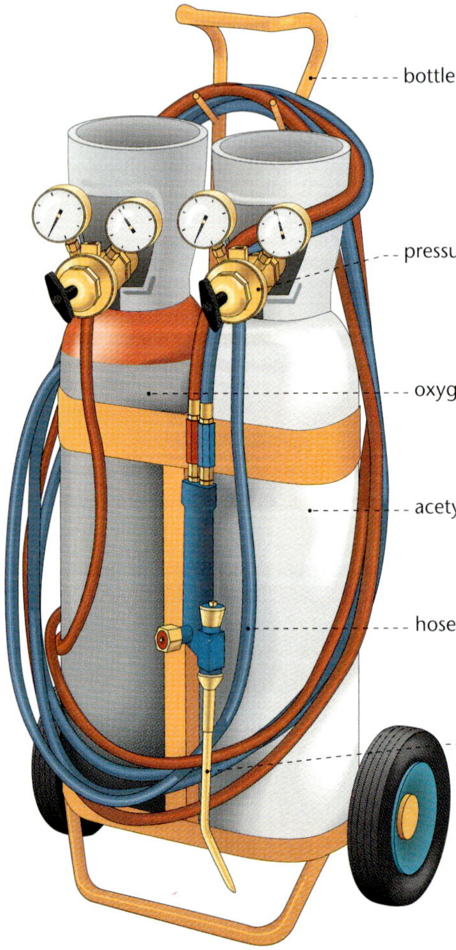

PRESSURE REGULATOR

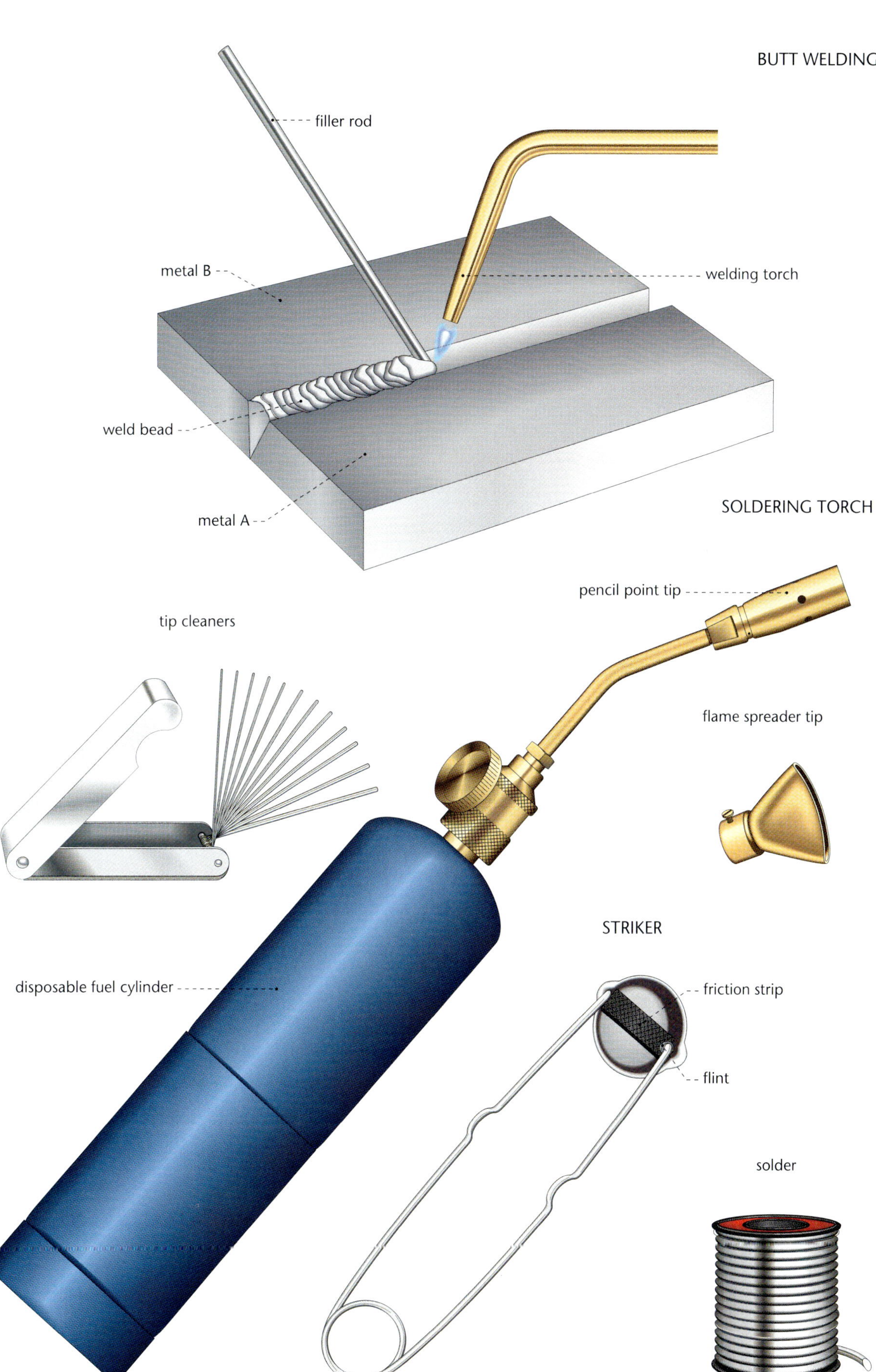
filler rod
welding torch
metal B
weld bead
metal A
SOLDERING TORCH
pencil point tip
tip cleaners
flame spreader tip
STRIKER
disposable fuel cylinder
friction strip
flint
solder

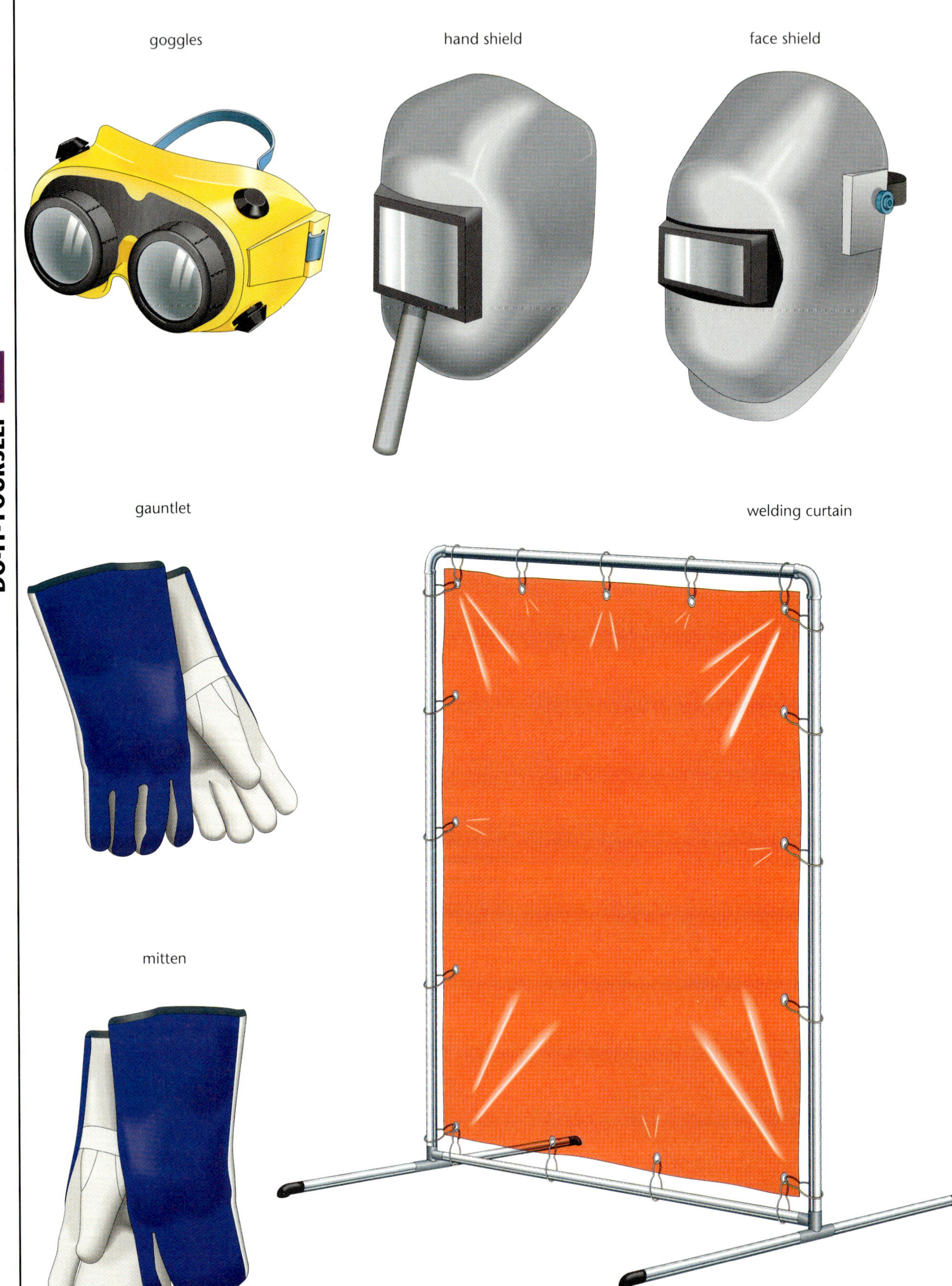

goggles
hand shield
face shield
gauntlet
welding curtain
mitten

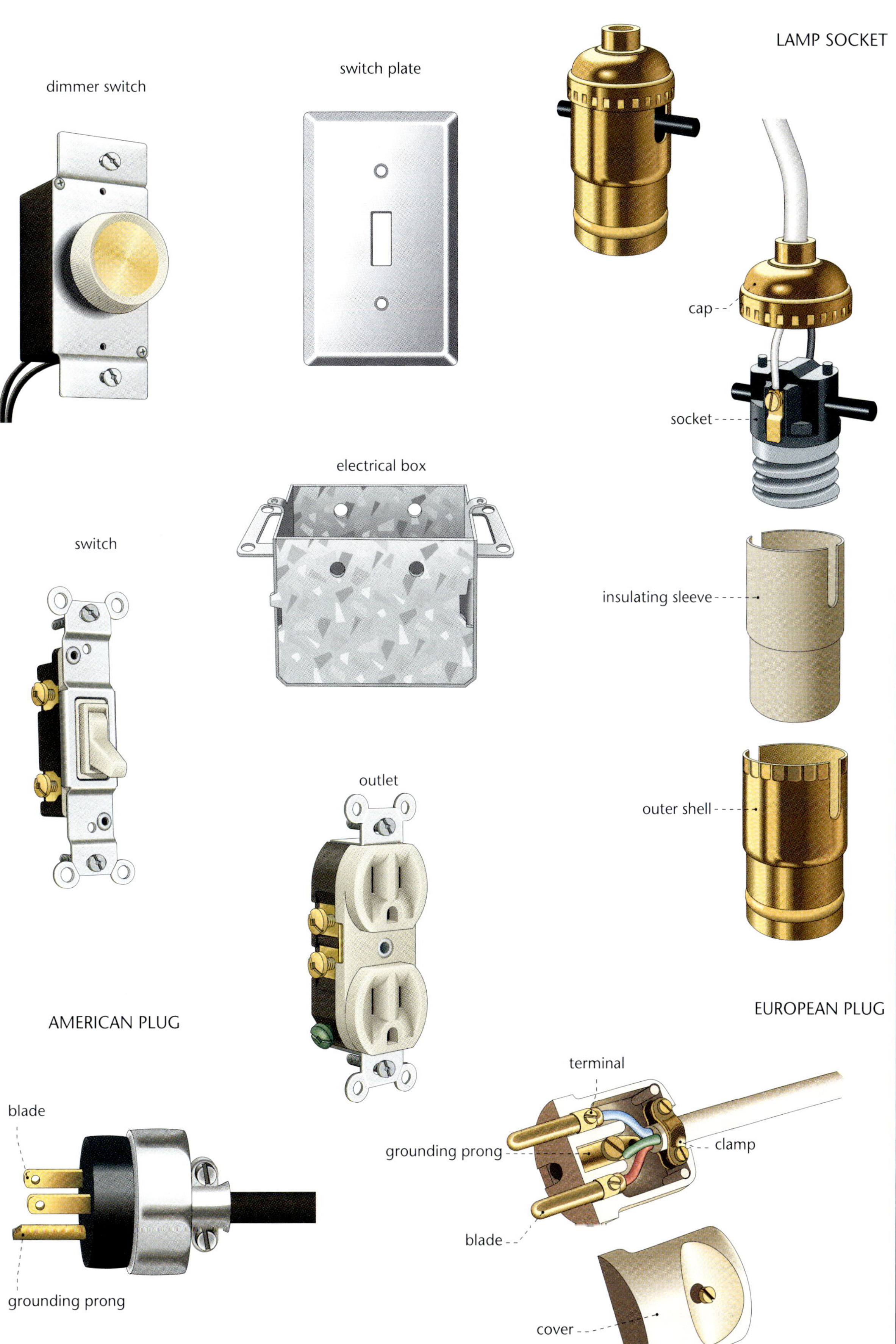

DO-IT-YOURSELF

ELECTRICIAN'S TOOLS

multimeter

voltage tester

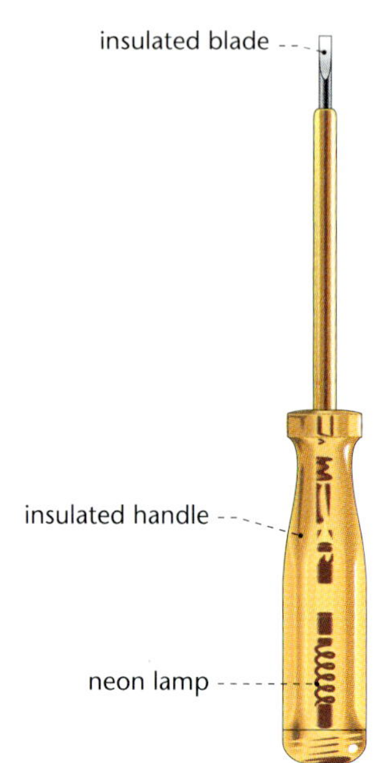

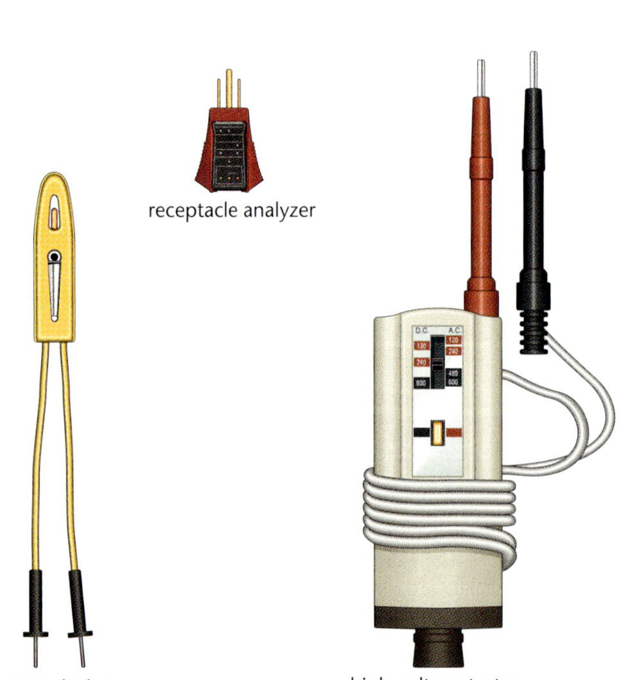

drop light

multipurpose tool
pivot
wire cutter
wire stripper
insulated handle
hammer
fuse puller
cable ripper
fish wire
needle-nose pliers
lineman's pliers
jaw
wire cutter
pivot
insulated handle
wire nut
cutter
adjustment wheel
wire stripper

FUSE BOX

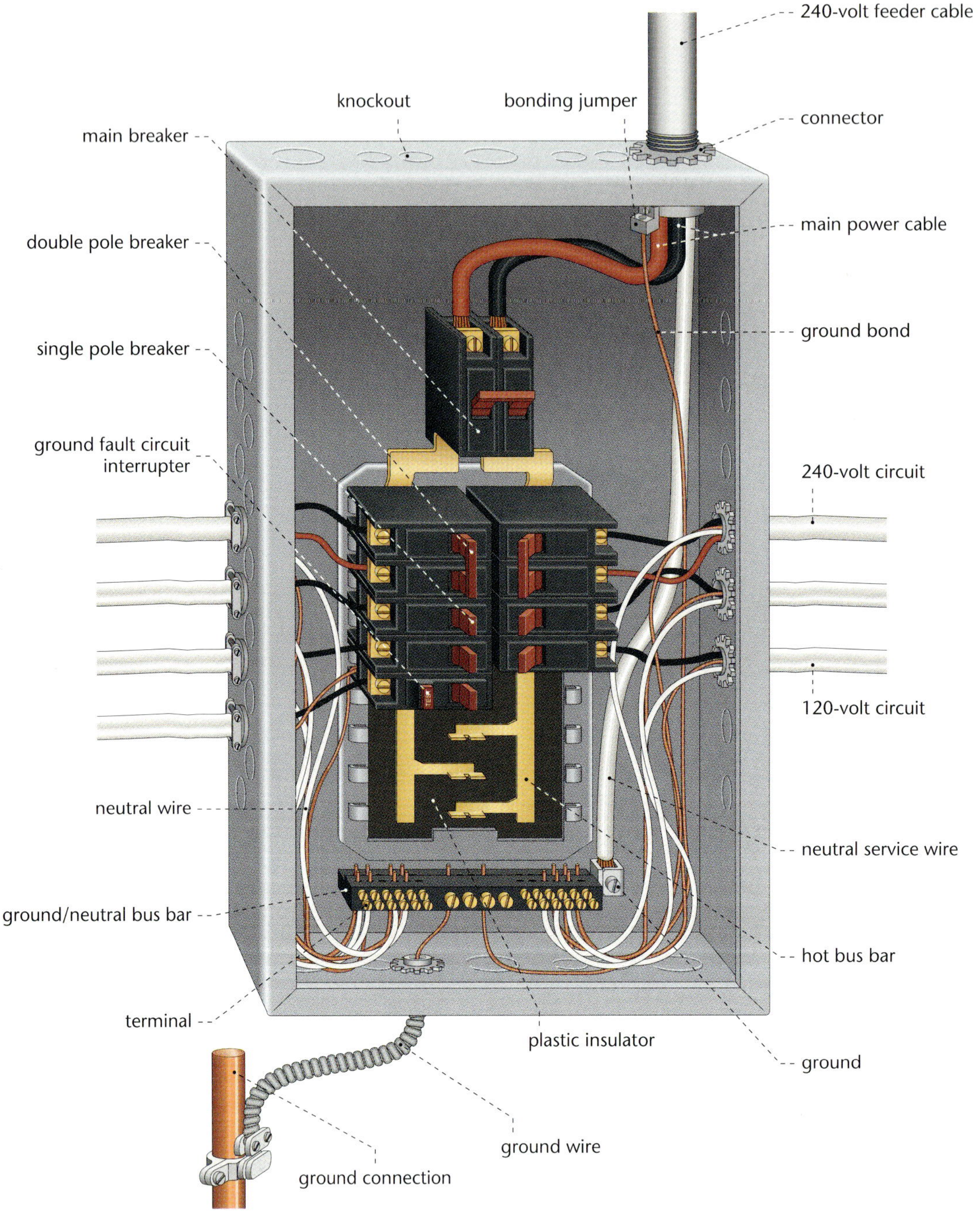

FUSES

cartridge fuse

plug fuse

knife-blade cartridge fuse

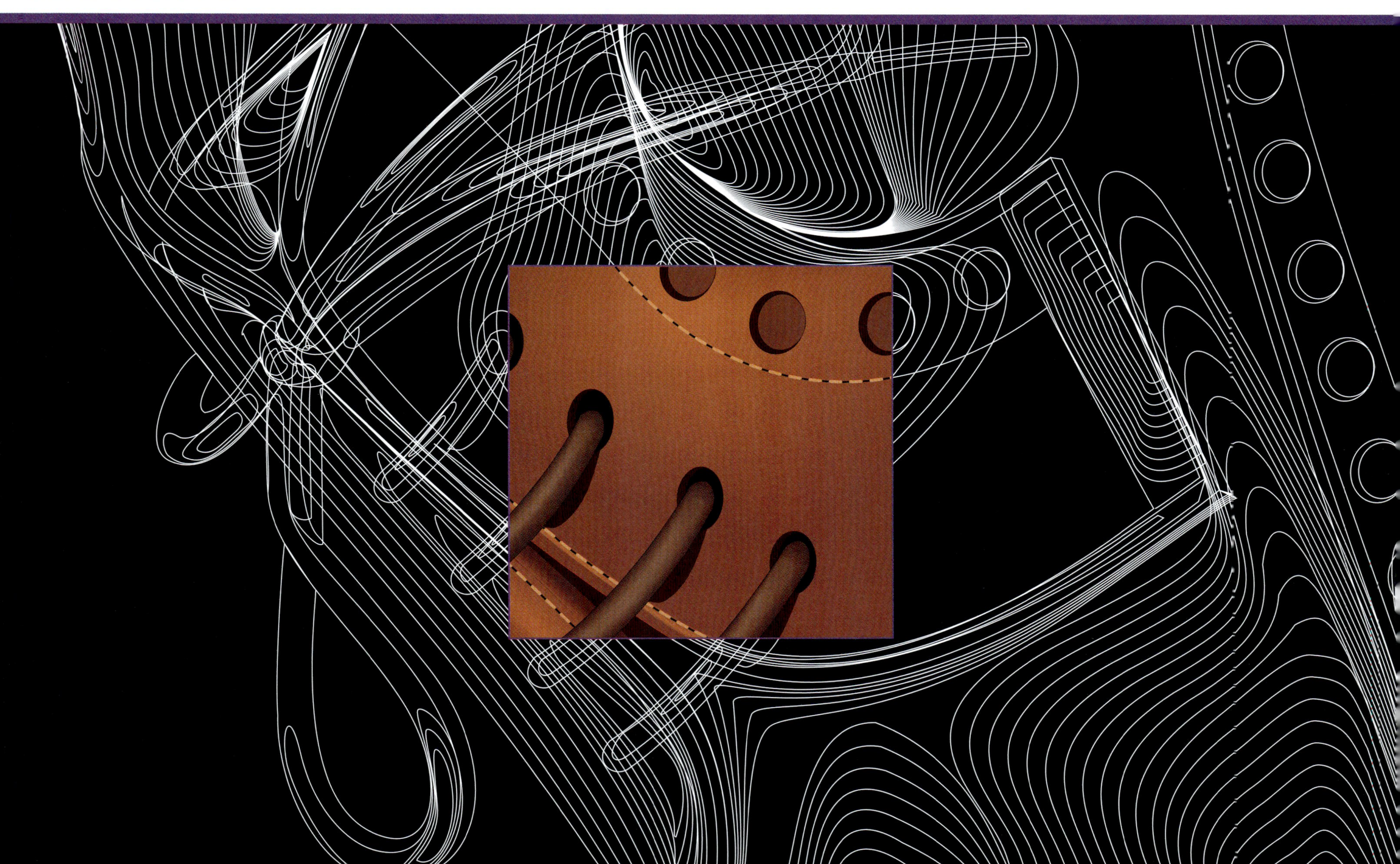

CONTENTS

ELEMENTS OF ANCIENT COSTUME

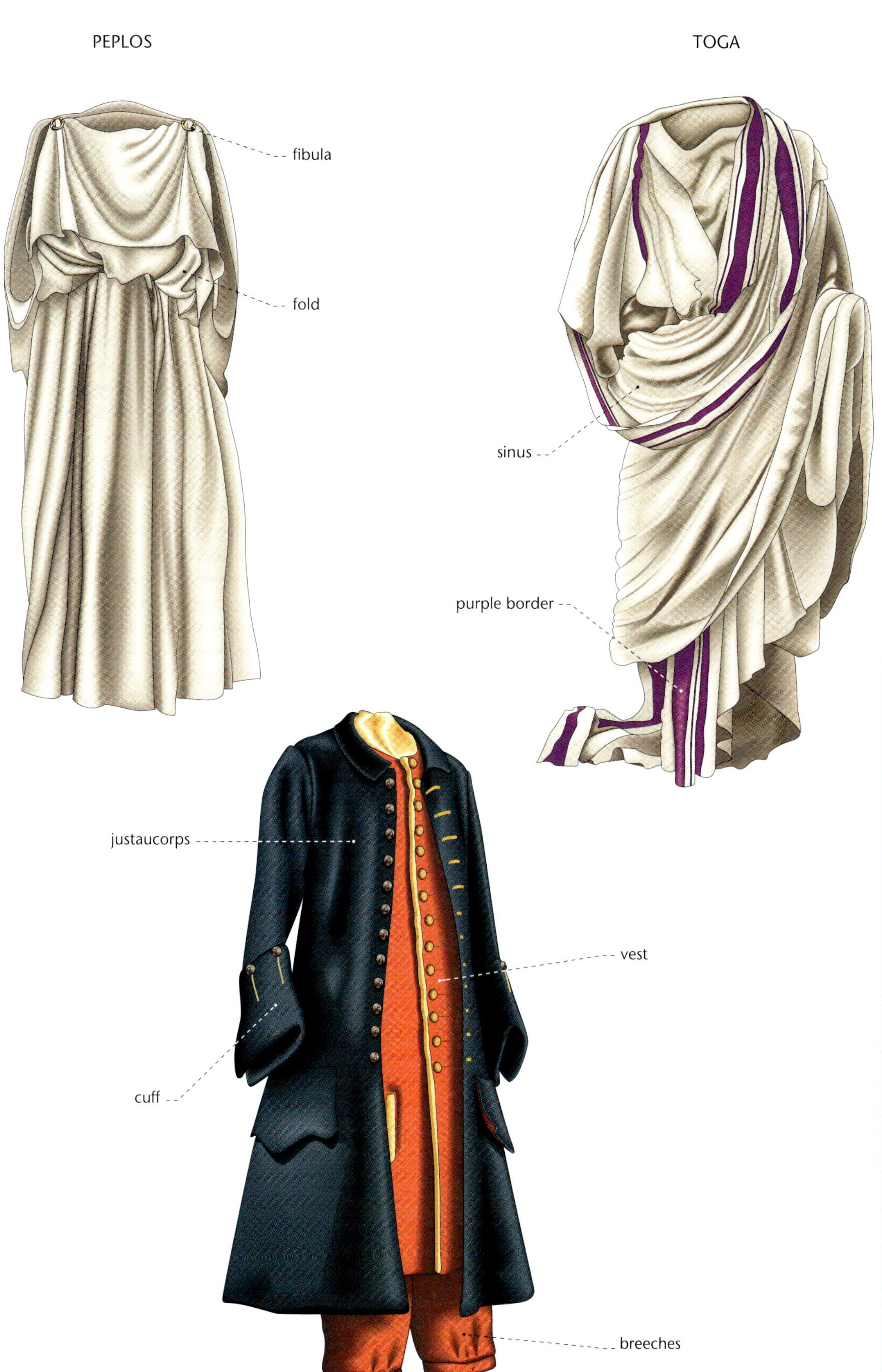

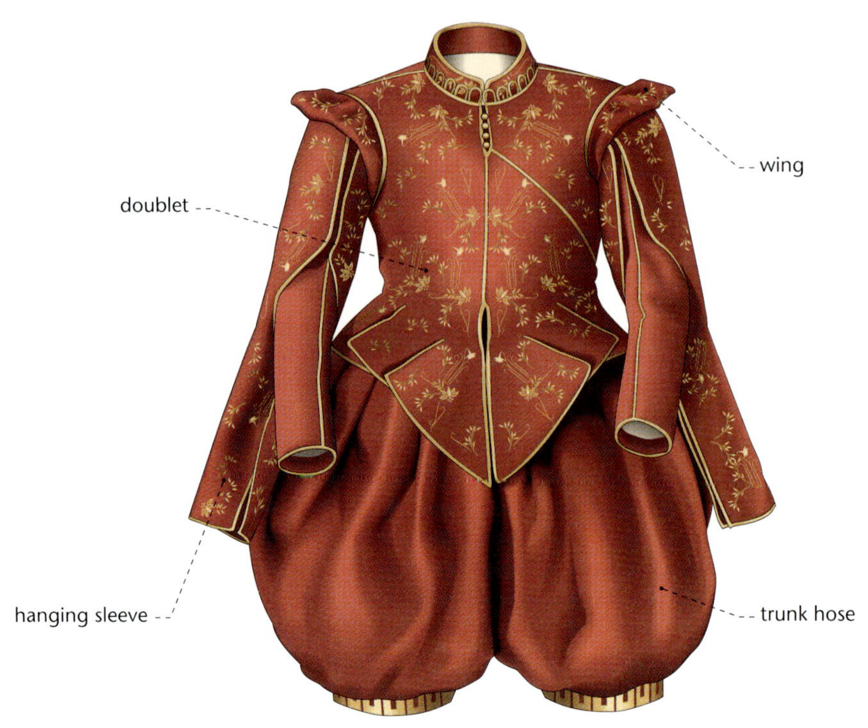

COTEHARDIE

DRESS WITH BUSTLE

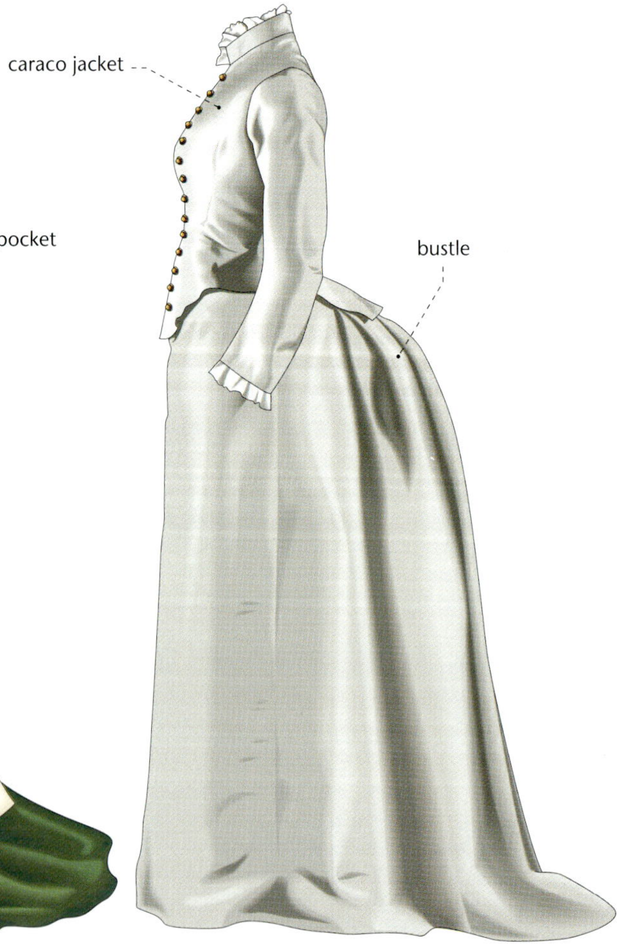

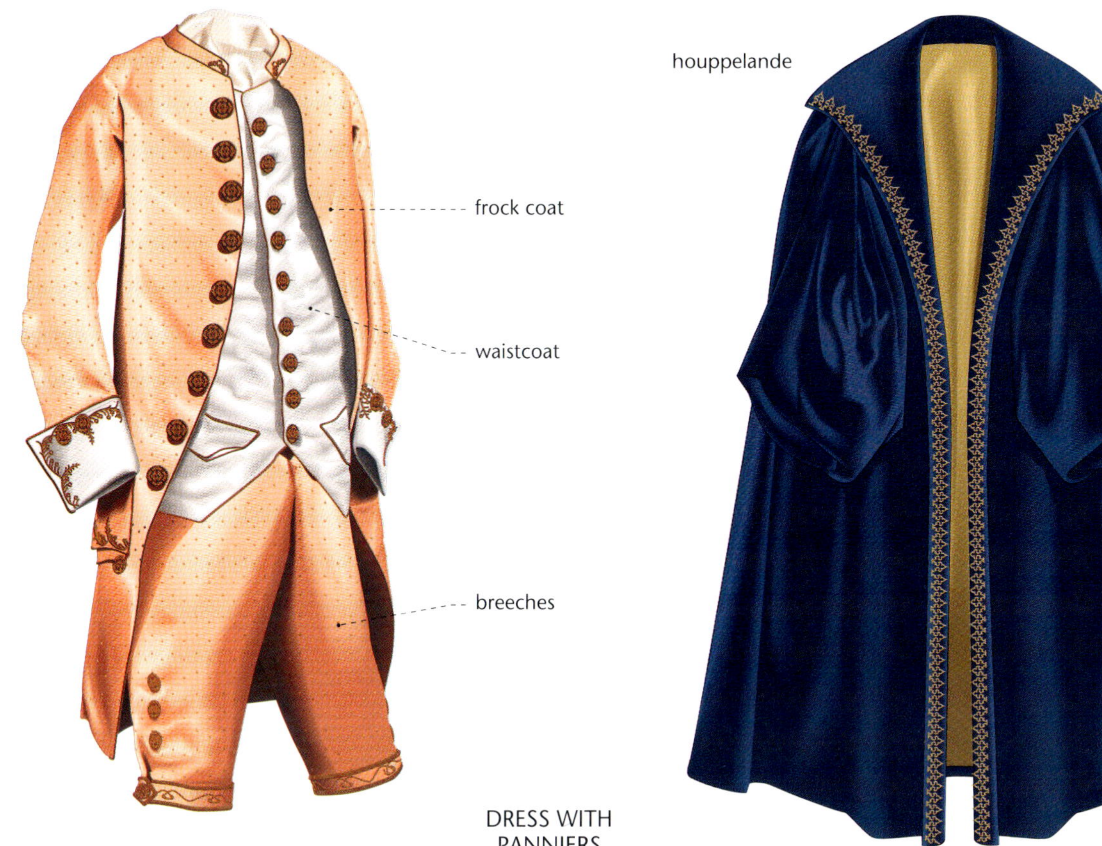

DRESS WITH
PANNIERS

ELEMENTS OF ANCIENT COSTUME

DRESS WITH CRINOLINE

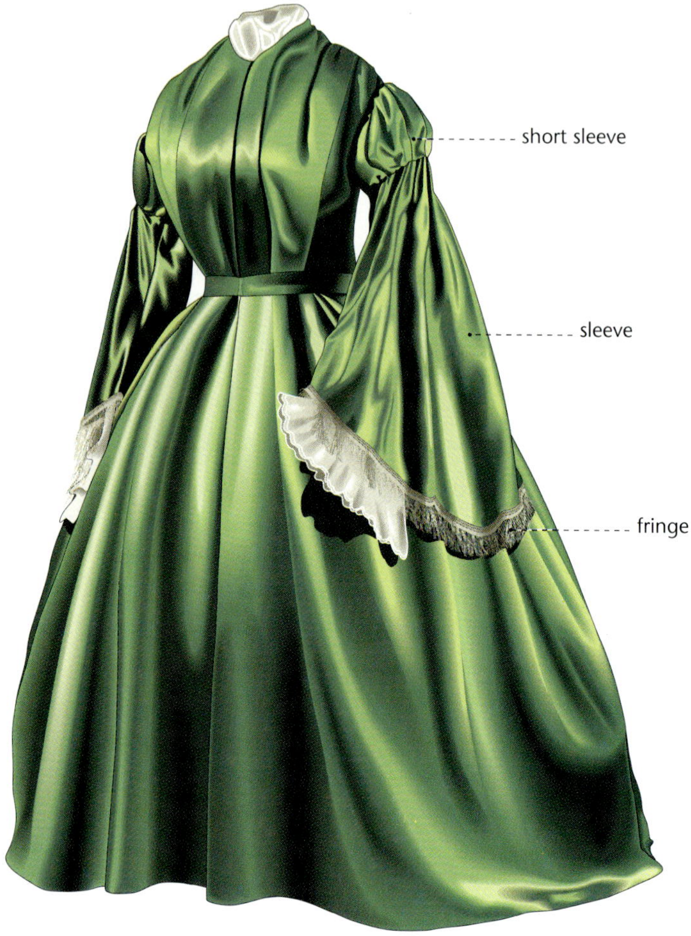

short sleeve

sleeve

fringe

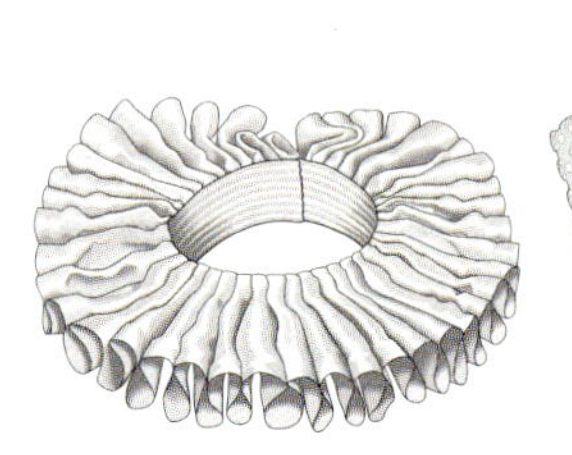

hennin

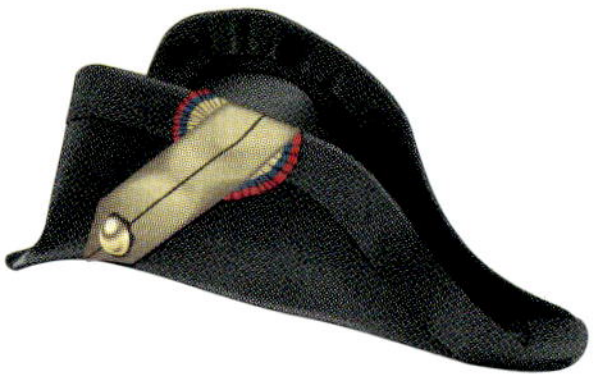

bicorne

tricorne

fraise

collaret

heeled shoe

crakow

RAINCOAT

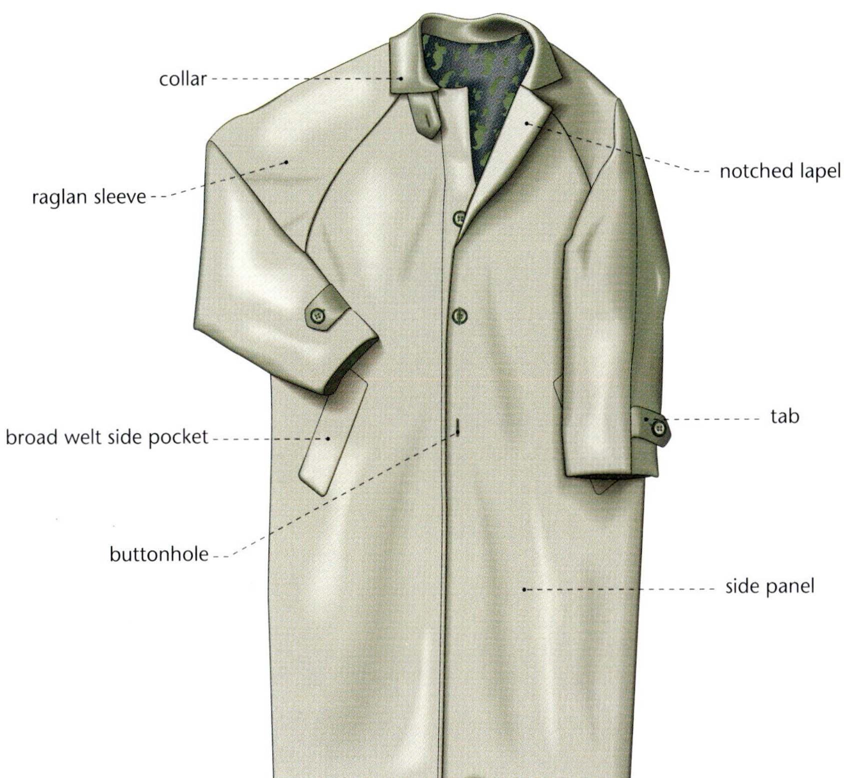

CLOTHING

TRENCH COAT

DUFFLE COAT
hood
yoke
frog
patch pocket
toggle fastening
OVERCOAT
notched lapel
breast pocket
breast dart
flap pocket
WINDBREAKER
waistband
drawstring

three-quarter coat

PARKA

zipper

snap-fastening tab

JACKET

sheepskin jacket

snap fastener

hand-warmer pocket

elastic waistband

DOUBLE-BREASTED JACKET
lining
peaked lapel
collar
breast welt pocket
sleeve
flap
outside ticket pocket
patch pocket
side back vent
VEST
V-neck
lining
welt
front
seaming
welt pocket
adjustable waist tab
SINGLE-BREASTED JACKET
lining
notch
back
lapel
pocket handkerchief
front
sleeve
flap pocket
center back vent

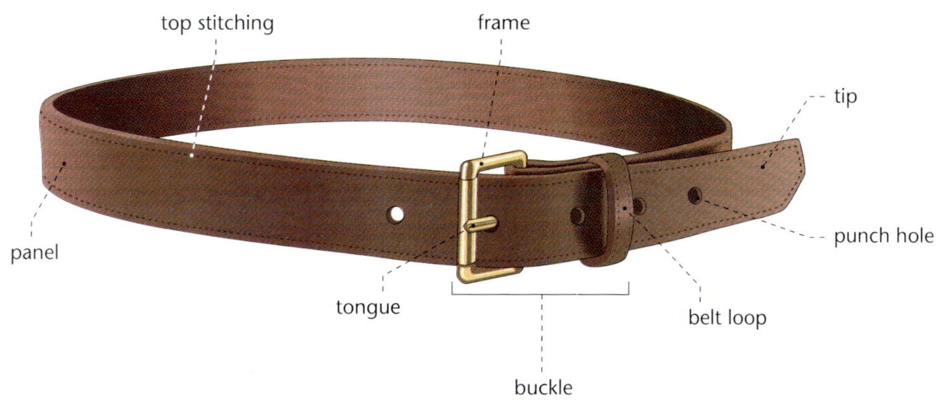

CLOTHING

SUSPENDERS

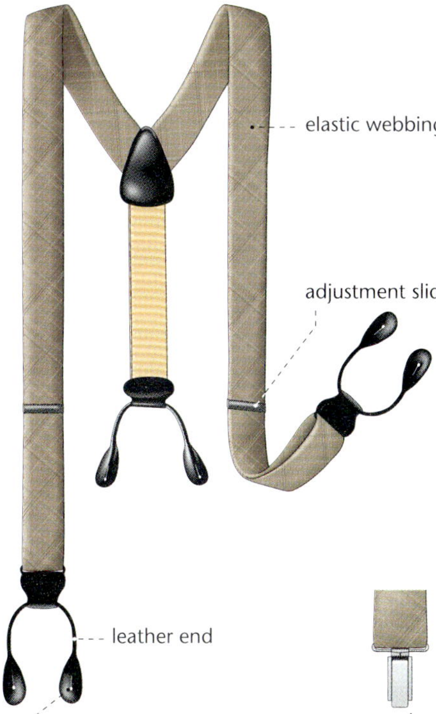

CLOTHING

SHIRT

NECKTIE

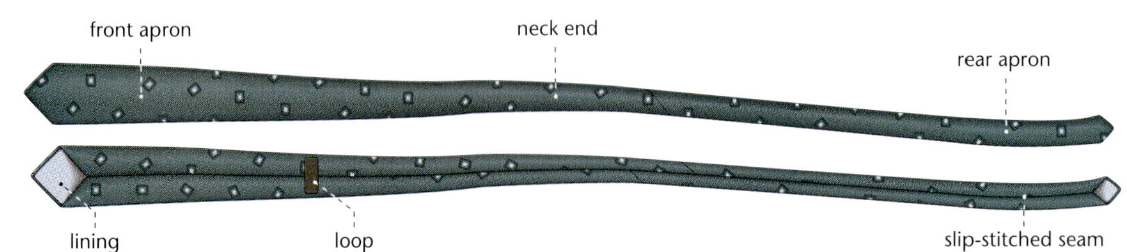

UNDERWEAR

athletic shirt

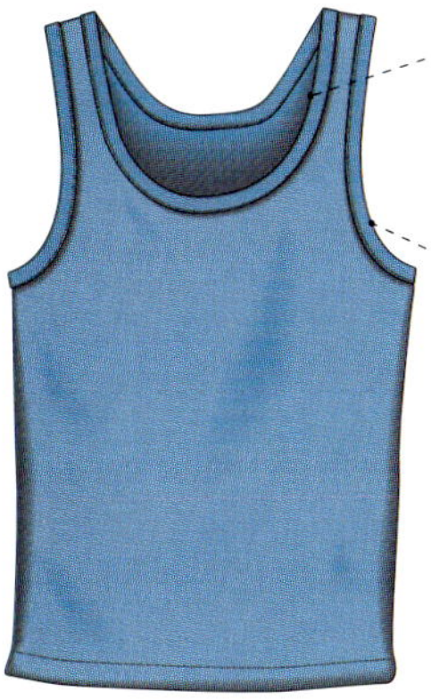

neckhole
armhole

briefs

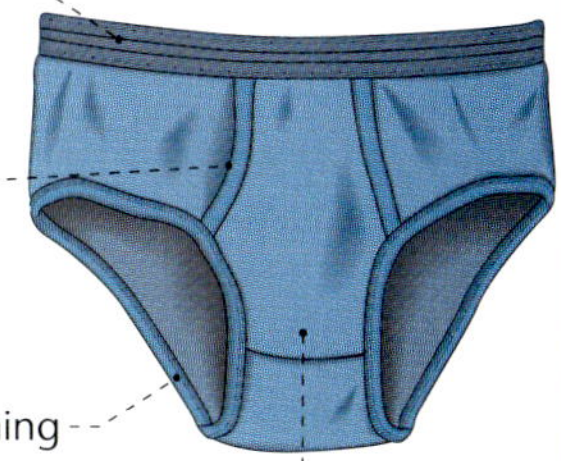

waistband
fly
elasticized leg opening
crotch

union suit

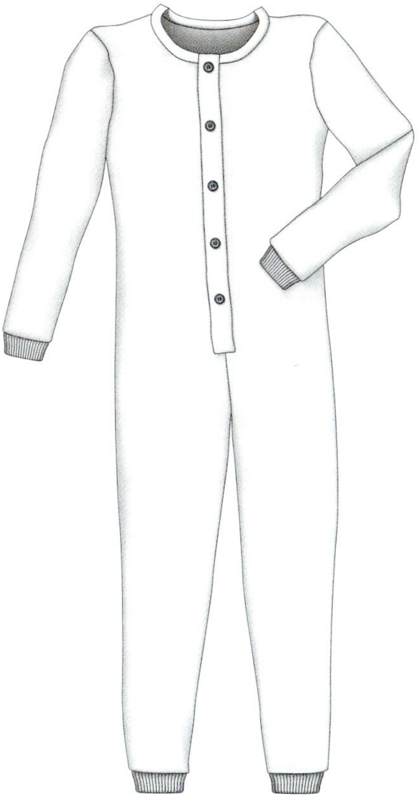

drawers

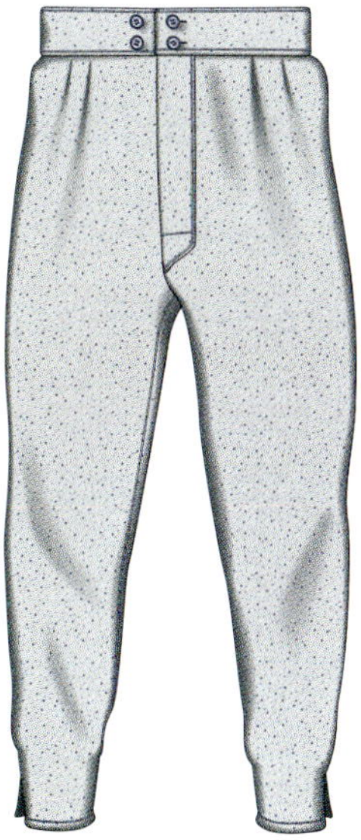

bikini briefs

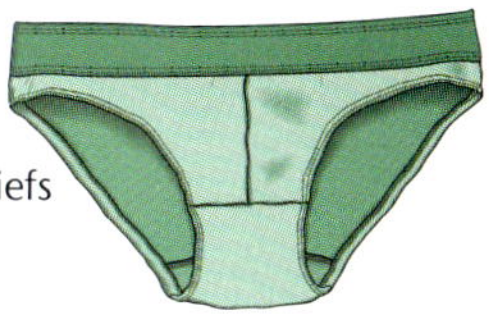

boxer shorts

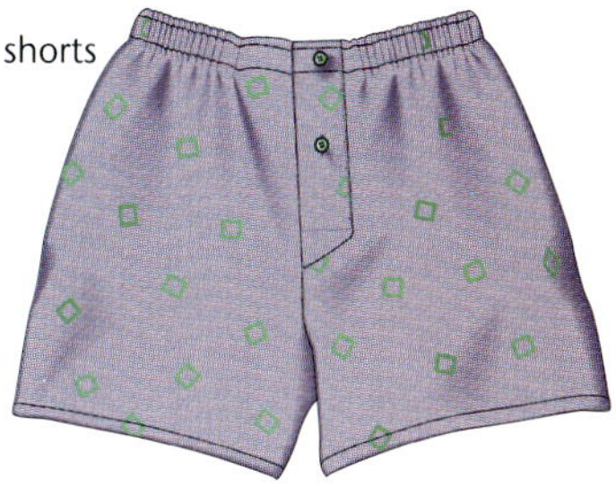

SOCKS

mid-calf length

ankle length

executive length

straight-up ribbed top
leg
heel
instep
sole
toe

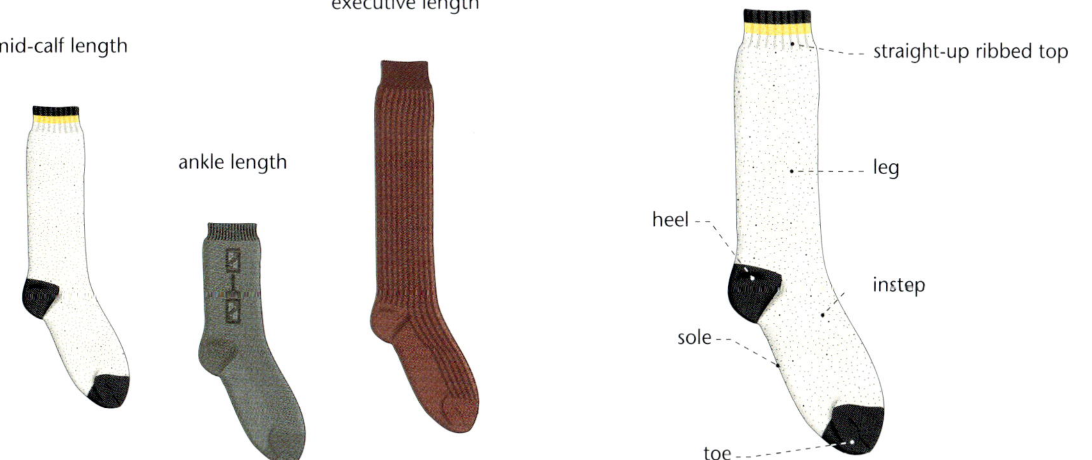

V-NECK CARDIGAN
hanger loop
set-in sleeve
V-neck
button
ribbing
welt pocket
turtleneck
KNIT SHIRT
buttoned placket
crew neck sweater
sweater
cardigan

GLOVES

thumb
fourchette
glove finger
palm
snap fastener
stitching
seam
DRIVING GLOVE
perforation
opening
mitten
MITT
gauntlet
evening glove
wrist-length glove
gauntlet
short glove

HEADGEAR

FELT HAT

crown
hatband
binding
bow
brim

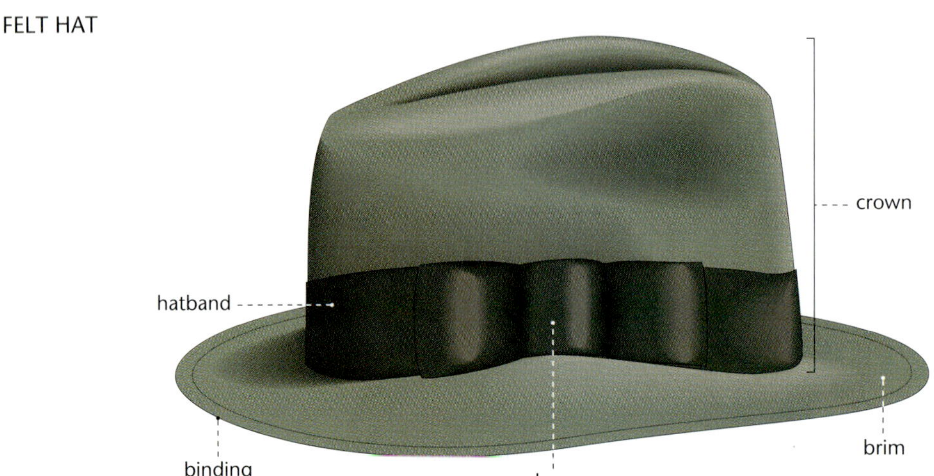

boater

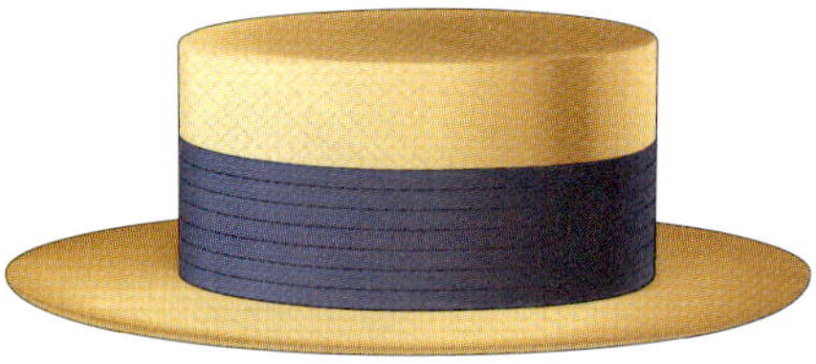

top hat

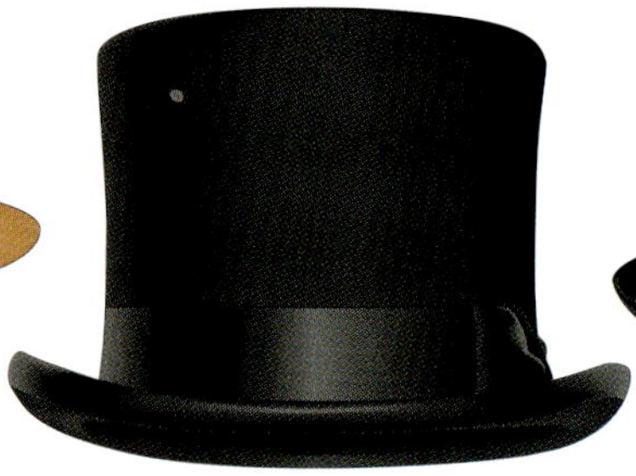

derby

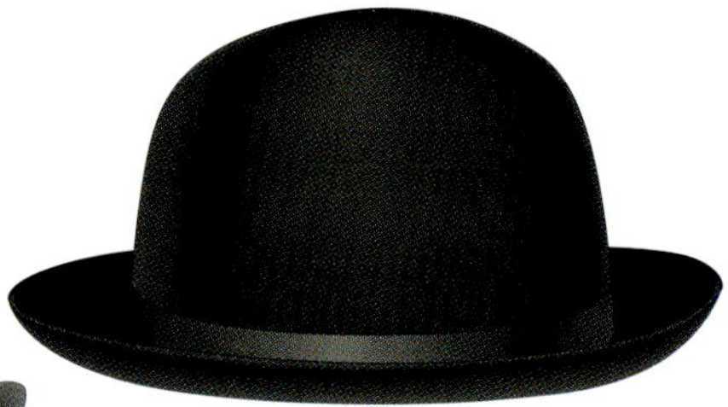

HUNTING CAP

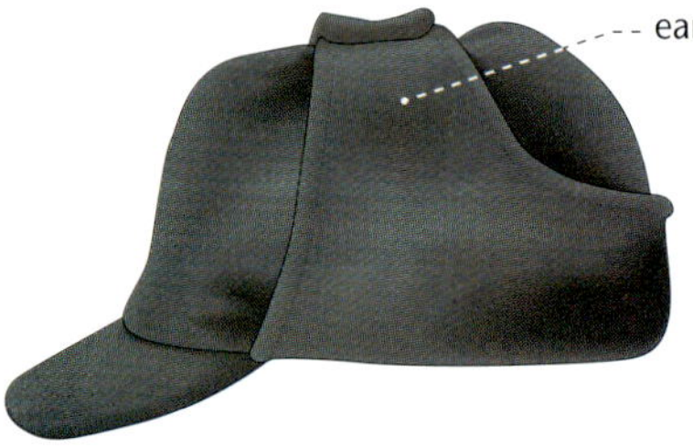
ear flap

shapka

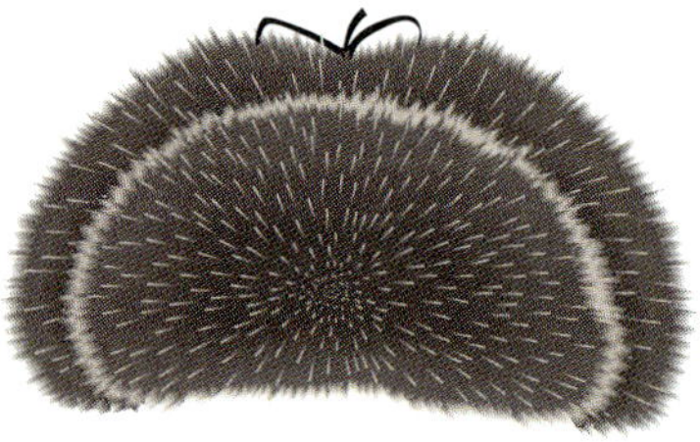

CAP

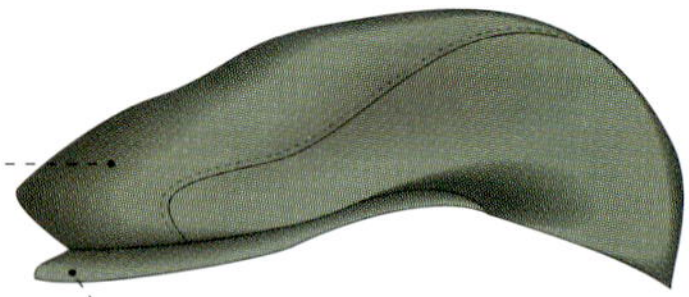
crown
peak

panama

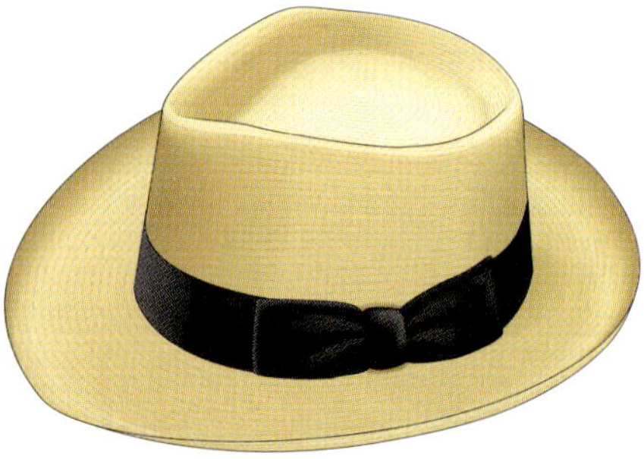

garrison cap

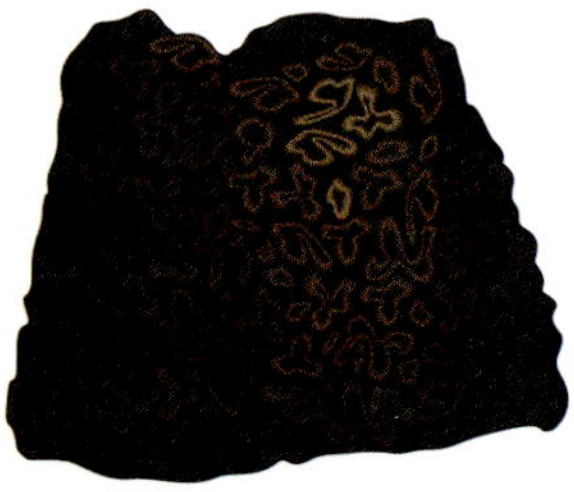

skullcap

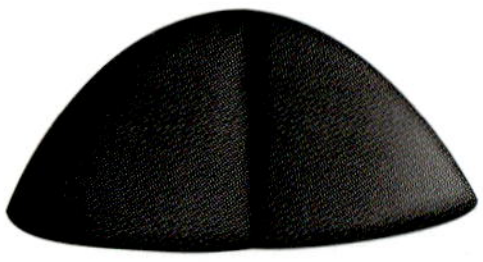

toque
pillbox hat
beret
turban
cloche
felt hat
BALACLAVA
southwester
peak
stocking cap
knit cap
GOB HAT
cartwheel hat
crown
brim

TYPES OF COATS

cape
overcoat
top coat
arm slit
poncho
suit
jacket
jacket
skirt

TYPES OF DRESSES

polo dress 
house dress 
shirtwaist dress 
jumper
wraparound dress
tunic dress

TYPES OF SKIRTS

kilt
gather skirt
inverted pleat
kick pleat
accordion pleat
knife pleat
top stitched pleat

TYPES OF PANTS

CLOTHING

classic blouse
middy
polo shirt
smock
yoke
gather
tunic
wrap-over top
mini shirtdress
body shirt
over-blouse
shirttail
crotch piece

CLOTHING

JACKETS, VEST AND SWEATERS

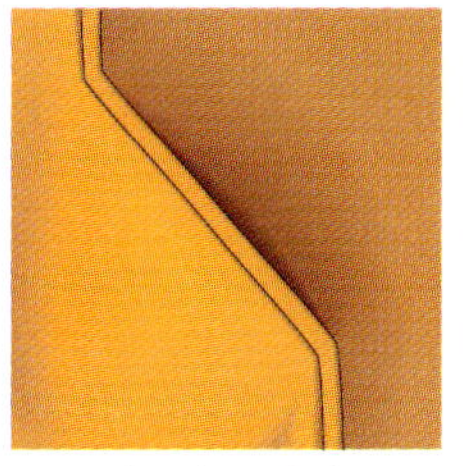

inset pocket

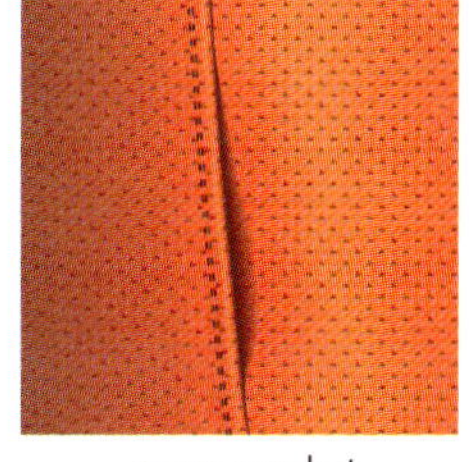

seam pocket

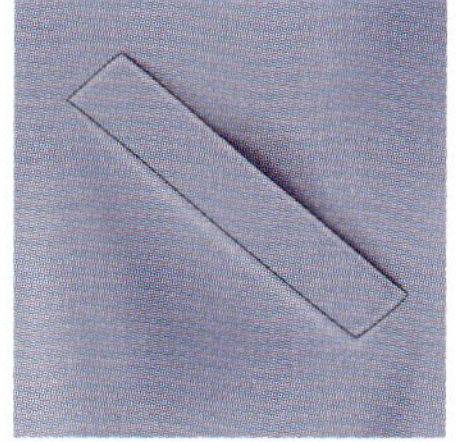

broad welt side pocket

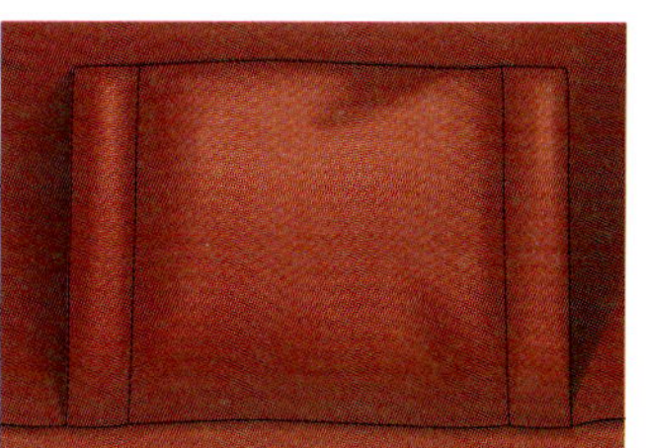

hand warmer pouch

gusset pocket

flap pocket

patch pocket

welt pocket

CLOTHING

TYPES OF SLEEVES

French cuff

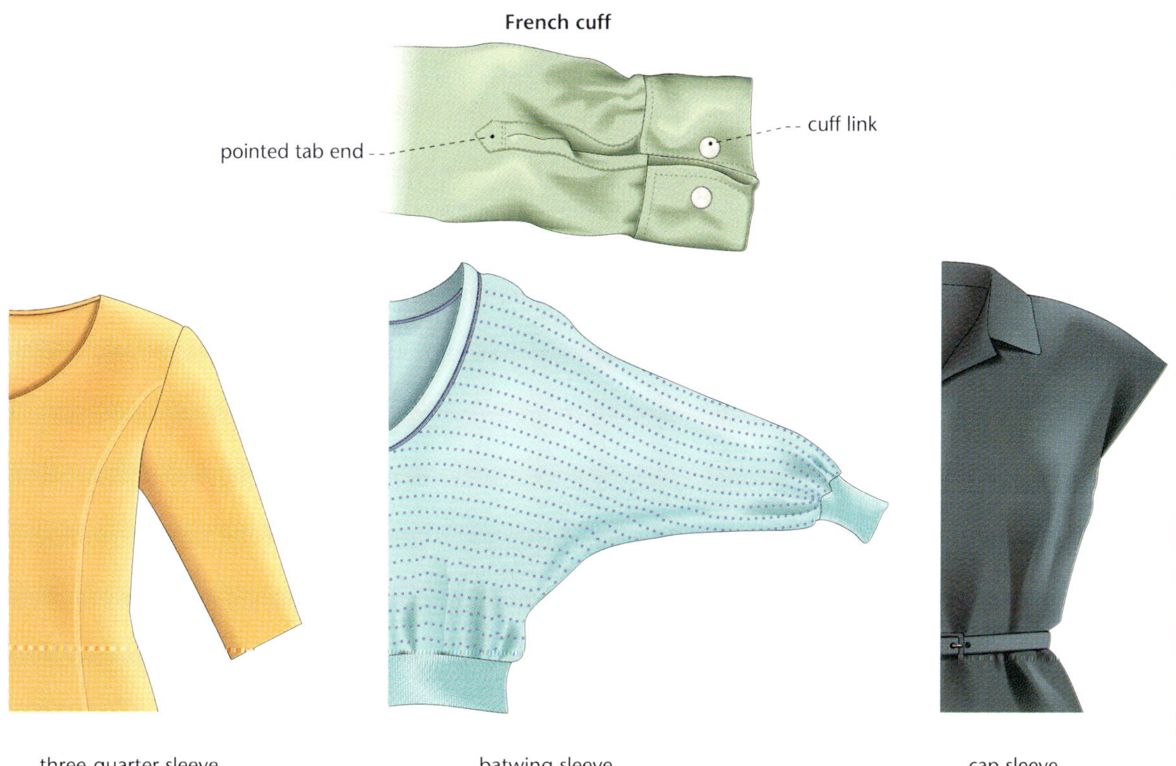

three-quarter sleeve

batwing sleeve

cap sleeve

TYPES OF SLEEVES

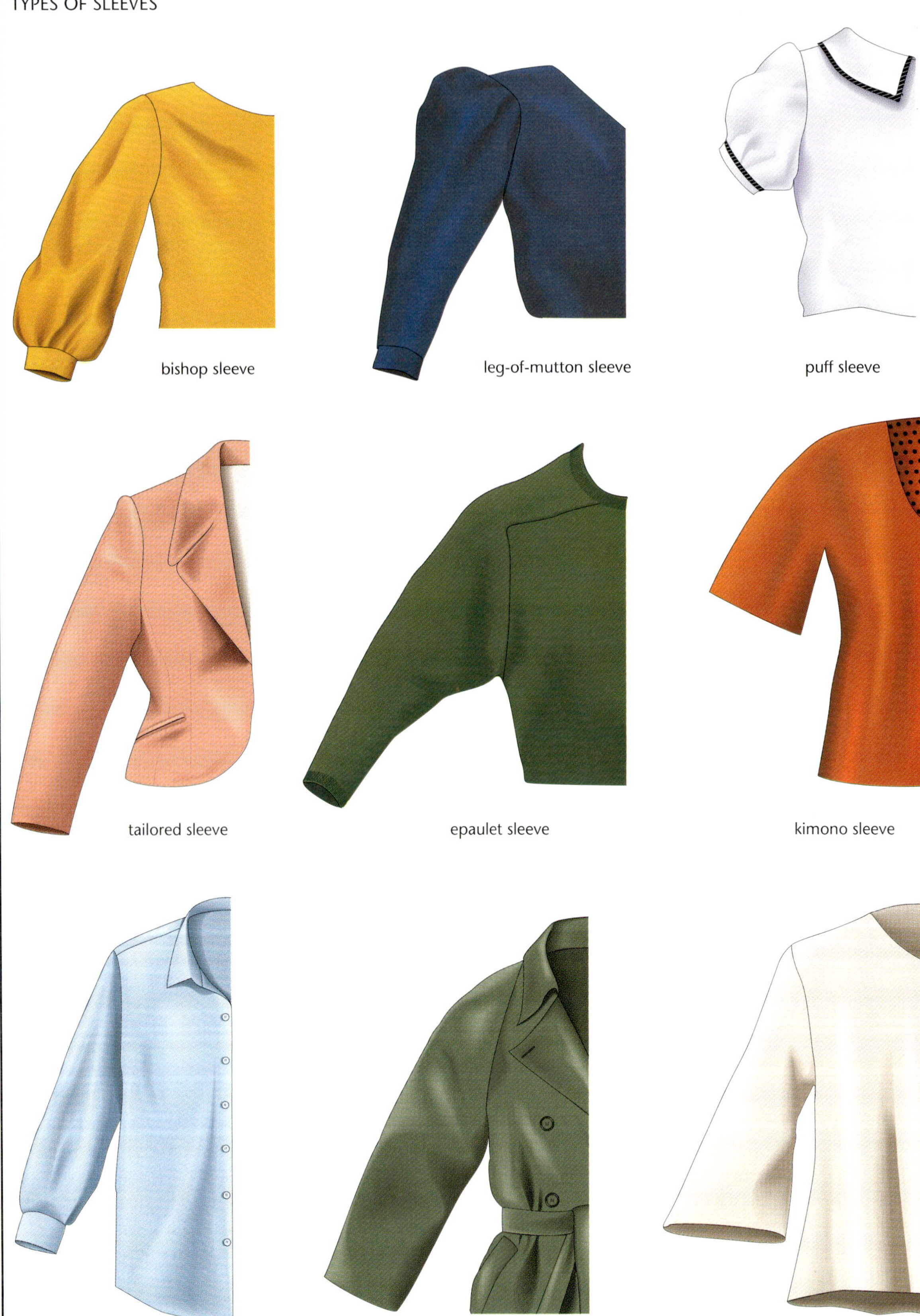

bishop sleeve

leg-of-mutton sleeve

puff sleeve

tailored sleeve

epaulet sleeve

kimono sleeve

shirt sleeve

raglan sleeve

pagoda sleeve

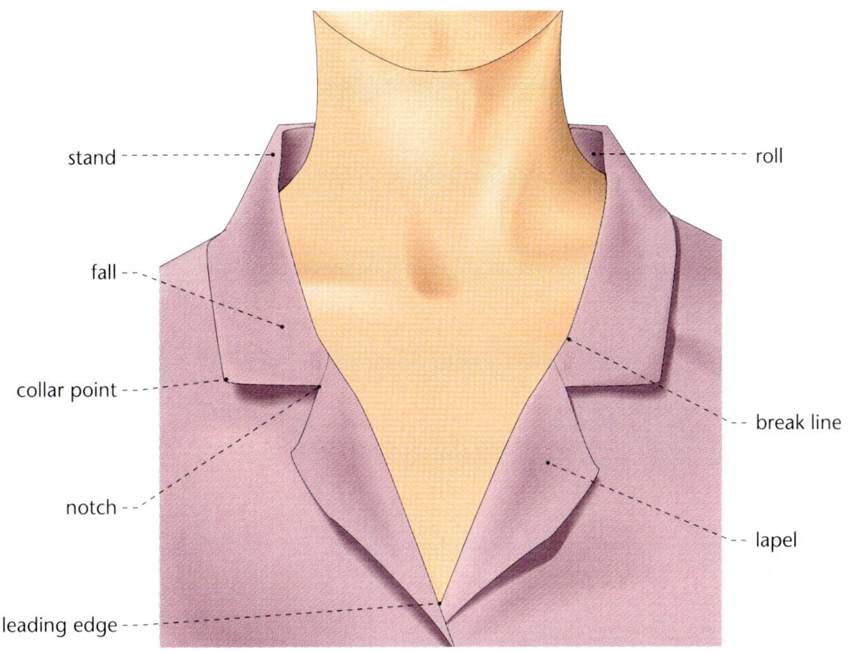

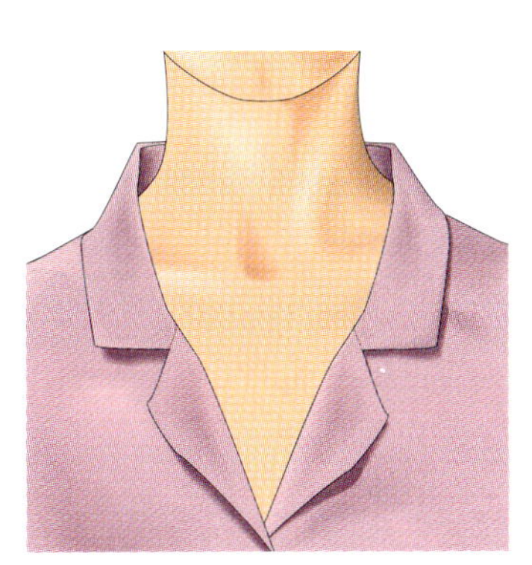
shirt collar

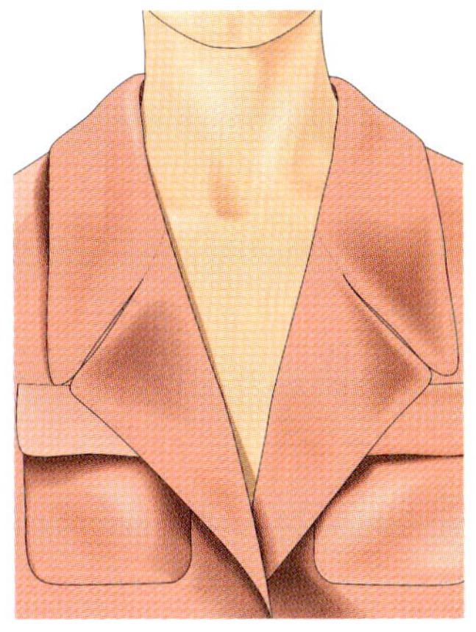
tailored collar

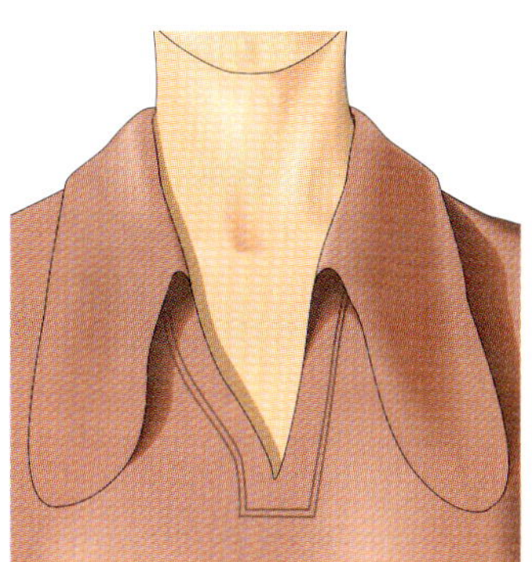
dog ear collar

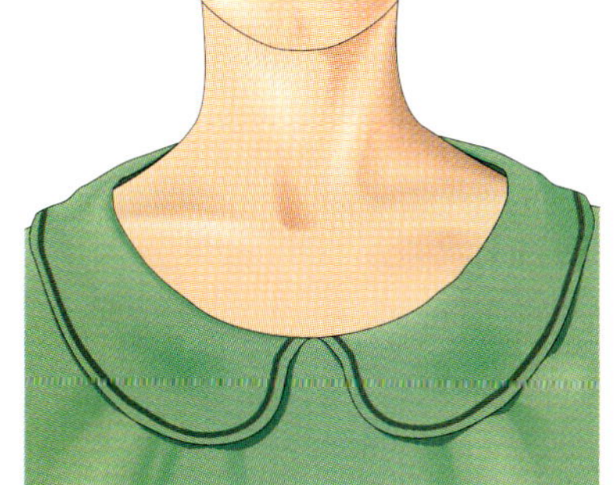
Peter Pan collar

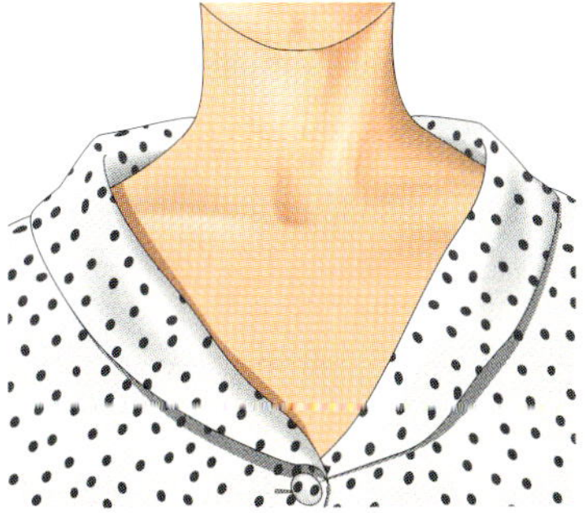
shawl collar

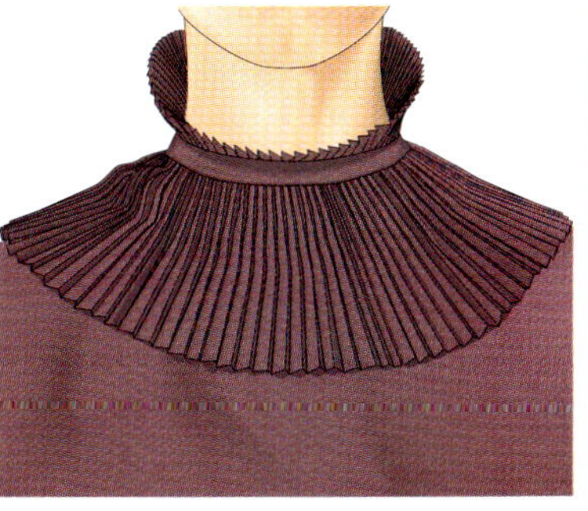
collaret

TYPES OF COLLARS

CLOTHING

bertha collar

bow collar

sailor collar

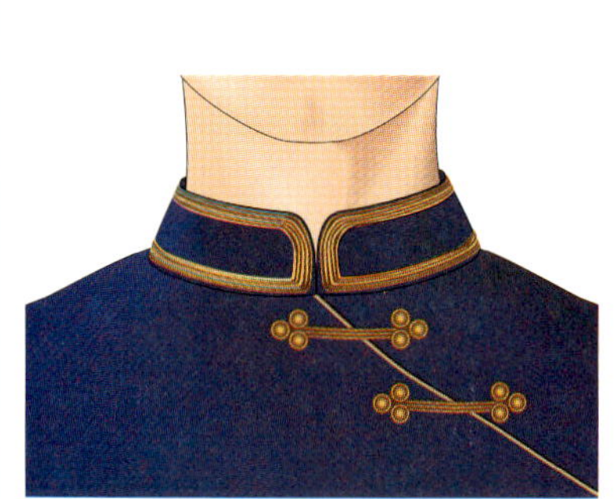

mandarin collar

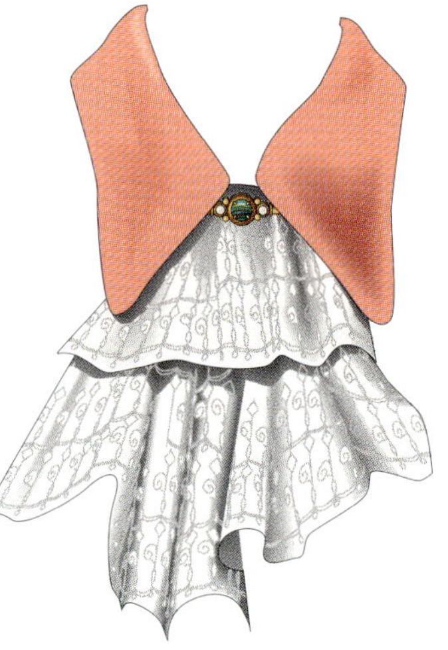

jabot

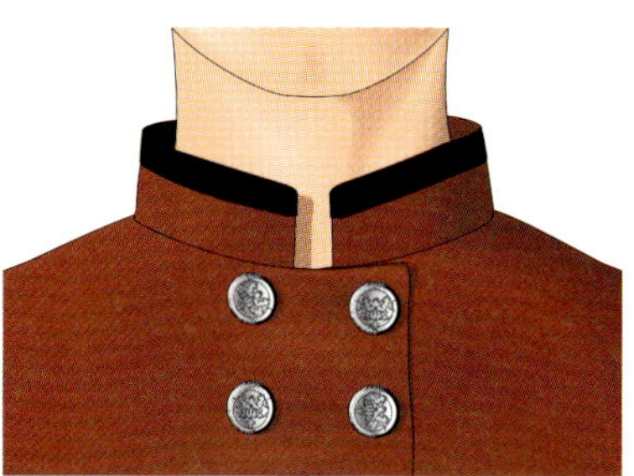

stand-up collar

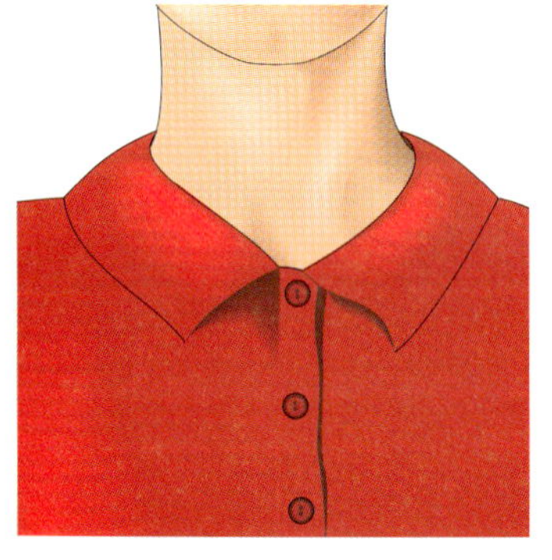

polo collar

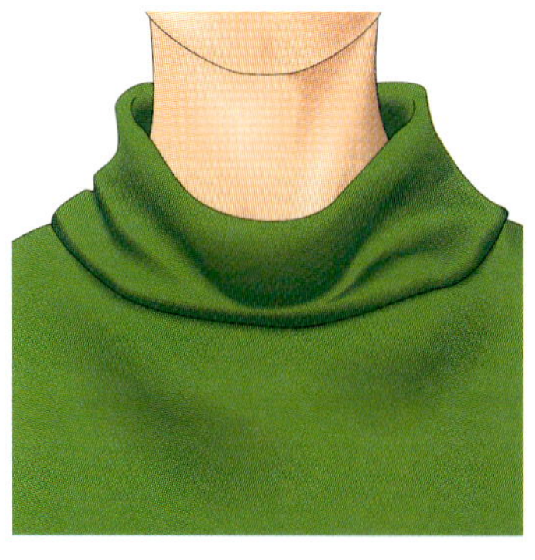

cowl neck

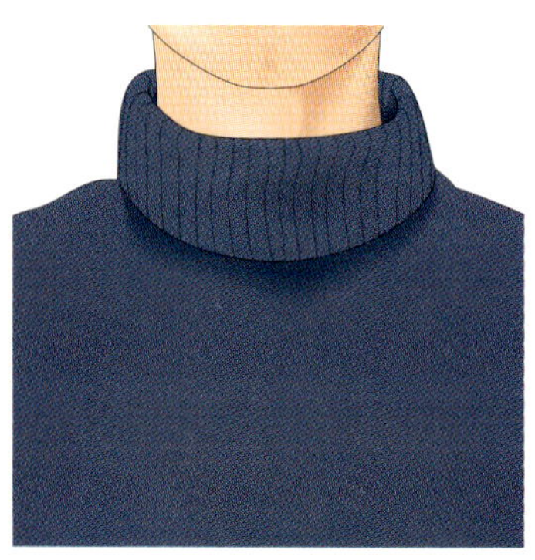

turtleneck

plunging neckline

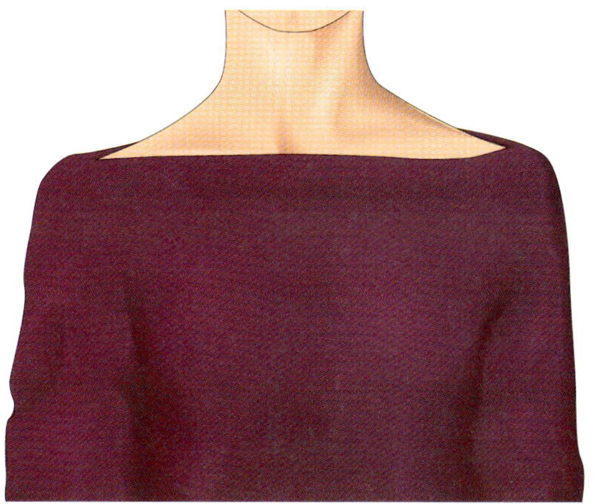

bateau neck

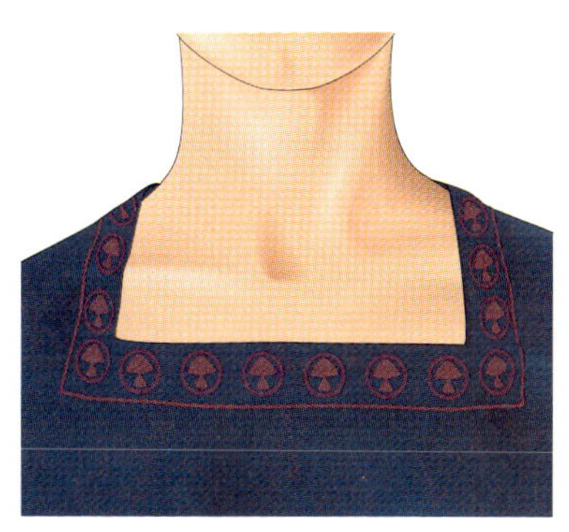

square neck

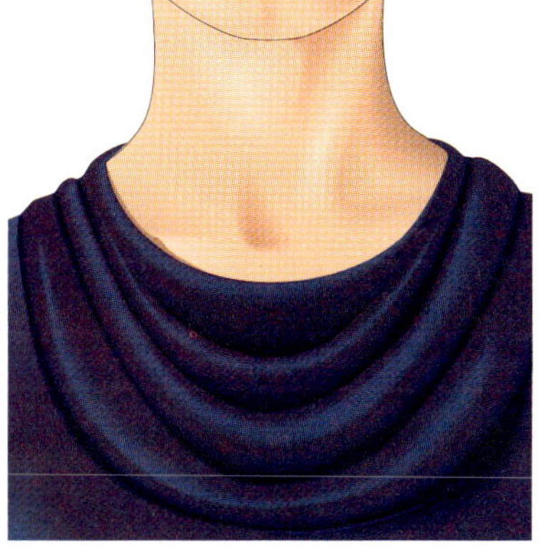

draped neck

round neck

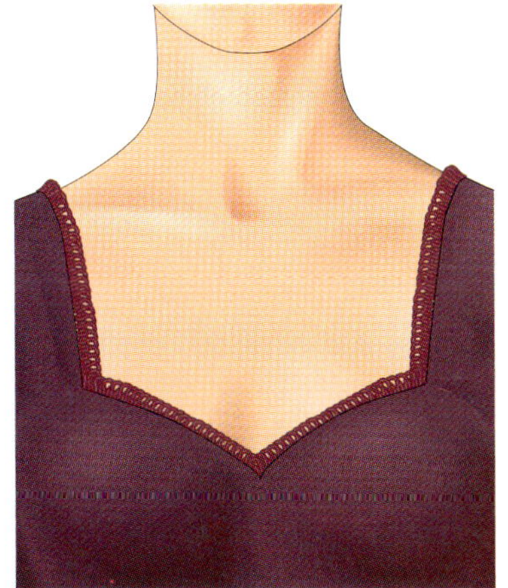

sweetheart neckline

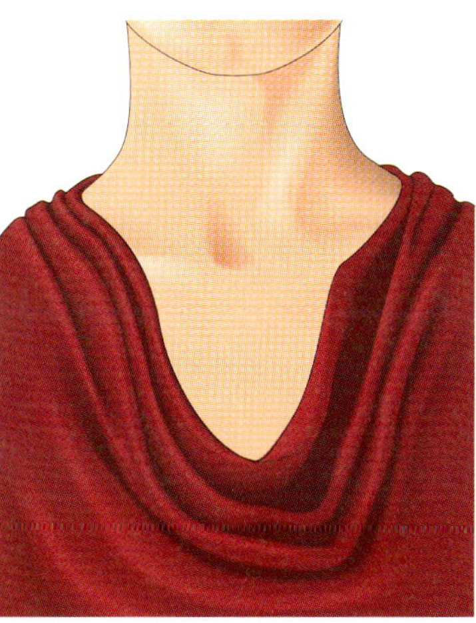

draped neckline

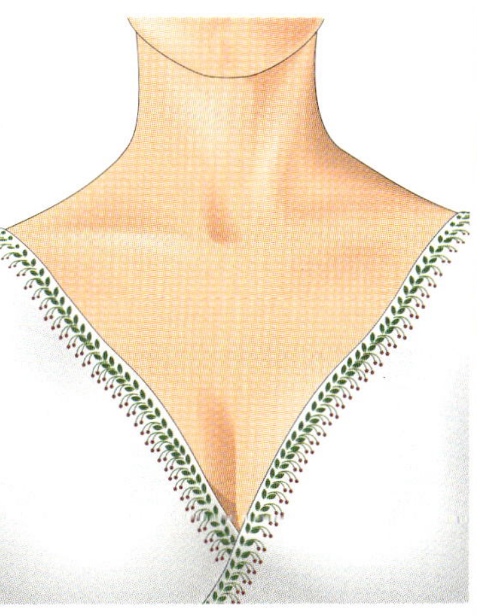

V-shaped neck

HOSE

short sock
anklet
sock
knee-high socks
panty hose
hose
thigh-high stocking
net stocking

body suit
teddy
camisole
foundation slip
slip
princess seaming
half-slip

CLOTHING

UNDERWEAR

corselette
push-up bra
underwiring
garter belt
bikini
garter
hose
panty corselette
wasp-waisted corset

NIGHTWEAR

kimono

nightgown

baby doll

pajamas

negligee

bathrobe

CLOTHING

BATHING WRAP
PLASTIC PANTS
decorative braid
hood
Velcro® closure
false tuck
nylon rumba tights
waterproof pants
bib
diaper
bunting bag
jumpsuit
shirt
RUFFLED RUMBA PANTS
ruching

BLANKET SLEEPERS

SLEEPERS

HIGH-BACK OVERALLS

GROW SLEEPERS

TRAINING SET
tank top
shorts
CROSSOVER BACK STRAPS OVERALLS
button strap
bib
polojama
SNOWSUIT
drawstring hood
fly front closing
rompers
T-shirt dress
jumpsuit

RUNNING SHOE

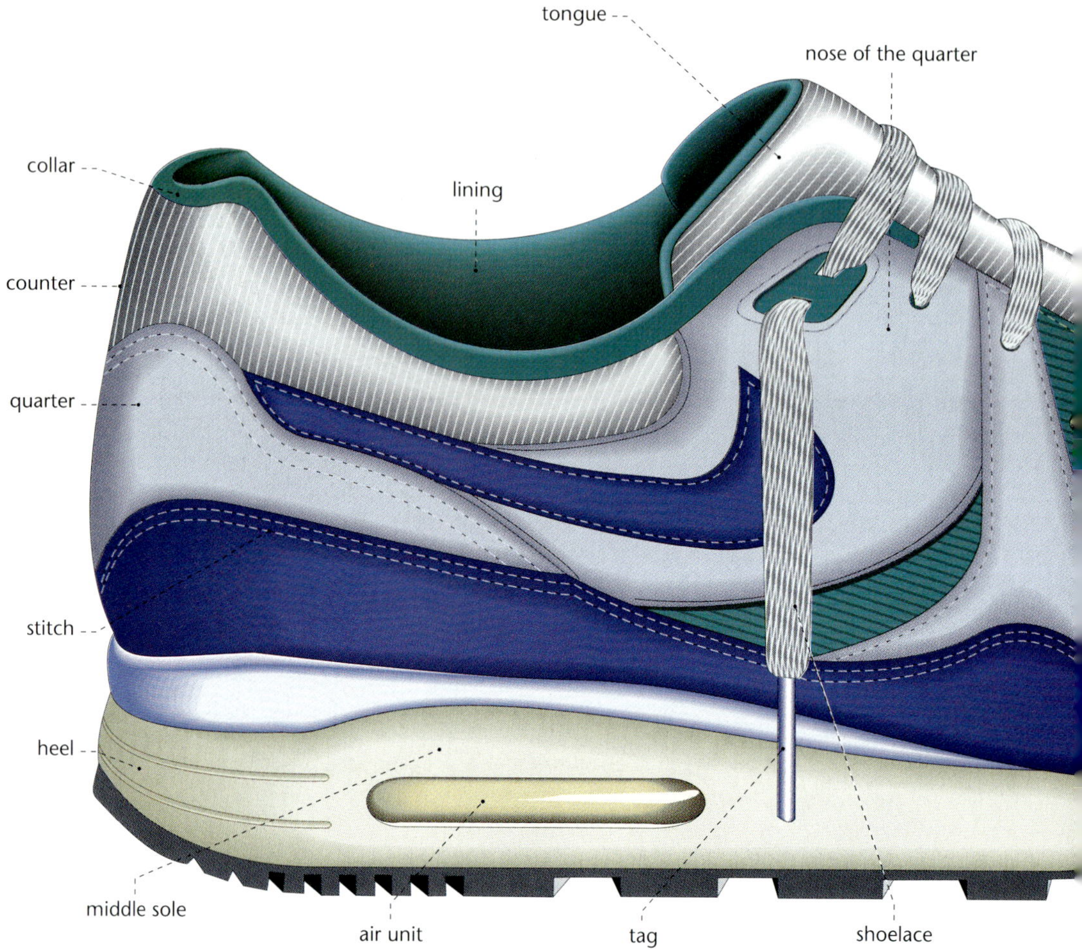

tongue

nose of the quarter

collar

lining

counter

quarter

stitch

heel

middle sole

air unit

tag

shoelace

TRAINING SUIT

hooded sweat shirt

sweat pants

sweat shirt

swimming trunks
swimsuit
eyelet
vamp
punch hole
leotard
footless tights
stud
outsole
leg-warmer
boxer shorts
pants
anorak
tank top

PARTS OF A SHOE

MAJOR TYPES OF SHOES

oxford shoe

chukka

bootee

tennis shoe

blucher oxford

moccasin

loafer

mule

heavy duty boot

rubber

MAJOR TYPES OF SHOES

sandal
thong
ankle boot
clog
espadrille
thigh-boot
sandal

ACCESSORIES

PERSONAL ADORNMENT

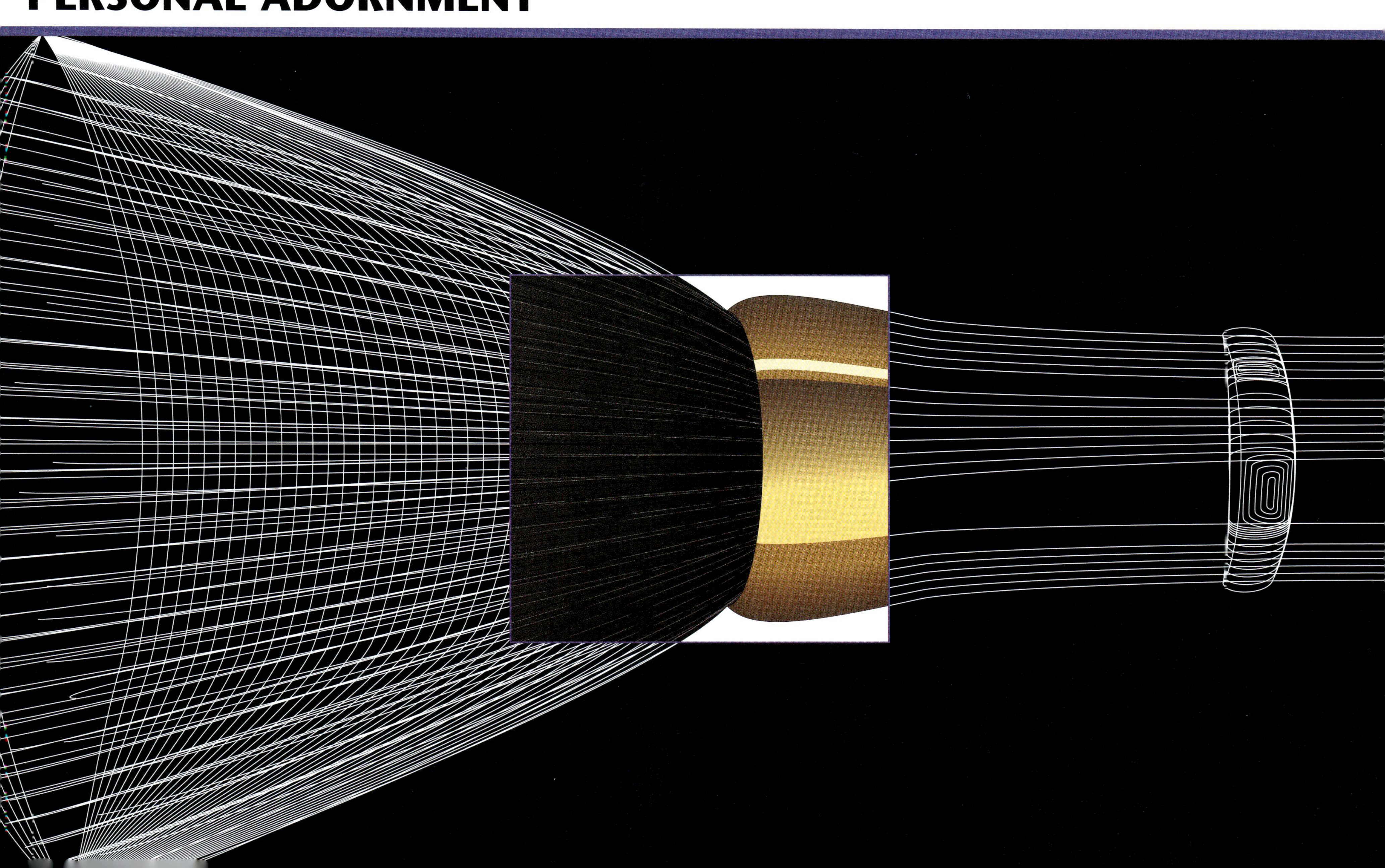

CONTENTS

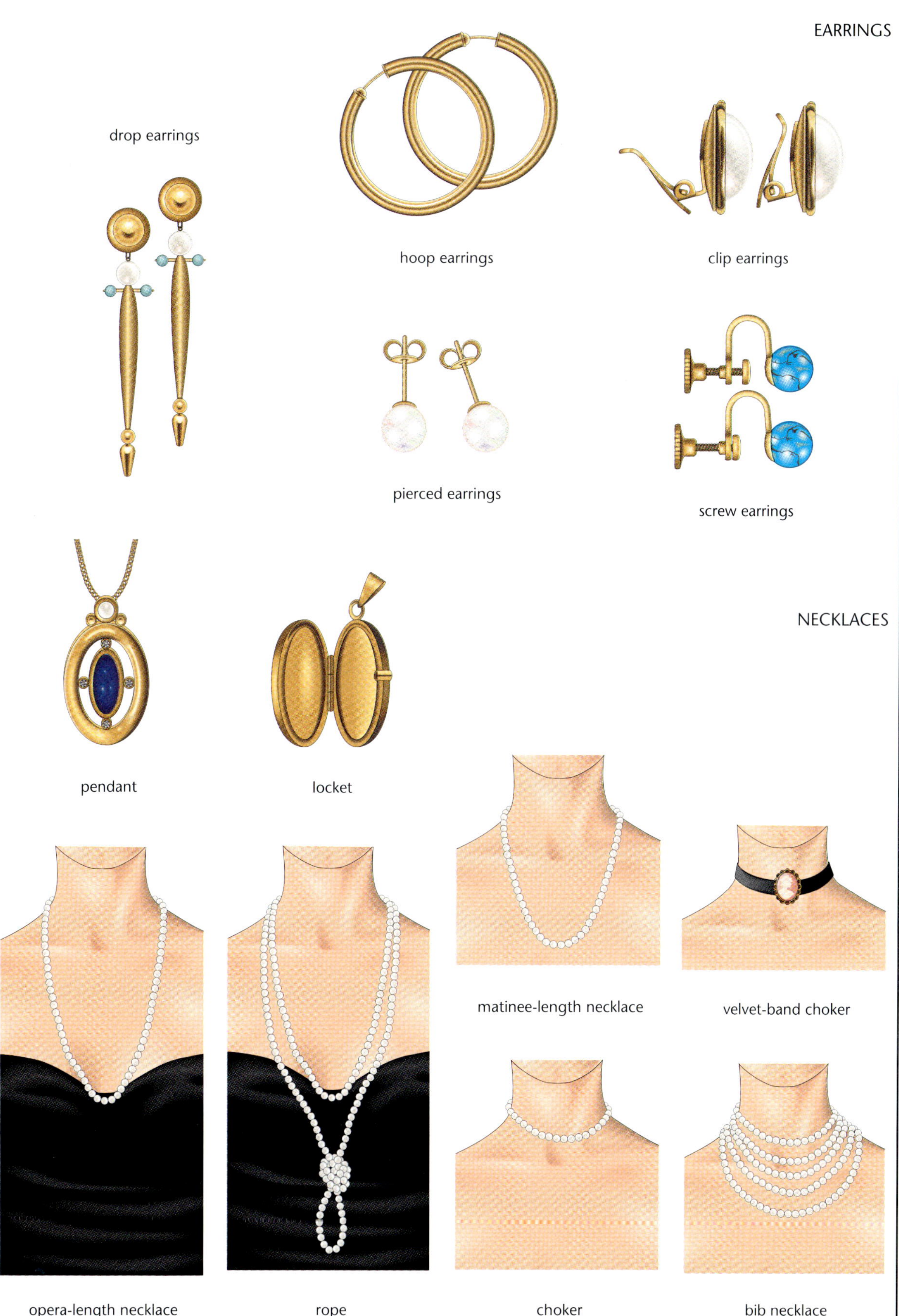

PERSONAL ADORNMENT

CUT FOR GEMSTONES

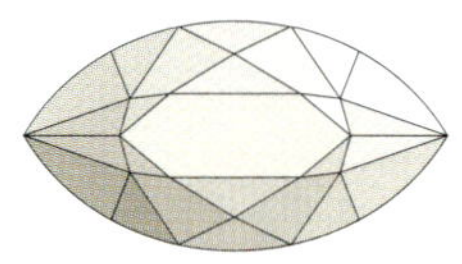

navette cut

baguette cut

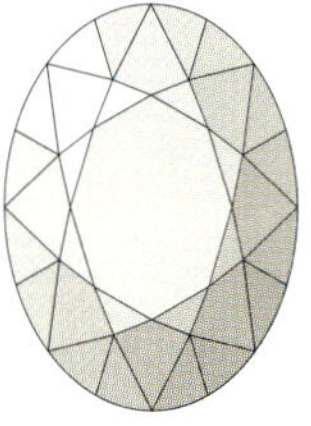

oval cut

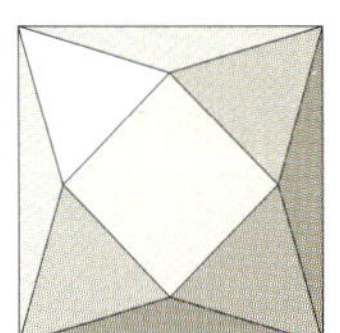

French cut

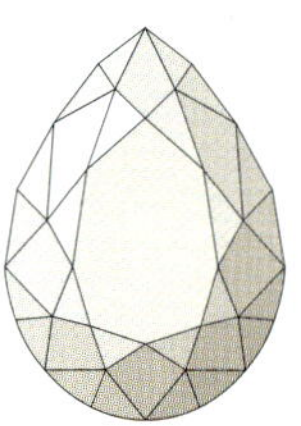

pear-shaped cut

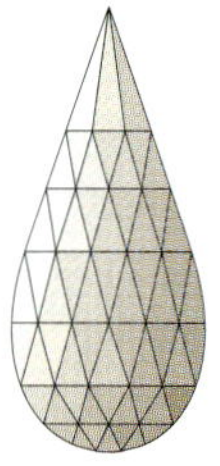

briolette cut

table cut

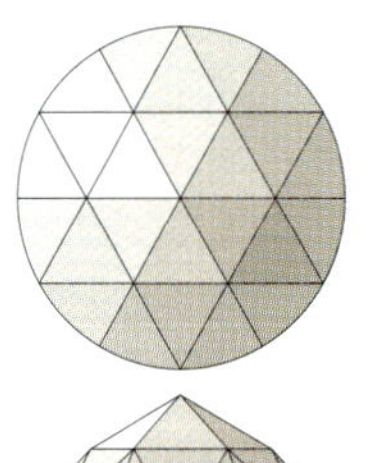

rose cut

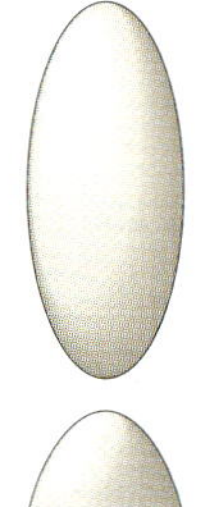

cabochon cut

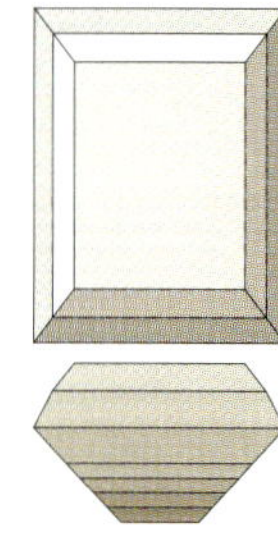

step cut

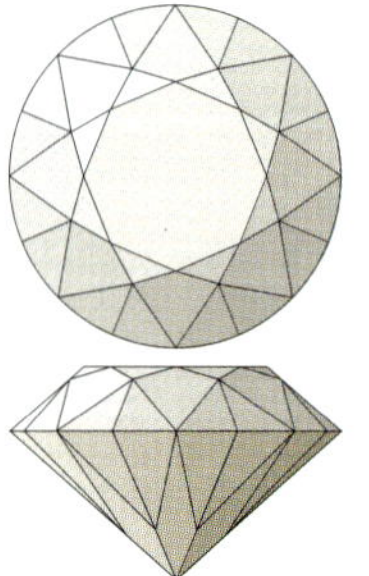

brilliant full cut

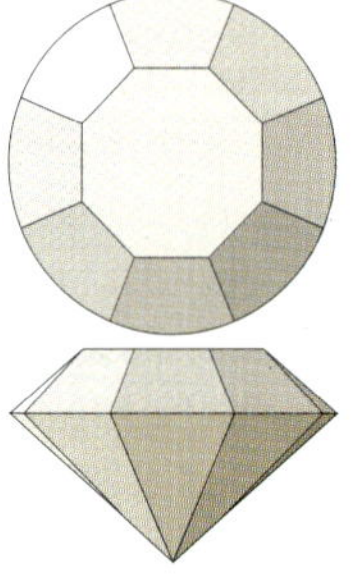

eight cut

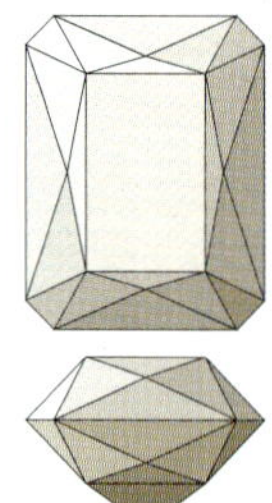

scissors cut

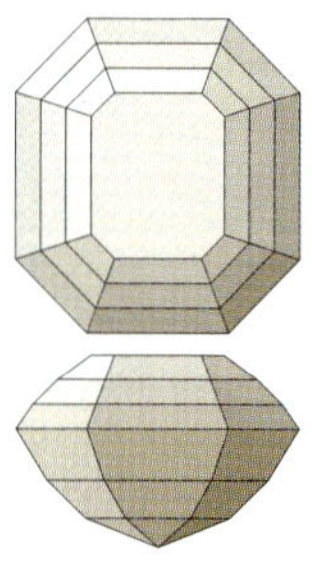

emerald cut

BRILLIANT CUT FACETS

BOTTOM FACE

pavilion facet (8)

culet

lower girdle facet (16)

TOP FACE

star facet (8)

table

bezel facet (8)

upper girdle facet (16)

SIDE FACE

table

girdle

crown

pavilion

culet

PRECIOUS STONES

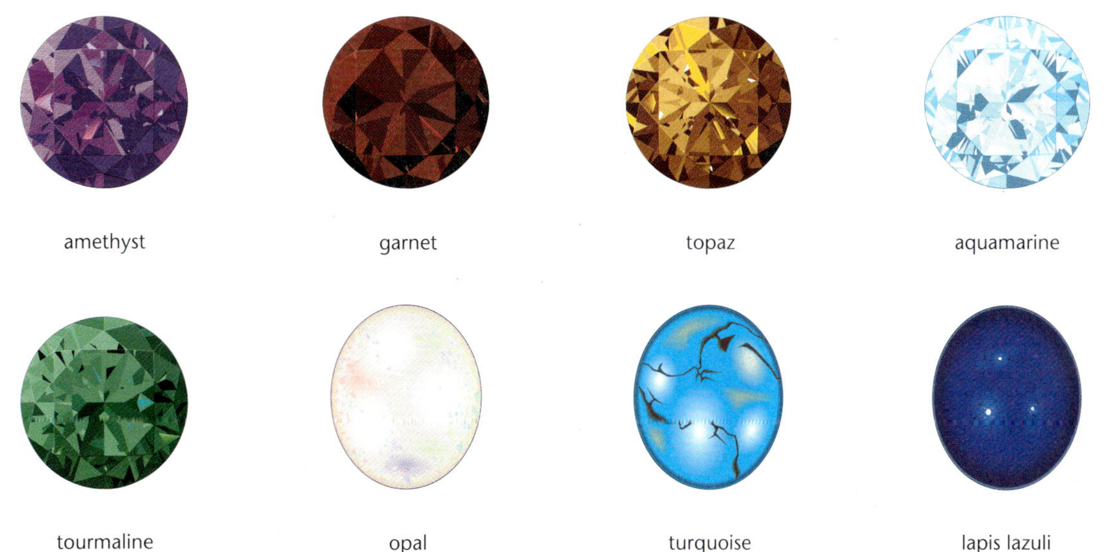

emerald

ruby

sapphire

diamond

SEMIPRECIOUS STONES

amethyst

garnet

topaz

aquamarine

tourmaline

opal

turquoise

lapis lazuli

JEWELRY

RINGS
signet ring
setting
claw
stone
bezel
class ring
band ring
wedding ring
engagement ring
solitaire ring
BRACELETS
identification bracelet
bangle
charm bracelet
CHARMS
PINS
brooch
stickpin
nameplate
horseshoe
tiepin
collar bar
tie bar
horn

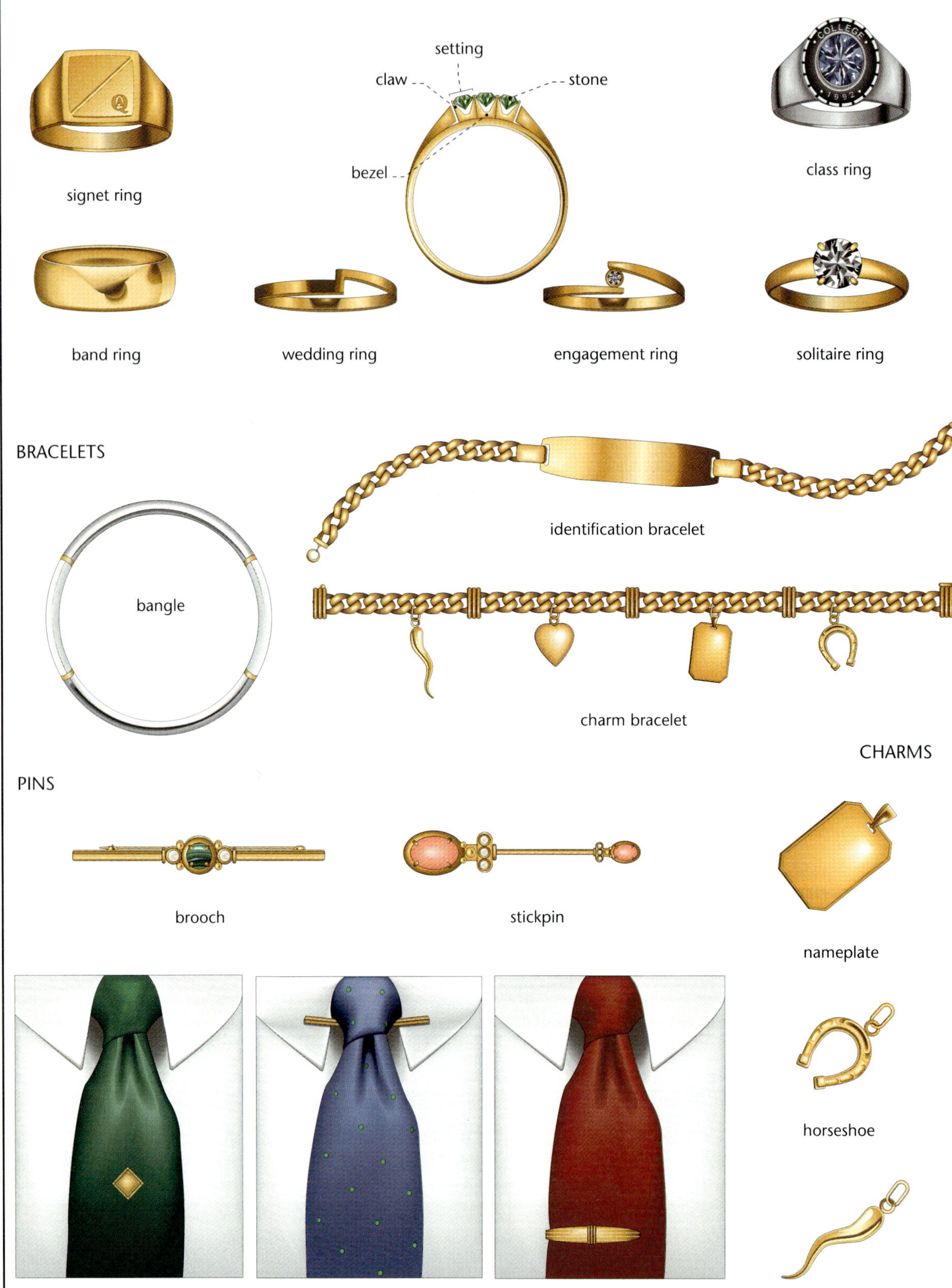

MANICURE SET

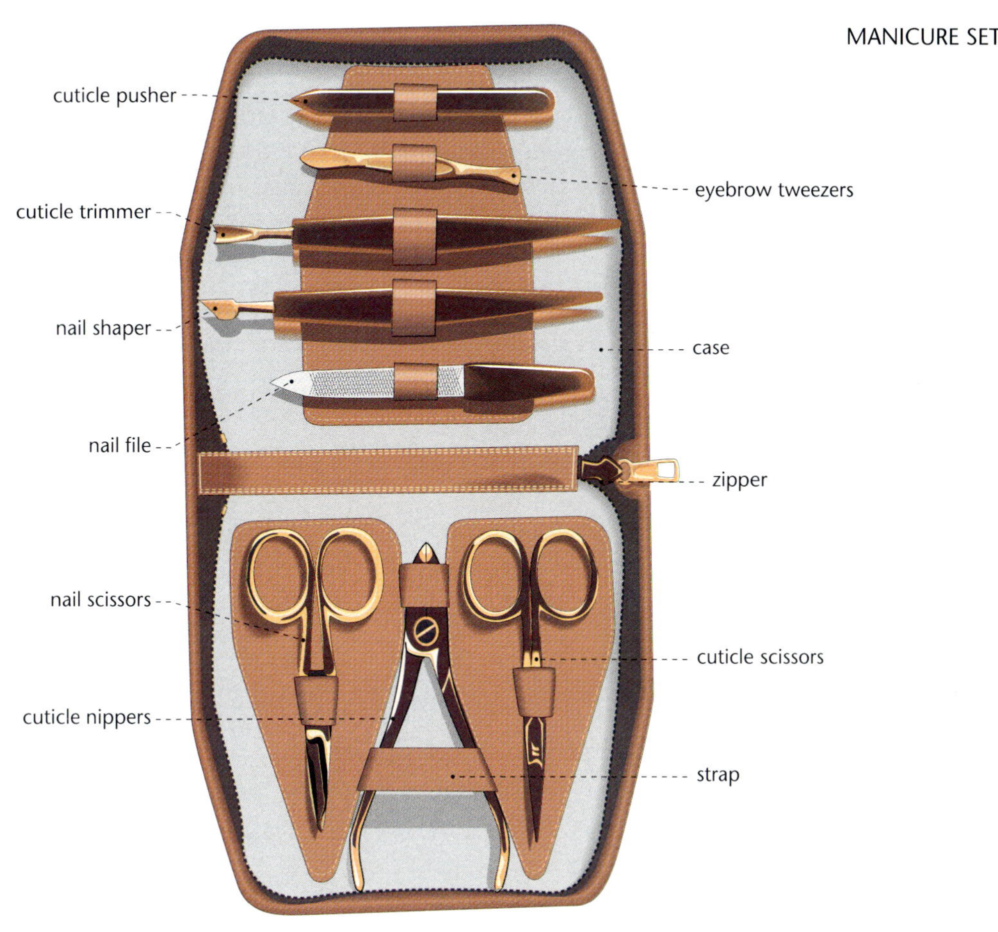

NAIL CLIPPERS

MANICURING IMPLEMENTS

FACIAL MAKEUP
fan brush
loose powder brush
loose powder
liquid foundation
powder puff
compact
pressed powder
blusher brush
powder blusher
LIP MAKEUP
lipbrush
lipstick
lipliner

EYE MAKEUP
eyebrow pencil
brow brush and lash comb
liquid eyeliner
liquid mascara
eyelash curler
mascara brush
sponge-tipped applicator
cake mascara
eyeshadow
SPONGES
vegetable sponge
natural sponge
synthetic sponge

PERSONAL ADORNMENT

LIGHTED MIRROR

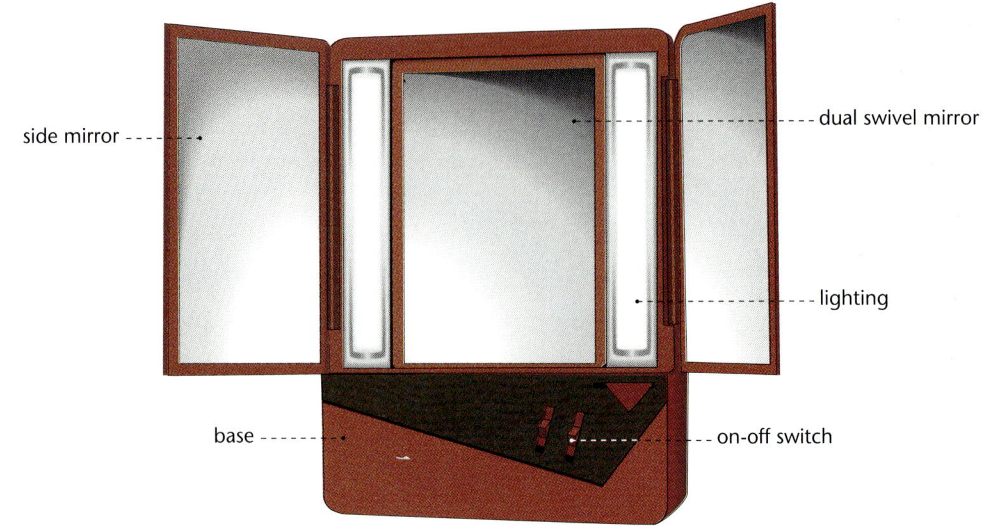

HAIRBRUSHES

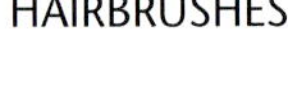

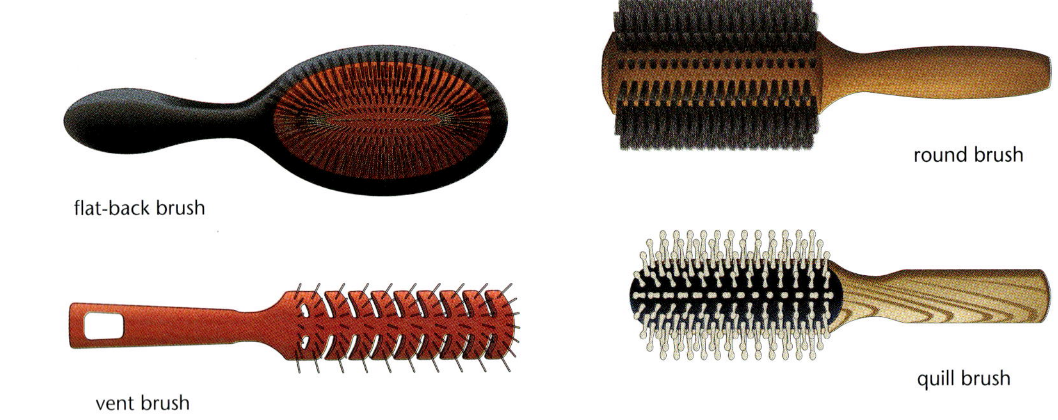

COMBS

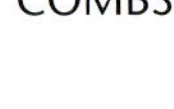

cutting edge
blade
ferrule
pivot
shank
blade close stop
clippers
thinning razor
NOTCHED DOUBLE-EDGED
THINNING SCISSORS
NOTCHED SINGLE-EDGED
THINNING SCISSORS
tooth
blade
notched edge
HAIRSTYLING IMPLEMENTS
bobby pin
hairpin
wave clip
HAIR ROLLER
roller
hair roller pin
hair clip
barrette

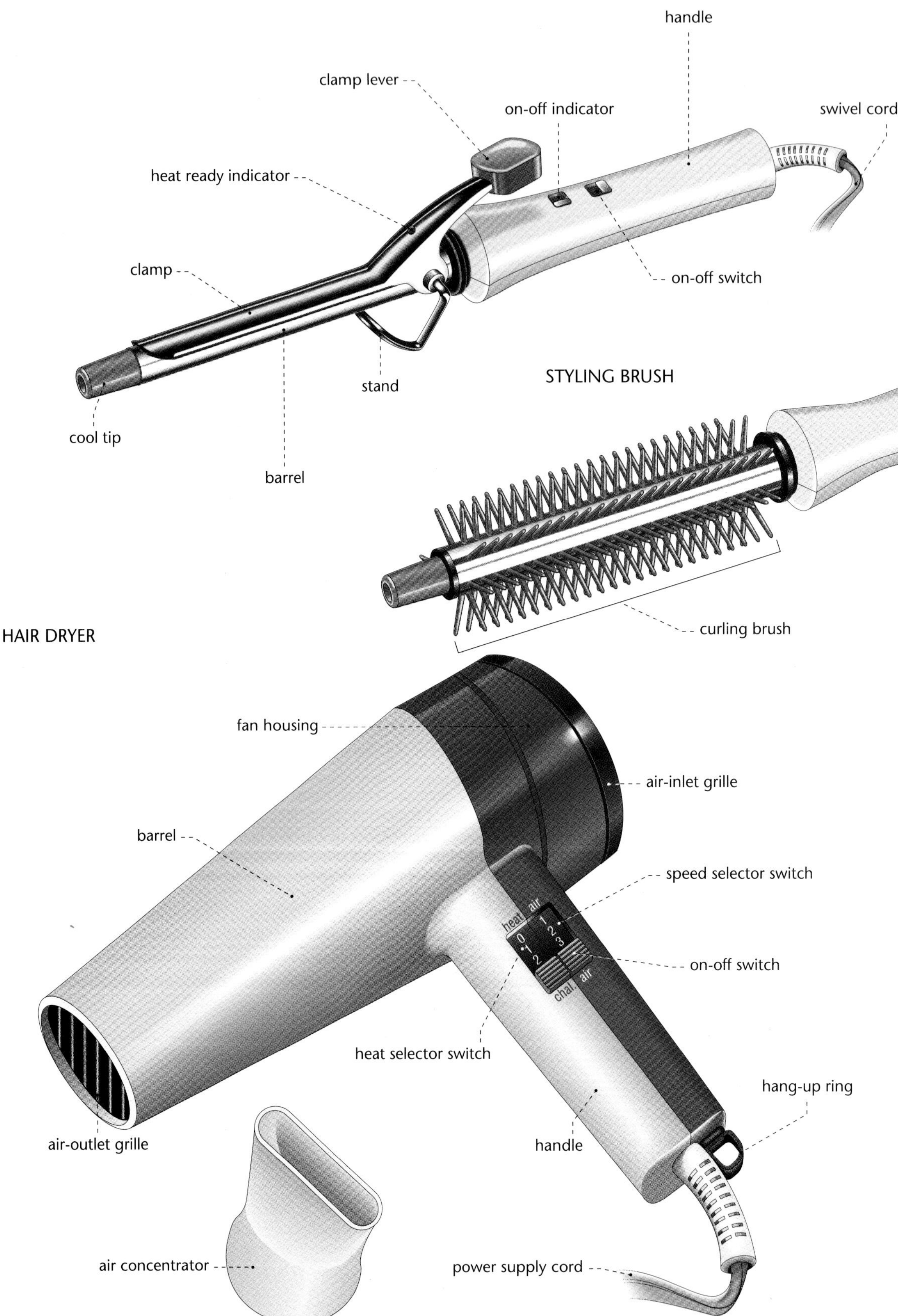

CURLING IRON
clamp lever
on-off indicator
handle
swivel cord
heat ready indicator
clamp
on-off switch
cool tip
stand
barrel
STYLING BRUSH
curling brush
HAIR DRYER
fan housing
air-inlet grille
barrel
speed selector switch
on-off switch
heat selector switch
heat air
0 1
1 2 3
2
chal air
air-outlet grille
hang-up ring
handle
air concentrator
power supply cord

PERSONAL ADORNMENT

PERSONAL ARTICLES

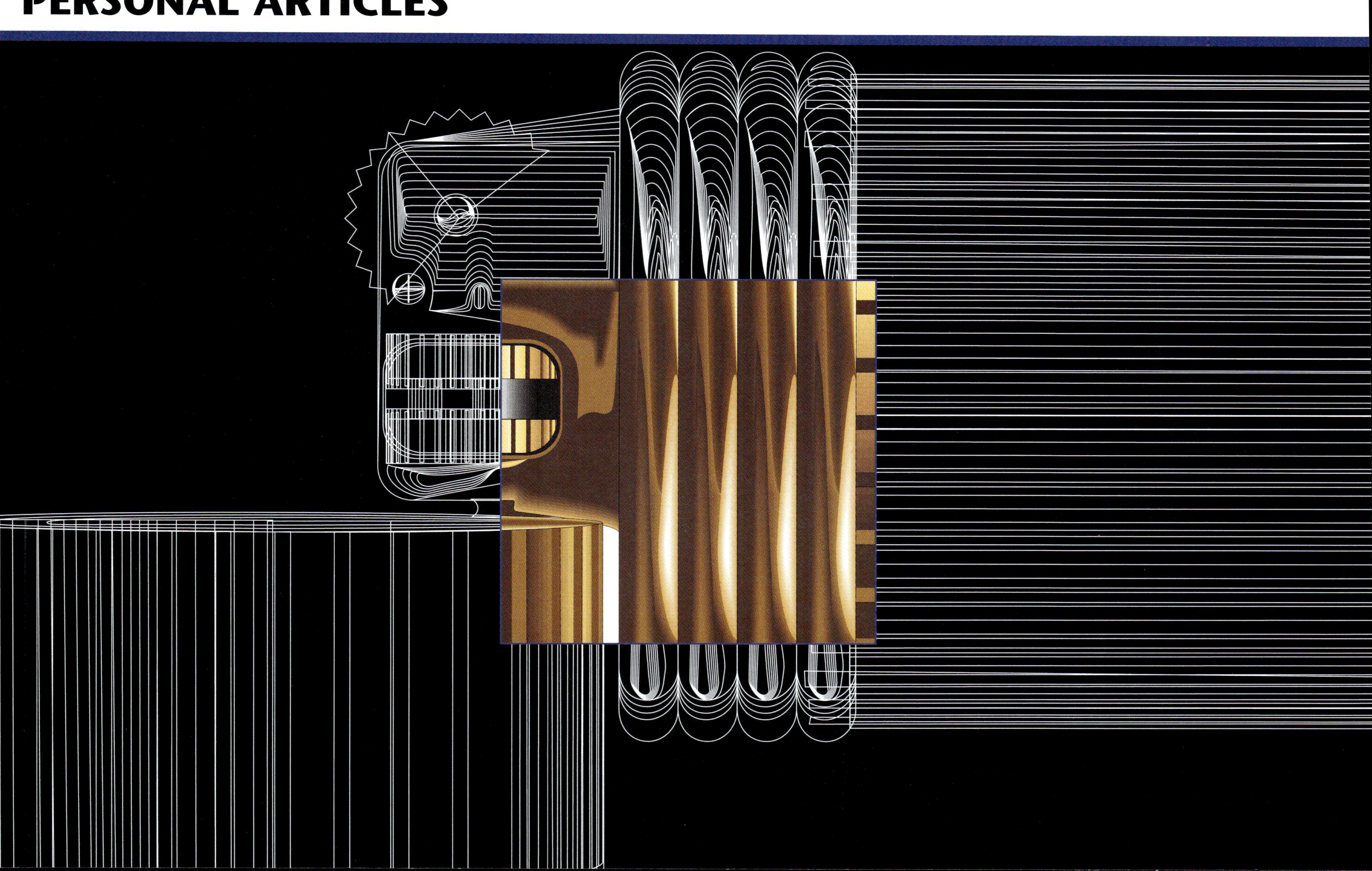

CONTENTS

DENTAL CARE

TOOTHBRUSH
stimulator tip
handle
bristle
row
head
toothpaste
dental floss
ORAL HYGIENE CENTER
brush
toothbrush shaft
on-off switch
handle
jet tip
toothbrush
water tank
oral irrigator
motor unit
toothbrush well
pressure control

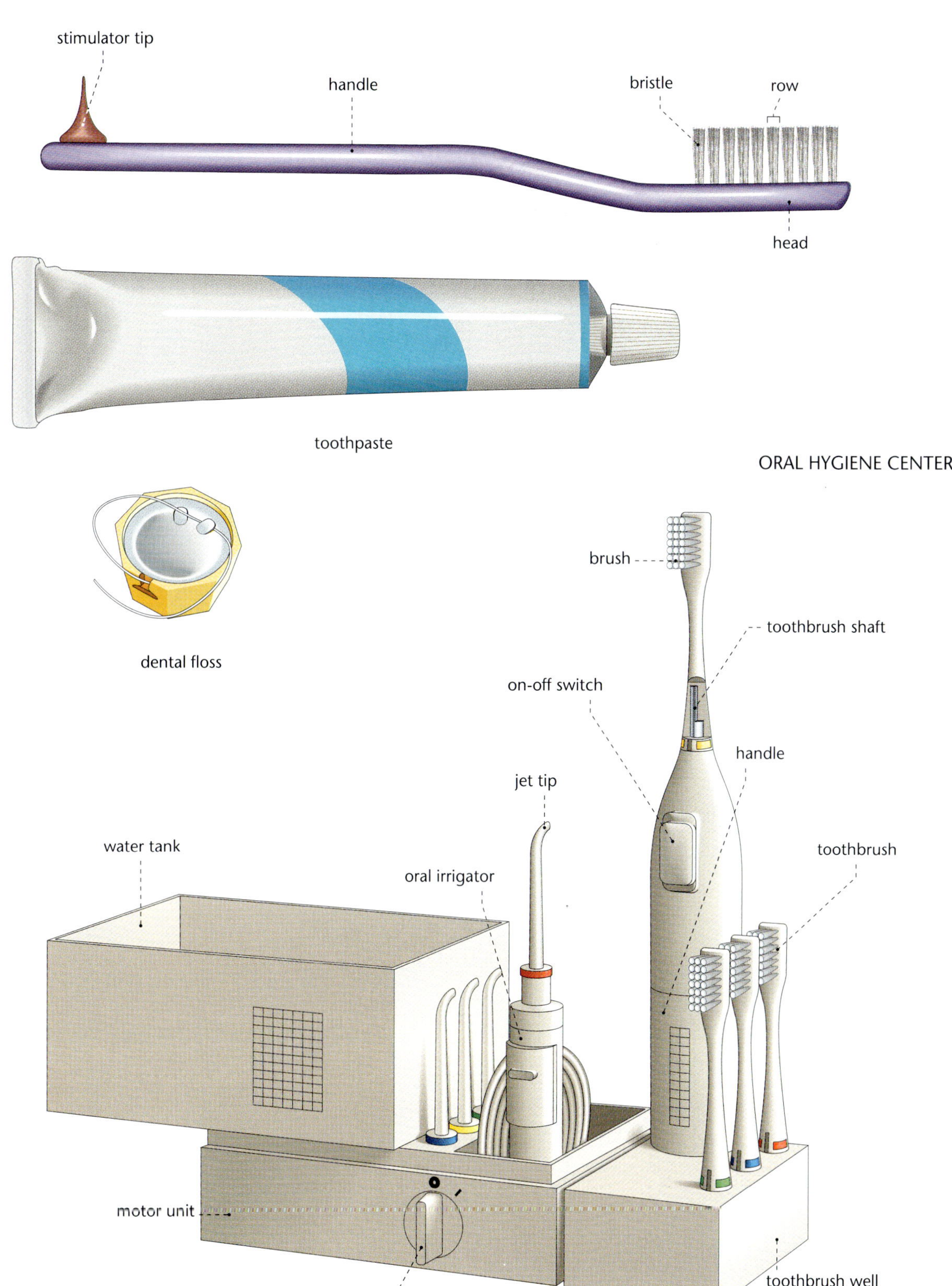

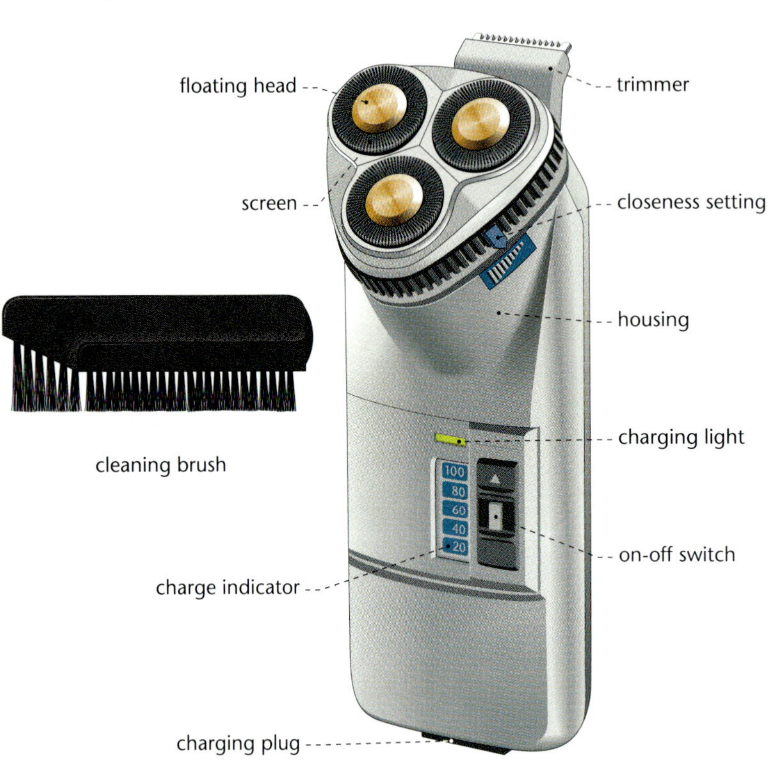

cleaning brush

power cord

plug adapter

STRAIGHT RAZOR

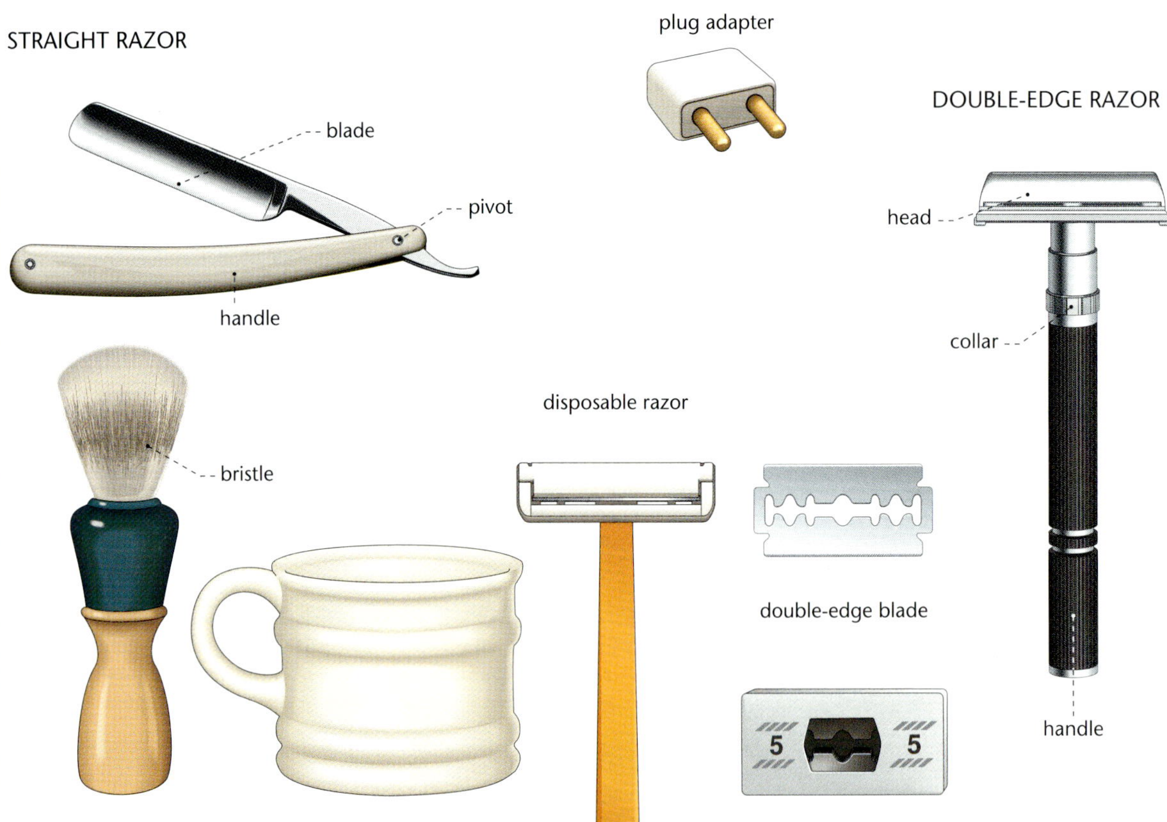

SHAVING BRUSH

shaving mug

UMBRELLA AND STICK

UMBRELLA

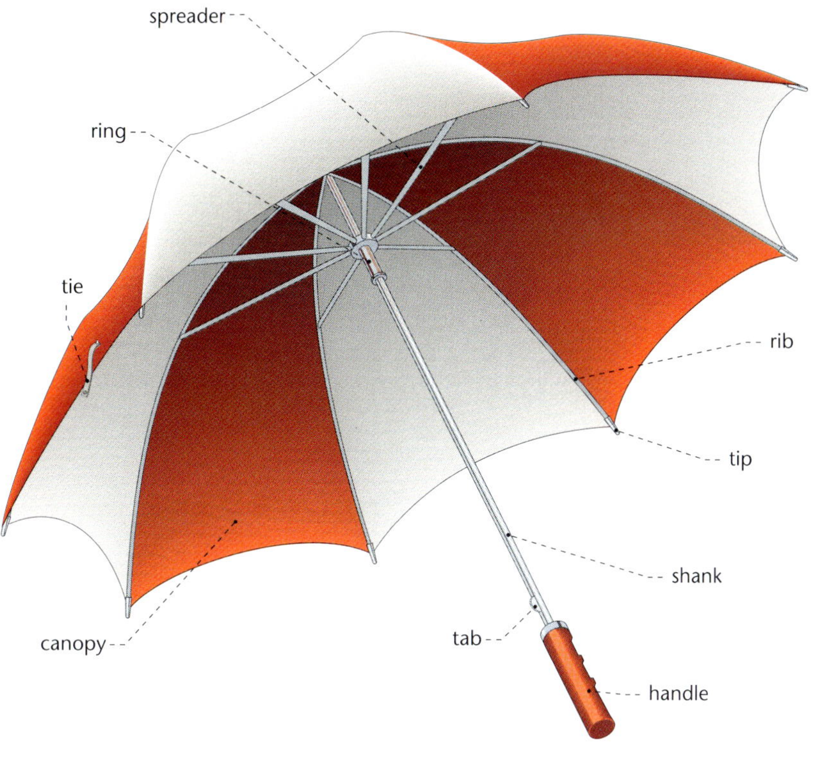

TELESCOPIC UMBRELLA

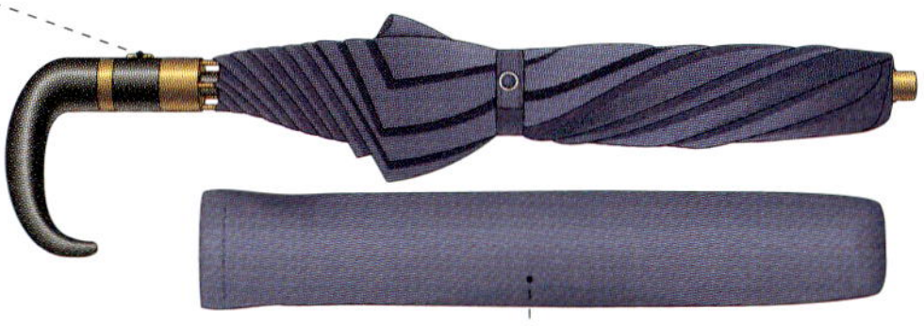

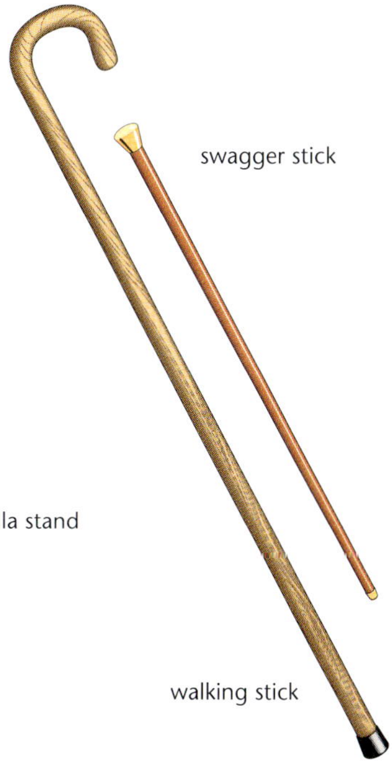

STICK UMBRELLA

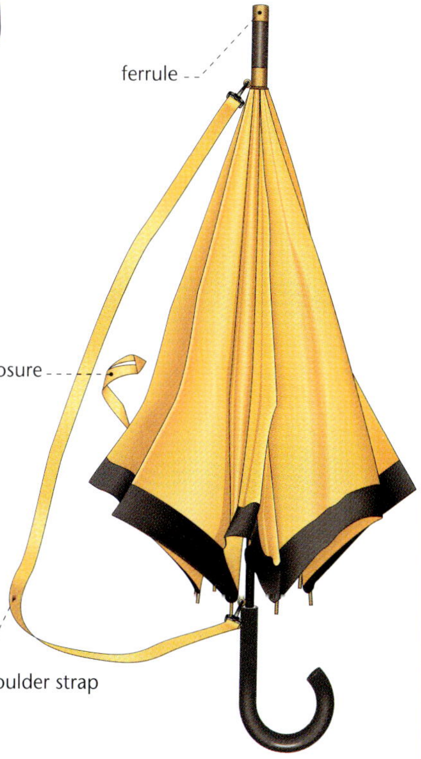

375

EYEGLASSES PARTS

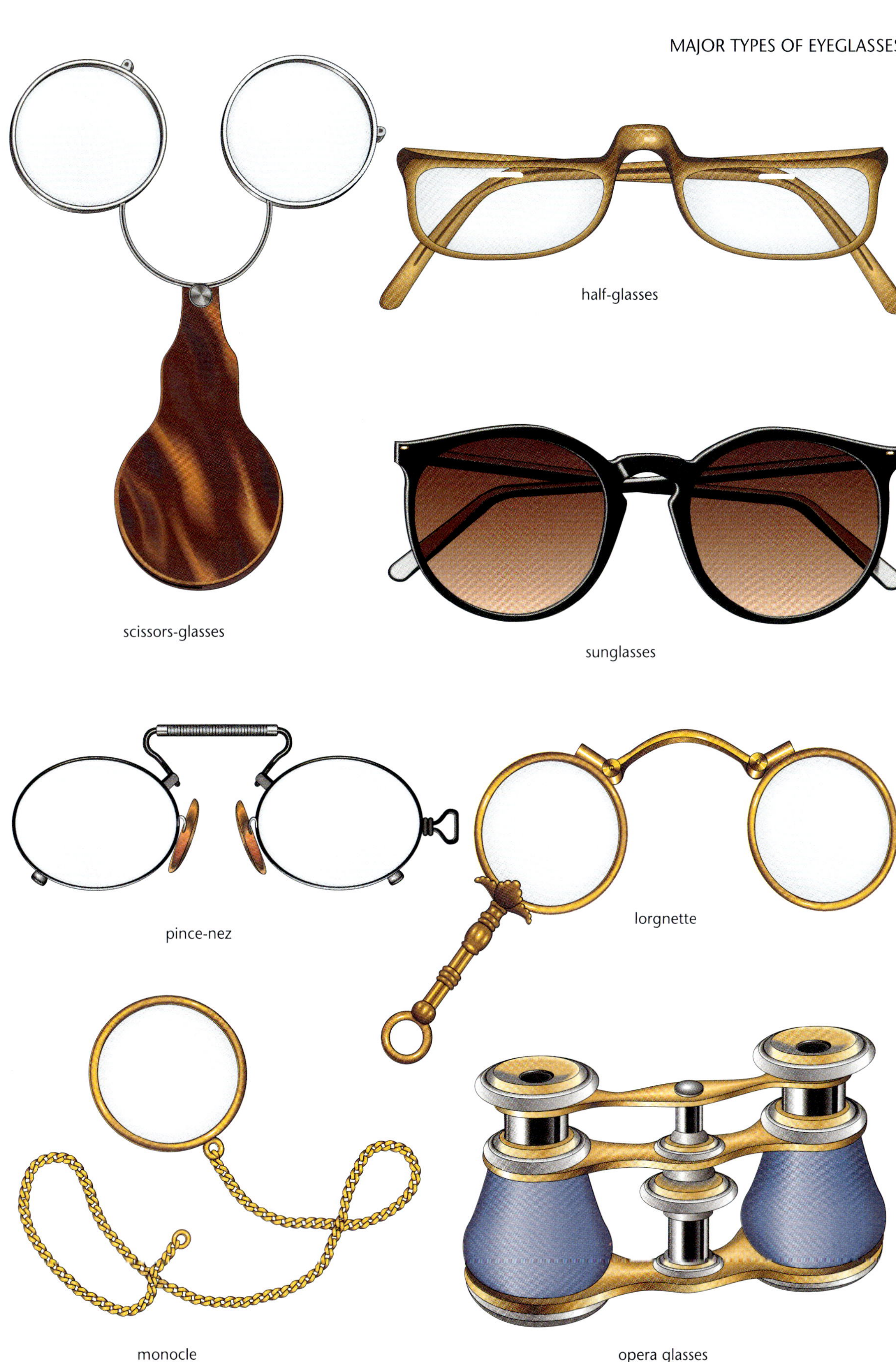
half-glasses
scissors-glasses
sunglasses
pince-nez
lorgnette
monocle
opera glasses

ATTACHÉ CASE

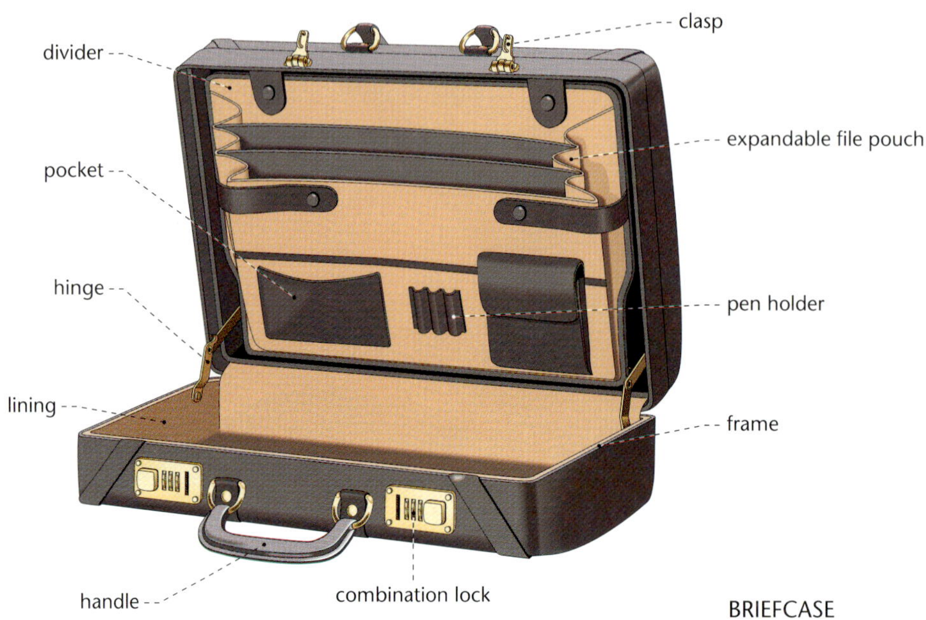

BOTTOM-FOLD PORTFOLIO

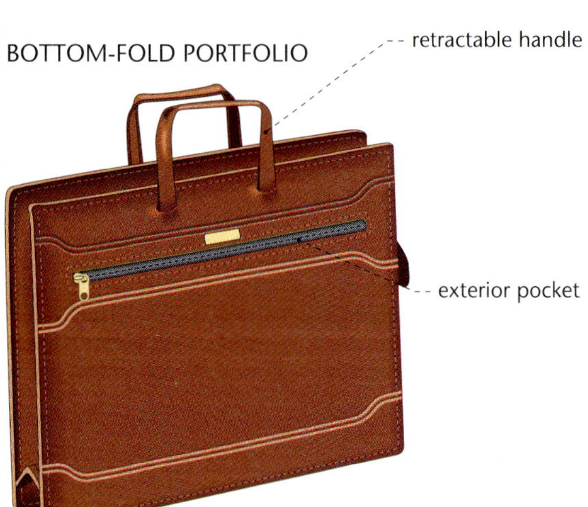

BRIEFCASE

underarm portfolio

writing case

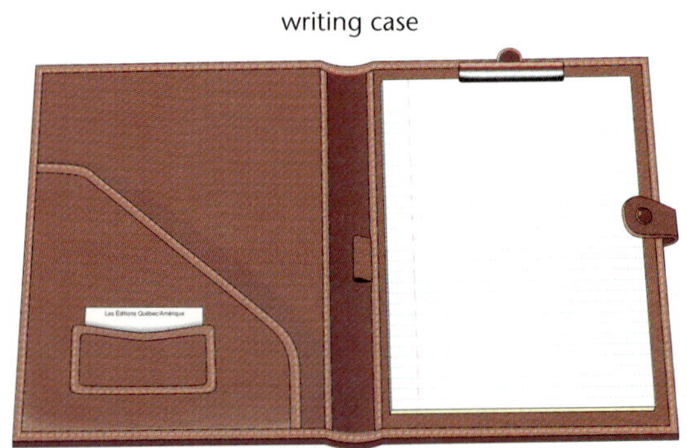

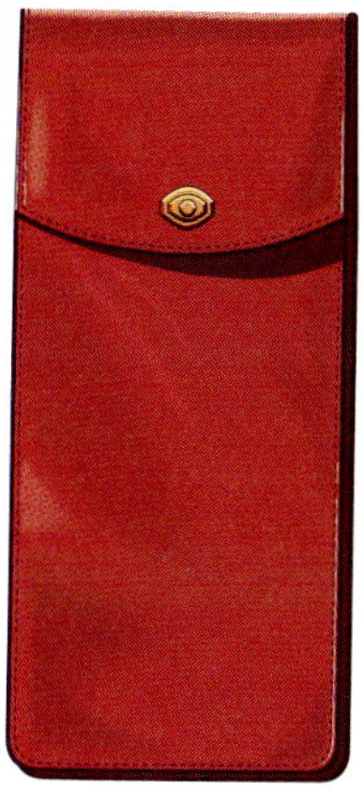

eyeglasses case

CHECKBOOK/SECRETARY CLUTCH

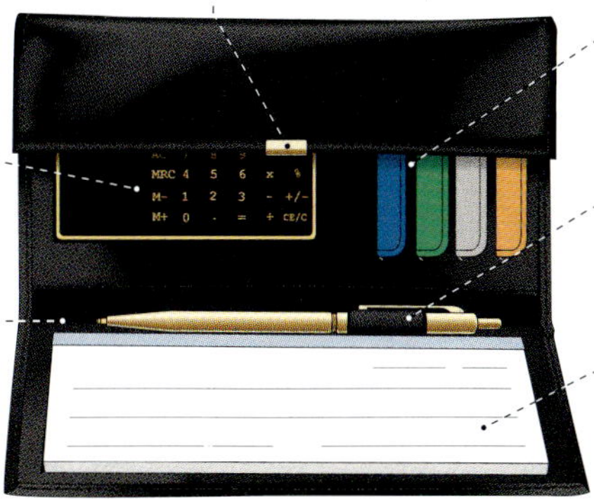
trimming
card case
calculator
pen holder
hidden pocket
checkbook

CARD CASE

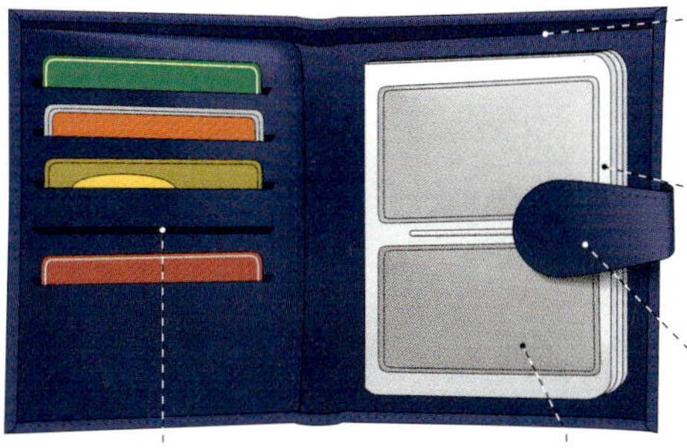
bill compartment
windows
tab
slot
window

key case

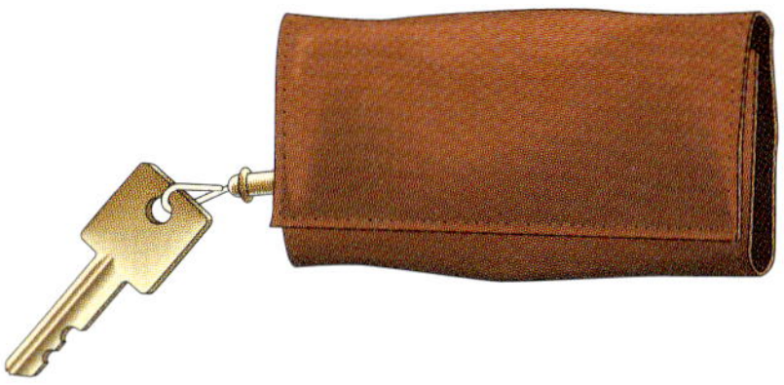

billfold

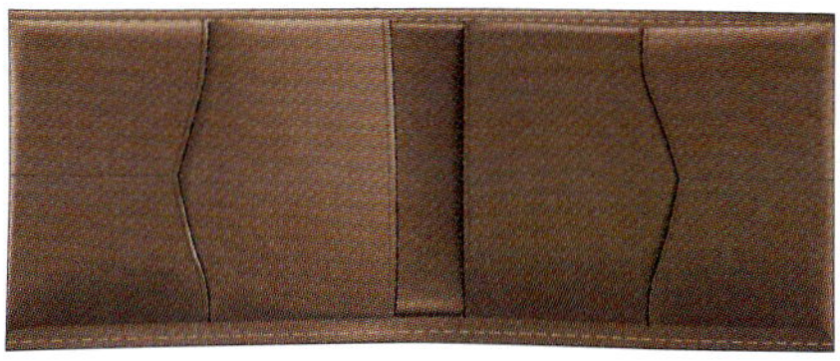

purse

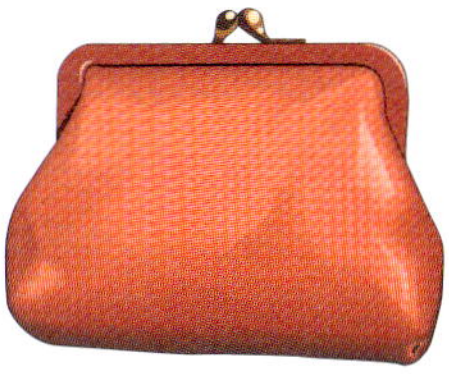

wallet

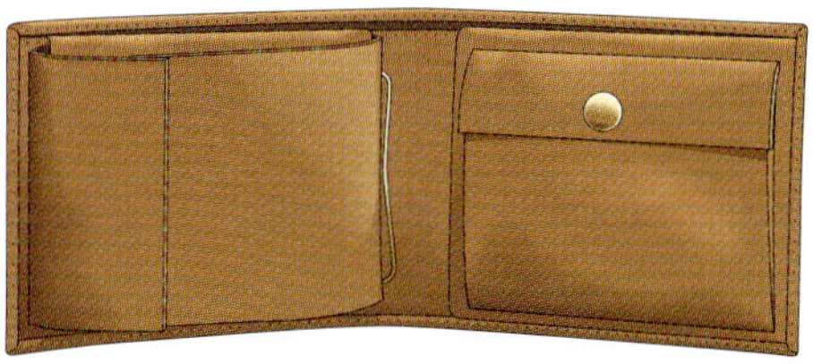

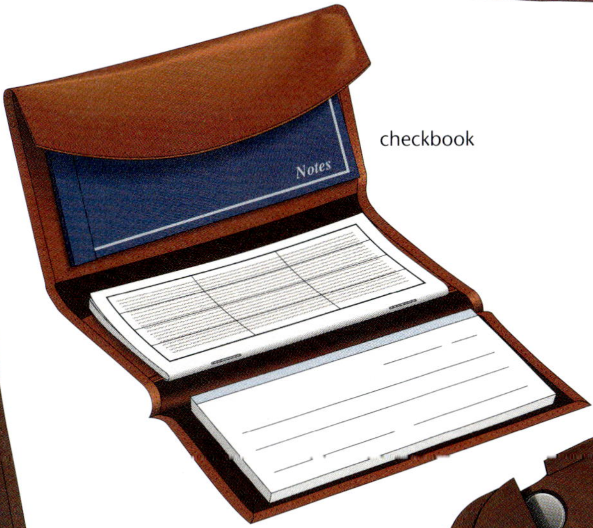
Notes

checkbook

passport case

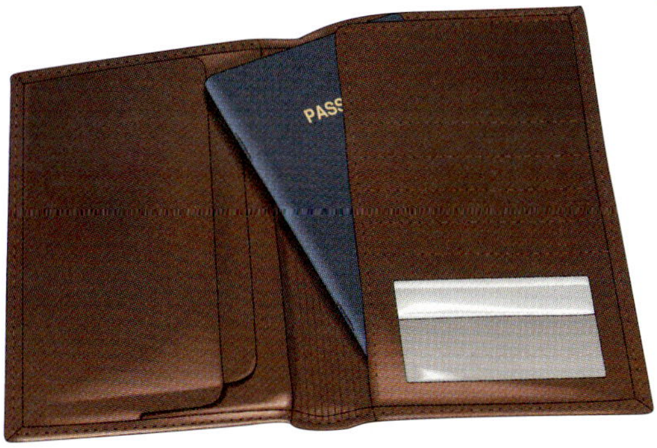
PASS

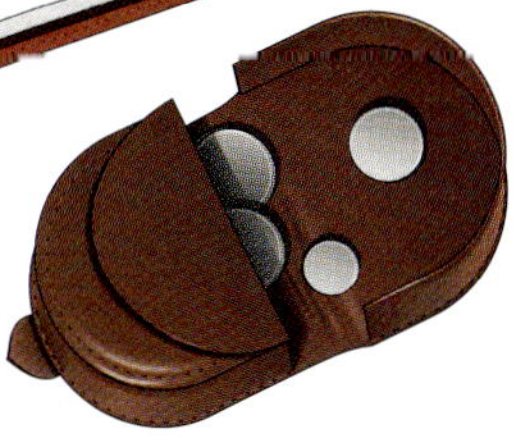

coin purse

men's bag
SATCHEL BAG
handle
flap
clasp
lock
pouch
SHOULDER BAG
buckle
shoulder strap
ACCORDION BAG
gusset
tote bag
duffel bag
hobo bag

clutch bag
box bag
DRAWSTRING BAG
eyelet
drawstring
front pocket
sea bag
duffel bag
muff
shopping bag
carrier bag

CARRY-ON BAG
tote bag
handle
exterior pocket
shoulder strap
VANITY CASE
mirror
hinge
cosmetic tray
GARMENT BAG
LUGGAGE CARRIER
utility case
frame
luggage elastic
zipper
stand

PULLMAN CASE 
handle
frame
pull strap
wheel
identification tag
trim
WEEKENDER 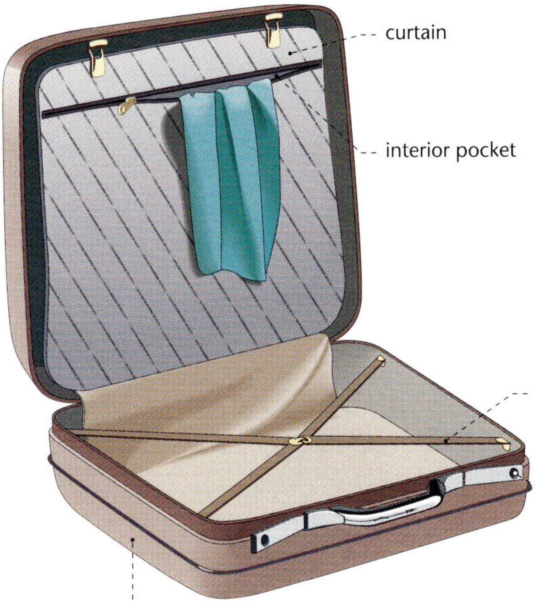
curtain
interior pocket
garment strap
lock
shell
TRUNK
hasp
tray
latch
handle
fittings
cornerpiece

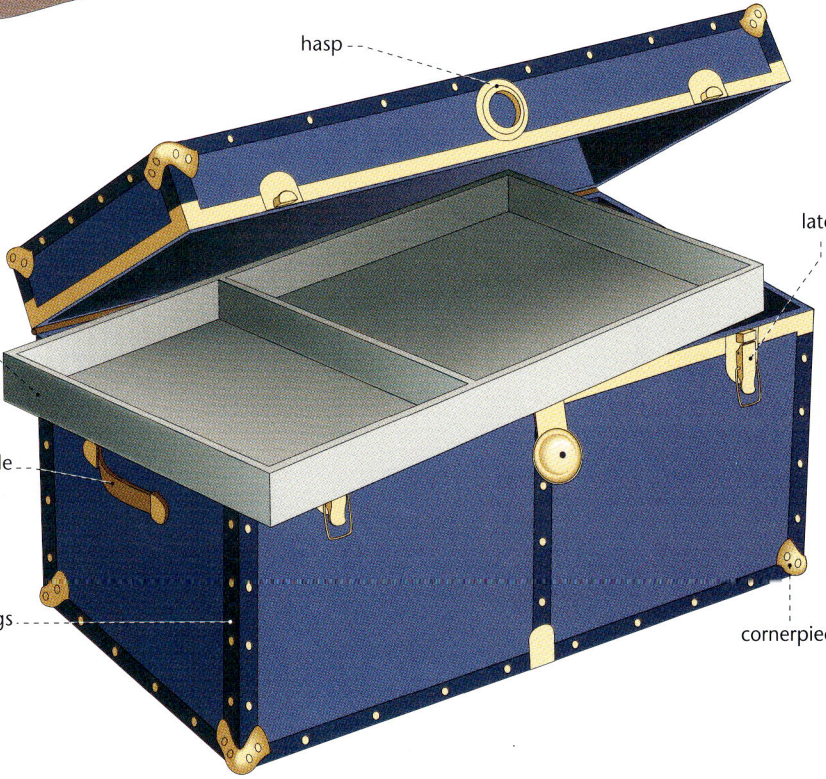

SMOKING ACCESSORIES

CIGAR

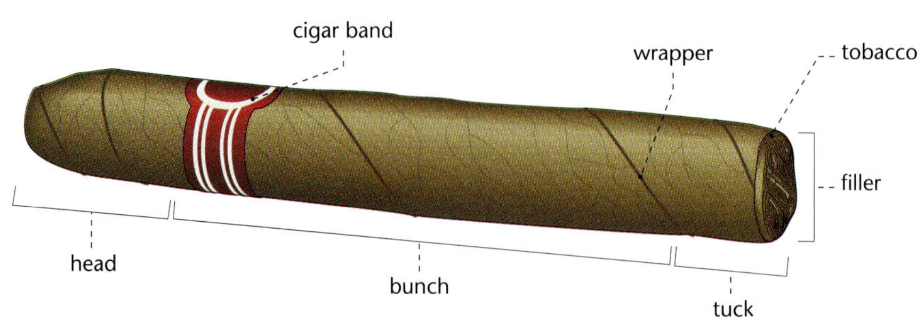

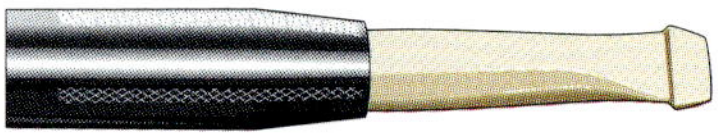

cigarette holder

CIGARETTE

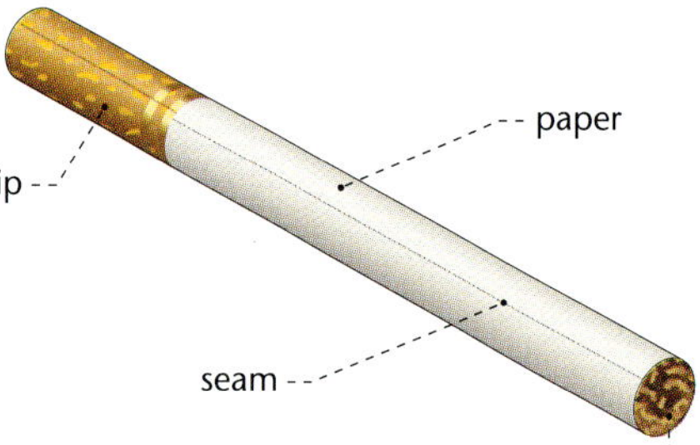

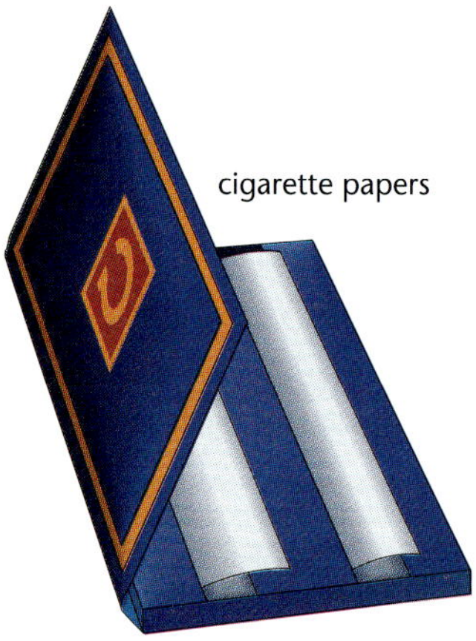

cigarette papers

CIGARETTE PACK

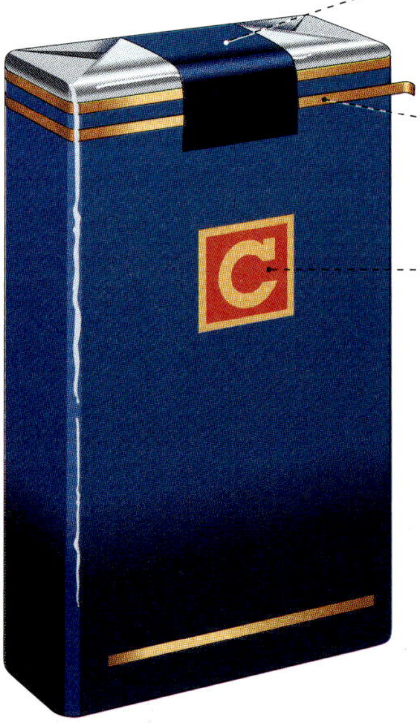

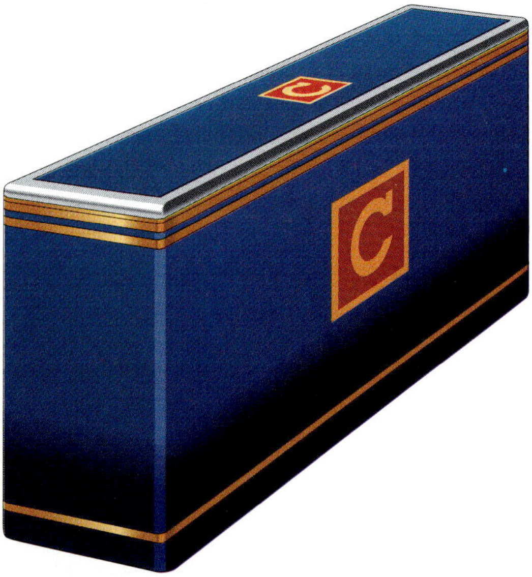

carton

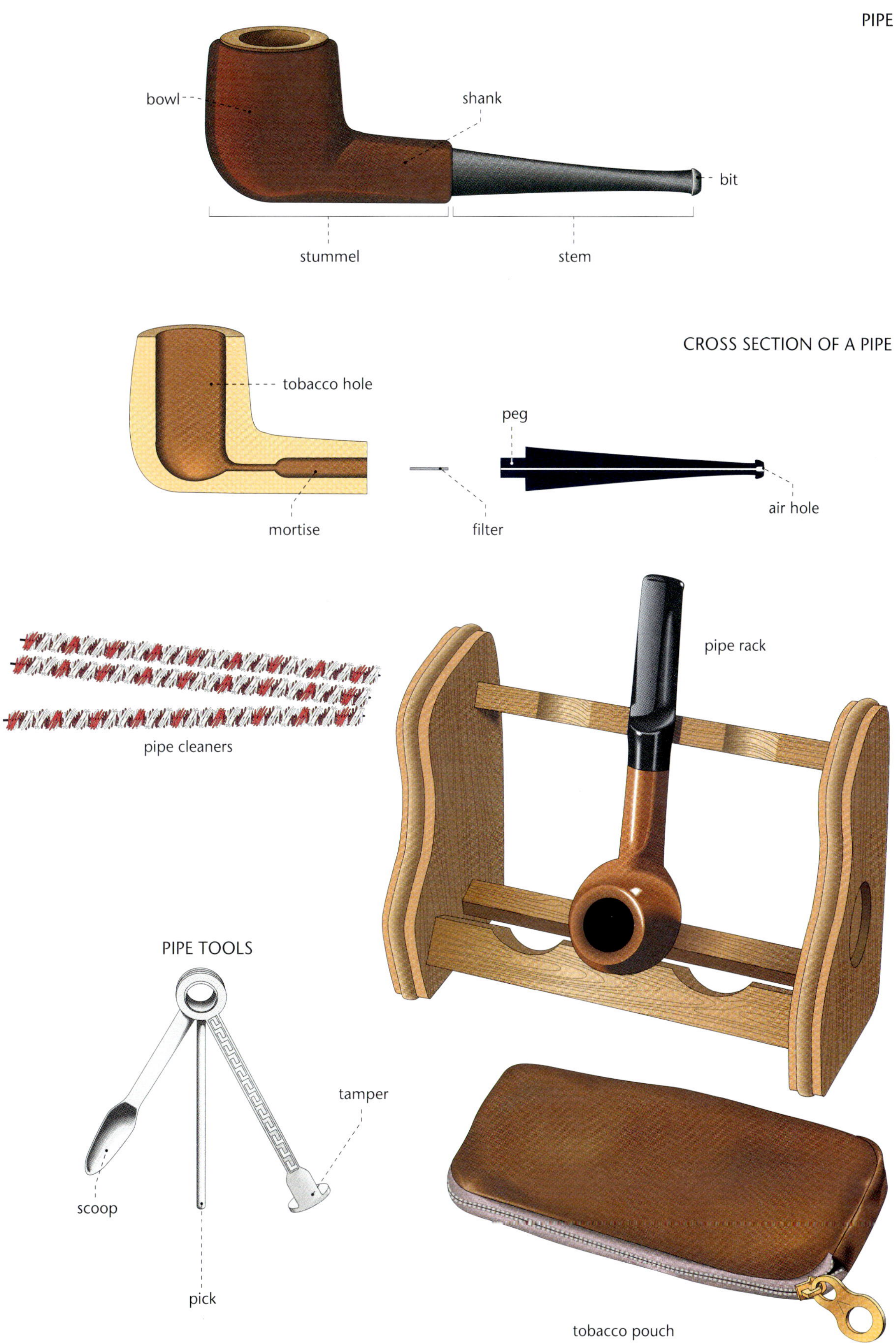

bowl
shank
bit
stummel
stem
CROSS SECTION OF A PIPE
tobacco hole
peg
mortise
filter
air hole
pipe cleaners
pipe rack
PIPE TOOLS
tamper
scoop
pick
tobacco pouch

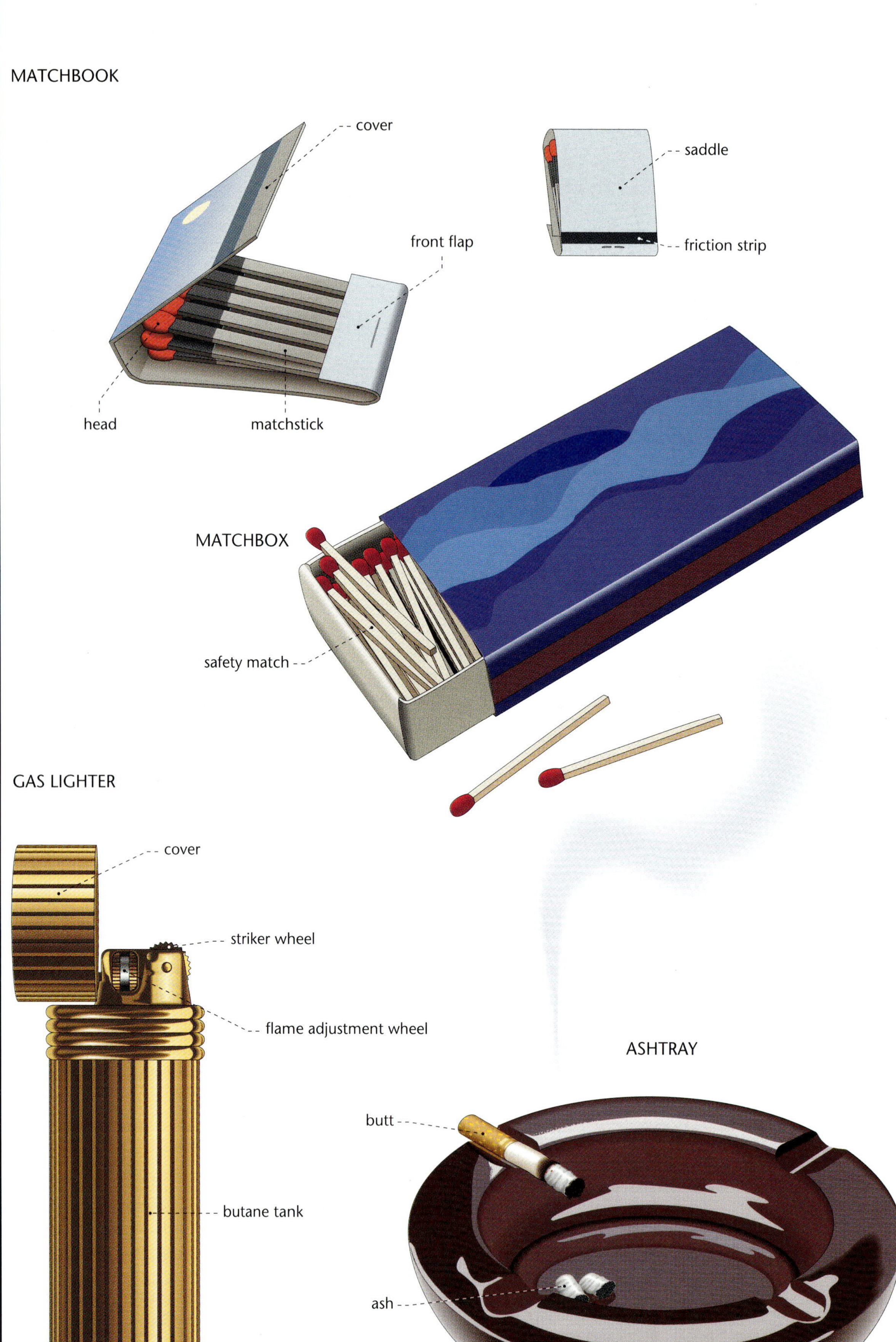

MATCHBOOK
cover
front flap
head
matchstick
saddle
friction strip
MATCHBOX
safety match
GAS LIGHTER
cover
striker wheel
flame adjustment wheel
butane tank
ASHTRAY
butt
ash

COMMUNICATIONS

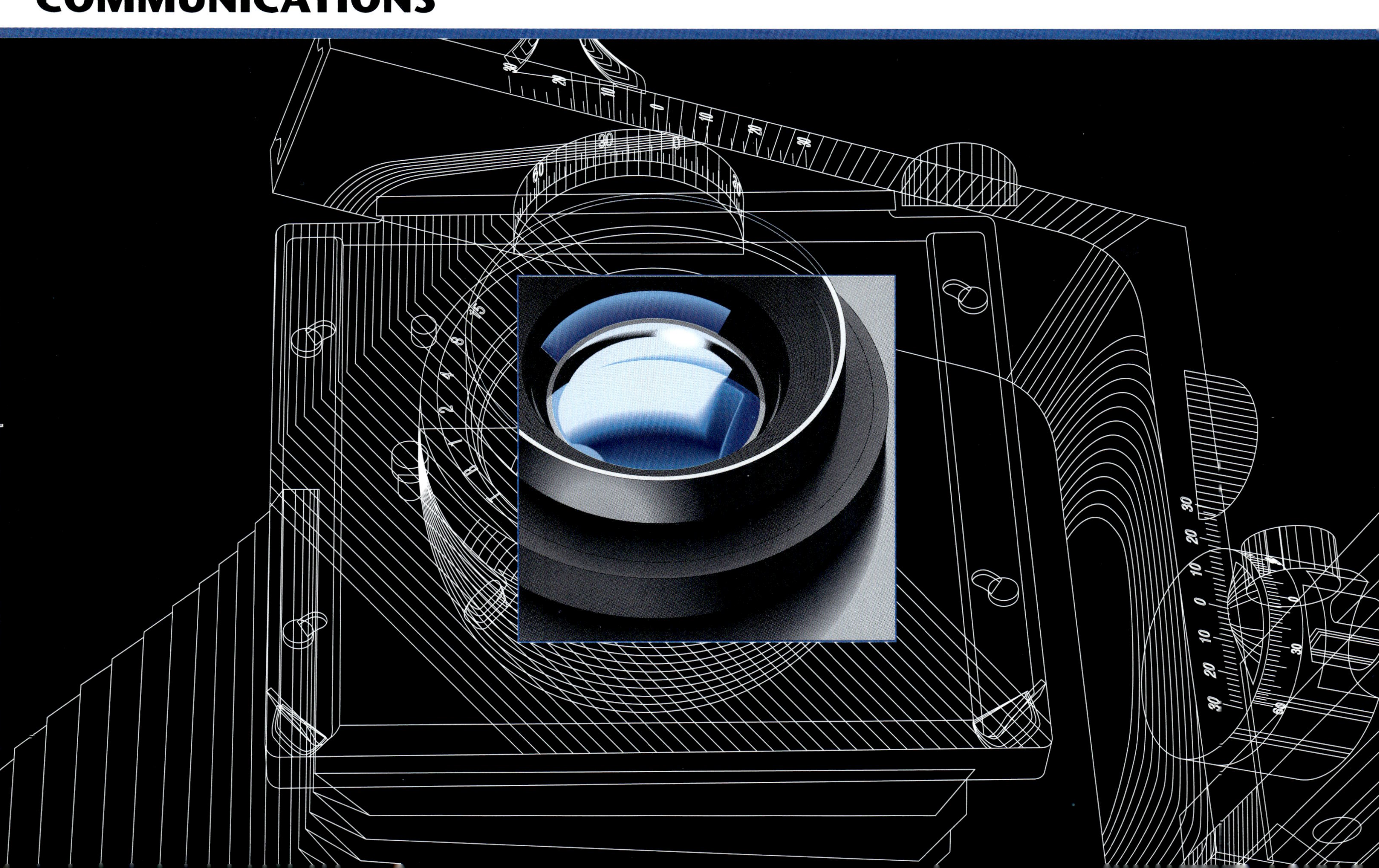

CONTENTS

COMMUNICATIONS

WRITING INSTRUMENTS

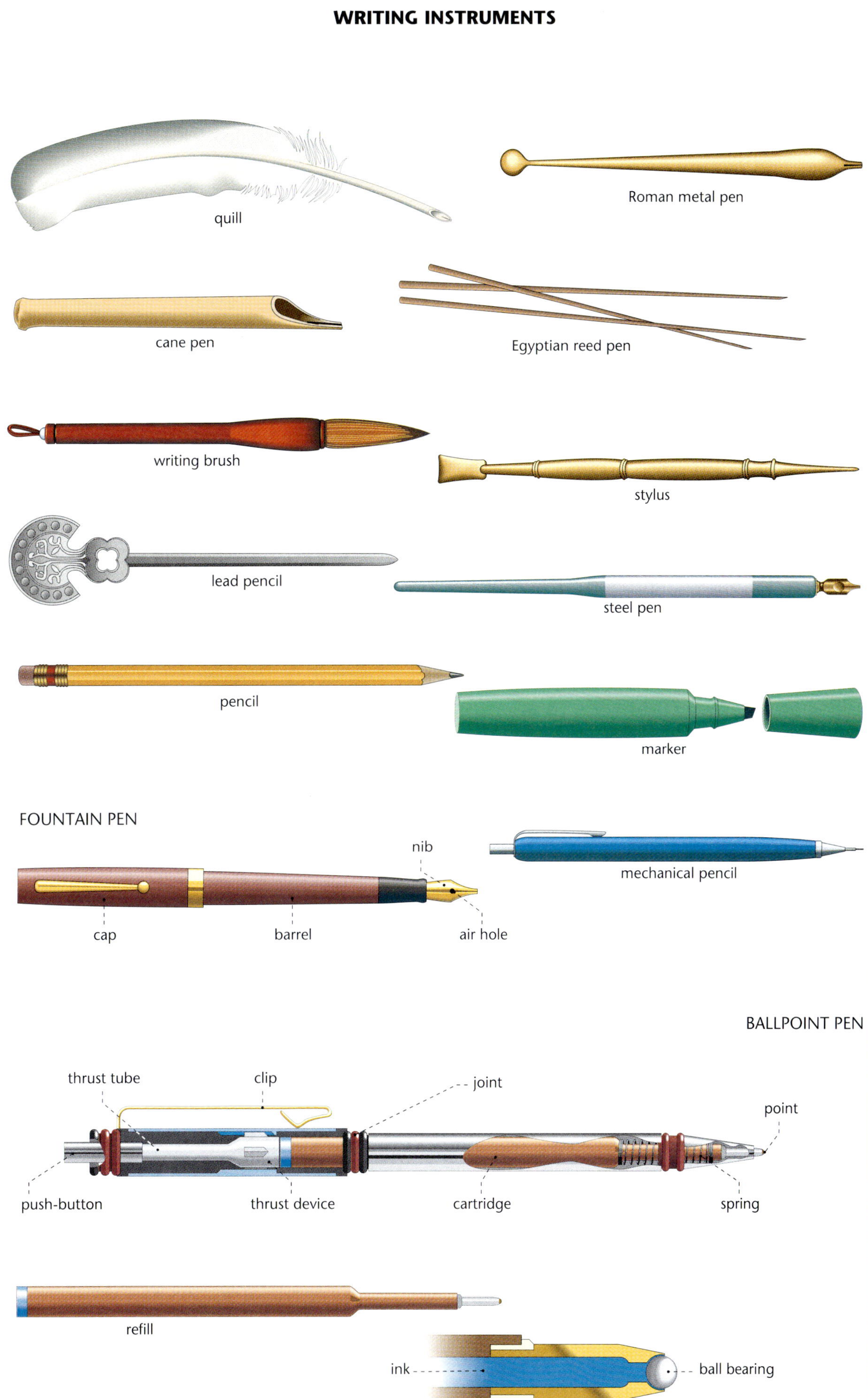

CROSS SECTION OF A REFLEX CAMERA

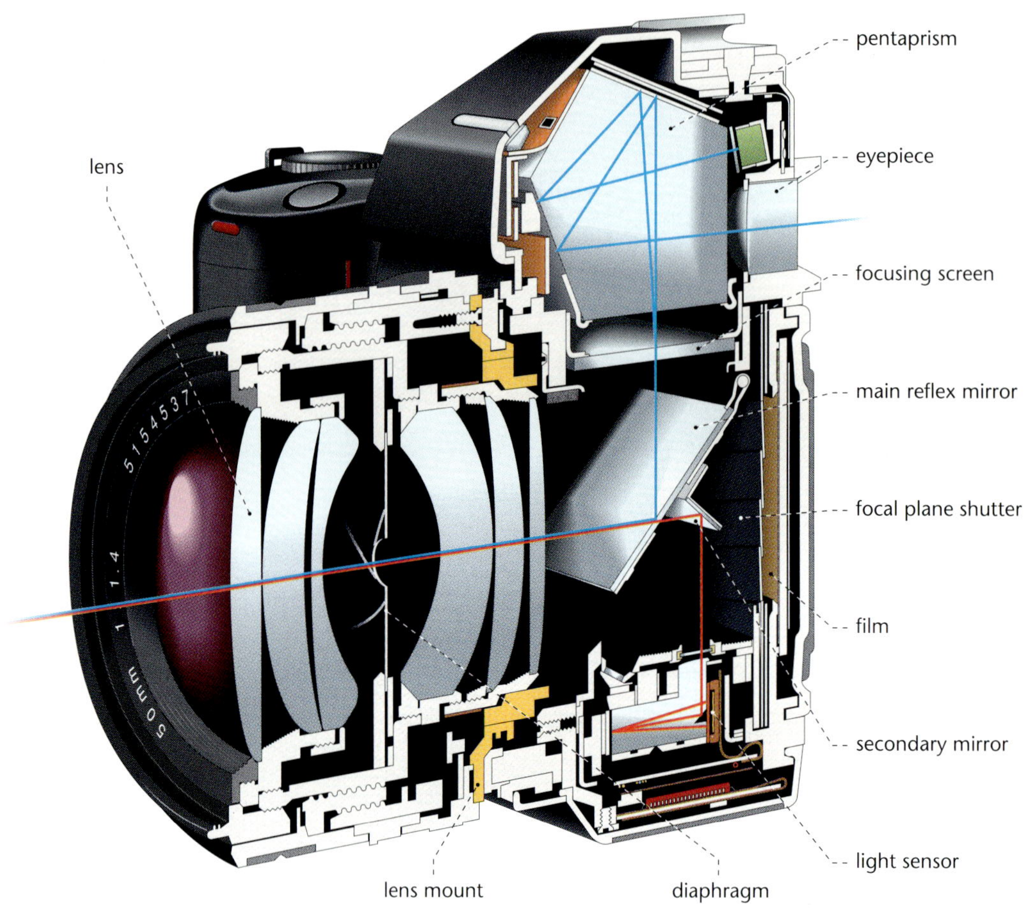

CAMERA BACK

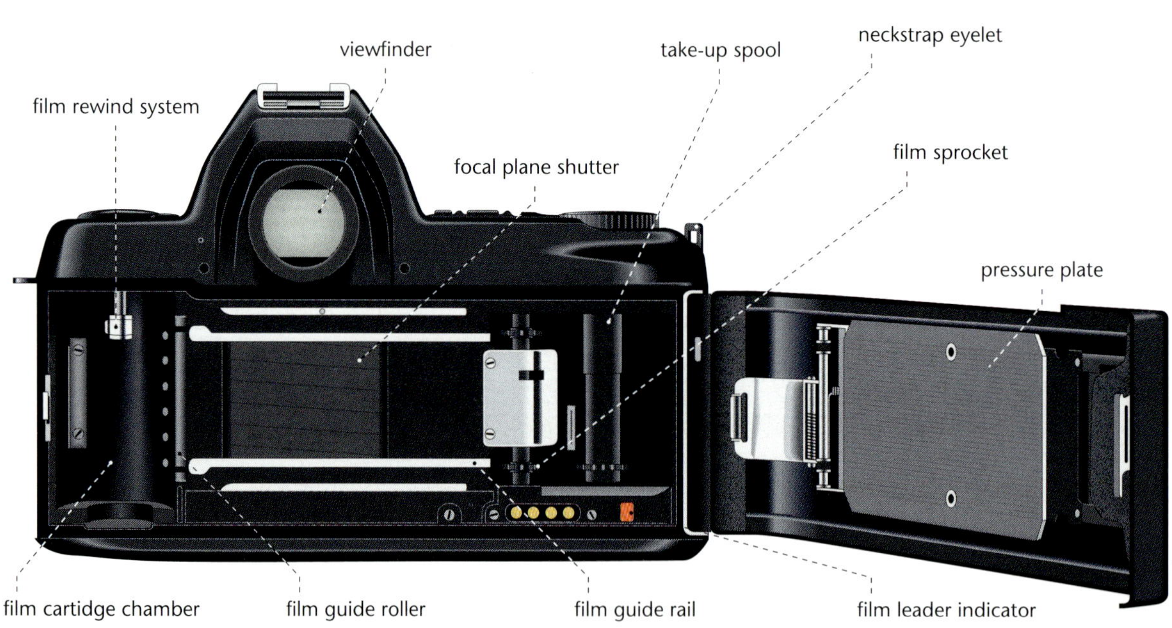

film rewind knob
control panel
exposure adjustment knob
on/off switch
command control dial
film advance mode
hot-shoe contact
film speed
accessory shoe
multiple exposure mode
exposure mode
self-timer indicator
shutter release button
camera body
lens release button
objective lens
remote control terminal
focus mode selector
depth-of-field preview button
50 mm
1 : 3.5
AUTO

391

LENSES

standard lens

lens

focus setting ring

distance scale

depth-of-field scale

lens aperture scale

wide-angle lens

bayonet mount

LENS ACCESSORIES

lens cap

lens hood

zoom lens

semi-fisheye lens

color filter

close-up lens

polarizing filter

objective lens

telephoto lens

fisheye lens

tele-converter

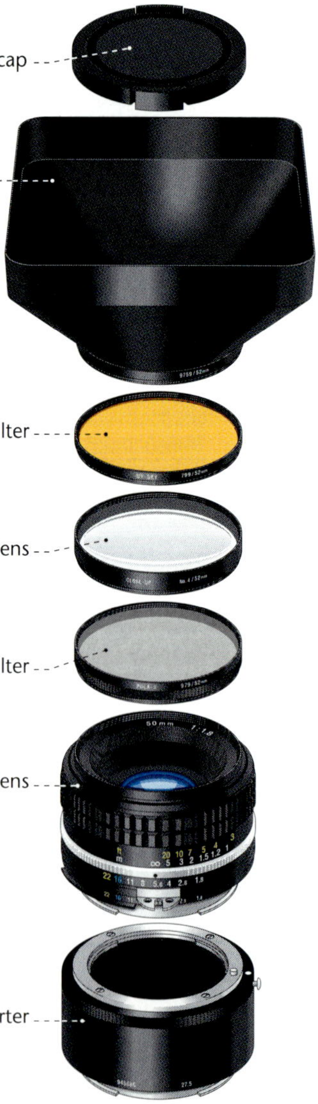

COMMUNICATIONS

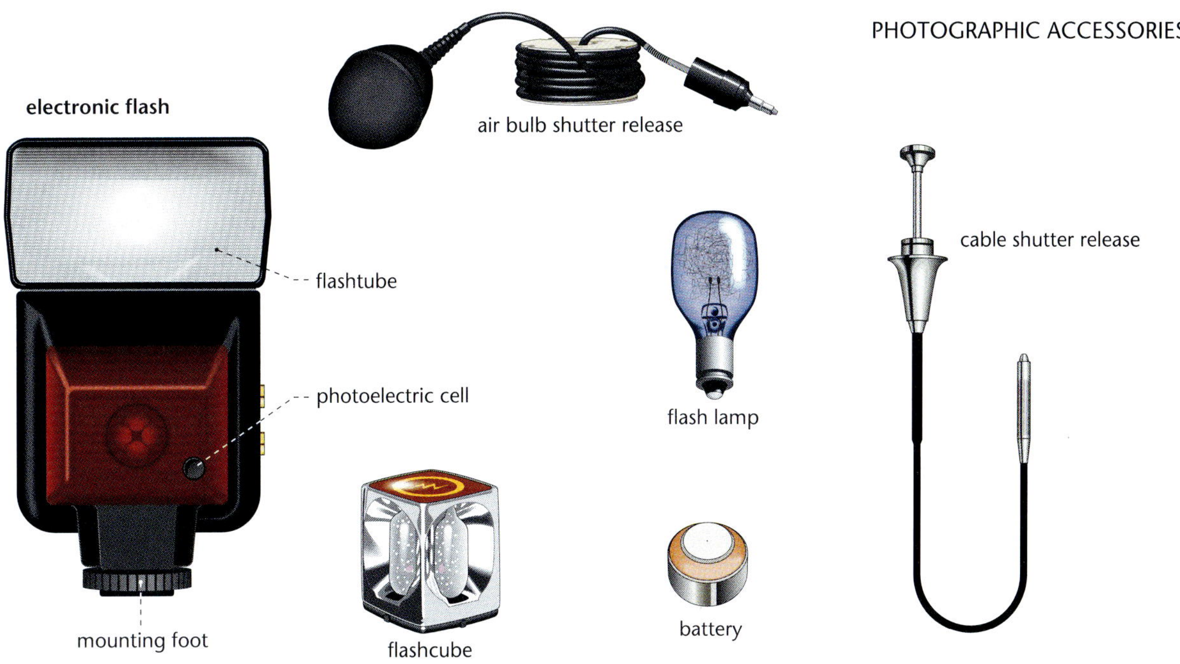

TRIPOD

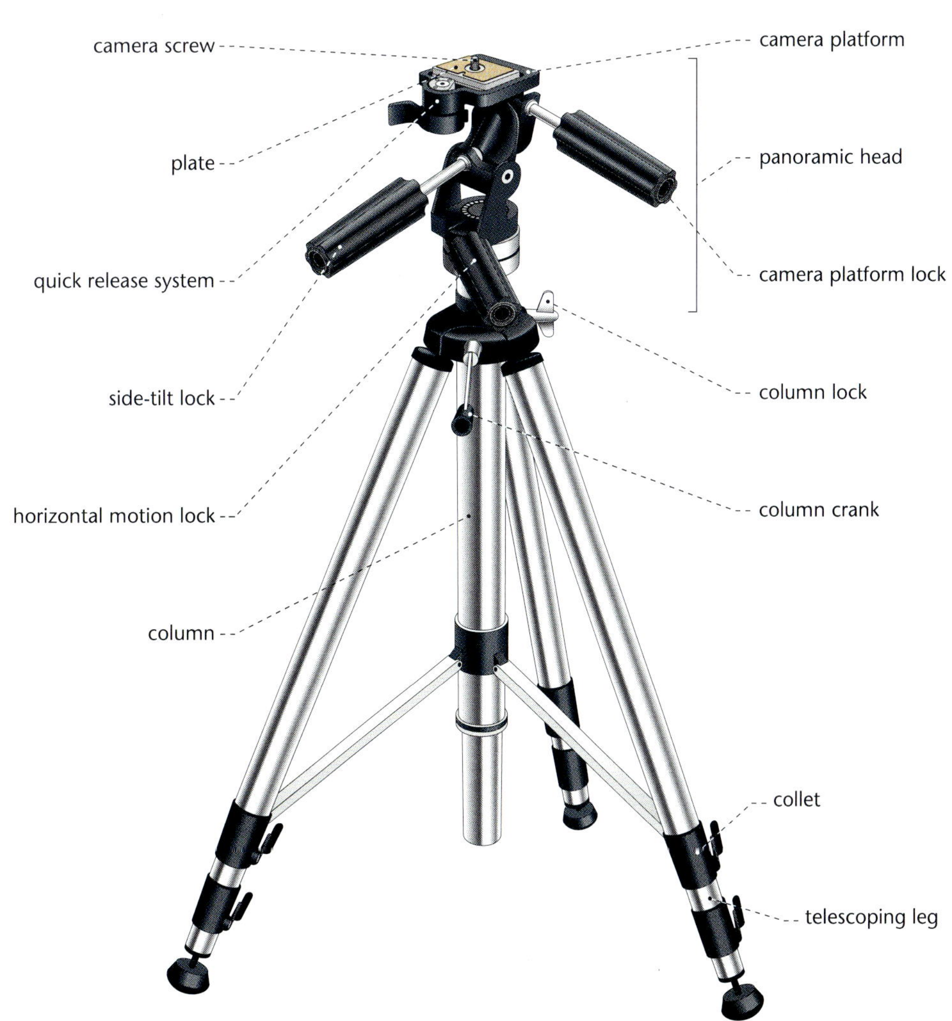

COMMUNICATIONS

STILL CAMERAS
rangefinder
underwater camera
Polaroid® Land camera
single-lens reflex camera
disposable camera
twin-lens reflex camera
view camera

medium format SLR (6 x 6)

pocket camera

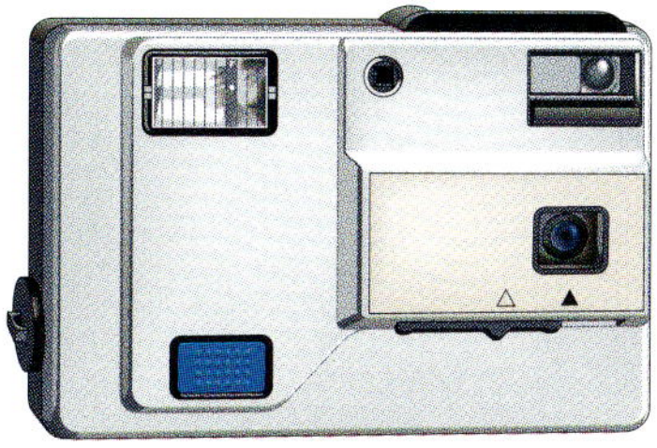

disk camera

stereo camera

still video camera

FILMS

film leader   perforation

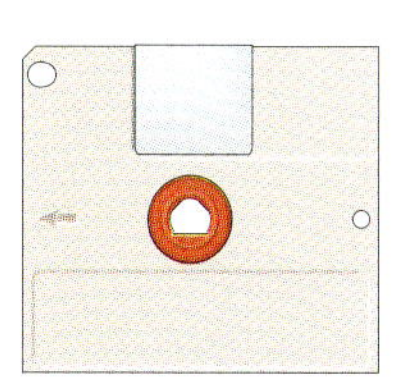

still video film disk

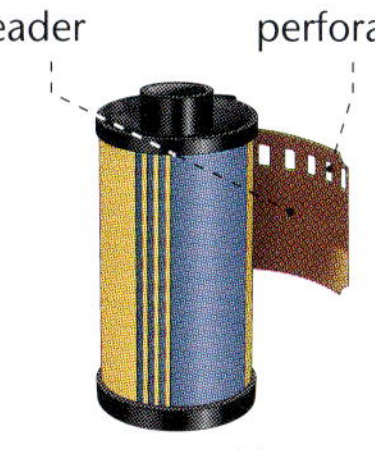

cassette film

film disk

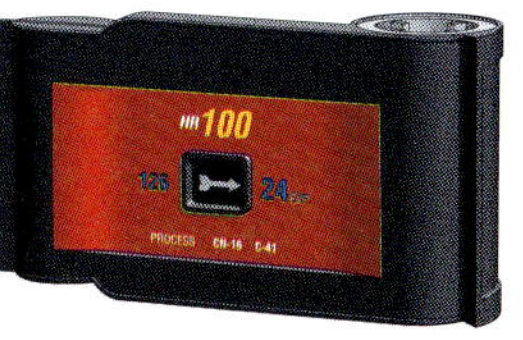

cartridge film

sheet film

roll film

film pack

COMMUNICATIONS

395

EXPOSURE METER

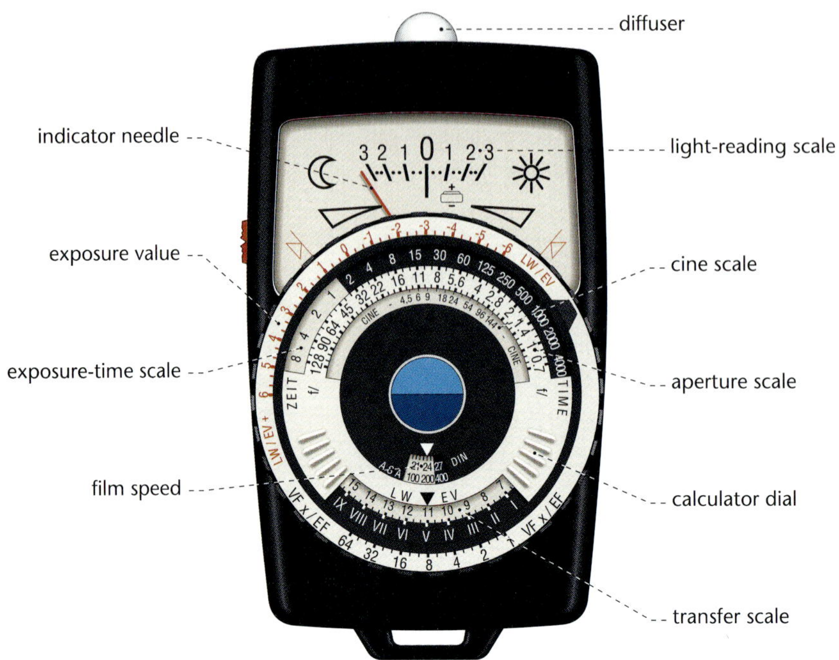

SPOTMETER

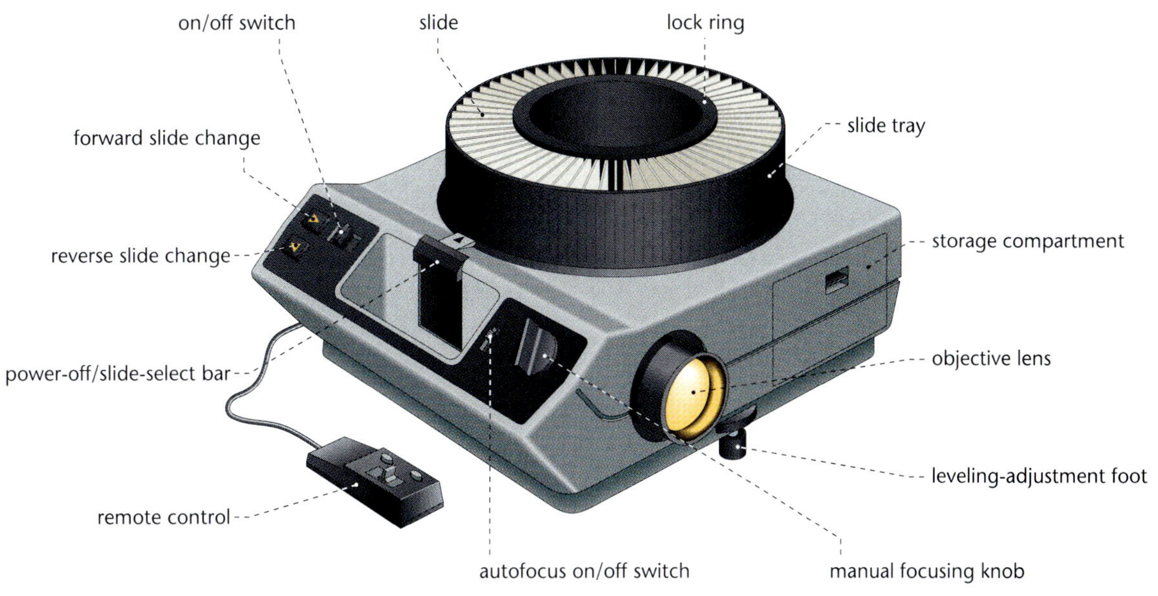

PROJECTION SCREEN

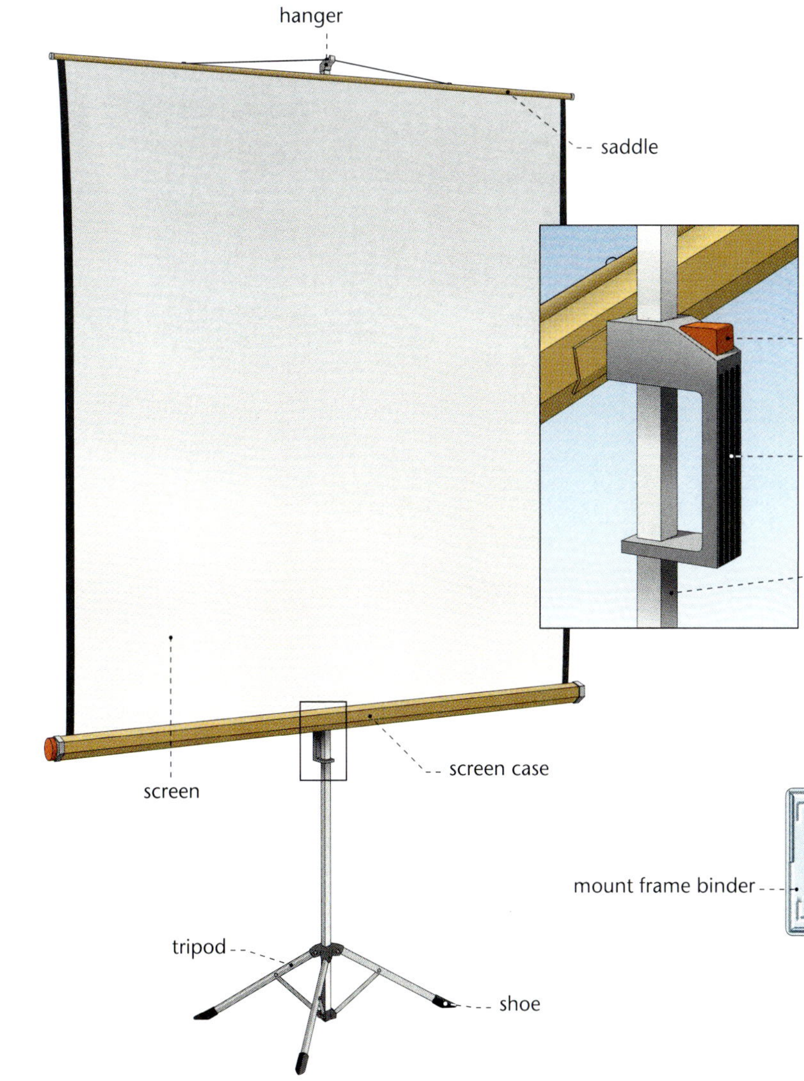

TRANSPARENCY SLIDE

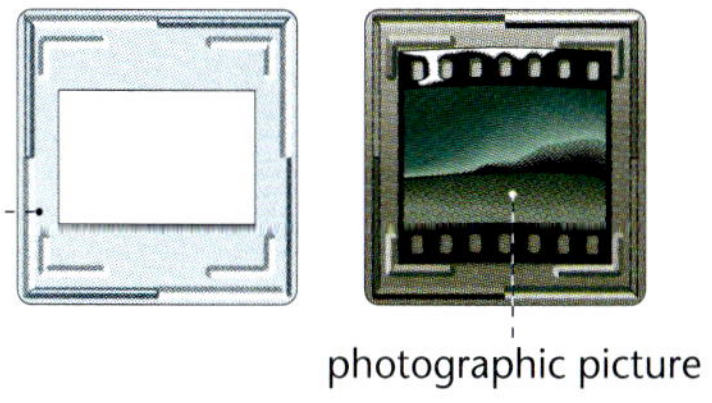

COMMUNICATIONS

397

DEVELOPING TANK
cap
lid
reel
tank
lightbox
timer
safelight
guillotine trimmer
film drying cabinet
easel
contact printer

NEGATIVE CARRIER

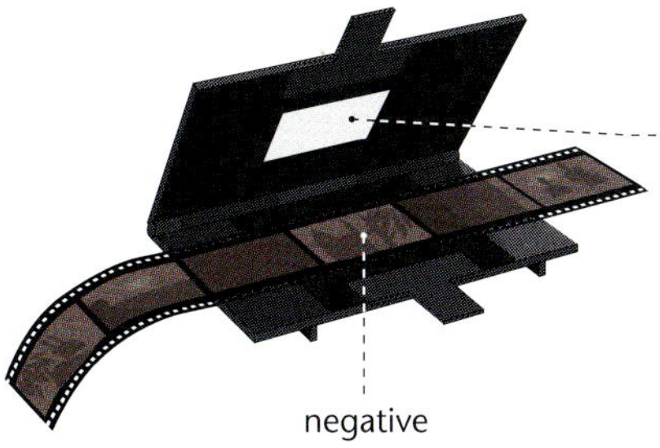

enlarger timer

ENLARGER

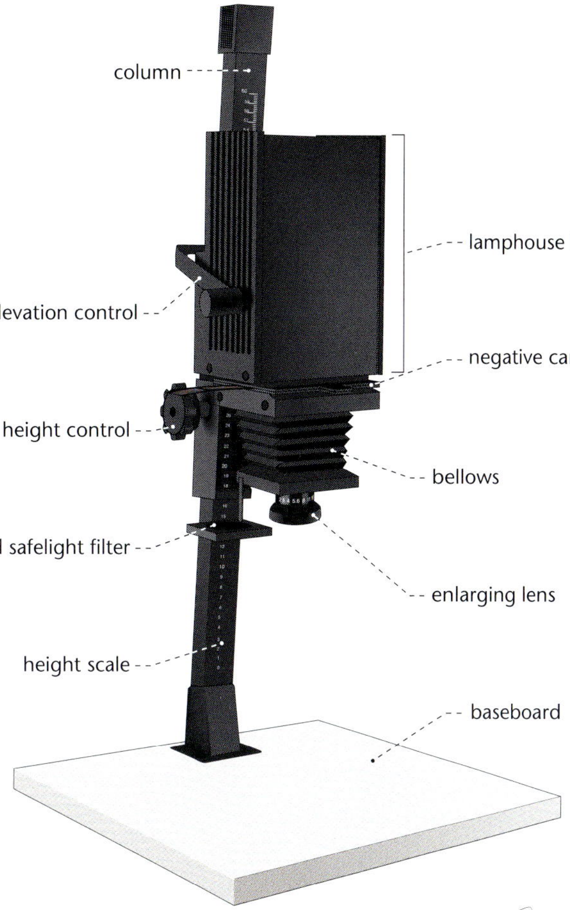

DEVELOPING BATHS

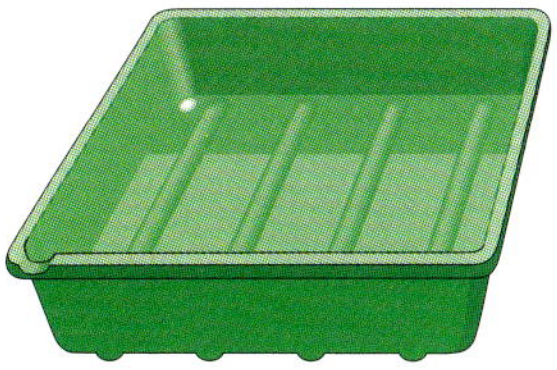

developer bath

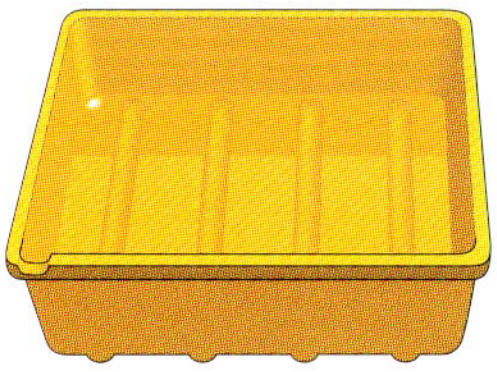

stop bath

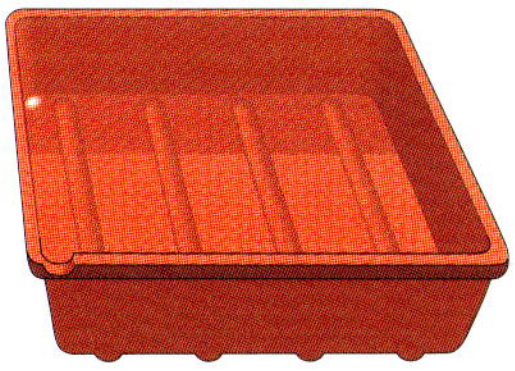

fixing bath

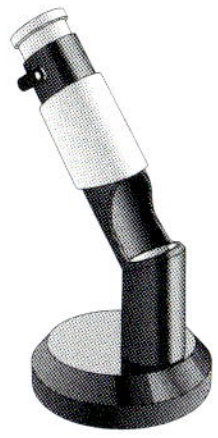

focusing magnifier

PRINT WASHER

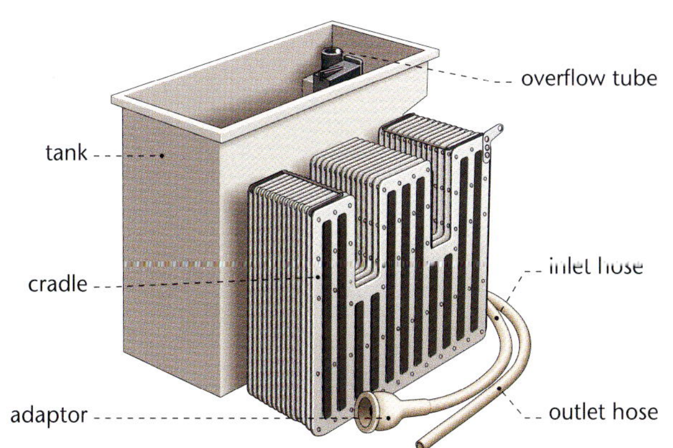

print drying rack

SOUND REPRODUCING SYSTEM

SYSTEM COMPONENTS

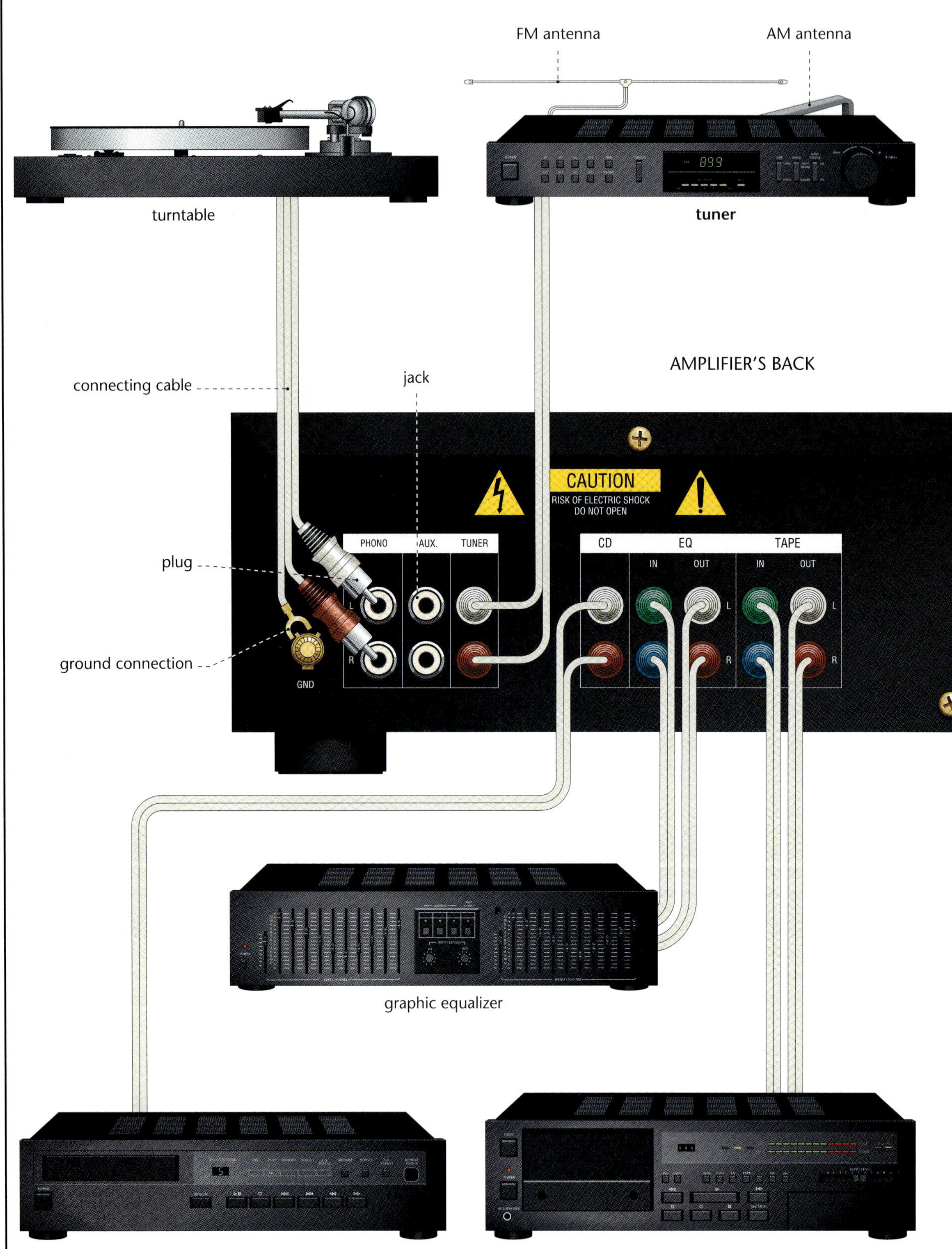

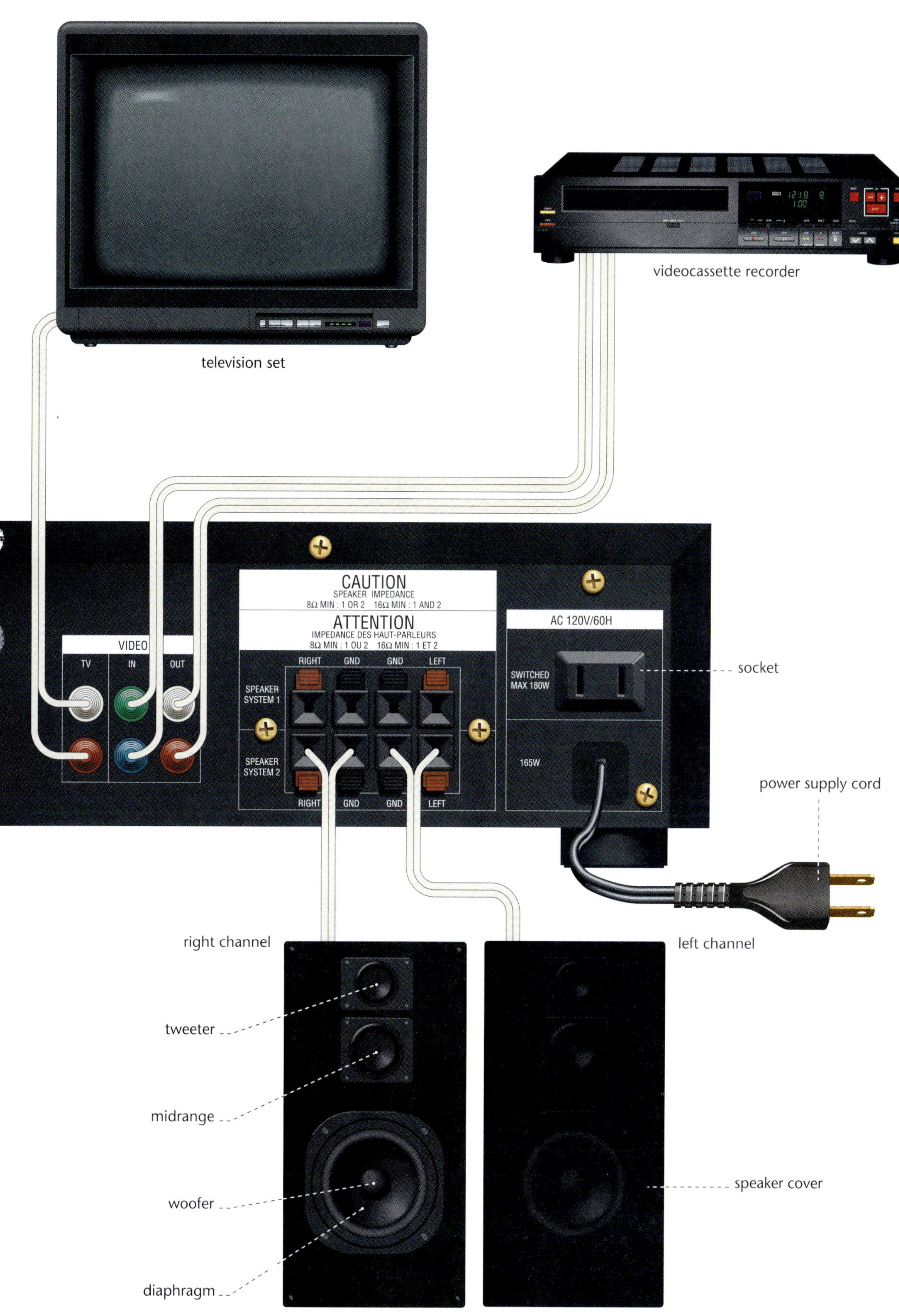

loudspeakers

SOUND REPRODUCING SYSTEM

TUNER

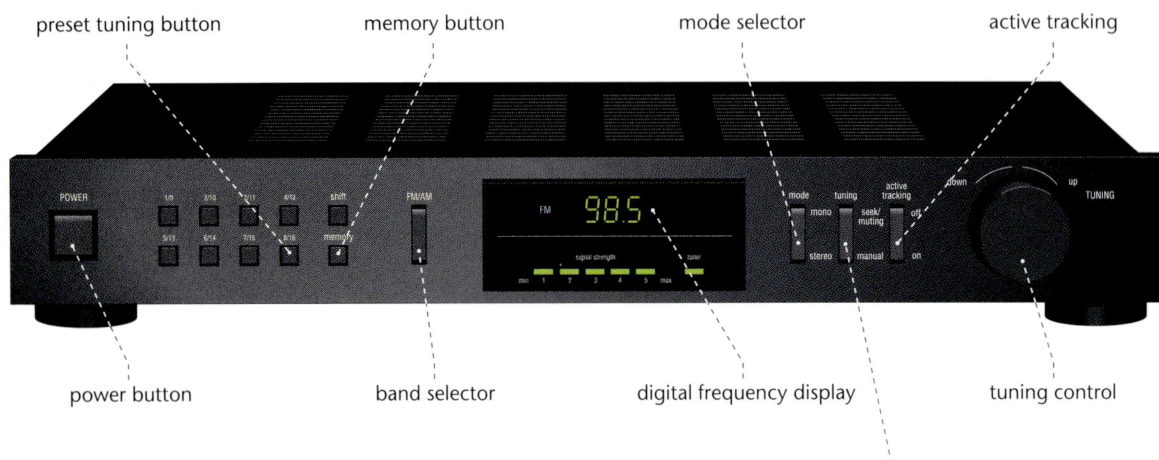

AMPLIFIER

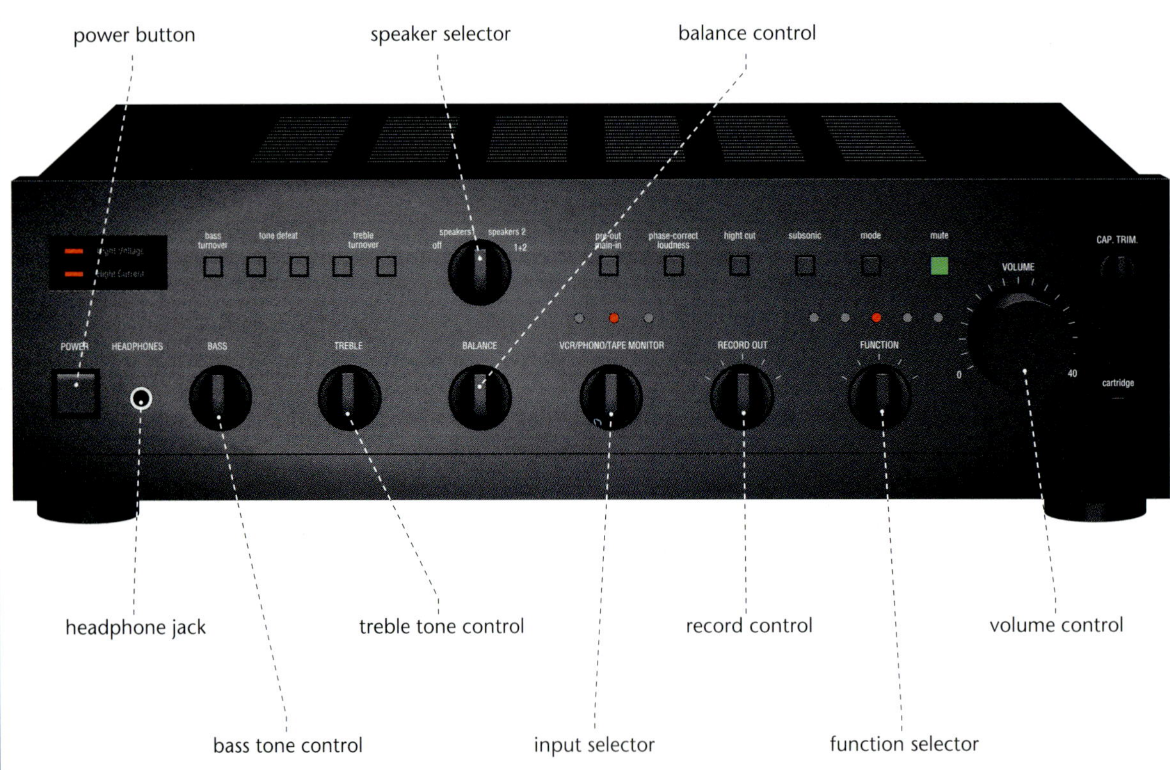

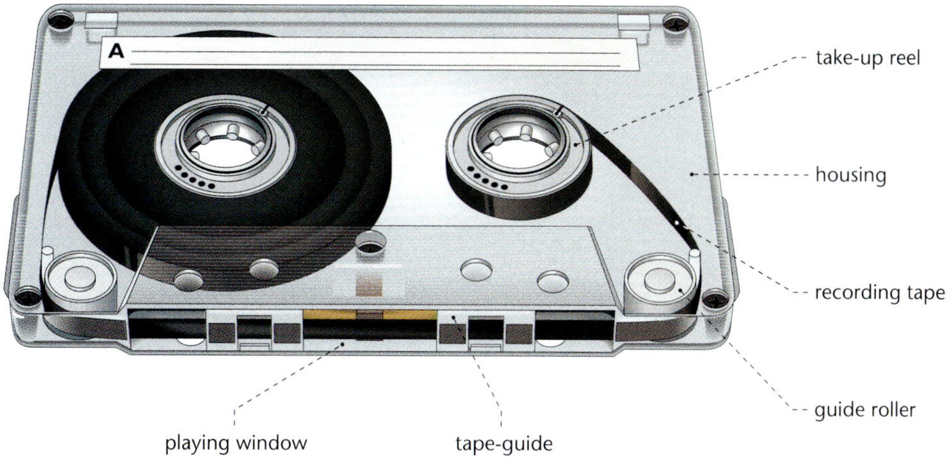

CASSETTE TAPE DECK

COMMUNICATIONS

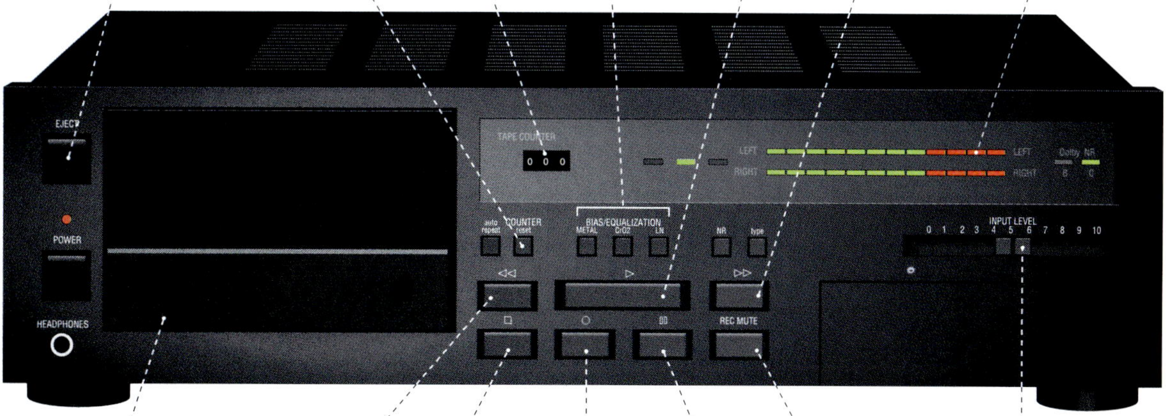

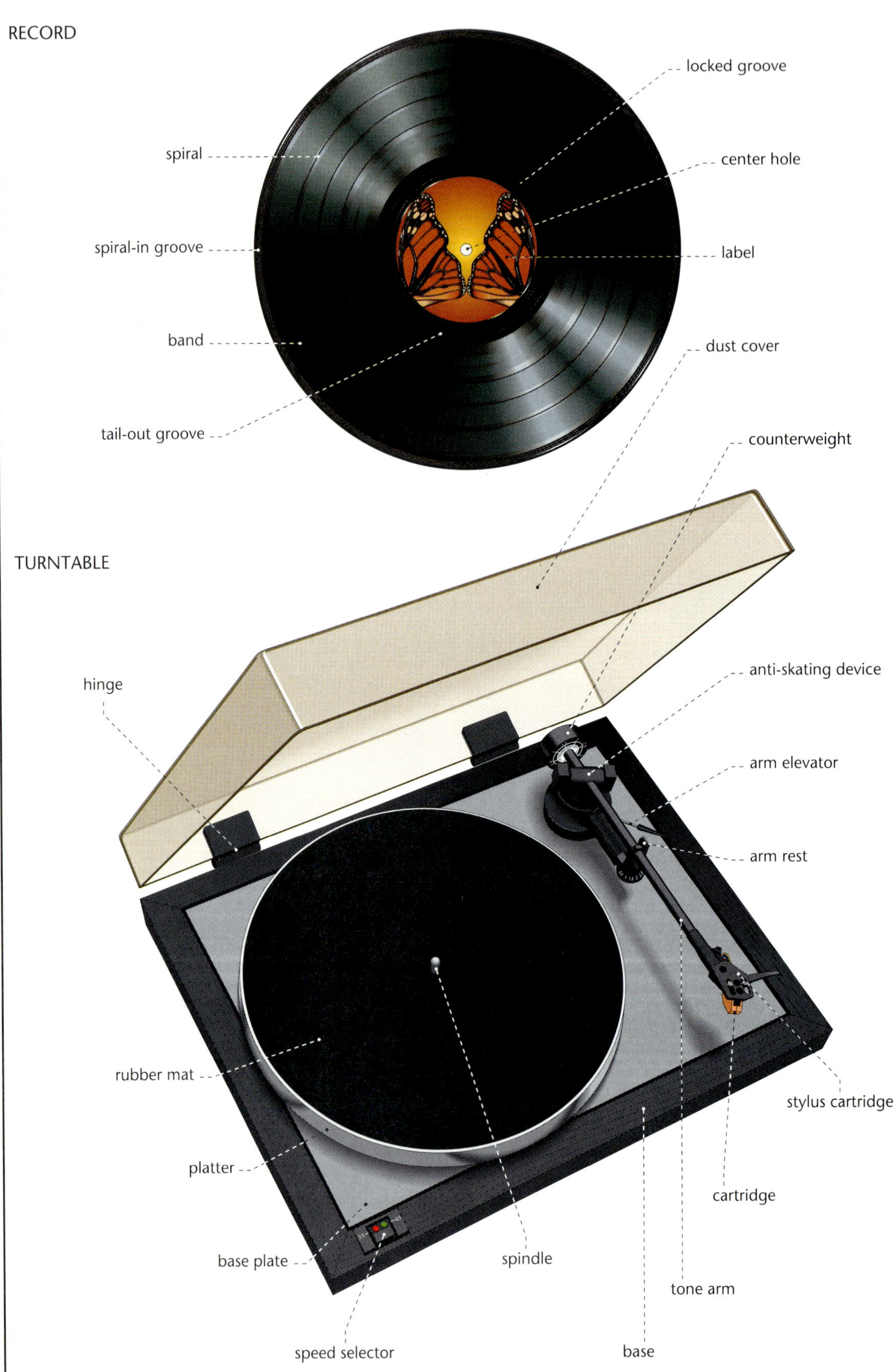

RECORD
locked groove
spiral
center hole
spiral-in groove
label
band
dust cover
tail-out groove
counterweight
TURNTABLE
hinge
anti-skating device
arm elevator
arm rest
rubber mat
stylus cartridge
platter
cartridge
base plate
spindle
tone arm
speed selector
base

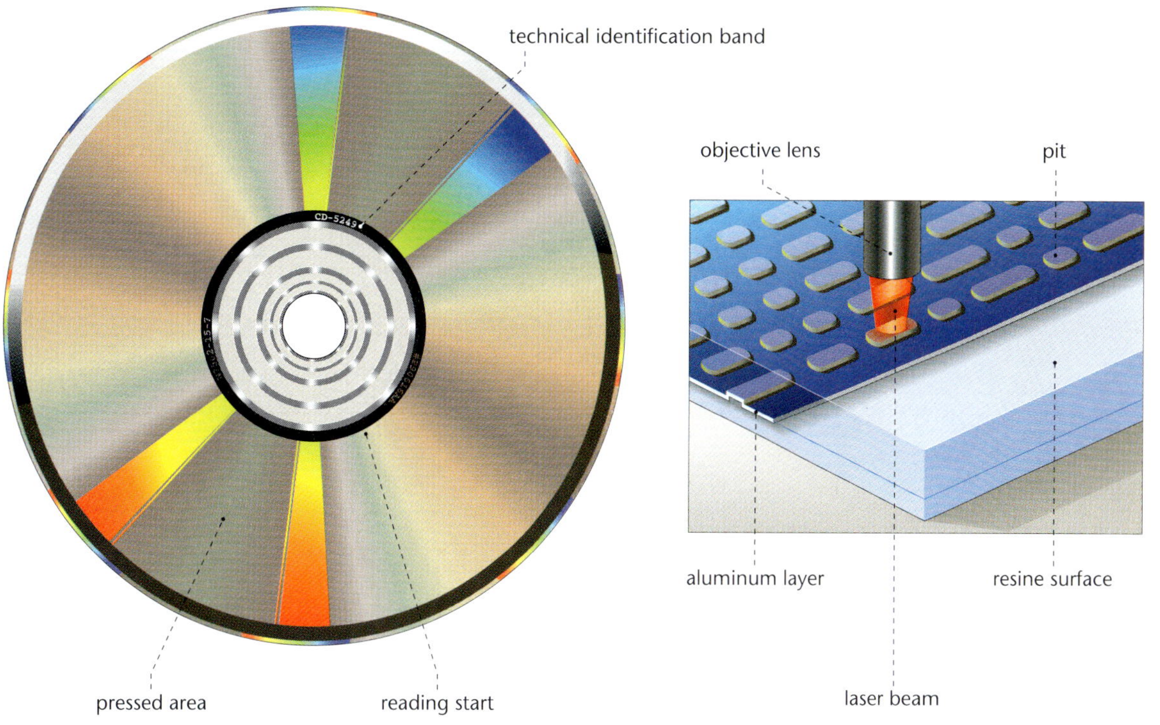

COMPACT DISK
technical identification band
objective lens
pit
CD-5245
aluminum layer
resine surface
pressed area
reading start
laser beam

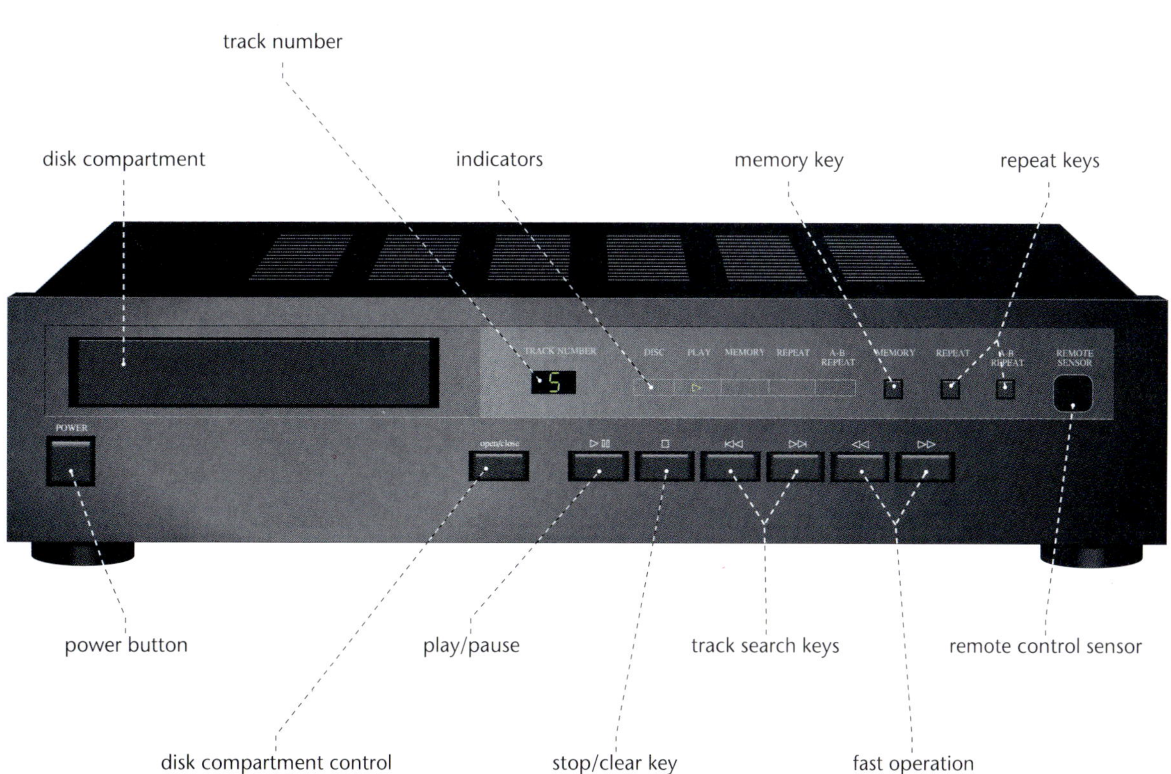

COMPACT DISK PLAYER
track number
disk compartment
indicators
memory key
repeat keys
TRACK NUMBER
DISC
PLAY
MEMORY
REPEAT
A-B REPEAT
MEMORY
REPEAT
A-B REPEAT
REMOTE SENSOR
POWER
open/close
power button
play/pause
track search keys
remote control sensor
disk compartment control
stop/clear key
fast operation

windscreen
diaphragm
moving coil
magnet
on/off switch
housing
connector
plug
cable

HEADPHONE

resonator
ear cushion
headband
adjusting band
connecting cable
earphone
plug

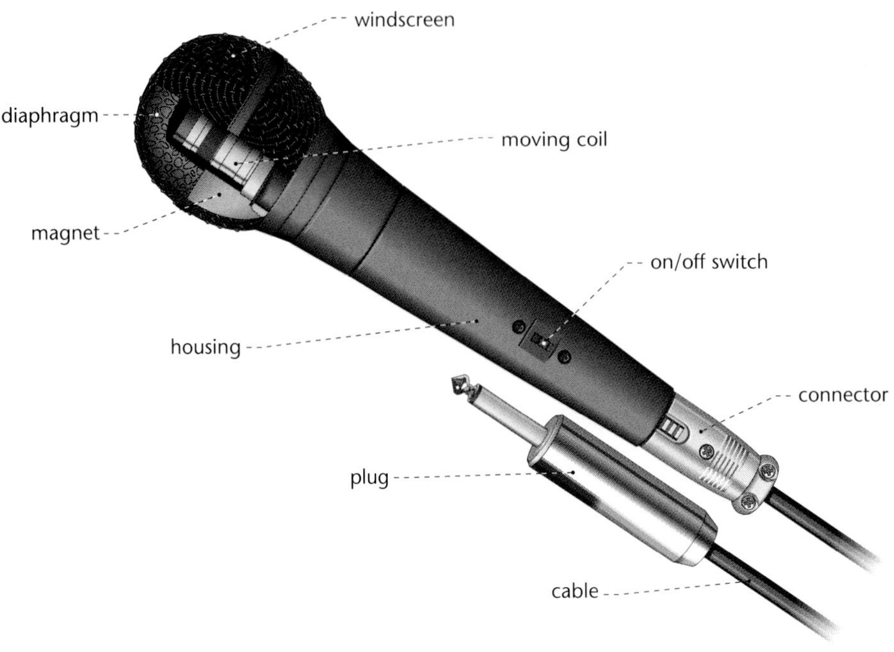

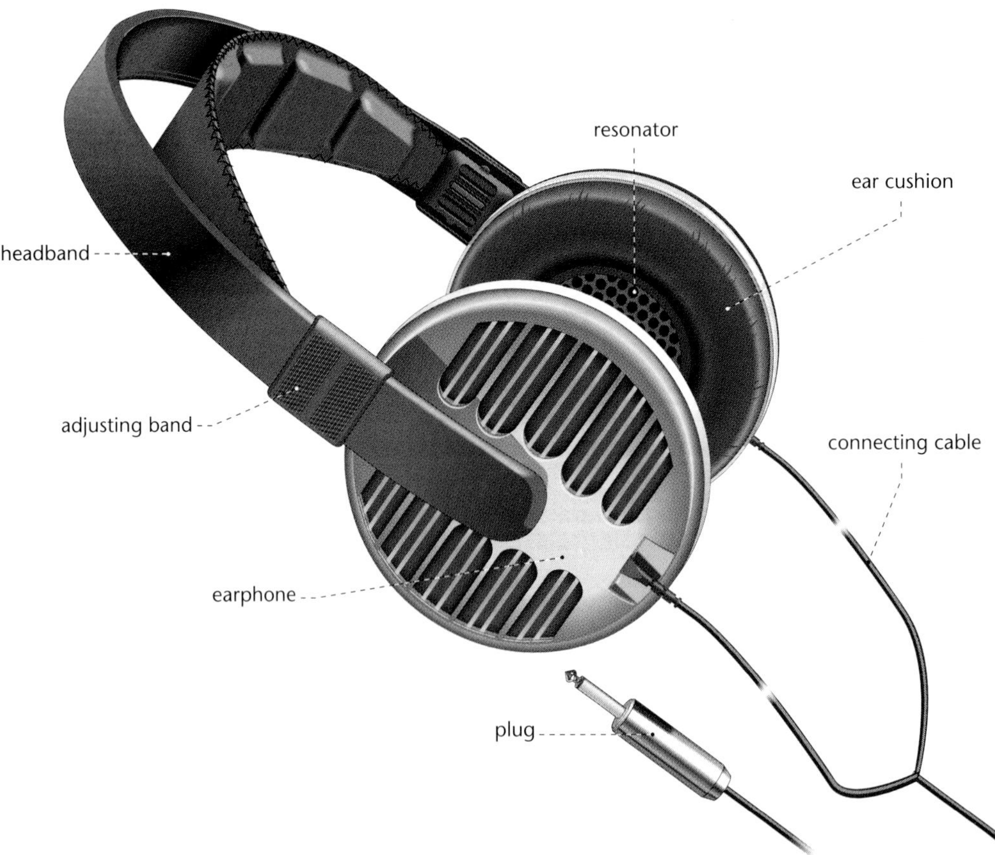

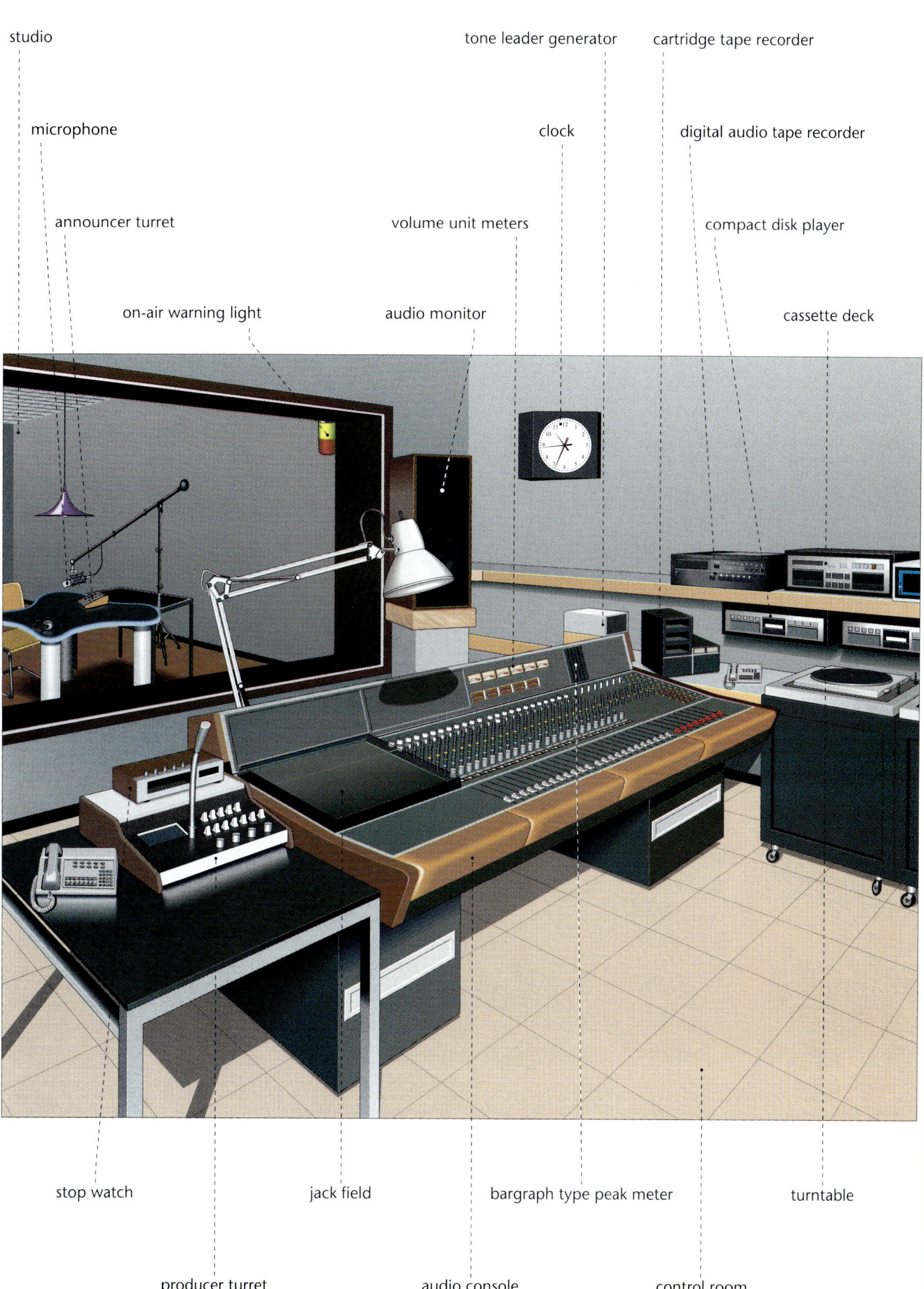
studio
microphone
announcer turret
on-air warning light
tone leader generator
clock
volume unit meters
audio monitor
cartridge tape recorder
digital audio tape recorder
compact disk player
cassette deck
stop watch
jack field
bargraph type peak meter
turntable
producer turret
audio console
control room

COMMUNICATIONS

PERSONAL AM-FM CASSETTE PLAYER

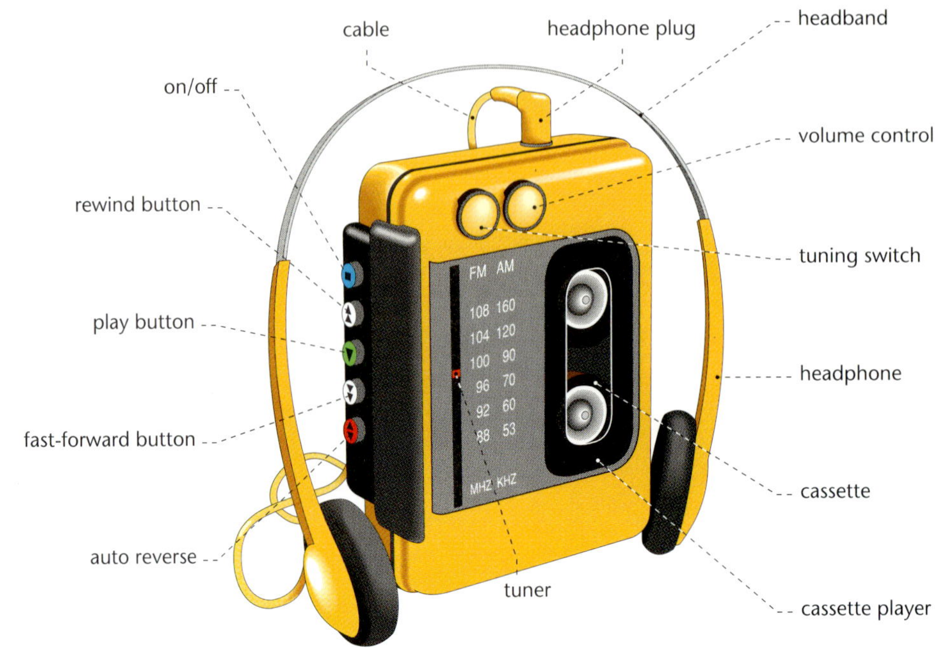

PORTABLE AM-FM CASSETTE RECORDER

eyepiece
power zoom button
white balance sensor
electronic viewfinder
accessory shoe
cassette eject switch
videotape operation controls
viewfinder adjustment keys
built-in microphone
DATA SET
ADJUST
ZERO MEM.
RESET
SELECT
BATT
00425
EXPOSURE
EDIT SEARCH
SPEED
FOCUS
WHITE BAL.
FADER
AUTO LOCK
macro set button
cassette compartment
zoom lens
data display
battery eject switch
lens hood
shooting adjustment keys
battery
edit/search buttons

TELEVISION SET

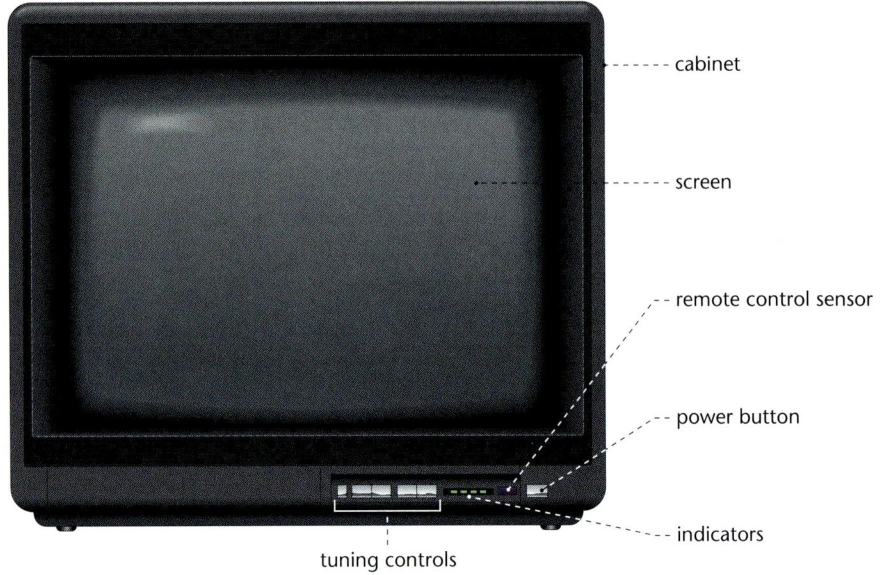

PICTURE TUBE

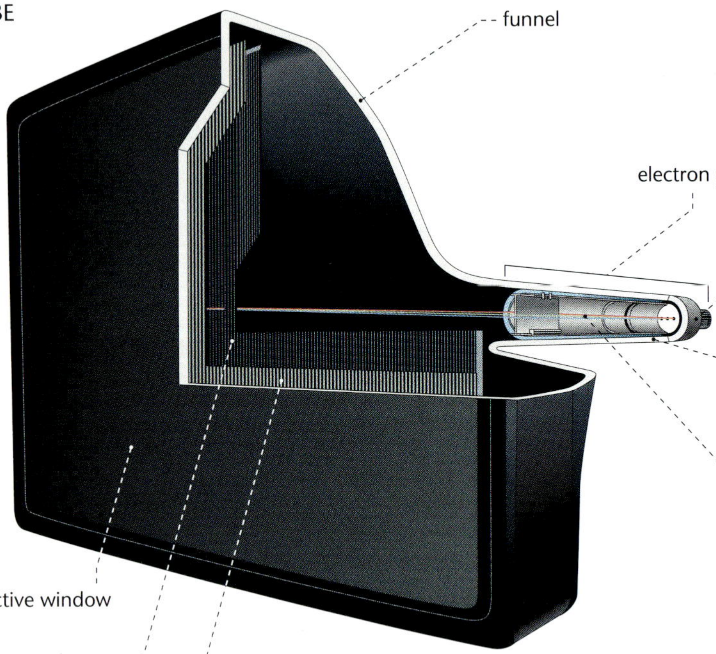

electron gun

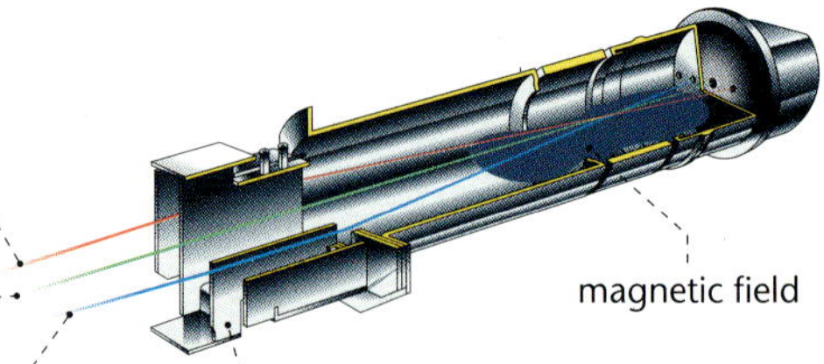

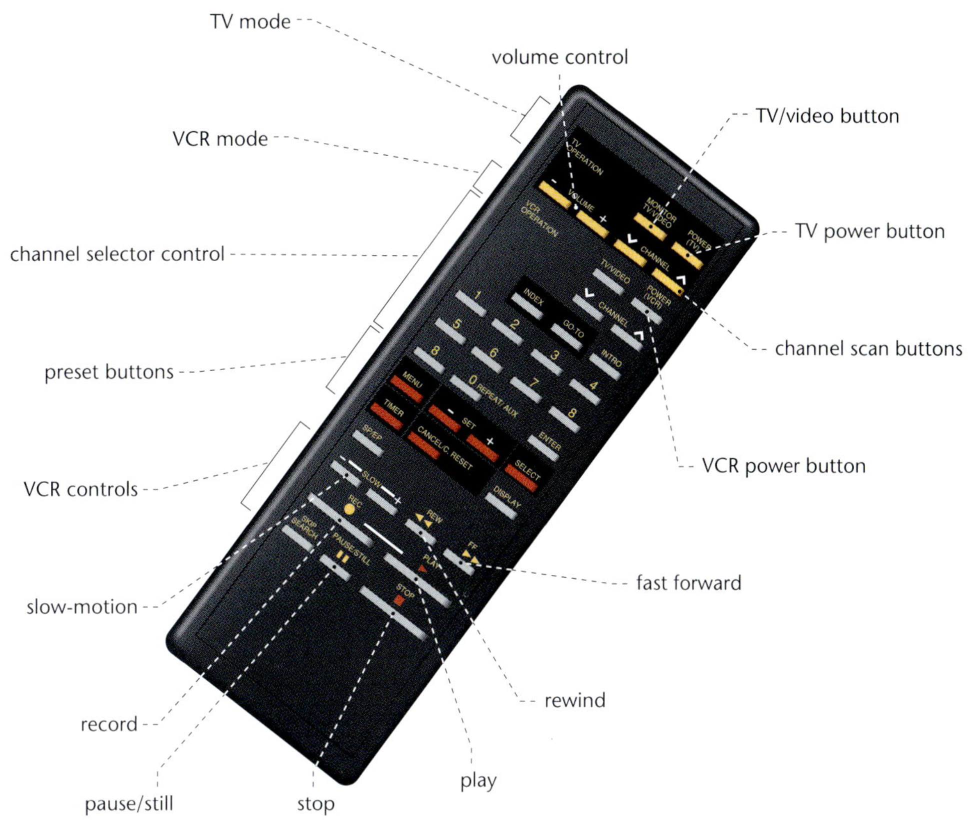

COMMUNICATIONS

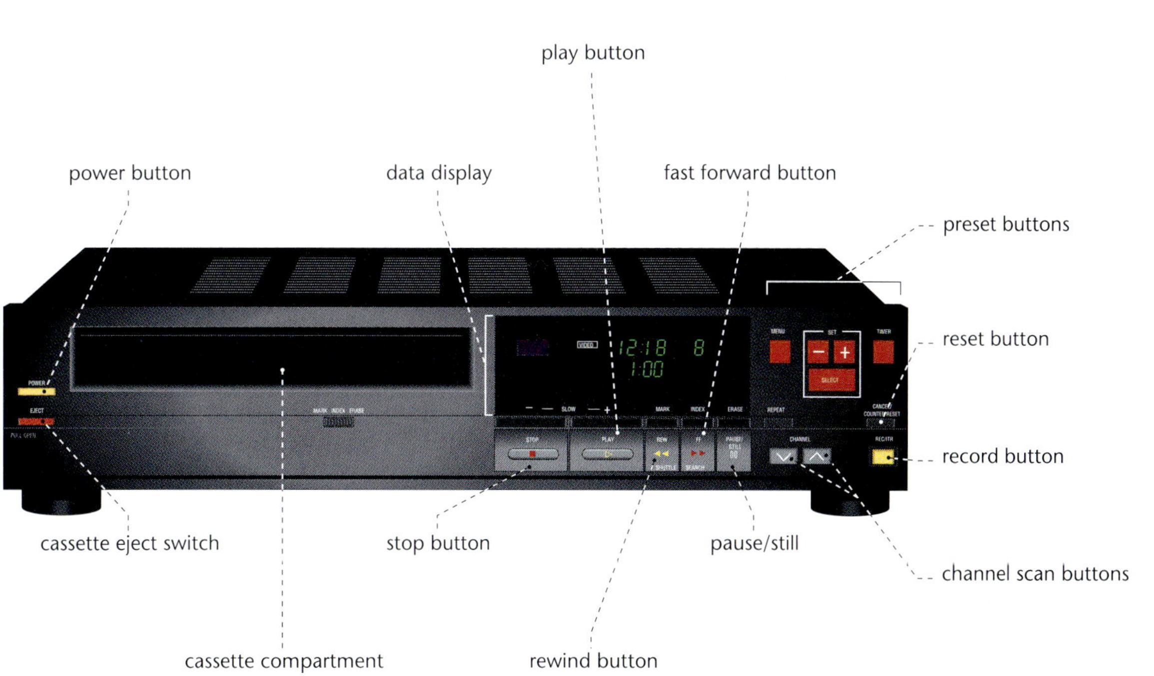

STUDIO AND CONTROL ROOMS

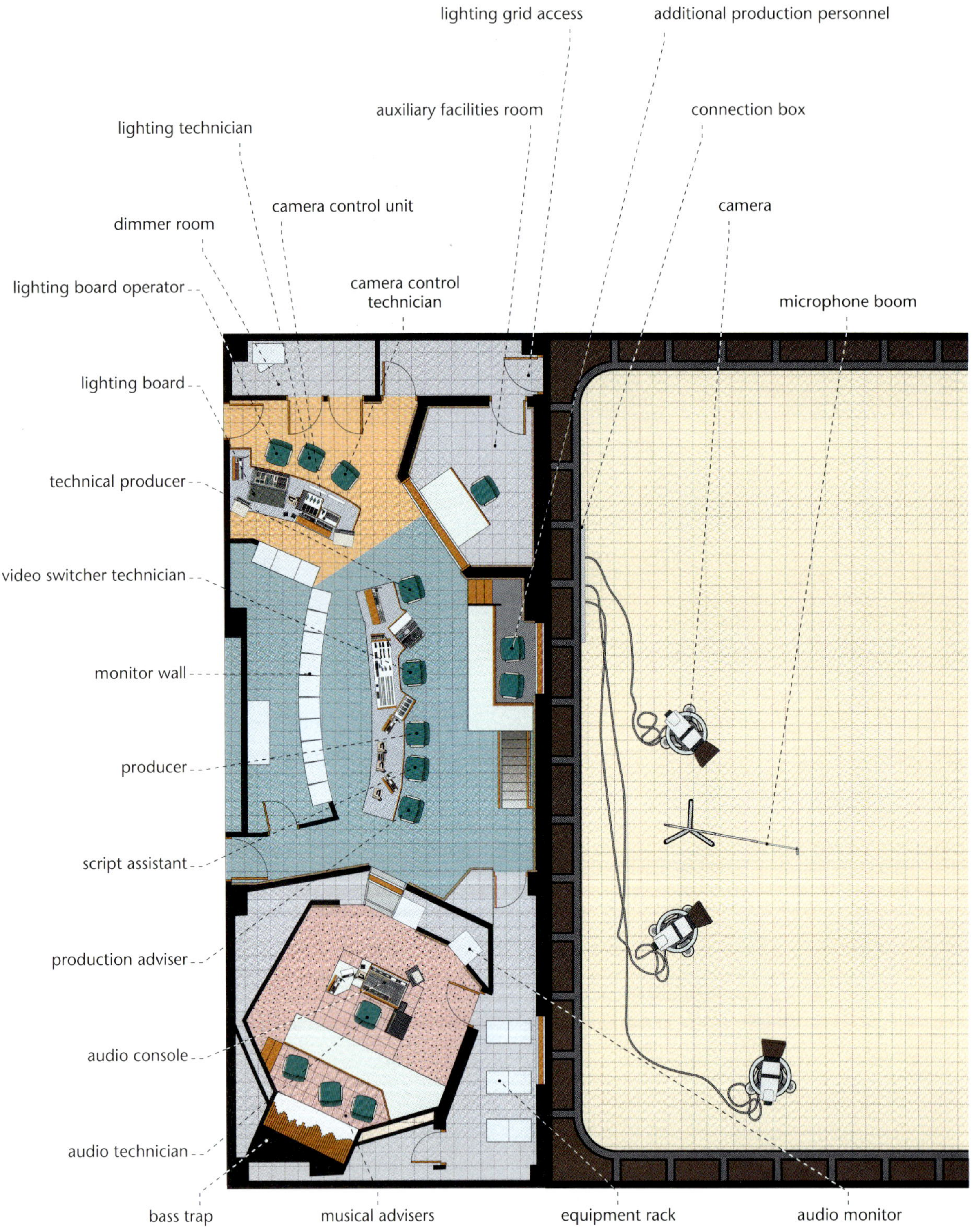

studio floor

lighting/camera control area

audio control room

production control room

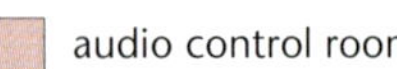

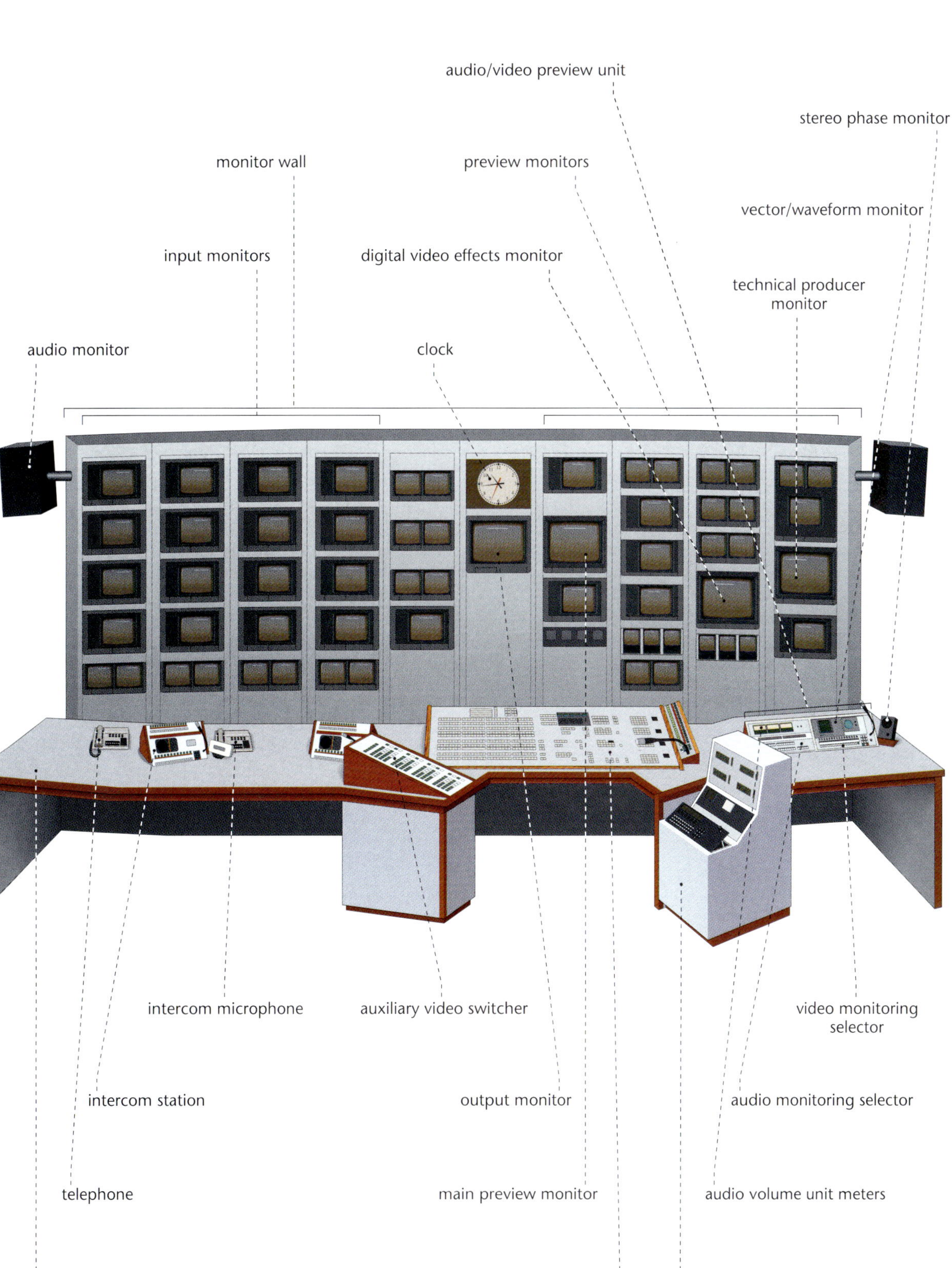
audio/video preview unit
stereo phase monitor
monitor wall
preview monitors
vector/waveform monitor
input monitors
digital video effects monitor
technical producer monitor
audio monitor
clock
intercom microphone
auxiliary video switcher
video monitoring selector
intercom station
output monitor
audio monitoring selector
telephone
main preview monitor
audio volume unit meters
production desk
production video switcher
digital video special effects

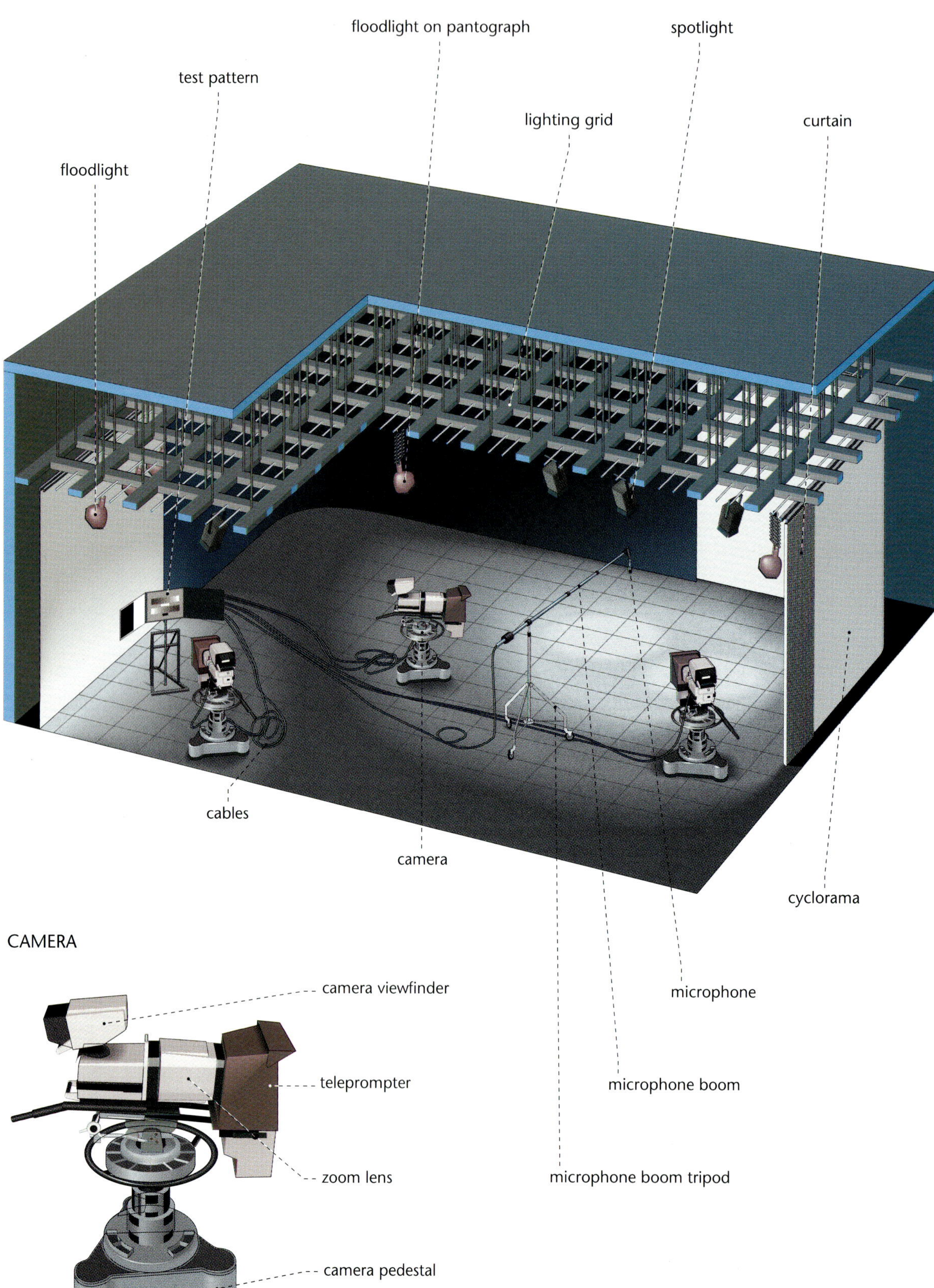
STUDIO FLOOR
floodlight
test pattern
floodlight on pantograph
lighting grid
spotlight
curtain
cables
camera
cyclorama
microphone
CAMERA
camera viewfinder
teleprompter
microphone boom
zoom lens
microphone boom tripod
camera pedestal
COMMUNICATIONS

MOBILE UNIT

microwave transmitter
wave guide
parabolic antenna
microwave dish
tripod
equipment rack
equipment rack
audio control room
camera control area
audio technician
production control room
camera control unit
telephone set
monitor wall
camera control technician
audio monitor
audio monitor
maintenance area
audio console
air conditioning unit
electrical connection panel
producer
video connection panel
technical equipment compartment
clock
preview monitor
technical producer
output monitor
video switcher technician
cable drum compartment

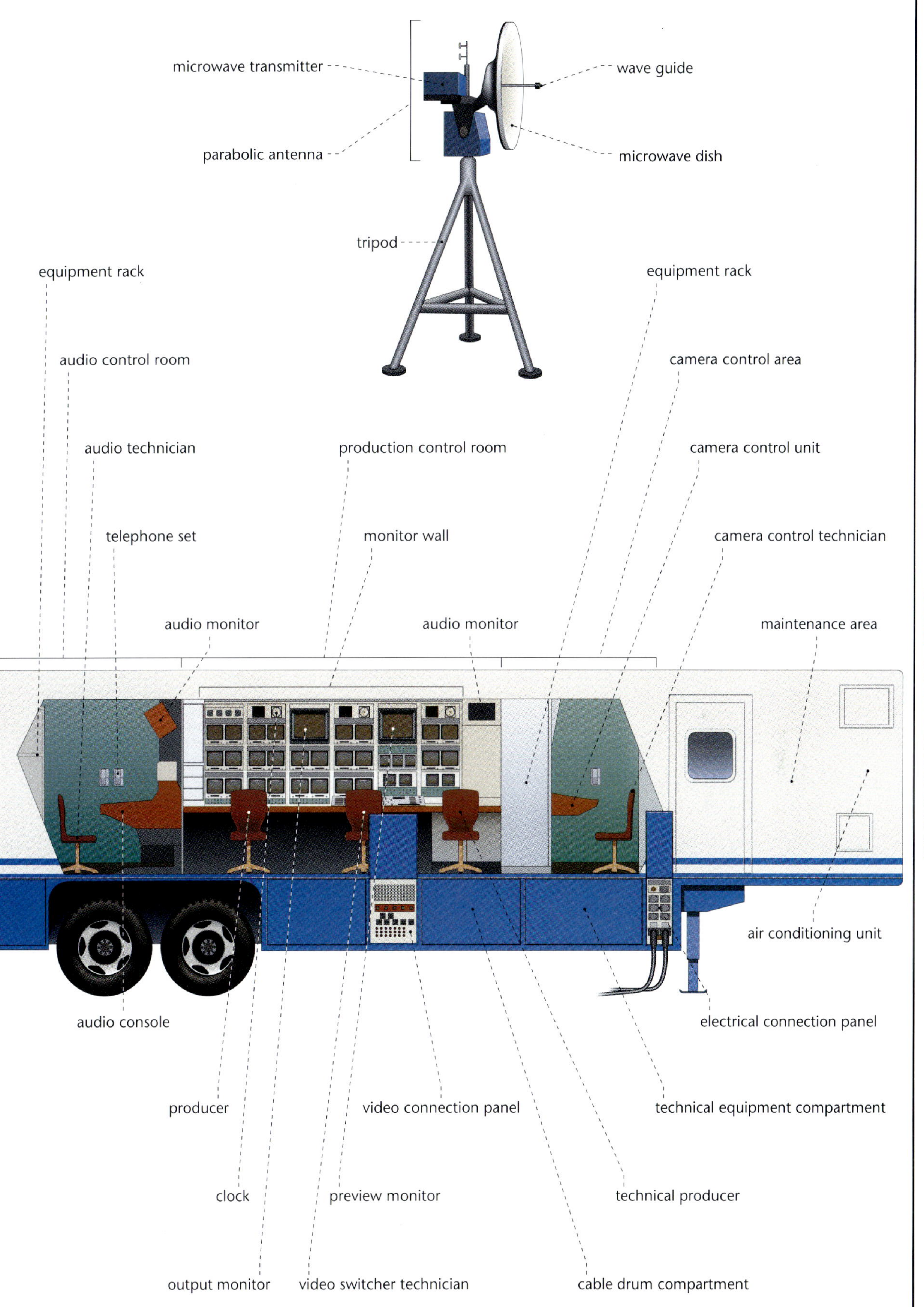

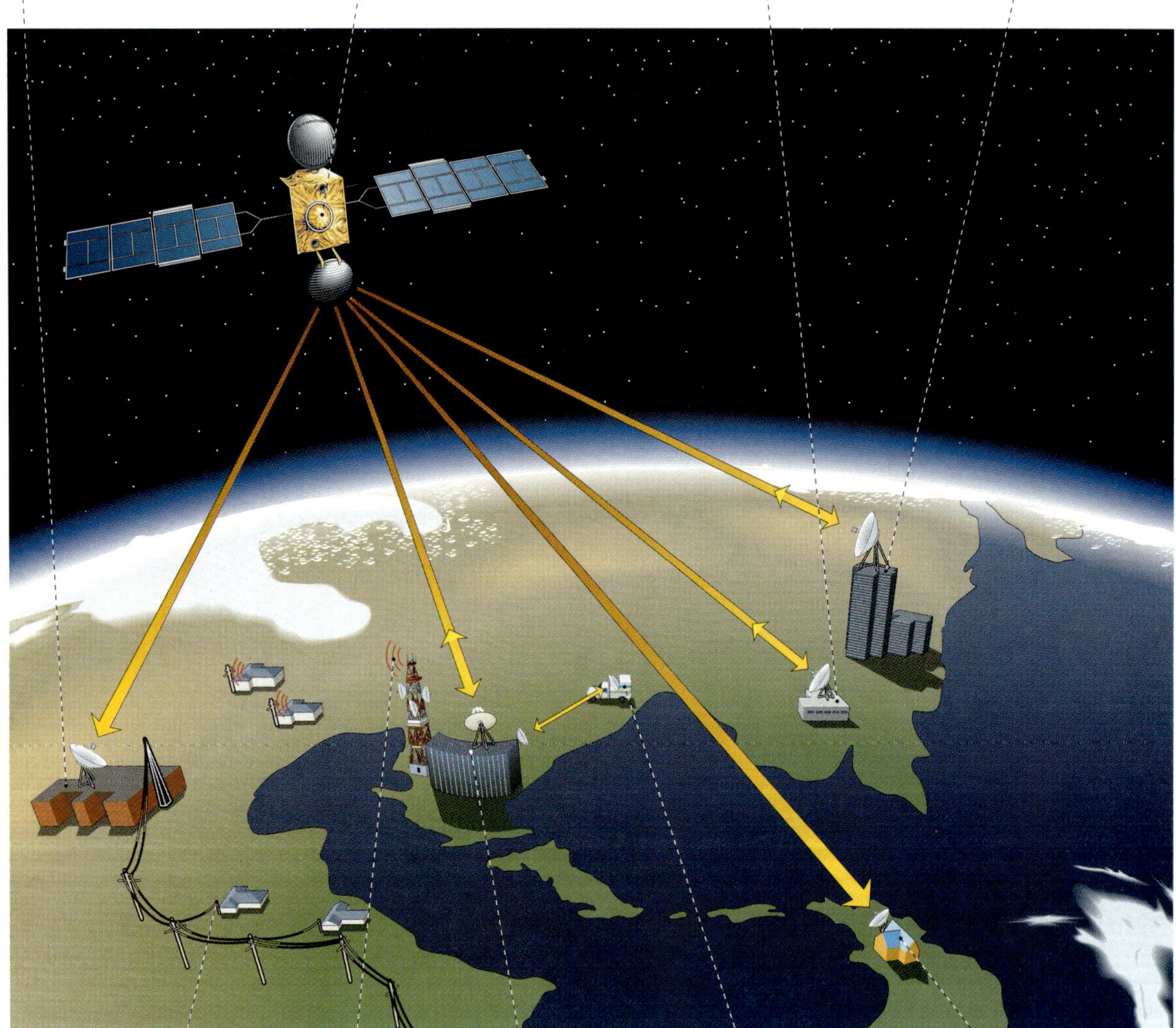
satellite
local station
cable distributor
private broadcasting network
distribution by cable network
direct home reception
Hertzian wave transmission
mobile unit
national broadcasting network

TELECOMMUNICATIONS BY SATELLITE

TELECOMMUNICATIONS BY TELEPHONE NETWORK

computer communication

facsimile machine

telex

cellular telephone

telephone set

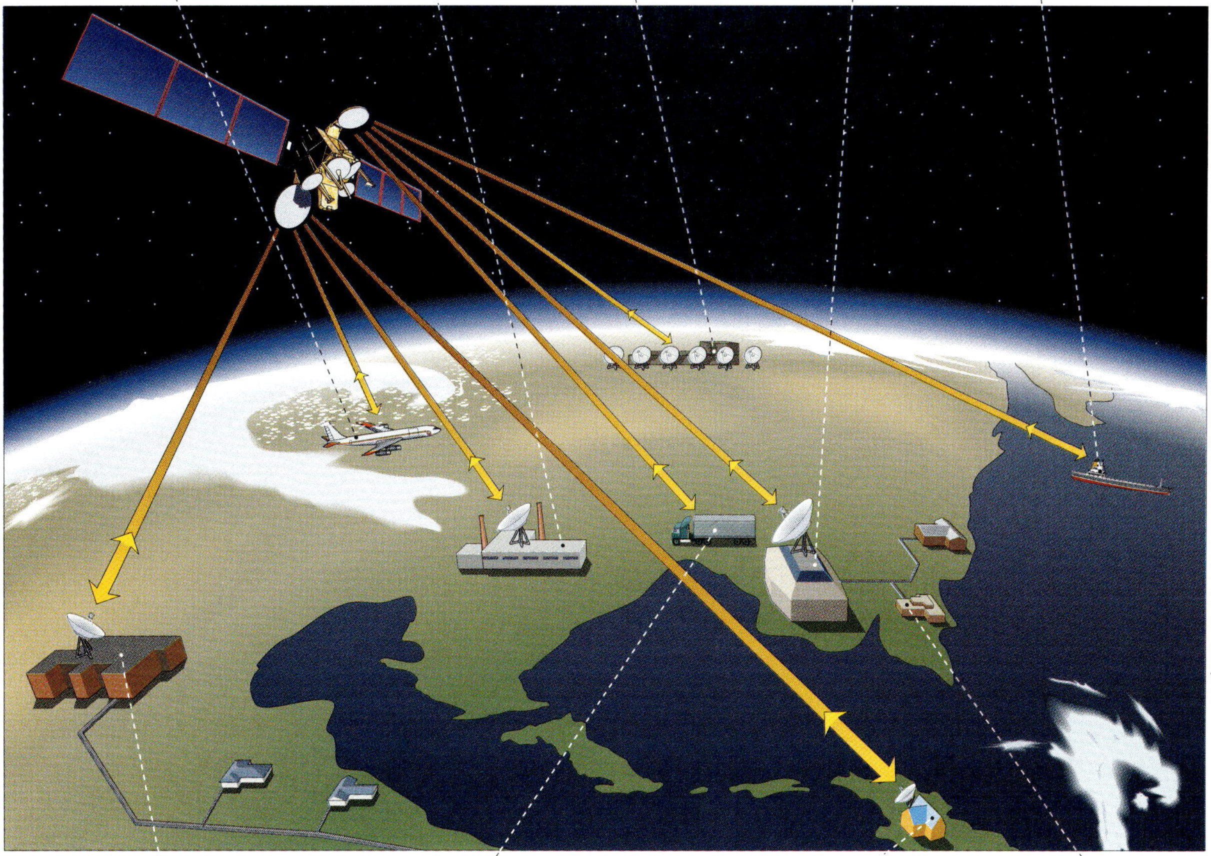

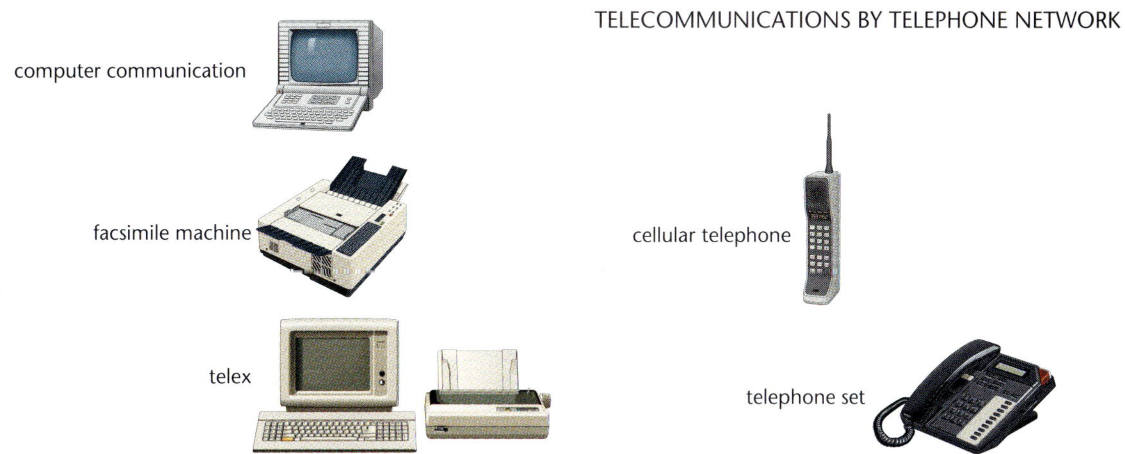

TELECOMMUNICATION SATELLITES

EXAMPLES OF SATELLITES

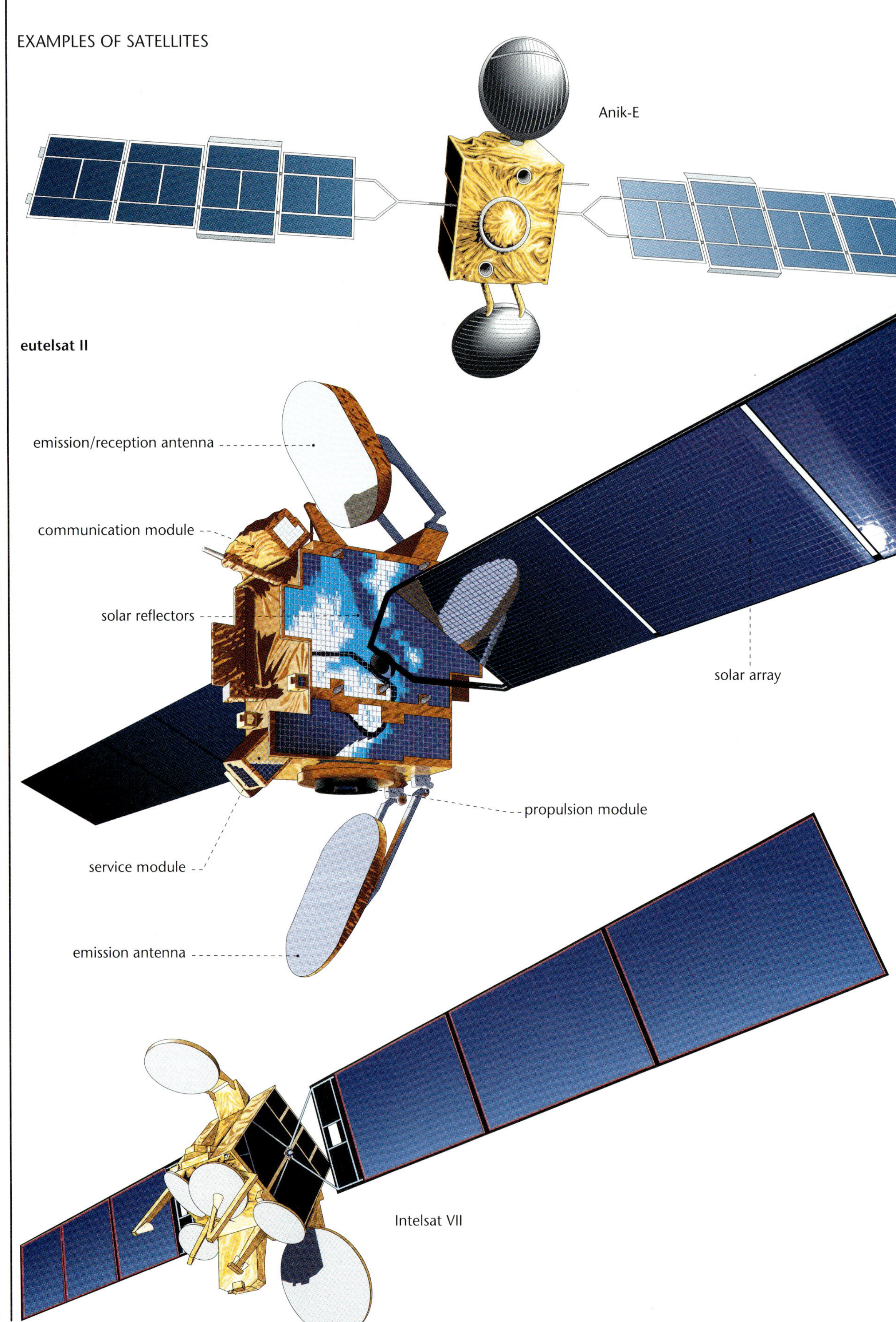

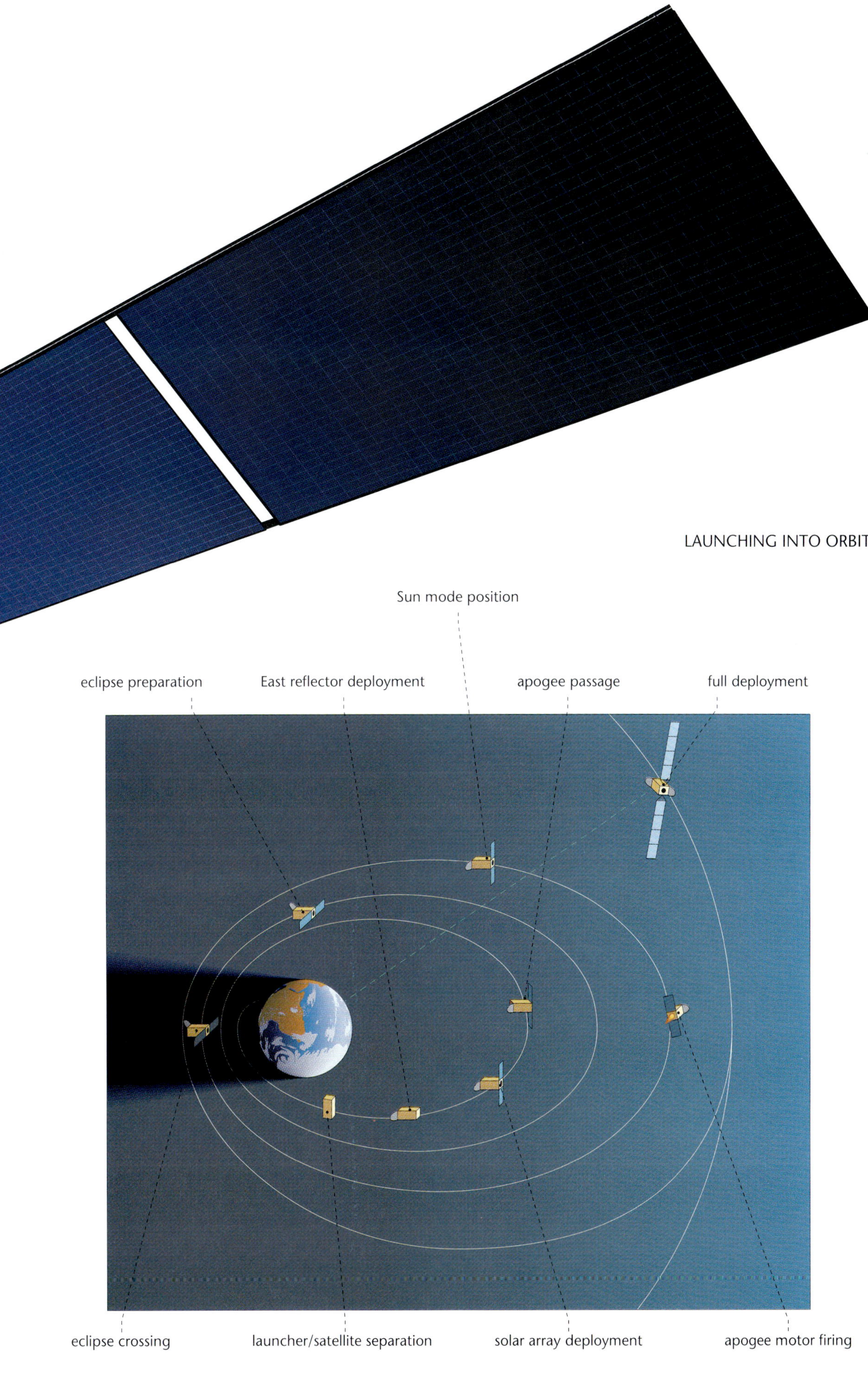

LAUNCHING INTO ORBIT
Sun mode position
eclipse preparation
East reflector deployment
apogee passage
full deployment
eclipse crossing
launcher/satellite separation
solar array deployment
apogee motor firing

COMMUNICATIONS

TELEPHONE ANSWERING MACHINE

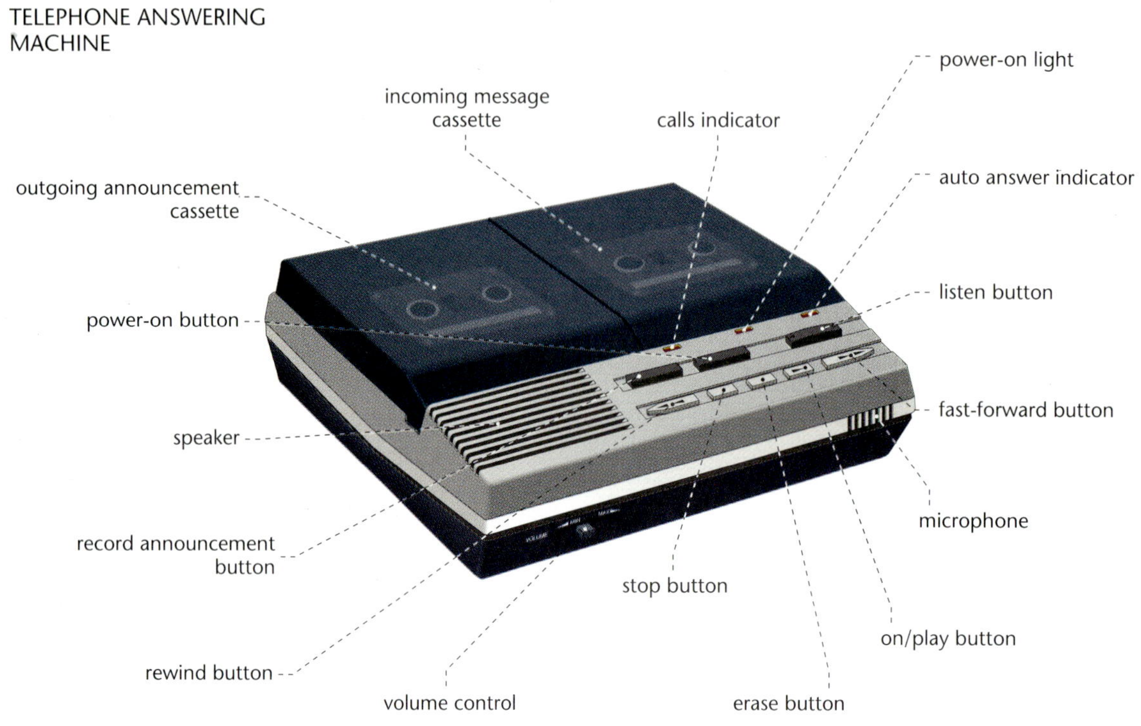

TELEPHONE SET

terminal

visual display unit
transmission/reception of messages

printer

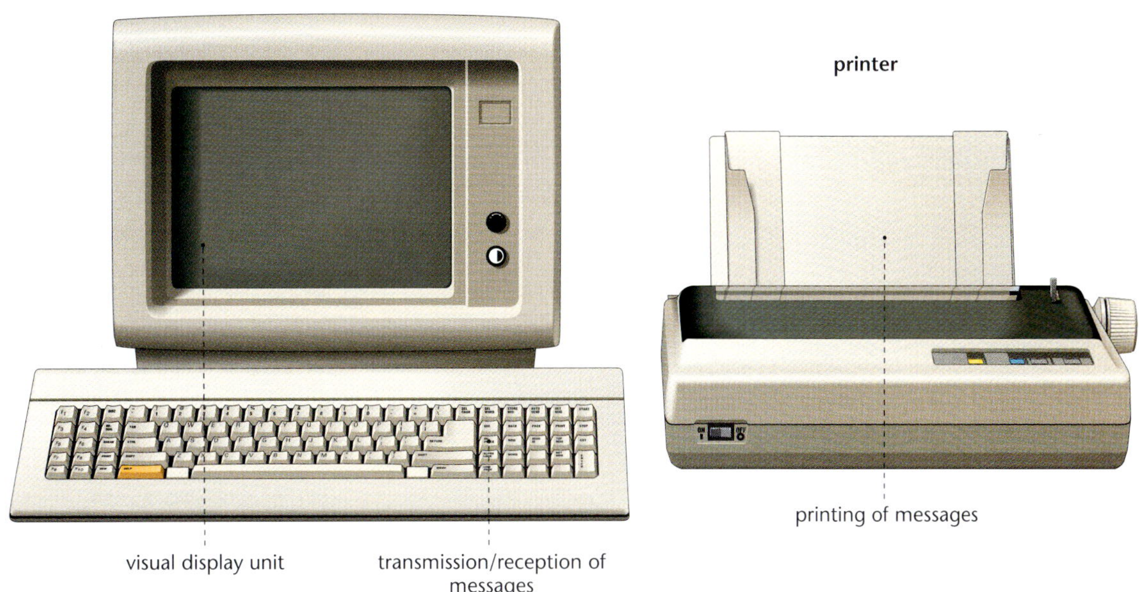

printing of messages

FACSIMILE MACHINE

data display
start key
sent document recovery
document receiving
document-to-be-sent position
paper guide
function keys
reset key
control keys
number key

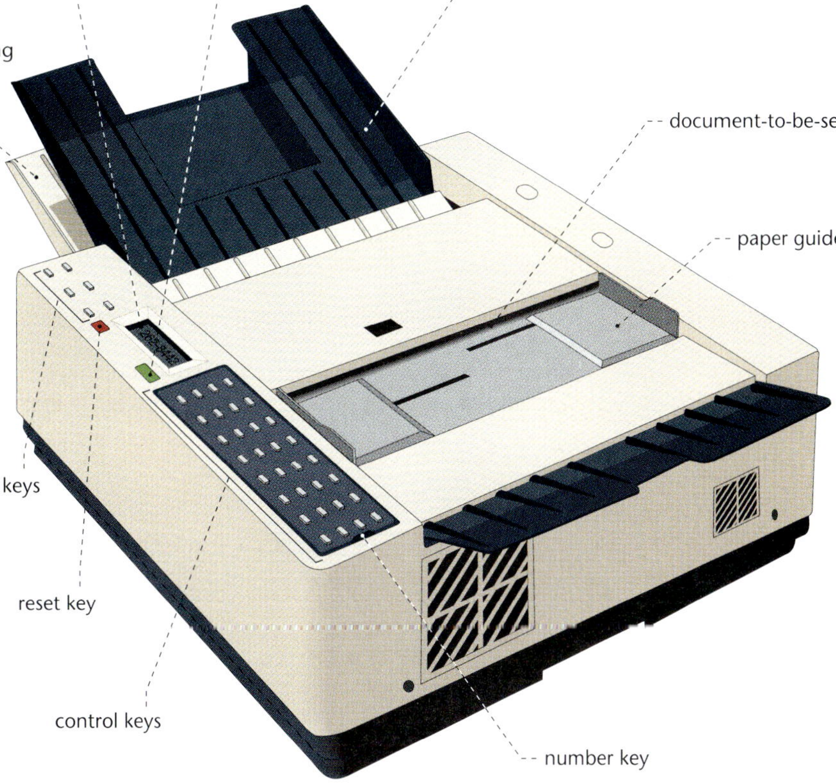

TYPES OF TELEPHONES

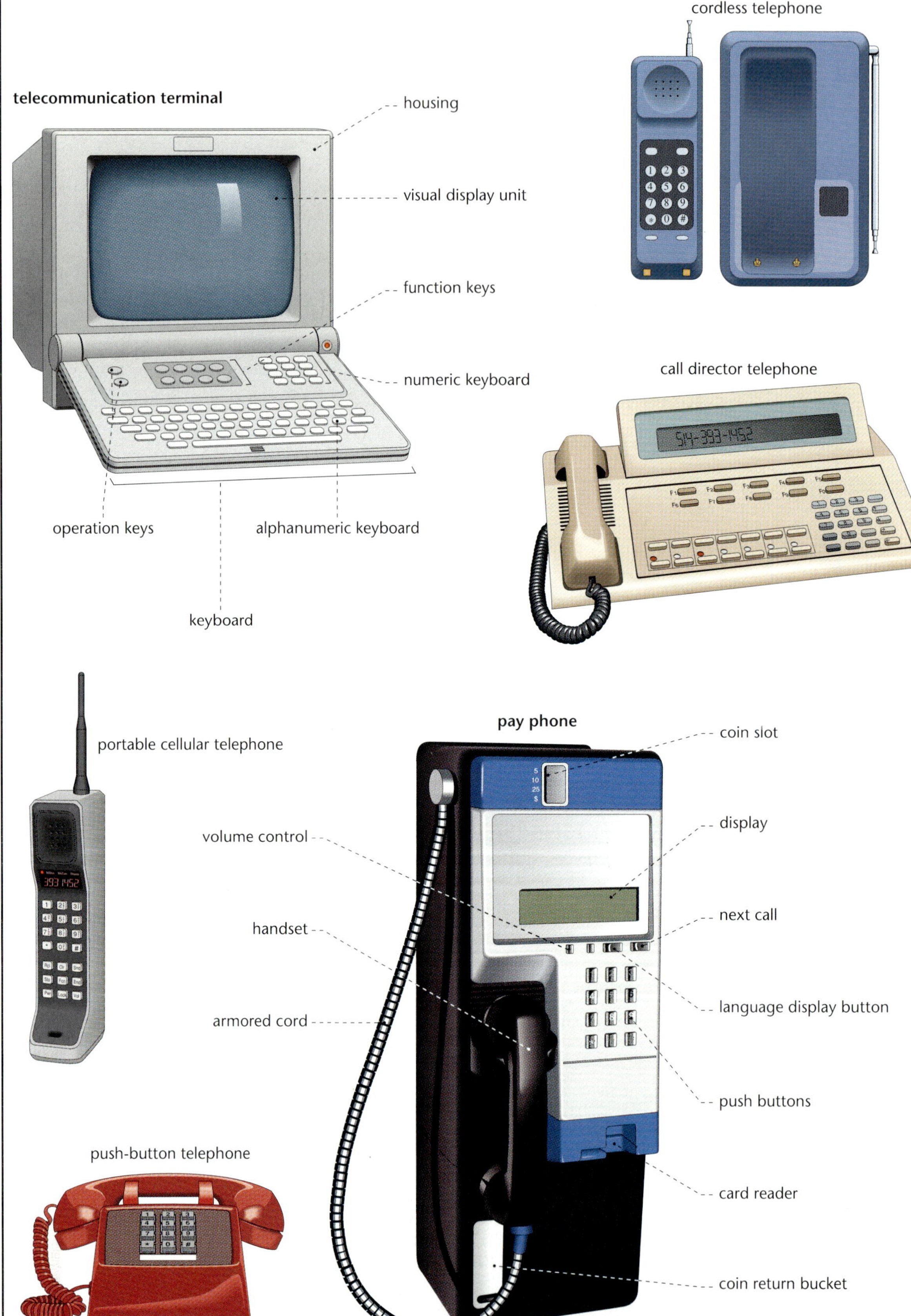

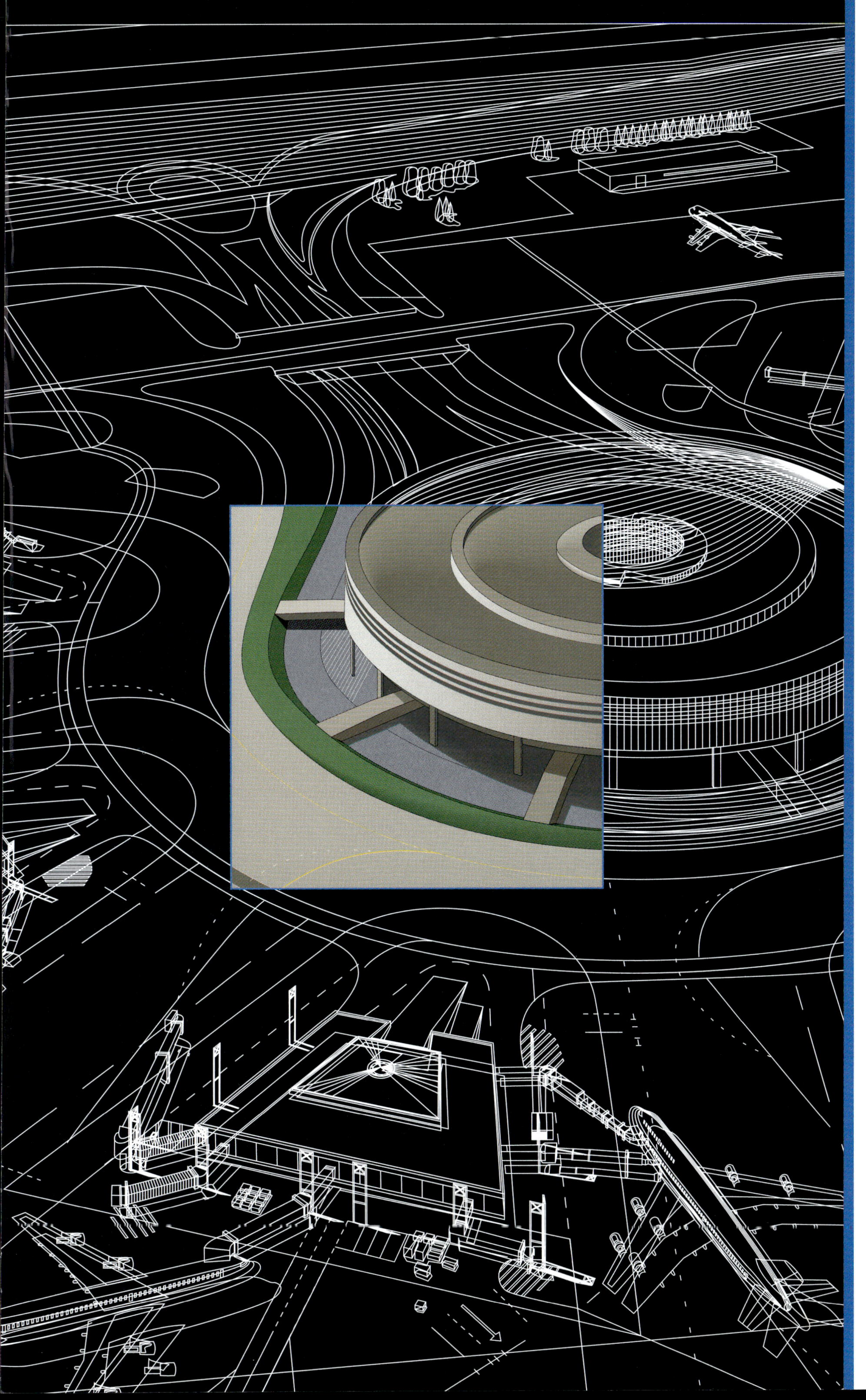

CONTENTS

sports car
two-door sedan
hatchback
station wagon
convertible
four-door sedan
pickup truck
minivan
multipurpose vehicle
limousine

BODY

windshield
windshield wiper
cowl
outside mirror
washer nozzle
hood
headlight
grille
bumper
shield
fender

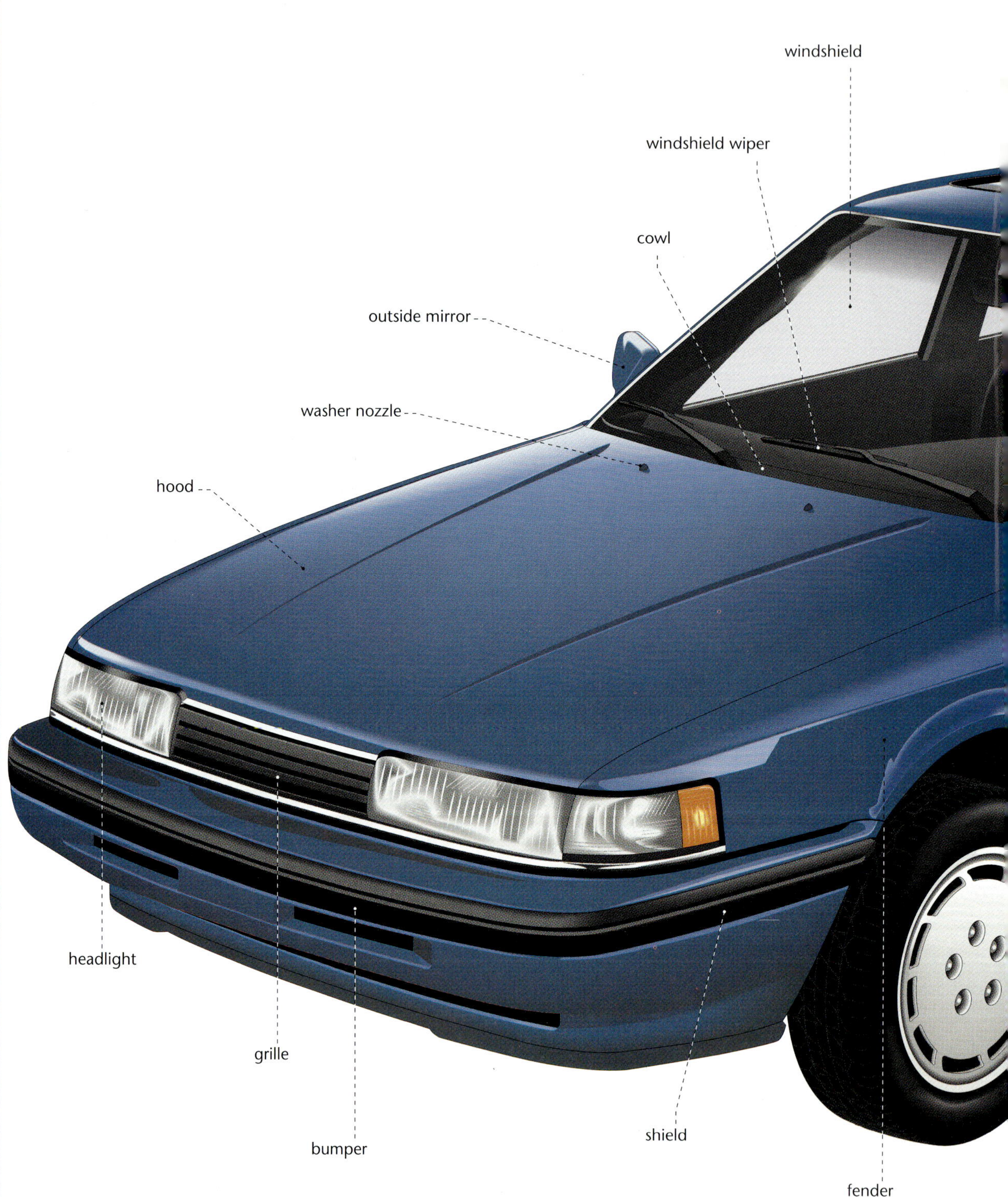

sliding sunroof
antenna
roof
center post
drip molding
quarter window
trunk
gas tank door
mud flap
window
wheel cover
door
door lock
wheel
body side molding
door handle

BUCKET SEAT

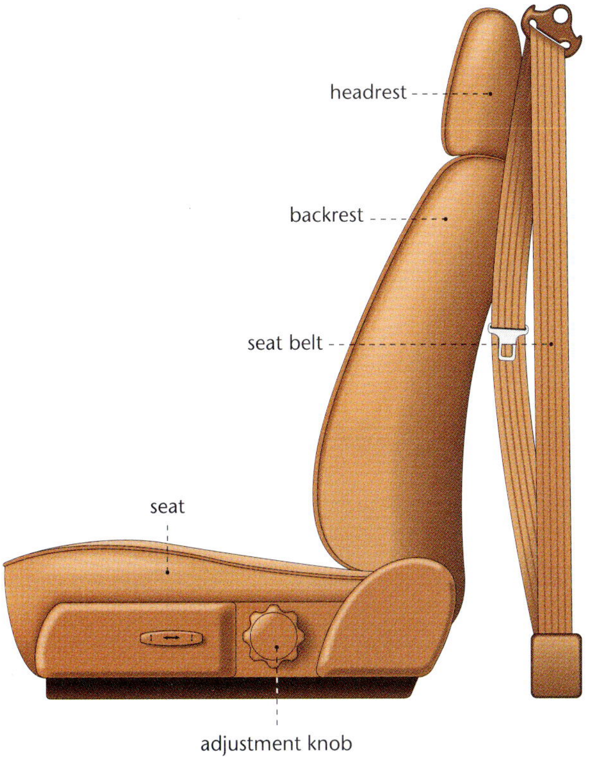

REAR SEAT

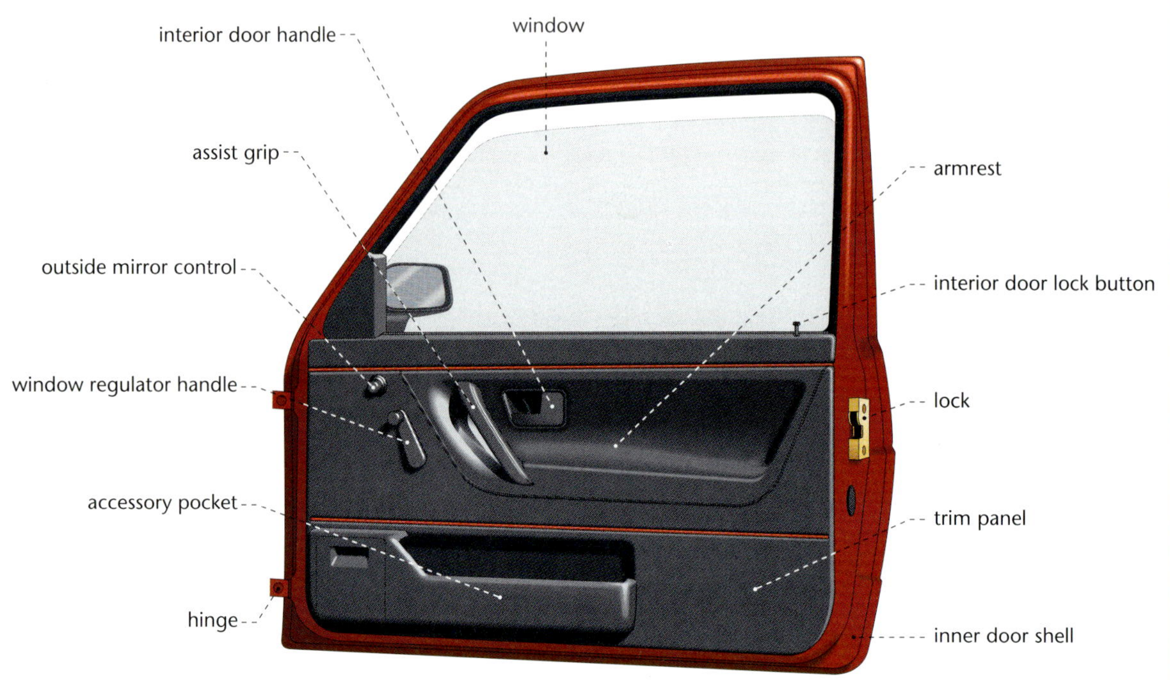

headlights

taillights

DASHBOARD

wiper switch
vanity mirror
clock
sun visor
horn
rearview mirror
vent
instrument panel
glove compartment
headlight/turn signal
climate control
steering wheel
audio system
parking brake lever
clutch pedal
gas pedal
gearshift lever
ignition switch
brake pedal
center console

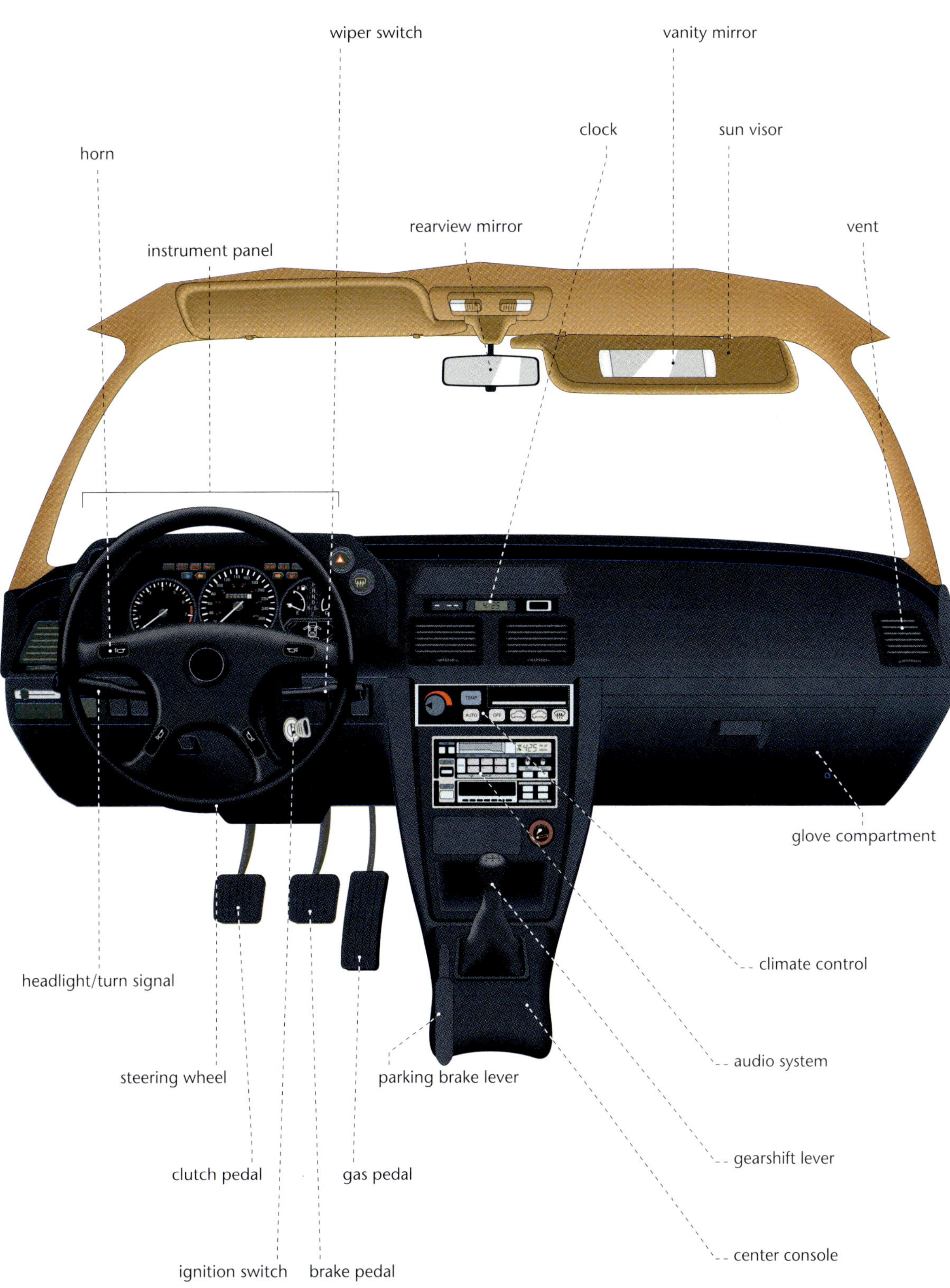

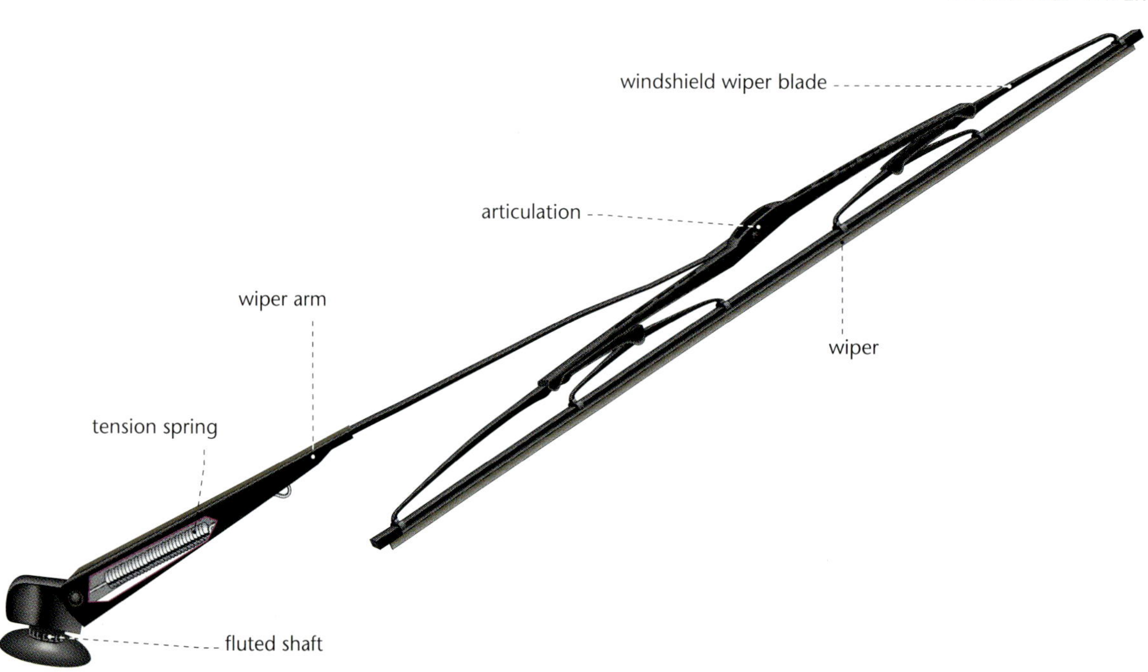
alternator warning light
high beam indicator light
oil warning light
low fuel warning light
fuel indicator
warning lights
turn signal indicator
temperature indicator
ENGINE MOTEUR
ALB
CRUISE CONTROL
120 140 160 180
100 200
80 220
60 240
40 260
20 280
m/h
km/h
F
E
C
H
tachometer
odometer
trip odometer
door open warning light
seat-belt warning light
speedometer
WINDSHIELD WIPER
windshield wiper blade
articulation
wiper arm
wiper
tension spring
fluted shaft

DISK BRAKE

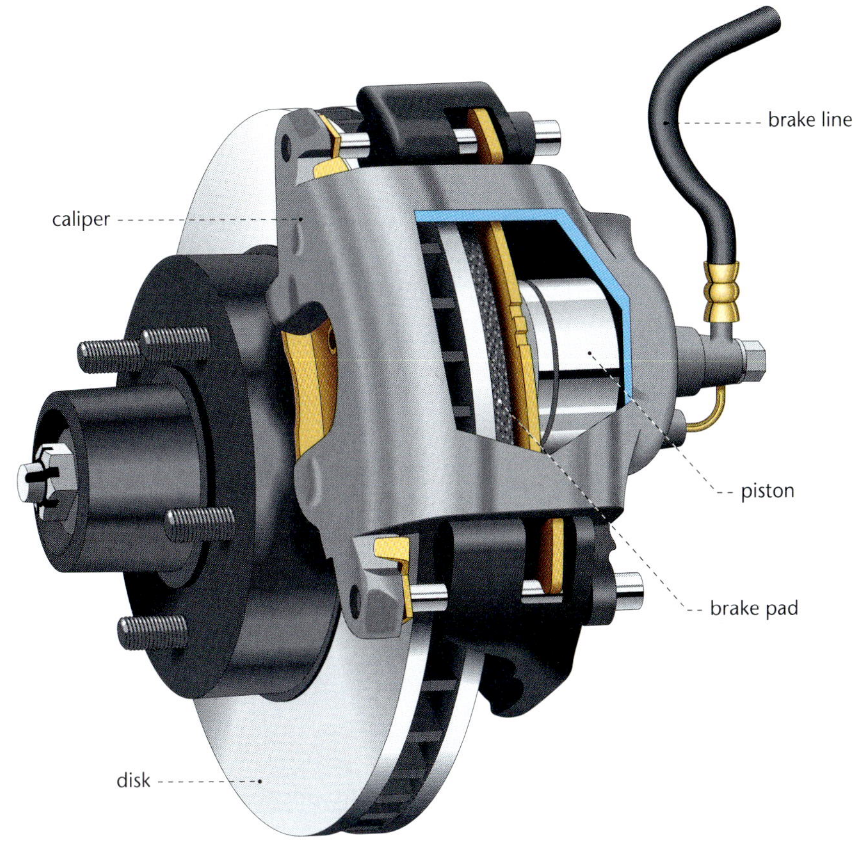

DRUM BRAKE

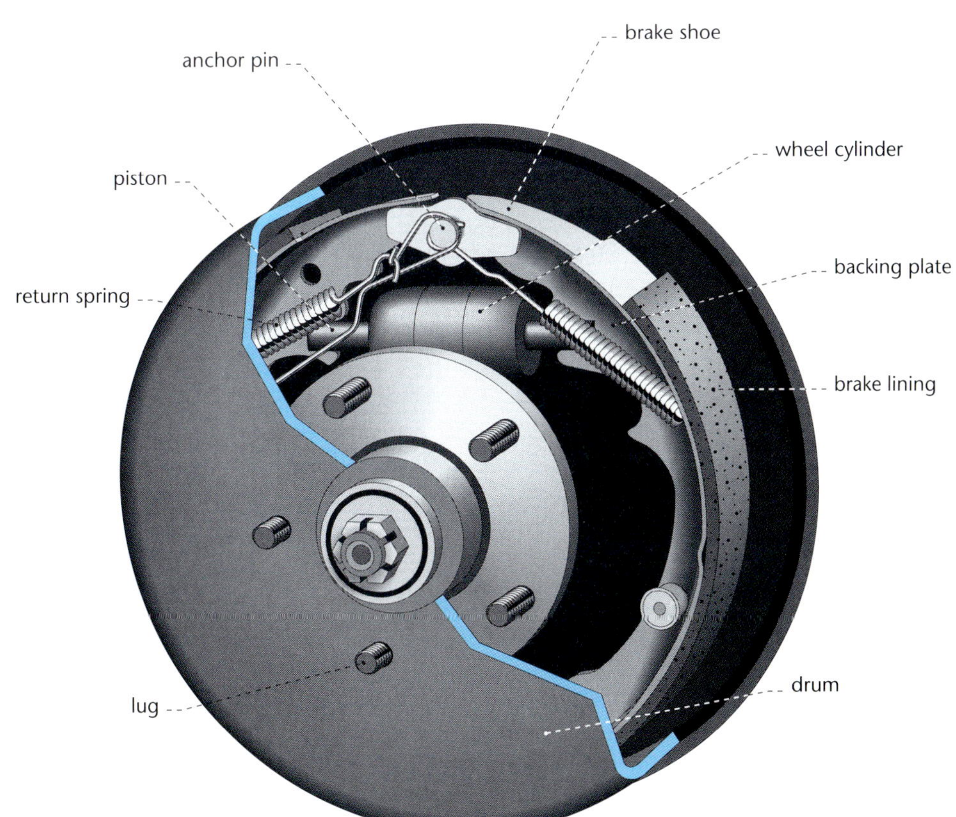

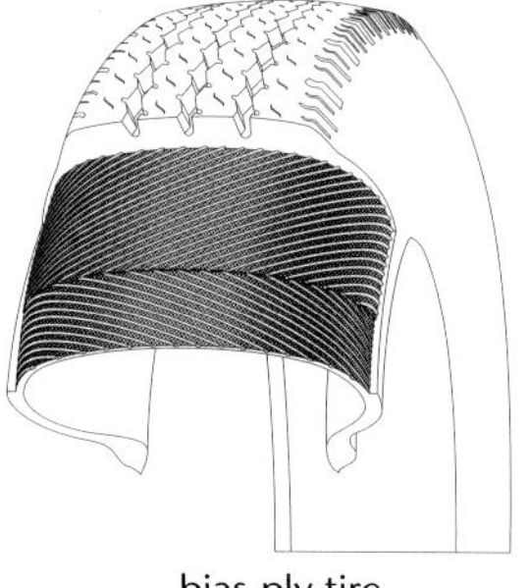

bias-ply tire

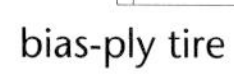

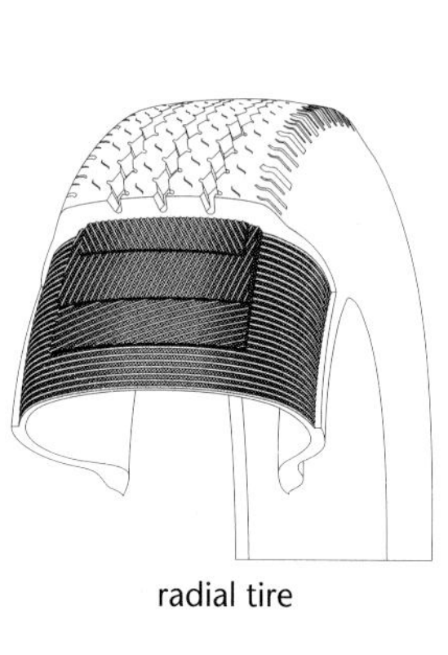

radial tire

STEEL BELTED RADIAL TIRE

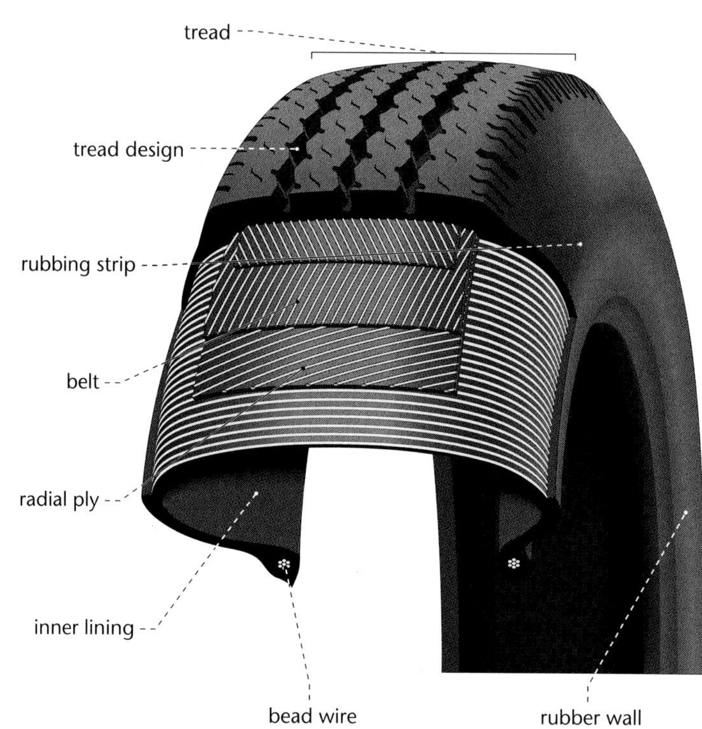

TIRE

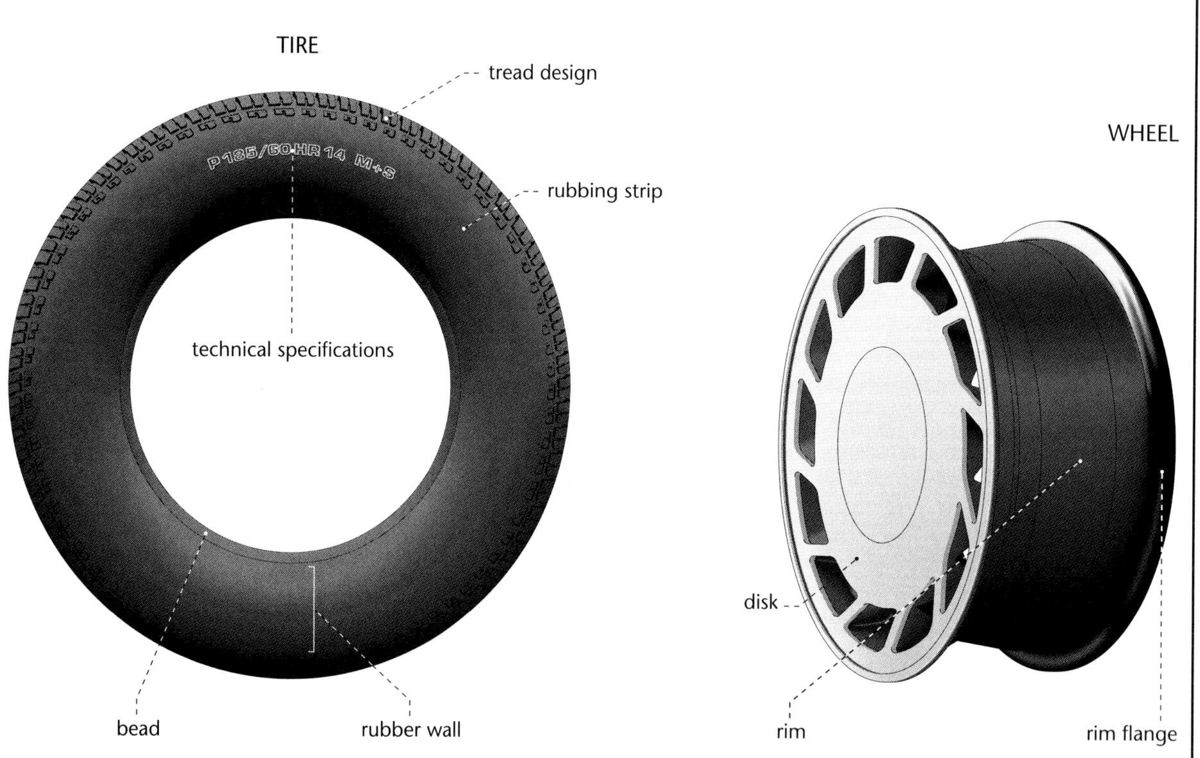

433

GASOLINE ENGINE

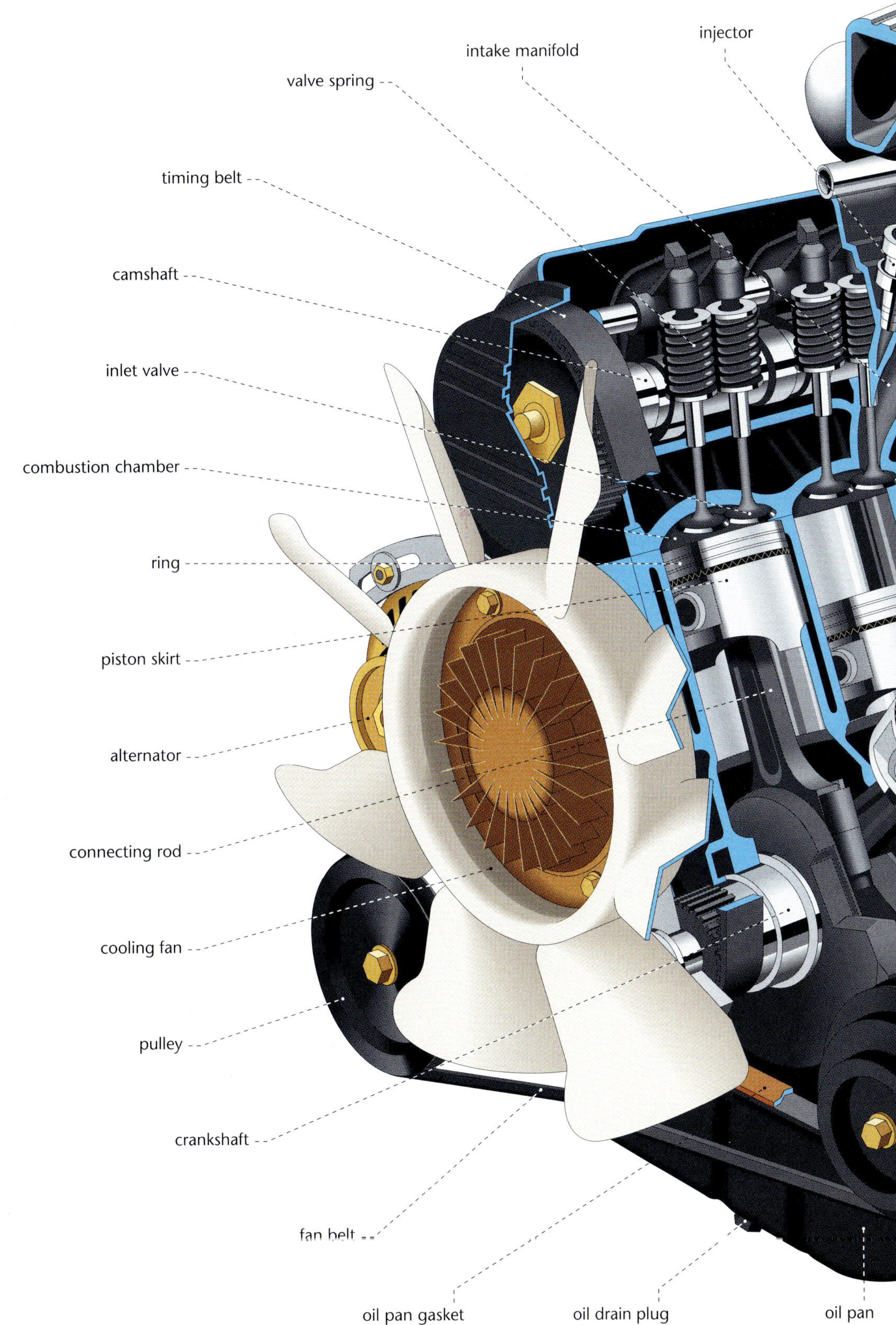

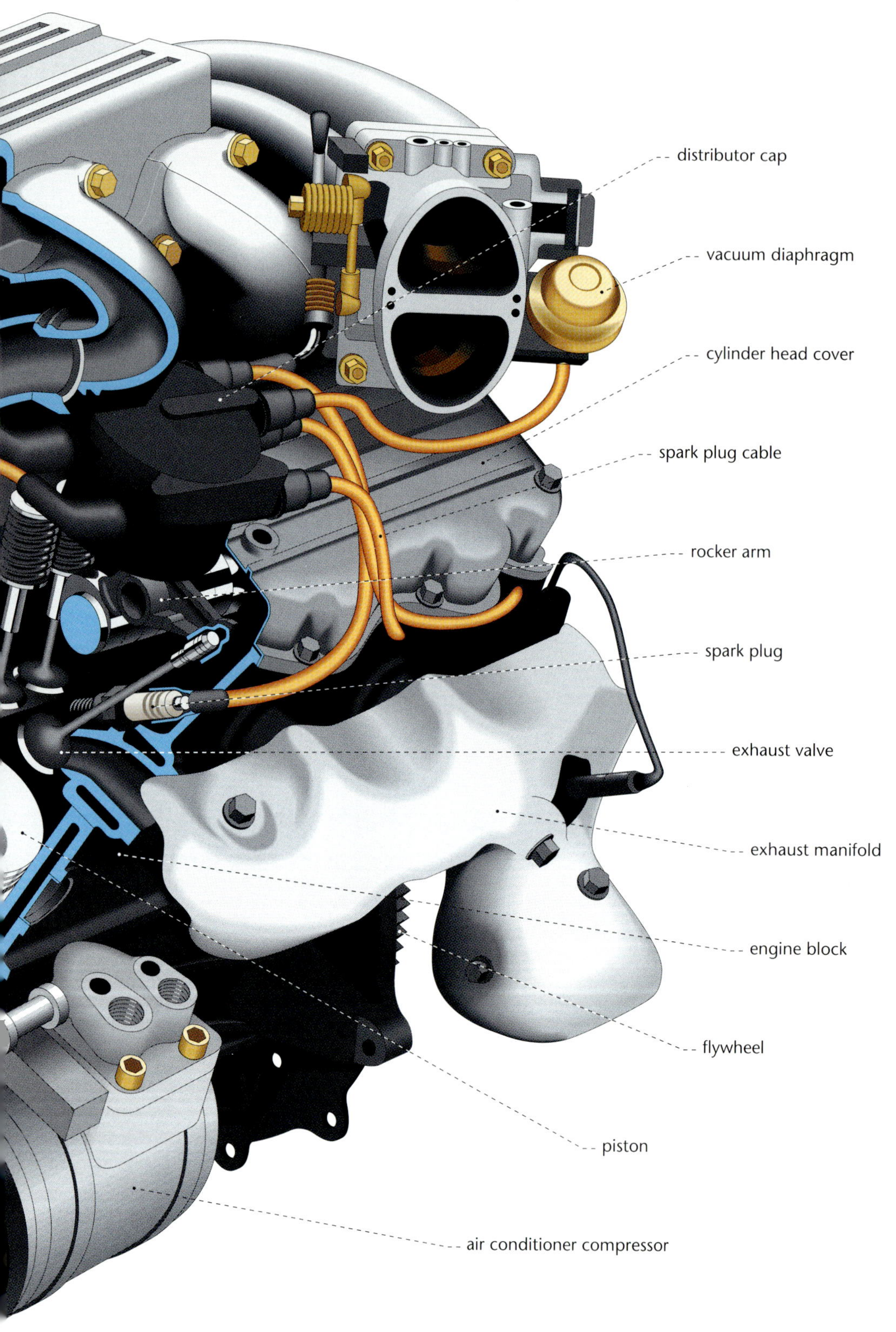

distributor cap
vacuum diaphragm
cylinder head cover
spark plug cable
rocker arm
spark plug
exhaust valve
exhaust manifold
engine block
flywheel
piston
air conditioner compressor

FOUR-STROKE-CYCLE ENGINE

TWO-STROKE-CYCLE ENGINE

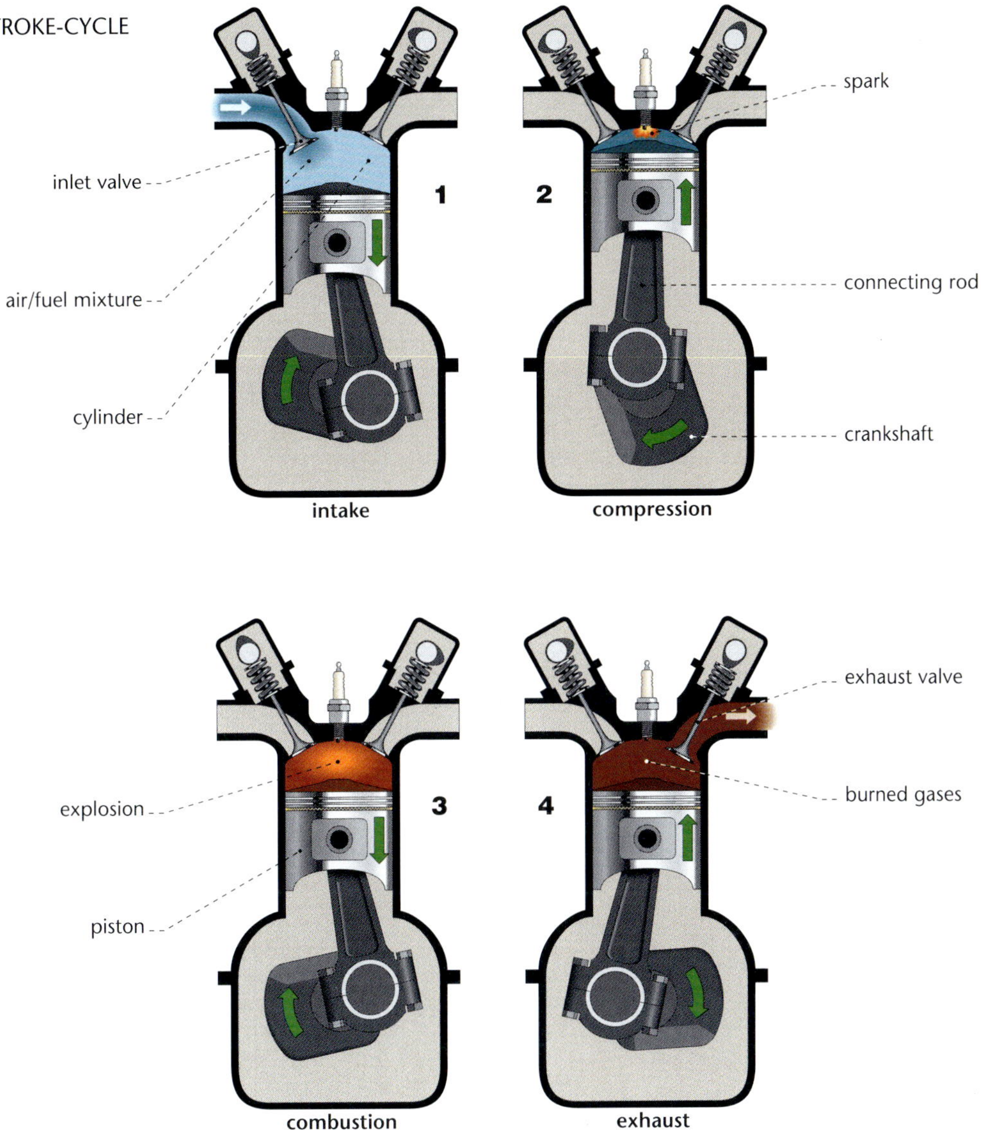

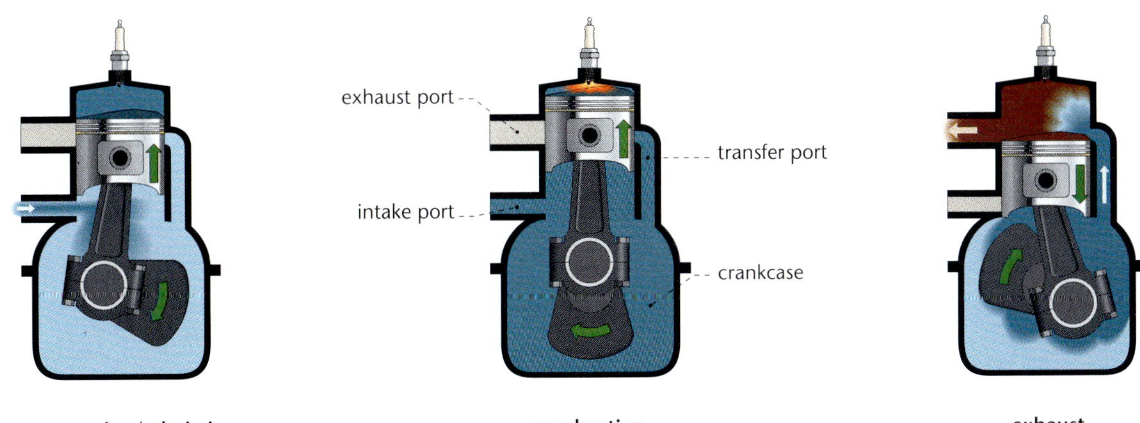

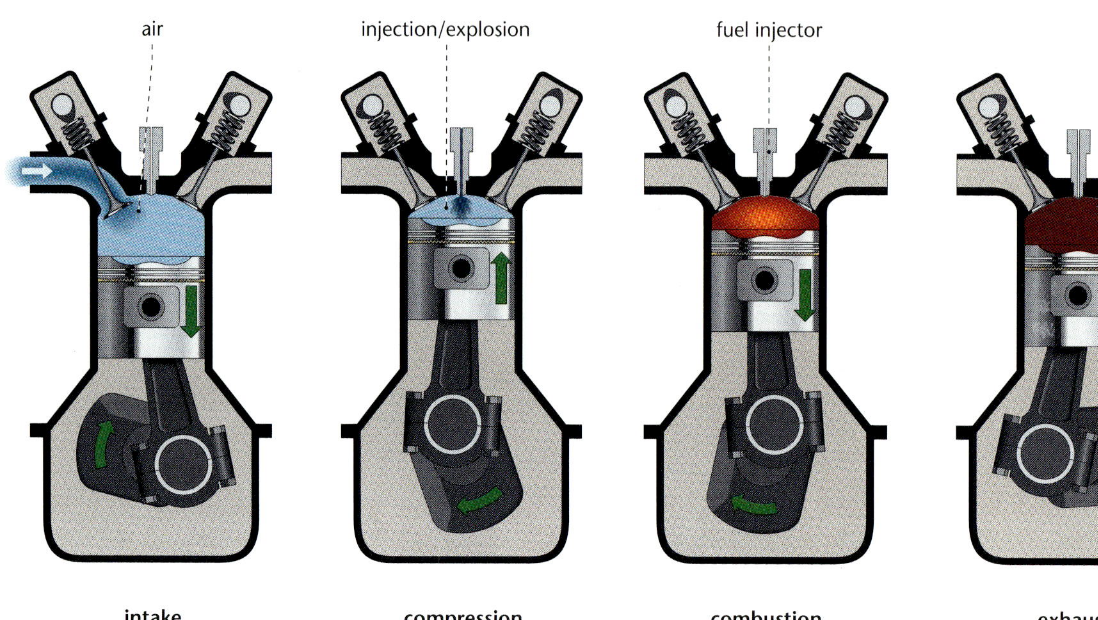

ROAD TRANSPORT

ROTARY ENGINE

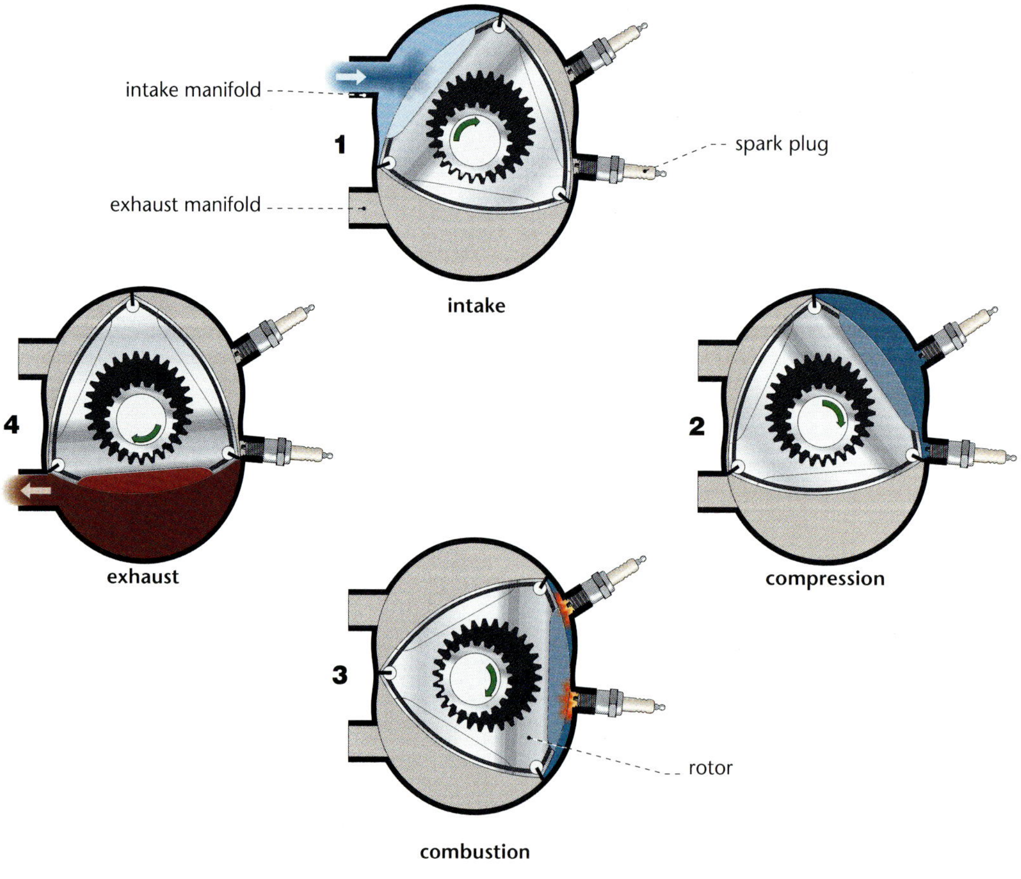

RADIATOR

TURBO-COMPRESSOR ENGINE

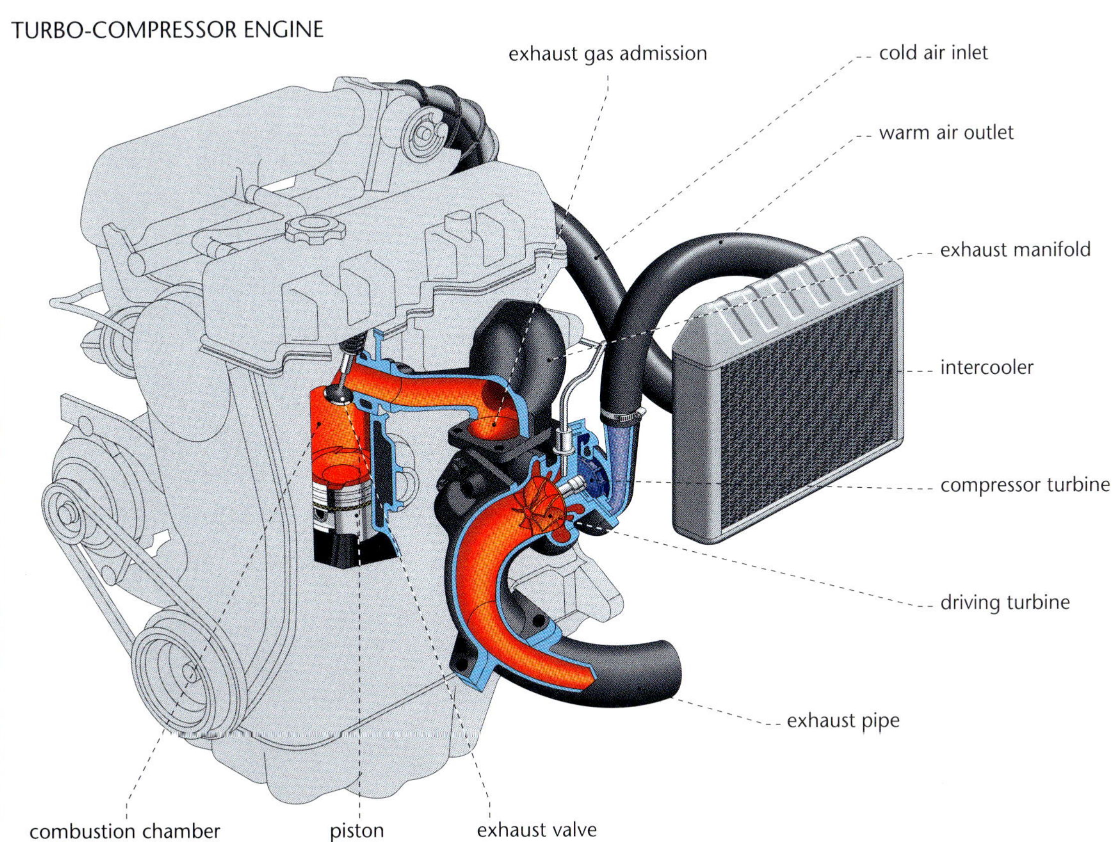

SPARK PLUG

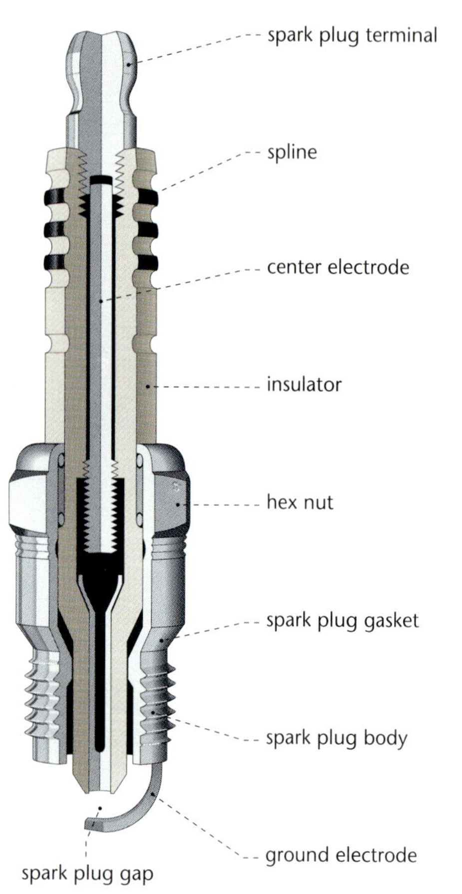

EXHAUST SYSTEM

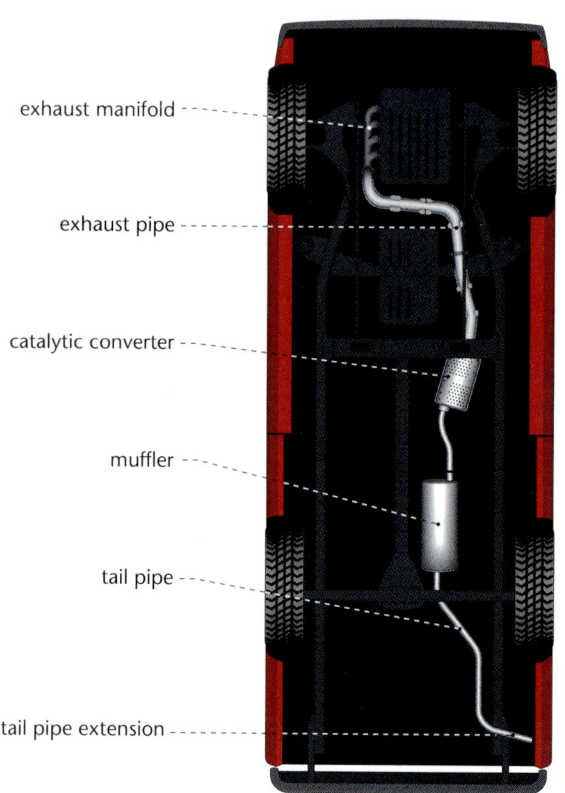

BATTERY

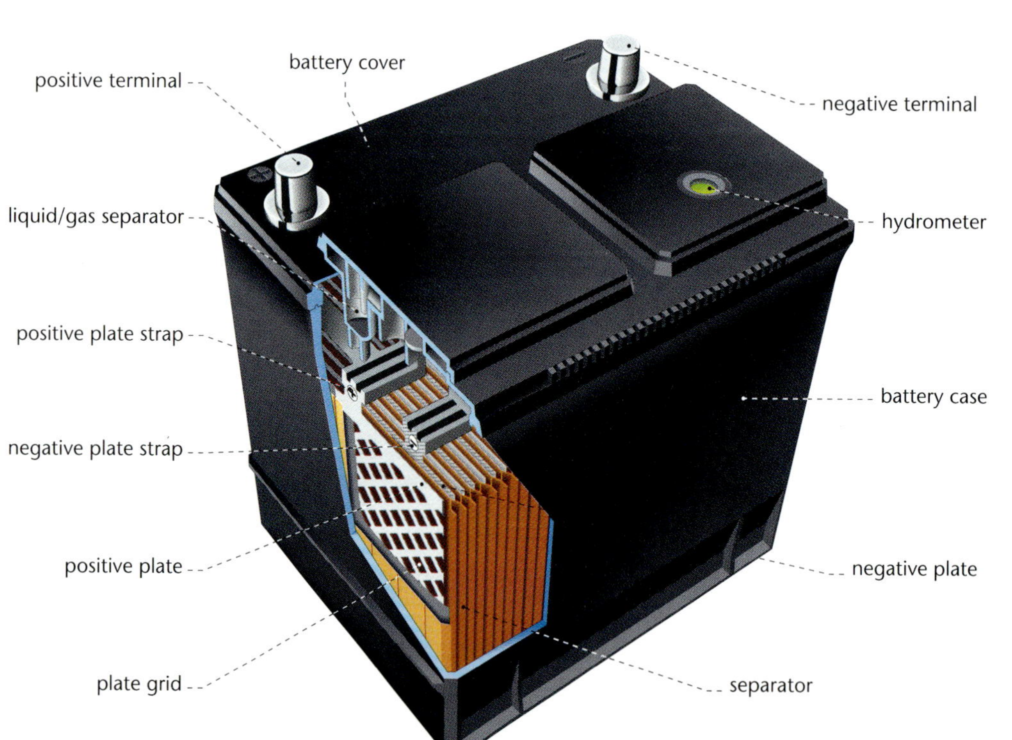

ROAD TRANSPORT

TRUCK TRACTOR

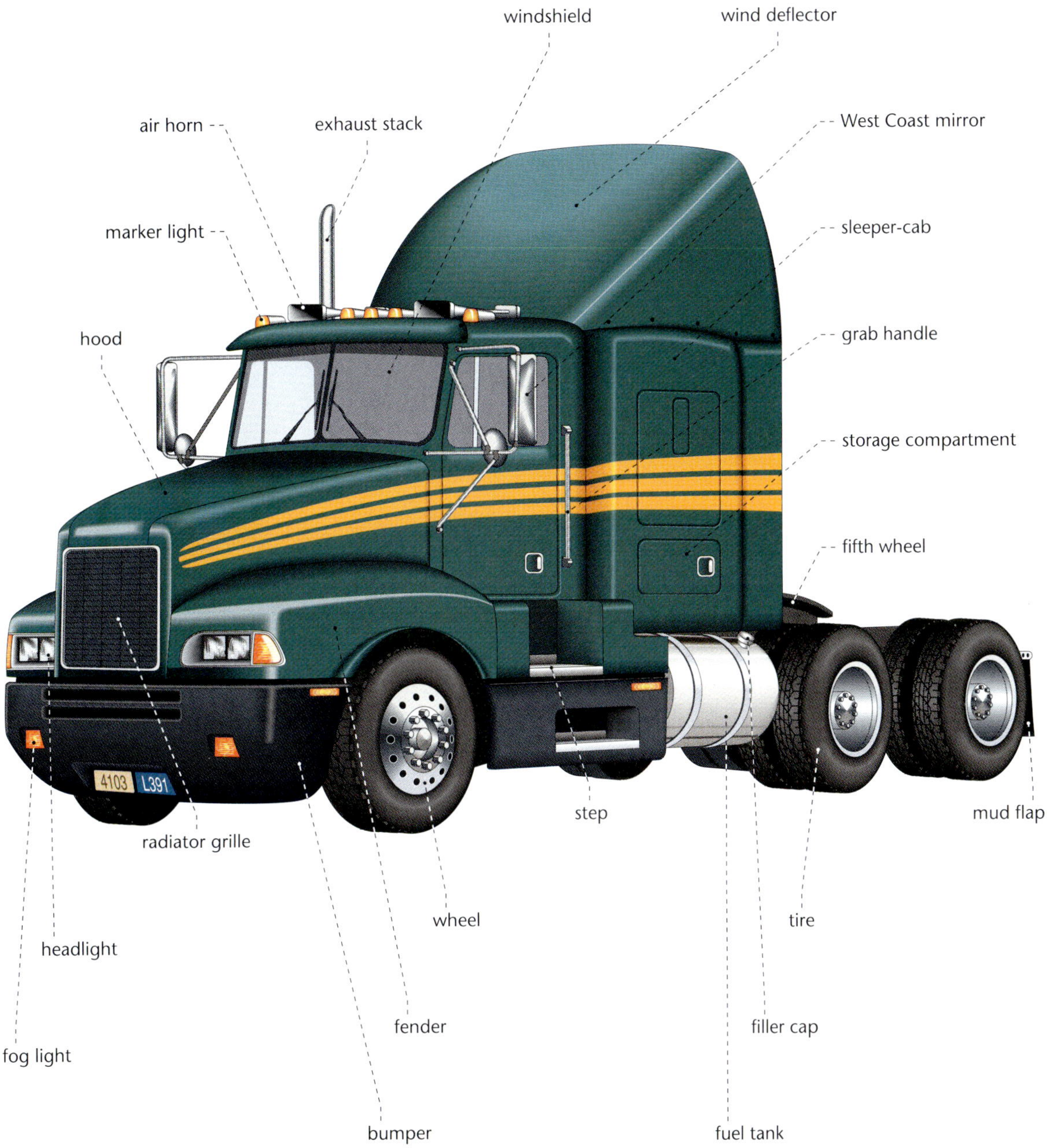

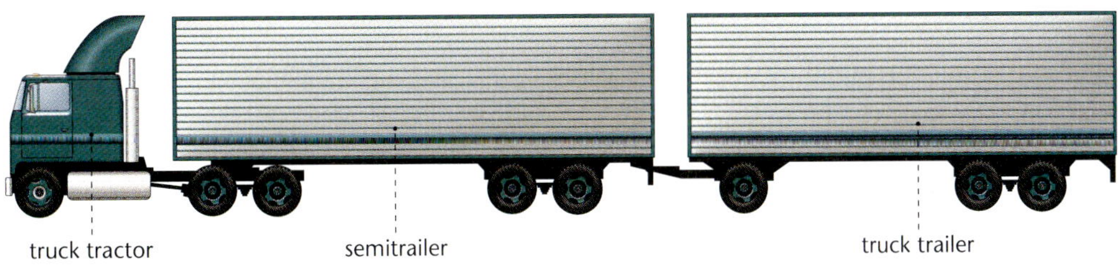

TANDEM TRACTOR TRAILER

SEMITRAILER

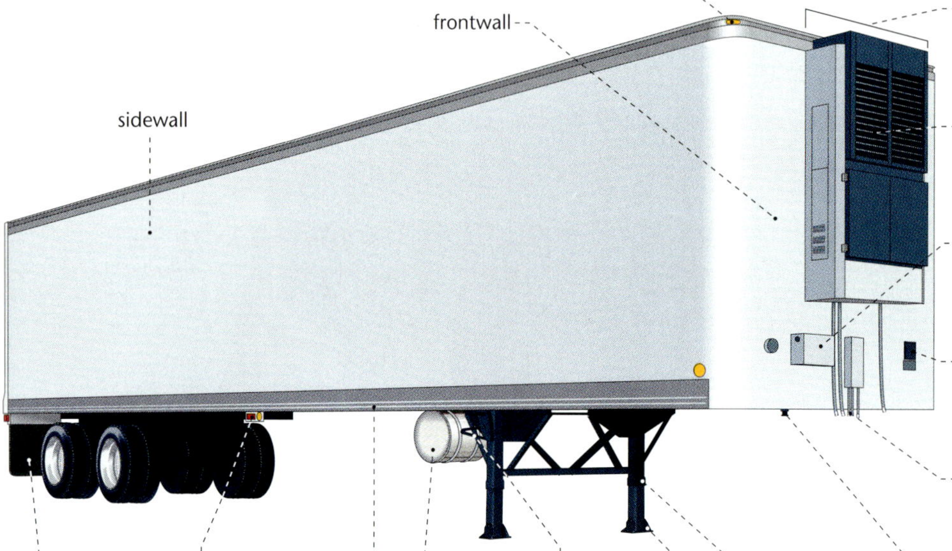

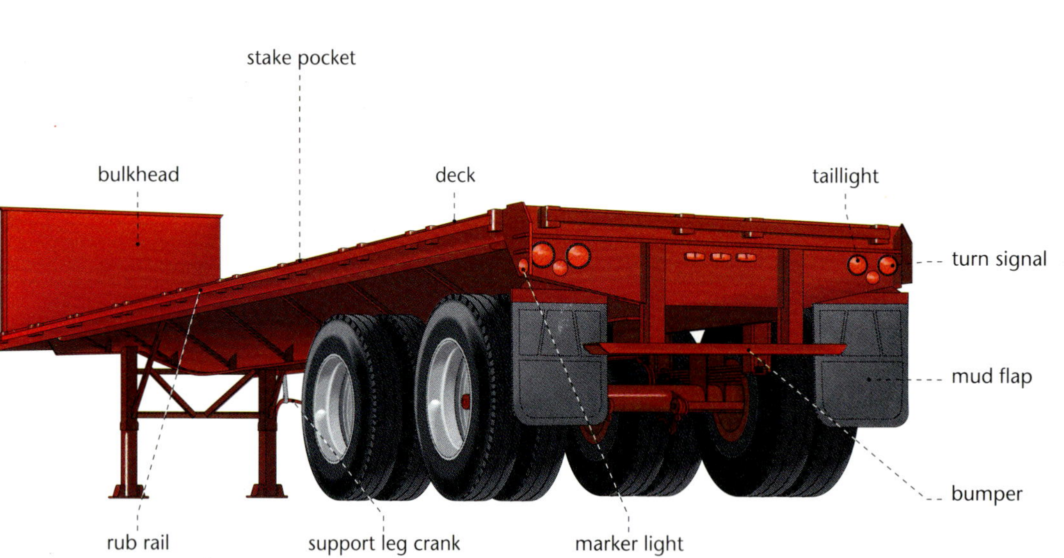

FLATBED

SIDE VIEW

mirror
windshield
fuel tank
clutch lever
dashboard
turn signal
headlight
handgrip
front fender
telescopic front fork
fairing
brake caliper
rim
disk brake
carburetor
spoiler
engine

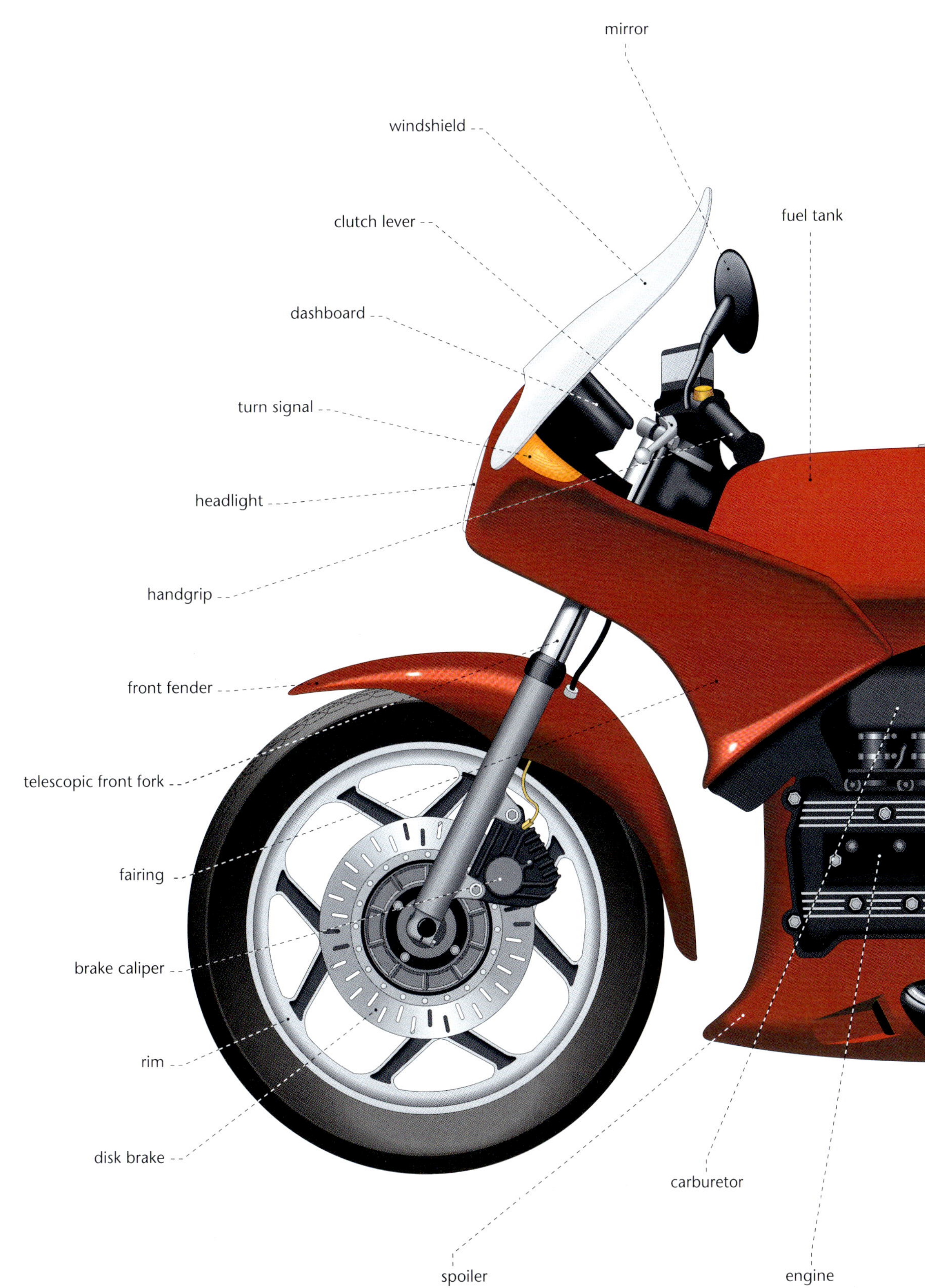

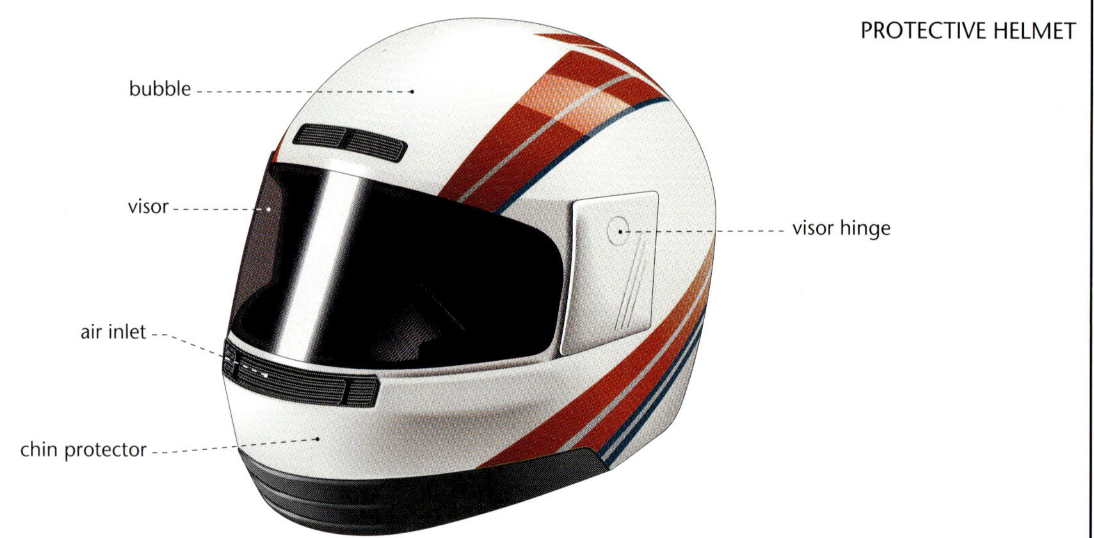

PROTECTIVE HELMET

bubble
visor
visor hinge
air inlet
chin protector

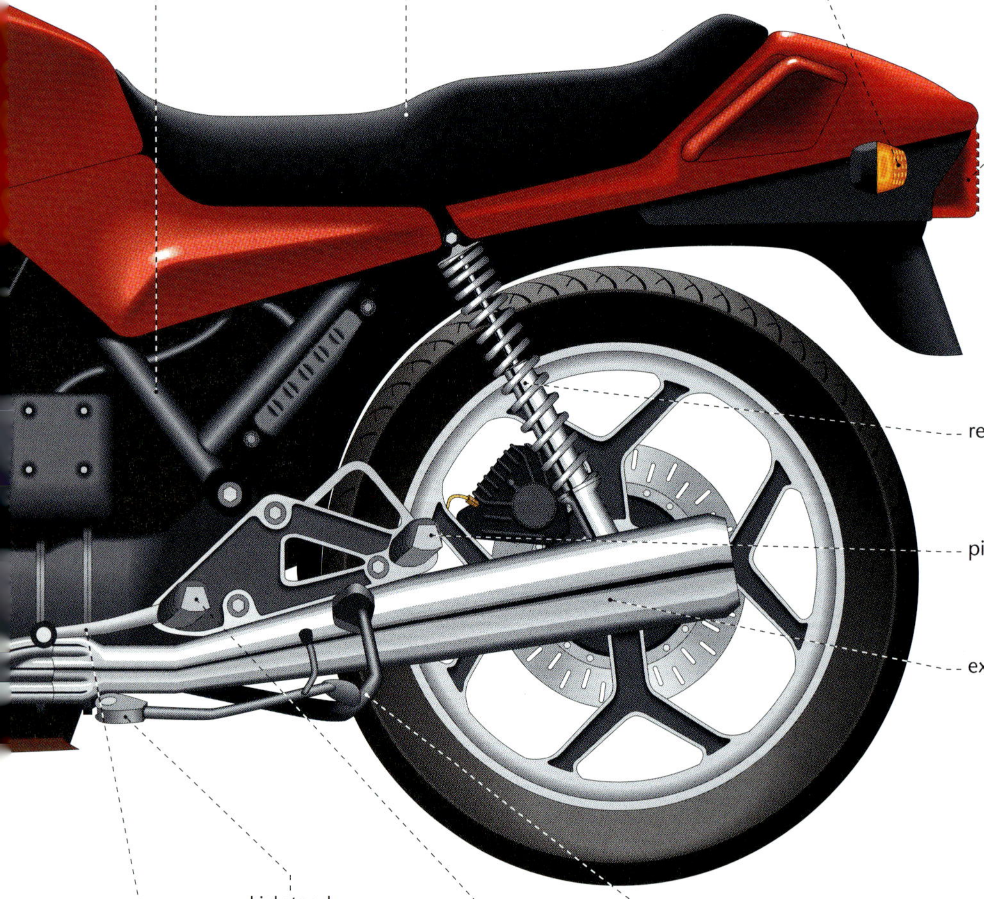
frame
dual seat
turn signal
taillight
rear shock absorber
pillion footrest
exhaust pipe
kickstand
main stand
gearshift lever
front footrest

VIEW FROM ABOVE

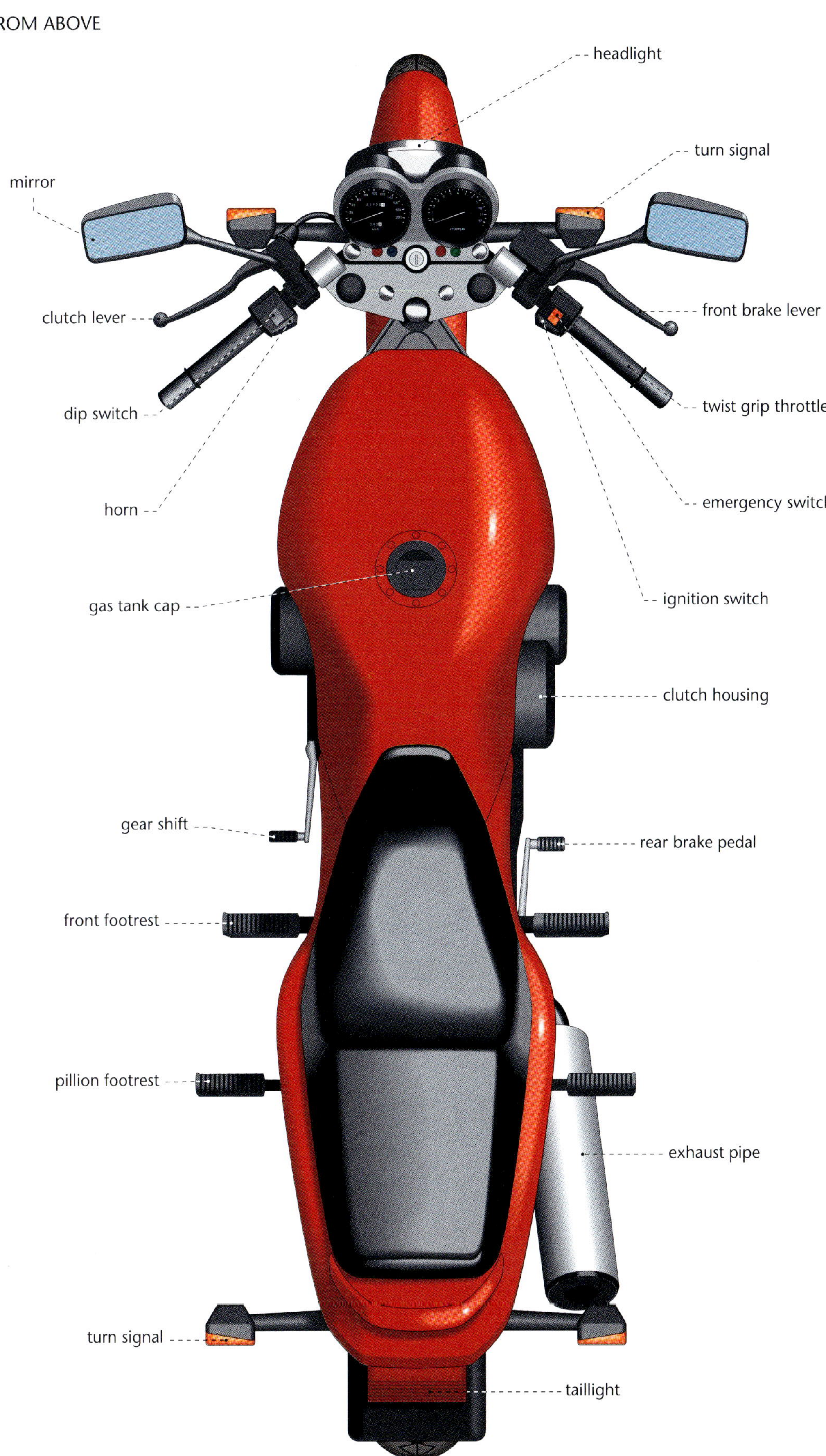

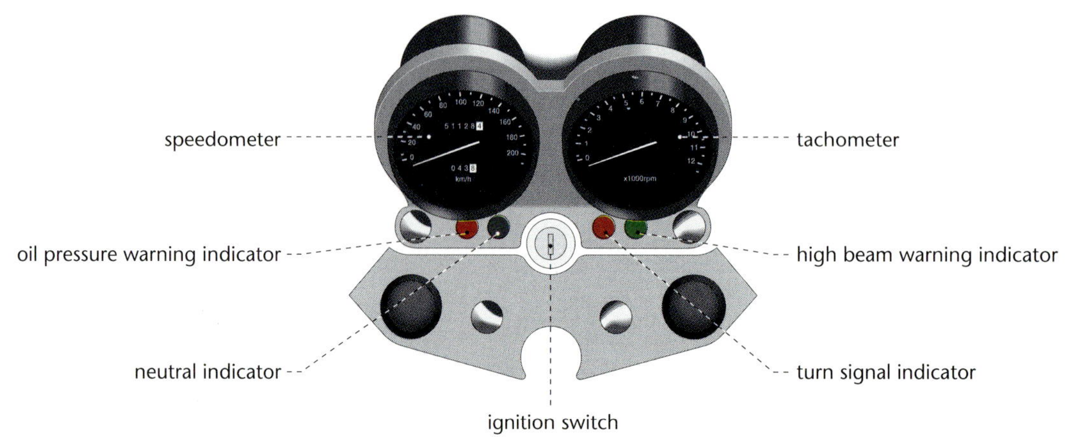

MOTORCYCLE DASHBOARD
speedometer
tachometer
oil pressure warning indicator
high beam warning indicator
neutral indicator
turn signal indicator
ignition switch

SNOWMOBILE
rear bumper
seat
handlebars
luggage rack
brake handle
windshield
backrest
cab
headlight
idler wheel
track
reflector
body
sprocket
footboard
air scoop
snow guard
shock absorber
ski

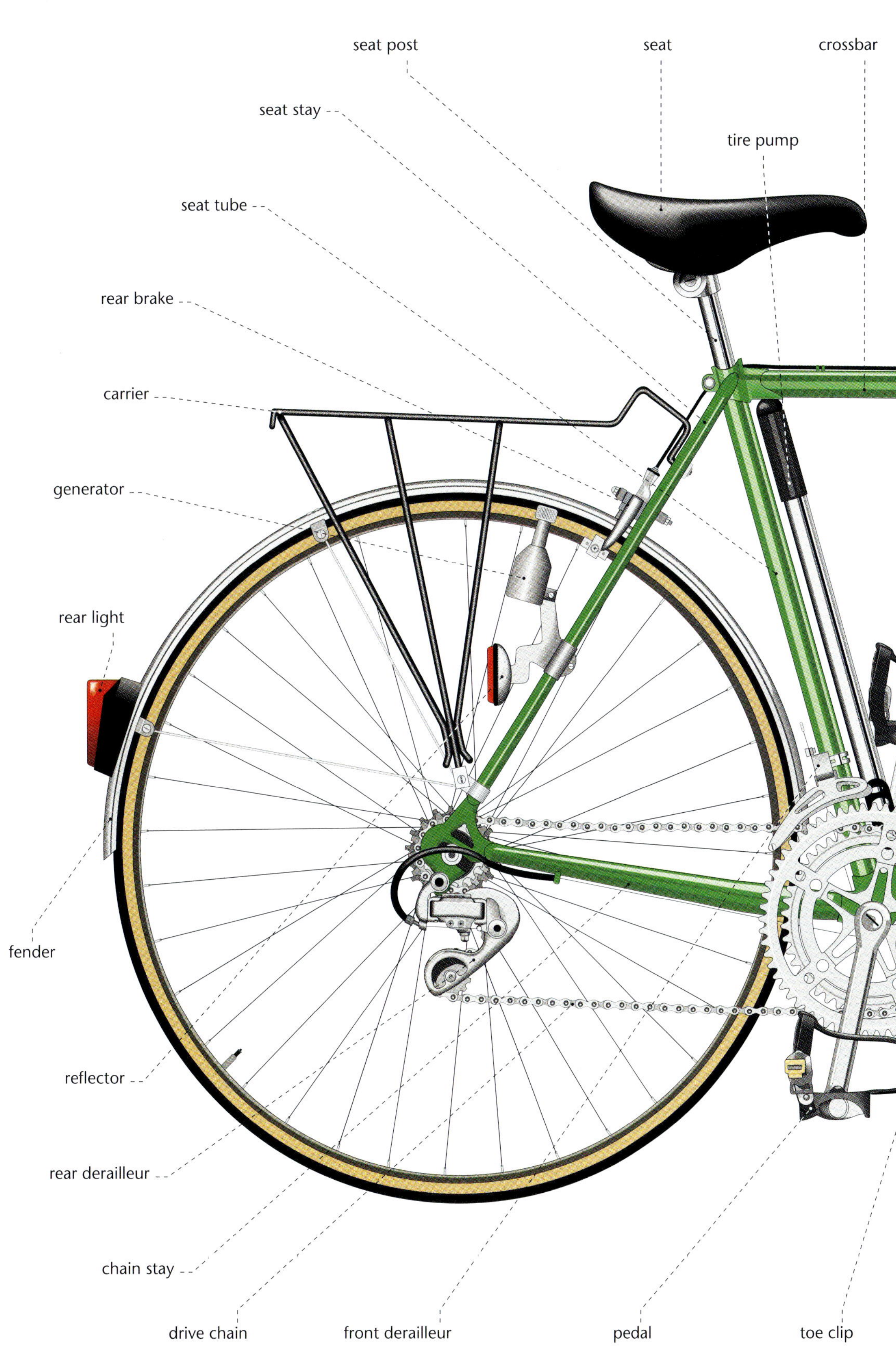
seat post
seat stay
seat tube
rear brake
carrier
generator
rear light
fender
reflector
rear derailleur
chain stay
drive chain
front derailleur
seat
crossbar
tire pump
pedal
toe clip

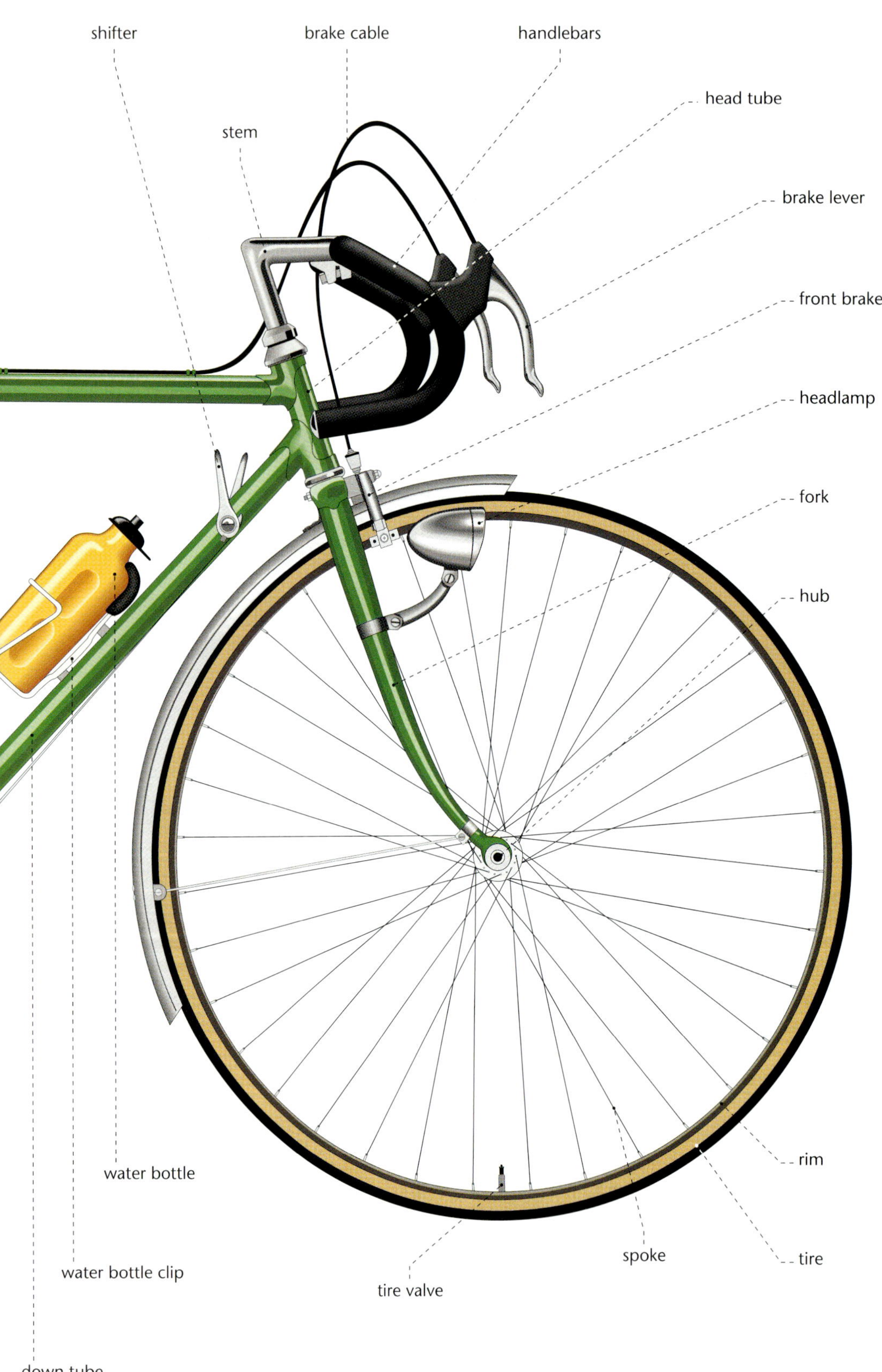

shifter
brake cable
handlebars
stem
head tube
brake lever
front brake
headlamp
fork
hub
water bottle
rim
water bottle clip
spoke
tire
tire valve
down tube

POWER TRAIN

ACCESSORIES

ROAD TRANSPORT

MOTOR HOME

CROSS SECTION OF A ROAD

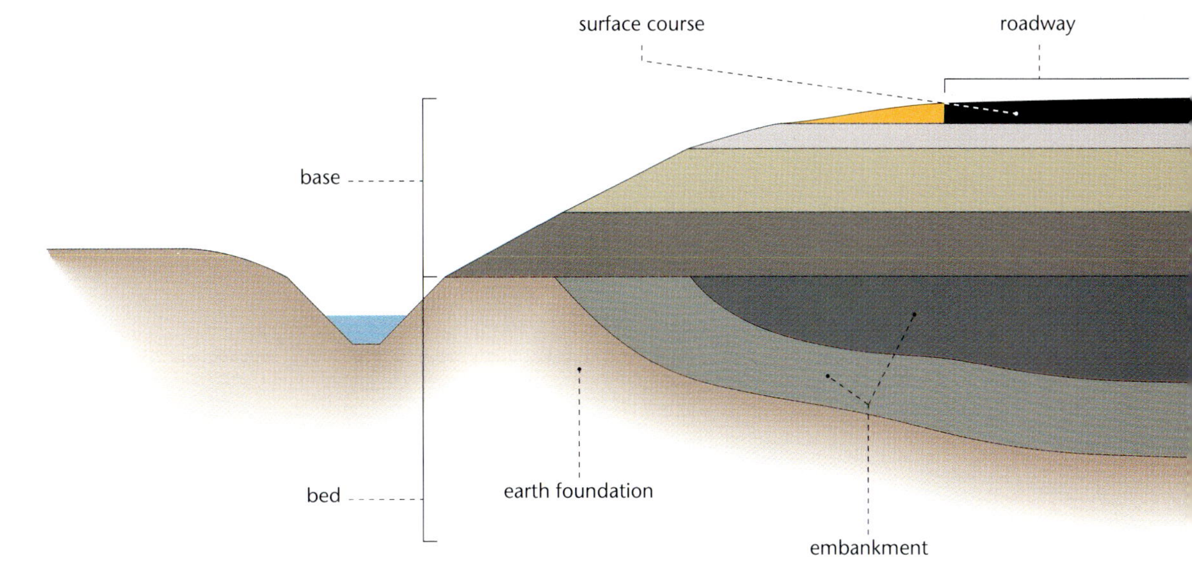

MAJOR TYPES OF INTERCHANGES

cloverleaf

traffic circle

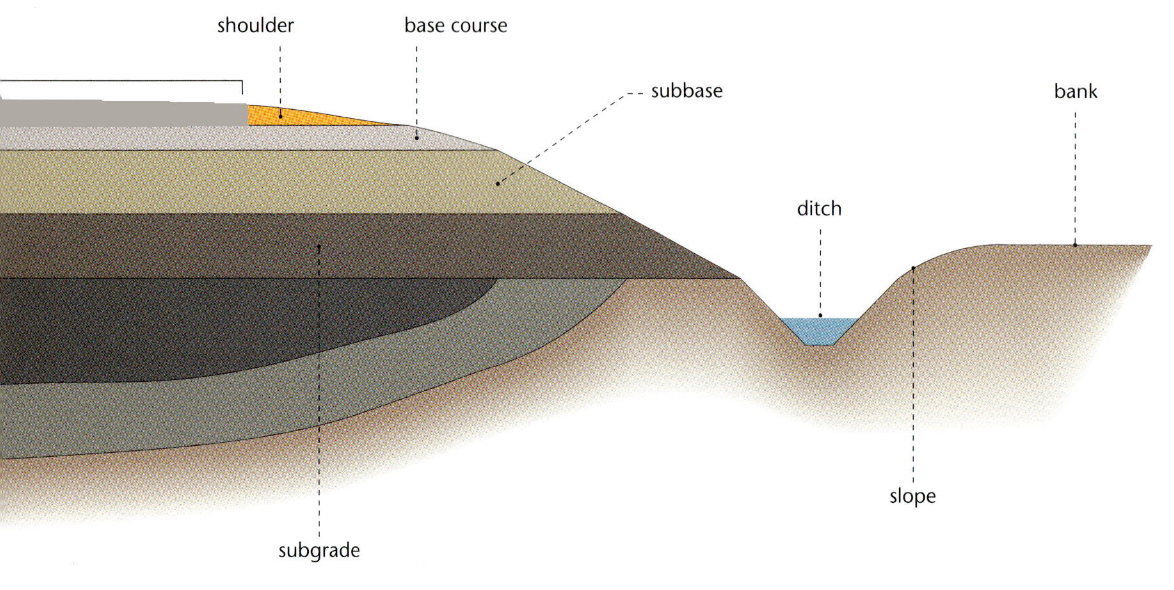

diamond interchange

trumpet interchange

ROAD TRANSPORT

CLOVERLEAF

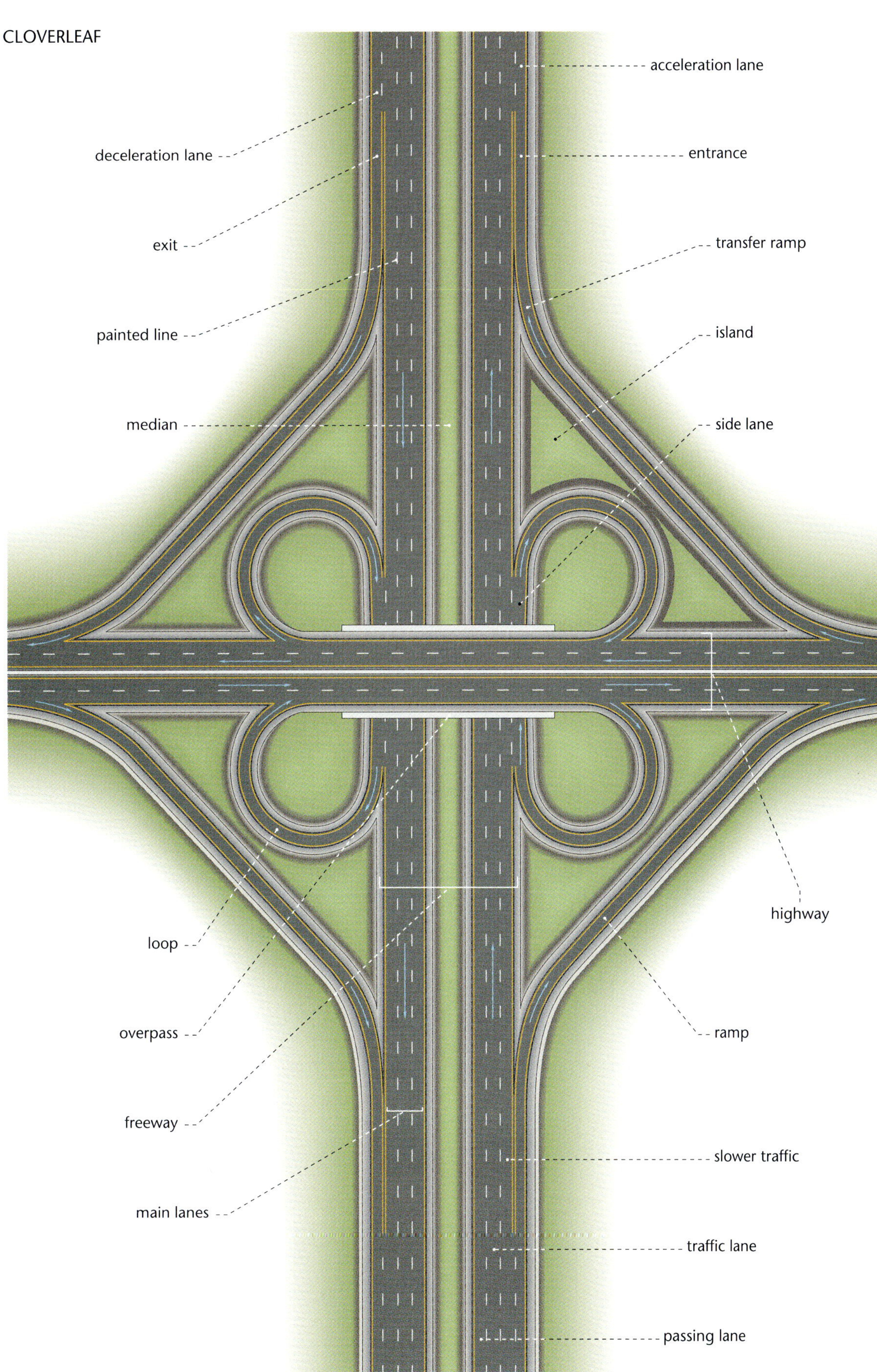

GASOLINE PUMP

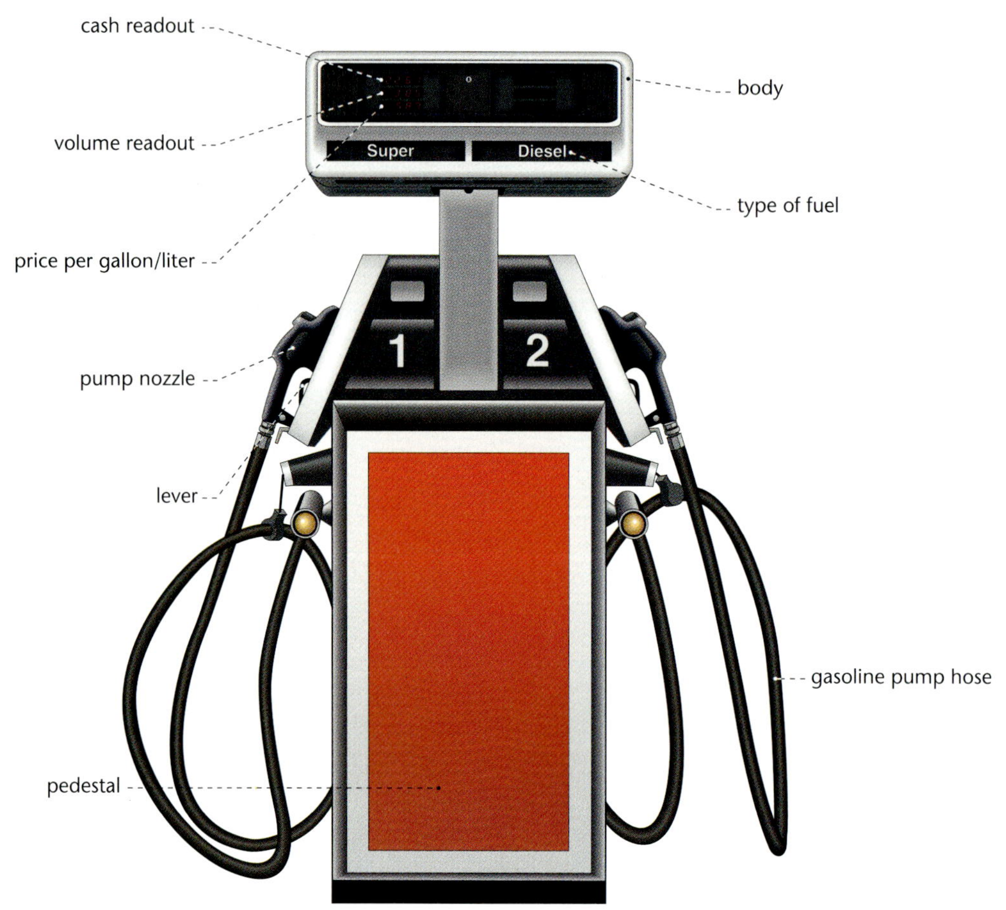

SERVICE STATION

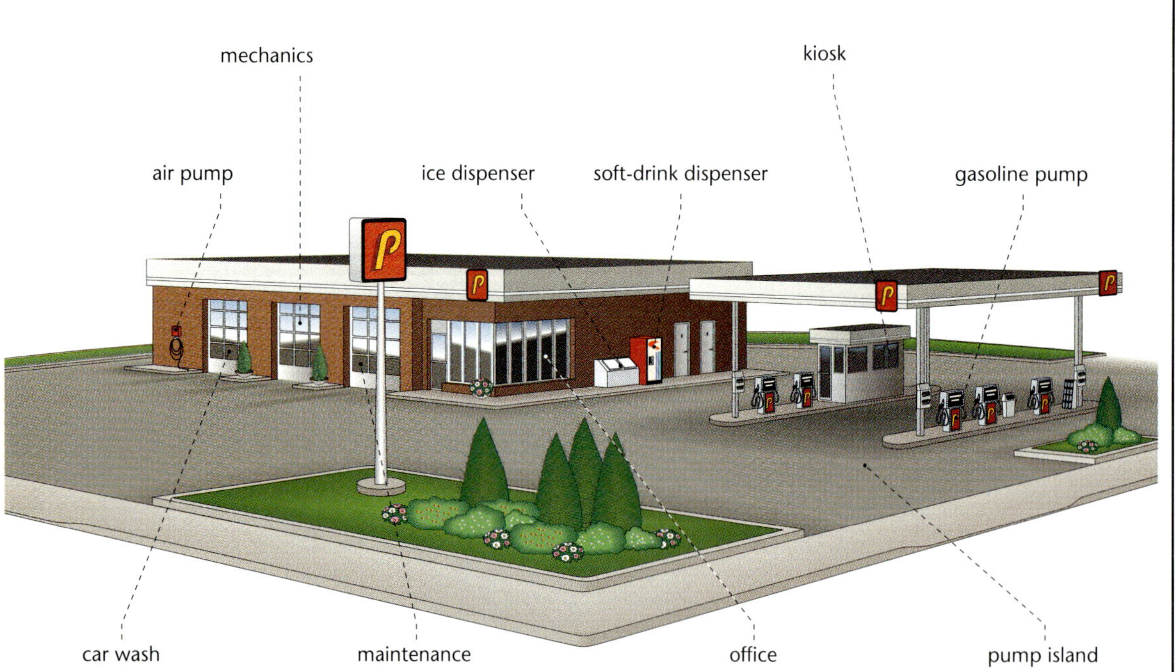

ROAD TRANSPORT

BEAM BRIDGE

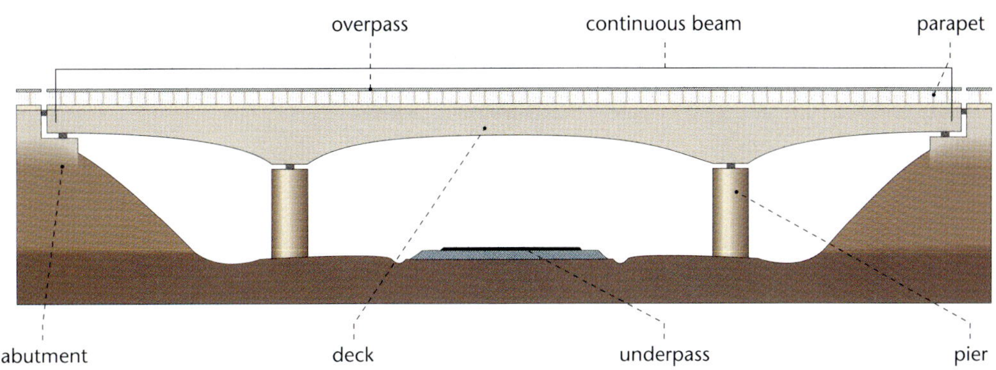

TYPES OF BEAM BRIDGES

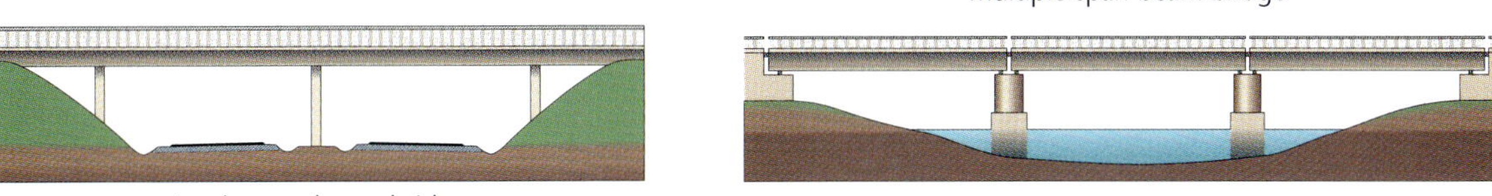

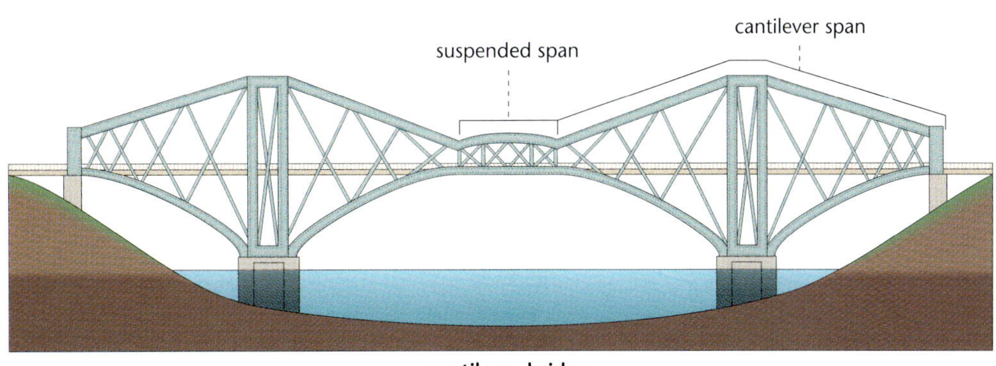

ARCH BRIDGE

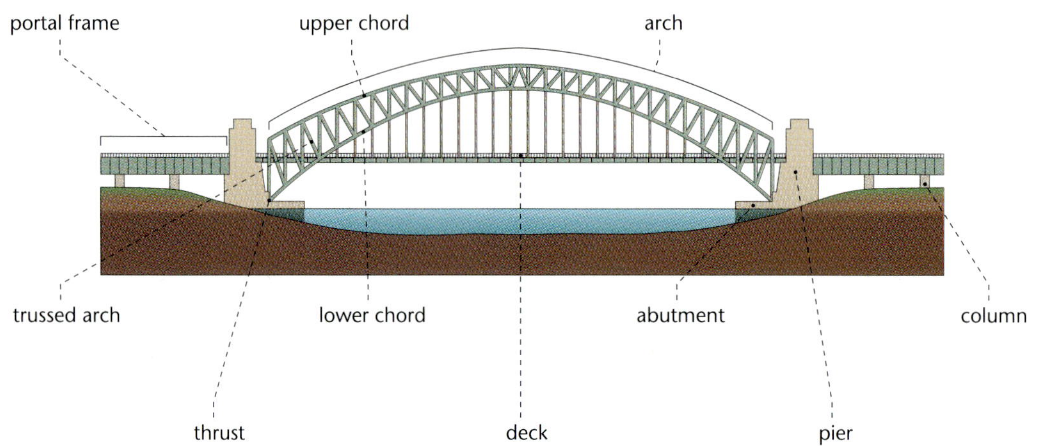

TYPES OF ARCH BRIDGES

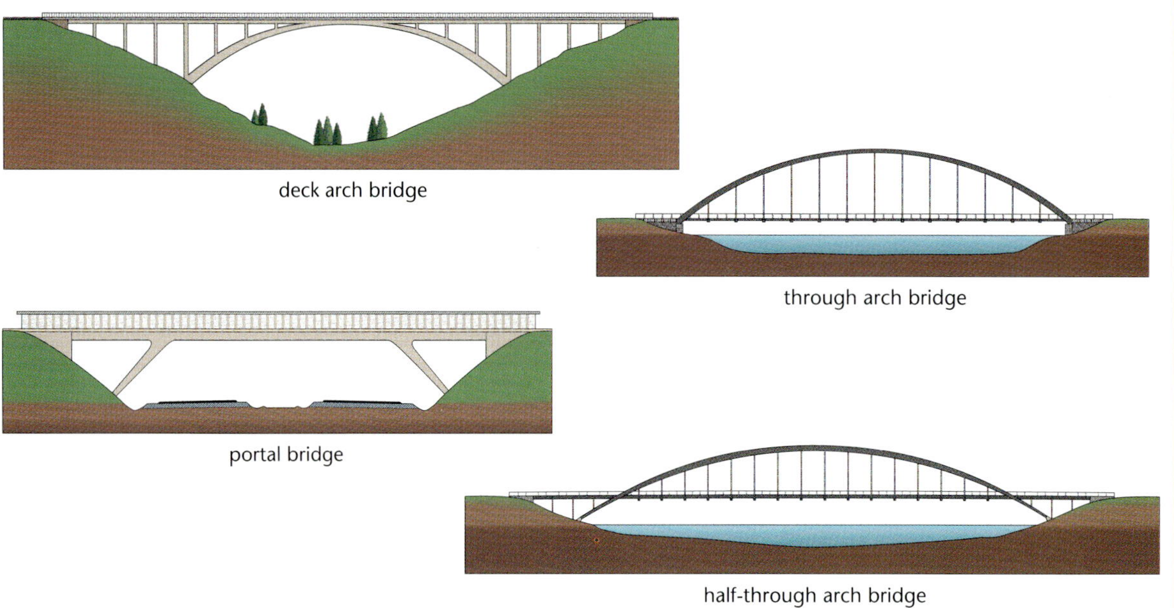

TYPES OF ARCHES

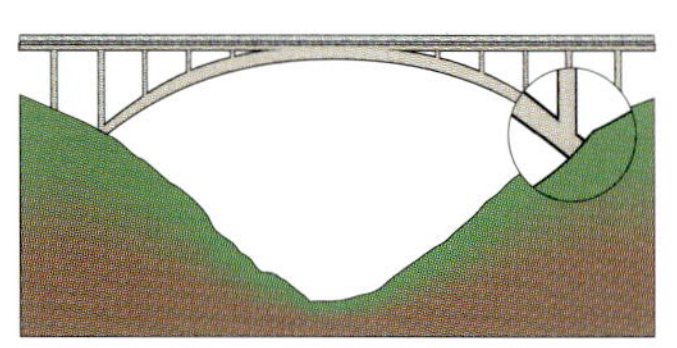

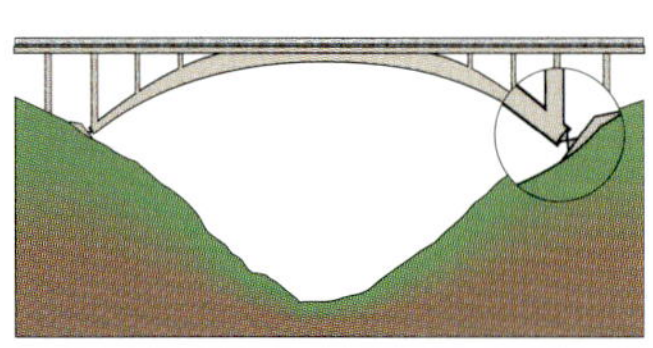

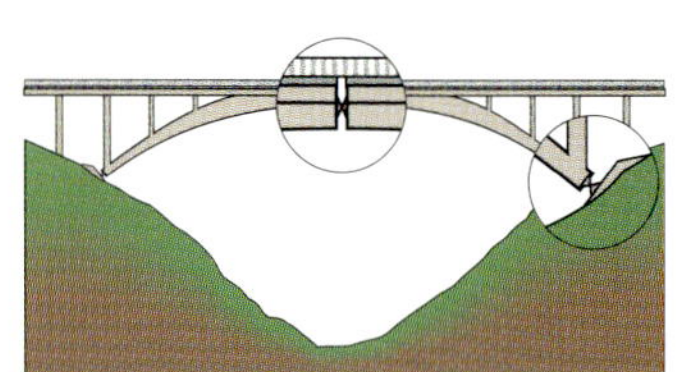

SUSPENSION BRIDGE

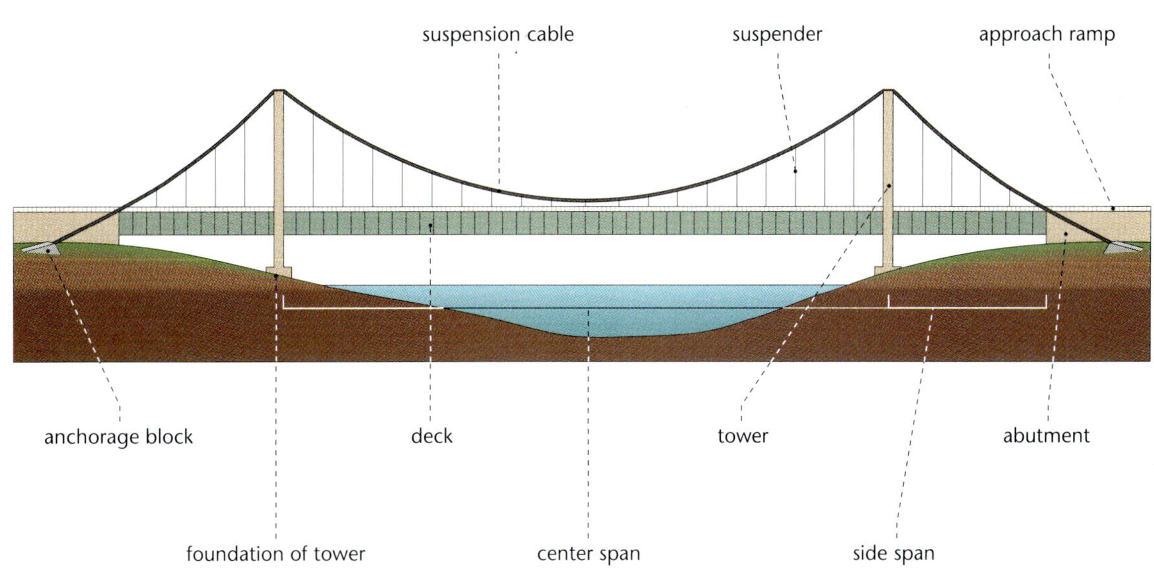

CABLE-STAYED BRIDGES

fan cable stays

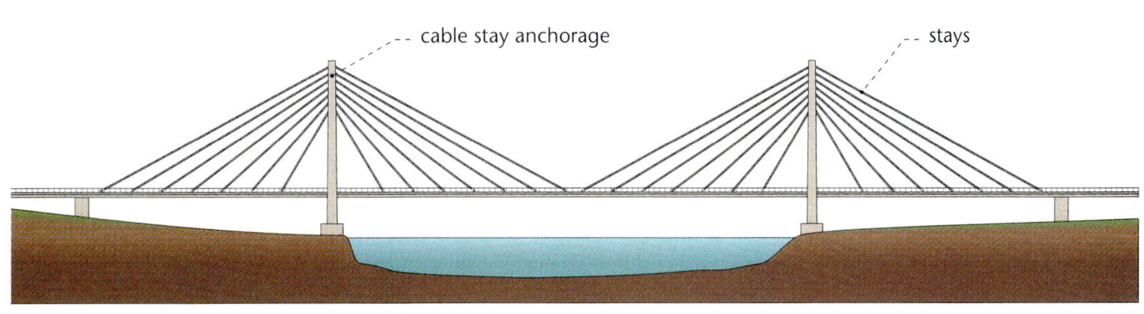

harp cable stays

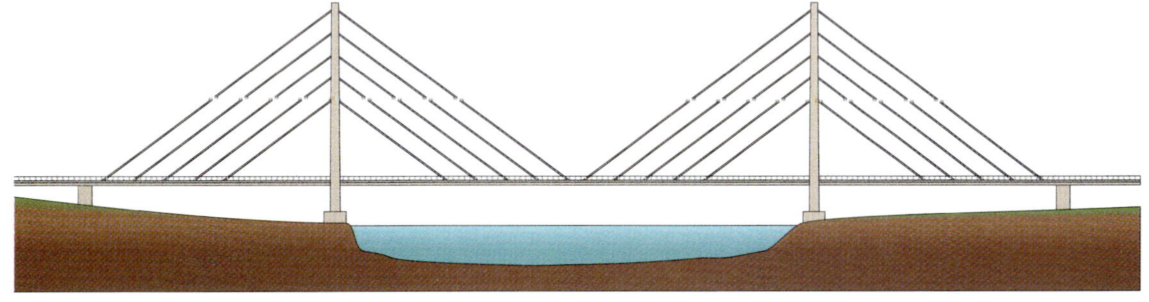

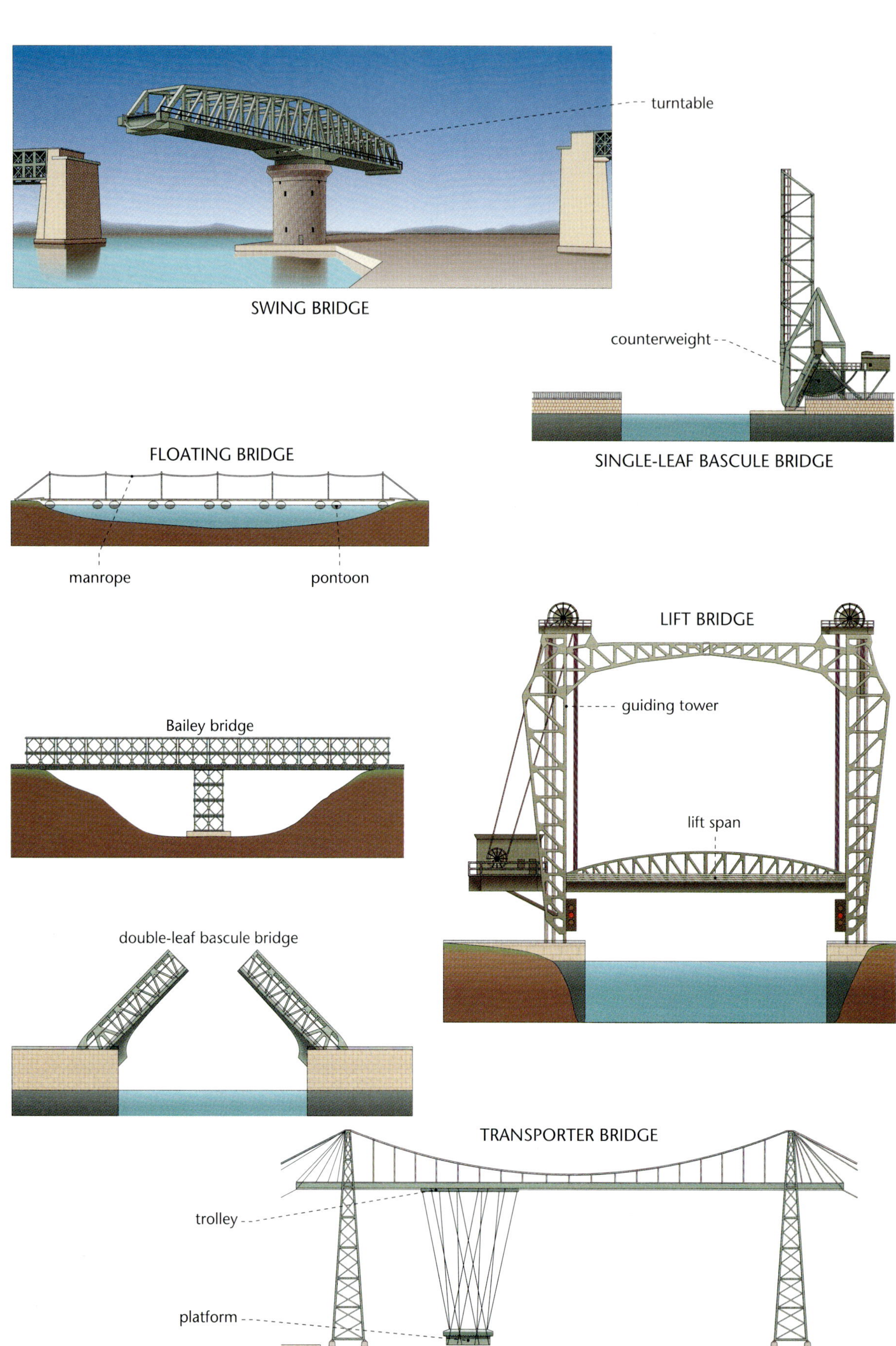
turntable
SWING BRIDGE
counterweight
SINGLE-LEAF BASCULE BRIDGE
FLOATING BRIDGE
manrope
pontoon
LIFT BRIDGE
guiding tower
lift span
Bailey bridge
double-leaf bascule bridge
TRANSPORTER BRIDGE
trolley
platform

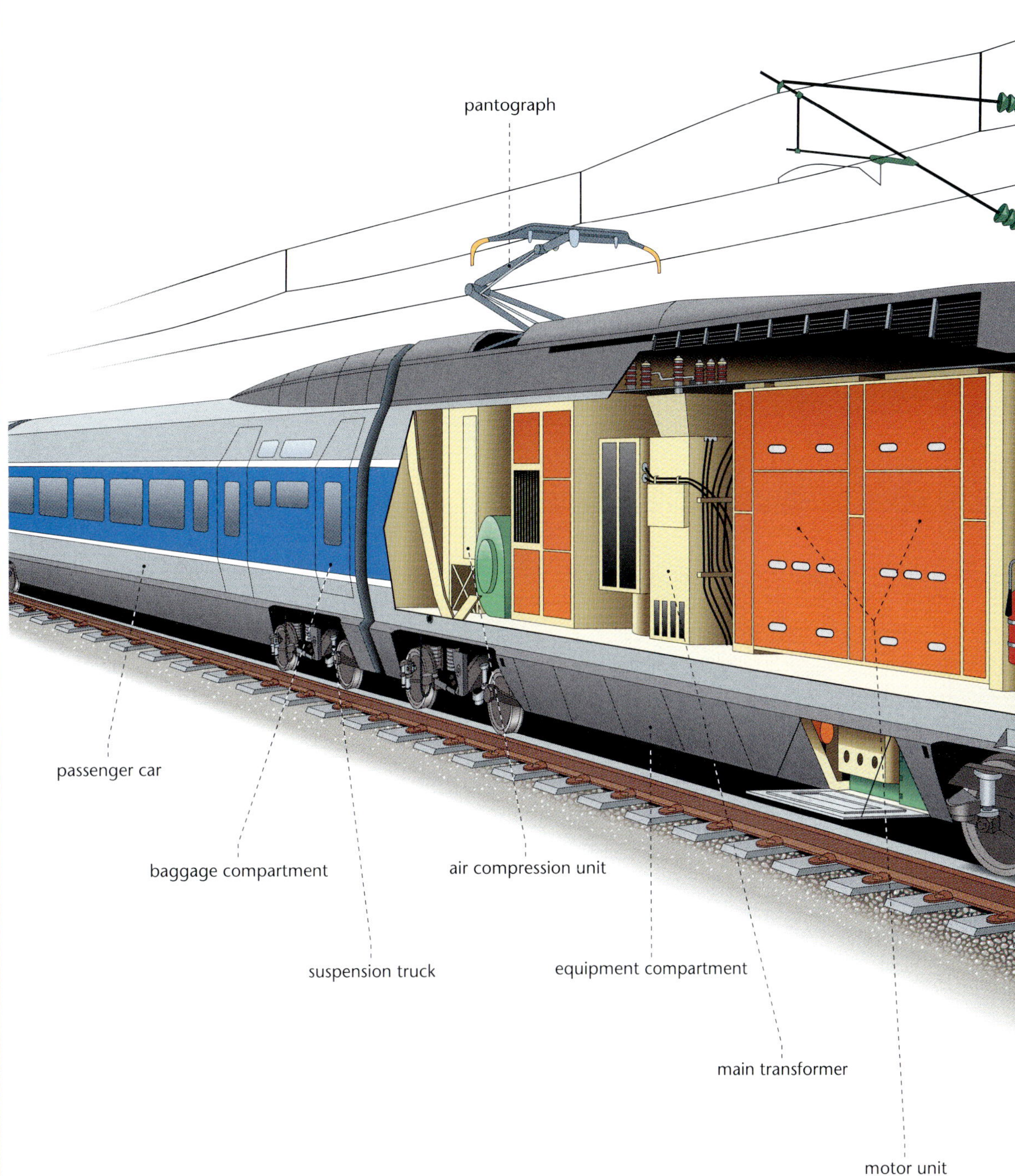

pantograph
passenger car
baggage compartment
air compression unit
suspension truck
equipment compartment
main transformer
motor unit

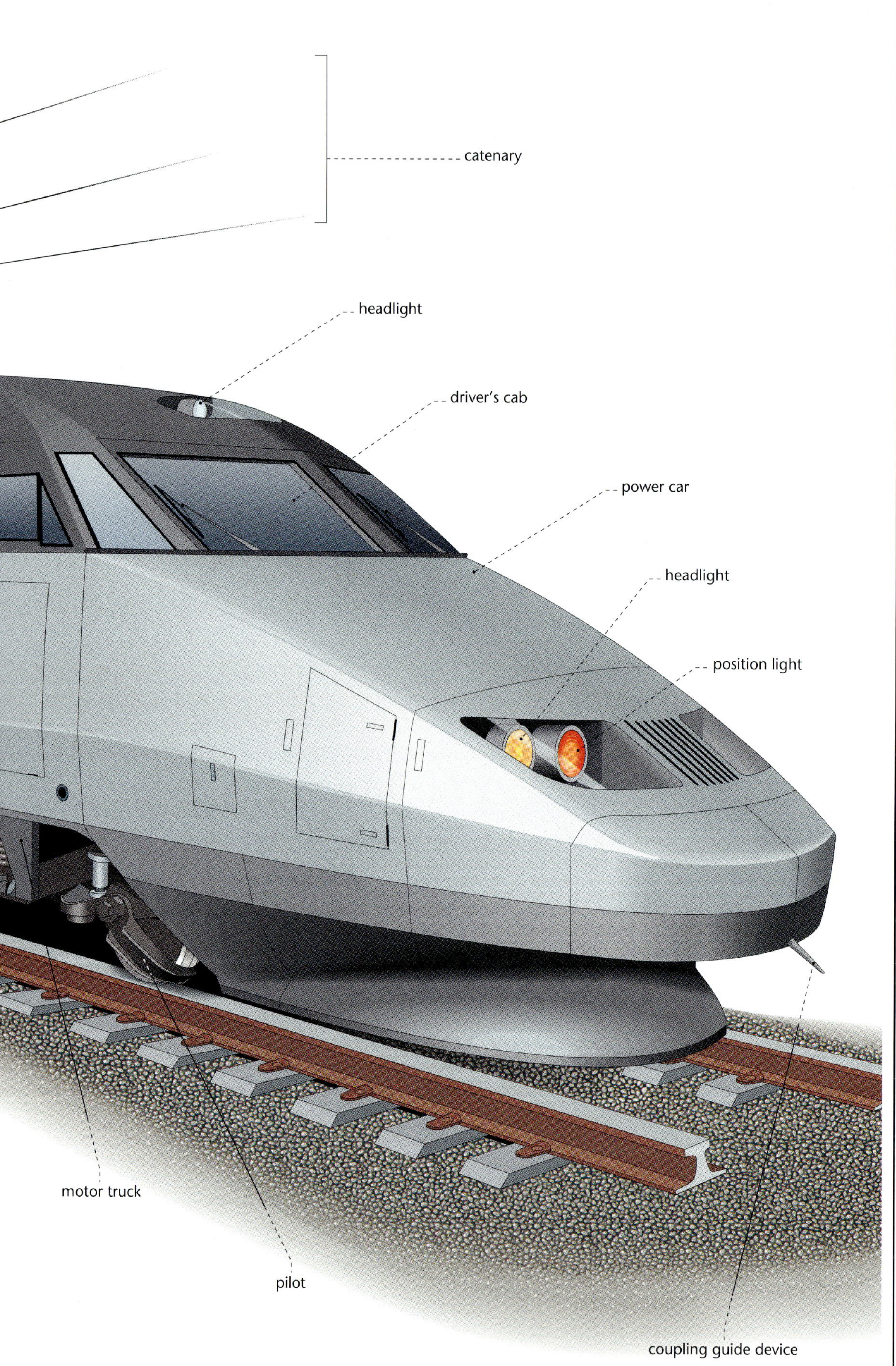

catenary
headlight
driver's cab
power car
headlight
position light
motor truck
pilot
coupling guide device

TYPES OF PASSENGER CARS

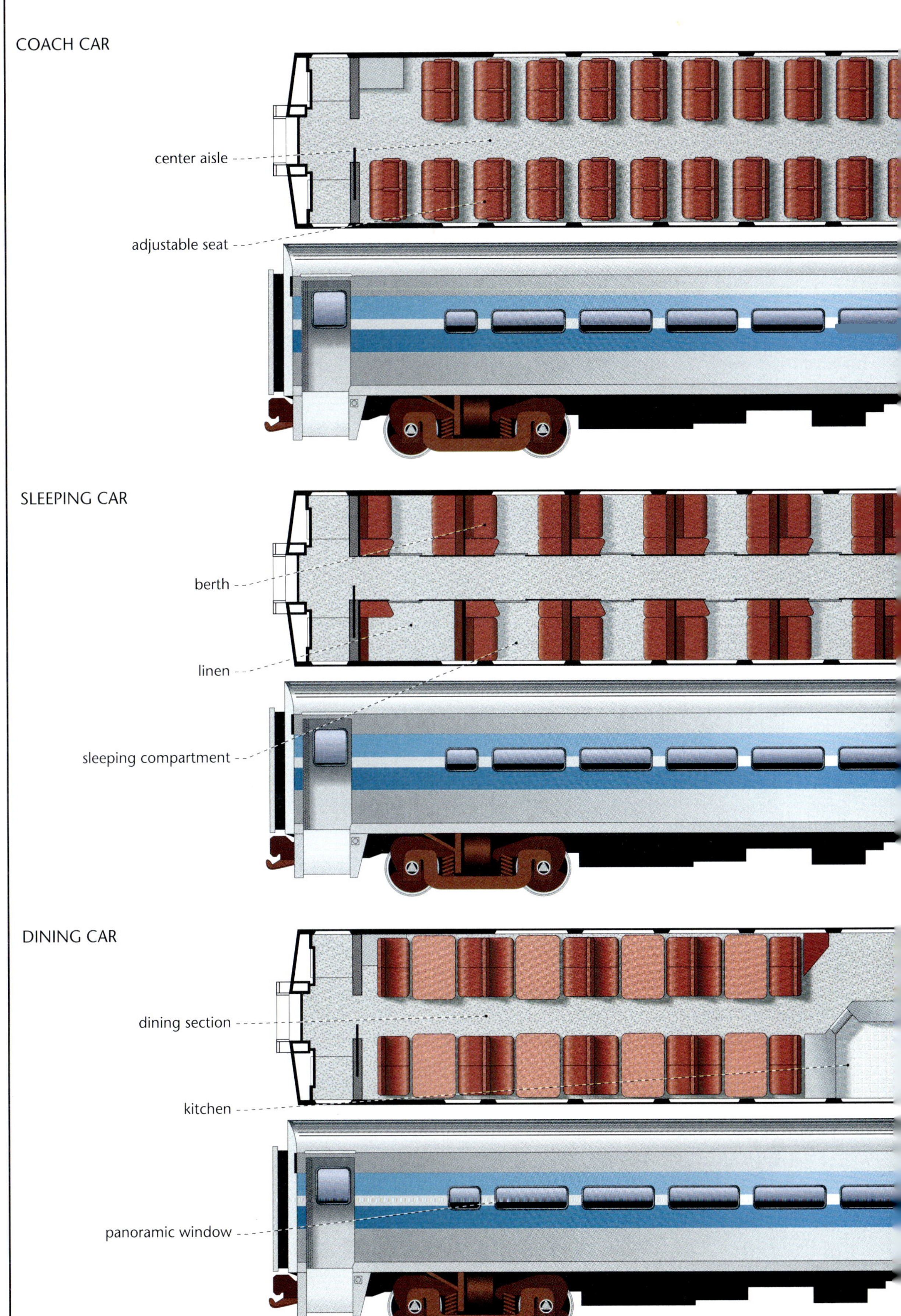

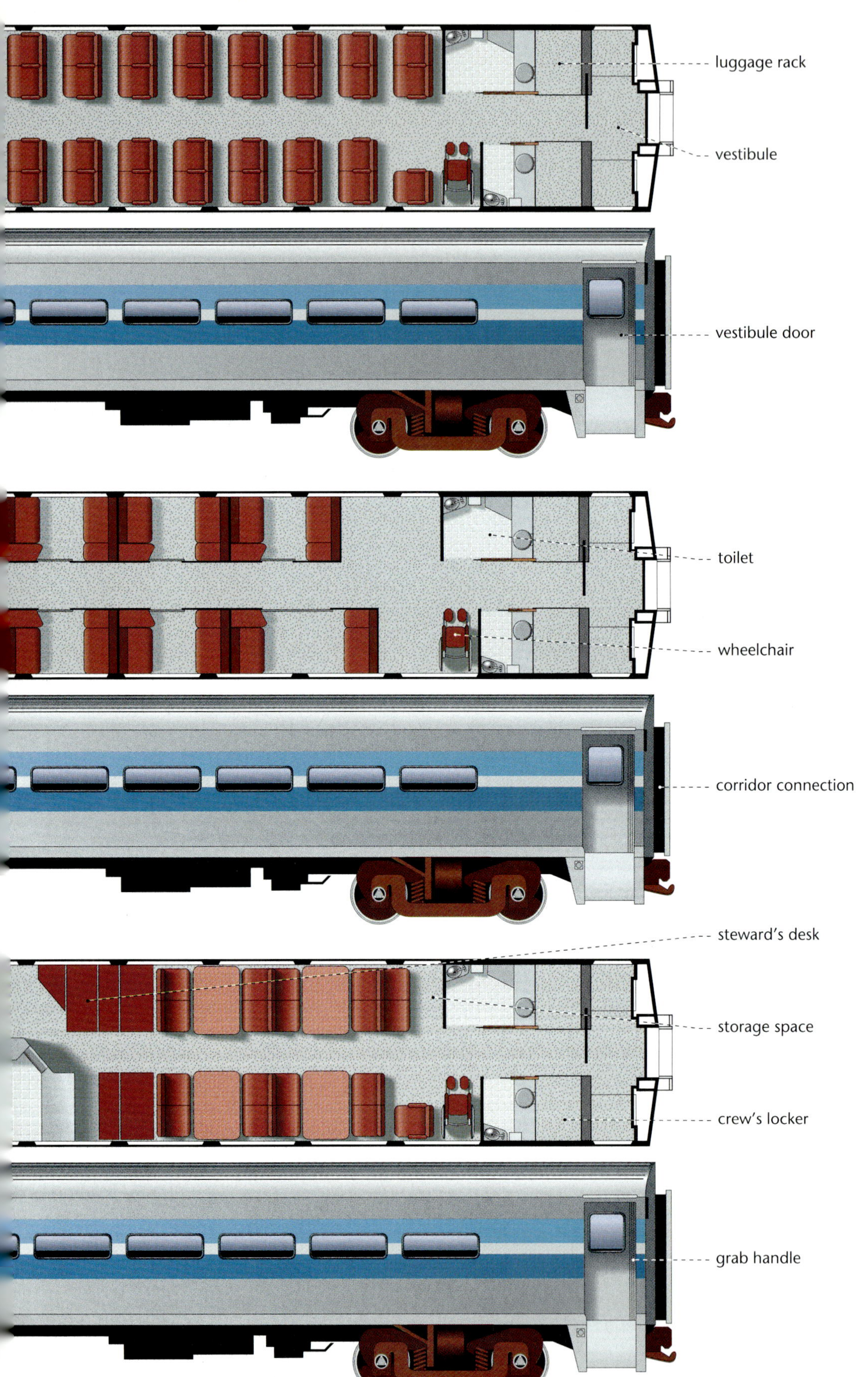
luggage rack
vestibule
vestibule door
toilet
wheelchair
corridor connection
steward's desk
storage space
crew's locker
grab handle

office
glassed roof
indicator board
parcels office
baggage room
passenger train
passenger platform
platform edge
gate
booking hall
platform number

metal structure
baggage cart
departure time indicator
ticket collector
baggage lockers
destination
platform entrance
track
schedules
ticket control

RAILROAD STATION

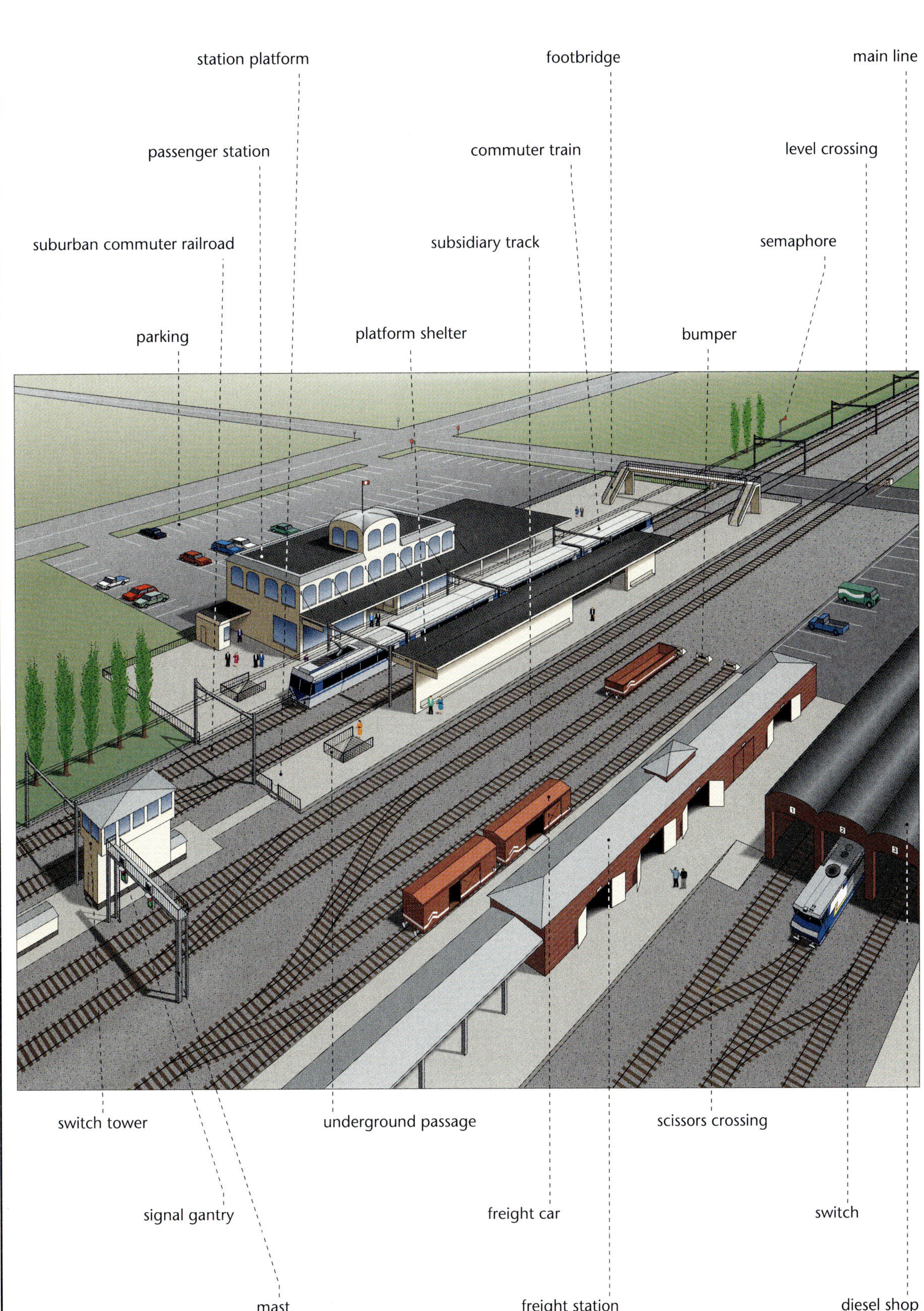

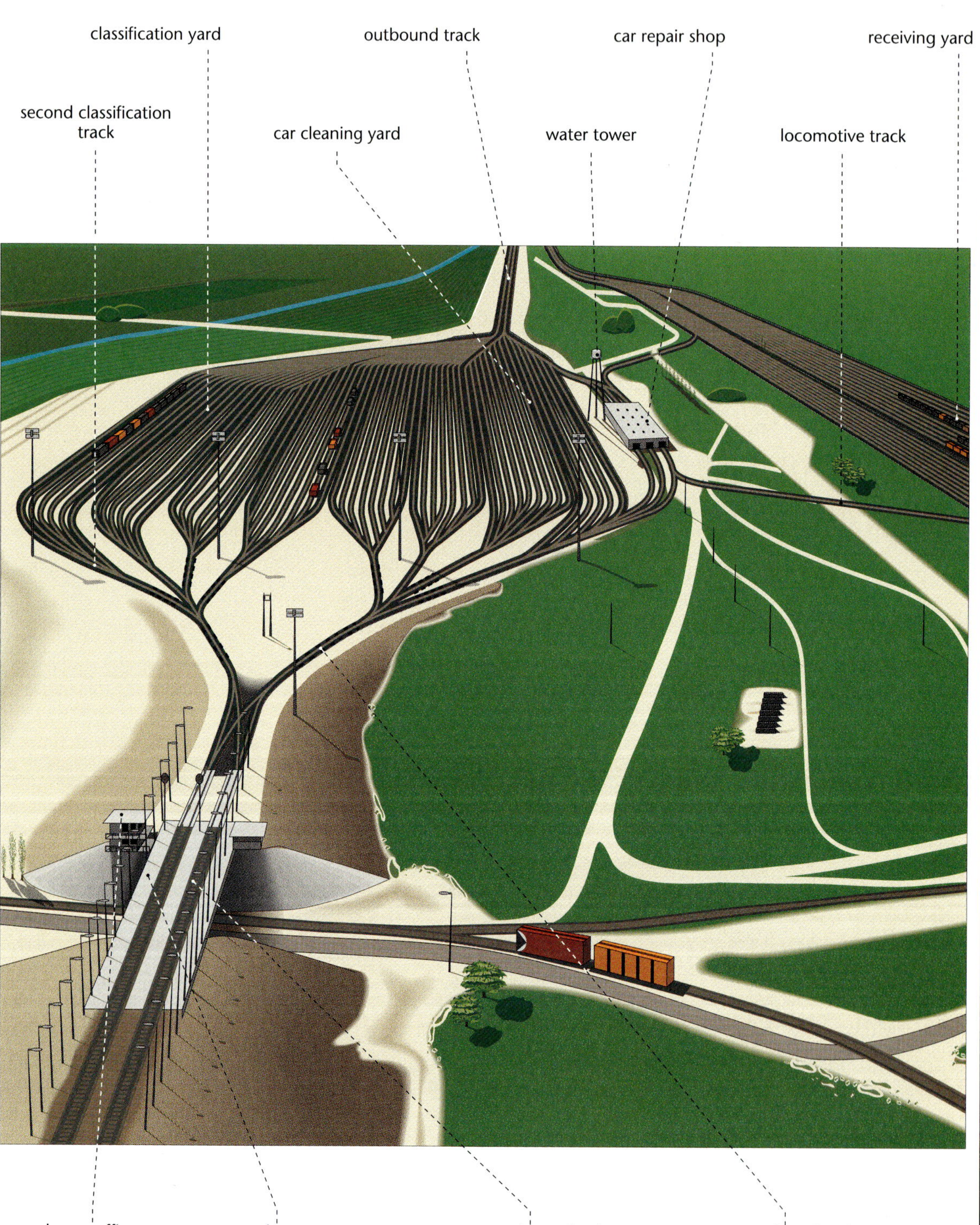
classification yard
outbound track
car repair shop
receiving yard
second classification track
car cleaning yard
water tower
locomotive track
hump office
hump
hump lead
first classification track

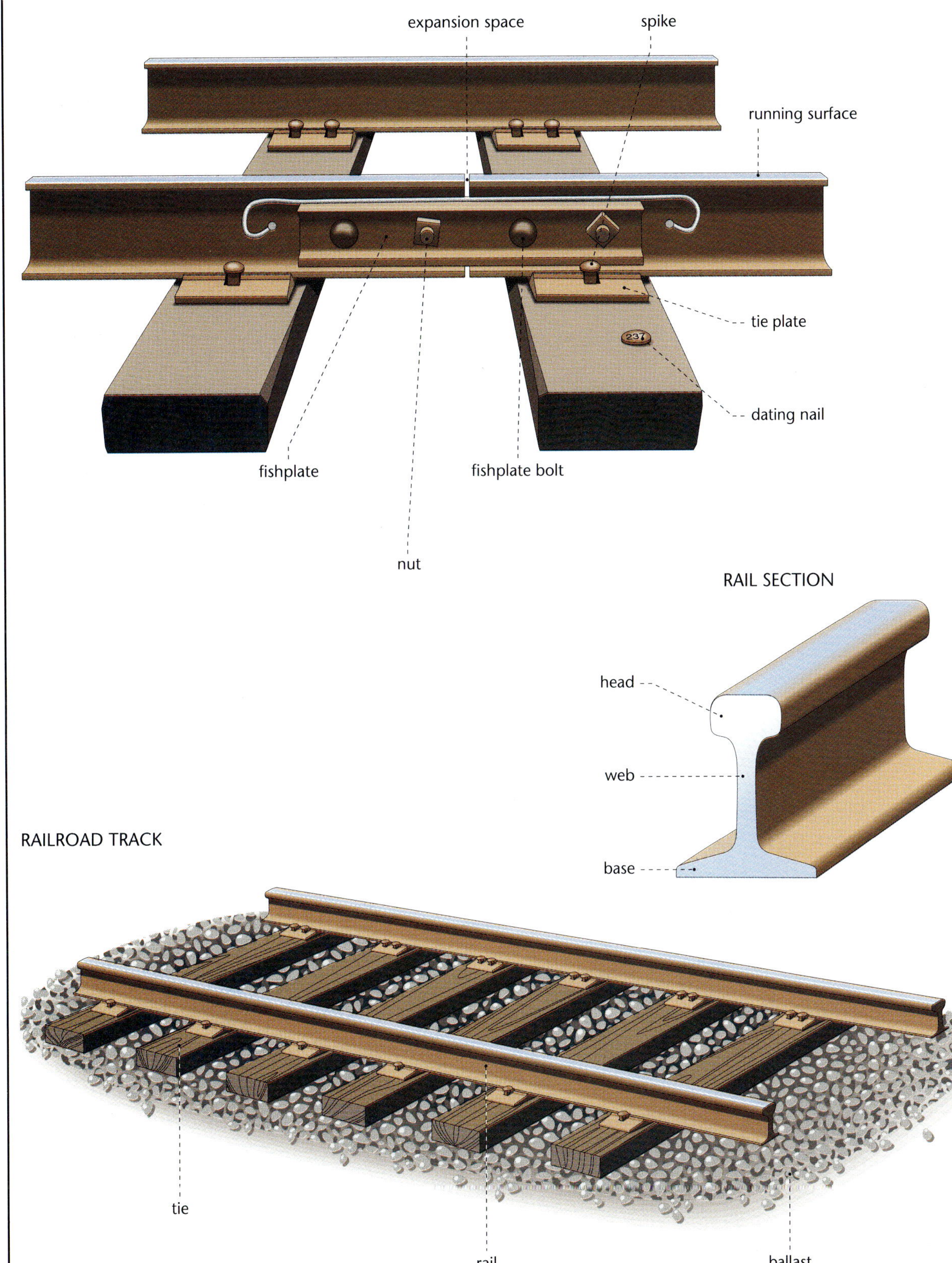

RAIL JOINT
expansion space
spike
running surface
tie plate
237
dating nail
fishplate
fishplate bolt
nut
RAIL SECTION
head
web
base
RAILROAD TRACK
tie
rail
ballast

REMOTE-CONTROLLED SWITCH

MANUALLY-OPERATED SWITCH

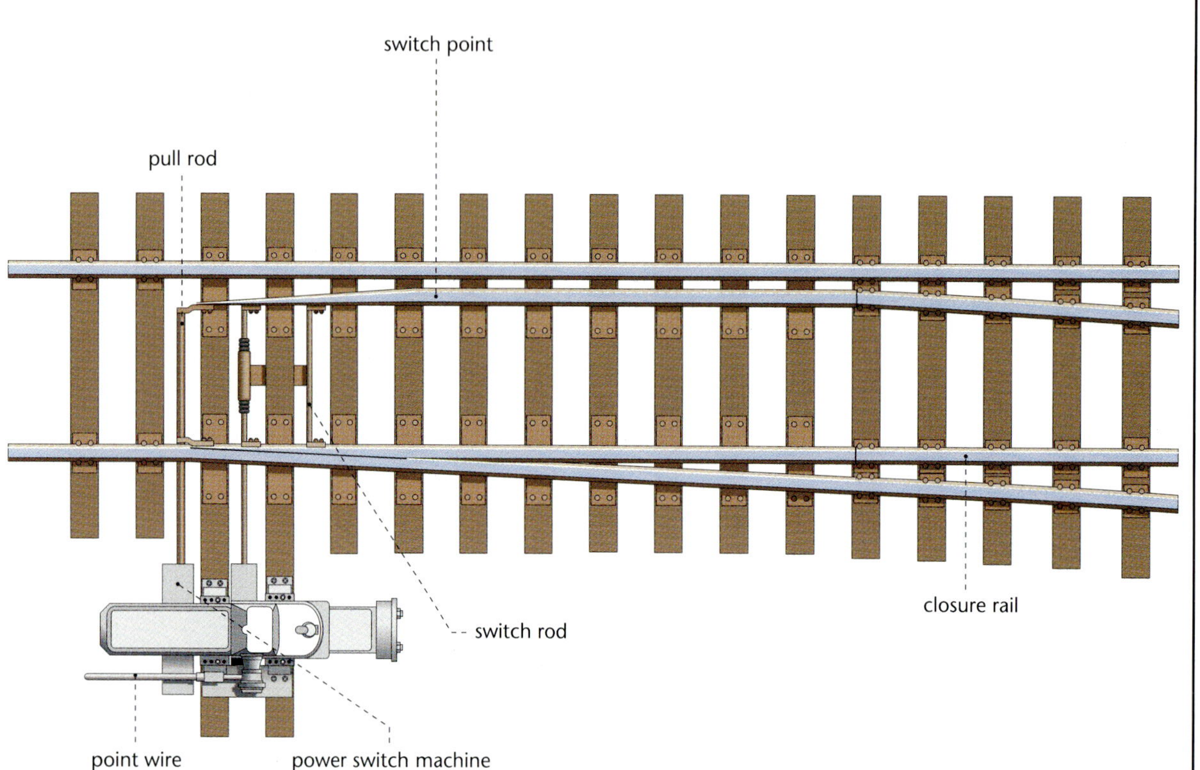

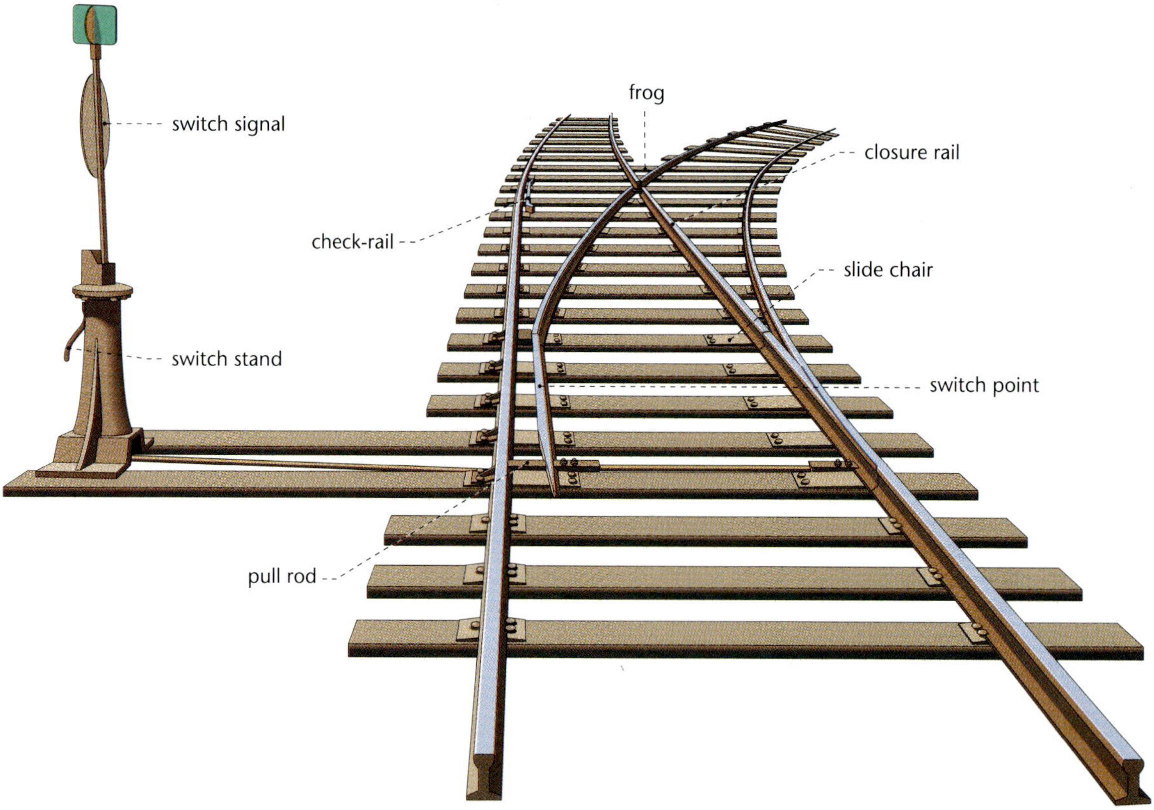

DIESEL-ELECTRIC LOCOMOTIVE

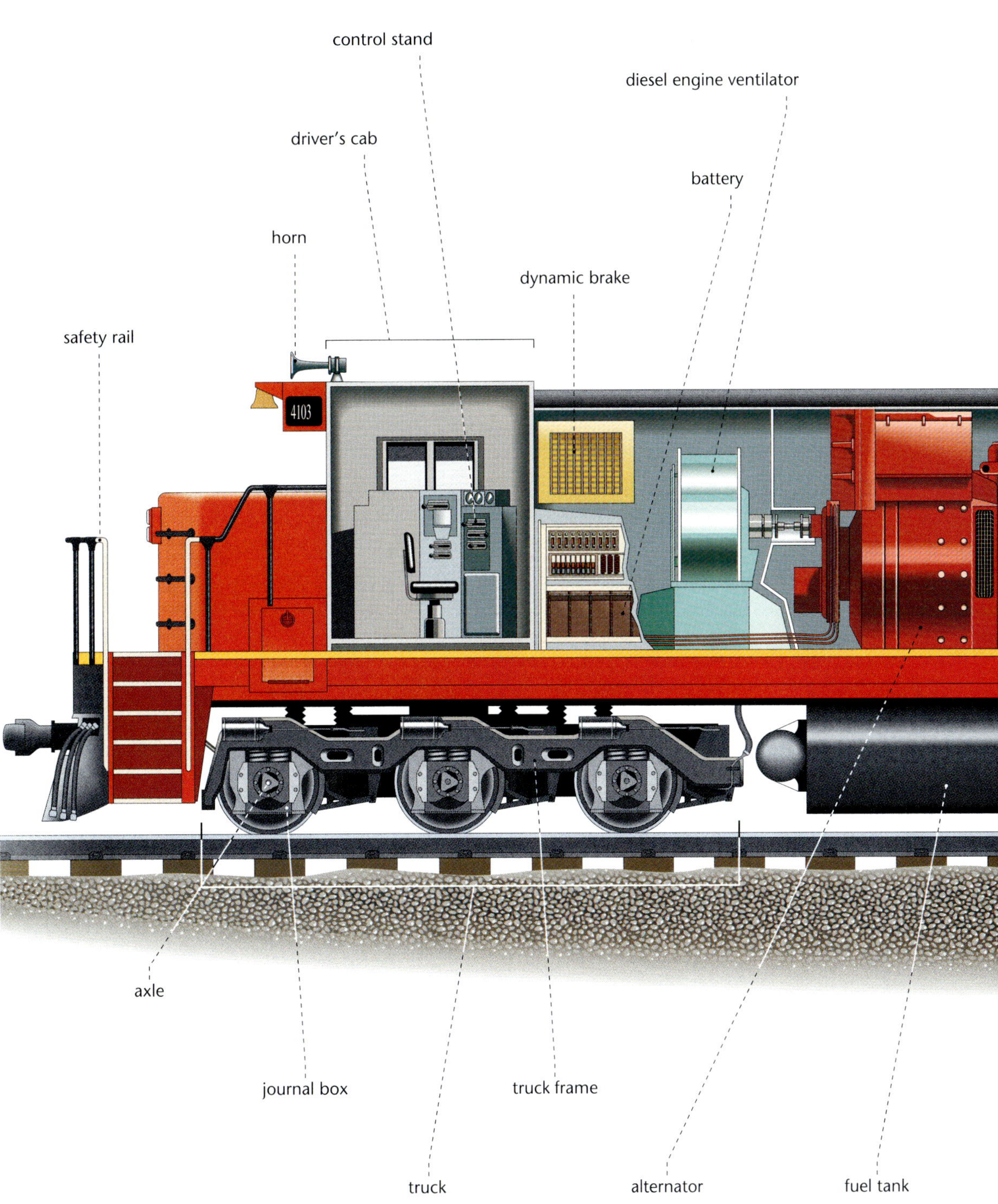

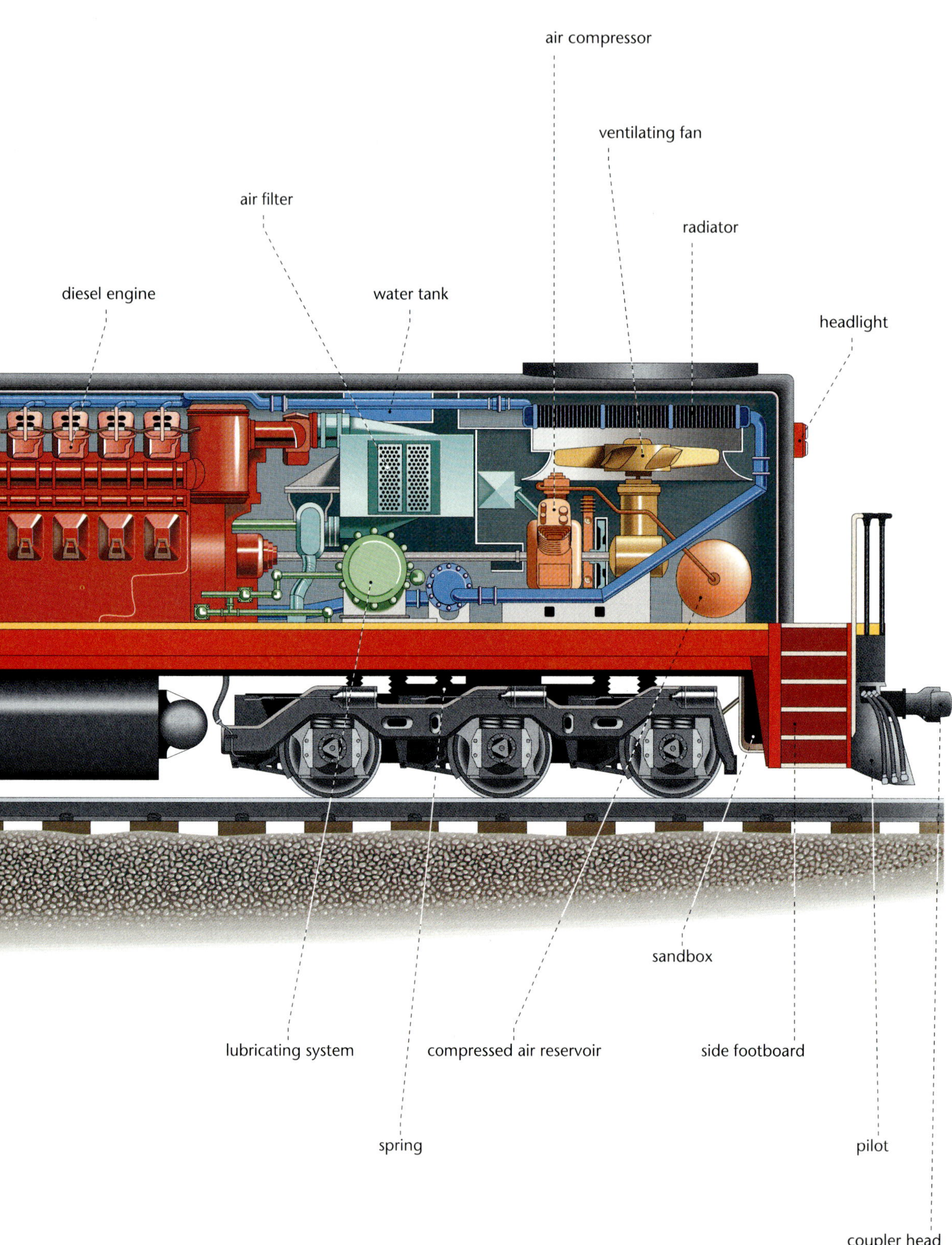

air compressor
ventilating fan
radiator
air filter
water tank
headlight
diesel engine
sandbox
lubricating system
compressed air reservoir
side footboard
spring
pilot
coupler head

RAIL TRANSPORT

BOX CAR

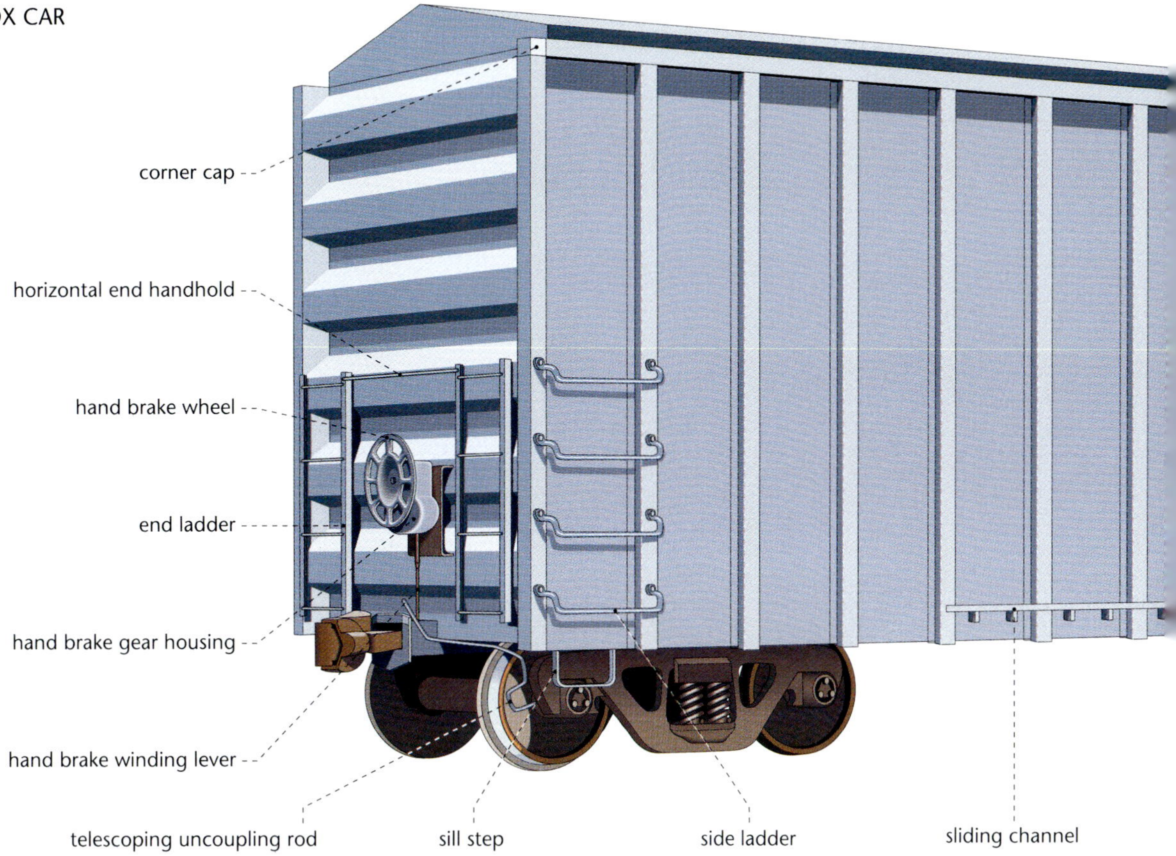

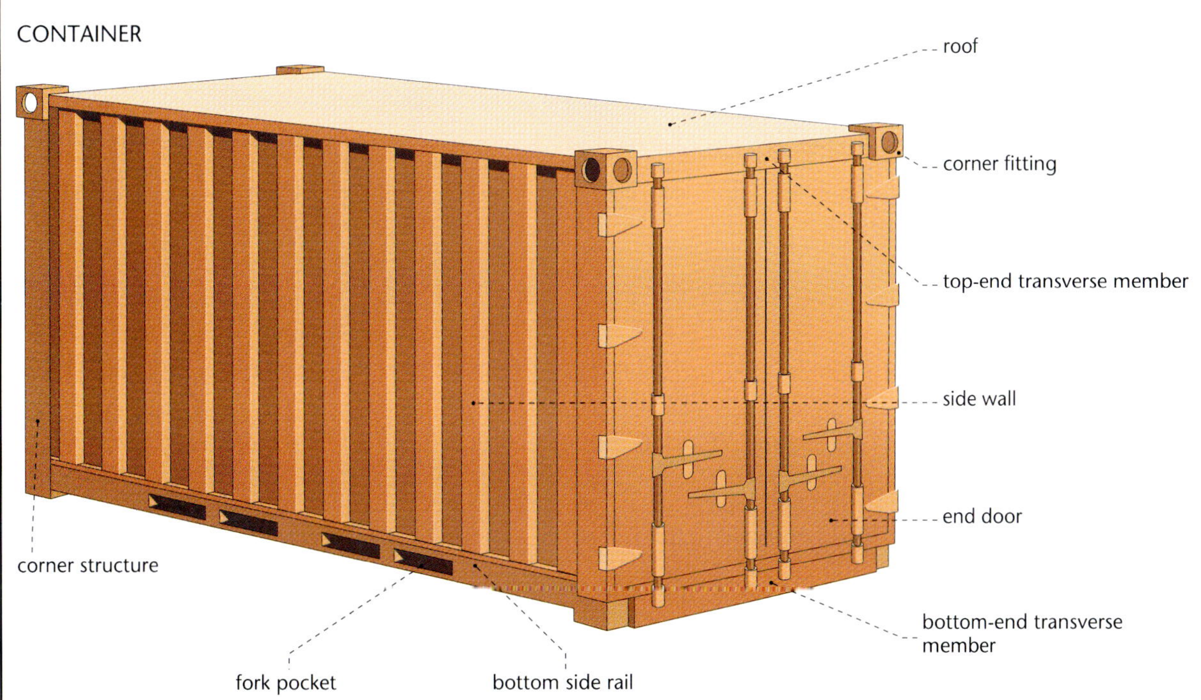

CONTAINER

RAIL TRANSPORT

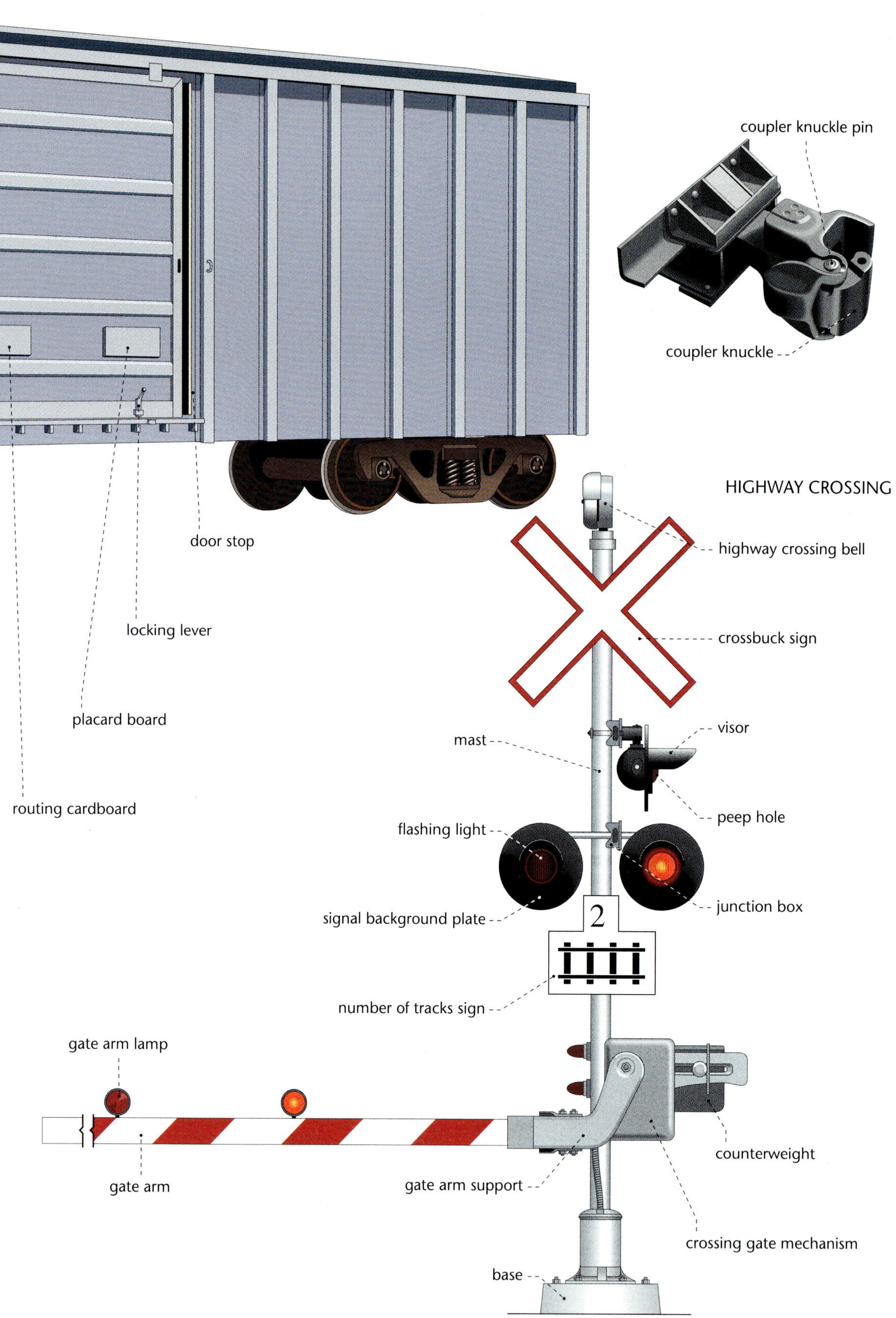
coupler knuckle pin
coupler knuckle
door stop
locking lever
placard board
routing cardboard
HIGHWAY CROSSING
highway crossing bell
crossbuck sign
mast
visor
peep hole
flashing light
junction box
signal background plate
2
number of tracks sign
gate arm lamp
counterweight
gate arm
gate arm support
crossing gate mechanism
base

TYPES OF FREIGHT CARS

box car

tank car

wood chip car

livestock car

hopper car

hard top gondola

hopper ore car

refrigerator car

automobile car

container car

piggyback car

flat car

bulkhead flat car

gondola car

depressed-center flat car

caboose

SUBWAY STATION

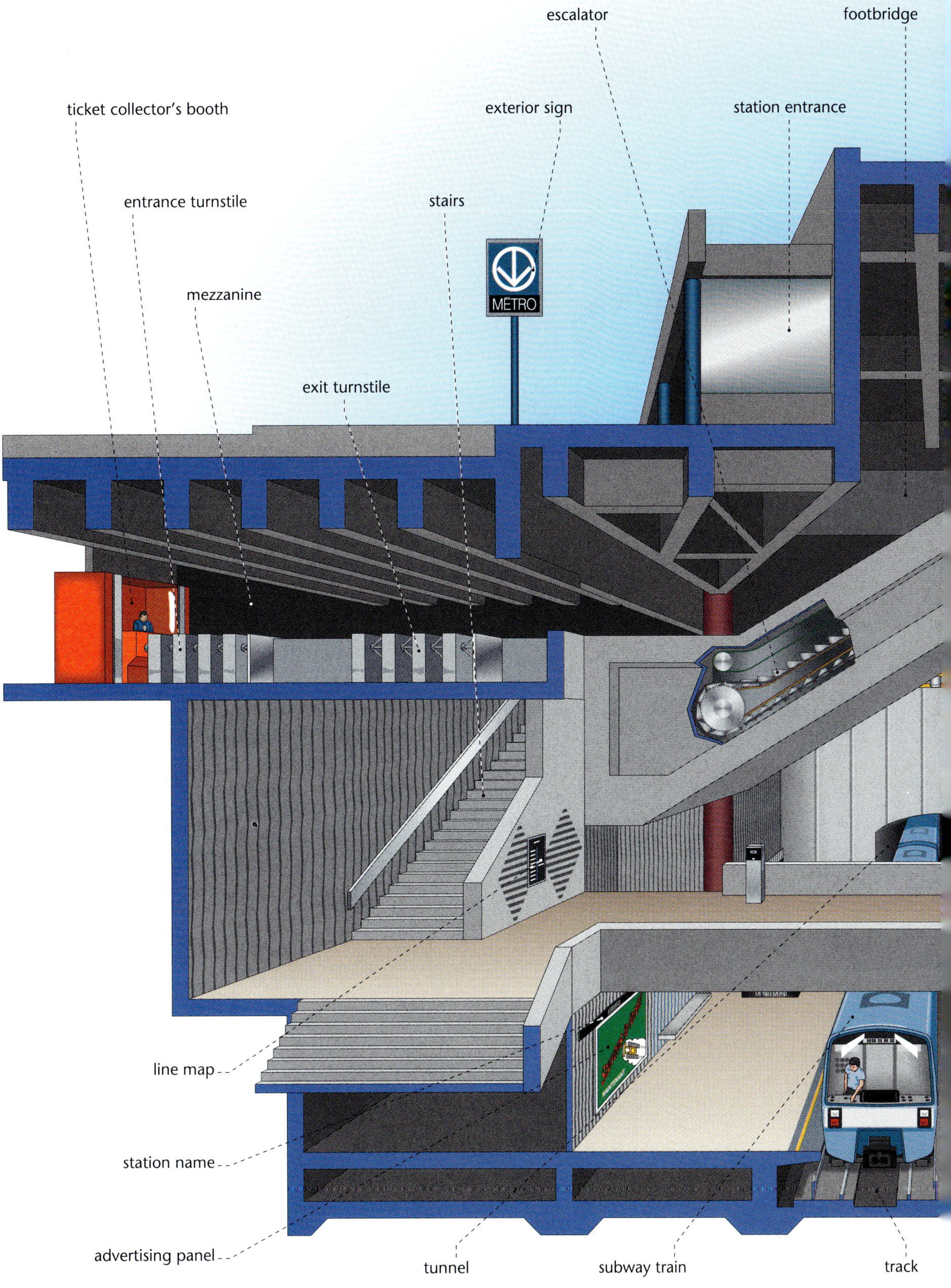

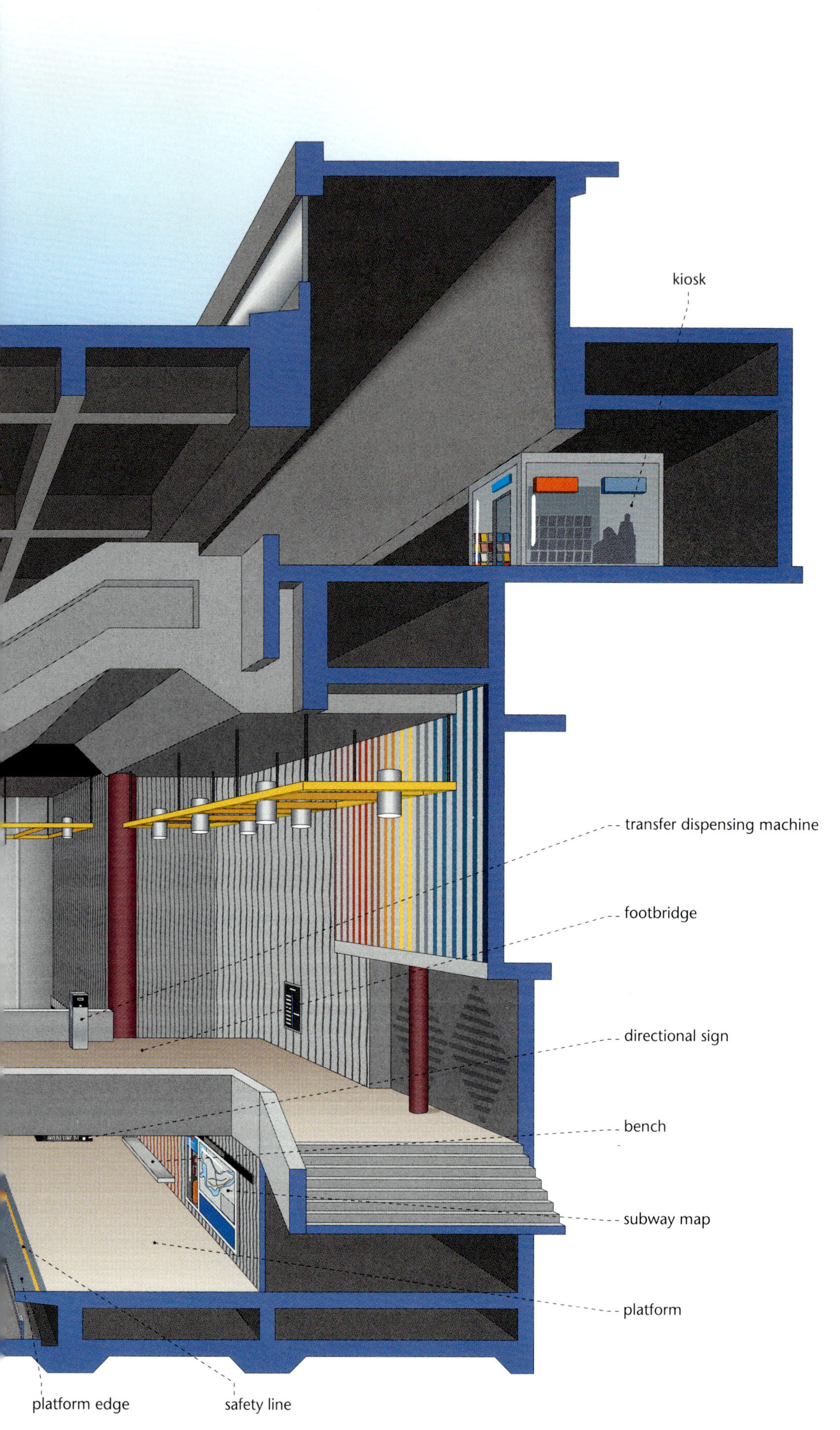
kiosk
transfer dispensing machine
footbridge
directional sign
bench
subway map
platform
platform edge
safety line

TRUCK AND TRACK

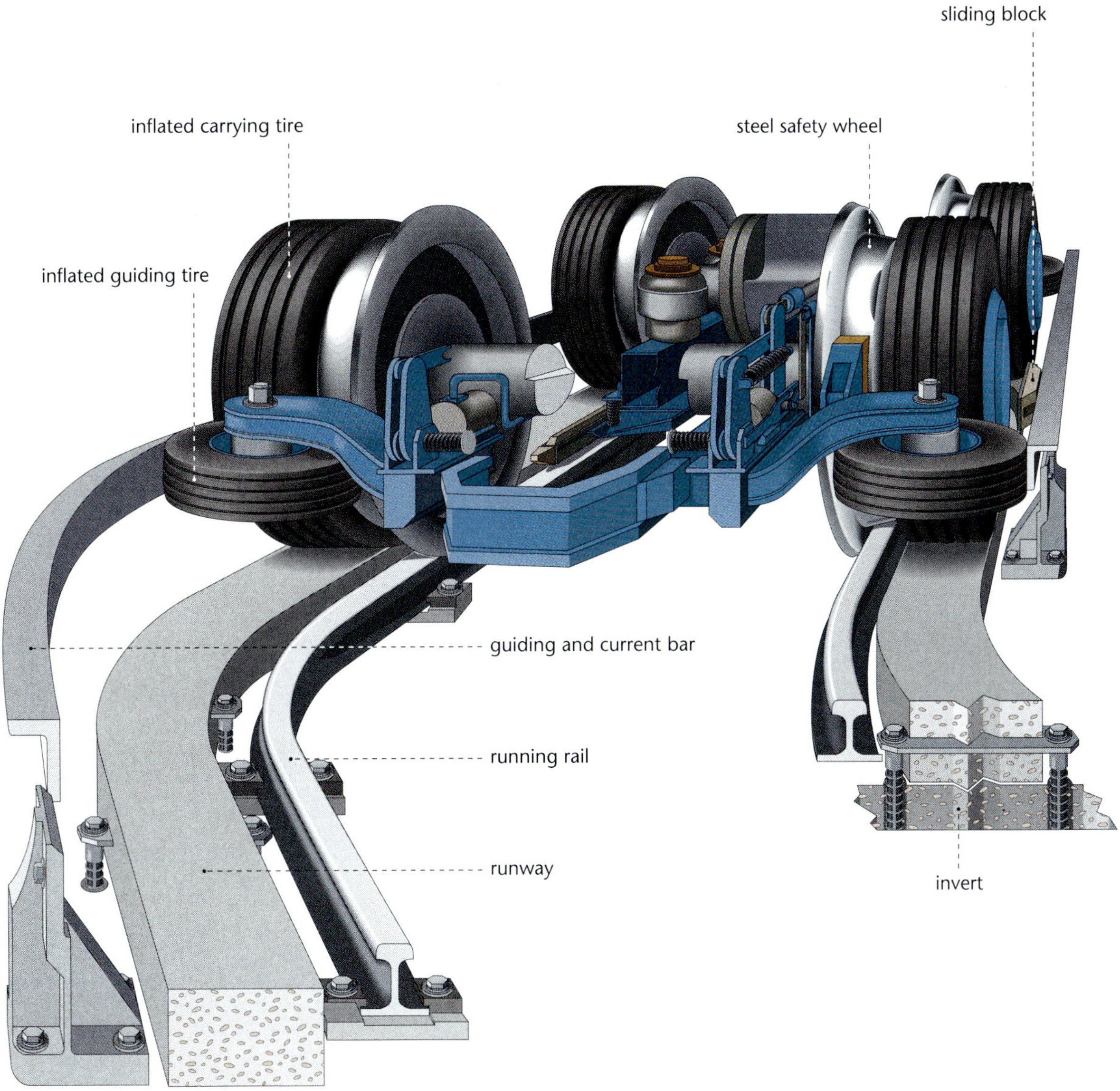

sliding block
inflated carrying tire
steel safety wheel
inflated guiding tire
guiding and current bar
running rail
runway
invert

SUBWAY TRAIN

motor car
passenger car

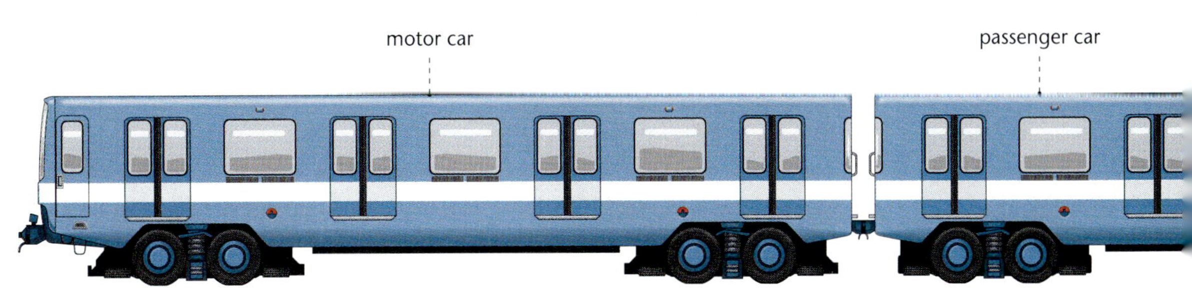

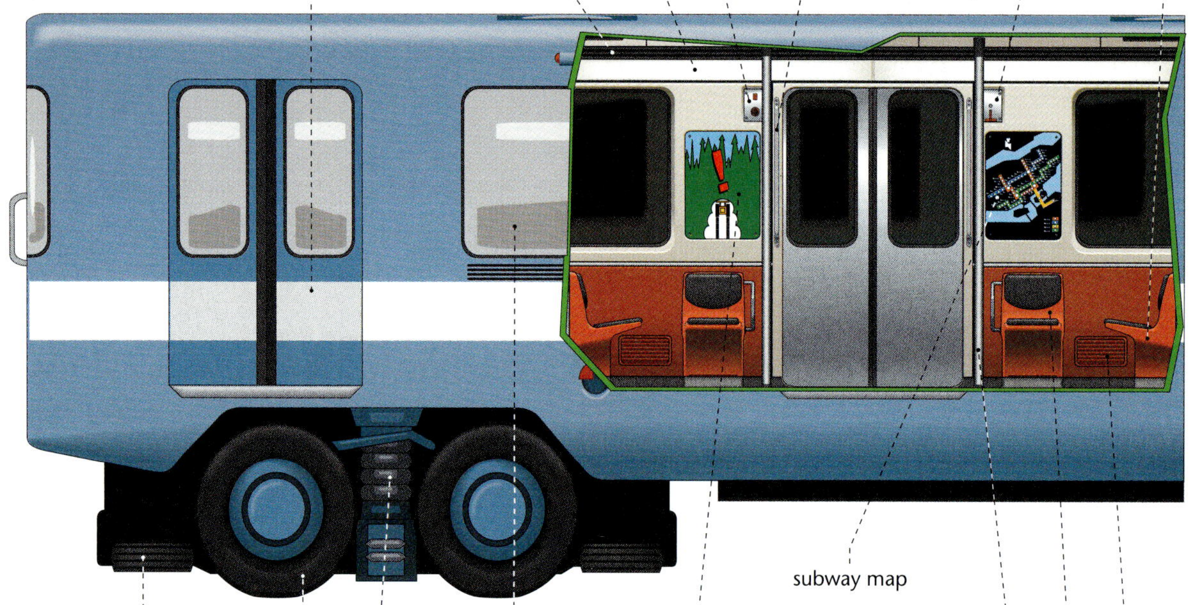

communication set
light
side handrail
double seat
side door
ventilator
emergency brake
subway map
inflated guiding tire
window
handrail
advertising sign
inflated carrying tire
single seat
suspension
heating grille
motor car

FOUR-MASTED BARK

MASTING AND RIGGING

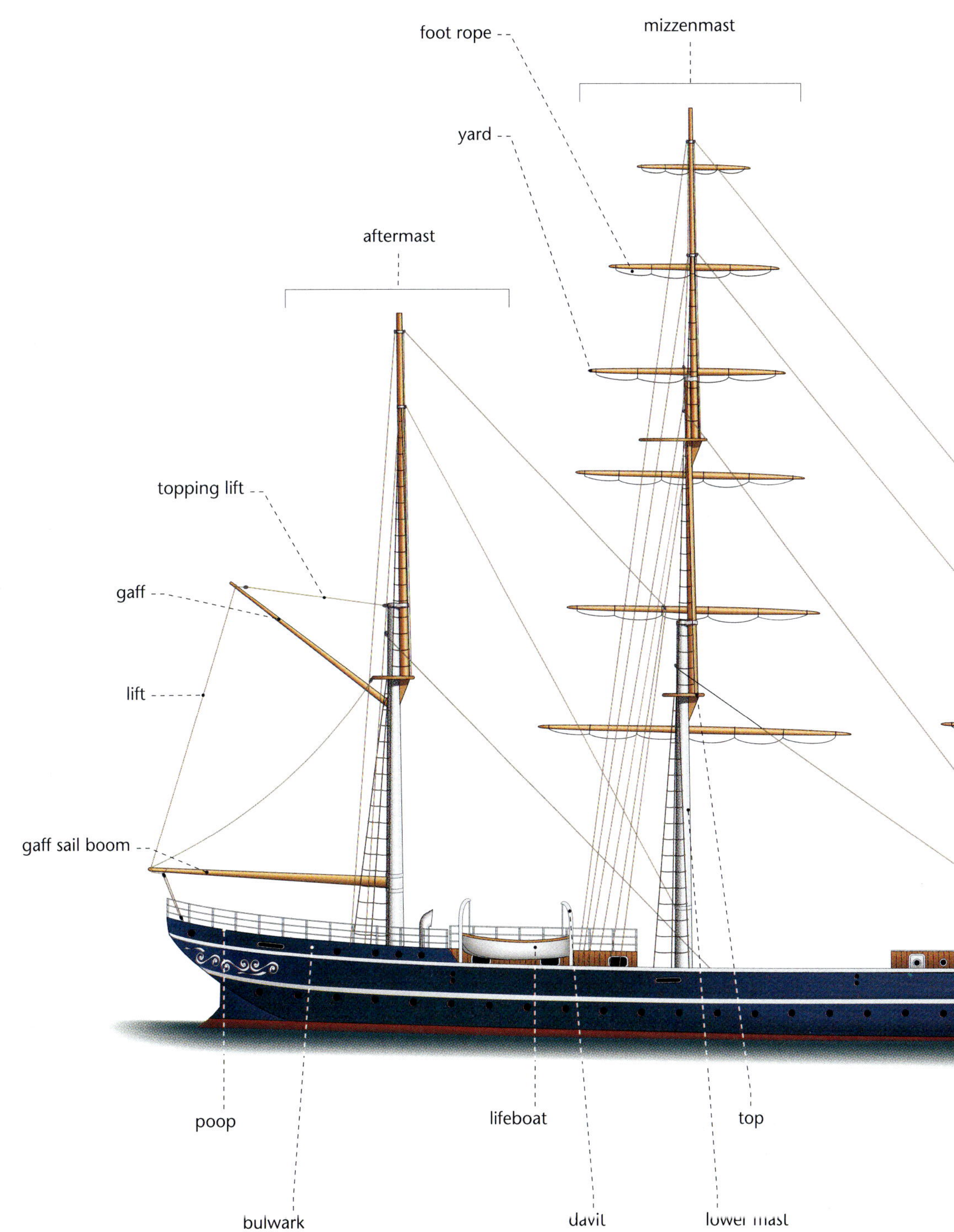

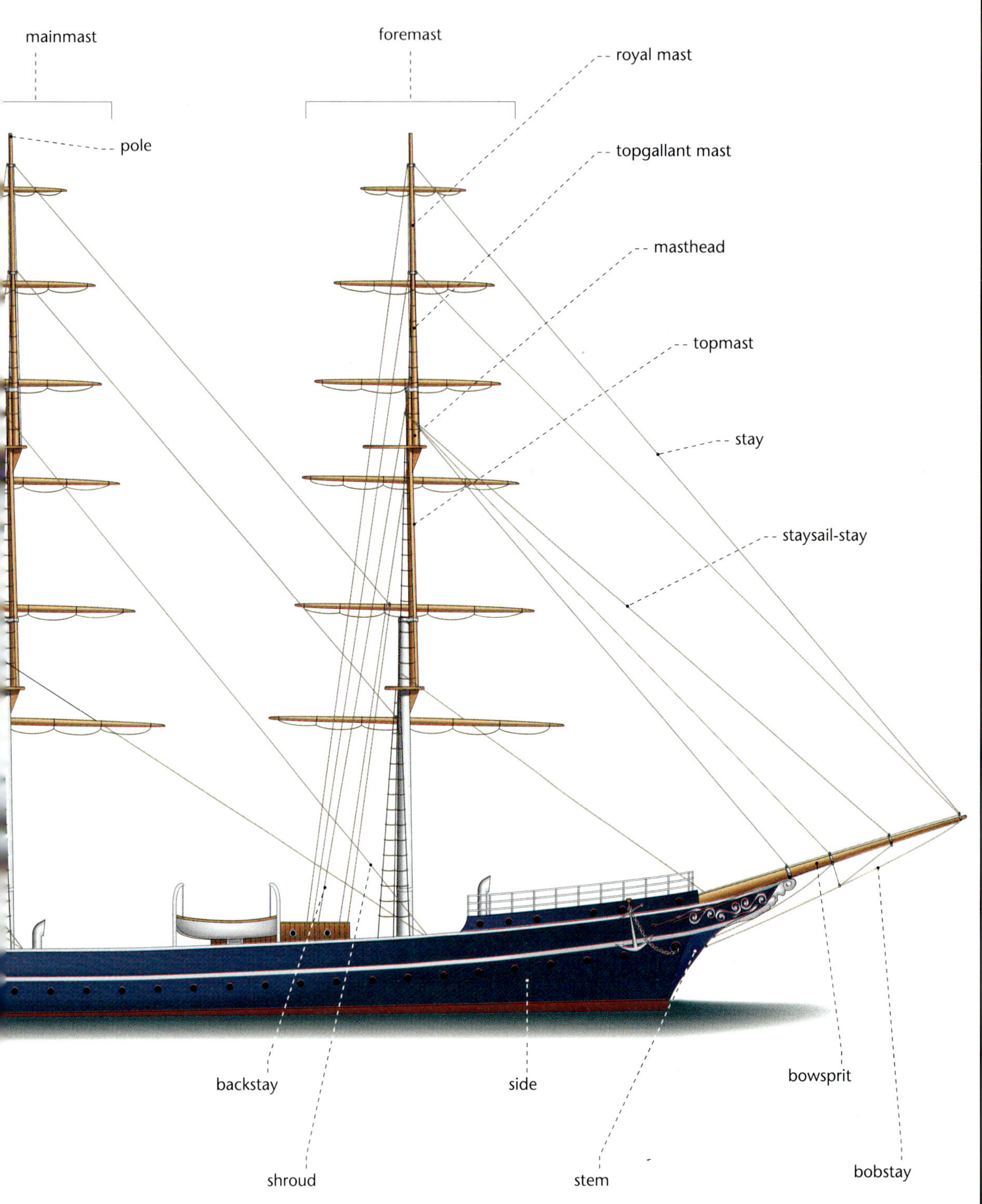

mainmast
foremast
royal mast
topgallant mast
pole
masthead
topmast
stay
staysail-stay
backstay
side
bowsprit
shroud
stem
bobstay

SAILS

mizzen royal staysail
mizzen topgallant staysail
mizzen topmast staysail
mizzen royal brace
jigger topgallant staysail
jigger topmast staysail
gaff topsail
spanker
brail
sheet
mizzen sail
halyard
reef band
reef point

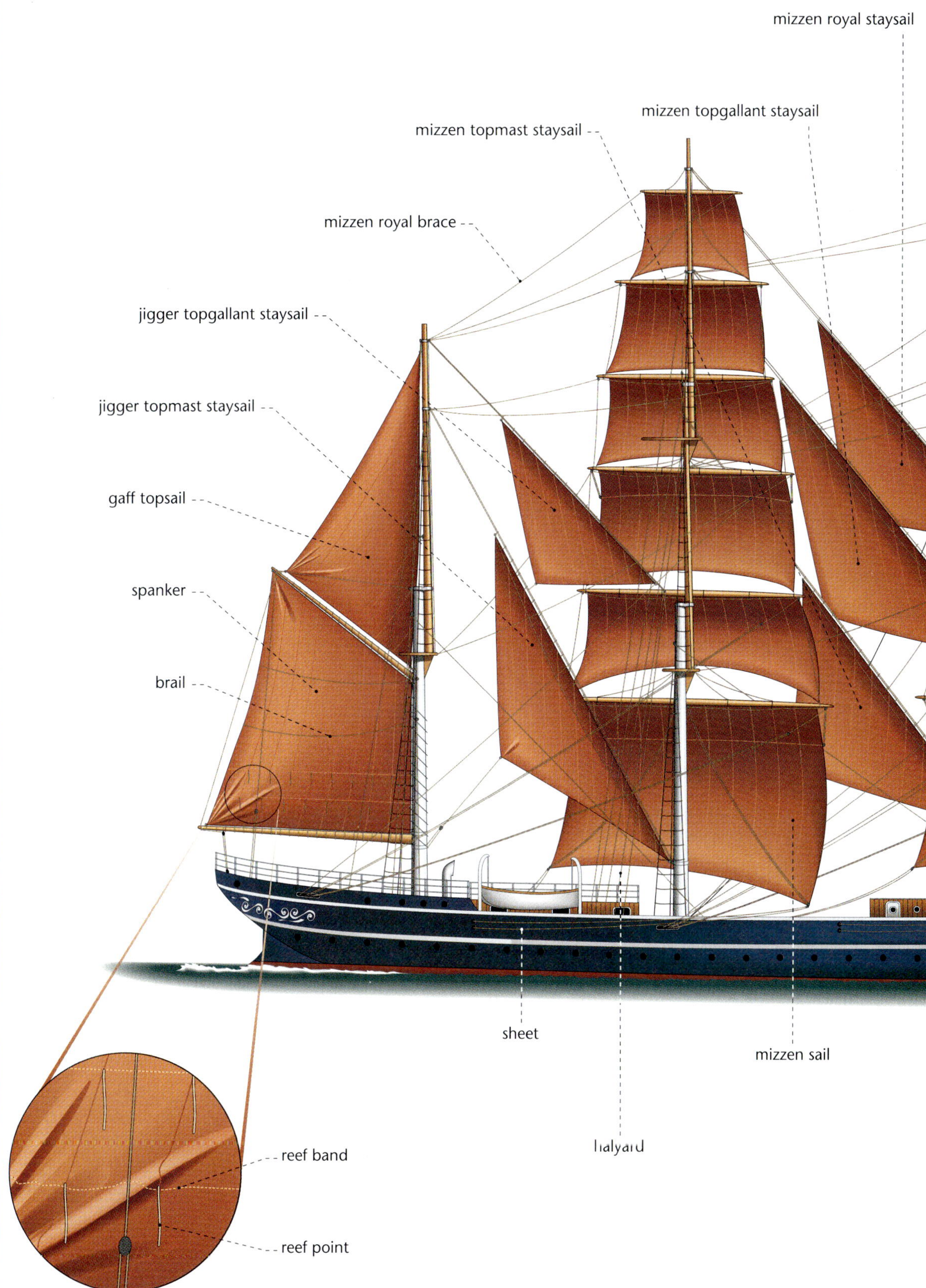

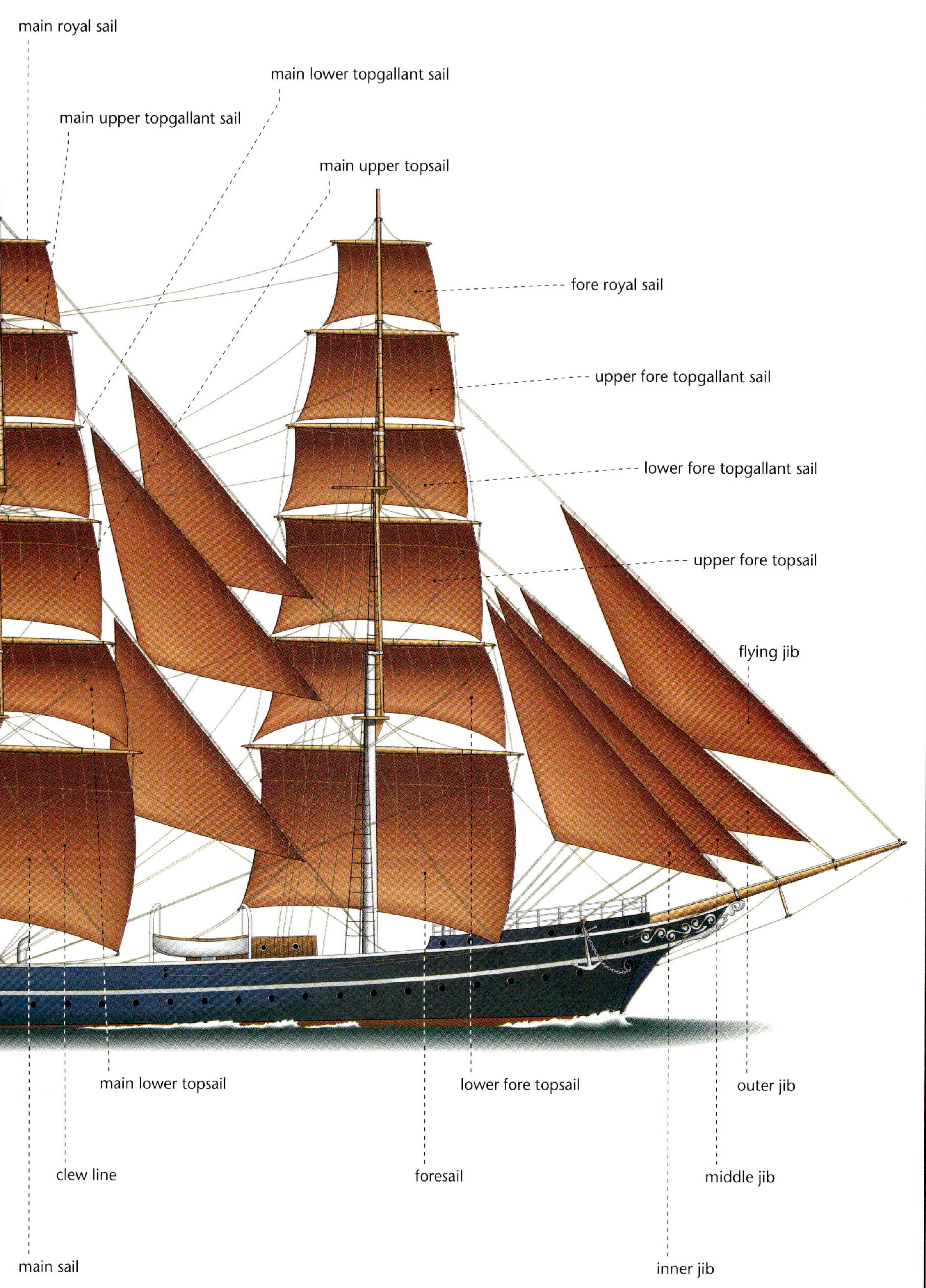

main royal sail
main upper topgallant sail
main lower topgallant sail
main upper topsail
fore royal sail
upper fore topgallant sail
lower fore topgallant sail
upper fore topsail
flying jib
main lower topsail
lower fore topsail
outer jib
clew line
foresail
middle jib
main sail
inner jib

TYPES OF SAILS

square sail

lateen sail

gaff sail

Bermuda sail

TYPES OF RIGS

whale boat

brigantine

ketch

Marconi cutter

brig

schooner

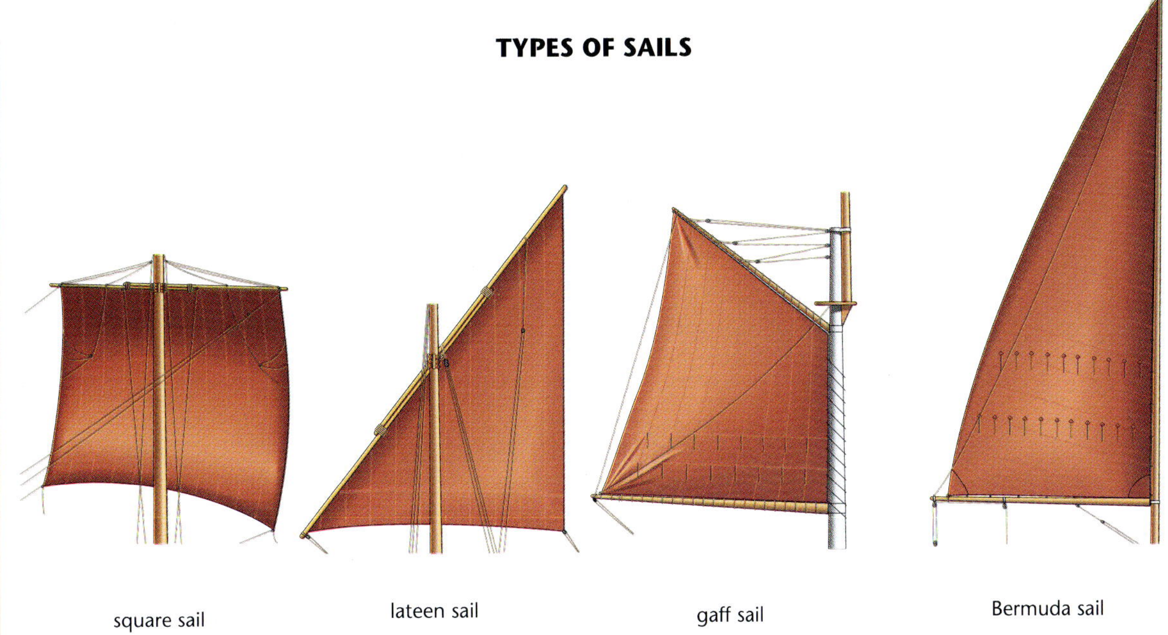

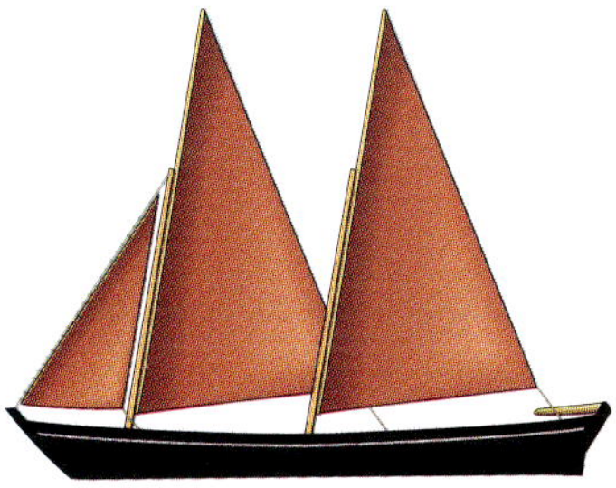

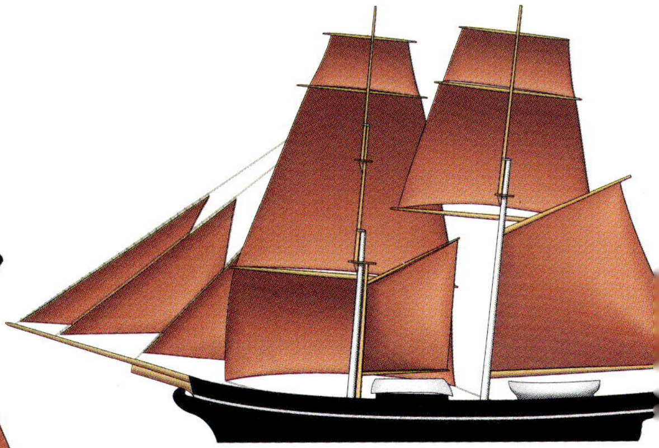

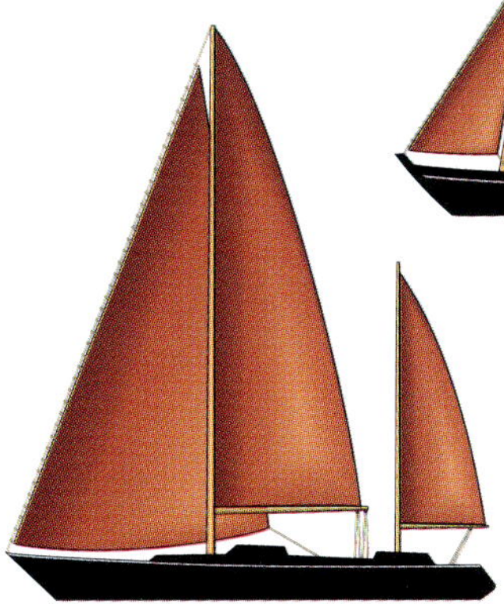

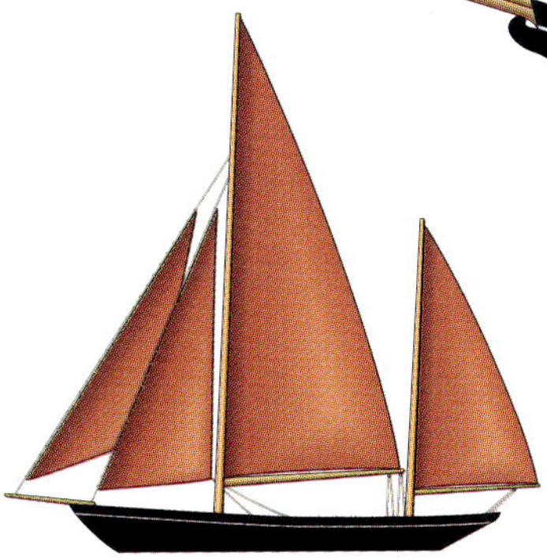

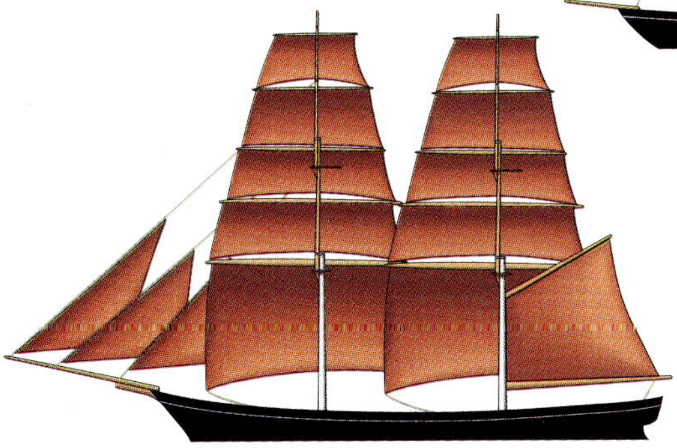

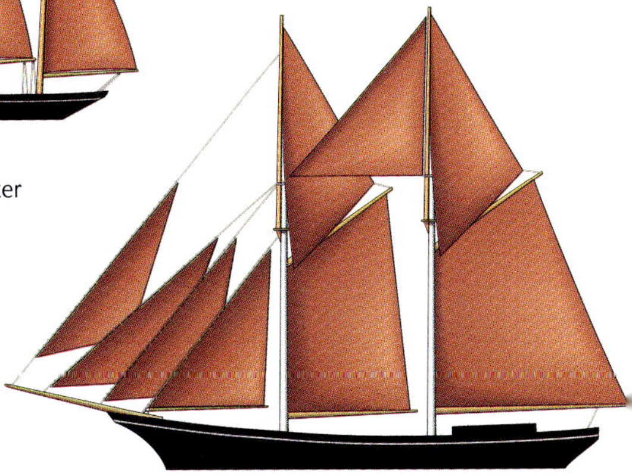

ANCHOR

SHIP'S ANCHOR
arm
crown
throat
gravity band
hoisting ring
ring
palm
fluke
shank
bill
stock
TYPES OF ANCHORS
stocked anchor
stockless anchor
mushroom anchor
sea anchor
plow anchor
grapnel

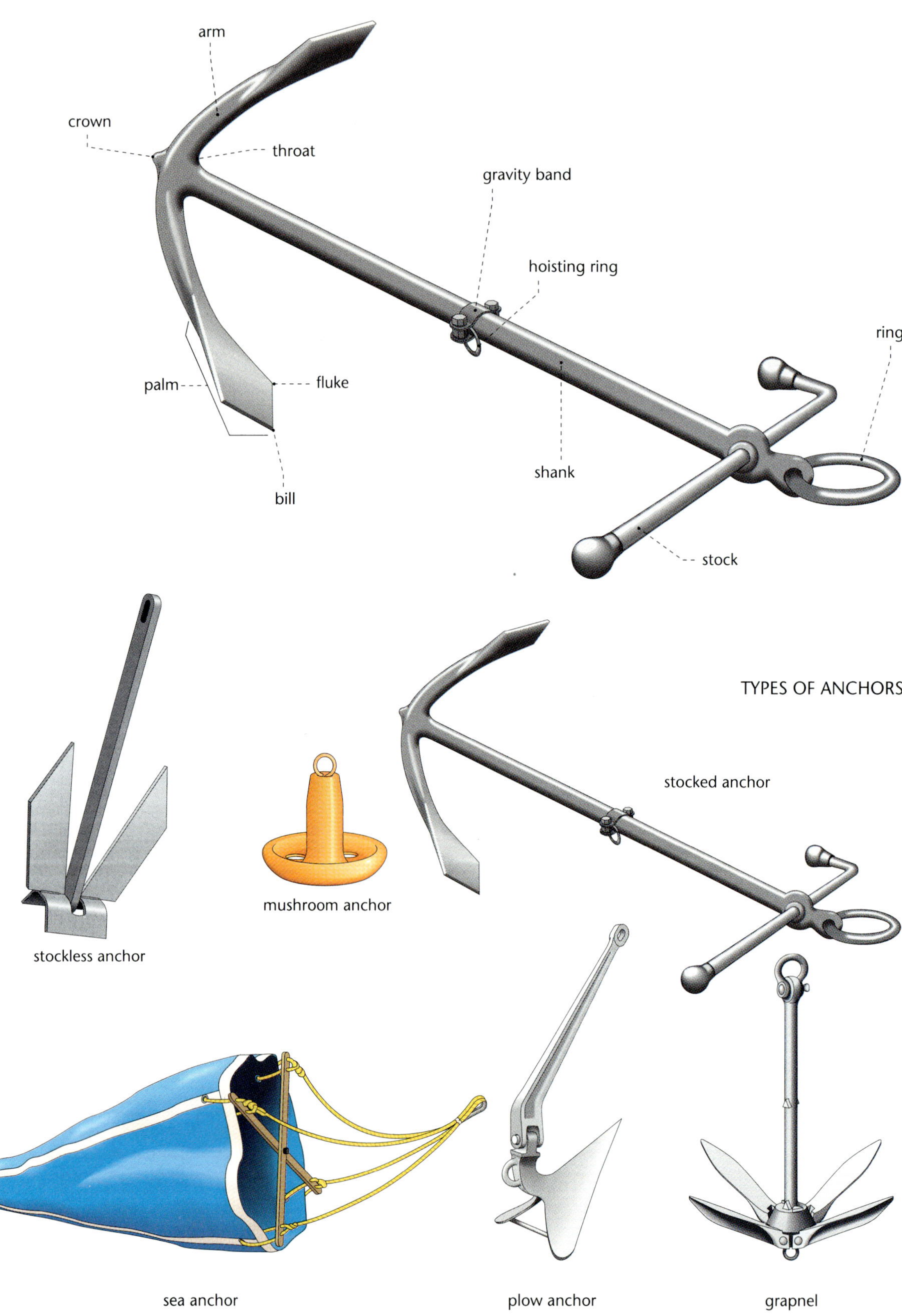

SEXTANT

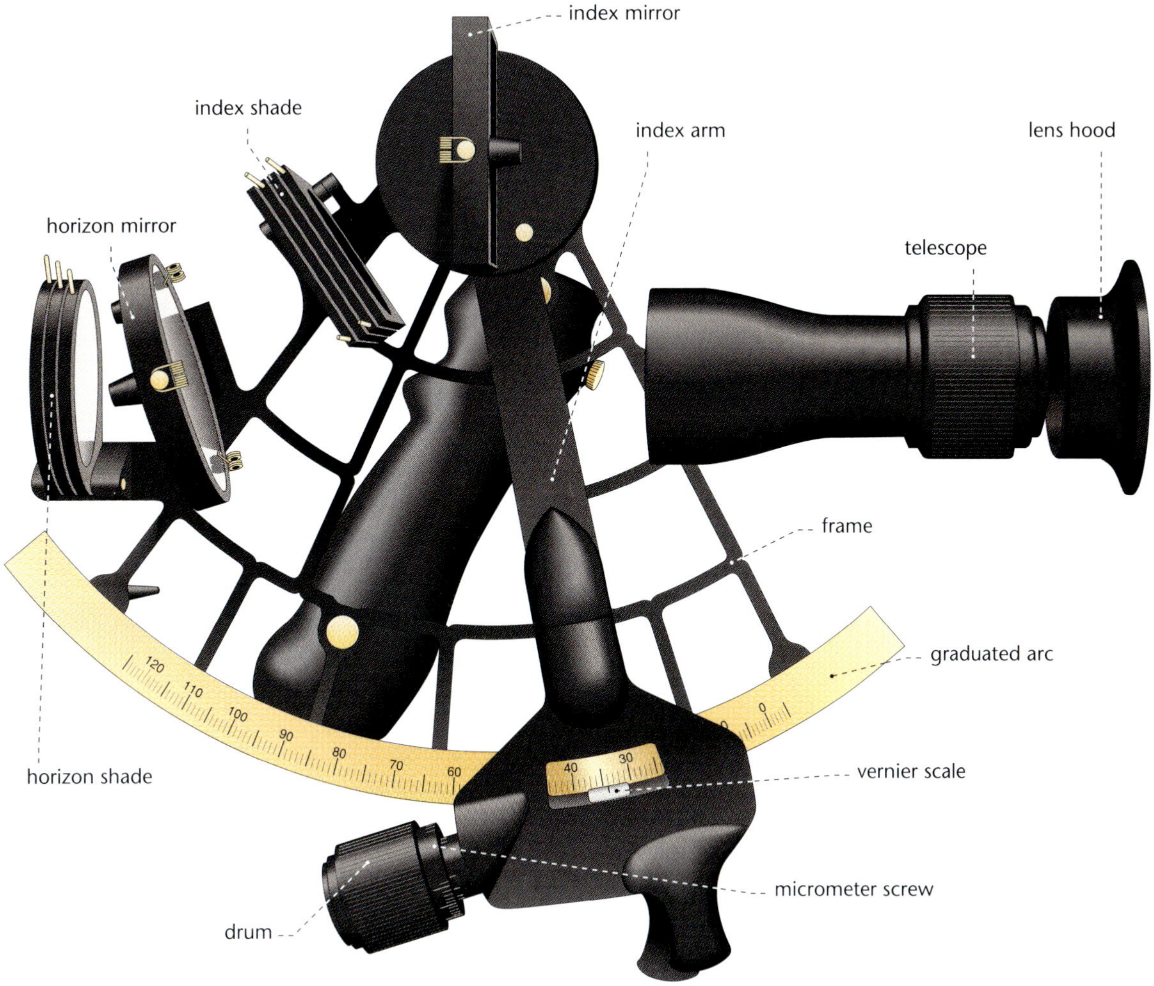

LIQUID COMPASS

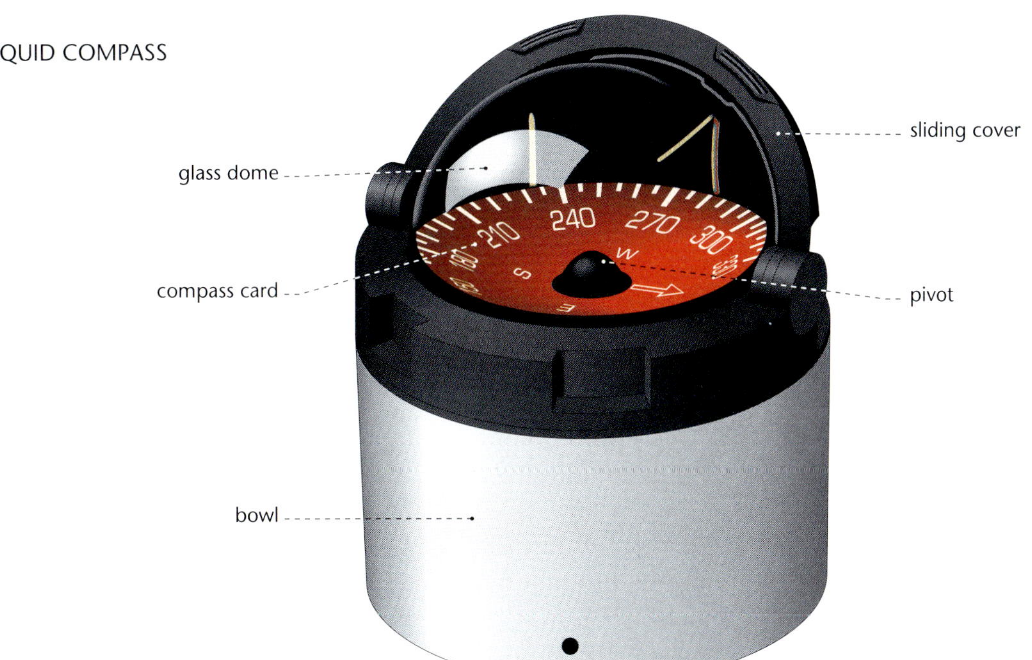

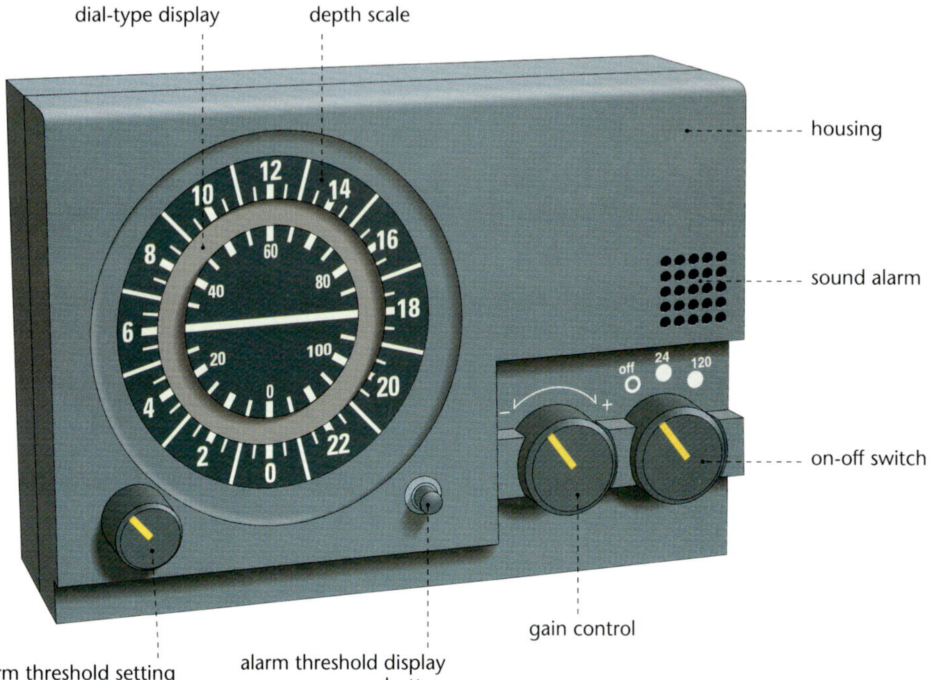

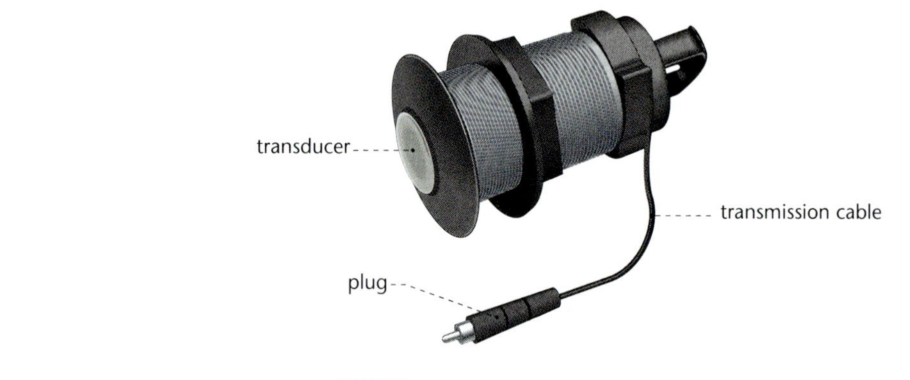

CROSS SECTION OF A LIQUID COMPASS

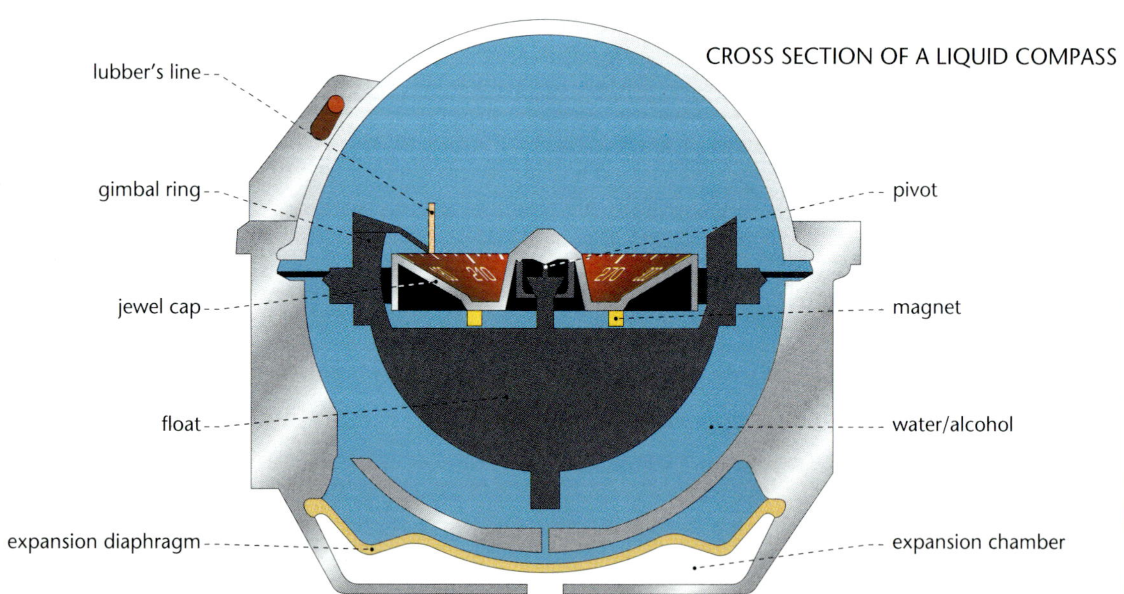

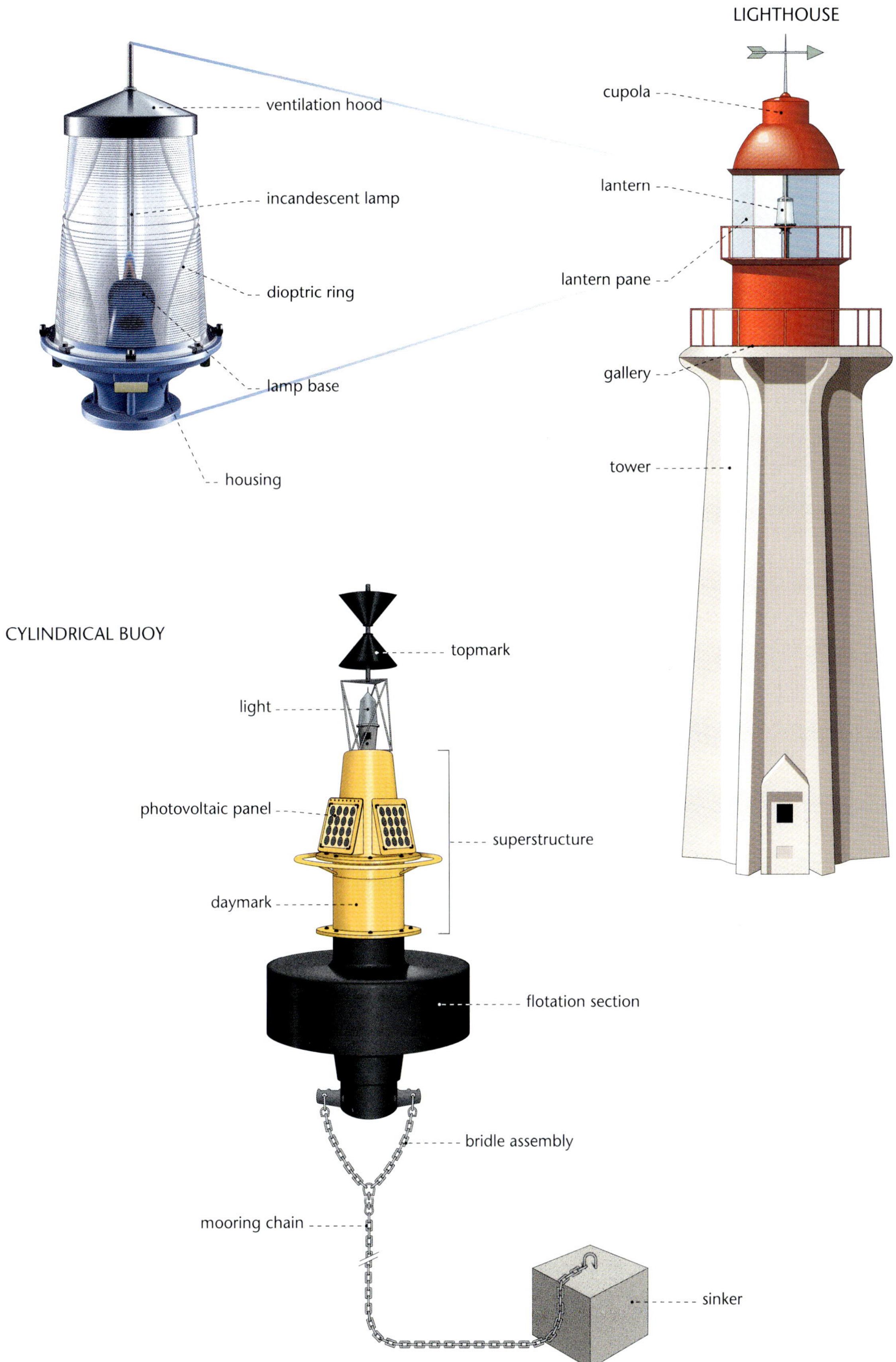

MARITIME SIGNALS
LIGHTHOUSE LANTERN
ventilation hood
incandescent lamp
dioptric ring
lamp base
housing
LIGHTHOUSE
cupola
lantern
lantern pane
gallery
tower
CYLINDRICAL BUOY
topmark
light
photovoltaic panel
superstructure
daymark
flotation section
bridle assembly
mooring chain
sinker

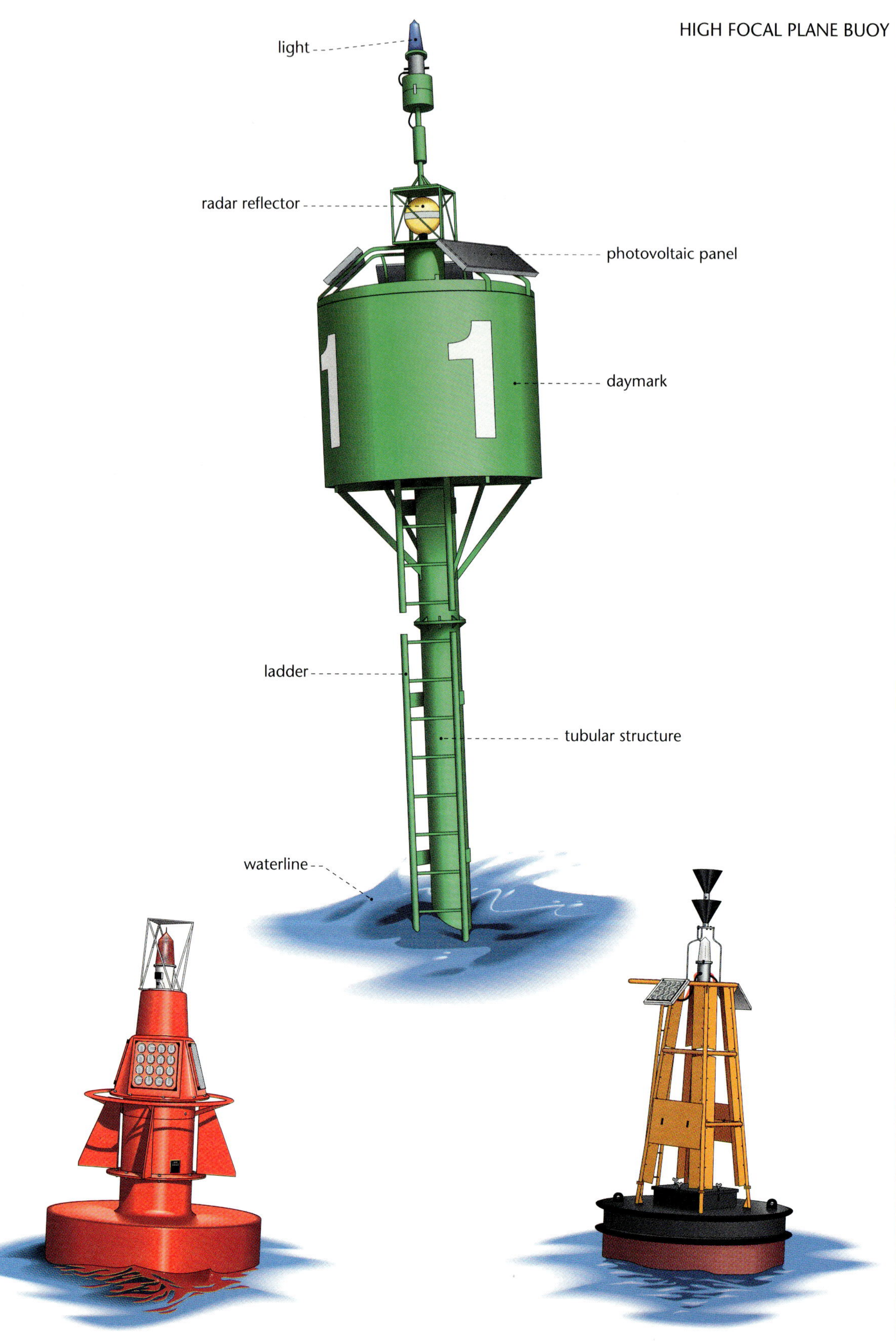
light
radar reflector
photovoltaic panel
daymark
ladder
tubular structure
waterline
conical buoy
pillar buoy

MARITIME BUOYAGE SYSTEM

CARDINAL MARKS

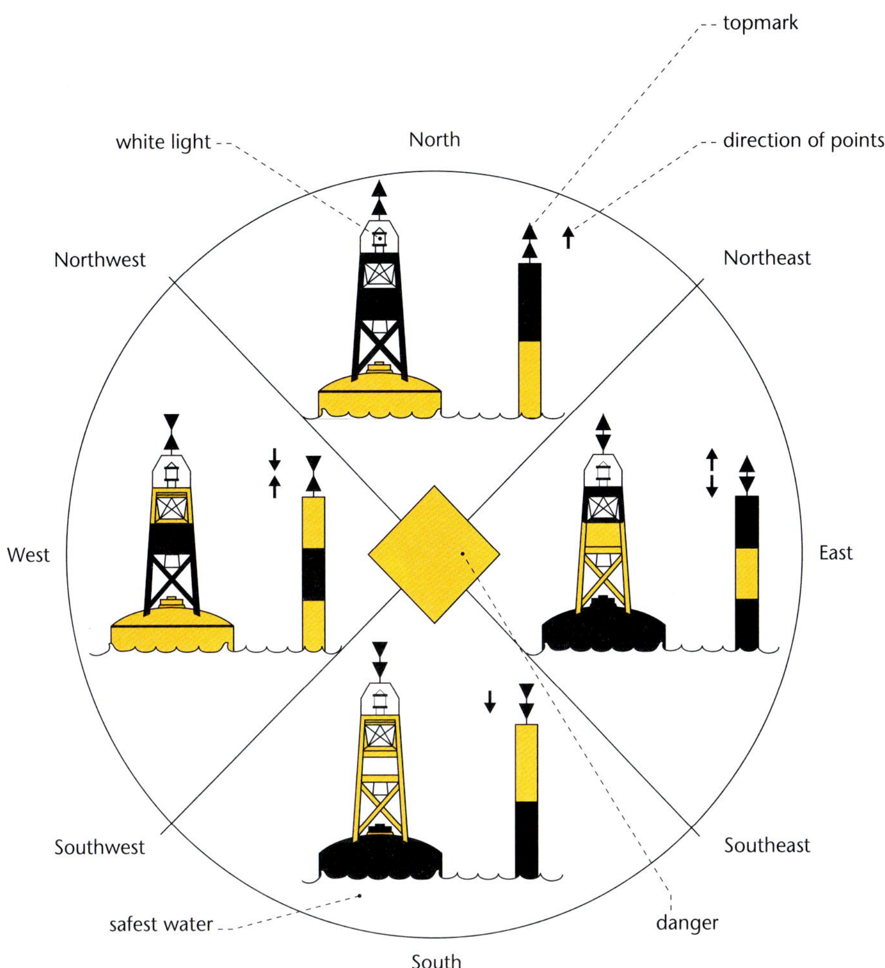

BUOYAGE REGIONS

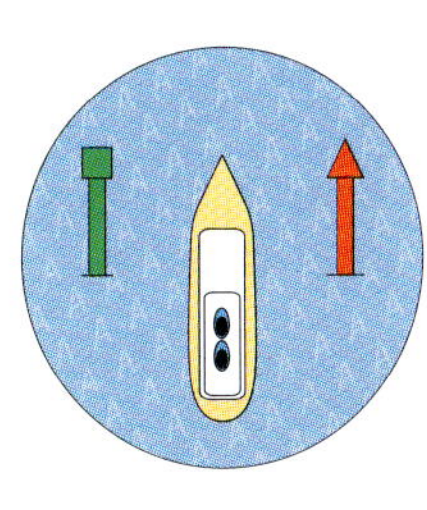

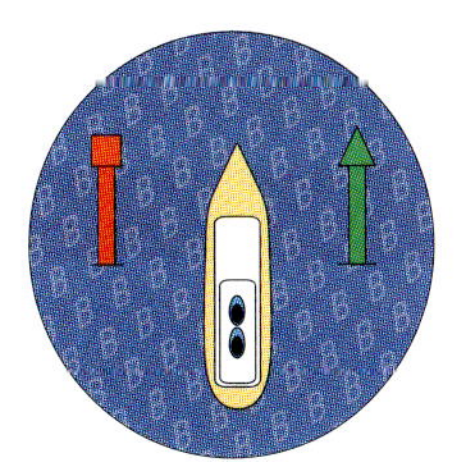

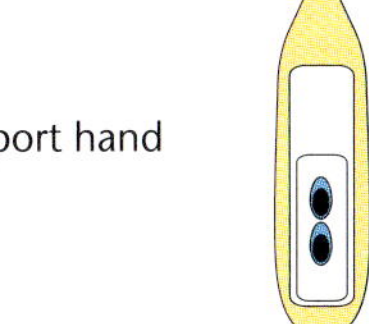

RHYTHM OF MARKS BY NIGHT

DAYMARKS (REGION B)

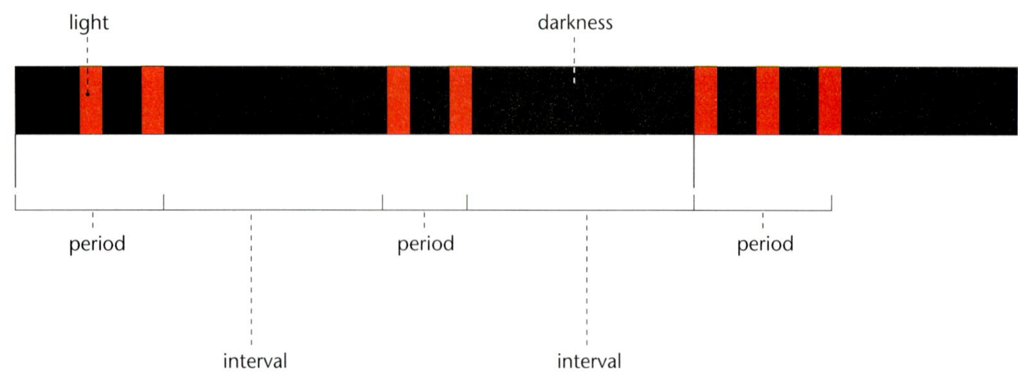

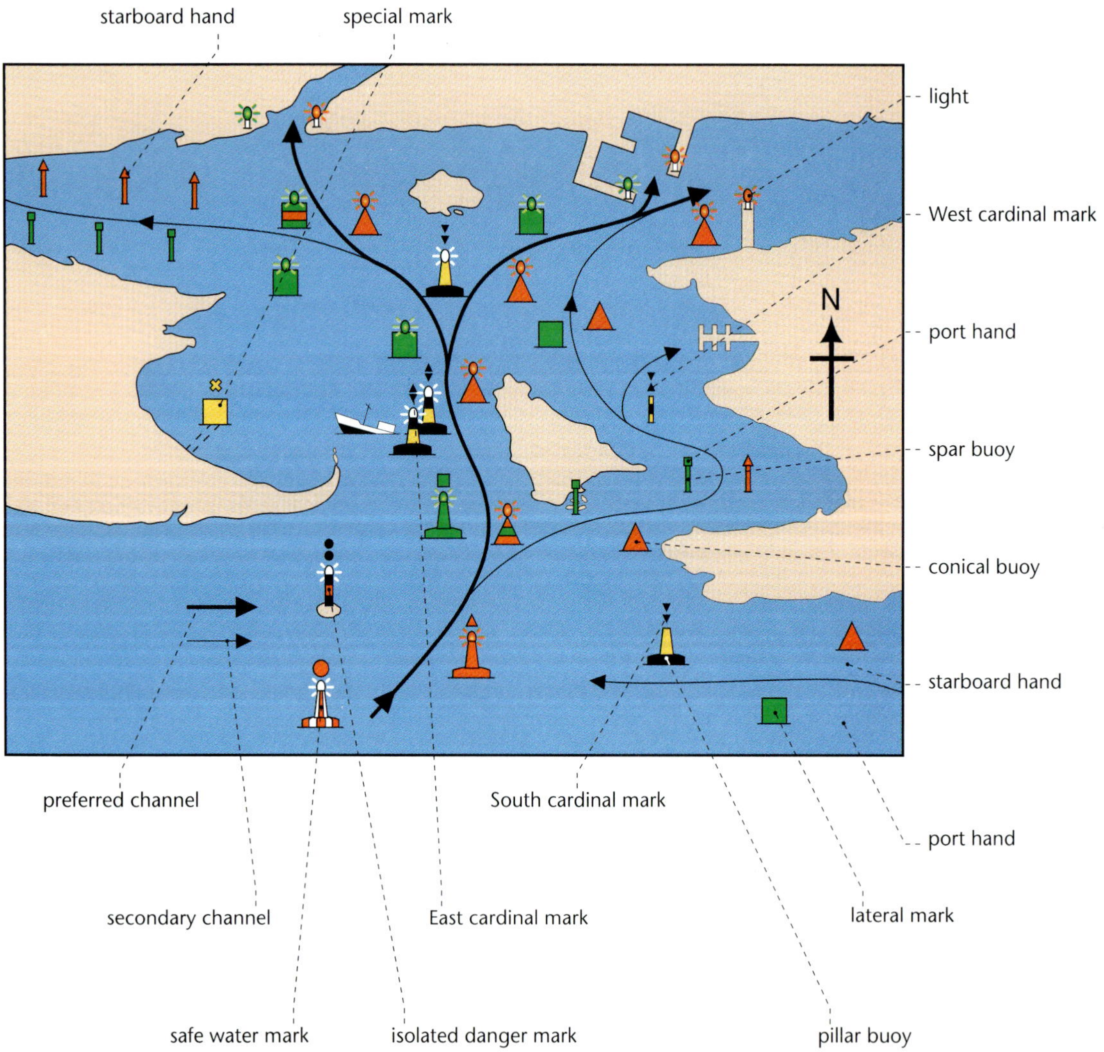

MARITIME TRANSPORT

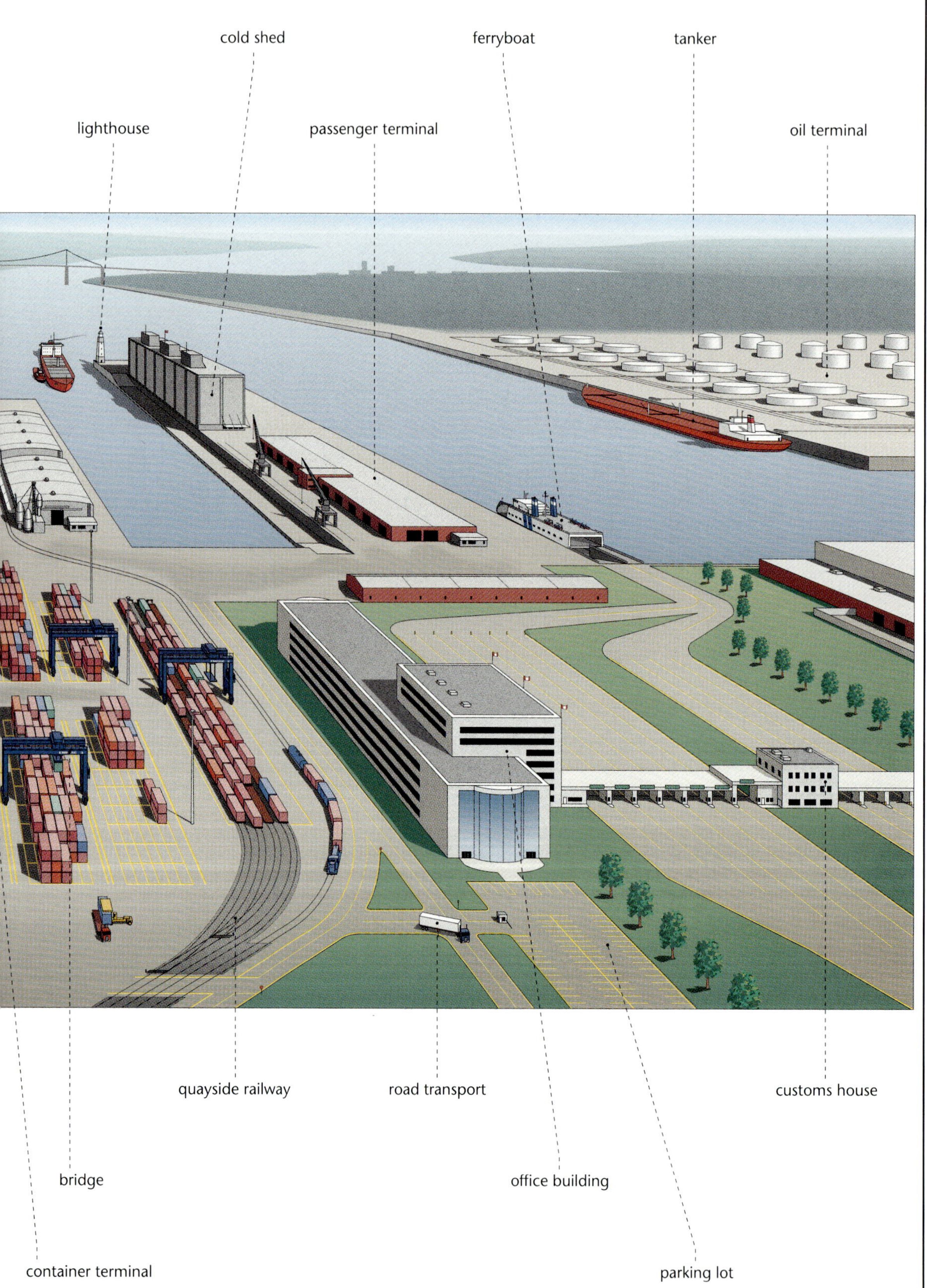

cold shed
ferryboat
tanker
lighthouse
passenger terminal
oil terminal
quayside railway
road transport
customs house
bridge
office building
container terminal
parking lot

CANAL LOCK

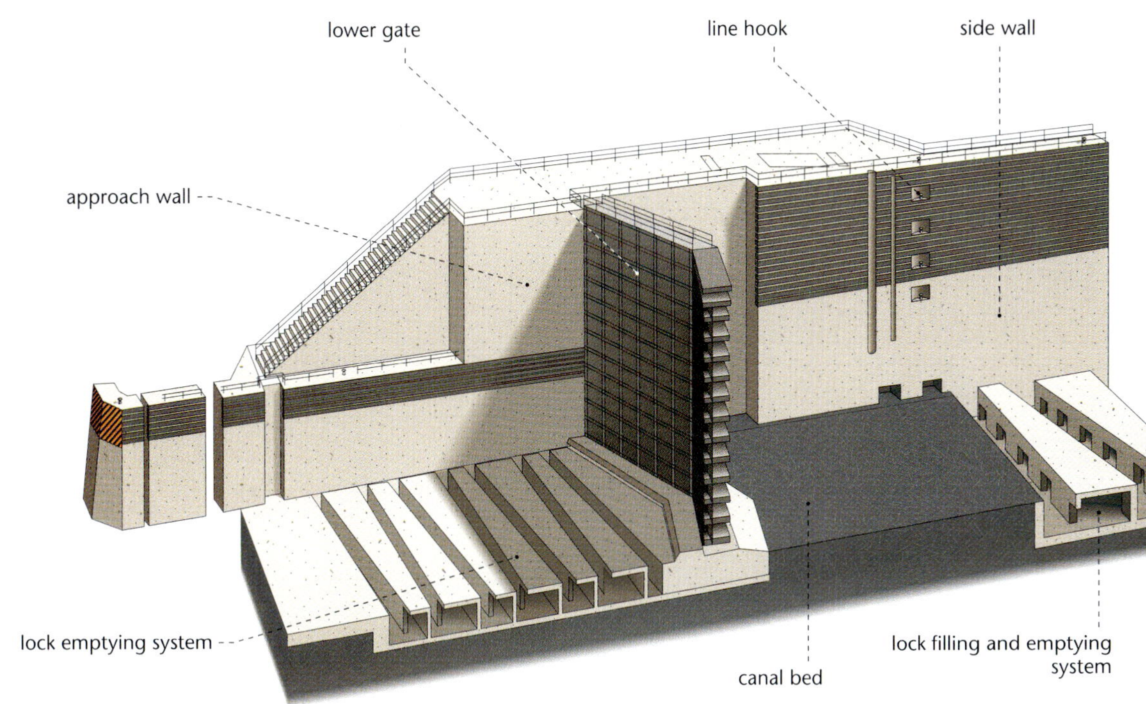

HOVERCRAFT

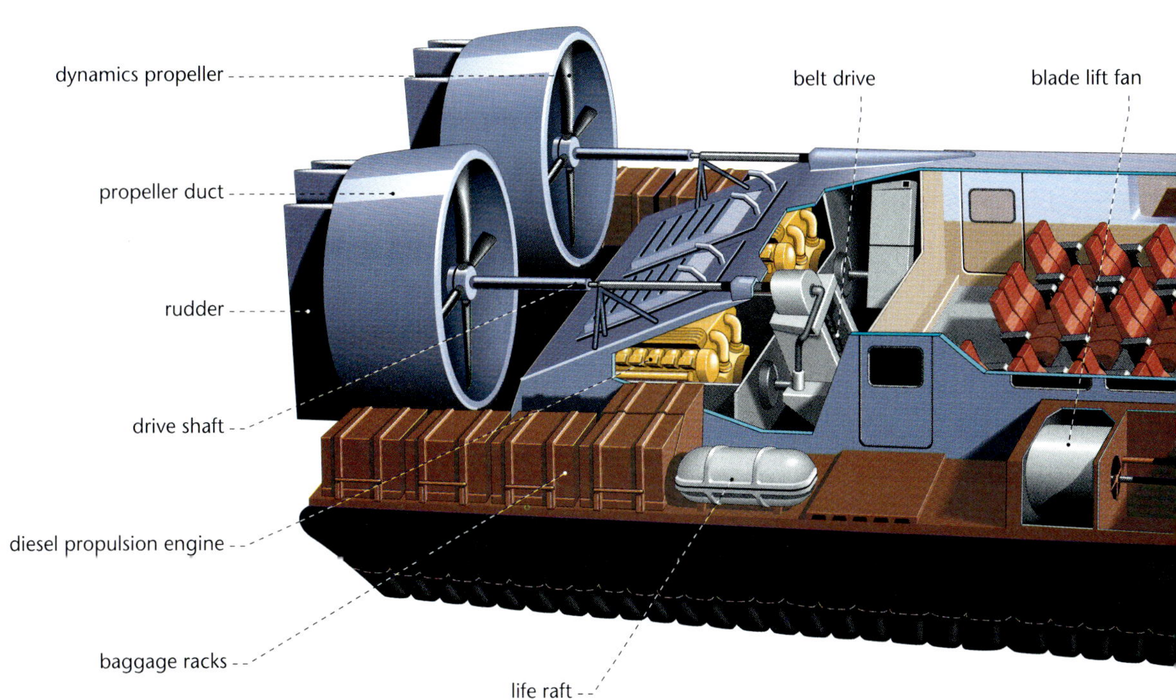

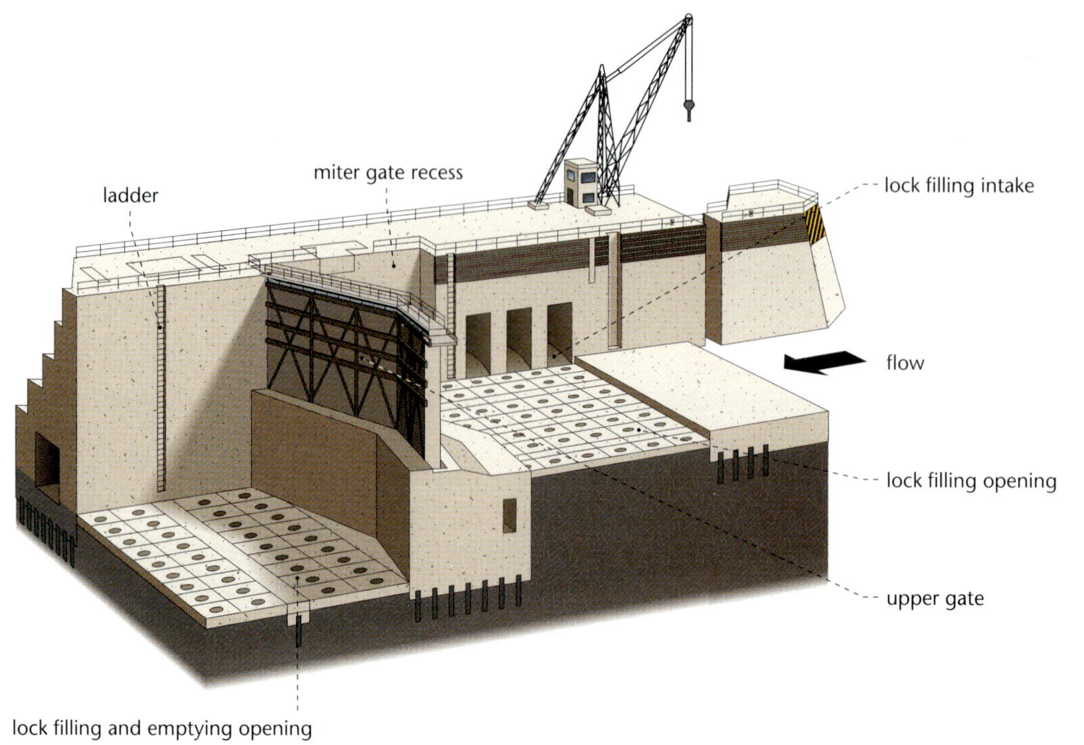

ladder
miter gate recess
lock filling intake
flow
lock filling opening
upper gate
lock filling and emptying opening

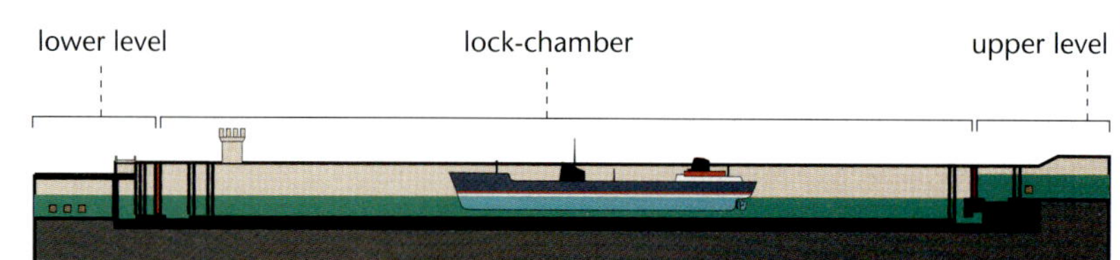

lower level
lock-chamber
upper level

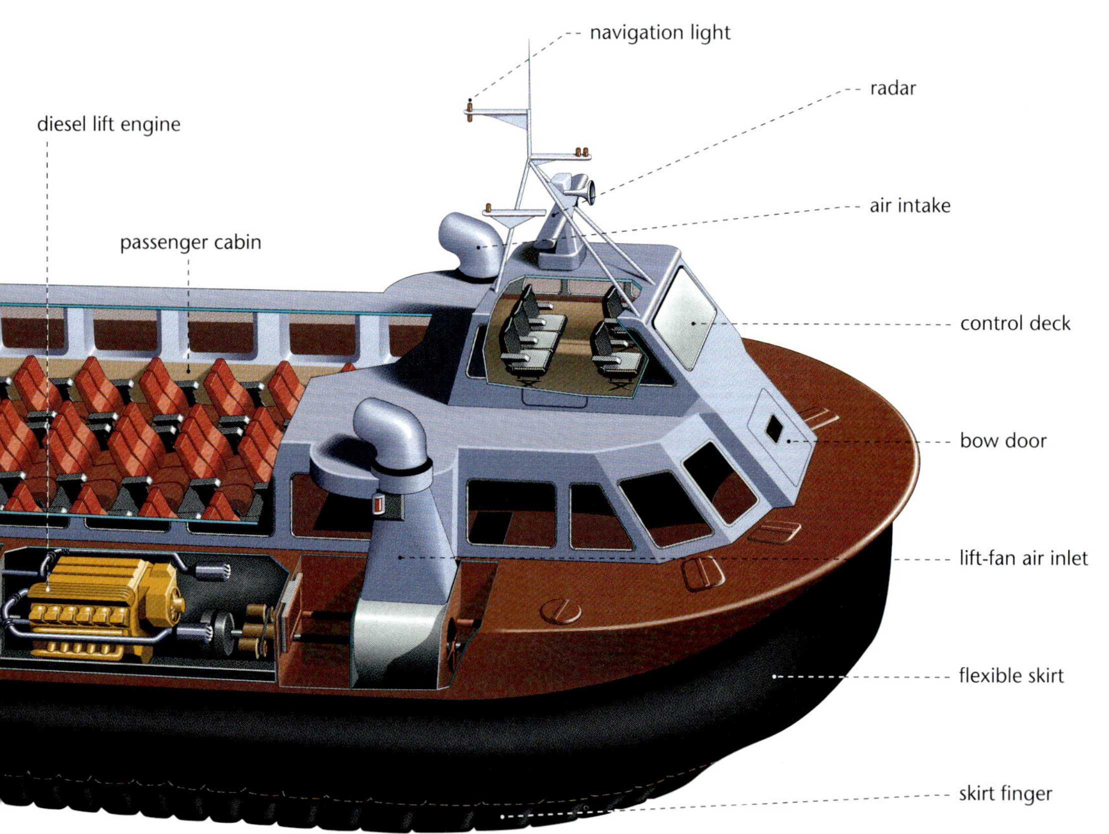

navigation light
radar
diesel lift engine
air intake
passenger cabin
control deck
bow door
lift-fan air inlet
flexible skirt
skirt finger

FERRY

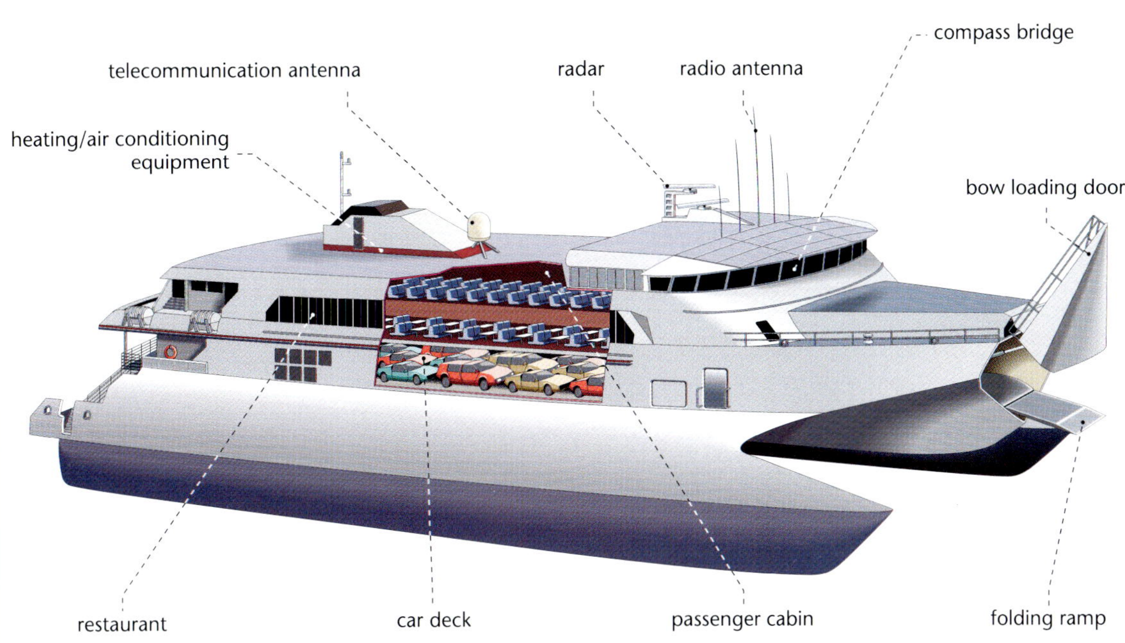

CONTAINER SHIP

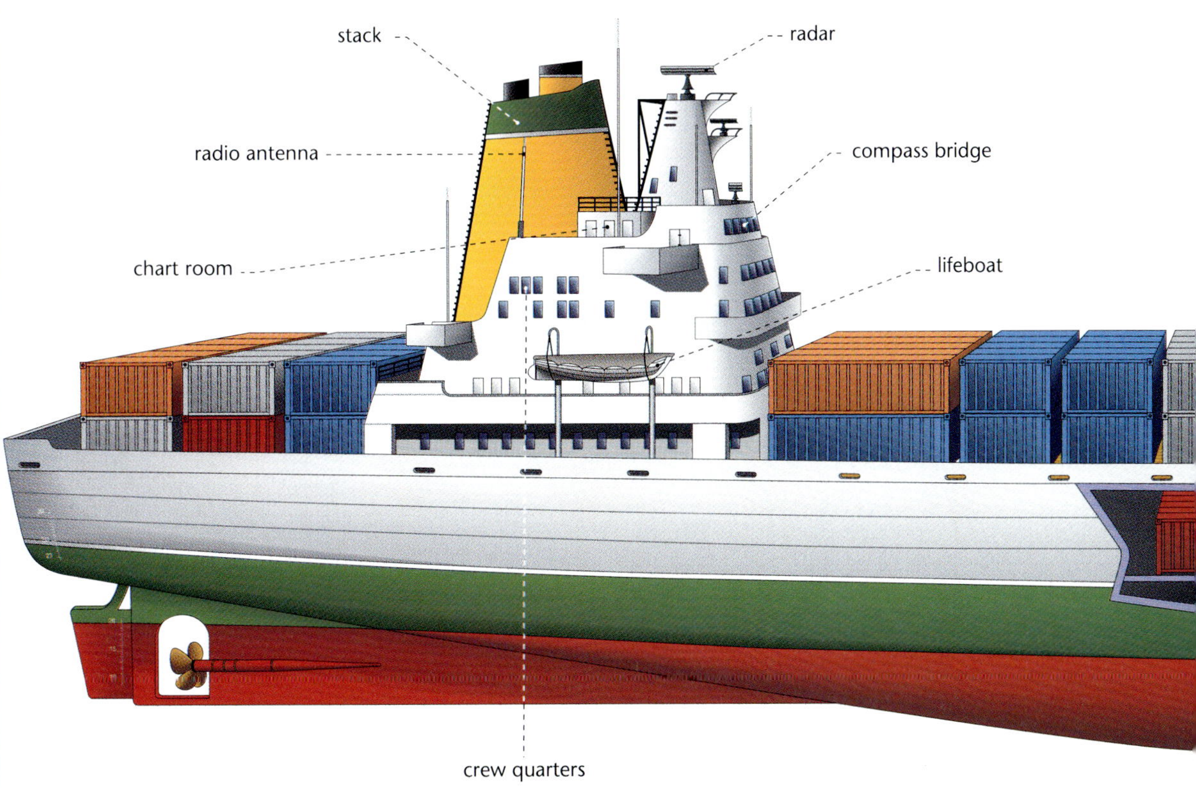

HYDROFOIL BOAT

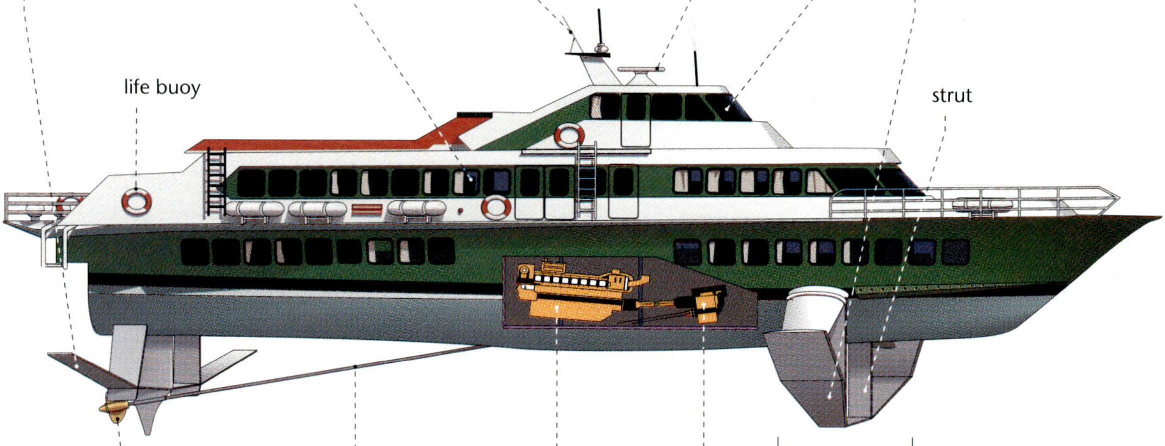

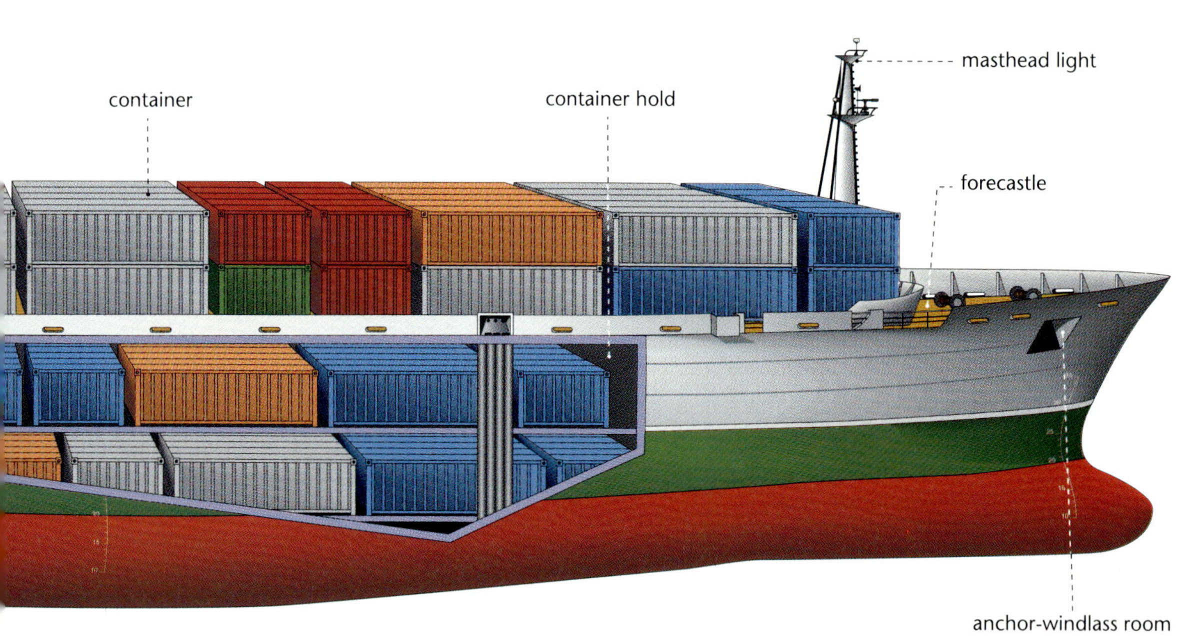

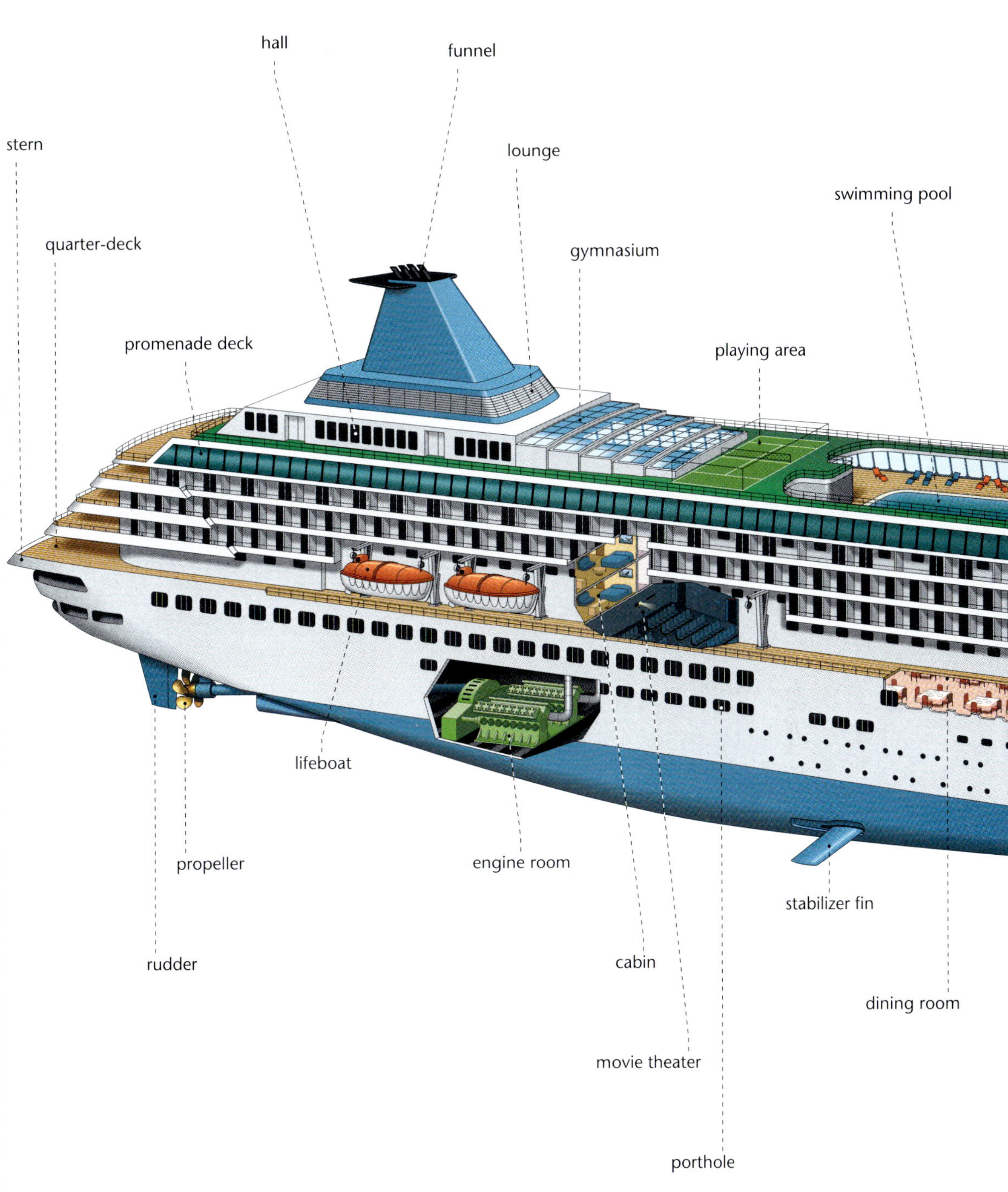

hall
funnel
lounge
swimming pool
stern
quarter-deck
gymnasium
promenade deck
playing area
lifeboat
propeller
engine room
rudder
cabin
stabilizer fin
movie theater
dining room
porthole

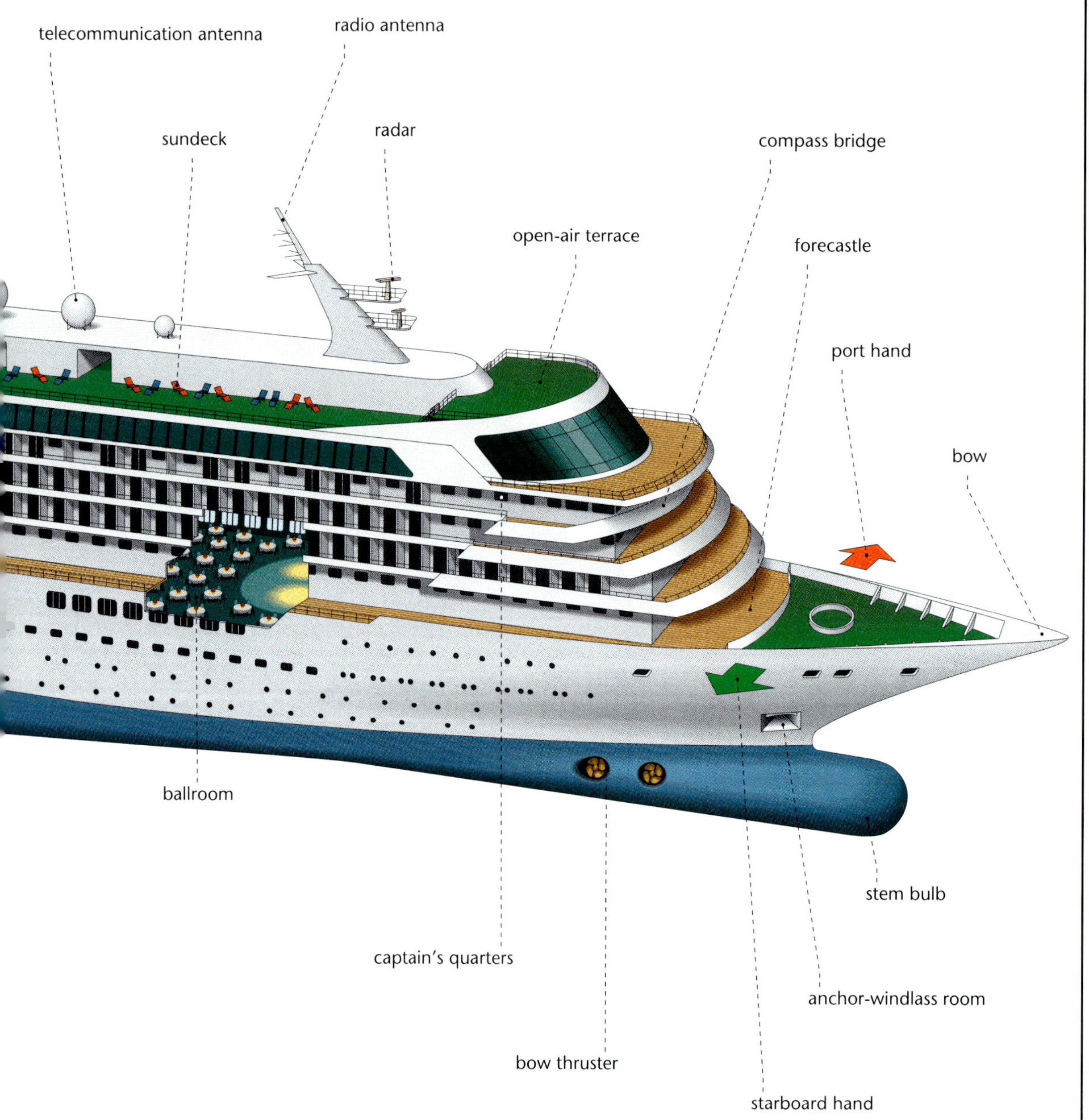

telecommunication antenna
radio antenna
sundeck
radar
open-air terrace
compass bridge
forecastle
port hand
bow
ballroom
stem bulb
captain's quarters
anchor-windlass room
bow thruster
starboard hand

LONG-RANGE JET

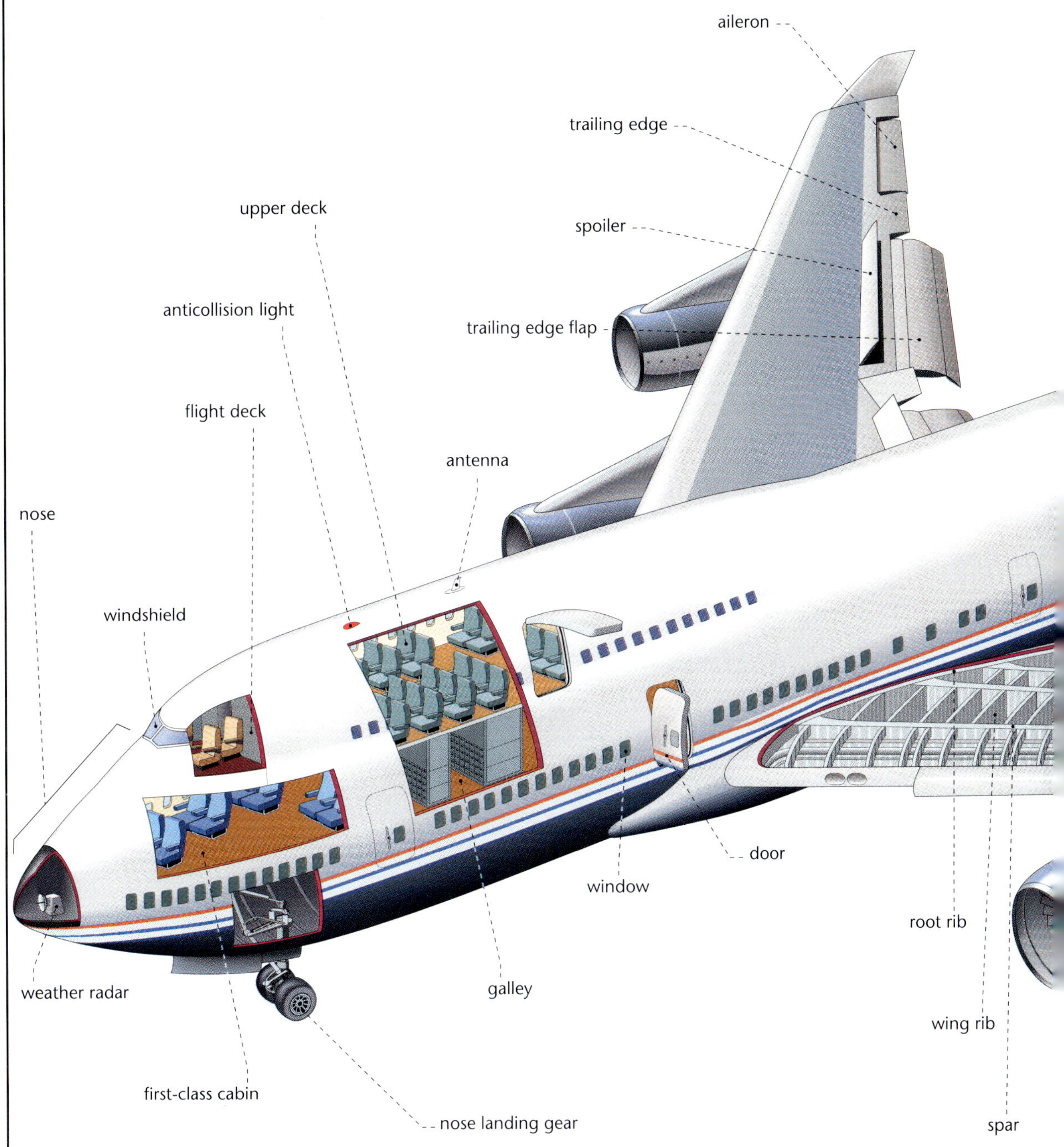

TYPES OF TAIL SHAPES

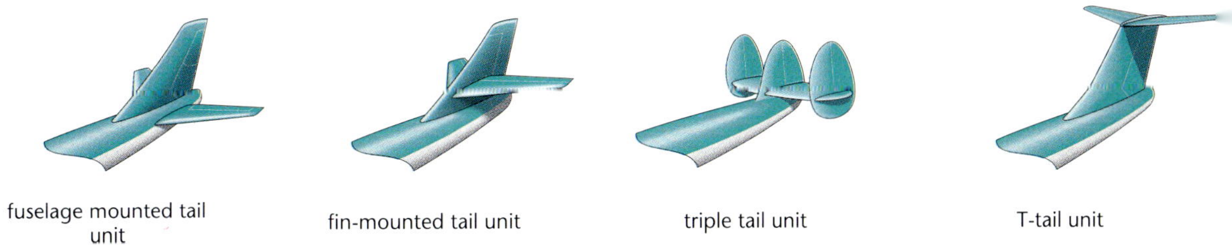

fuselage mounted tail unit

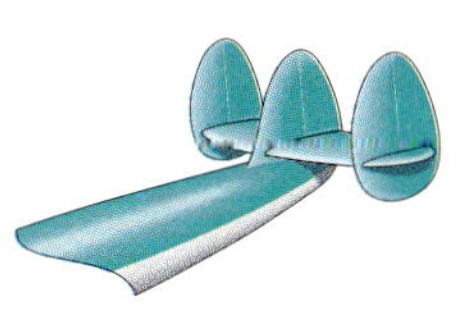

fin-mounted tail unit

triple tail unit

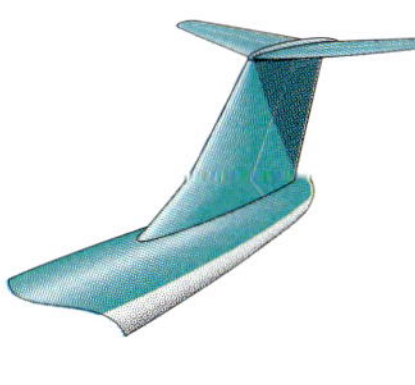

T-tail unit

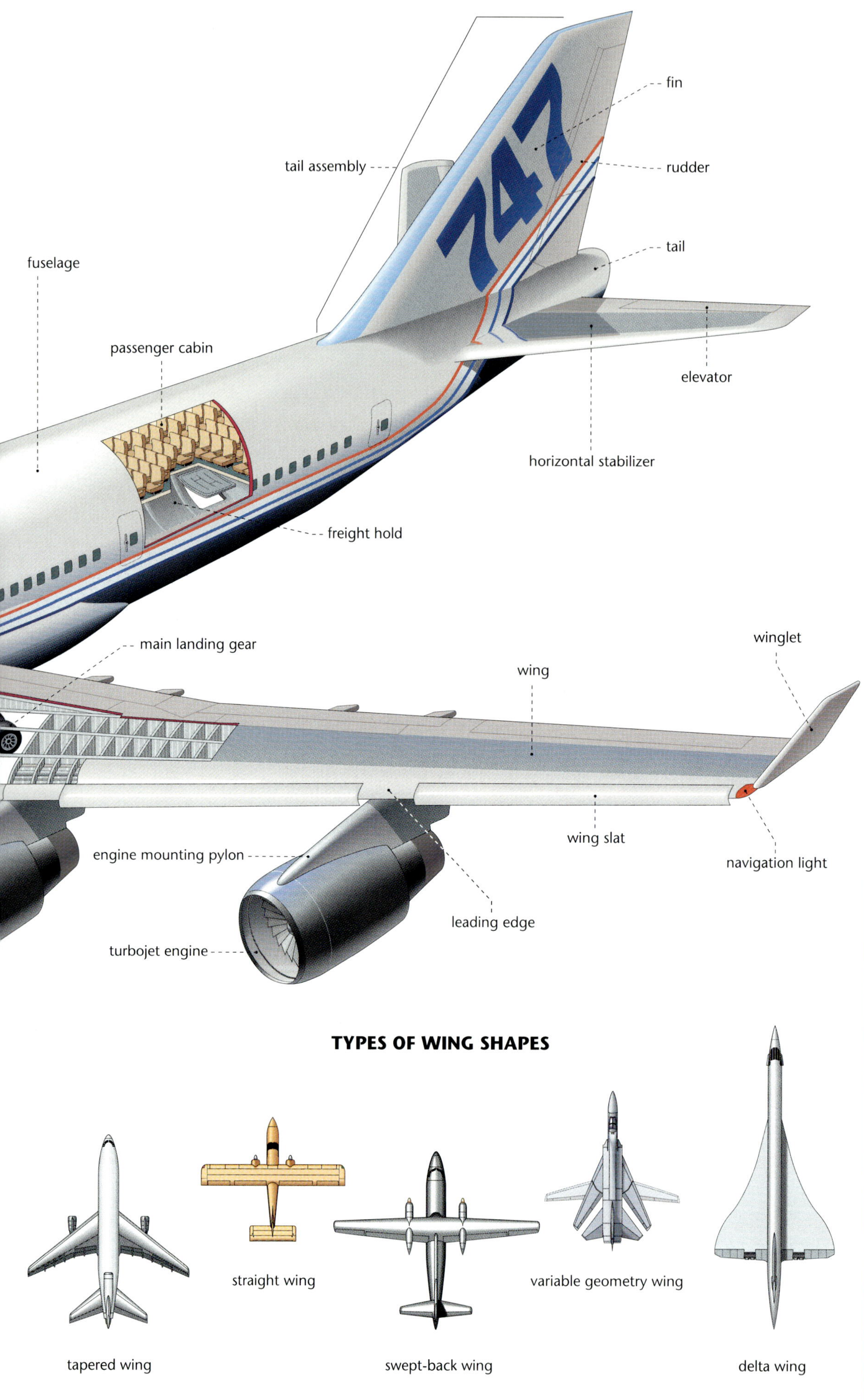

TYPES OF WING SHAPES

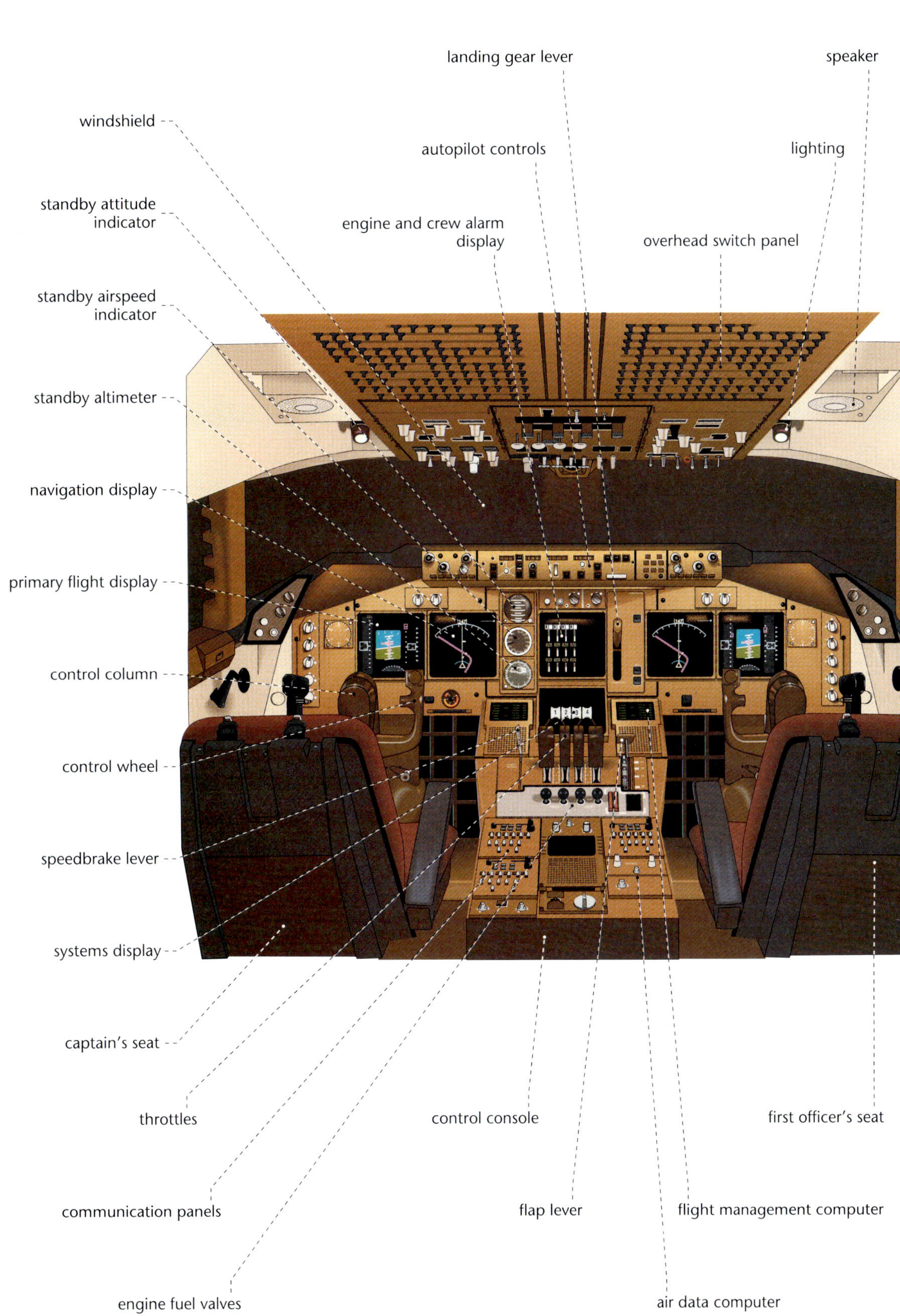
landing gear lever
speaker
autopilot controls
lighting
windshield
engine and crew alarm
display
overhead switch panel
standby attitude
indicator
standby airspeed
indicator
standby altimeter
navigation display
primary flight display
control column
control wheel
speedbrake lever
systems display
captain's seat
throttles
control console
first officer's seat
communication panels
flap lever
flight management computer
engine fuel valves
air data computer

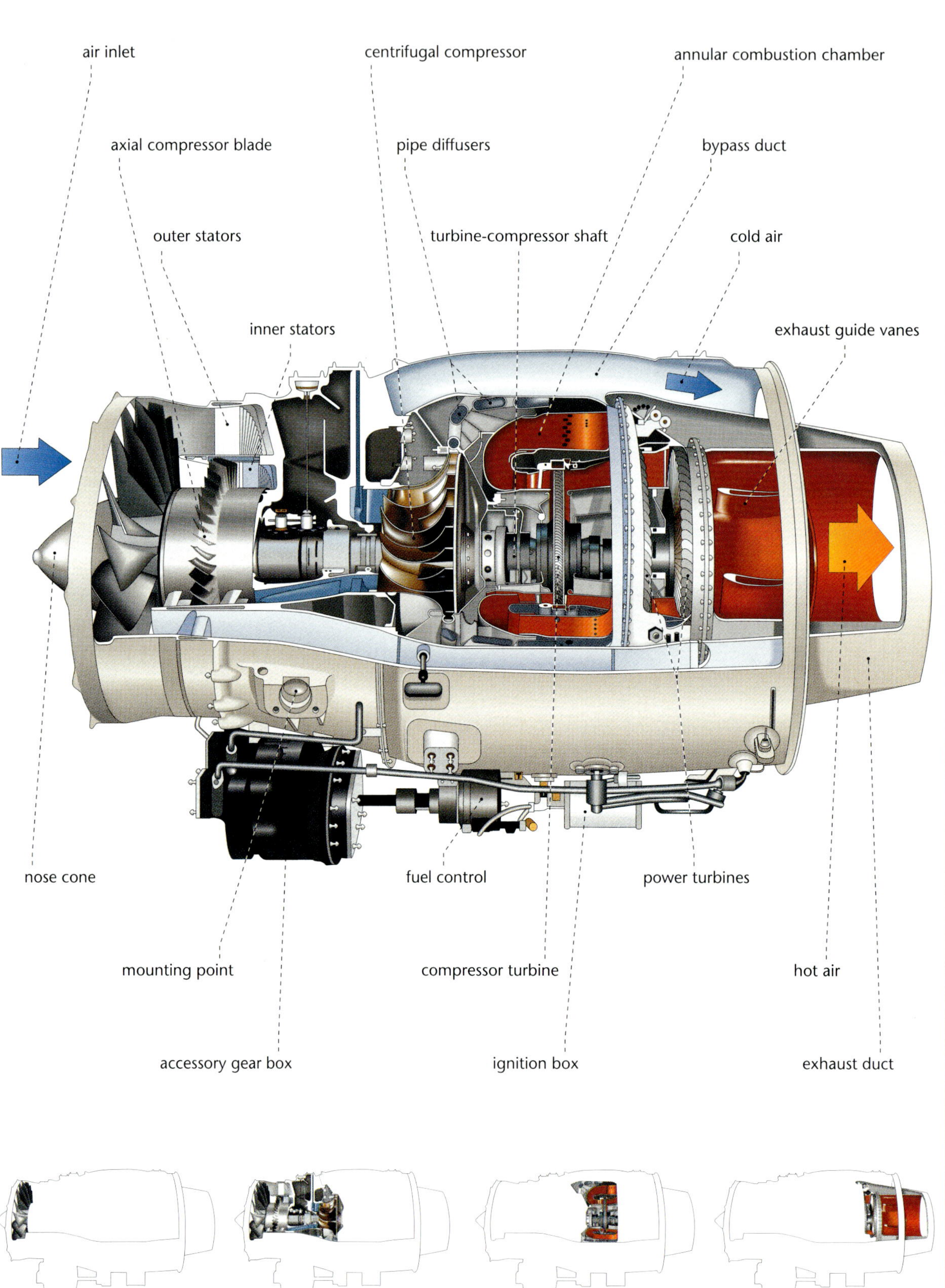
air inlet
centrifugal compressor
annular combustion chamber
axial compressor blade
pipe diffusers
bypass duct
outer stators
turbine-compressor shaft
cold air
inner stators
exhaust guide vanes
nose cone
fuel control
power turbines
mounting point
compressor turbine
hot air
accessory gear box
ignition box
exhaust duct
fan
compression
combustion
exhaust

control tower cab
access road
high-speed exit taxiway
control tower
taxiway
by-pass taxiway
apron
apron
taxiway
service road

maintenance hangar
passenger terminal
parking area
telescopic corridor
boarding walkway
radial passenger loading area
service area
taxiway line

PASSENGER TERMINAL

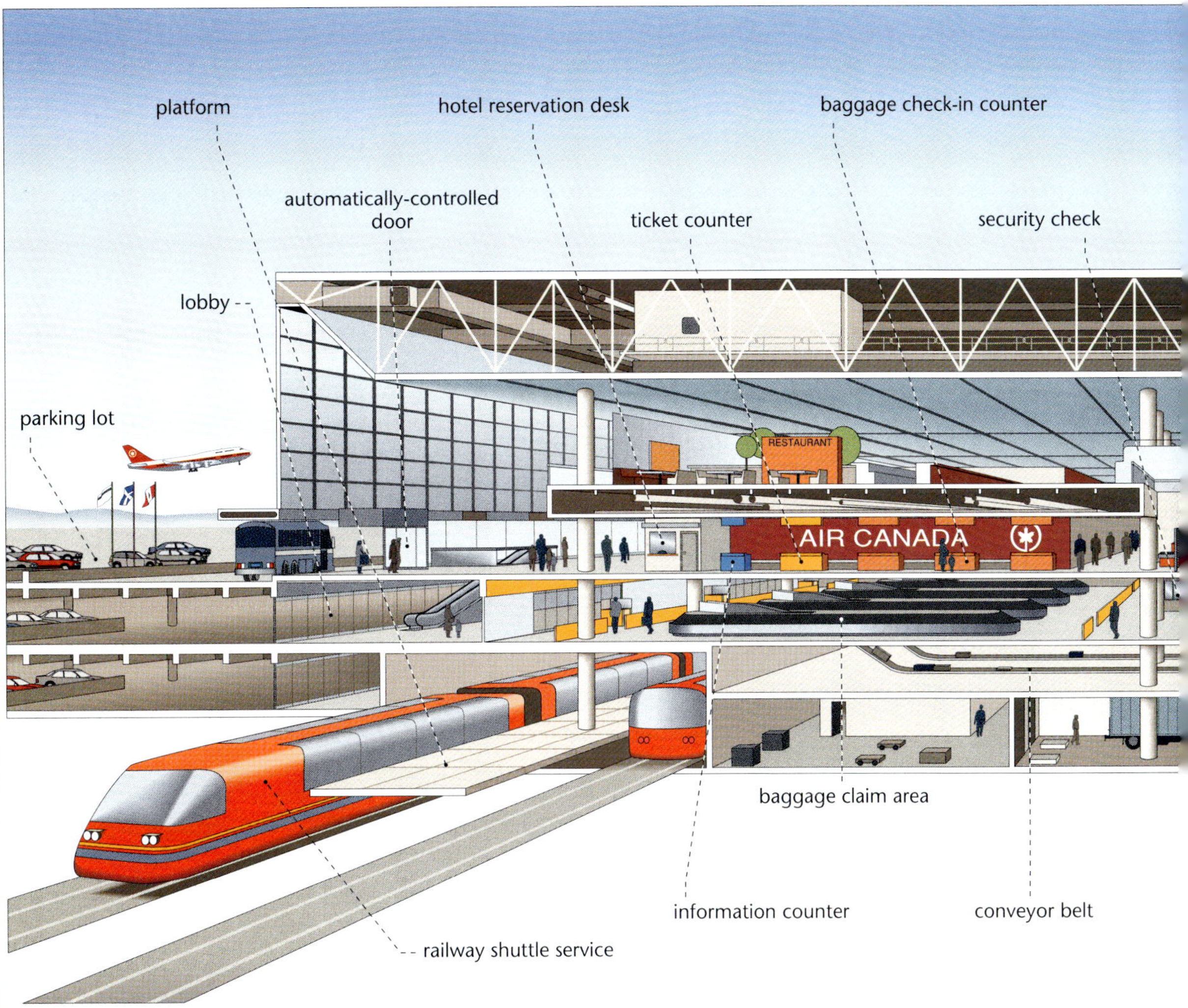

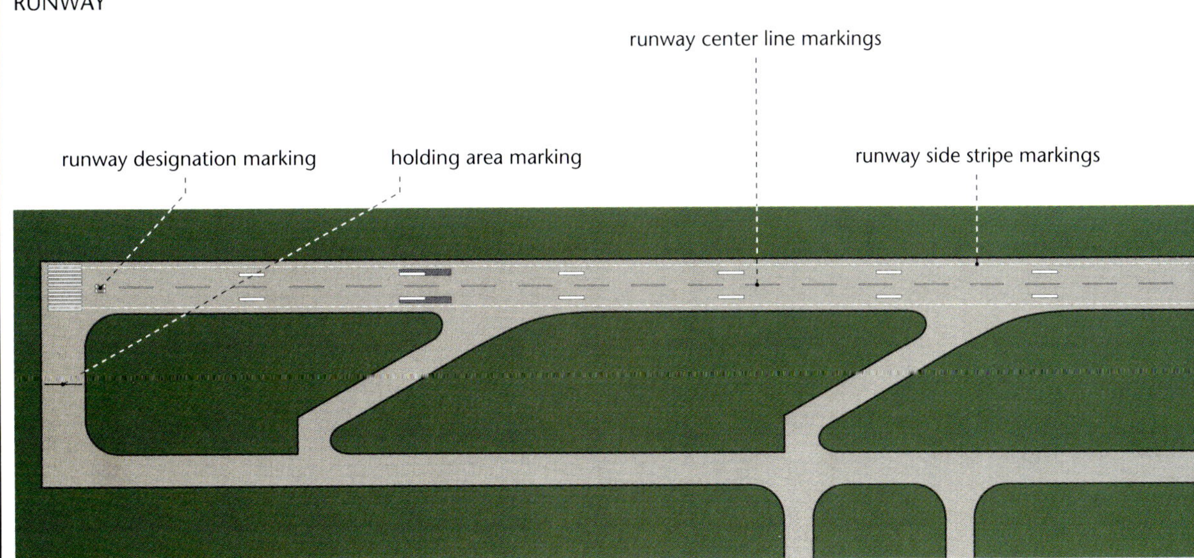

RUNWAY

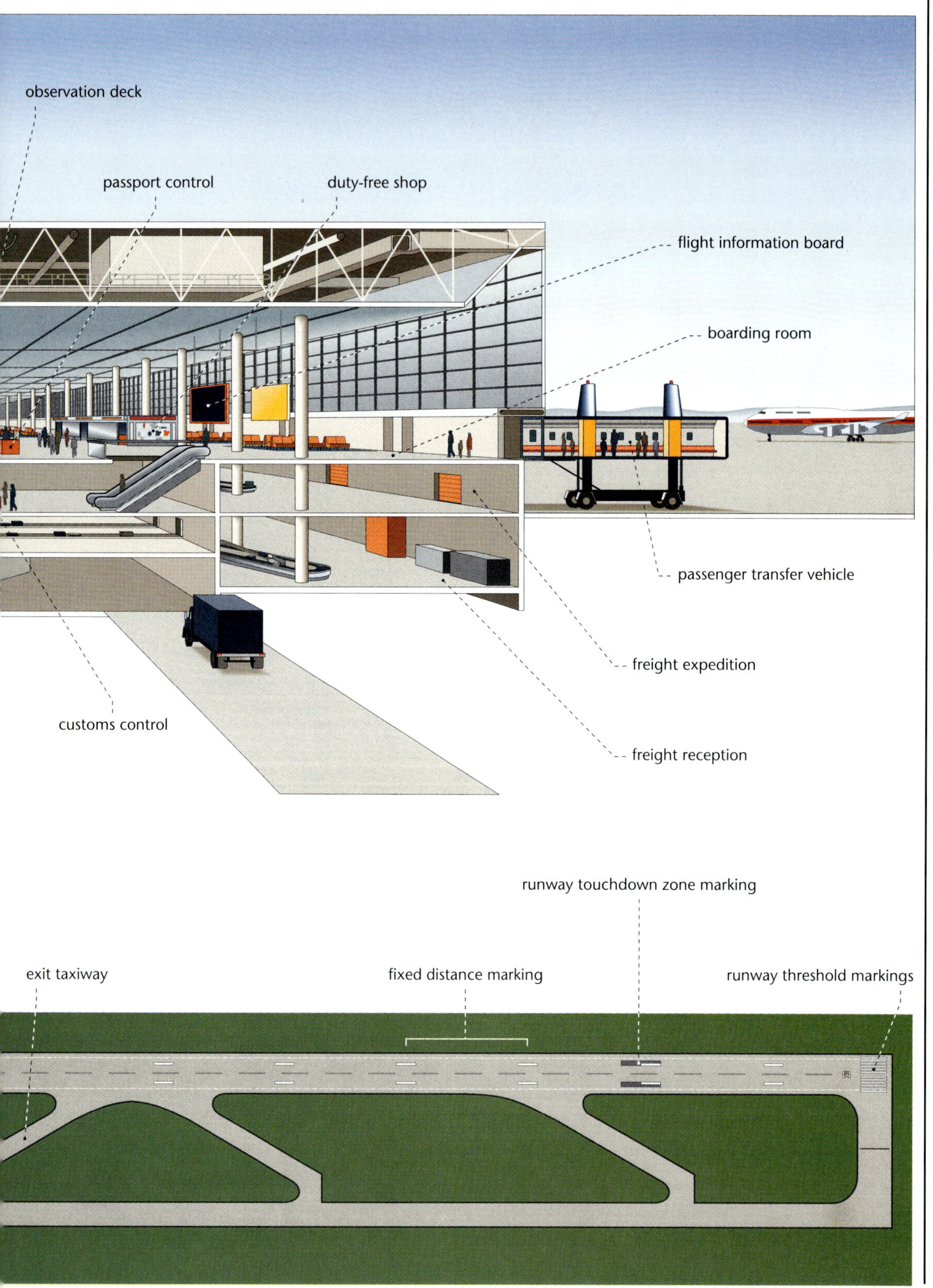

observation deck
passport control
duty-free shop
flight information board
boarding room
customs control
passenger transfer vehicle
freight expedition
freight reception
runway touchdown zone marking
exit taxiway
fixed distance marking
runway threshold markings

AIR TRANSPORT

GROUND AIRPORT EQUIPMENT

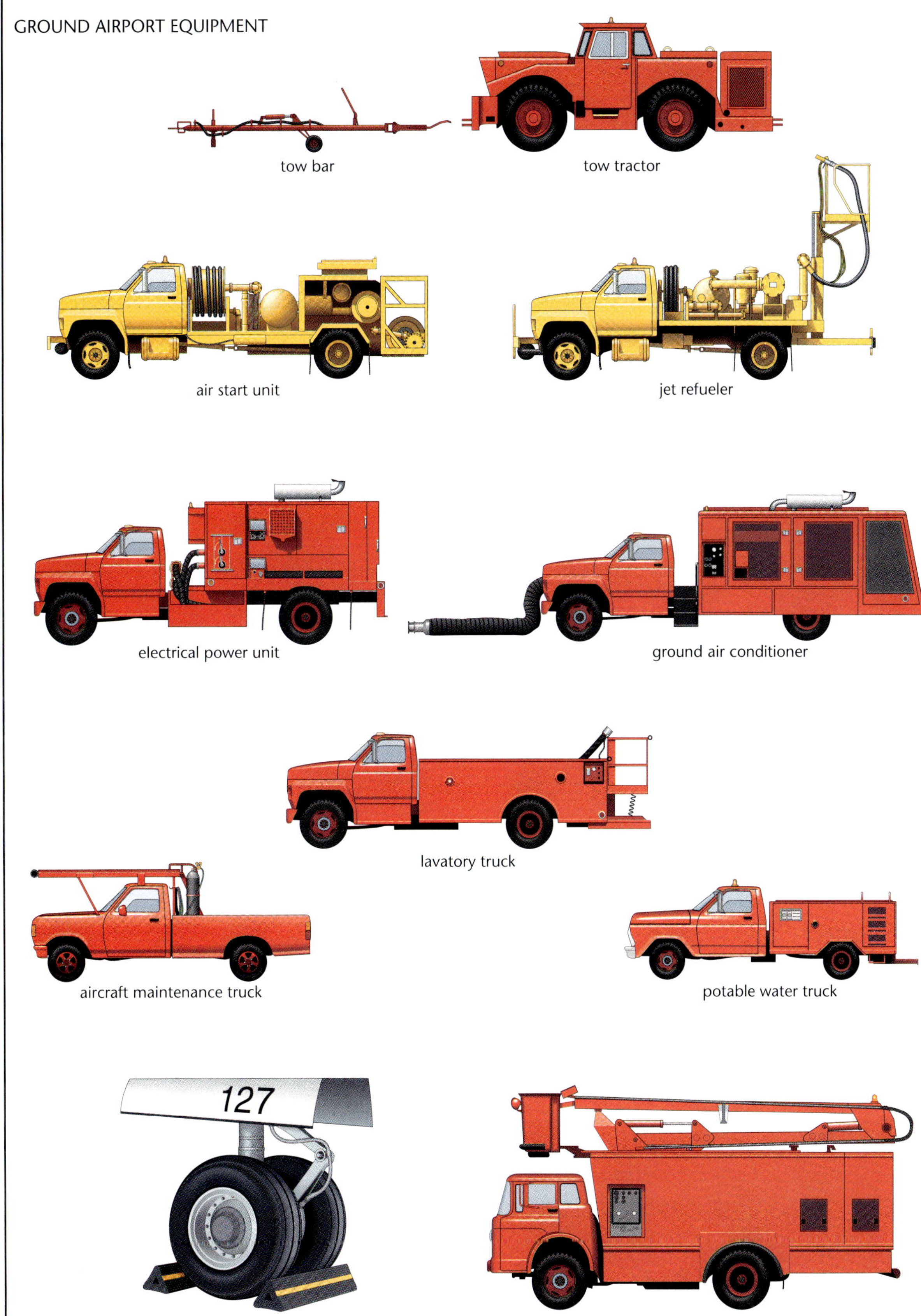

tow bar

tow tractor

air start unit

jet refueler

electrical power unit

ground air conditioner

lavatory truck

aircraft maintenance truck

potable water truck

wheel chock

boom truck

tripod tail support

baggage trailer

tow tractor

baggage conveyor

container/pallet loader

catering vehicle

mobile passenger stairs

universal step

passenger transfer vehicle

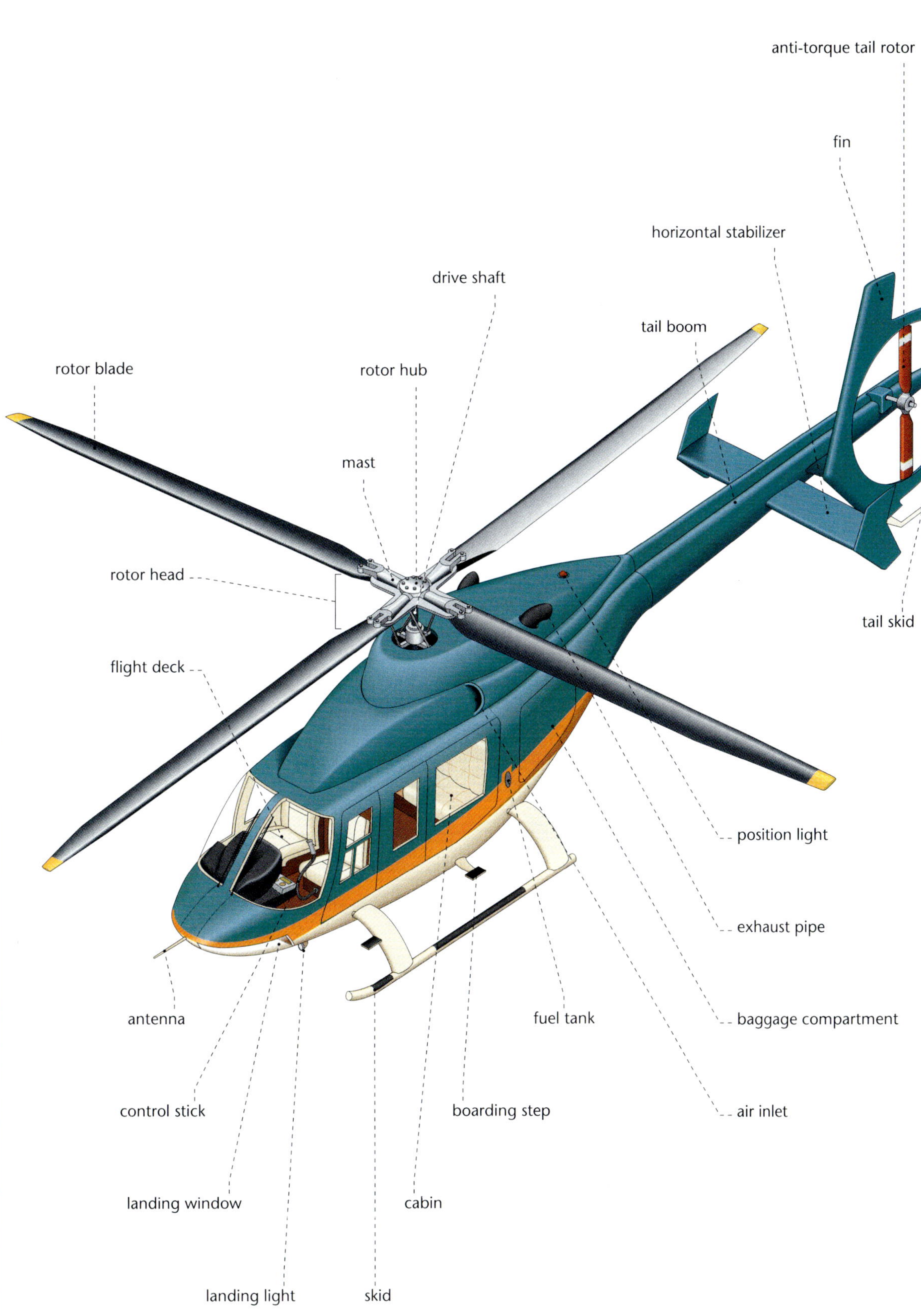
anti-torque tail rotor
fin
horizontal stabilizer
drive shaft
tail boom
rotor blade
rotor hub
mast
tail skid
rotor head
flight deck
position light
exhaust pipe
antenna
fuel tank
baggage compartment
control stick
boarding step
air inlet
landing window
cabin
landing light
skid

ROCKET

launch escape system
command module
service module
lunar module
instrument unit
helium sphere
J-2 engine
liquid hydrogen tank
liquid oxygen tank
liquid oxygen tank baffle
kerosene tank
fuel transfer pipe
stabilizing fin
nozzle
F-1 engine
payload
third stage
second stage
first stage

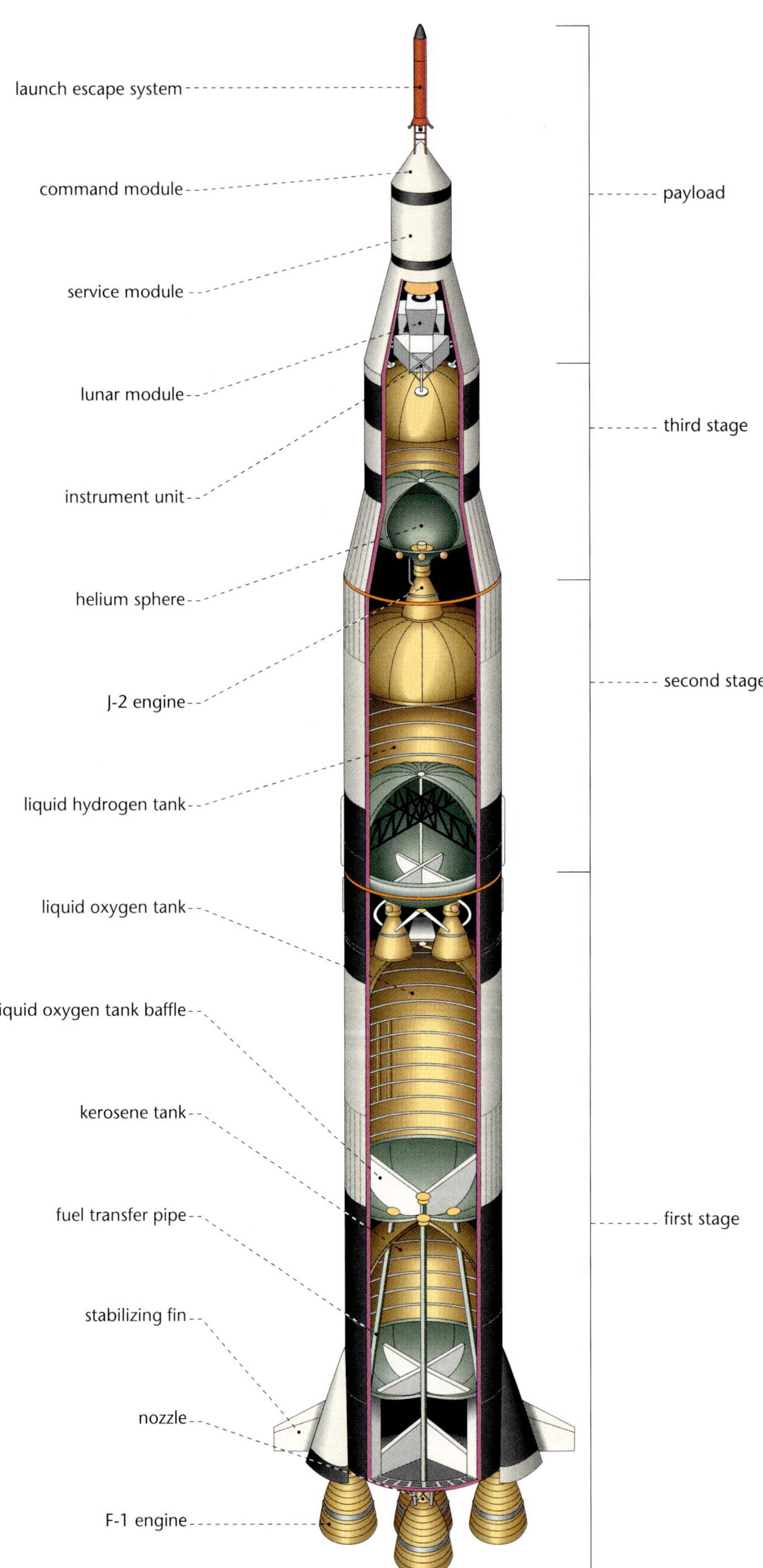

SPACE SHUTTLE

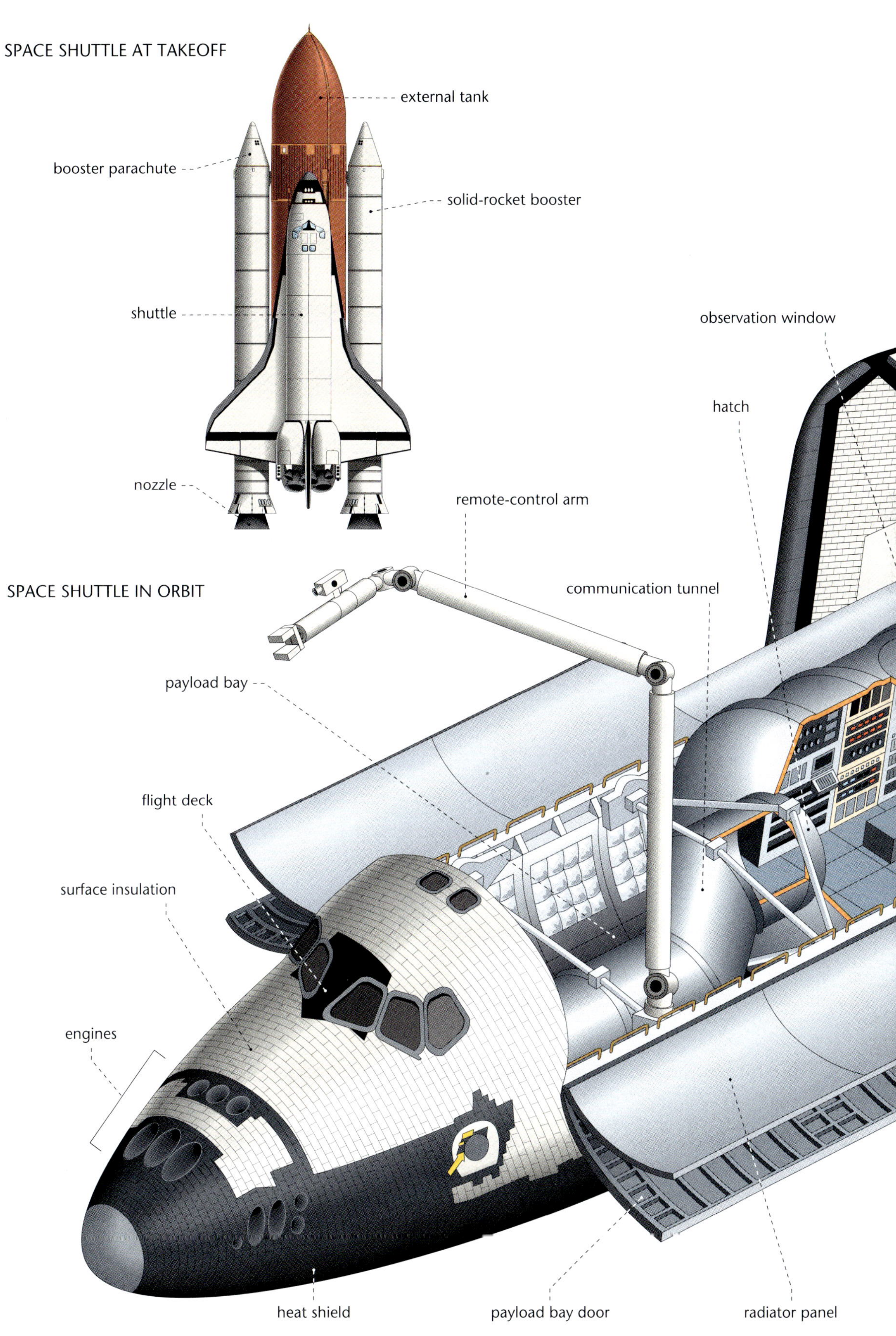

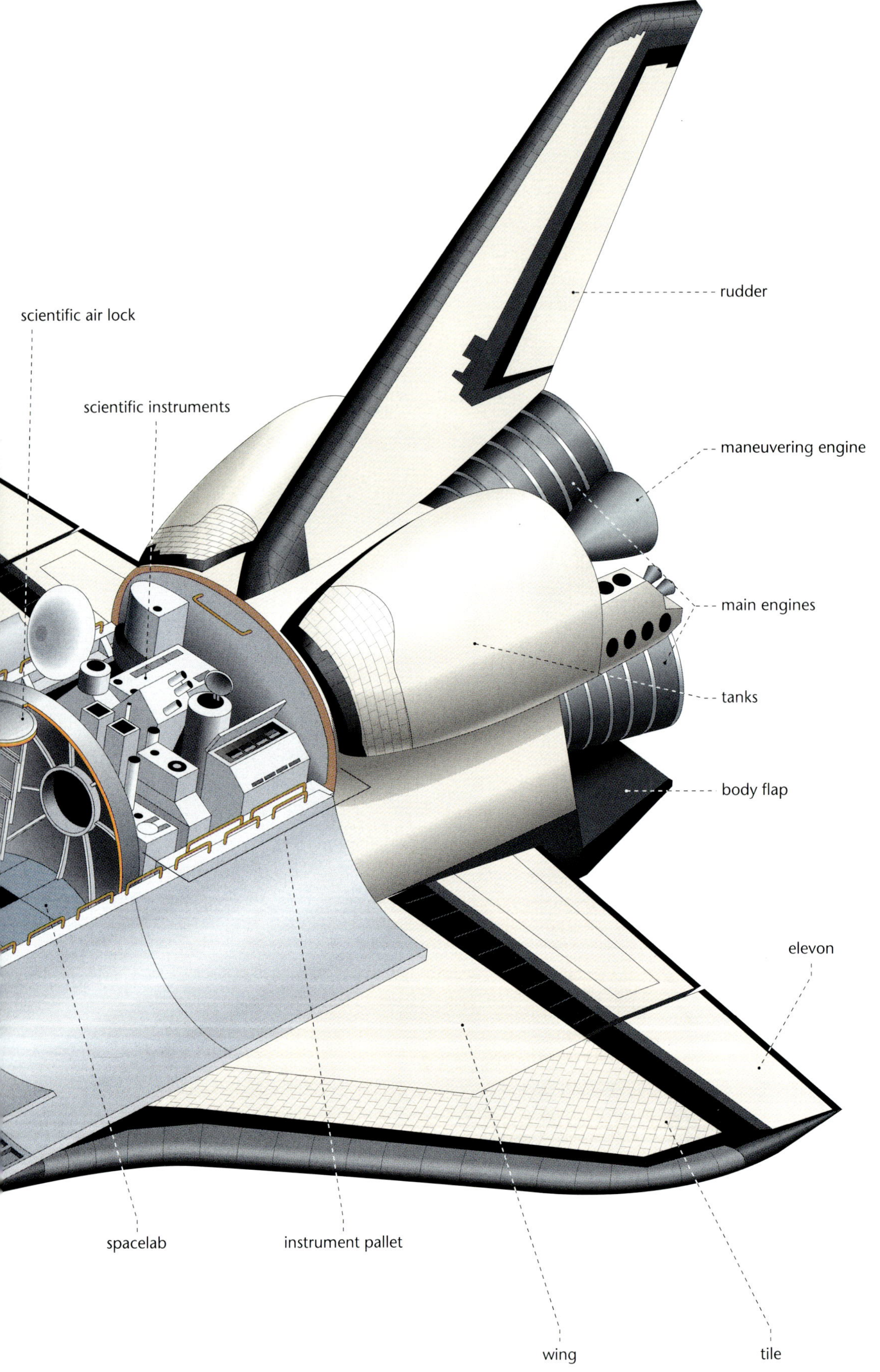

scientific air lock
scientific instruments
rudder
maneuvering engine
main engines
tanks
body flap
elevon
spacelab
instrument pallet
wing
tile

SPACESUIT

35 mm still camera
propellant level gauge
life support system
solar shield
helmet ring
helmet
computer screen intensity controls
color television camera
communications volume controls
procedure checklist
glove
safety suit connection
safety tether
tool tether
reading mirror
life support system controls
body temperature control unit
manned maneuvering unit
oxygen pressure actuator
thruster
protection layer
biomedical monitoring sensor
liquid cooling and ventilation garment
insulation layers
EV1
EV1

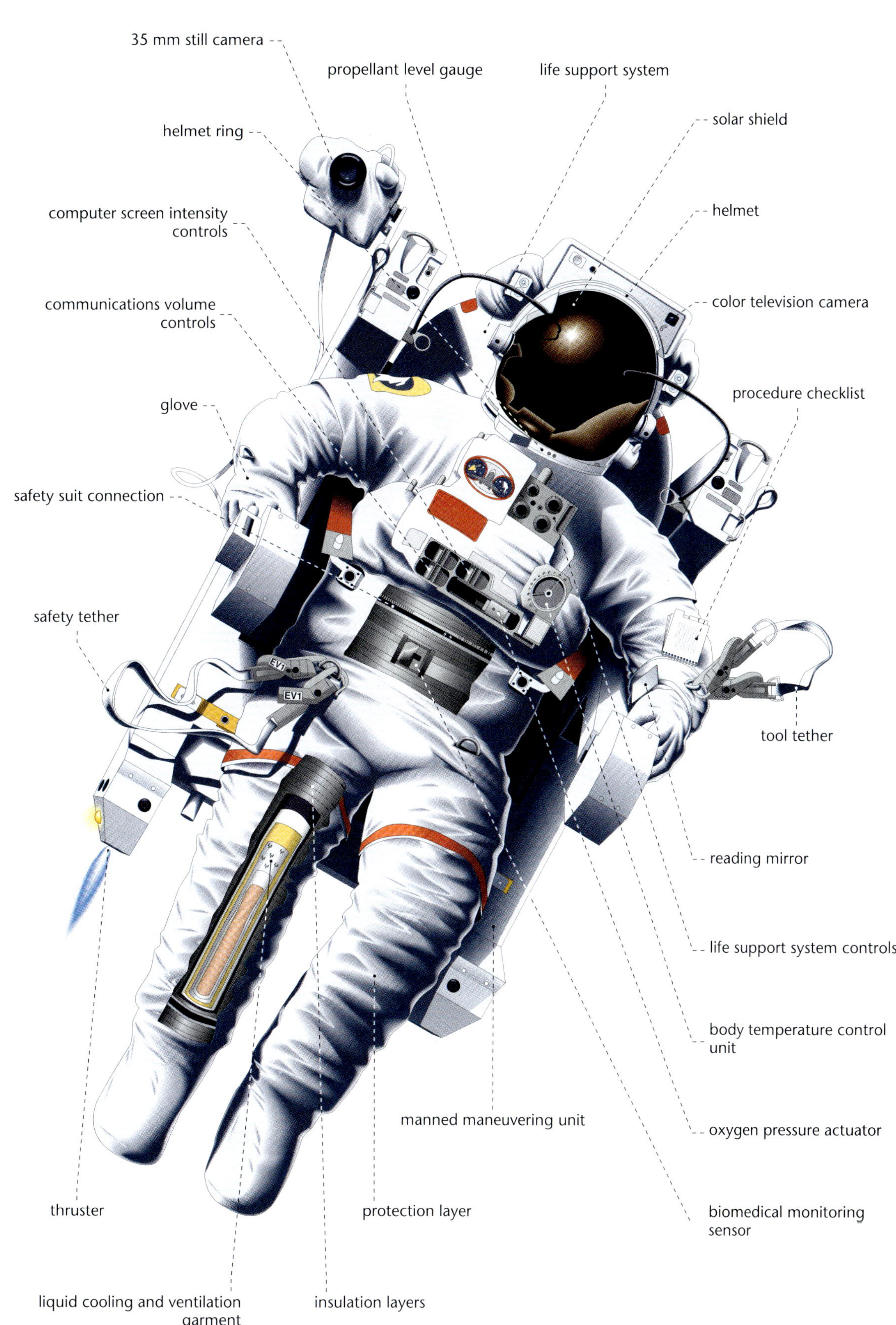

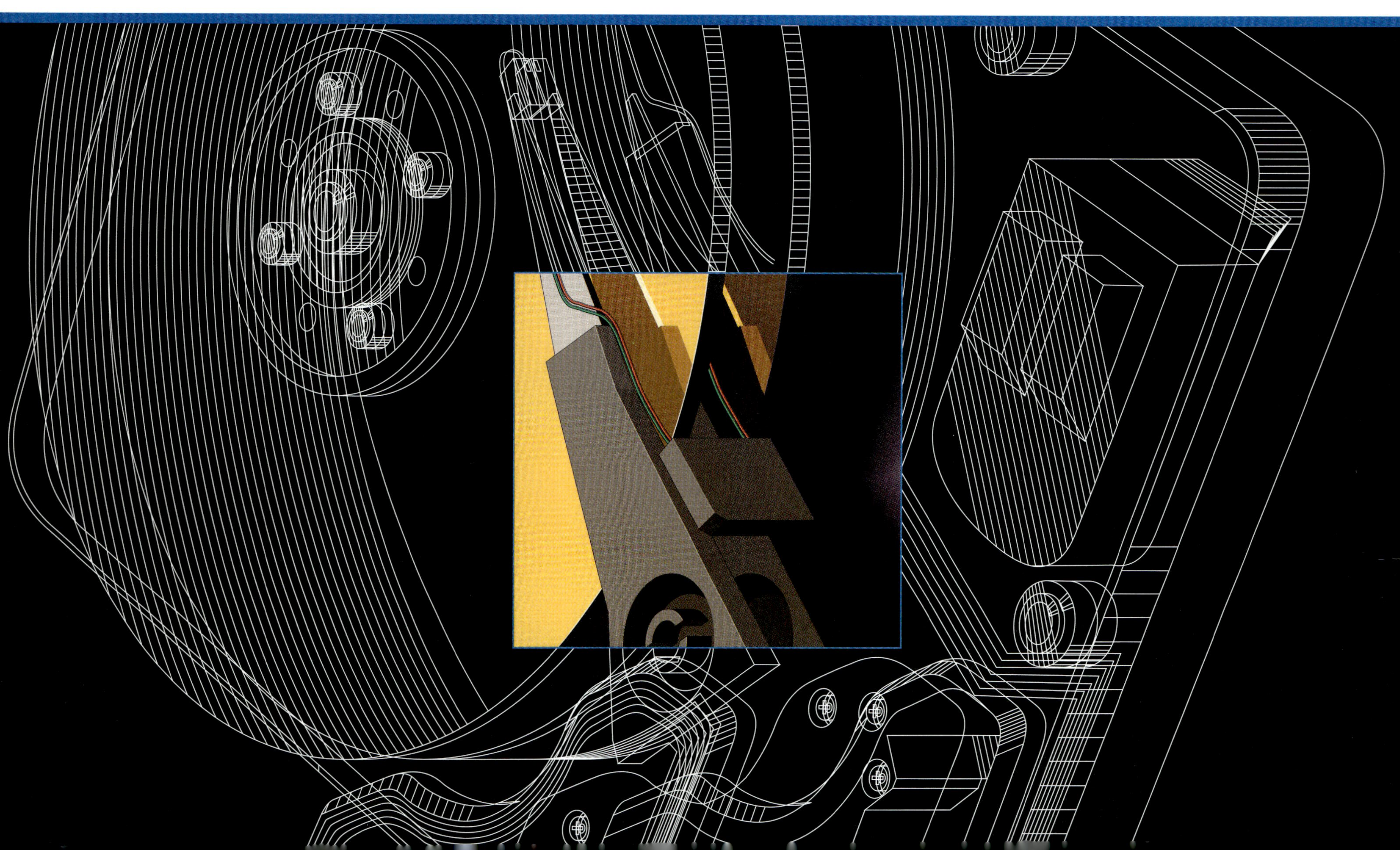

CONTENTS

OFFICE SUPPLIES

mechanical pencil

ballpoint pen

pencil

fountain pen

eraser holder

stick eraser

marker

glue stick

eraser

correction fluid

highlighter pen

clip

paper clips

stapler

letter opener

paper fasteners

staples

thumb tacks

pencil sharpener

correction paper

staple remover

rubber stamp
stamp pad
tape dispenser
bill-file
numbering machine
dater
stamp rack
paper punch
label maker
QUEBE
moistener
rotary file
letter scale
pencil sharpener
telephone index

INDEX CARD DRAWER

tear-off calendar
appointment book
calendar pad
account book
memo pad
self-adhesive labels
tab
archboard
window tab
folder
file guides
hanging file

clipboard
post binder
spring binder
document folder
ring binder
dividers
spiral binding
clamp binder
fastener binder

executive desk
swivel-tilter armchair
desk mat
credenza
partition
lateral filing cabinet

COMPUTER TABLE
PRINTER TABLE
paper catcher
adjustable platen
paper tray
modesty panel
paper feed channel
mobile filing unit
mobile drawer unit
typist's chair
return
SECRETARIAL DESK

OFFICE FURNITURE

CALCULATOR

POCKET CALCULATOR

PRINTING CALCULATOR

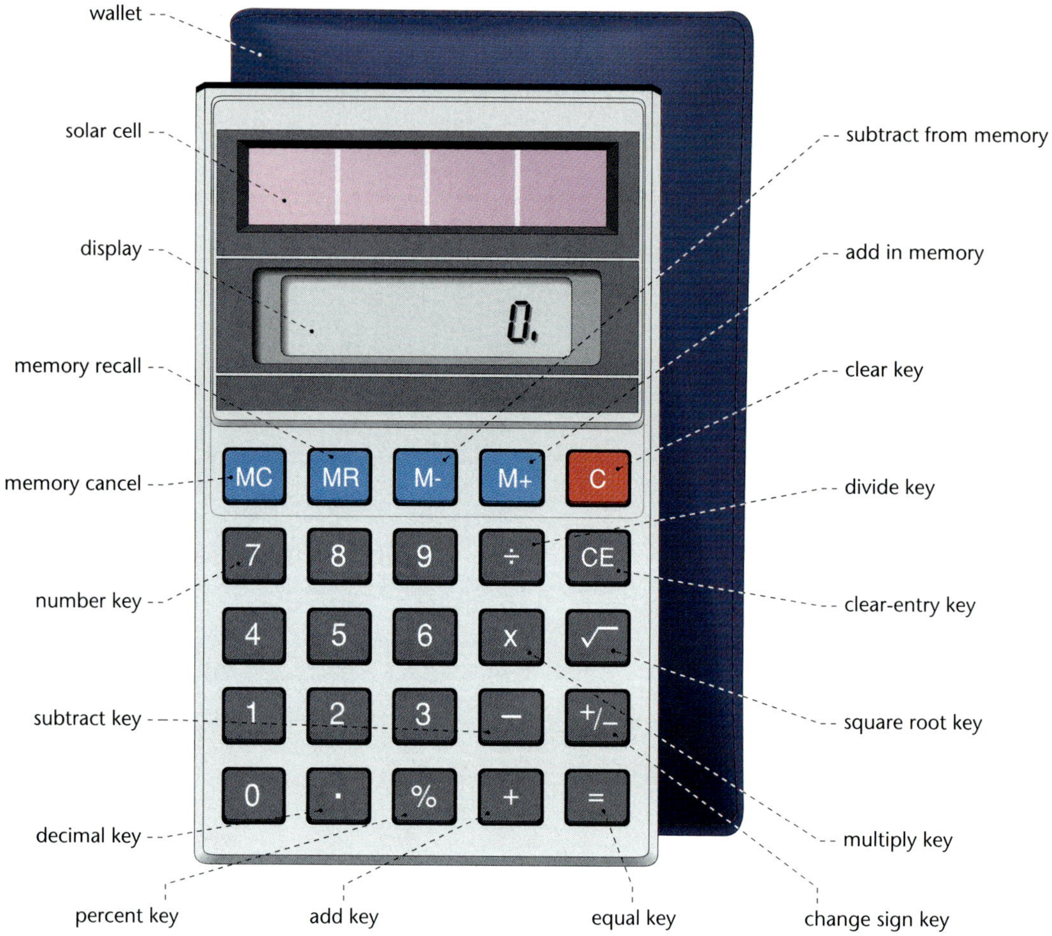

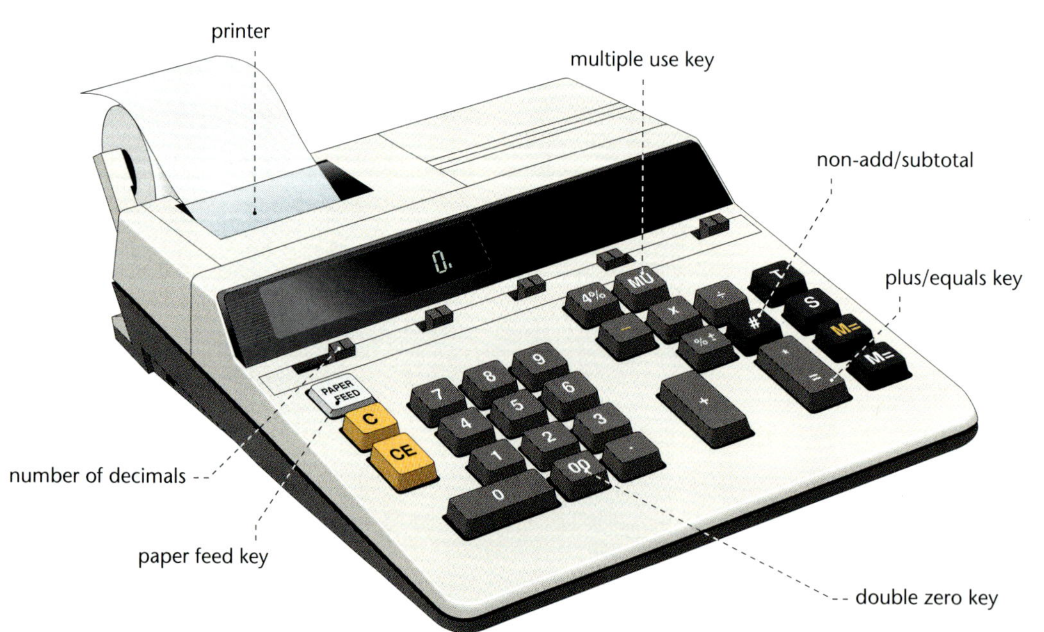

ELECTRONIC TYPEWRITER

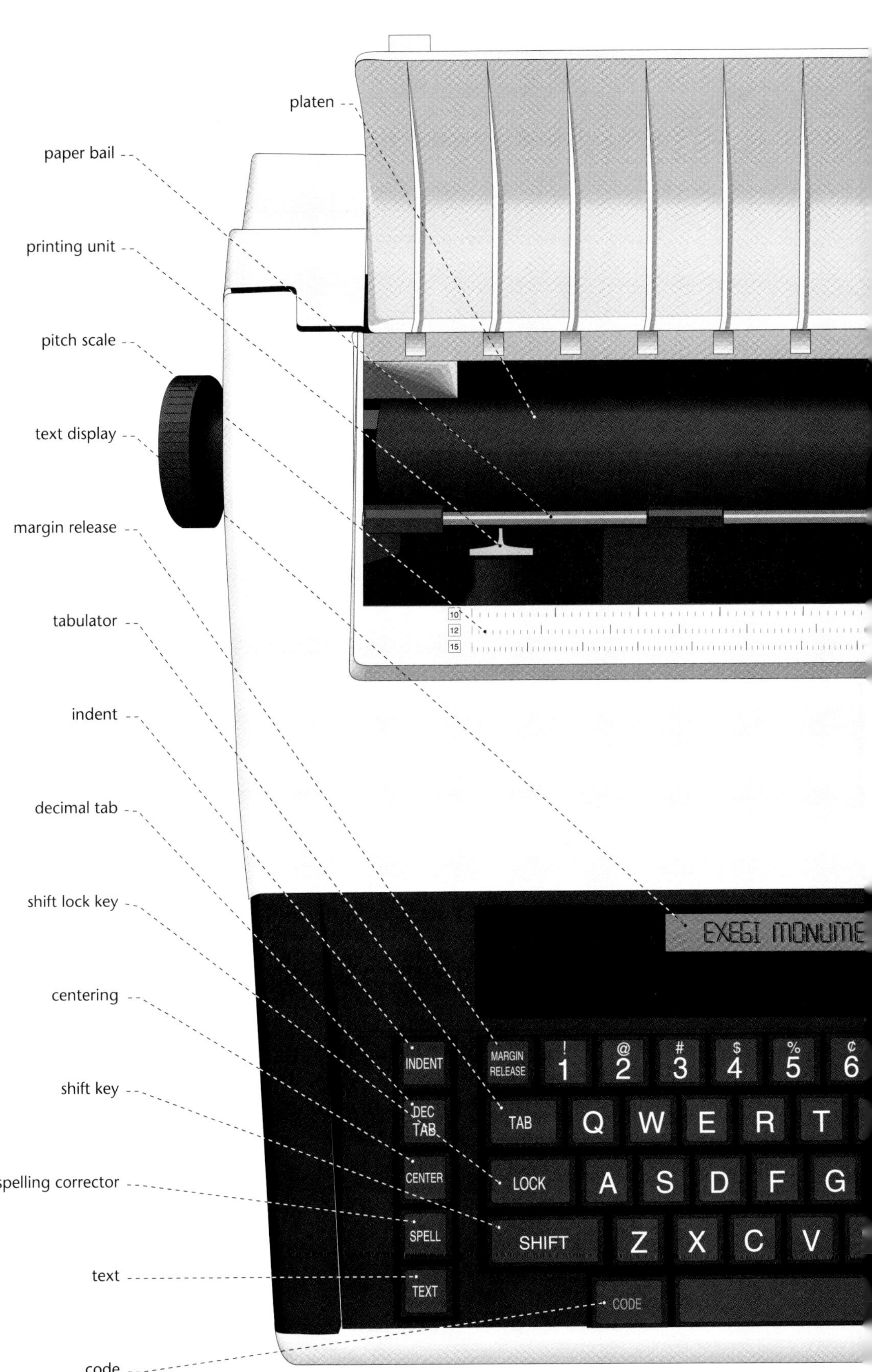

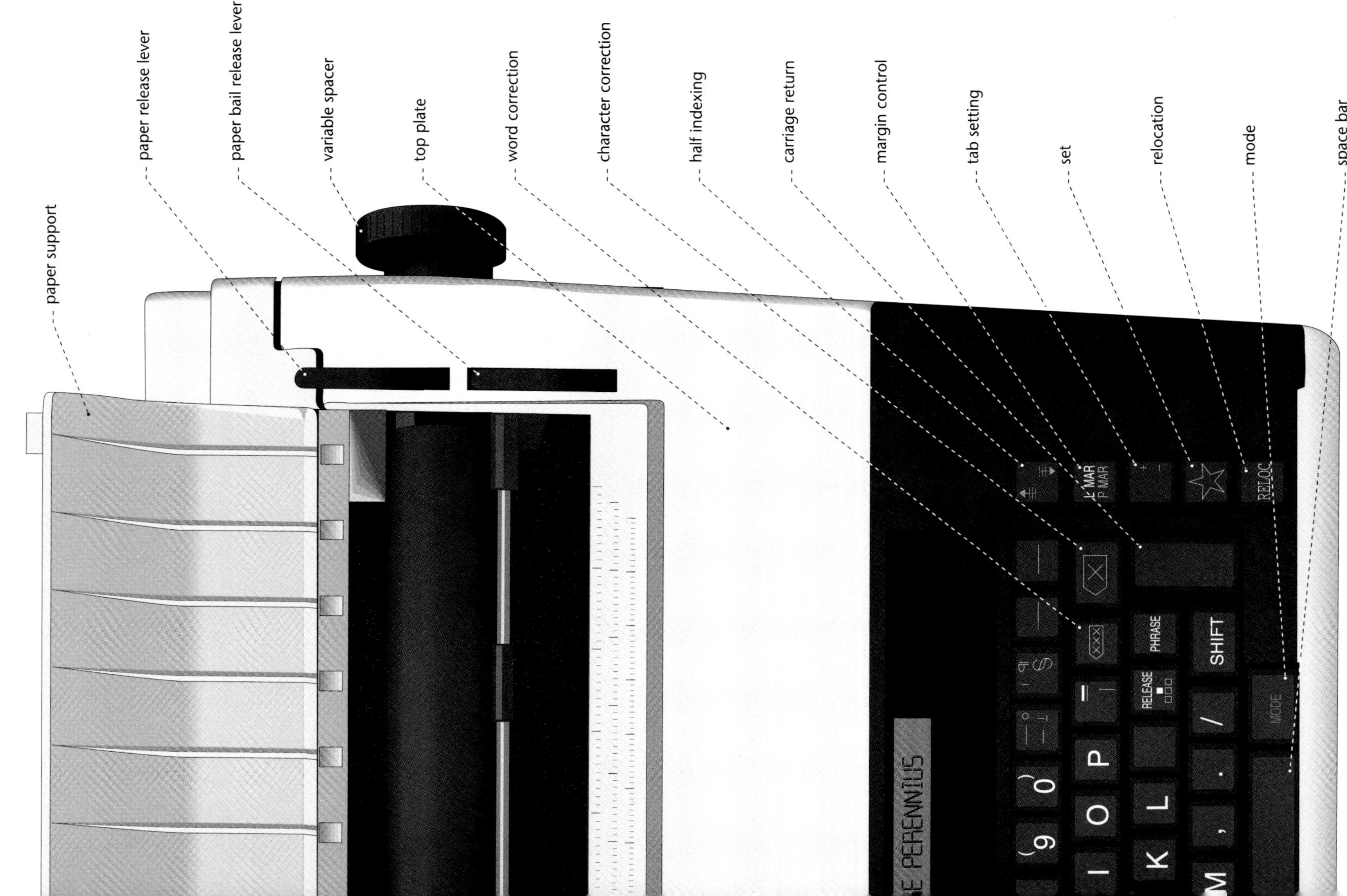

paper support
paper release lever
paper bail release lever
variable spacer
top plate
word correction
character correction
half indexing
carriage return
margin control
tab setting
set
relocation
mode
space bar
E PERENNIUS
L MAR
P MAR
RELEASE
PHRASE
SHIFT
MODE
RELOC
9 0
I O P
K L
M , . /

CONFIGURATION OF AN OFFICE AUTOMATION SYSTEM

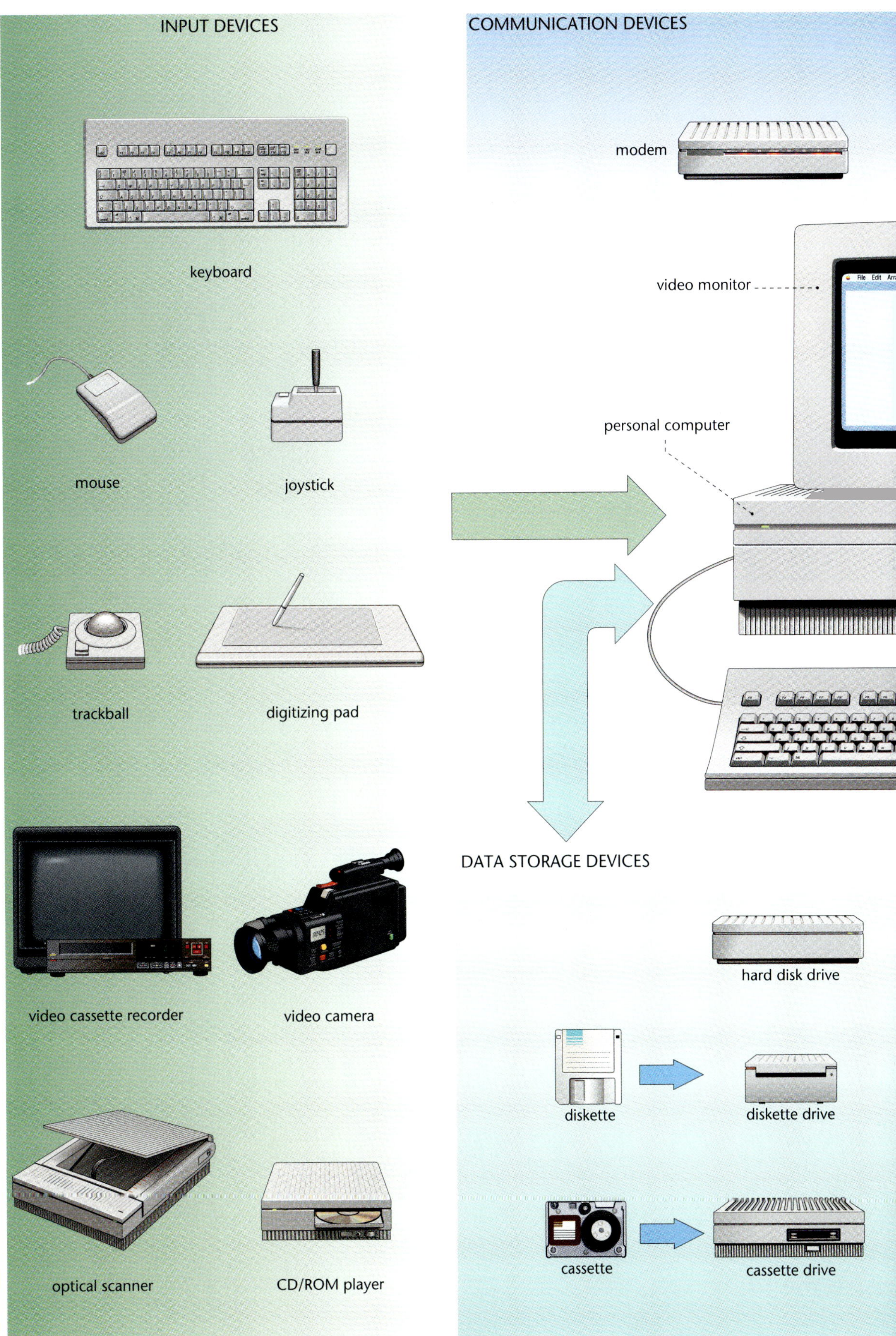

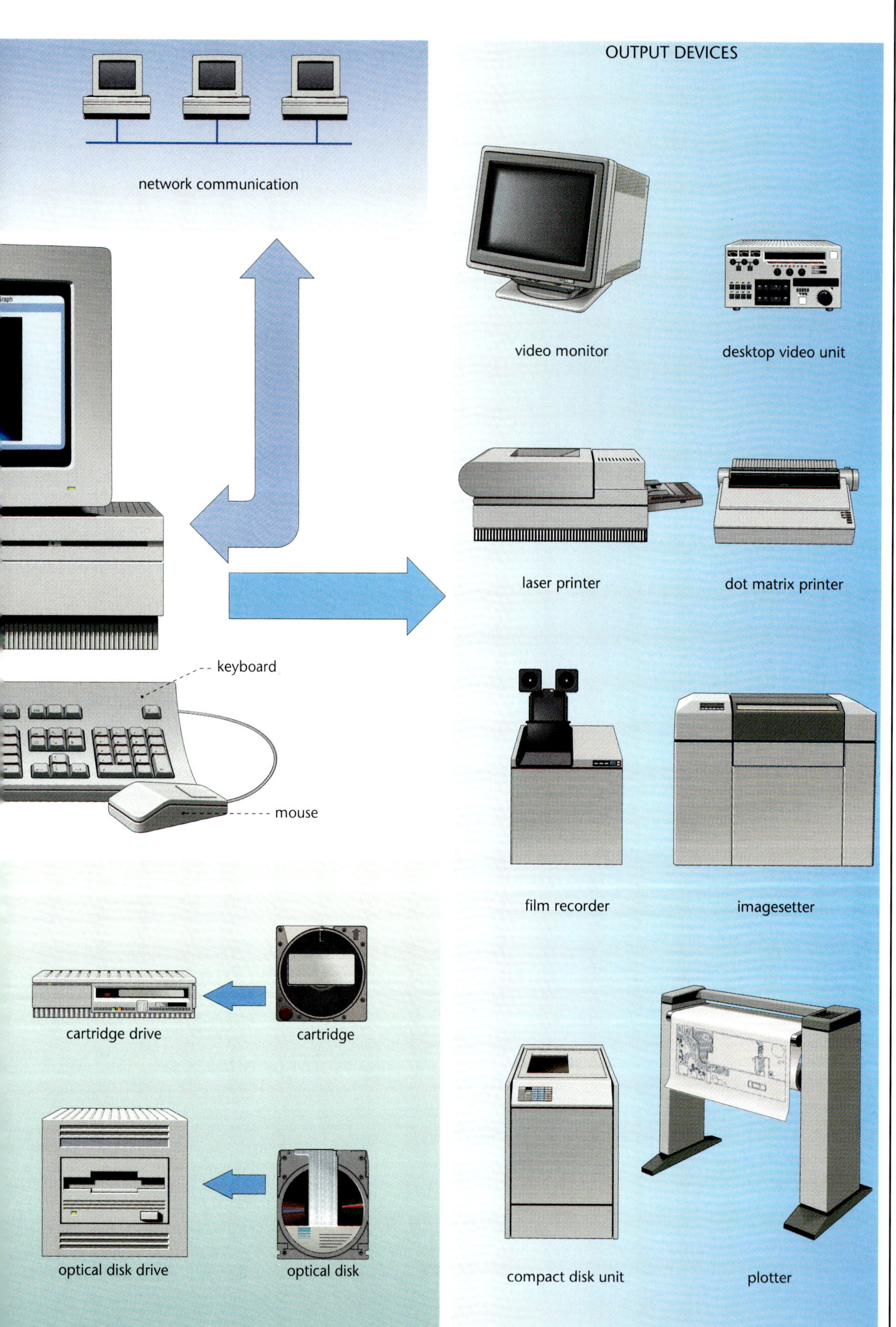

network communication
OUTPUT DEVICES
video monitor
desktop video unit
laser printer
dot matrix printer
film recorder
imagesetter
keyboard
mouse
cartridge drive
cartridge
optical disk drive
optical disk
compact disk unit
plotter

PERSONAL COMPUTER (VIEW FROM ABOVE)

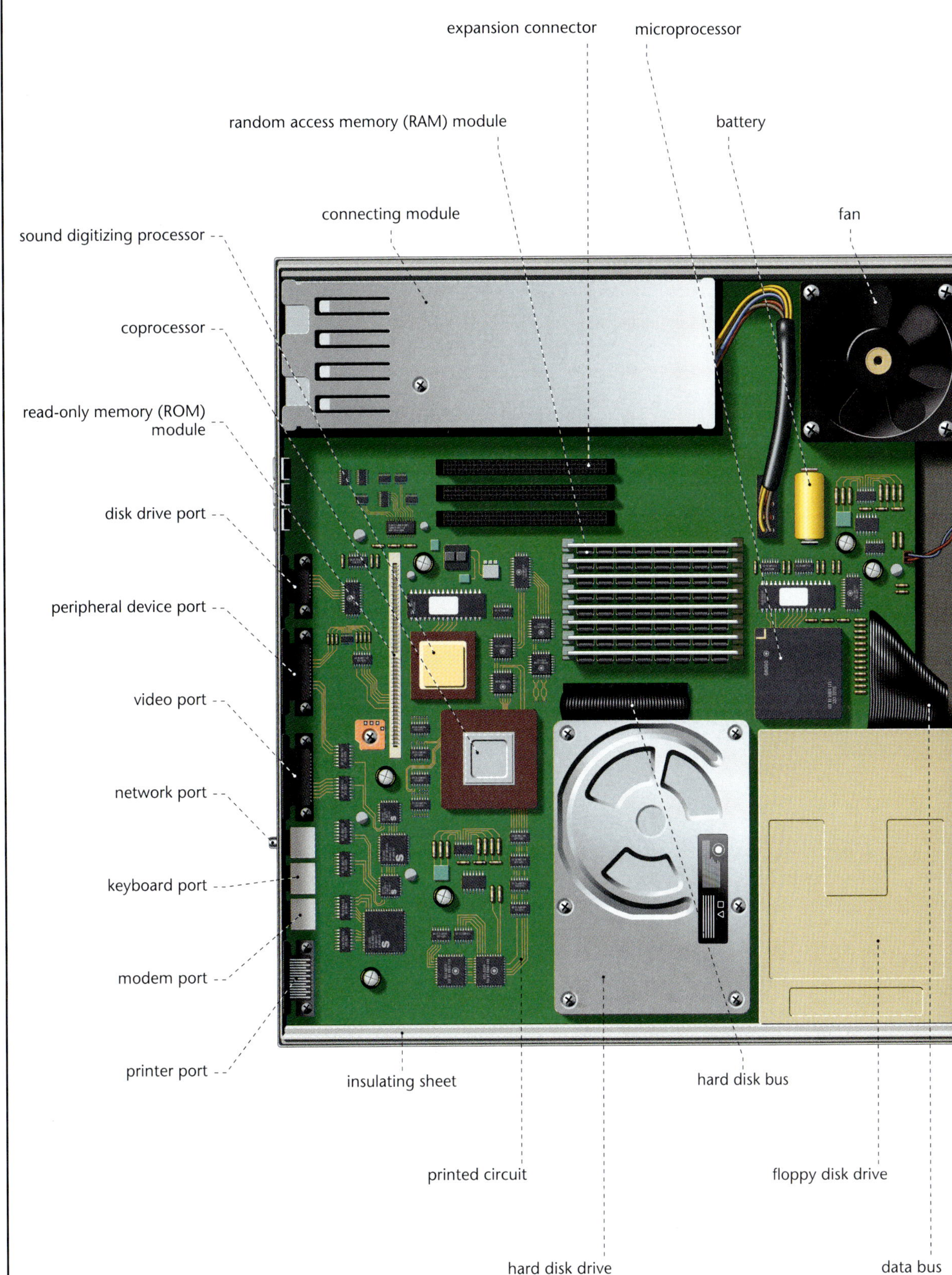

FLOPPY DISK

MINI-FLOPPY DISK

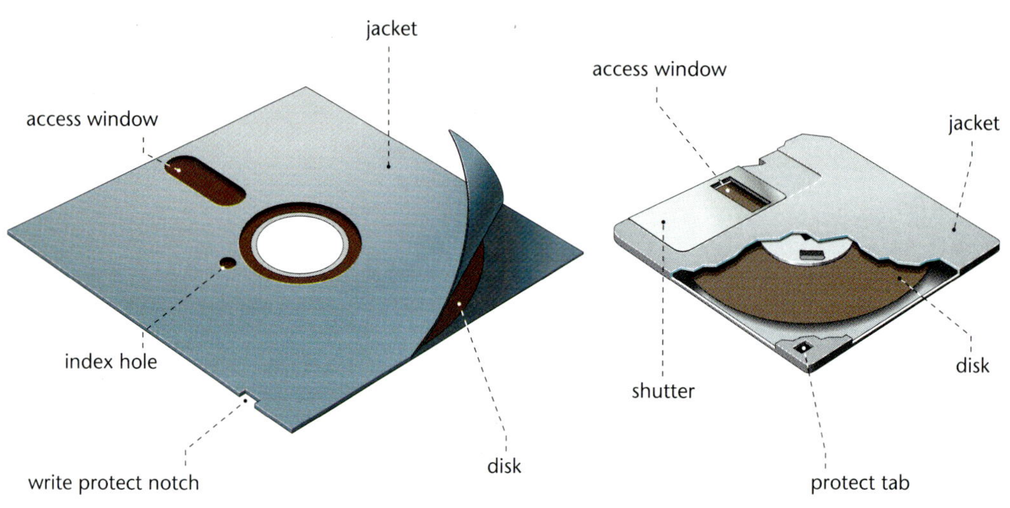

HARD DISK DRIVE

KEYBOARD

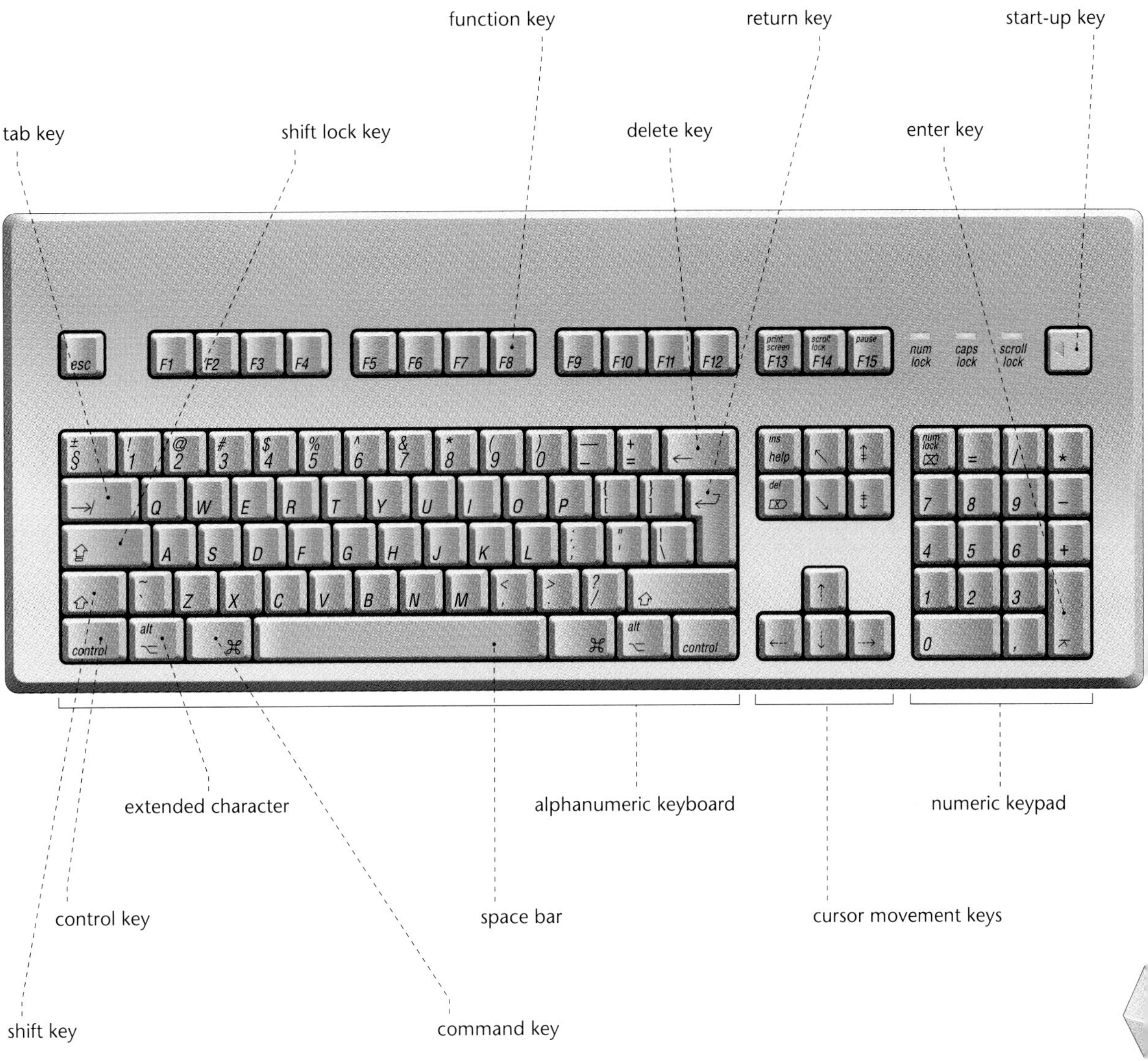

MOUSE

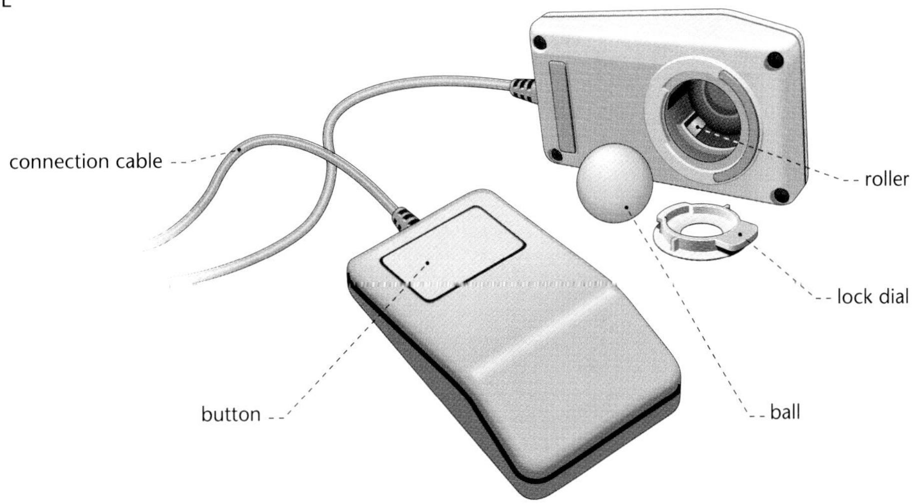

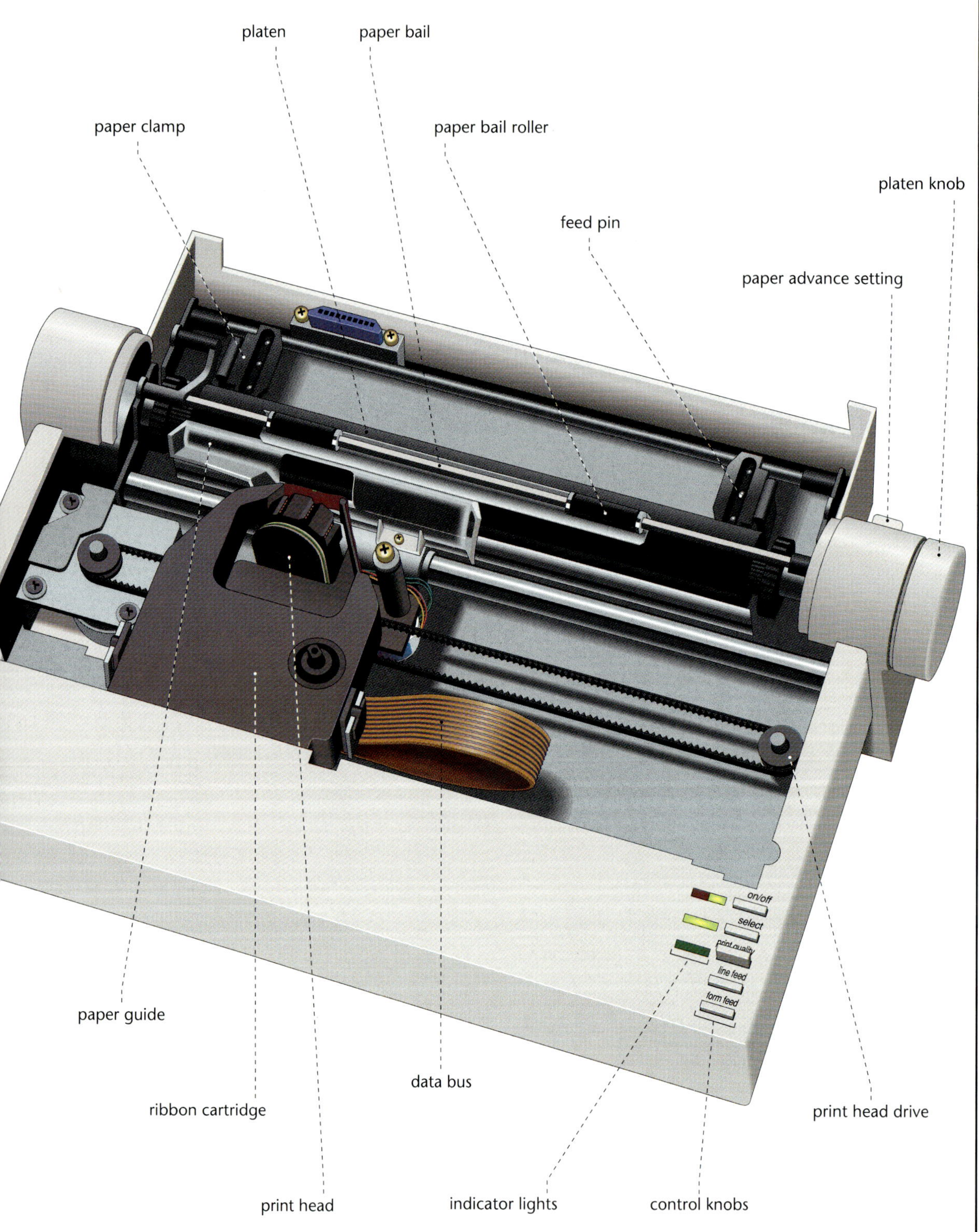
platen
paper bail
paper clamp
paper bail roller
feed pin
platen knob
paper advance setting
on/off
select
print quality
line feed
form feed
paper guide
data bus
print head drive
ribbon cartridge
print head
indicator lights
control knobs

PHOTOCOPIER

CONTROL PANEL

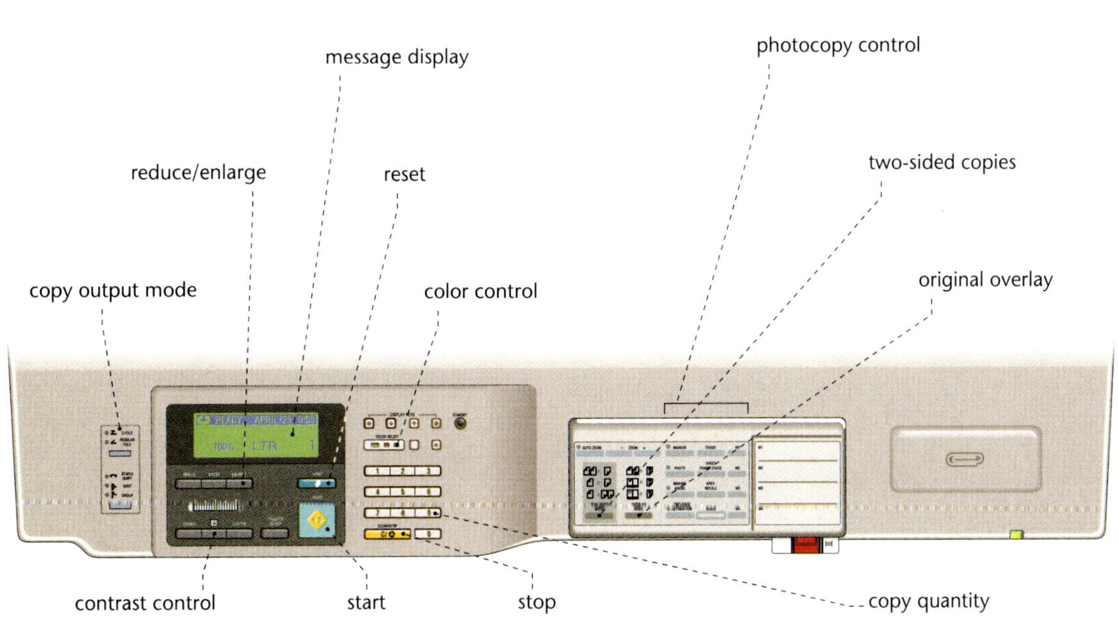

MUSIC

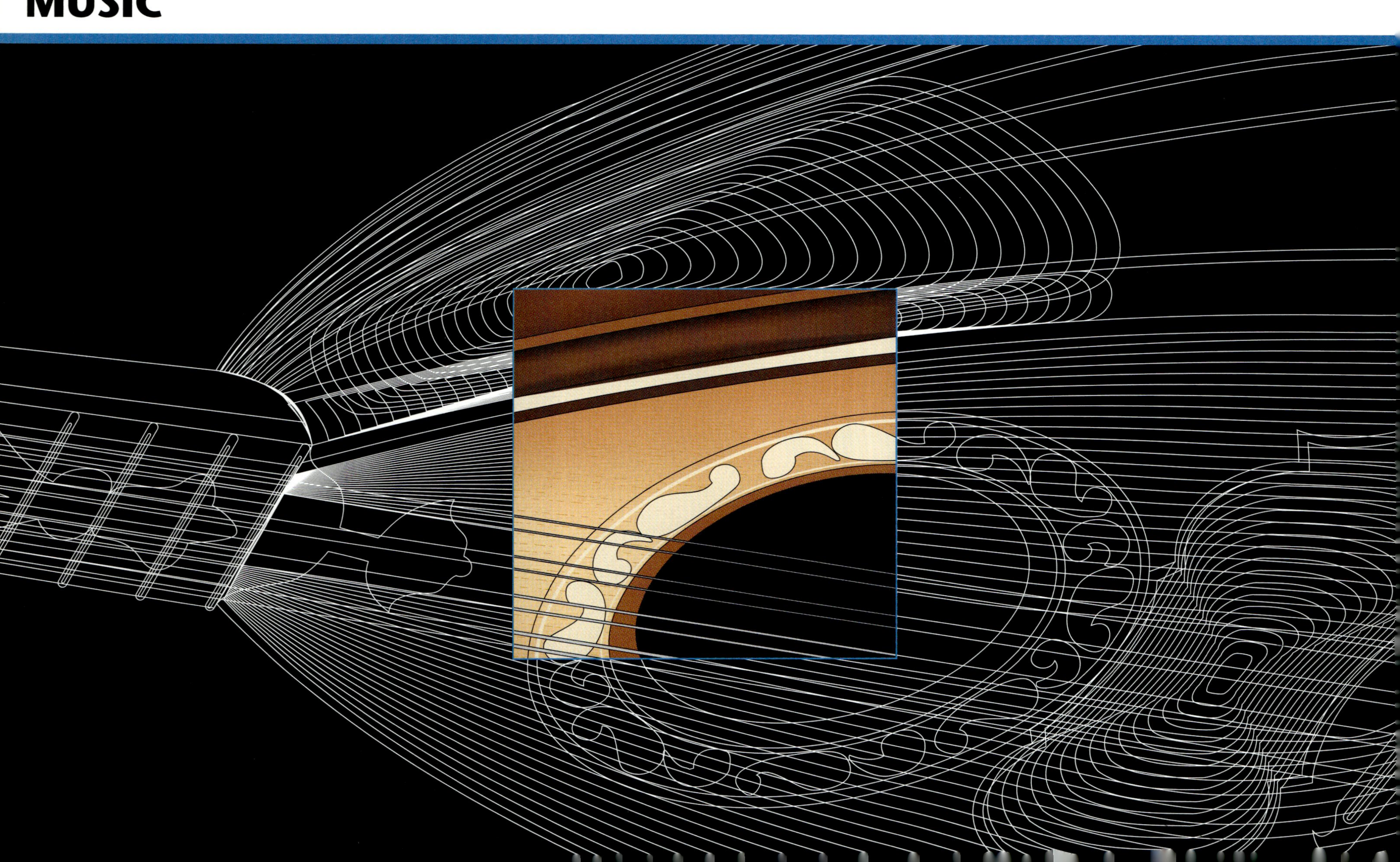

CONTENTS

TRADITIONAL MUSICAL INSTRUMENTS

ACCORDION

BAGPIPES

MUSIC

MUSICAL NOTATION

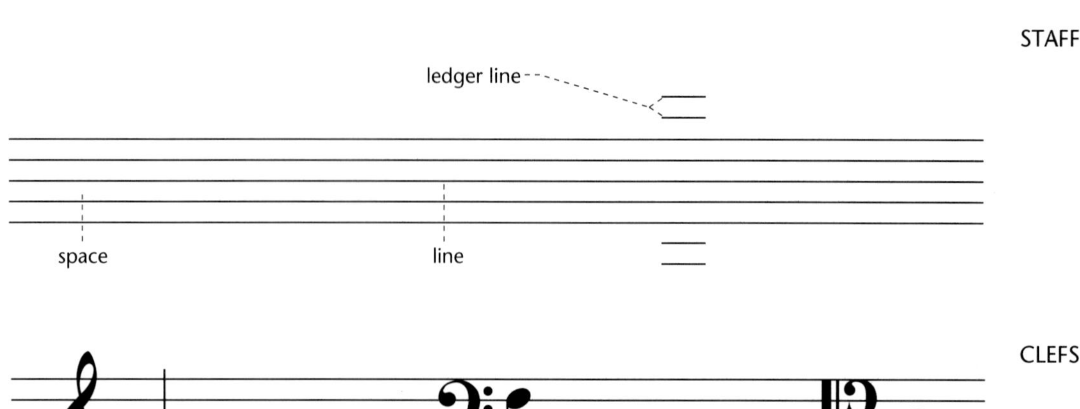

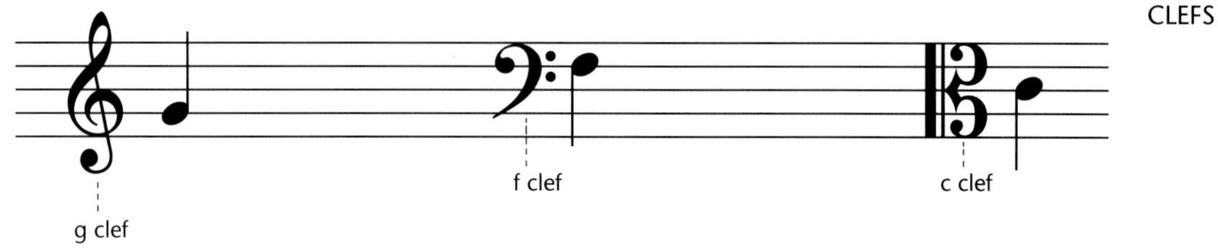

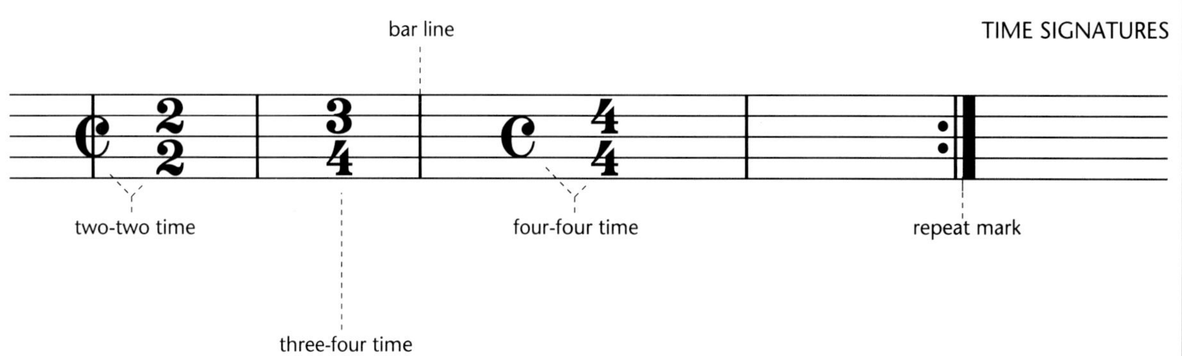

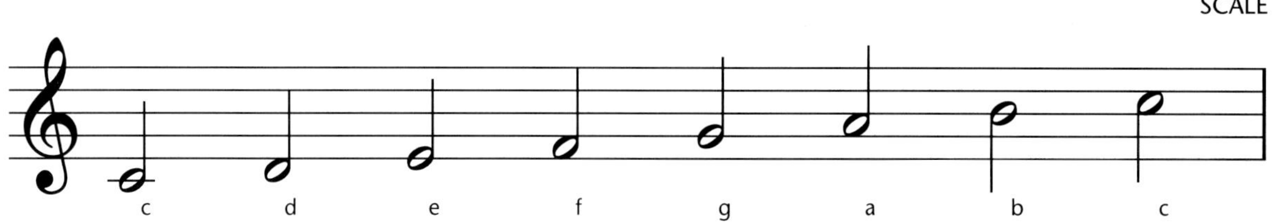

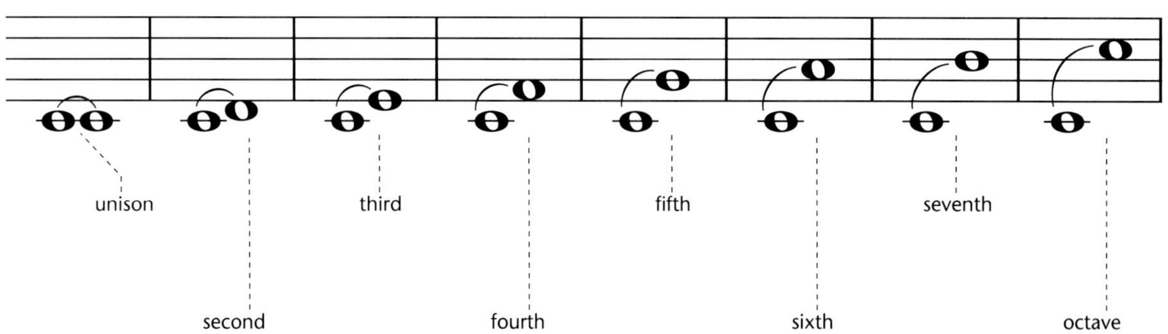

MUSICAL NOTATION

NOTE SYMBOLS

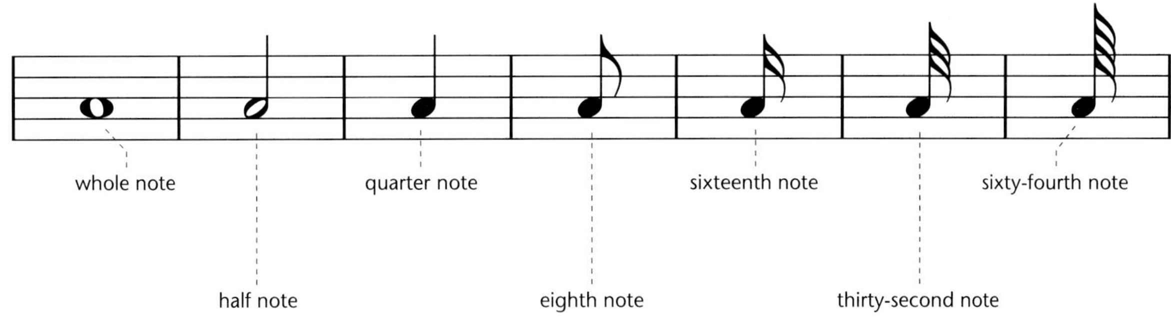

REST SYMBOLS

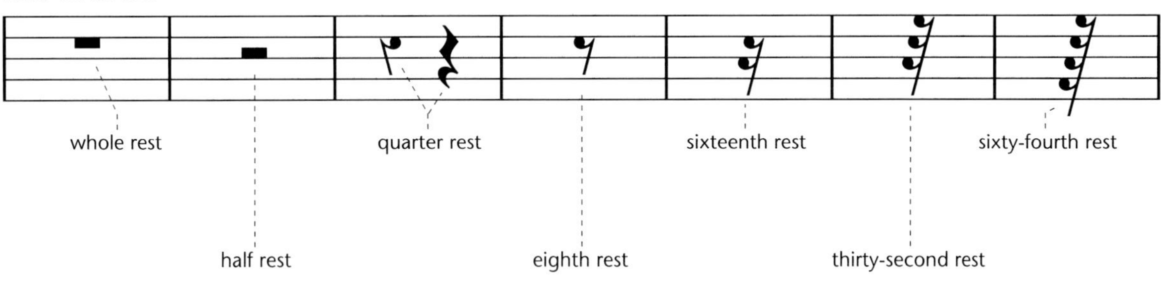

ACCIDENTALS

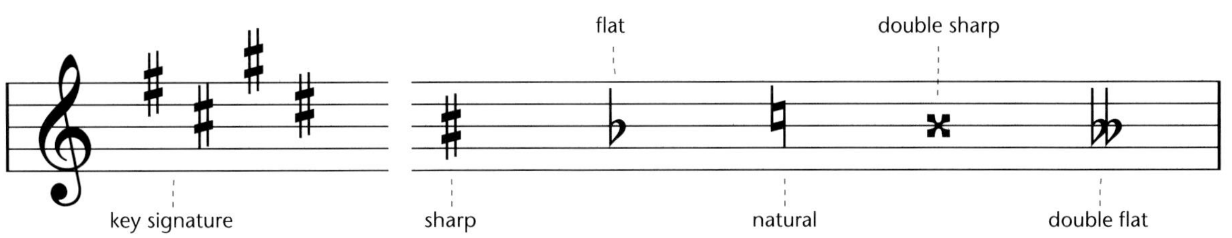

ORNAMENTS

CHORD

OTHER SIGNS

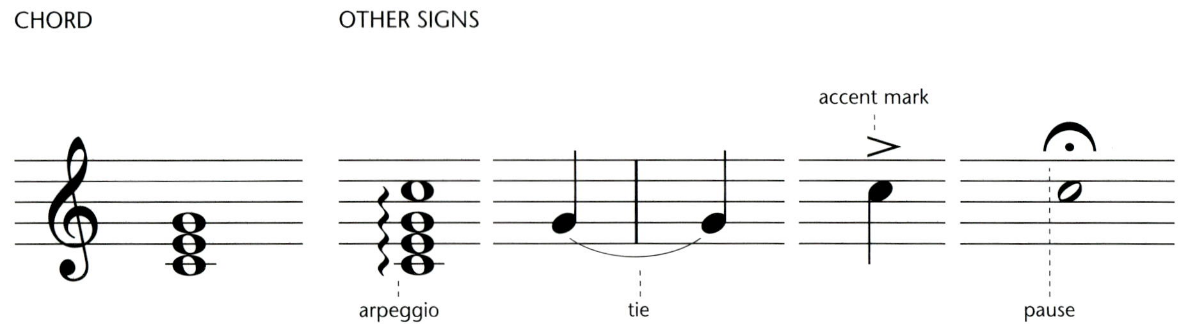

MUSICAL ACCESSORIES

MUSIC STAND

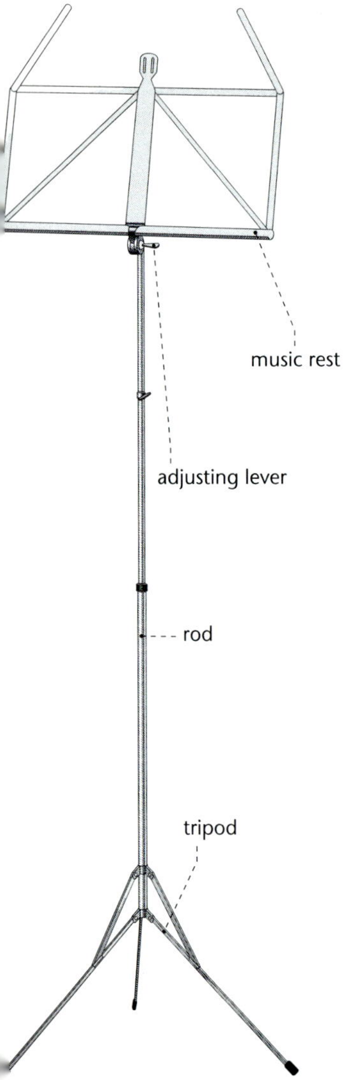

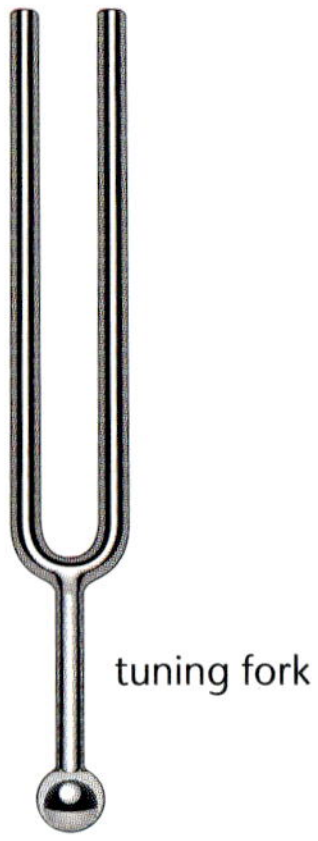

QUARTZ METRONOME

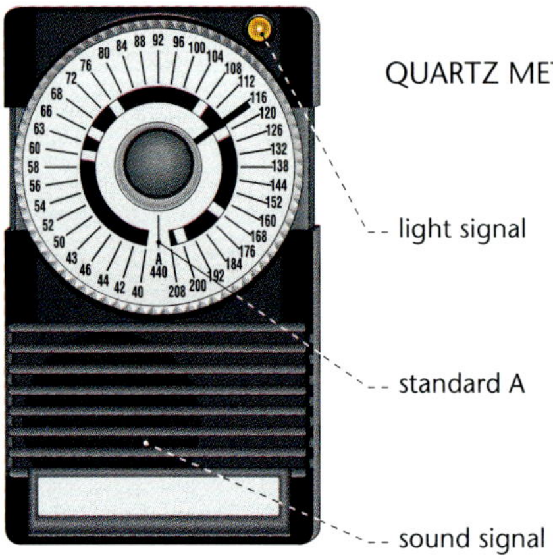

METRONOME

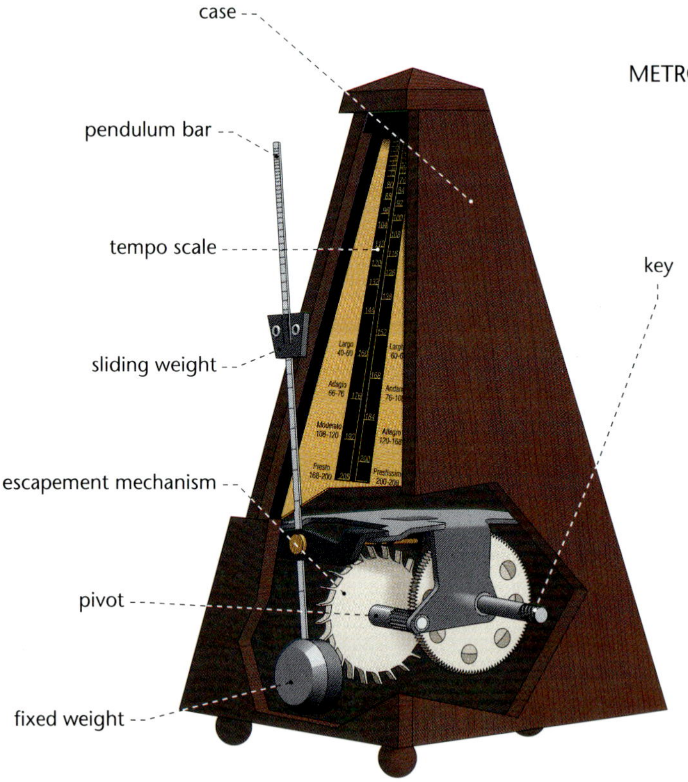

UPRIGHT PIANO

MUSIC

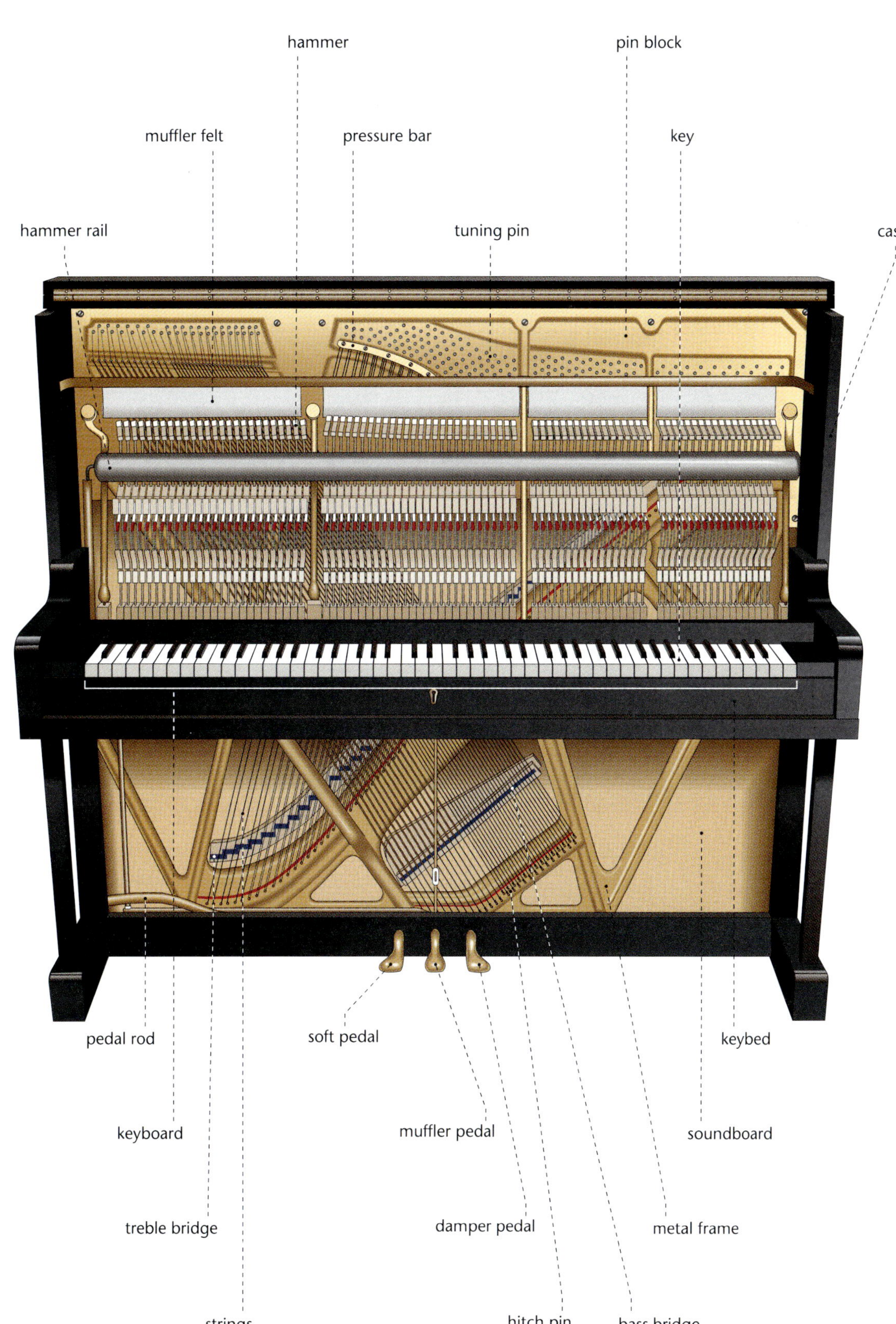

MUSIC

string
damper
hammer felt
hammer
damper rail
hammer rail
hammer shank
hammer butt
catcher
back check
bridle tape
regulating button
jack spring
damper lever
action lever
key
jack
capstan button
balance rail

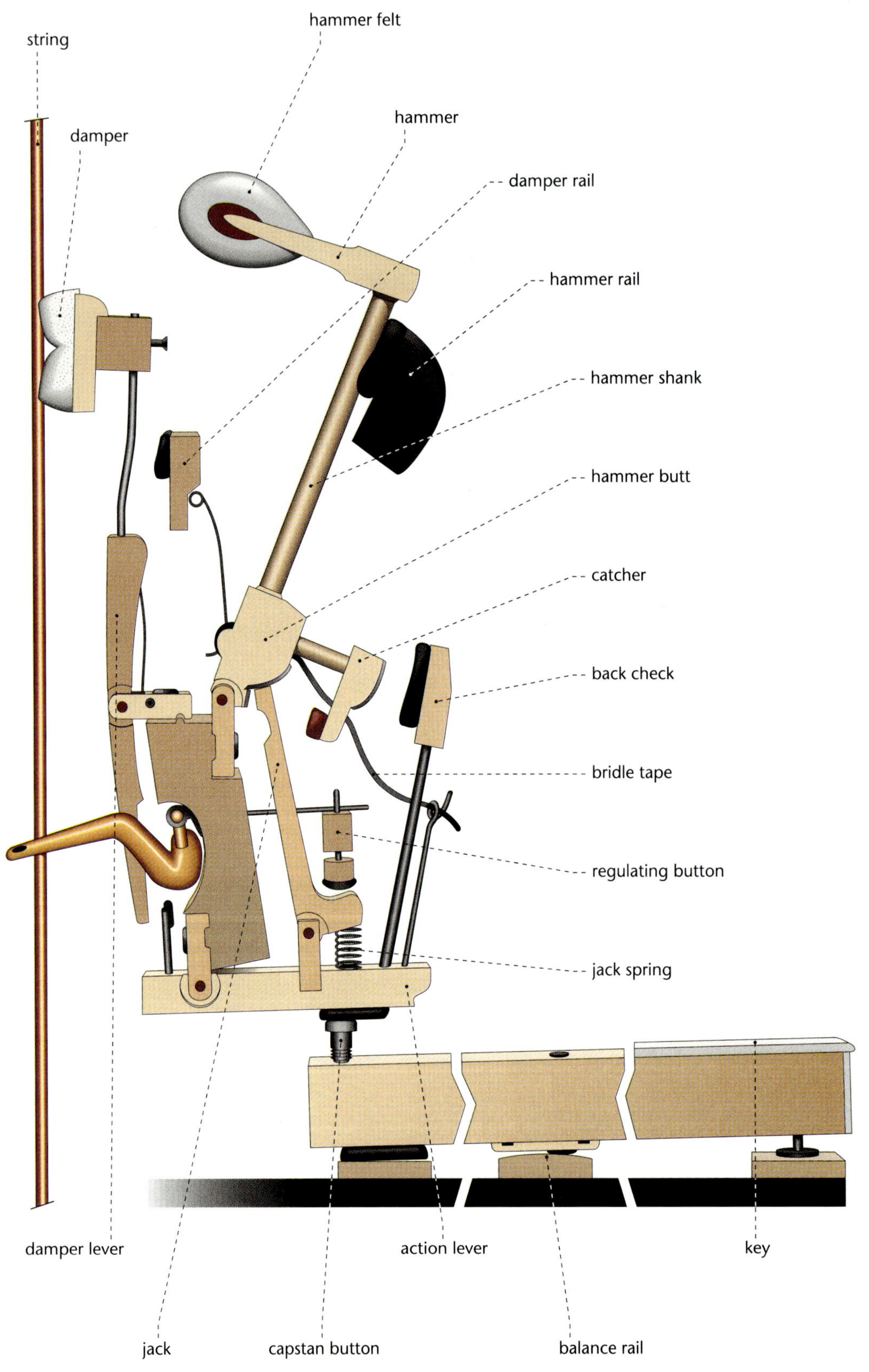

ORGAN

ORGAN CONSOLE

FLUE PIPE

REED PIPE

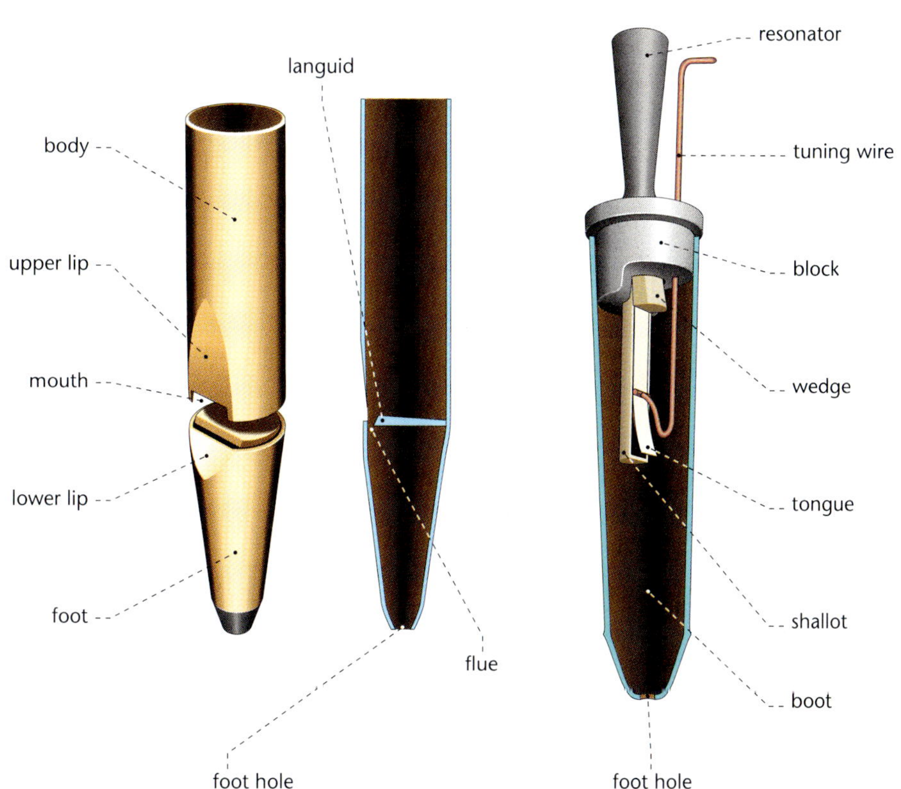

MECHANISM OF THE ORGAN

PRODUCTION OF SOUND

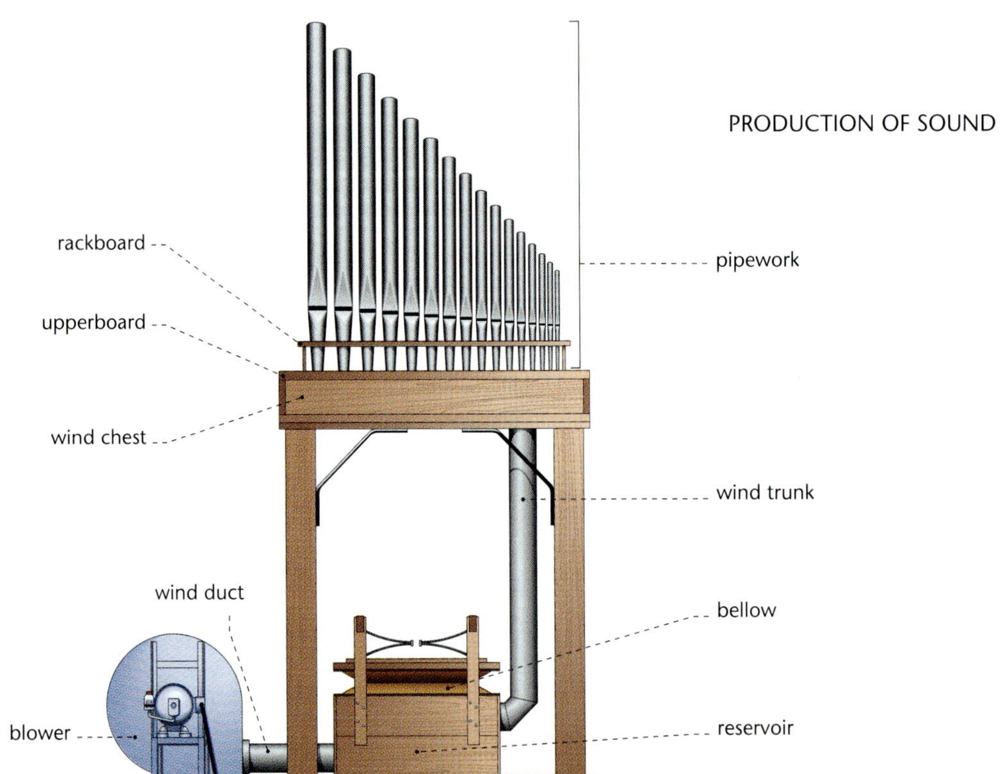

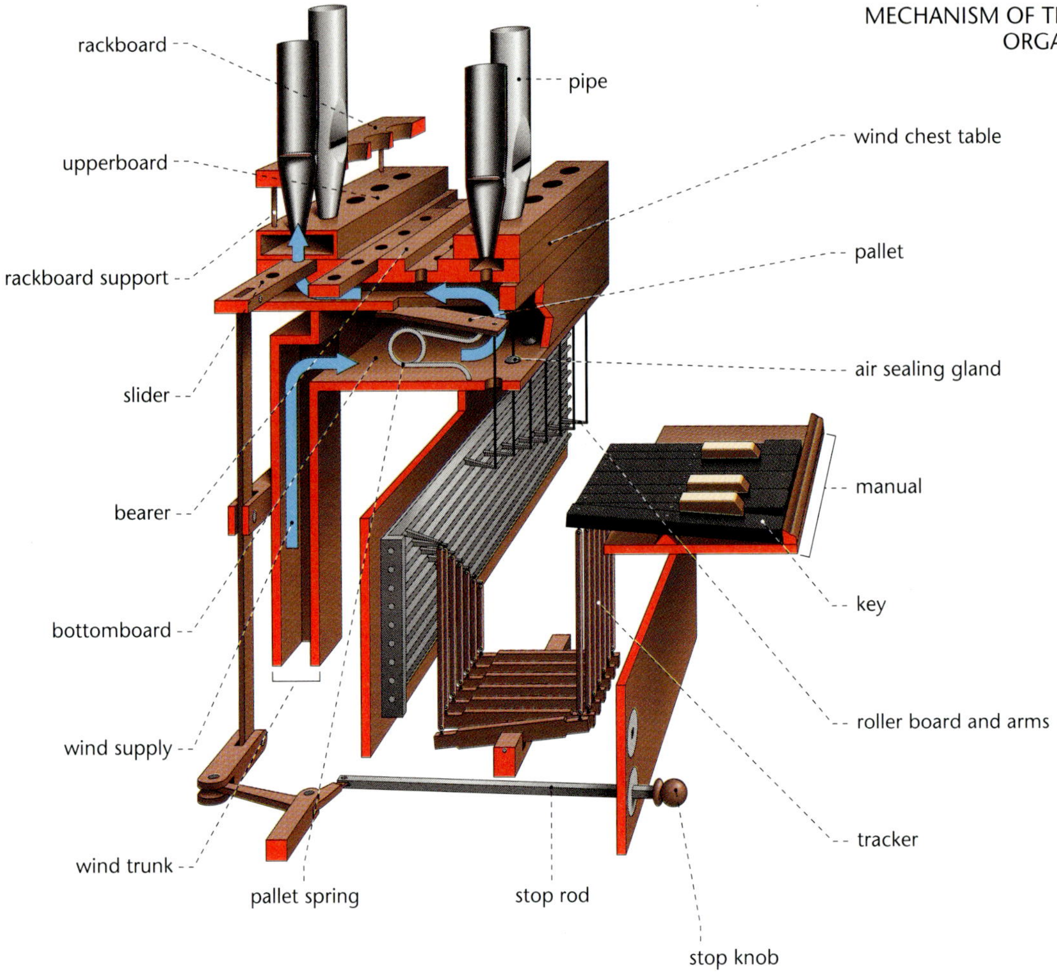

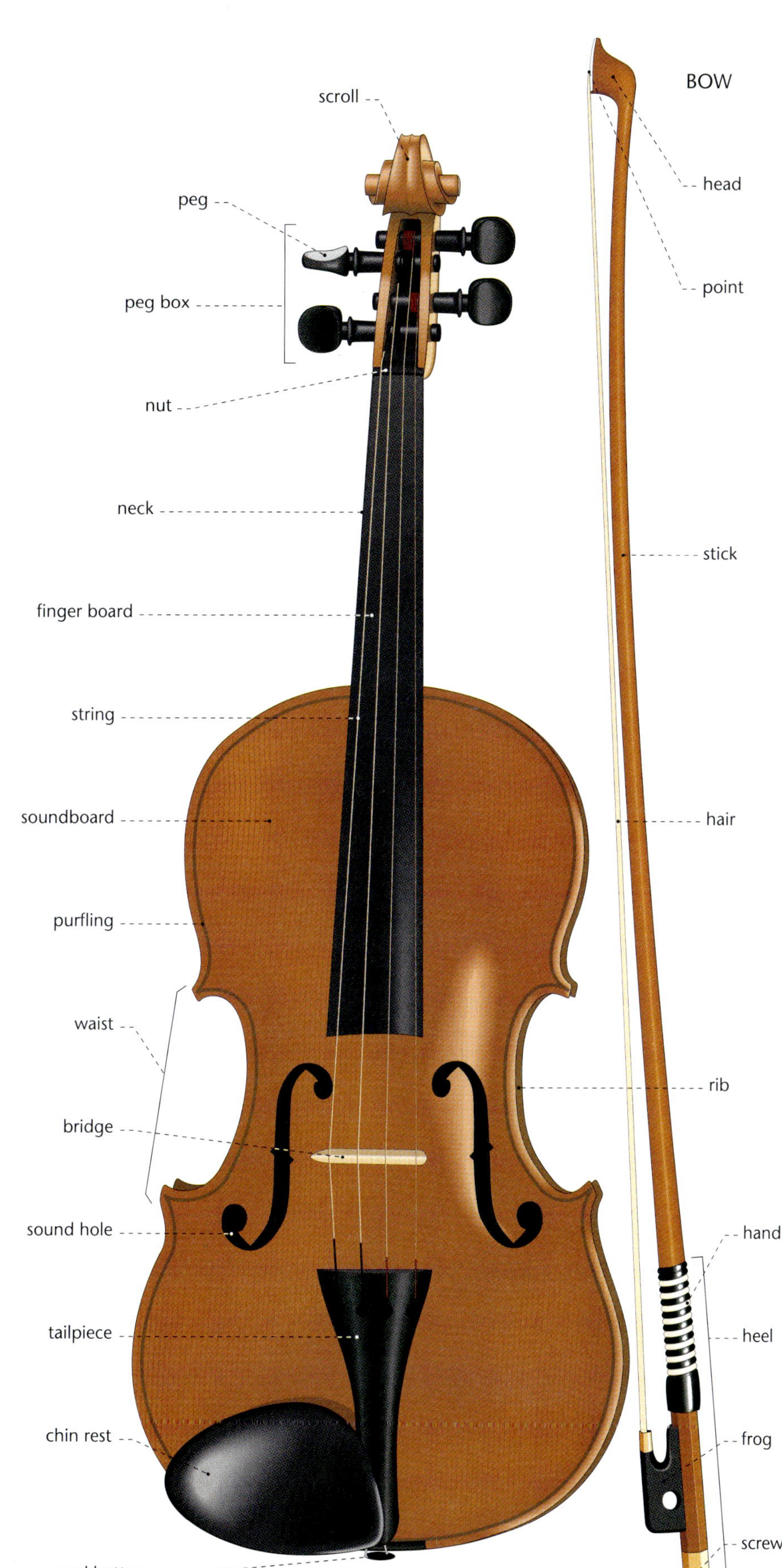

VIOLIN
BOW
scroll
peg
peg box
nut
neck
finger board
string
soundboard
purfling
waist
bridge
sound hole
tailpiece
chin rest
end button
head
point
stick
hair
rib
handle
heel
frog
screw

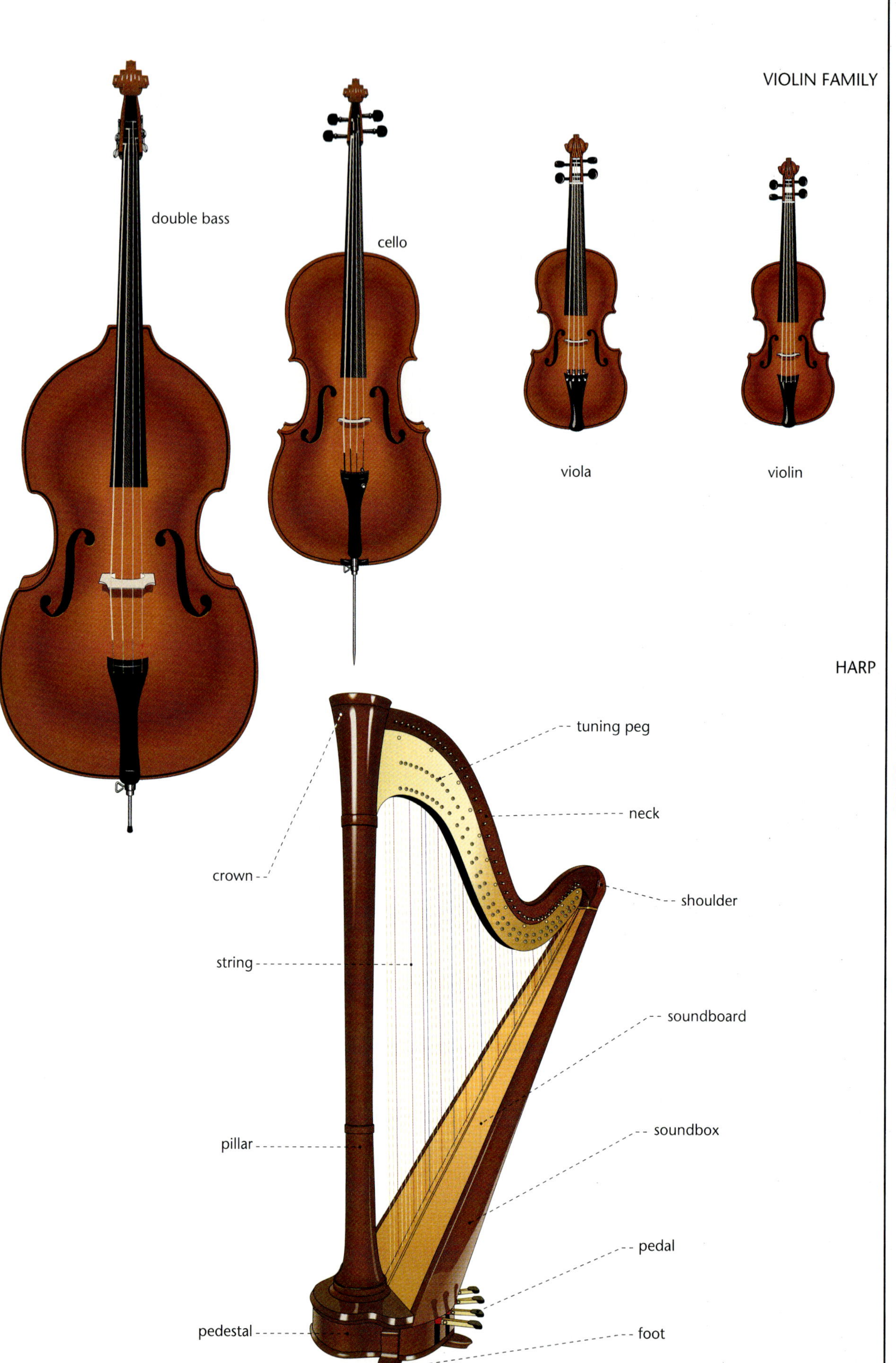
double bass
cello
viola
violin
HARP
tuning peg
neck
shoulder
crown
string
soundboard
pillar
soundbox
pedal
pedestal
foot
MUSIC

ACOUSTIC GUITAR

tuning peg
head
nut
finger board
position marker
fret
neck
pickguard
bass pickup
vibrato arm
midrange pickup
pickup selector
treble pickup
volume control
bridge assembly
tone control
solid body
output jack

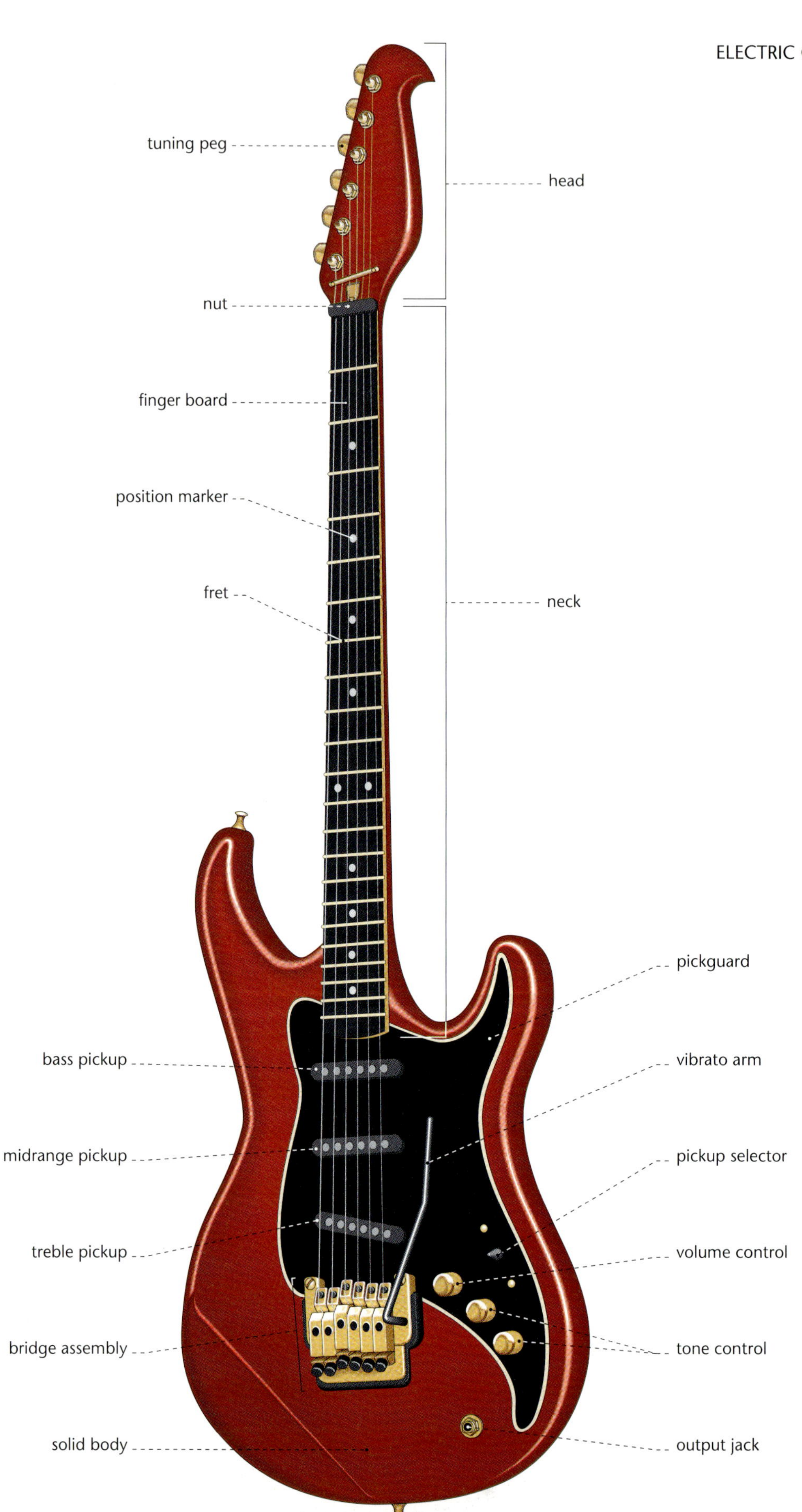

MUSIC

SAXOPHONE
crook key
mouthpiece
crook
reed
ligature
octave mechanism
WOODWIND FAMILY
piccolo
clarinet
oboe
flute
bassoon
saxophone
English horn

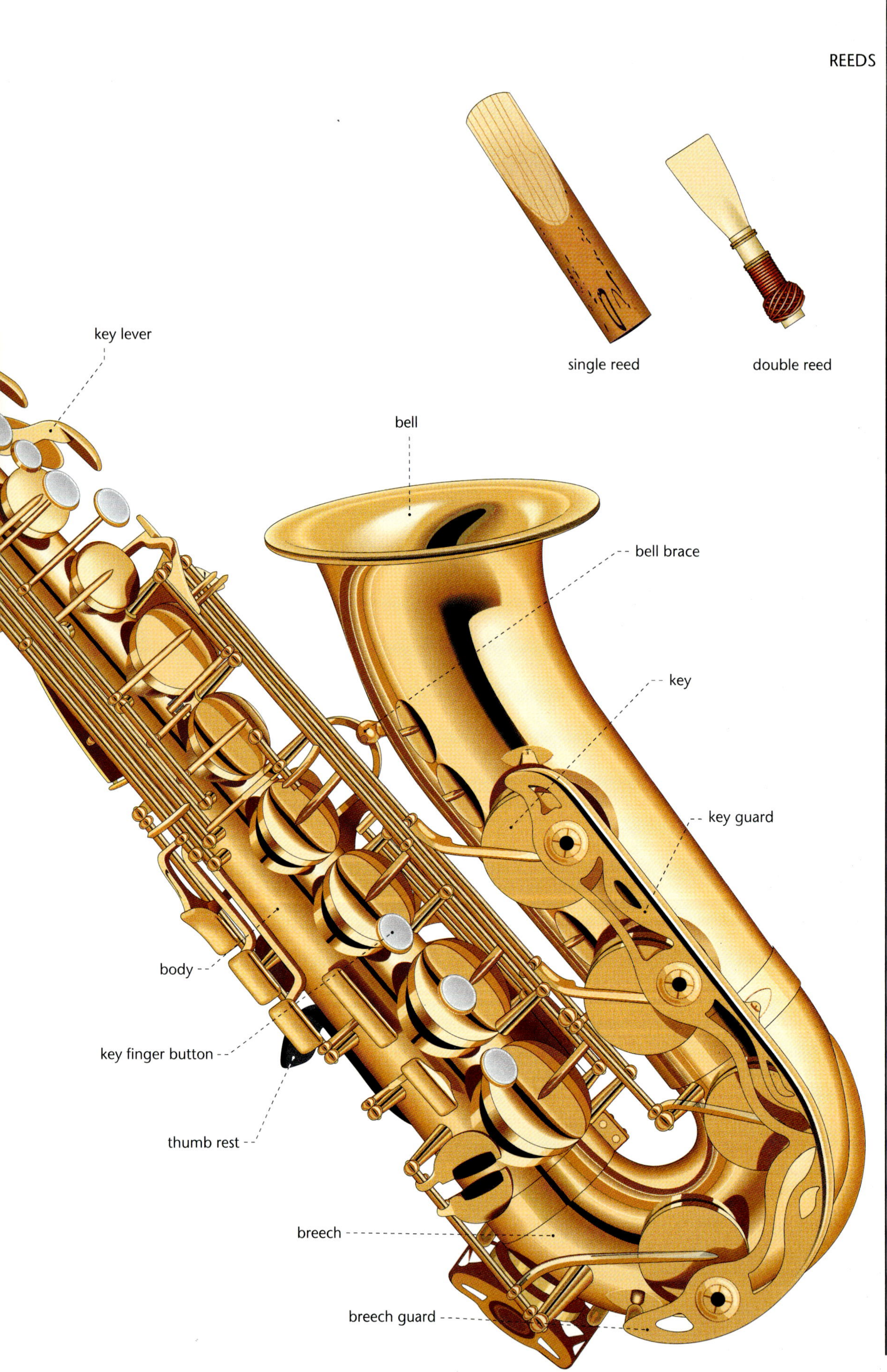

REEDS
single reed
double reed
key lever
bell
bell brace
key
key guard
body
key finger button
thumb rest
breech
breech guard
MUSIC

TRUMPET
finger button
mouthpipe
mouthpiece
mouthpiece receiver
thumb hook
first valve slide
valve casing
second valve slide
valve
BRASS FAMILY
cornet
trumpet
bugle
trombone

little finger hook
ring
bell
tuning slide
third valve slide
water key
mute
tuba
saxhorn
French horn

DRUMS

cymbal
tom-tom
Charleston cymbal
superior cymbal
inferior cymbal
batter head
snare drum
tripod stand
bass drum
tension screw
stand
mallet
pedal
spur

SNARE DRUM
lug
tension rod
snare
snare strainer
snare head
sticks
wire brush
mallets
tenor drum
KETTLEDRUM
batter head
metal counterhoop
tie rod
tuning gauge
shell
strut
leg
tension rod
crown
caster
foot
pedal
MUSIC

PERCUSSION INSTRUMENTS

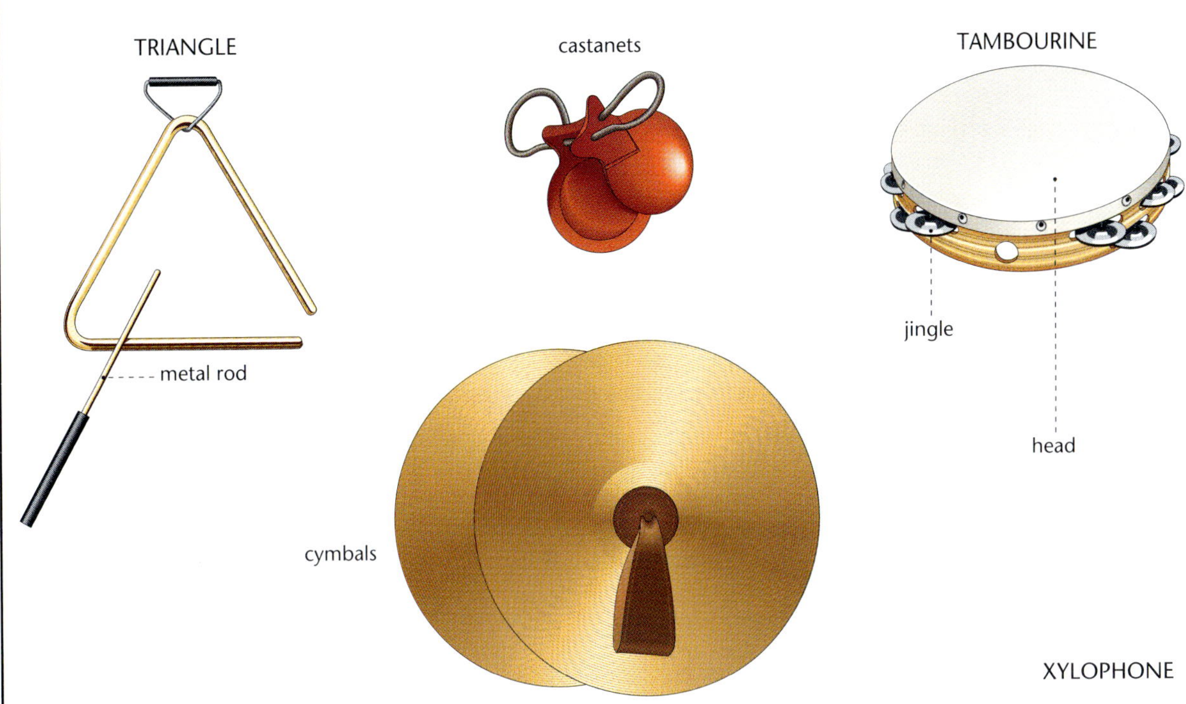

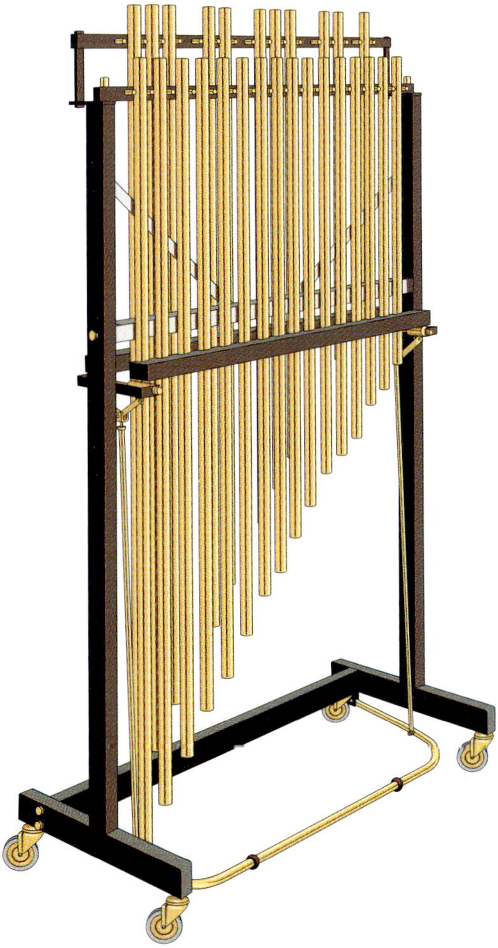

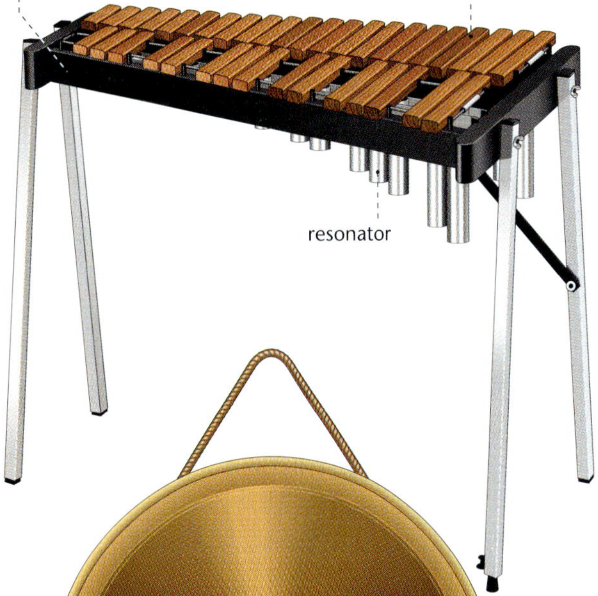

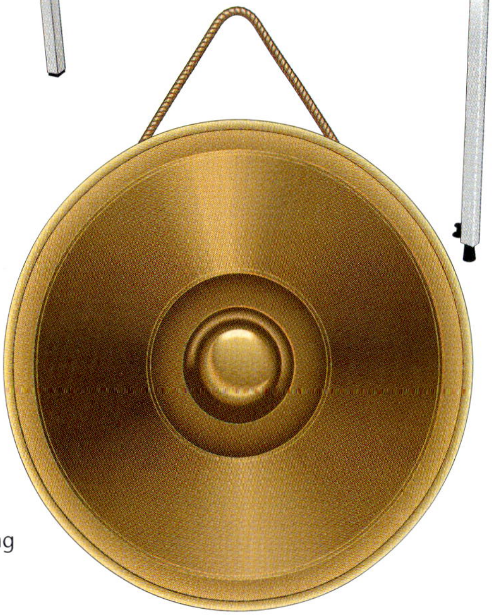

ELECTRONIC INSTRUMENTS

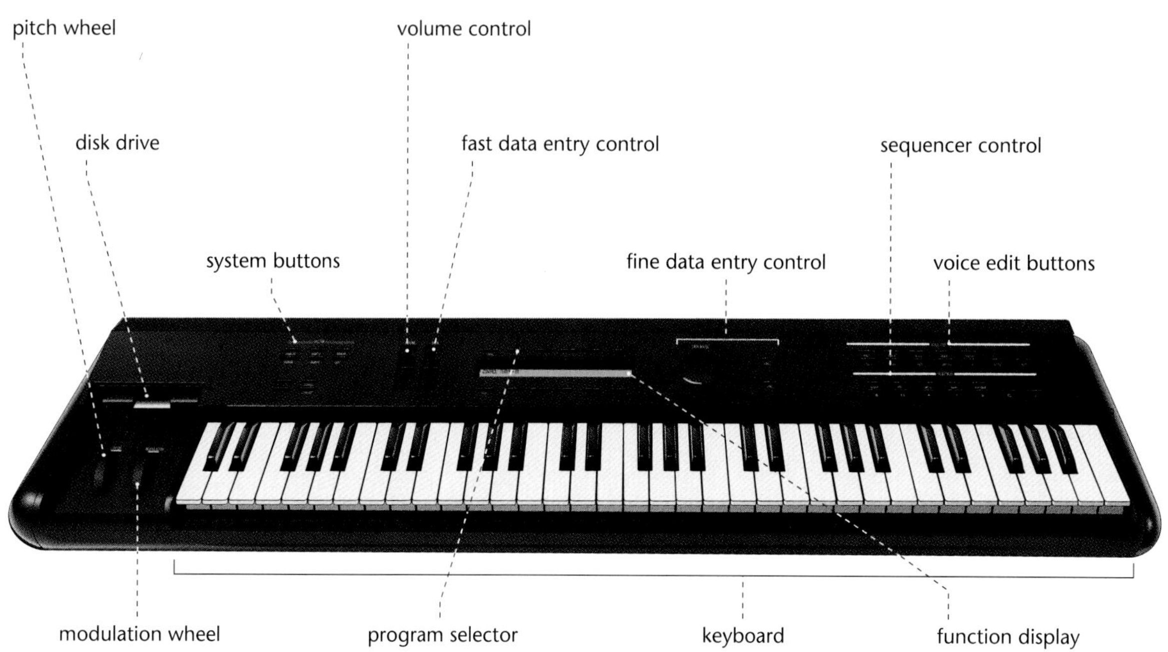

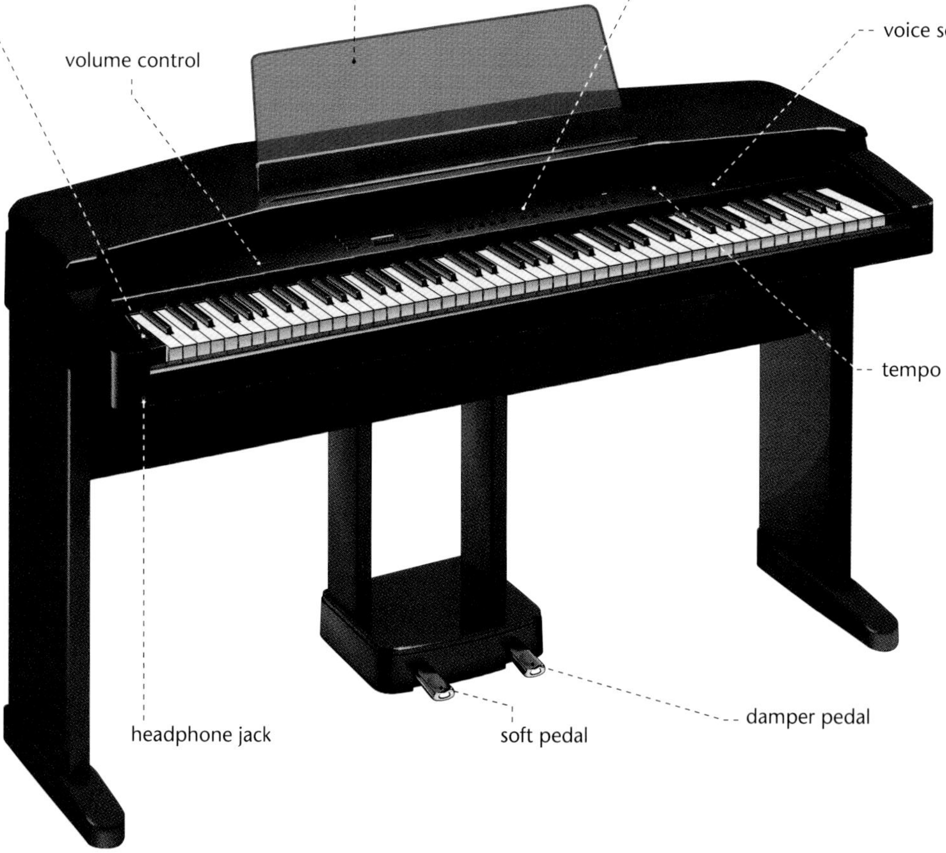

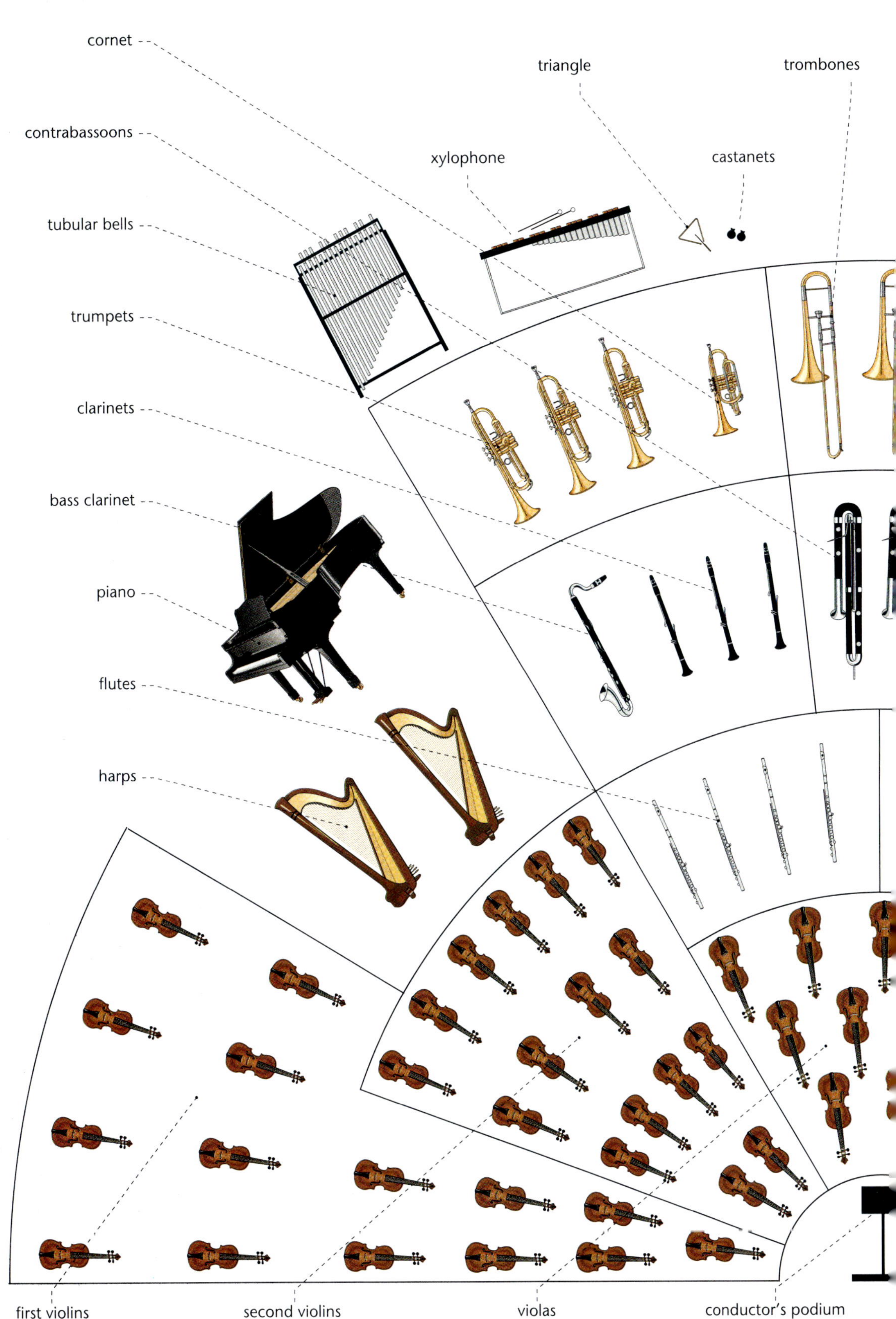
cornet
contrabassoons
tubular bells
trumpets
clarinets
bass clarinet
piano
flutes
harps
triangle
xylophone
castanets
trombones
first violins
second violins
violas
conductor's podium

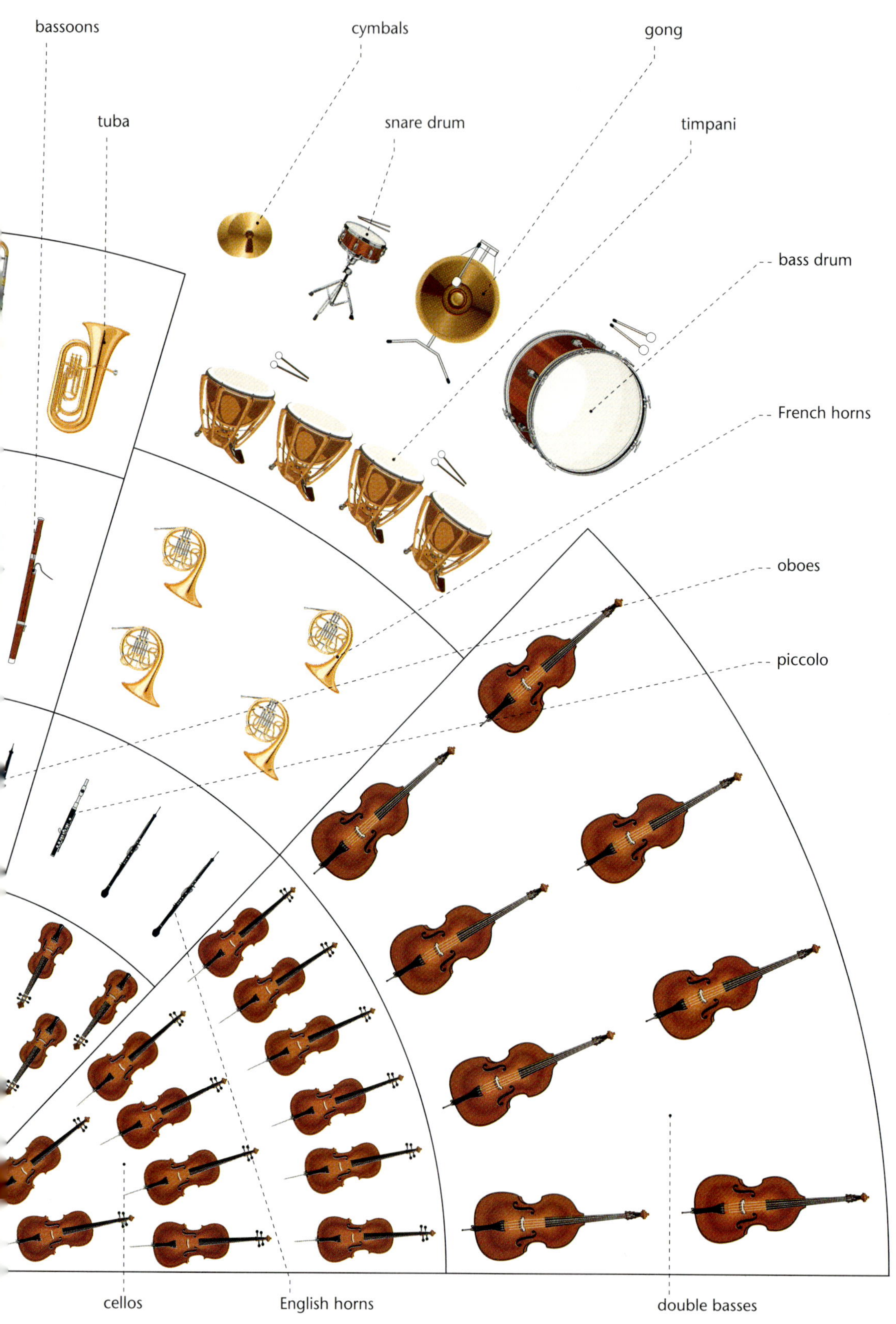

bassoons
tuba
cymbals
snare drum
gong
timpani
bass drum
French horns
oboes
piccolo
cellos
English horns
double basses

EXAMPLES OF INSTRUMENTAL GROUPS

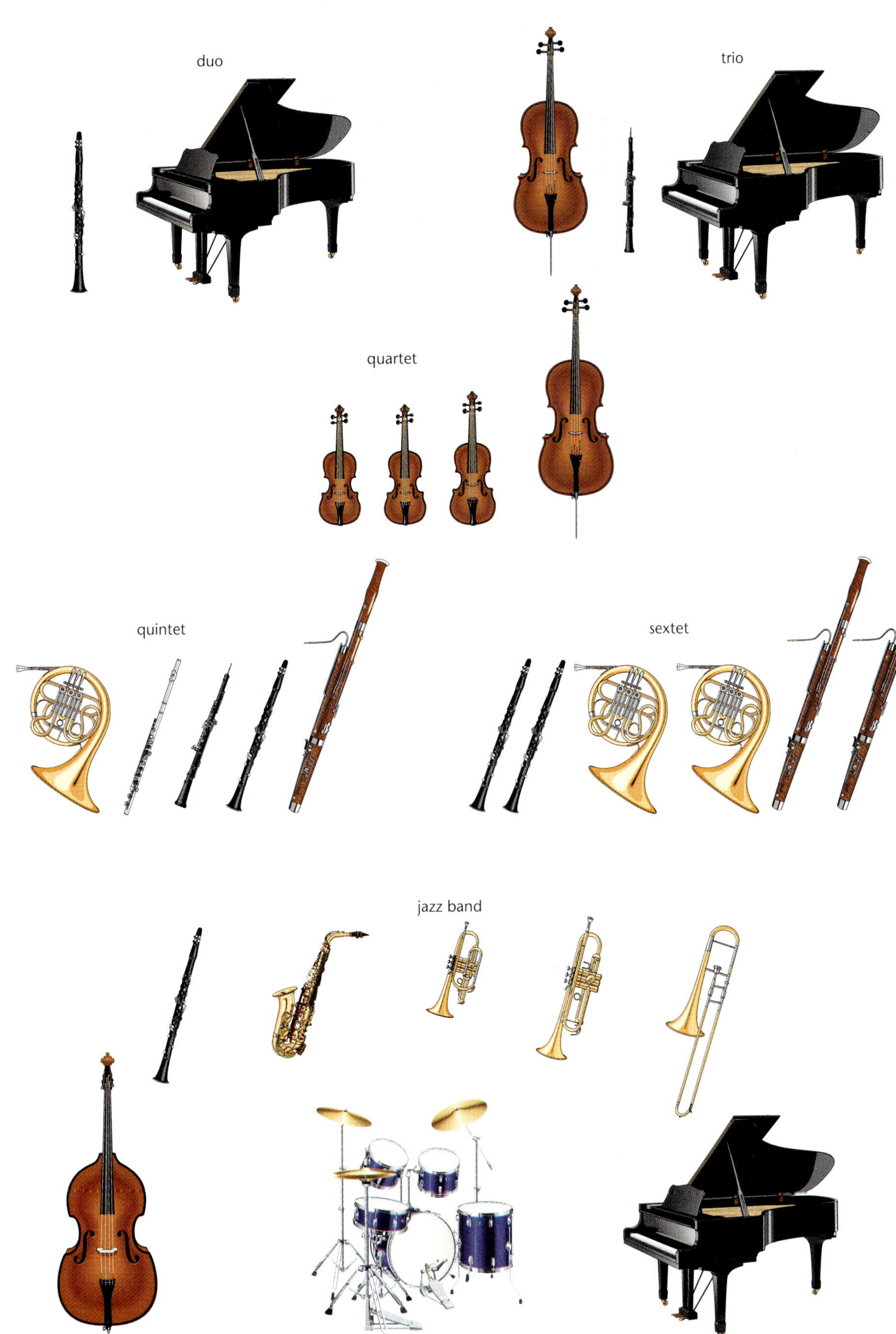

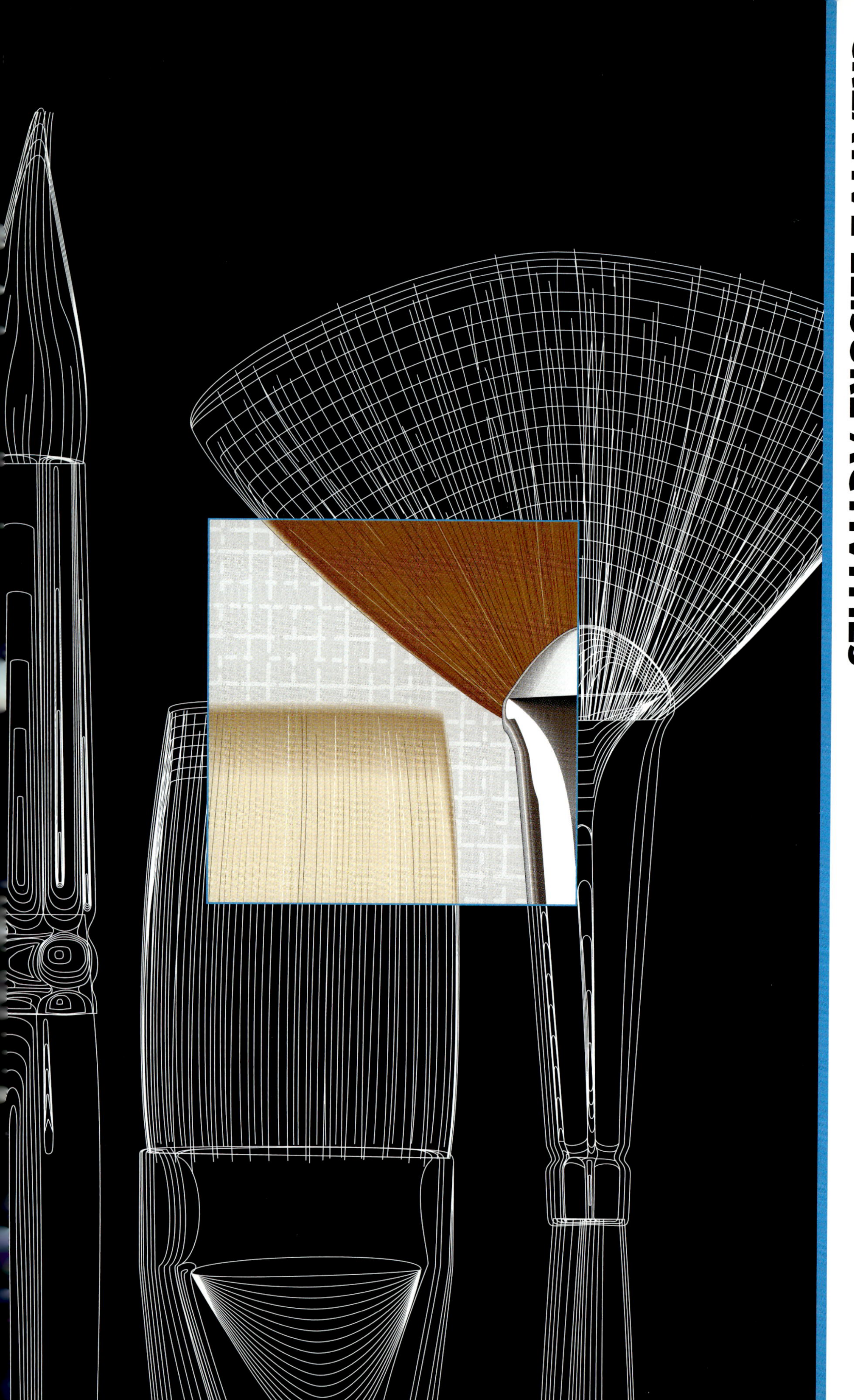
CREATIVE LEISURE ACTIVITIES

CONTENTS

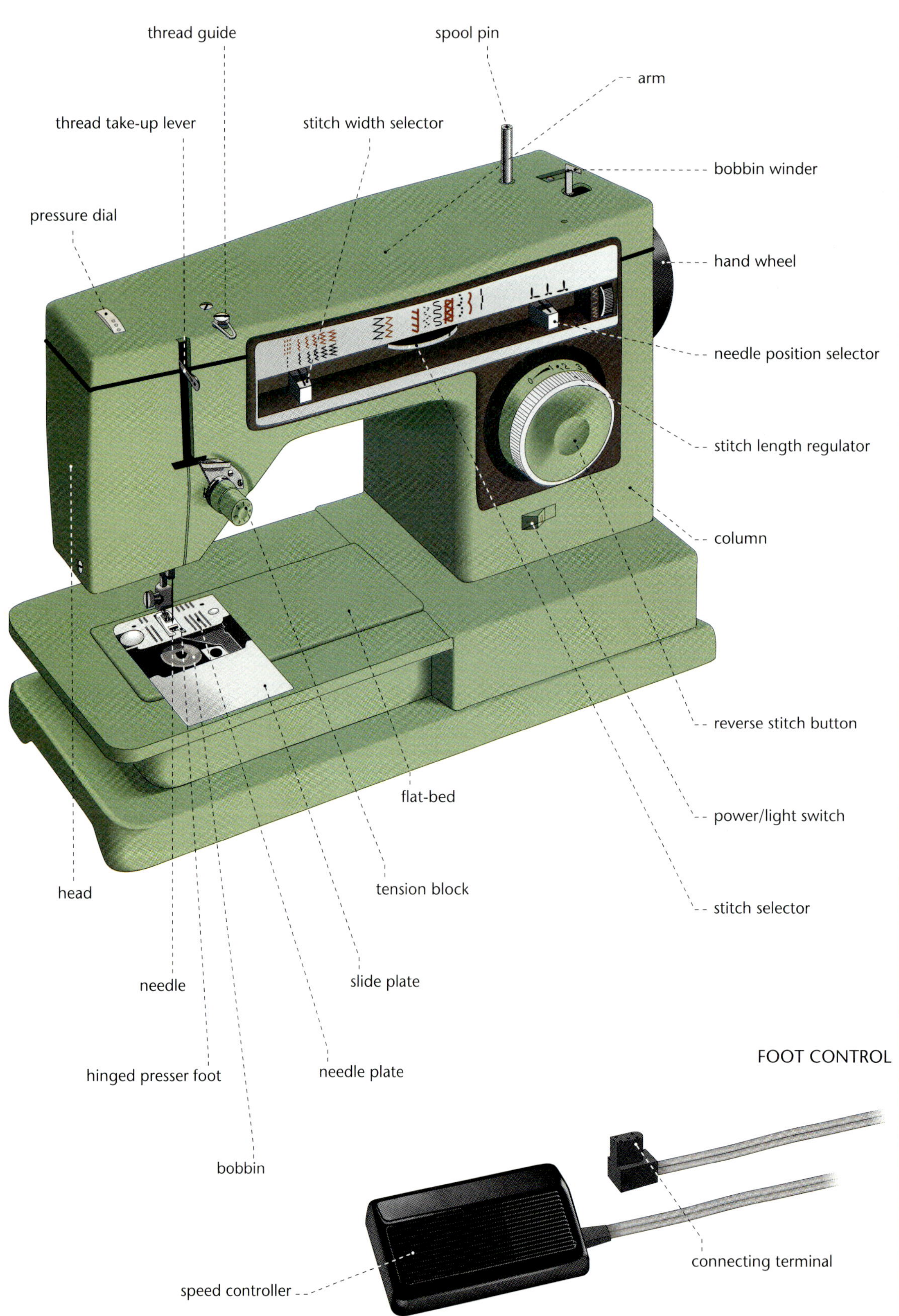
SEWING MACHINE
thread guide
spool pin
arm
thread take-up lever
stitch width selector
bobbin winder
pressure dial
hand wheel
needle position selector
stitch length regulator
column
reverse stitch button
flat-bed
power/light switch
head
tension block
stitch selector
needle
slide plate
hinged presser foot
needle plate
bobbin
FOOT CONTROL
connecting terminal
speed controller

PRESSER FOOT

presser bar

needle bar

needle clamp

thread guide

needle clamp screw

thread trimmer

needle

feed dog

hinged presser foot

bobbin

slide plate

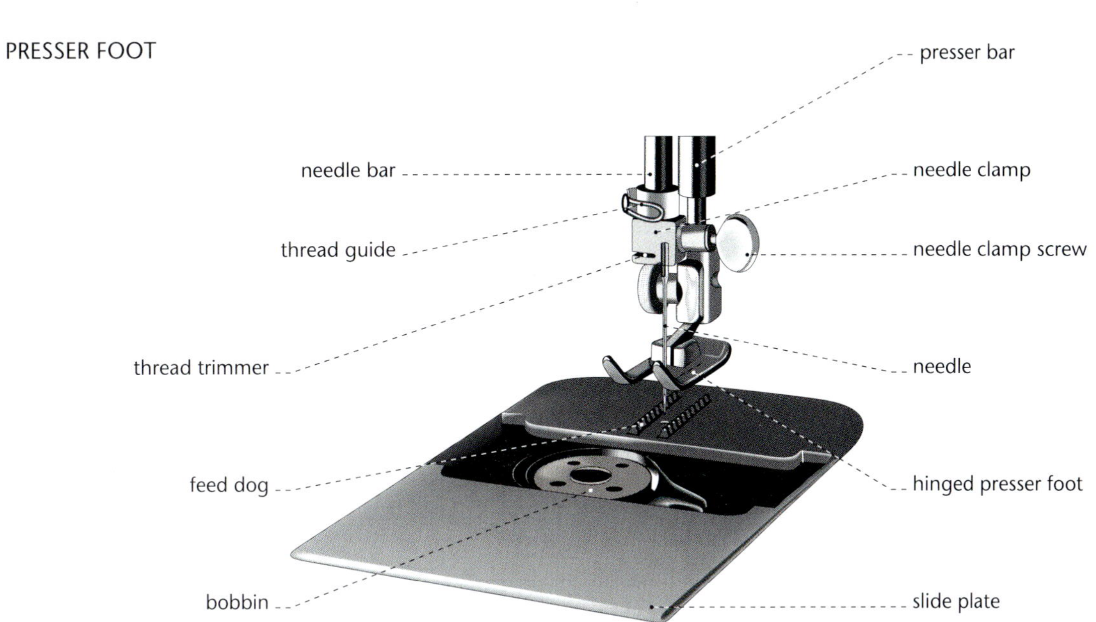

NEEDLE

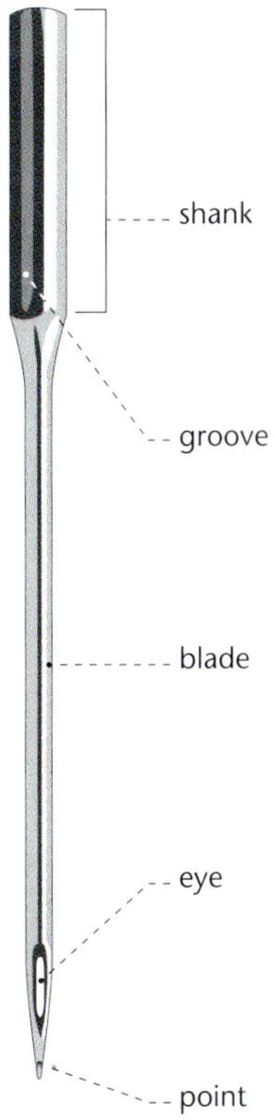

TENSION BLOCK

shank

thread guide

tension disk

groove

tension spring

blade

tension dial

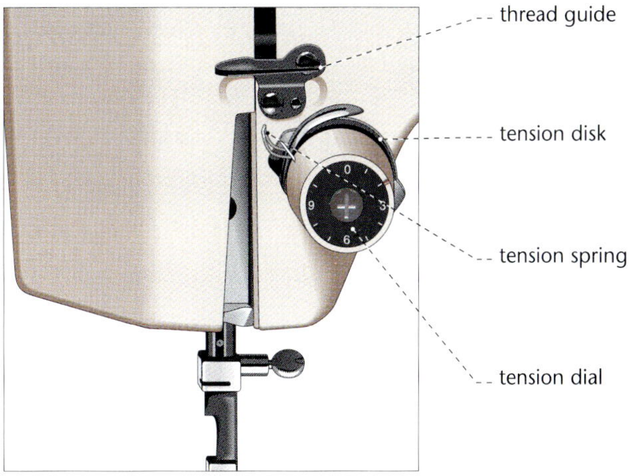

BOBBIN CASE

eye

point

latch lever

bobbin

hook

PIN CUSHION

pin
eye
needle
emery pack
thimble
needle threader
magnet
seam gauge
TRACING WHEEL
wheel
shank
handle
tape measure

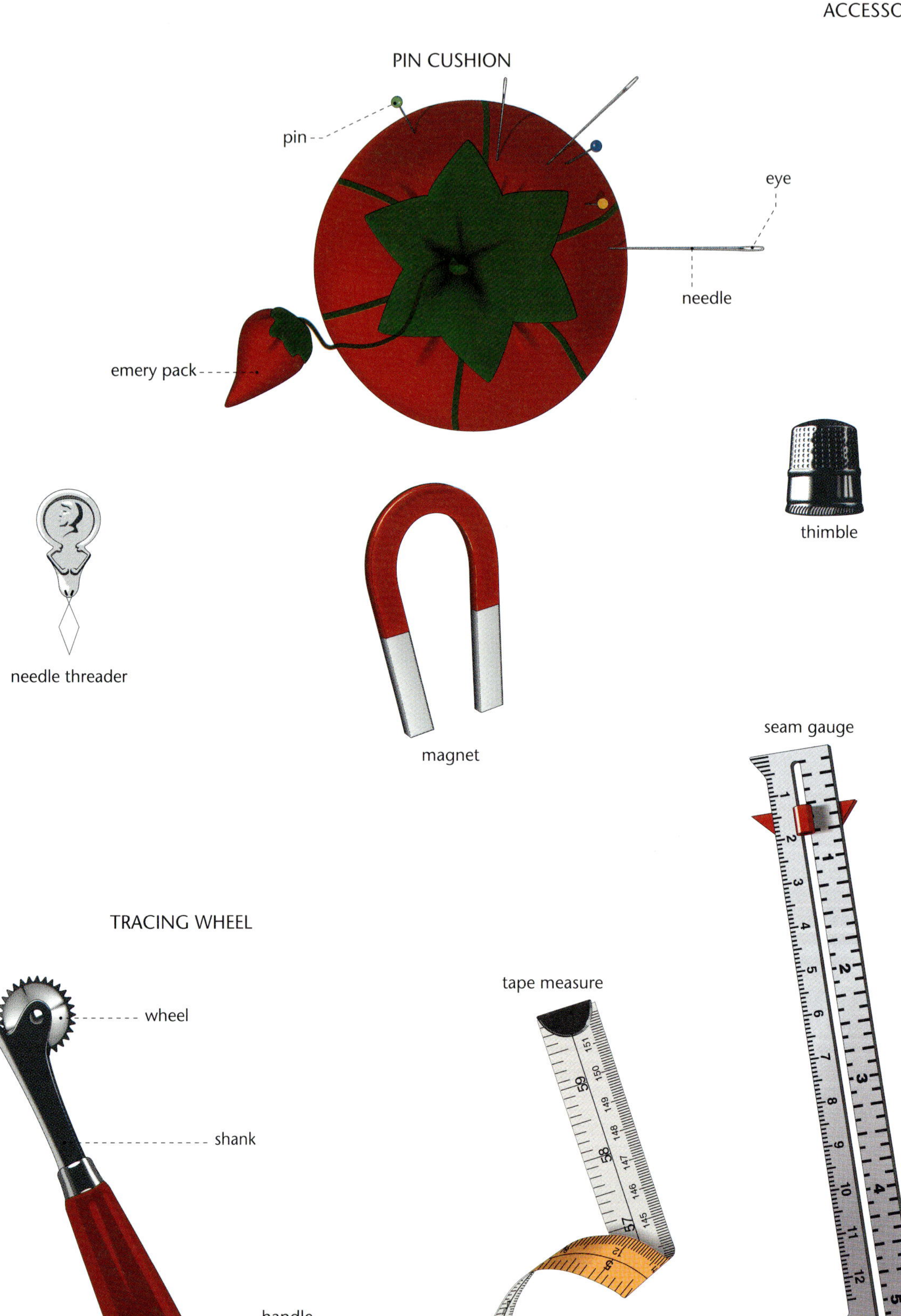

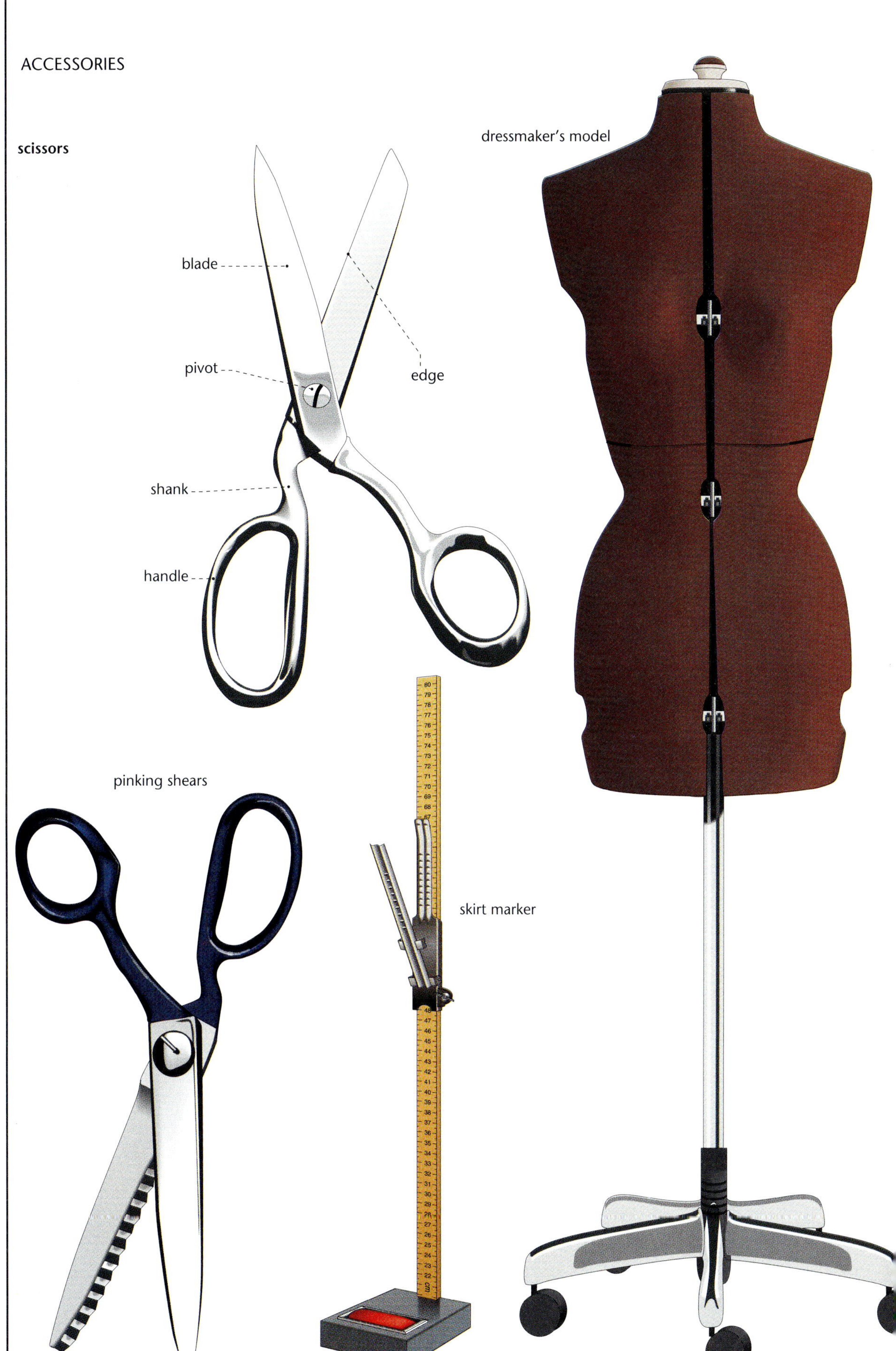

ACCESSORIES

scissors

blade

pivot

edge

shank

handle

pinking shears

skirt marker

dressmaker's model

garment fabric
interlining
lining
interfacing
underlining

PATTERN

cutting line
seam line
notch
fold line
marking dot
zipper line
seam allowance
alteration line
dart
lengthwise grain
hemline

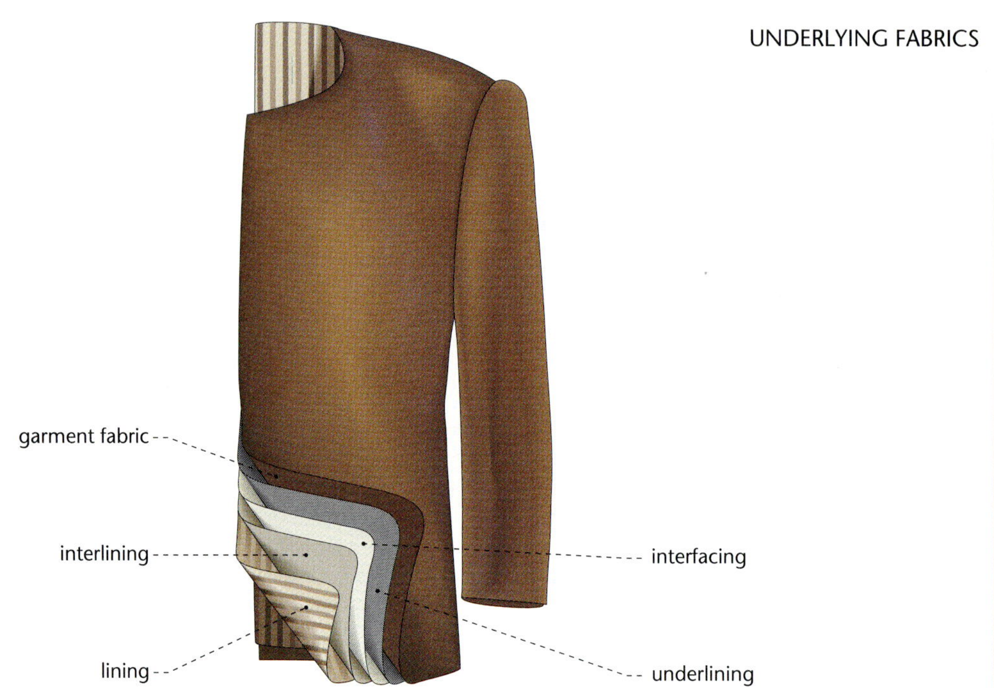

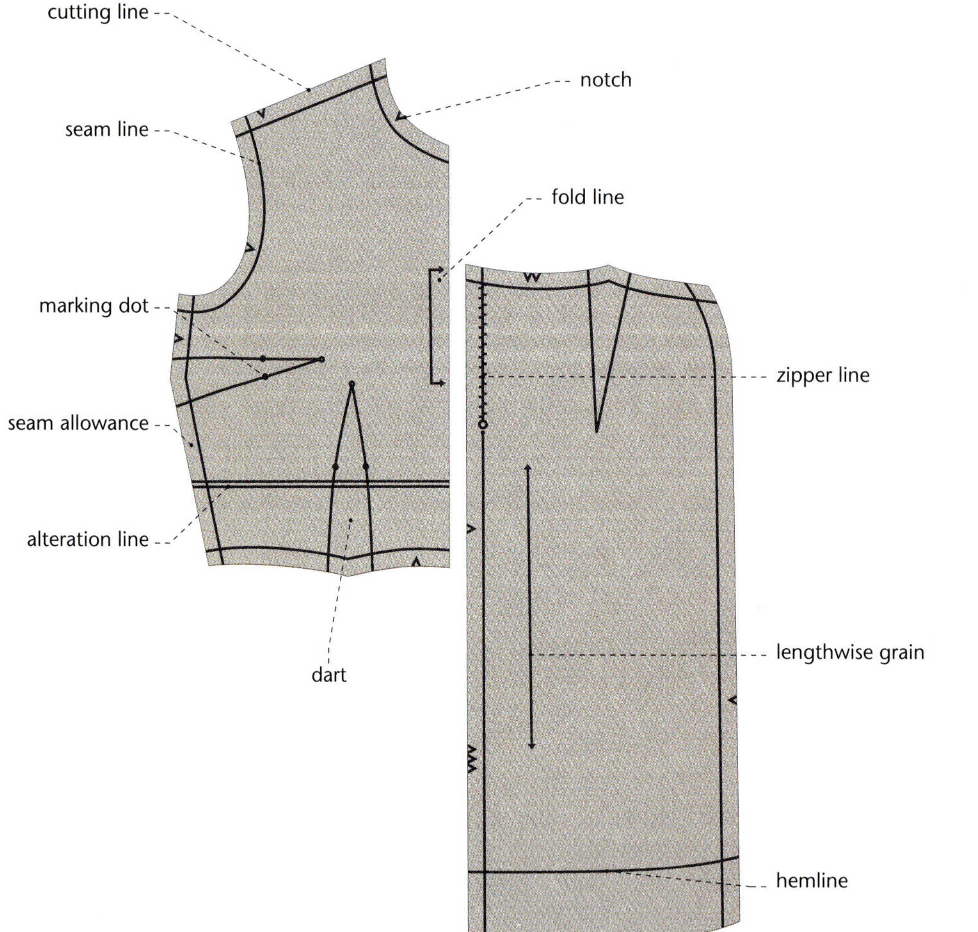

FASTENERS

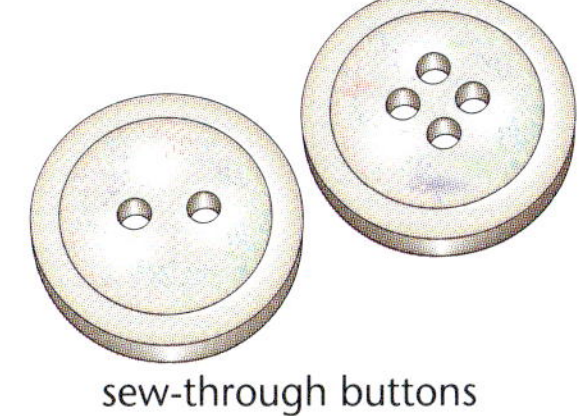

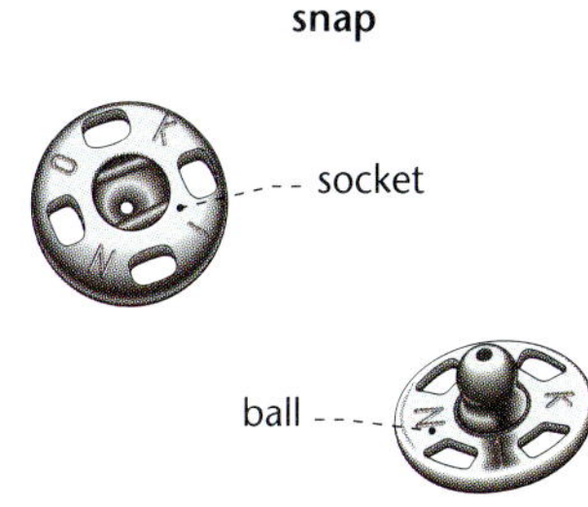

hook and eyes

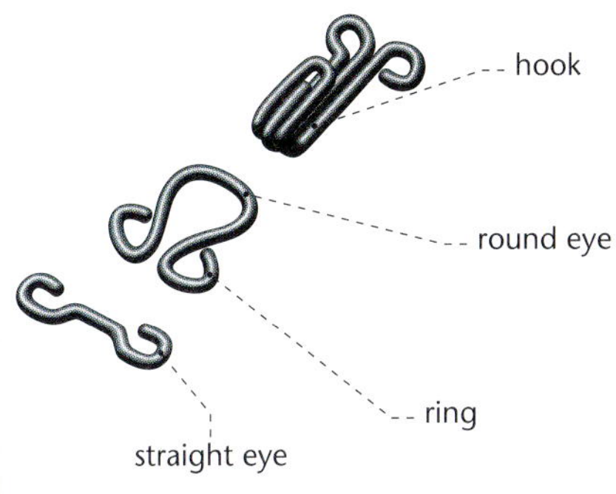

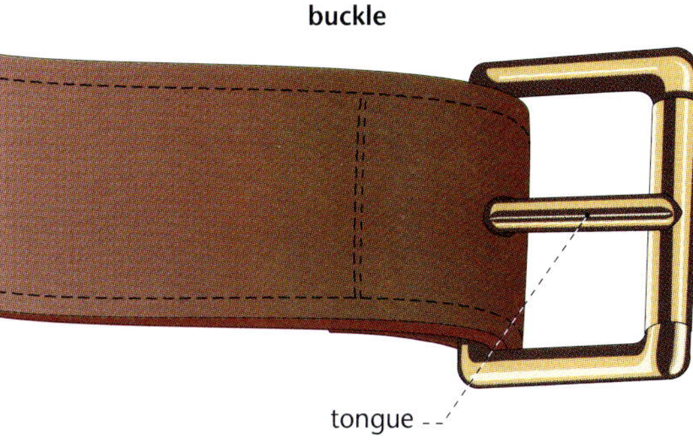

FABRIC STRUCTURE

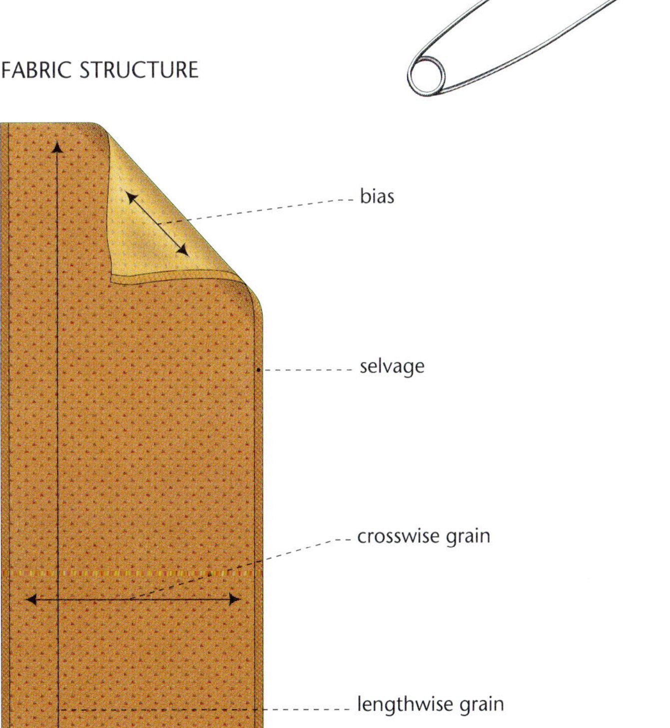

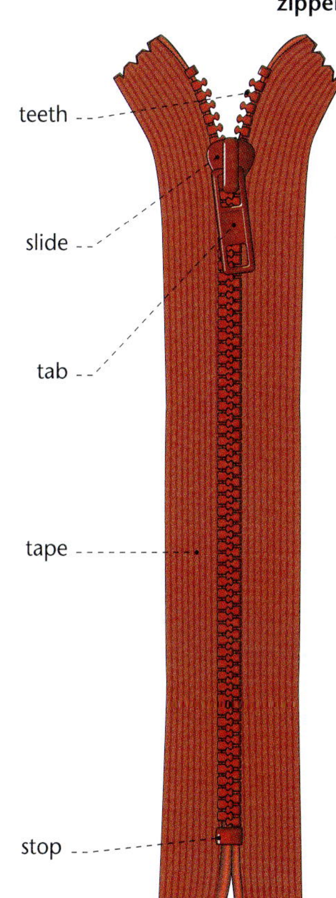

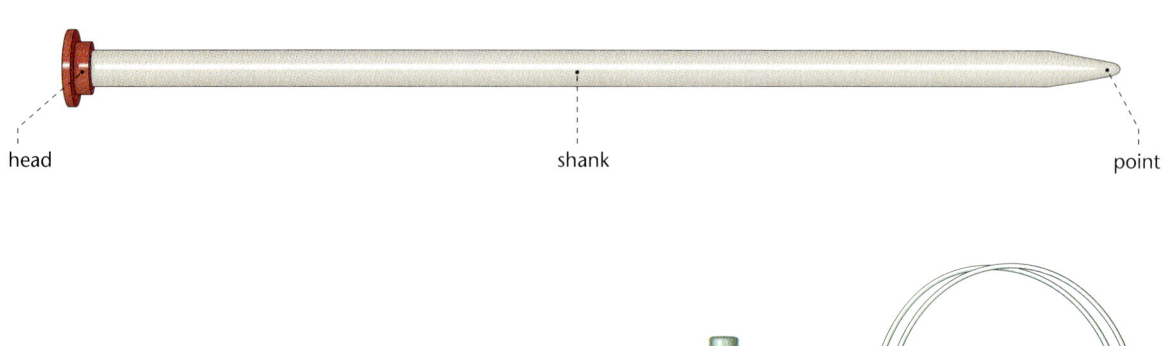

KNITTING NEEDLES

head

shank

point

crochet hook

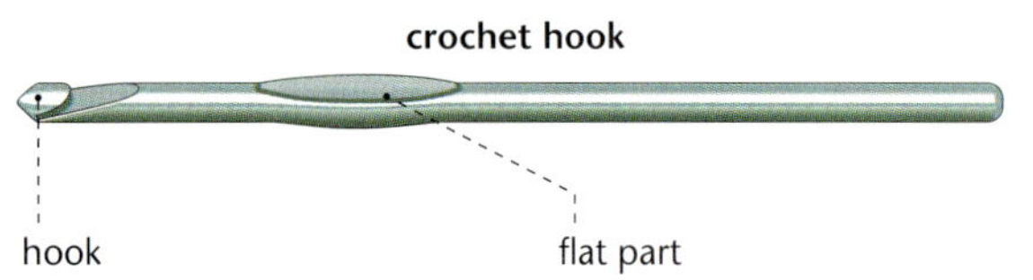

hook

flat part

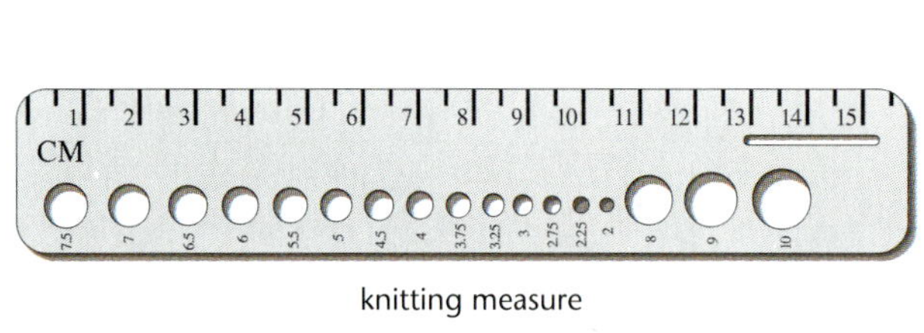

knitting measure

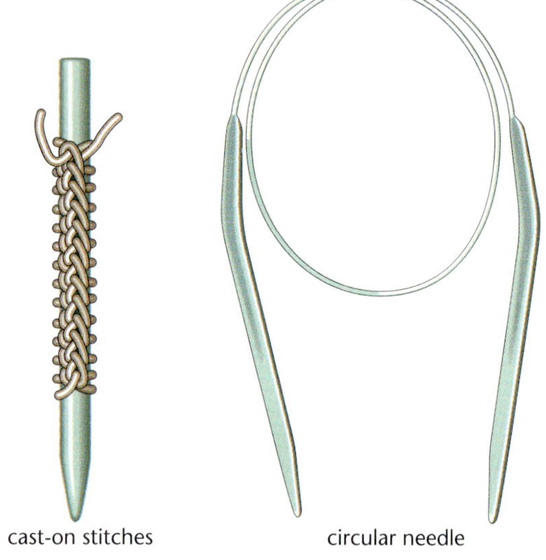

cast-on stitches

circular needle

STITCH PATTERNS

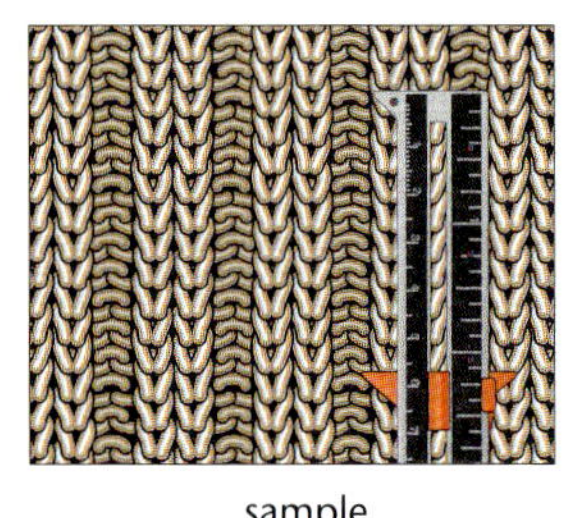

sample

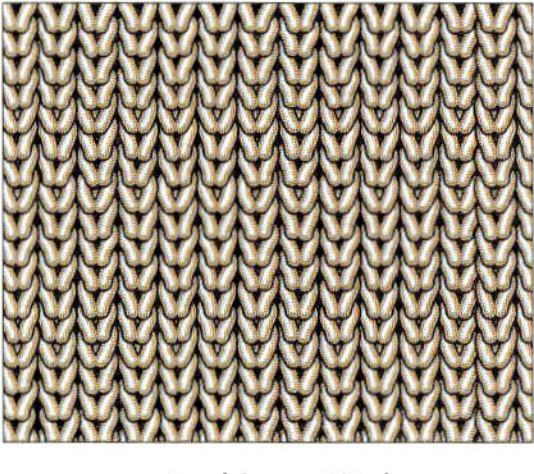

stocking stitch

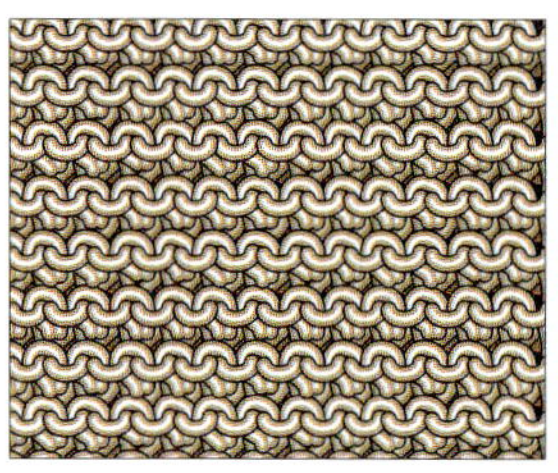

garter stitch

moss stitch

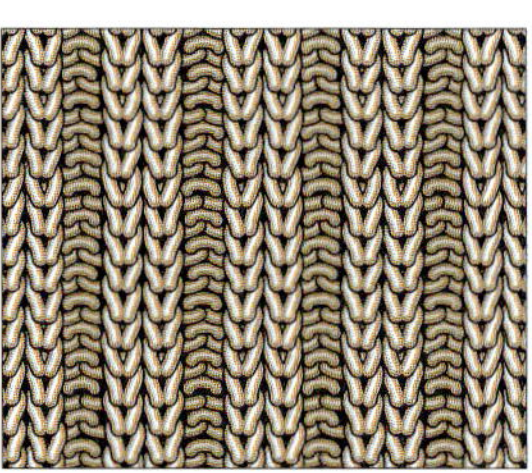

rib stitch

basket stitch

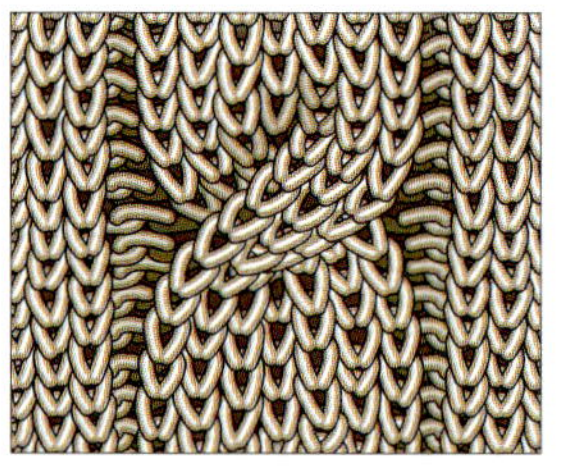

cable stitch

KNITTING MACHINE

NEEDLE BED AND CARRIAGES

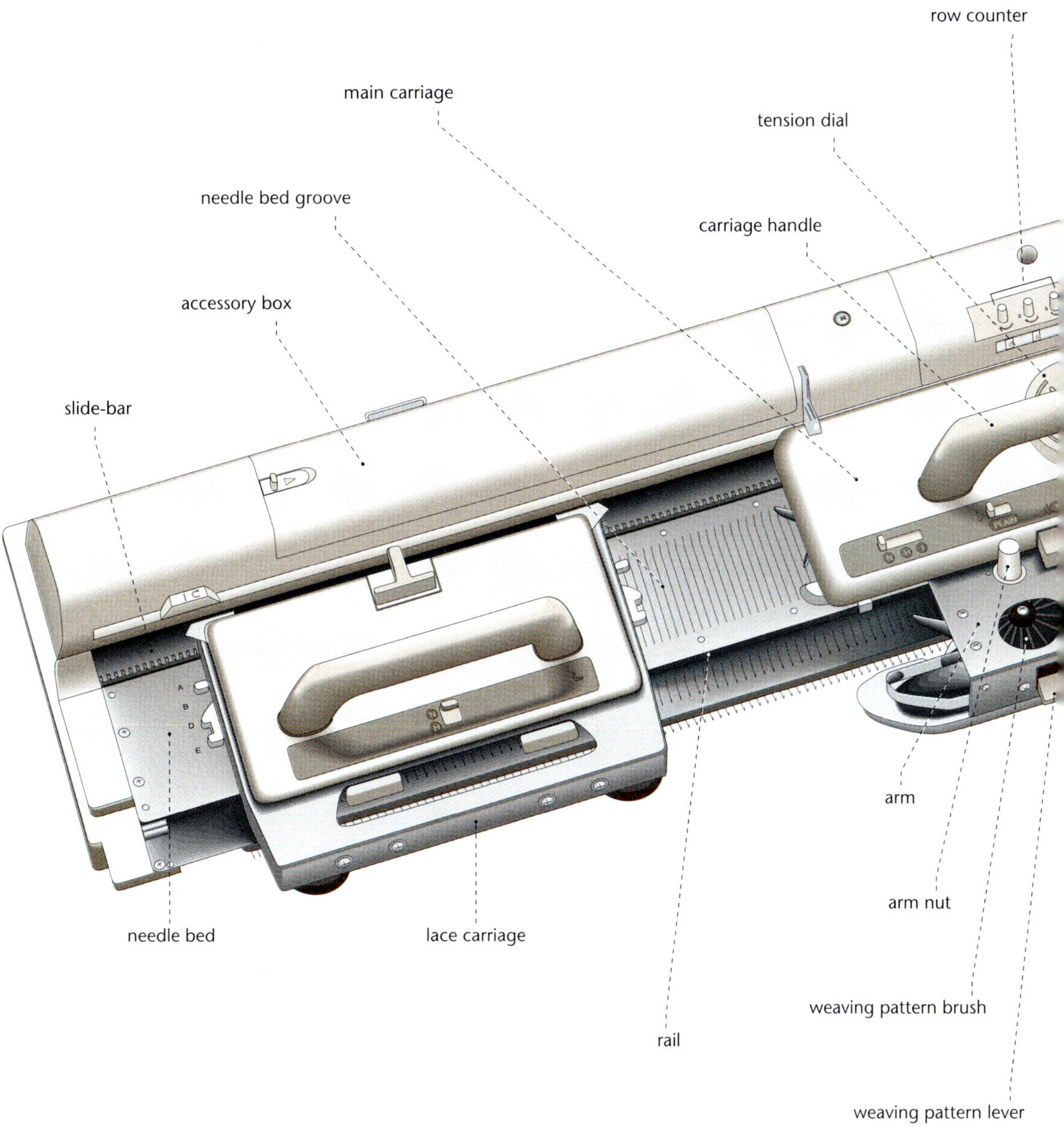

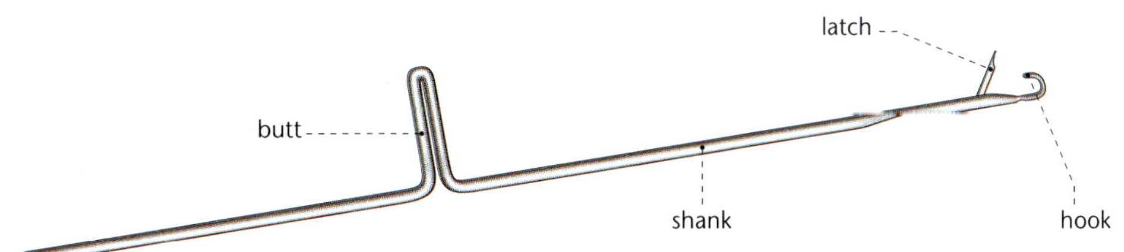

LATCH NEEDLE

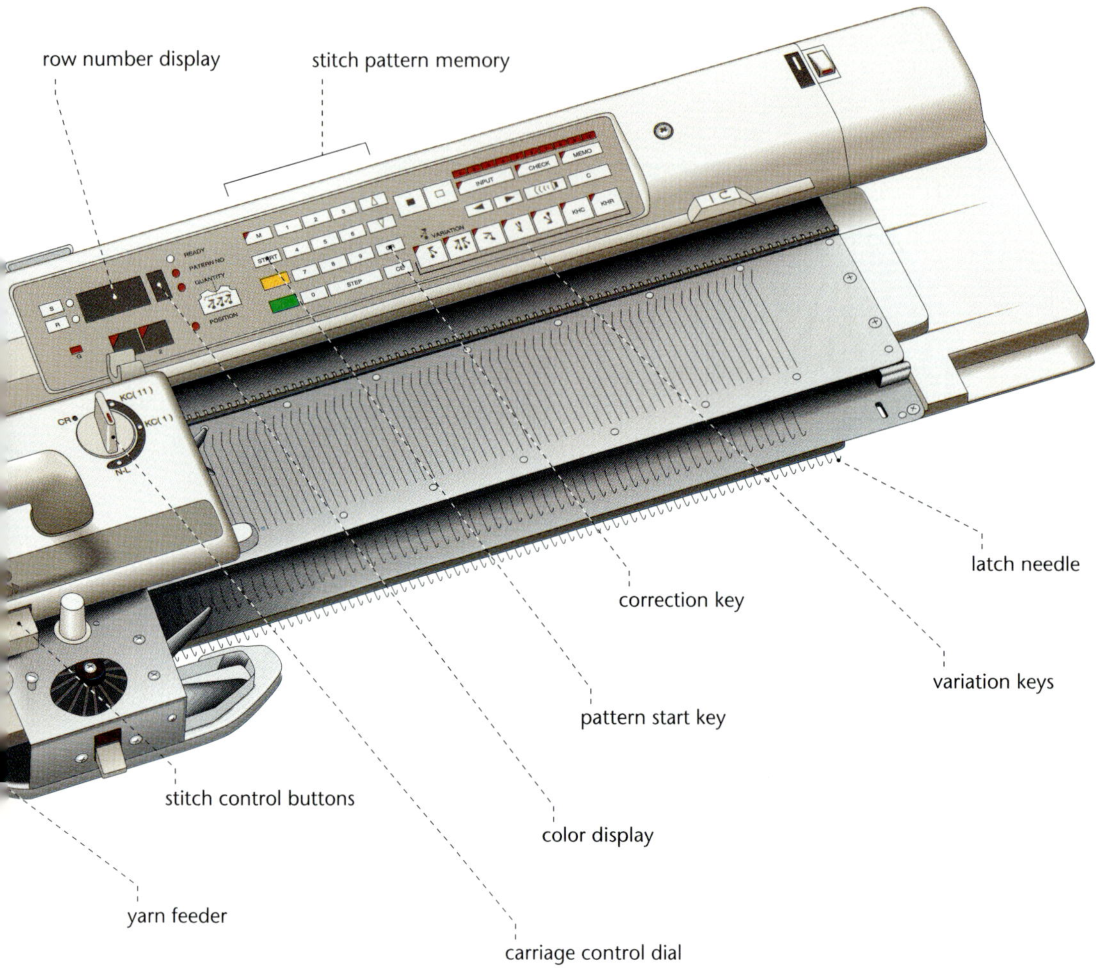

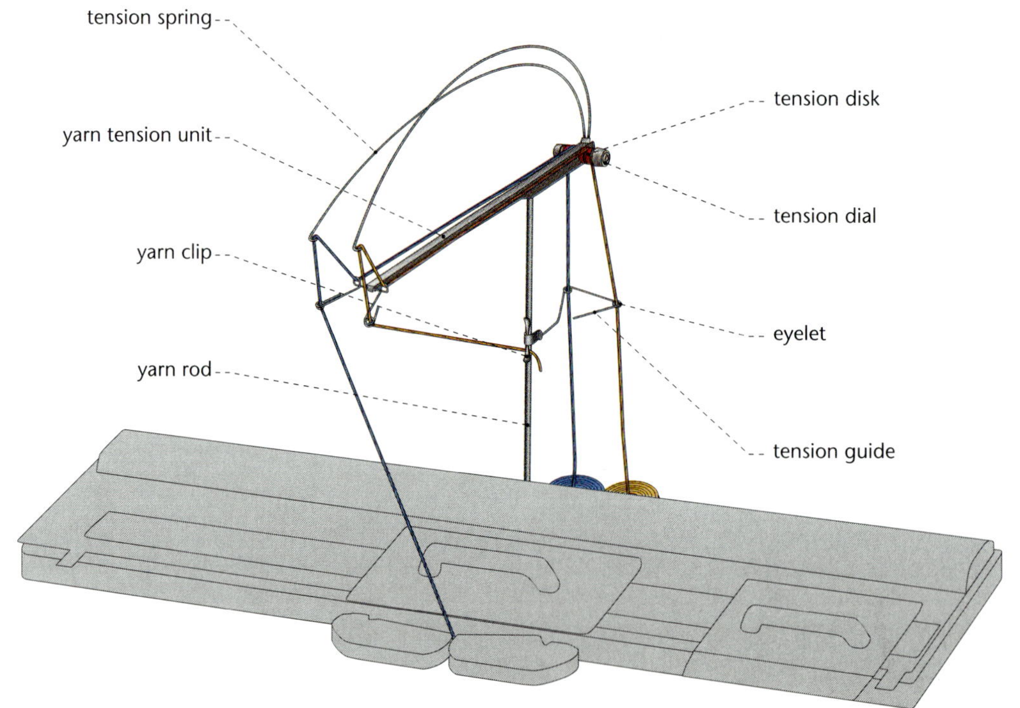

TENSION BLOCK

PILLOW

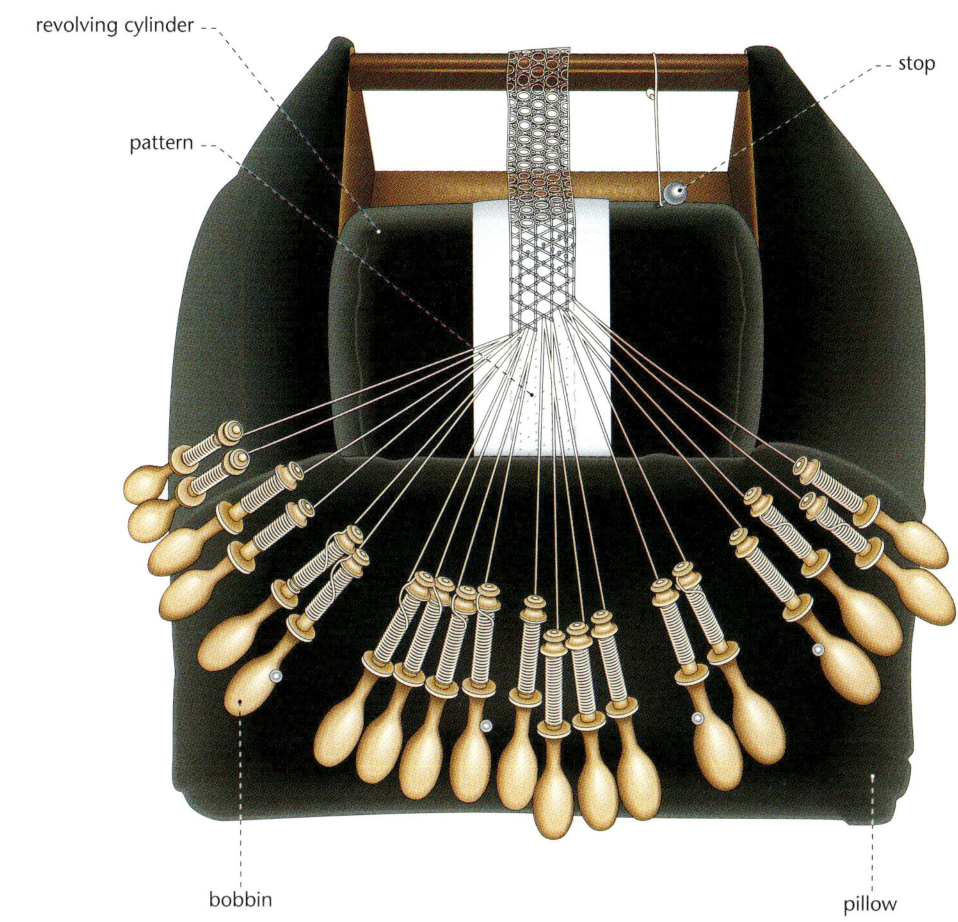

pricker

BOBBIN

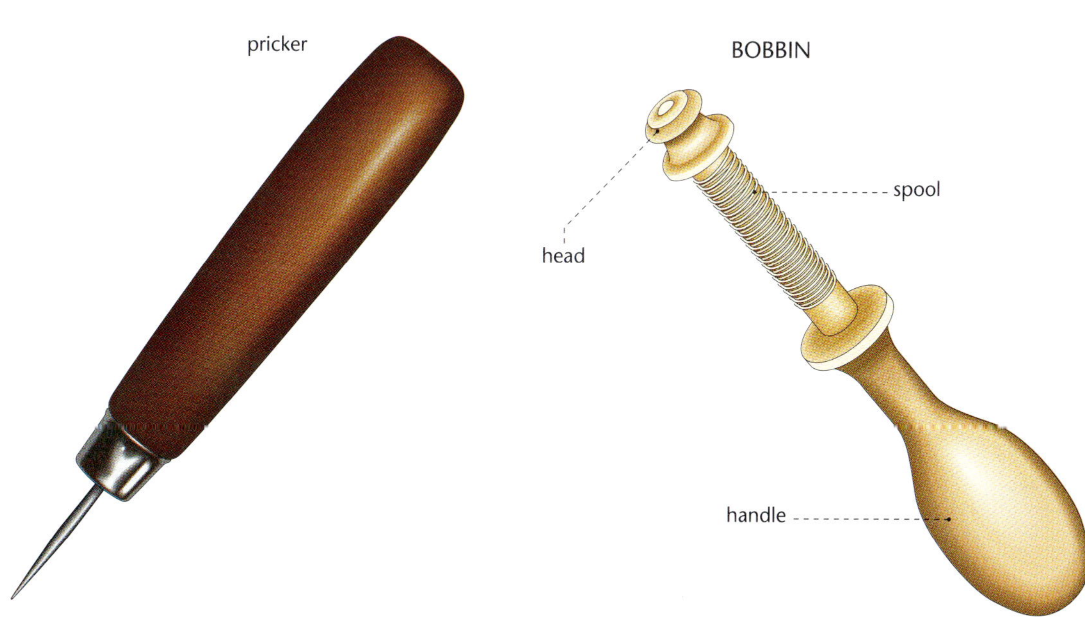

EMBROIDERY

FRAME

embroidered fabric
peg
tape
slat
webbing

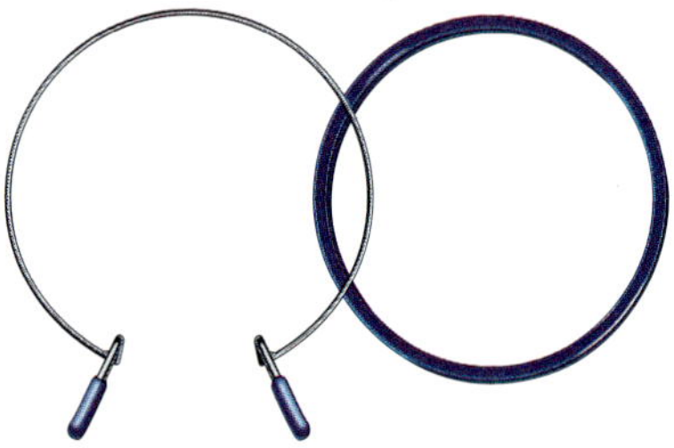

hoop

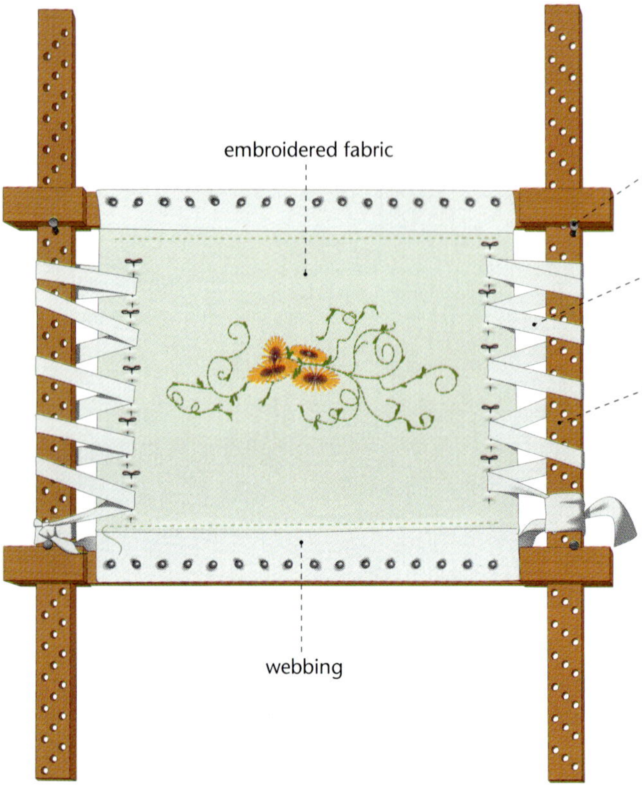

STITCHES

cross stitches

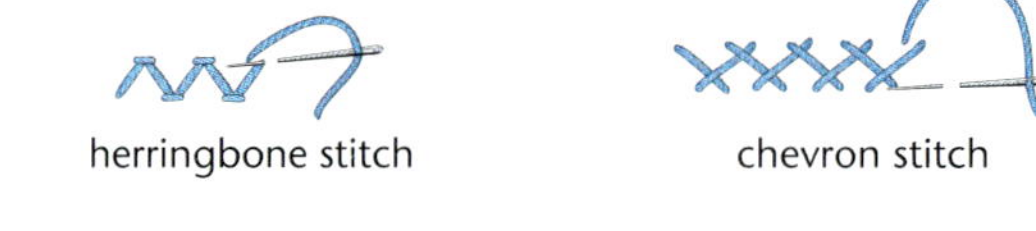

herringbone stitch

chevron stitch

flat stitches

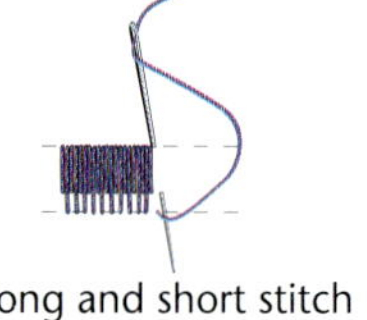

long and short stitch

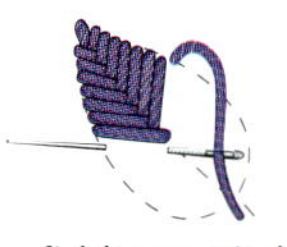

fishbone stitch

couched stitches

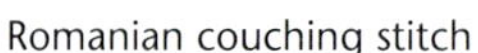

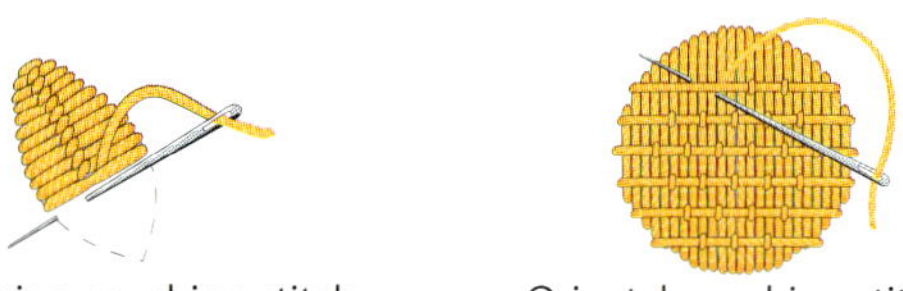

Romanian couching stitch

Oriental couching stitch

knot stitches

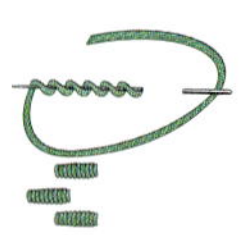

bullion stitch

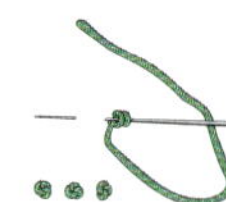

French knot stitch

loop stitches

chain stitch

feather stitch

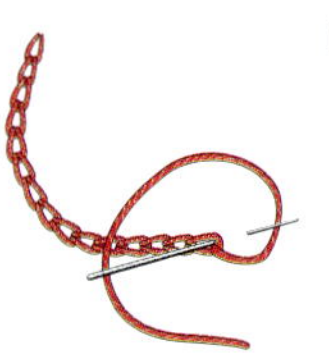

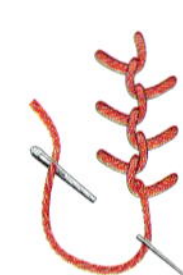

LOW WARP LOOM

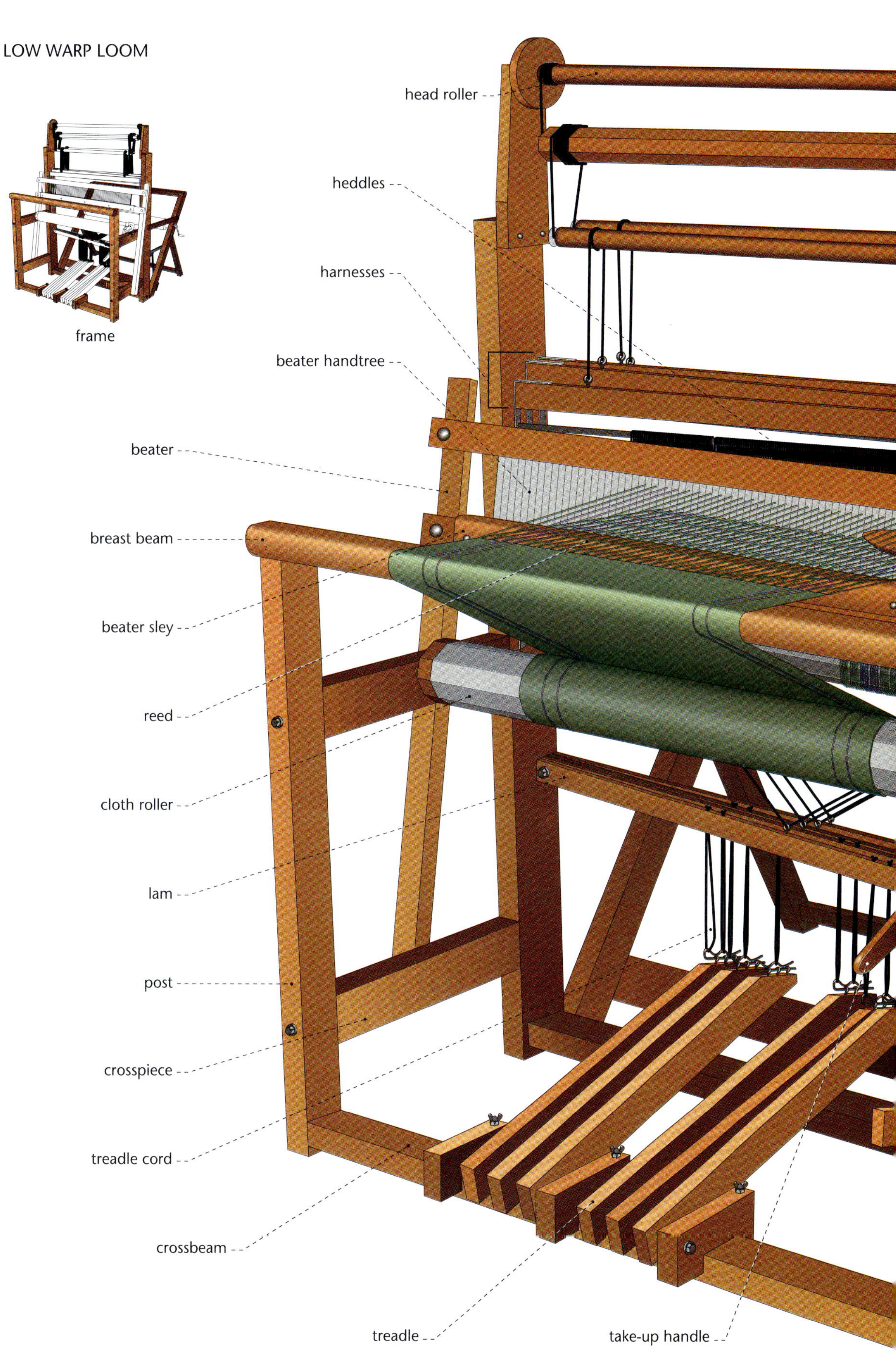

upright
harness
weft
back beam
warp
handle
warp roller
ratchet
ratchet wheel
release treadle
HEDDLES
eye
flat shuttle
reed hooks
temple
SHUTTLE
rod
bobbin
eye

HIGH WARP LOOM
vertical frame
upright
warp
shed stick
heddle rod
heddles
tapestry bobbin
weft
support
crossbar
leash rod
comb
tapestry bobbin

bobbin winder
worm
gear
shaft
swift
ball winder
driving wheel
clamp
ball
warping frame
peg
spool rack

DIAGRAM OF WEAVING PRINCIPLE

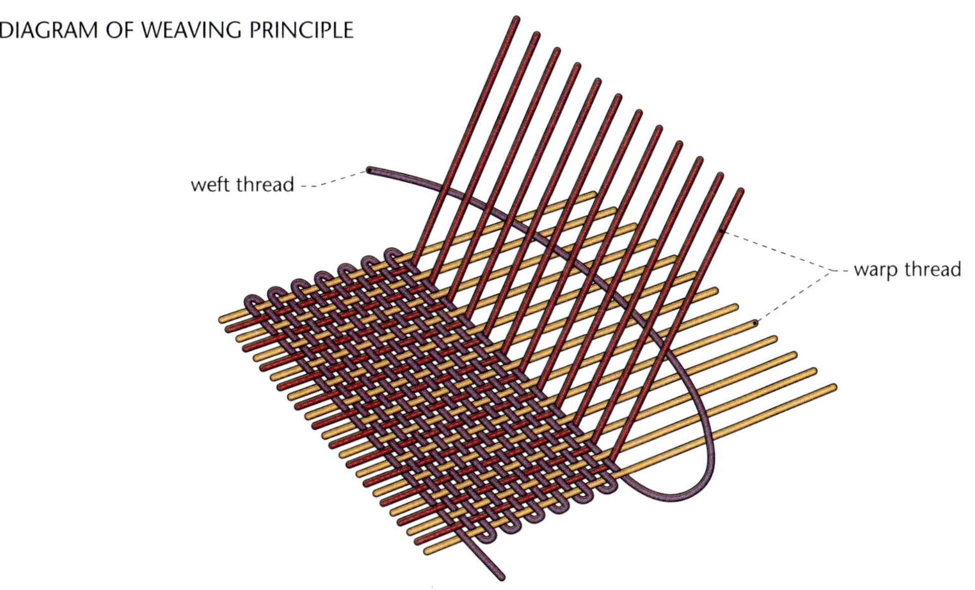

BASIC WEAVES

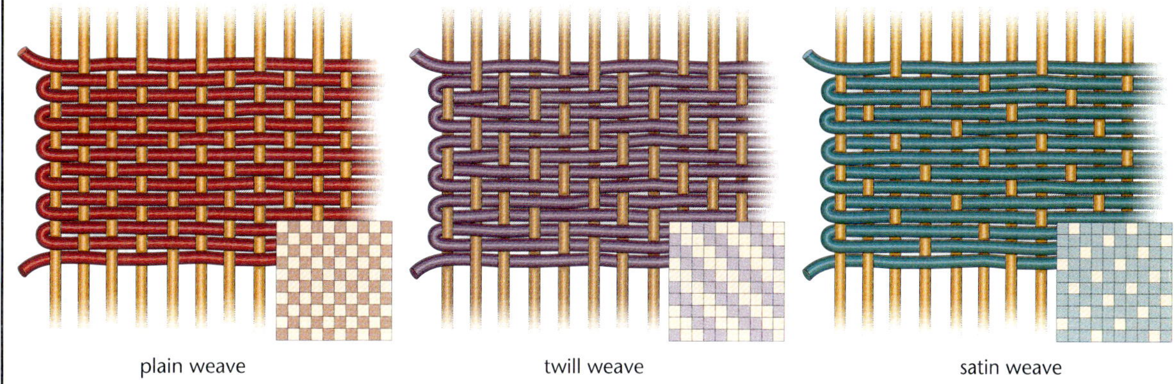

OTHER TECHNIQUES

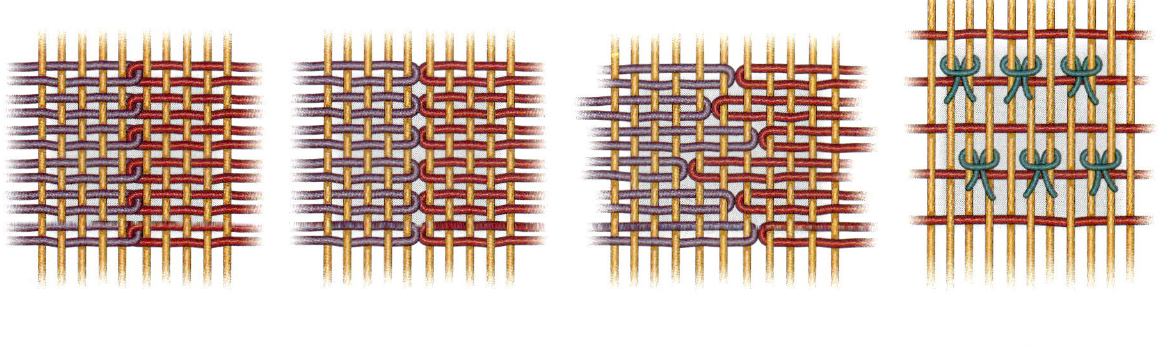

FINE BOOKBINDING

BOUND BOOK

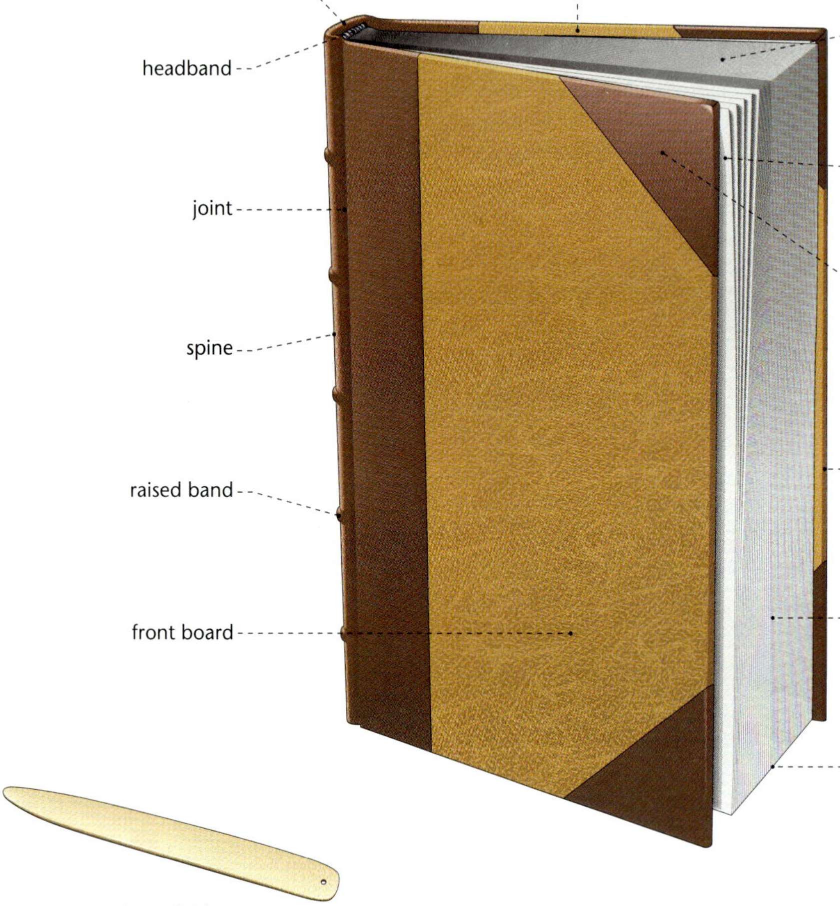

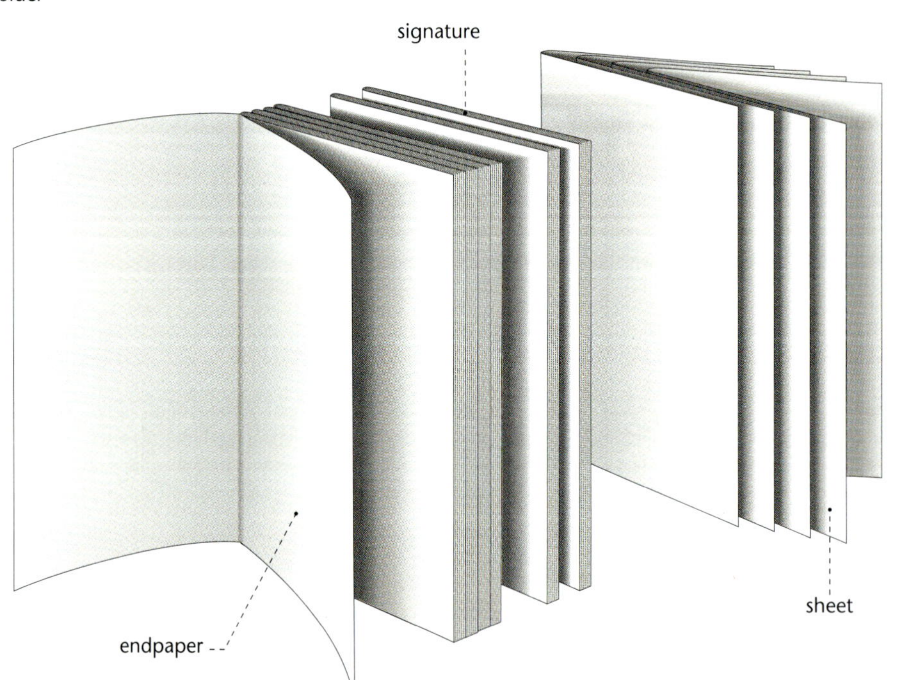

GATHERING

FINE BOOKBINDING

TRIMMING

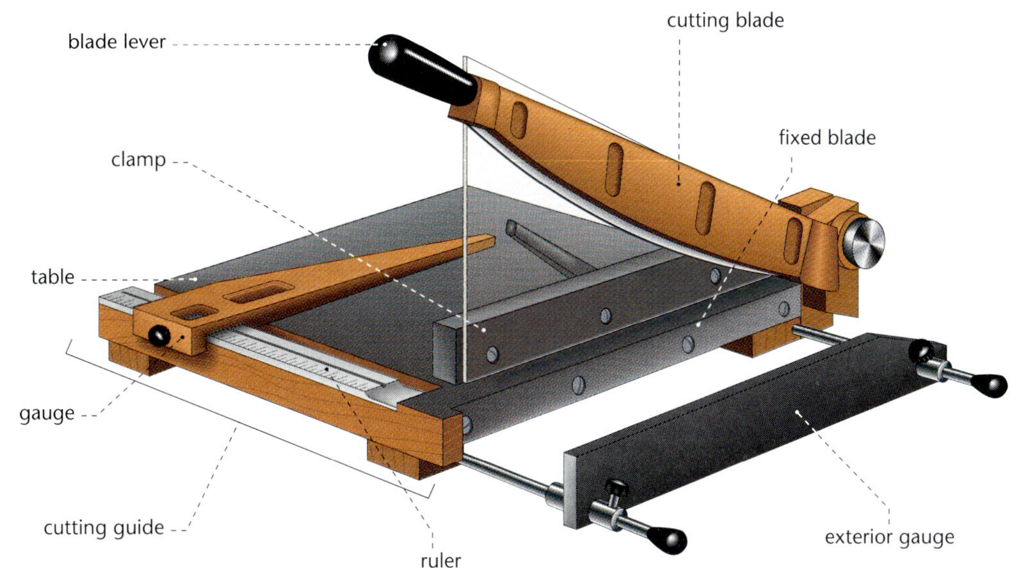

SAWING-IN

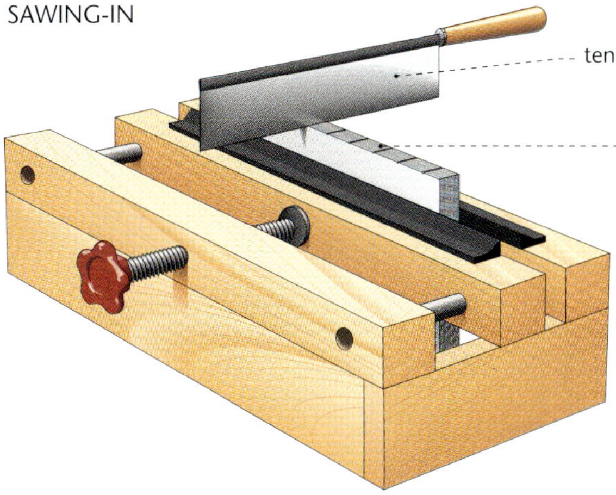

SEWING

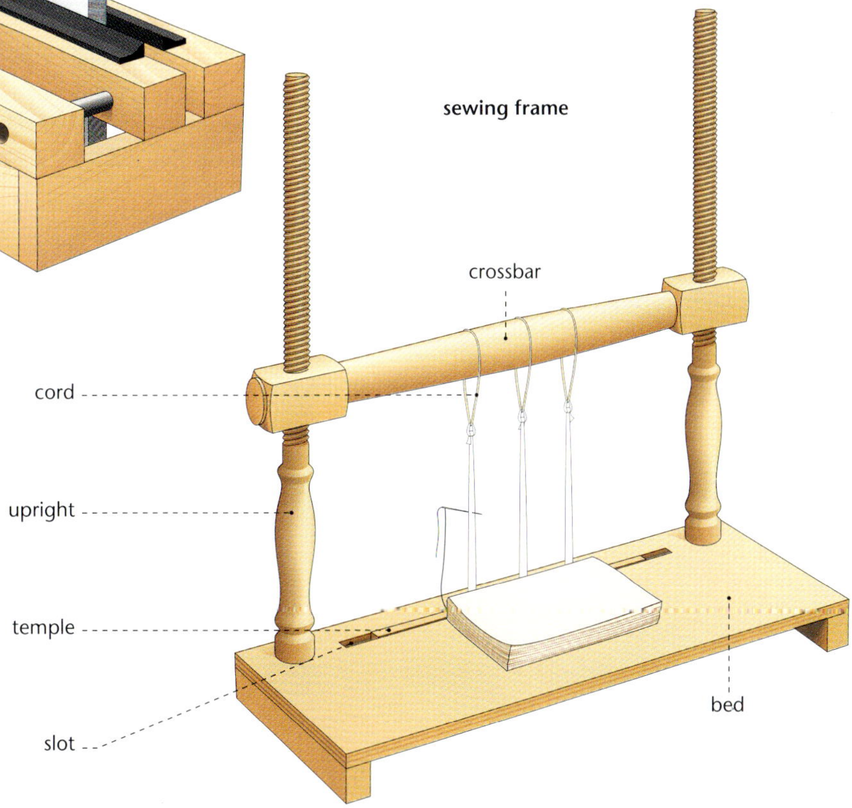

PRESSING

standing press

upright

central screw

hand-wheel

platen

pressing board

base

BACKING PRESS

backing board

spine of the book

BACKING HAMMER

claw

handle

face

COVERING

bookbinding leather

head

neck

flank

feet

tail

butt

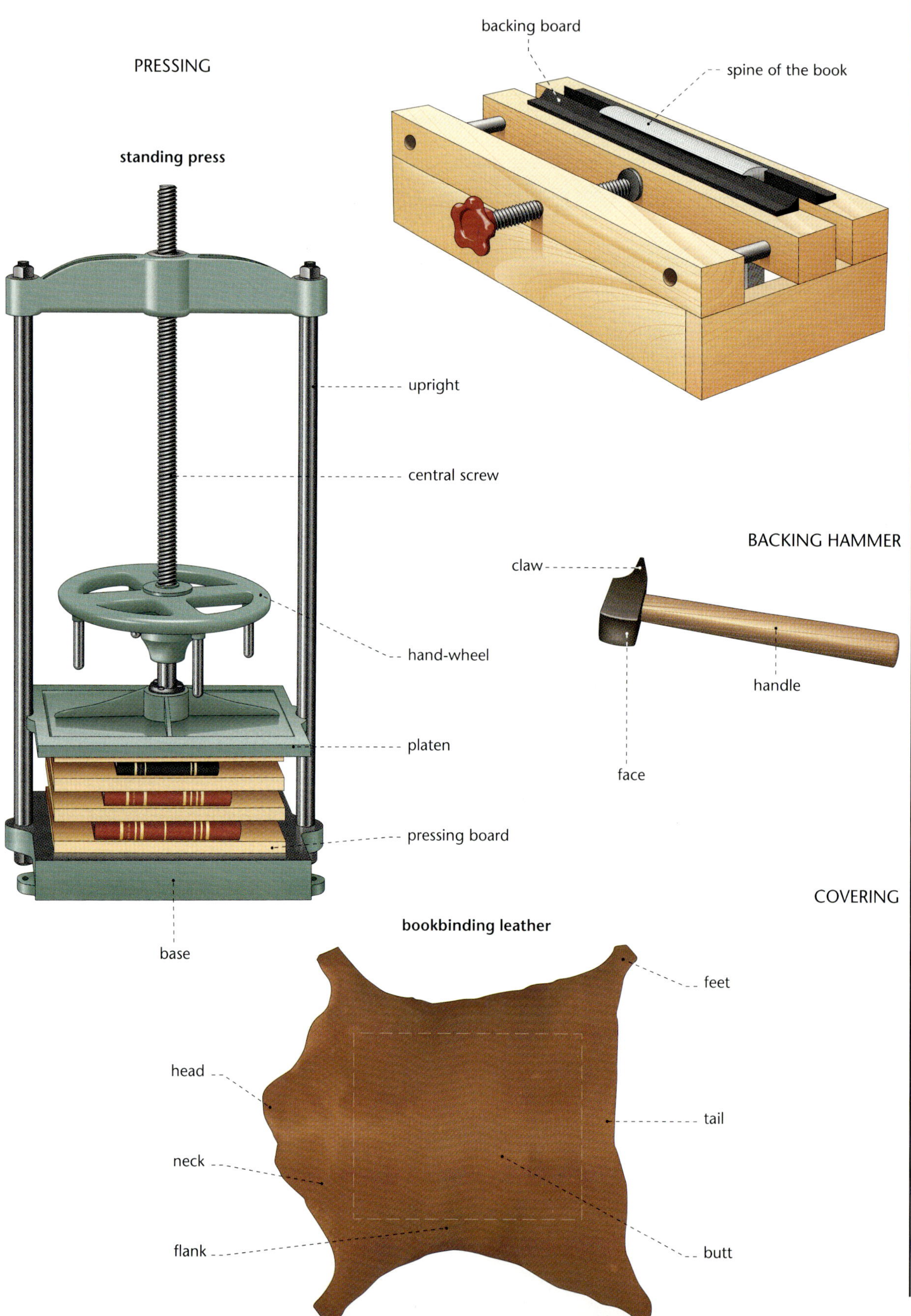

579

RELIEF PRINTING

INTAGLIO PRINTING

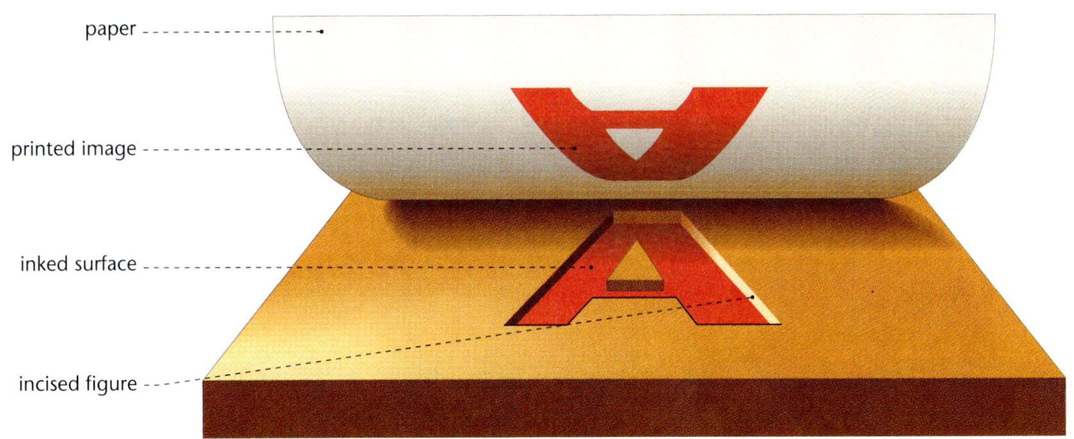

LITHOGRAPHIC PRINTING

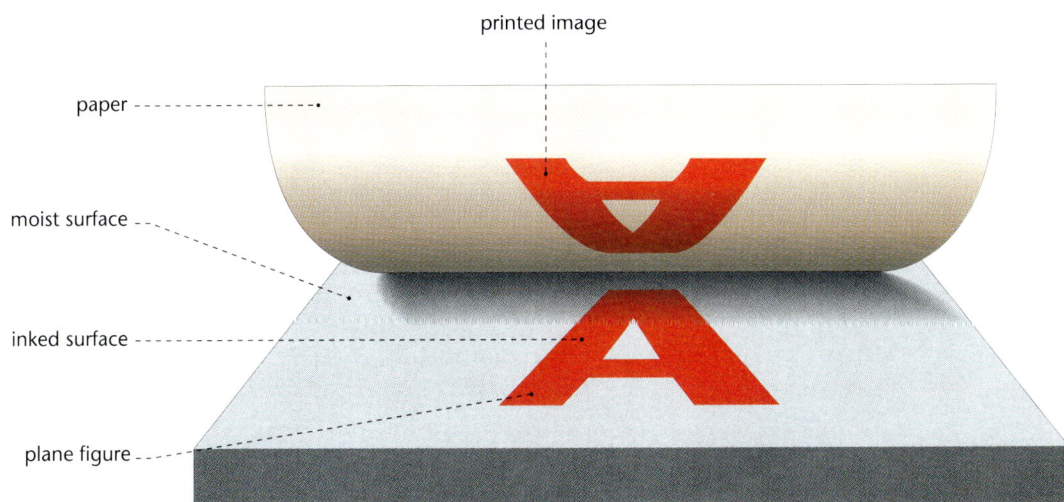

RELIEF PRINTING PROCESS

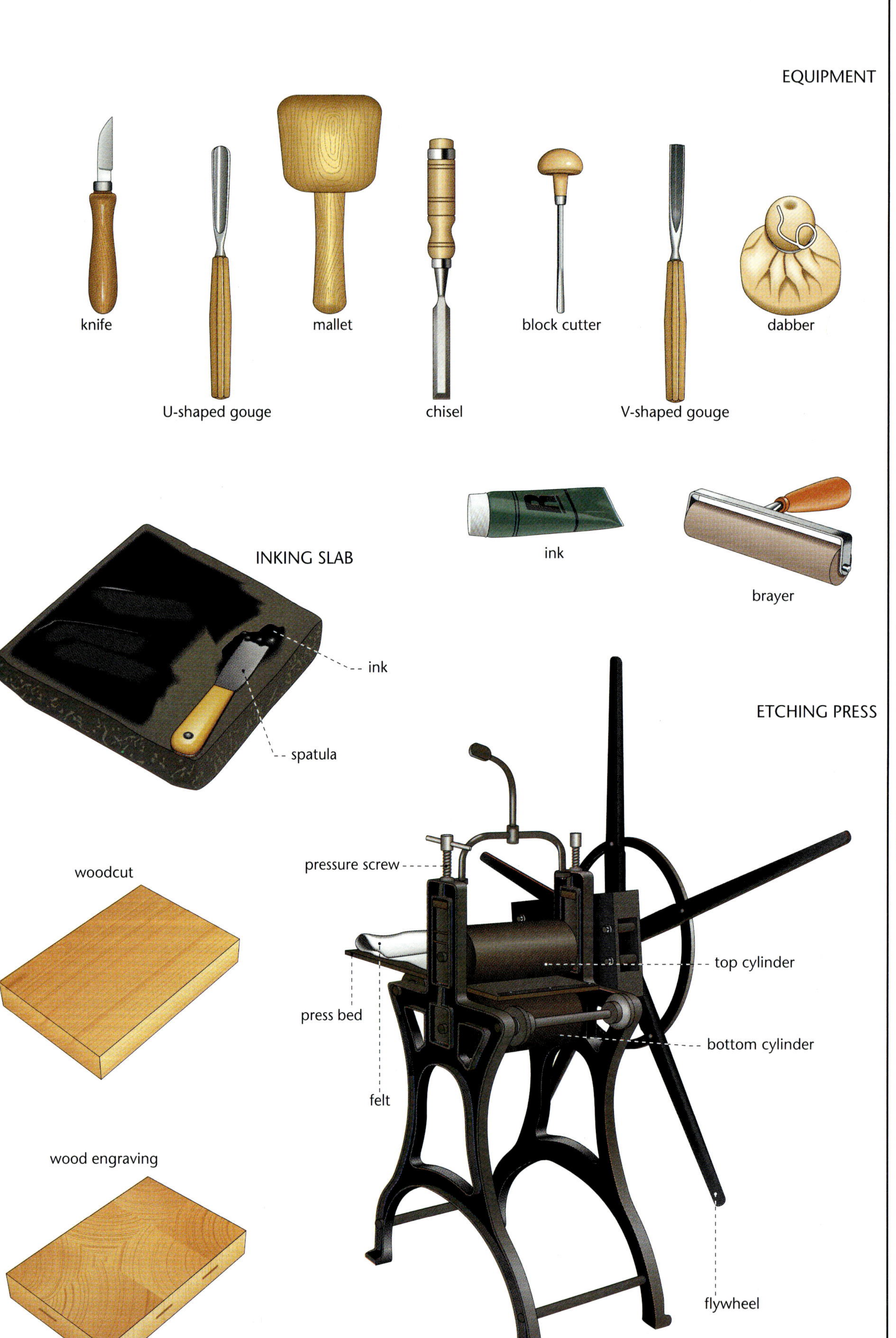

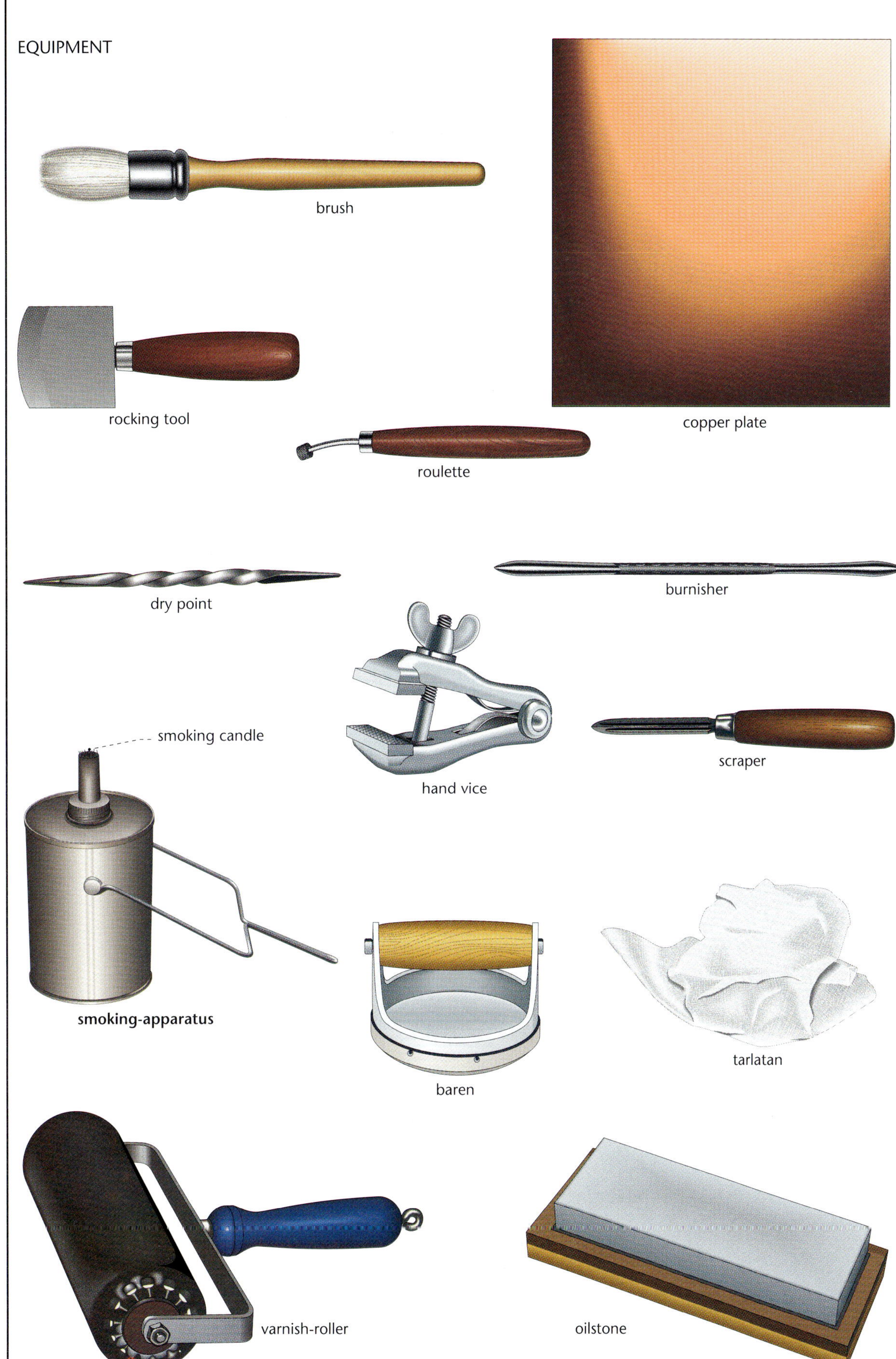
EQUIPMENT
brush
copper plate
rocking tool
roulette
dry point
burnisher
smoking candle
hand vice
scraper
smoking-apparatus
baren
tarlatan
varnish-roller
oilstone

LITHOGRAPHY

TURNING

coiling

slab building

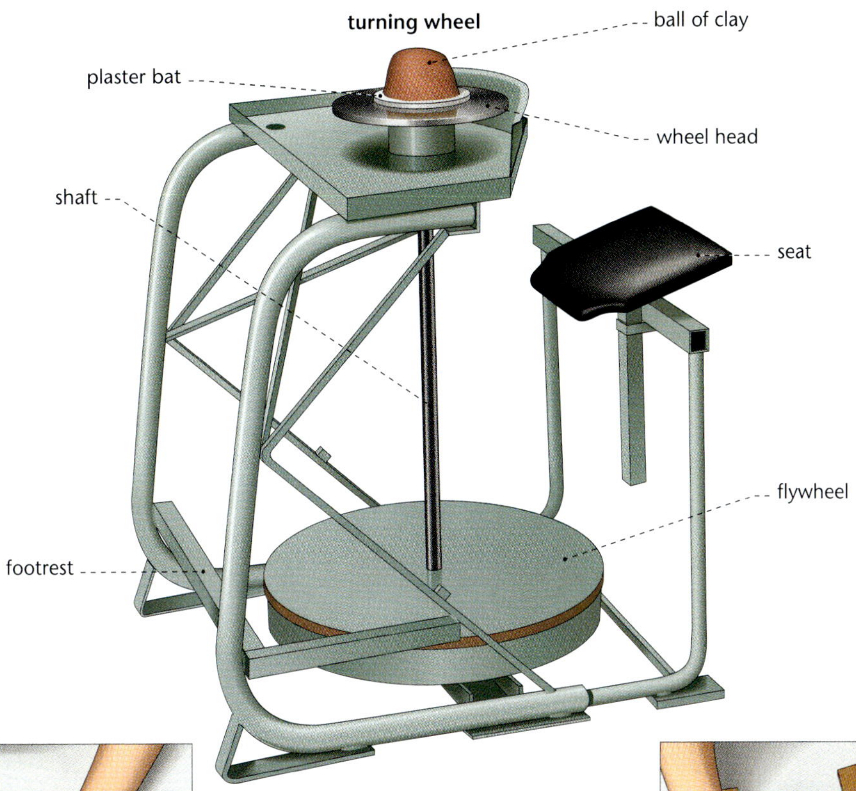

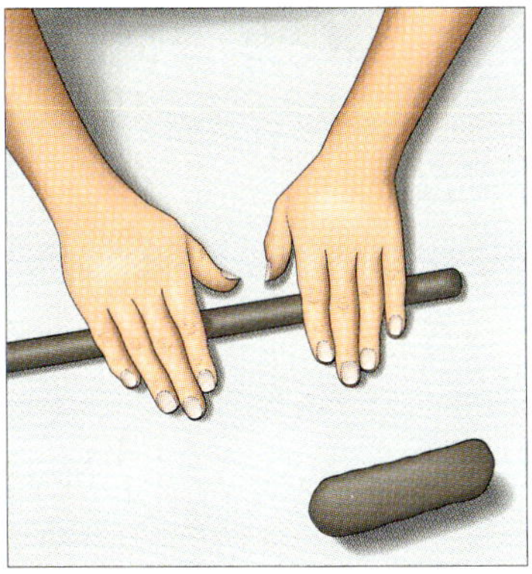

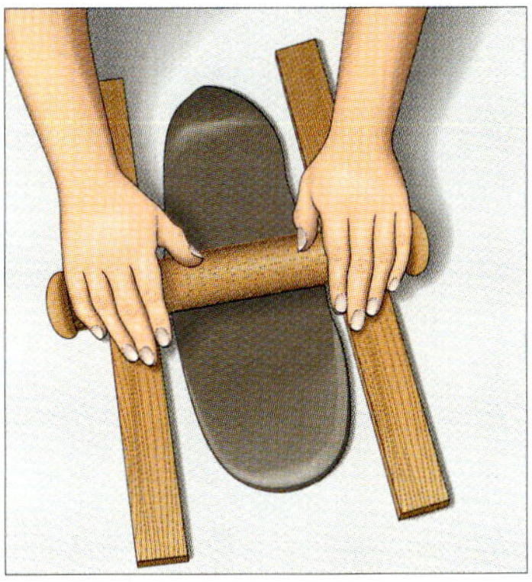

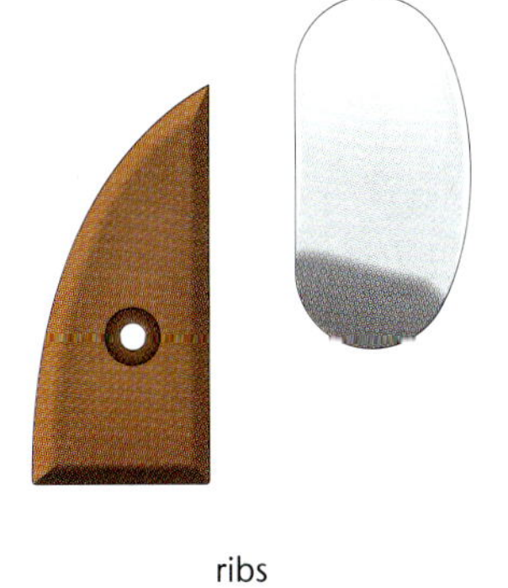

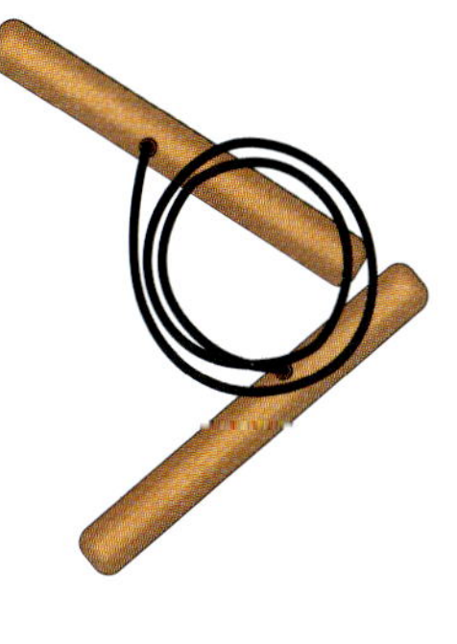

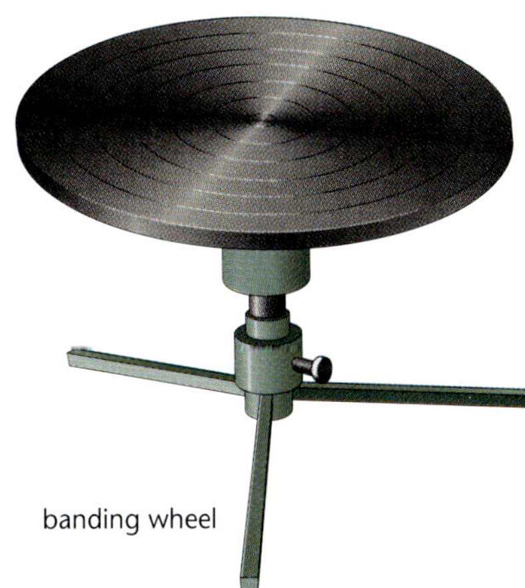

TOOLS

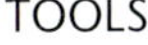

ribs

cutting wire

banding wheel

wooden modeling tools
fettling knife
needle tool
trimming tool
pyrometric cone
stilt
electric kiln
refractory brick
lid
lid brace
hinge
heating element
firing chamber
damper
temperature control knob
manual/automatic mode
signal lamp
timer
electrical inlet
connecting cable

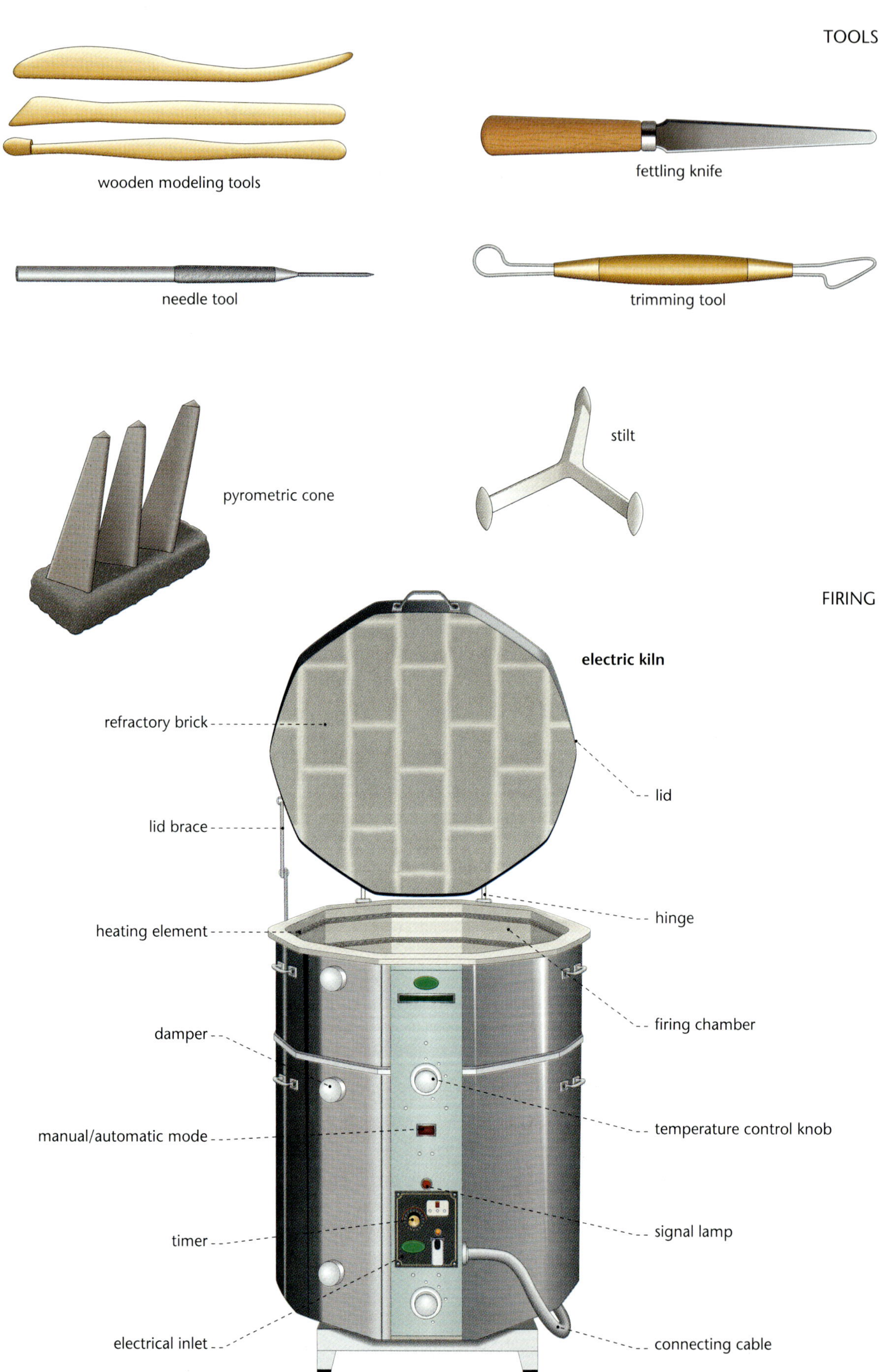

FIRING

WOOD CARVING

STEPS

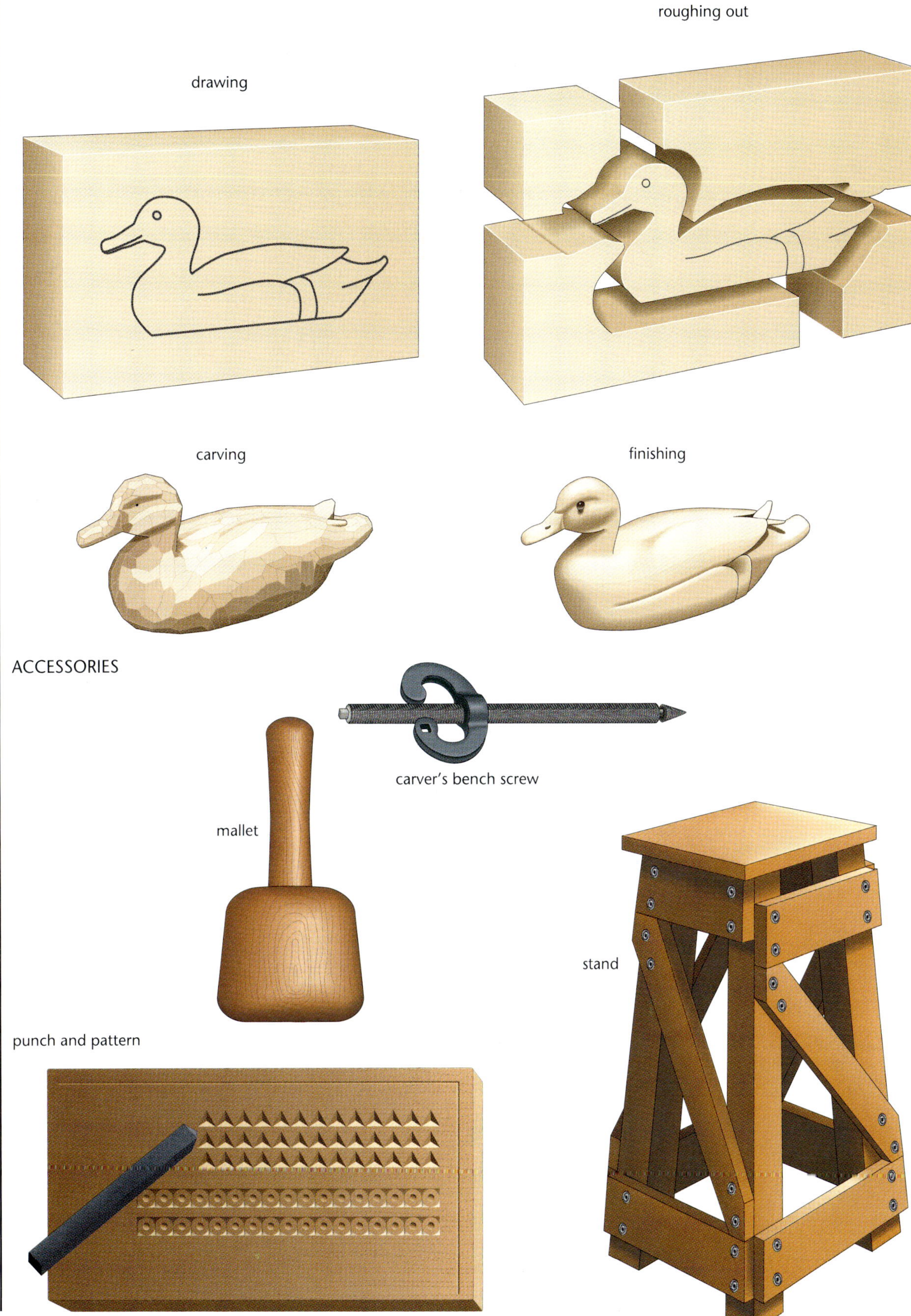

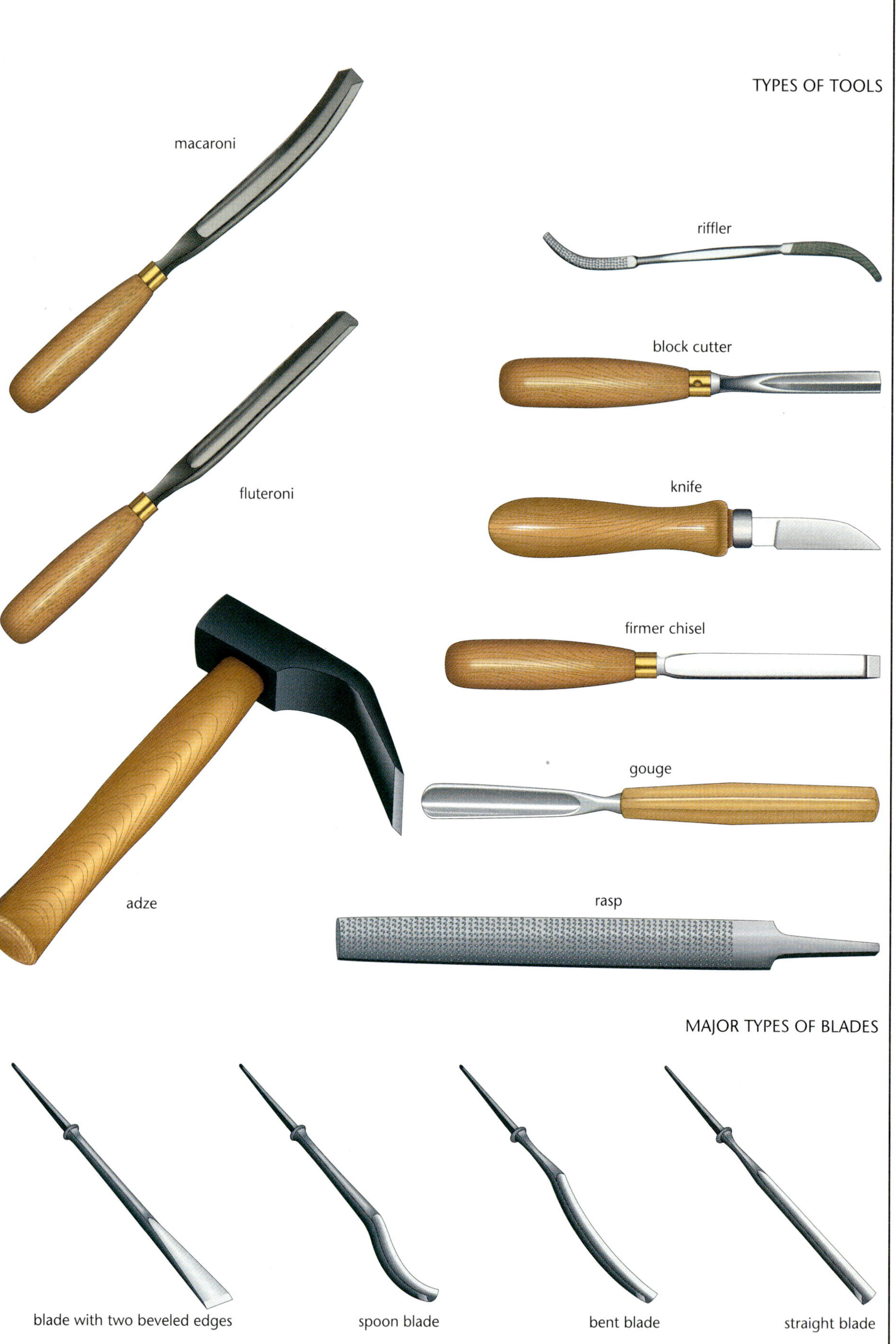

MAJOR TYPES OF BLADES

MAJOR TECHNIQUES

EQUIPMENT

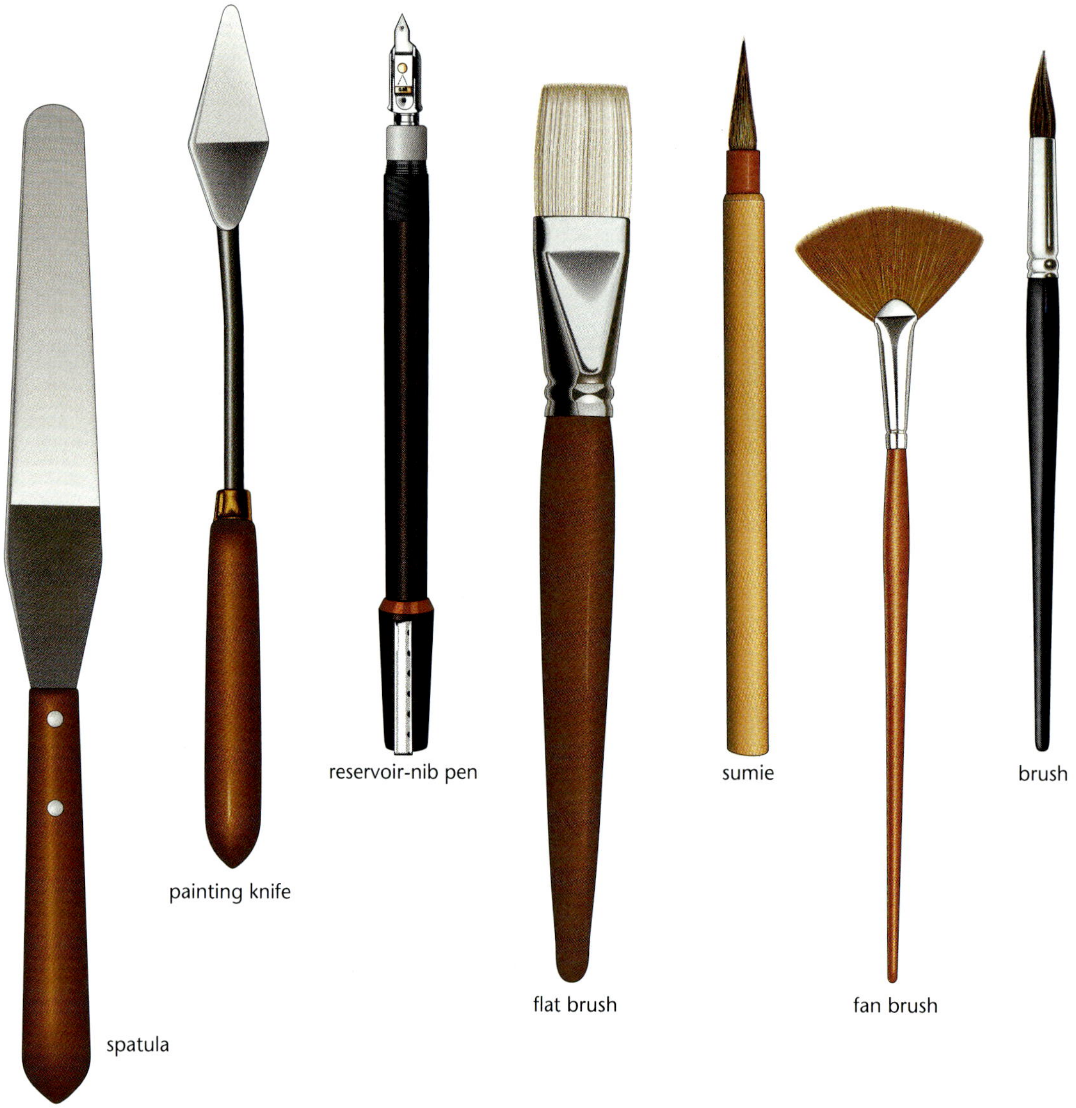
reservoir-nib pen
sumie
brush
painting knife
flat brush
fan brush
spatula

SUPPORTS

paper
cardboard
canvas
panel

AIRBRUSH

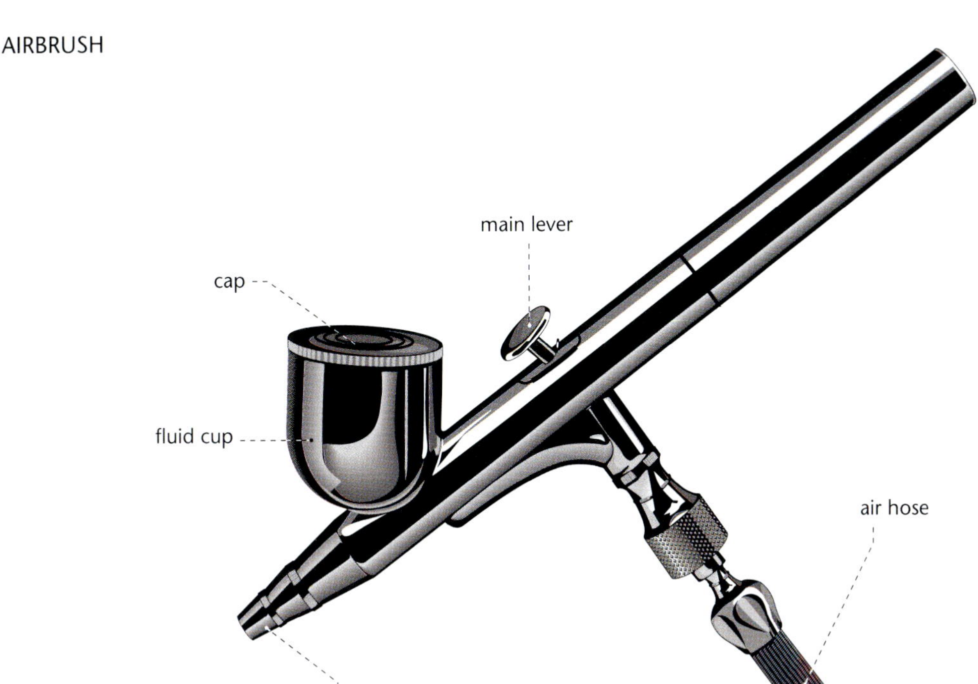

CROSS SECTION OF AN AIRBRUSH

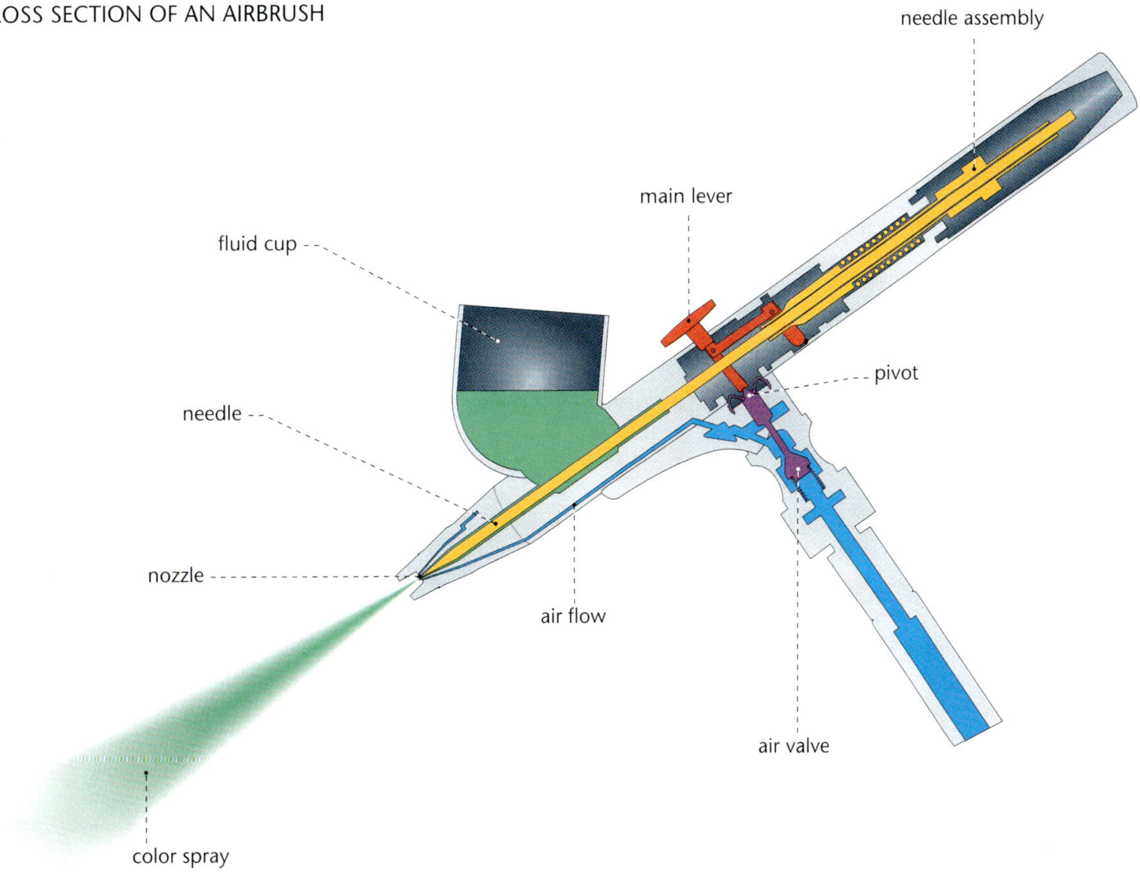

CREATIVE LEISURE ACTIVITIES

ACCESSORIES

color chart

palette with hollows

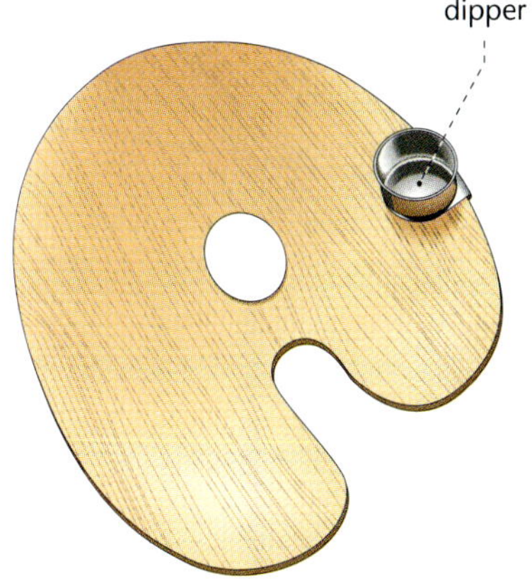

palette with dipper

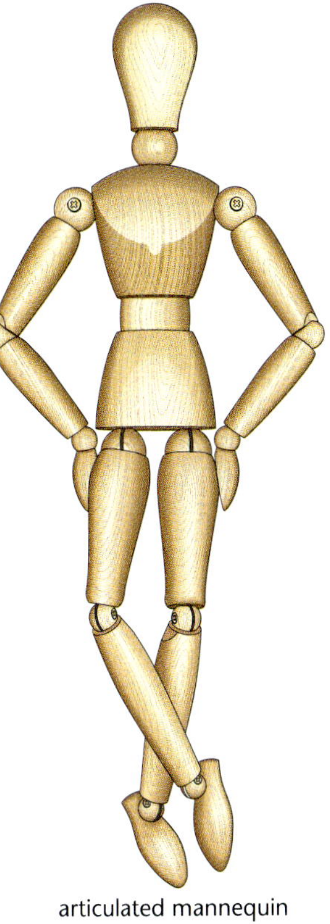

articulated mannequin

UTILITY LIQUIDS

varnish

linseed oil

turpentine

fixative

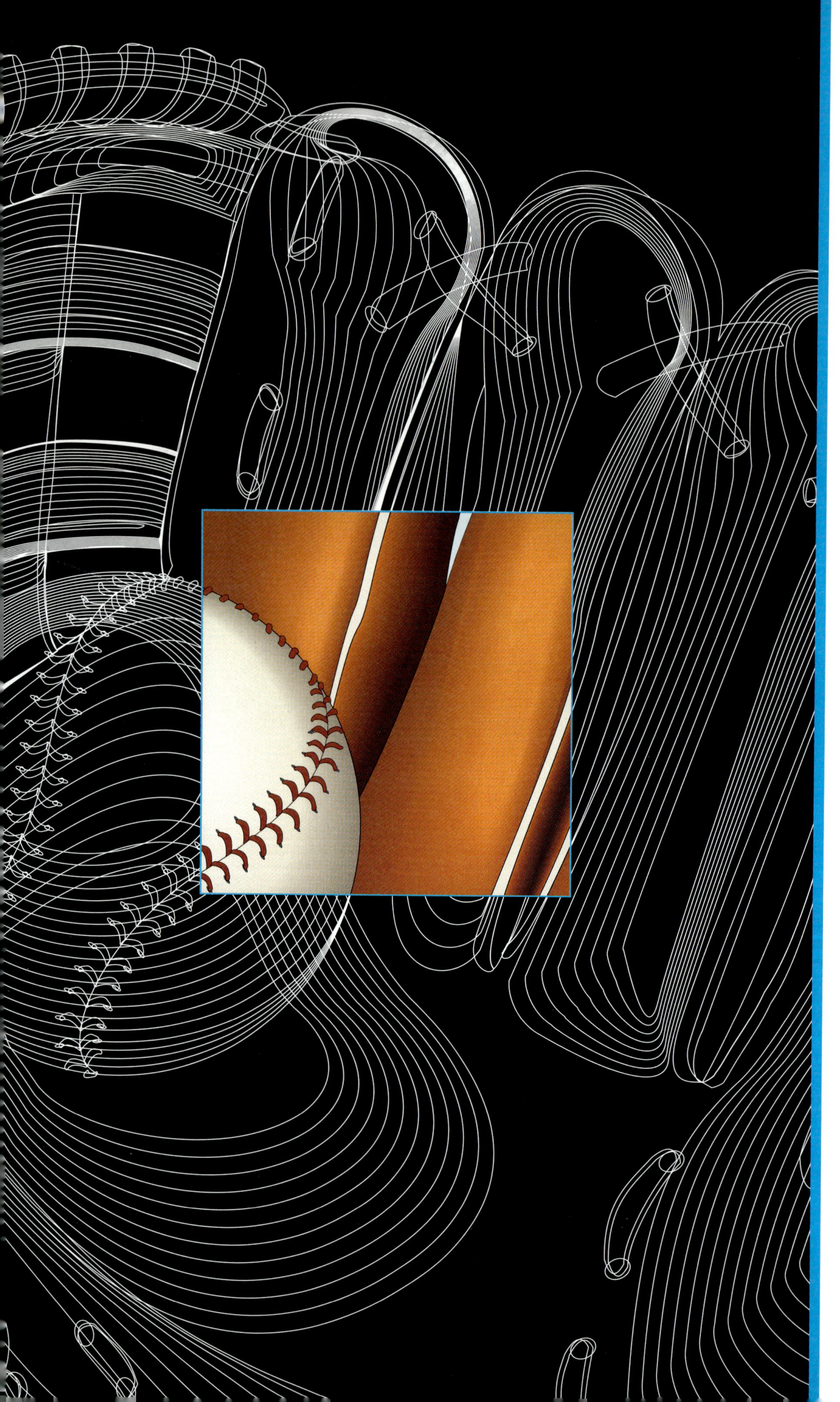

SPORTS

CATCHER
BATTER
throat protector
mask
frame
batting glove
batter's helmet
team shirt
bat
catcher's glove
undershirt
shin guard
chest protector
stirrup sock
toe guard
knee pad
pants
spiked shoe

TEAM GAMES

BAT
knob
handle
crest
hitting area
BASEBALL
2 13/16 – 2 29/32 in
BASEBALL, CROSS SECTION
yarn ball
cork ball
cover
stitches
FIELDER'S GLOVE
web
finger
strap
thumb
palm
heel
lace

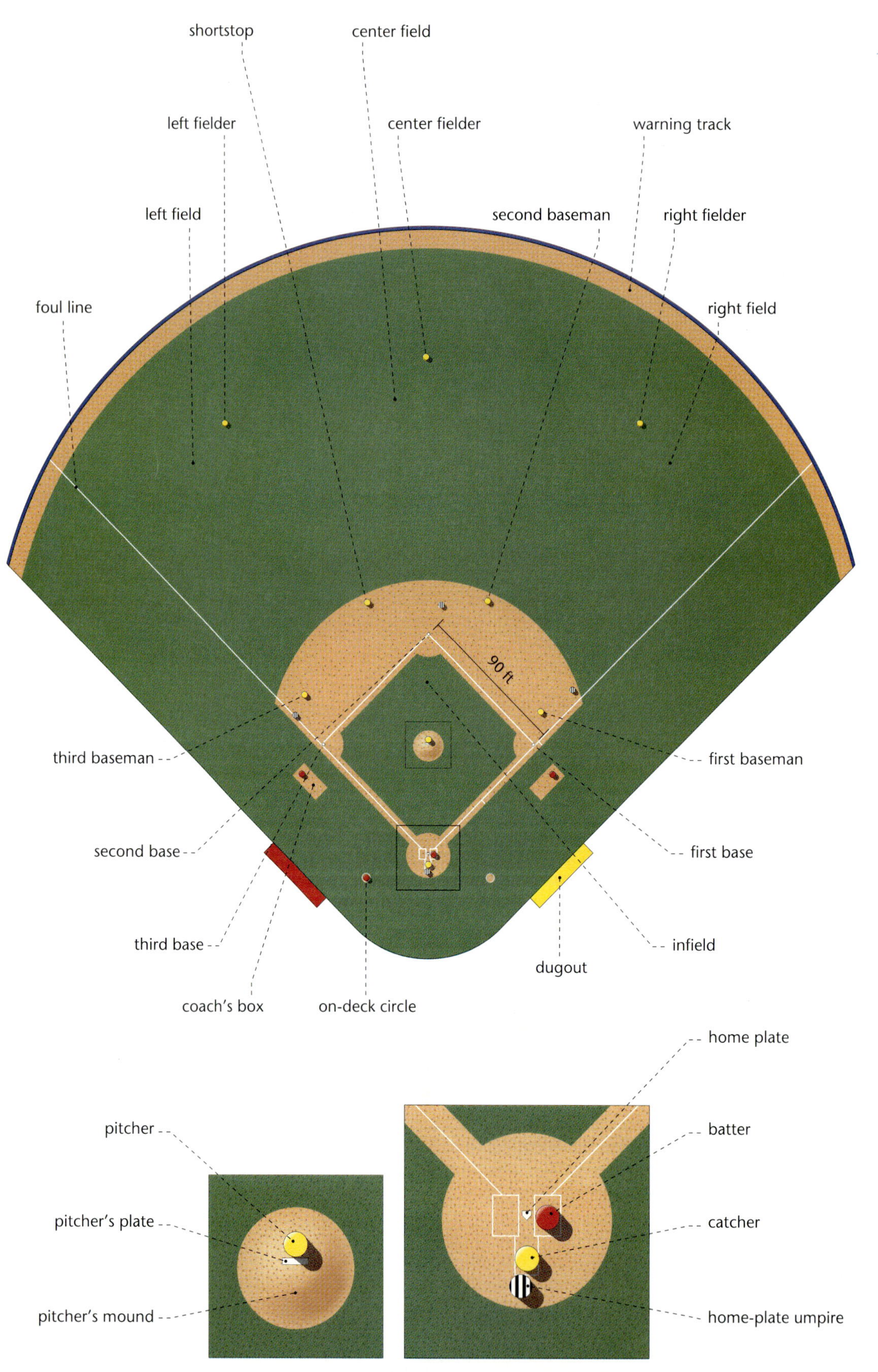

shortstop
center field
left fielder
center fielder
warning track
left field
second baseman
right fielder
right field
foul line
90 ft
third baseman
first baseman
second base
first base
third base
infield
coach's box
on-deck circle
dugout
home plate
pitcher
batter
pitcher's plate
catcher
pitcher's mound
home-plate umpire

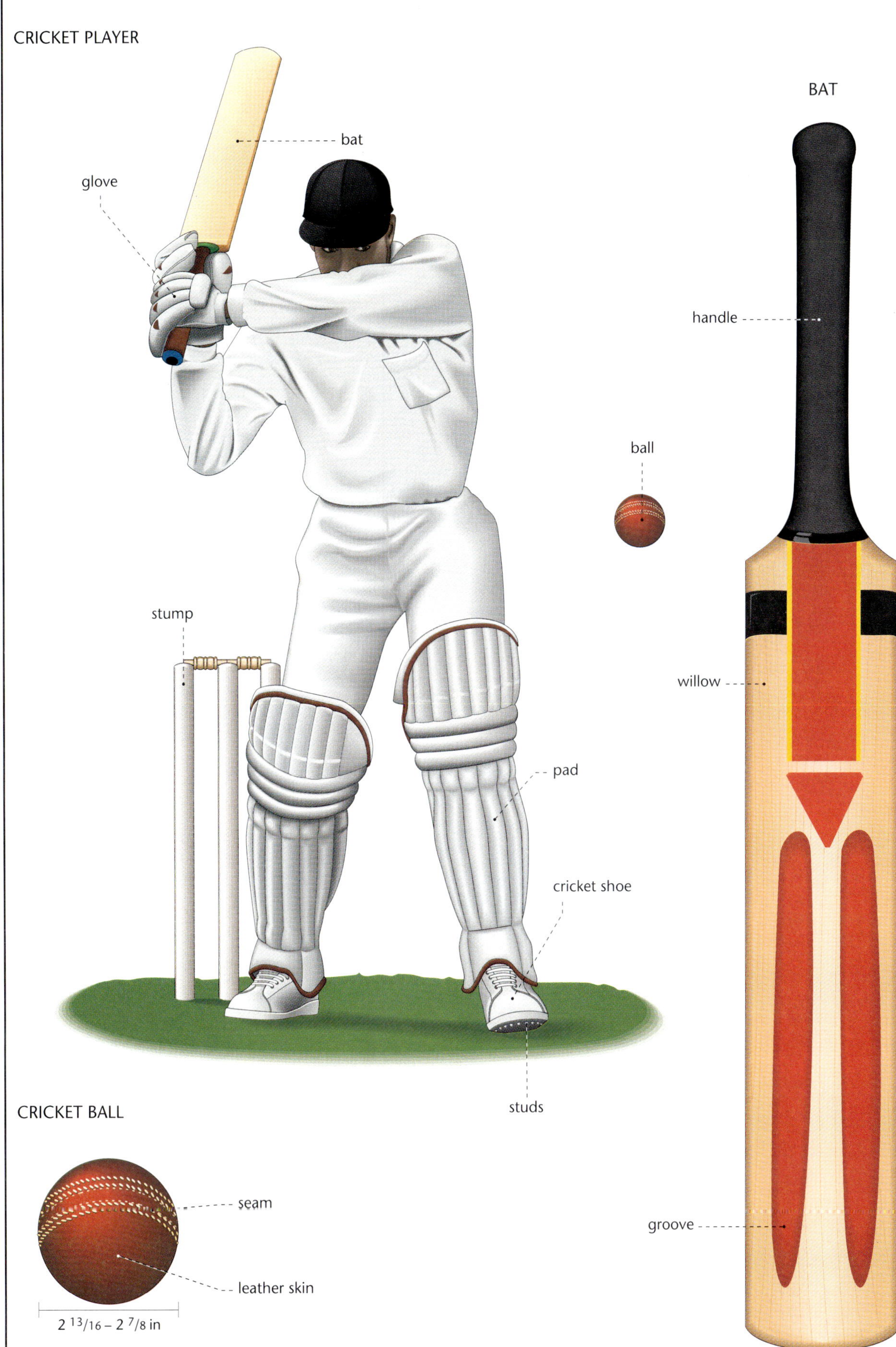
CRICKET PLAYER
bat
glove
BAT
handle
ball
stump
willow
pad
cricket shoe
studs
CRICKET BALL
seam
leather skin
2 13/16 – 2 7/8 in
groove
TEAM GAMES

WICKET

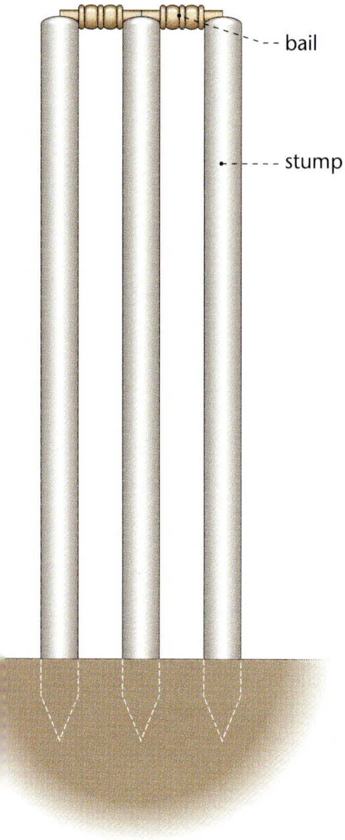

FIELD

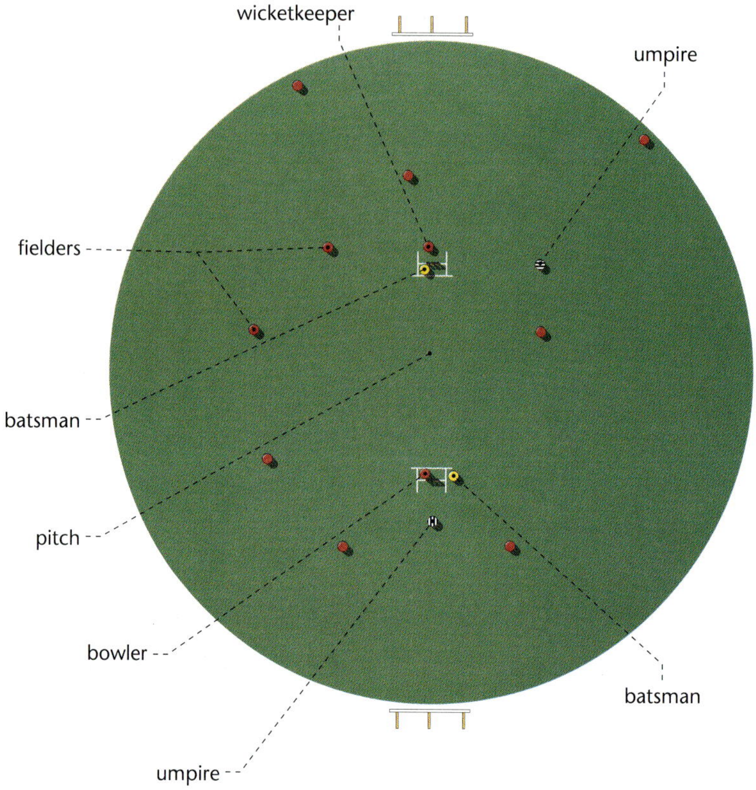

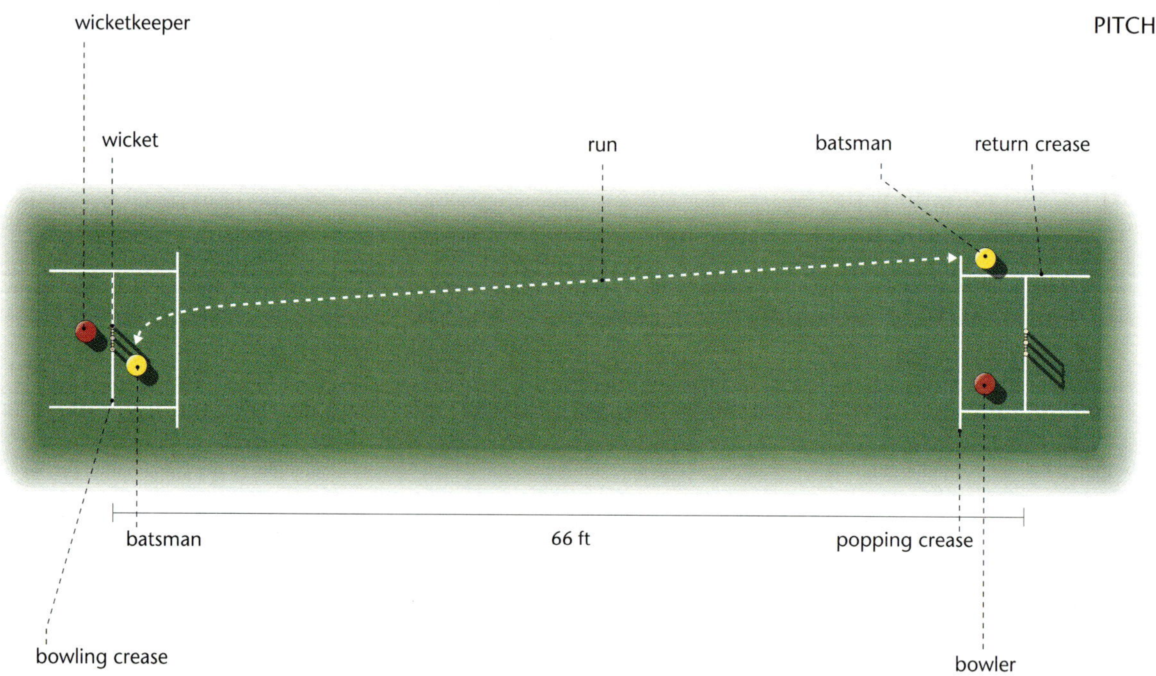

PITCH

SOCCER PLAYER
SOCCER BALL
team shirt
8 1/2 in
shorts
shin guard
soccer shoe
interchangeable studs

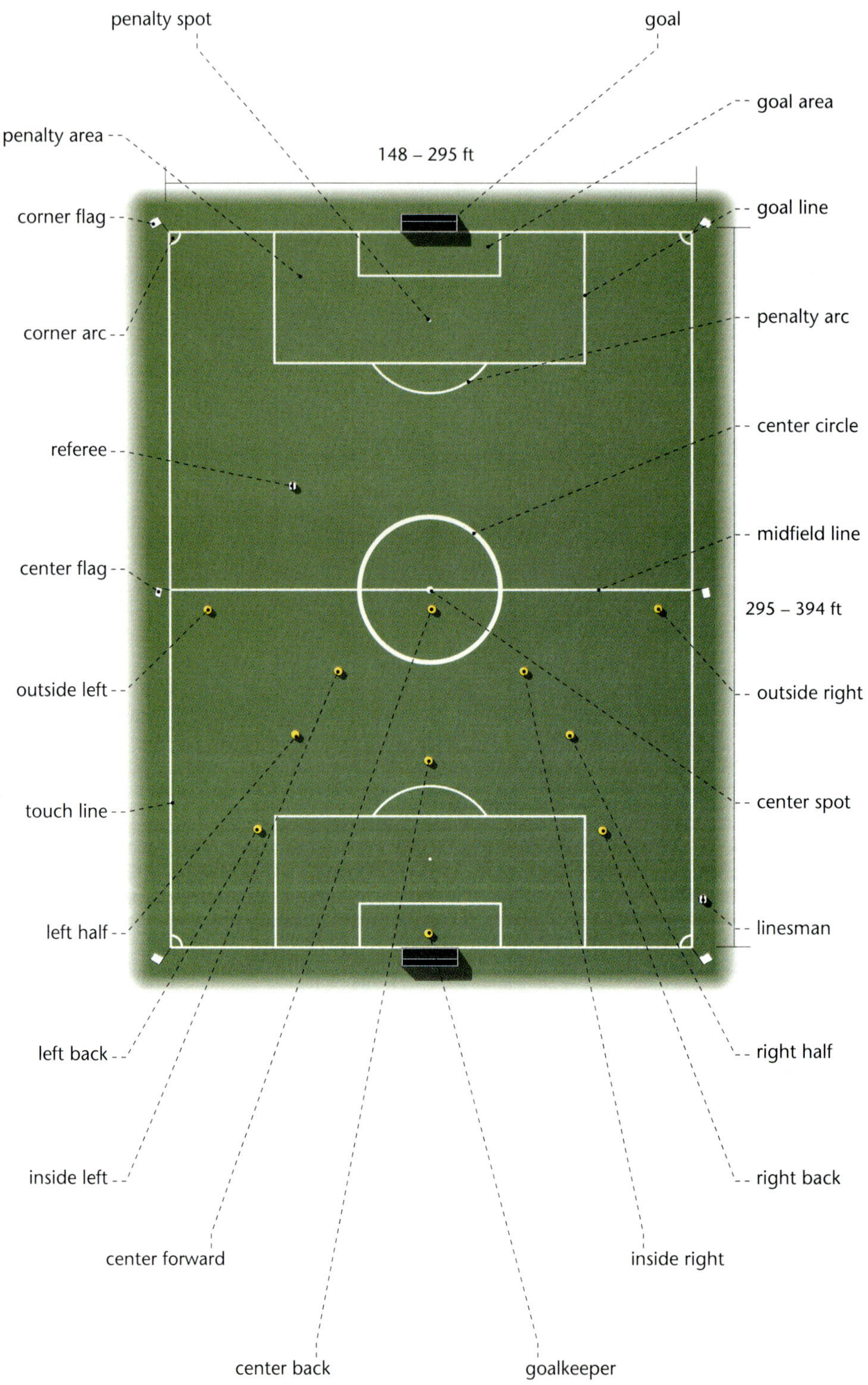

TEAM GAMES

601

FOOTBALL PLAYER

OFFENSE

DEFENSE

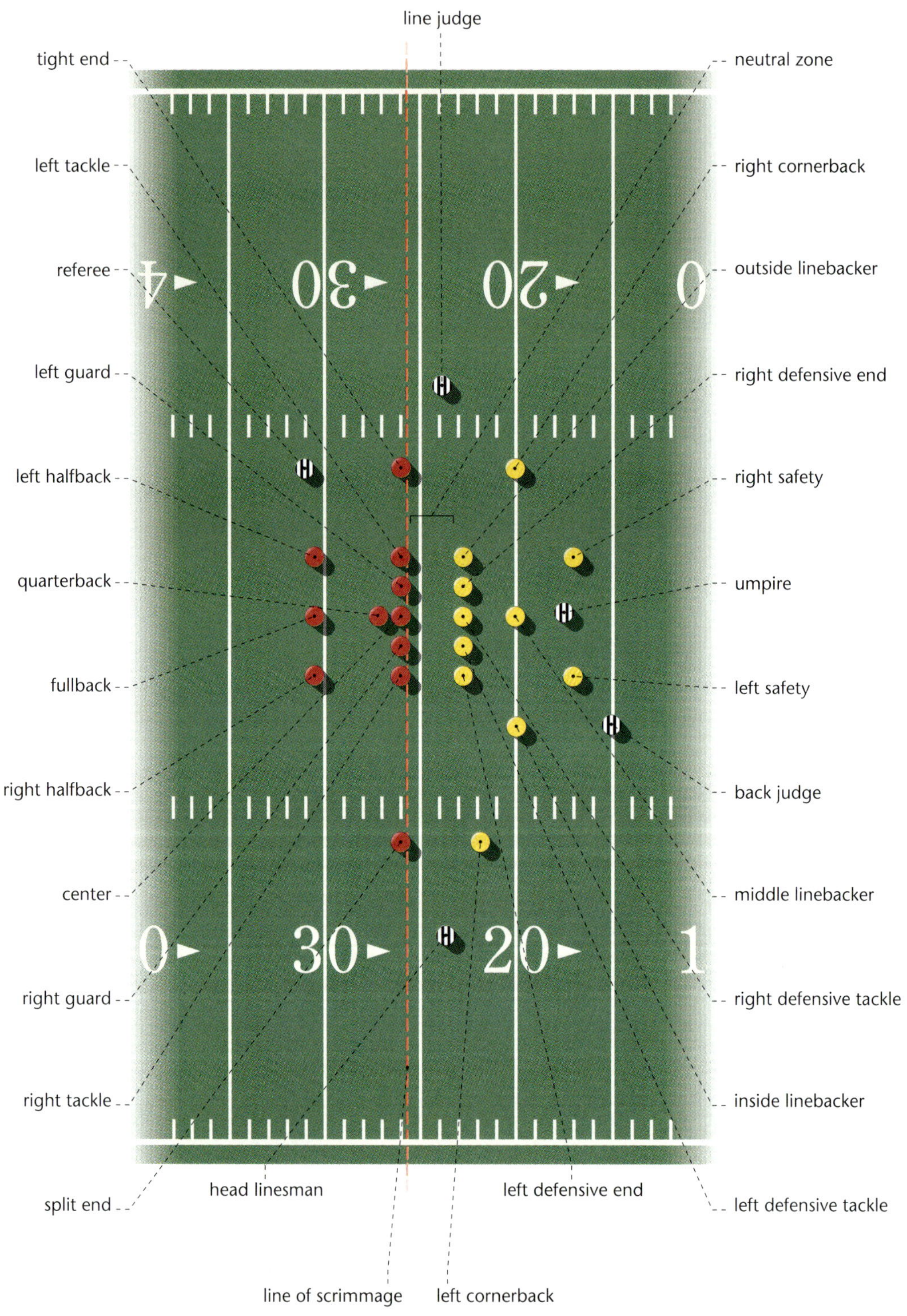

line judge
tight end
neutral zone
left tackle
right cornerback
referee
outside linebacker
left guard
right defensive end
left halfback
right safety
quarterback
umpire
fullback
left safety
right halfback
back judge
center
middle linebacker
right guard
right defensive tackle
right tackle
inside linebacker
split end
head linesman
left defensive end
left defensive tackle
line of scrimmage
left cornerback

PLAYING FIELD FOR AMERICAN
FOOTBALL

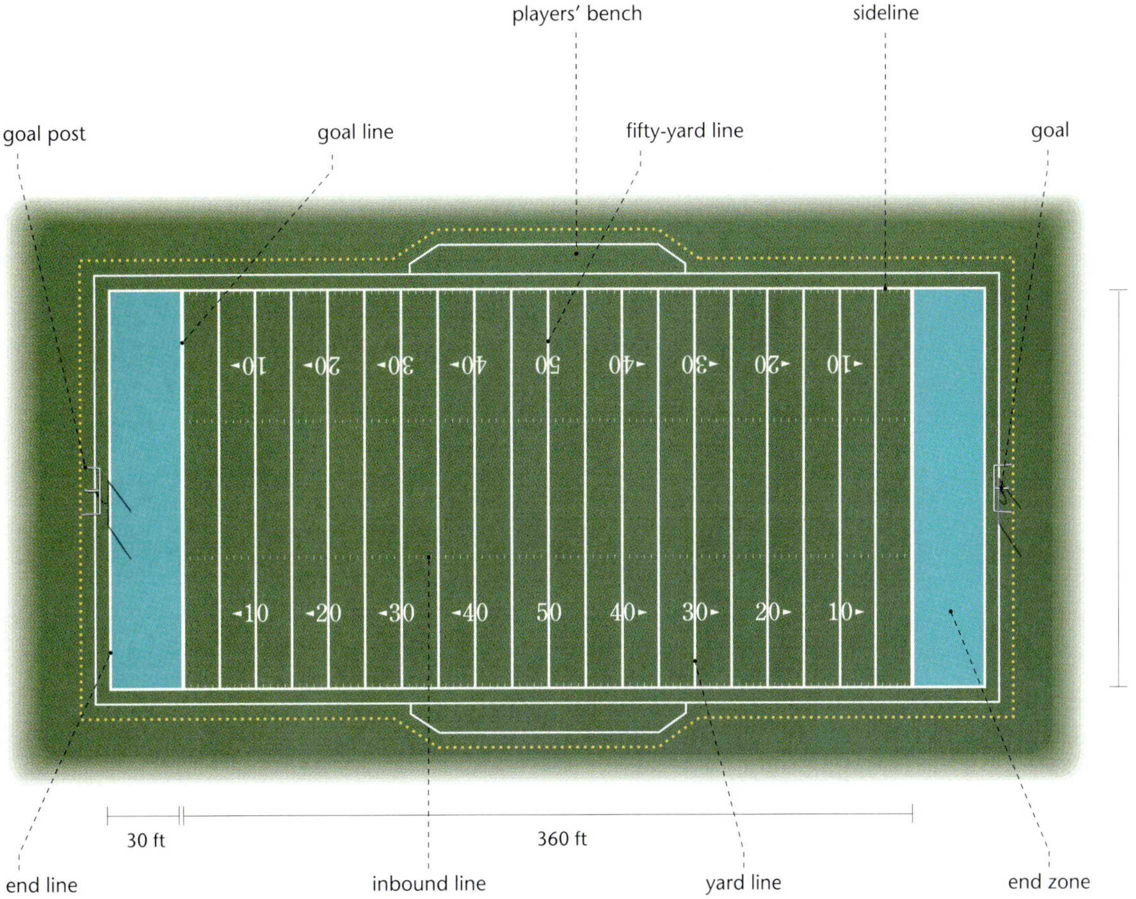

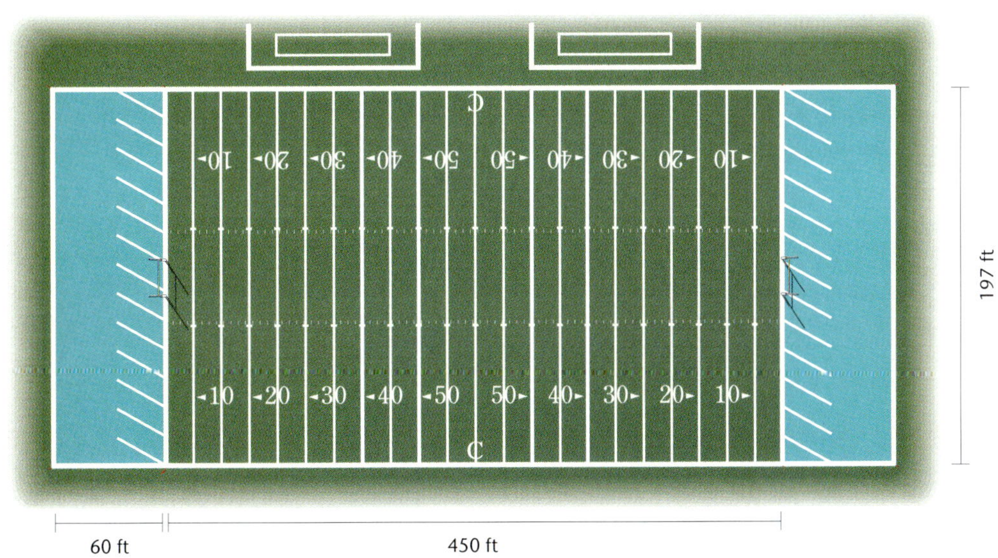

PLAYING FIELD FOR CANADIAN FOOTBALL

offense
defense
line of scrimmage
line judge
tight end
neutral zone
right outside linebacker
back judge
left tackle
right cornerback
referee
right defensive end
left guard
right defensive tackle
slotback
umpire
fullback
right safety back
halfback
monster
flanker
left safety back
quarterback
middle linebacker
center
field judge
right guard
left defensive tackle
right tackle
split end
left outside linebacker
left cornerback
linesman
left defensive end
side judge

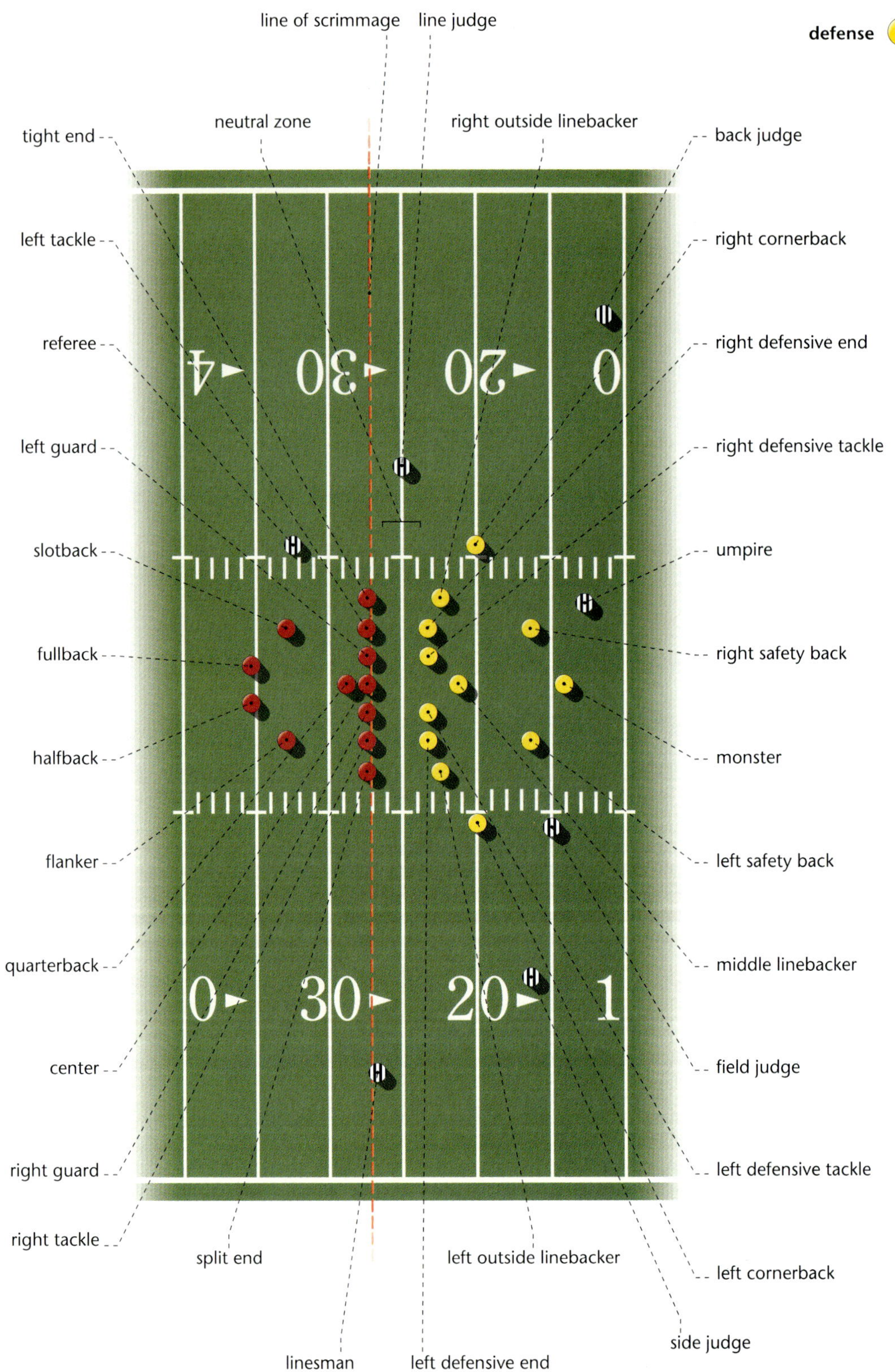

TEAM GAMES

RUGBY

FIELD

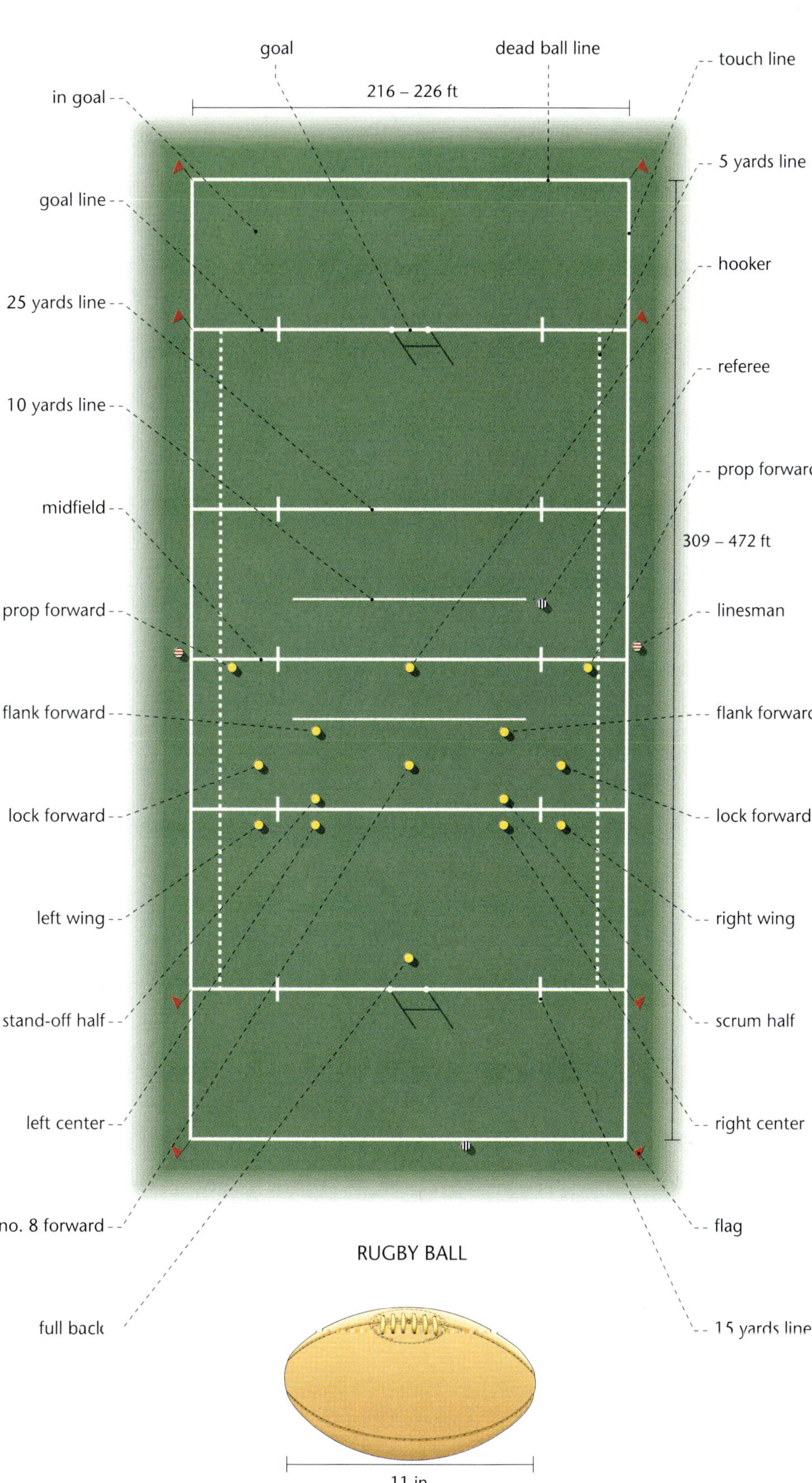

RUGBY BALL

FIELD HOCKEY

PLAYING FIELD

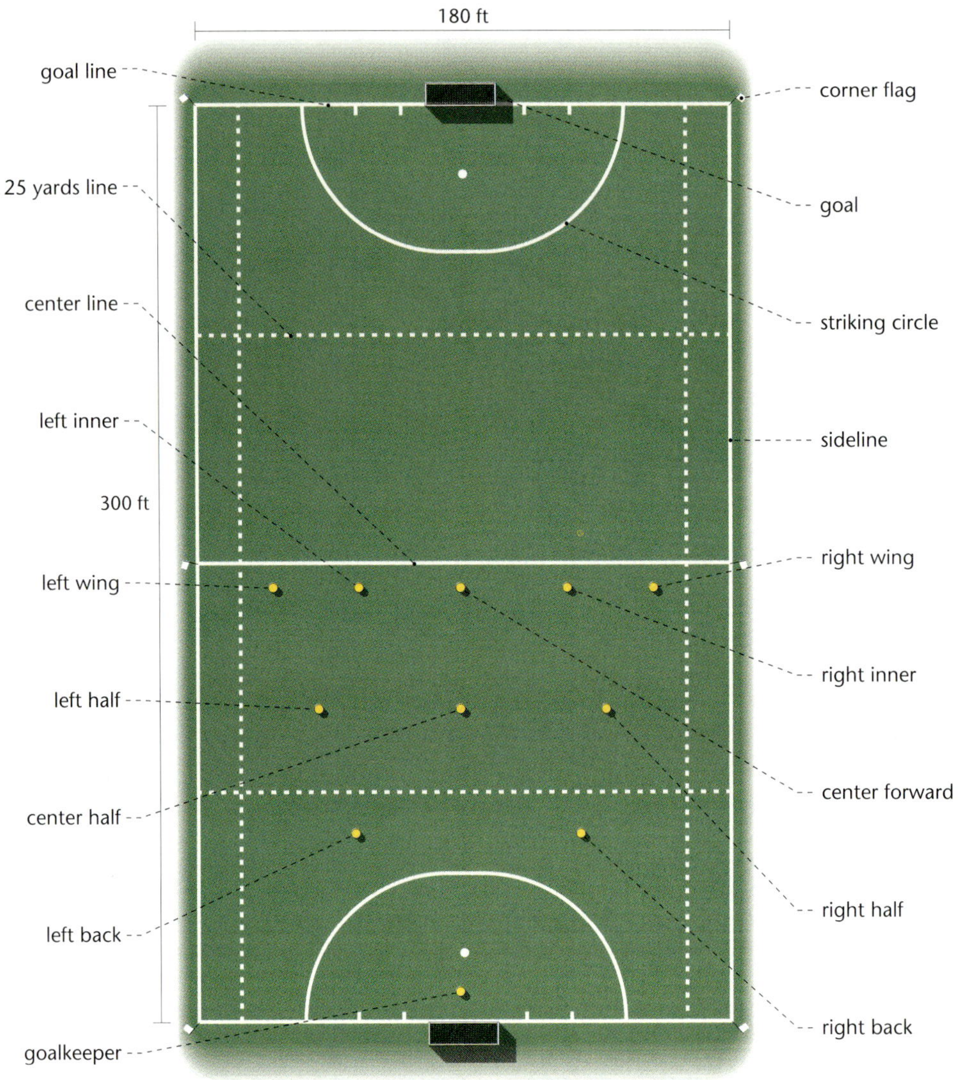

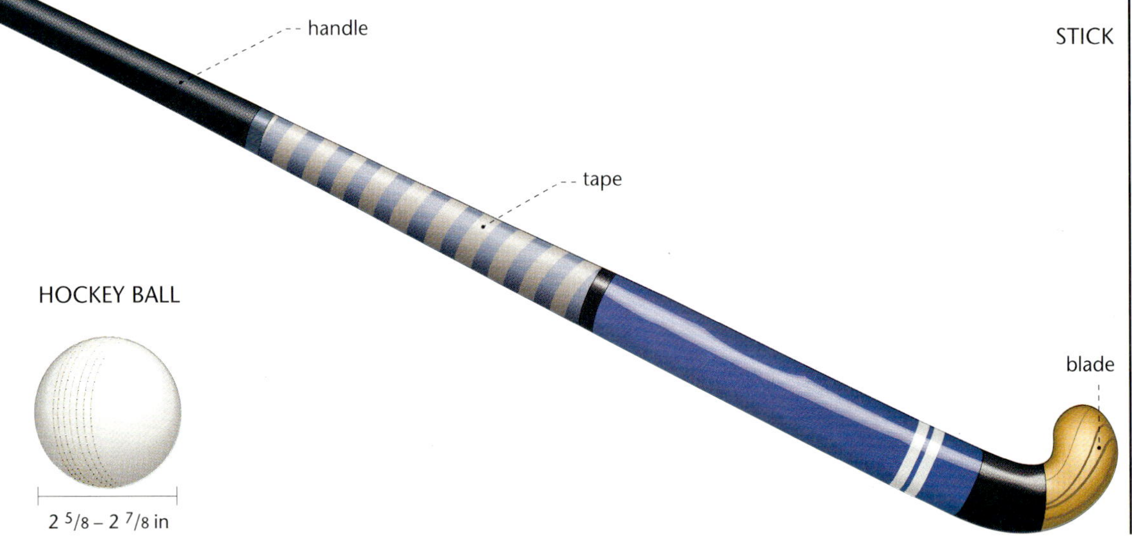

STICK

HOCKEY BALL

RINK
85 – 100 ft
goal line
goal
goal crease
face-off spot
attacking zone
face-off circle
blue line
neutral zone
left wing
referee
penalty bench
players' bench
200 ft
officials' bench
center line
center
right wing
center face-off circle
linesman
left defense
right defense
defending zone
goalkeeper
boards
rink corner
goal judge
PUCK
1 in
3 in

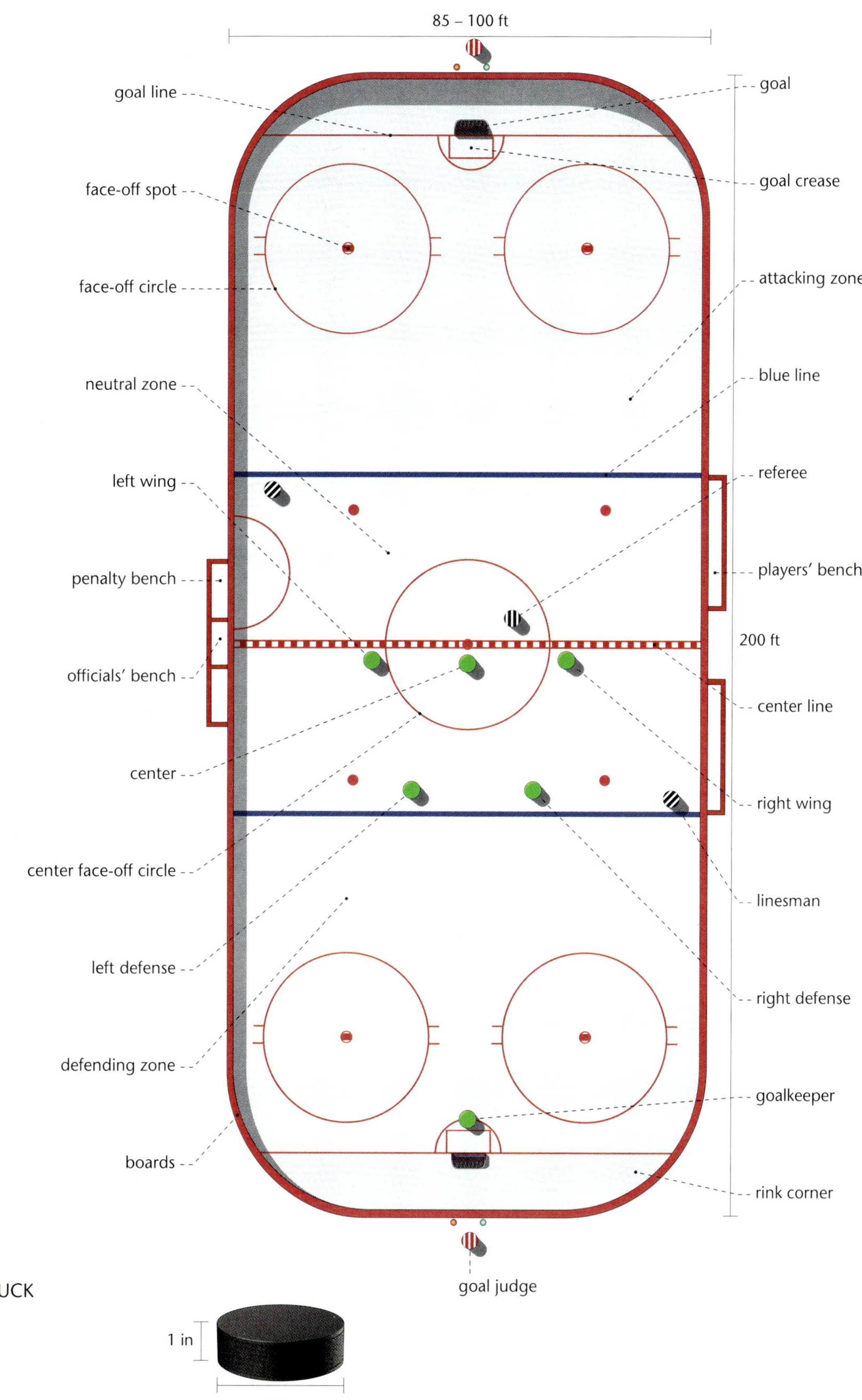

TEAM GAMES

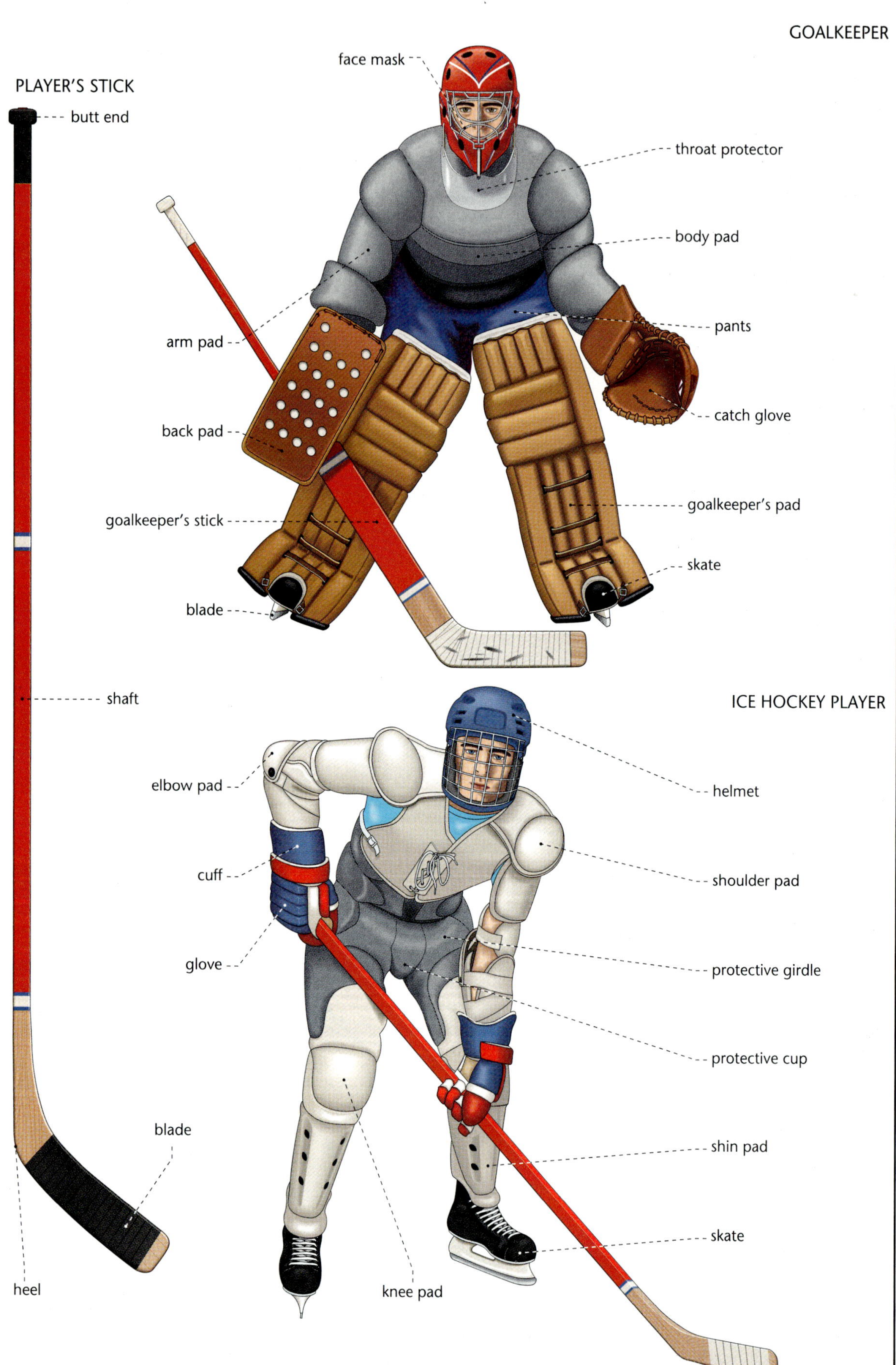
PLAYER'S STICK
butt end
shaft
blade
heel
GOALKEEPER
face mask
throat protector
body pad
pants
catch glove
arm pad
back pad
goalkeeper's stick
blade
goalkeeper's pad
skate
ICE HOCKEY PLAYER
helmet
elbow pad
shoulder pad
cuff
protective girdle
glove
protective cup
shin pad
skate
blade
knee pad

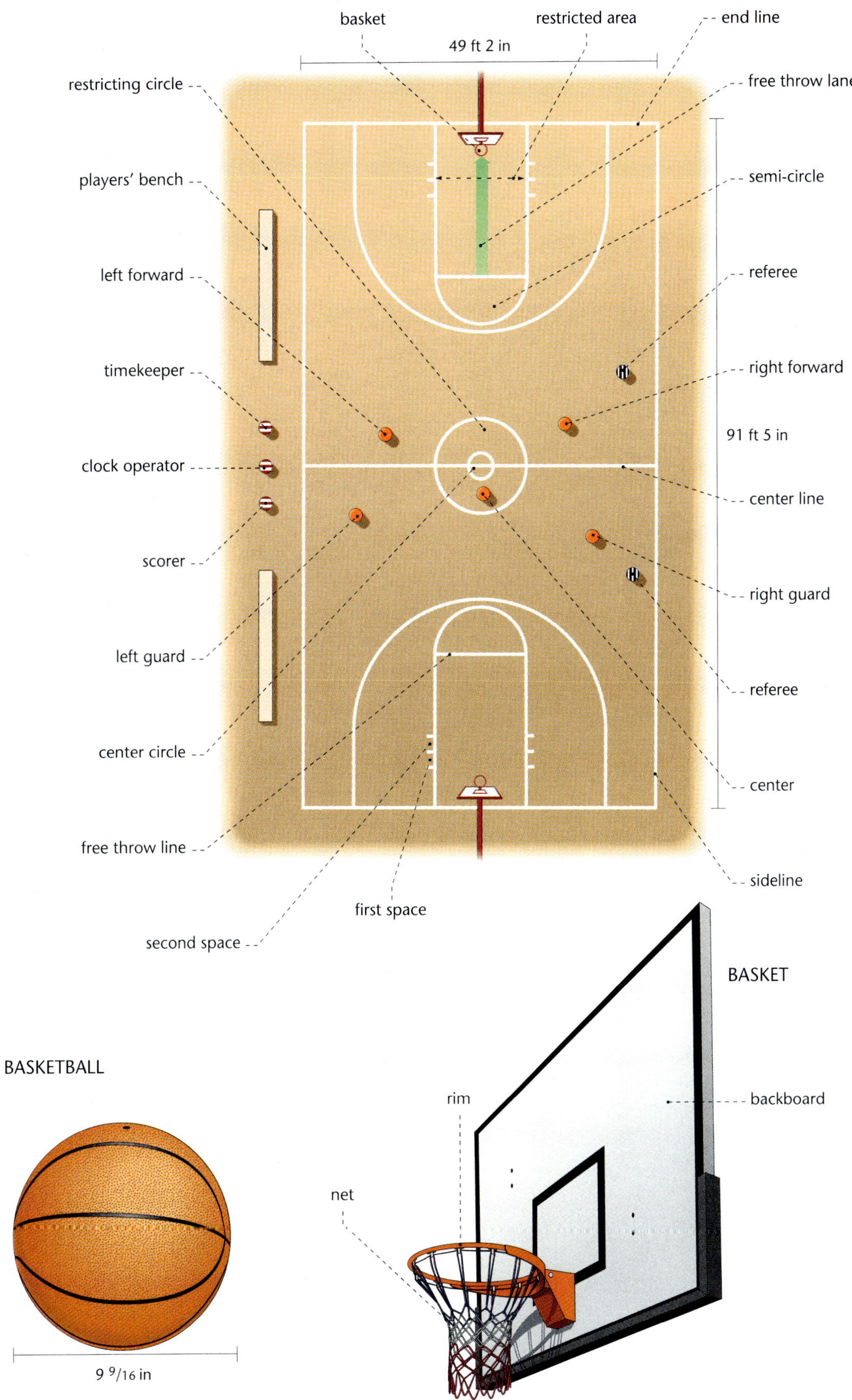
COURT
basket
restricted area
end line
49 ft 2 in
restricting circle
free throw lane
players' bench
semi-circle
left forward
referee
timekeeper
right forward
clock operator
91 ft 5 in
center line
scorer
right guard
left guard
referee
center circle
center
free throw line
sideline
first space
second space
BASKETBALL
BASKET
rim
backboard
net
9 9/16 in

NETBALL

goal post
goalkeeper
back line
defense third
goal circle
goal defense
umpire
central circle
wing defense
100 ft
center third
center
wing attack
goal attack
goal third
sideline
goal shooter
50 ft

2 1/2 – 2 5/8 in

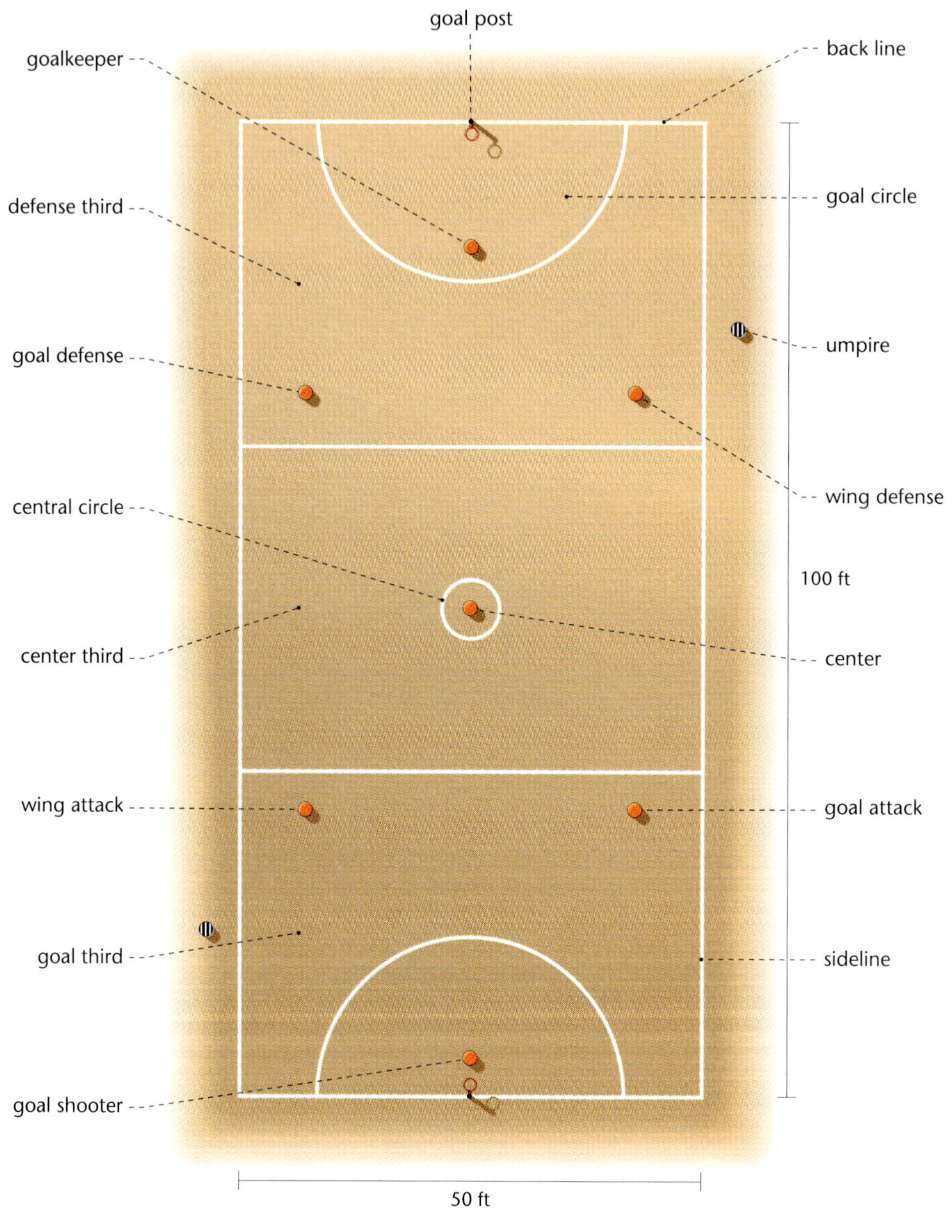

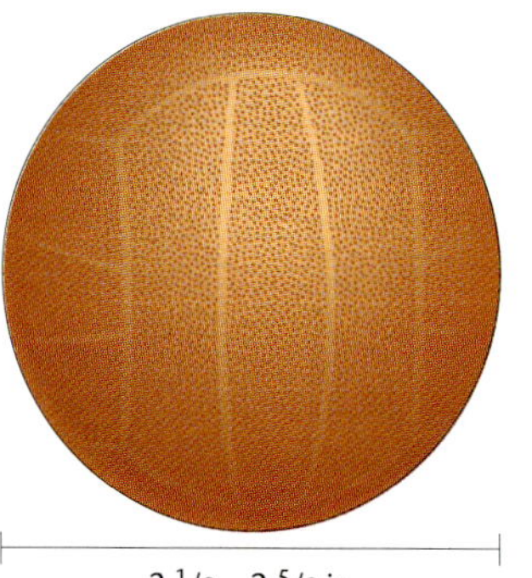

TEAM GAMES

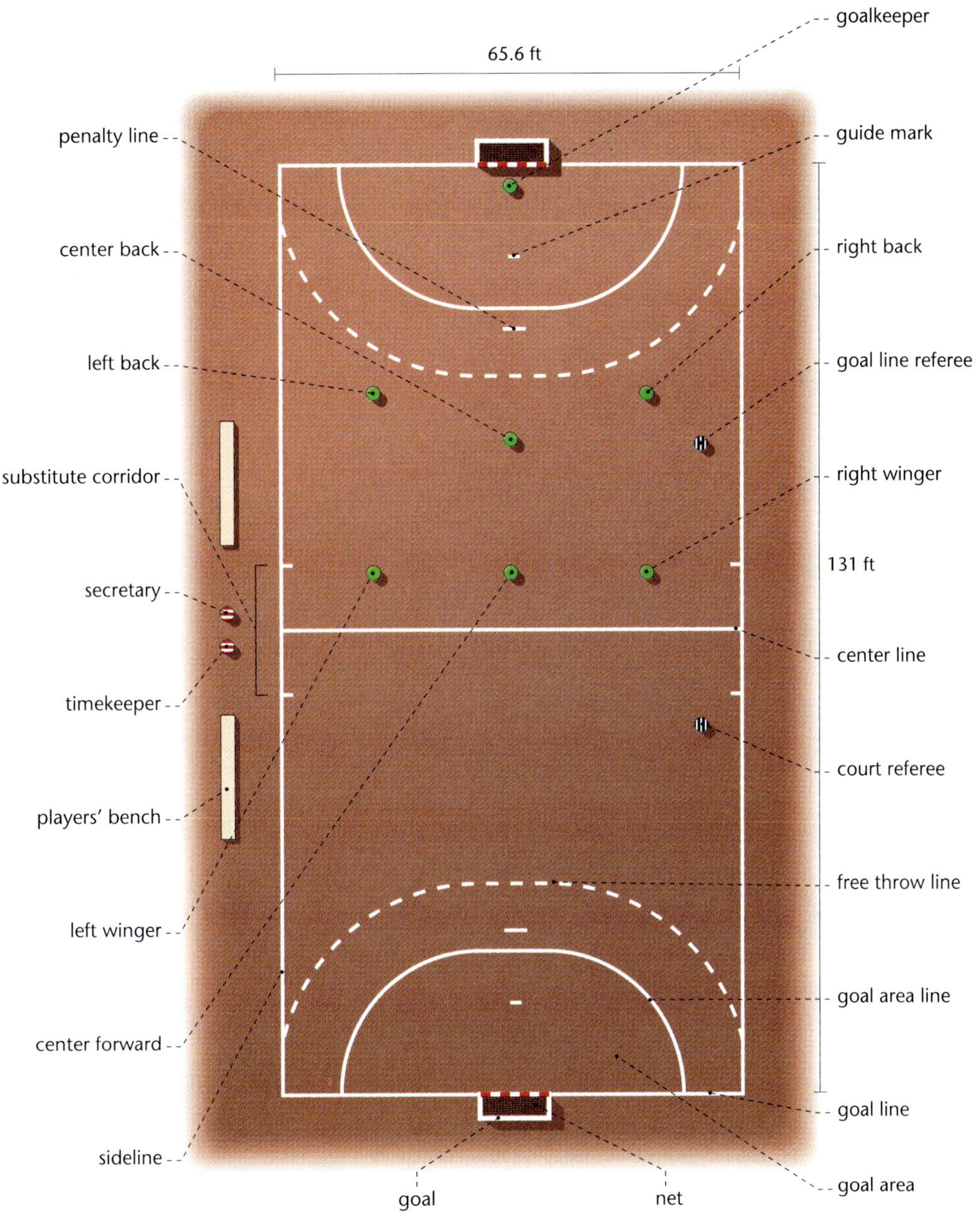

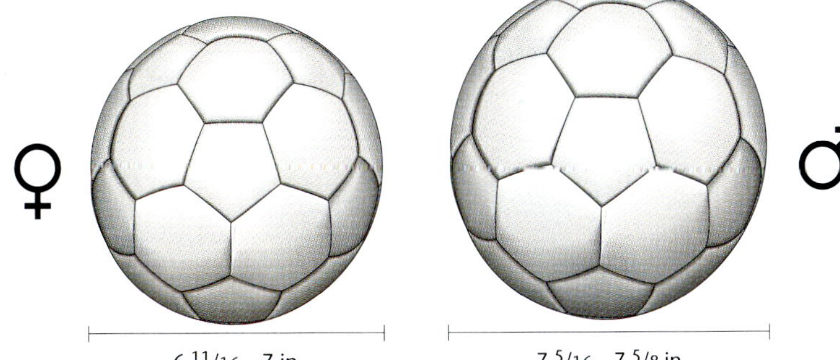

HANDBALL

VOLLEYBALL

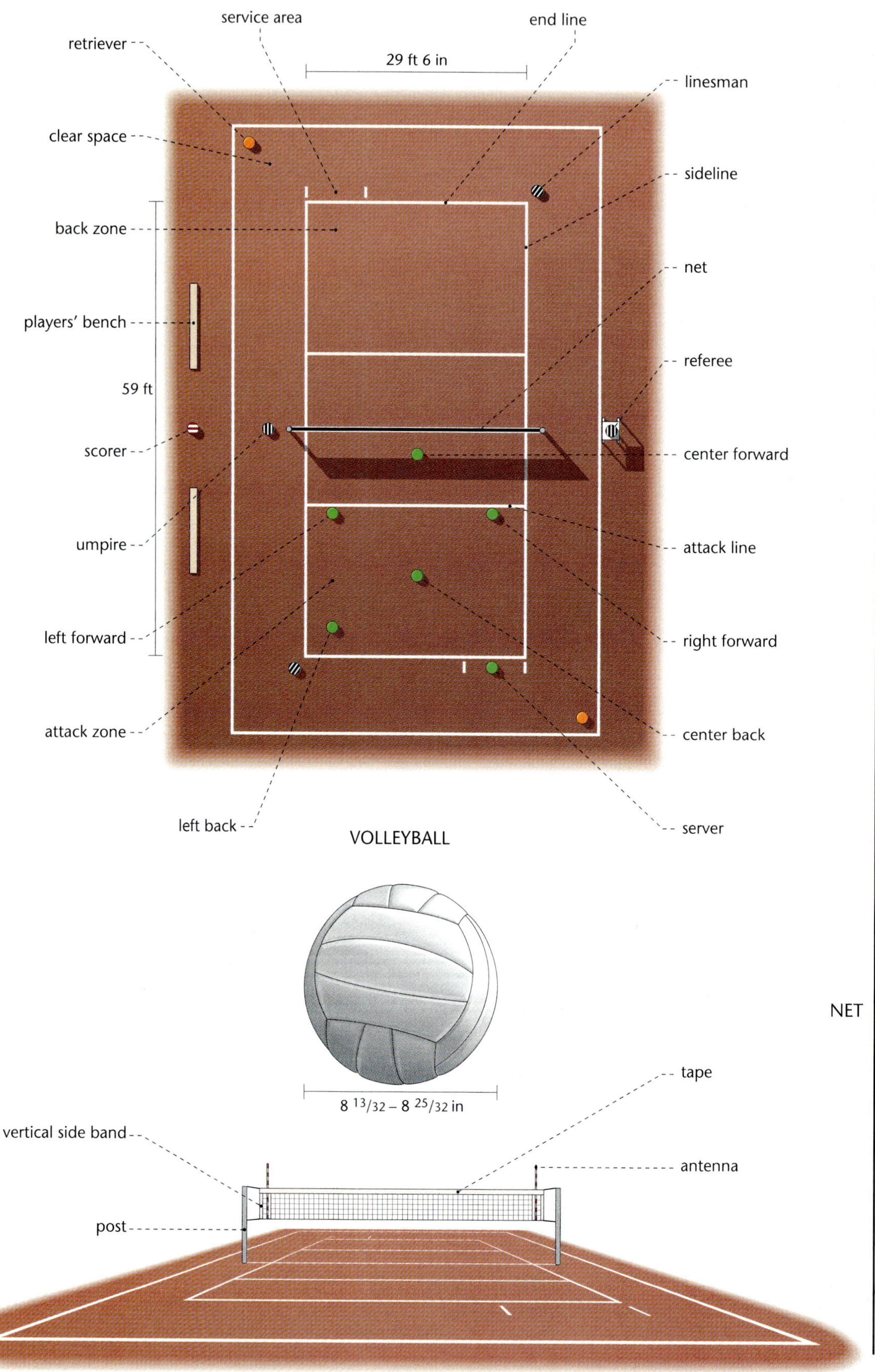

VOLLEYBALL

COURT

TEAM GAMES

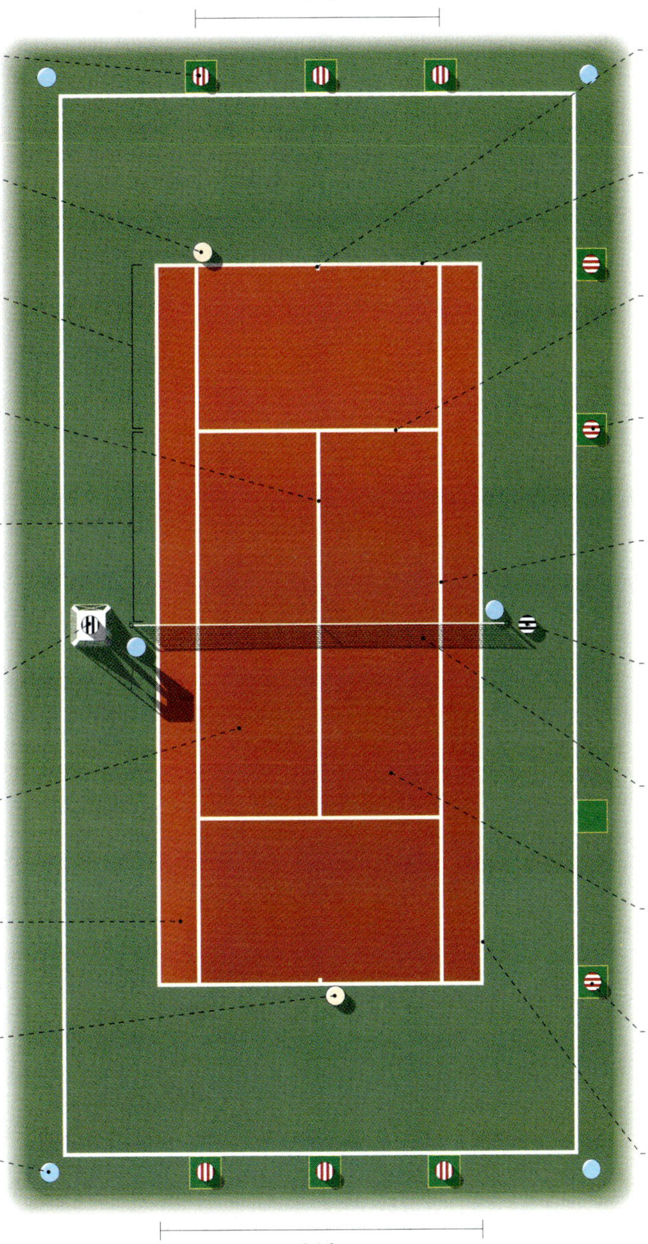

NET

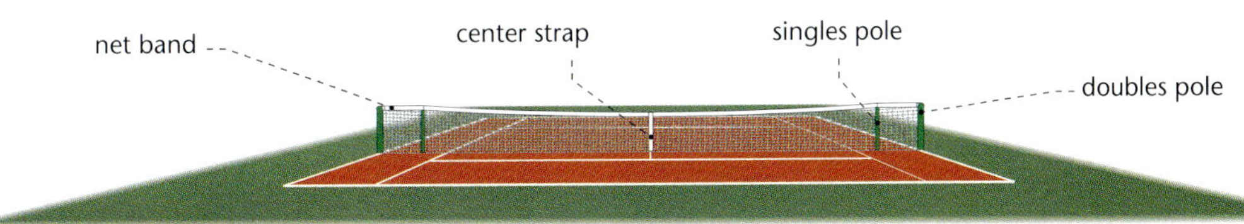

headband
polo shirt
wristband
skirt
sock
tennis shoe
TENNIS BALL
2 1/2 – 2 5/8 in
TENNIS RACKET
frame
head
stringing
shoulder
throat
shaft
handle
butt
TEAM GAMES

SQUASH

SQUASH BALL

SQUASH RACKET

INTERNATIONAL SINGLES COURT

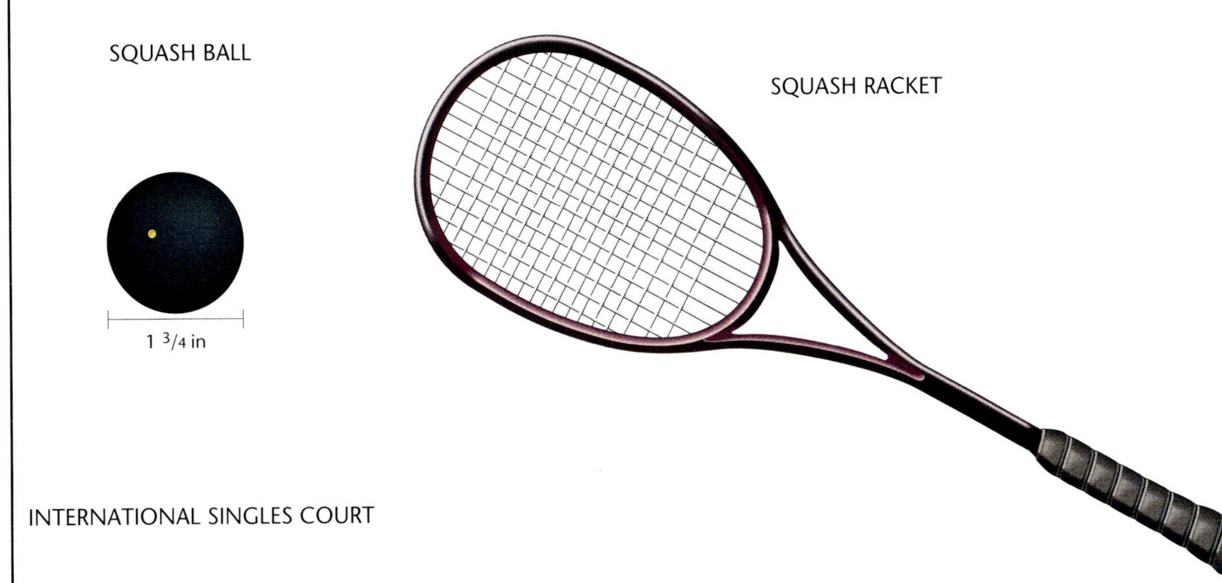

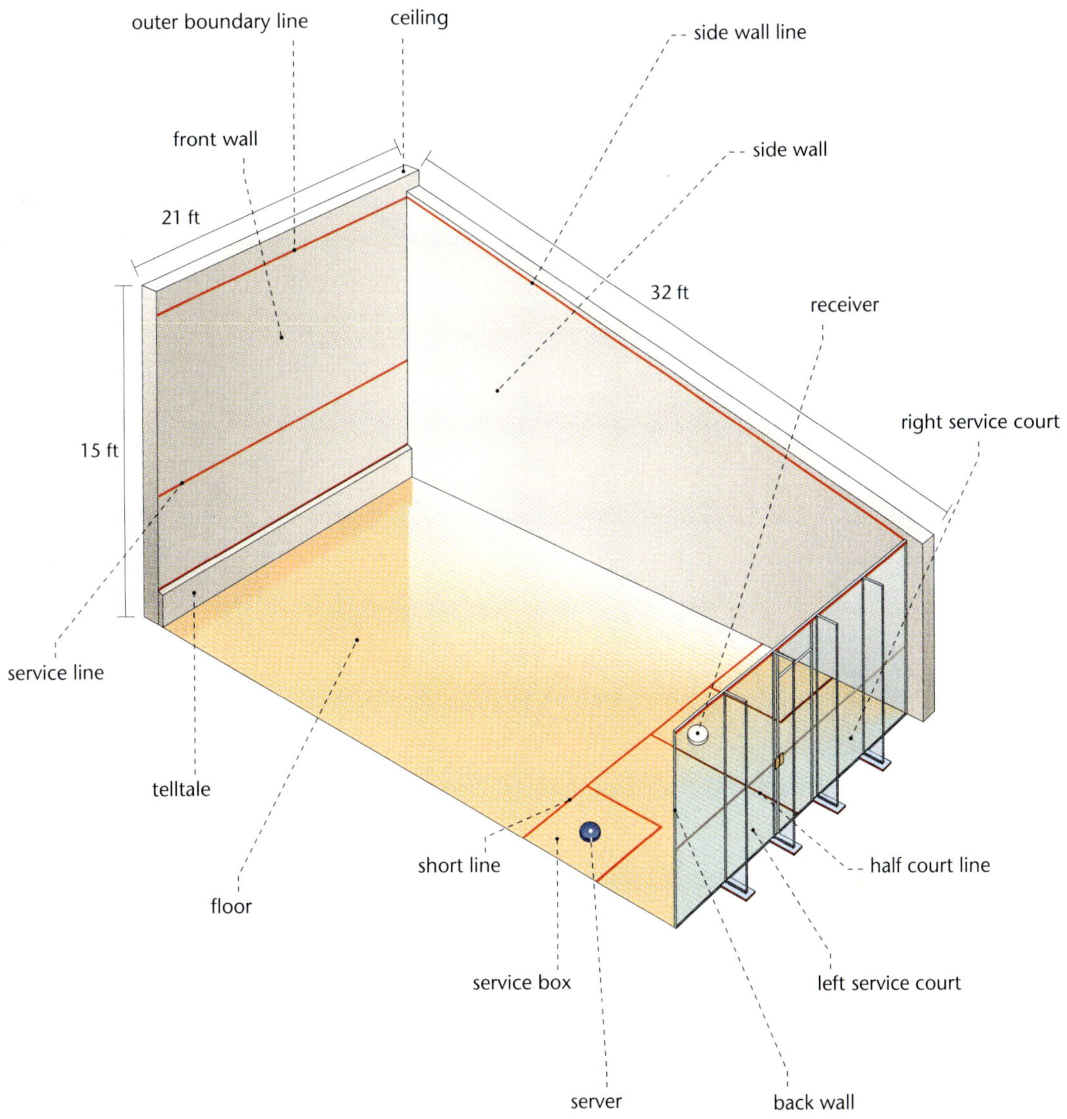

RACQUETBALL

RACQUETBALL RACKET

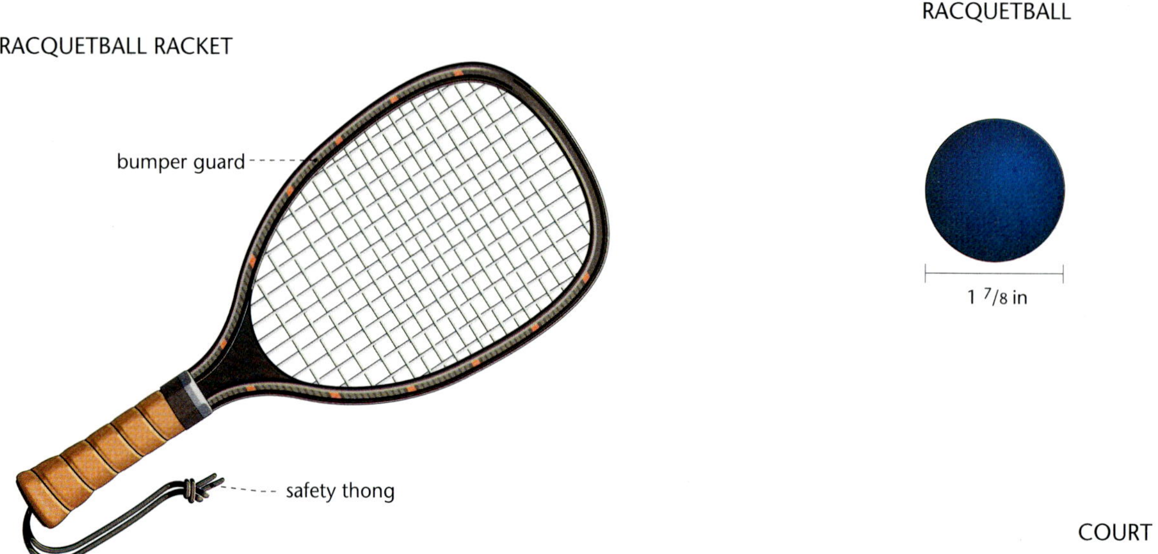

RACQUETBALL

COURT

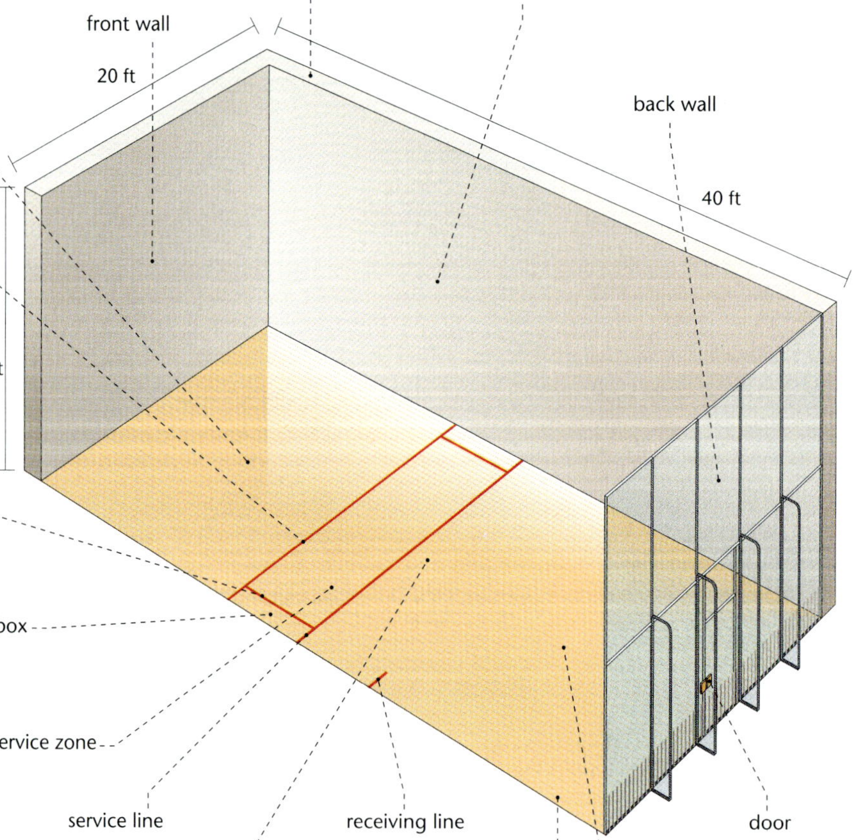

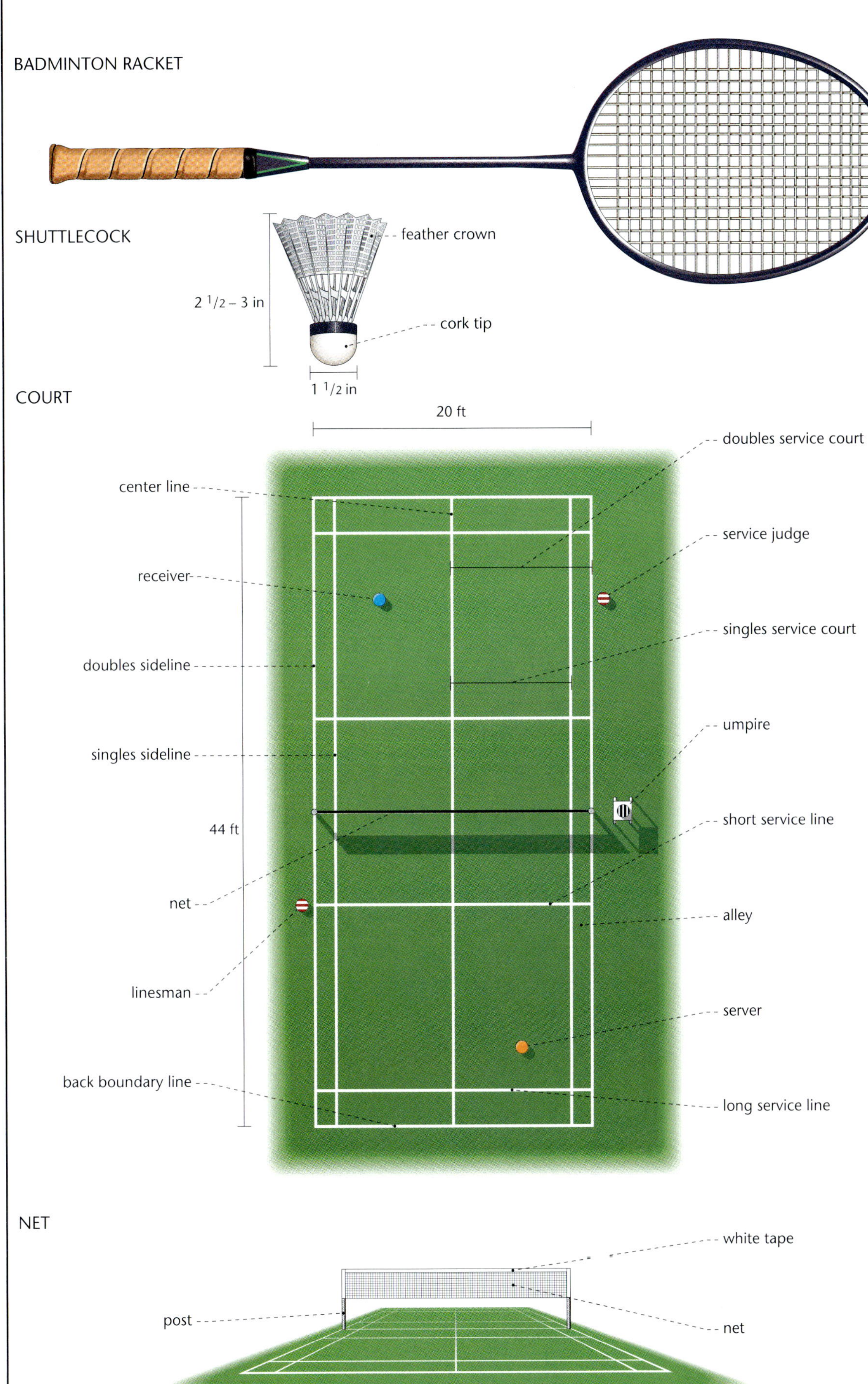
BADMINTON RACKET
SHUTTLECOCK
feather crown
2 1/2 – 3 in
cork tip
1 1/2 in
COURT
20 ft
center line
doubles service court
receiver
service judge
doubles sideline
singles service court
singles sideline
umpire
44 ft
short service line
net
alley
linesman
server
back boundary line
long service line
NET
white tape
post
net

TABLE

mesh
side line
net
upper edge
white tape
playing surface
center line
end line
net support
6 in
5 ft
9 ft
leg
1 1/2 in
TYPES OF GRIPS
TABLE TENNIS PADDLE
table tennis ball
face
penholder grip
handle
covering
blade
shake-hands grip

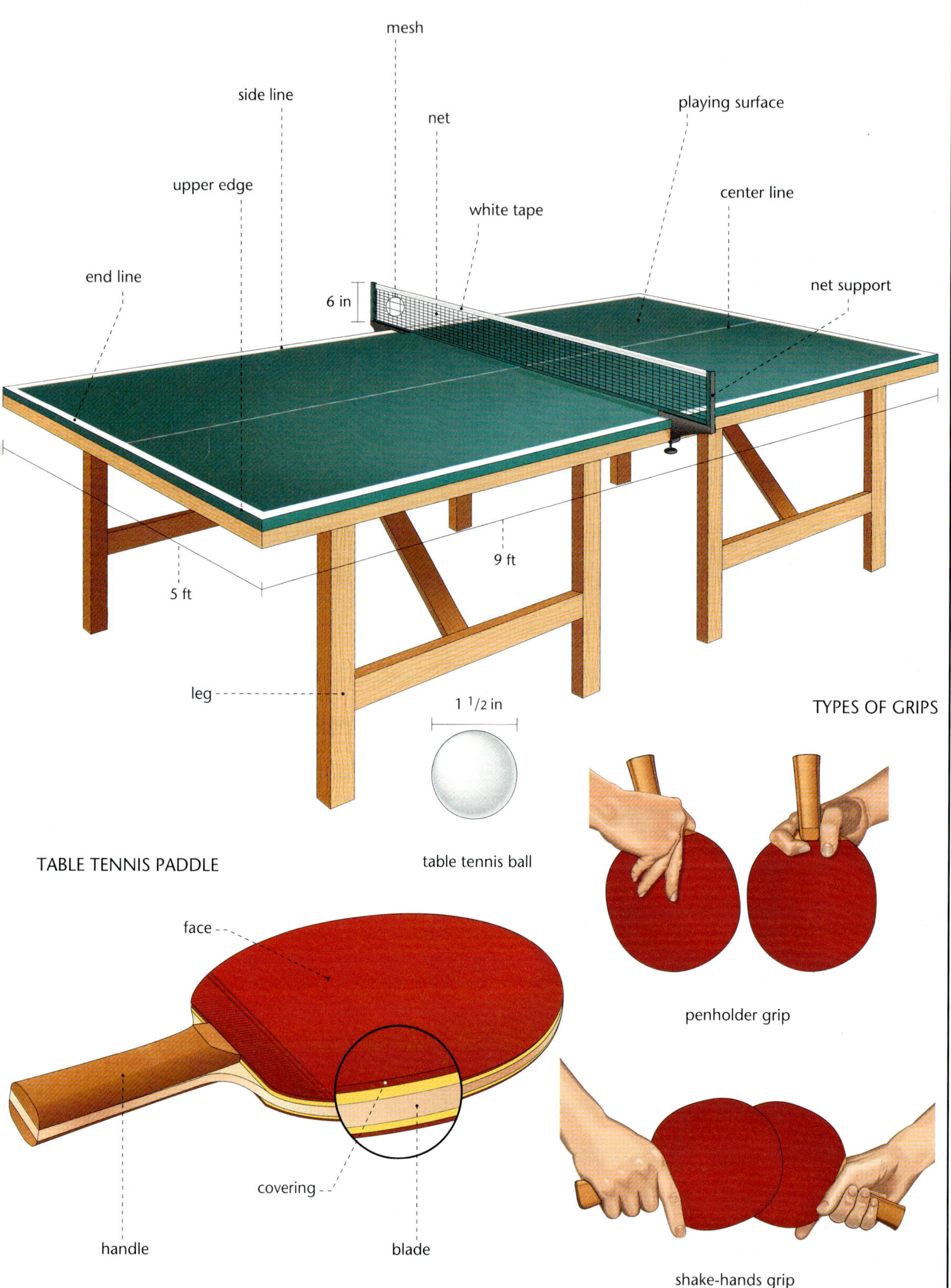

CURLING

CURLING STONE
handle
4 1/2 in
11 1/2 in
CURLING BROOMS
TEAM GAMES
RINK
rink
number two
lead
sweeping score line
back score line
hog score line
number three
skip
138 ft
center line
area of ice
lateral line
outer circle
tee
inner circle
house
curler
foot score line
hack
14 ft

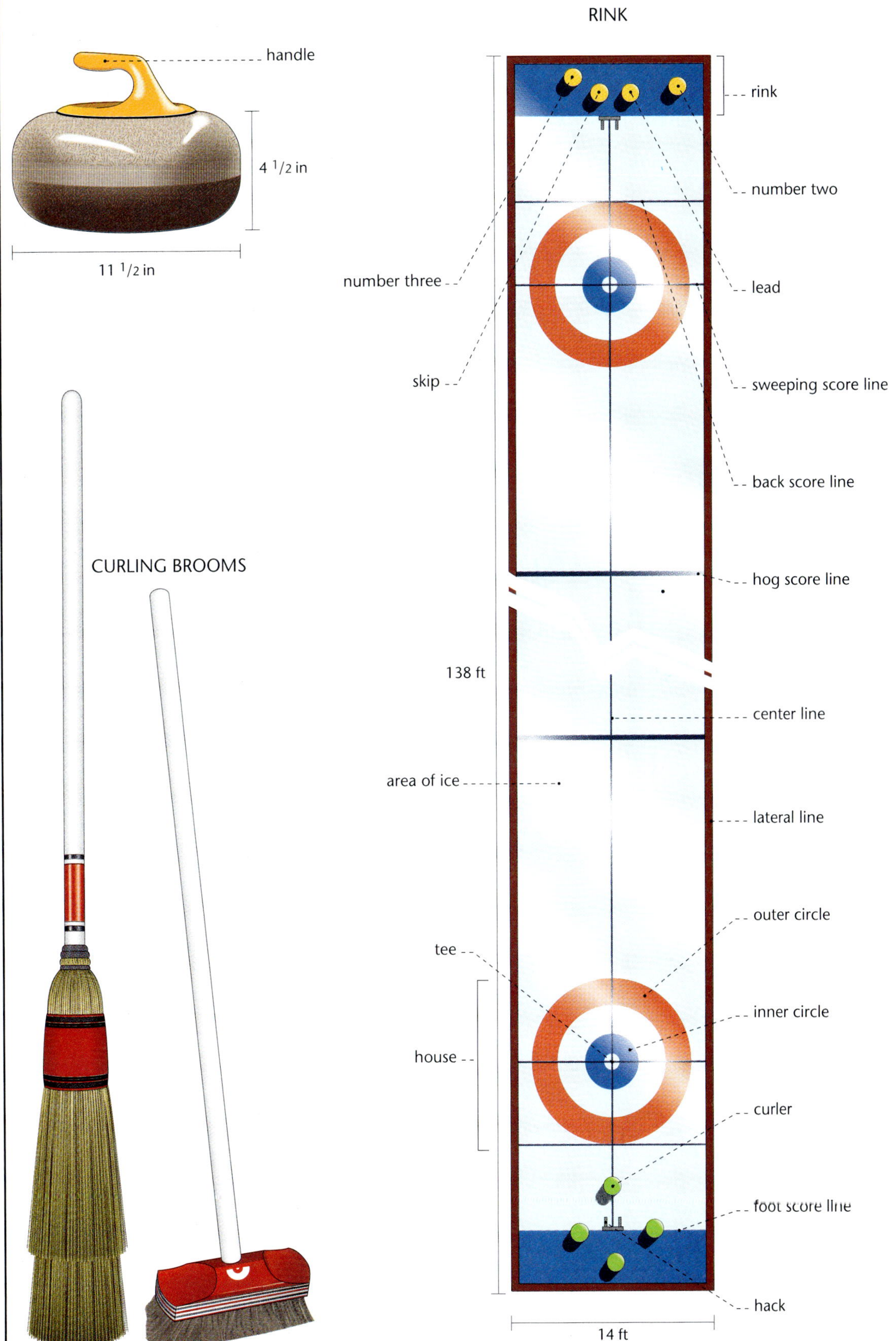

COMPETITIVE COURSE

STARTING BLOCK

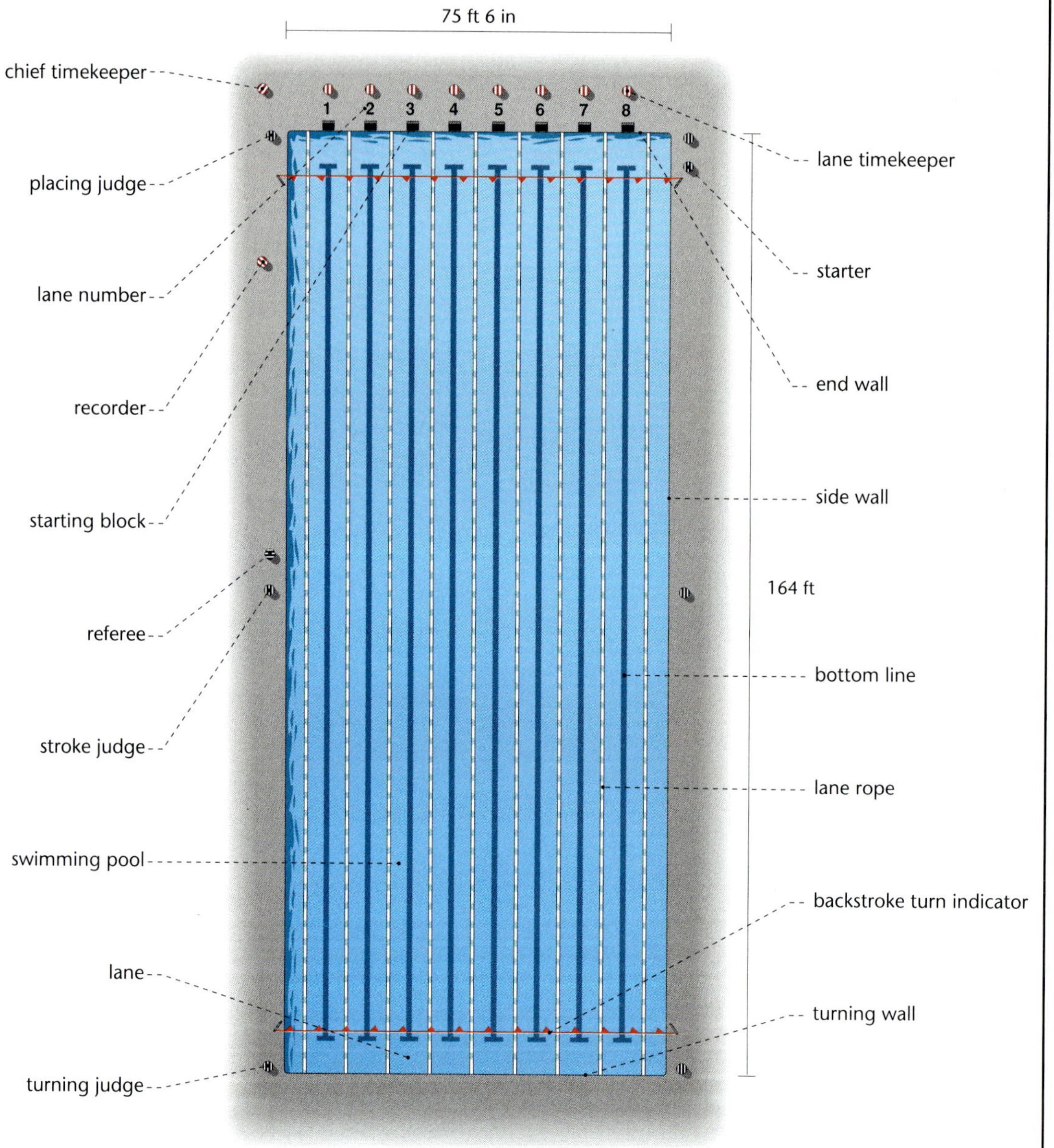

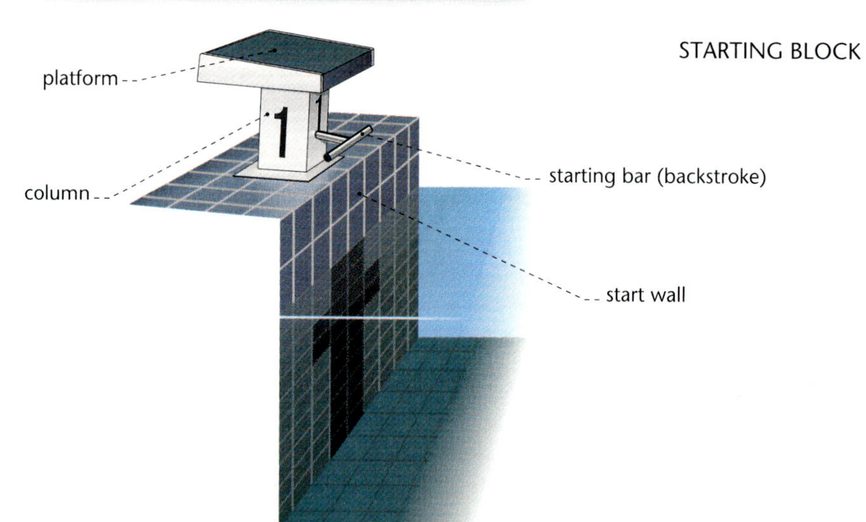

SWIMMING

TYPES OF STROKES

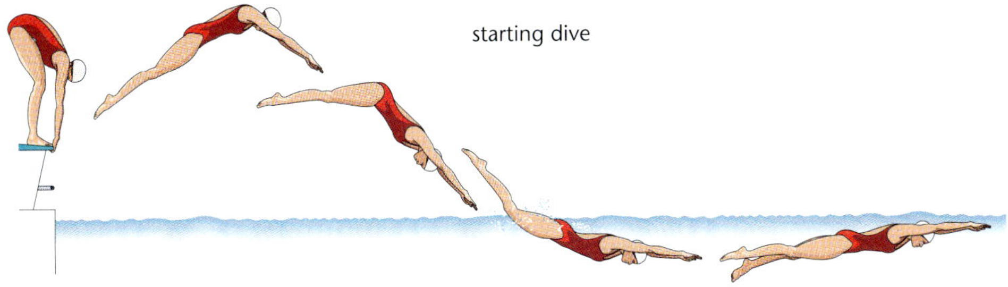

FRONT CRAWL STROKE

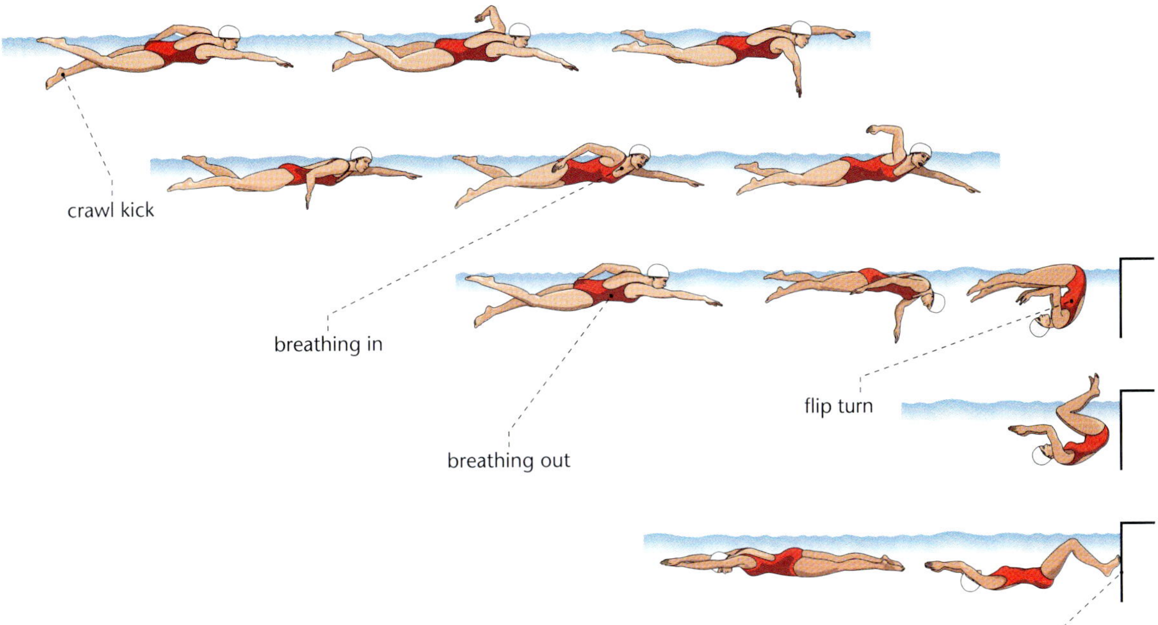

BREASTSTROKE

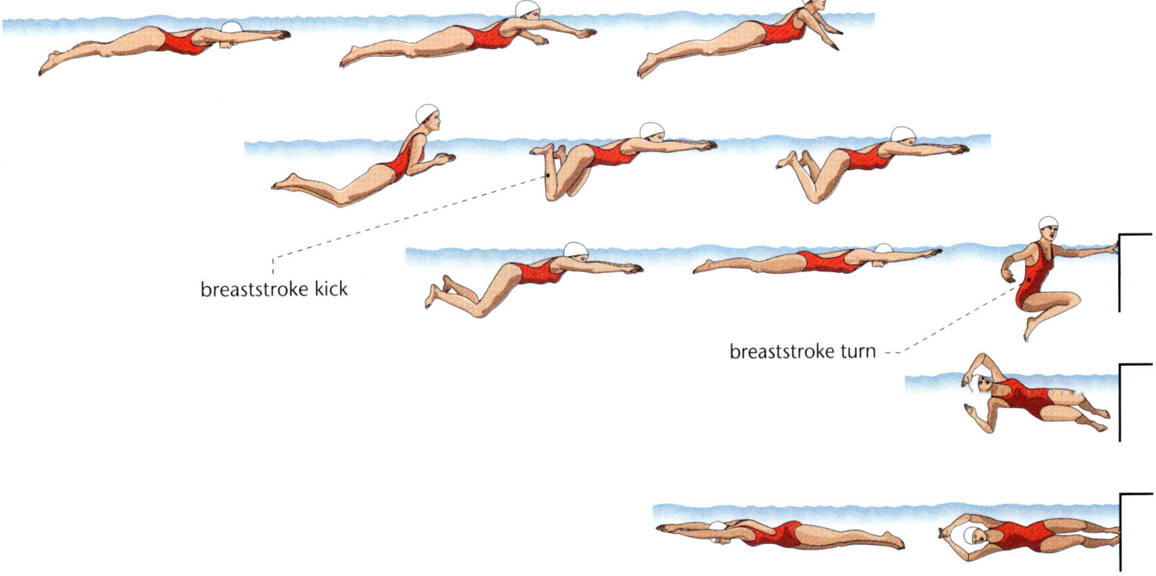

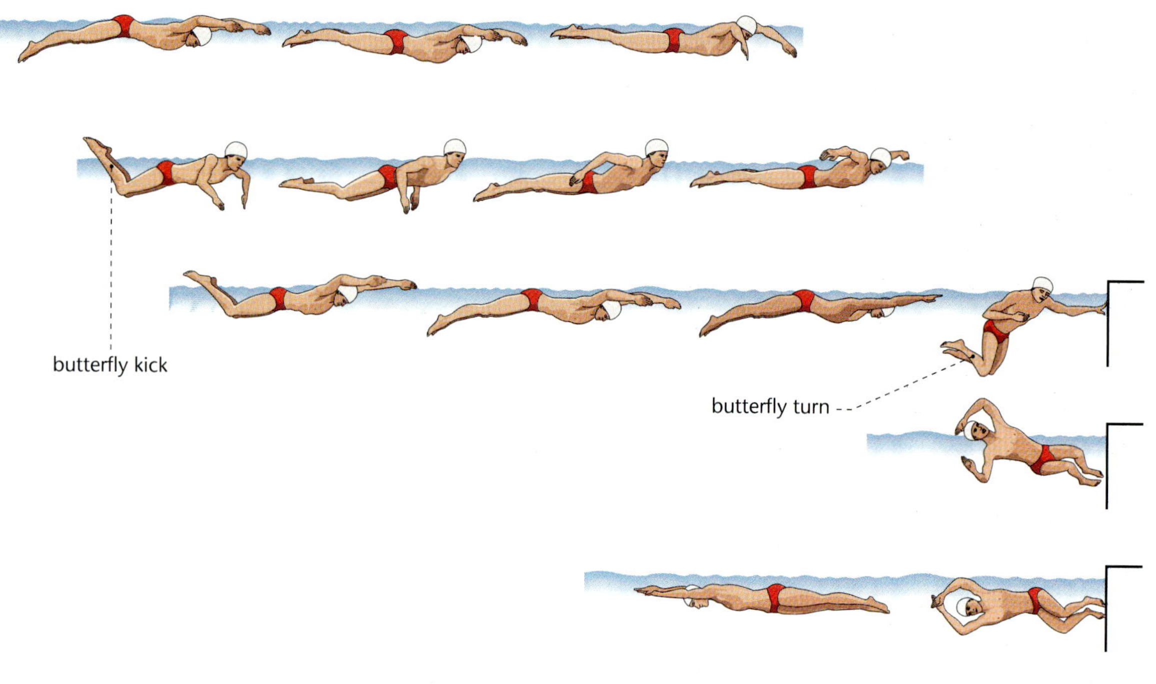
BUTTERFLY STROKE
butterfly kick
butterfly turn

BACKSTROKE START

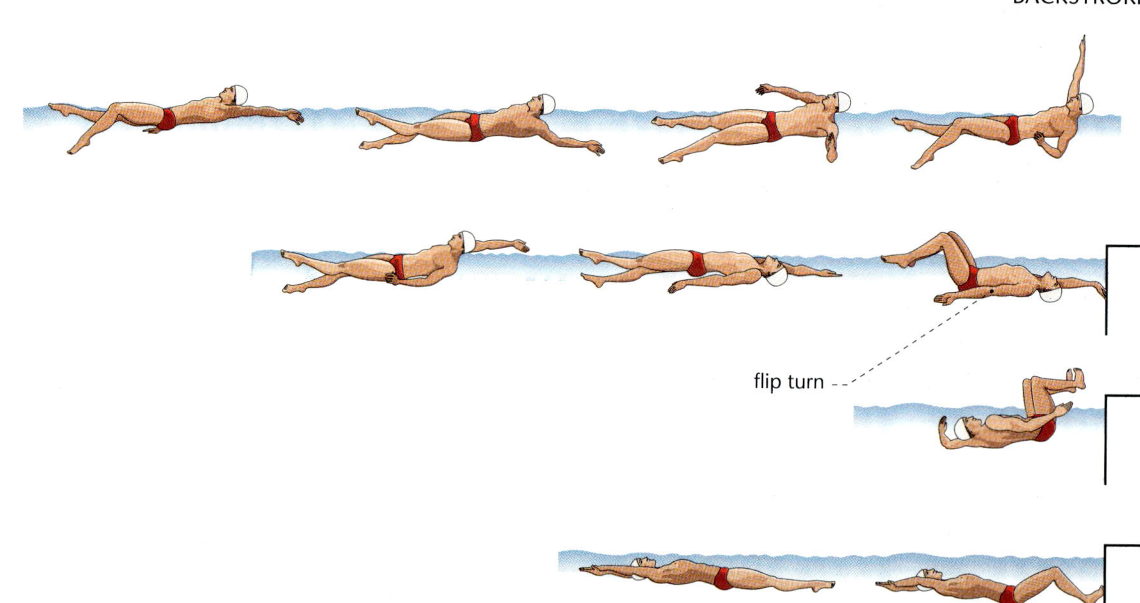
BACKSTROKE
flip turn

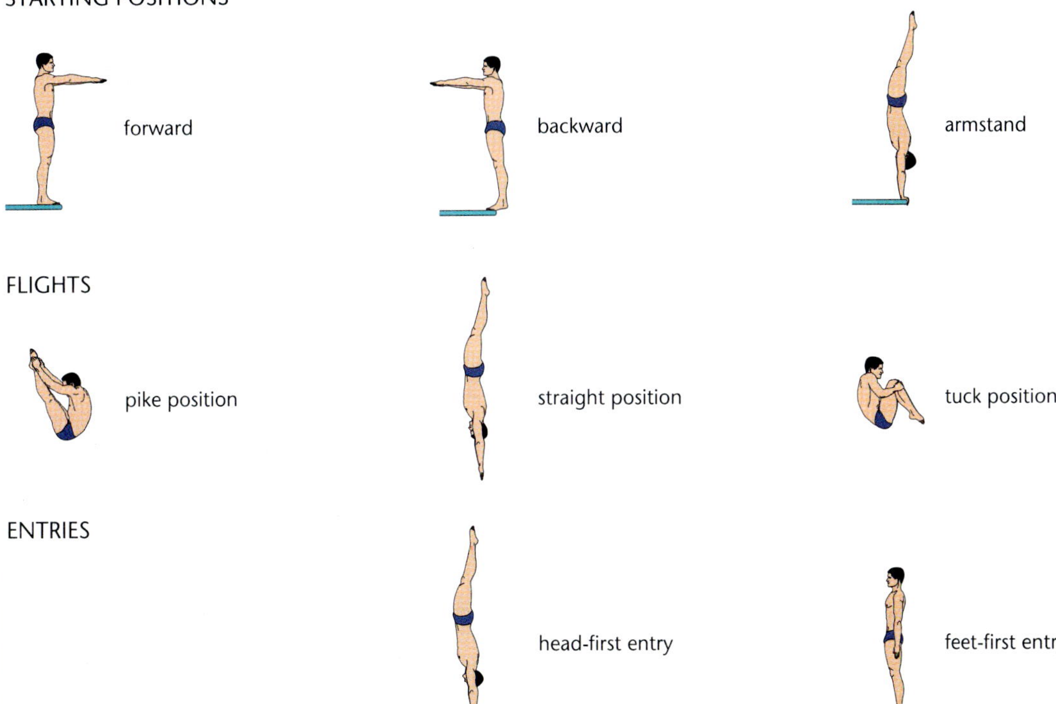
DIVING INSTALLATIONS 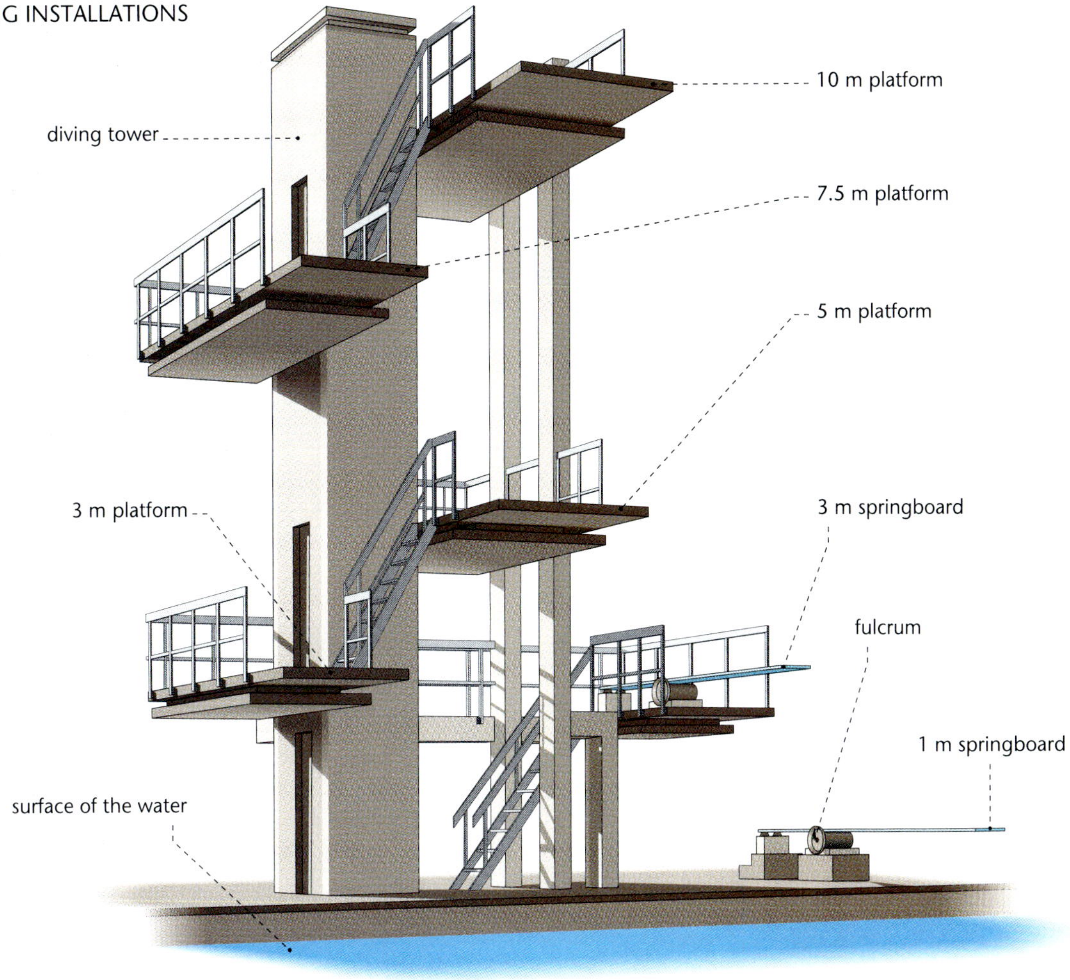
10 m platform
diving tower
7.5 m platform
5 m platform
3 m platform
3 m springboard
fulcrum
1 m springboard
surface of the water
STARTING POSITIONS
forward
backward
armstand
FLIGHTS
pike position
straight position
tuck position
ENTRIES
head-first entry
feet-first entry

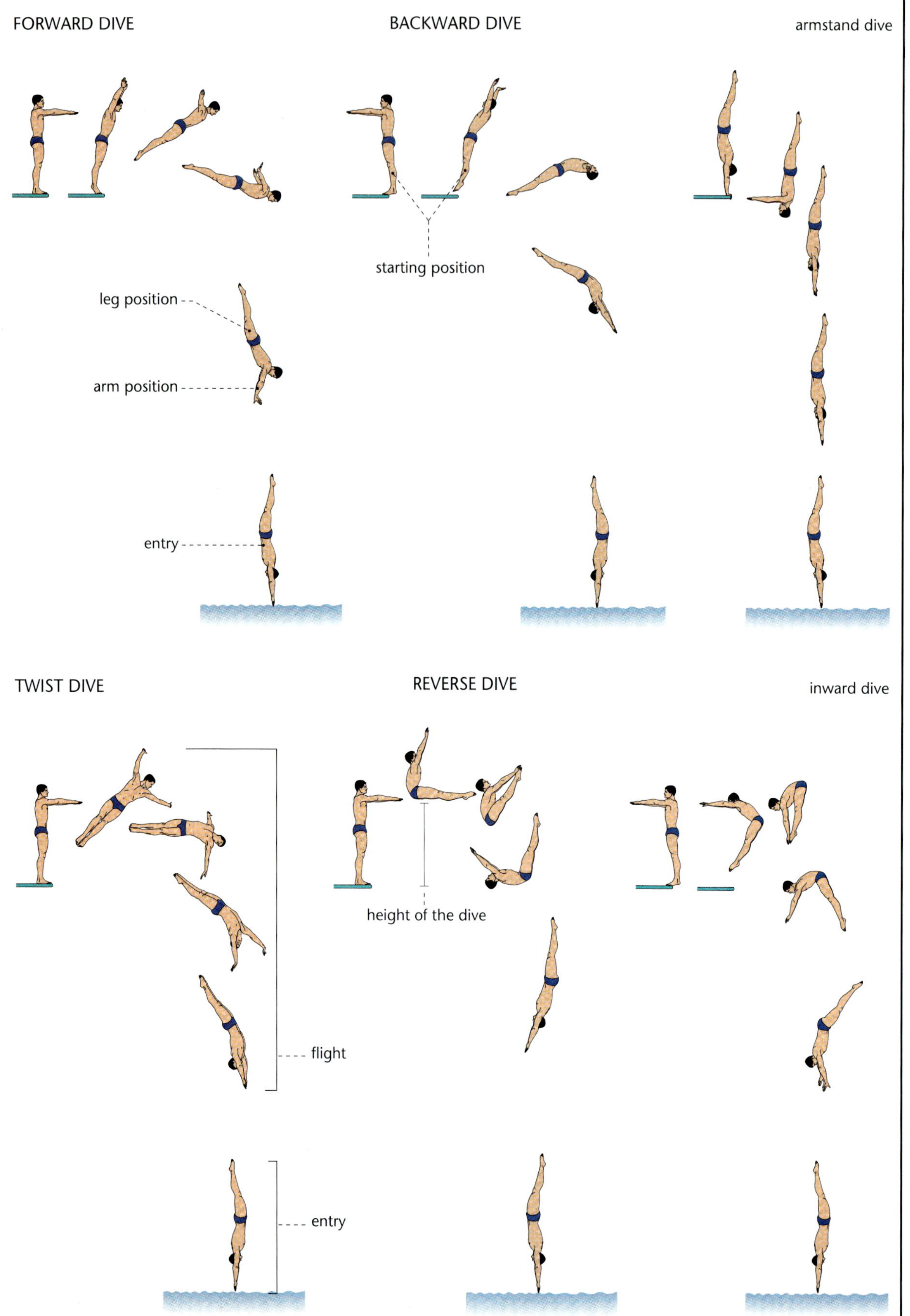

FORWARD DIVE
BACKWARD DIVE
armstand dive
starting position
leg position
arm position
entry
TWIST DIVE
REVERSE DIVE
inward dive
height of the dive
flight
entry

WATER POLO

PLAYING AREA
player
goalkeeper
goal
blue cap
white flag
team bench
red flag
blue flag
75 – 100 ft
secretary
referee
assistant timer
white flag
timekeeper
half-distance line
goal judge
4 m line
swimming pool
2 m line
26 – 66 ft
white cap
goal line
GOAL
crossbar
net
post
floater
bottom of the pool
WATER POLO BALL
8 9/16 – 8 15/16 in

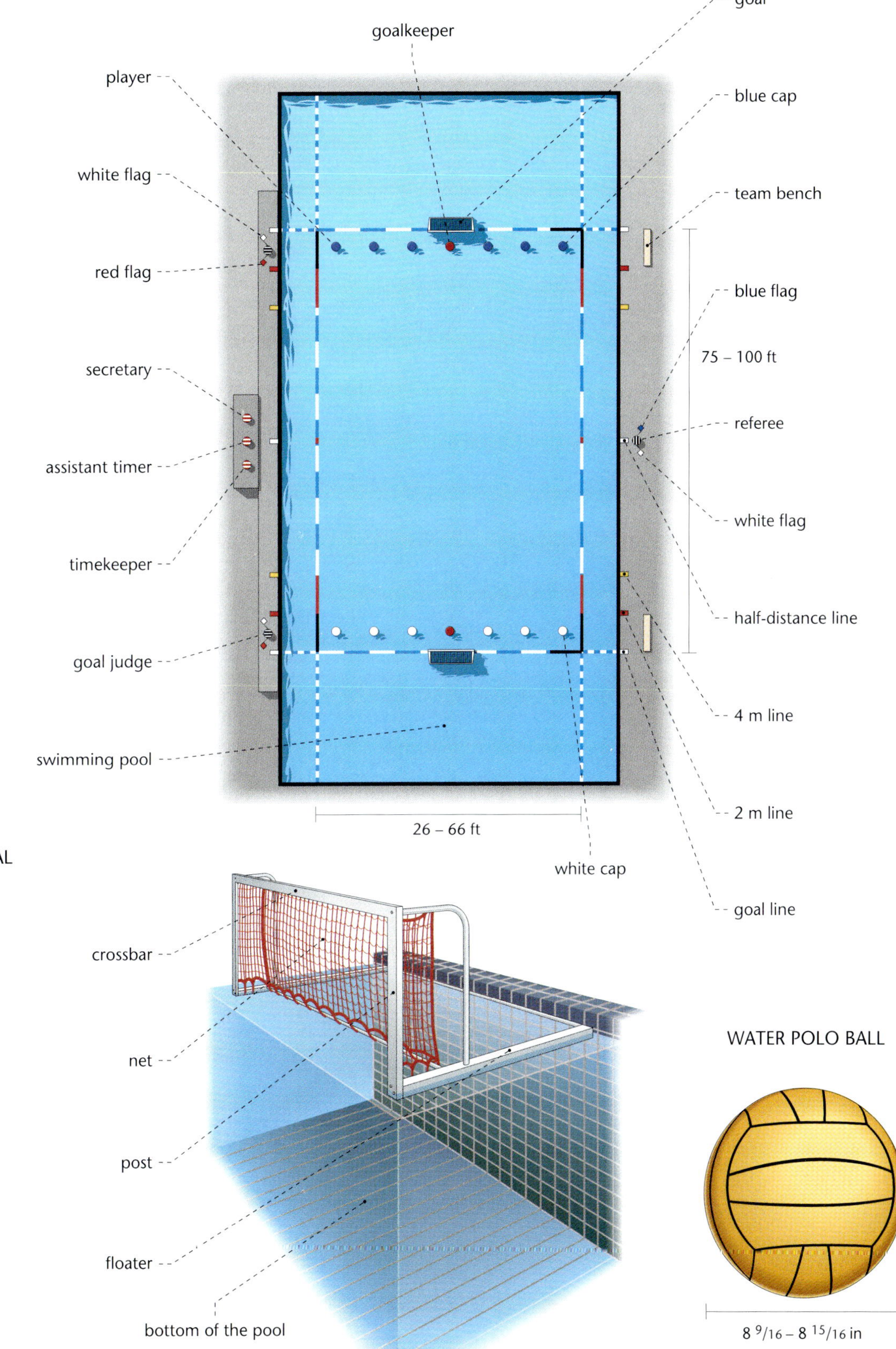

SCUBA DIVER

hood
snorkel
mask
regulator second stage
harness
inflator
regulator first stage
inflator valve
air hose
mouthpiece
weight belt
purge valve
buoyancy compensator
information console
compressed-air cylinder
thermometer
emergency regulator
pressure gauge
diving glove
depth gauge
wet suit
fin
boot
blade
foot pocket
rail
speargun

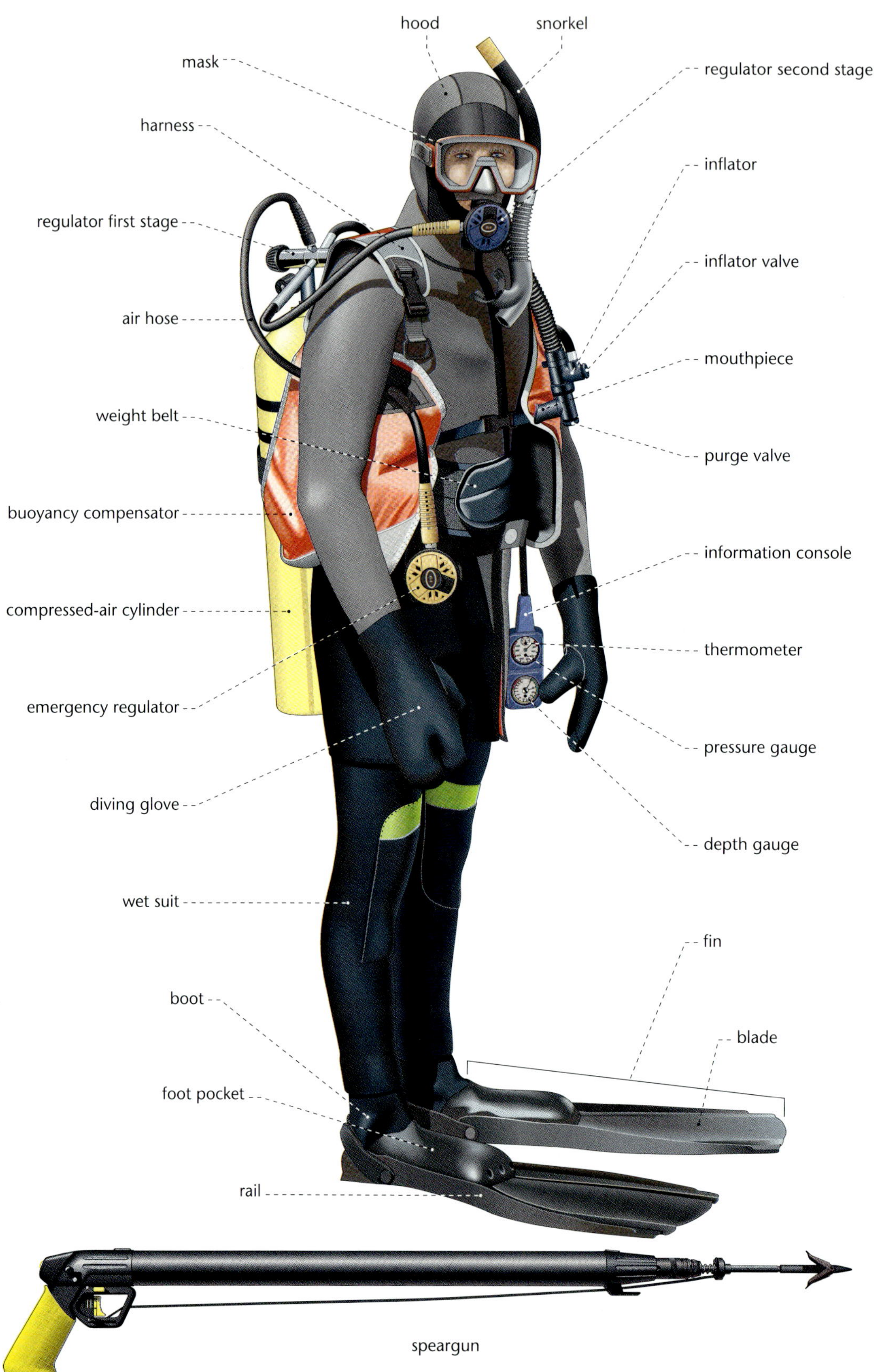

SAILBOAT

WATER SPORTS

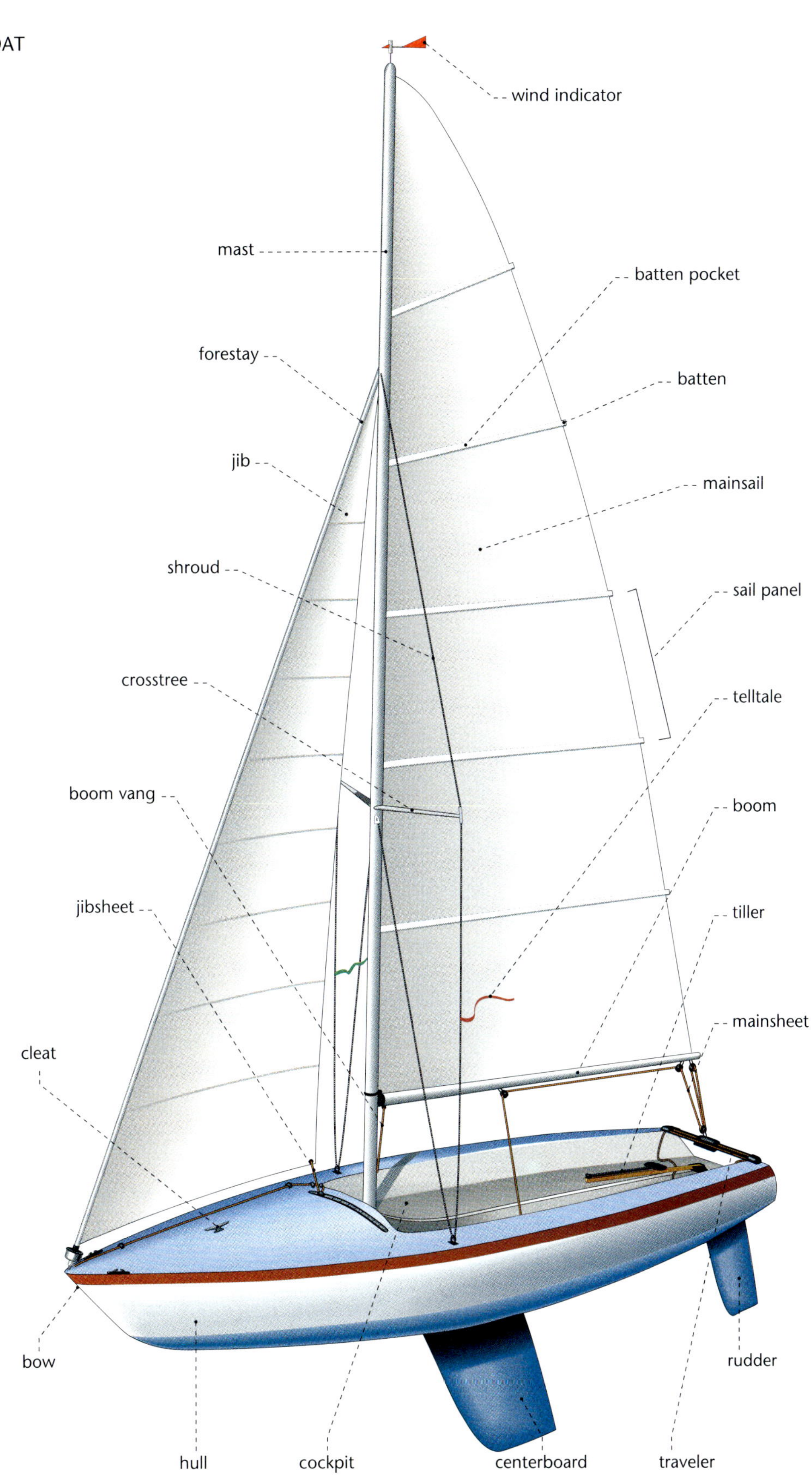

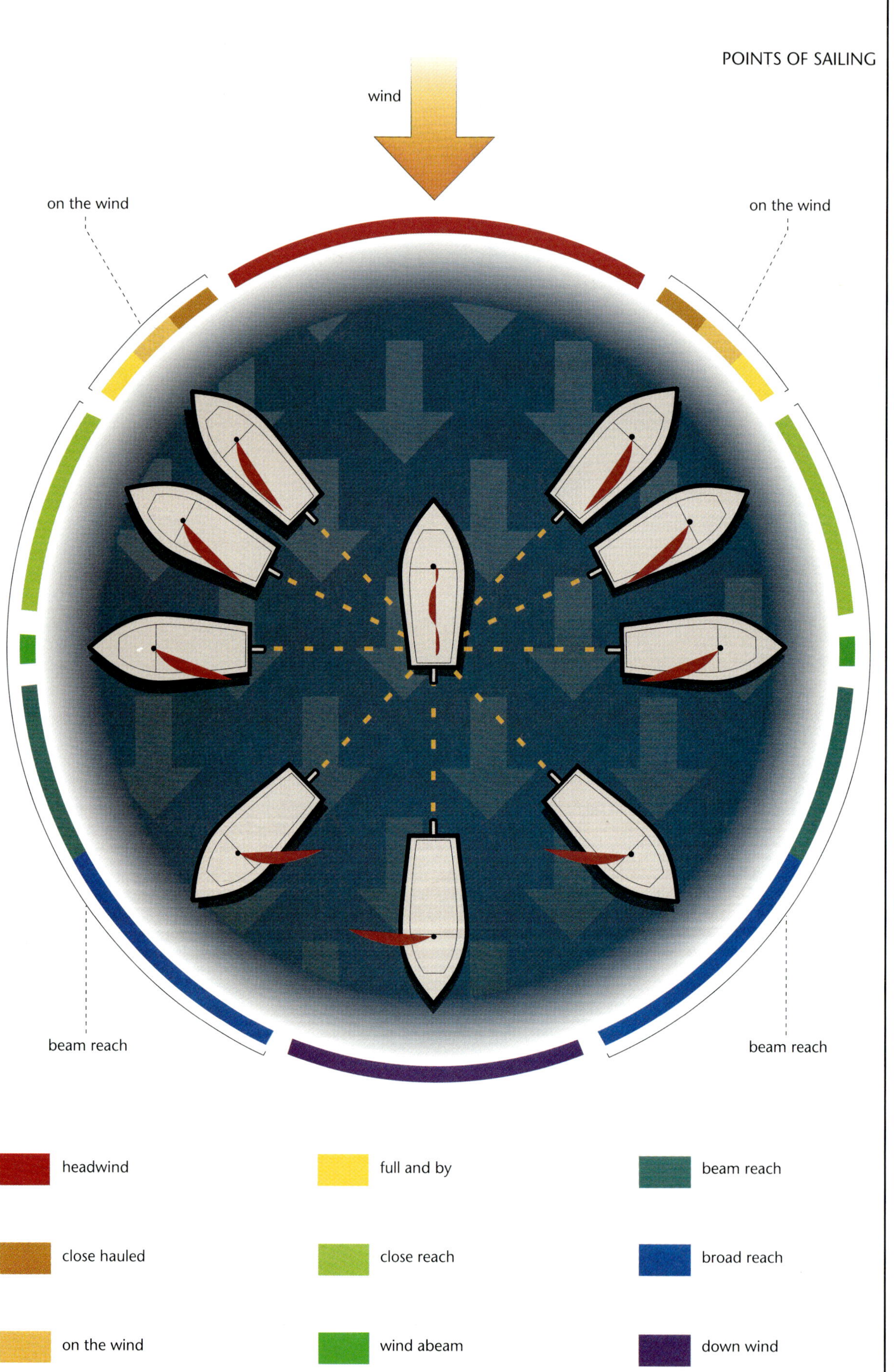

WATER SPORTS

■ headwind	■ full and by	■ beam reach
■ close hauled	■ close reach	■ broad reach
■ on the wind	■ wind abeam	■ down wind

UPPERWORKS

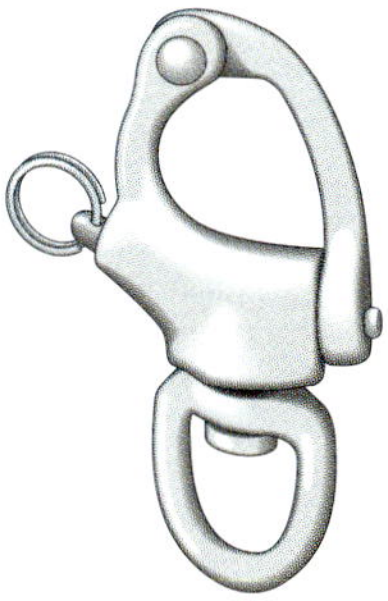

hank

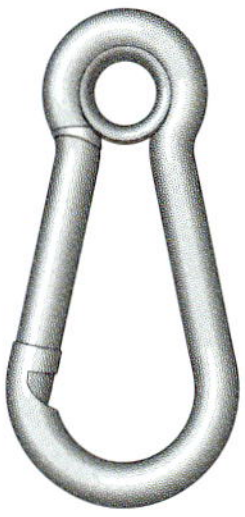

snap shackle

shackle

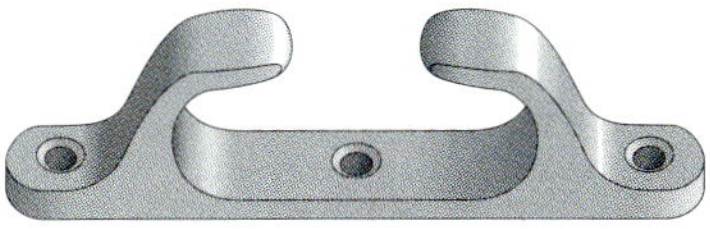

fairlead

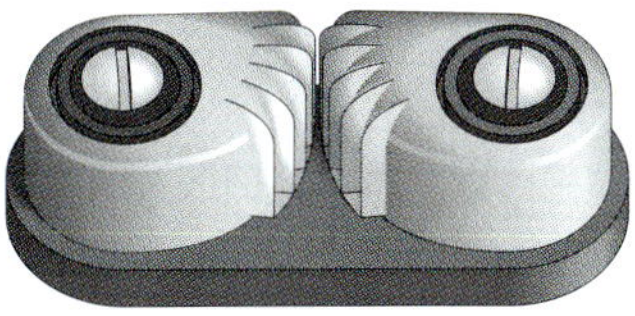

cleat

clam cleat

turnbuckle

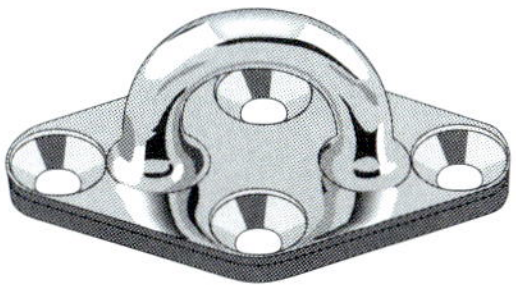

sheet lead

winch

TRAVELER

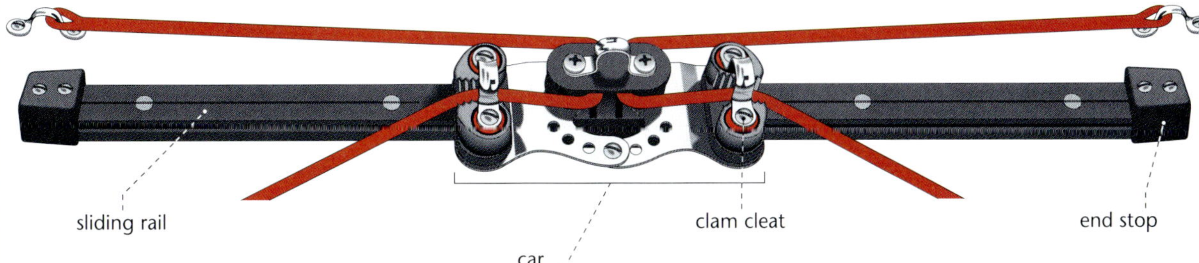

WATER SPORTS

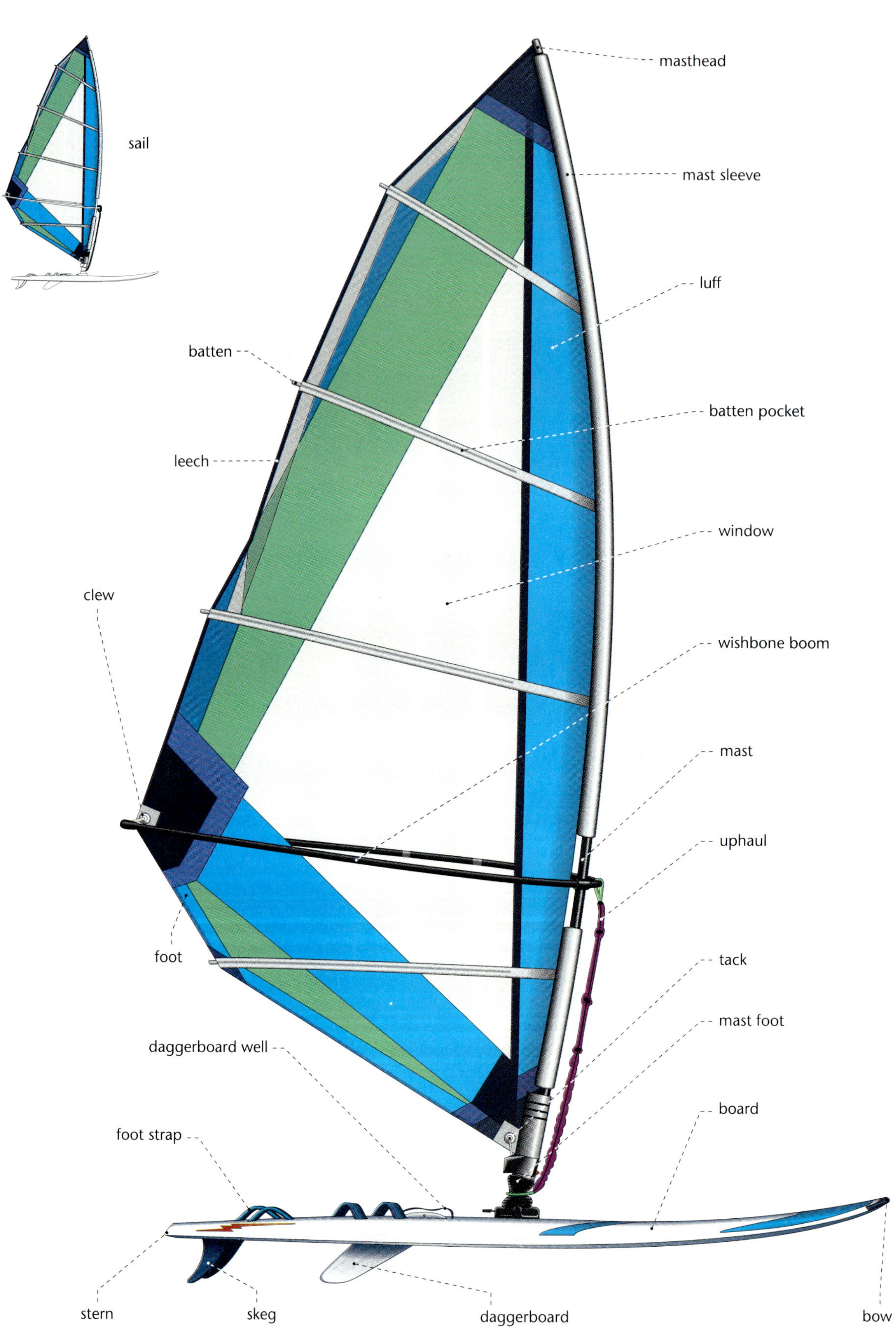
sail
masthead
mast sleeve
luff
batten
batten pocket
leech
window
clew
wishbone boom
mast
uphaul
tack
foot
mast foot
daggerboard well
board
foot strap
stern
skeg
daggerboard
bow

WATER SPORTS

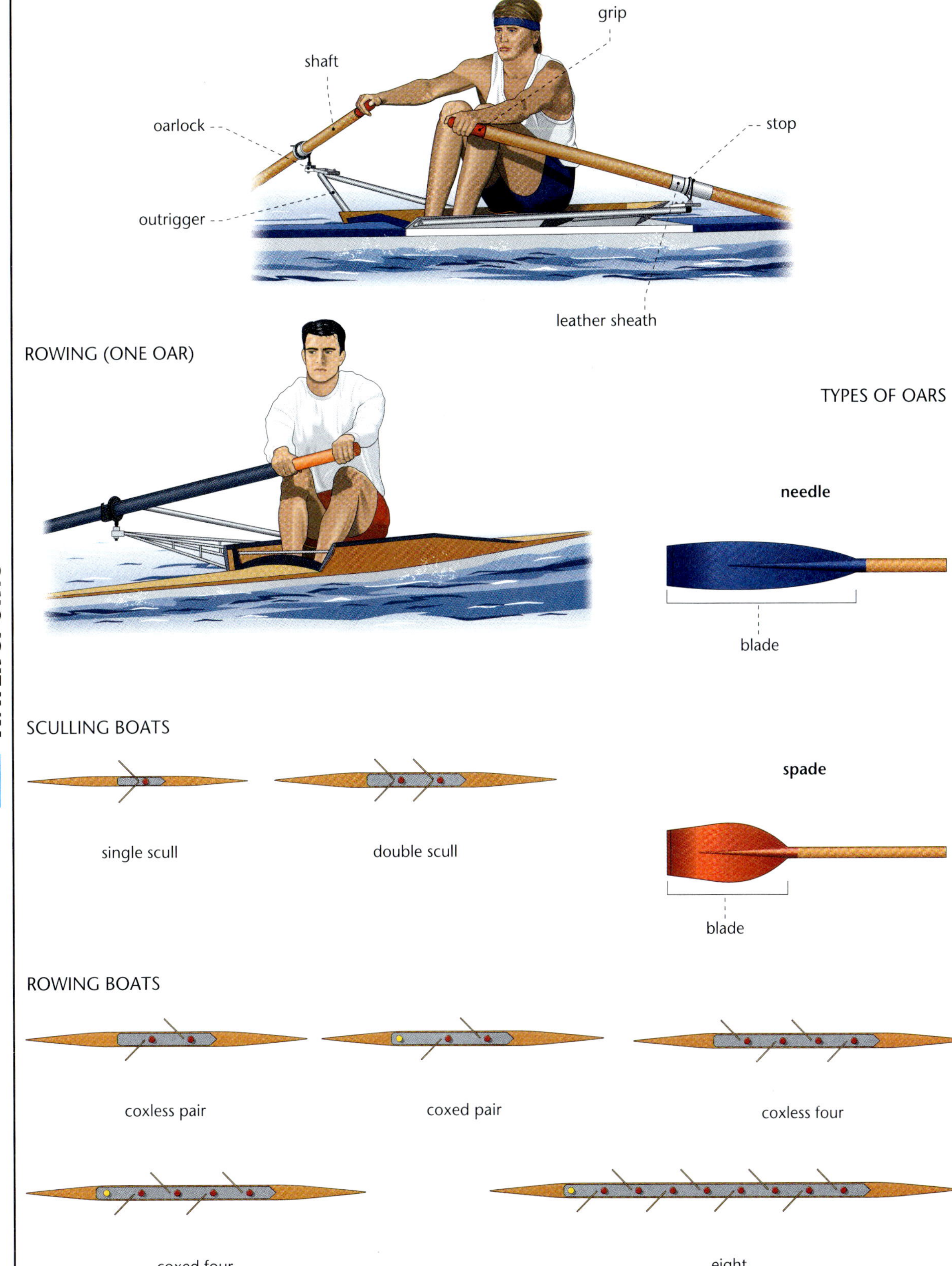

TYPES OF SKIS

twin skis

tip

jump ski

toe piece

bindings

heel piece

fin

figure ski

slalom ski

bottom

front binding

back binding

tail

WATER SPORTS

TYPES OF HANDLES

figure skiing handle

double handles

handle

tow line

toe strap

tow bar

BALLOON
parachute valve
panel
webbing
envelope
balloon
wind guard
basket suspension cables
burner
basket

SKY DIVING

SKY DIVER

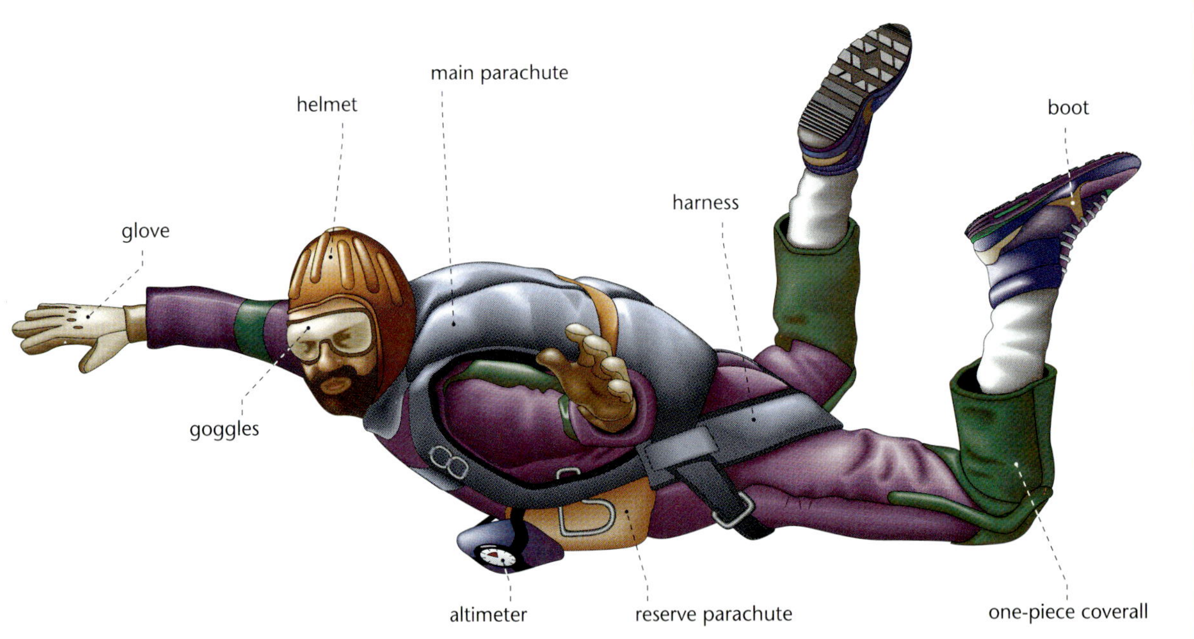

CANOPY
canopy 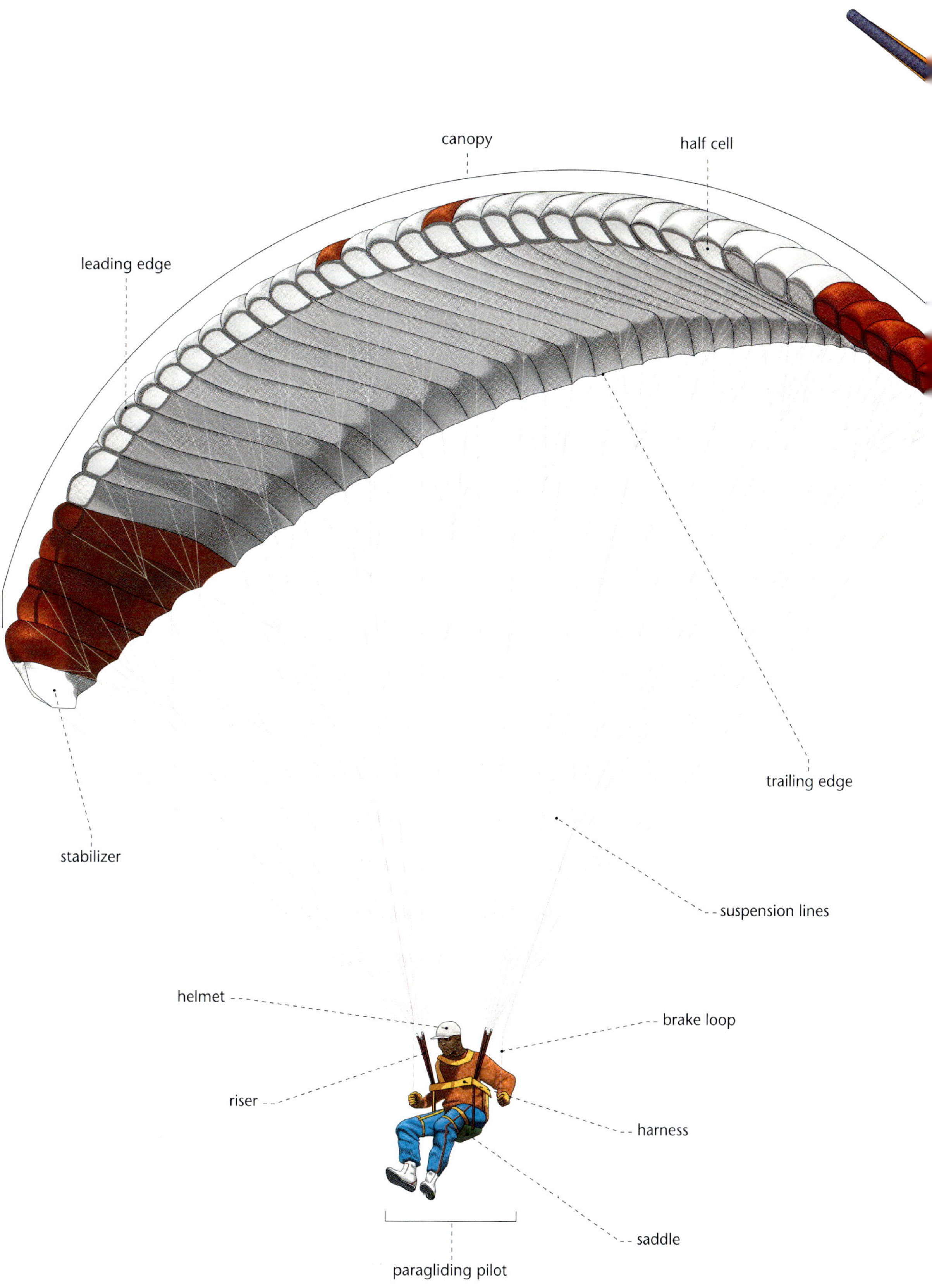
half cell
leading edge
trailing edge
stabilizer
suspension lines
helmet
brake loop
riser
harness
saddle
paragliding pilot

HANG GLIDER

crossbar
sail
batten
leading edge tube
keel
king post
nose
rigging wire
wing
airframe
control bar
flight bag
harness
pilot
hang point
trailing edge
tip

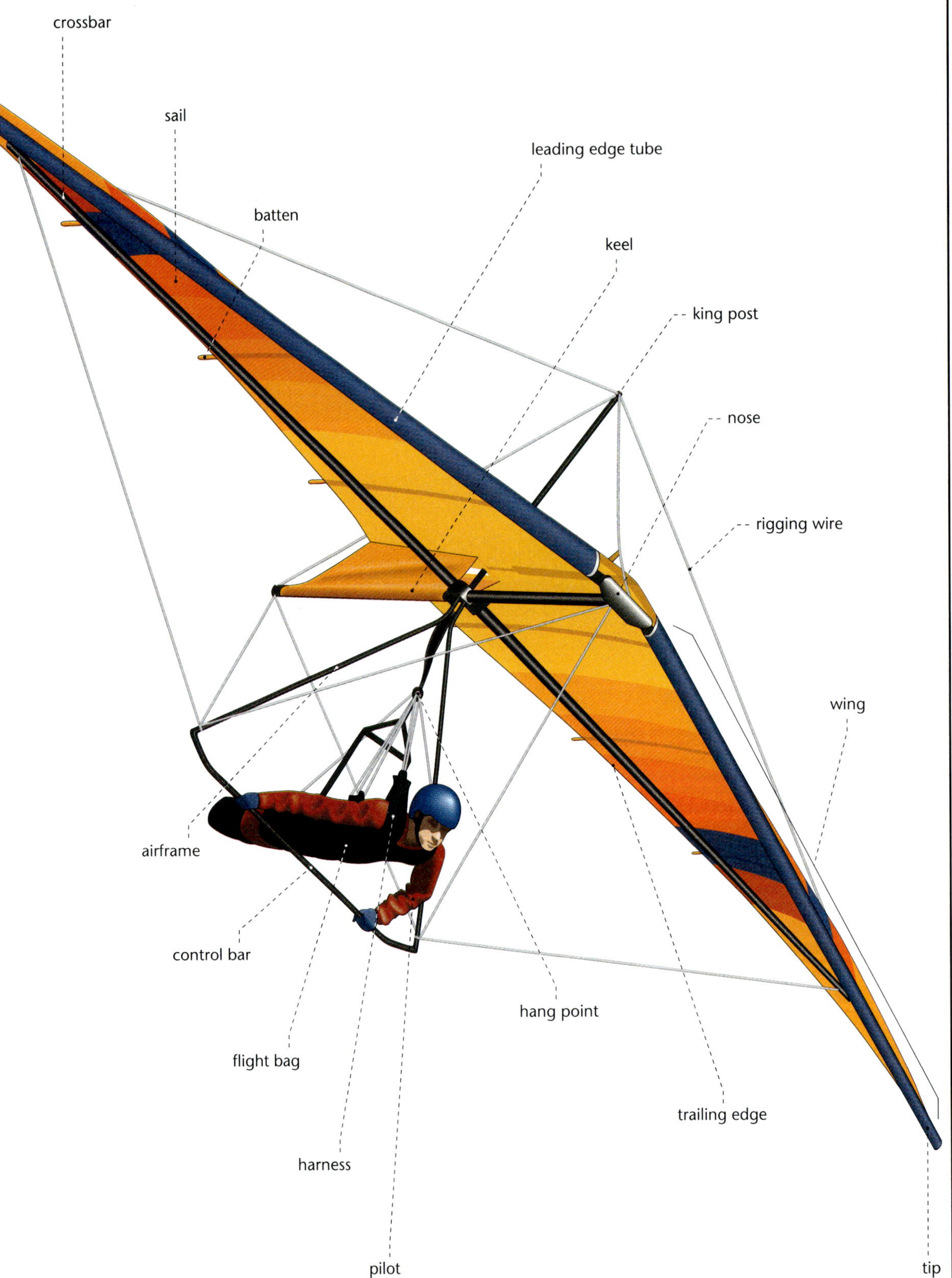

GLIDER

air brake
aileron
cockpit canopy
nose
leading edge
trailing edge
wing tip
wings
tail

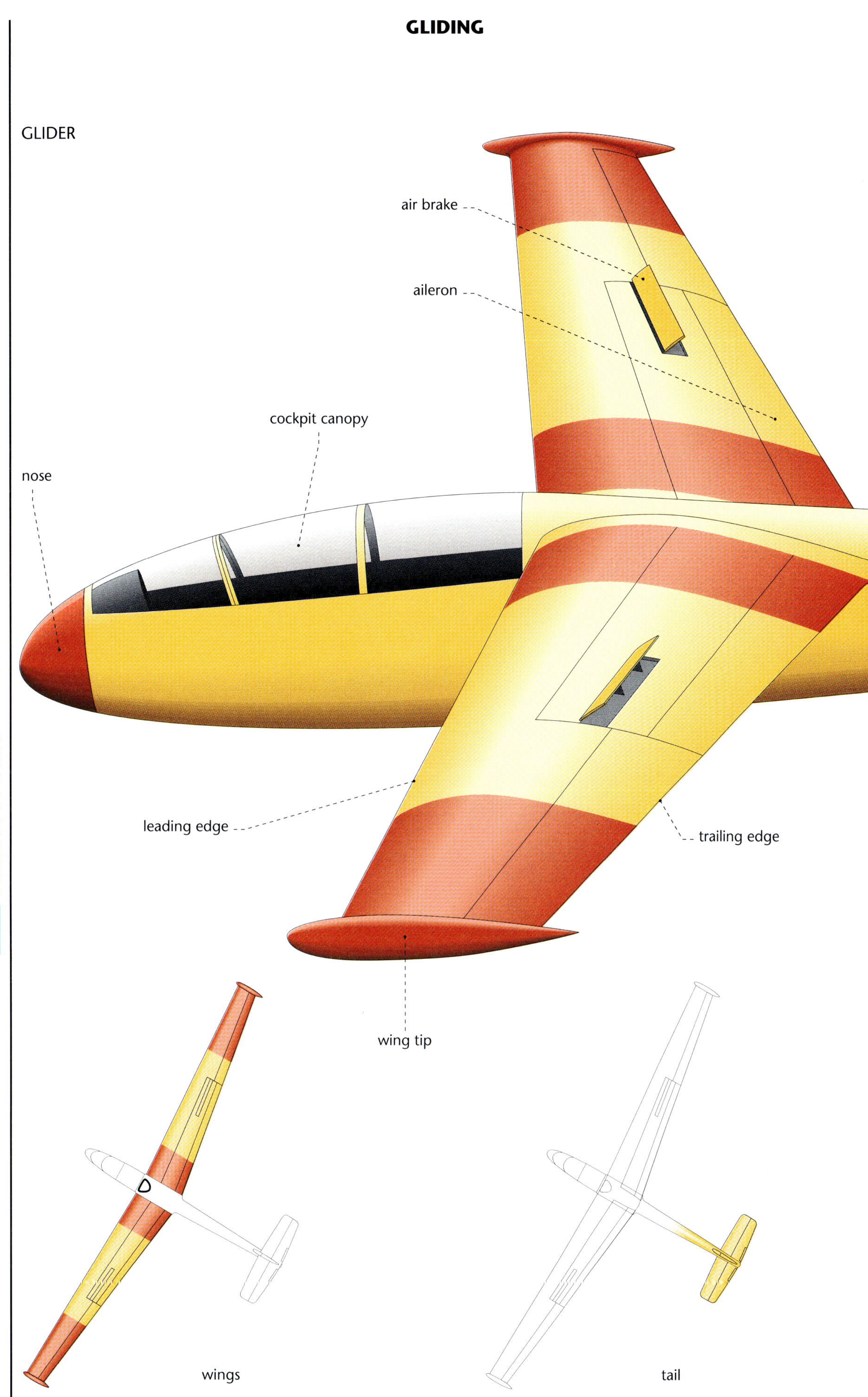

rudder
vertical stabilizer
elevator
fuselage
horizontal stabilizer

COCKPIT

altimeter
airspeed indicator
turn and slip indicator
compass
cockpit ventilation
electric variometer
mechanical variometer
oxygen feeding control
tow release knob
oxygen feeding knob
rudder pedal
microphone
air brake handle
canopy release knob
turn and slip knob
control stick
radio
seat

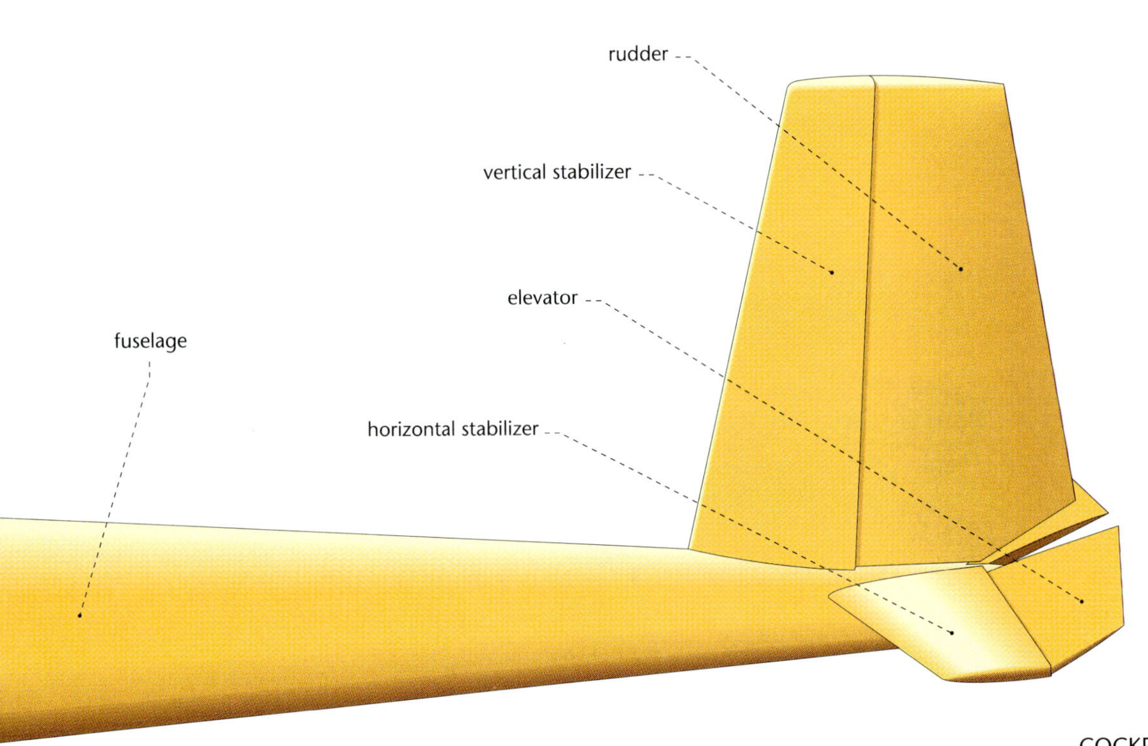

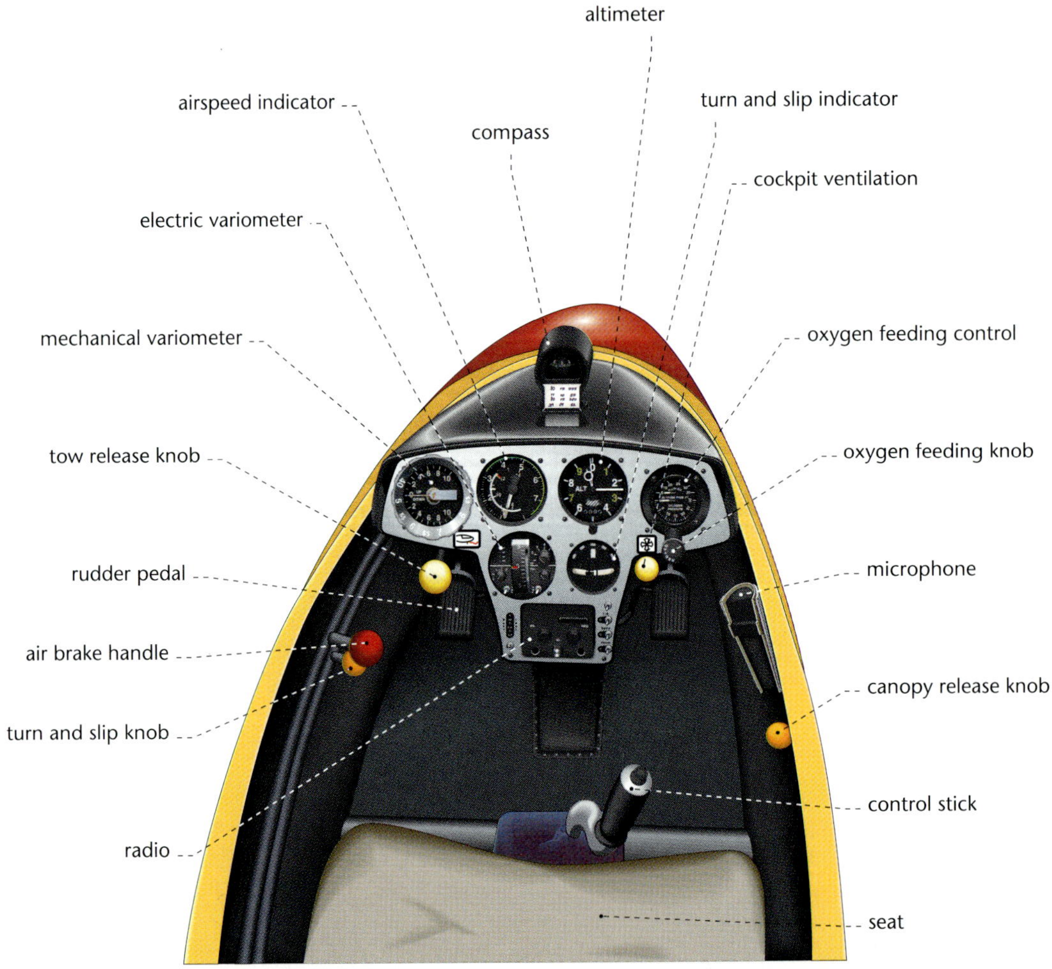

ALPINE SKIER

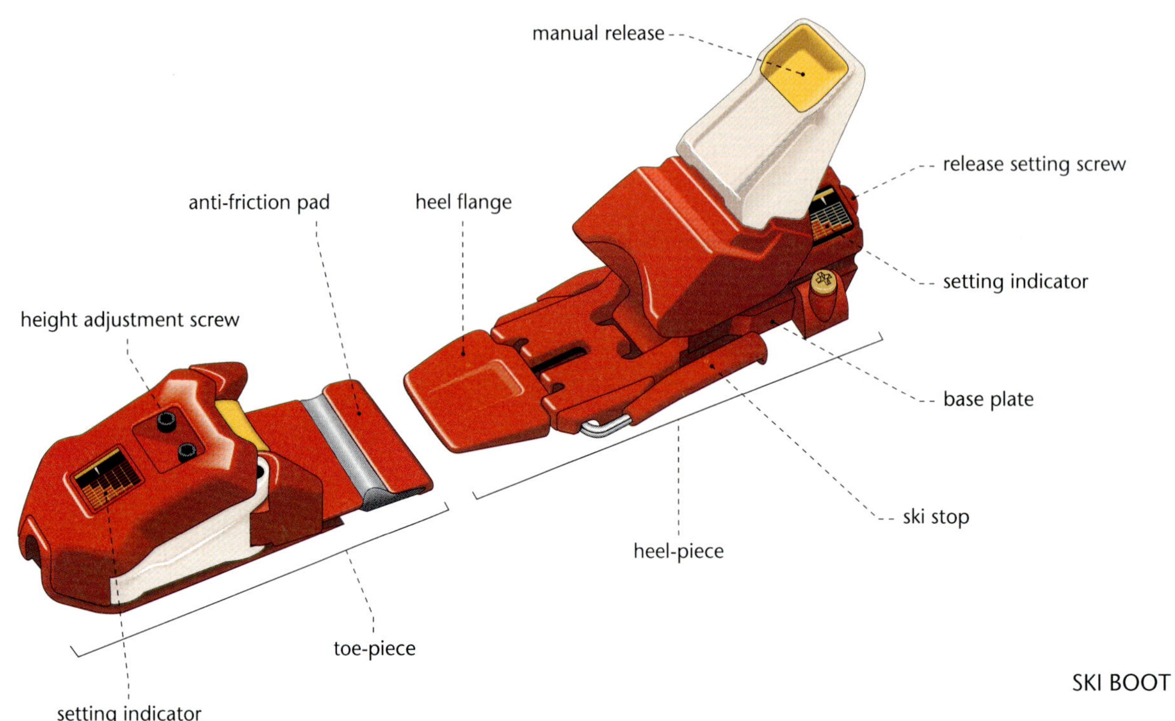

SAFETY BINDING

manual release
release setting screw
anti-friction pad
heel flange
setting indicator
height adjustment screw
base plate
ski stop
heel-piece
toe-piece
setting indicator

SKI BOOT

inner boot
upper cuff
tongue
upper
upper strap
buckle
upper shell
wire
adjusting catch
hinge
lower shell
sole

basket

tail
groove
ski

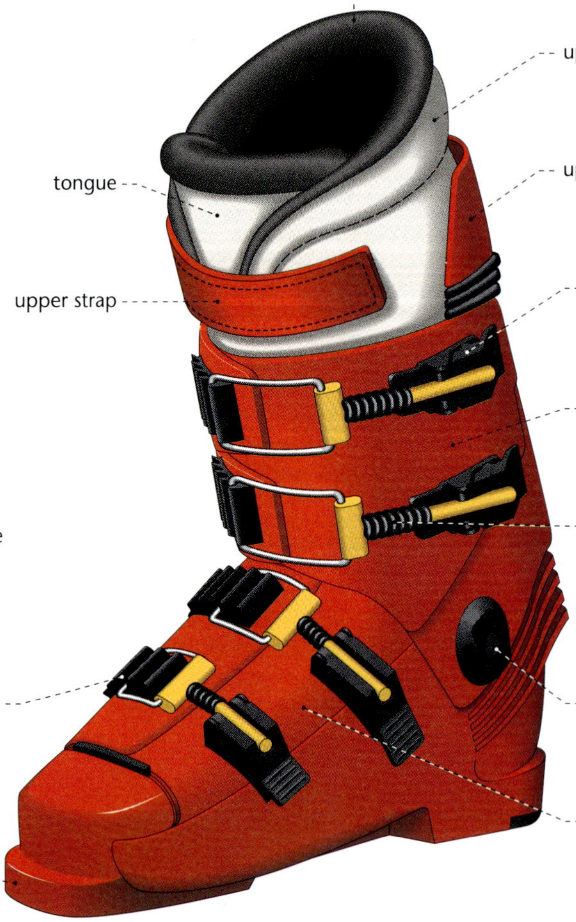

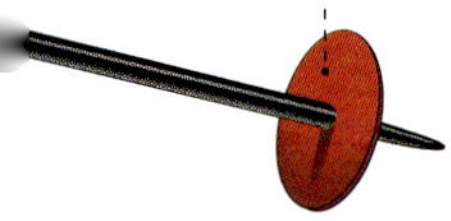

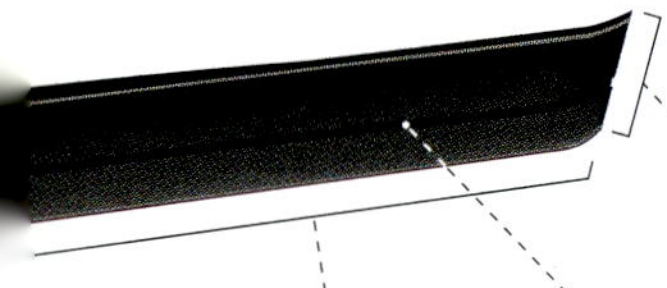

CROSS-COUNTRY SKIER

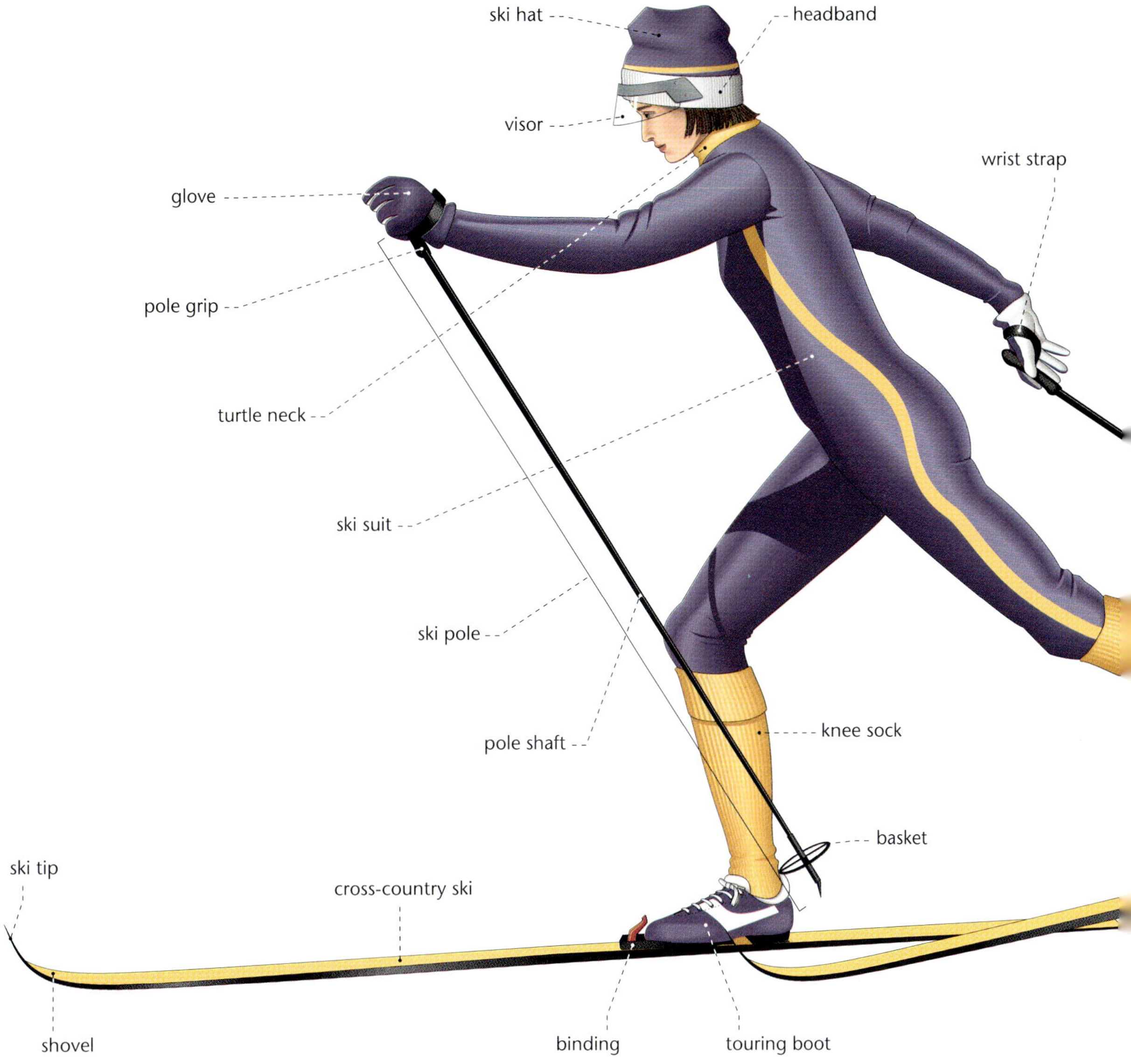

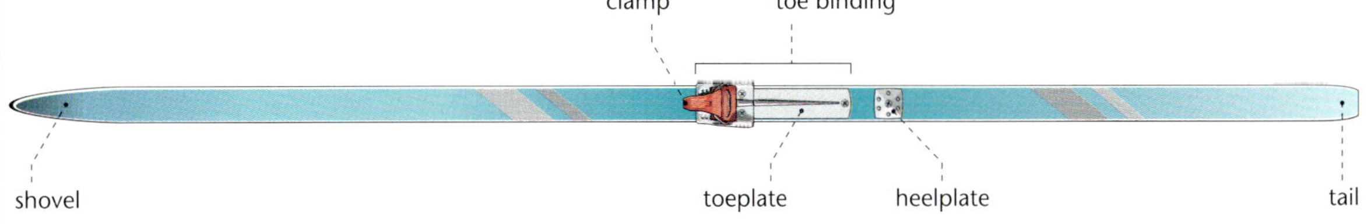

CROSS-COUNTRY SKI

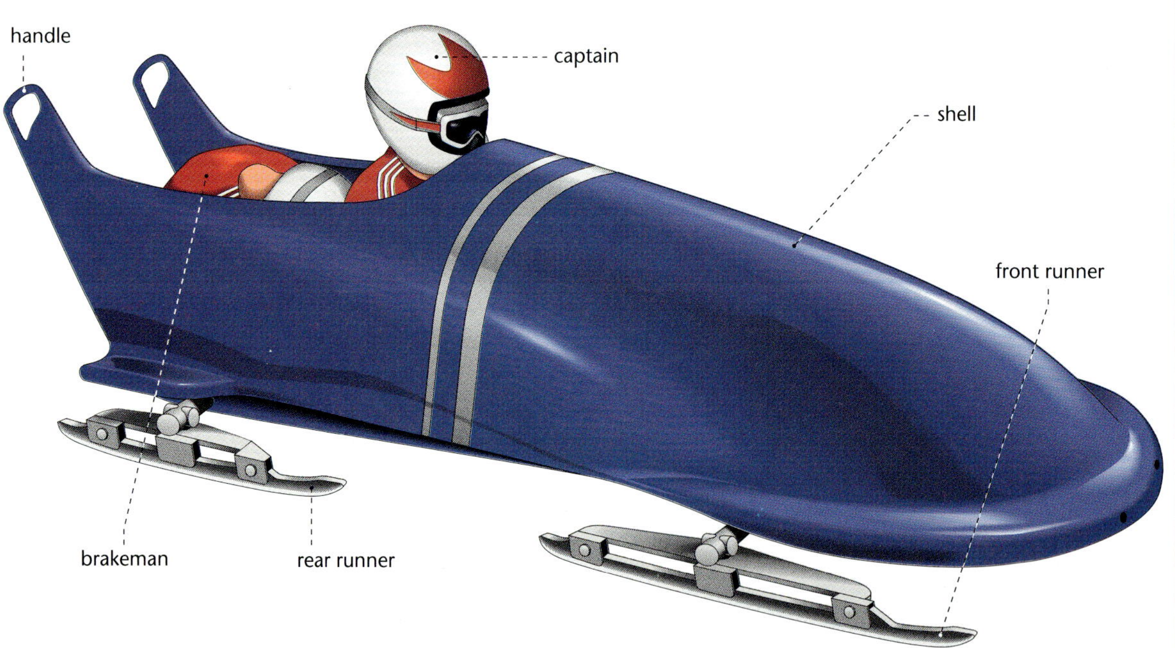

LUGE 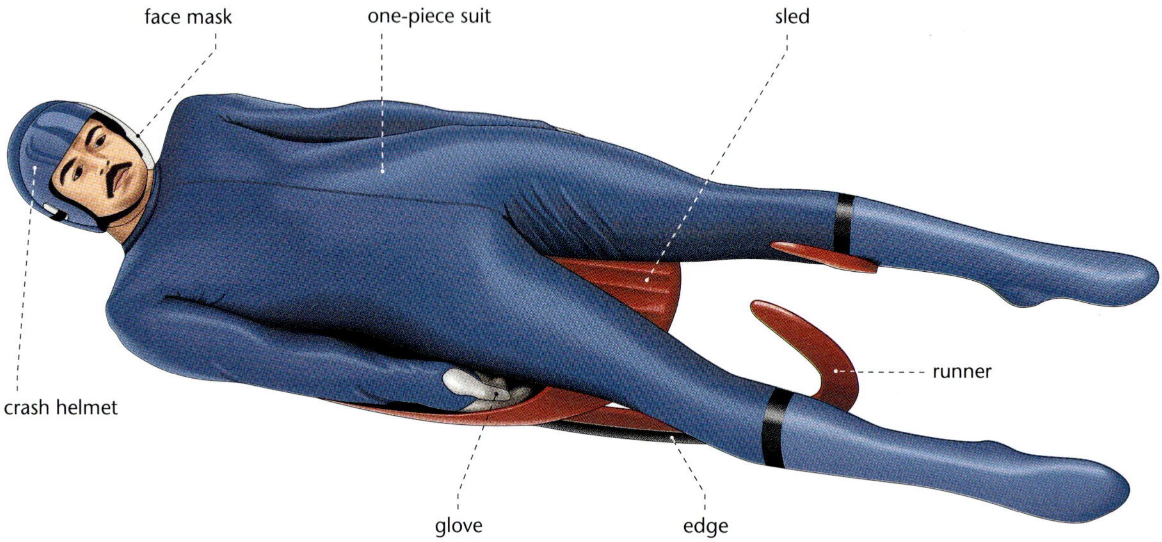 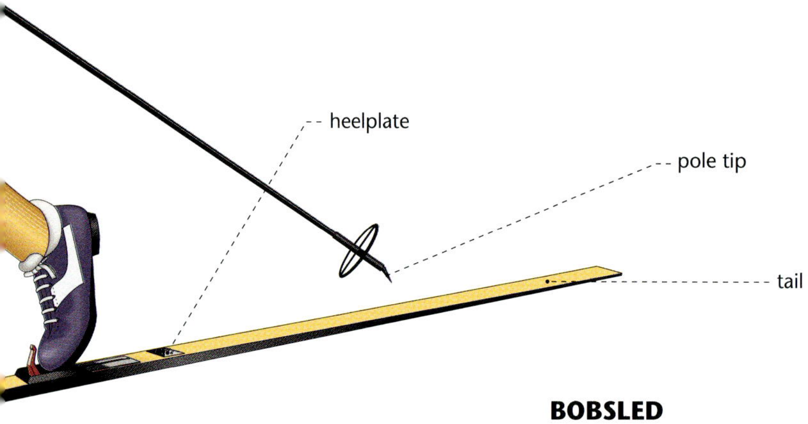
face mask
one-piece suit
sled
crash helmet
runner
glove
edge
heelplate
pole tip
tail
BOBSLED
handle
captain
shell
front runner
brakeman
rear runner

SKATING

FIGURE SKATE

HOCKEY SKATE

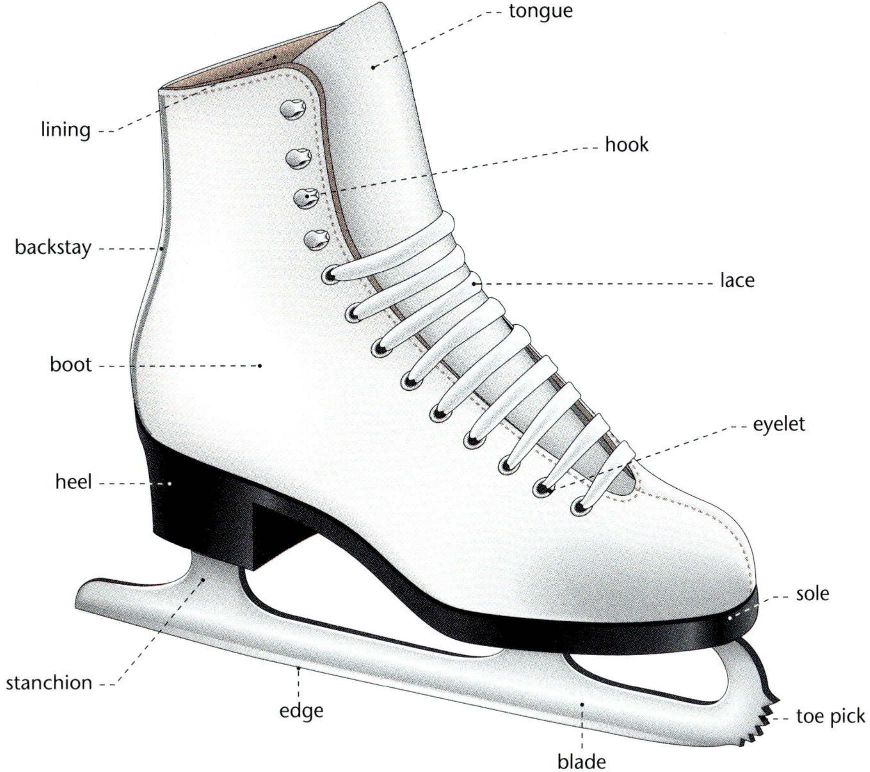

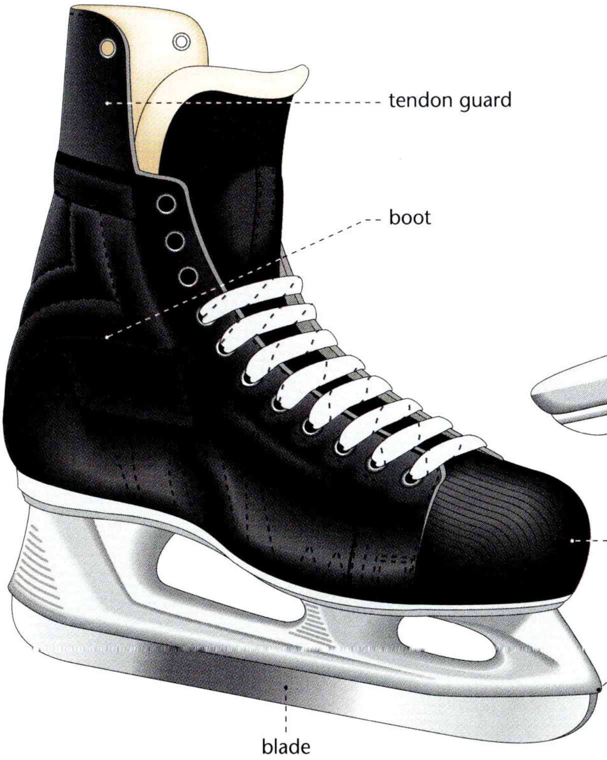

speed skate

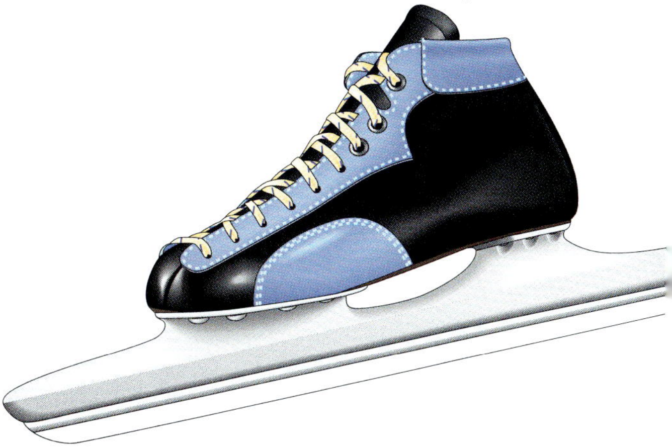

skate guard

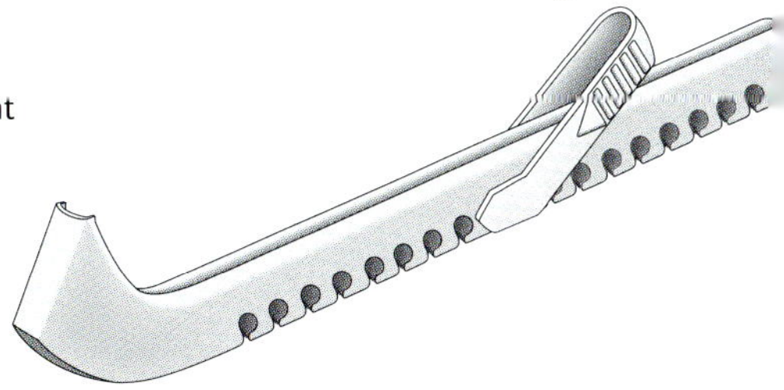

SNOWSHOE

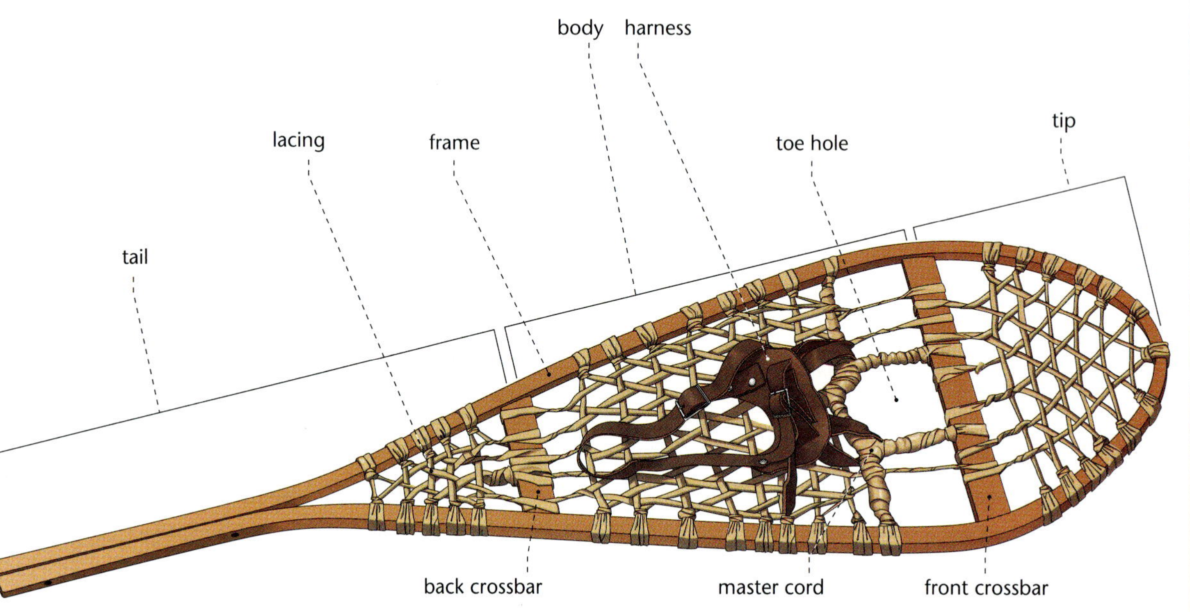

ROLLER SKATE

COMPETITION RING

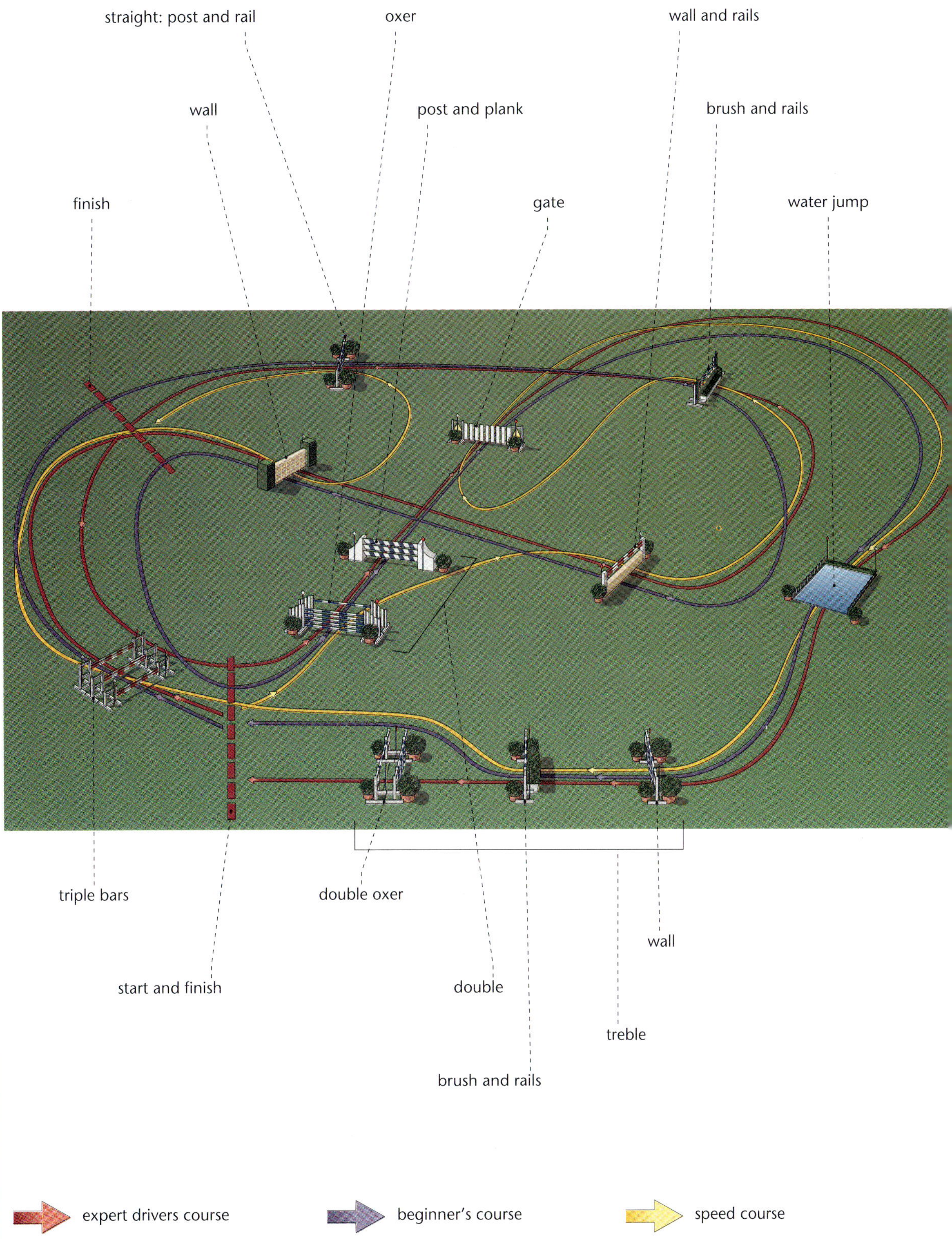

EQUESTRIAN SPORTS

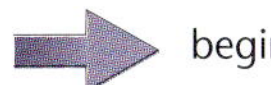

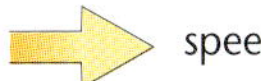

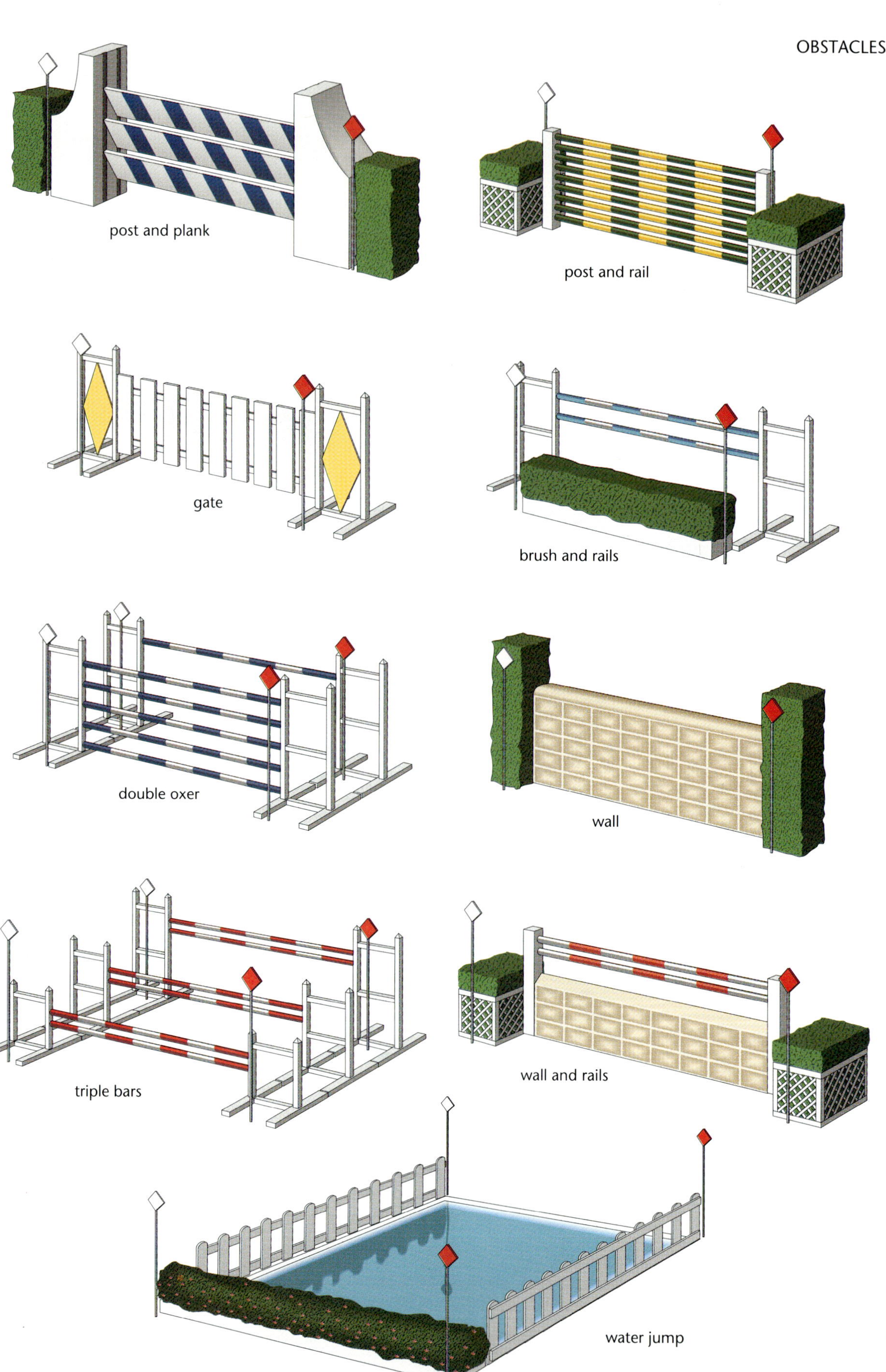

post and plank
post and rail
gate
brush and rails
double oxer
wall
triple bars
wall and rails
water jump

RIDER

riding cap
riding jacket
jodhpur
riding glove
saddle
bit
riding crop
saddle pad
boot
stirrup iron
shin boot
spur
saddlecloth

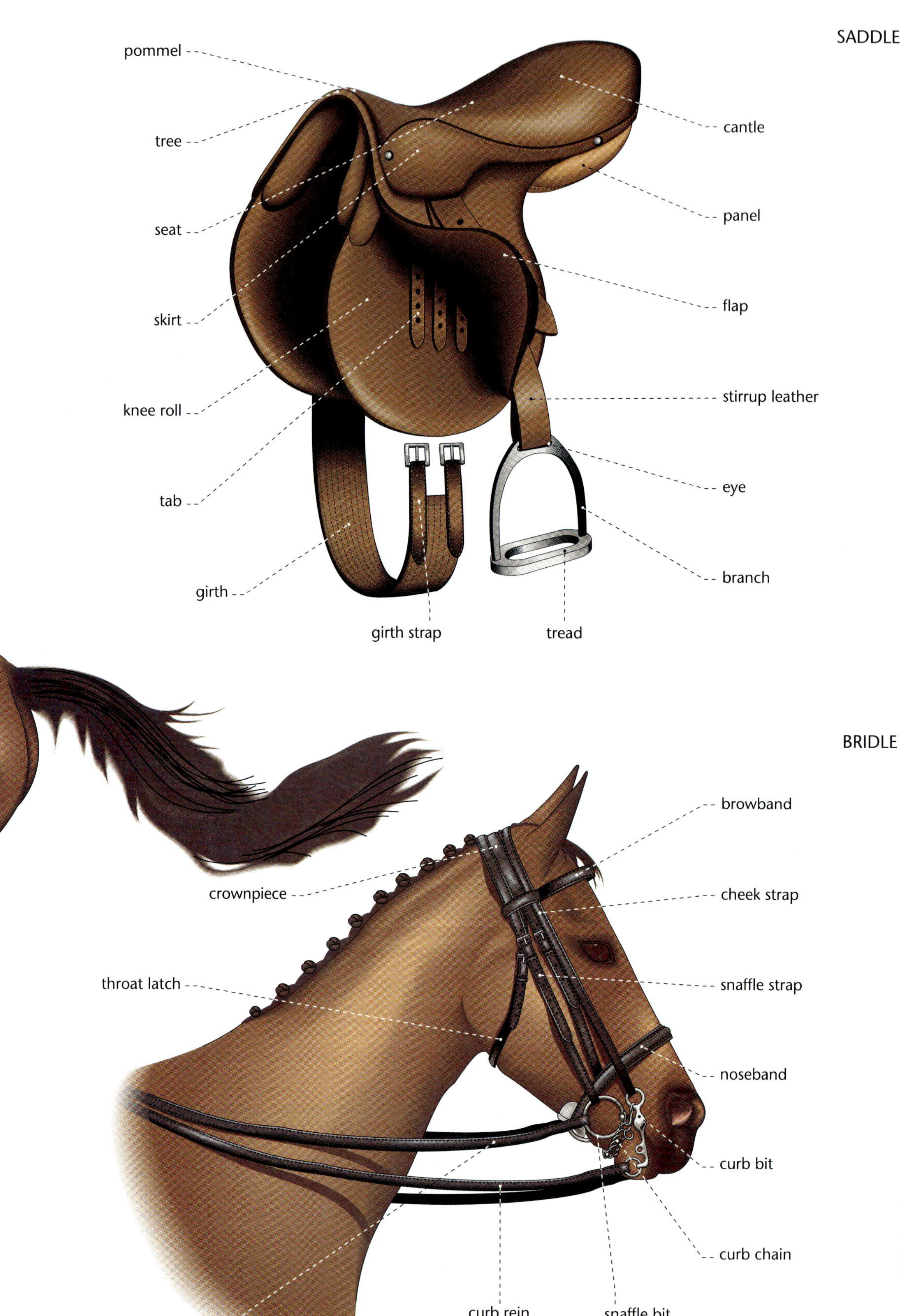

EQUESTRIAN SPORTS

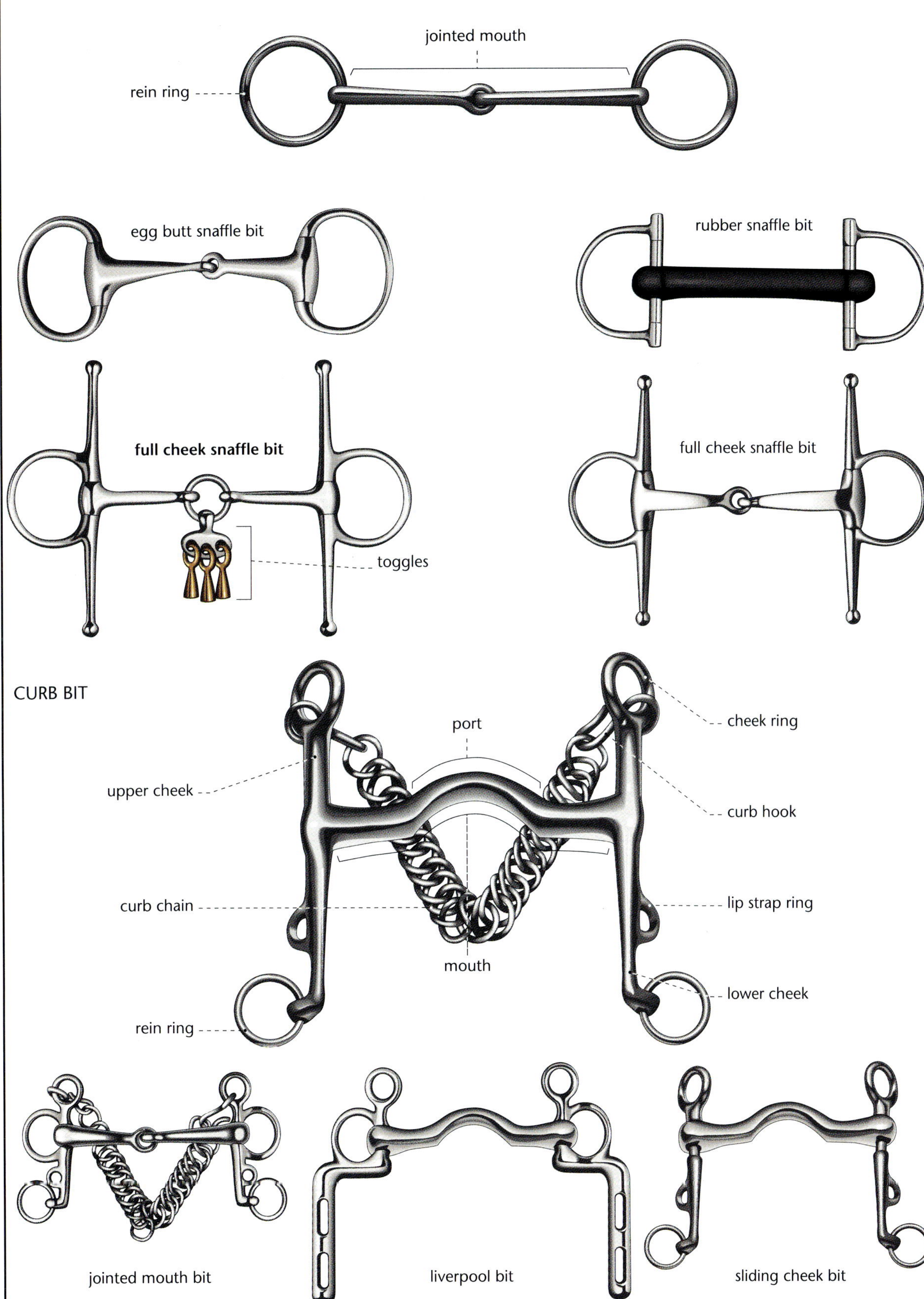
SNAFFLE BIT
jointed mouth
rein ring
egg butt snaffle bit
rubber snaffle bit
full cheek snaffle bit
full cheek snaffle bit
toggles
CURB BIT
port
cheek ring
upper cheek
curb hook
curb chain
lip strap ring
mouth
lower cheek
rein ring
jointed mouth bit
liverpool bit
sliding cheek bit

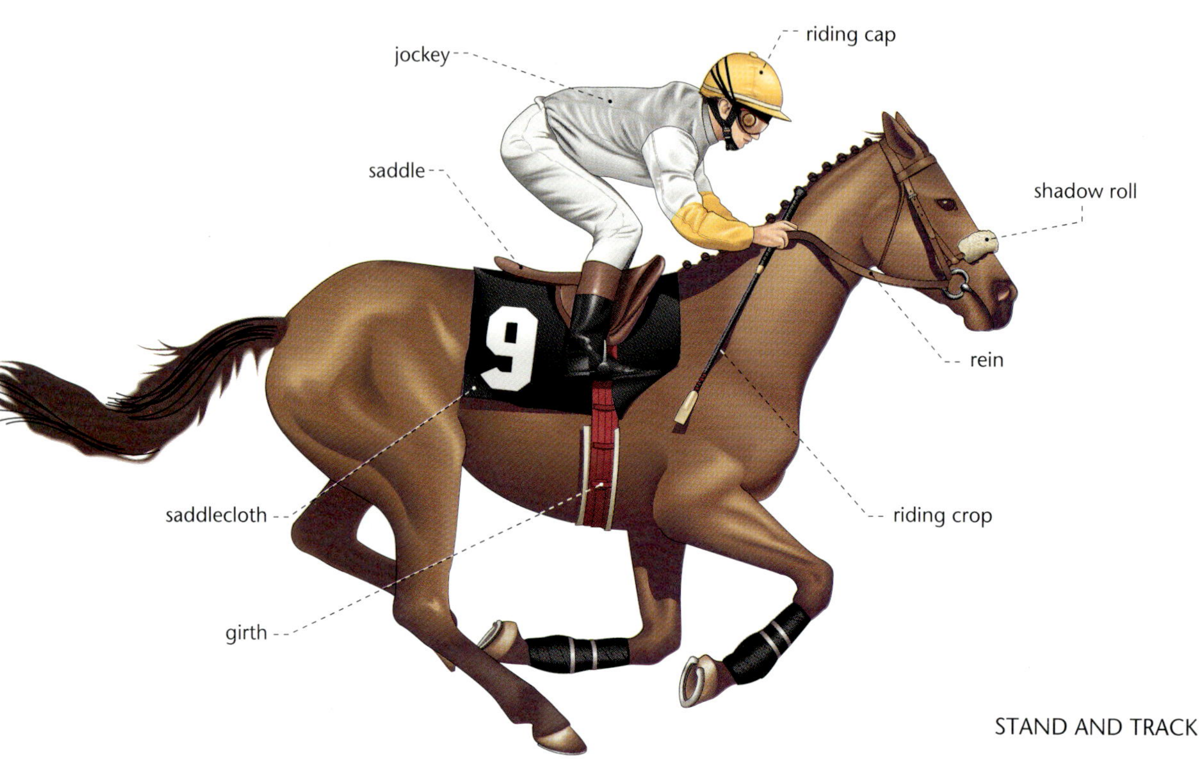

STAND AND TRACK

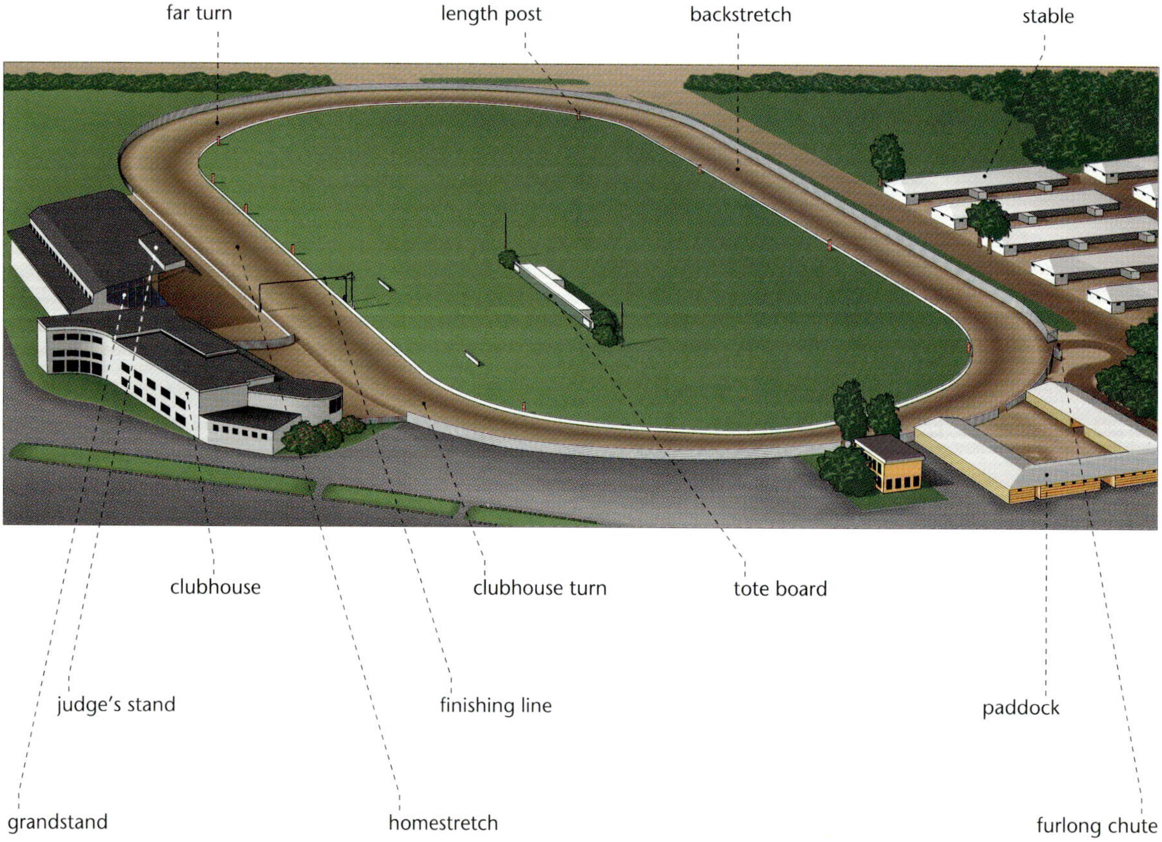

STANDARDBRED PACER

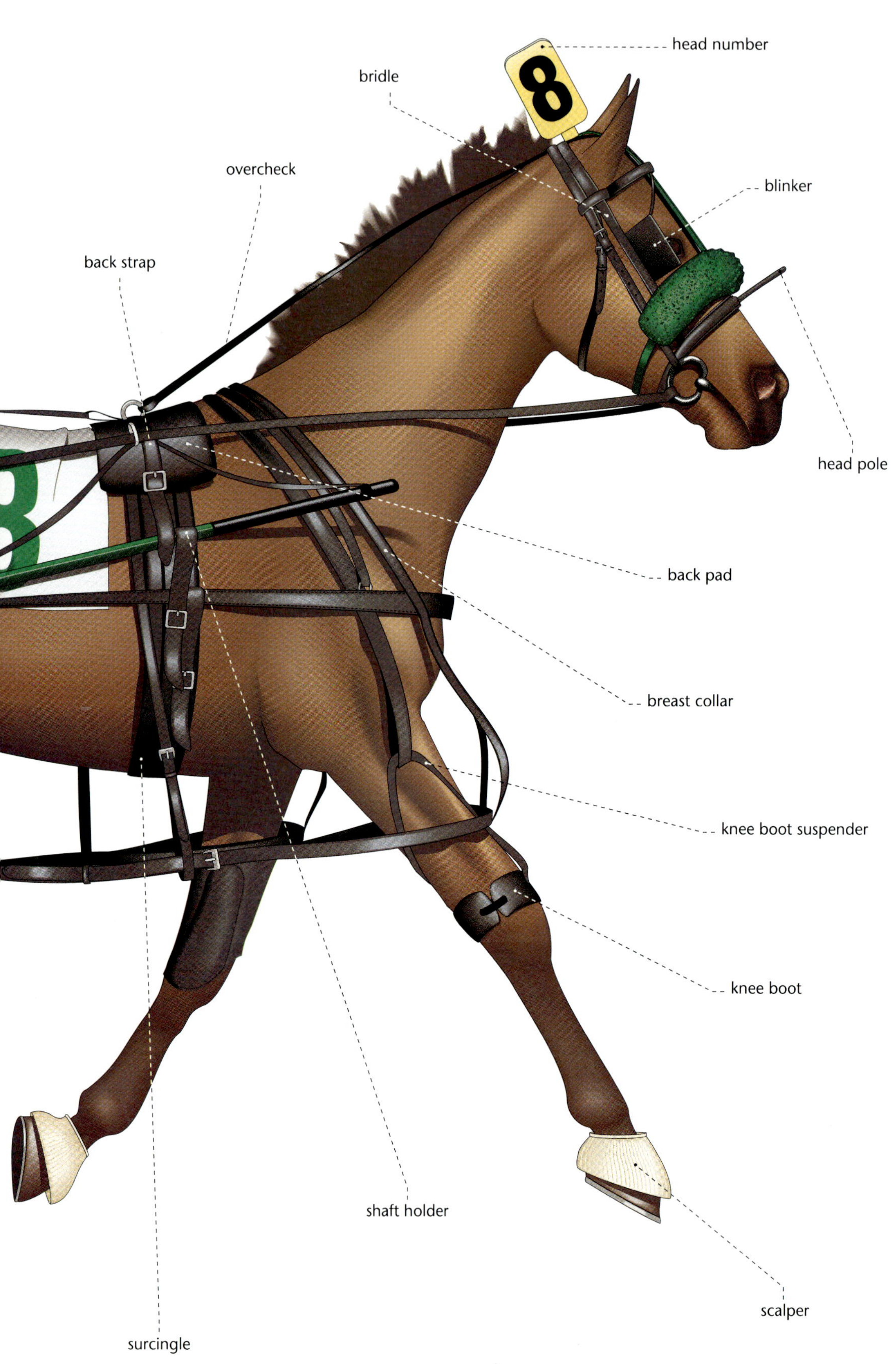

head number
bridle
blinker
overcheck
back strap
head pole
back pad
breast collar
knee boot suspender
knee boot
shaft holder
scalper
surcingle
8

ARENA

high jump
javelin throw
approach
finish line
finishing post
running
throwing circle
safety cage
discus and hammer throw
triple jump take-off board
triple jump take-off line
indicator board

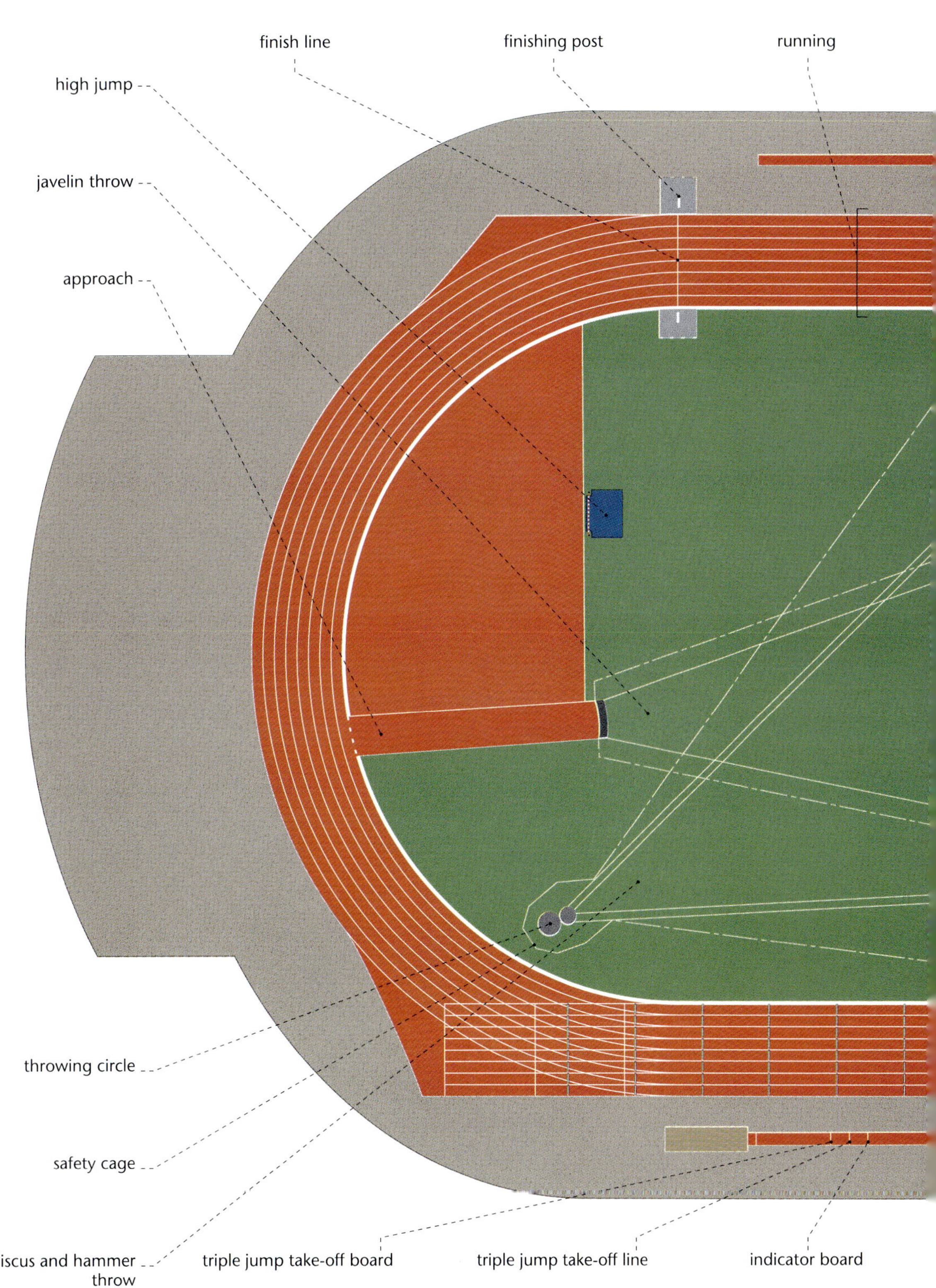

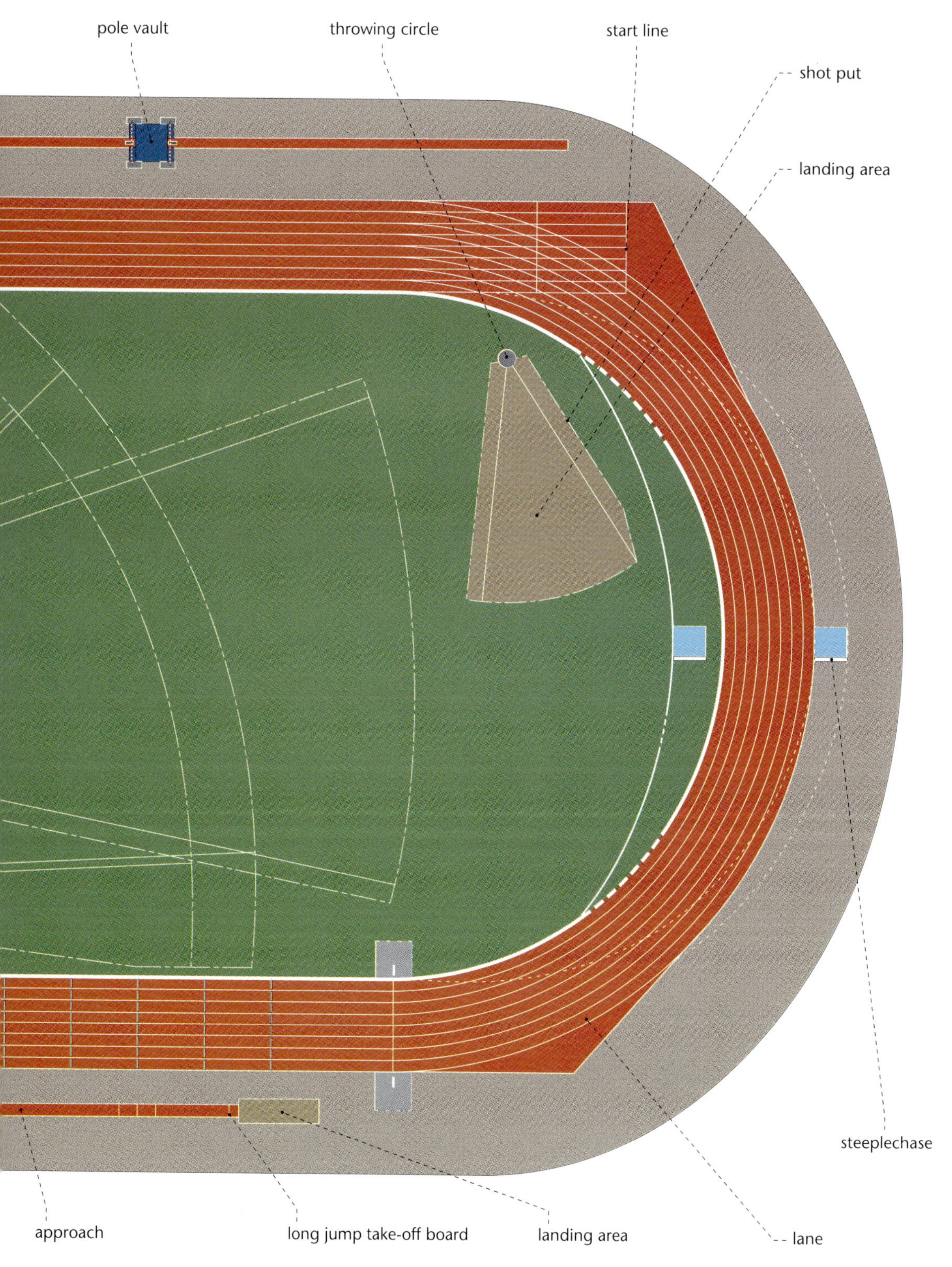

pole vault
throwing circle
start line
shot put
landing area
approach
long jump take-off board
landing area
lane
steeplechase

STARTING BLOCK

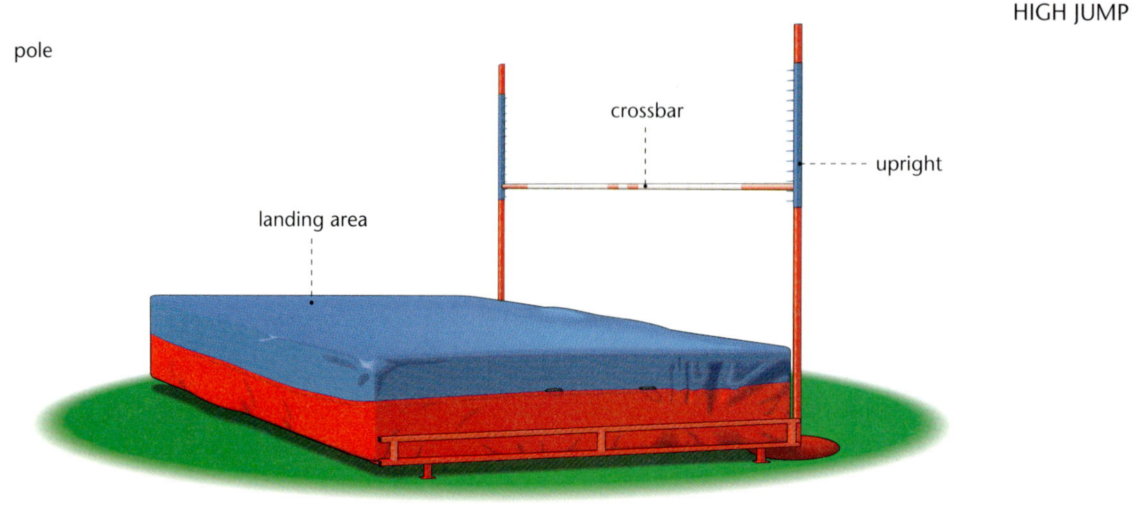

POLE VAULT

ATHLETICS

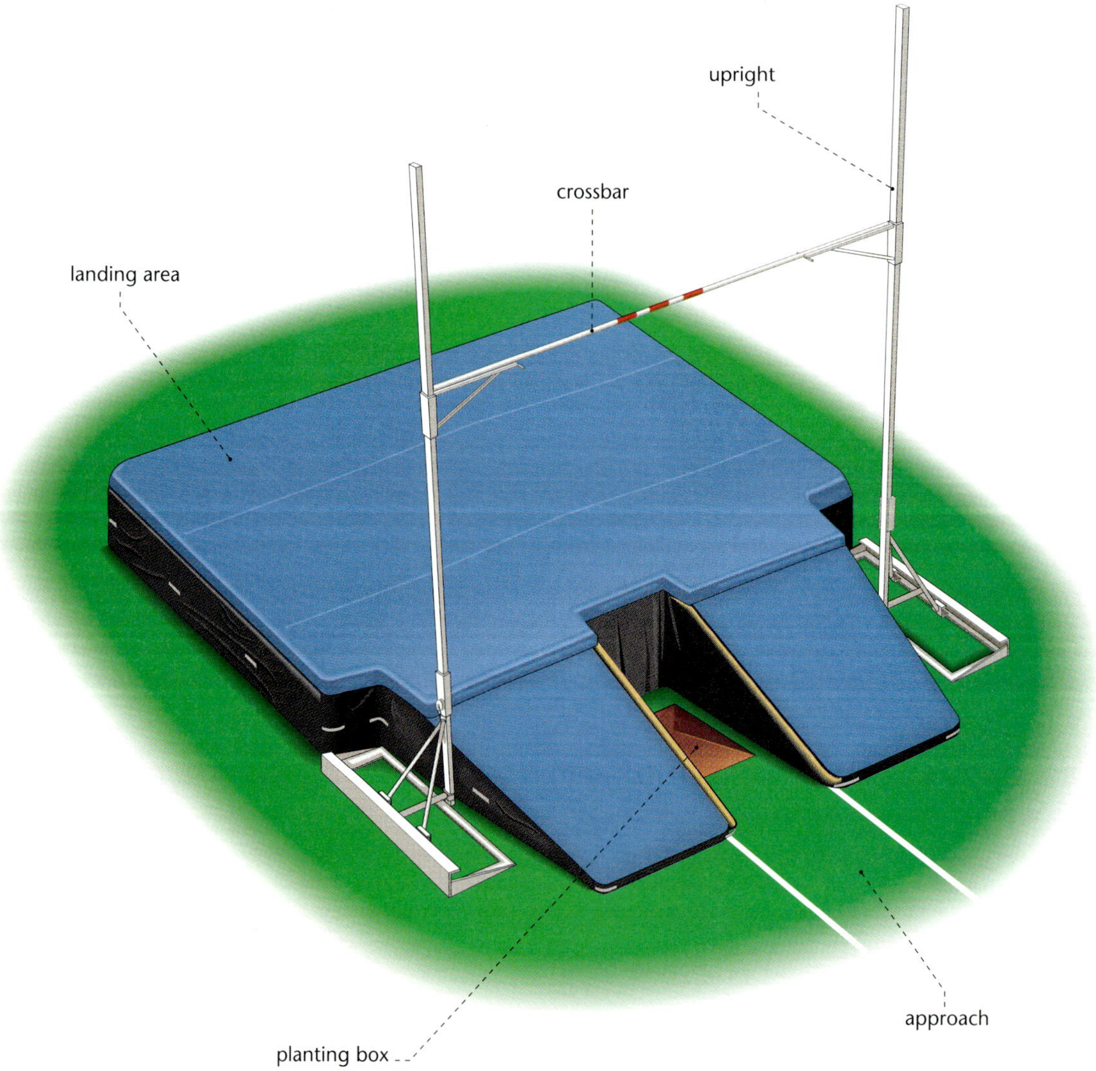

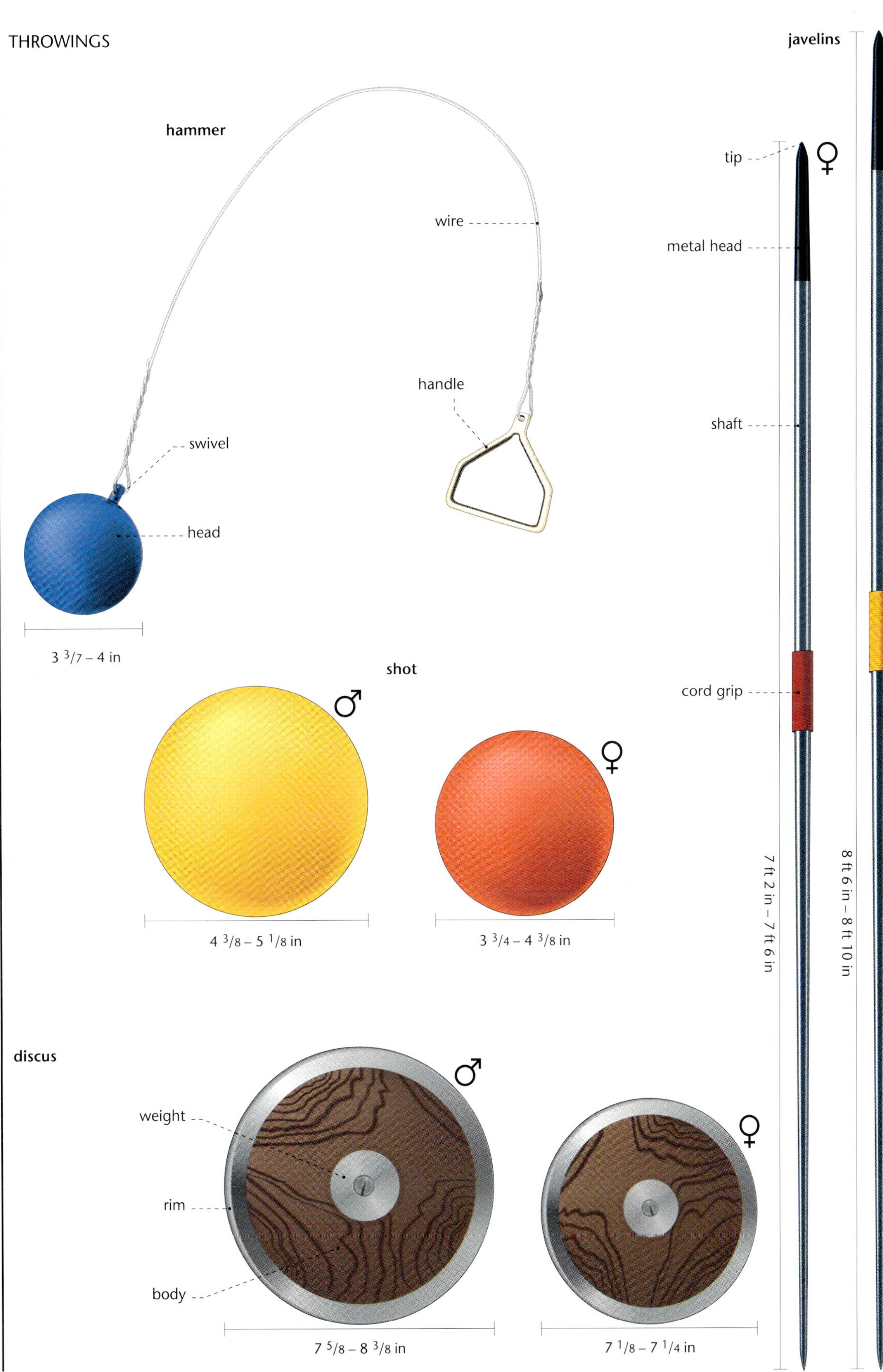
ATHLETICS
THROWINGS
javelins
hammer
wire
handle
tip
metal head
shaft
swivel
head
cord grip
3 3/7 – 4 in
shot
4 3/8 – 5 1/8 in
3 3/4 – 4 3/8 in
7 ft 2 in – 7 ft 6 in
8 ft 6 in – 8 ft 10 in
discus
weight
rim
body
7 5/8 – 8 3/8 in
7 1/8 – 7 1/4 in

vaulting horse
ASYMMETRICAL BARS
top bar
low bar
adjusting tube
springboard
BALANCE BEAM
beam
upright
height adjustment
TRAMPOLINE
safety pad
bed
spring
frame
leg

RINGS

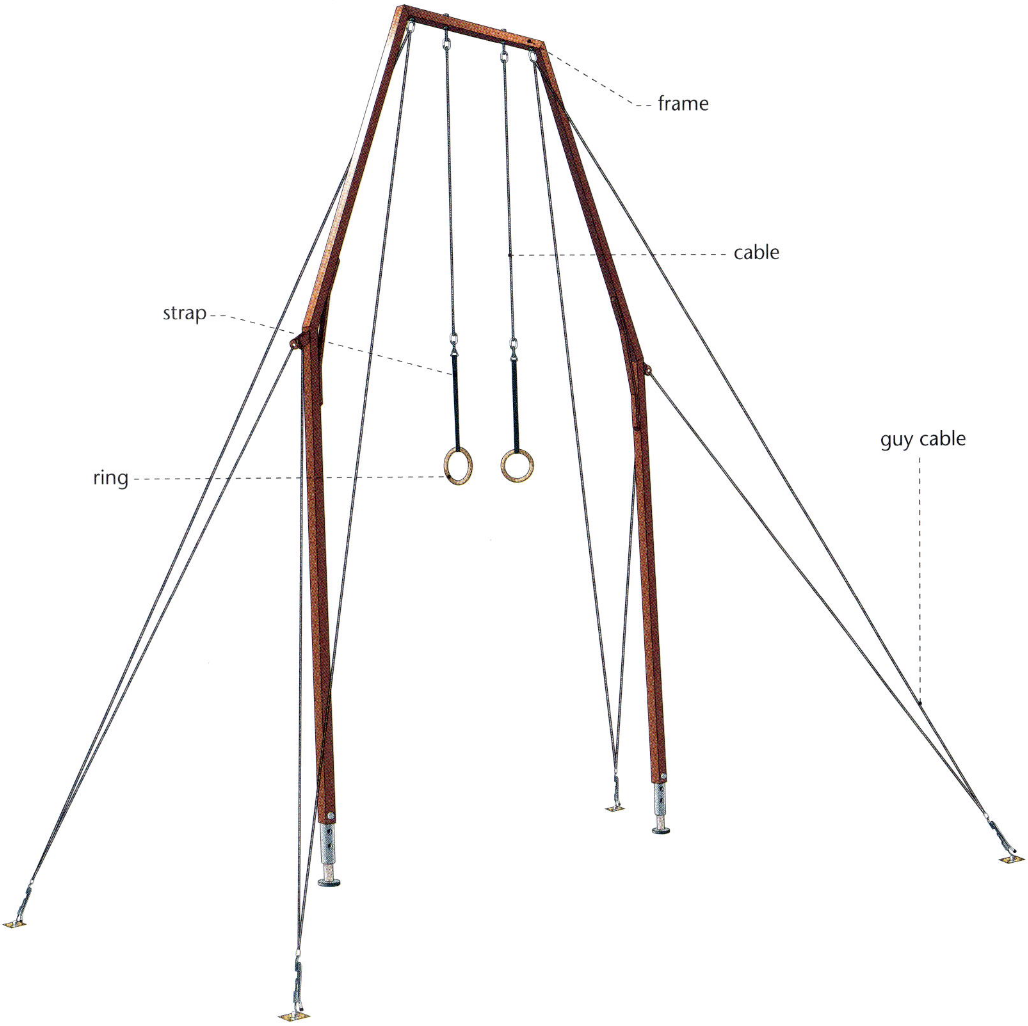

HORIZONTAL BAR

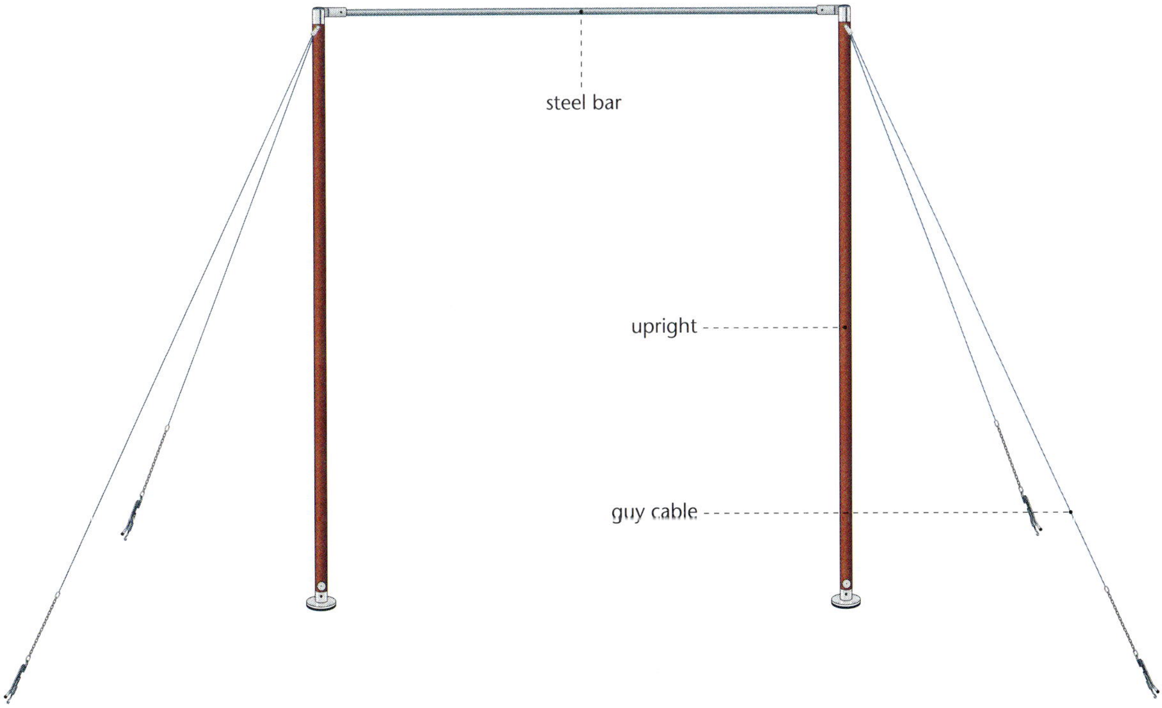

neck
saddle
croup
pommel
height adjustment
chain
upright
anti-slip shoe
tightener
fastening system
horse
base

ATHLETICS

wooden bar
adjusting tube
base

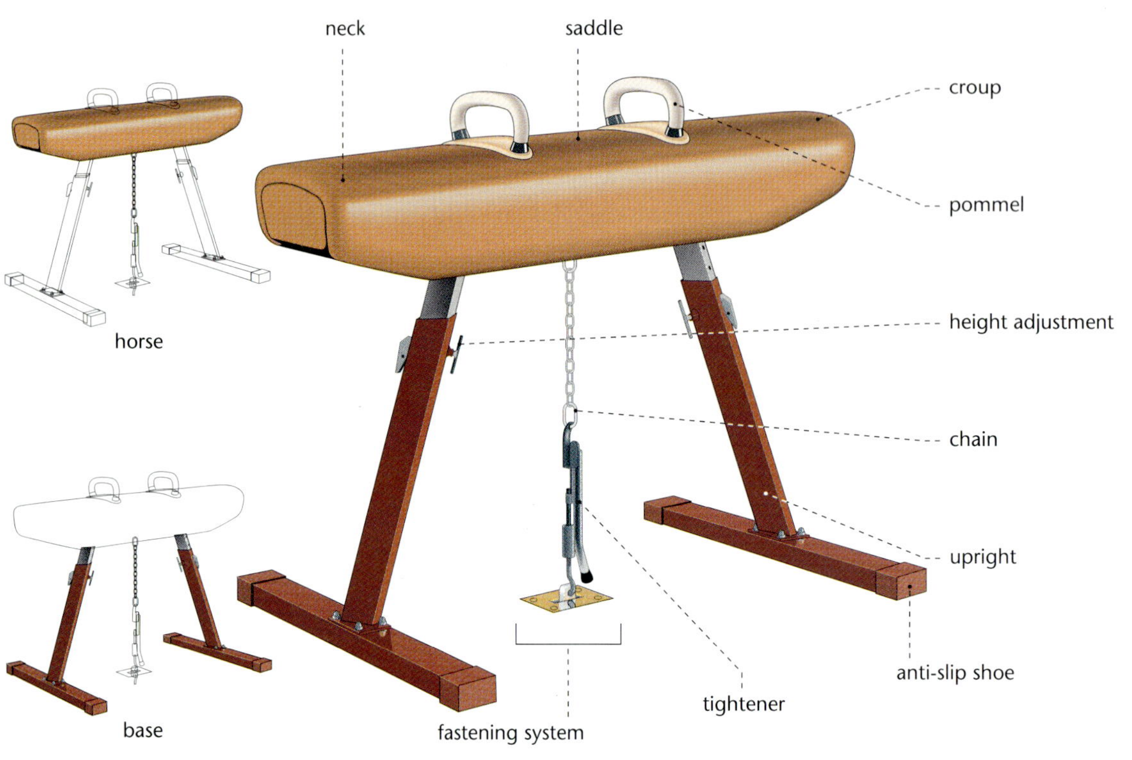

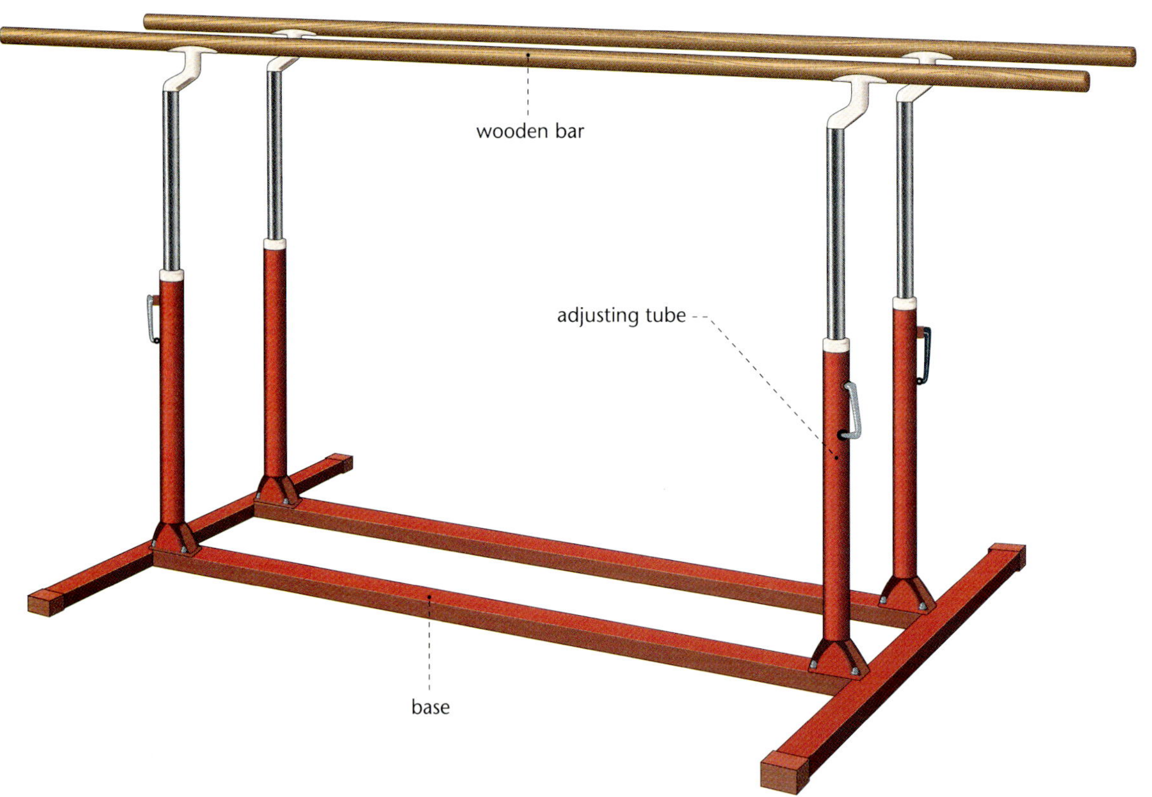

WEIGHTLIFTING

WEIGHTLIFTER

TWO-HAND SNATCH

TWO-HAND CLEAN AND JERK

WEIGHT STACK EXERCISE UNIT

ATHLETICS

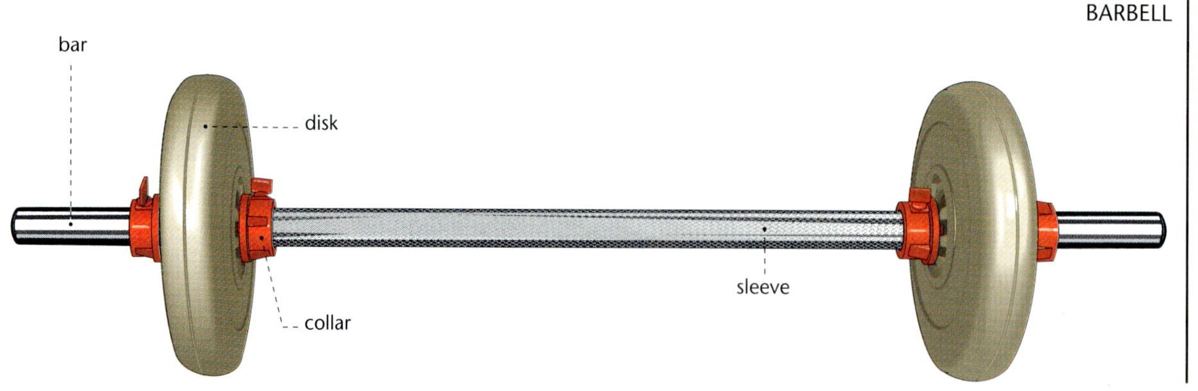

ATHLETICS

STATIONARY BICYCLE
resistance adjustment
handlebar
seat
timer
speedometer
height adjustment
climber
footstrap
pedal
brake
flywheel
ROWER
oar
push-up stand
hydraulic resistance
foot support
free-rolling seat

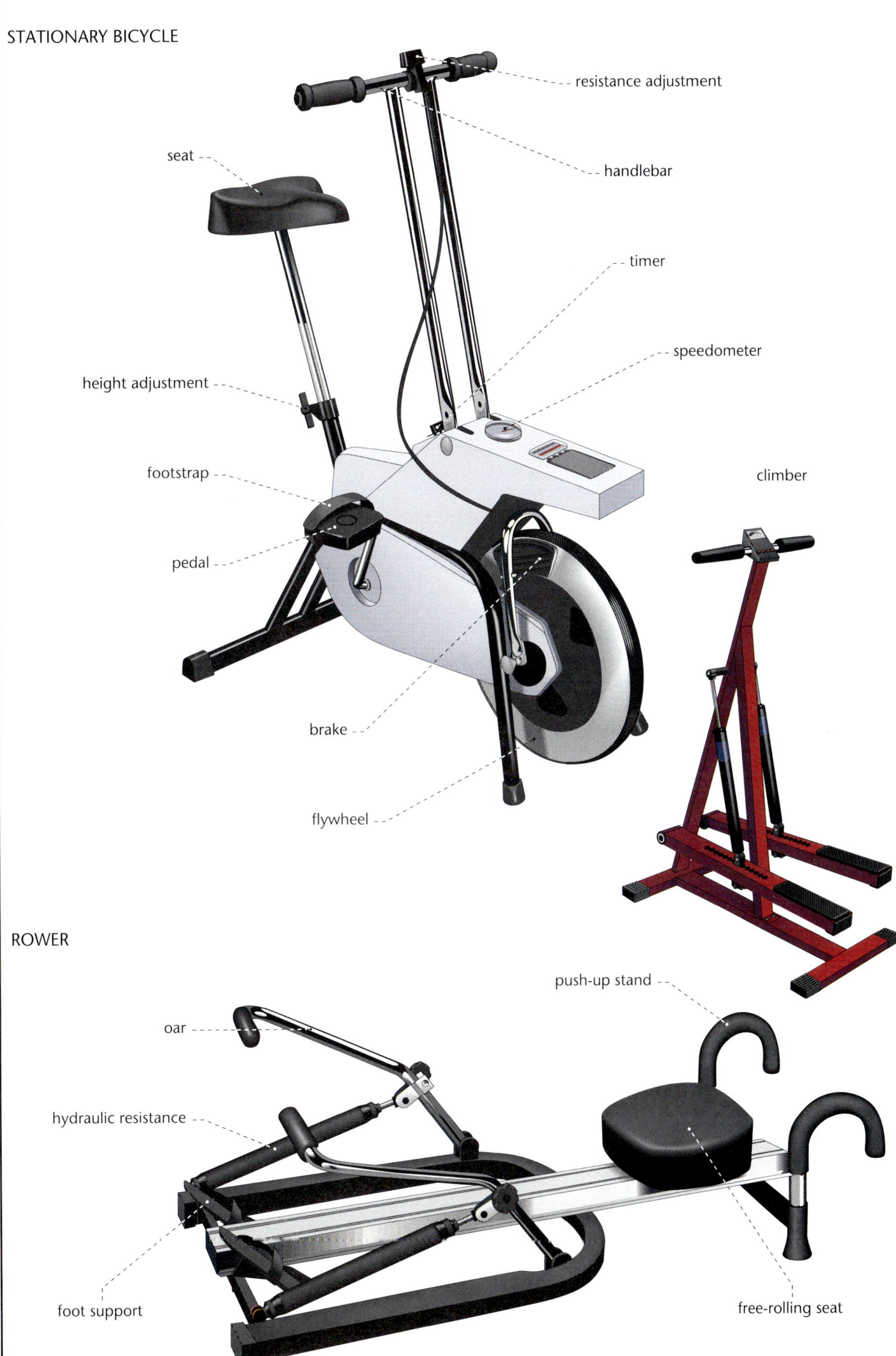

DUMBBELL
weight
bar
handgrips
ankle/wrist weight
jump rope
TWIST BAR
grip
tension spring
chest expander

PARTS OF THE WEAPON

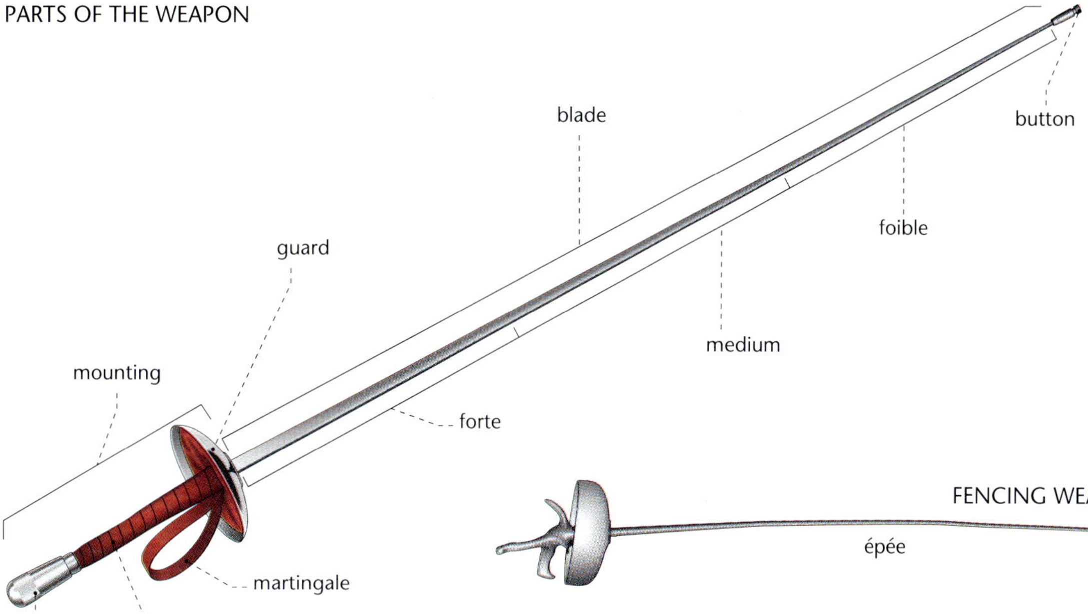

blade

button

foible

guard

medium

mounting

forte

FENCING WEAPONS

épée

martingale

handle

foil

pommel

saber

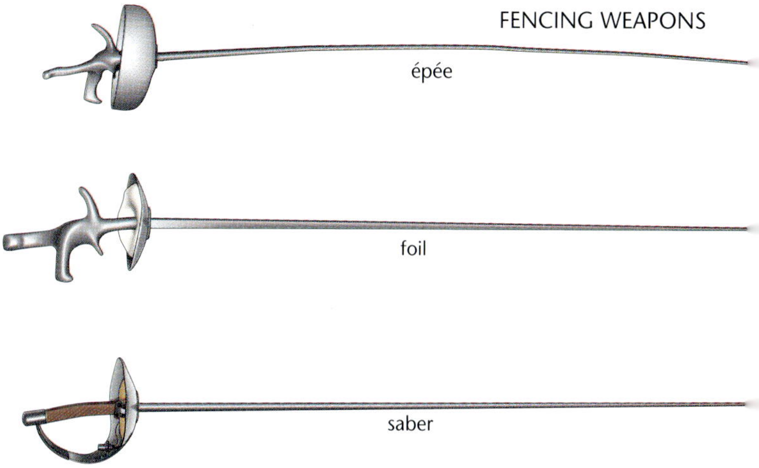

PISTE

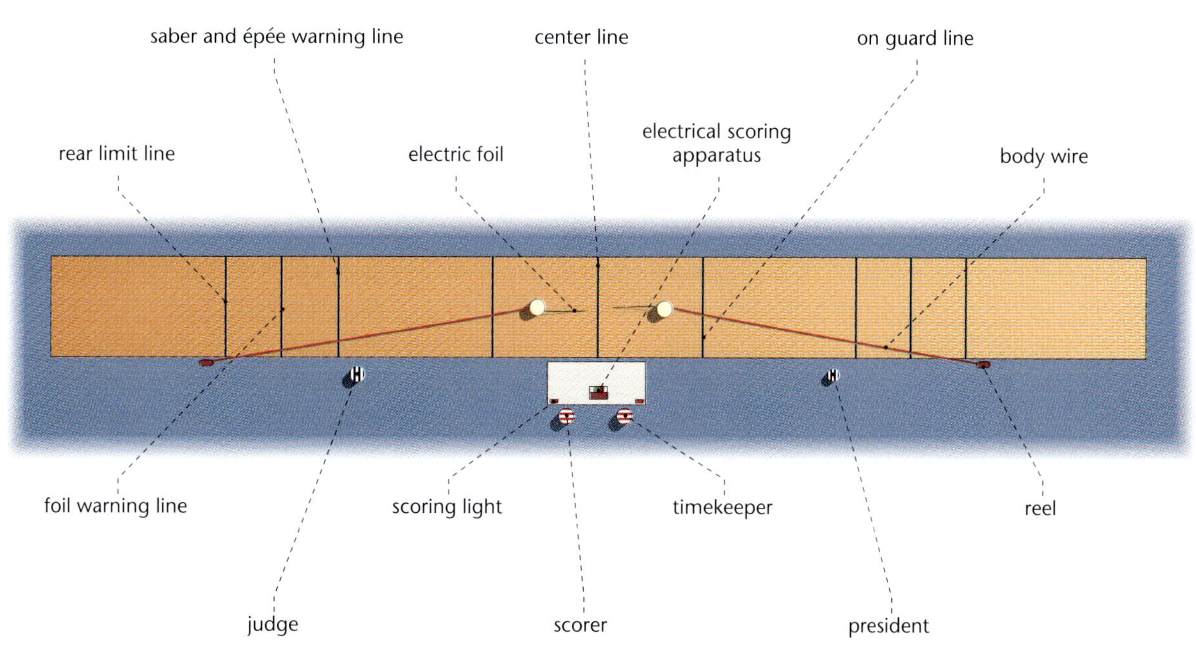

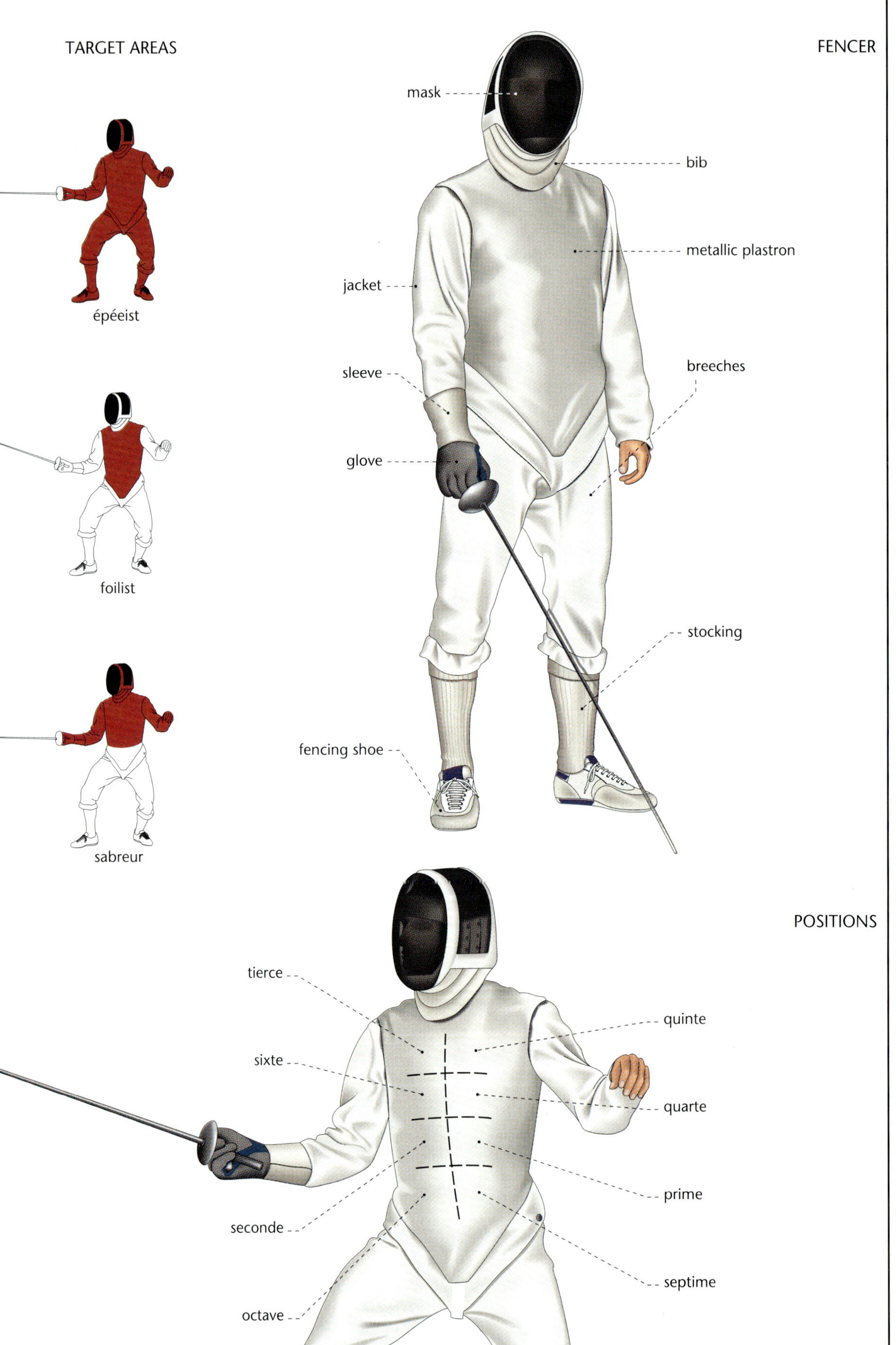

TARGET AREAS

épéeist

foilist

sabreur

FENCER

mask

bib

metallic plastron

jacket

breeches

sleeve

glove

stocking

fencing shoe

POSITIONS

tierce

quinte

sixte

quarte

prime

seconde

septime

octave

JUDO

JUDO SUIT

EXAMPLES OF HOLDS

arm lock

holding

major outer reaping throw

one-arm shoulder throw

major inner reaping throw

naked strangle

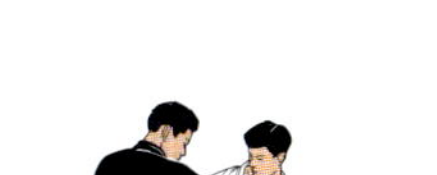

stomach throw

sweeping hip throw

MAT

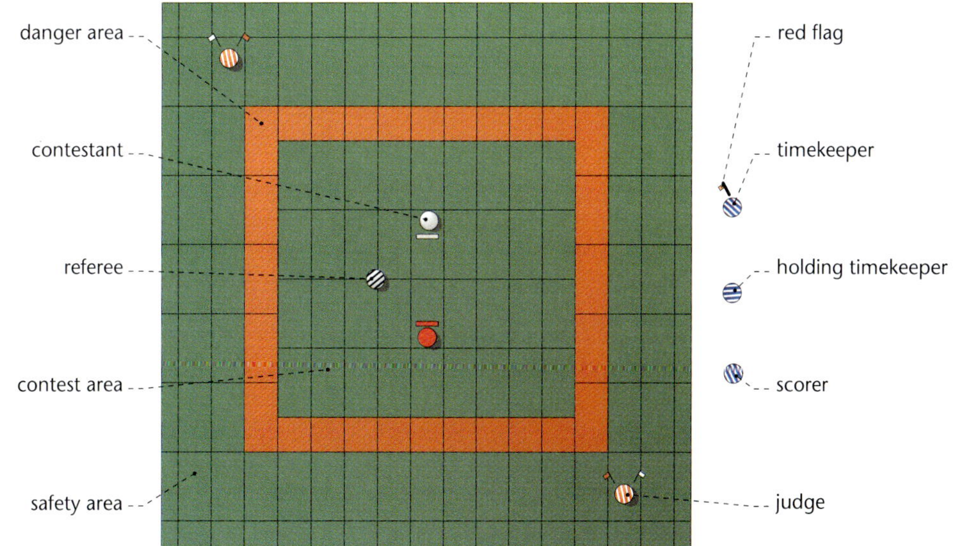

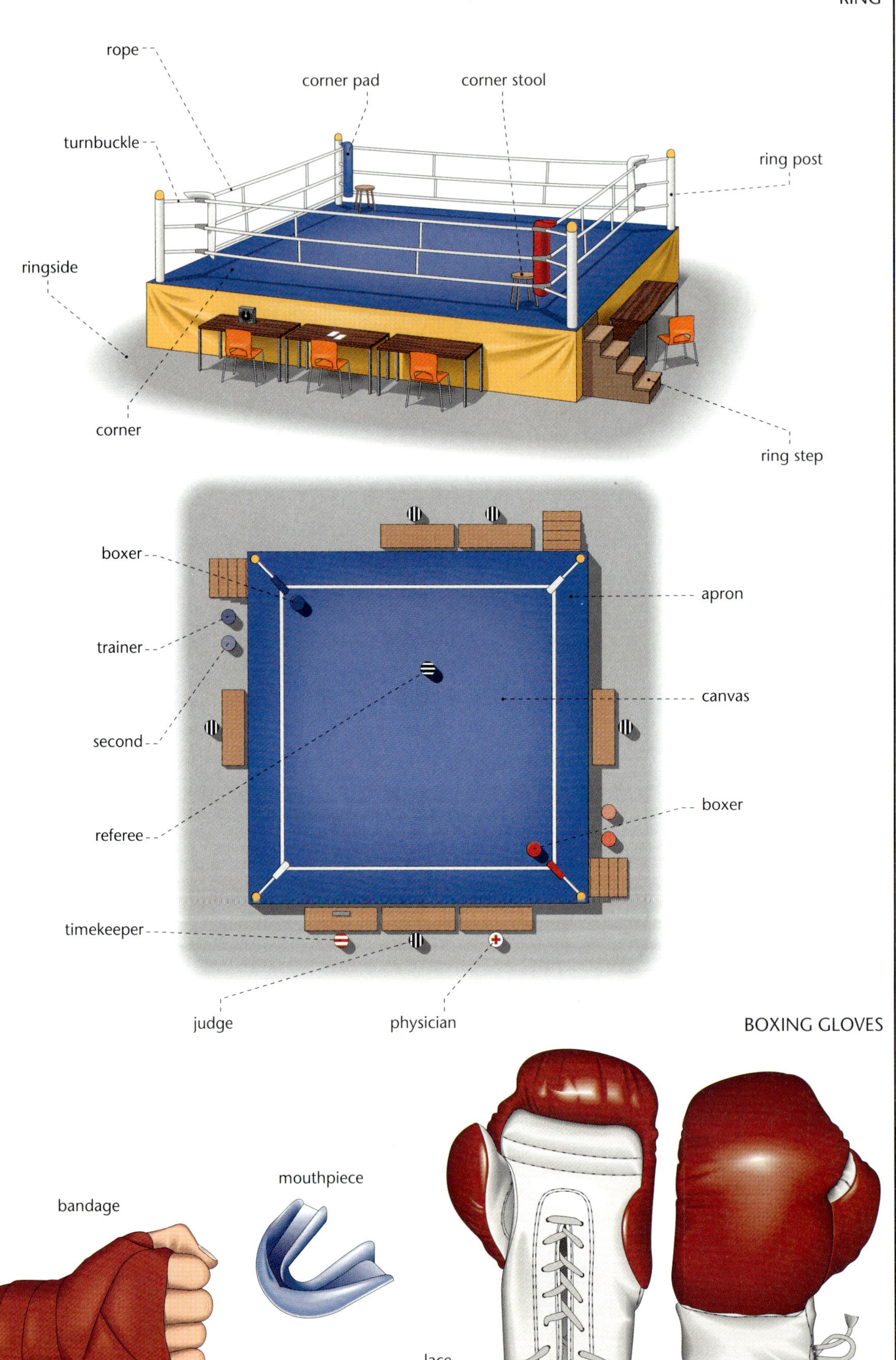
RING
rope
corner pad
corner stool
turnbuckle
ring post
ringside
corner
ring step
boxer
apron
trainer
second
canvas
referee
boxer
timekeeper
judge
physician
bandage
mouthpiece
BOXING GLOVES
lace
14 OZ

FLY ROD

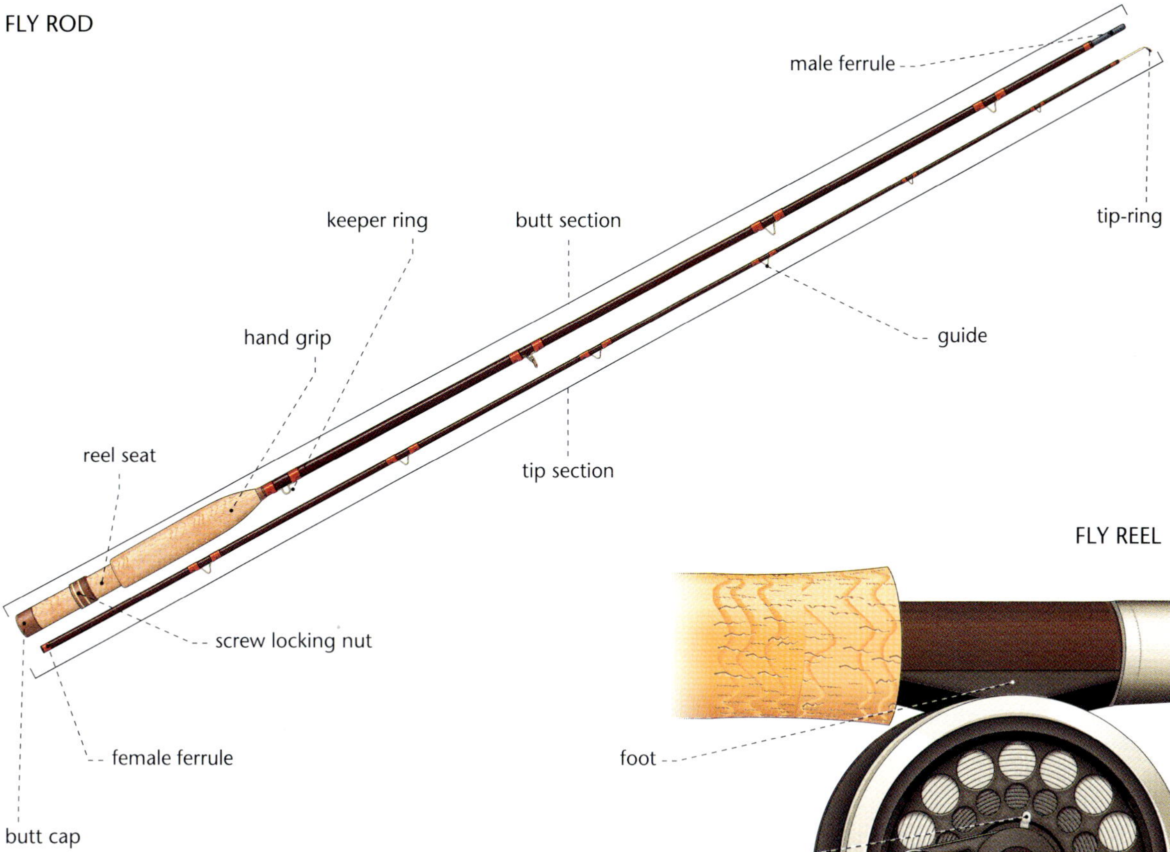

male ferrule
keeper ring
butt section
tip-ring
hand grip
guide
reel seat
tip section
screw locking nut
female ferrule
butt cap

FLY REEL

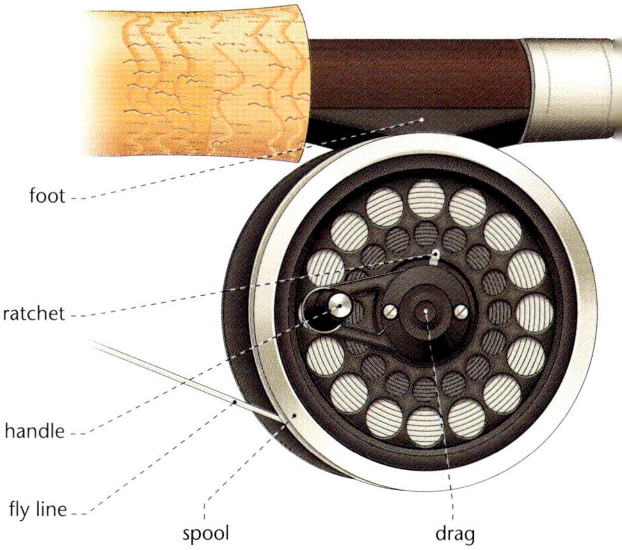

foot
ratchet
handle
fly line
spool
drag

ARTIFICIAL FLY

veil
wing
topping
cheek
tail
shoulder
tip
head
butt
hackle
fishhook
body
ribbing
joint

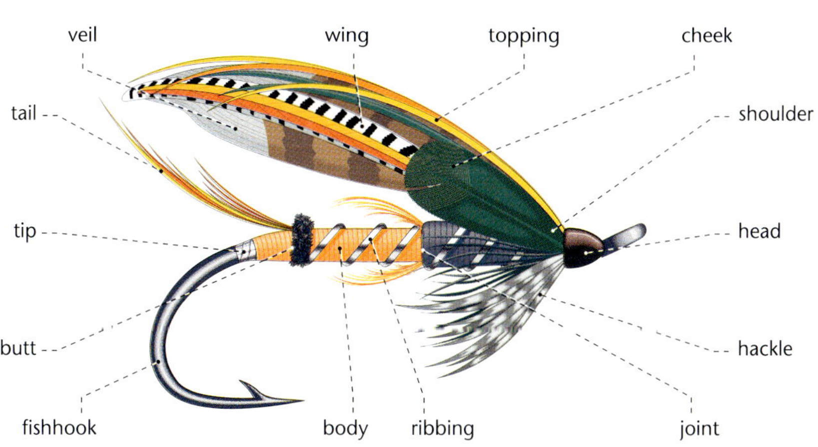

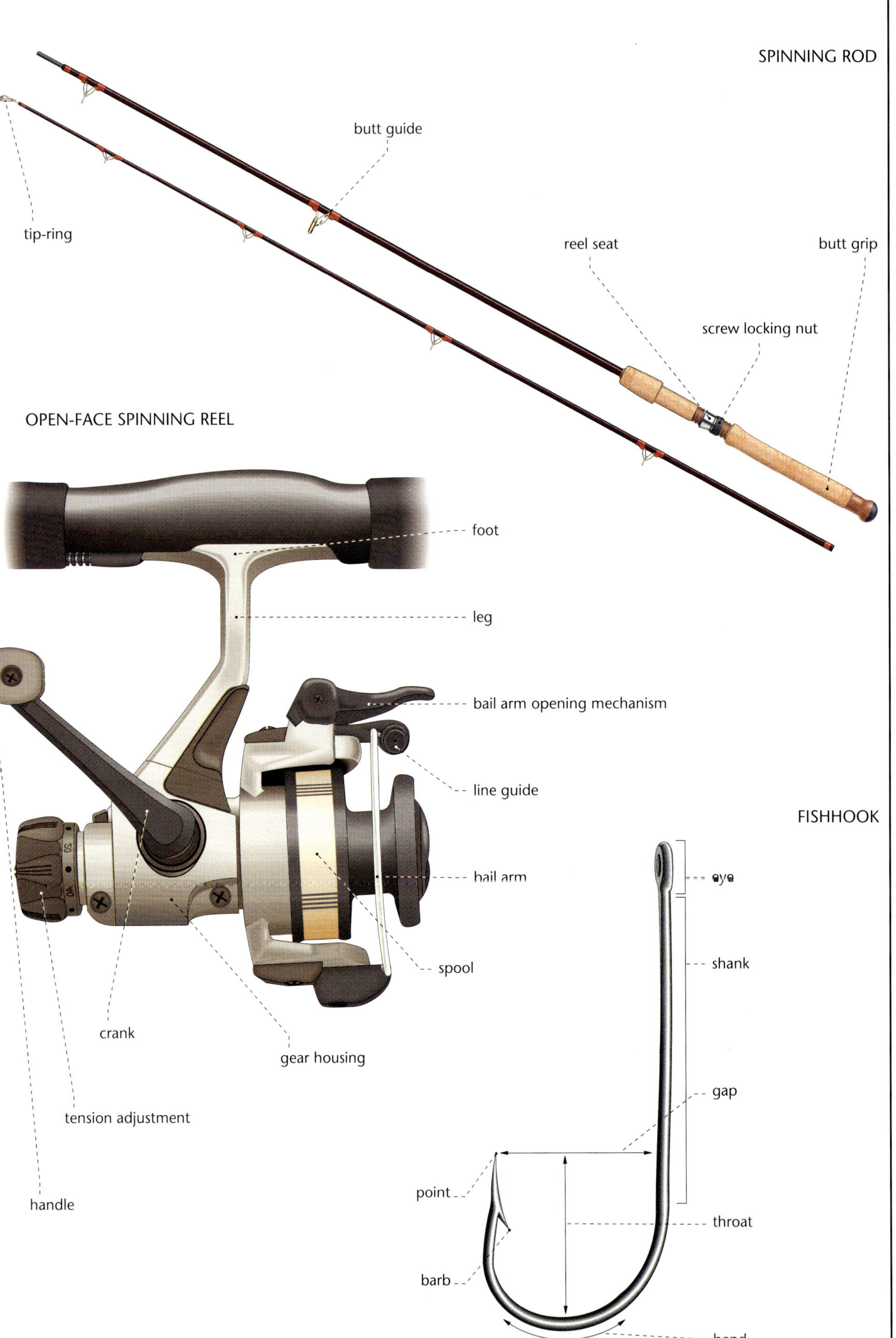

SPINNING ROD
butt guide
tip-ring
reel seat
butt grip
screw locking nut
OPEN-FACE SPINNING REEL
foot
leg
bail arm opening mechanism
line guide
bail arm
spool
crank
gear housing
tension adjustment
handle
FISHHOOK
eye
shank
gap
throat
point
barb
bend

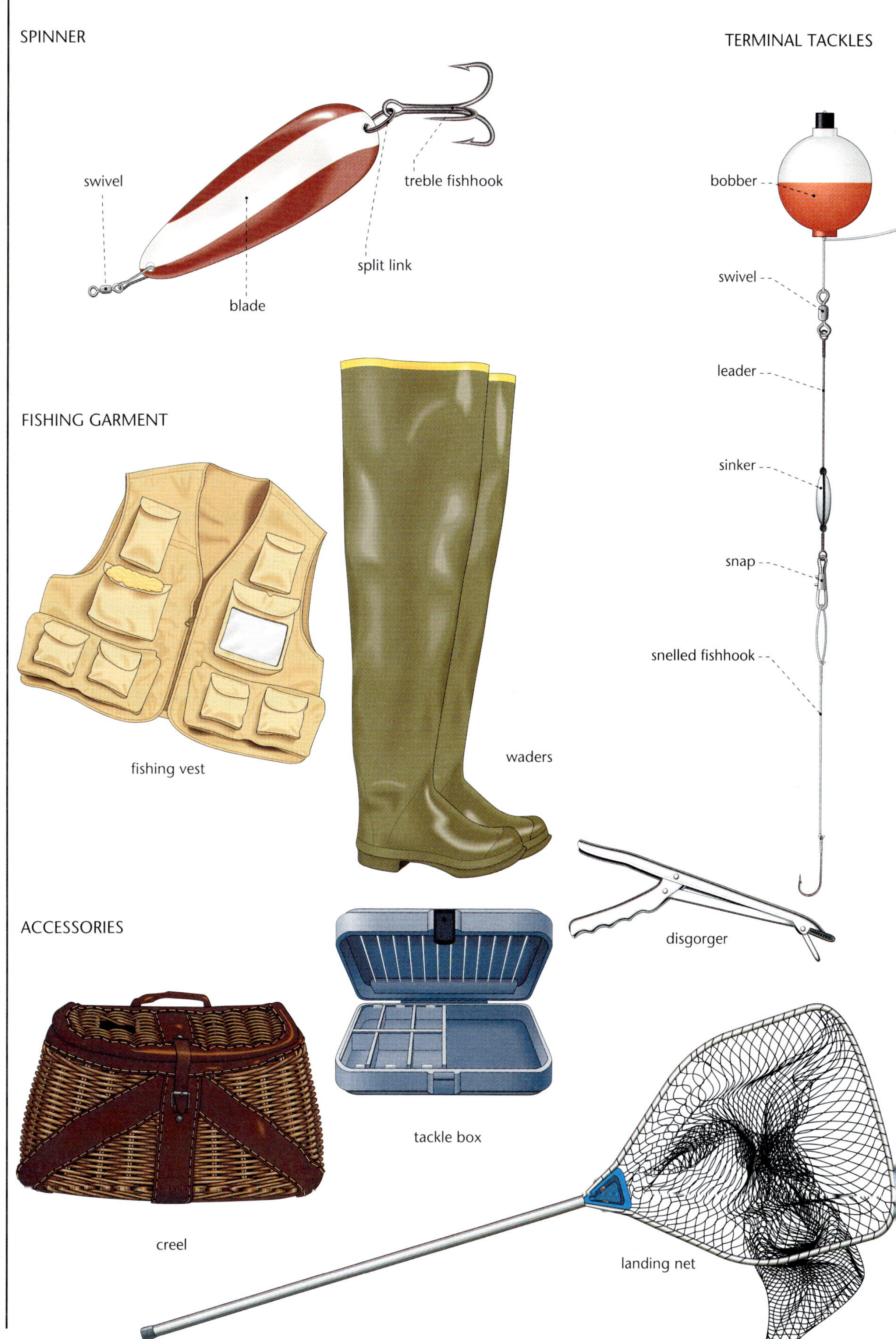

SPINNER
TERMINAL TACKLES
swivel
treble fishhook
split link
blade
bobber
swivel
leader
sinker
snap
snelled fishhook
FISHING GARMENT
fishing vest
waders
disgorger
ACCESSORIES
creel
tackle box
landing net
LEISURE SPORTS

BILLIARDS

CAROM BILLIARDS

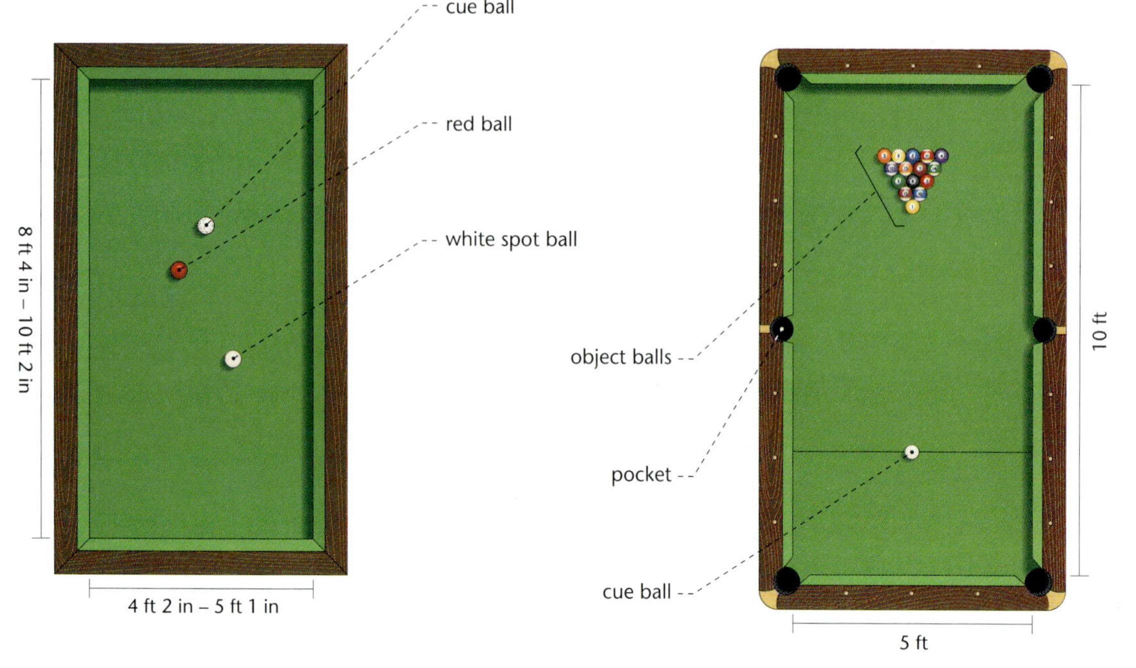

POOL

ENGLISH BILLIARDS

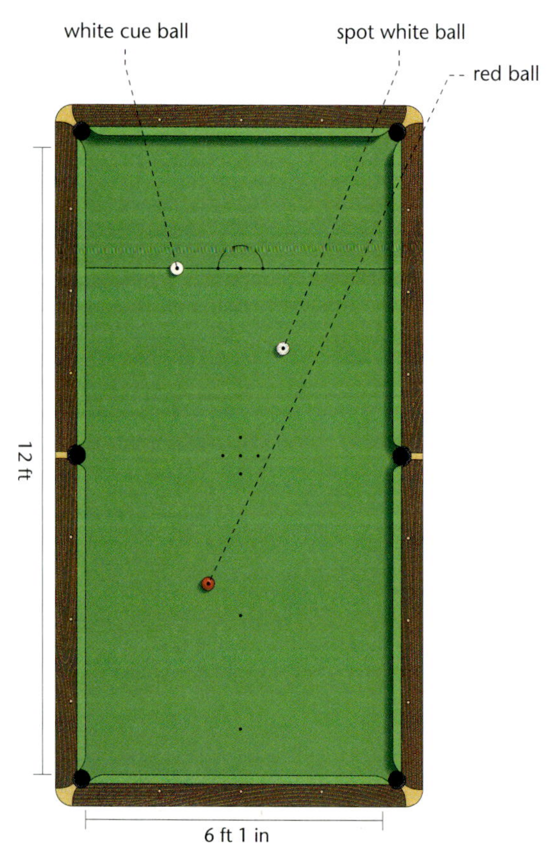

SNOOKER

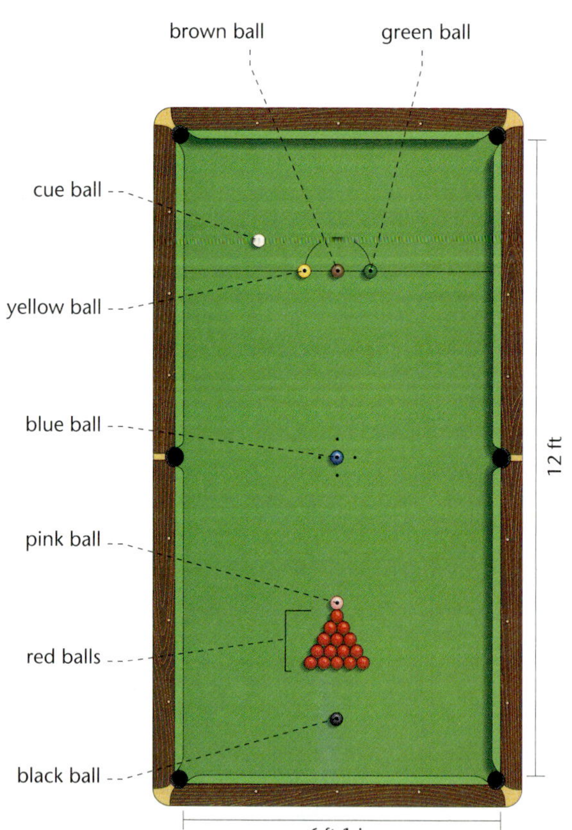

TABLE

BRIDGE

baize
pyramid spot
billiard spot
foot cushion
bottom pocket
rail
chalk
BILLIARDS CUE
tip
ferrule
shaft
joint
butt
675
LEISURE SPORTS

COURSE

hole
clubhouse
cart path
practice green
putting green
fairway
rough
bunker
trees
water hazard
teeing ground
brook
GOLF

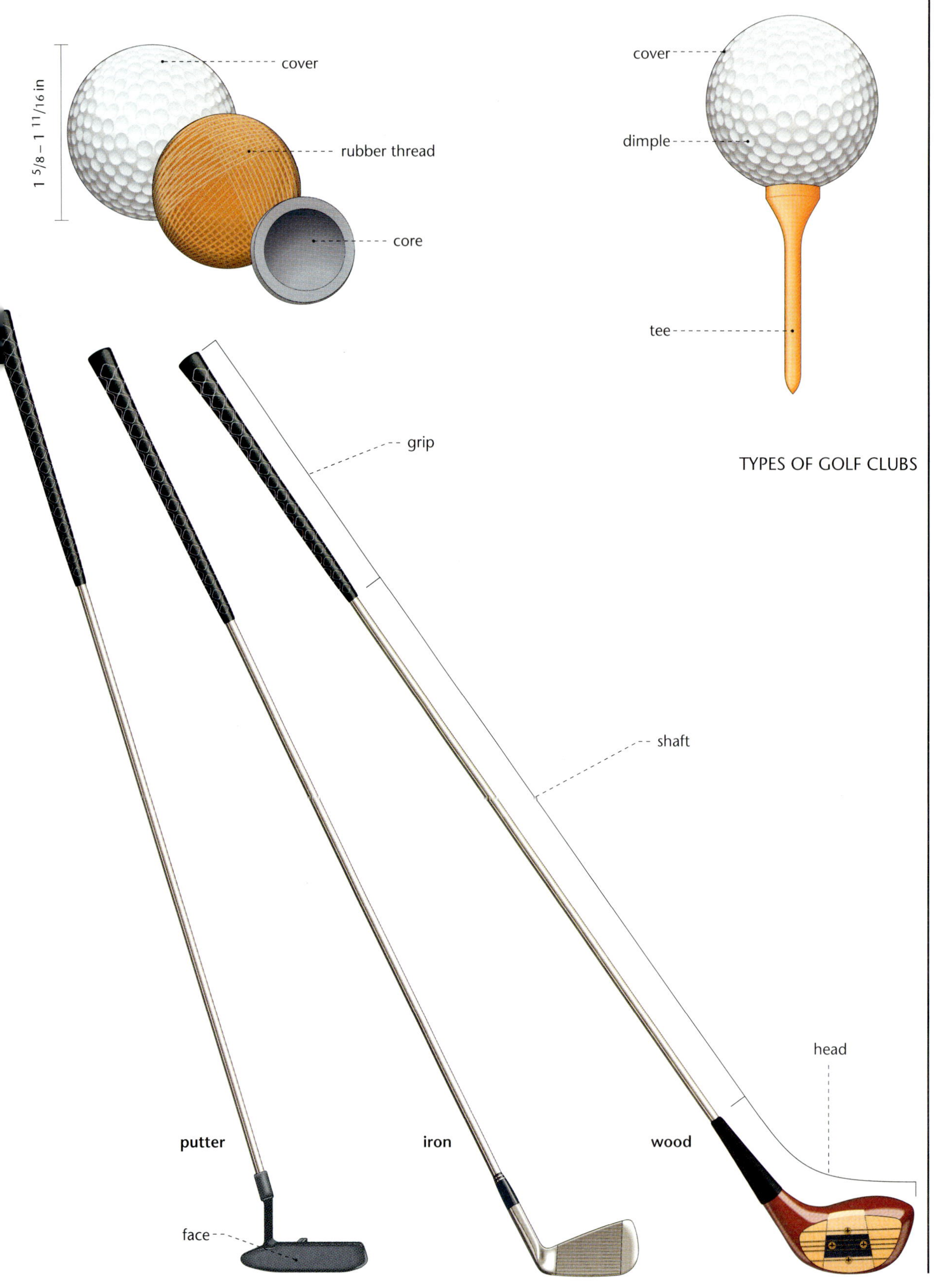

TYPES OF GOLF CLUBS

LEISURE SPORTS

WOOD

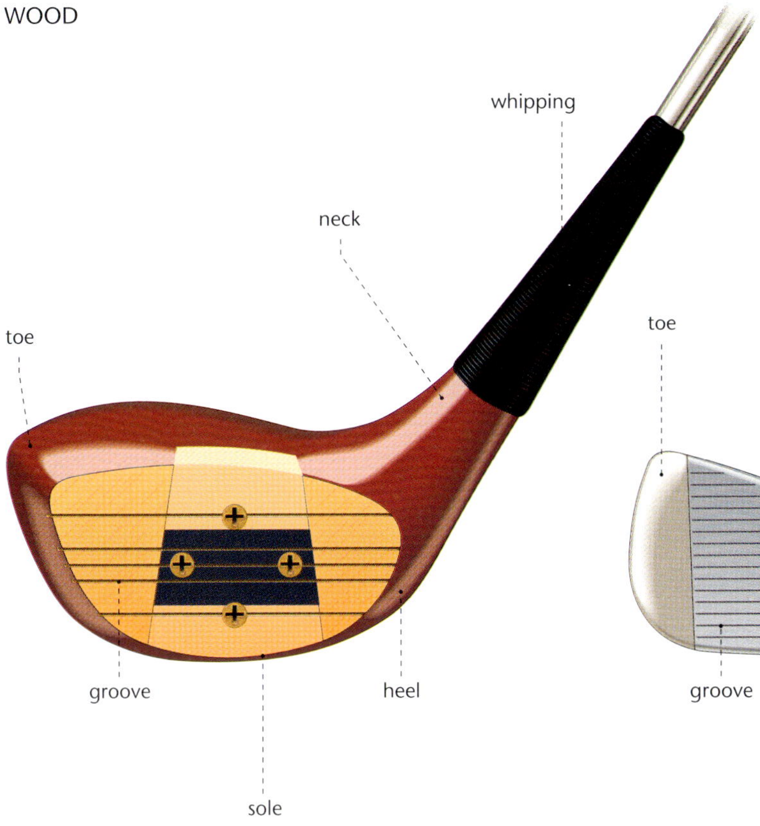

IRON

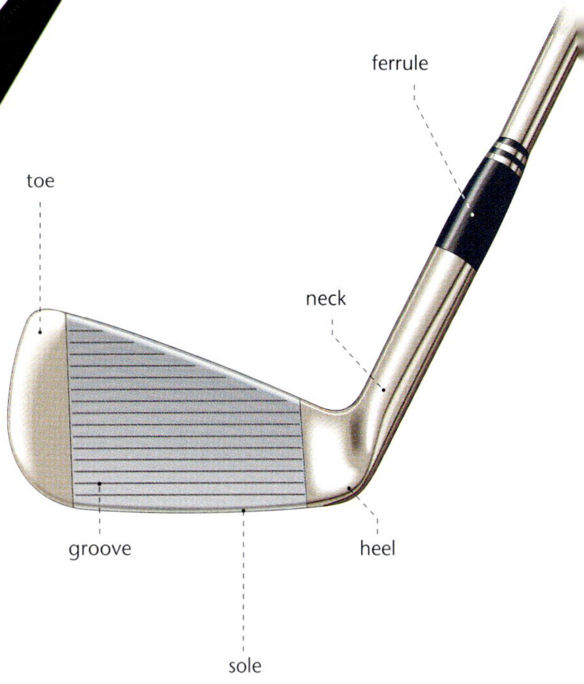

whipping

neck

toe

ferrule

toe

neck

groove

heel

groove

heel

sole

sole

GOLF CLUBS

driver

no. 3 wood

no. 5 wood

no. 3 iron

no. 4 iron

no. 5 iron

no. 6 iron

no. 7 iron

no. 8 iron

no. 9 iron

pitching wedge

sand wedge

putter

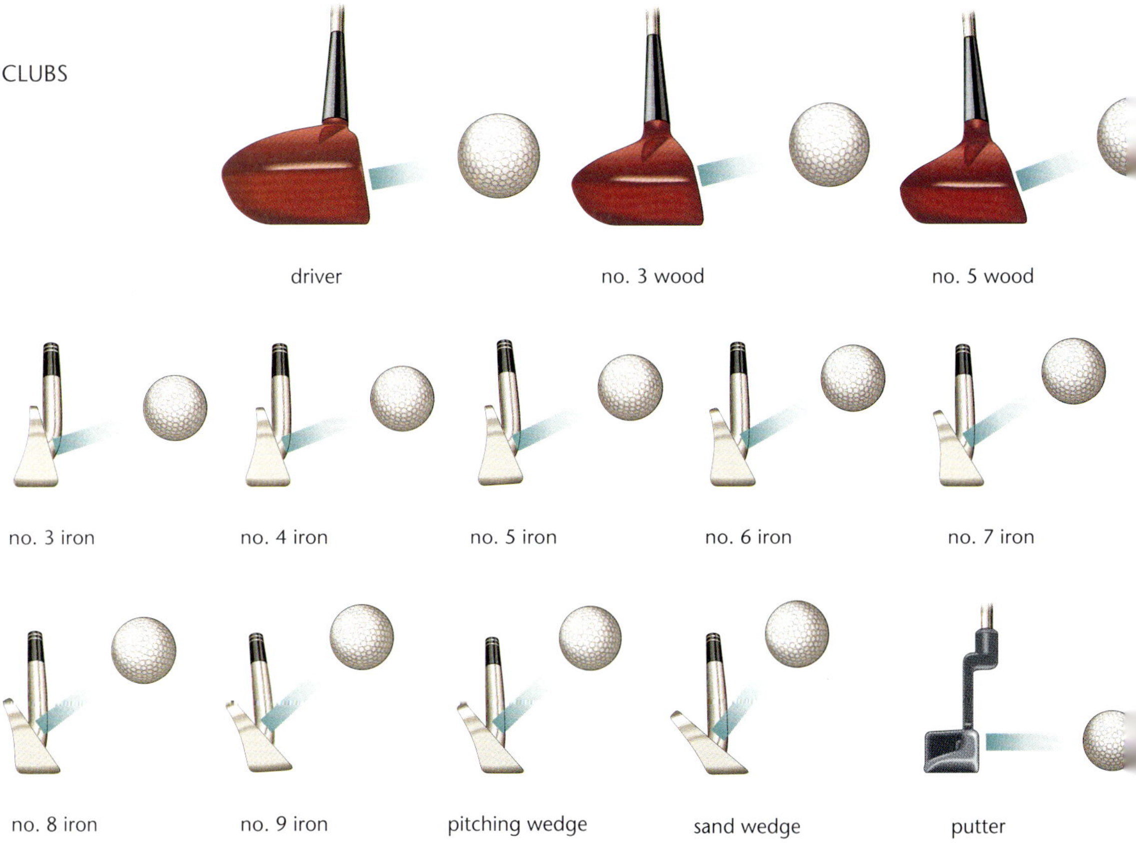

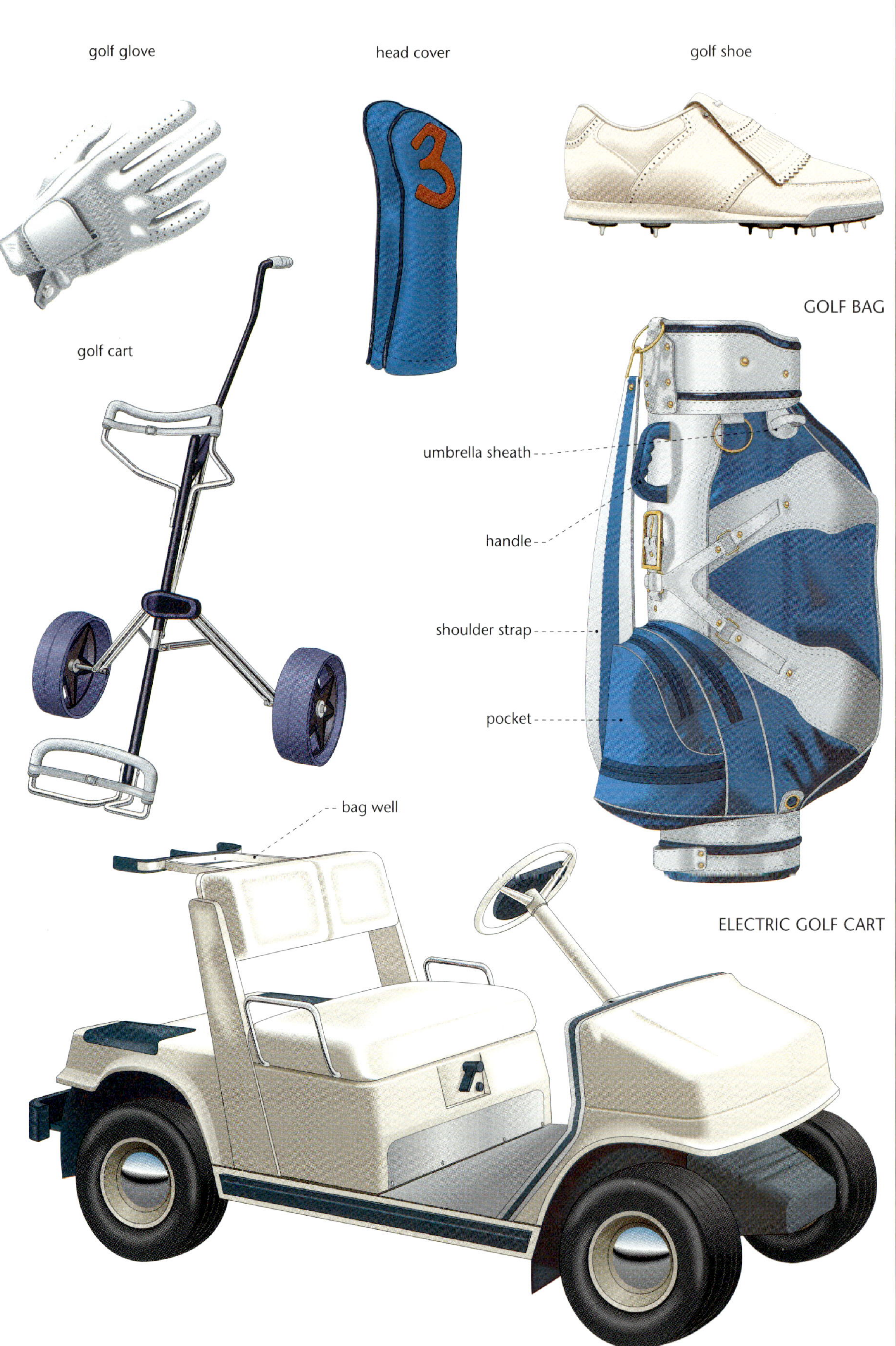

golf glove
head cover
golf shoe
3
golf cart
GOLF BAG
umbrella sheath
handle
shoulder strap
pocket
bag well
ELECTRIC GOLF CART

MOUNTAINEER

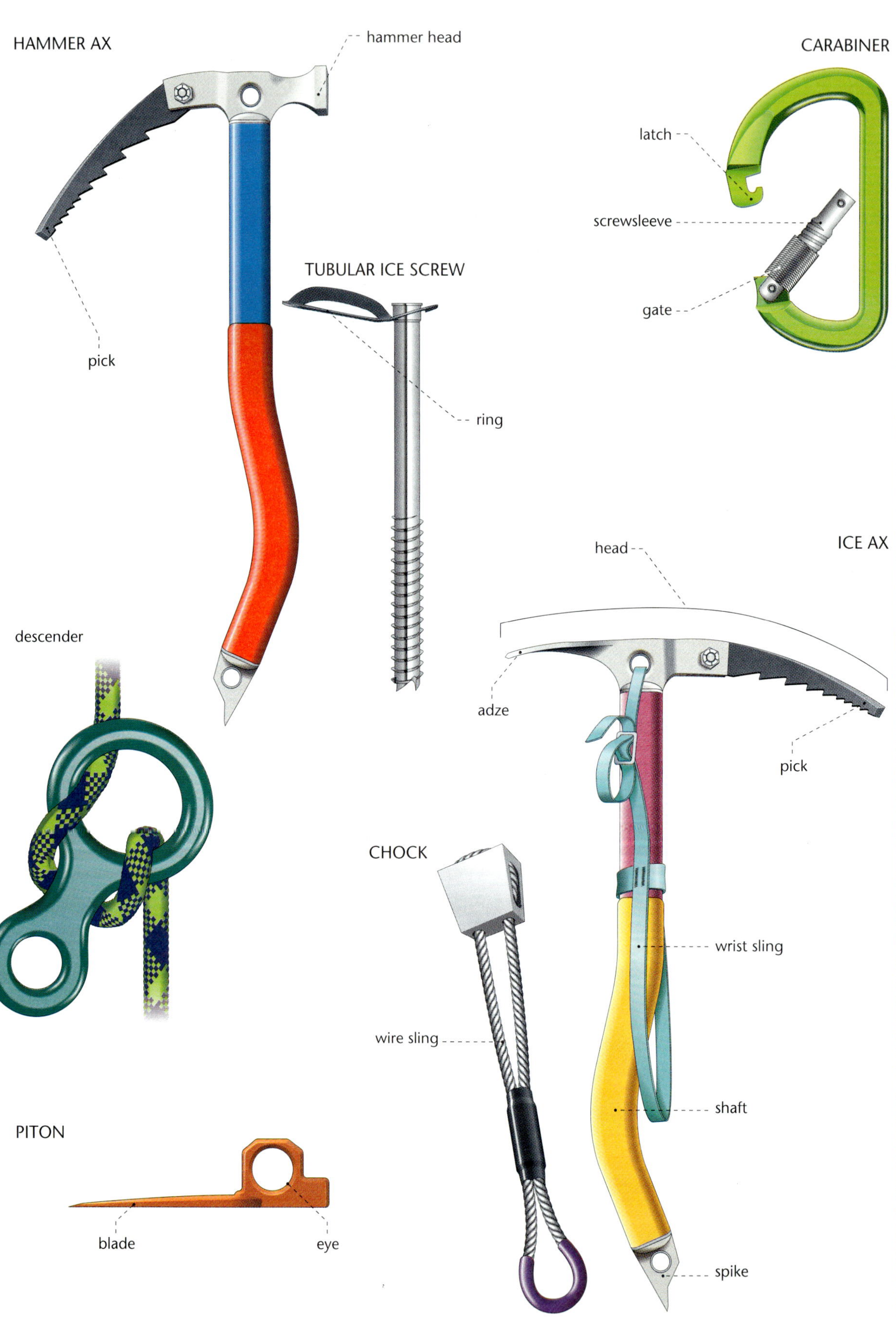

EQUIPMENT
CARABINER
HAMMER AX
hammer head
latch
screwsleeve
gate
pick
TUBULAR ICE SCREW
ring
ICE AX
head
descender
adze
pick
CHOCK
wrist sling
wire sling
shaft
PITON
blade
eye
spike

GREEN

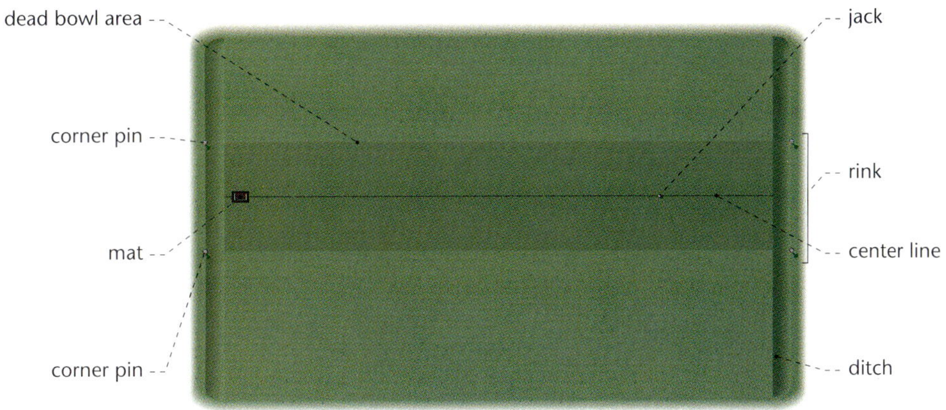

DELIVERY

LEISURE SPORTS

BOWLING

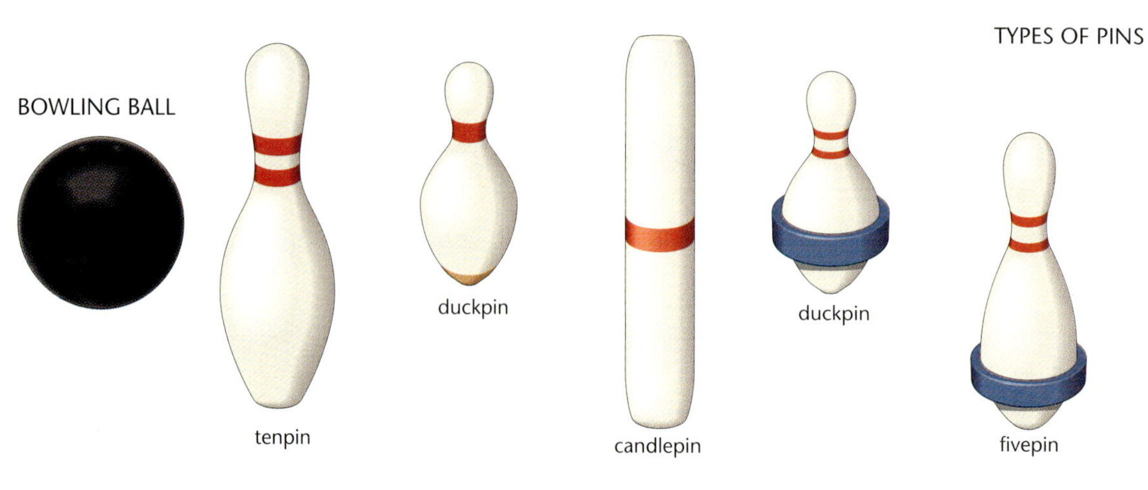

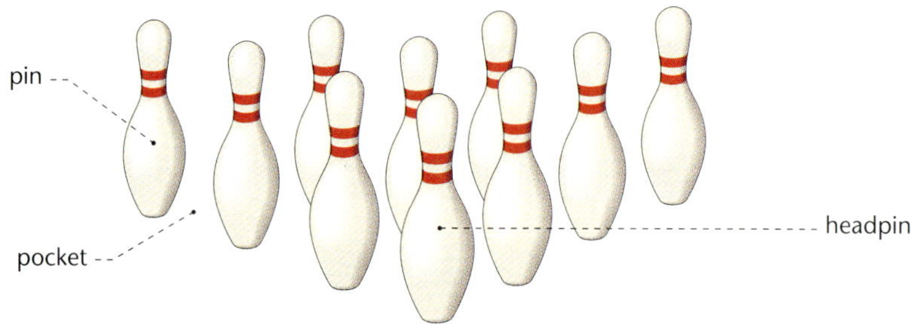

LEISURE SPORTS

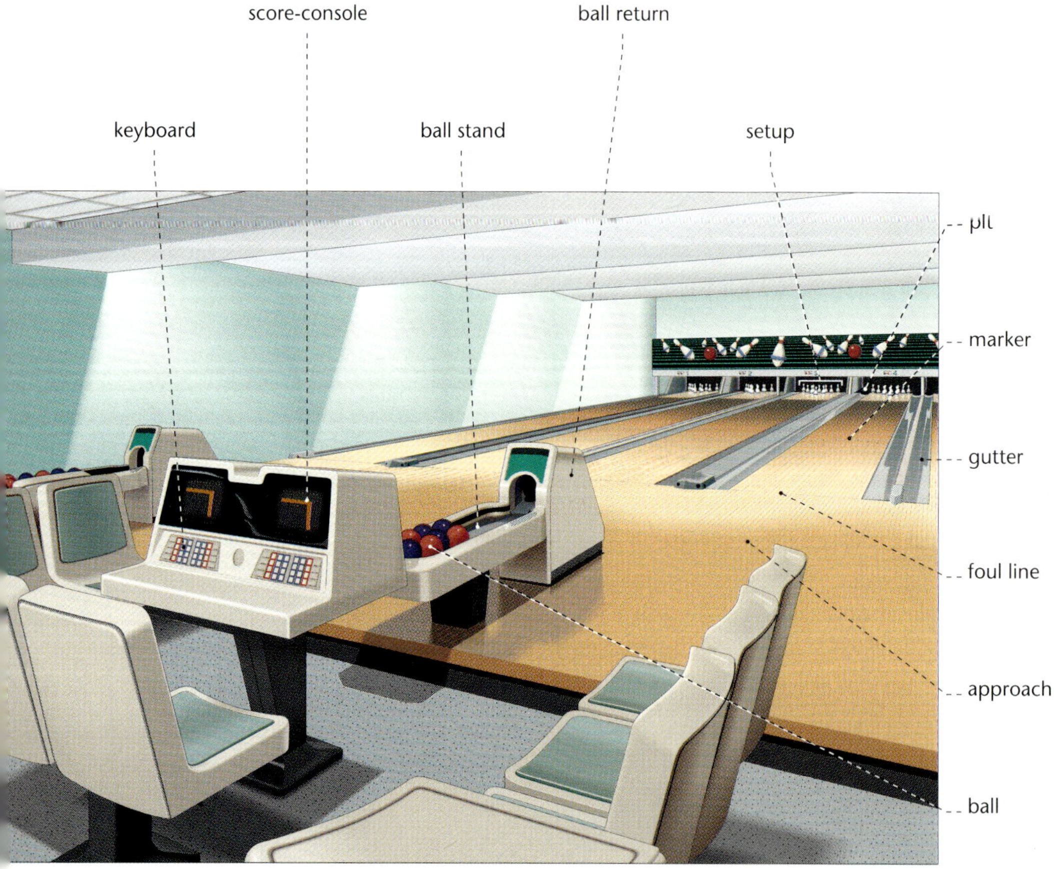

ARCHERY

ARROW

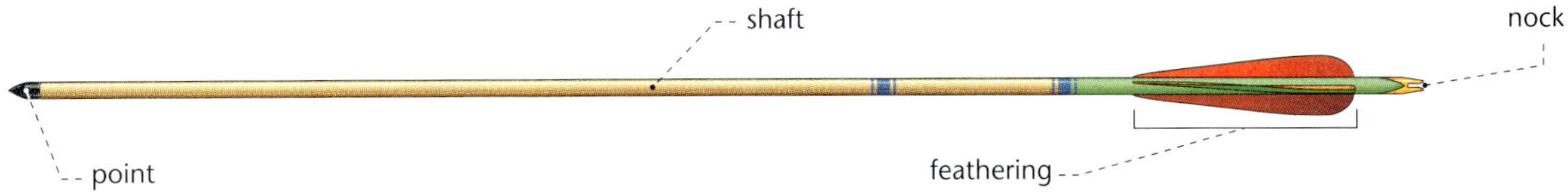

ARCHER

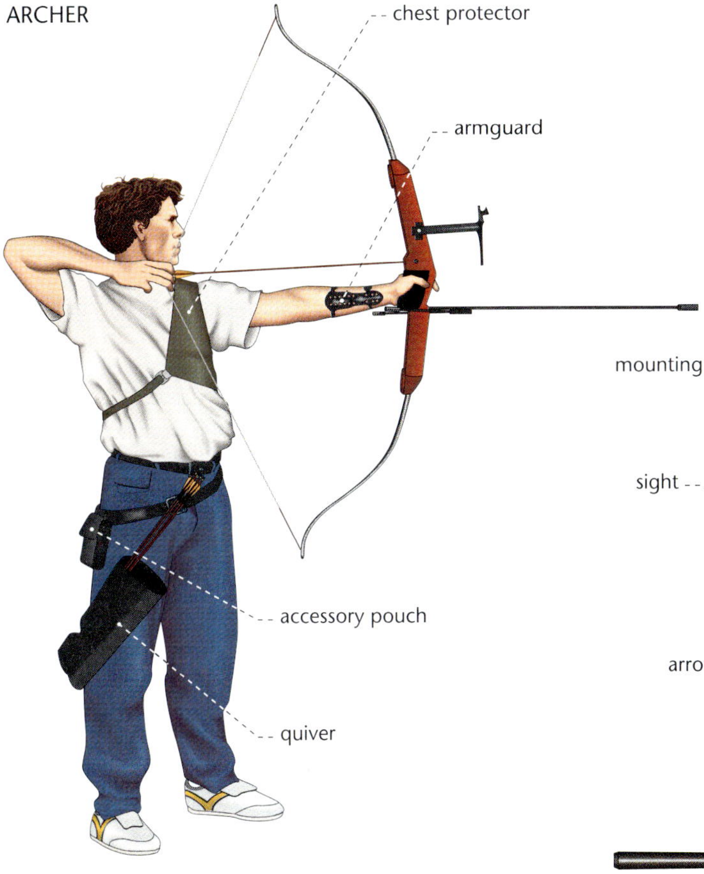

COMPOUND BOW

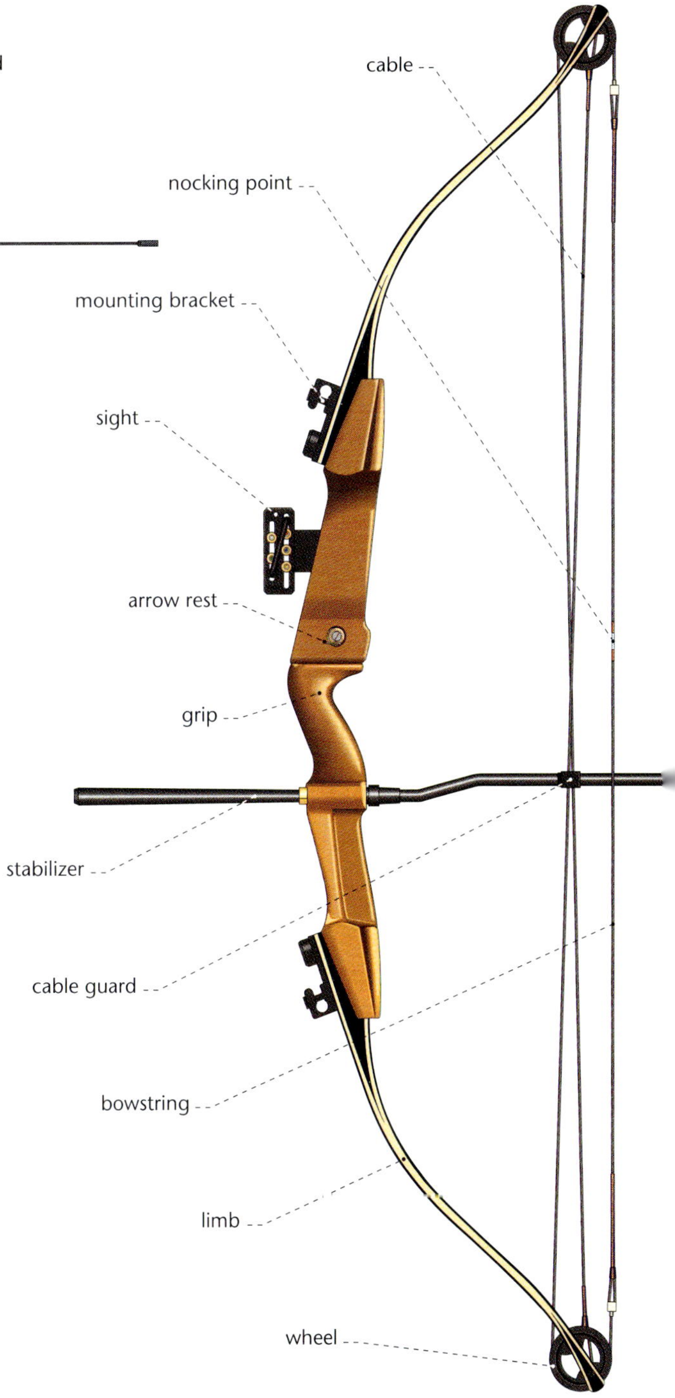

TARGET

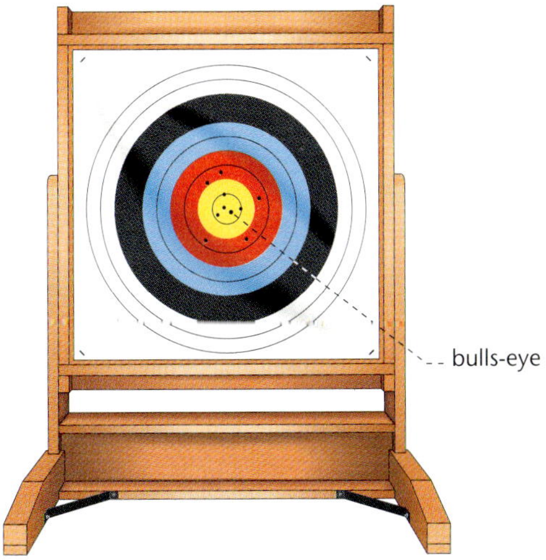

LEISURE SPORTS

TWO-PERSON TENT

FAMILY TENT

PUP TENT

MAJOR TYPES OF TENTS

wall tent

wagon tent

one-person tent

dome tent

pop-up tent

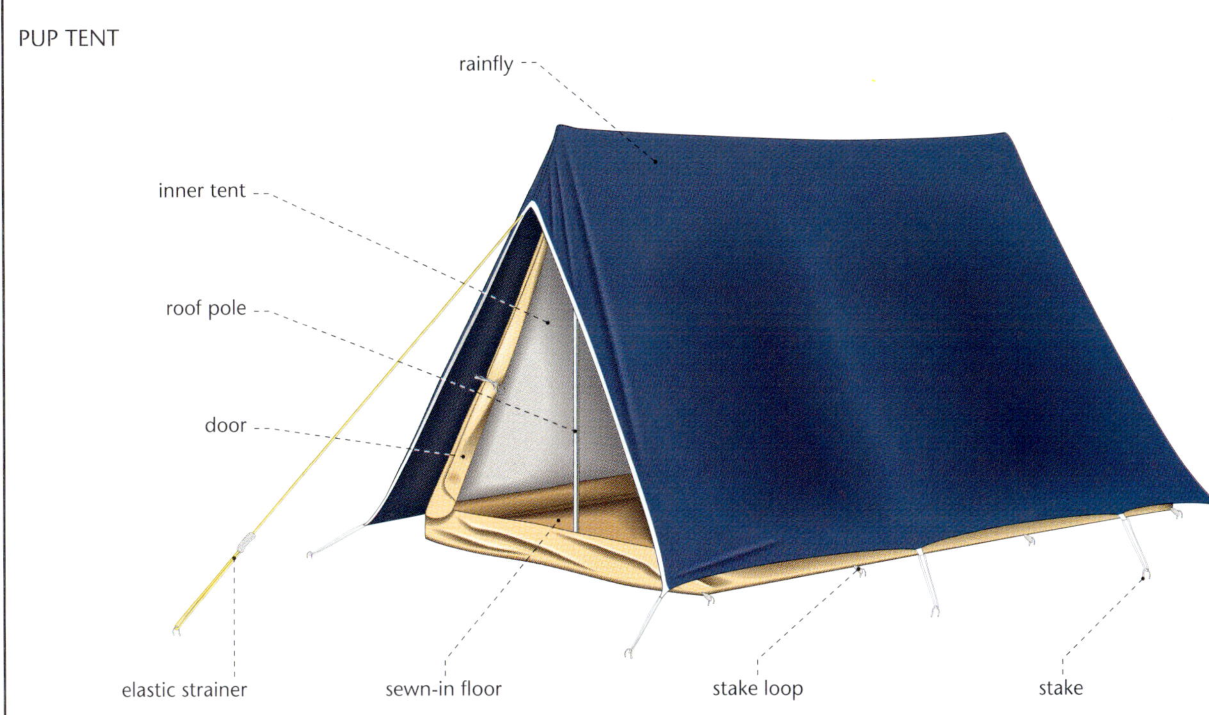

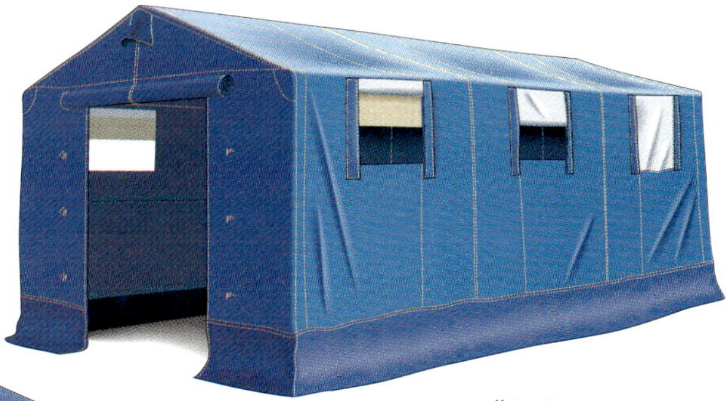

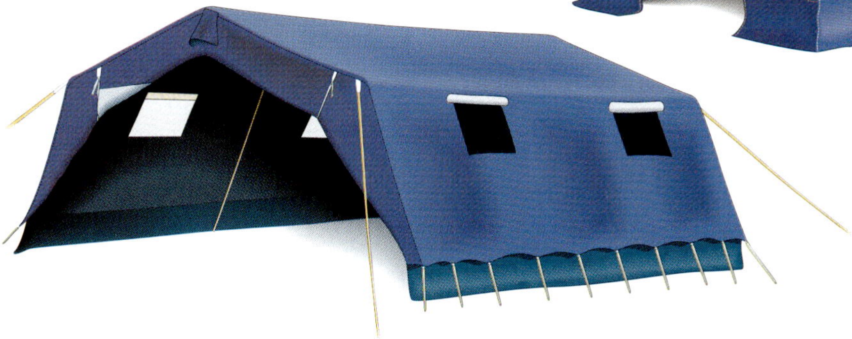

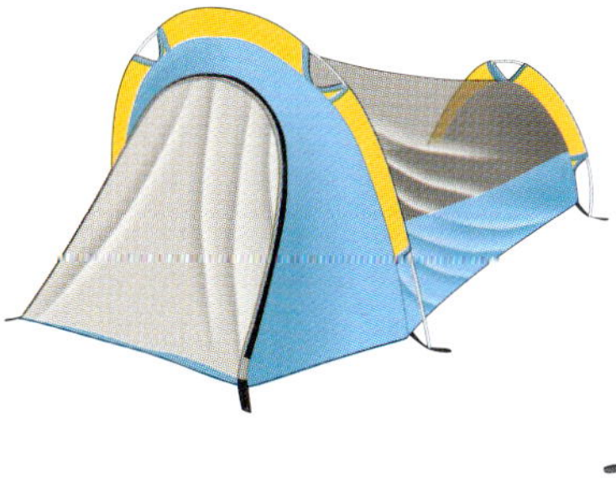

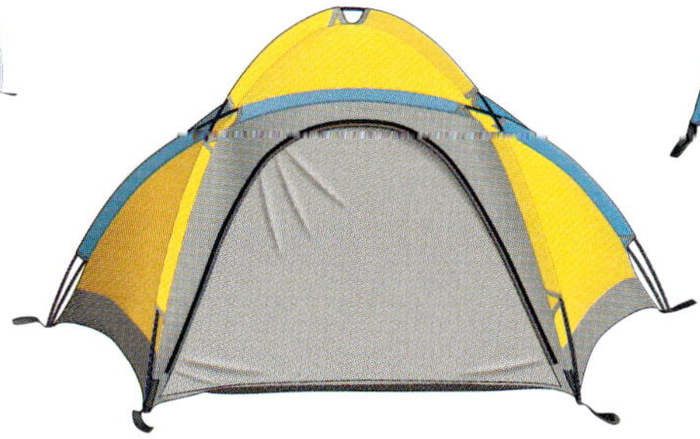

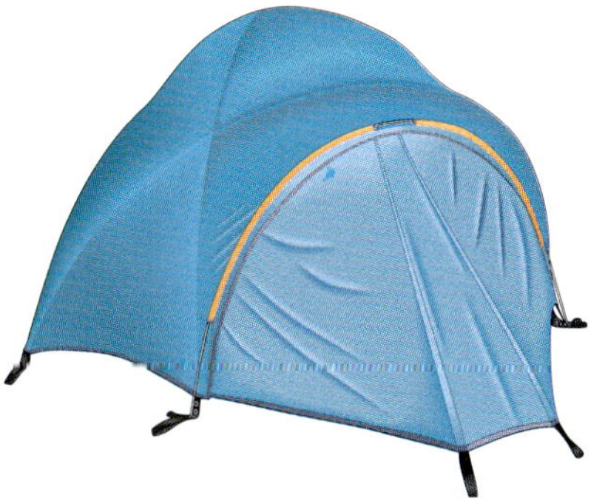

SLEEPING BAGS

CAMPING

CAMPING EQUIPMENT

SWISS ARMY KNIFE

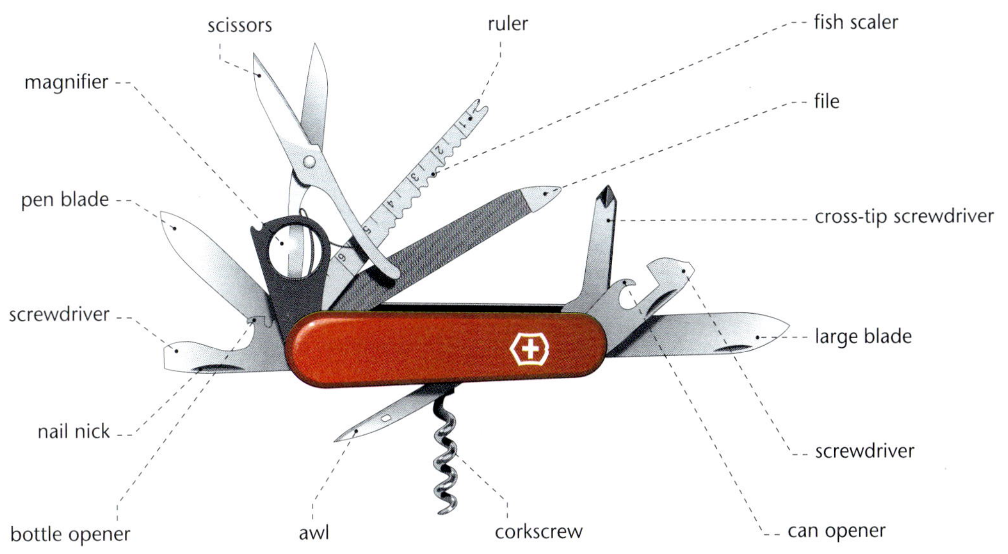

COOKING SET

CUTLERY SET

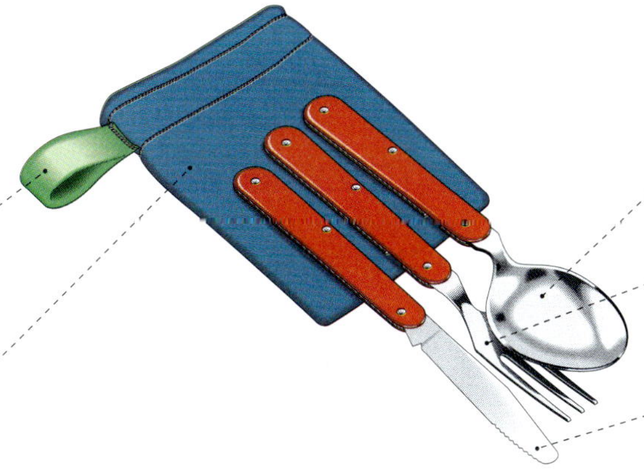

lantern
globe
burner frame
pressure regulator
leakproof cap
tank
pump
heater
single-burner camp stove
two-burner camp stove
burner
control valve
wire support
tank

CAMPING

CAMPING EQUIPMENT

TOOLS

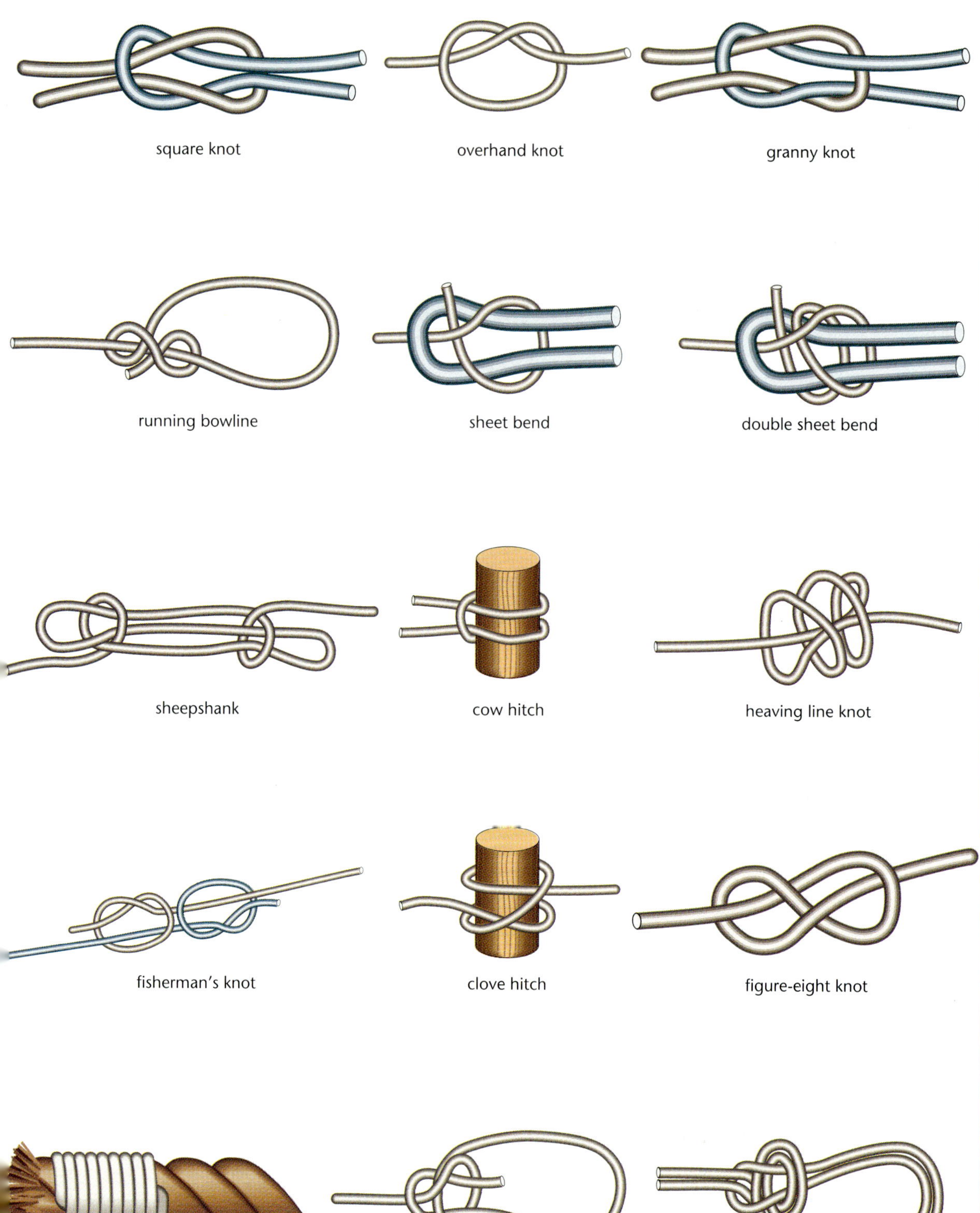

square knot
overhand knot
granny knot
running bowline
sheet bend
double sheet bend
sheepshank
cow hitch
heaving line knot
fisherman's knot
clove hitch
figure-eight knot
common whipping
bowline
bowline on a bight

SHORT SPLICE

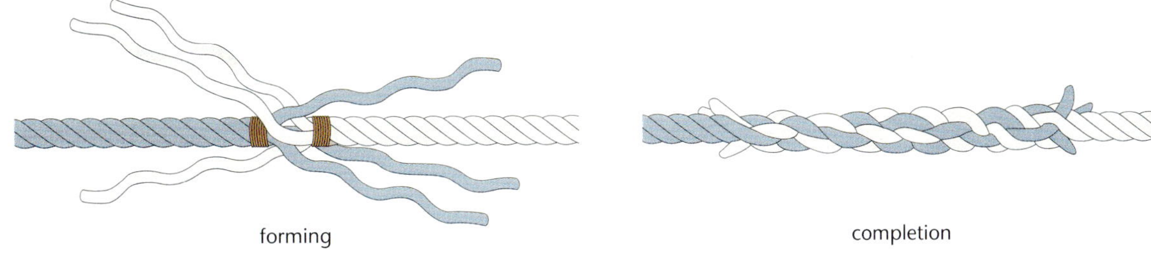

CABLE

TWISTED ROPE

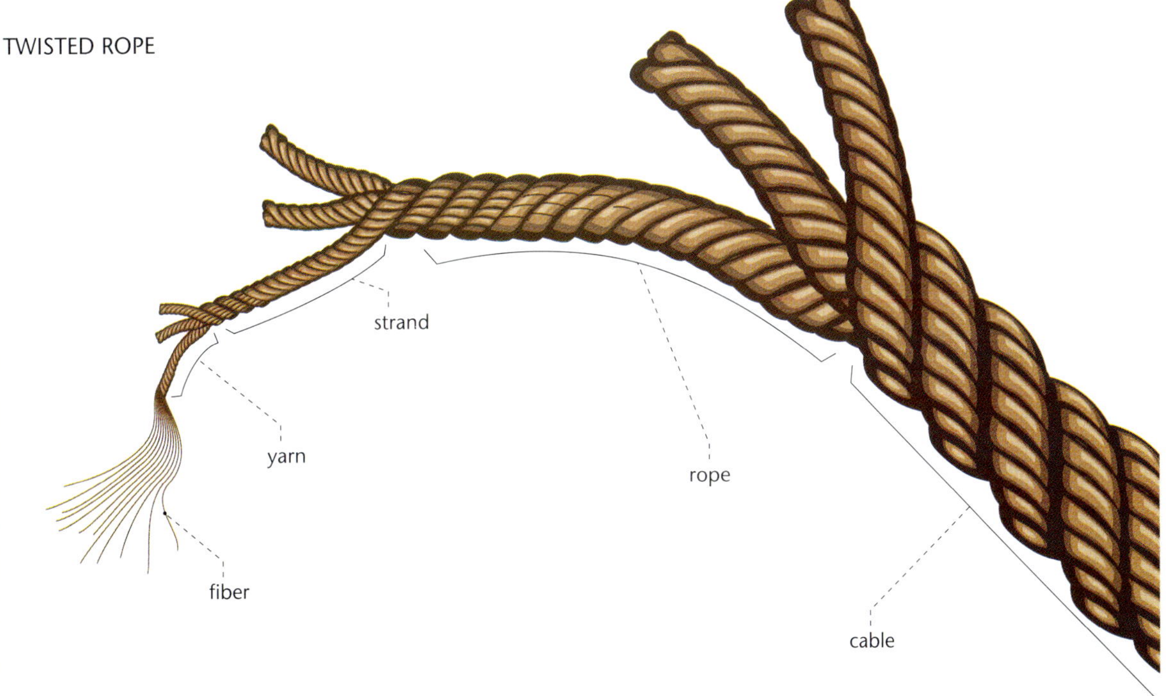

BRAIDED ROPE

CAMPING

INDOOR GAMES

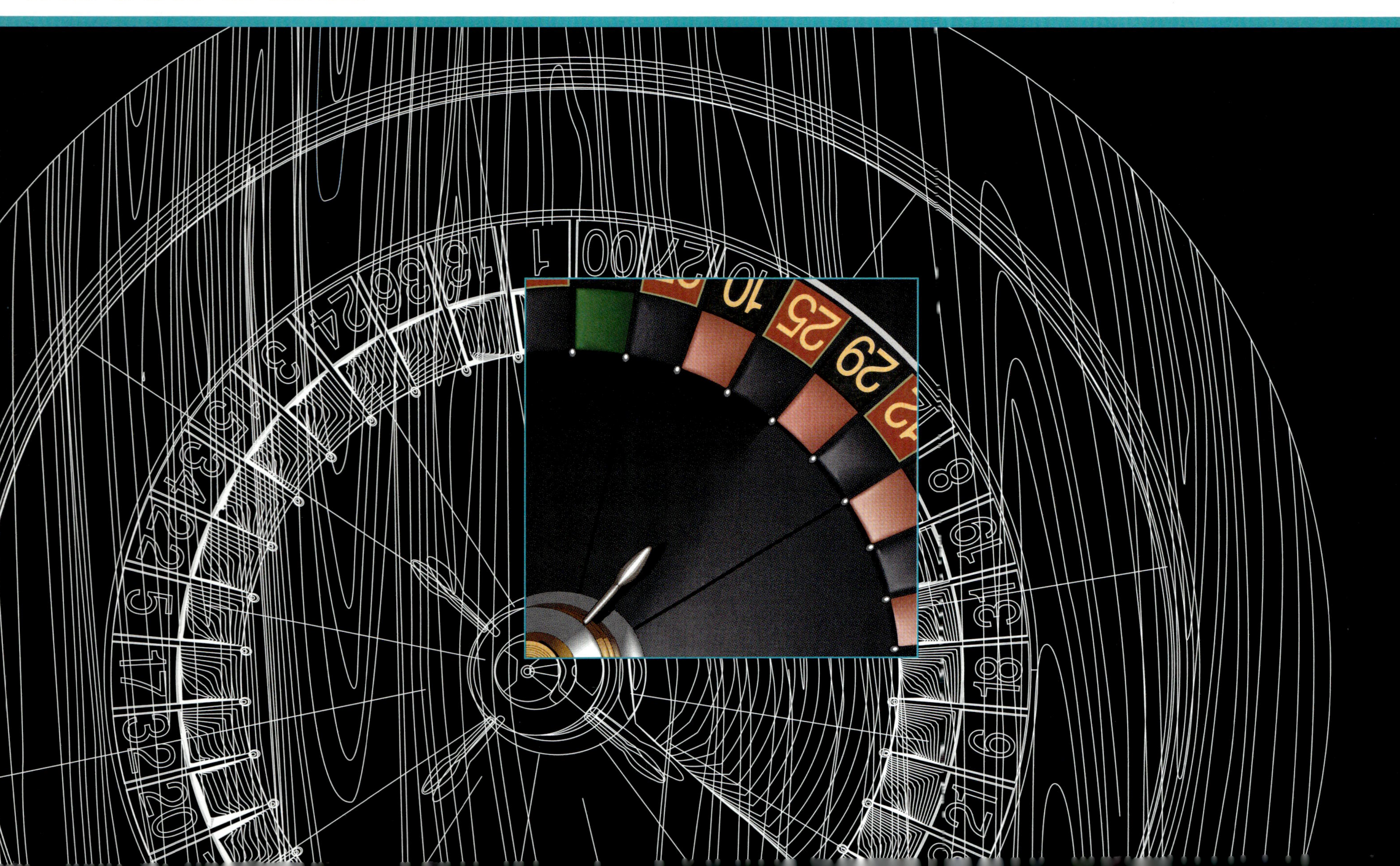

CONTENTS

CARD GAMES

SYMBOLS

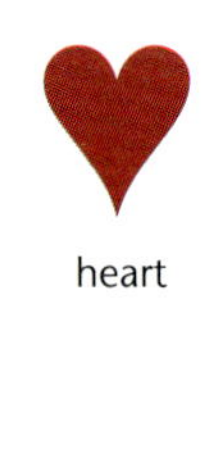
heart

diamond

club

spade

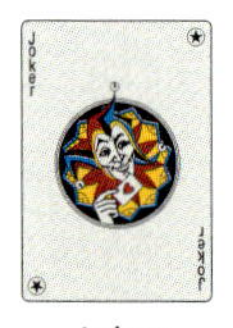
Joker

Ace

King

Queen

Jack

STANDARD POKER HANDS

royal flush

straight flush

four-of-a-kind

full house

flush

straight

three-of-a-kind

two pairs

one pair

high card

DOMINOES

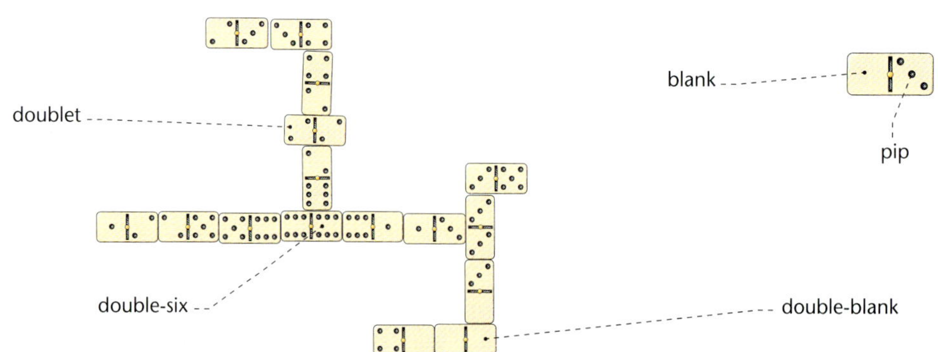

CHESS

CHESSBOARD

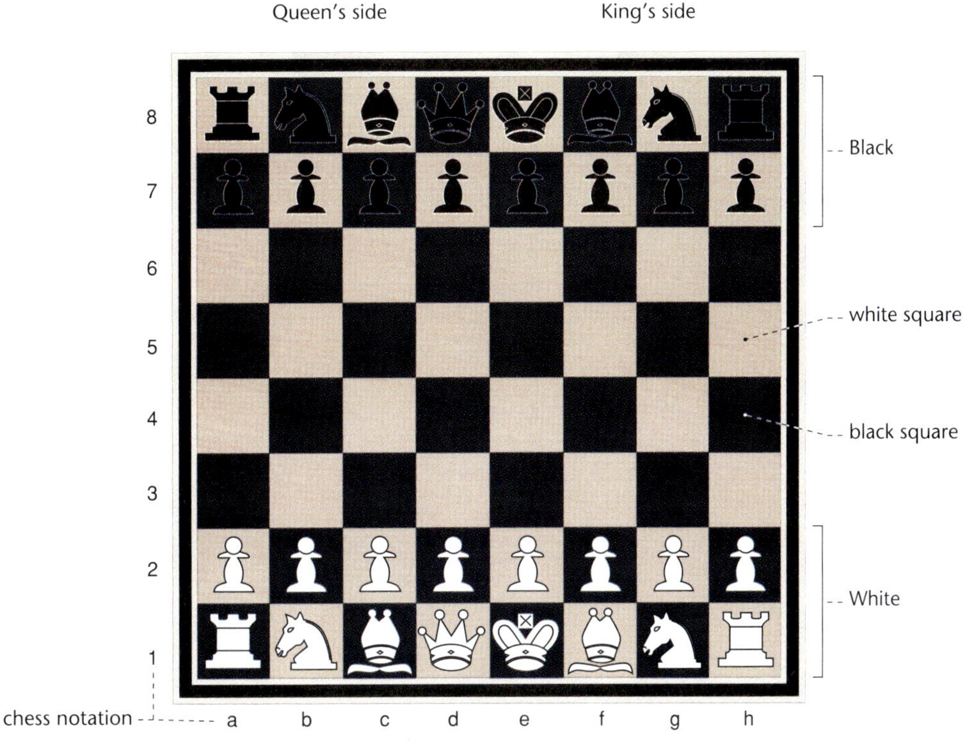

TYPES OF MOVEMENTS

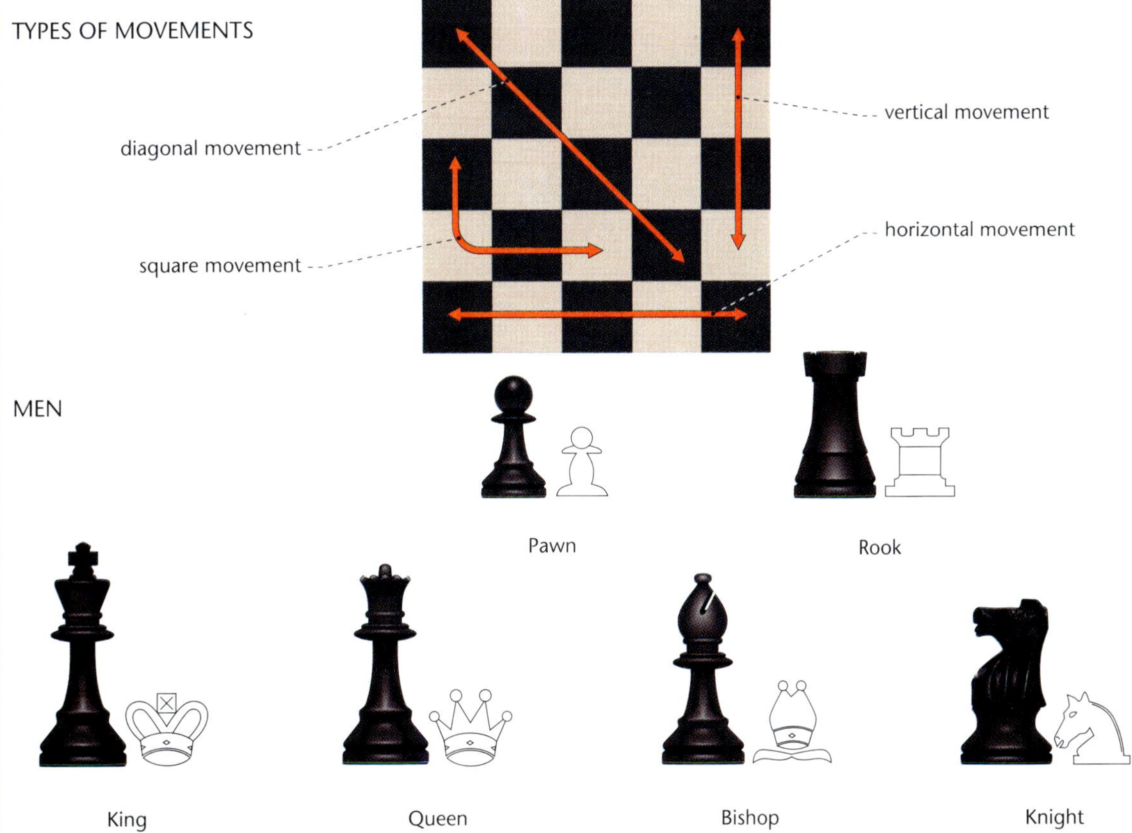

MEN

Pawn

Rook

King

Queen

Bishop

Knight

BACKGAMMON

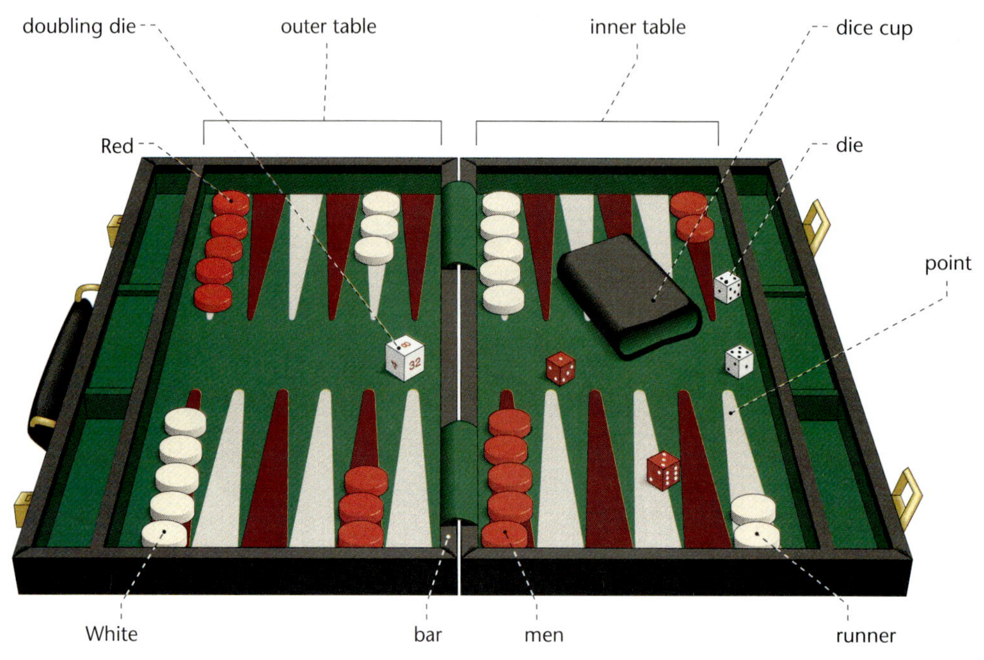

GO

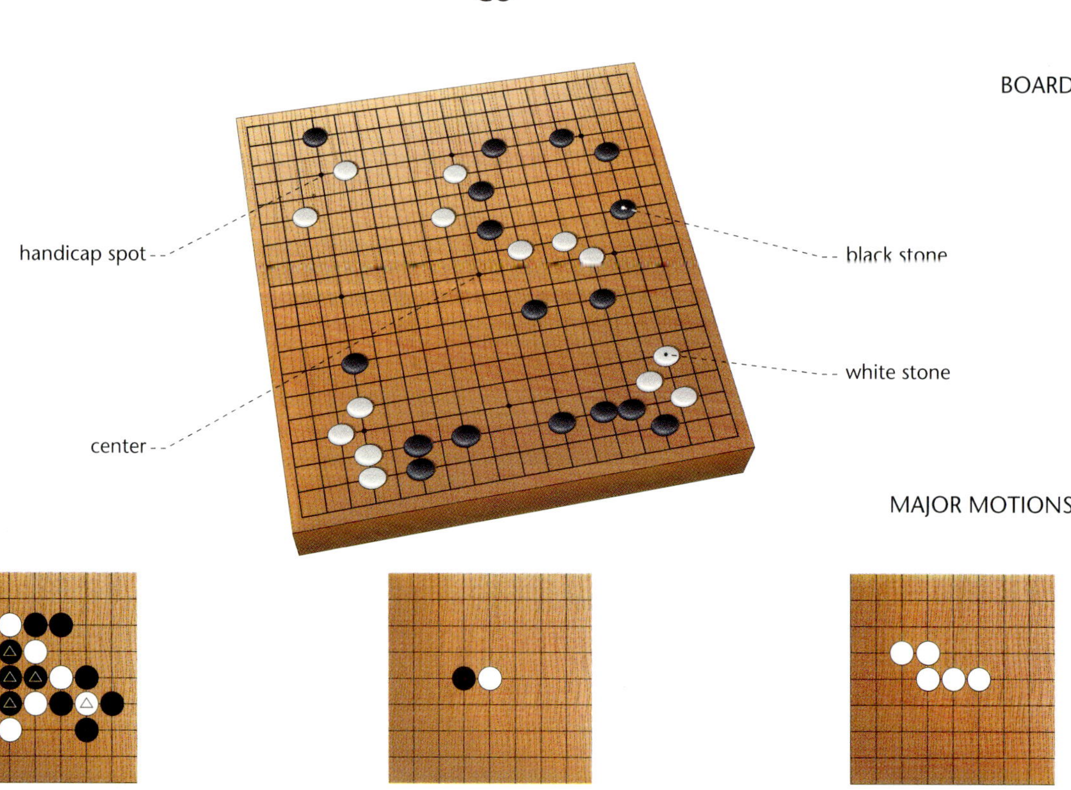

DARTBOARD

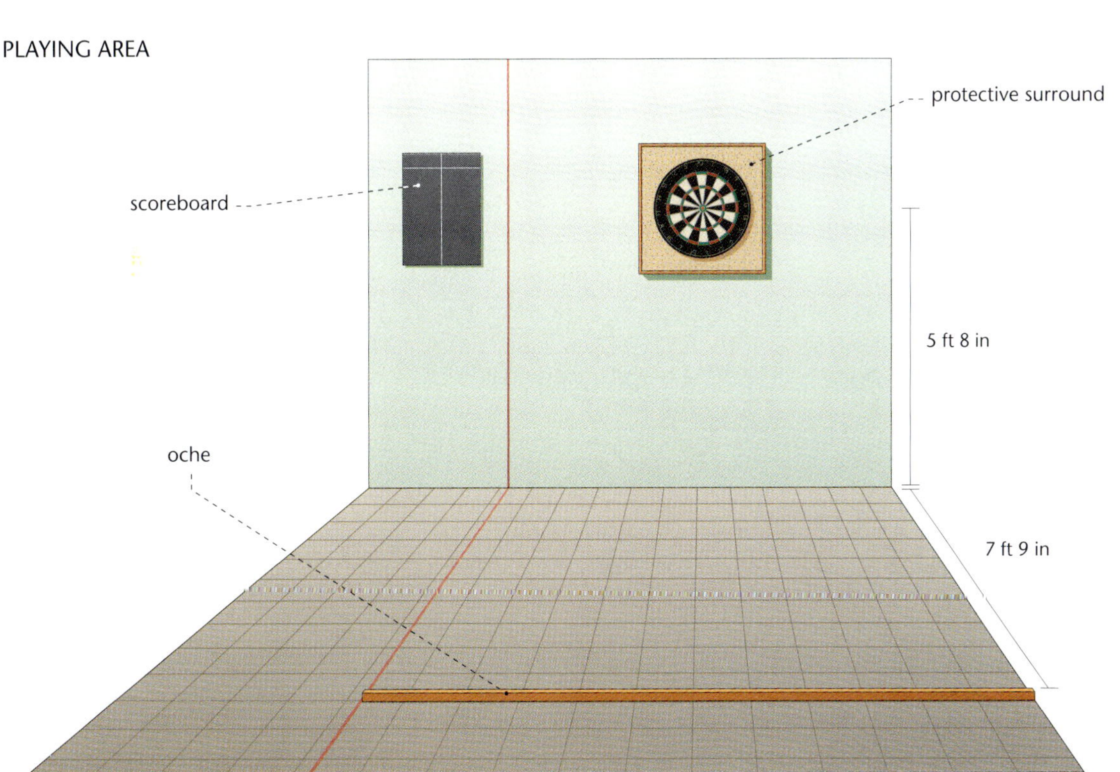

DART

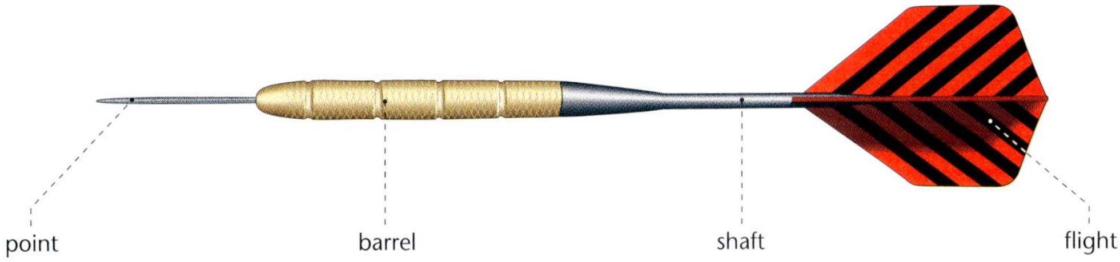

PLAYING AREA

698

VIDEO ENTERTAINMENT SYSTEM

DICE

poker die

ordinary die

ROULETTE TABLE

AMERICAN ROULETTE WHEEL

AMERICAN BETTING LAYOUT

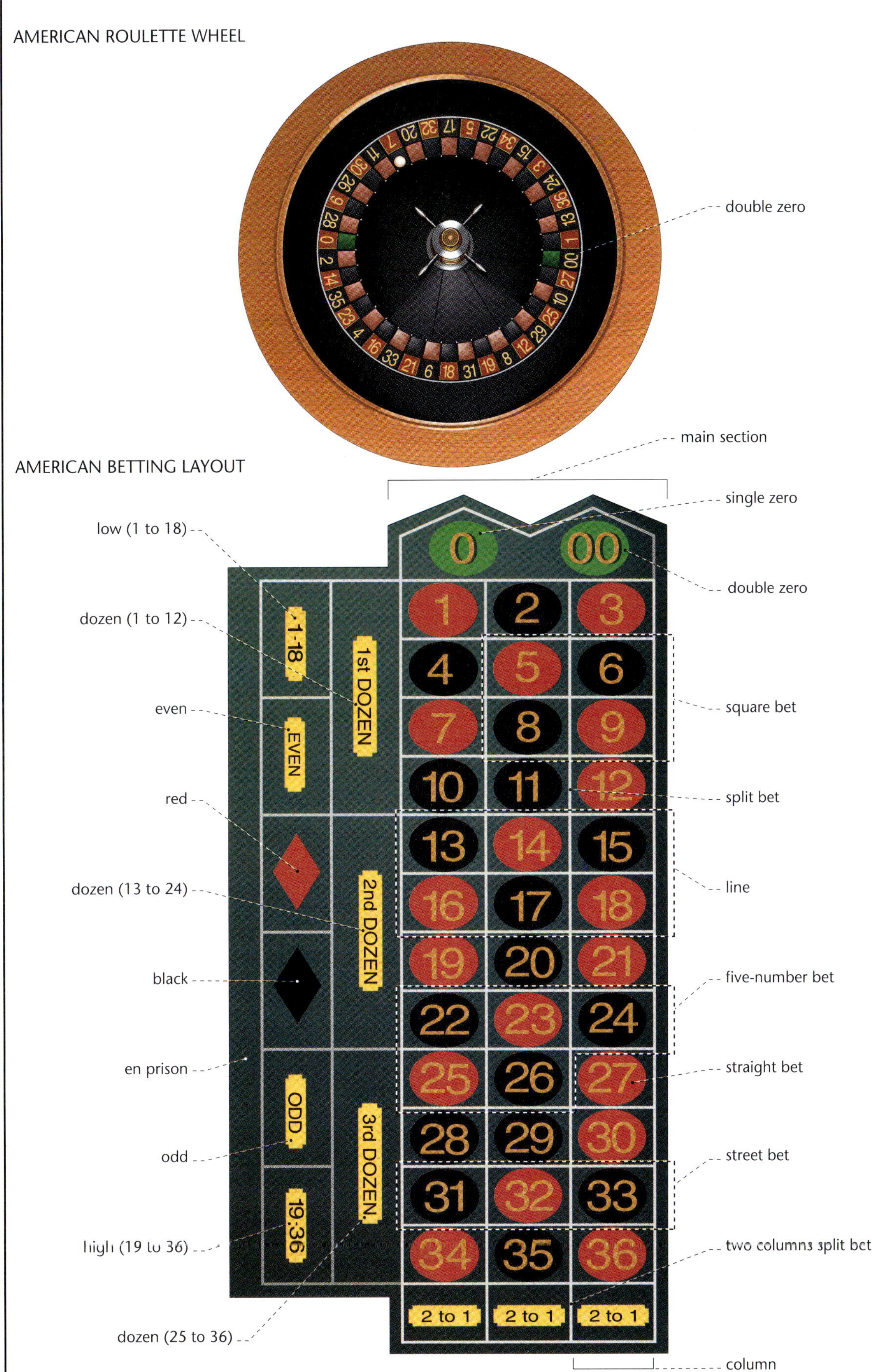

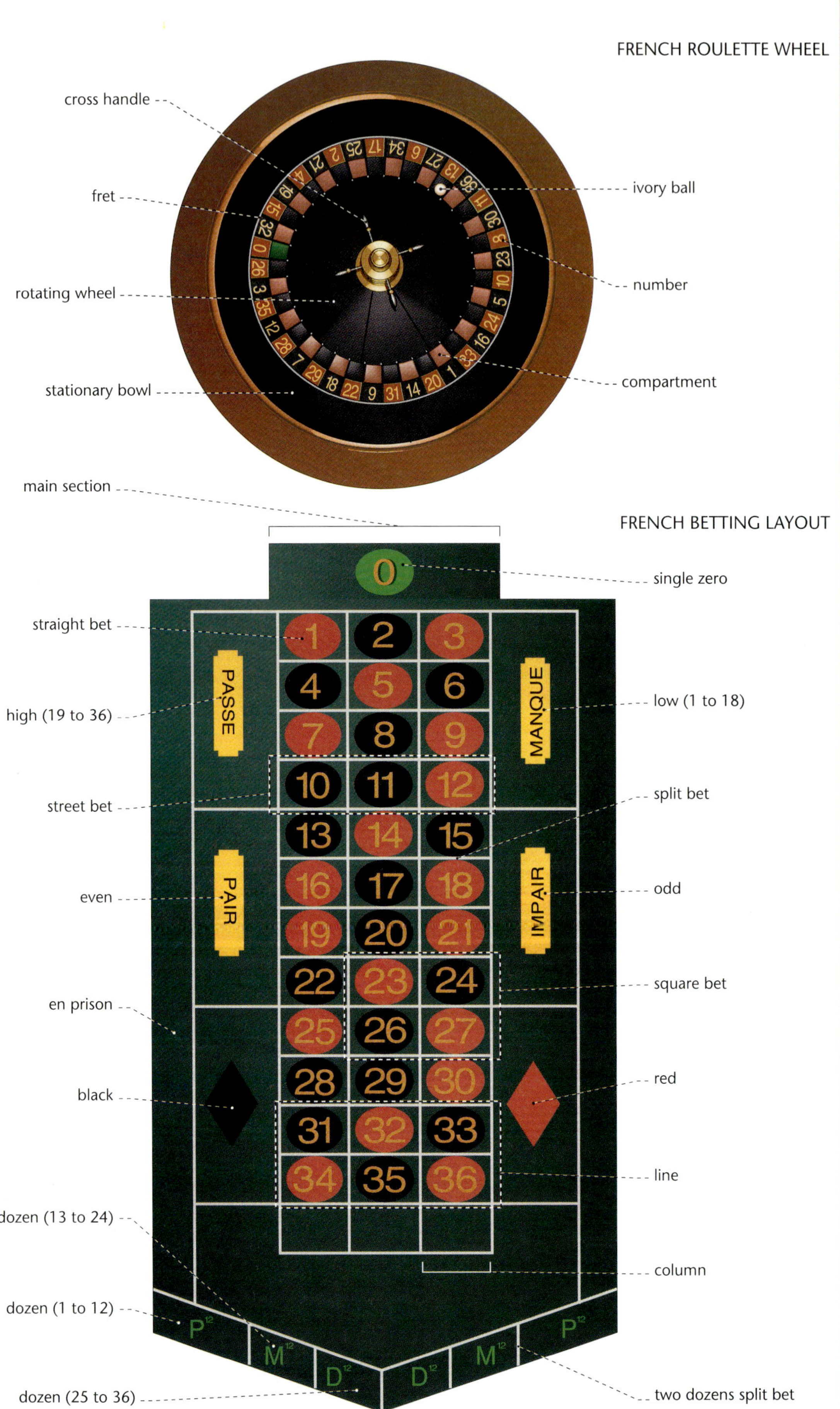

FRENCH ROULETTE WHEEL
cross handle
fret
rotating wheel
stationary bowl
ivory ball
number
compartment
main section
FRENCH BETTING LAYOUT
single zero
straight bet
PASSE
MANQUE
high (19 to 36)
low (1 to 18)
street bet
split bet
even
PAIR
IMPAIR
odd
square bet
en prison
black
red
line
dozen (13 to 24)
column
dozen (1 to 12)
two dozens split bet
dozen (25 to 36)

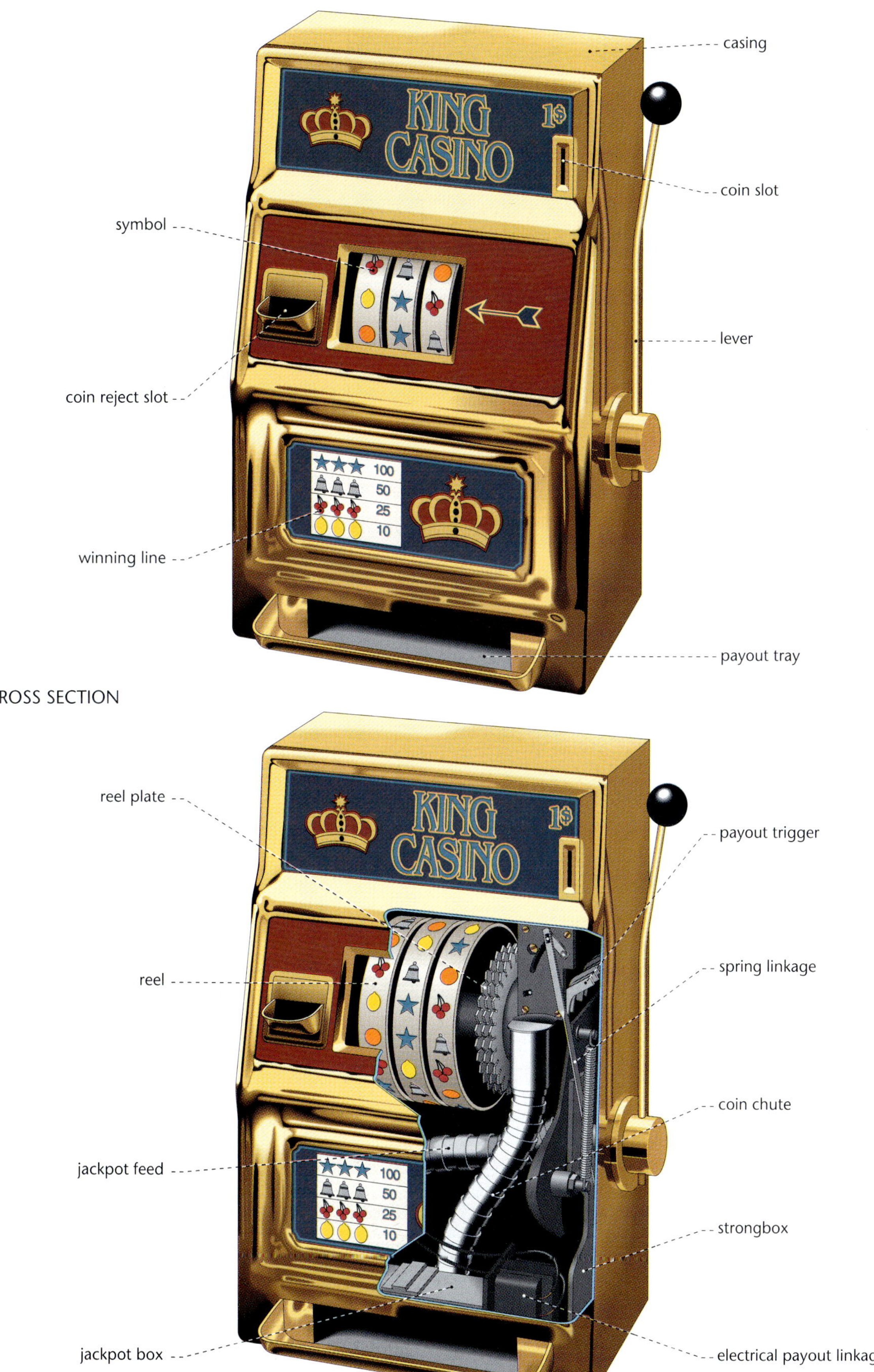

CROSS SECTION

CONTENTS

MEASURE OF TEMPERATURE

THERMOMETER

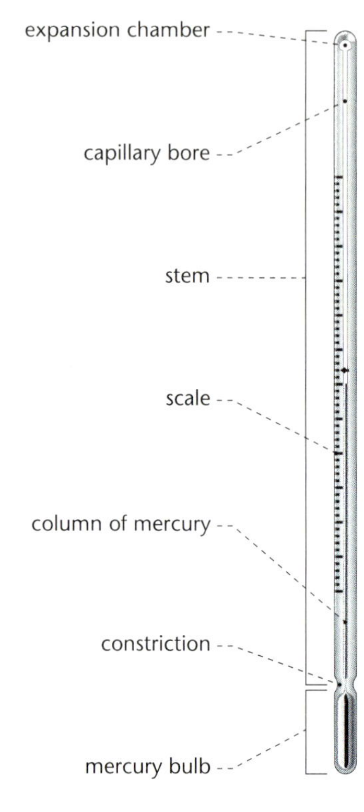

CLINICAL THERMOMETER

BIMETALLIC THERMOMETER

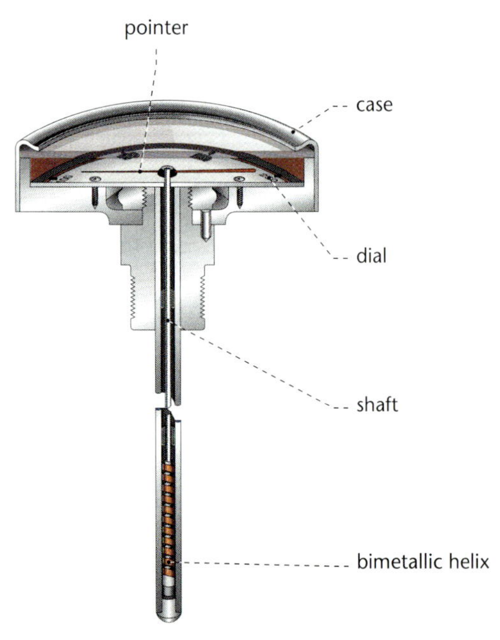

ROOM THERMOSTAT

STOPWATCH

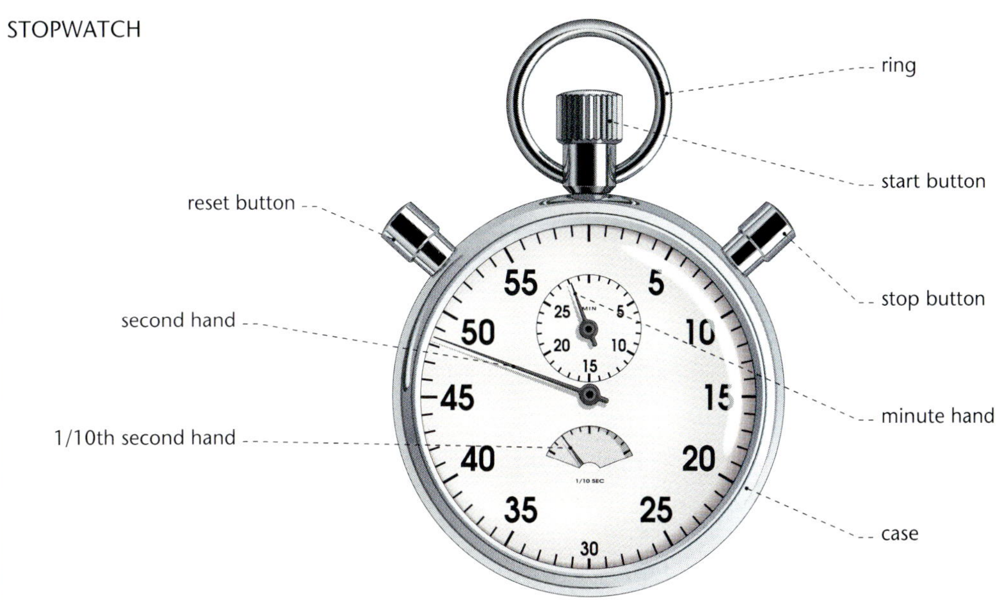

MECHANICAL WATCH

ANALOG WATCH

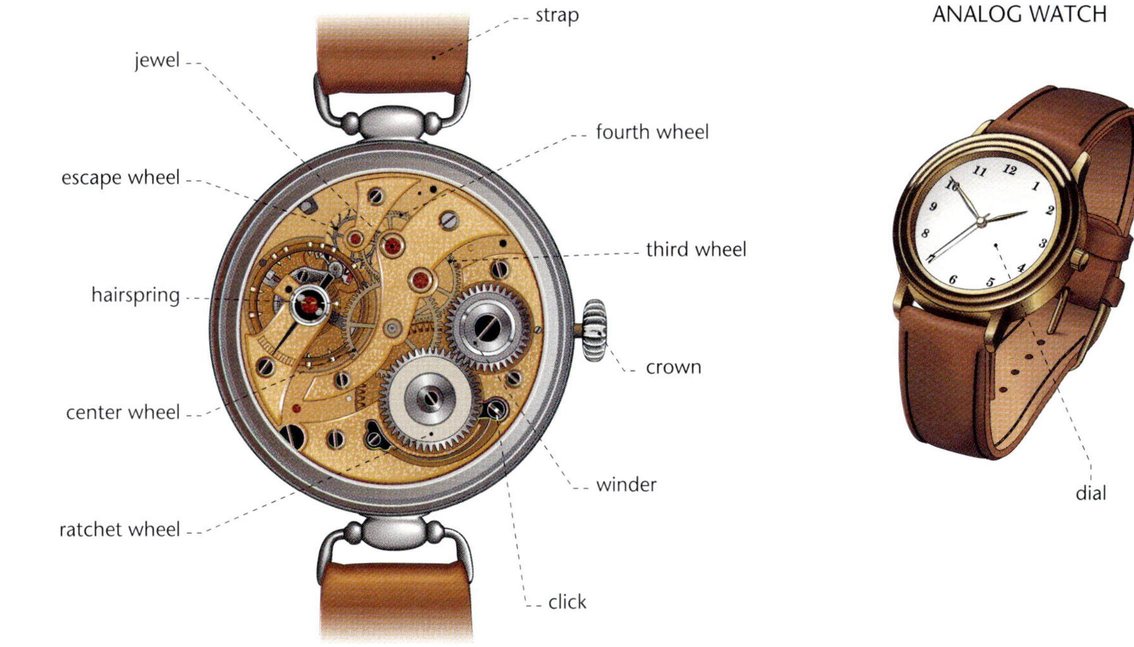

DIGITAL WATCH

SUNDIAL

GRANDFATHER CLOCK

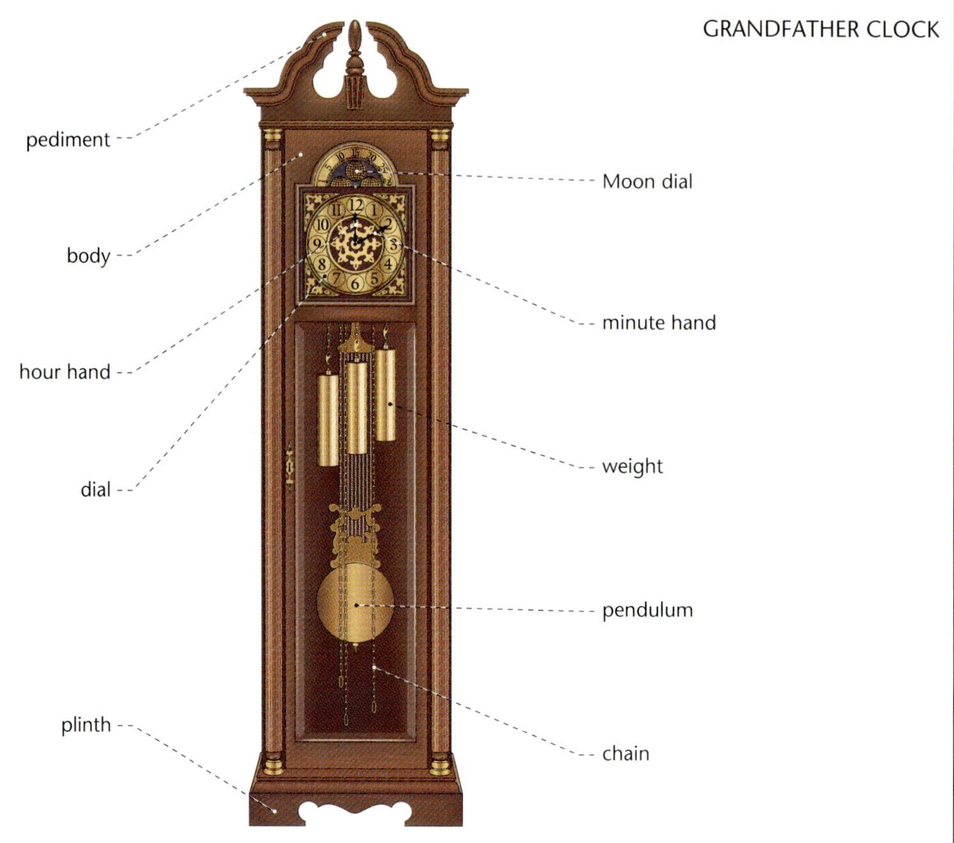

pediment
body
hour hand
dial
plinth
Moon dial
minute hand
weight
pendulum
chain

WEIGHT-DRIVEN CLOCK MECHANISM

suspension spring
pinion
fork
center wheel
pendulum rod
click
pendulum
main wheel
ratchet wheel
pallet
escape wheel
spindle
third wheel
minute hand
hour hand
winding mechanism
weight
drum

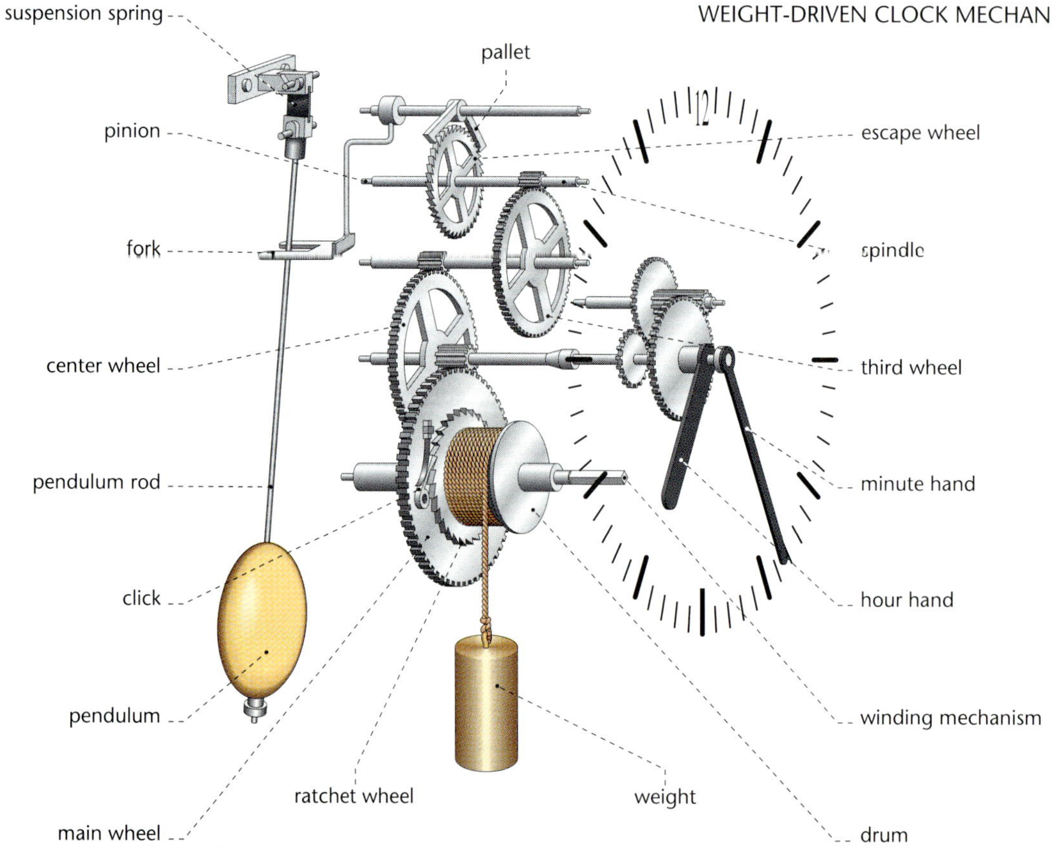

BEAM BALANCE

STEELYARD

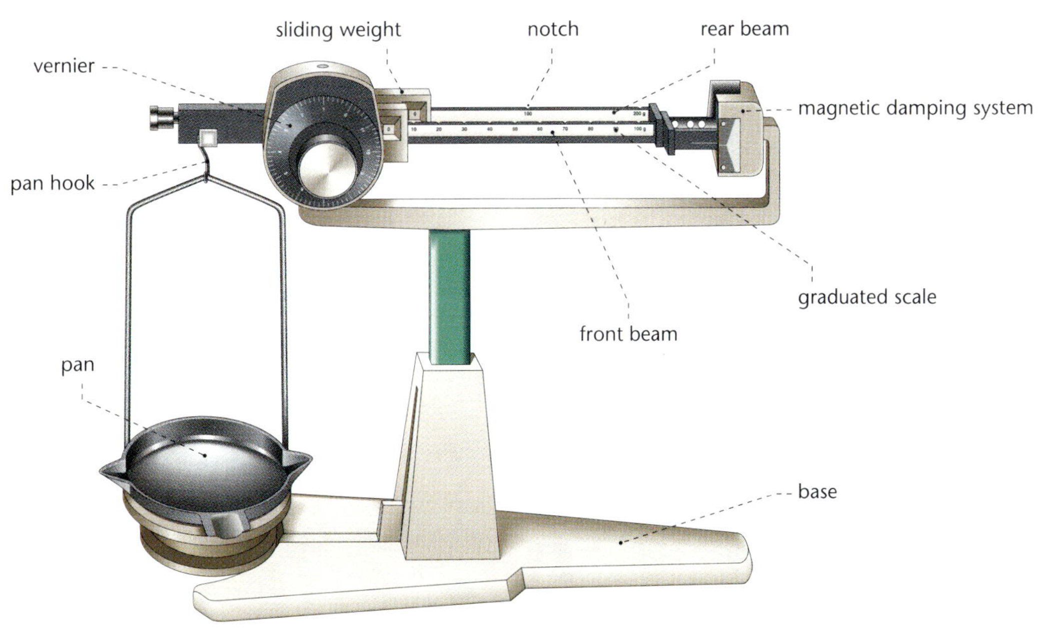

ROBERVAL'S BALANCE

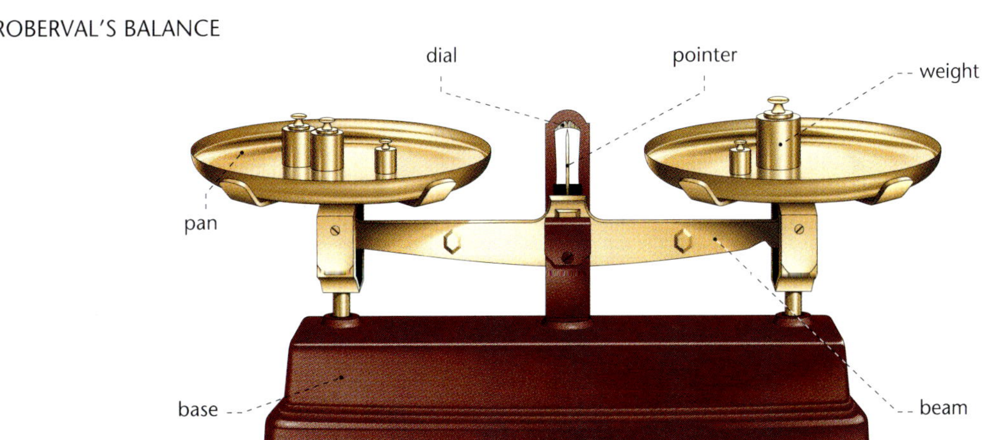

SPRING BALANCE

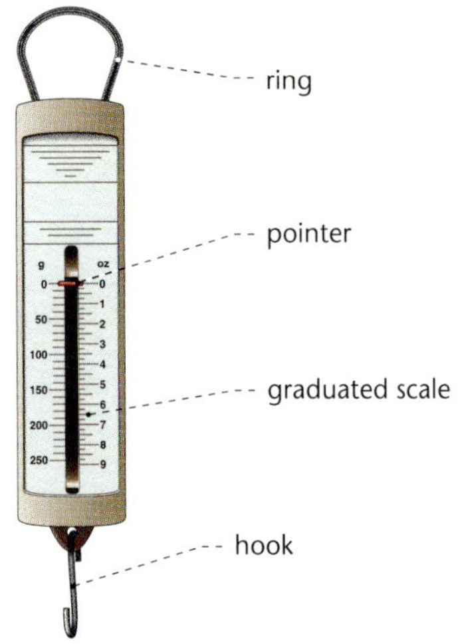

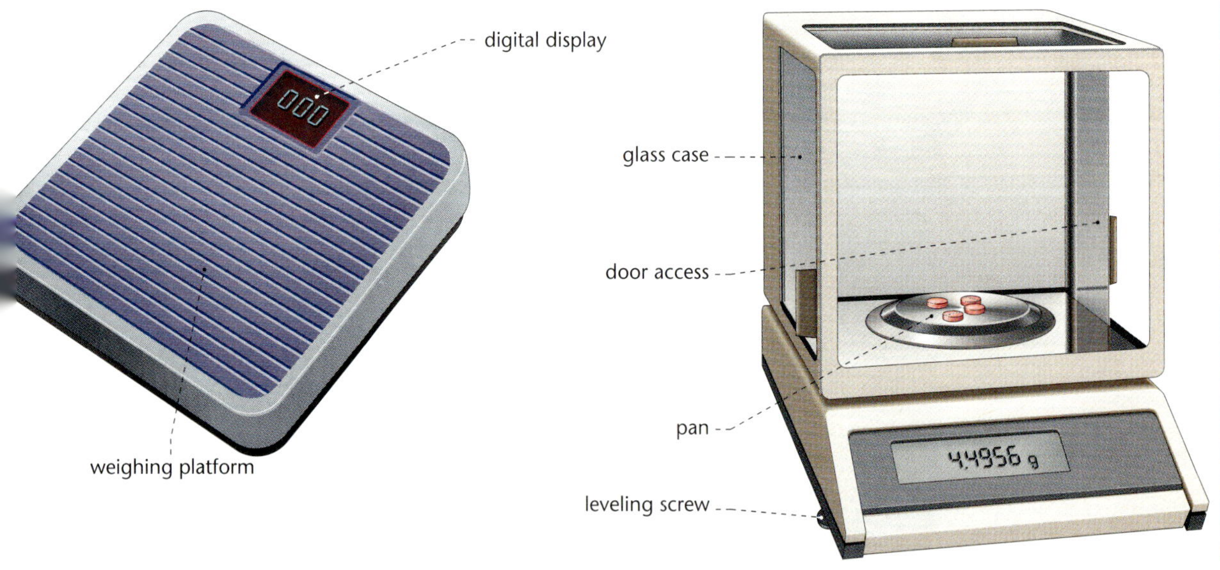

ELECTRONIC SCALE

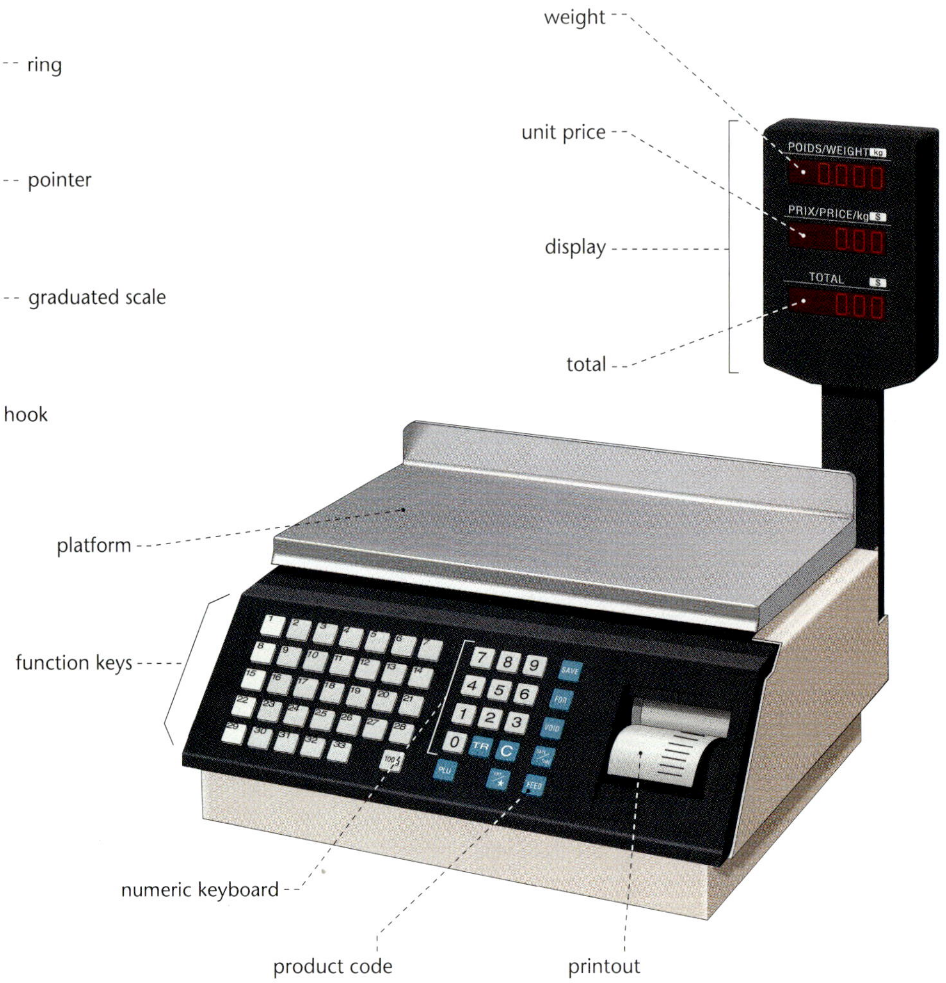

BATHROOM SCALE

ANALYTICAL BALANCE

BAROMETER/THERMOMETER

TENSIOMETER

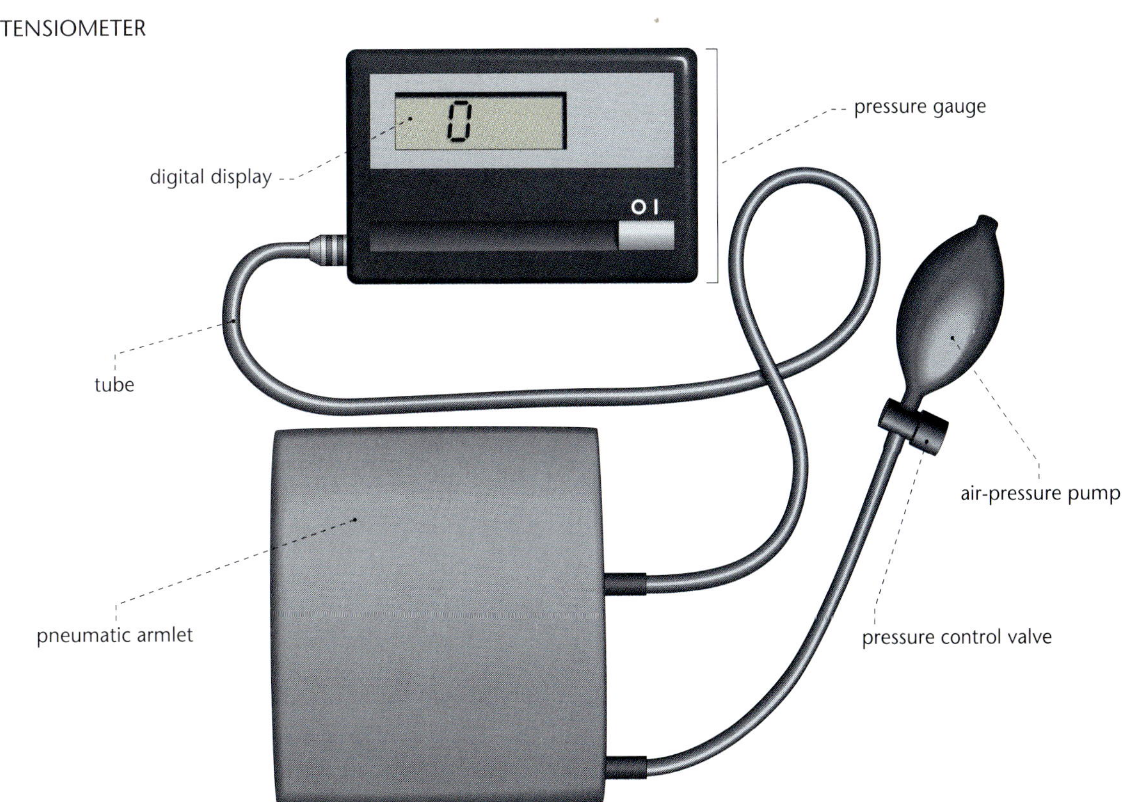

MEASURE OF LENGTH

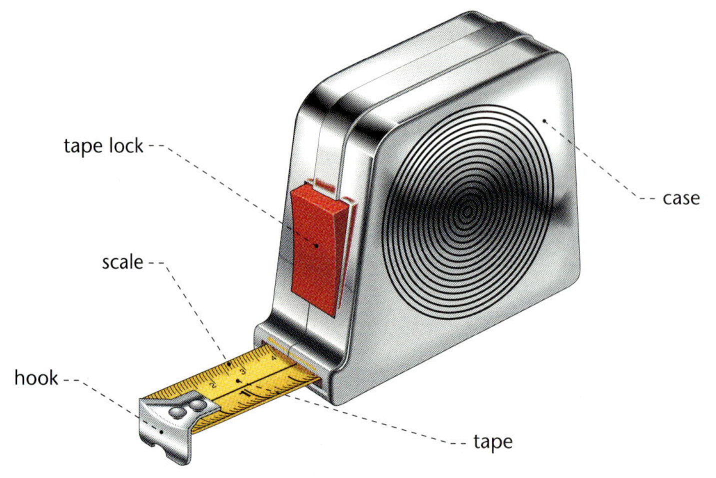

MEASURE OF DISTANCE

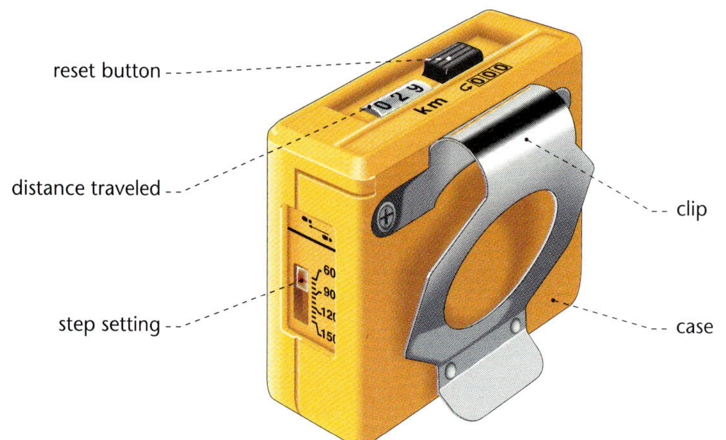

MEASURE OF THICKNESS

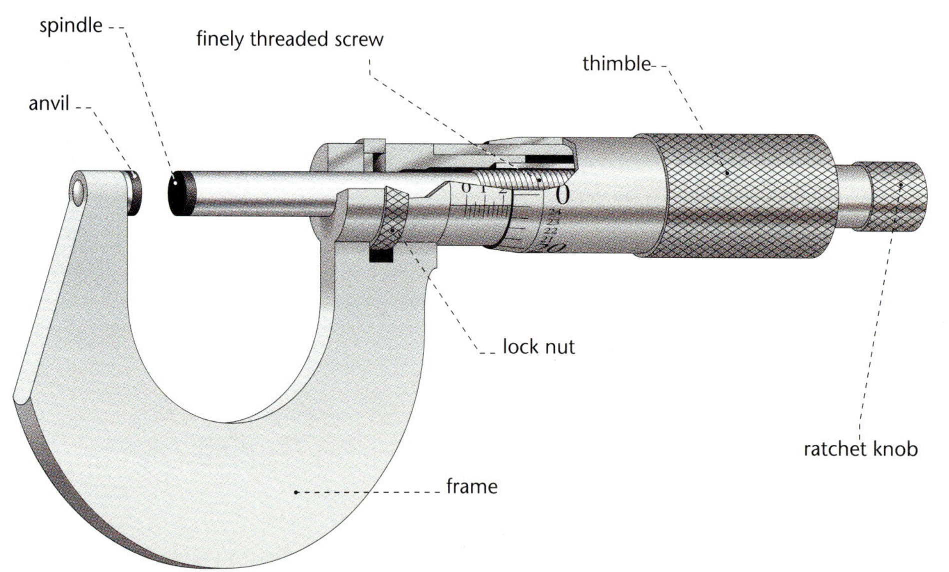

WATT-HOUR METER

EXTERIOR VIEW

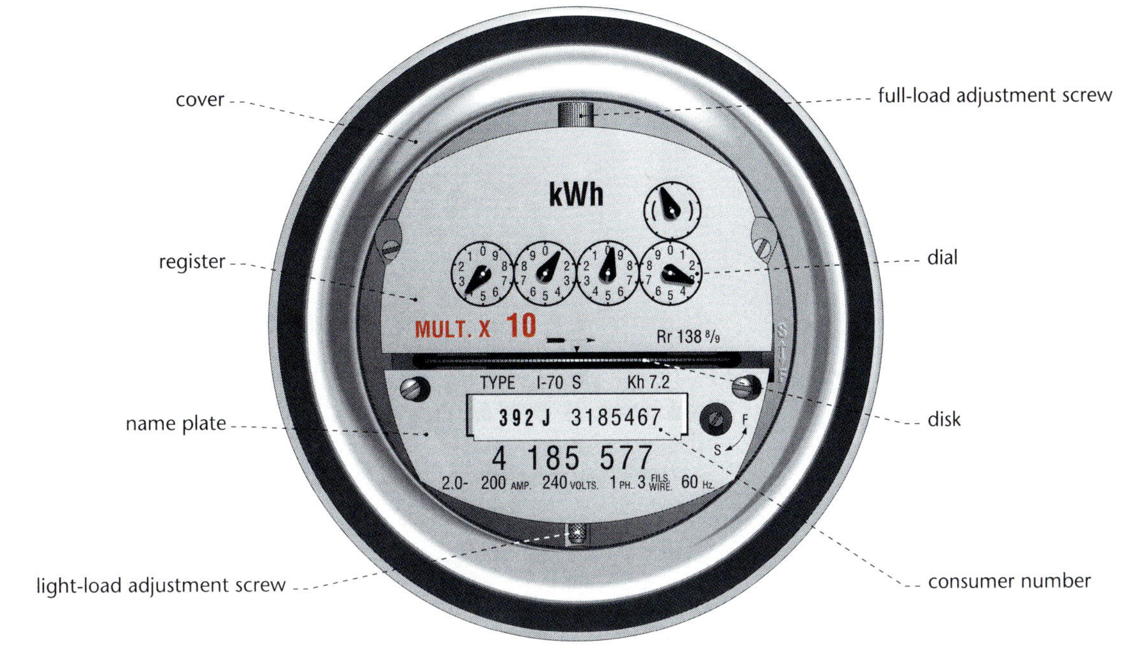

MECHANISM

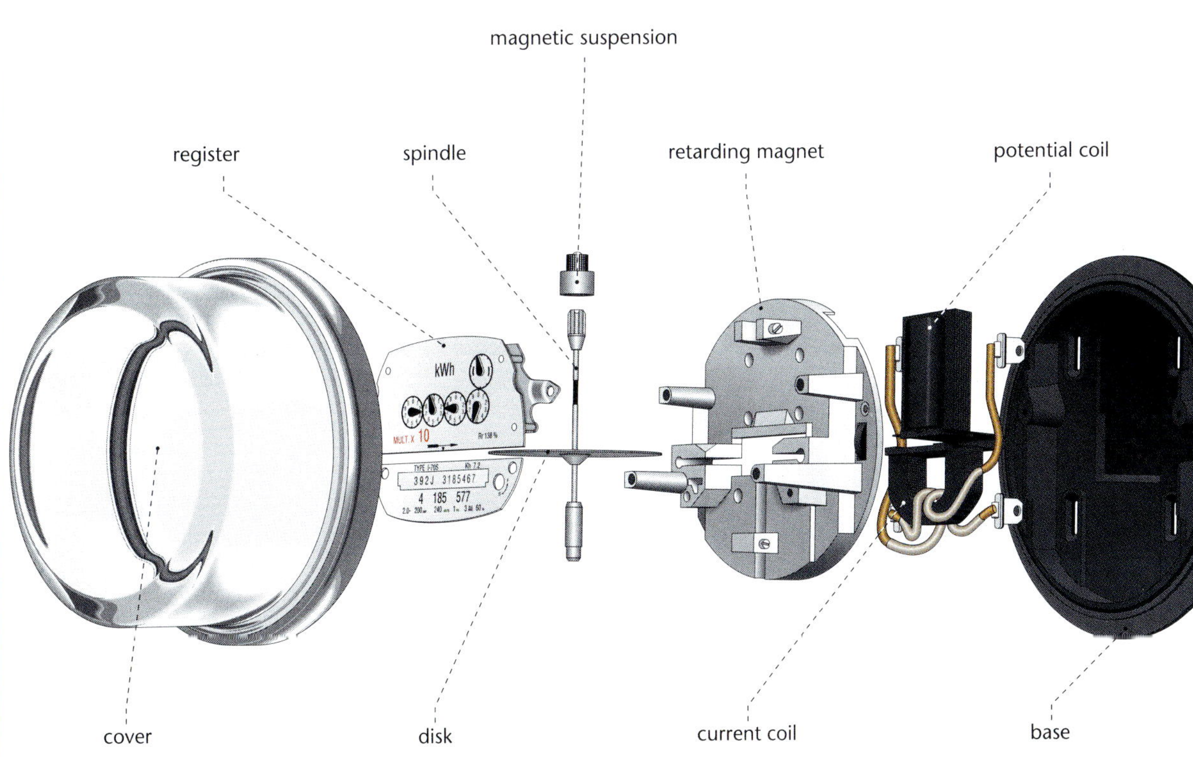

THEODOLITE

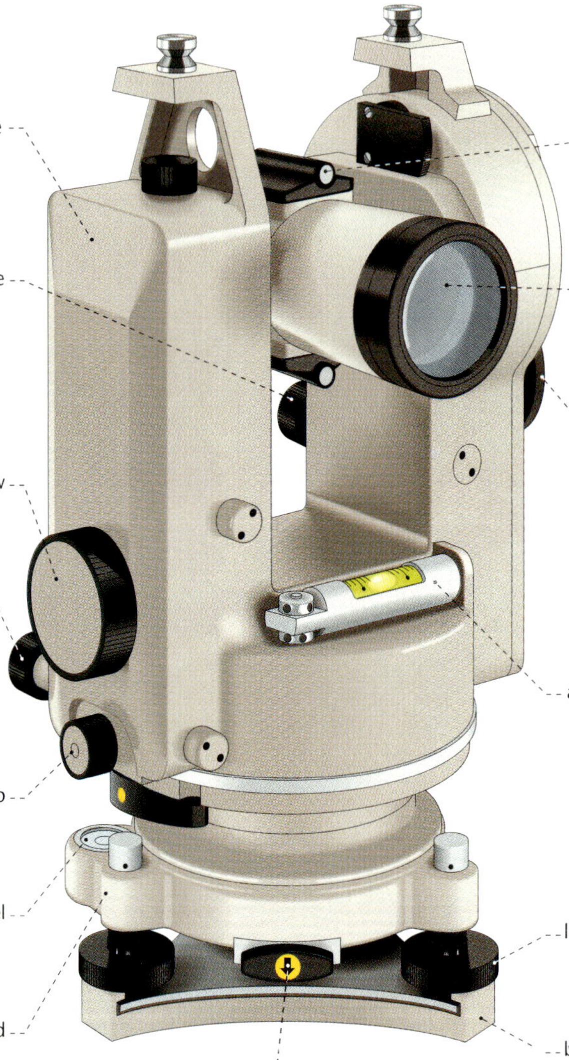

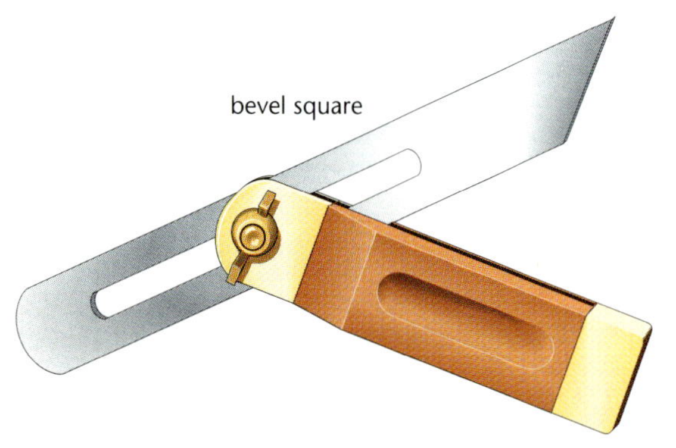

bevel square

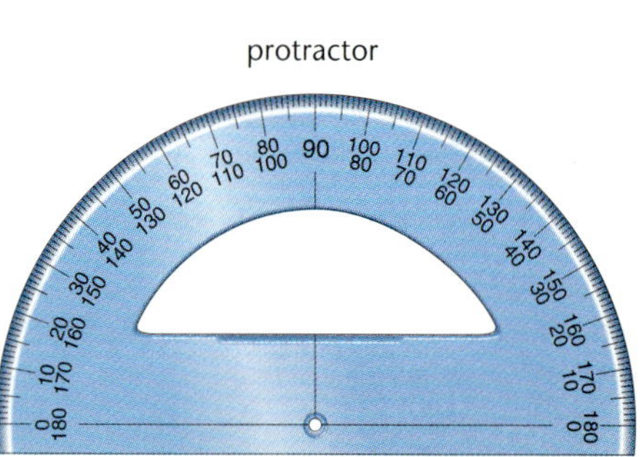

protractor

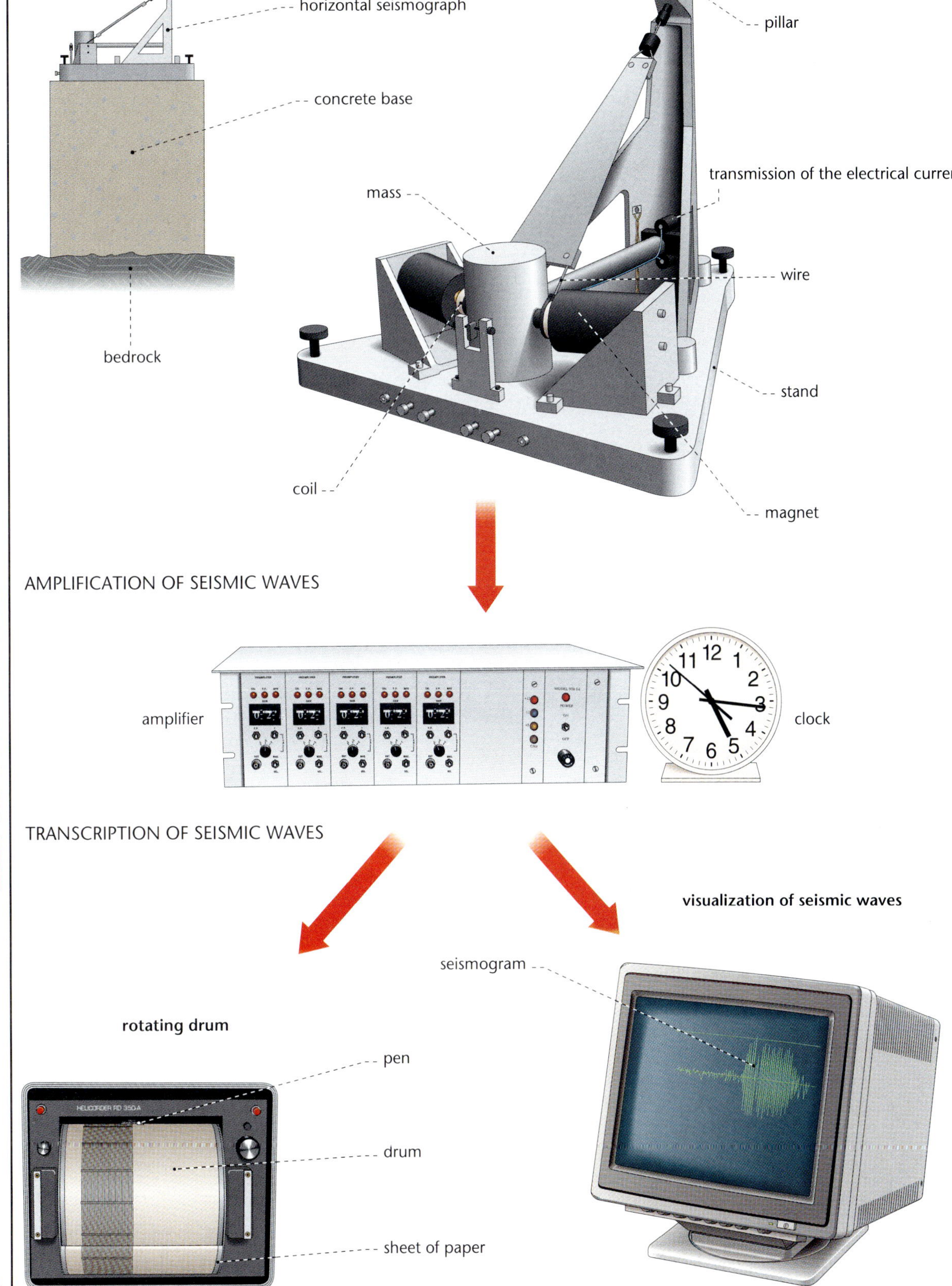
DETECTION OF SEISMIC WAVES
horizontal seismograph
concrete base
bedrock
pillar
mass
transmission of the electrical current
wire
stand
coil
magnet
AMPLIFICATION OF SEISMIC WAVES
amplifier
clock
12
TRANSCRIPTION OF SEISMIC WAVES
visualization of seismic waves
seismogram
rotating drum
pen
HELICORDER RD 350-A
drum
sheet of paper

OPTICAL INSTRUMENTS

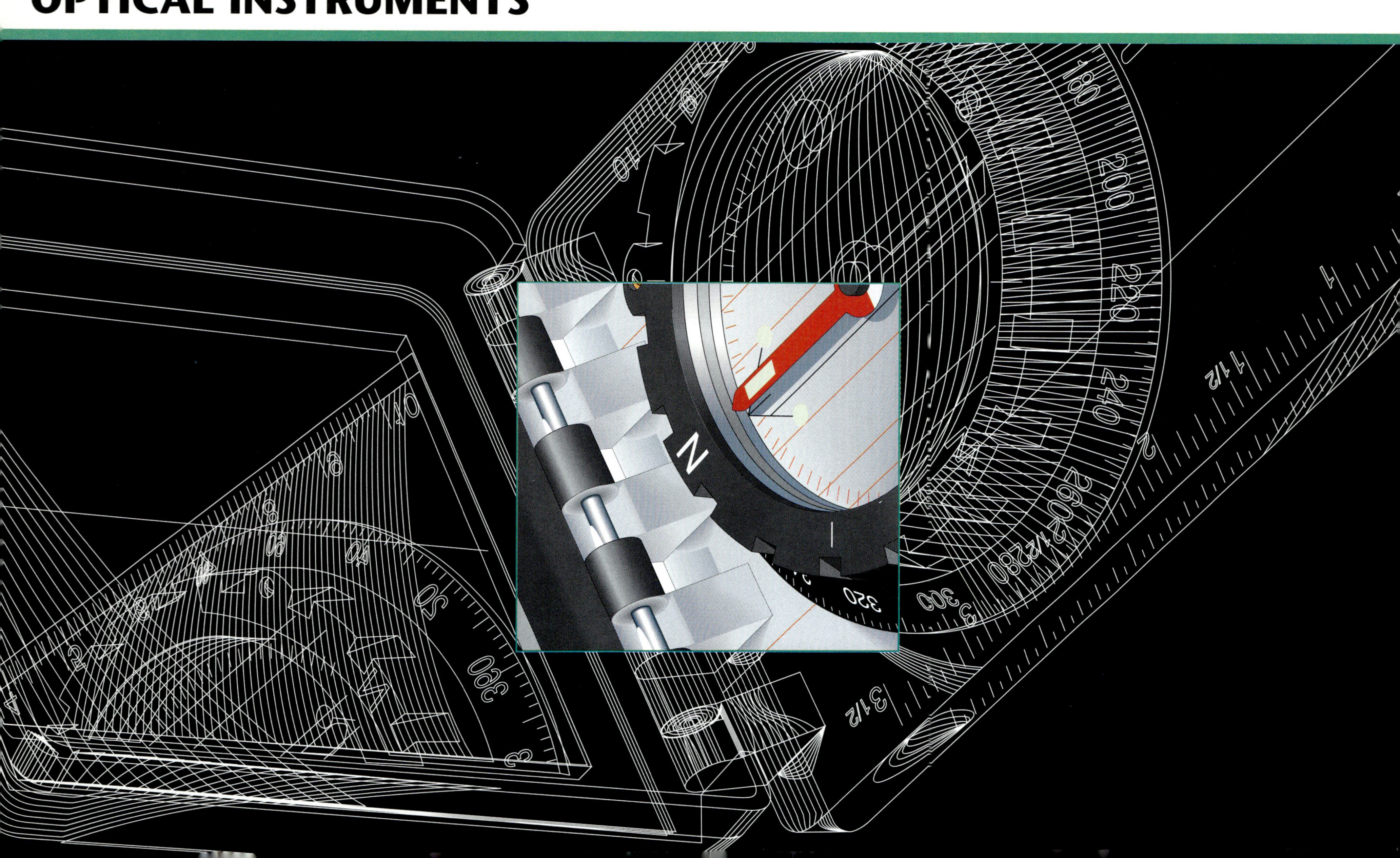

CONTENTS

OPTICAL INSTRUMENTS

ELECTRON MICROSCOPE

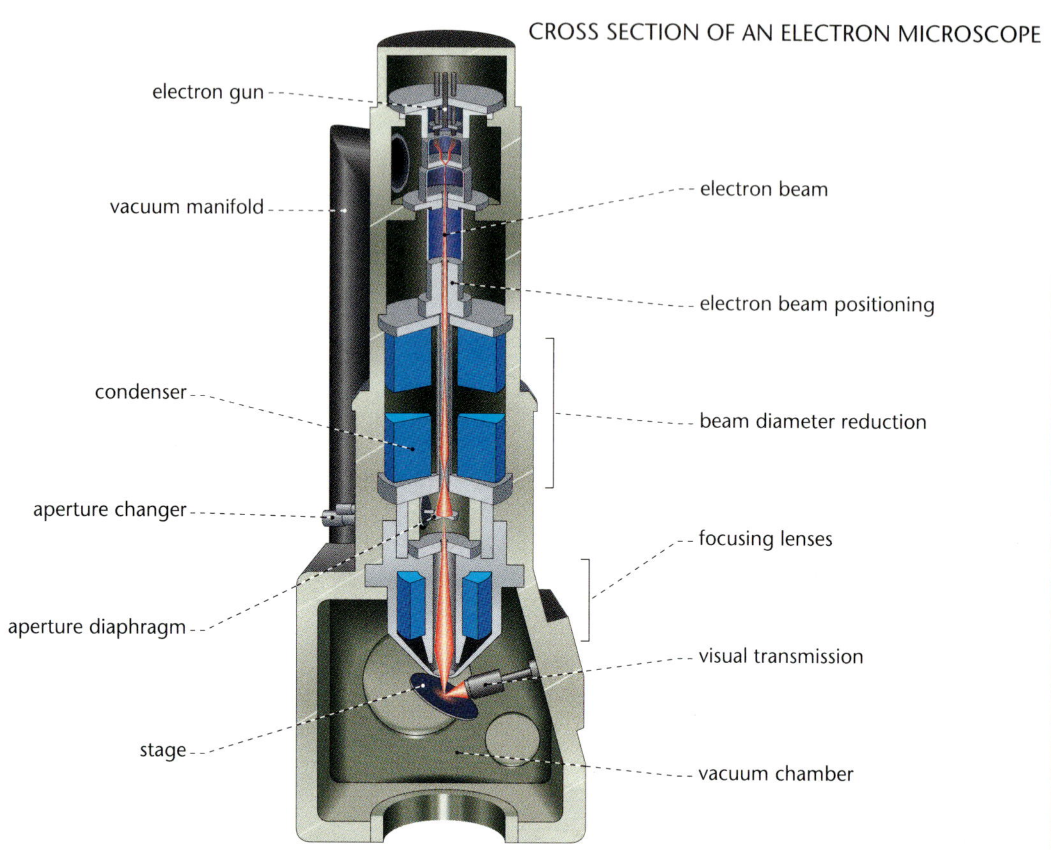

CROSS SECTION OF AN ELECTRON MICROSCOPE

electron gun
vacuum manifold
condenser
aperture changer
aperture diaphragm
stage
electron beam
electron beam positioning
beam diameter reduction
focusing lenses
visual transmission
vacuum chamber

ELECTRON MICROSCOPE ELEMENTS

liquid nitrogen tank
spectrometer
specimen chamber
vacuum system console
specimen positioning control
control panel
photographic chamber
data record system
electron gun
control visual display

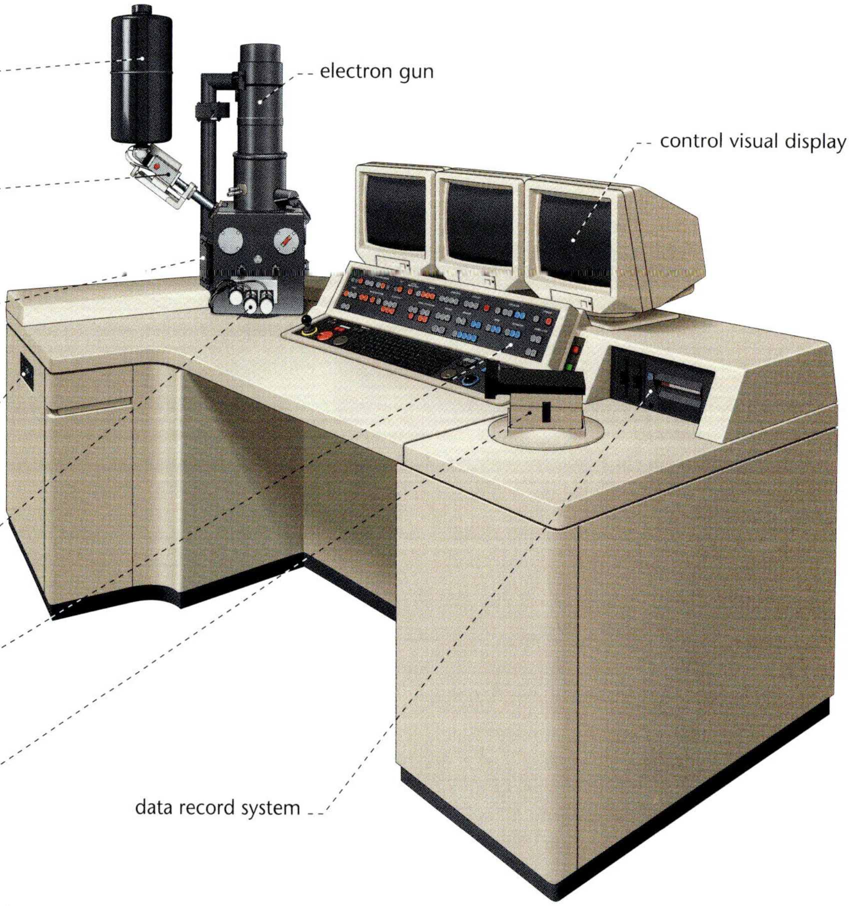

BINOCULAR MICROSCOPE

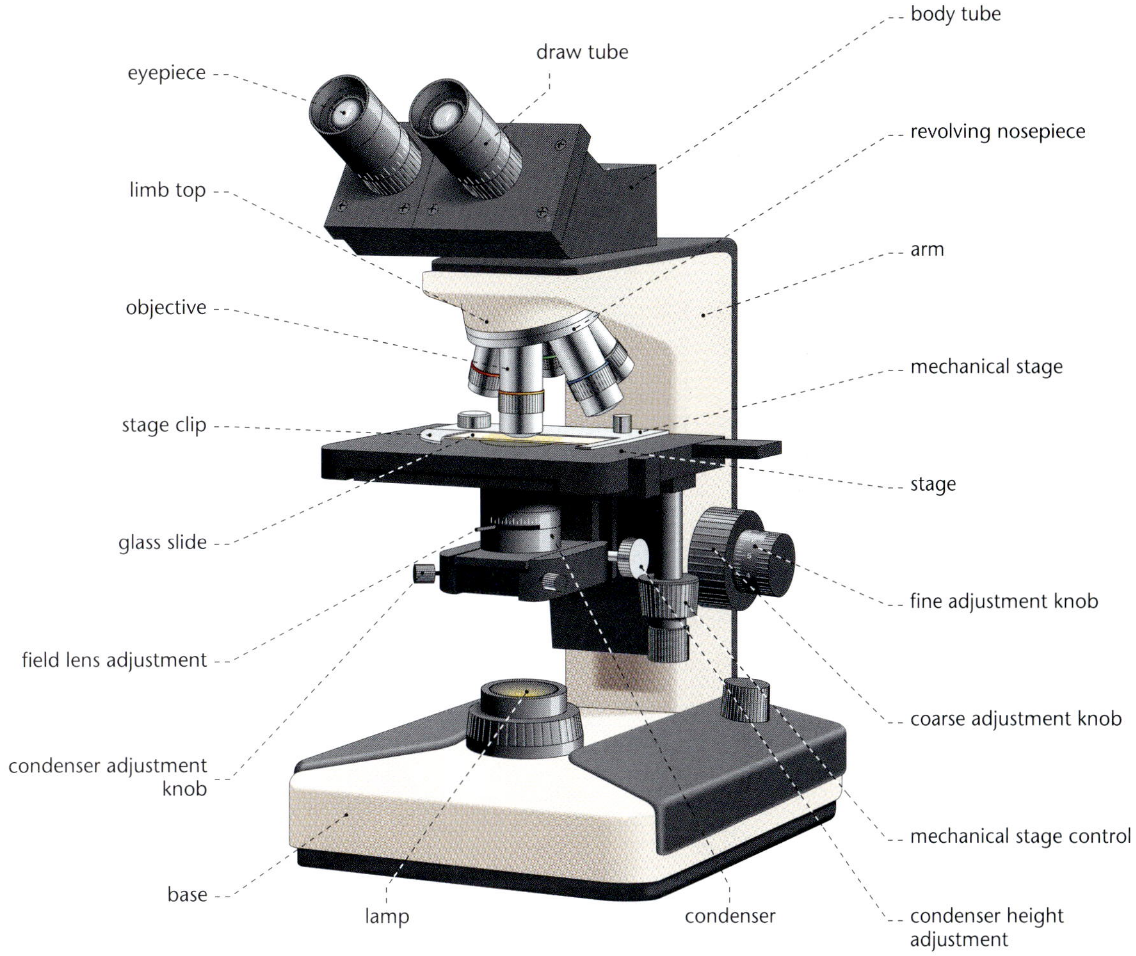

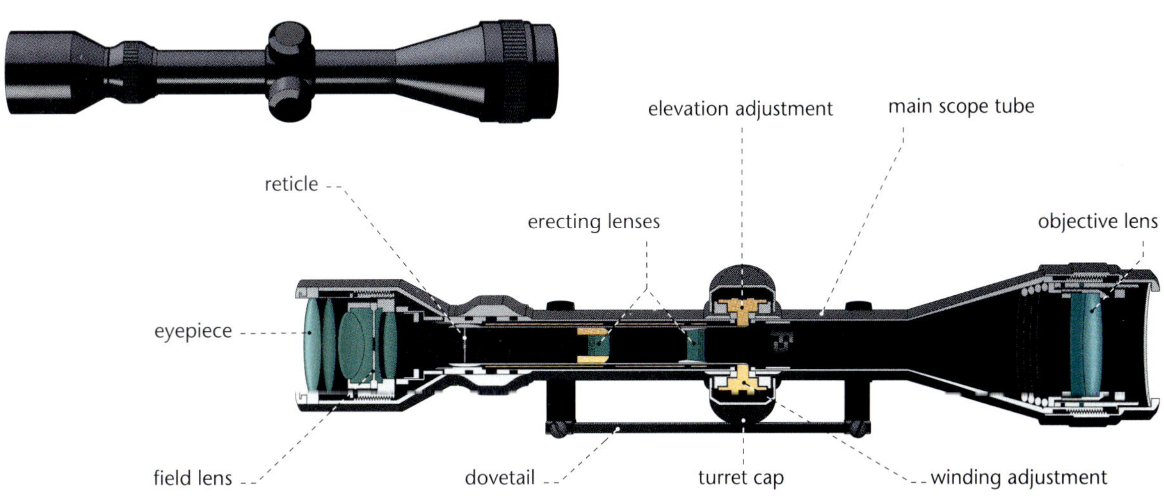

TELESCOPIC SIGHT

PRISM BINOCULARS

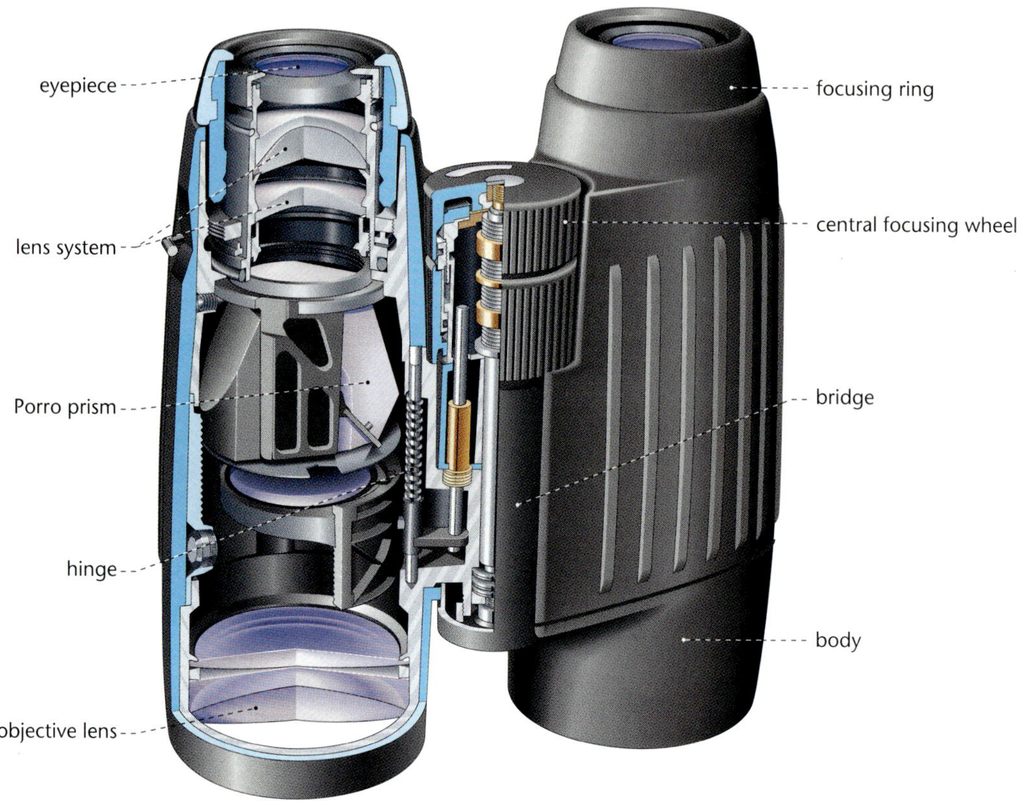

MAGNETIC COMPASS

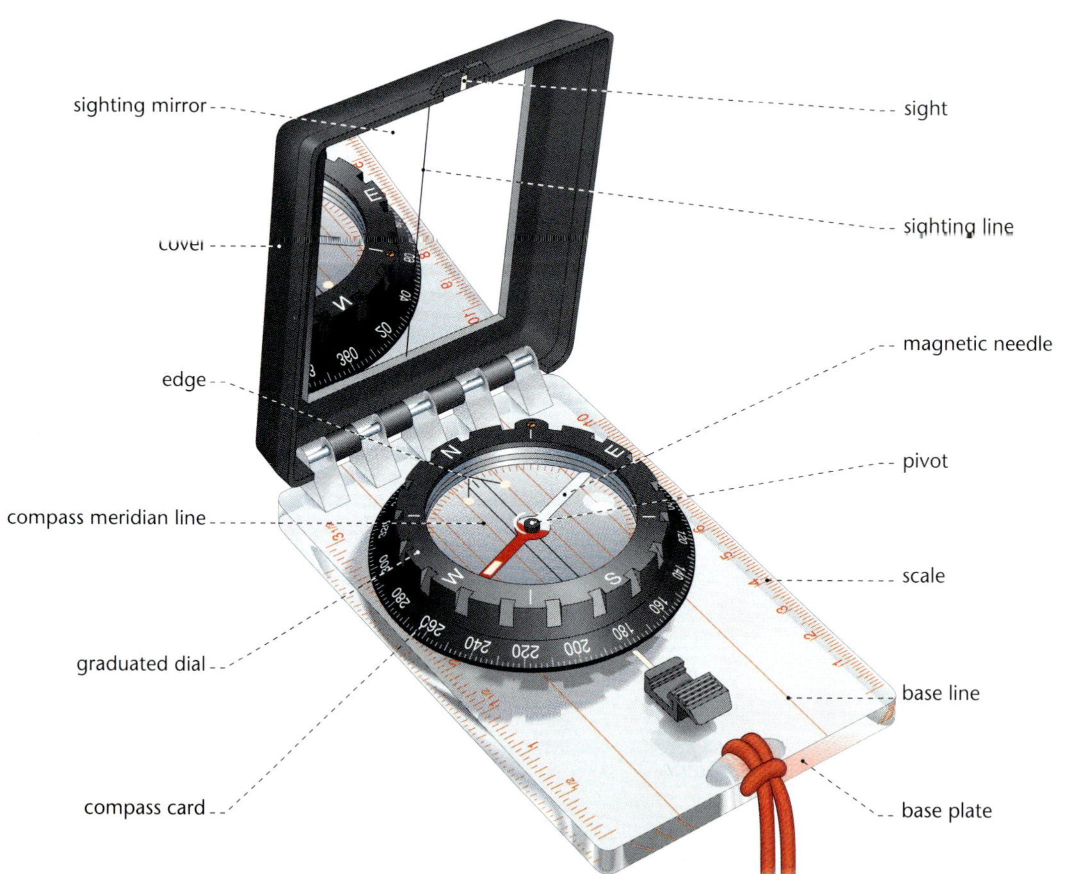

OPTICAL INSTRUMENTS

CROSS SECTION OF A REFLECTING TELESCOPE

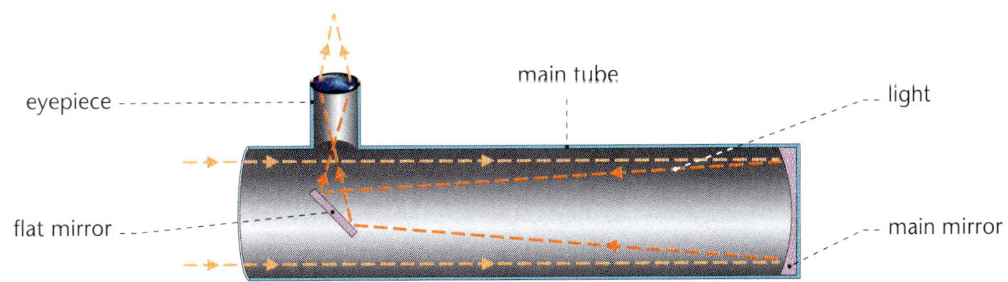

REFRACTING TELESCOPE

CROSS SECTION OF A REFRACTING TELESCOPE

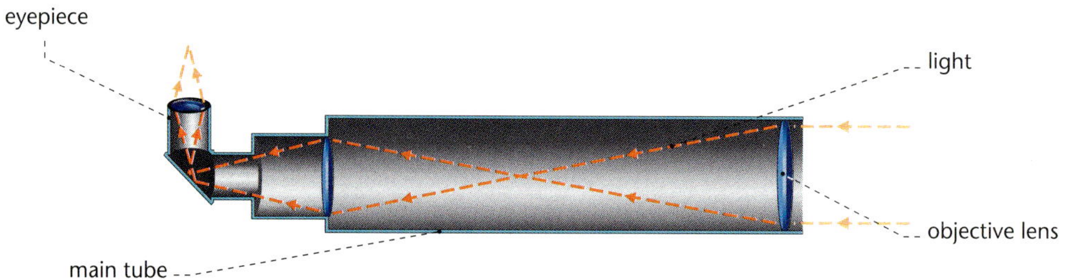

LENSES

CONVERGING LENSES

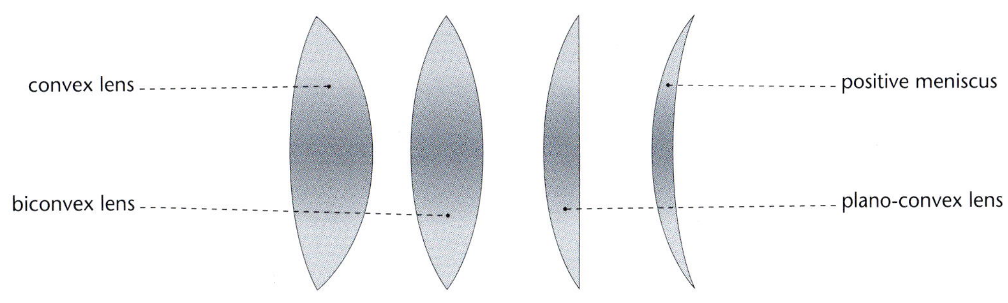

DIVERGING LENSES

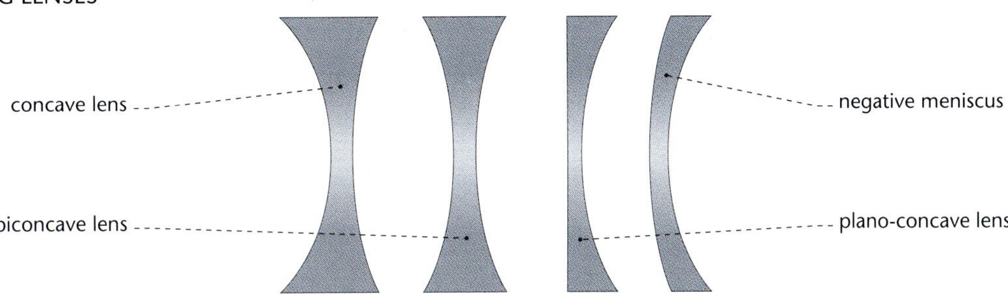

RADAR

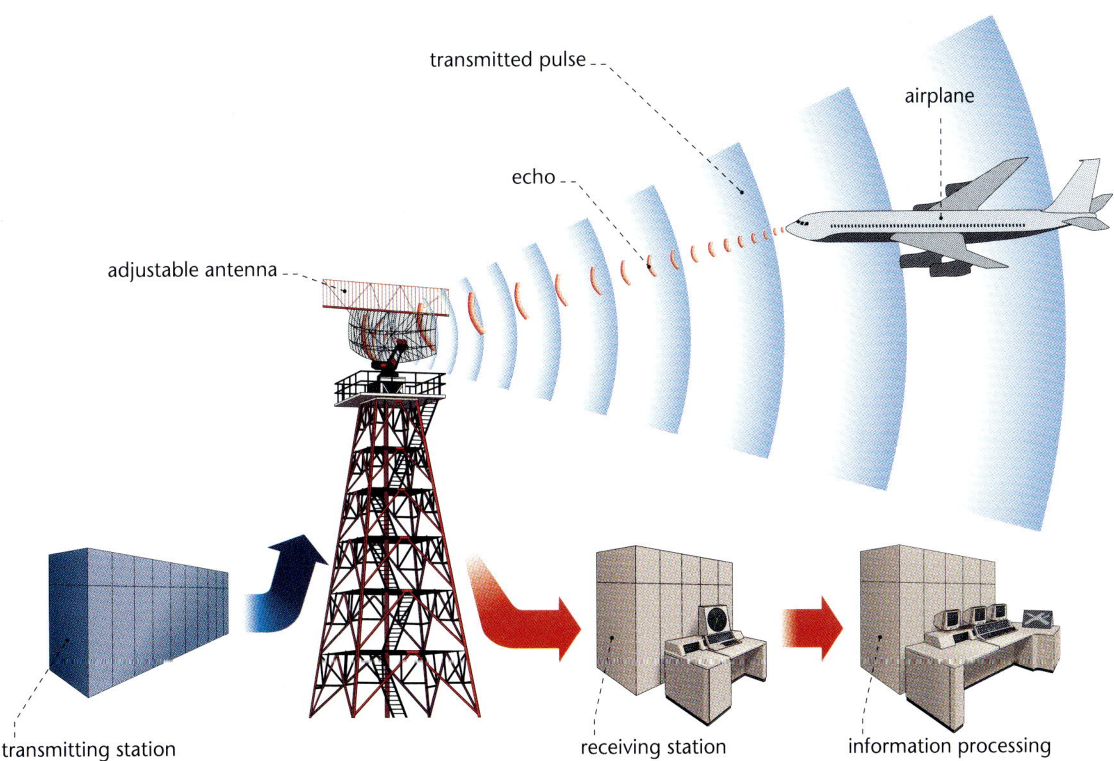

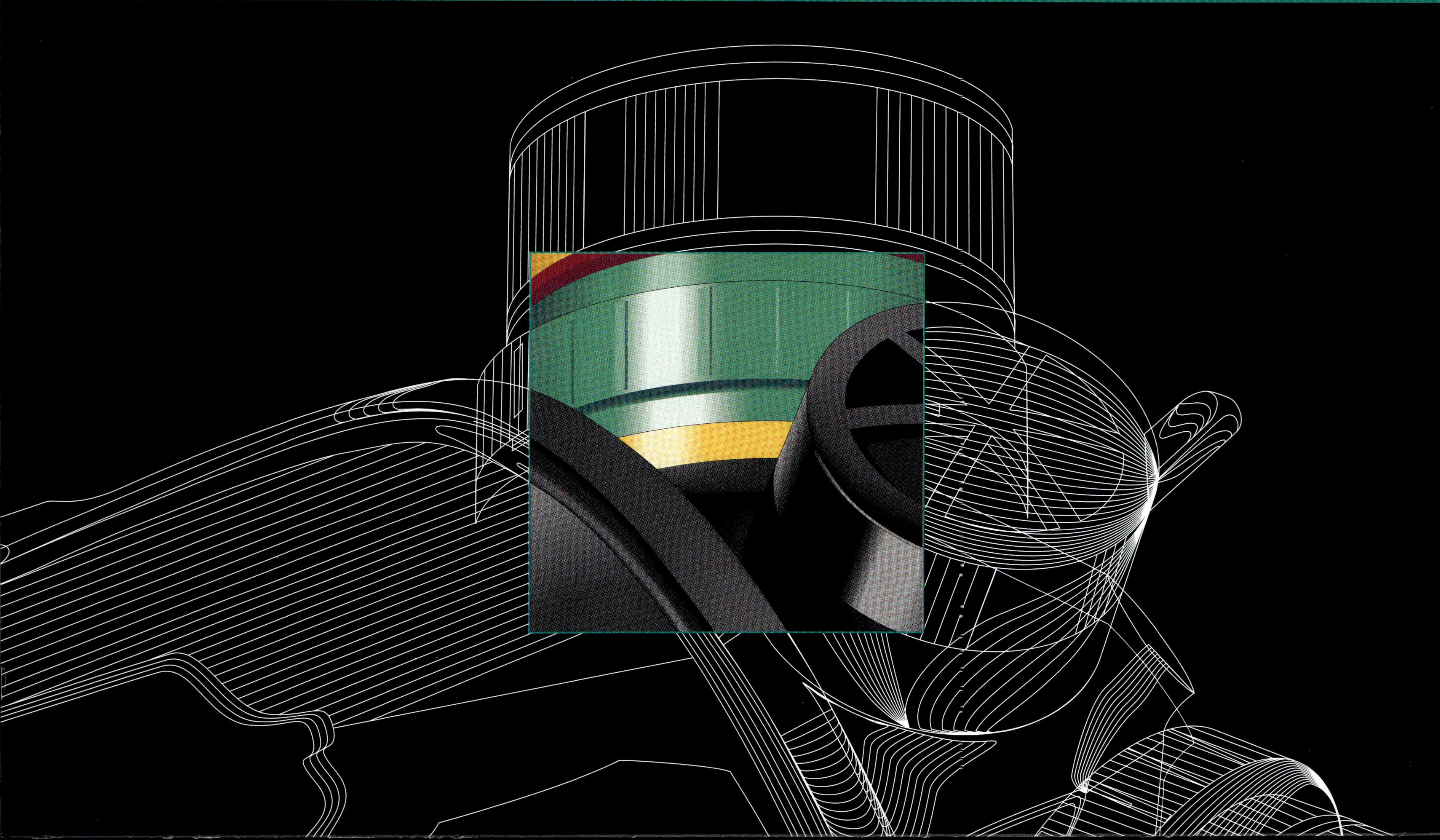

CONTENTS

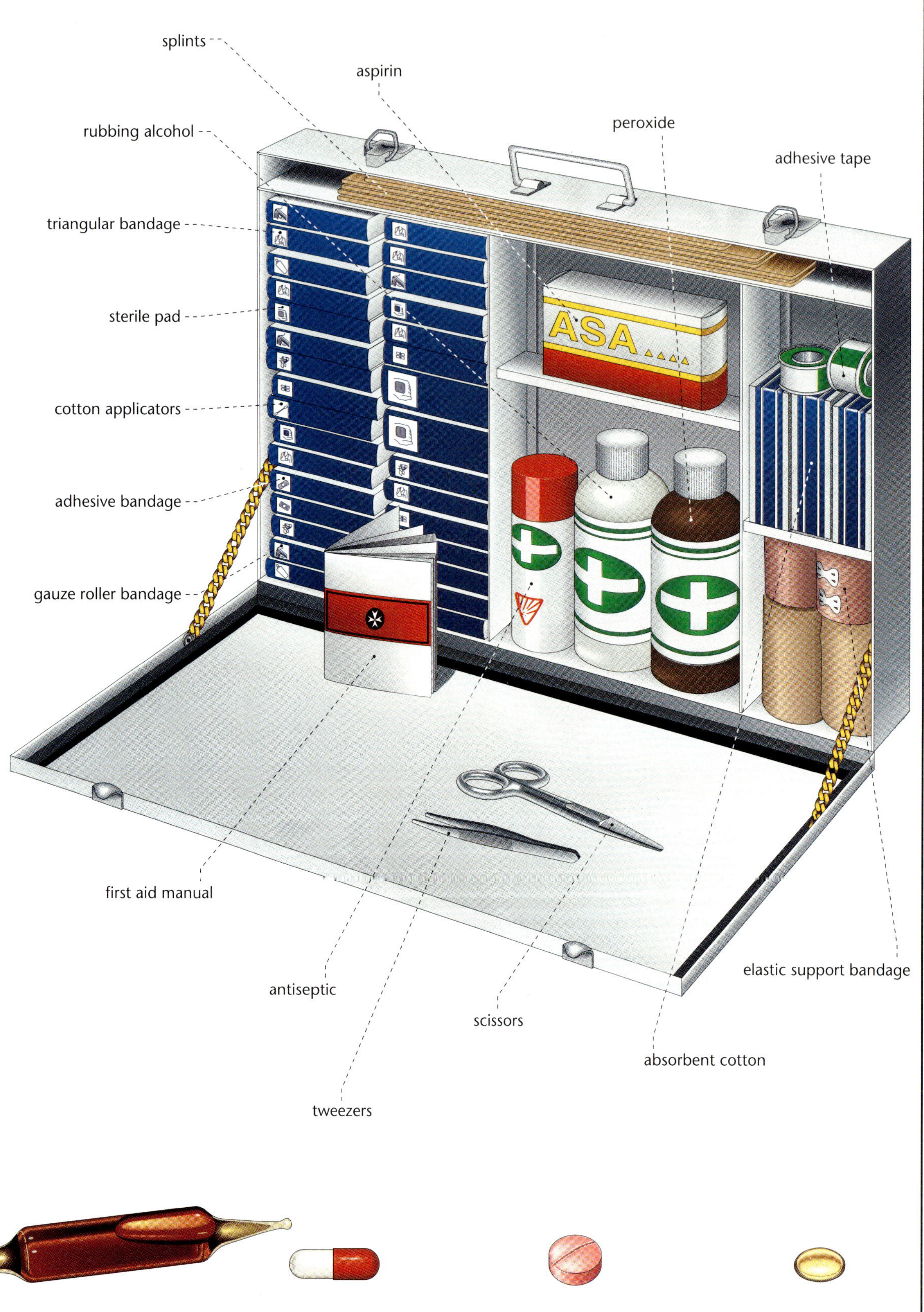

splints
aspirin
peroxide
rubbing alcohol
adhesive tape
triangular bandage
sterile pad
ASA
cotton applicators
adhesive bandage
gauze roller bandage
first aid manual
antiseptic
scissors
absorbent cotton
tweezers
elastic support bandage
vial
capsule
tablet
gelatin capsule

STETHOSCOPE

SYRINGE

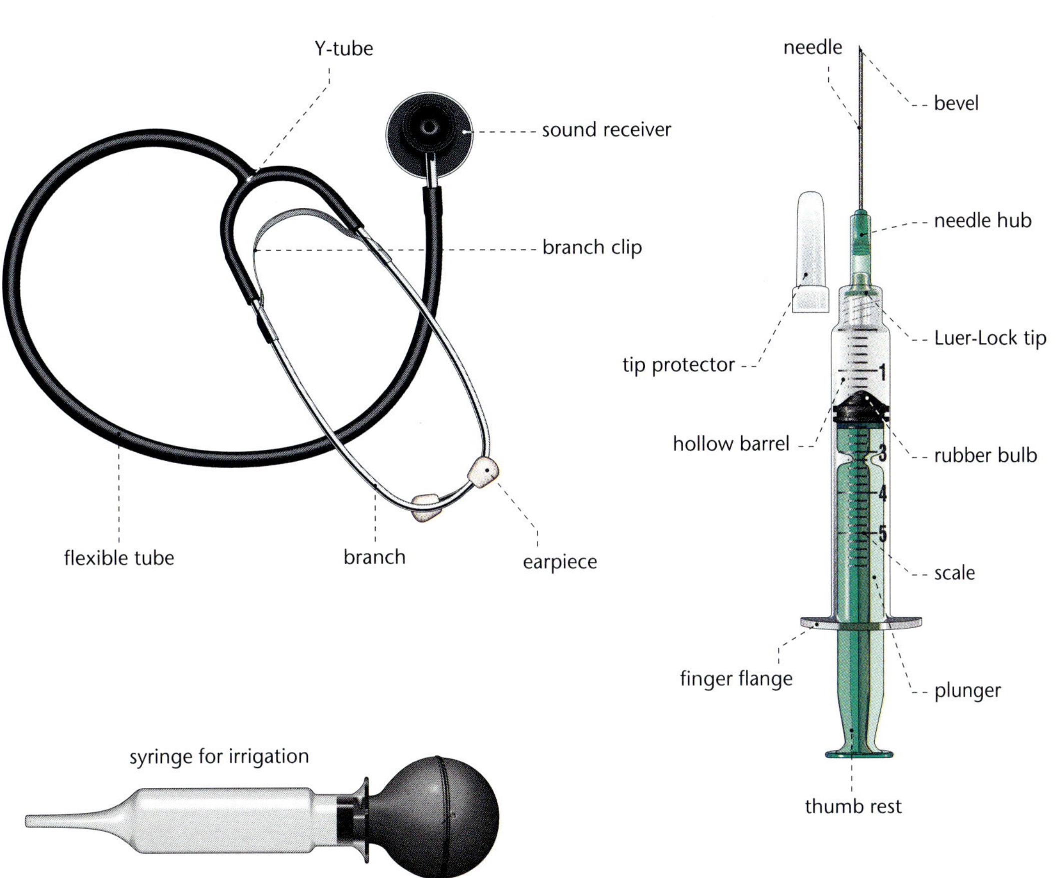

COT

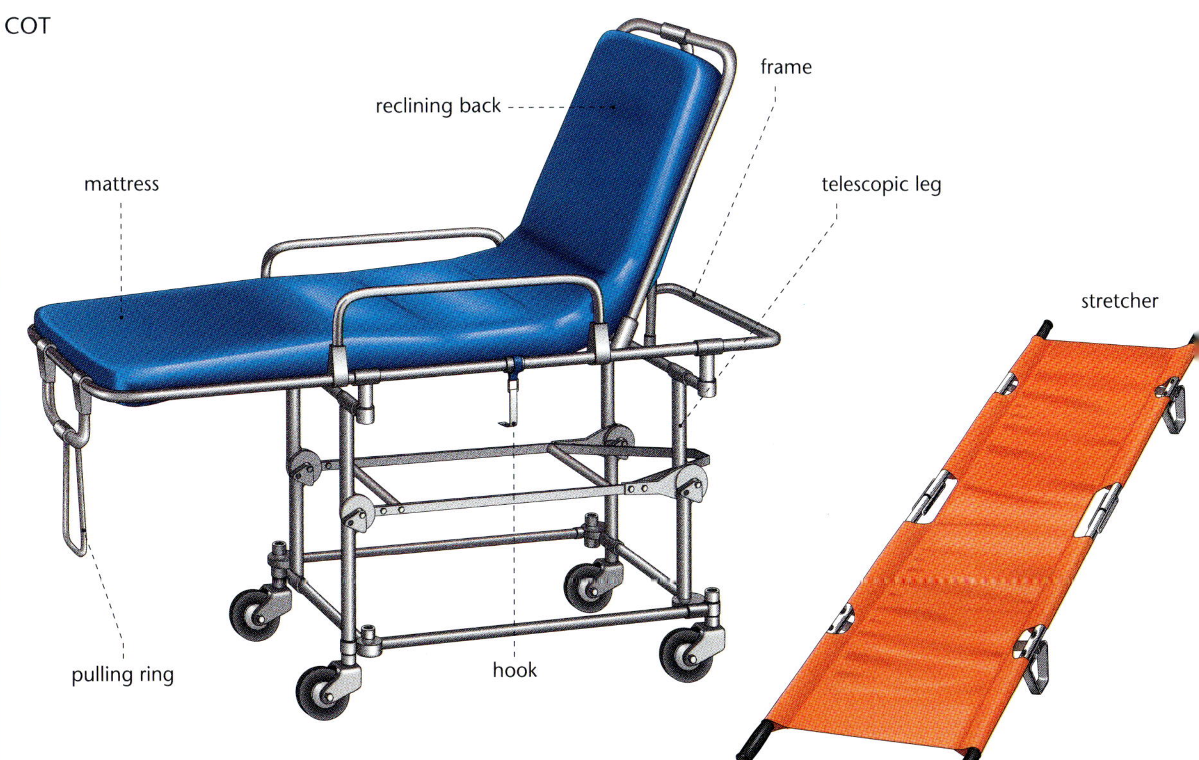

back
handle
seat
armrest
clothing guard
arm
brake
spacer
hub
push rim
large wheel
cross brace
front wheel
tipping lever
heel loop
footrest
hanger bracket

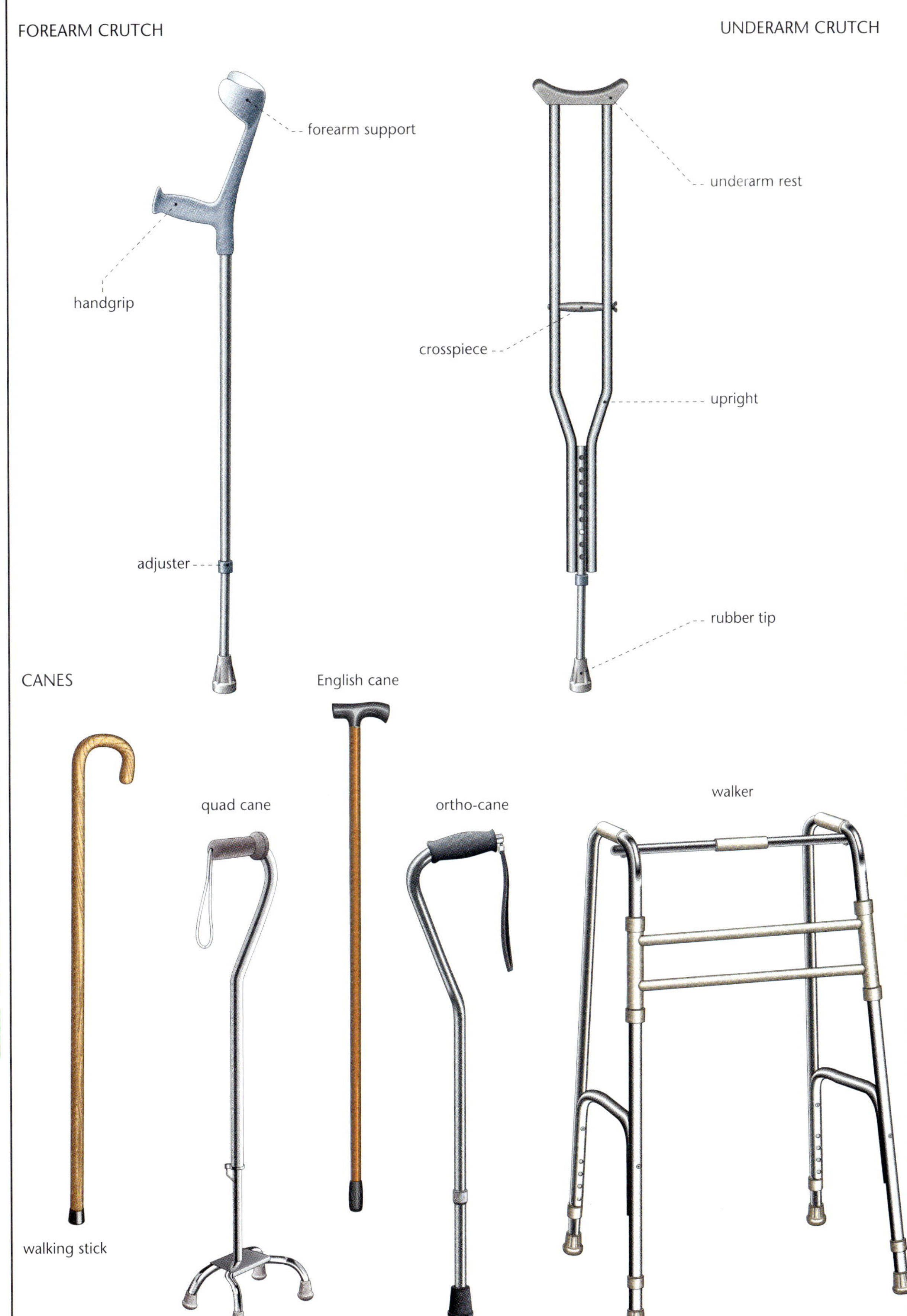

FOREARM CRUTCH
UNDERARM CRUTCH
forearm support
underarm rest
handgrip
crosspiece
upright
adjuster
rubber tip
CANES
English cane
quad cane
ortho-cane
walker
walking stick

EAR PROTECTION

EYE PROTECTION

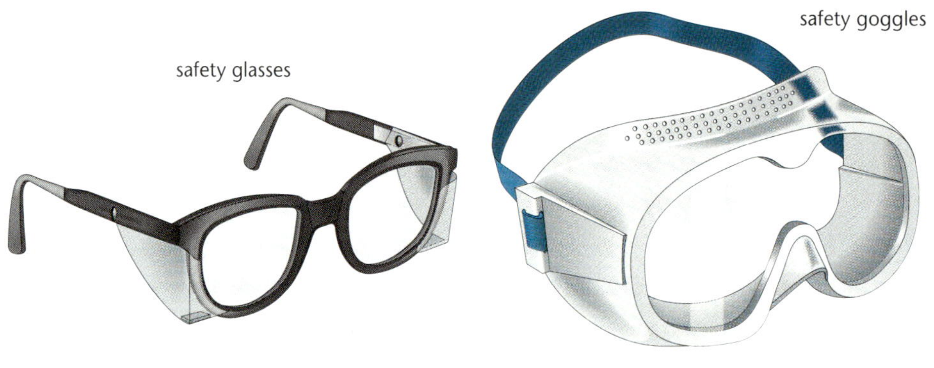

HEAD PROTECTION

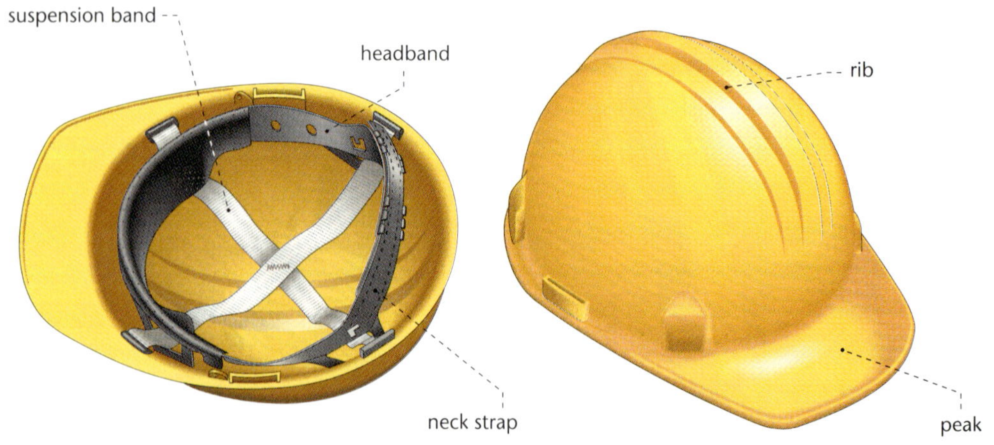

RESPIRATORY SYSTEM PROTECTION

RESPIRATOR

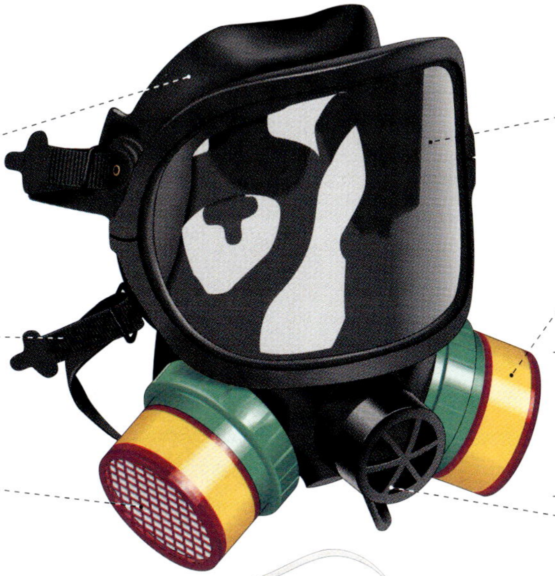

HALF-MASK RESPIRATOR

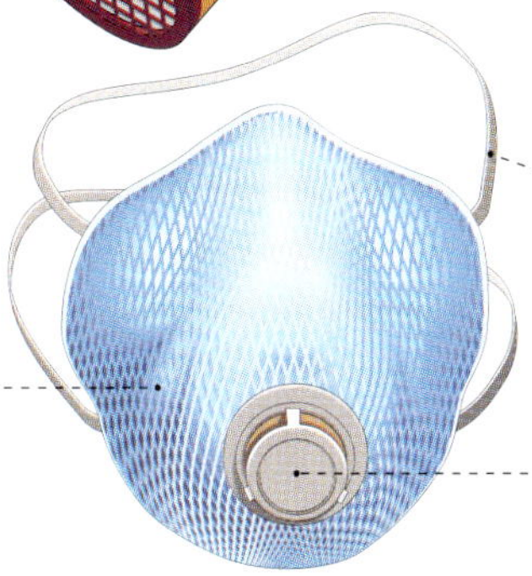

SAFETY VEST

FEET PROTECTION

toe guard

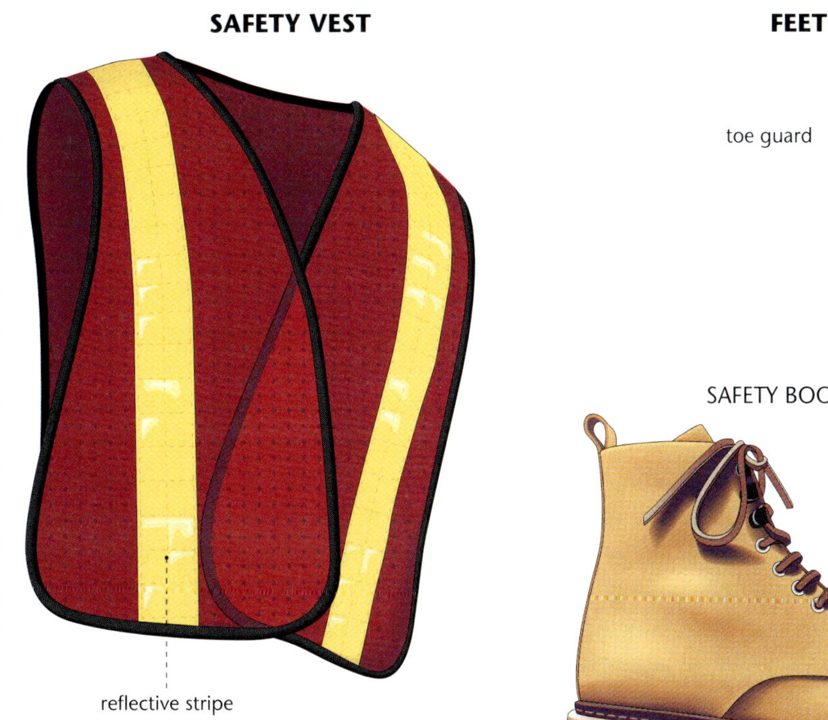

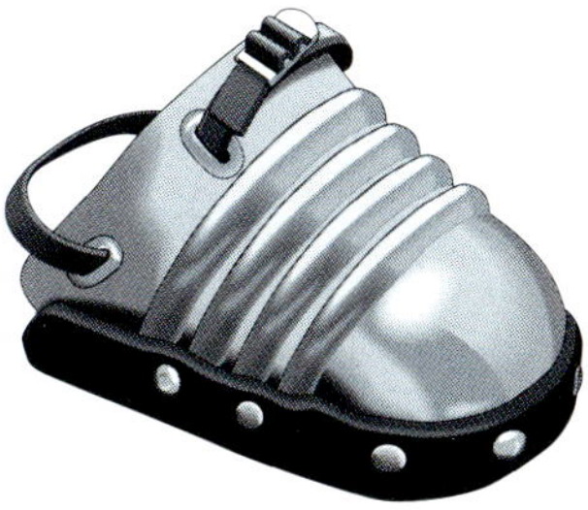

SAFETY BOOT

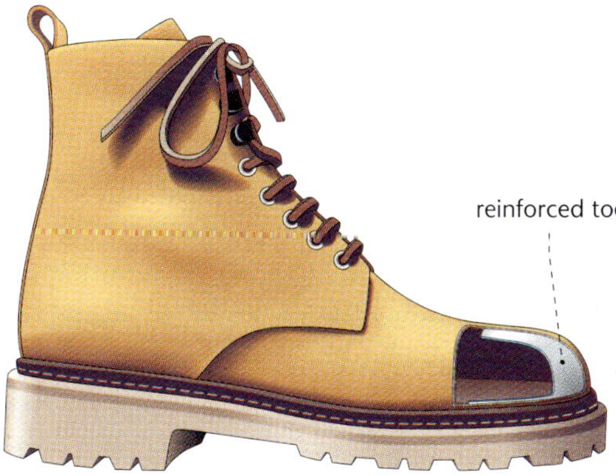

ENERGY

CONTENTS

COAL MINE

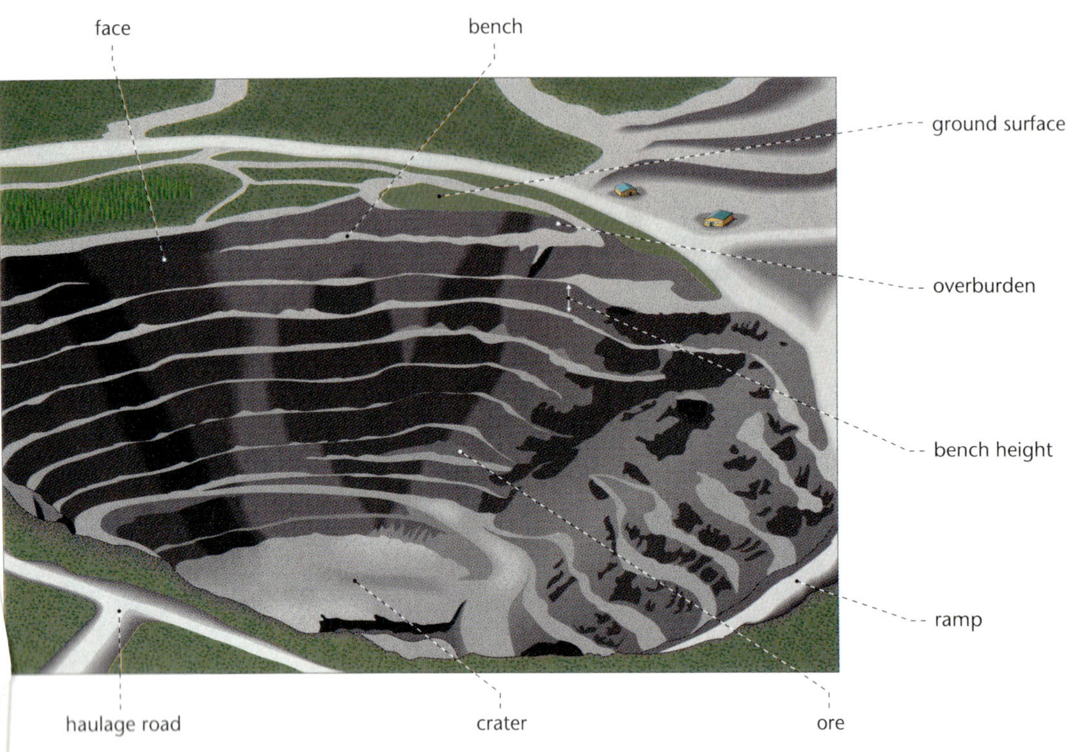

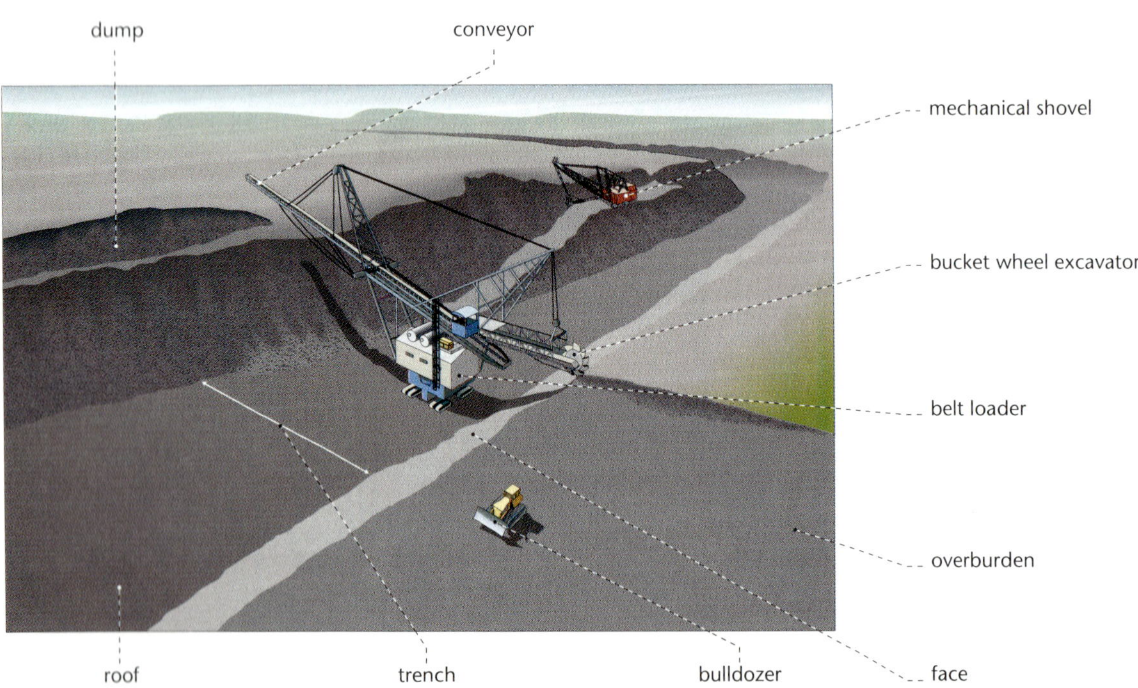

ENERGY

JACKLEG DRILL

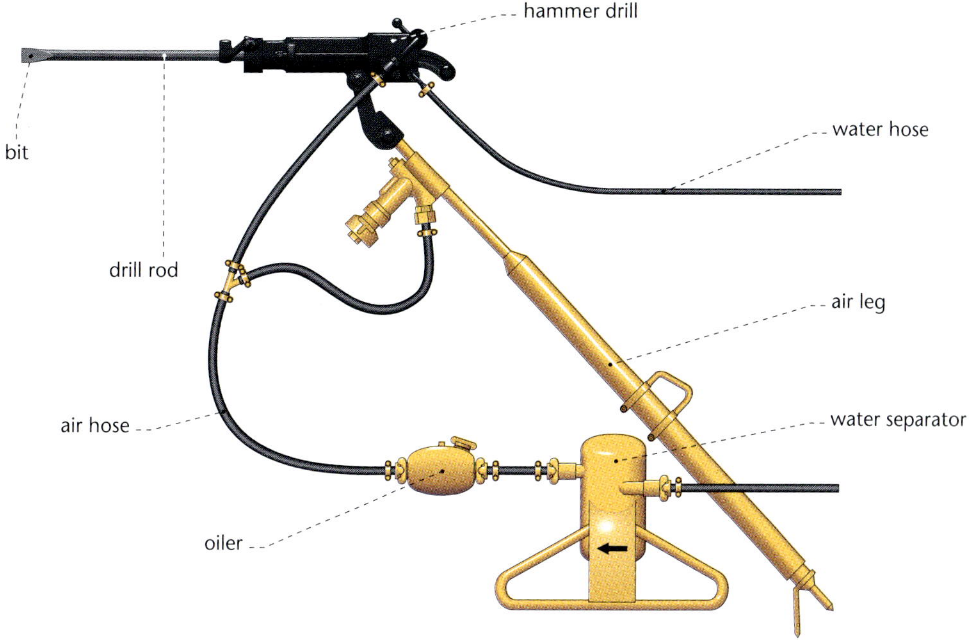

PITHEAD

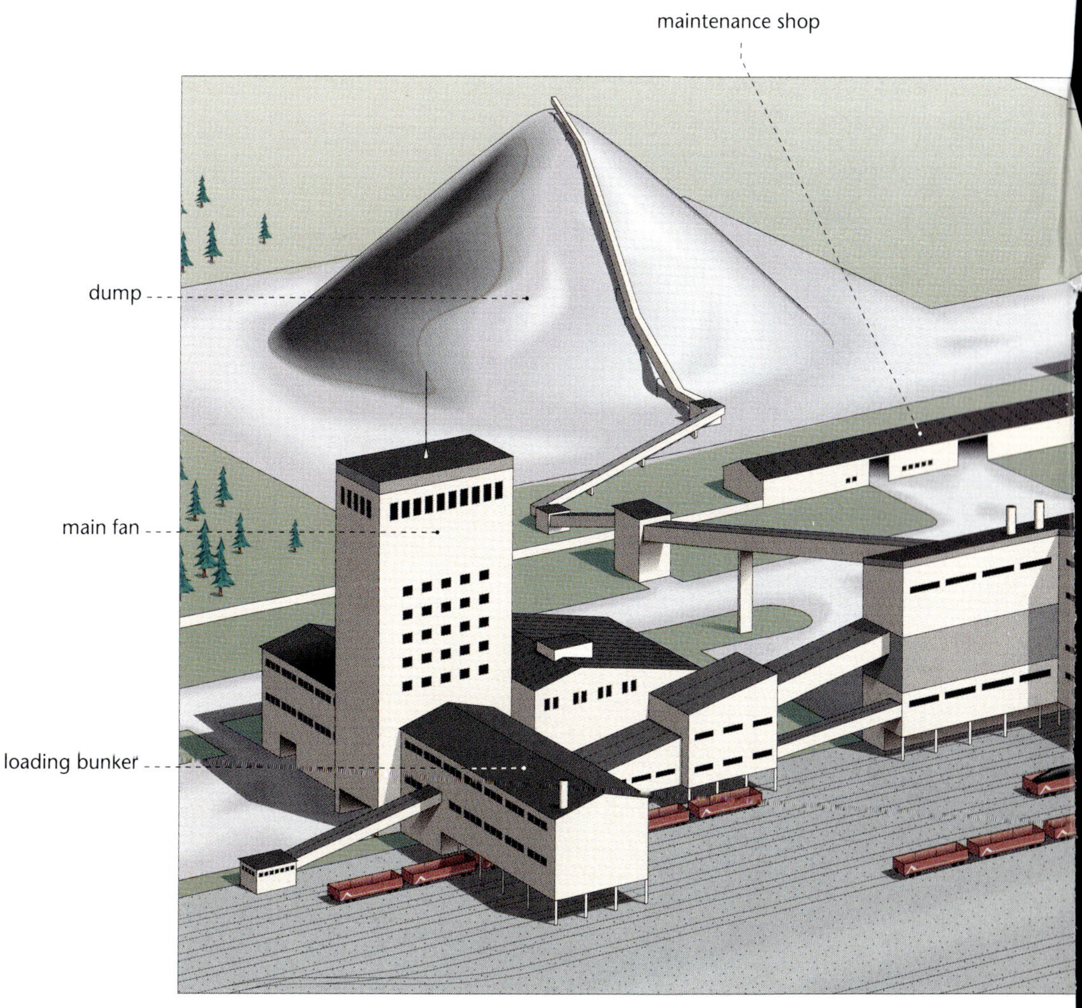

ENERGY

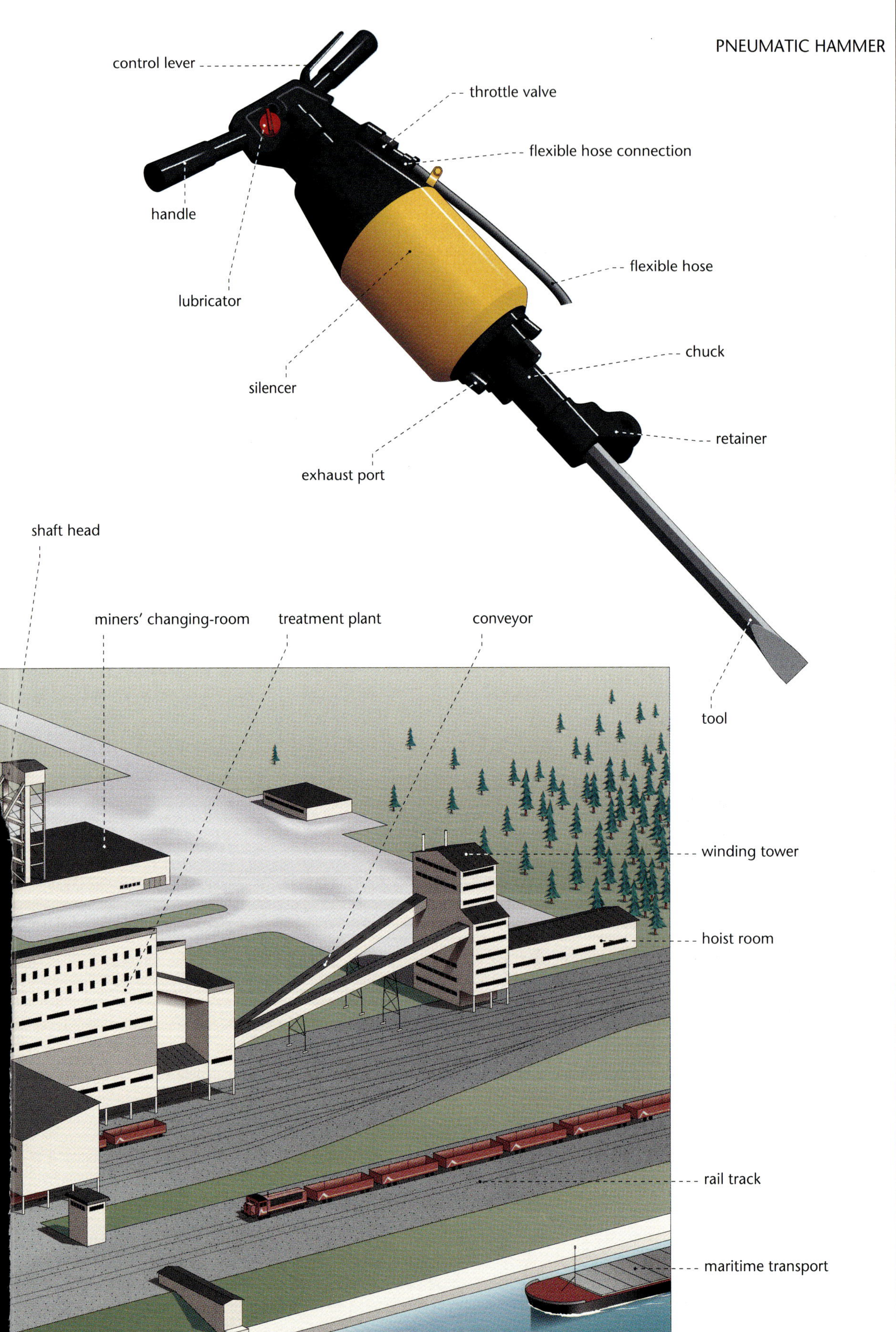
control lever
throttle valve
flexible hose connection
handle
flexible hose
lubricator
chuck
silencer
retainer
exhaust port
shaft head
tool
miners' changing-room
treatment plant
conveyor
winding tower
hoist room
rail track
maritime transport

UNDERGROUND MINE

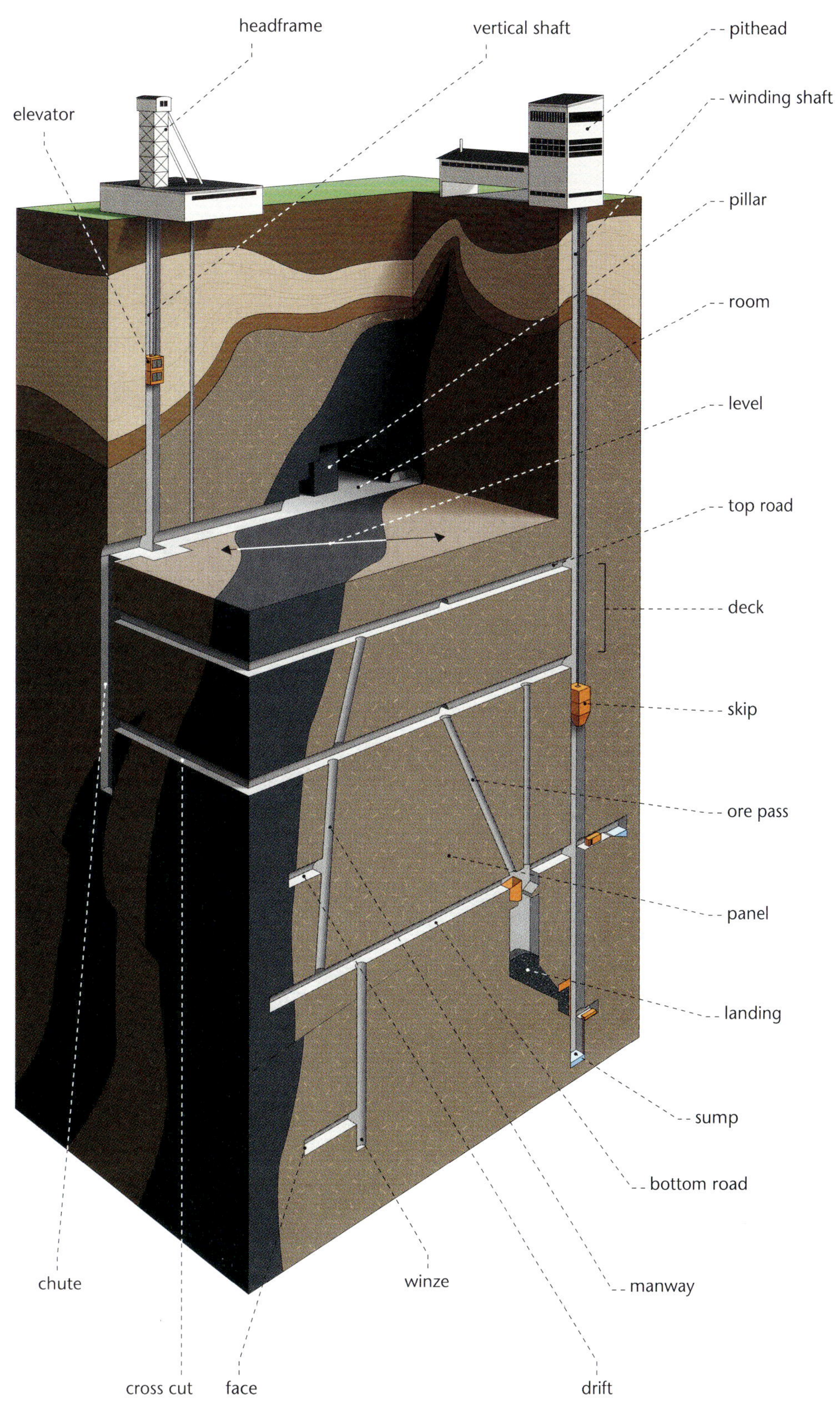

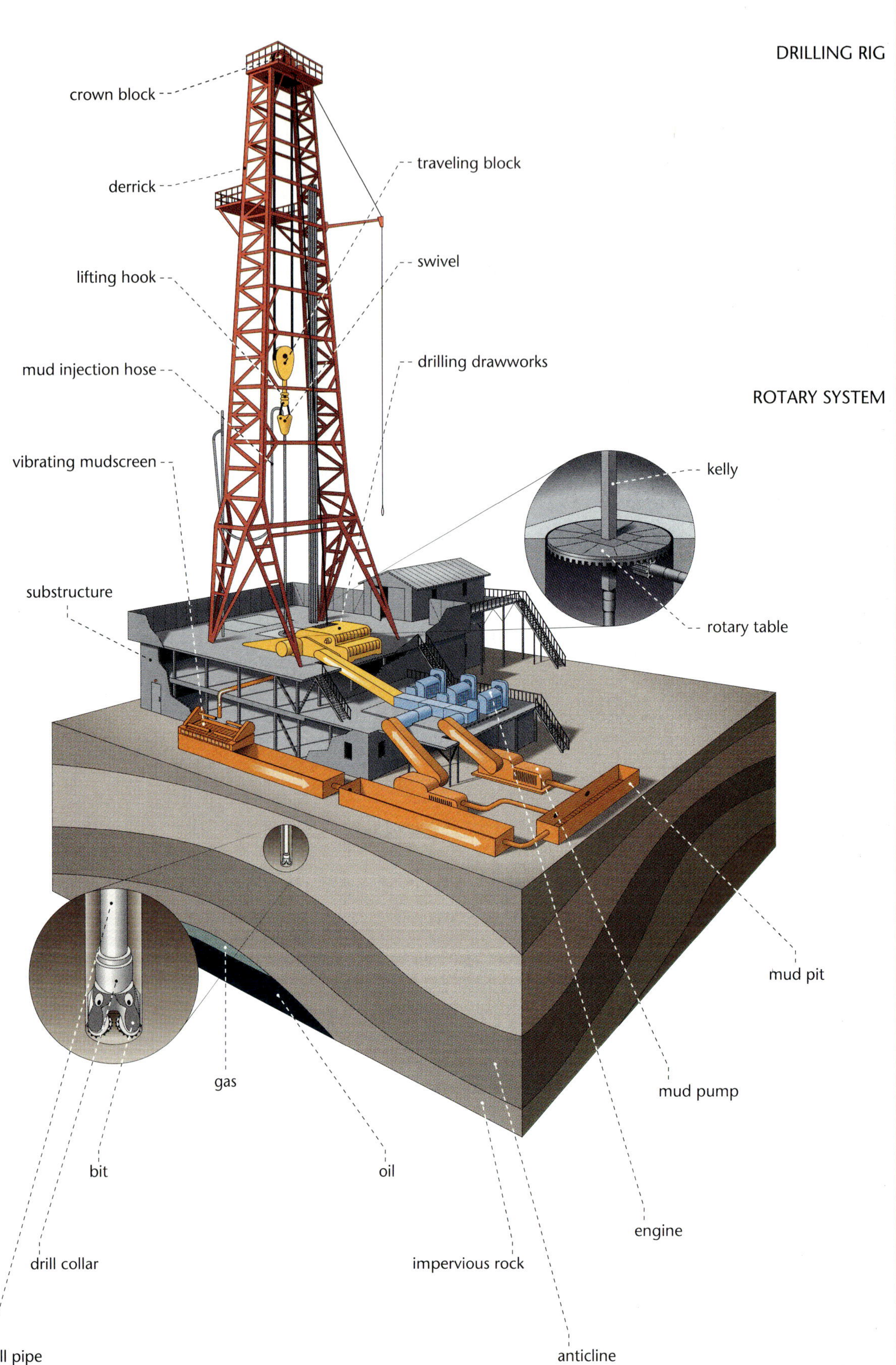
crown block
derrick
lifting hook
mud injection hose
vibrating mudscreen
substructure
traveling block
swivel
drilling drawworks
kelly
rotary table
drill pipe
drill collar
bit
gas
oil
impervious rock
anticline
engine
mud pump
mud pit

PRODUCTION PLATFORM

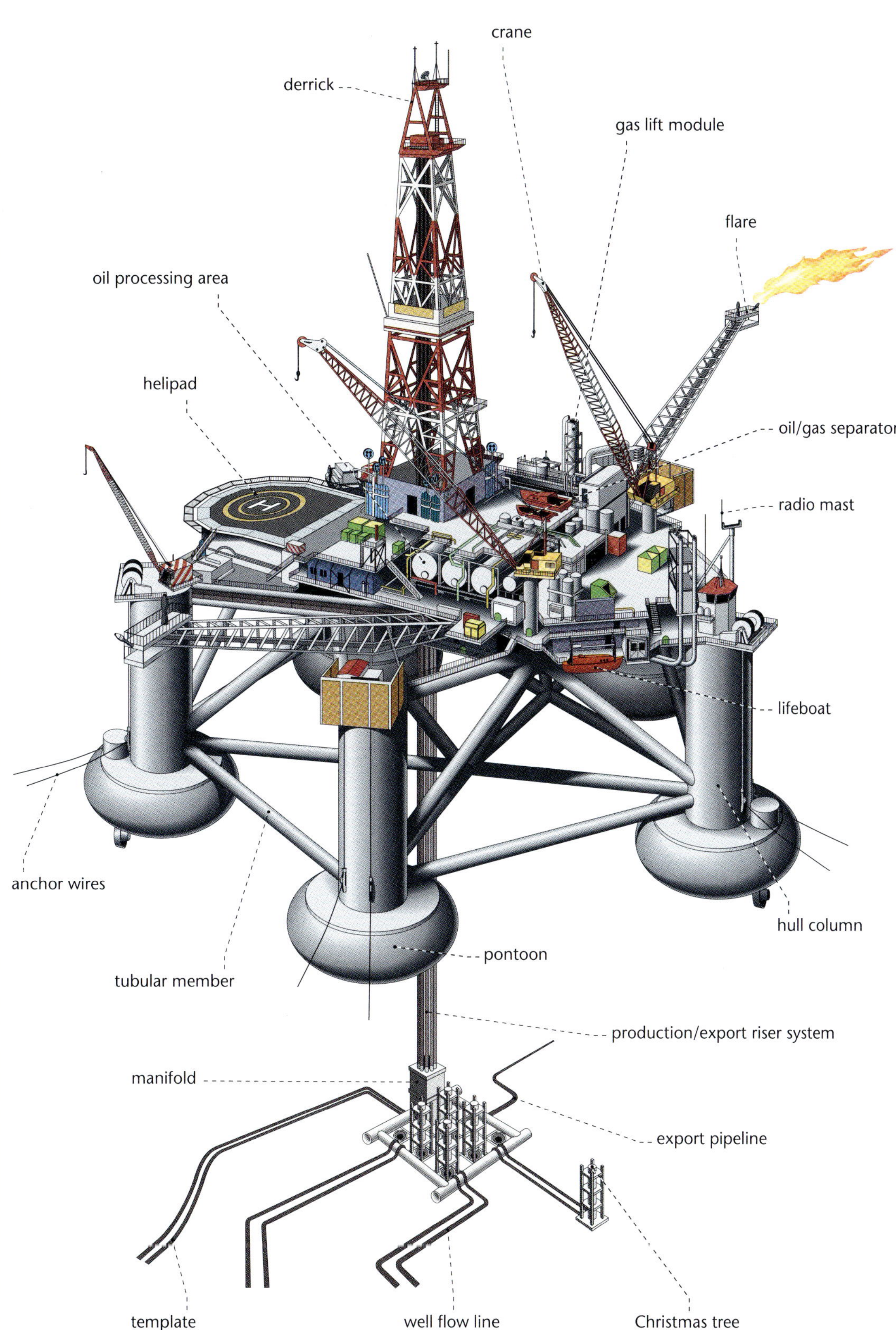

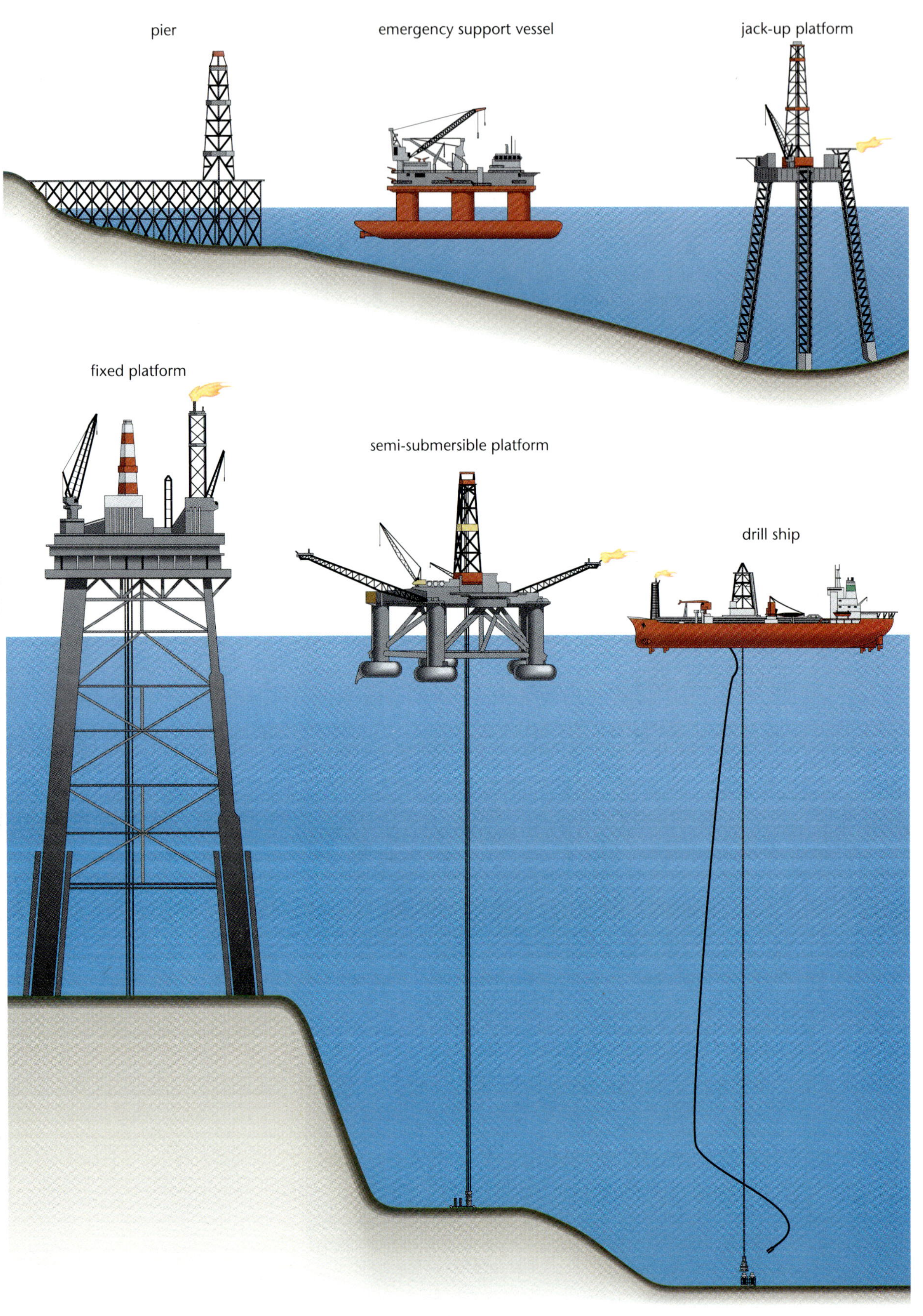

pier
emergency support vessel
jack-up platform
fixed platform
semi-submersible platform
drill ship

CHRISTMAS TREE

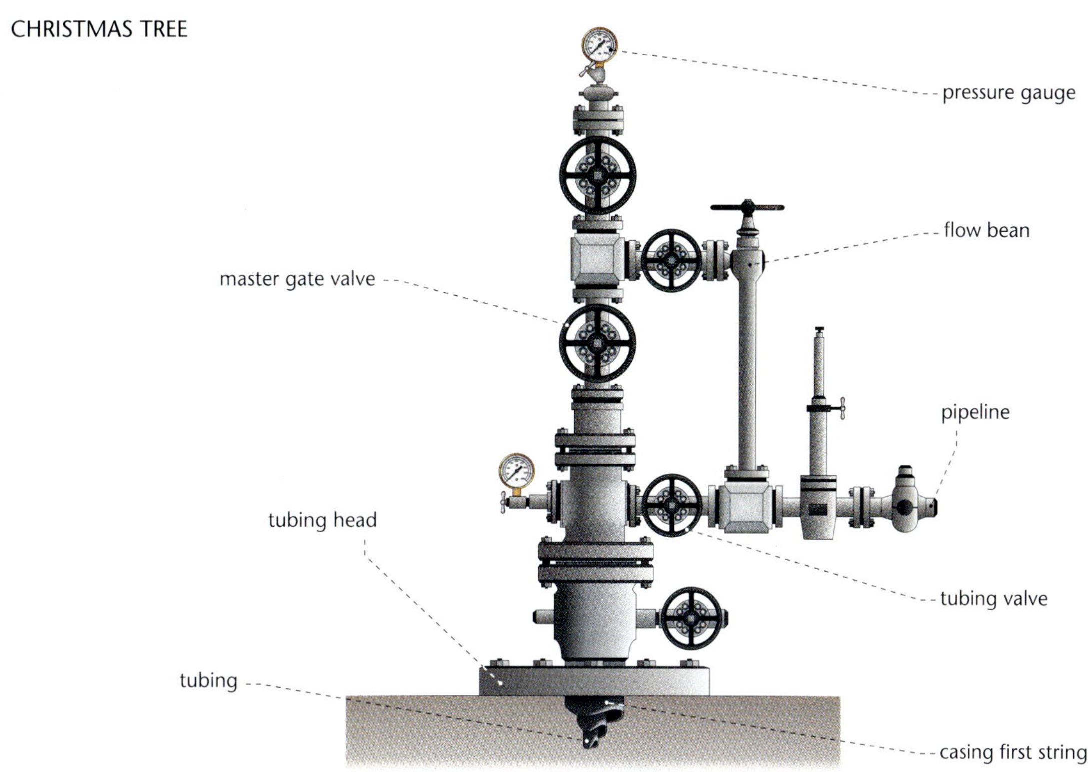

CRUDE-OIL PIPELINE

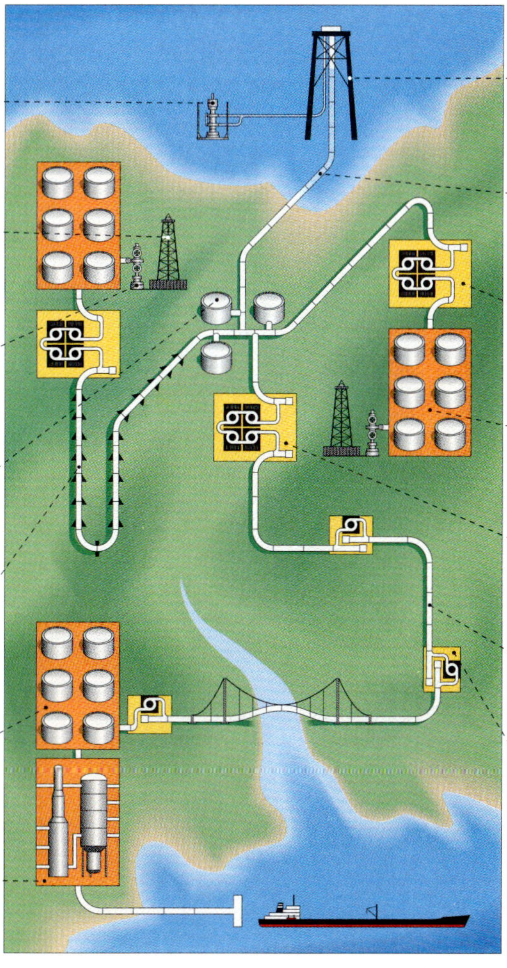

ENERGY

740

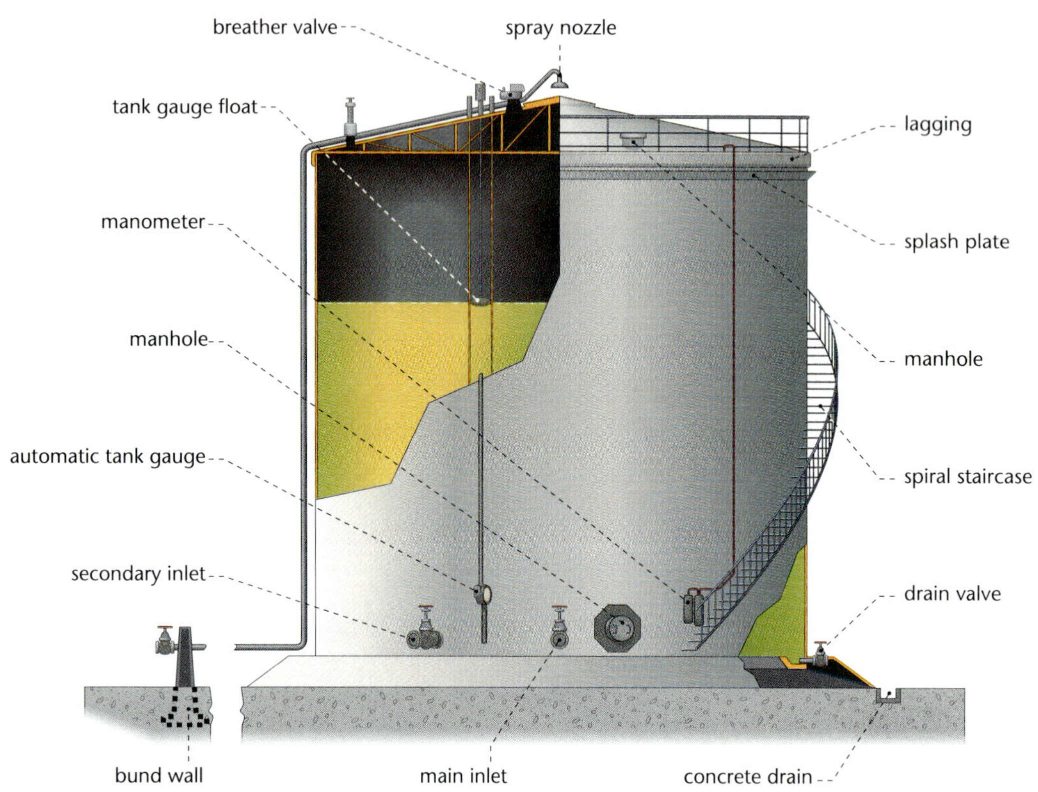

FLOATING-ROOF TANK

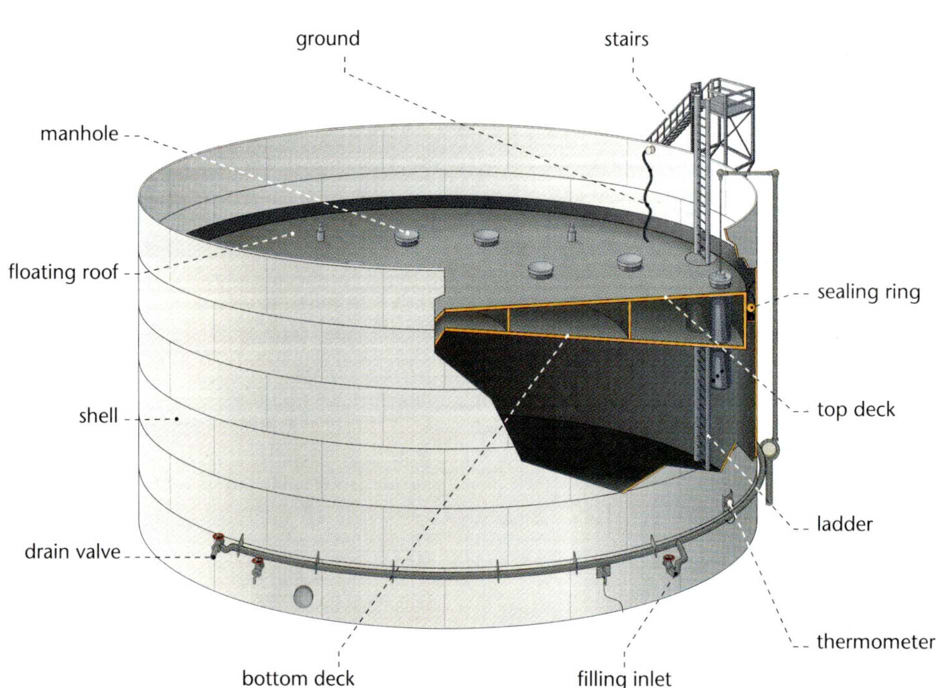

TANK TRAILER

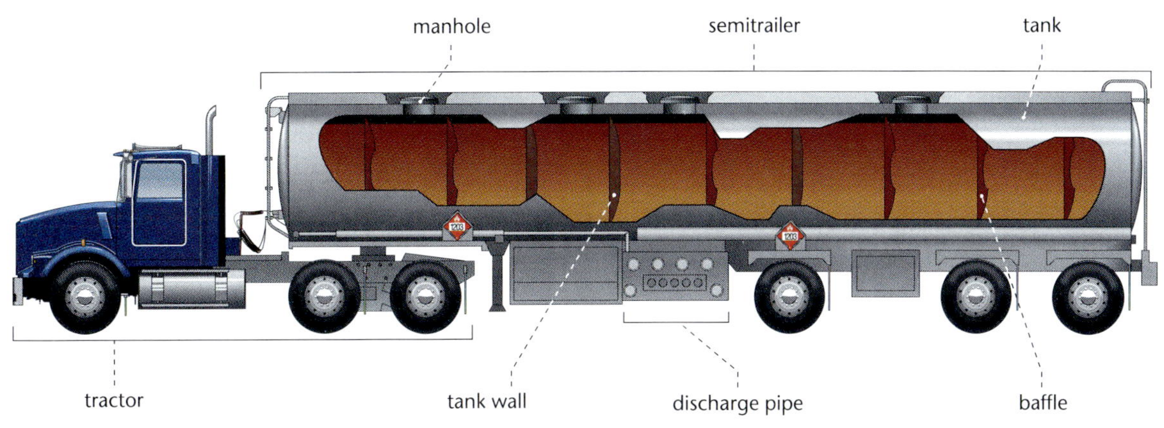

TANKER

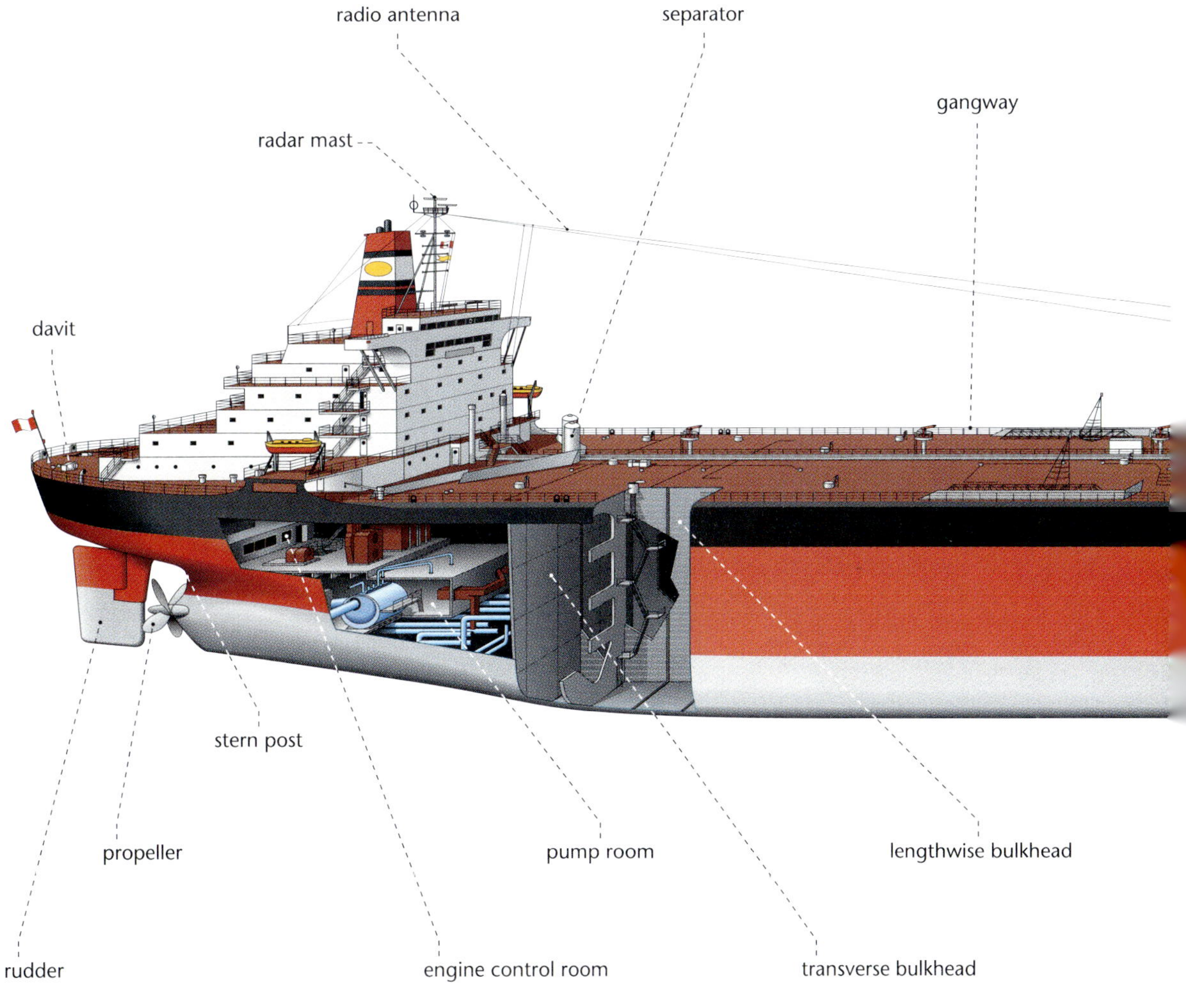

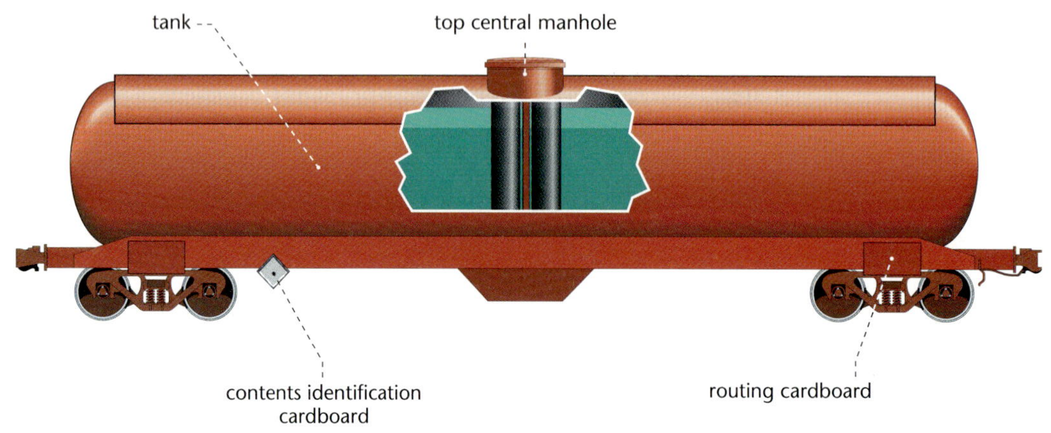

tank
top central manhole
contents identification cardboard
routing cardboard

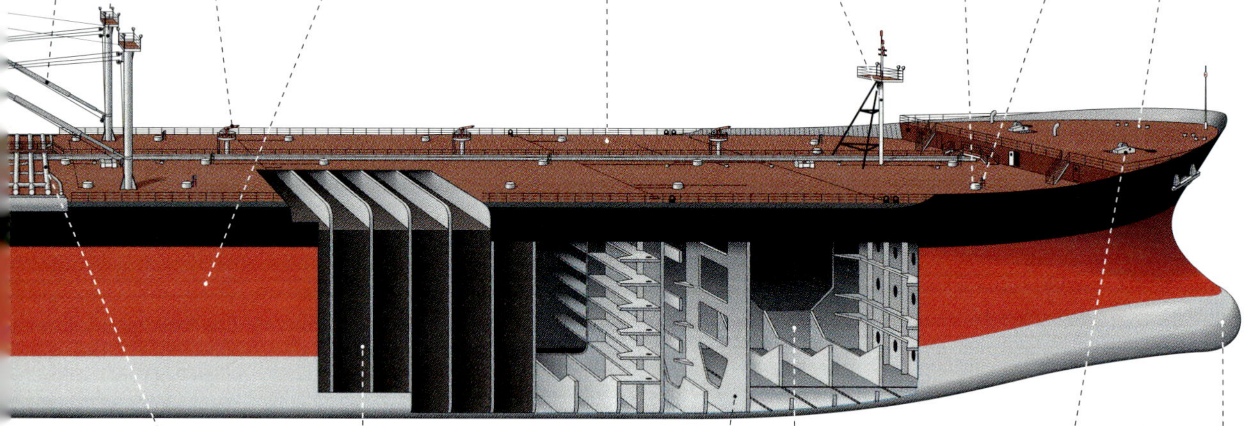

derrick
bitt
derrick mast
air relief valve
foam monitor
foremast
tank hatch
wall side
main deck
crossover cargo deck line
web frame
mooring winch
tank
center keelson
bulb

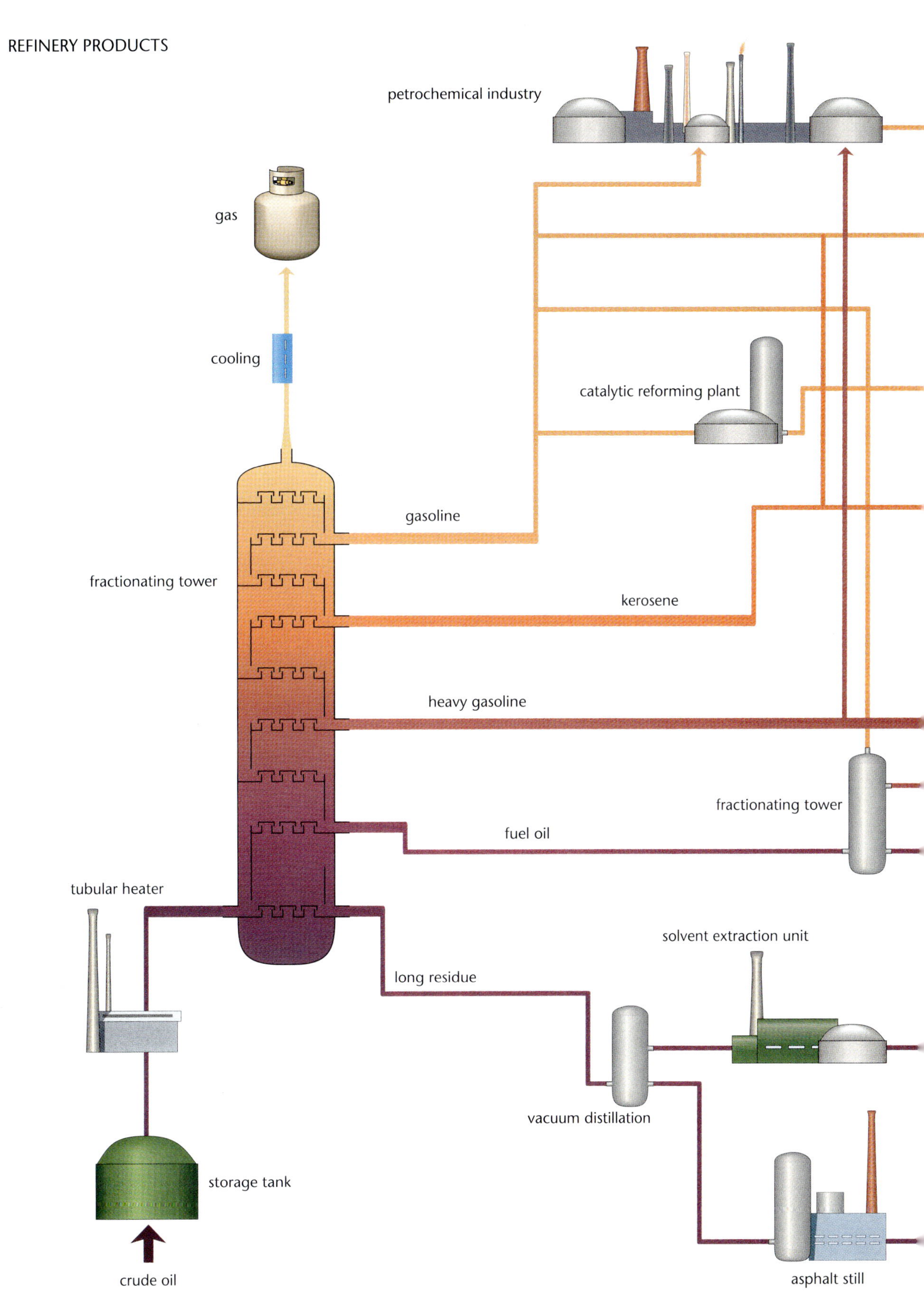

REFINERY PRODUCTS
petrochemical industry
gas
cooling
catalytic reforming plant
fractionating tower
gasoline
kerosene
heavy gasoline
fractionating tower
fuel oil
tubular heater
solvent extraction unit
long residue
vacuum distillation
storage tank
crude oil
asphalt still

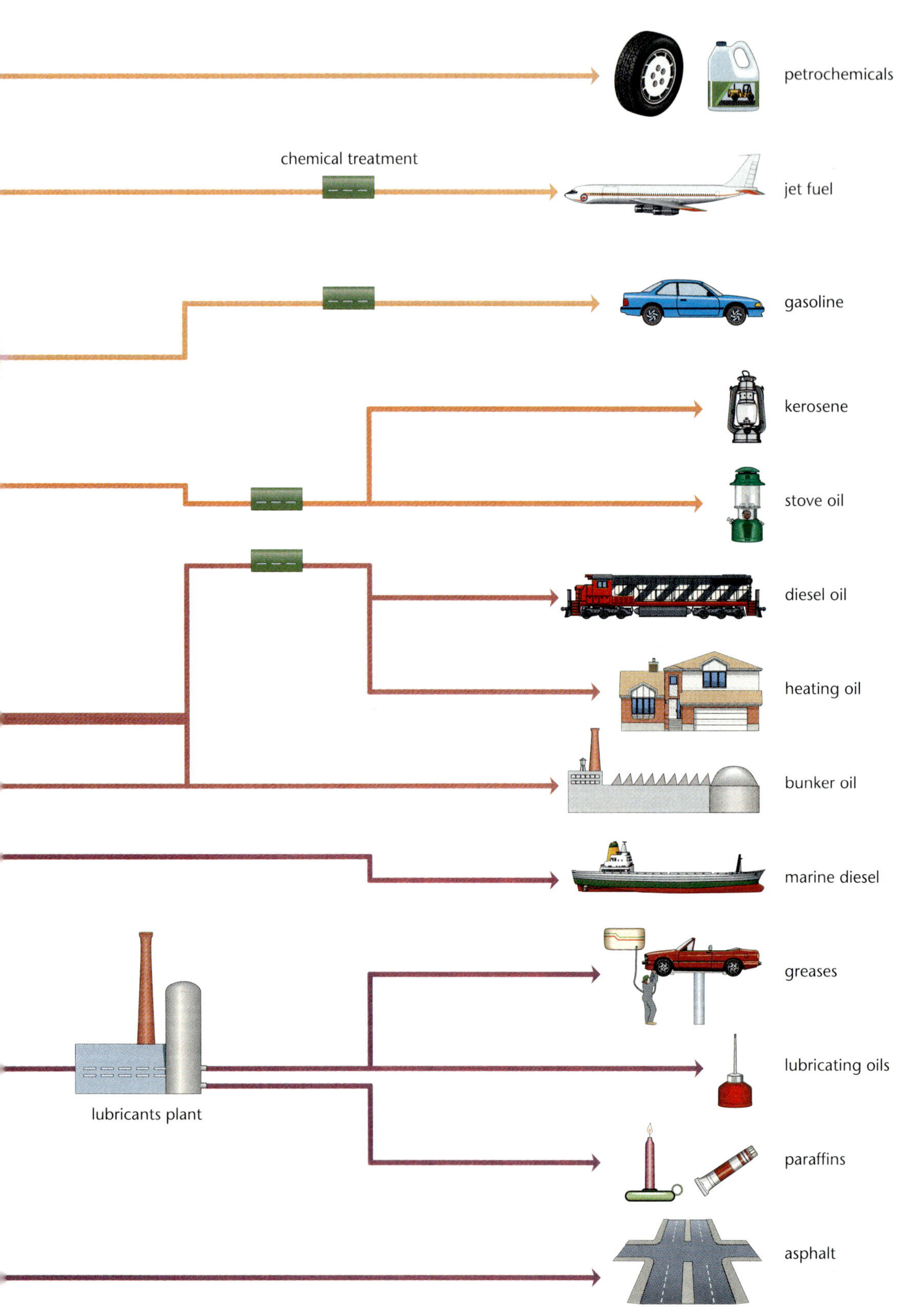

petrochemicals
chemical treatment
jet fuel
gasoline
kerosene
stove oil
diesel oil
heating oil
bunker oil
marine diesel
greases
lubricating oils
lubricants plant
paraffins
asphalt

HYDROELECTRIC COMPLEX

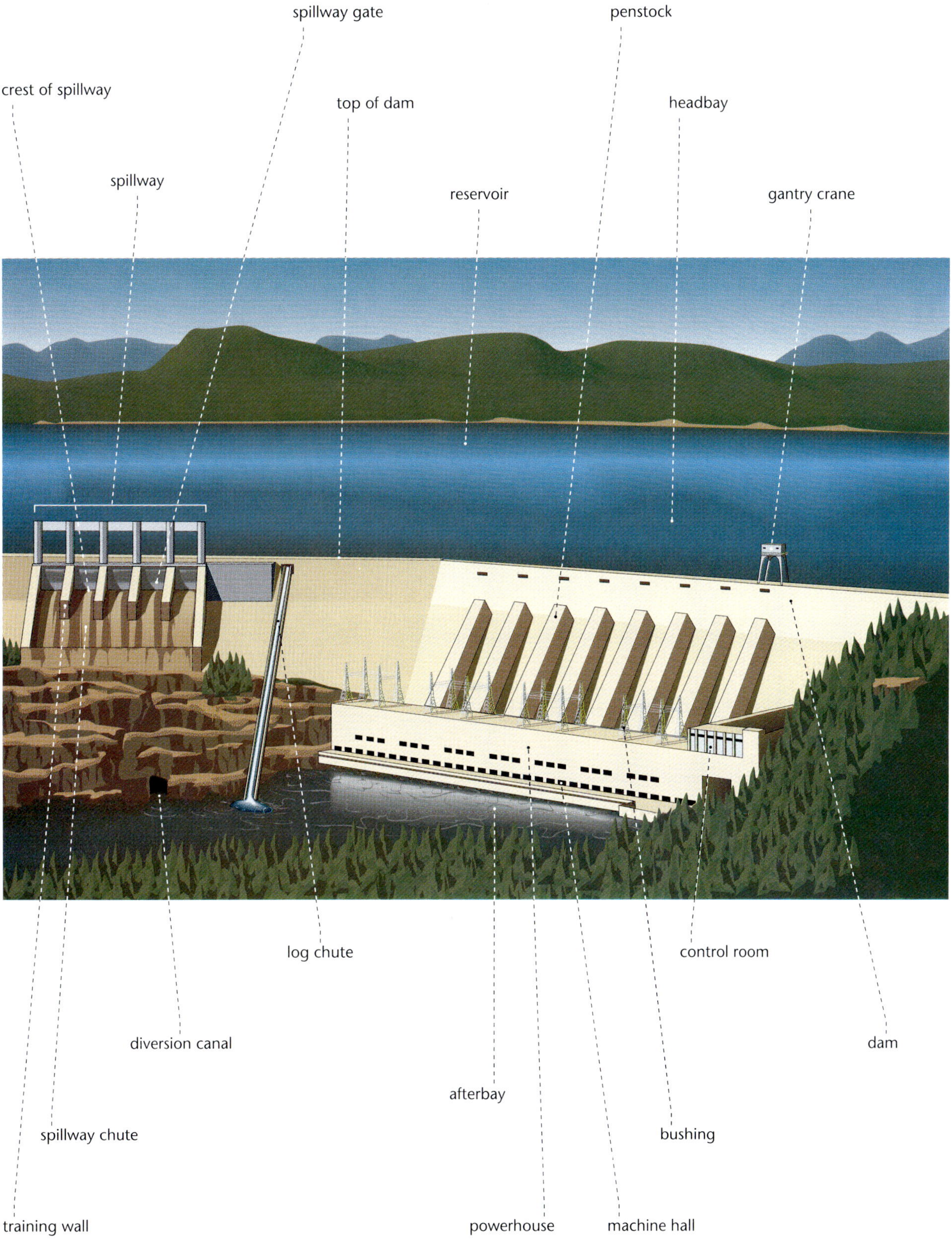

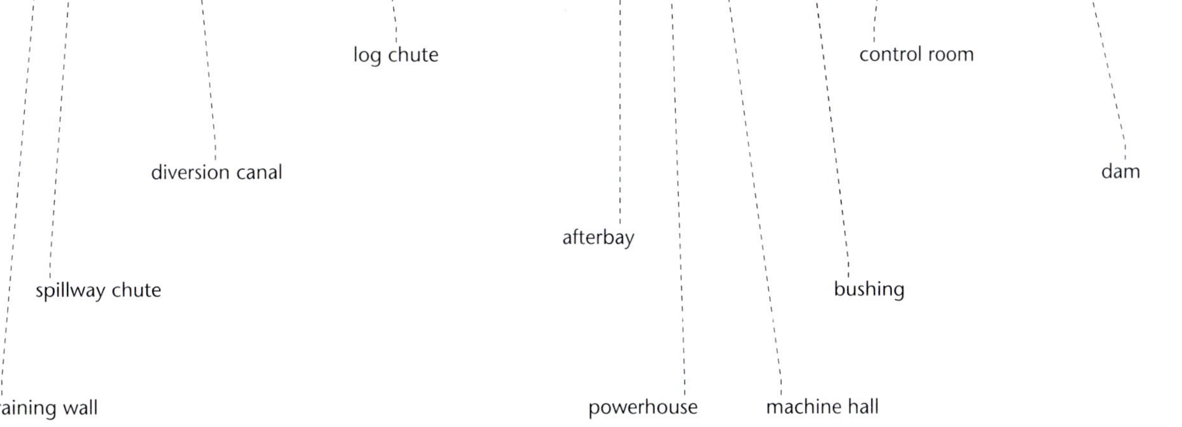

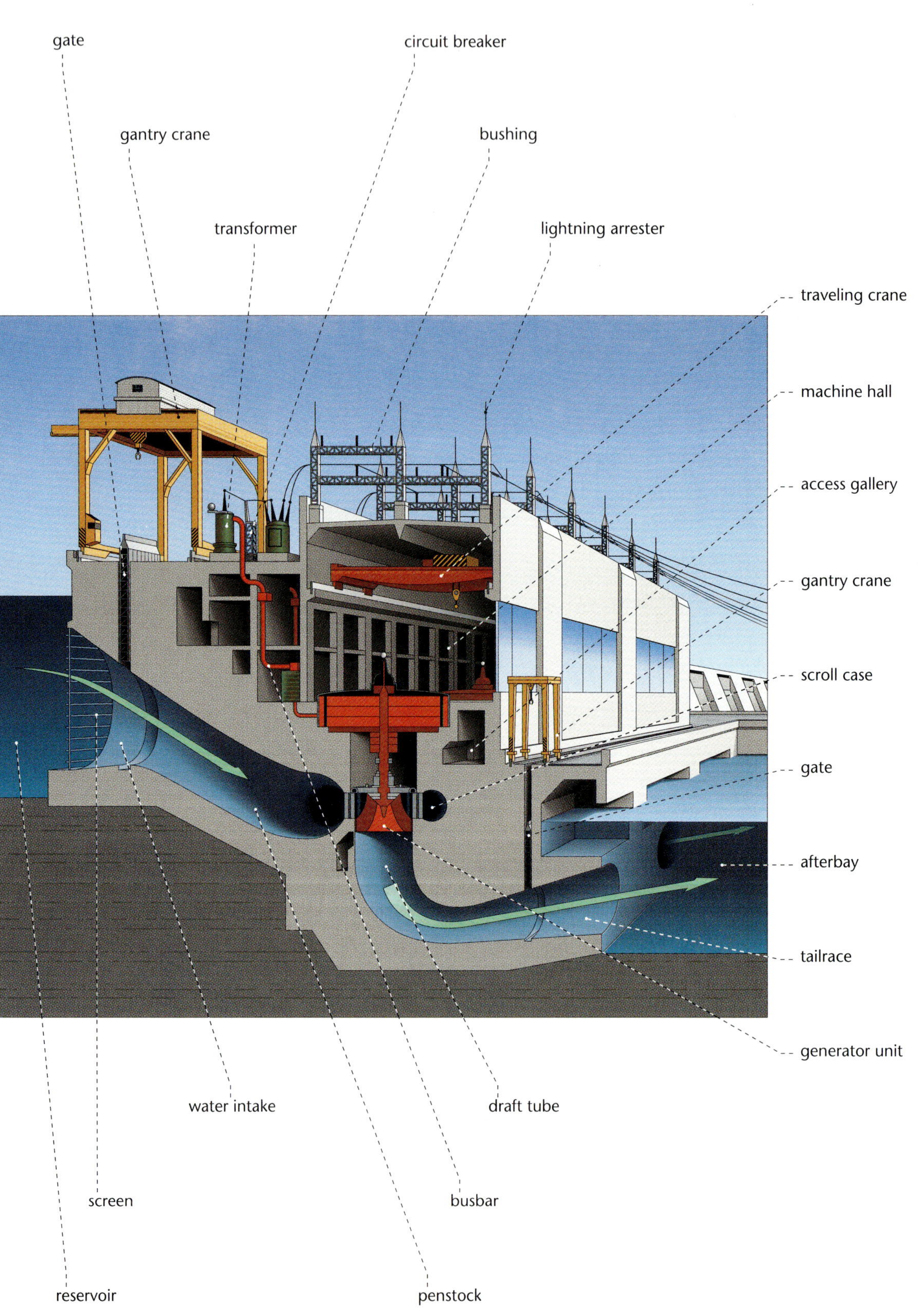

gate
gantry crane
circuit breaker
bushing
transformer
lightning arrester
traveling crane
machine hall
access gallery
gantry crane
scroll case
gate
afterbay
tailrace
generator unit
water intake
draft tube
screen
busbar
reservoir
penstock

embankment dam

CROSS SECTION OF AN EMBANKMENT DAM

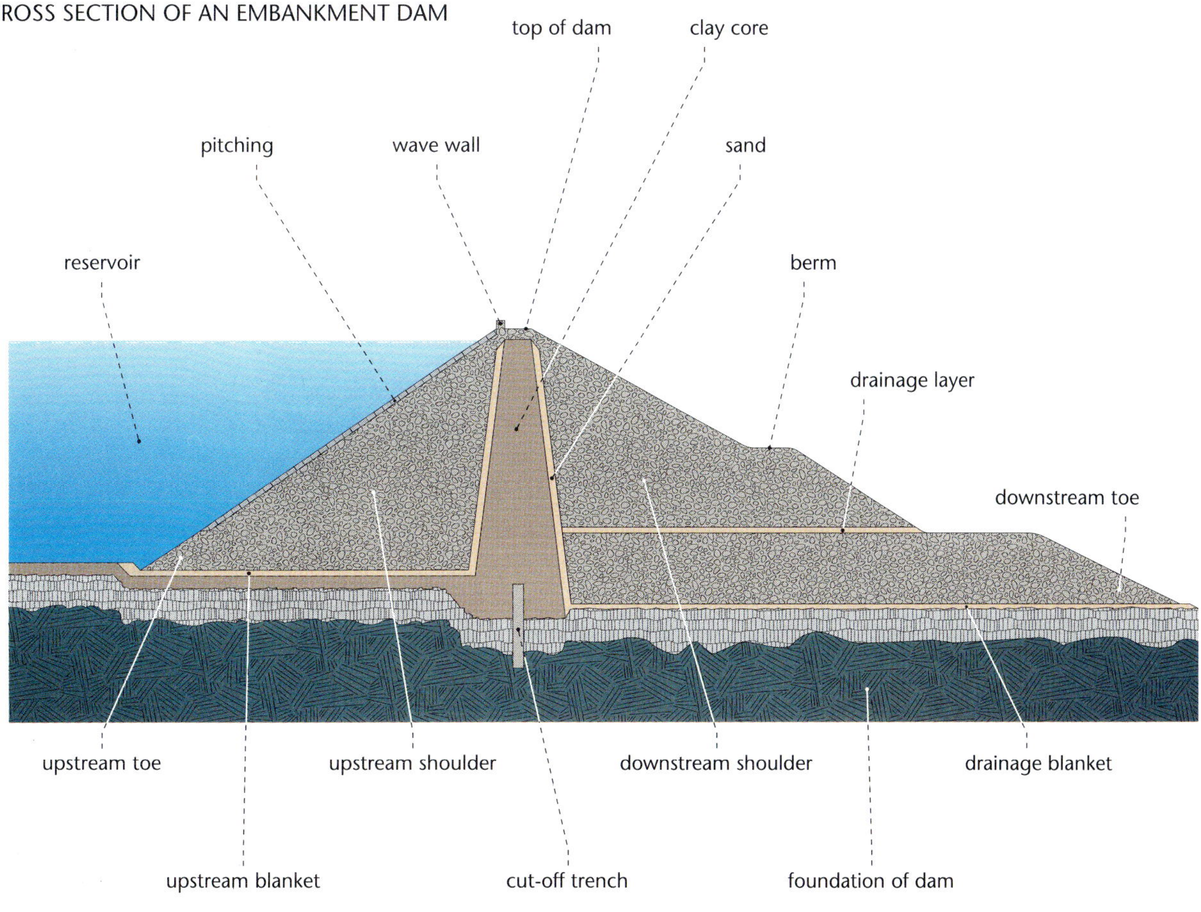

CROSS SECTION OF A GRAVITY DAM

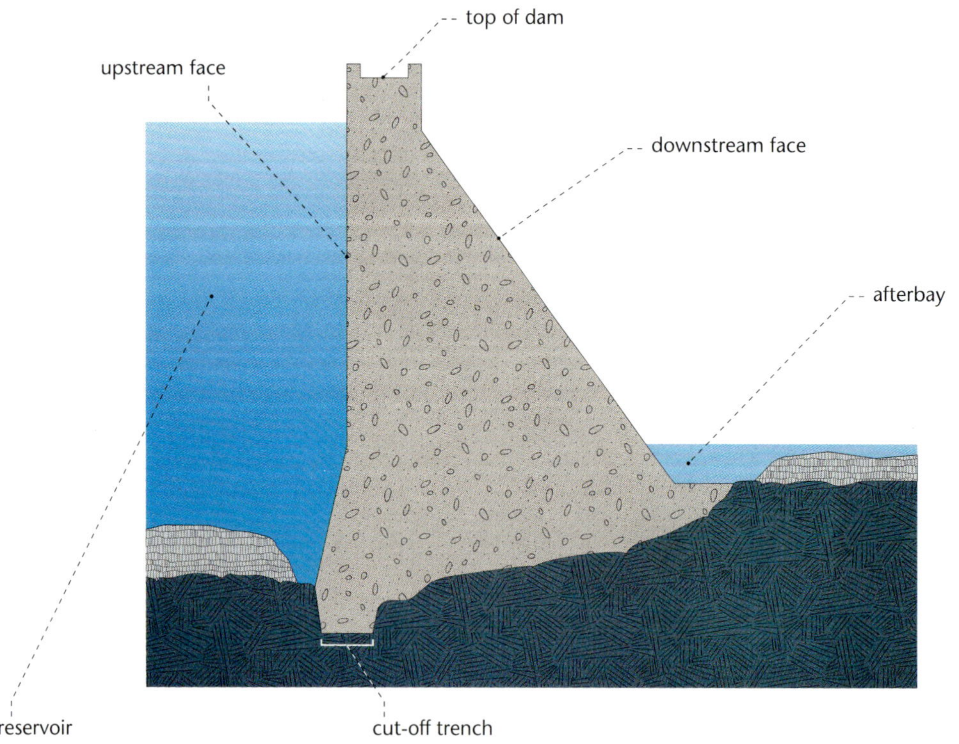

arch dam

CROSS SECTION OF AN ARCH DAM

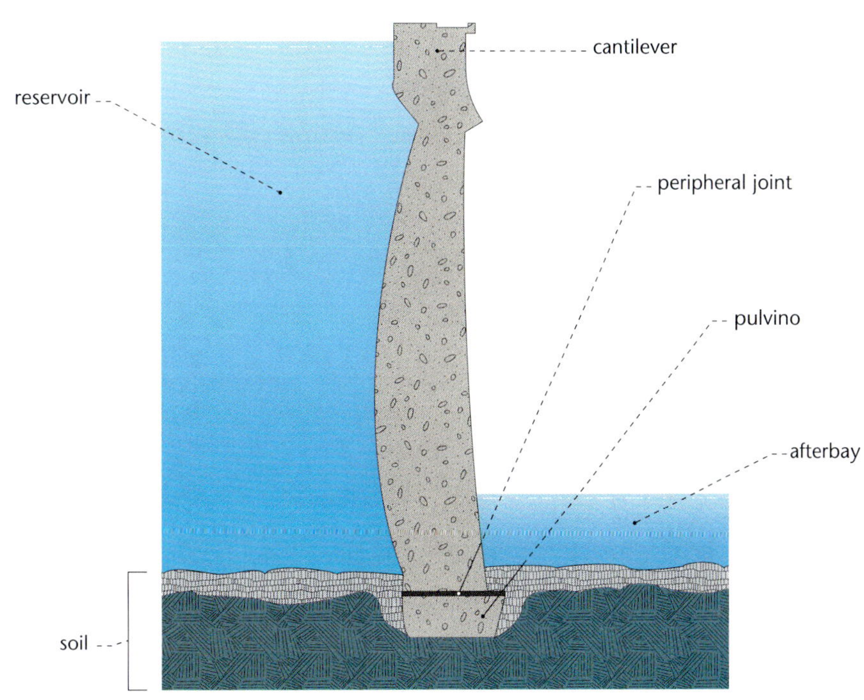

CROSS SECTION OF A BUTTRESS DAM

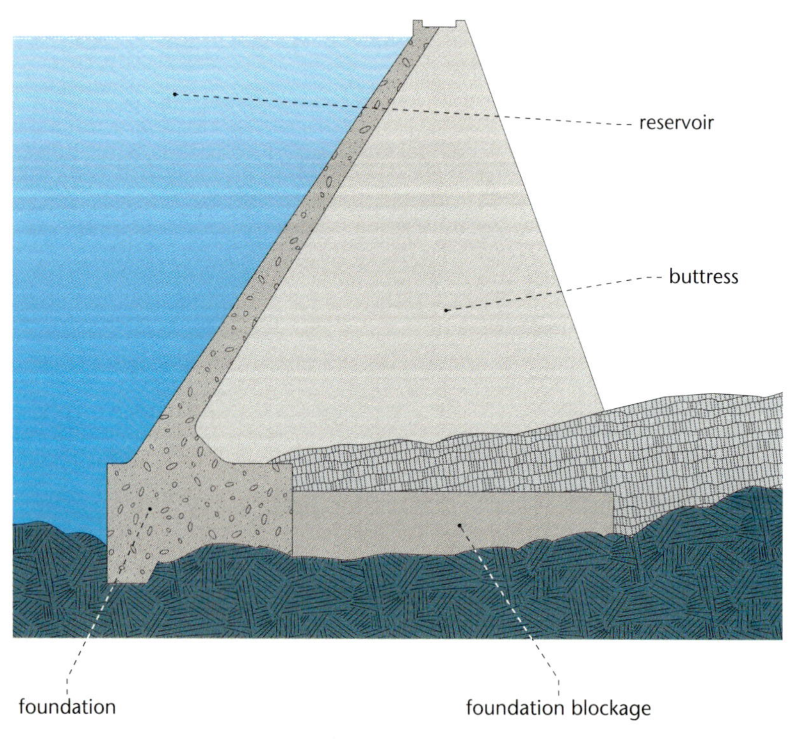

TIDAL POWER PLANT

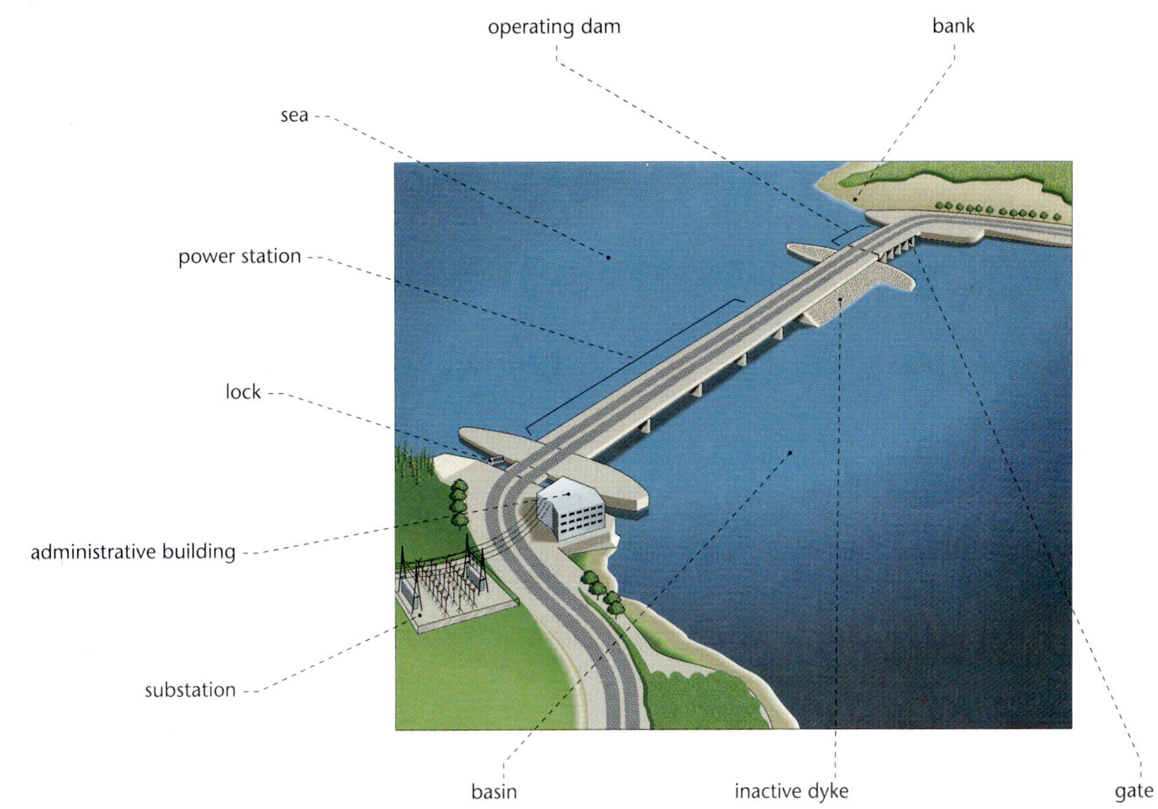

CROSS SECTION OF POWER PLANT

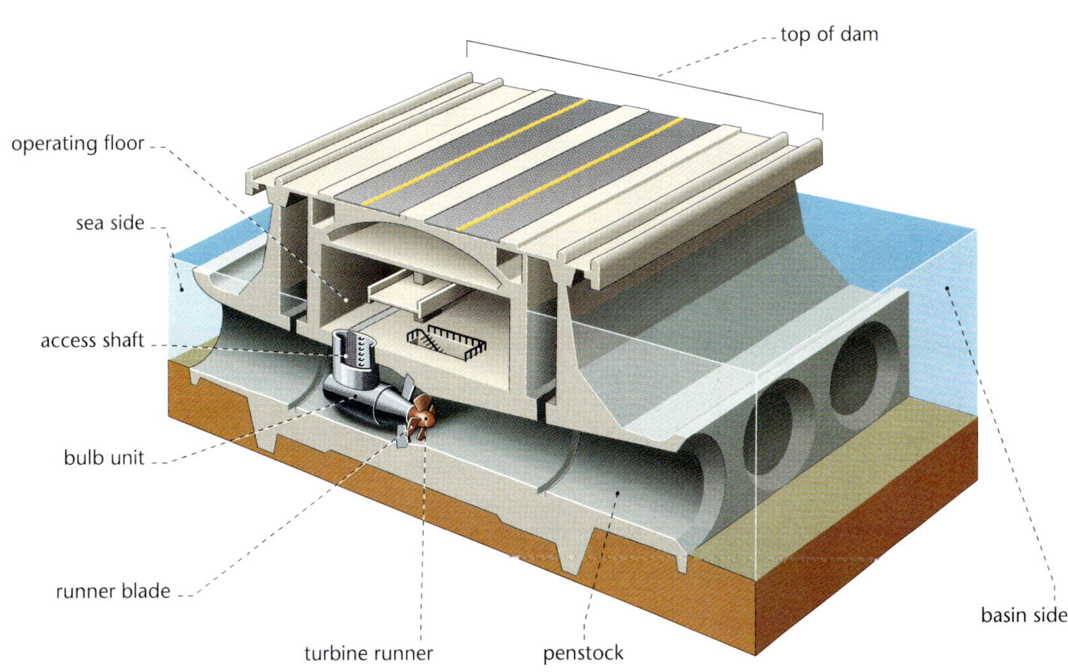

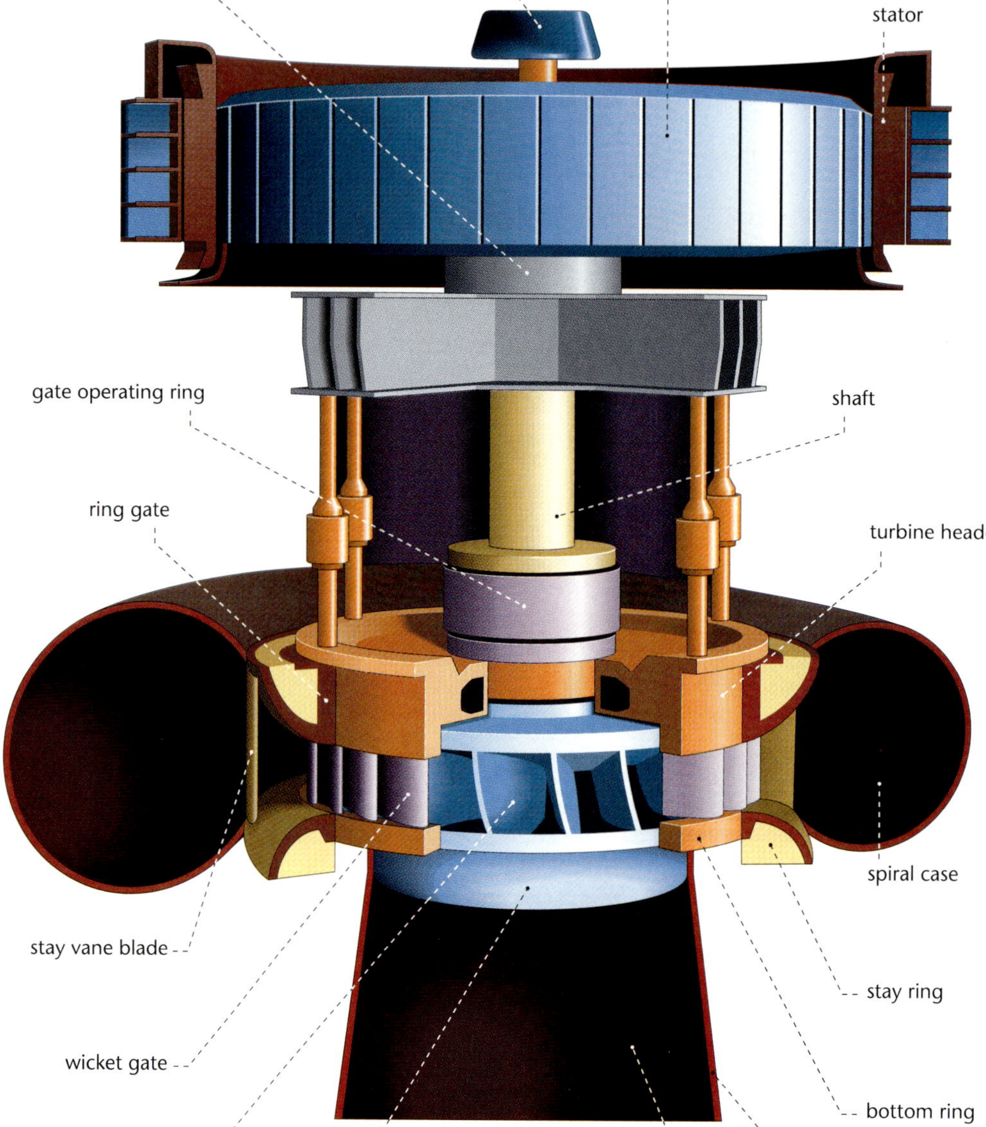

collector
rotor
thrust bearing
stator
gate operating ring
shaft
ring gate
turbine headcover
spiral case
stay vane blade
stay ring
wicket gate
bottom ring
runner blade
runner
draft tube
discharge liner
generator 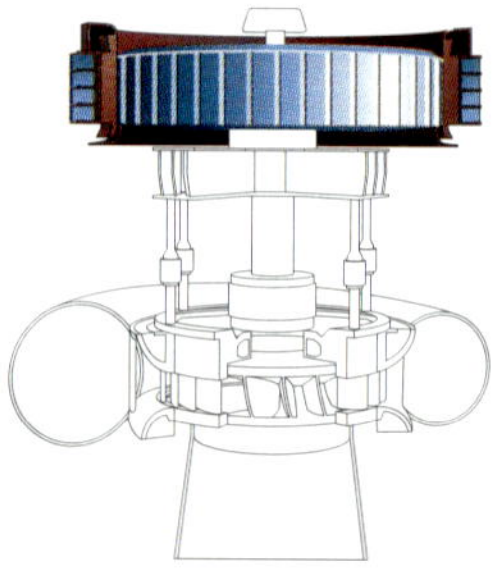
turbine

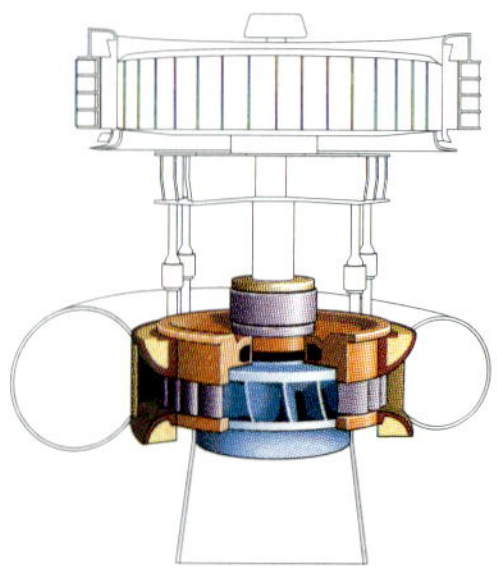

FRANCIS TURBINE

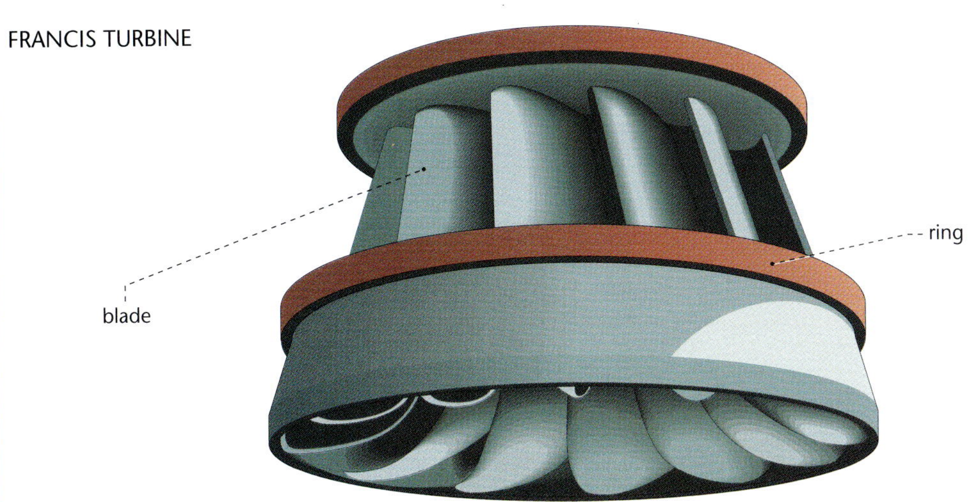

KAPLAN TURBINE

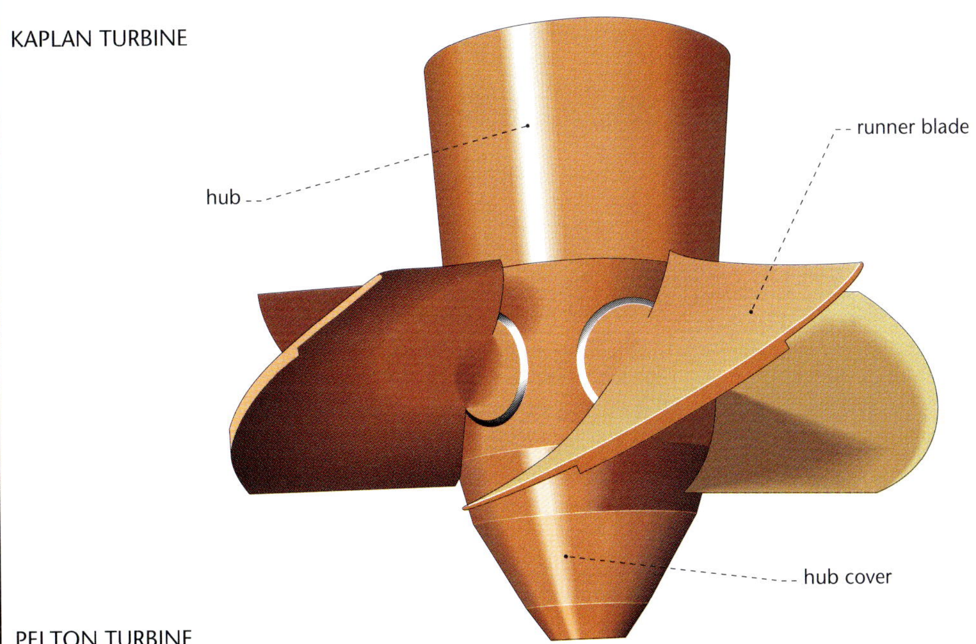

PELTON TURBINE

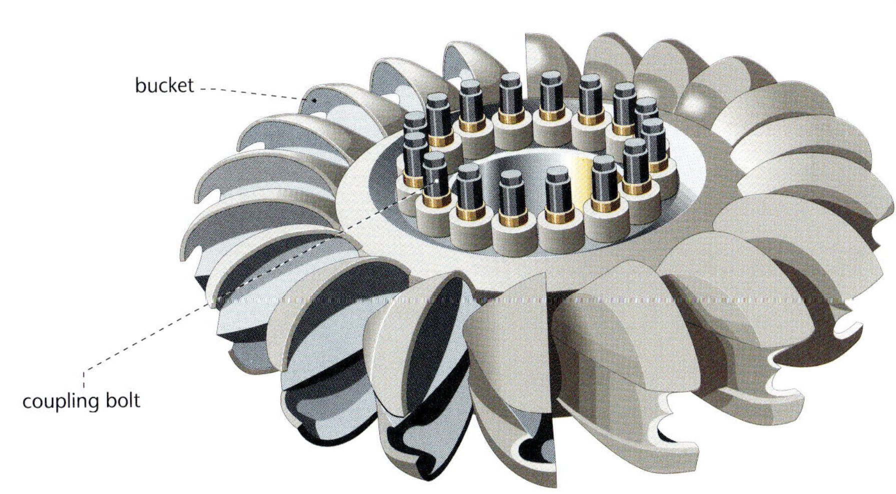

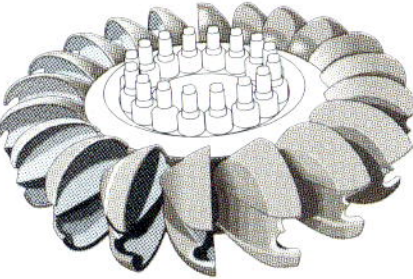

bucket ring

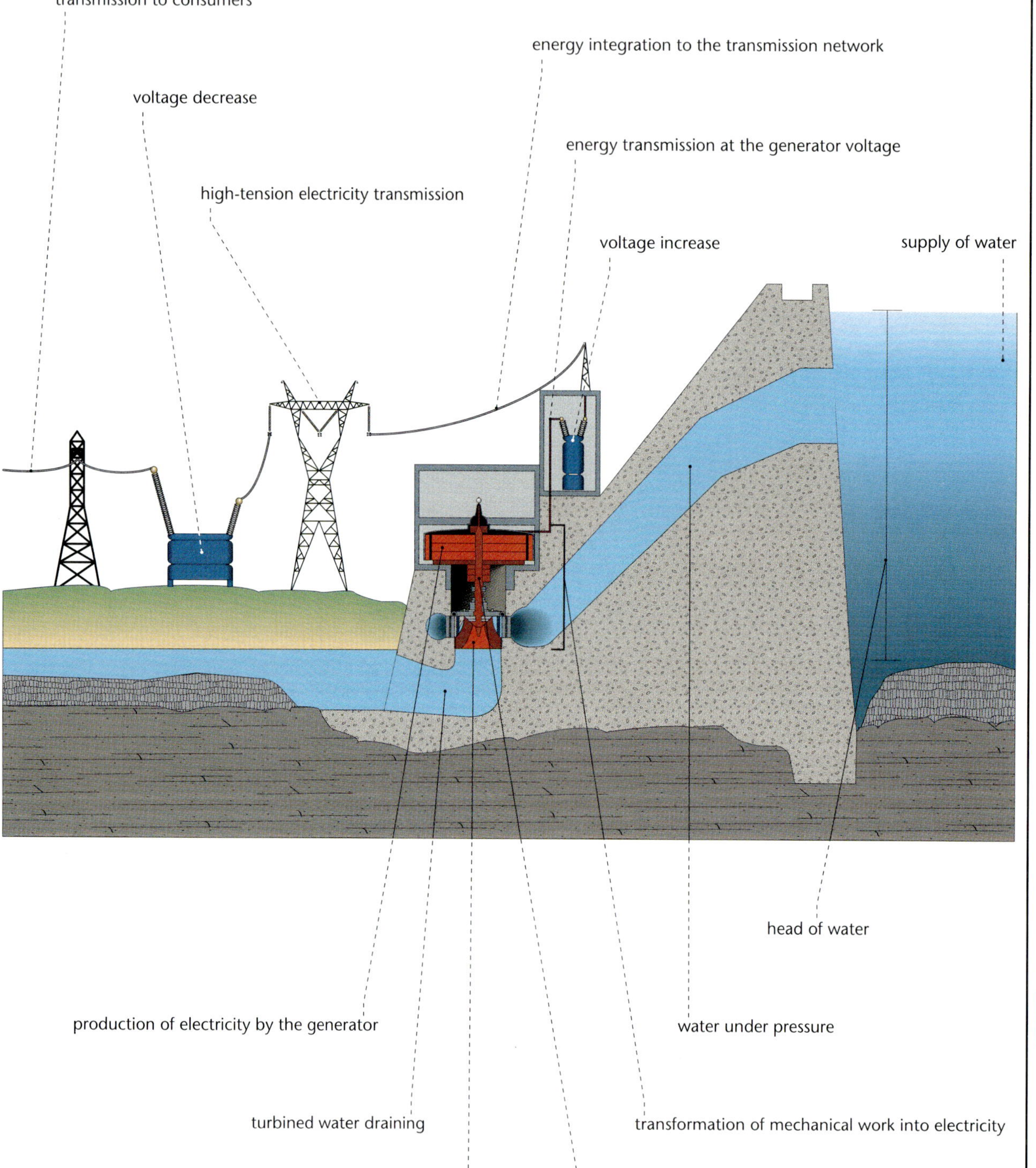
transmission to consumers
voltage decrease
high-tension electricity transmission
energy integration to the transmission network
energy transmission at the generator voltage
voltage increase
supply of water
head of water
production of electricity by the generator
water under pressure
turbined water draining
transformation of mechanical work into electricity
rotation of the turbine
transmission of the rotative movement to the rotor

TOWER

overhead ground wire
beam gantry
crossarm
ground-wire peak
tower top
tower window
suspension insulator string
K-frame
node
bundle
redundant bracing
waist
panel
diagonal
horizontal member
tower body
main leg
tower foot
base width

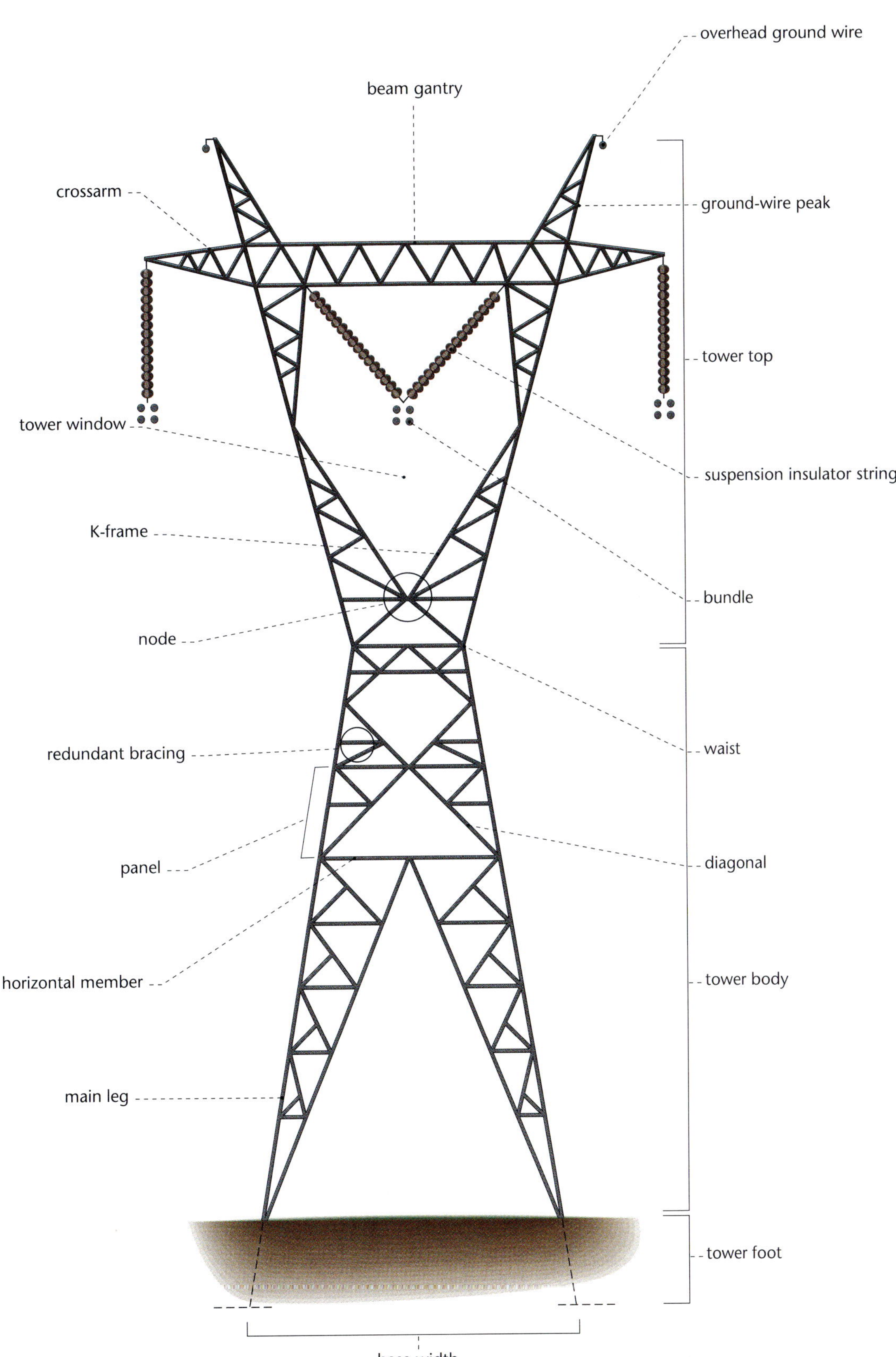

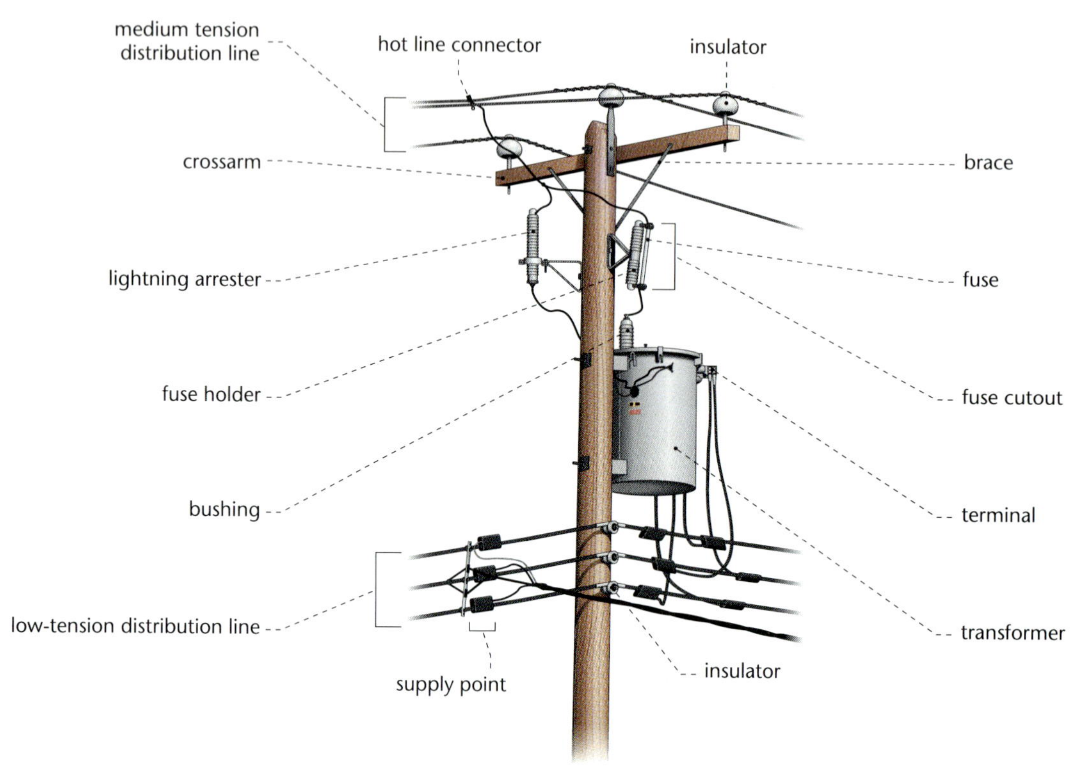

OVERHEAD CONNECTION

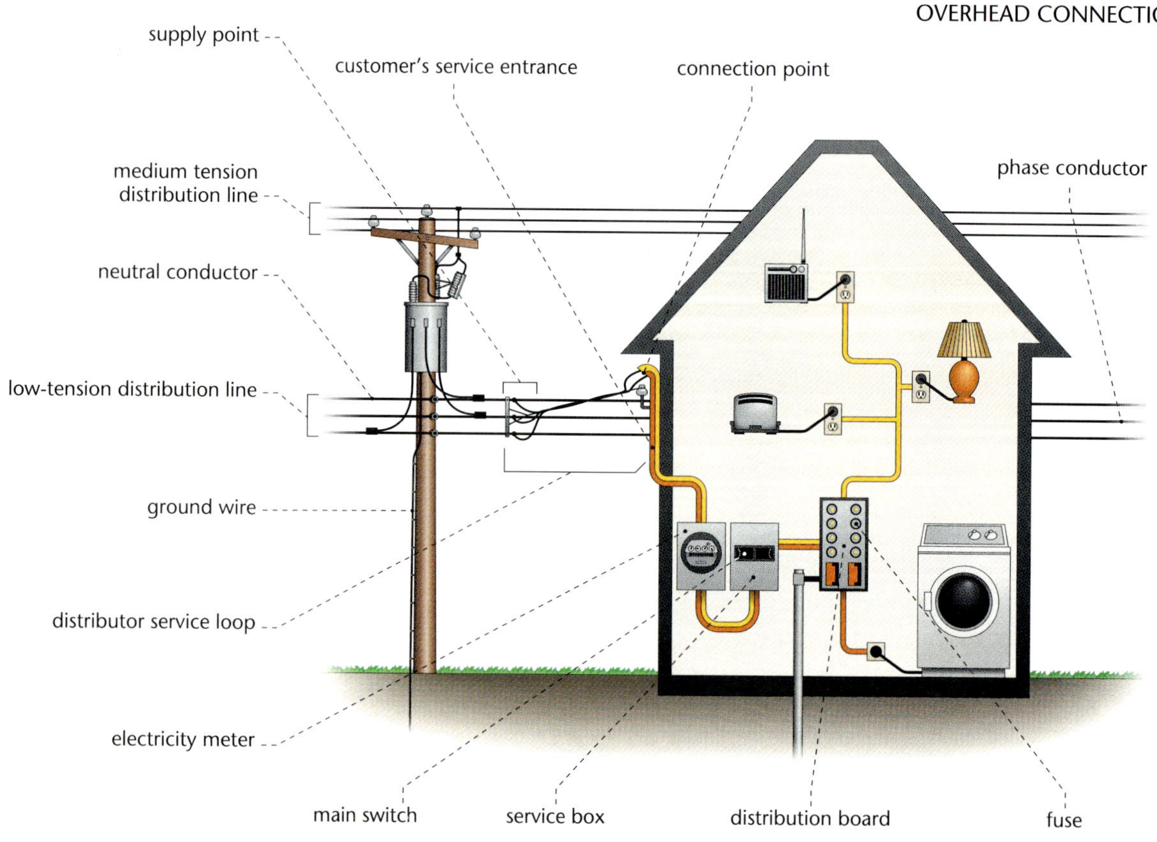

ENERGY

NUCLEAR GENERATING STATION

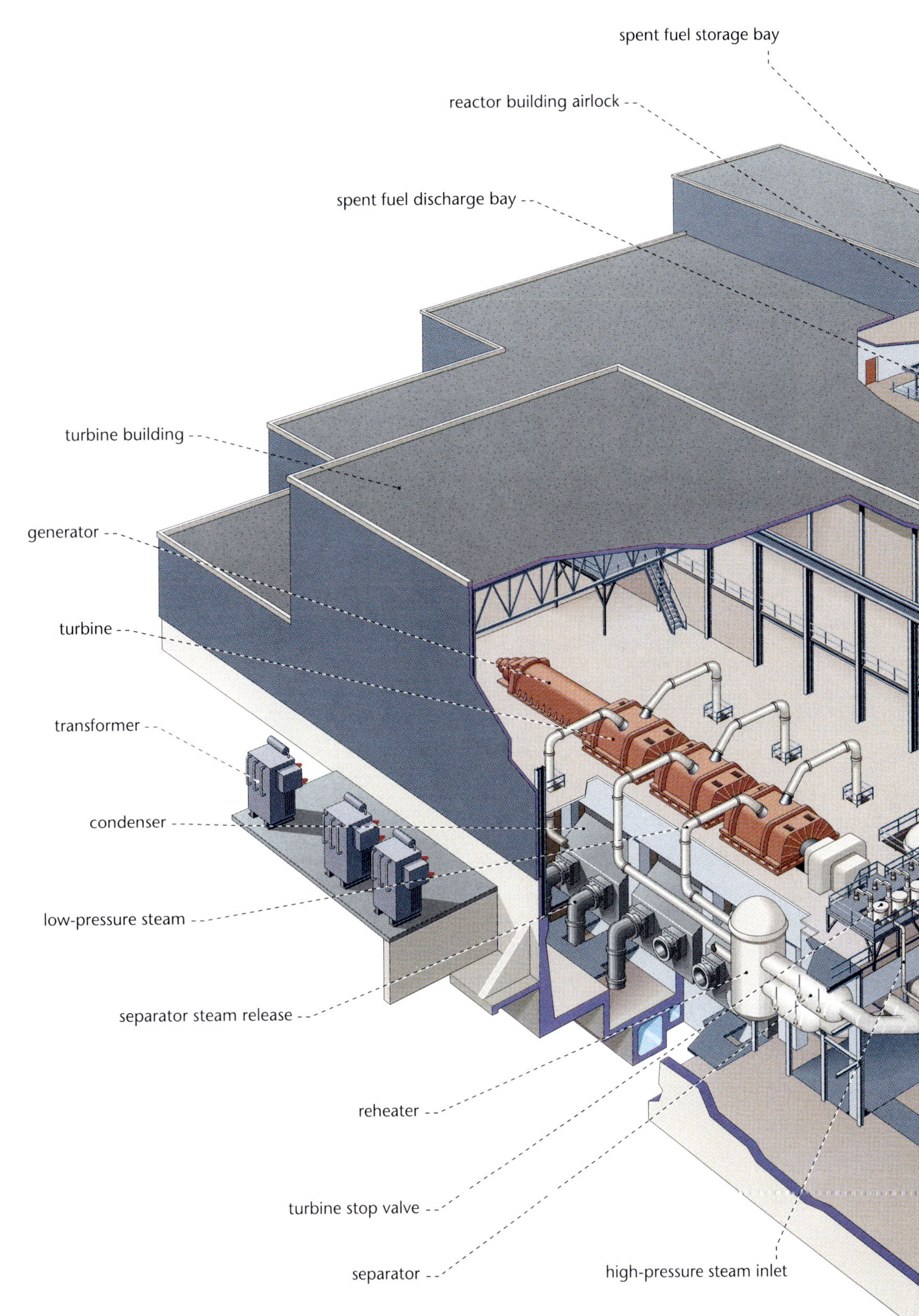

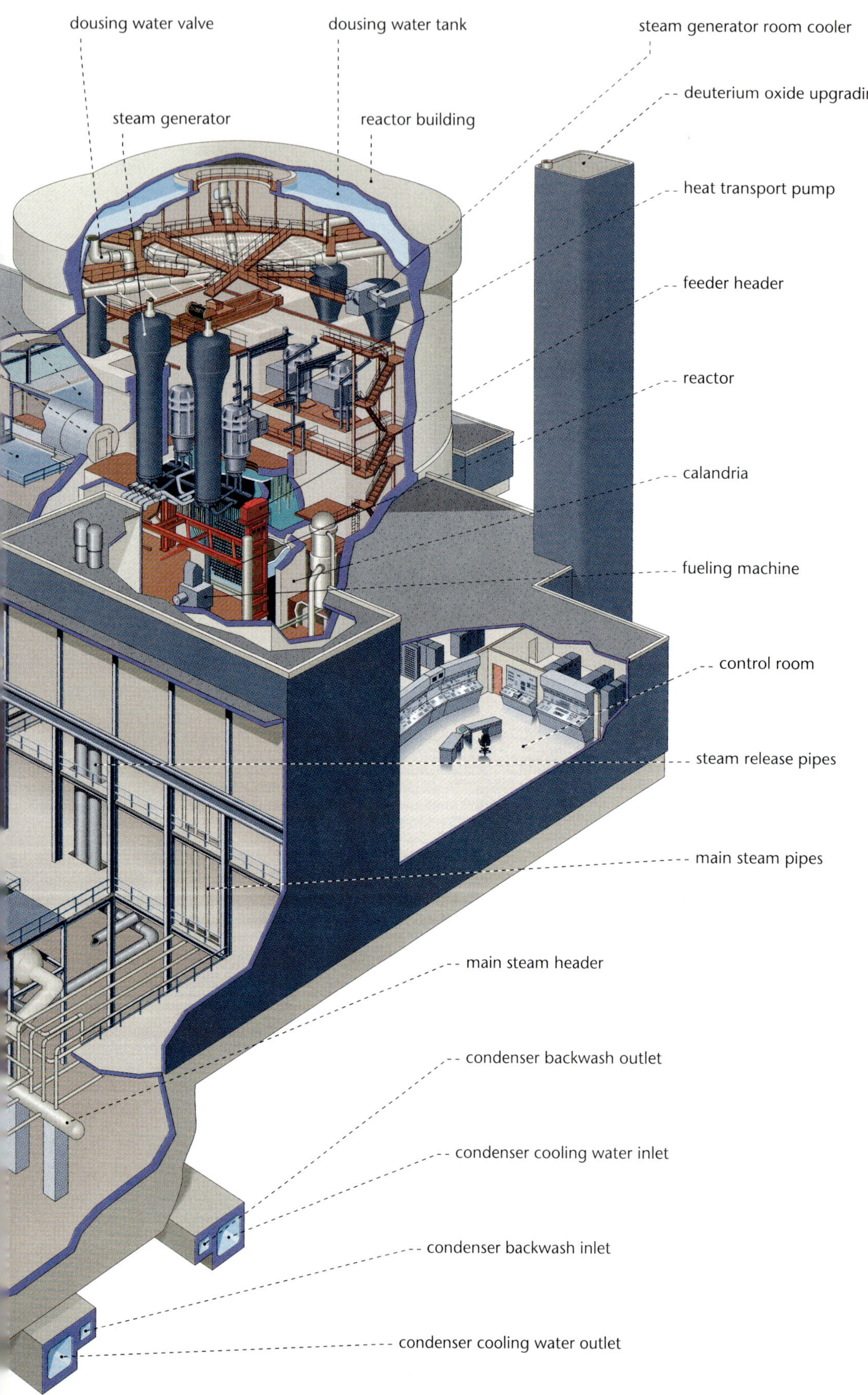

dousing water valve
dousing water tank
steam generator room cooler
deuterium oxide upgrading
steam generator
reactor building
heat transport pump
feeder header
reactor
calandria
fueling machine
control room
steam release pipes
main steam pipes
main steam header
condenser backwash outlet
condenser cooling water inlet
condenser backwash inlet
condenser cooling water outlet

CARBON DIOXIDE REACTOR

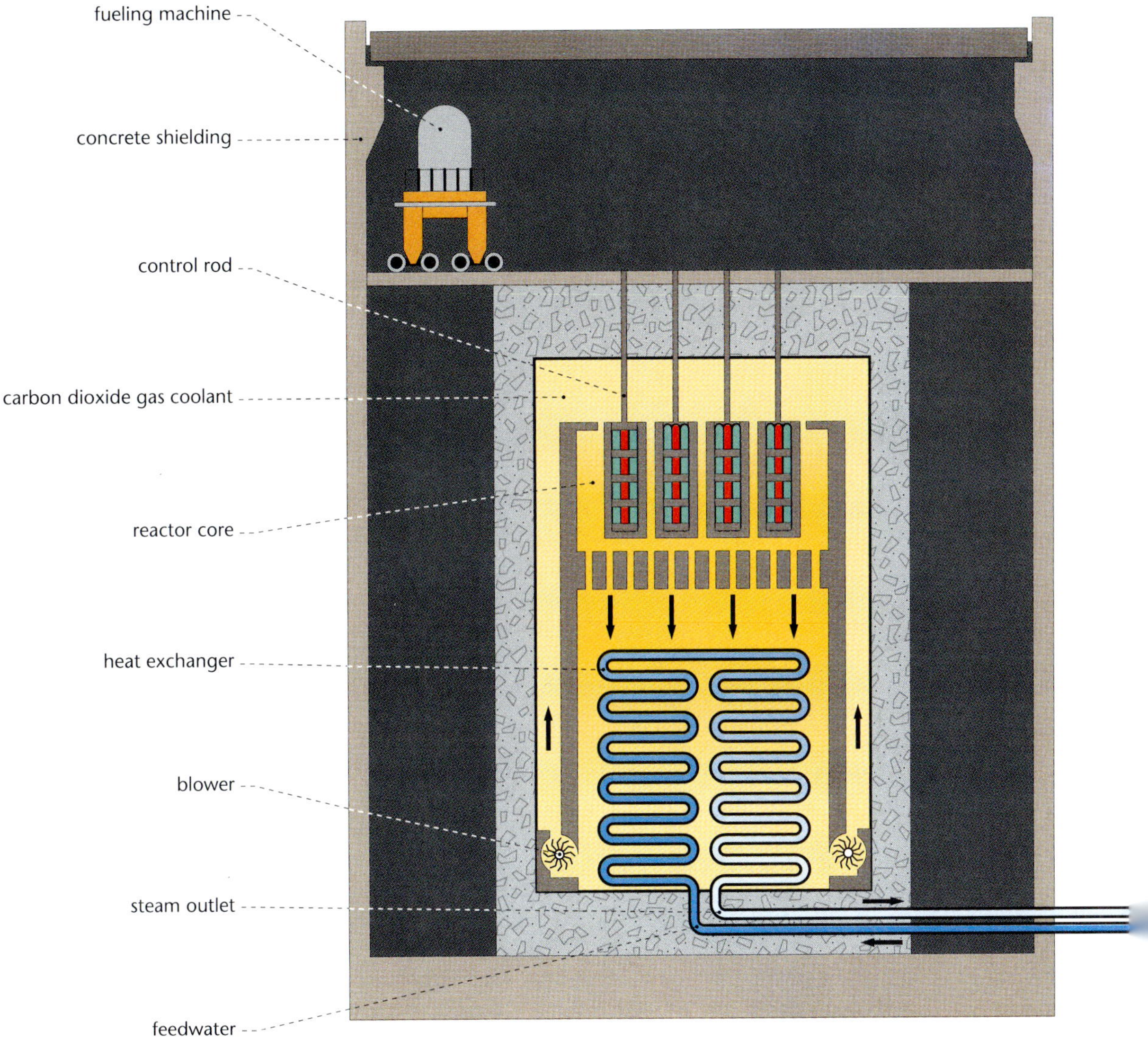

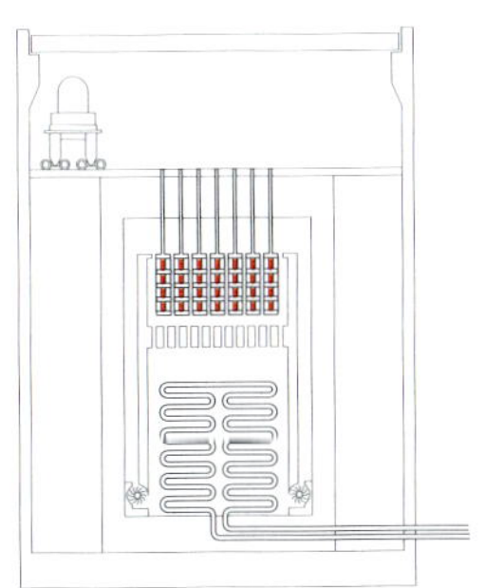

fuel: natural uranium

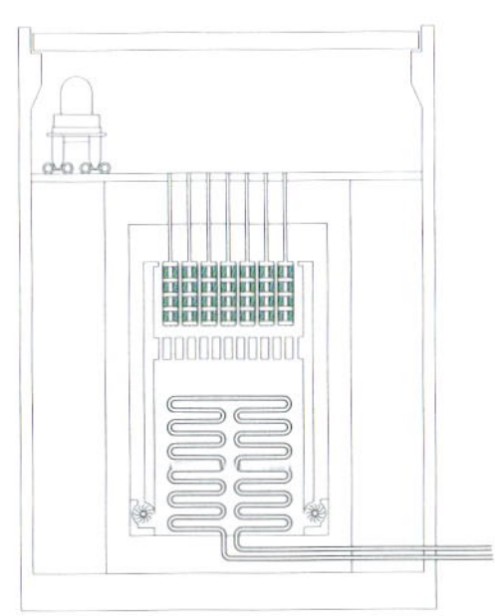

moderator: graphite

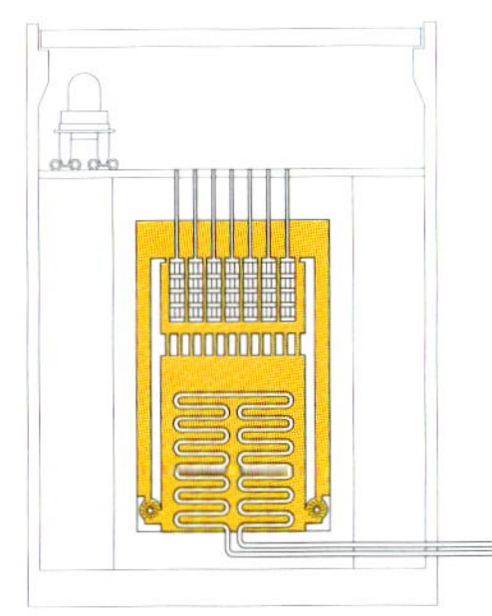

coolant: carbon dioxide

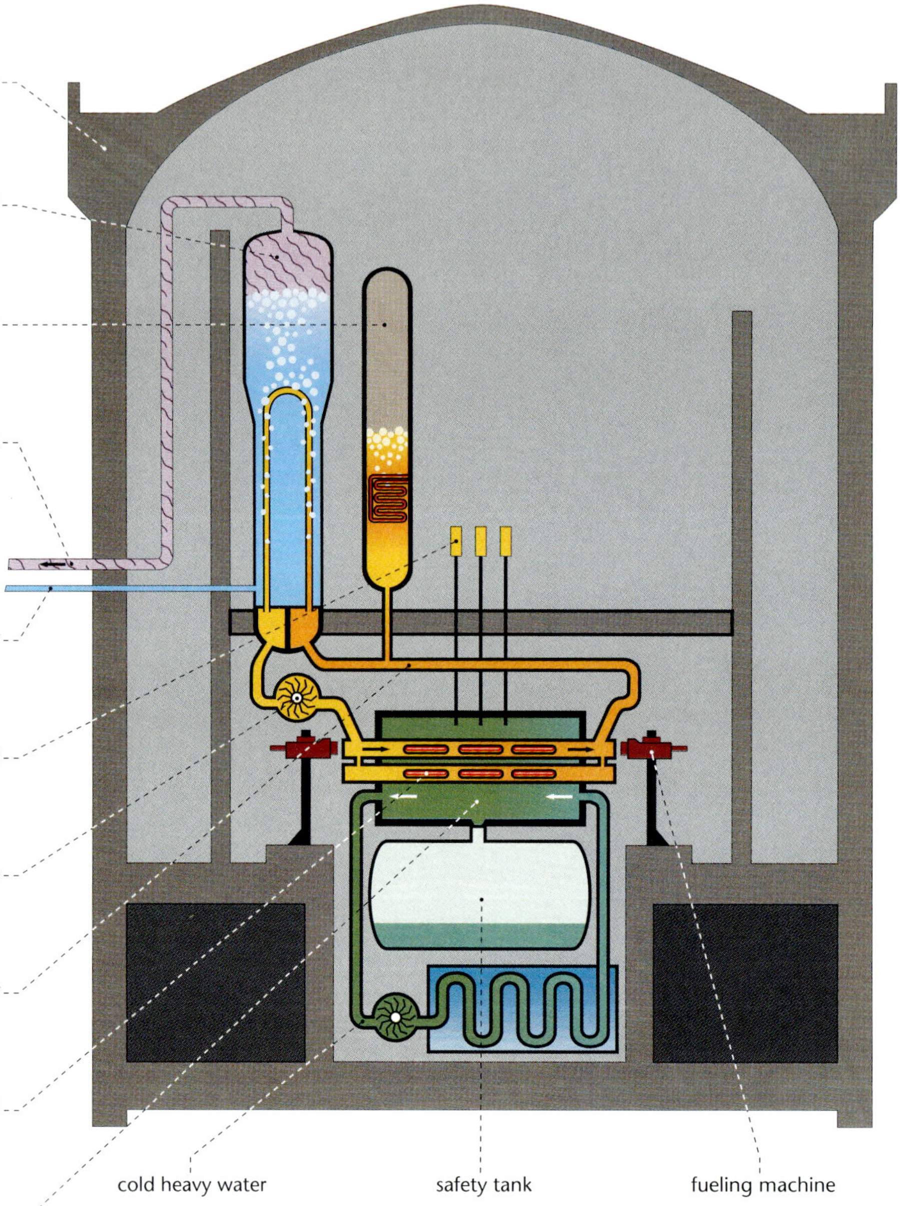

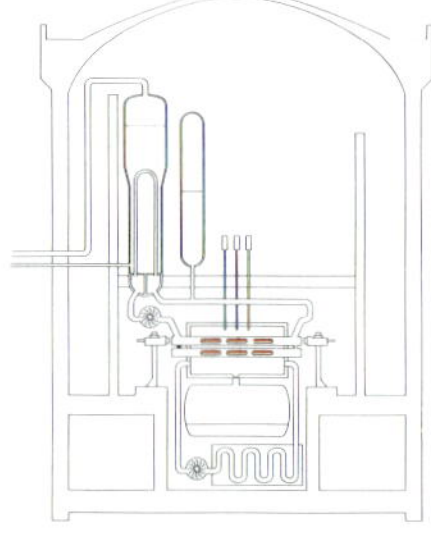
fuel: natural uranium

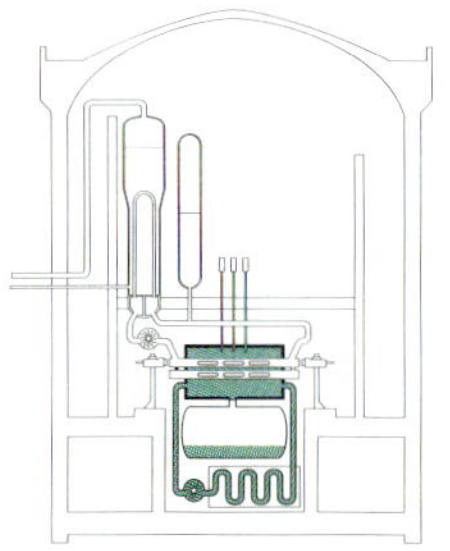
moderator: heavy water

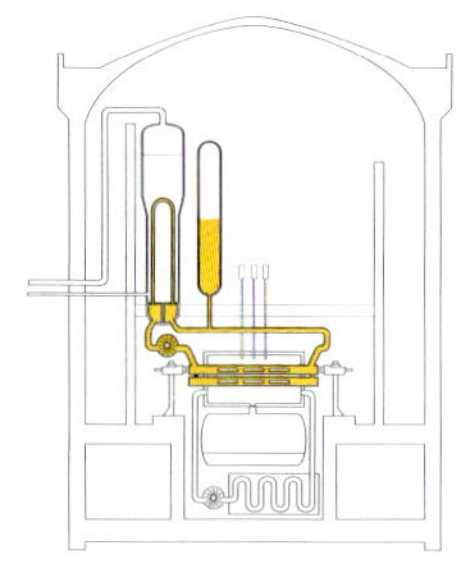
coolant: pressurized heavy water

PRESSURIZED-WATER REACTOR

fuel: enriched uranium

moderator: natural water

coolant: pressurized water

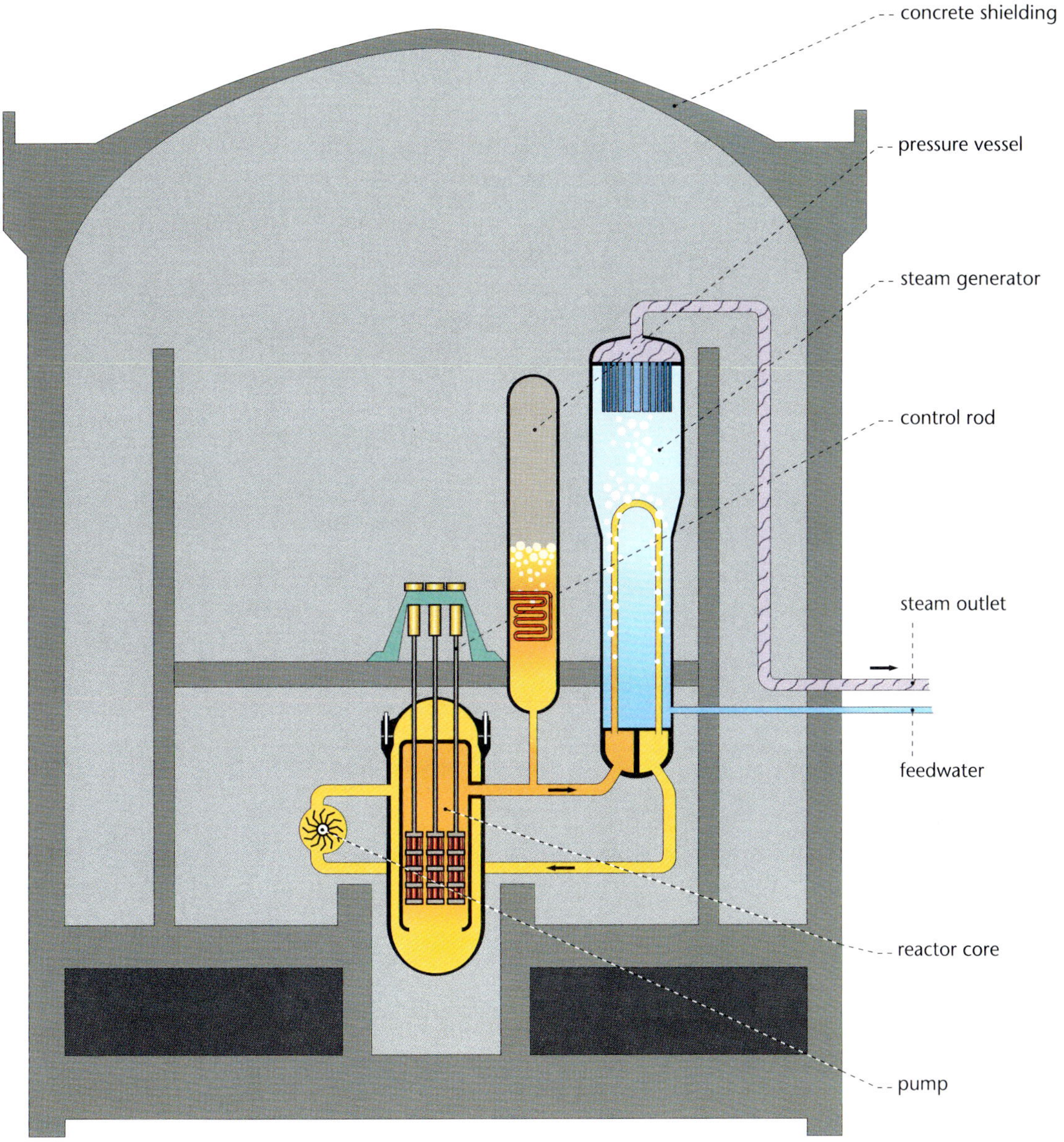

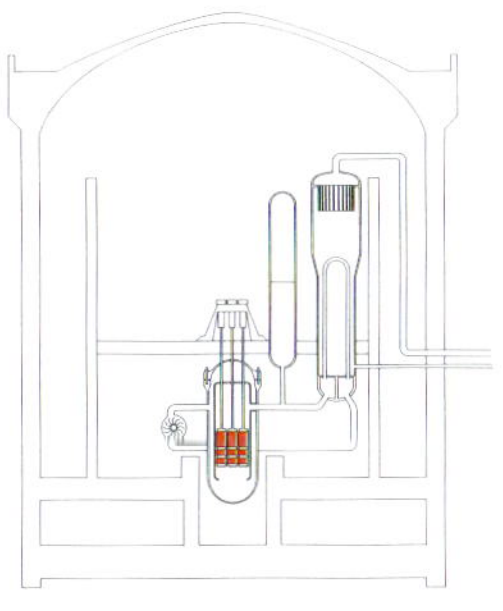

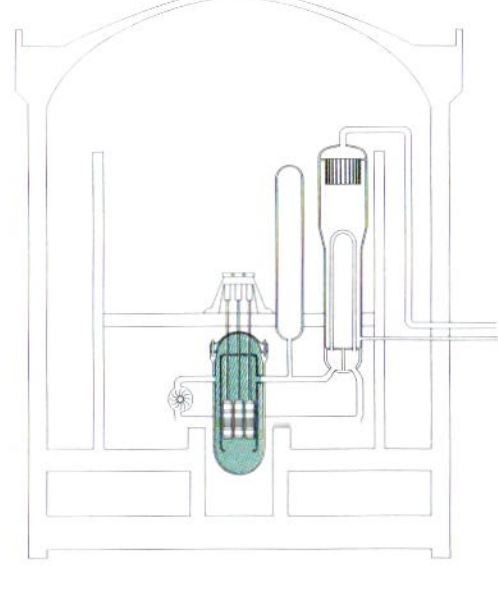

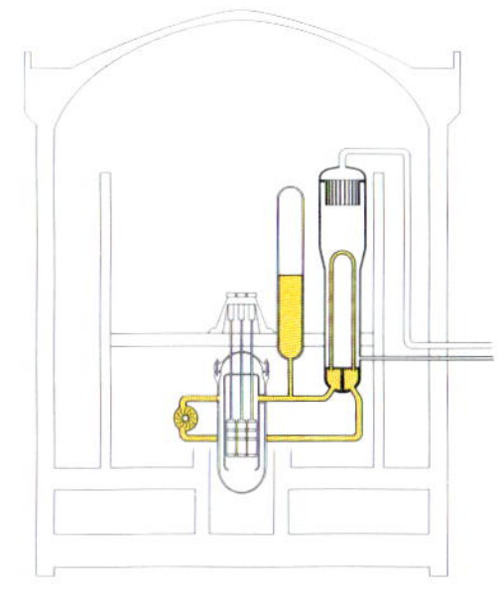

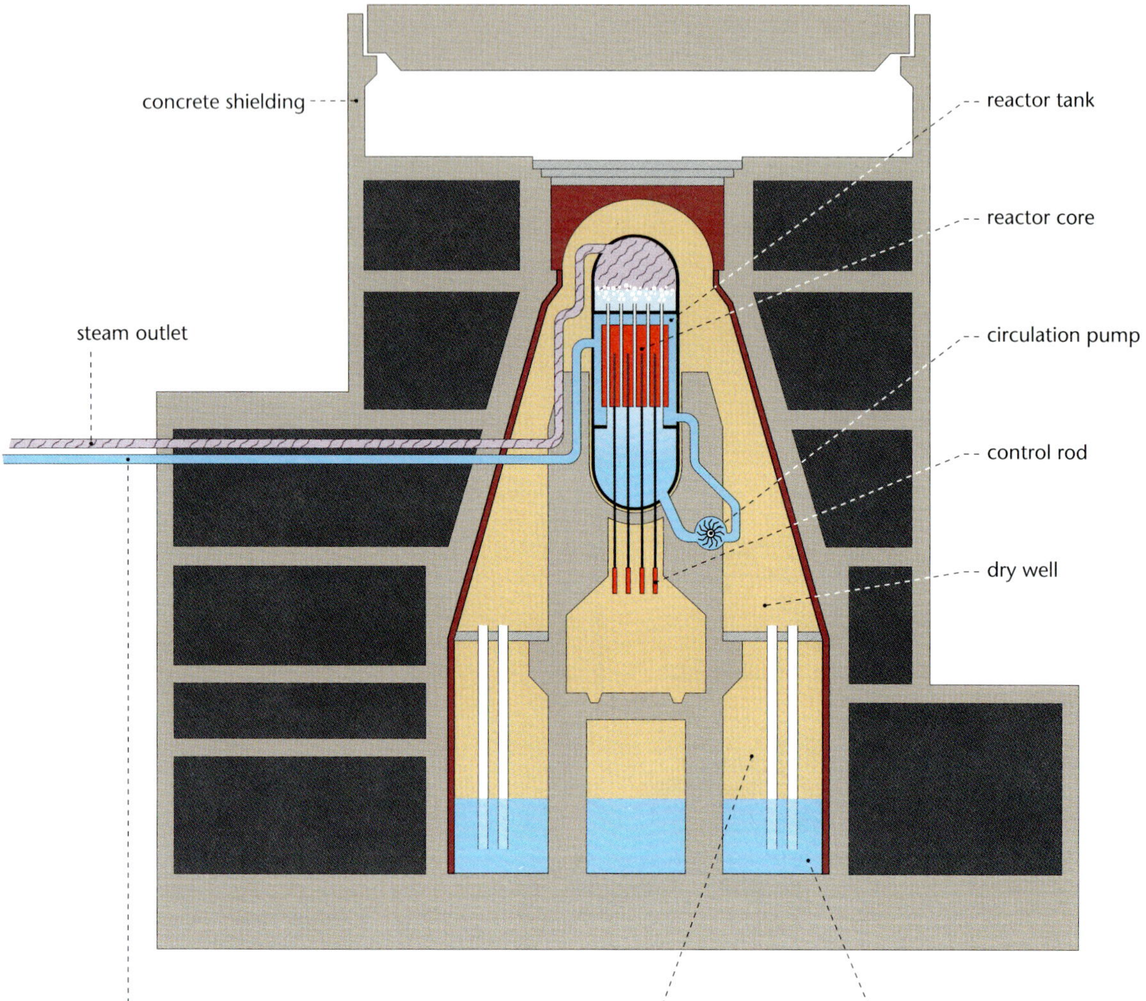

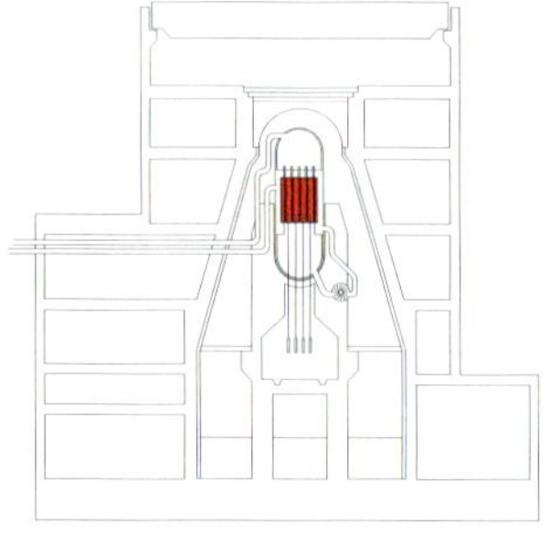

fuel: enriched uranium

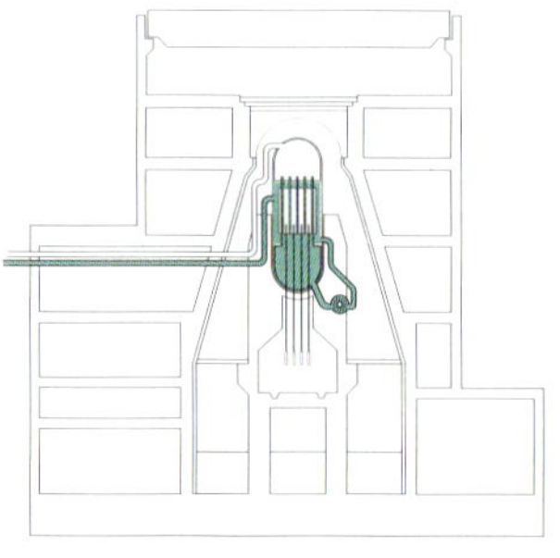

moderator: natural water

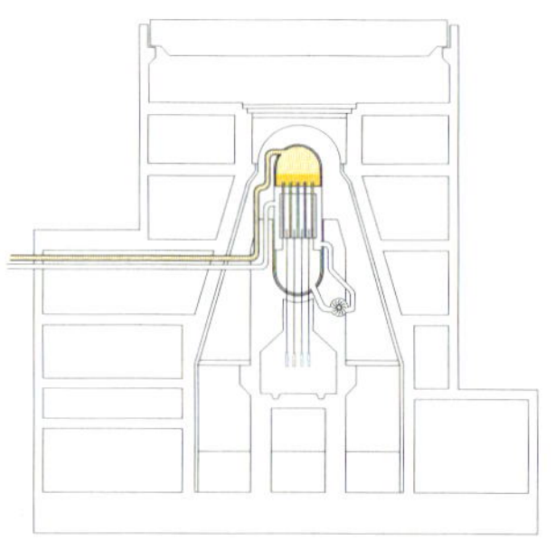

coolant: boiling water

FUEL HANDLING SEQUENCE

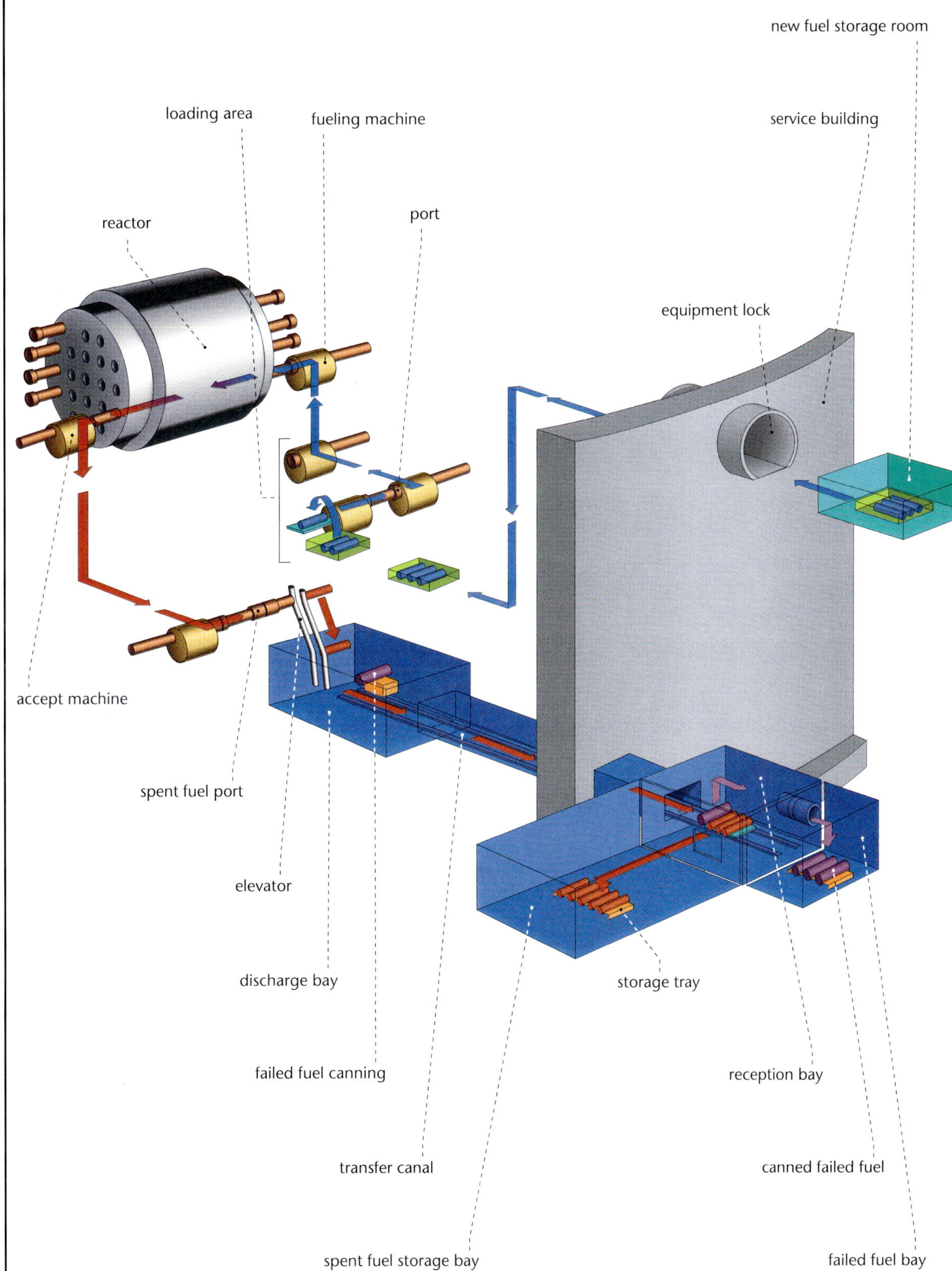

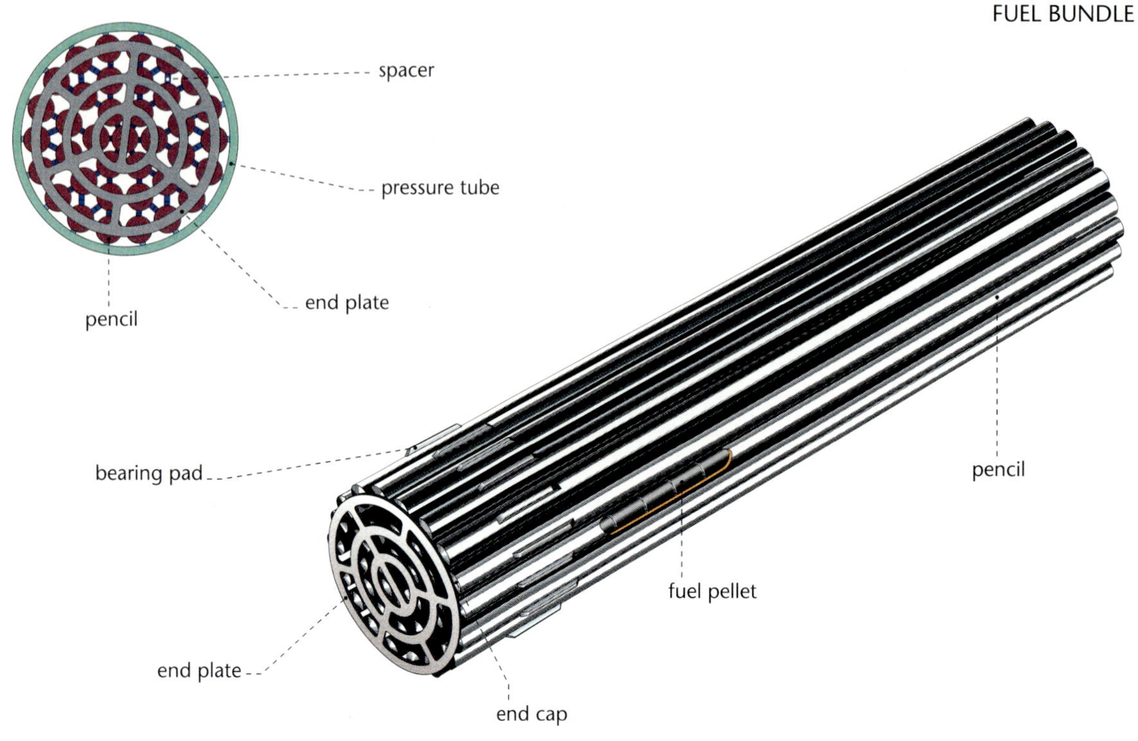
spacer
pressure tube
end plate
pencil
bearing pad
pencil
fuel pellet
end plate
end cap

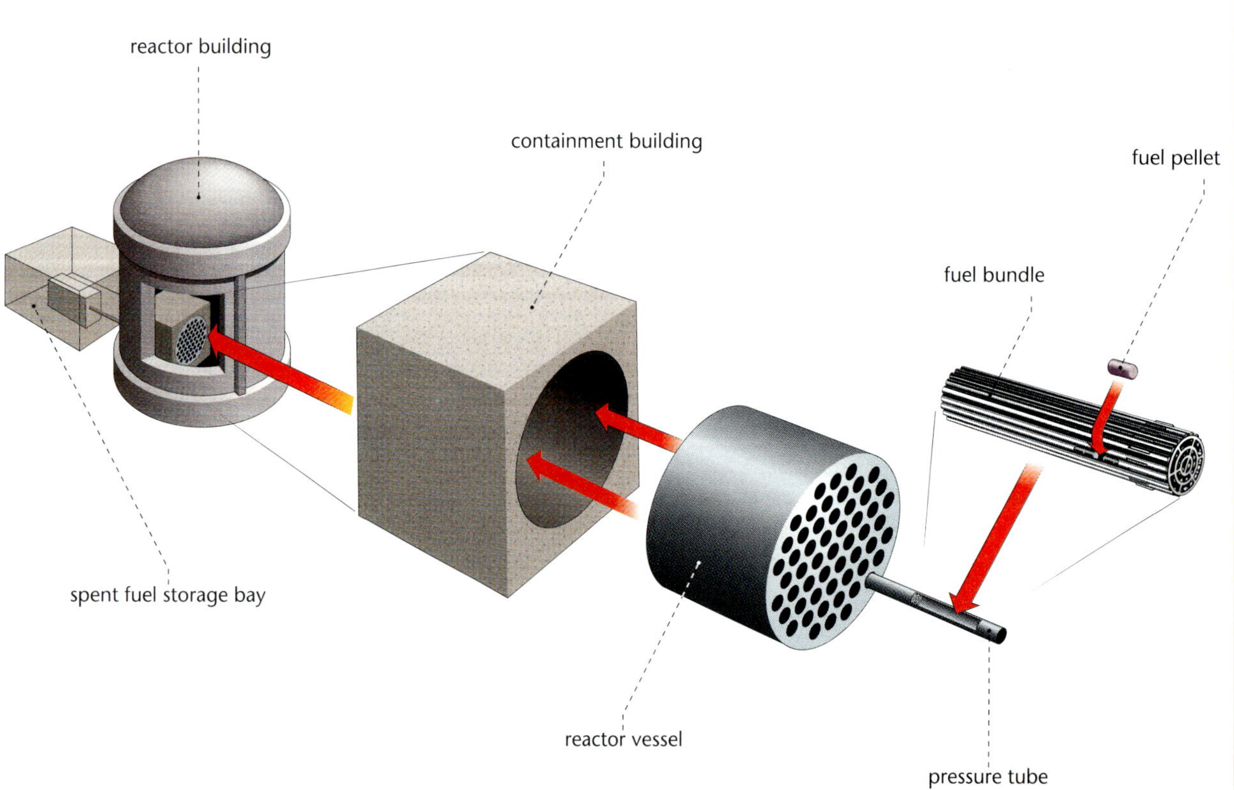
reactor building
containment building
fuel pellet
fuel bundle
spent fuel storage bay
reactor vessel
pressure tube

PRODUCTION OF ELECTRICITY FROM NUCLEAR ENERGY

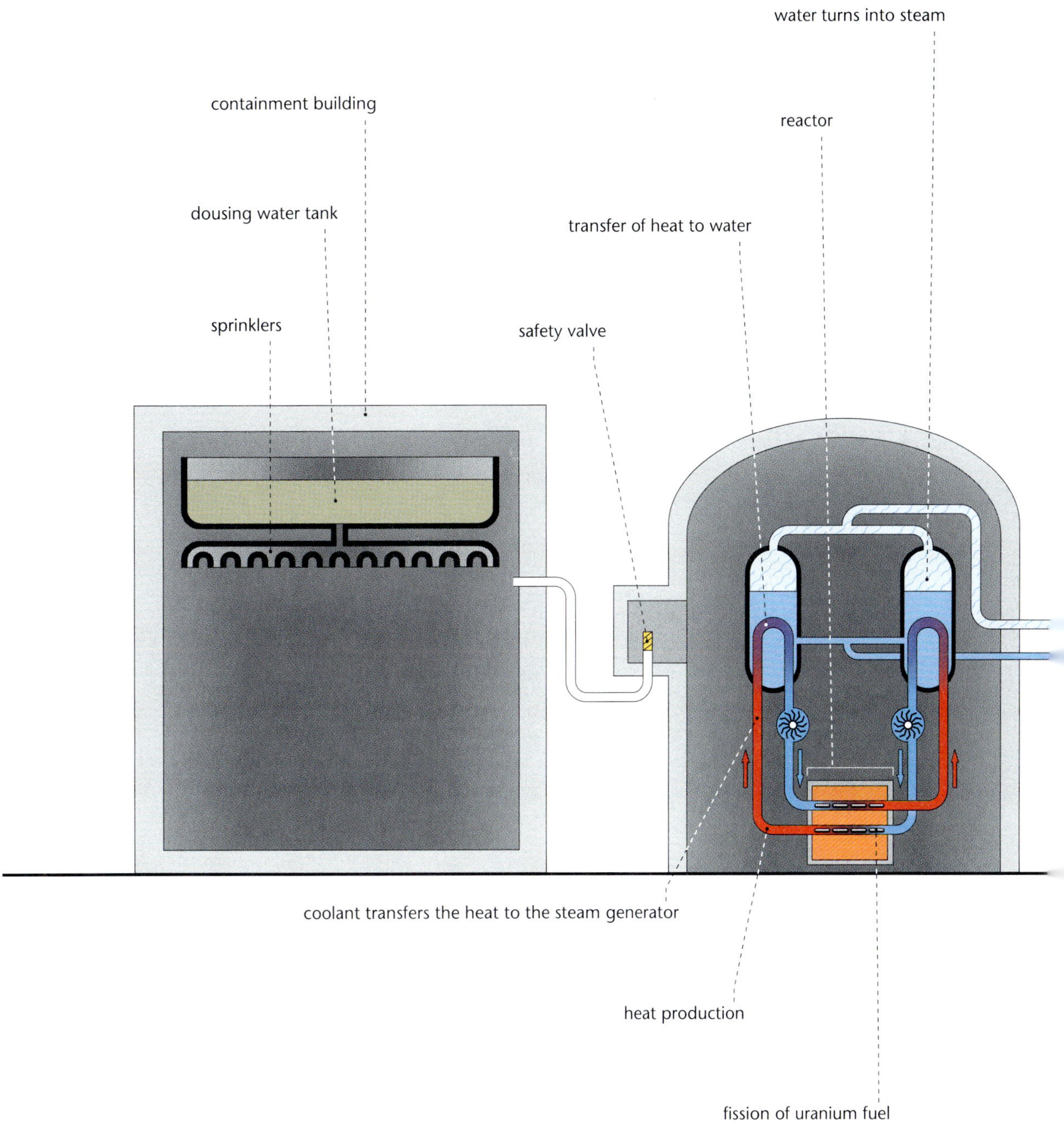

water turns into steam
containment building
reactor
dousing water tank
transfer of heat to water
sprinklers
safety valve
coolant transfers the heat to the steam generator
heat production
fission of uranium fuel

fuel

moderator

coolant

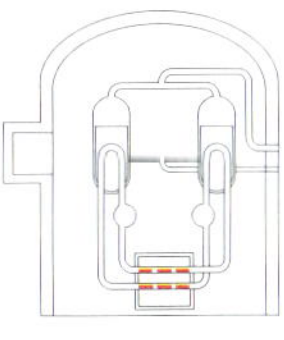

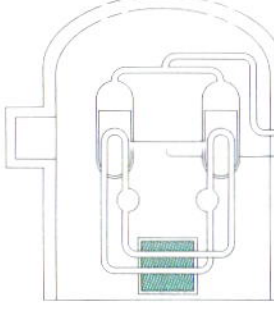

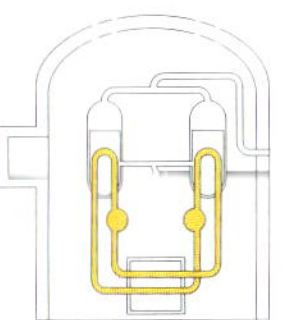

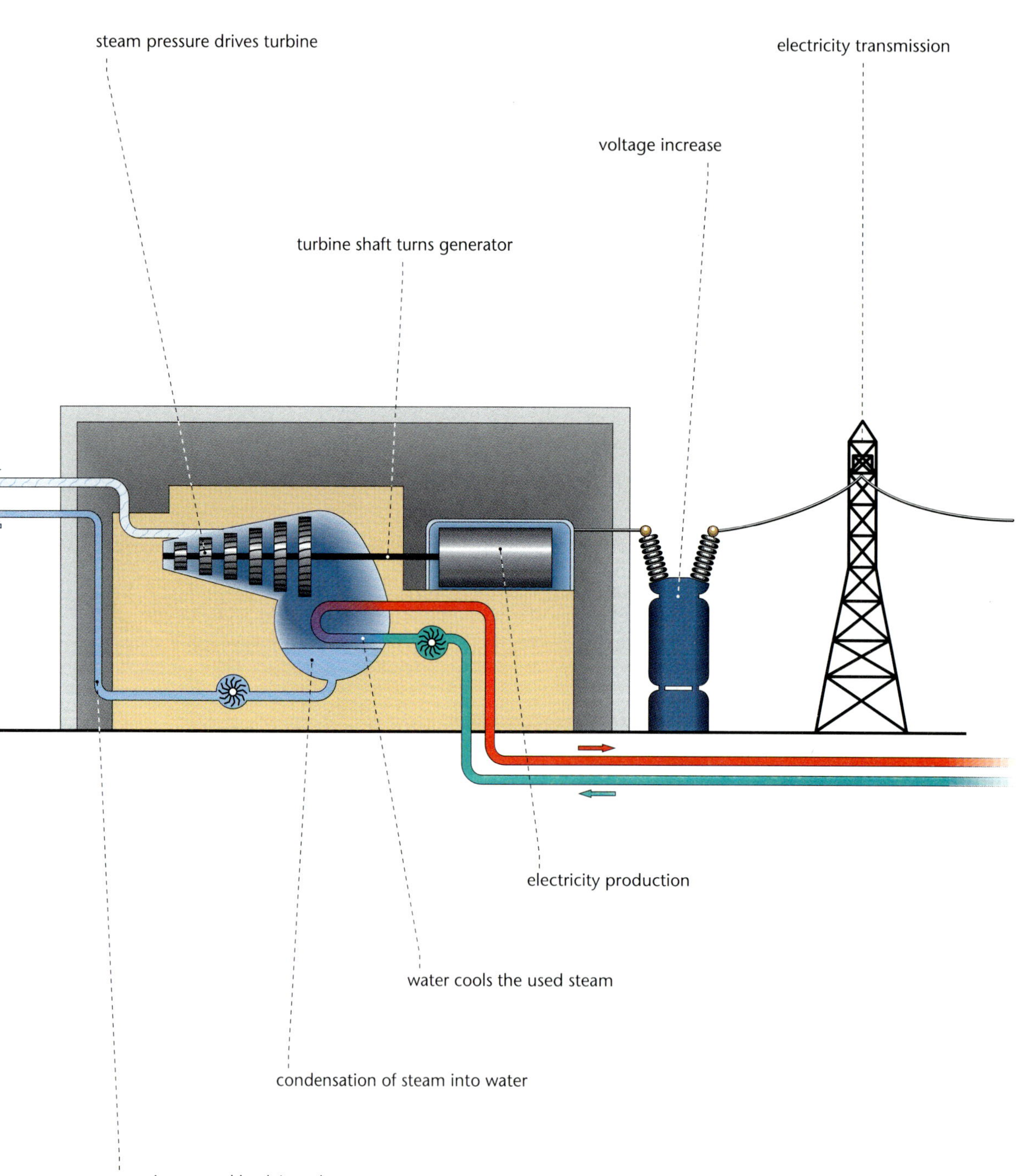

steam pressure drives turbine
electricity transmission
voltage increase
turbine shaft turns generator
electricity production
water cools the used steam
condensation of steam into water
water is pumped back into the steam generator

SOLAR CELL

solar radiation
antireflection coating
metallic contact grid
positive region
negative contact
positive/negative junction
positive contact
negative region
FLAT-PLATE SOLAR COLLECTOR
solar radiation
glass
coolant outlet
frame
flow tube
absorbing plate
coolant inlet
insulation

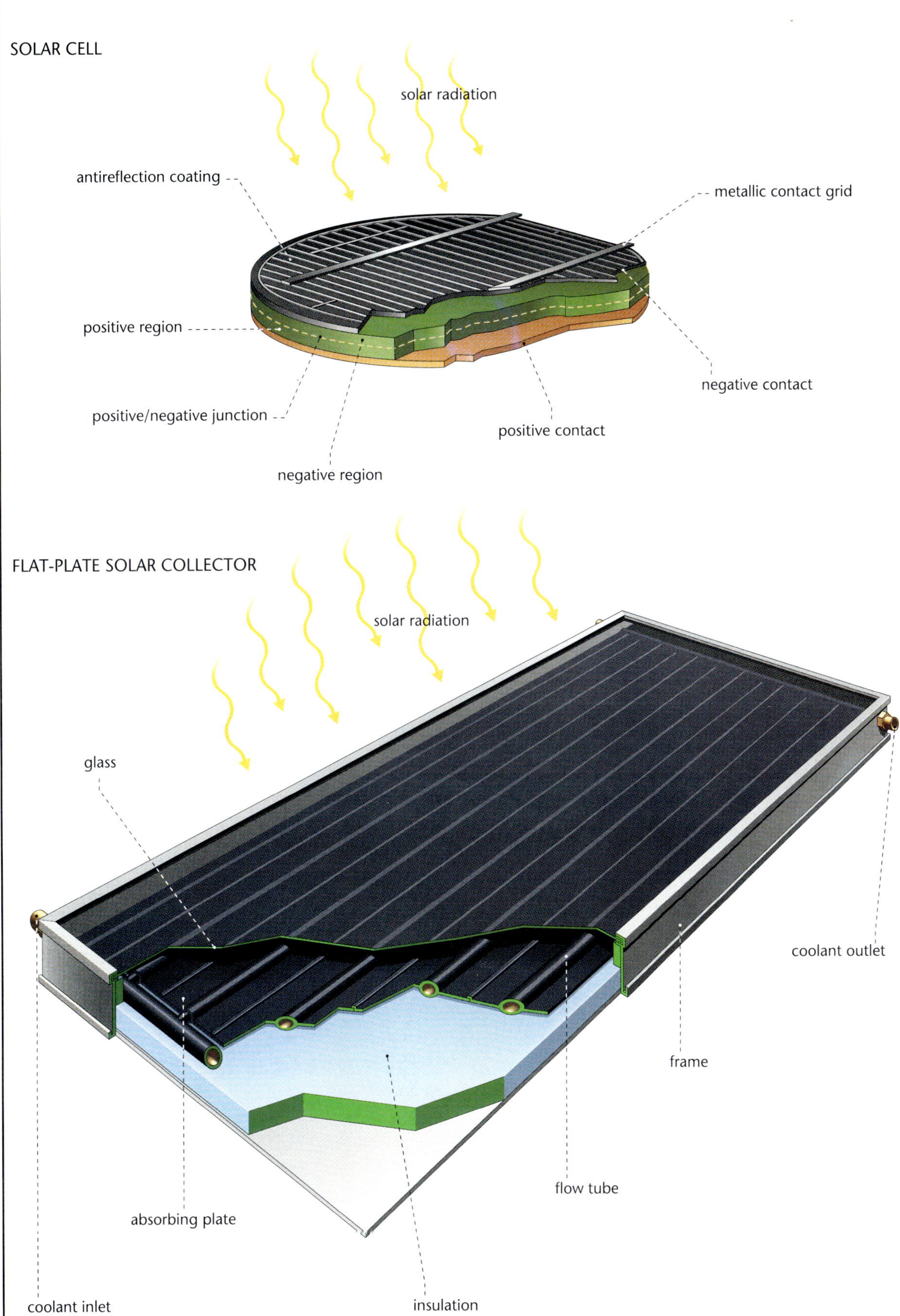

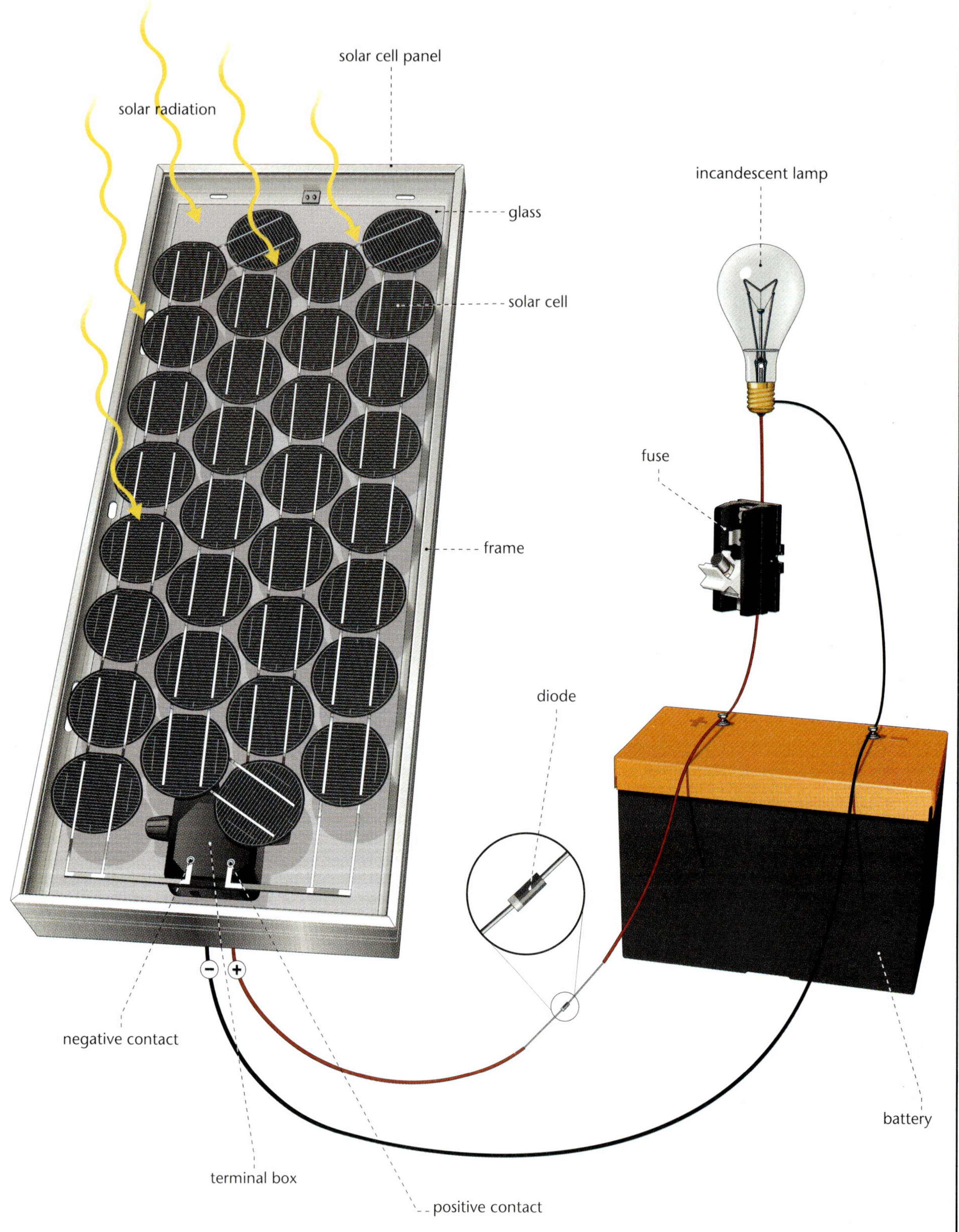

solar cell panel
solar radiation
glass
solar cell
frame
incandescent lamp
fuse
diode
negative contact
terminal box
positive contact
battery
−
+

SOLAR FURNACE

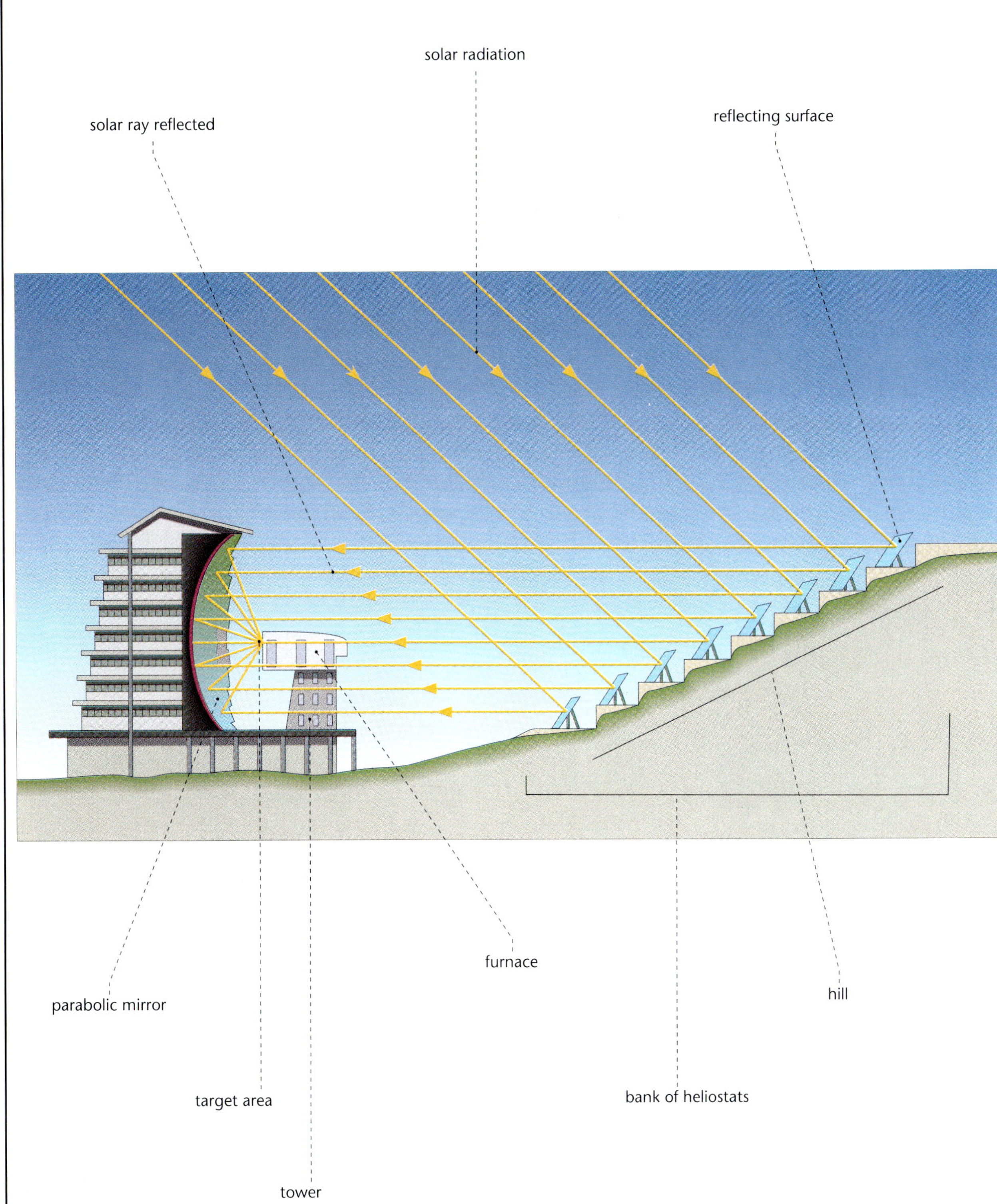

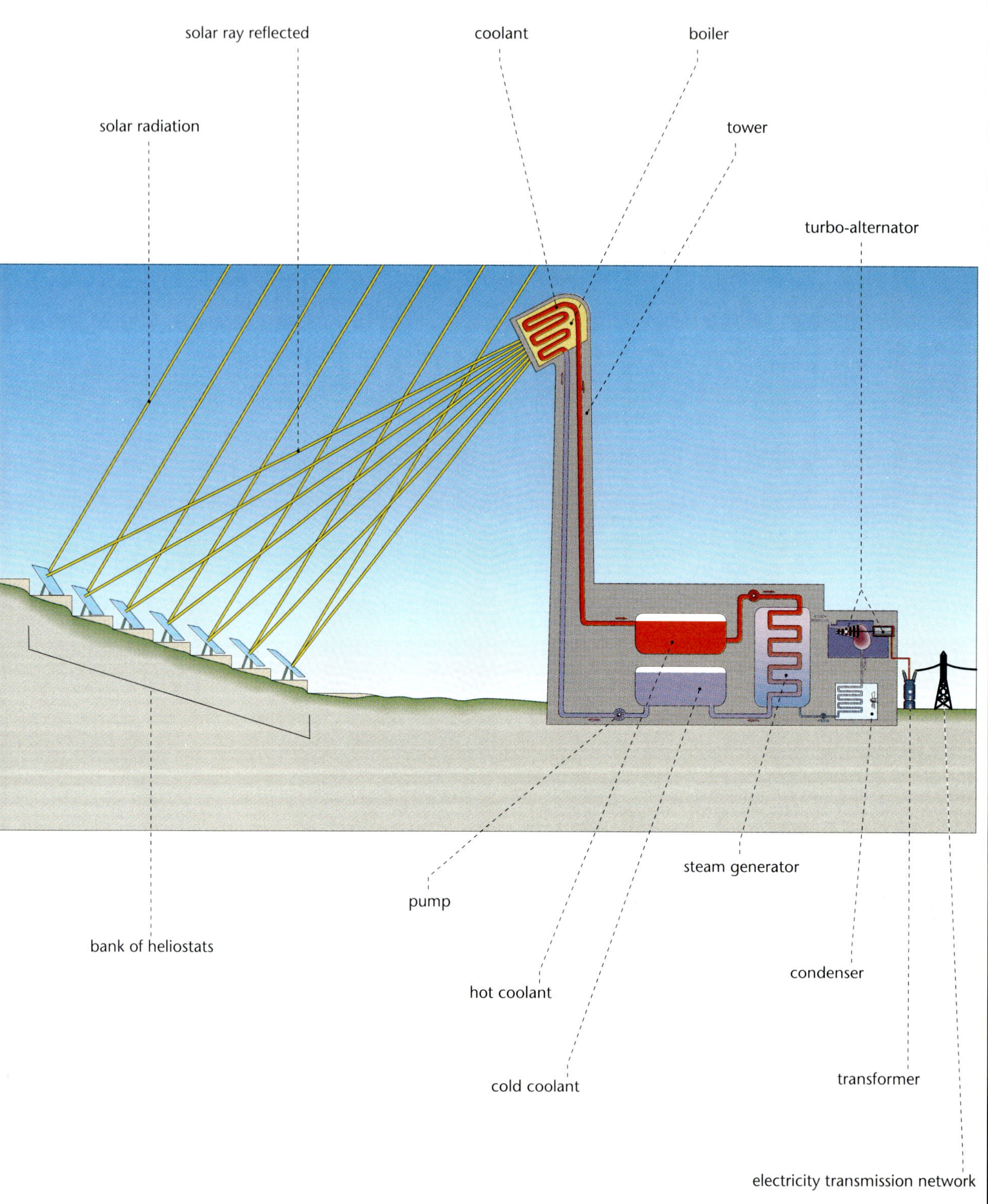

solar ray reflected
coolant
boiler
solar radiation
tower
turbo-alternator
bank of heliostats
pump
hot coolant
cold coolant
steam generator
condenser
transformer
electricity transmission network

SOLAR ENERGY

SOLAR HOUSE

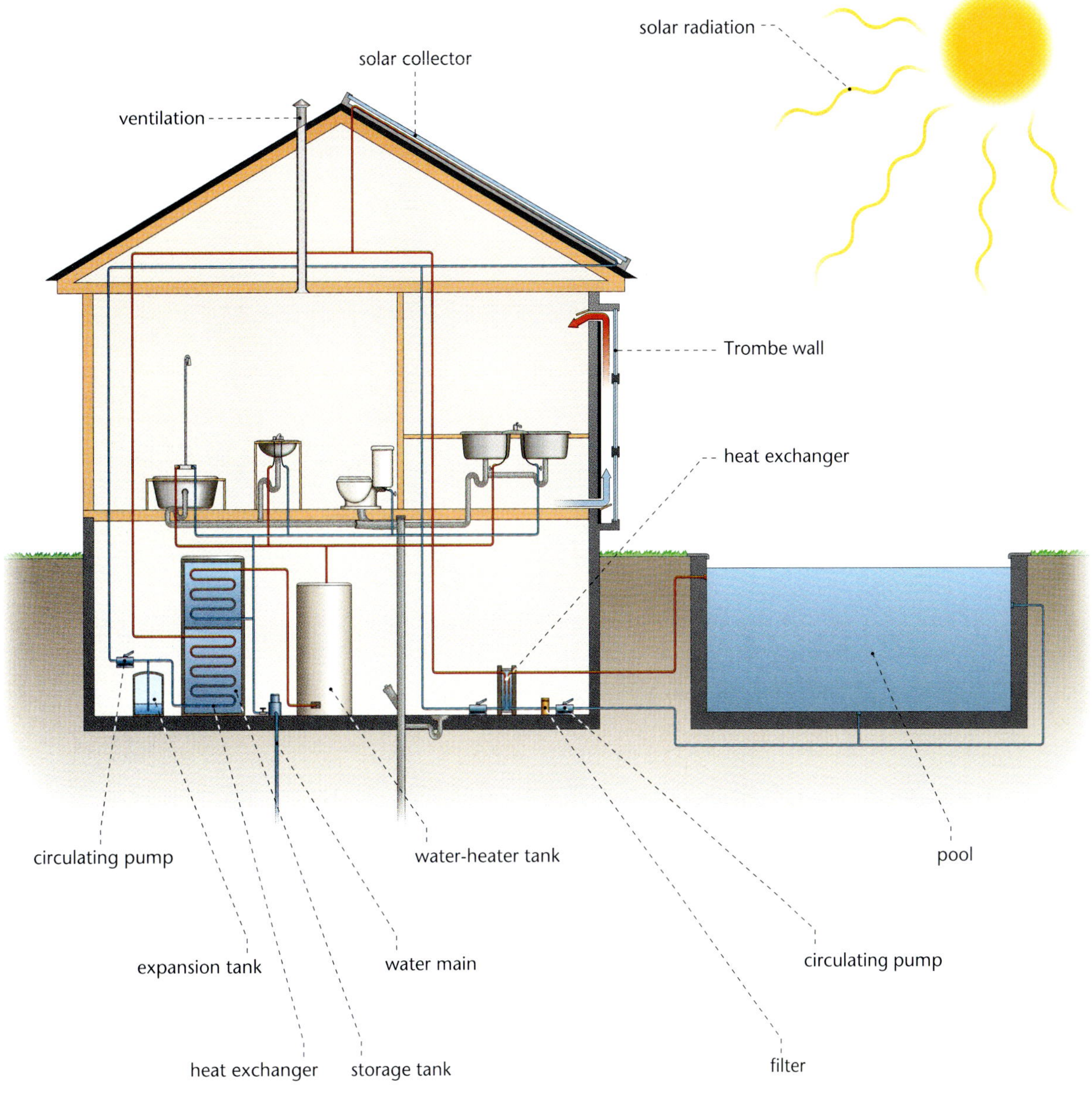

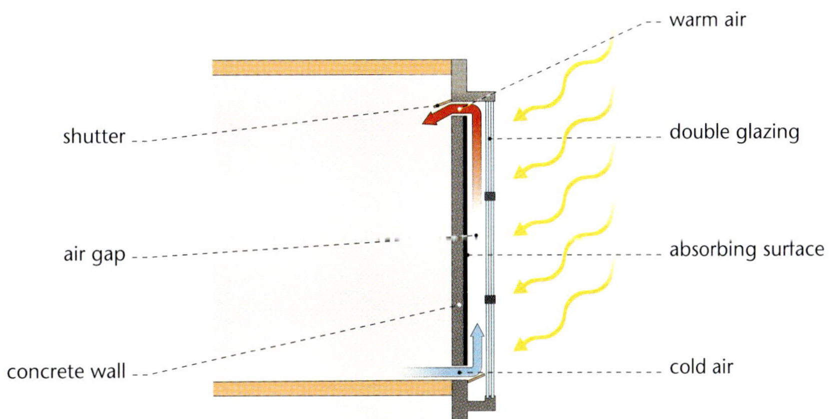

TROMBE WALL

WIND ENERGY

stock
sail
windshaft
cap
tower
floor
gallery
fantail
sail cloth
hemlath
sailbar
frame

ladder
tail pole
rotor
post

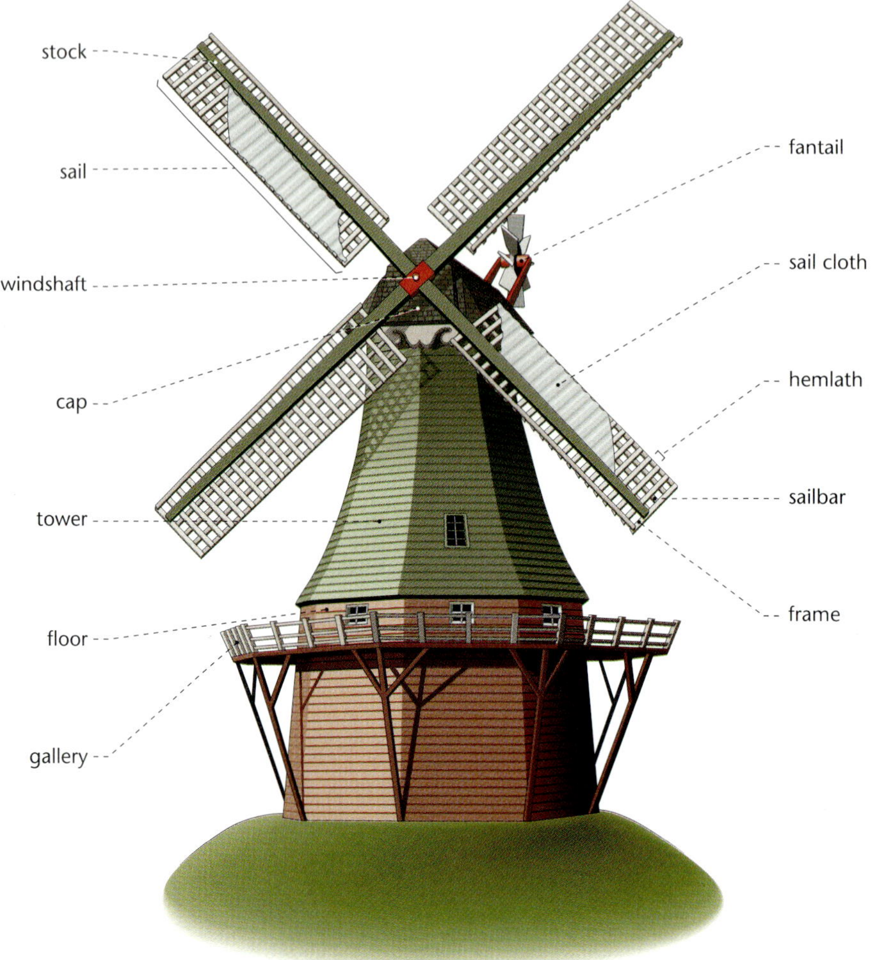

HORIZONTAL-AXIS WIND TURBINE

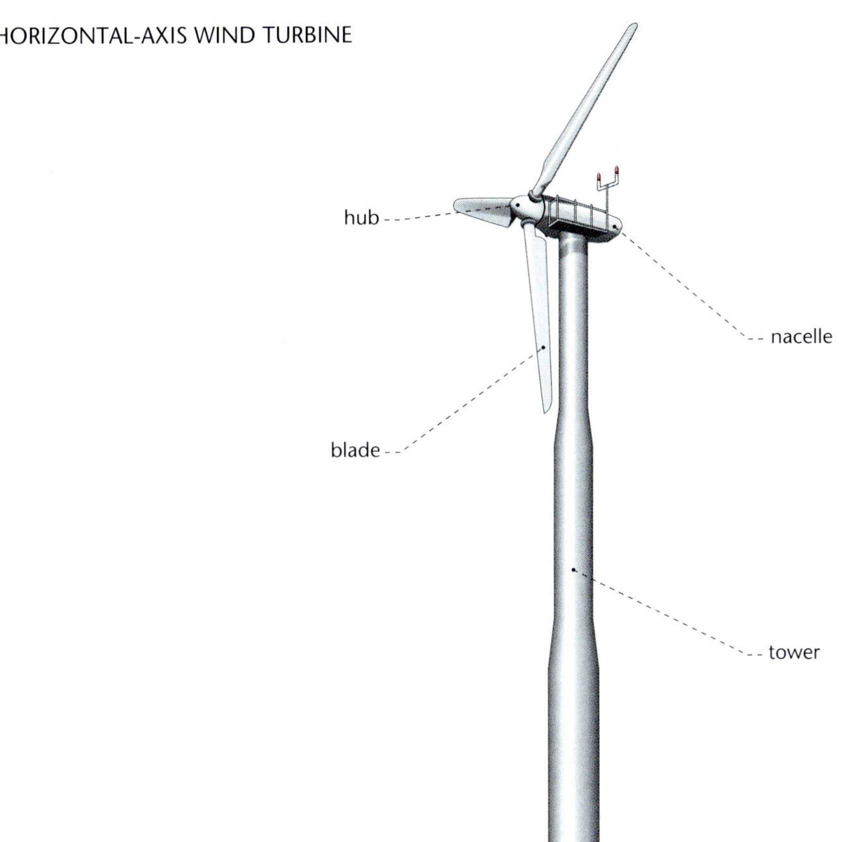

VERTICAL-AXIS WIND TURBINE

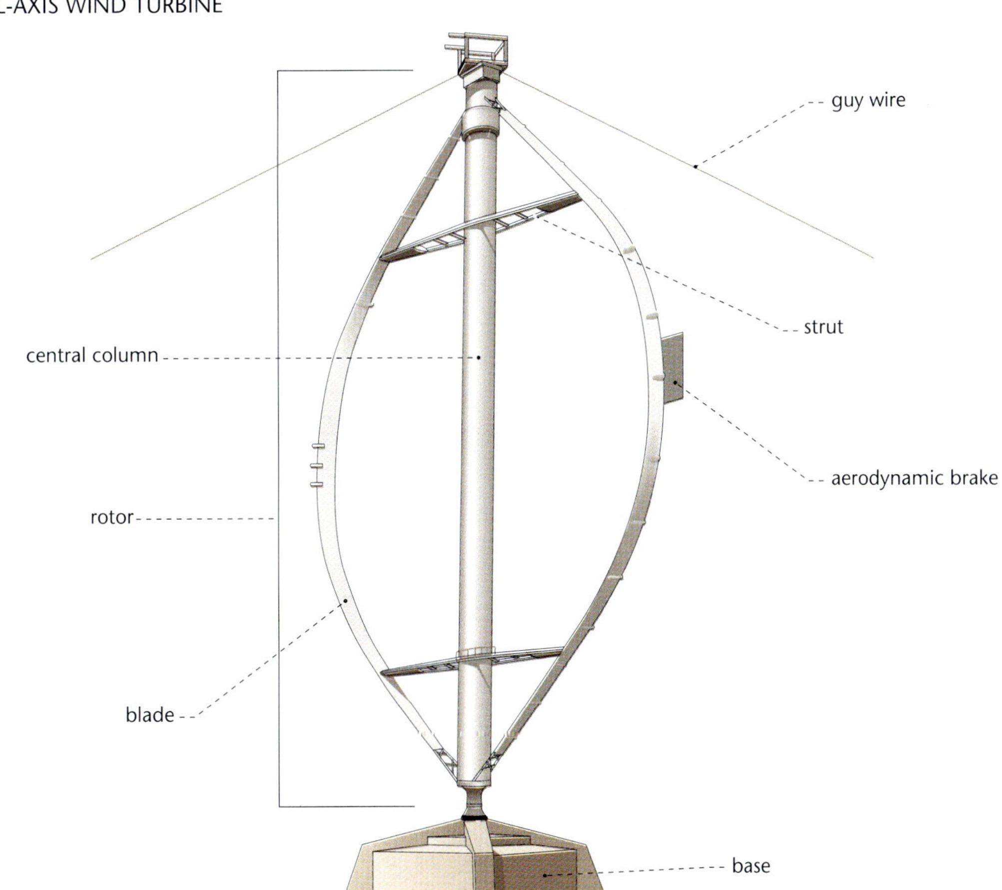

HEAVY MACHINERY

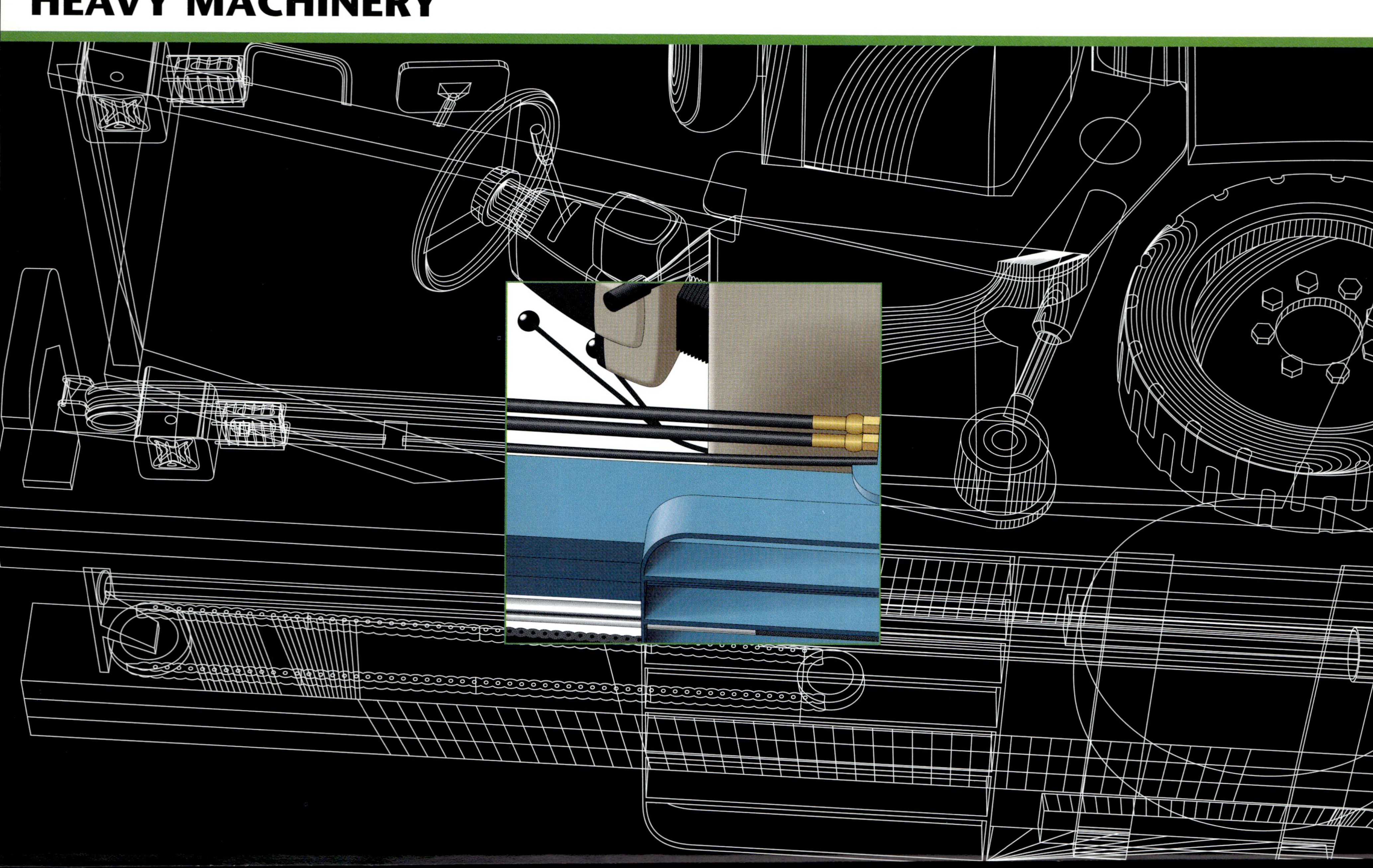

CONTENTS

FIRE PREVENTION

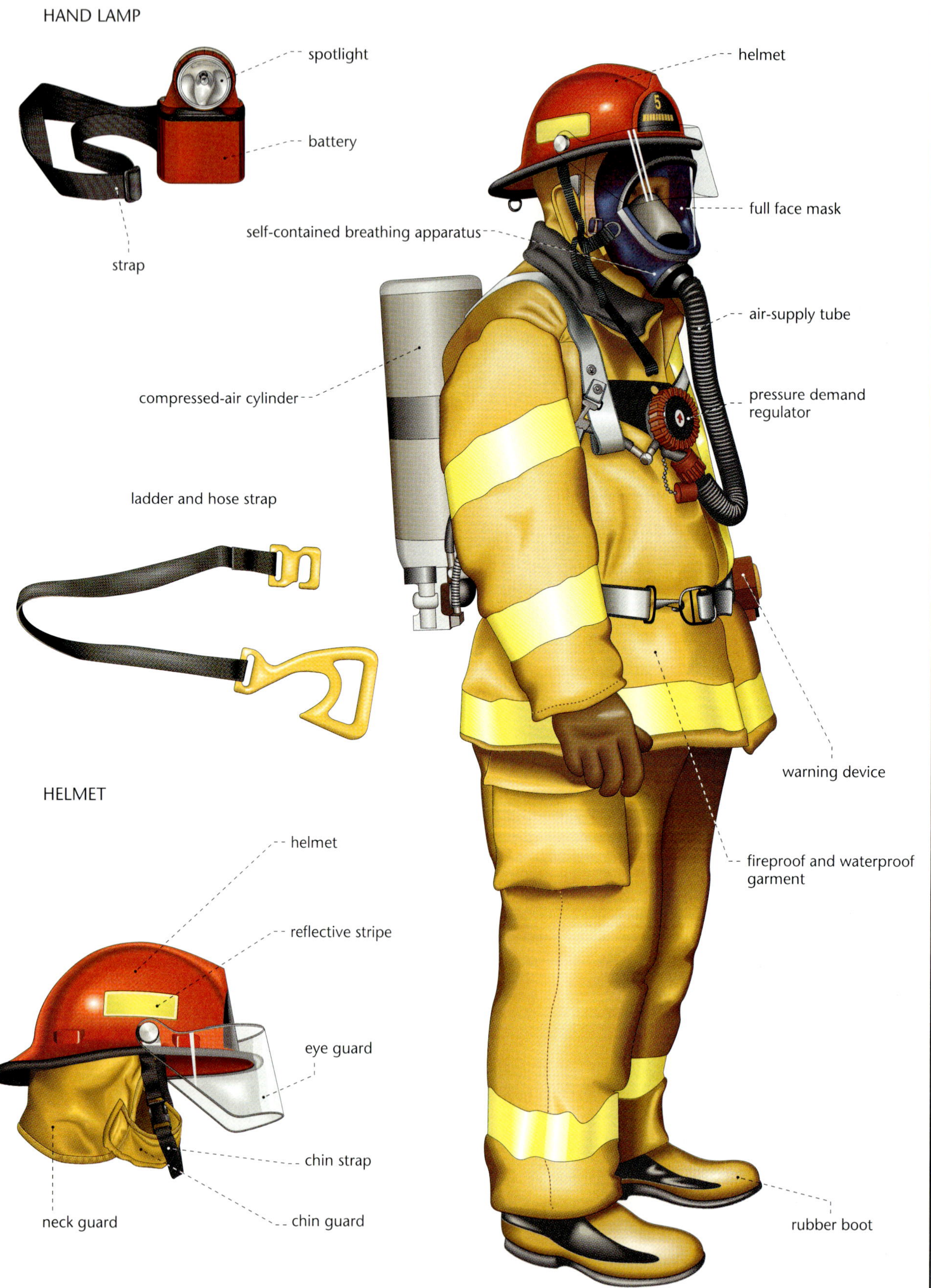

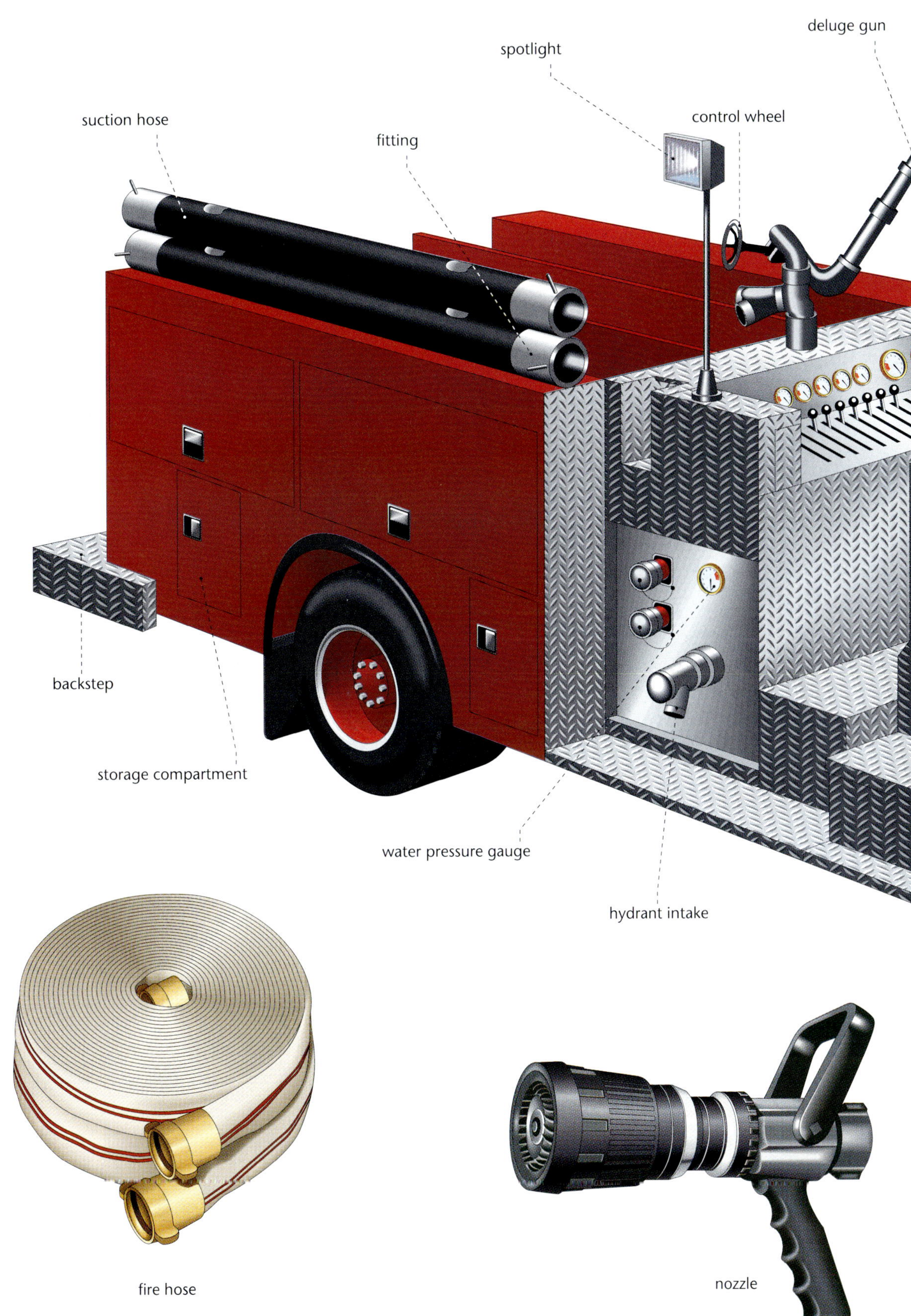

PUMPER
deluge gun
spotlight
control wheel
suction hose
fitting
backstep
storage compartment
water pressure gauge
hydrant intake
fire hose
nozzle

control panel
light bar
horn
dividing breeching
loudspeaker
grab handle
hydrant intake
fire hydrant wrench

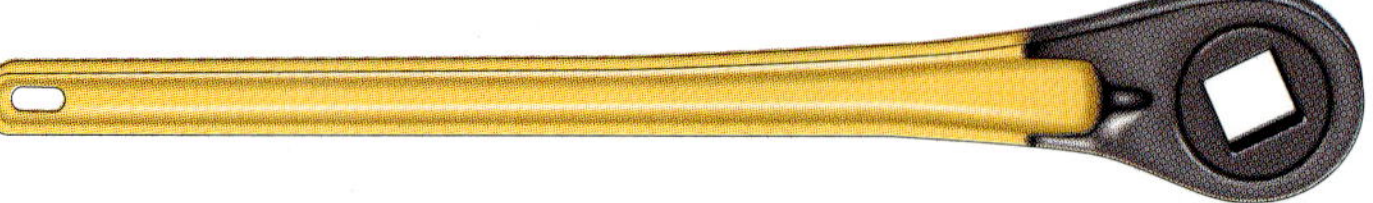

AERIAL LADDER TRUCK

PORTABLE FIRE EXTINGUISHER

pike pole

percussion bar

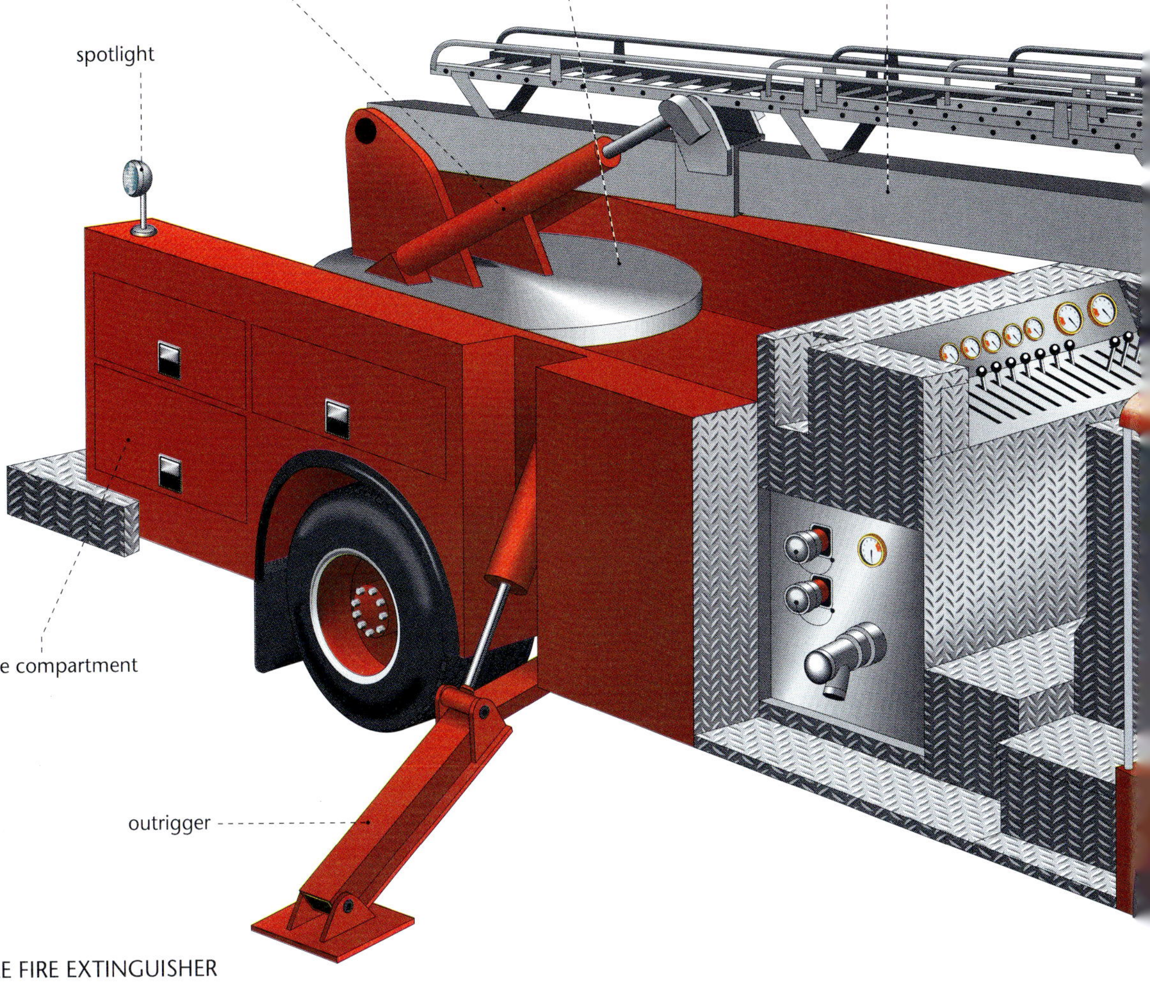

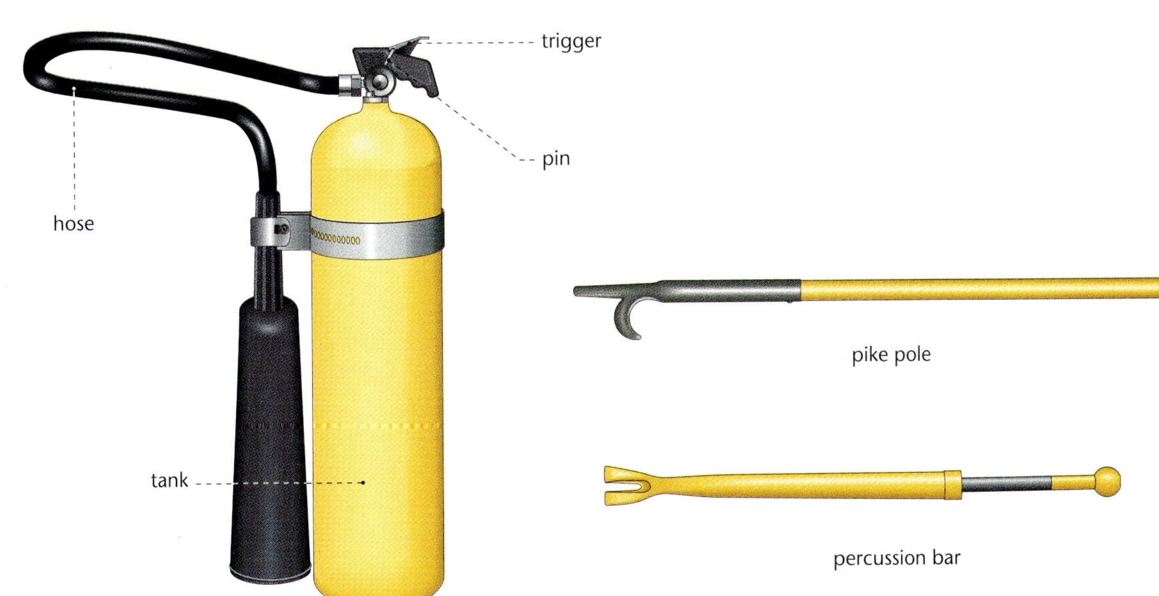

tower ladder
mars light
top ladder
ladder pipe nozzle
fireman's hatchet
hook ladder

WHEEL LOADER

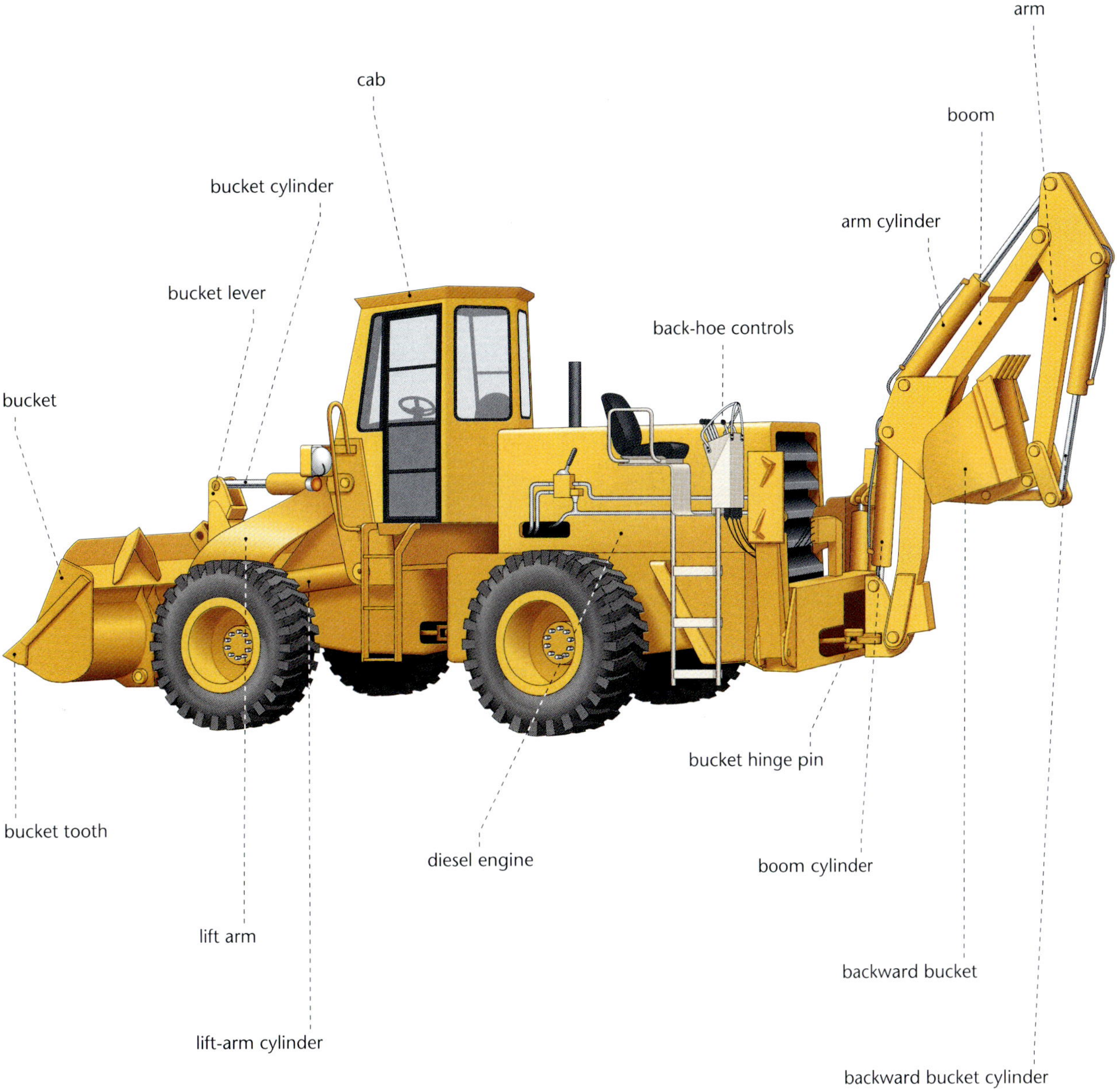

front-end loader

wheel tractor

back-hoe

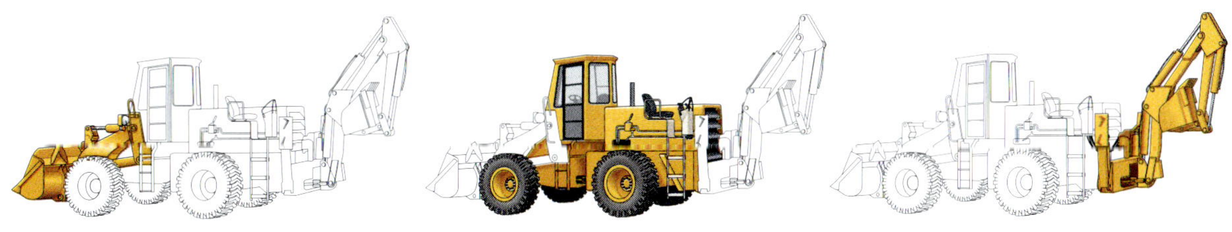

blade

crawler tractor

ripper

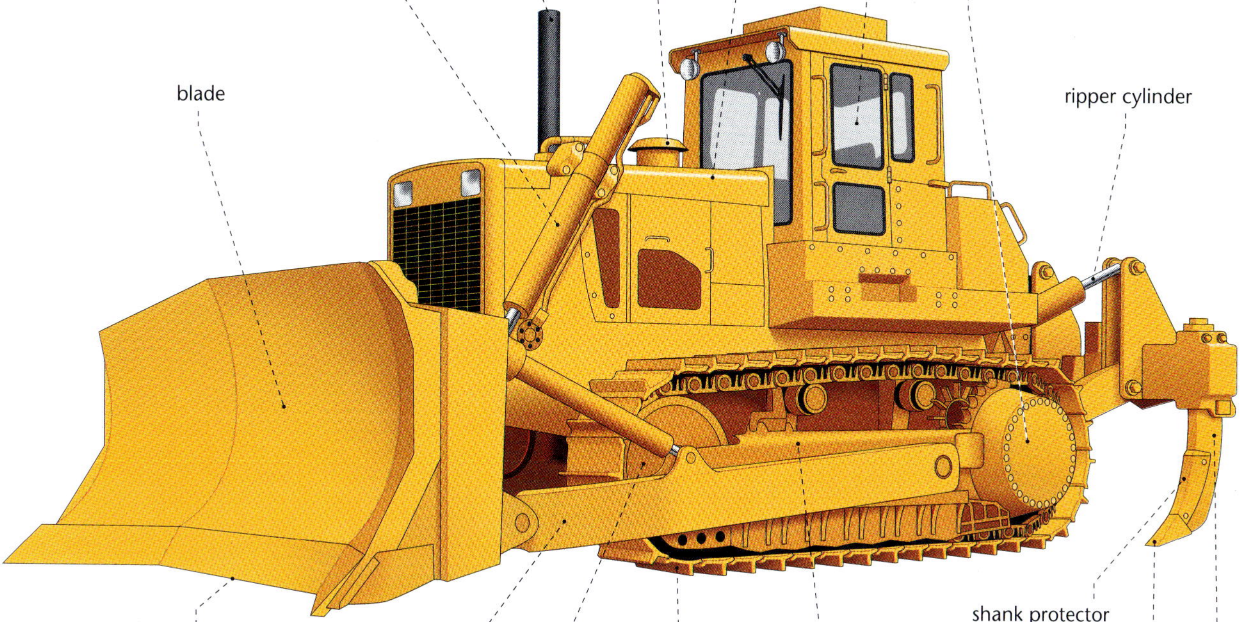

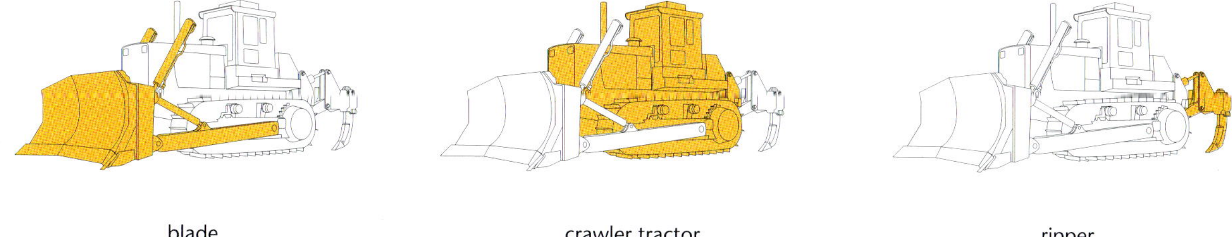

SCRAPER

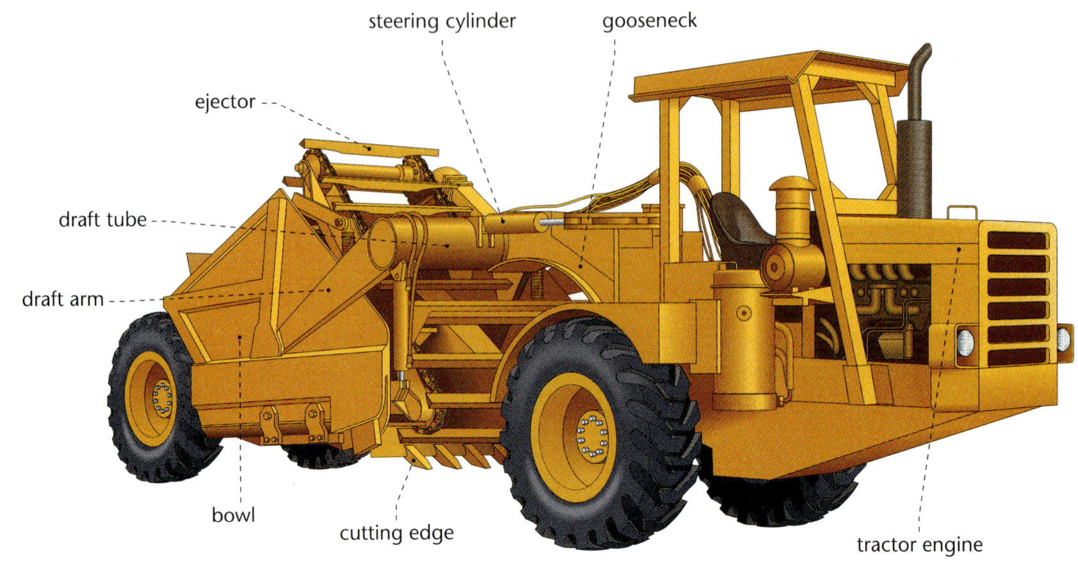

GRADER

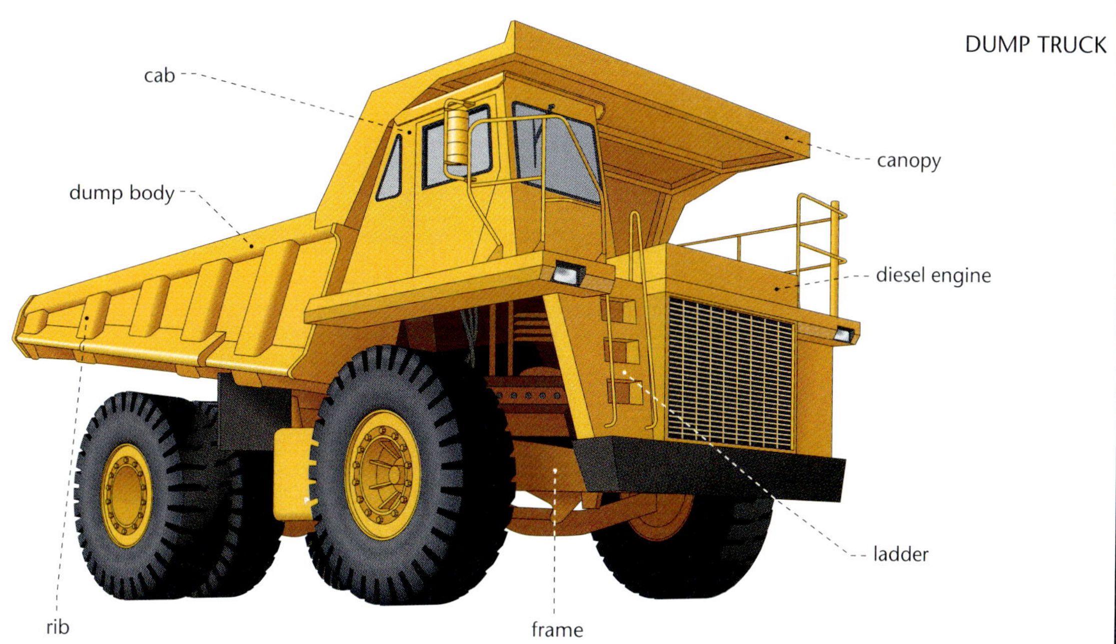
DUMP TRUCK
cab
dump body
canopy
diesel engine
ladder
rib
frame

HYDRAULIC SHOVEL
boom cylinder
boom
arm cylinder
cab
hinge pin
counterweight
arm
diesel engine
bucket cylinder
pivot cab
turntable
frame
outrigger
tooth
dipper bucket

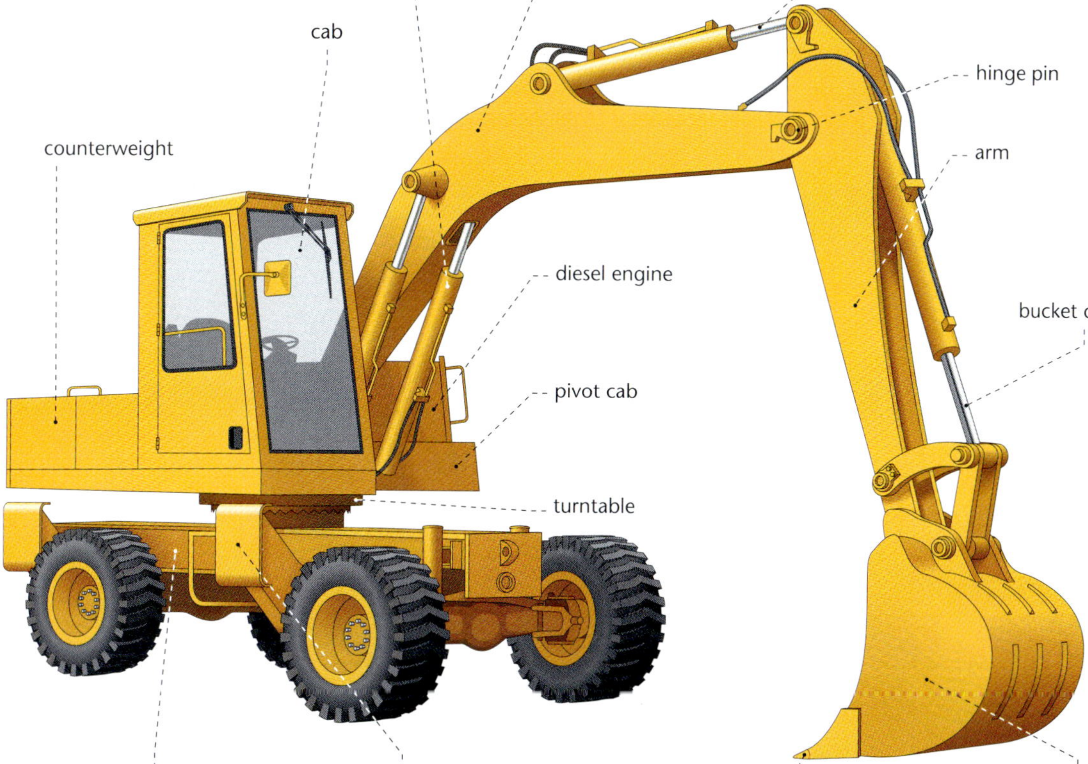

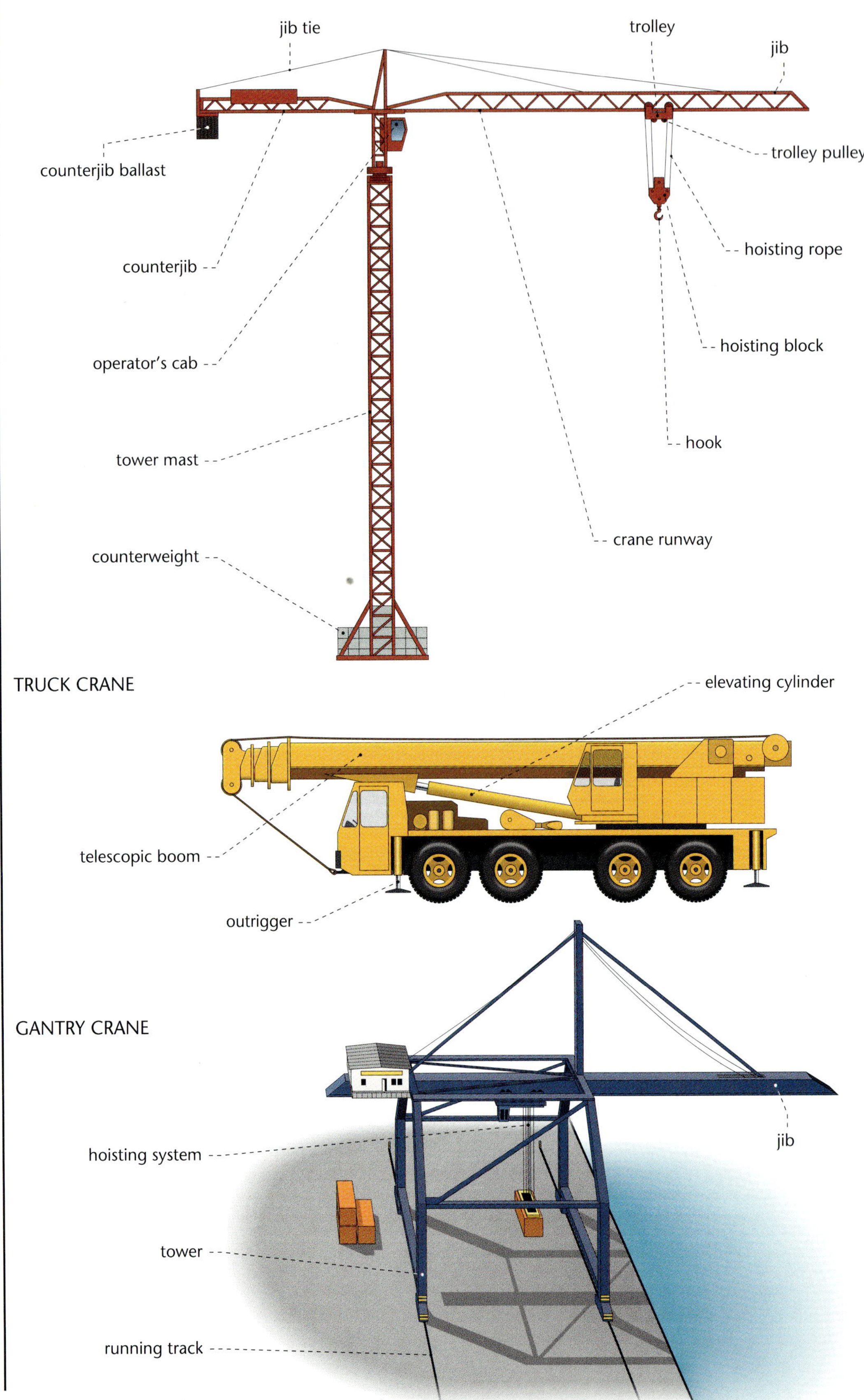
TOWER CRANE
jib tie
trolley
jib
counterjib ballast
trolley pulley
counterjib
operator's cab
hoisting rope
hoisting block
tower mast
hook
counterweight
crane runway
TRUCK CRANE
elevating cylinder
telescopic boom
outrigger
GANTRY CRANE
jib
hoisting system
tower
running track

WING PALLET

BOX PALLET

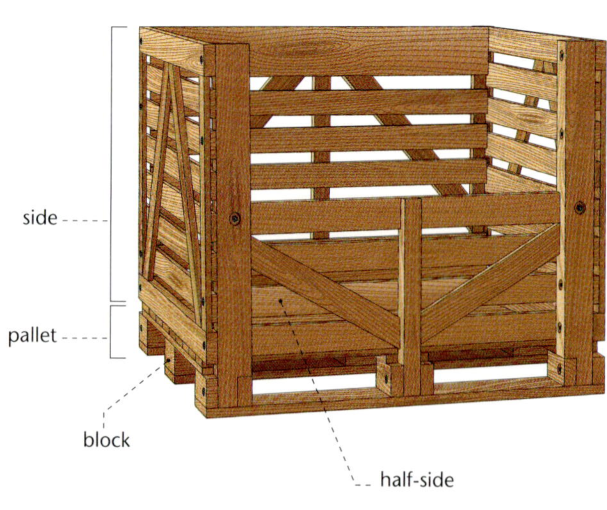

HYDRAULIC PALLET TRUCK
pallet truck
maneuvering lever
steering lever
mast
hydraulic cylinder
hand truck
forks
solid rubber tire
stabilizing shaft
steering axle
frame
roller
platform pallet truck
flatbed pushcart

WEAPONS

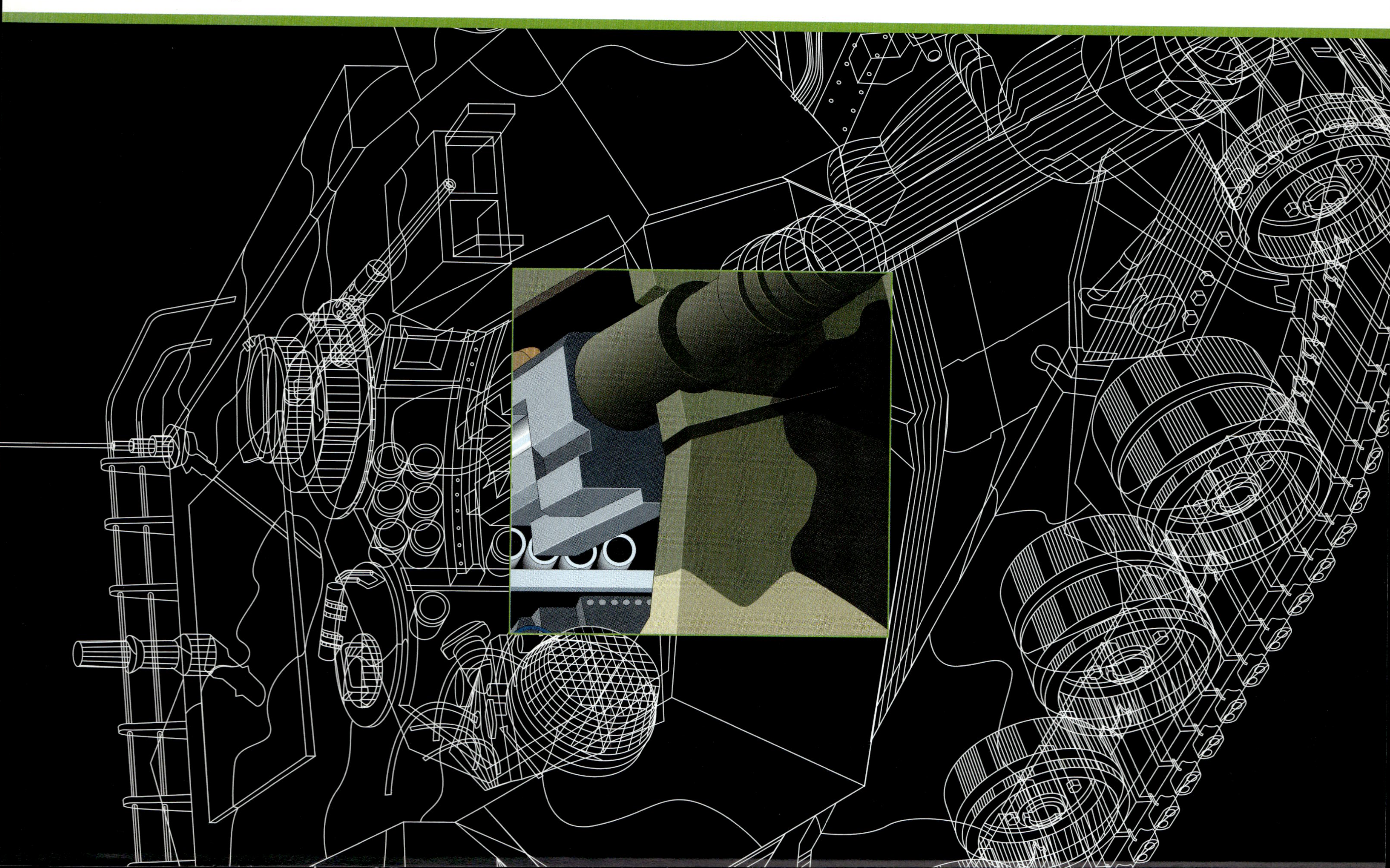

CONTENTS

STONE AGE ARMS

polished stone hand axe

flint arrowhead

flint knife

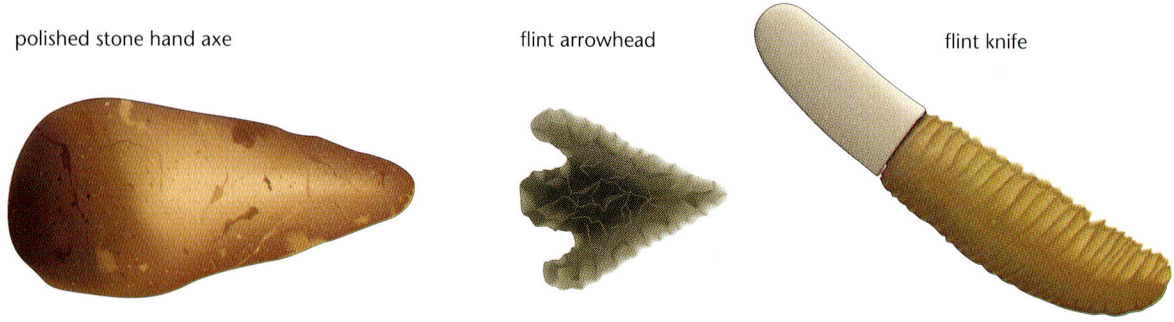

WEAPONS IN THE AGE OF THE ROMANS

GALLIC WARRIOR

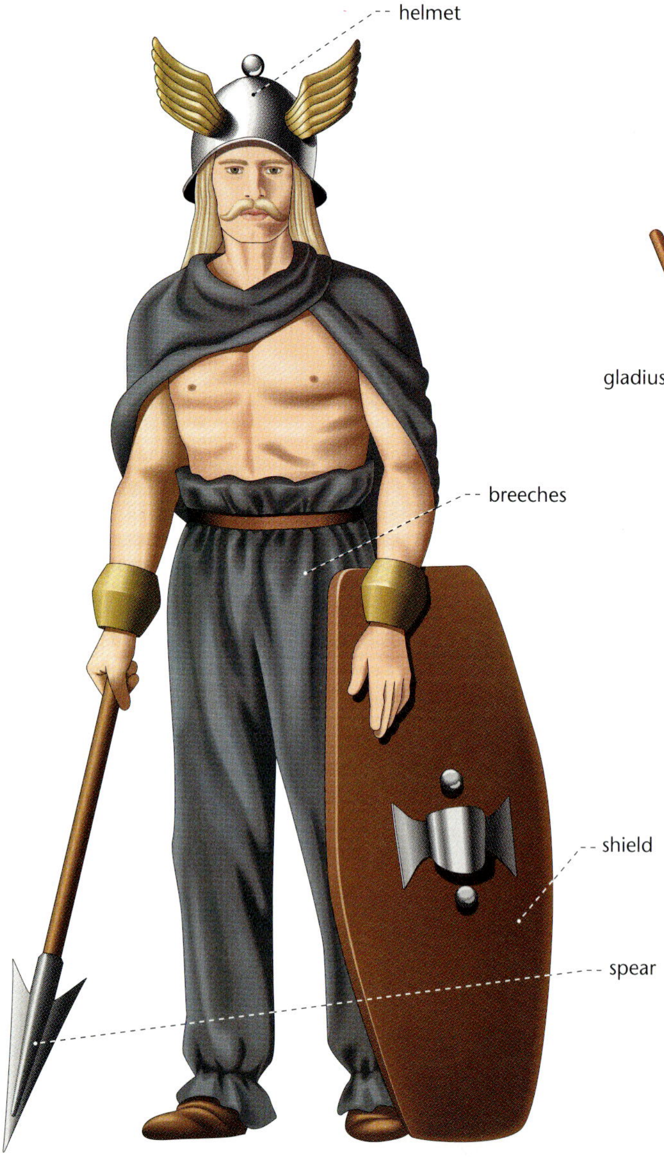

ROMAN LEGIONARY

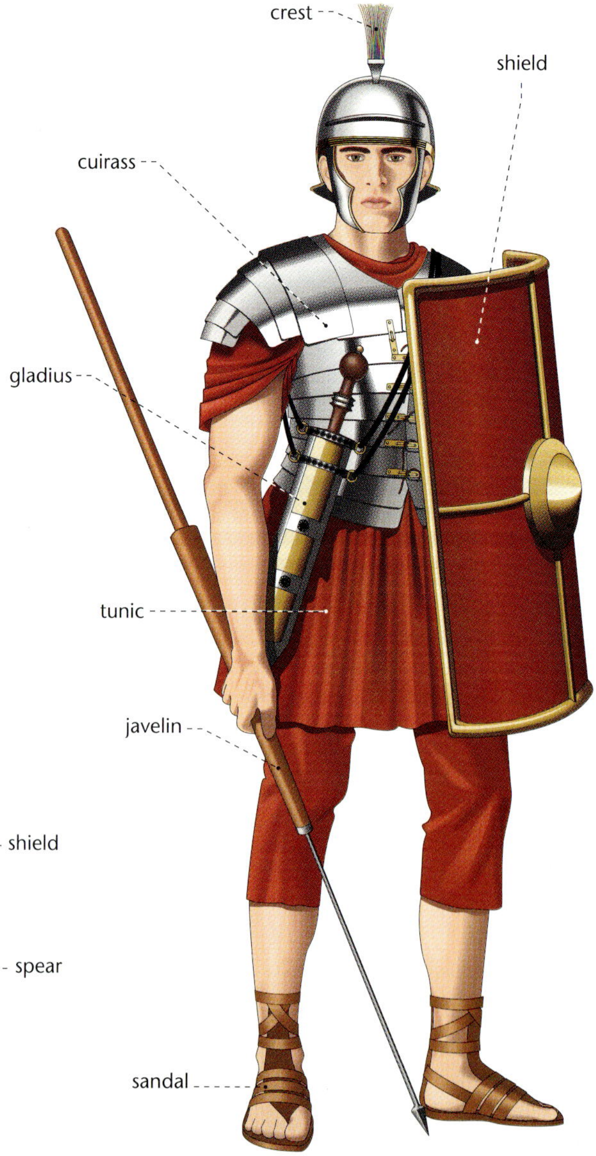

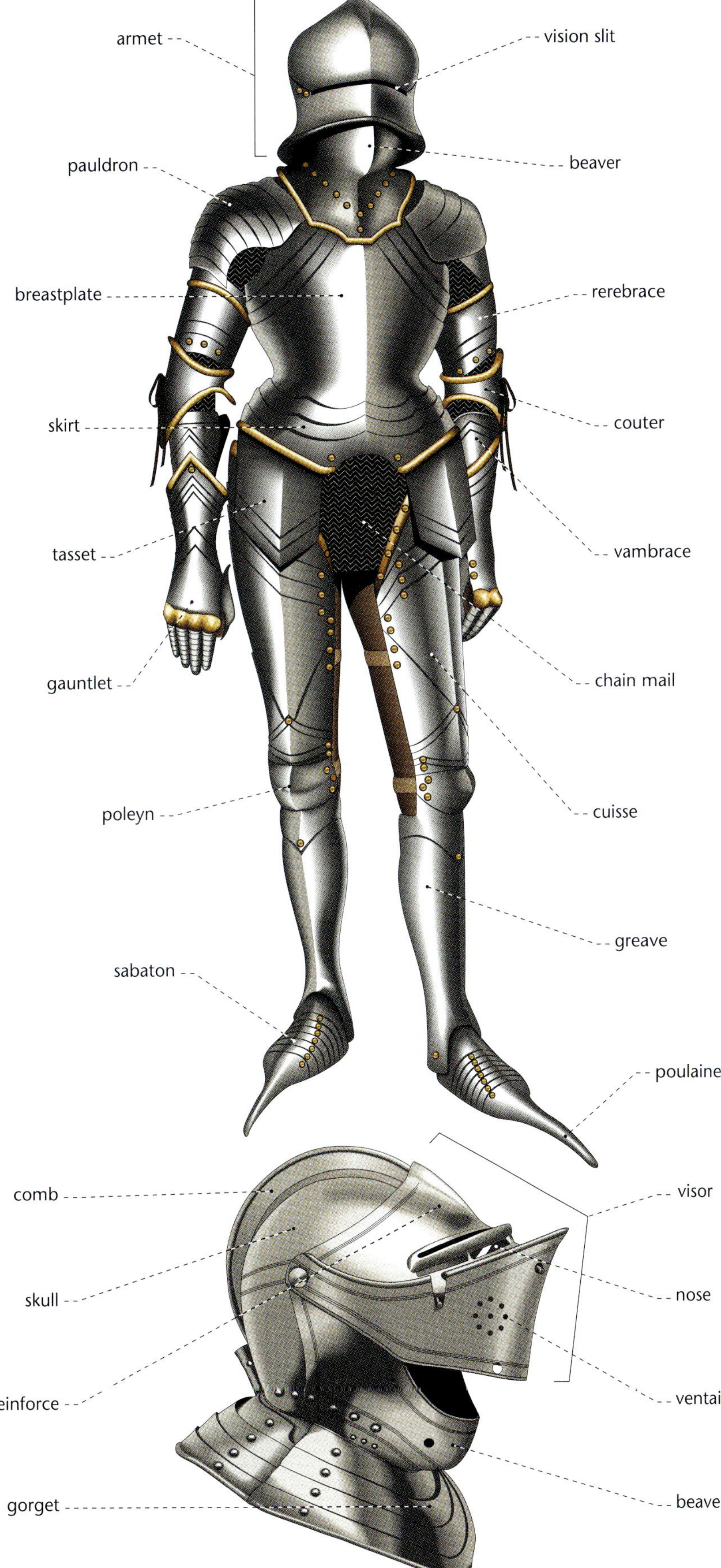
armet
vision slit
pauldron
beaver
breastplate
rerebrace
skirt
couter
tasset
vambrace
gauntlet
chain mail
poleyn
cuisse
greave
sabaton
poulaine
ARMET
comb
visor
skull
nose
brow reinforce
ventail
gorget
beaver

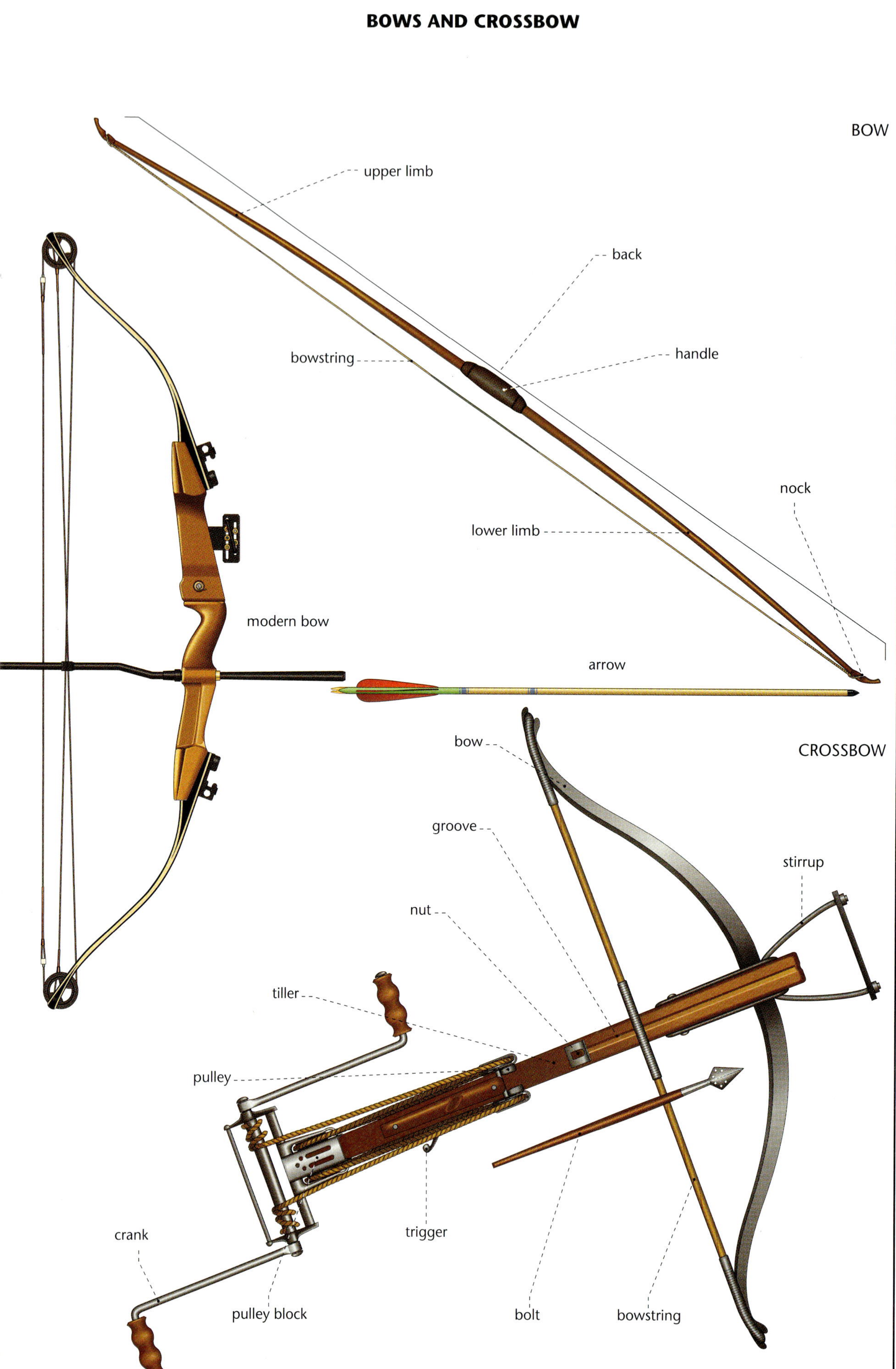
BOW
upper limb
back
handle
bowstring
nock
lower limb
modern bow
arrow
CROSSBOW
bow
groove
stirrup
nut
tiller
pulley
crank
trigger
pulley block
bolt
bowstring
WEAPONS

saber
rapier
broadsword
stiletto
poniard
dagger
machete
commando knife
hilted bayonet
plug bayonet
integral bayonet
socket bayonet

HARQUEBUS

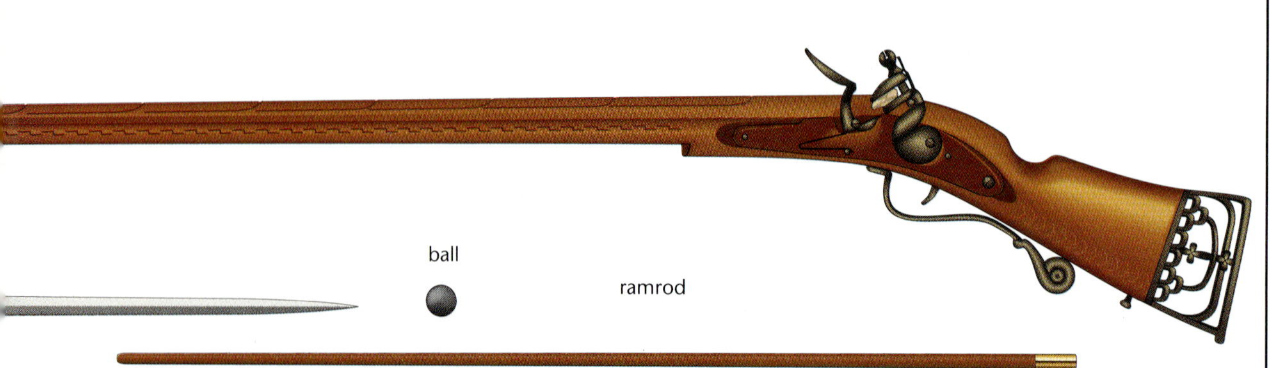

ball

ramrod

FLINTLOCK

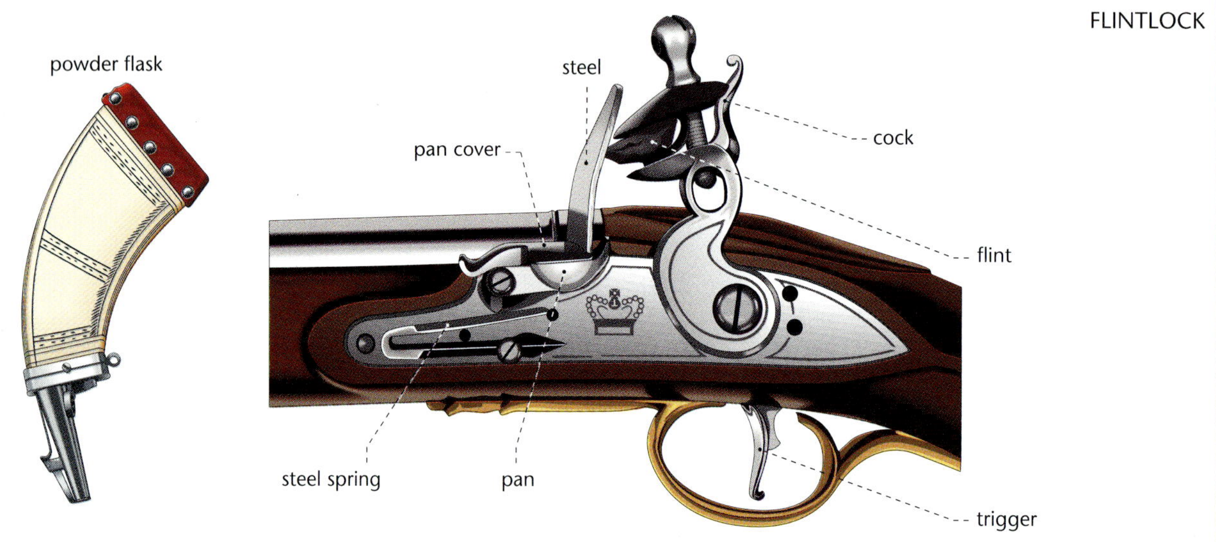

SUBMACHINE GUN

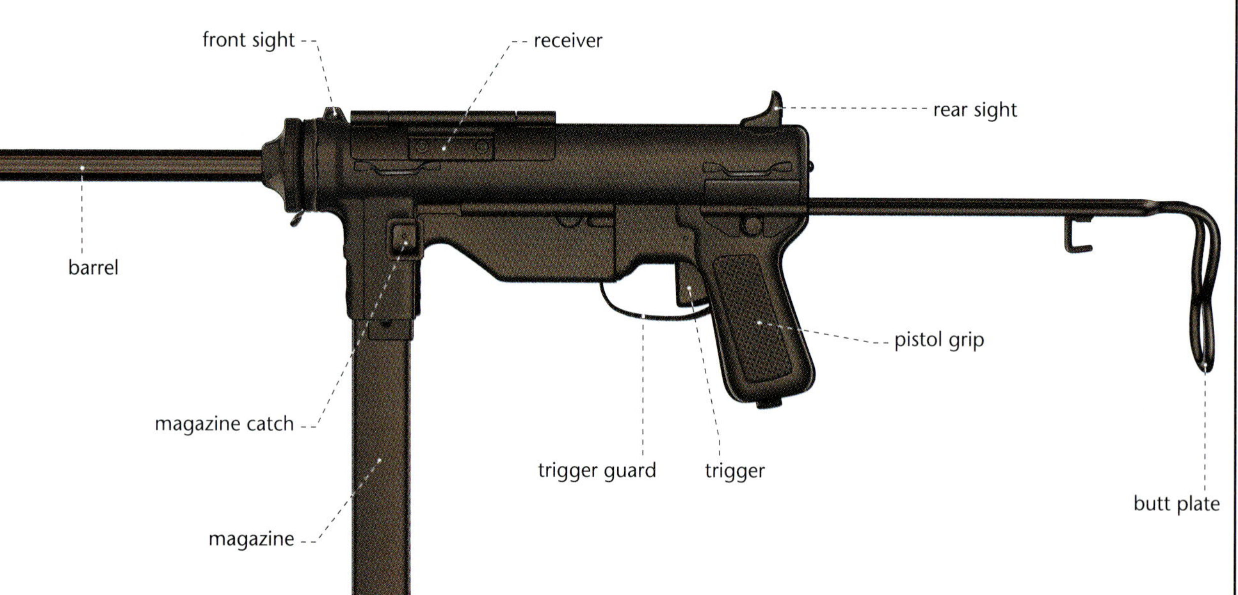

AUTOMATIC RIFLE

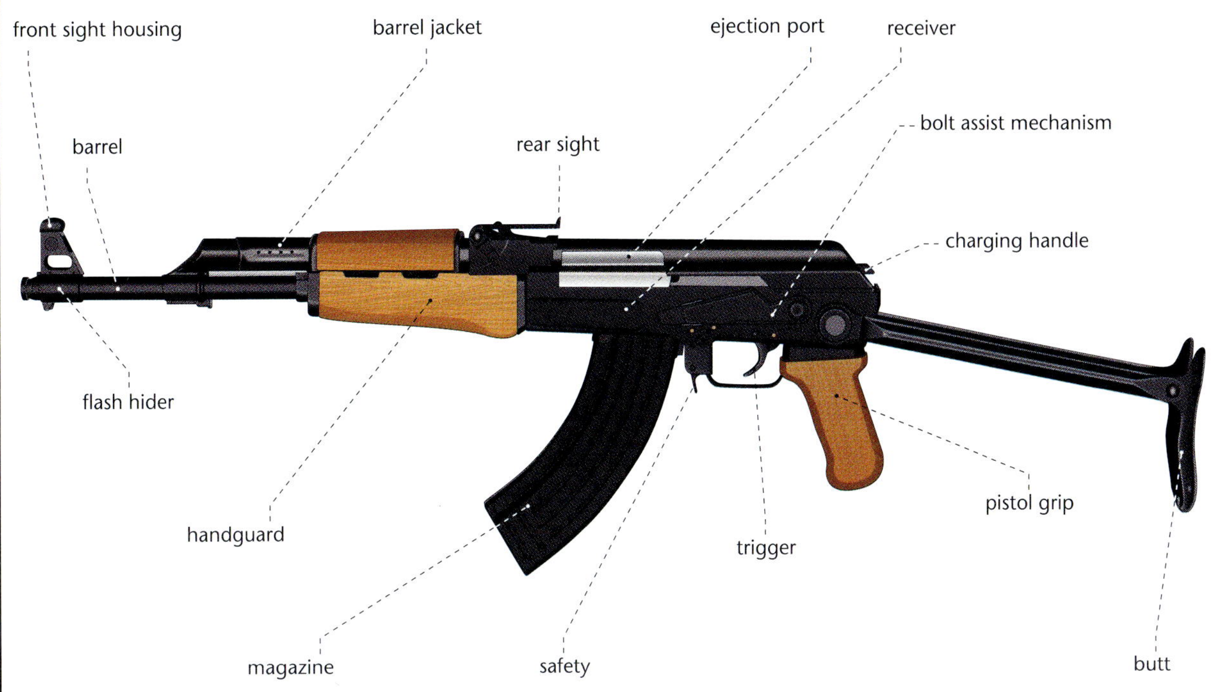

LIGHT MACHINE GUN

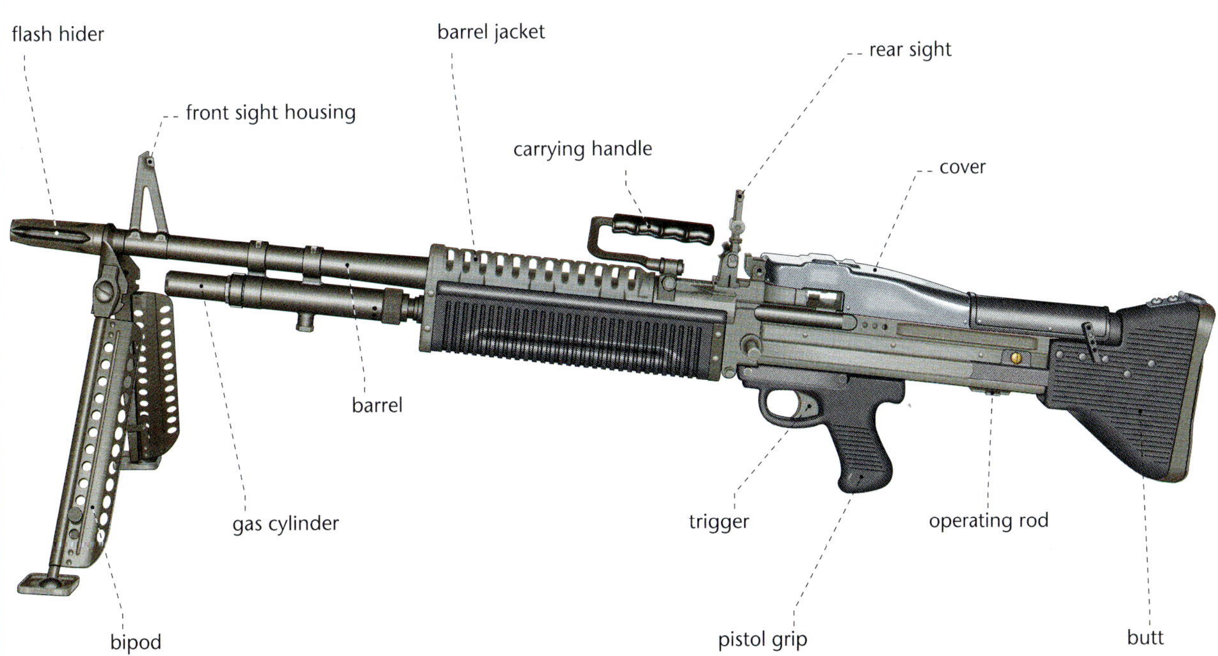

hammer
barrel
front sight
muzzle
cylinder
trigger guard
butt
trigger

PISTOL

hammer
rear sight
barrel
front sight
magazine
slide
trigger guard
trigger
magazine base
butt
magazine catch
cartridge

HUNTING WEAPONS

CARTRIDGE (RIFLE)

RIFLE (RIFLED BORE)

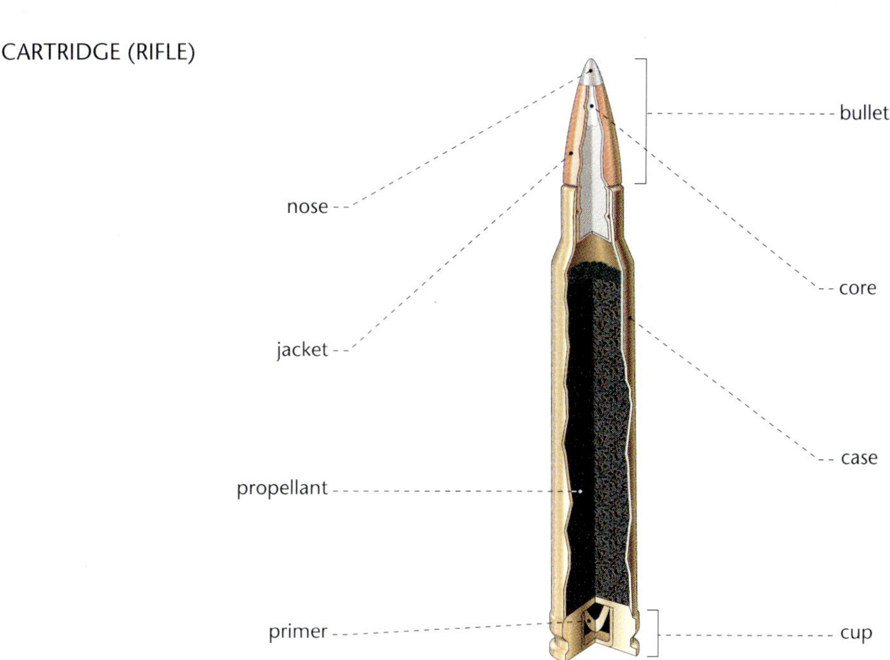

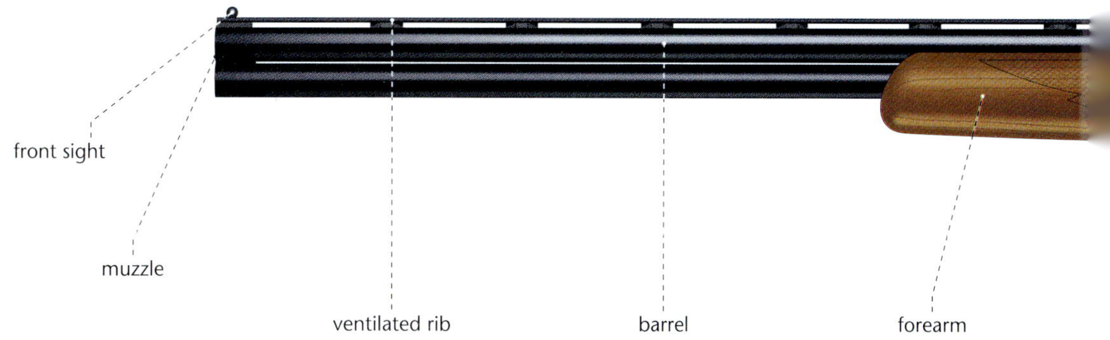

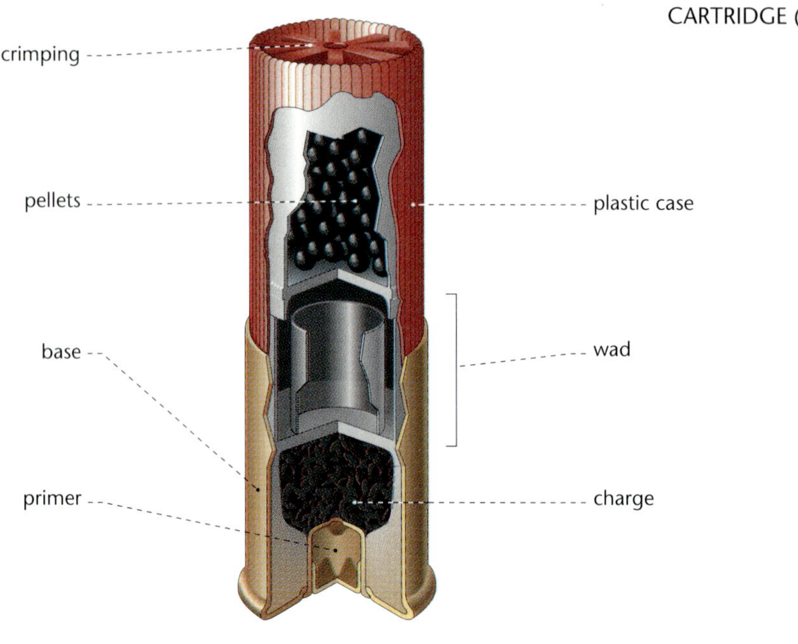

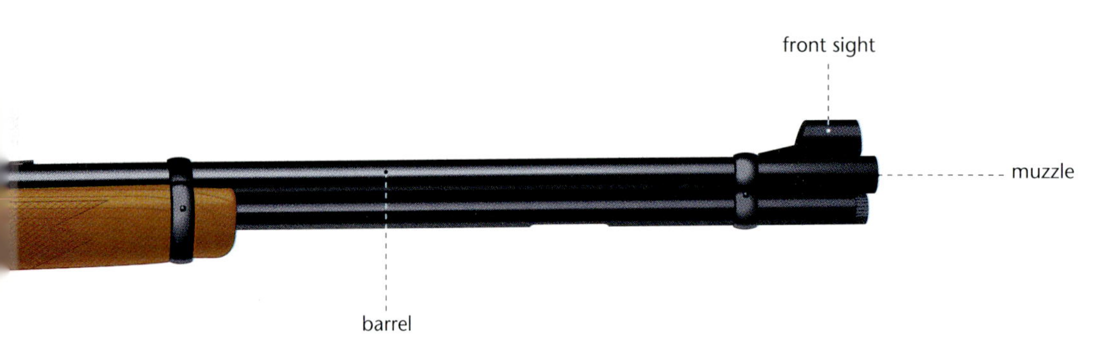

SHOTGUN (SMOOTH-BORE)

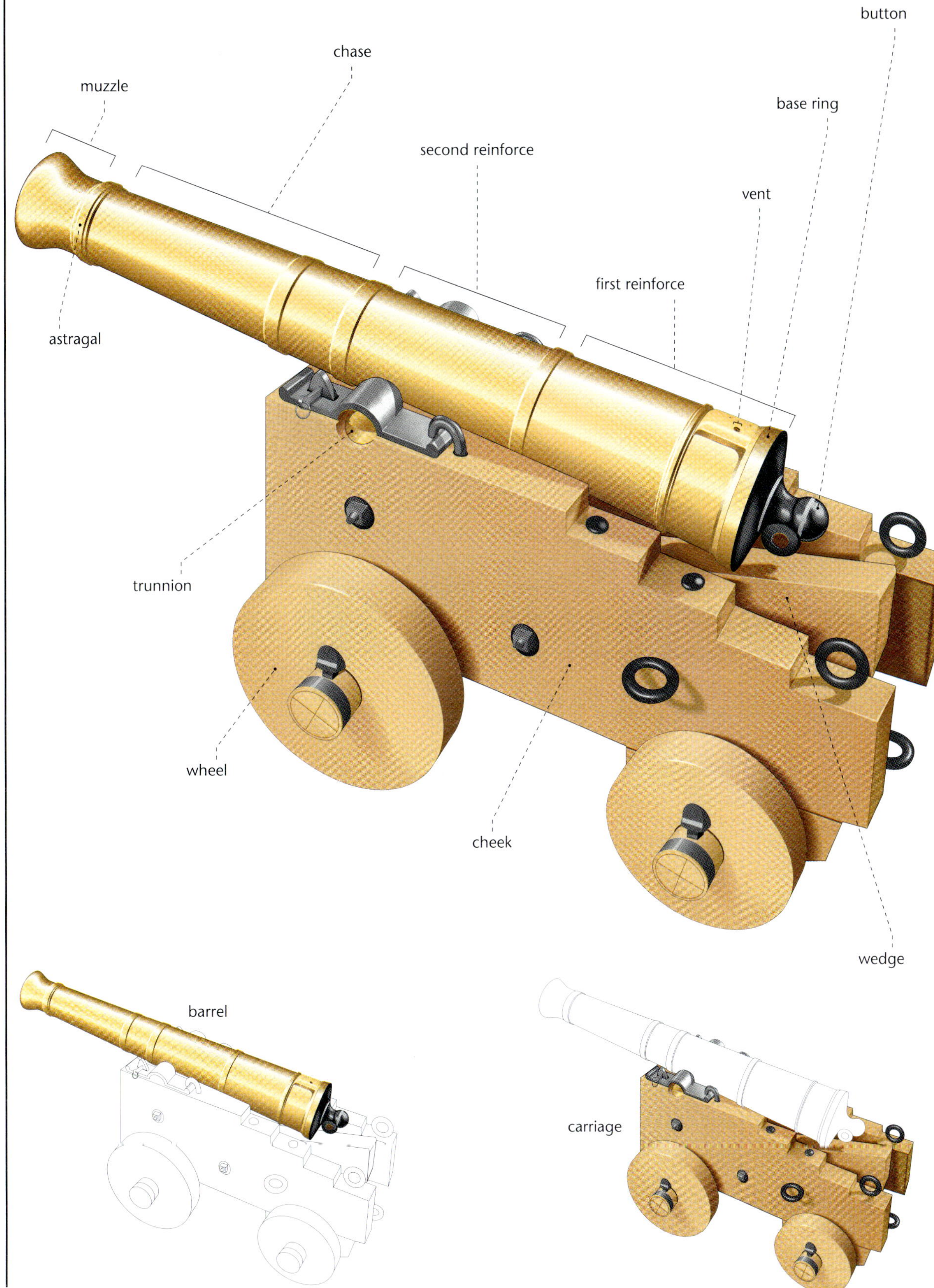

MUZZLE LOADING
muzzle
chase
button
base ring
second reinforce
vent
first reinforce
astragal
trunnion
wheel
cheek
wedge
barrel
carriage

CROSS SECTION OF A MUZZLE LOADING

FIRING ACCESSORIES

PROJECTILES

MODERN HOWITZER

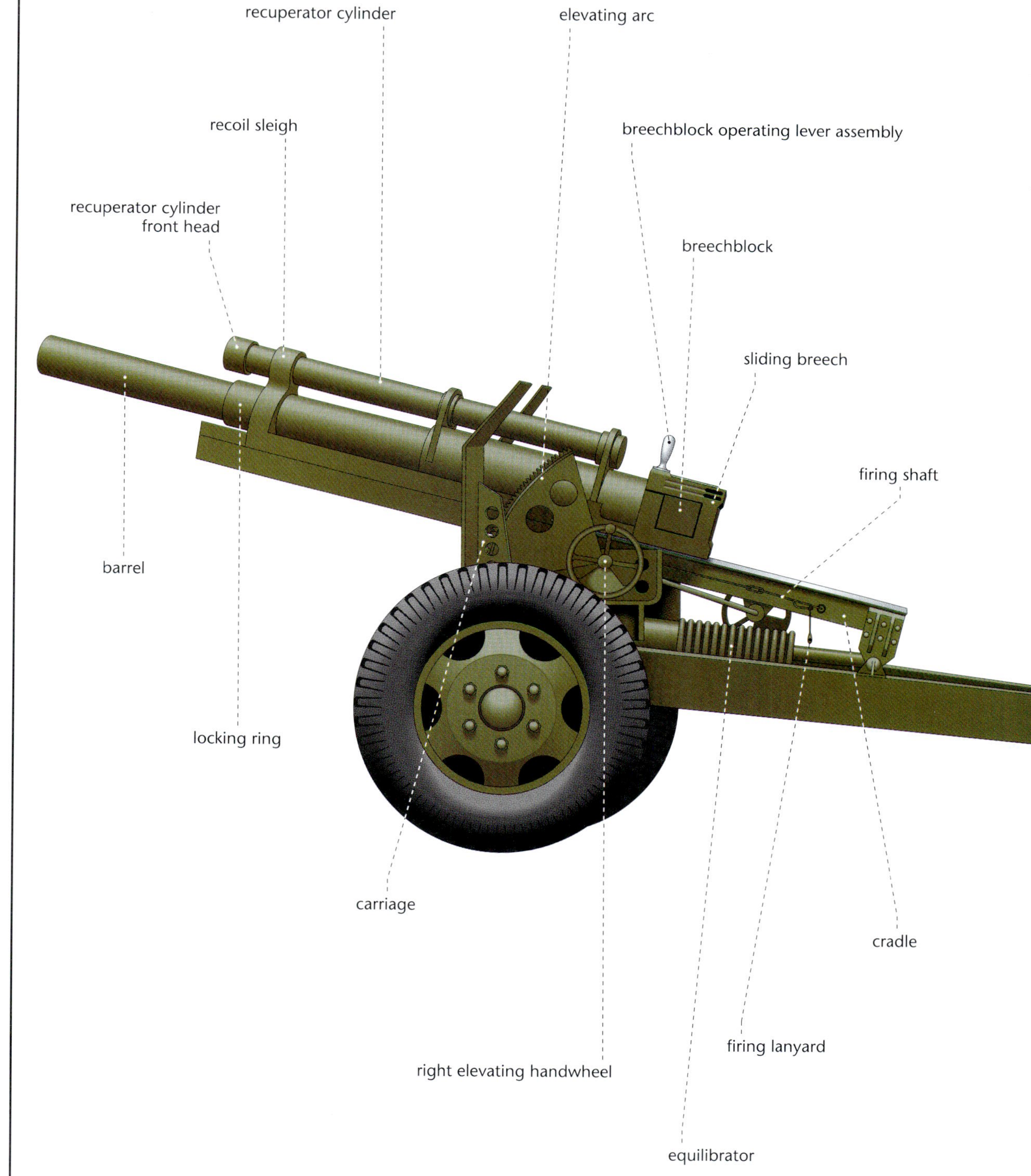

MORTAR

MODERN MORTAR
muzzle
sight
elevating handle
traversing handle
tube
bipod
baseplate
drawbar
drawbar lock
towing eye
right trail
lifting handle
spade
float
SEVENTEENTH-CENTURY MORTAR

HAND GRENADE

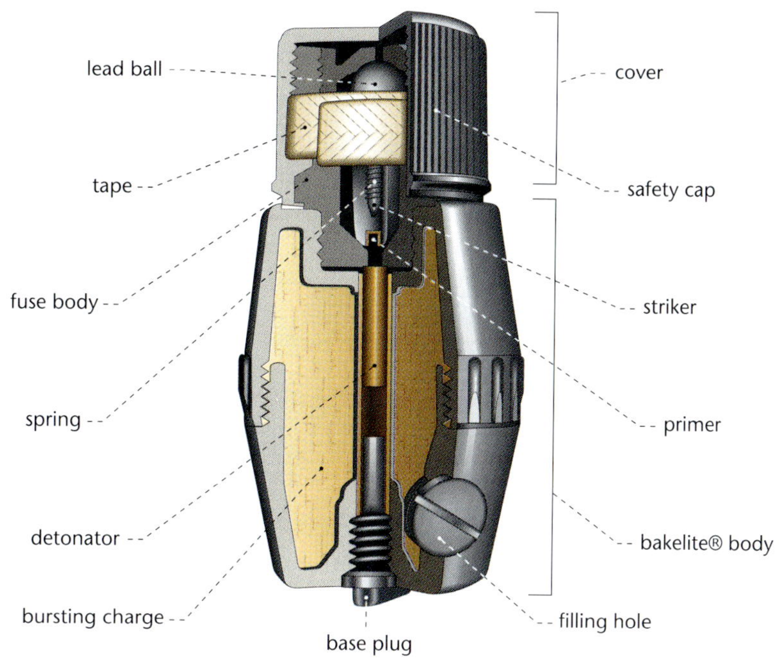

BAZOOKA

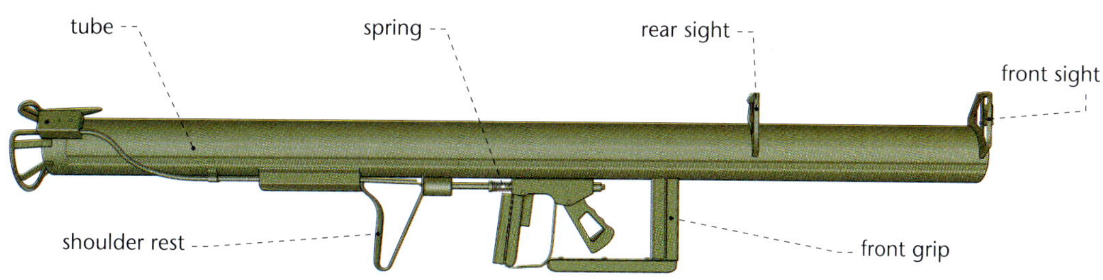

RECOILLESS RIFLE

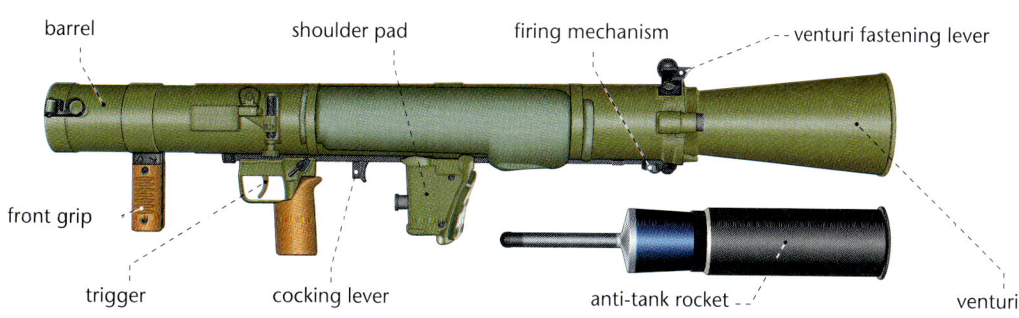

TANK

gunner's sight
antenna
machine gun
commander's seat
periscopic sight
ammunition stowage
smoke bomb discharger
hatch
driver's seat
sprocket wheel
fuel tank
track shoe
armored plate
armor
headlight
track link
engine
cannon
wheel
turret
fume extractor

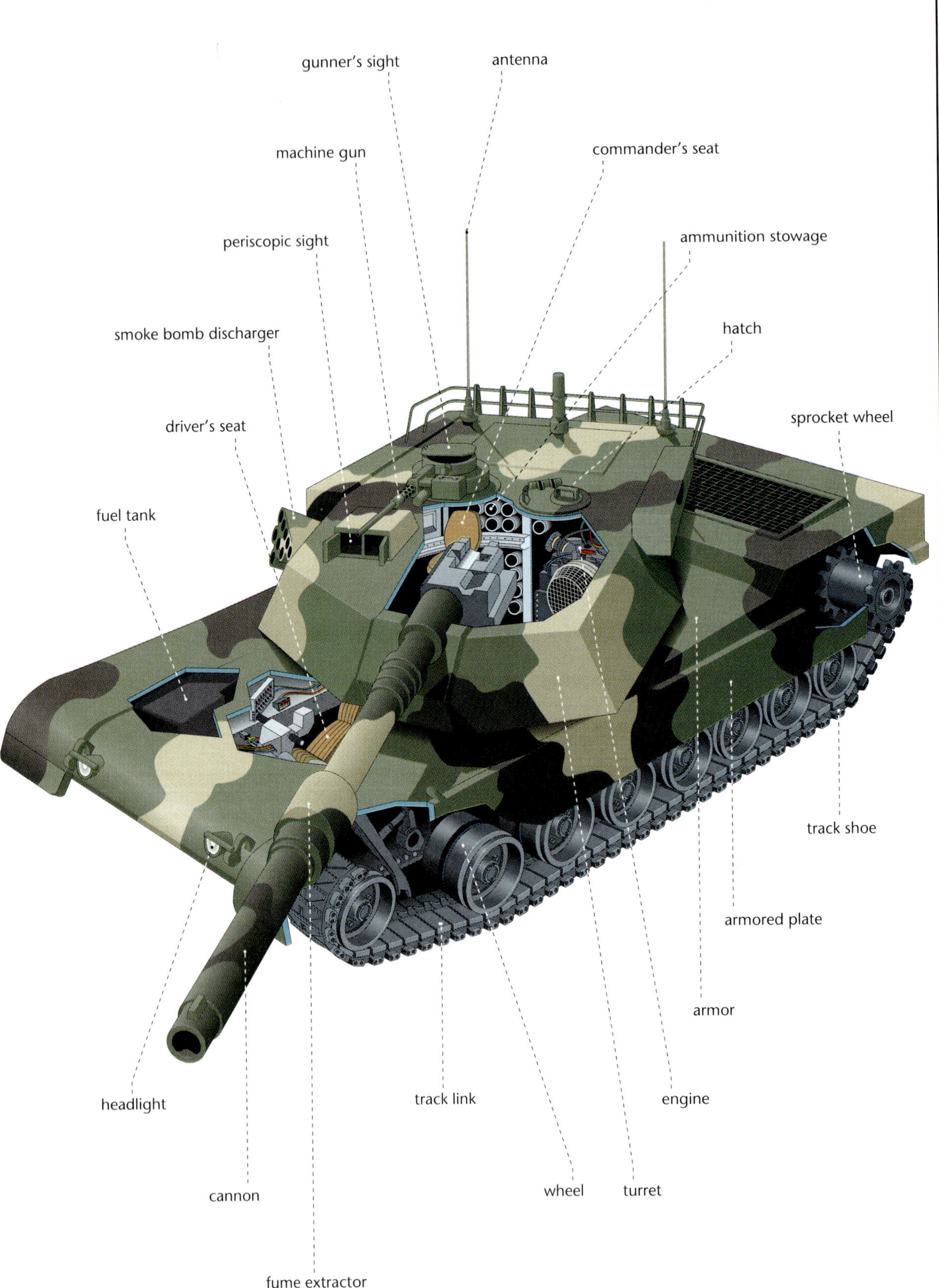

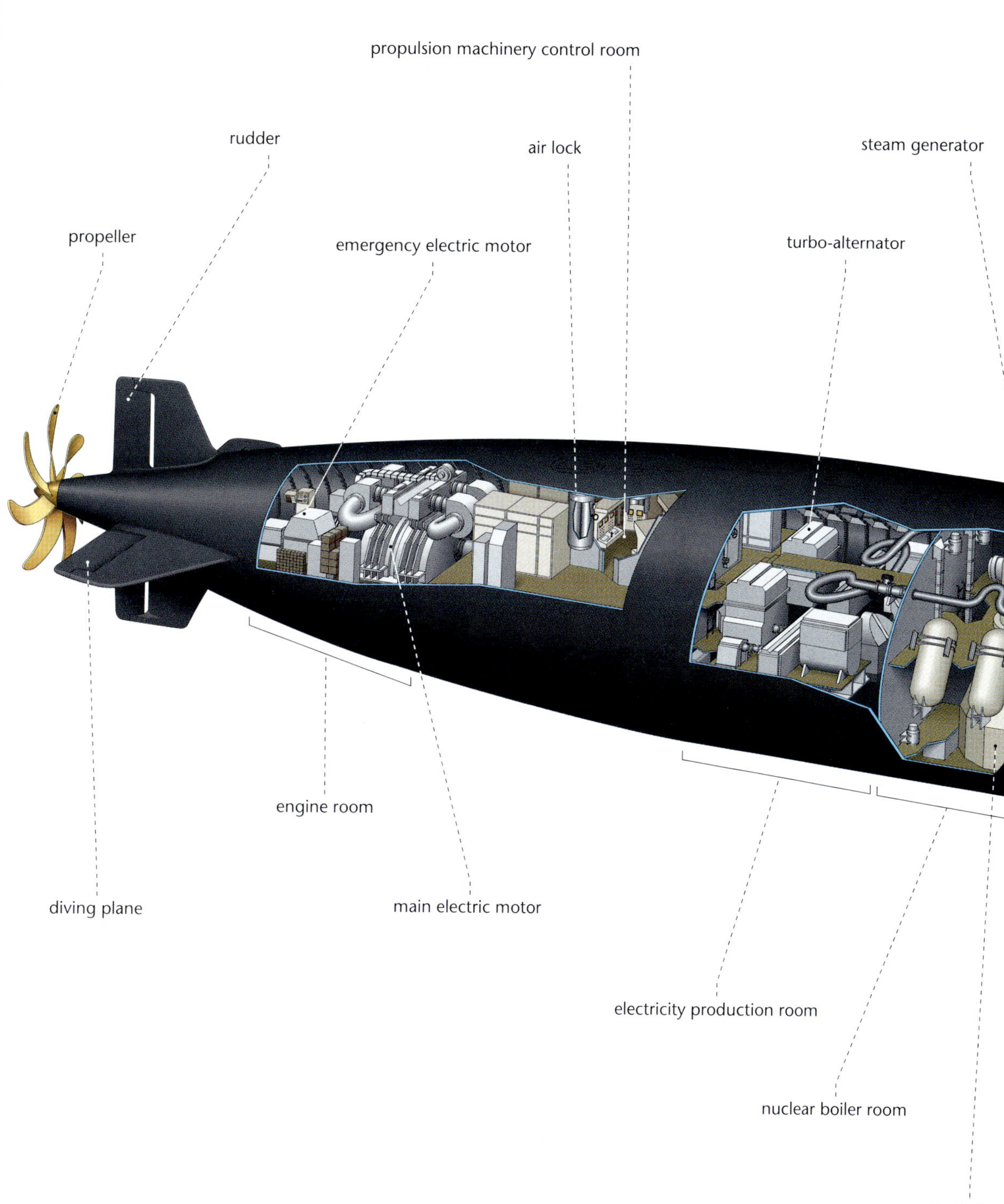
propulsion machinery control room
rudder
air lock
steam generator
propeller
emergency electric motor
turbo-alternator
engine room
main electric motor
diving plane
electricity production room
nuclear boiler room
reactor

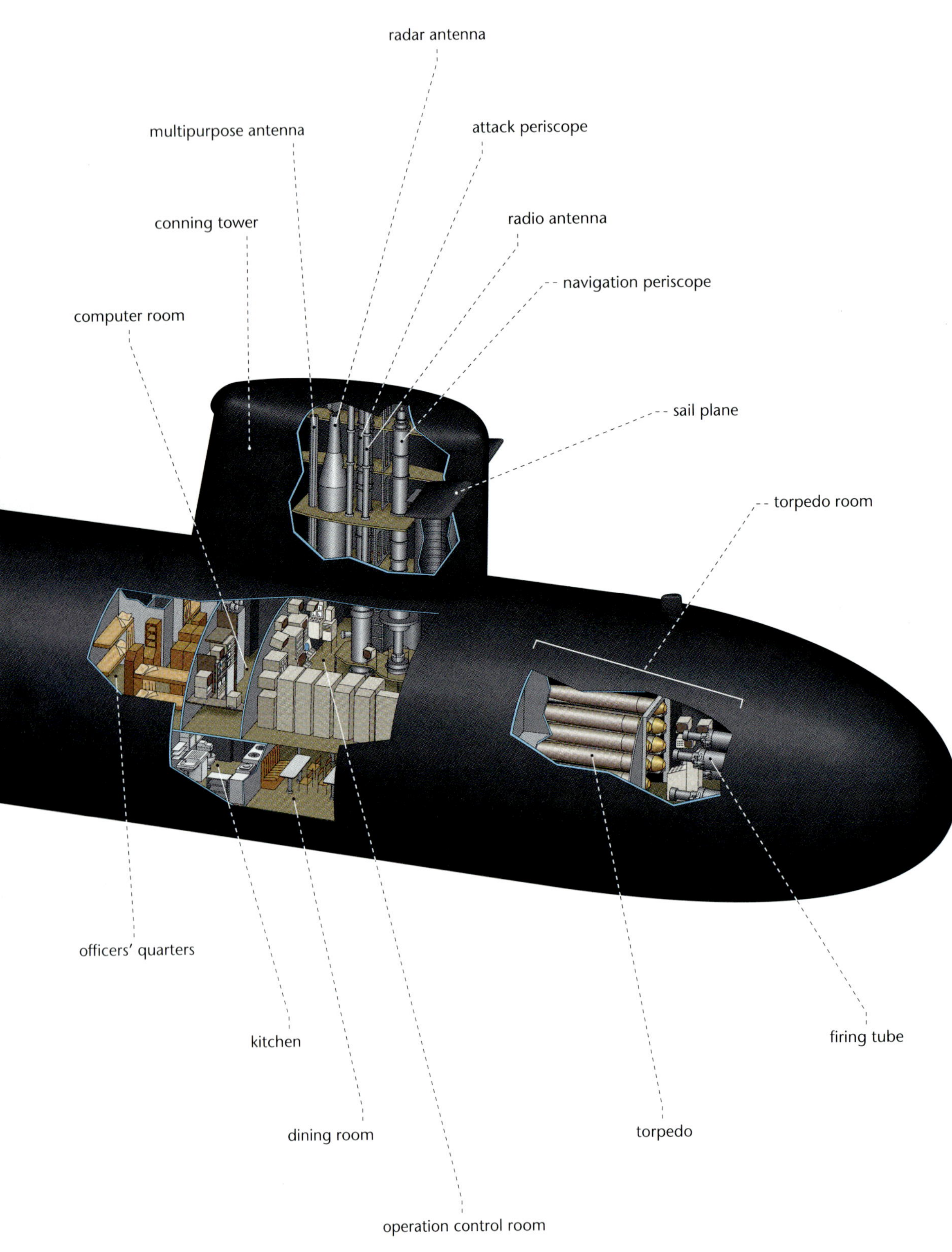

radar antenna
multipurpose antenna
attack periscope
conning tower
radio antenna
navigation periscope
computer room
sail plane
torpedo room
officers' quarters
kitchen
dining room
operation control room
torpedo
firing tube

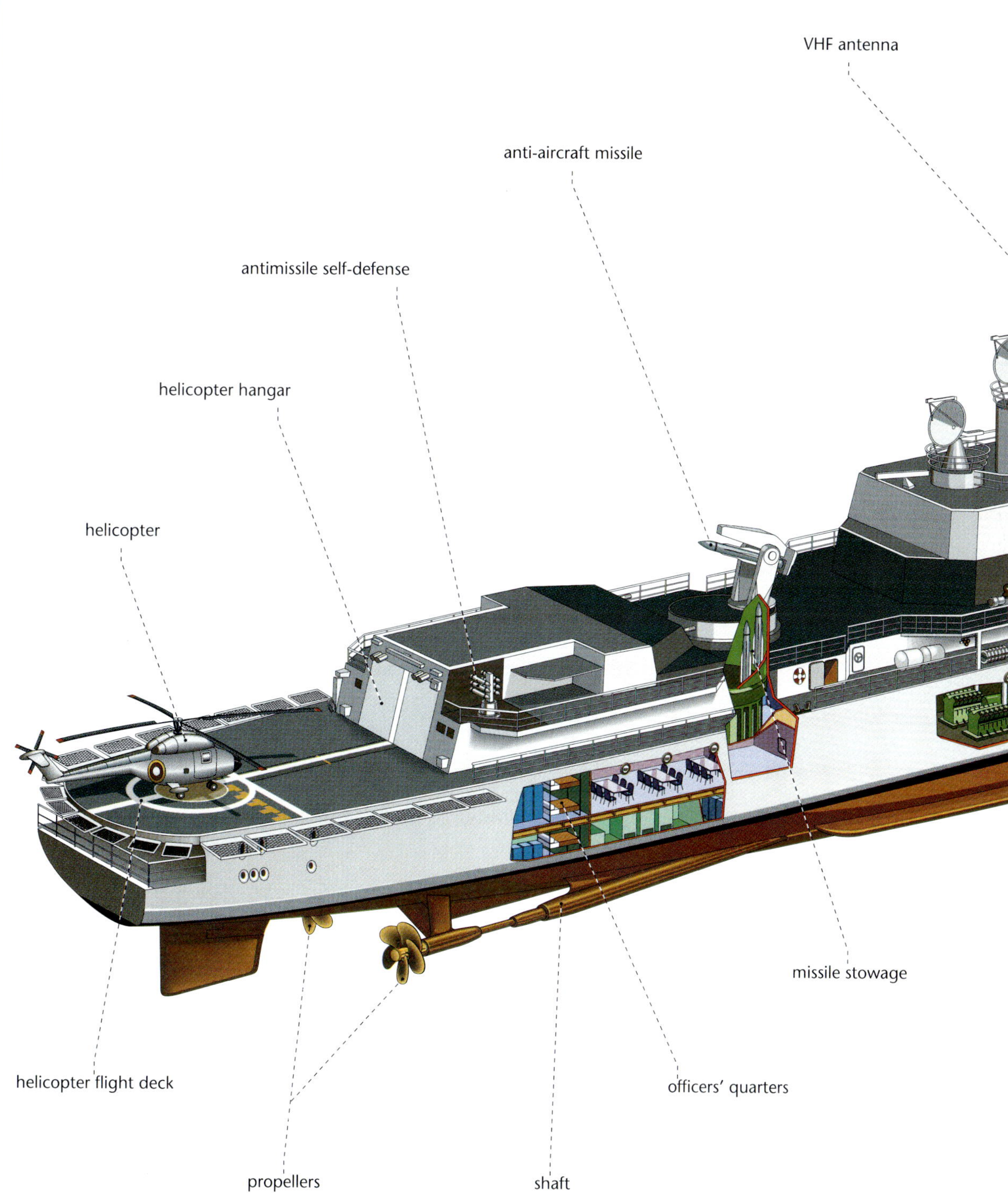

VHF antenna
anti-aircraft missile
antimissile self-defense
helicopter hangar
helicopter
helicopter flight deck
propellers
shaft
officers' quarters
missile stowage

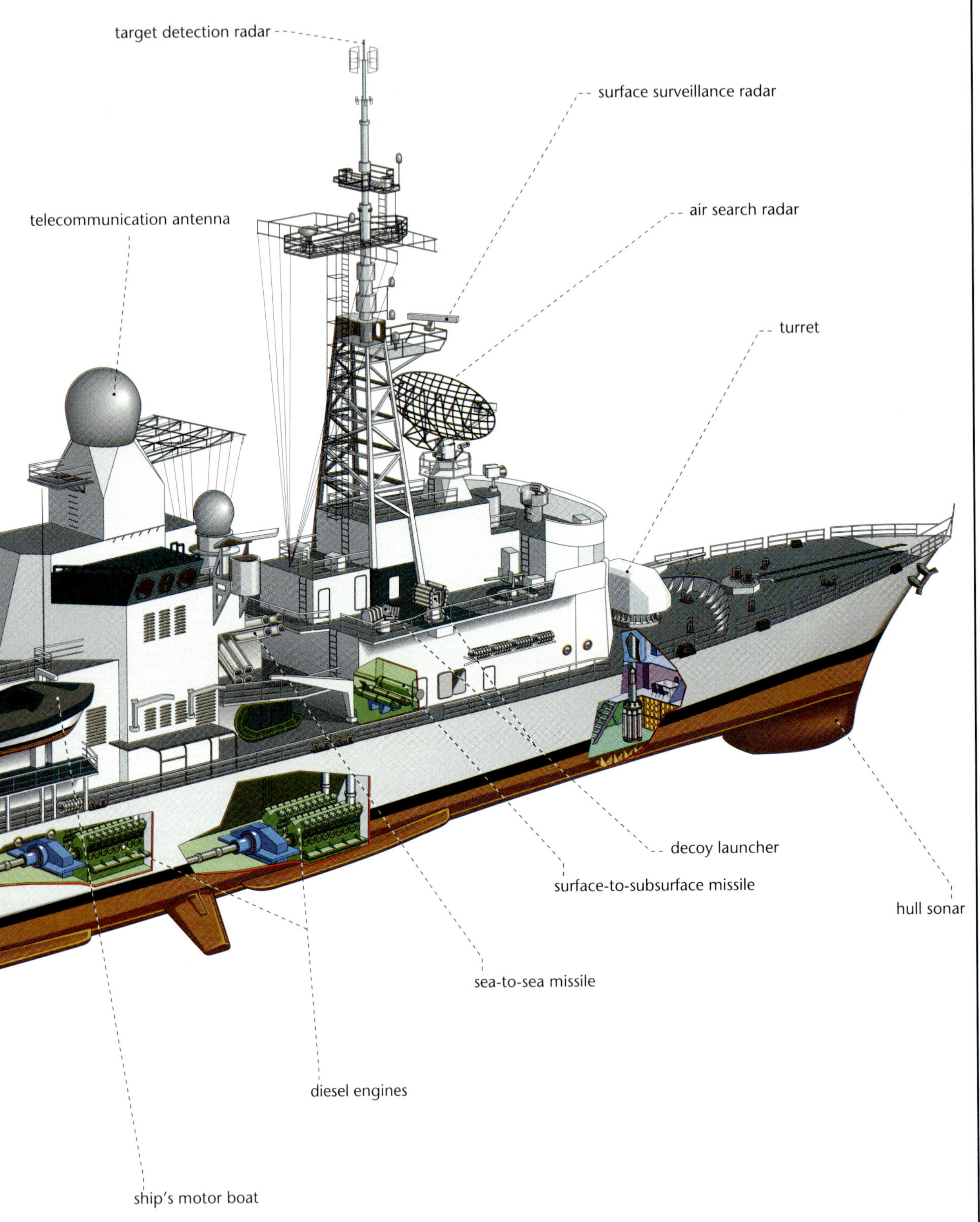

target detection radar
surface surveillance radar
telecommunication antenna
air search radar
turret
decoy launcher
surface-to-subsurface missile
hull sonar
sea-to-sea missile
diesel engines
ship's motor boat

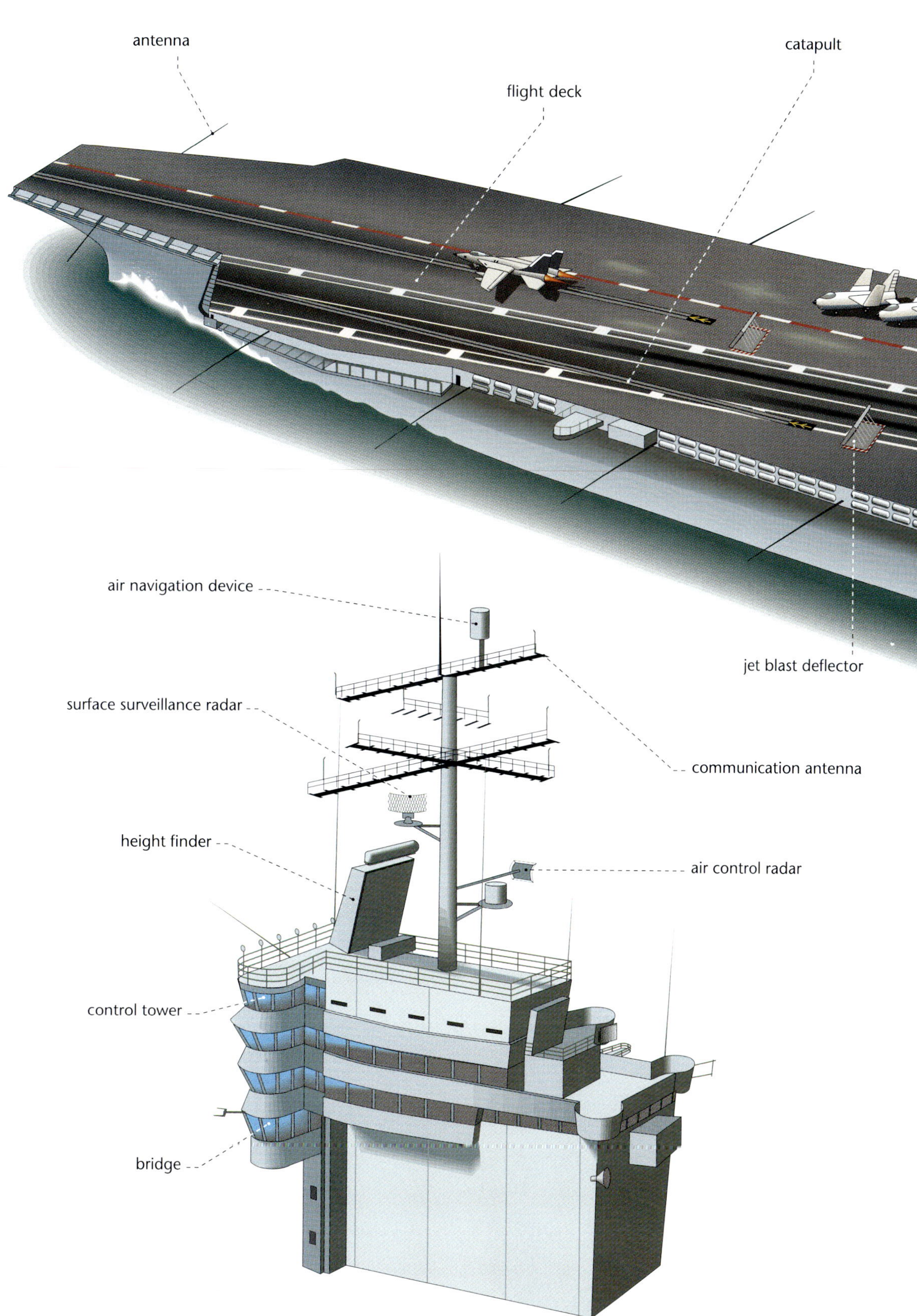

antenna
flight deck
catapult
air navigation device
jet blast deflector
surface surveillance radar
communication antenna
height finder
air control radar
control tower
bridge

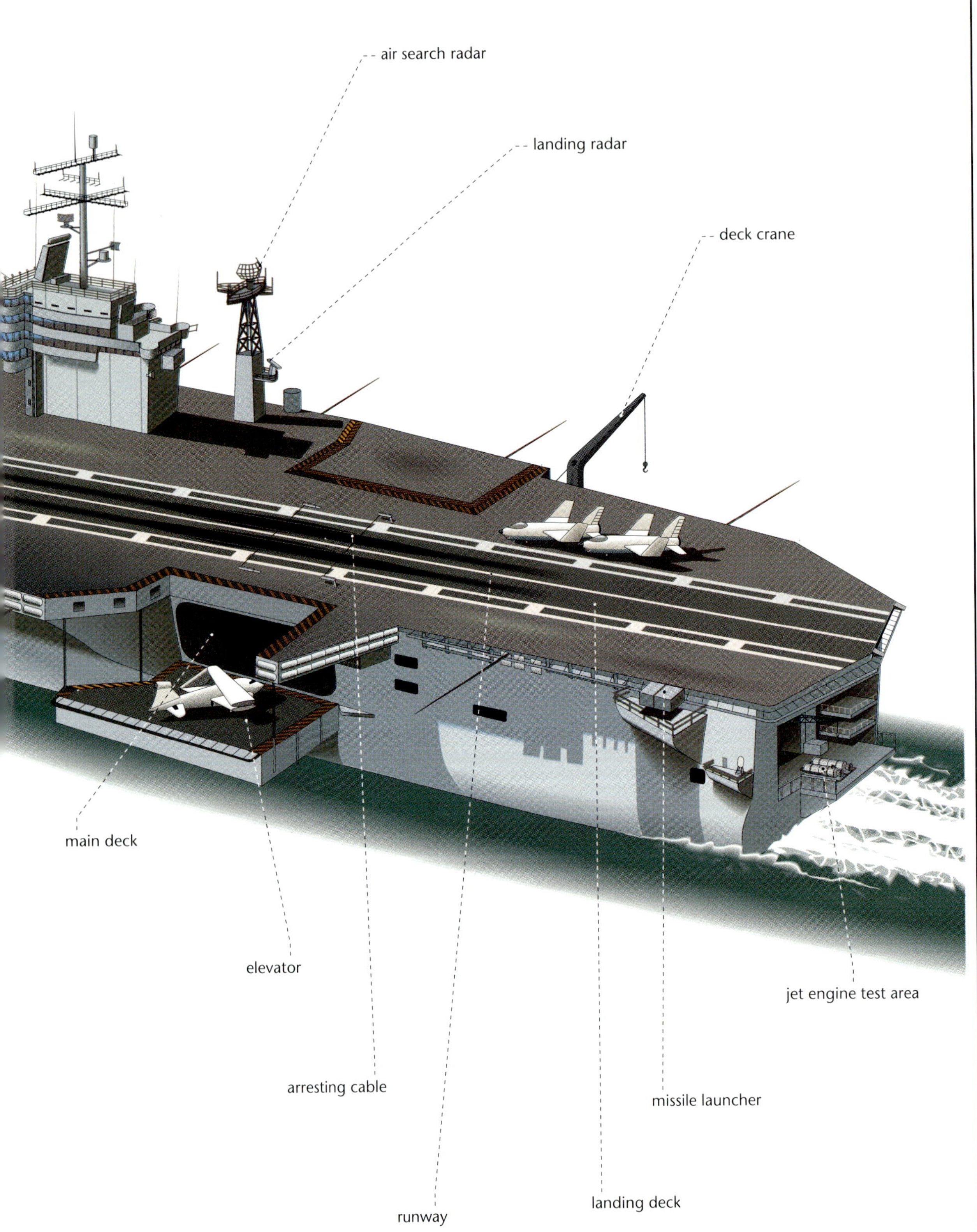

air search radar
landing radar
deck crane
main deck
elevator
arresting cable
runway
landing deck
missile launcher
jet engine test area

COMBAT AIRCRAFT

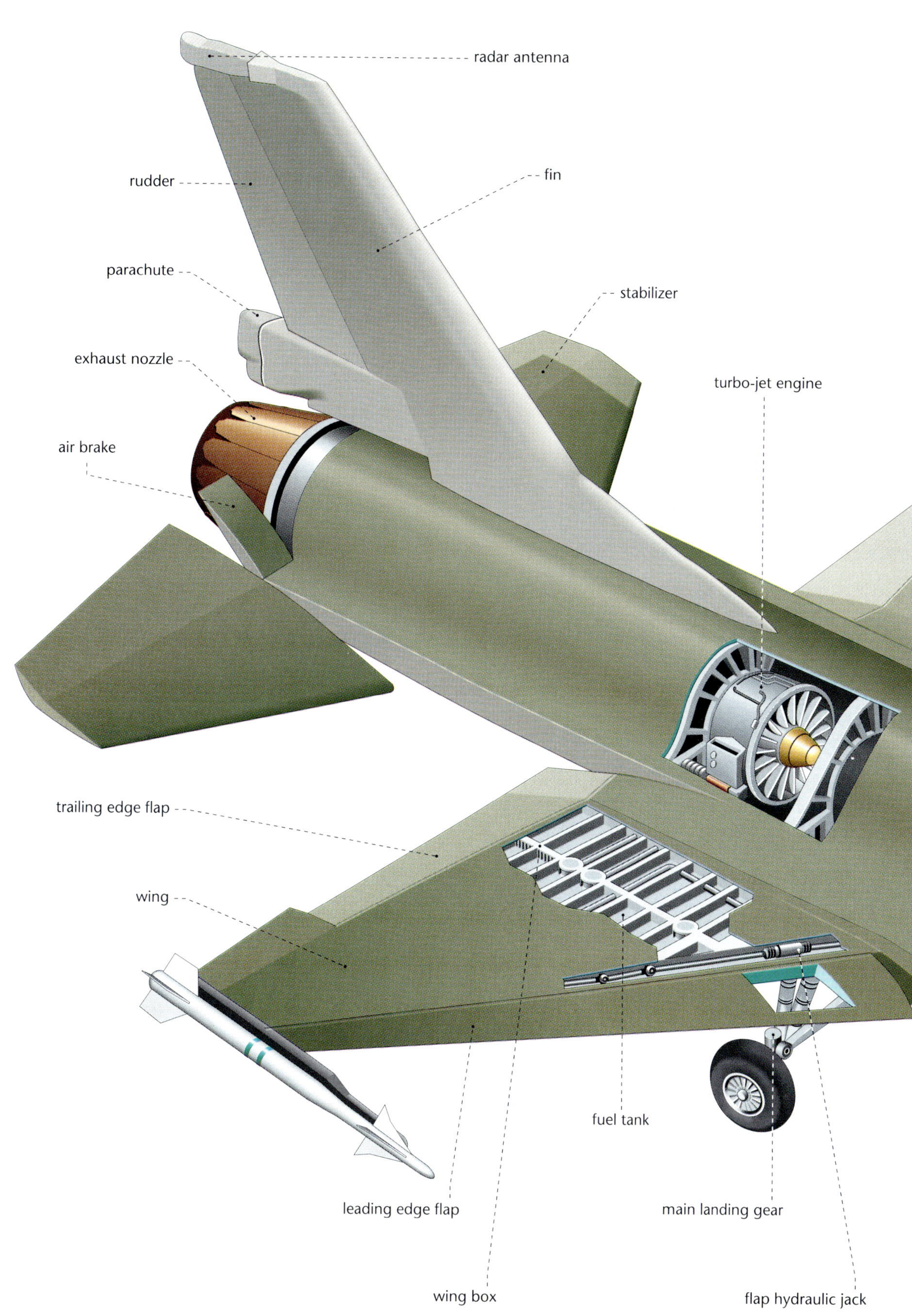

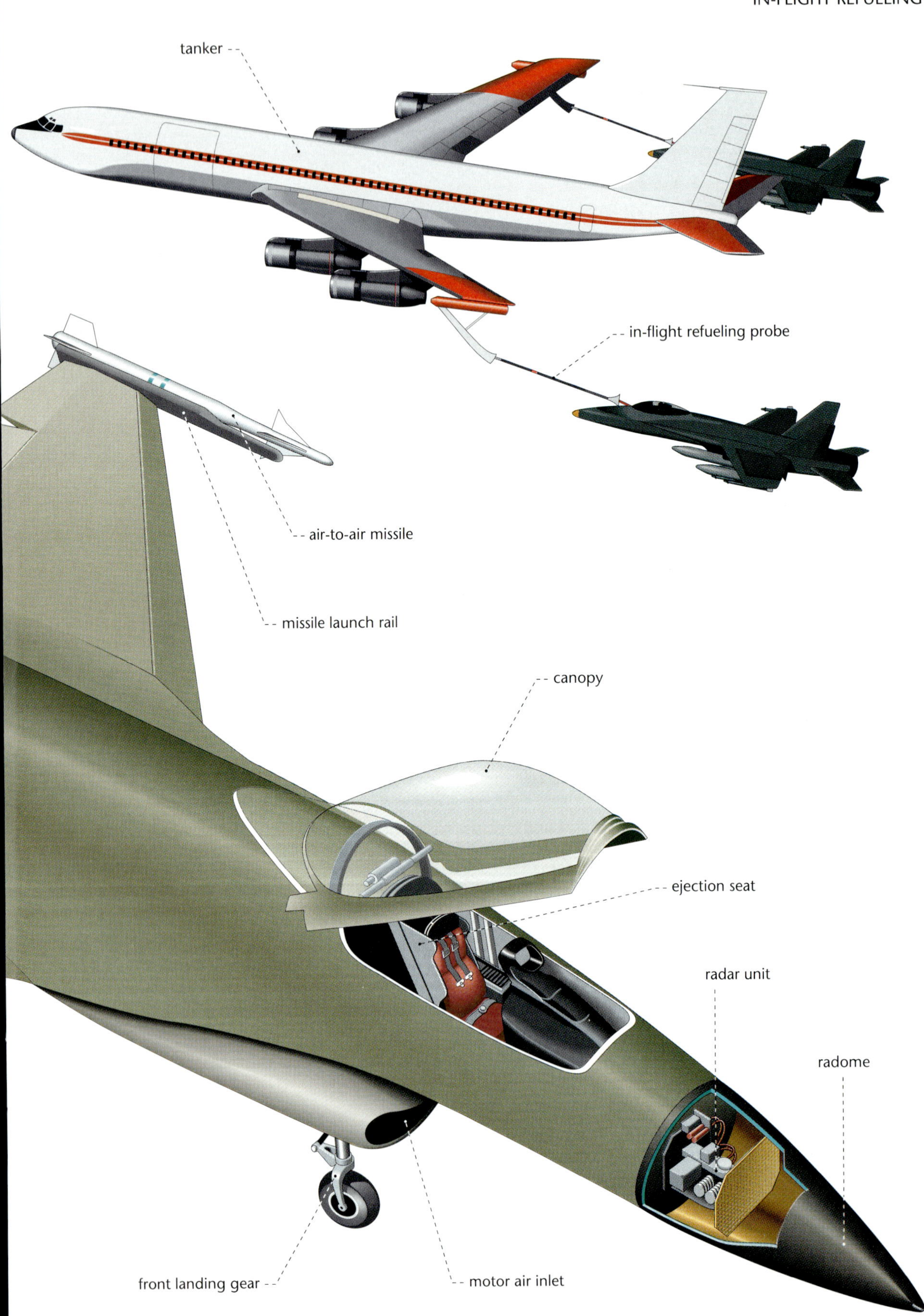
tanker
in-flight refueling probe
air-to-air missile
missile launch rail
canopy
ejection seat
radar unit
radome
front landing gear
motor air inlet

STRUCTURE OF A MISSILE

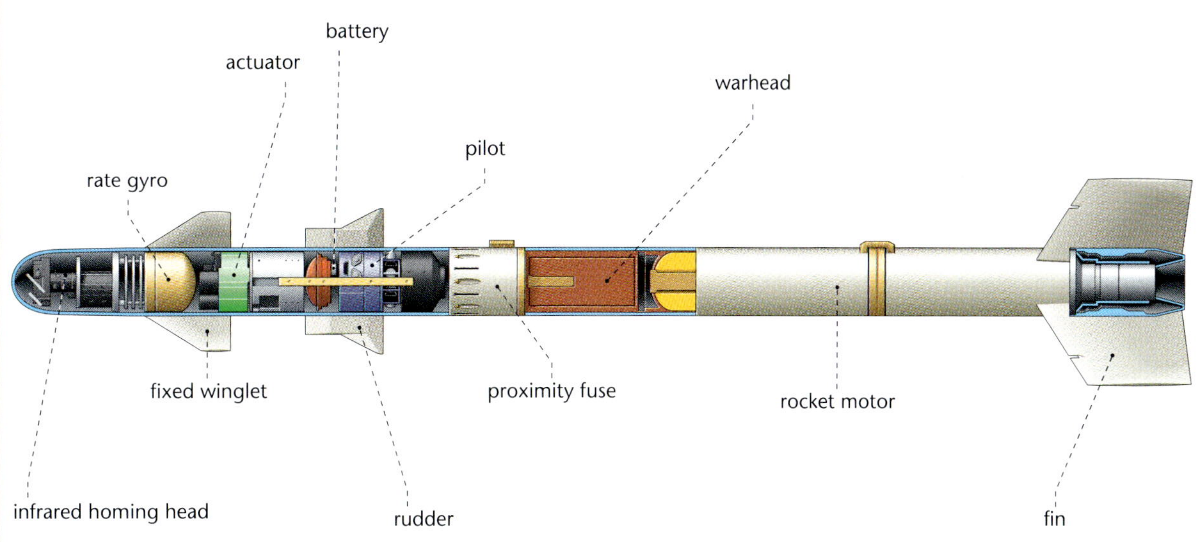

MAJOR TYPES OF MISSILES

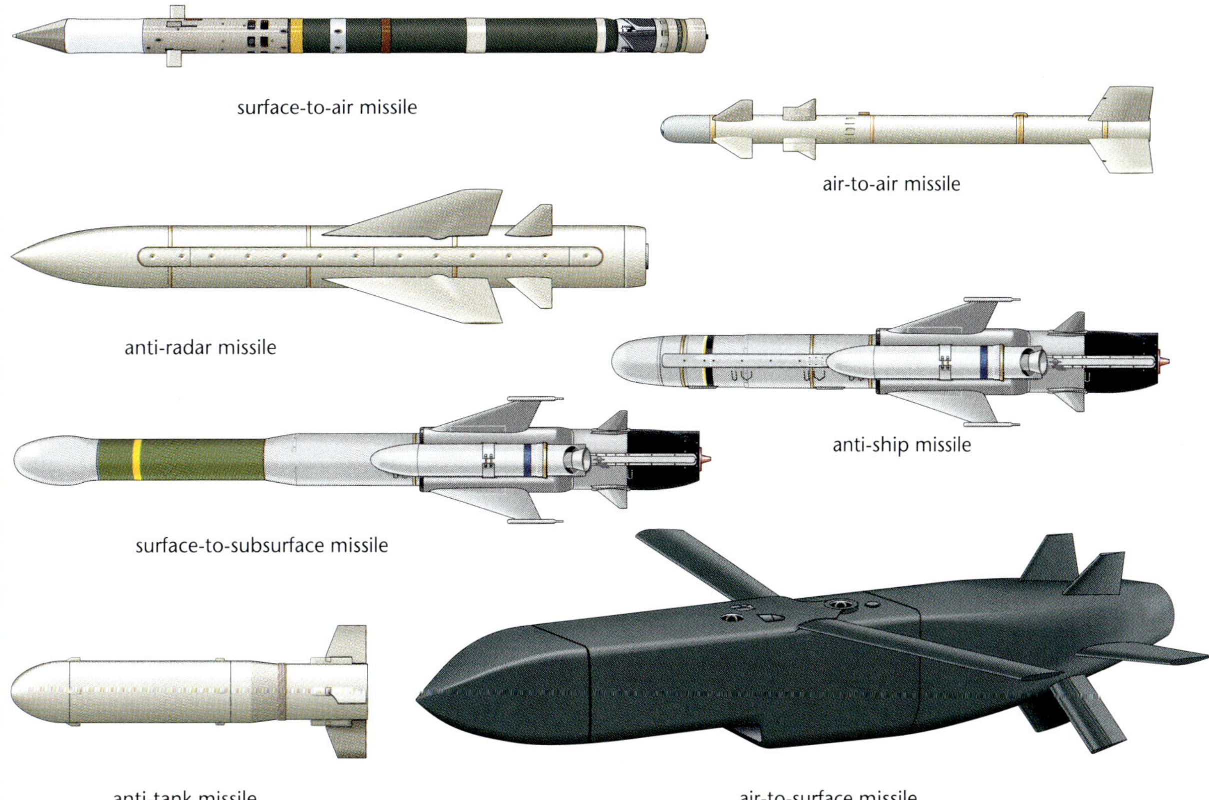

PARTS OF A FLAG

FLAG SHAPES

finial

emblem

hoist

fly

halyard

toggle

staff

base

streamer

square flag

rectangular flag

pennant

double pennant

swallowtail

swallowtail and tongue

burgee

wind sock

flag with Schwenkel

gonfalon

oriflamme

bunting

fanion

SHIELD DIVISIONS

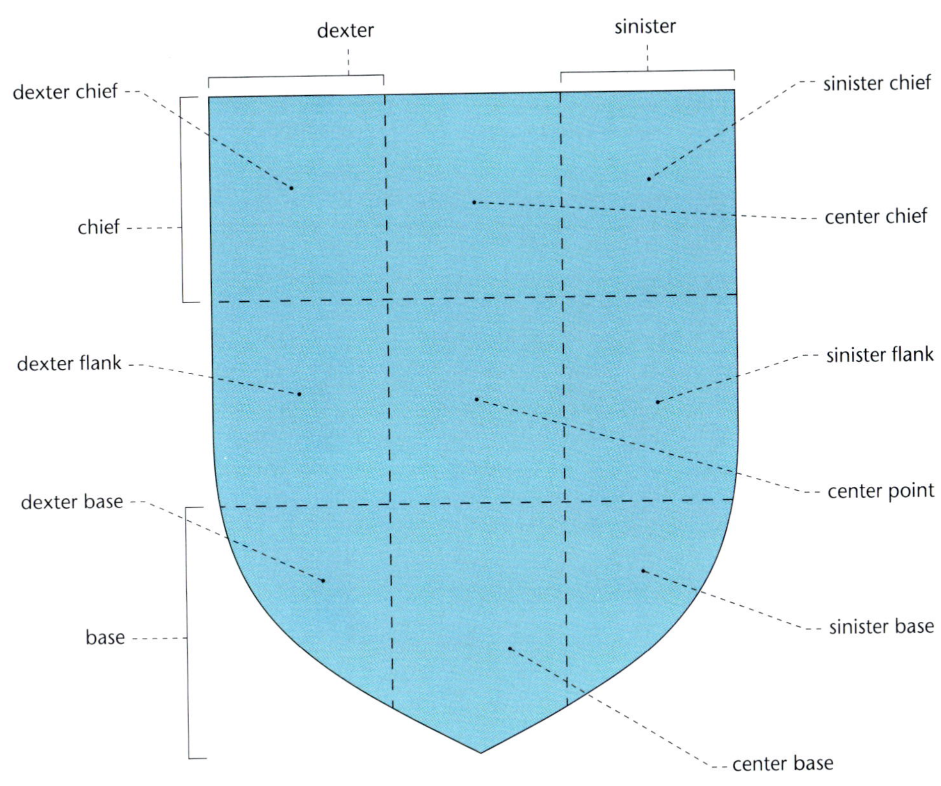

EXAMPLES OF PARTITIONS

per fess

party

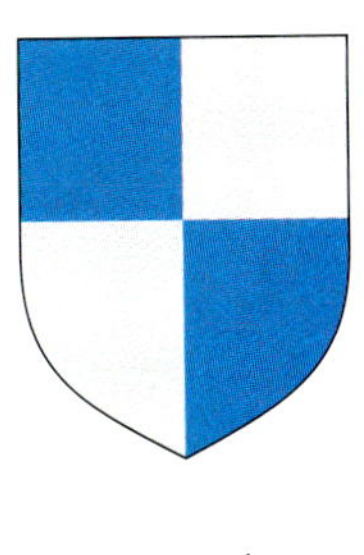

per bend

quarterly

EXAMPLES OF ORDINARIES

chief

chevron

pale

cross

fleur-de-lis

crescent

lion passant

eagle

mulet

EXAMPLES OF METALS

argent

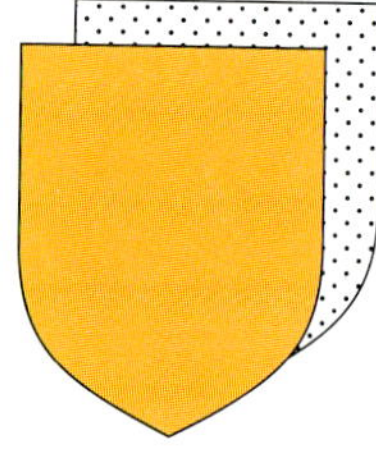

or

EXAMPLES OF FURS

ermine

vair

EXAMPLES OF COLORS

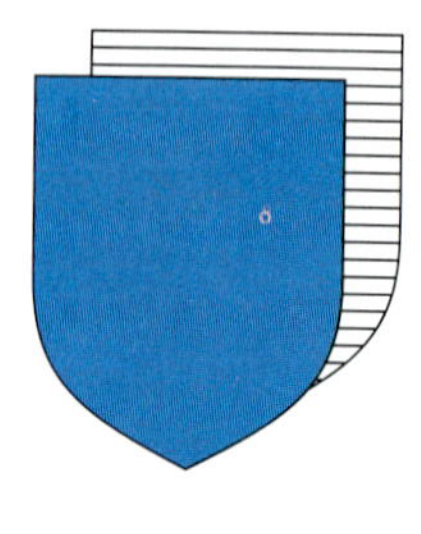

azure

gules

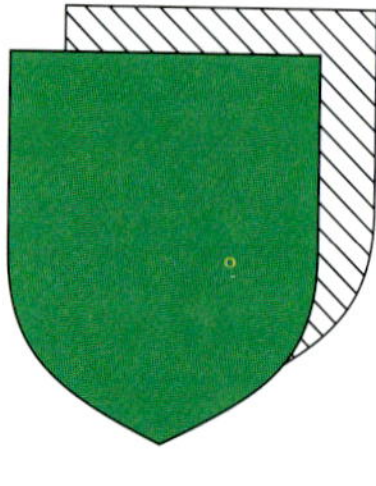

vert

purpure

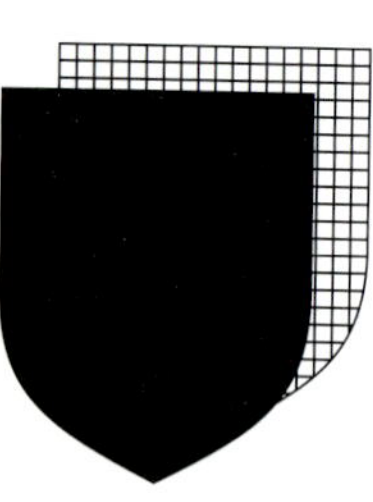

sable

FIRE SIGNS

Aries the Ram (March 21)

Leo the Lion (July 23)

Sagittarius the Archer (November 22)

EARTH SIGNS

Taurus the Bull (April 20)

Virgo the Virgin (August 23)

Capricorn the Goat (December 22)

AIR SIGNS

Libra the Balance (September 23)

Aquarius the Water Bearer (January 20)

Gemini the Twins (May 21)

WATER SIGNS

Cancer the Crab (June 22)

Scorpio the Scorpion (October 24)

Pisces the Fishes (February 19)

SAFETY SYMBOLS

corrosive

electrical hazard

explosive

flammable

radioactive

poison

PROTECTION

eye protection

ear protection

head protection

hand protection

feet protection

respiratory system protection

coffee shop

telephone

restaurant

men's rest room

women's rest room

access for physically handicapped

pharmacy

no access for wheelchairs

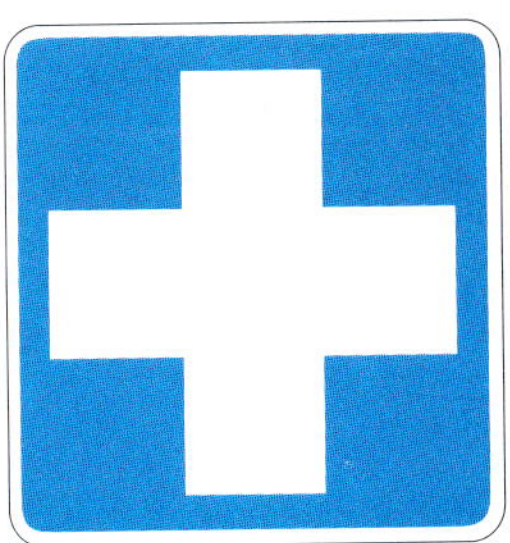

first aid

hospital

police

taxi transportation

camping (tent)

camping prohibited

camping (trailer)

camping (trailer and tent)

picnics prohibited

picnic area

service station

information

information

currency exchange

lost and found articles

fire extinguisher

MAJOR NORTH AMERICAN ROAD SIGNS

stop at intersection

no entry

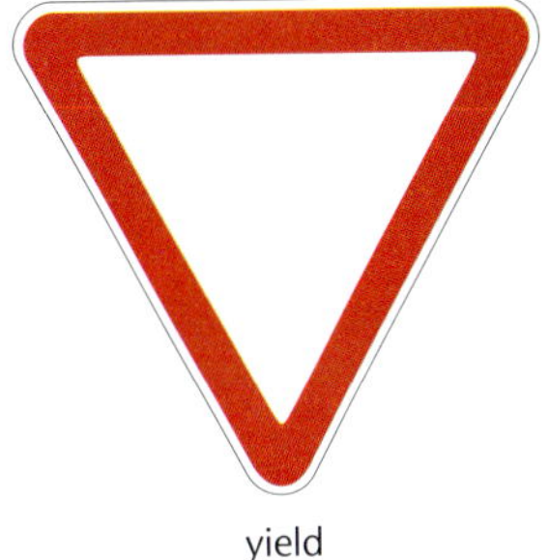

yield

one-way traffic

direction to be followed

direction to be followed

direction to be followed

direction to be followed

no U-turn

passing prohibited

two-way traffic

merging traffic

stop at intersection

no entry

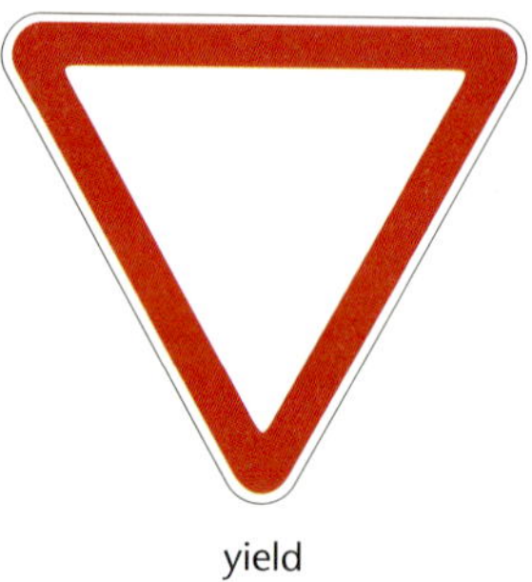

yield

one-way traffic

direction to be followed

direction to be followed

direction to be followed

direction to be followed

no U-turn

passing prohibited

two-way traffic

priority intersection

MAJOR NORTH AMERICAN ROAD SIGNS

right bend

double bend

roadway narrows

slippery road

bumps

steep hill

falling rocks

overhead clearance

signal ahead

school zone

pedestrian crossing

road work ahead

right bend

double bend

roadway narrows

slippery road

bumps

steep hill

falling rocks

overhead clearance

signal ahead

school zone

pedestrian crossing

road work ahead

MAJOR NORTH AMERICAN ROAD SIGNS

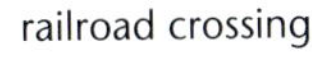

railroad crossing

deer crossing

closed to pedestrians

closed to bicycles

closed to motorcycles

closed to trucks

MAJOR INTERNATIONAL ROAD SIGNS

railroad crossing

deer crossing

closed to pedestrians

closed to bicycles

closed to motorcycles

closed to trucks

FABRIC CARE

WASHING

do not wash

hand wash in lukewarm water

machine wash in lukewarm water at a gentle setting/reduced agitation

machine wash in warm water at a gentle setting/reduced agitation

machine wash in warm water at a normal setting

machine wash in hot water at a normal setting

do not use chlorine bleach

use chlorine bleach as directed

DRYING

hang to dry

dry flat

tumble dry at medium to high temperature

tumble dry at low temperature

drip dry

IRONING

do not iron

iron at low setting

iron at medium setting

iron at high setting

COMMON SCIENTIFIC SYMBOLS

MATHEMATICS

subtraction

addition

multiplication

division

is equal to

is not equal to

is approximately equal to

is equivalent to

is identical with

is not identical with

plus or minus

empty set

is greater than

is equal to or greater than

is less than

is equal to or less than

union

intersection

is contained in

percent

belongs to

does not belong to

square root of

sum

infinity

integral

factorial

GEOMETRY

degree

minute

second

pi

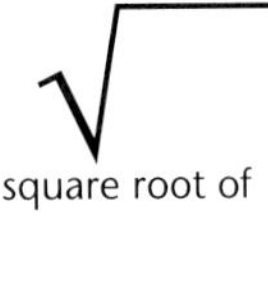
perpendicular

acute angle

right angle

obtuse angle

is parallel to

is not parallel to

male

female

birth

blood factor positive

Rh-

blood factor negative

death

negative charge

positive charge

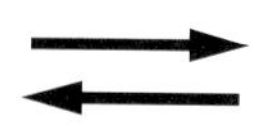
reversible reaction

reaction direction

recycled

recyclable

ampersand

registered trademark

copyright

prescription

pause/still

stop

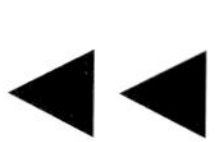
rewind

play

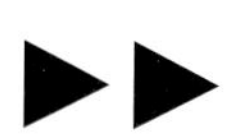
fast forward

DIACRITIC SYMBOLS

acute accent

umlaut

grave accent

circumflex accent

cedilla

tilde

PUNCTUATION MARKS

;
semicolon

.
period

,
comma

. . .
ellipses

:
colon

*
asterisk

« »
quotation marks
(French)

' '
single quotation marks

" "
quotation marks

—
dash

( )
parentheses

/
virgule

!
exclamation point

?
question mark

[ ]
square brackets

EXAMPLES OF CURRENCY ABBREVIATIONS

$
dollar

¢
cent

£
pound

¥
yen

F
franc

DM
deutsche mark

Dr
drachma

L
lira

Kr
krone

IS
shekel

ECU
European Community
Currency

Esc
escudo

Pta
peseta

Fl
florin

INDEX

The terms in **bold type** indicate the title of an illustration.

INDEX

The terms in **bold type** indicate the title of an illustration.

bevel, 726
bevel square, 713
bezel, 364
bezel facet (8), 363
bias, 566
bias-ply tire, 433
bib, 349
bib, 350, 351, 667
bib necklace, 361
biceps of arm, 120
biceps of thigh, 121
biconcave lens, 722
biconvex lens, 722
bicorne, 318
bicycle, 446, 448
bicycle bag, 448
bicycle, accessories, 448
bidet, 292
bifocal lens, 376
bikini, 347
bikini briefs, 325
bill, 108, 483
bill compartment, 379
bill-file, 516
billfold, 379
billhook, 269
billiard spot, 675
billiards, 673
billiards cue, 675
bills, principal types, 111
bimetallic helix, 705
bimetallic thermometer, 705
binder, 159
binding, 328, 633, 642
binocular microscope, 718
biology, 831
biomedical monitoring sensor, 512
biosphere, structure, 31
biparous cyme, 60
bipod, 796, 803
bird, 108, 110
Bird of Paradise, 13
bird of prey, 111
bird of prey, 111
bird, morphology, 108
birth, 831
Bishop, 696
bishop sleeve, 340
bit, 385, 648, 734, 737
bits, types, 650
bitt, 743
bitter taste, 143
bivalve shell, 95
Black, 696, 700, 701
black ball, 673
black currant, 62
black rye bread, 153
black salsify, 71
Black Sea, 21
black square, 696
black stone, 697
blade, 783
blade, 57, 214, 239, 242, 251, 256,
    268, 271, 276, 277, 284, 285, 291,
    304, 309, 369, 374, 562, 564, 607,
    609, 619, 627, 632, 644, 666, 672,
    681, 754, 774, 783, 784
blade close stop, 369
blade guard, 285
blade height adjustment, 285
blade injector, 374
blade lever, 578
blade lift cylinder, 783
blade lift fan, 492
blade lifting mechanism, 784
blade locking bolt, 284
blade rotation mechanism, 784
blade tilting lock, 284
blade tilting mechanism, 284, 285
blade with two beveled edges, 587
blades, major types, 587
blank, 695
blanket, 224
blanket insulation, 287
blanket sleepers, 350
blast valve, 635
blastodisc, 109
blazer, 338
bleeder valve, 208
blender, 250
blending attachment, 250
blinker, 653
block, 542, 656, 787
block bracket, 230
block cutter, 581, 587
blockboard, 288
blood circulation, 124, 126
blood circulation, schema, 124
blood factor negative, 831
blood factor positive, 831

blood vessel, 136
blood vessels, 112
blouses, types, 337
blow pipe, 536
blower, 207, 213, 543, 760
blower motor, 207, 214
blucher oxford, 355
blue ball, 673
blue beam, 410
blue cap, 626
blue flag, 626
blue line, 608
blue mussel, 93
blueberry, 62
blueprint reading, 193, 195
blusher brush, 366
board, 288
board, 288, 631
board cutter, 578
board insulation, 287
boarding room, 505
boarding step, 508
boarding walkway, 503
boards, 608
boater, 328
bobber, 672
bobbin, 570
bobbin, 561, 562, 570, 573
bobbin case, 562
bobbin lace, 570
bobbin winder, 575
bobbin winder, 561
bobby pin, 369
bobeche, 236
bobsled, 643
bobstay, 479
bodies, types, 425
body, 426
body, 143, 252, 281, 294, 295, 445,
    449, 453, 542, 546, 549, 645, 658,
    670, 707, 719
body flap, 511
body guard molding, 449
body of fornix, 134
body of nail, 137
body pad, 609
body shirt, 337
body side molding, 427
body suit, 345
body temperature control unit, 512
body tube, 718
body whorl, 94
body wire, 666
boiler, 209
boiler, 208, 771
boiling-water reactor, 763
bole, 59
bolero, 338
boletus, 55
bolster, 224, 239, 242
bolt, 279
bolt, 278, 282, 290, 793
bolt assist mechanism, 796
bonding jumper, 312
bone folder, 577
boning knife, 242
bonnet, 294, 295
book ends, 517
bookbinding leather, 579
booking hall, 462
boom, 628, 782, 785
boom cylinder, 782, 785
boom truck, 506
boom vang, 628
booster intermediate station, 740
booster parachute, 510
boot, 356
boot, 542, 627, 635, 644, 645, 648
boot jack, 358
bootee, 354
Bootes, 11
borage, 74
bordeaux glass, 237
border, 188, 189
bore, 801
bottle cart, 306
bottle opener, 244, 688
bottom, 633, 640
bottom bracket axle, 448
bottom cylinder, 581
bottom deck, 741
bottom deckboard, 787
bottom line, 621
bottom of the pool, 626
bottom pocket, 675
bottom rail, 202, 225, 231
bottom ring, 753
bottom road, 736
bottom side rail, 470
bottom-end transverse member, 470

bottom-fold portfolio, 378
bottomboard, 543
boulevard, 52, 184
bound book, 577
bow, 544, 793
bow, 328, 497, 628, 631, 793
bow collar, 342
bow door, 493
bow loading door, 494
bow saw, 690
bow thruster, 497
bow tie, 324
bow window, 197
bowl, 682
bowl, 241, 251, 385, 484, 784
bowl with serving spout, 251
bowler, 599
bowline, 691
bowline on a bight, 691
bowling, 683
bowling ball, 683
bowling crease, 599
bowling lane, 683
bowls and petanque, 682
bows, 793
bowsprit, 479
bowstring, 684, 793
box, 156, 189, 204, 209
box bag, 381
box car, 470, 472
box end wrench, 279
box pallet, 787
box pleat, 228
box spring, 224
boxer, 669
boxer shorts, 325
boxer shorts, 353
boxing, 669
boxing gloves, 669
bra, 346
brace, 281
brace, 198, 302, 757
bracelets, 364
brachial, 120
brachial artery, 126
brachial plexus, 133
brachioradialis, 120, 121
bracket, 231
bracket base, 225
bract, 66
braided rope, 692
brail, 480
brain, 88
brake, 664, 727
brake cable, 447
brake caliper, 442
brake handle, 445
brake lever, 447
brake line, 432
brake lining, 432
brake loop, 636
brake pad, 432
brake pedal, 430
brake shoe, 432
brakelight, 429
brakeman, 643
branch, 58
branch, 59, 61, 72, 104, 215, 649, 726
branch clip, 726
branch duct, 206
branch return pipe, 208
branch supply pipe, 208
branches, 59
branching, plumbing, 298
brandy snifter, 237
brass family, 550
brassiere cup, 346
brattice, 181
brayer, 581
Brazil nut, 66
bread, 153
bread and butter plate, 238
bread guide, 252
bread knife, 242
break line, 341
breaker, 30
breast, 129
breast, 108, 116, 118
breast beam, 572
breast collar, 653
breast dart, 320
breast pocket, 320, 324
breast welt pocket, 322
breastplate, 792
breaststroke, 622
breaststroke kick, 622
breaststroke turn, 622
breather valve, 741
breathing in, 622
breathing out, 622

breech, 549
breech guard, 549
breechblock, 798, 799, 802
breechblock operating lever assembly,
    802
breeches, 315
breeches, 317, 667, 791
brick, 286
brick wall, 199
bricklayer's hammer, 291
bridge, 674
bridge, 52, 230, 376, 491, 544, 546,
    719, 810
bridge assembly, 547
bridging, 198
bridle, 649
bridle, 653
bridle assembly, 486
bridle tape, 541
briefcase, 378
briefs, 325, 346
brig, 482
brigantine, 482
brightness control, 529
brilliant cut facets, 363
brilliant full cut, 362
brim, 328, 329
briolette cut, 363
bristle, 373, 374
bristles, 304
broad beans, 72
broad ligament of uterus, 129
broad reach, 629
broad welt side pocket, 339
broad welt side pocket, 319, 330
broad-leaved endive, 73
**broadcast satellite
    communication**, 416
broadest of back, 121
broadsword, 794
broccoli, 69
brooch, 364
brood chamber, 82
brook, 676
broom, 205
brow brush and lash comb, 367
brow reinforce, 792
brow tine, 105
browband, 649
brown ball, 673
Brunn's membrane, 142
brush, 304, 582, 589
brush, 152, 373
brush and rails, 647
brush and rails, 646
Brussels sprouts, 73
bubble, 443
bucket, 754, 782
bucket cylinder, 782, 785
bucket hinge pin, 782
bucket lever, 782
bucket ring, 754
bucket seat, 428
bucket tooth, 782
bucket wheel excavator, 733
buckle, 566
buckle, 323, 380, 428, 641
buckwheat, 152
bud, 70
buffer tank, 740
buffet, 227
bugle, 550
building materials, 286, 288
building server, 216
building sewer, 215
built-in microphone, 409
bulb, 72, 104, 232, 233, 310, 743
bulb dibble, 268
bulb unit, 752
bulb vegetables, 70
bulbil, 70
bulbocavernous muscle, 127
bulk terminal, 490
bulkhead, 441
bulkhead flat car, 473
Bull, 11
bull's-eye, 698
bulldozer, 783
bulldozer, 733
bullet, 798
bullion stitch, 571
bulls-eye, 684
bulwark, 478
bumper, 260, 426, 440, 441, 464
bumper guard, 617
bumps, 826, 827
bunch, 384
bunch of grapes, 61
bund wall, 741
bundle, 72, 756

The terms in **bold type** indicate the title of an illustration.

The terms in **bold type** indicate the title of an illustration.

The terms in **bold type** indicate the title of an illustration.

The terms in **bold type** indicate the title of an illustration.

The terms in **bold type** indicate the title of an illustration.

The terms in **bold type** indicate the title of an illustration.

INDEX

The terms in **bold type** indicate the title of an illustration.

INDEX

The terms in **bold type** indicate the title of an illustration.

The terms in **bold type** indicate the title of an illustration.

The terms in **bold type** indicate the title of an illustration.

INDEX

851

The terms in **bold type** indicate the title of an illustration.

The terms in **bold type** indicate the title of an illustration.

The terms in **bold type** indicate the title of an illustration.

The terms in **bold type** indicate the title of an illustration.

The terms in **bold type** indicate the title of an illustration.

The terms in **bold type** indicate the title of an illustration.

slope, 451
sloped turret, 183
sloping cornice, 168
slot, 188, 240, 252, 276, 379, 578
slot machine, 702
slotback, 605
slow-burning stove, 204
slow-motion, 411
slower traffic, 452
sludge, 216
small decanter, 237
small hand cultivator, 268
small intestine, 131
smaller round, 121
smell, 141
smock, 337
smoke, 39
smoke baffle, 204
smoke bomb discharger, 805
smoking accessories, 384, 386
smoking candle, 582
smoking-apparatus, 582
snaffle bit, 650
snaffle bit, 649
snaffle rein, 649
snaffle strap, 649
snail, 83
snail dish, 246
snail tongs, 246
snap, 566
snap, 672
snap fastener, 321, 327
snap shackle, 630
snap-fastening front, 350
snap-fastening tab, 321
snap-fastening waist, 350
snare, 553
snare drum, 553
snare drum, 552, 557
snare head, 553
snare strainer, 553
snelled fishhook, 672
snooker, 673
snorkel, 627
snout, 84
snow, 34
snow crystals, classification, 36
snow gauge, 41
snow guard, 445
snow pellet, 37
snow shower, 39
snowfall, measure, 41
snowmobile, 445
snowshoe, 645
snowsuit, 351
soap dish, 292
soccer, 600
soccer ball, 600
soccer player, 600
soccer shoe, 600
soccer, playing field, 601
sock, 344
sock, 602, 615
socket, 309, 401, 566
socket bayonet, 794
socket head, 276
socks, 325
sofa, 221
soft palate, 141, 142
soft pastel, 588
soft pedal, 540, 555
soft ray, 87
soft shell clam, 93
soft-drink dispenser, 453
soil, 750
solar array, 42, 48, 418
solar array deployment, 419
solar array drive, 42
solar cell, 768
solar cell, 523, 769
solar cell panel, 769
solar cells, 42
solar collector, 772
solar eclipse, 8
solar energy, 768, 770, 772
solar furnace, 770
solar house, 772
solar panel, 16
solar radiation, 768, 769, 770, 771,
  772
solar ray reflected, 770, 771
solar reflectors, 418
solar shield, 512
solar system, 4
solar-cell system, 769
solder, 307
soldering, 305, 306, 308
soldering gun, 305
soldering iron, 305
soldering torch, 299, 307

sole, 104, 325, 641, 644, 678
soleplate, 256
soleus, 120
solid body, 547
solid rubber tire, 788
solid shot, 801
solid-rocket booster, 510
solitaire ring, 364
solvent extraction unit, 744
sorghum, 152
sound alarm, 485
sound digitizing processor, 528
sound hole, 544
sound receiver, 726
sound reproducing system, 400,
  402, 404
**sound reproducing system,
  components**, 400
sound signal, 539
soundboard, 535, 540, 544, 545, 546
soundbox, 545
soup bowl, 238
soup spoon, 241
soup tureen, 238
sour taste, 143
sources of pollution, 34
South, 488
South America, 20
South cardinal mark, 489
South celestial pole, 3
South Pole, 3
Southeast, 488
Southern Cross, 13
Southern Crown, 13
Southern Fish, 13
Southern hemisphere, 3, 47
Southern Triangle, 13
Southwest, 488
southwester, 329
sow, 151
soybeans, 72
space, 537
space bar, 525, 530
space probe, 19
space shuttle, 510
space shuttle at takeoff, 510
space shuttle in orbit, 510
spacelab, 511
spacer, 727, 765
spacesuit, 512
spade, 266, 632, 695
spade, 803
spading fork, 266
spadix, 60
spaghetti tongs, 246
spandrel, 174
spanker, 480
spar, 498
spar buoy, 489
spark, 436
spark plug, 439
spark plug, 271, 435, 437
spark plug body, 439
spark plug cable, 435
spark plug gap, 439
spark plug gasket, 439
spark plug terminal, 439
sparkling wine glass, 237
spatial dendrite, 36
spatula, 589
spatula, 244, 581
spatulate, 56
speaker, 408, 420, 500
speaker cover, 400
speaker selector, 402
spear, 72, 791
speargun, 627
special mark, 489
specimen chamber, 717
specimen positioning control, 717
spectrometer, 717
speed control, 250, 271
speed controller, 561
speed course, 646
speed selector, 251, 404
speed selector switch, 370
speed skate, 644
speedbrake lever, 500
speedometer, 431, 445, 664
spelling corrector, 524
spencer, 338
spent fuel discharge bay, 758
spent fuel port, 764
spent fuel storage bay, 758, 764, 765
spermatic cord, 127
spermatozoon, 127
sphenoidal sinus, 141
sphere support, 40
sphincter muscle of anus, 131
spicules, 6

spider, 77
spider, 77
spike, 60, 466, 656, 680, 681
spiked shoe, 595
spillway, 746
spillway chute, 746
spillway gate, 746
spinach, 73
spinal cord, 89, 134, 135
spinal ganglion, 135
spinal nerve, 135
spindle, 223, 251, 290, 294, 404, 707,
  711, 712
spine, 577
spine of scapula, 123
spine of the book, 579
spinner, 672
spinning rod, 671
spinous process, 135
spiny lobster, 91
spiny ray, 86
spiracle, 78, 79
spiral, 276, 404
spiral arm, 9
spiral beater, 250
spiral binder, 519
spiral case, 753
spiral galaxy, 9
spiral rib, 94
spiral screwdriver, 276
spiral staircase, 741
spiral-in groove, 404
spire, 94, 175
spirit level, 291
spit, 30
splash plate, 741
splat, 220
splay, 175
spleen, 88, 124
splenius muscle of head, 121
spline, 439
splints, 725
split bet, 700, 701
split end, 603, 605
split link, 672
spoiler, 442, 498
spoke, 447
spoked wheel, 652
sponge, 801
sponge-tipped applicator, 367
sponges, 367
spool, 570, 670, 671
spool pin, 561
spool rack, 575
spoon, 241
spoon, 688
spoon blade, 587
spoons, major types, 241
spores, 55
sports car, 425
sportswear, 352
spot, 235
spot white ball, 673
spotlight, 414, 777, 778, 780
spotmeter, 396
spout, 162, 247, 252, 294, 295
spout assembly, 296
spray, 267
spray arm, 257
spray button, 256
spray control, 256
spray head, 292
spray hose, 292, 296
spray nozzle, 264
spray nozzle, 741
spray paint gun, 304
sprayer, 264
spread collar, 324
spreader, 270
spreader, 375
spreader adjustment valve, 304
spring, 8, 234, 258, 278, 290, 294,
  389, 469, 659, 804
spring balance, 709
spring binder, 519
spring housing, 230
spring linkage, 702
spring wing, 276
spring-metal insulation, 287
springboard, 659
springer, 174
sprinkler hose, 265
sprinklers, 766
sprocket, 445
sprocket wheel, 783, 805
spur, 27, 80, 281, 552, 648
squall, 39
square, 184, 577
square bet, 700, 701
square brackets, 832

square flag, 817
square head plug, 301
square knot, 691
square movement, 696
square neck, 343
square root key, 523
square root of, 830
square sail, 482
square trowel, 291
square-headed tip, 276
squash, 616
squash ball, 616
squash racket, 616
squash, court, 616
stabilizer, 636, 684, 812
stabilizer fin, 496
stabilizing fin, 509
stabilizing shaft, 788
stable, 651
stack, 30, 494
stacking chairs, 223
stadium, 185
staff, 537
staff, 817
stage, 189
stage, 188, 717, 718
stage clip, 718
stage curtain, 188, 189
stained glass, 175
stairs, 201
stairs, 194, 474, 741
stairwell, 194
stake, 263, 685, 686
stake loop, 685, 686
stake pocket, 441
stalactite, 24
stalagmite, 24
stalk, 62, 63, 64, 72
stalk vegetables, 72
stamen, 60, 64
stamp, 384
stamp pad, 516
stamp rack, 516
stanchion, 644
stand, 651
stand, 236, 248, 250, 341, 370, 382,
  552, 586, 714
stand-off half, 606
stand-up collar, 342
standard A, 539
standard lens, 392
standardbred pacer, 652
standby airspeed indicator, 500
standby altimeter, 500
standby attitude indicator, 500
standing press, 579
standpipe, 298
stapes, 138
staple remover, 515
stapler, 515
staples, 515
star anise, 67
star diagonal, 721
star facet (8), 363
star tracker, 16
starboard diving plane, 806
starboard hand, 488, 489, 497
starch, 152
starch granule, 115
start, 532
start and finish, 646
start button, 706
start key, 421
start line, 655, 656
start switch, 259
start wall, 621
start-up key, 530
starter, 271, 272, 621
starter handle, 272
starting bar (backstroke), 621
starting block, 621, 656
starting block, 621
starting cable, 270
starting dive, 622
starting position, 625
starting step, 201
state, 51
station circle, 38
station entrance, 474
station name, 474
station platform, 464
station wagon, 425
stationary bicycle, 664
stationary bowl, 701
stationary front, 39
stationery, 515, 516, 518
stationery cabinet, 522
stator, 290, 753
stay, 479
stay ring, 753

857

The terms in **bold type** indicate the title of an illustration.

The terms in **bold type** indicate the title of an illustration.

INDEX